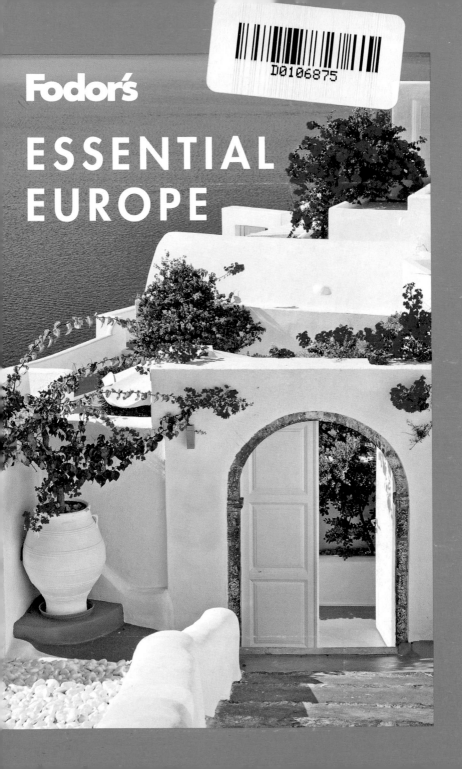

D0106875

Fodor's
ESSENTIAL
EUROPE

WELCOME TO EUROPE

Many first-time travelers seek out Europe's top destinations, including Rome, Paris, London, and Barcelona, for their famous sights and rich cultural offerings. What keeps people coming back is the spectacular variety of experiences, whether it's relaxing on a Greek island, hiking in the Swiss Alps, or shopping in Turkey's bazaars. Unique local pleasures also abound throughout Europe: you may travel to see the Eiffel Tower or the Acropolis, but what you remember as fondly is dining alfresco at a Roman café or lingering over a cup of Viennese coffee.

TOP REASONS TO GO

★ **History:** From ancient times to World War II, Europe has shaped Western culture.

★ **Food:** French, Italian, Greek, Spanish, Nordic— these cuisines resonate around the world.

★ **Arts and Culture:** Some of the world's finest music, dance, and opera companies.

★ **Natural Beauty:** Snowcapped mountains, iconic rivers, dazzling beaches, green forests.

★ **Museums:** No other region has such a high concentration of world-class institutions.

★ **Active Adventures:** Biking in the Netherlands, kayaking in the Aegean, skiing in Austria.

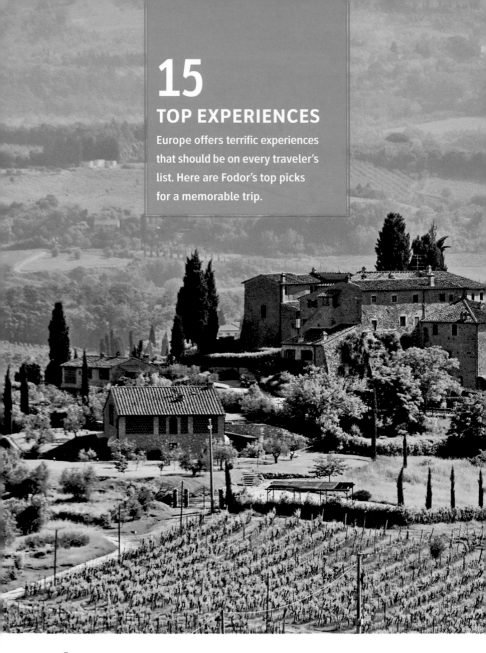

15

TOP EXPERIENCES

Europe offers terrific experiences that should be on every traveler's list. Here are Fodor's top picks for a memorable trip.

1 Wine and Wineries

Tastings and vineyard visits are now highlights of many trips. Whether it's Tuscan Chianti, French Bordeaux, Spanish Rioja, Hungarian Tokaji, or Portuguese Vinho Verde, wine has quenched the thirst of visitors to Europe for centuries.

2 Festivals and Events

Europe is packed with events to plan a trip around. August's Edinburgh International Festival has music, including bagpipes, and more; Munich's Oktoberfest is beer heaven.

3 Great Cities

Any of Europe's major capitals—such as fast-changing Berlin—can occupy you for a week. Easy rail and air connections allow you to combine several on a single short trip.

4 Modern Architecture

Almost any city here dazzles with exciting architectural achievements. Spain's Guggenheim Bilbao is one place that has helped inspire other vibrant new developments.

5 Cafés

One of Europe's greatest pleasures is to sit quietly and enjoy a cup of coffee or tea and a pastry. The café culture extends from Paris and Copenhagen to Madrid and Florence.

6 Music

From a grand opera performance in Vienna to chamber-music concerts in countless exquisite churches, the music of Mozart, Verdi, Debussy, and Beethoven fills the air.

7 Great Walks

One of the best ways to see Europe is on foot. Urbane city expanses such as London's Regent's Park are delightful for strolling, or you can hike magnificent mountains.

8 Churches

Take your pick among standouts in splendid styles from Renaissance to rococo to baroque. In France, the Gothic spires of Chartres Cathedral and its breathtaking interior are unforgettable.

9 Romance

Europe is for lovers, whether you are serenaded on a gondola in Venice, secluded in a room in Prague's Old Town, or drowsing in a hammock for two in a Greek-island villa.

10 Picturesque Towns

Postcard-perfect spots beckon, from peaceful hillside villages to breezy seaside favorites. Medieval, canal-laced Brugge in Belgium epitomizes Continental charm.

11 Classic Architecture

Architectural treasures from throughout the ages fill Europe, where landmarks from plazas to palaces reward attention. Istanbul's Byzantine Hagia Sophia is utterly majestic.

12 Visible History

Study the origins of Western civilization in ruins from the Romans and Greeks, and view the legacy of Vikings and Visigoths. Rome's Forum provides perspective on the past.

13 Art

From the Louvre to the Prado to the Uffizi, magnificent art museums are a highlight. But some churches have collections that are almost as grand as any gallery's holdings.

14 Shopping

Grand department stores like Galeries Lafayette in Paris carry famous luxury brands. Around Europe you can also buy Bohemian crystal, British tea, and Belgian chocolates.

15 Outdoor Activities

Find fun year-round. In winter, ski slopes in Switzerland and elsewhere attract international travelers. In summer beaches draw swimmers to the French Riviera and beyond.

16
FAVORITE PLACES
Europe has so many fabulous places to visit that it can be hard to choose. Here are Fodor's favorite destinations.

1 Amalfi Coast

The azure waters and picturesque towns of the Amalfi Coast have been a draw for writers, artists, and now tourists. The area is easy to explore by car or ferry; Positano is one of Fodor's favorite seaside spots in Italy. *(Ch. 12)*

2 Paris

From Notre Dame to the Eiffel Tower, the City of Light rewards repeat visits, whether you want to climb Montmartre, shop on Avenue Montaigne, or dine in great bistros. *(Ch. 7)*

3 Amsterdam

A city of narrow houses, myriad canals, and flower markets, Amsterdam remains a great capital. Don't miss the magnificently restored Rijksmuseum and Anne Frank's House. *(Ch. 13)*

4 Provence

Fields of lavender, bustling farmer's markets, and beautiful medieval villages have made Provence popular. Ancient Arles and Avignon's Palais des Papes are stunning. *(Ch. 7)*

5 County Kerry, Ireland

Plenty of green helps make the countryside here quintessentially Irish. Drive the 110-mile Ring of Kerry but also visit the market town of Kenmare or the Skellig Islands. *(Ch. 11)*

6 Copenhagen

Cafés and modern design shops abound in this walkable city. Tivoli Gardens is a top pick; the National Museum is one of Europe's underrated treasures. *(Ch. 15)*

7 Scotland

A trip to Edinburgh and the Great Glen will leave you wanting more. Ruined Urquhart Castle on Loch Ness is as deeply memorable as a wee dram of Scotch whisky. *(Ch. 20)*

8 Barcelona

Gaudí's creations, including colorful Park Guell, dominate the Catalonian capital. Stroll through El Barri Gòtic and take in excellent museums devoted to Picasso and Miró. *(Ch. 17)*

9 Prague

The city's Old Town is one of the best-preserved in Europe. Explore magnificent Prague Castle and the Jewish Quarter, and be sure to lift a glass of Czech pilsner. (Ch. 6)

10 London

The British capital can keep you occupied for weeks with iconic sights such as Big Ben. You can also shop, dine at trendy restaurants, or see West End shows. *(Ch. 20)*

11 Berner Oberland

Once you see this beautiful, mountainous region, you'll understand Switzerland's allure, whether in winter for skiing or in summer for hiking and sheer relaxation. *(Ch. 18)*

12 Rome

With sights from the splendid Piazza Navona to magnificent churches to evocative ancient ruins, the Eternal City remains a top draw for travelers in Europe for good reason. *(Ch. 12)*

13 Bavaria

Castles such as Neuschwanstein make mountainous southern Germany worth a trip. Bavaria is beautiful year round, including in winter when Christmas markets fill town squares. (Ch. 8)

14 Dubrovnik

Croatia's most popular destination is one of the world's most beautiful fortified cities. This former Venetian outpost also stars as King's Landing in *Game of Thrones*. *(Ch. 5)*

15 Iceland

Come to see the northern lights, the famous "Blue Lagoon," the weirdly beautiful volcanic landscape, or vibrant Reykjavik. Once you've been here, you will never forget it. *(Ch. 15)*

16 Santorini

Skeptics need only visit Oia to see why a view is so important. Everyone's favorite Greek island has great wine, comfortable small hotels, and loads of charm. *(Ch. 9)*

CONTENTS

MAPS

ABOUT THIS GUIDE

Fodor's Recommendations

Everything in this guide is worth doing—we don't cover what isn't—but exceptional sights, hotels, and restaurants are recognized with additional accolades. Fodor'sChoice★ indicates our top recommendations; and **Best Bets** calls attention to notable hotels and restaurants in various categories. Care to nominate a new place? Visit Fodors.com/contact-us.

Trip Costs

We list prices wherever possible to help you budget well. Hotel and restaurant price categories from $ to $$$$ are noted alongside each recommendation. For hotels, we include the lowest cost of a standard double room in high season. For restaurants, we cite the average price of a main course at dinner or, if dinner isn't served, at lunch. For attractions, we always list adult admission fees; discounts are usually available for children, students, and senior citizens.

Hotels

Our local writers vet every hotel to recommend the best overnights in each price category, from budget to expensive. Unless otherwise specified, you can expect private bath, phone, and TV in your room. For expanded hotel reviews, facilities, and deals visit Fodors.com.

Restaurants

Unless we state otherwise, restaurants are open for lunch and dinner daily. We mention dress code only when there's a specific requirement and reservations only when they're essential or not accepted. To make restaurant reservations, visit Fodors.com.

Credit Cards

The hotels and restaurants in this guide typically accept credit cards. If not, we'll say so.

Top Picks
★ Fodor'sChoice

Listings
⊠ Address
⊠ Branch address
☎ Telephone
🖶 Fax
⊕ Website
✉ E-mail
🎫 Admission fee
🕐 Open/closed times
Ⓜ Subway
⊹ Directions or Map coordinates

Hotels & Restaurants
🏨 Hotel
🛏 Number of rooms
🍽 Meal plans
✕ Restaurant
🔖 Reservations
🎩 Dress code
🚫 No credit cards
Ⓢ Price

Other
⇨ See also
☞ Take note
⛳ Golf facilities

EXPERIENCE
EUROPE

Visit Fodors.com for advice, updates, and bookings

WHAT'S WHERE

1 Ireland. While isolated at Europe's westernmost extreme, Ireland still holds a powerful allure. Modern Dublin has trendy hotels and hipster cafés, but the old stuff is still best—from the ancient pubs to the Georgian elegance. More classical experiences lie to the south and west, where the Blarney Stone, the Ring of Kerry, and the Rock of Cashel are set in a land of emerald glory. Belfast, in Northern Ireland, is another up-and-coming tourist destination. (⇨ *Chapter 11.*)

2 United Kingdom. London, one of the world's most exciting cities, is filled with ancient pageantry and contemporary buzz. Many top destinations are within two hours of it, including Oxford and Cambridge, centuries-old university towns. Stratford-upon-Avon is Shakespeare's birthplace. Farther west is Bath, rich with Palladian architecture. Four hundred miles north of London, Edinburgh's landmarks include a medieval castle and a modern Parliament building; farther north still is the Great Glen and its lochs. (⇨ *Chapter 20.*)

3 Scandinavia and the Baltic States. The northernmost countries of Europe, collectively known as Scandinavia, share a Viking heritage and a sturdy disposition.

Residents of the main cities (Copenhagen, Helsinki, Oslo, and Stockholm) are at once urbane and outdoorsy. The nearby Baltic States of Estonia and Latvia are well connected by rail and ferry to Scandinavia; the capitals Talinn and Rīga are increasingly popular destinations in their own right. Iceland, with its Scandinavian roots, is often grouped with these countries. (⇨ *Chapter 15.*)

4 The Netherlands. The Netherlands really is a land of windmills, tulips, and canals, while being a progressive 21st-century nation. The capital, Amsterdam, is famous for its waterways and its laid-back atmosphere. The Hague is home to the queen and a center for international diplomacy. And Delft and Haarlem are smaller, character-rich cities. (⇨ *Chapter 13.*)

5 Belgium. Diminutive Belgium is split between the Flemish-speaking north and French-speaking south. The two most cosmopolitan cities are Brussels, the multicultural capital, and Antwerp, a bustling port and fashion hotbed. The picture-book town of Brugge has a staggering wealth of fine art. (⇨ *Chapter 4.*)

0   100 mi

0   100 km

Barents Sea

Hammerfest

Zapolyarnyy

Polyarnyy

Tromsø

Harstad

Kovdor

Narvik

Kiruna

Bodø

Kemimärvi

Mo i Rana

Malmberget

Rovaniemi

Norwegian Sea

SWEDEN

Kemi

Pitea   Lulea

Namsos

Skelleftea   Raahe   Oulu

Stenkjaer

Lycksele

Trondheim

3   Umeå

FINLAND

Kristiansund

Ostersund

Kokkola

Alesund

Jakobstad

Kuopio

NORWAY

Vaasa

SHETLAND ISLANDS

Sundsvall

Jyvaskyla

Mikkeli

Lerwick

S C A N D I N A V I A

Tampere

Bergen

Gjovik

Bollnäs

Pori

Lappeenranta

Haugesund

OSLO

Gavle

Turku

HELSINKI

Stavanger

Sauda

Espoo

Skien

Vasteras

TALLINN   Jarve

Aberdeen

Egersund

Arendal

Orebro

STOCKHOLM   **ESTONIA**

Mandal

Uddevalla

Linköping

Tartu

Göteborg

Jönköping

Thisted

Alborg

Ljungby

LATVIA

DENMARK

Kalmar

Liepaja

RIGA   Balvi

Viborg

Århus

North Sea

COPENHAGEN   Malmö

Klaipeda

LITHUANIA

Baltic Sea

Schleswig   Kiel

Taurage

NETHERLANDS

Rostock

Gdánsk

VILNIUS

4

Hamburg

Szczecin

MINSK

HE HAGUE   **AMSTERDAM**

Hannover

BERLIN

POLAND

BELARUS

Dover

Poznań

WARSAW

Brest

Antwerp

GERMANY

Brugge   **BRUSSELS**

Łódź

Prypyat

BELGIUM

Dresden

Wrocław

Lublin

Rivne

Reims

5   **LUXEMBOURG**

PRAGUE

UKRAINE

LUXEMBOURG

PARIS   Metz   Nancy

Nürnberg

CZECH REPUBLIC

Ostrava

Kraków

L'viv

Strasbourg

Stuttgart

Brno

SLOVAKIA

WHAT'S WHERE

6 France. A trip to France should include Paris, the City of Light, to see the Eiffel Tower, Notre-Dame, the Louvre, and scores of other treasures. Yet just on the other side of the *Périphérique* is the French countryside, where châteaux— including Versailles—and some of the world's best food and wine await. And thanks to the country's high-speed trains, you can whisk down to Provence or the French Riviera in a little more than three hours. (⇨ *Chapter 7.*)

7 Switzerland. Switzerland packs abundant attractions into a tiny space. Among the cities, Zürich mixes Old World charm with a youthful vibe, while Luzern encompasses the best of the country in a nutshell. But outdoors is where you find Switzerland's scenic masterpieces, such as the lakes, valleys, and peaks of the Berner Oberland region. (⇨ *Chapter 15.*)

8 Germany. Bordered by nine countries and two seas, Germany sits at the heart of Europe. Its top cities exemplify the country's diversity: The capital, Berlin, is the essence of hip, with cutting-edge art and a "poor but sexy" attitude. In the southeast, Munich is famed for its Oktoberfest and beer gardens. To the north is Hamburg, known for its historic harbor and colorful red-light

district. Outside the cities, roads wind past half-timber towns, hillside vineyards, picturesque castles, and soaring mountains. (⇨ *Chapter 8.*)

9 Austria. It's not a large country, but Austria's land-scape is almost as varied as its cultural offerings. To some, Austria is synonymous with skiing and hiking in the Tyrolean Alps. To others it means the old-world charms of Vienna—with its magnifi-cent opera houses, grand art museums, and unmistakable coffee houses. And if you love *The Sound of Music,* you won't want to pass up Salzburg. (⇨ *Chapter 3.*)

10 Czech Republic. After years of Communist rule, the Czech Republic is now finishing its second decade beyond the Iron Curtain. The most popular destination is Prague, where Gothic splendors, including the Charles Bridge and Prague Castle, are dazzling relics of Europe's past. The castles in southern Bohemia are also rewarding. (⇨ *Chapter 6.*)

11 Hungary. Hungary sits at the crossroads of Central Europe, having been ruled by the Turks, Habsburgs, and the Soviets. Today, Budapest is an emerging capital, but the Danube Bend region and Eger offer additional highlights for those with more time. (⇨ *Chapter 10.*)

OTLAND

THE HAGUE

NETHERLANDS
AMSTERDAM

NDON

Dover

Calais

Rouen

PARIS

Orleans

Nancy

BELGIUM
BRUSSELS
Liège
Antwerp

LUXEMBOURG
LUXEMBOURG

Strasbourg

FRANCE

Dijon

Lausanne

Geneva

Lyon

Grenoble

Valence

Nîmes

Avignon

Marseille

Nice

Monte Carlo

MONACO

North Sea

ottingham

Göteborg

Thisted

DENMARK

Viborg

Arhus

COPENHAGEN

Malmo

SWEDEN

Jönköping

Schleswig

Kiel

Baltic Sea

Rostock

Gdánsk

Hamburg

Bremen

Hannover

BERLIN

Szczecin

POLAND

Poznań

8

GERMANY

Kassel

Dresden

Wrocław

Łódź

Frankfurt

Nürnberg

PRAGUE

10

CZECH
REPUBLIC

Ostrava

Brno

Stuttgart

Zurich

Munich

Danube

SLOVAKIA

BRATISLAVA

LIECHTENSTEIN

Linz

VIENNA

BERN

7

Salzburg

AUSTRIA

BUDAPEST

SWITZERLAND

Innsbruck

Graz

HUNGARY

Martigny

Novara

ITALY

LJUBLJANA

11

Turin

Milan

SLOVENIA

ZAGREB

Venice

CROATIA

Genoa

Po

Ravenna

Sava

BOSNIA &
HERZEGOVINA

Florence

Pisa

Ancona

SARAJEVO

Mediterranean Sea

CORSICA

Ajaccio

Perugia

PODGORICA

0   100 mi

0   100 km

Sassari

Siniscola

ROME

Bari

6

9

Rhine

Meuse

Loire

WHAT'S WHERE

12 Portugal. Portugal's long Atlantic coastline means that much of the country's history and culture have been strongly influenced by the sea. The capital, Lisbon, is a port city that mixes modernity and mellow age. Northwest is Sintra, a town that was a summer home for Portuguese royals and aristocrats. The country's second-largest city, Porto, is the cultural center of the northern region. (⇨ *Chapter 14.*)

13 Spain. Spain's largest cities, Barcelona and Madrid, vie with each other for preeminence. Both have fabulous restaurants, famous museums, and their own distinctive charms. Venture farther afield—to postcard lovely Andalusia, medieval Toledo, or Bilbao with its renowned museum—and you'll be struck by how the regions differ while still sharing the Spanish zest for life. (⇨ *Chapter 17.*)

14 Italy. It's fair to say that no other country in Europe is so packed with cultural and natural treasures. The top draws are three remarkable cities: In the northeast, waterborne Venice woos you with its opulent, East-meets-West architecture and its unique canals. Due south, Florence is a Renaissance museum come to life, where the works of Michelangelo, Leonardo, and Brunelleschi

compete for your attention. Farther south, halfway down the boot, stands Rome, one of the world's greatest cities for more than 2,000 years. (⇨ Chapter 12.)

15 Slovenia. Small but picturesque Slovenia offers a particularly lovely capital, Ljubljana, as well as excellent alpine scenery and one of Europe's longest cave systems. (⇨ Chapter 16.)

16 Croatia. The EU's newest member state is also one of Europe's favorite vacation destinations. And no wonder with the beauty and history of Dubrovnik and Split, not to mention thousands of islands, including the inviting Hvar. (⇨ Chapter 5.)

17 Greece. Greece has a continent's worth of extraordinary sights and timeless landscapes in a space the

size of New York State. All roads lead to Athens, but for a true Grecian escape, head to the islands of Mykonos and Santorini. (⇨ Chapter 9.)

18 Turkey. Istanbul beckons with both exoticism and modernity. Shoppers won't want to miss the bazaars, but the city also offers beautiful architecture, top-notch hotels, and great food. (⇨ Chapter 19.)

TOP ATTRACTIONS: LANDMARKS

Schönbrunn Palace, Vienna, Austria
One of Austria's premier attractions, the palace built by Empress Maria Theresa is one of Vienna's top landmarks. (⇨ *Chapter 3.*)

Grand'Place, Brussels, Belgium
(A) In Brussels's main square the spectacular 15th-century town hall is a stunning example of medieval Flemish architecture. (⇨ *Chapter 4.*)

Eiffel Tower, Paris, France
(B) There's no monument that better symbolizes Paris than Gustav Eiffel's Iron Lady. (⇨ *Chapter 7.*)

Mont-St-Michel, Normandy, France
(C) From its silhouette against the horizon to its magnificent church, you'll never forget the crowning glory of medieval France. (⇨ Chapter 7.)

Neuschwanstein Castle, Germany
(D) Walt Disney modeled the castle in *Sleeping Beauty* and later the Disneyland castle itself on "Mad" King Ludwig II's Neuschwanstein. (⇨ *Chapter 8.*)

Tower of London, United Kingdom
(E) This extraordinary minicity of 20 towers has been the scene of much blood and gore since the 11th century. The Crown Jewels are here, too. (⇨ *Chapter 20.*)

Acropolis, Athens, Greece
(F) The great emblem of classical Greece has loomed above Athens for 2,500 years. (⇨ *Chapter 9.*)

The Colosseum, Rome, Italy
(G) This mammoth amphitheater was begun by Emperor Vespasian and inaugurated by Titus in the year 80. For "the grandeur that was Rome," it can't be topped. (⇨ *Chapter 12.*)

Duomo, Florence, Italy
The massive dome of Florence's Cathedral of Santa Maria del Fiore (aka the Duomo) is one of the world's great feats of engineering. (⇨ *Chapter 12.*)

La Sagrada Familia, Barcelona, Spain
(H) *The* symbol of Barcelona, Gaudí's extraordinary unfinished cathedral should be included on everyone's must-see list. (⇨ *Chapter 17.*)

Alhambra, Granada, Spain
Nothing can prepare you for the Moorish grandeur of Andalusia's greatest monument. (⇨ *Chapter 17.*)

Charles Bridge, Prague, The Czech Republic
Prague's greatest landmark is as much a town square as a bridge. It's also the optimum place for spectacular views of the city, particularly at night. (⇨ *Chapter 6.*)

Aya Sofya, Istanbul, Turkey
This soaring edifice may be the greatest work of Byzantine architecture. (⇨ *Chapter 19.*)

Operahuset, Oslo, Norway
Oslo's modernist opera house is a wonder for both its artistry and sound quality. (⇨ *Chapter 15.*)

Kungliga Slottet, Stockholm, Sweden
The Swedish royal palace dates from 1760 and is one of the highlights of a visit to Stockholm. (⇨ *Chapter 15.*)

Tivoli Gardens, Copenhagen, Denmark
Copenhagen's top attraction is an amusement park, and much more. There are gardens with glorious flowers, ponds, concerts, theater, and more than 30 restaurants. Visit twice—once during the day, once at night. (⇨ *Chapter 15.*)

TOP ATTRACTIONS: MUSEUMS AND ART

Louvre, Paris, France
(A) This former palace was transformed into the home for the young Republic's art collection after the French Revolution. The Big Three—*Mona Lisa, Winged Victory,* and *Venus de Milo*—should not be missed (⇨ *Chapter 7.*)

Museum Island, Berlin, Germany
(B) Germany's capital has more than 150 museums, but this spot holds five state museums with world-class collections ranging from classical antiquities to 20th-century paintings and sculpture. (⇨ *Chapter 8.*)

British Museum, London, United Kingdom
(C) This vast museum is packed to bursting with antiquities and alluring objects. Among the greatest hits are the Parthenon Marbles, the Rosetta Stone, and Egyptian mummies. (⇨ *Chapter 20.*)

Book of Kells, Trinity College, Dublin, Ireland
(D) Often called "the most beautiful book in the world," this manuscript dating from the 8th or 9th century is a marvel of intricacy and creativity, executed by monks working with reed pens. (⇨ *Chapter 11.*)

Vatican Museums, Rome, Italy
(E) The lines waiting for entry here can be intimidating, but the reward—a vast collection of masterpieces, highlighted by the Sistine Chapel—makes it well worth the wait. (⇨ *Chapter 12.*)

Galleria degli Uffizi, Florence, Italy
The Uffizi—Renaissance art's hall of fame—contains masterpieces by Leonardo, Michelangelo, Raphael, Botticelli, Caravaggio, and dozens of other luminaries. (⇨ *Chapter 12.*)

Rijksmuseum, Amsterdam, The Netherlands

(F) This is the place to go when you're looking for Dutch masters, including Rembrandt, Vermeer, Hals, and a slew of others. (⇨ *Chapter 13.*)

Museu Calouste Gulbenkian, Lisbon, Portugal

(G) The collection here—one part devoted to Egyptian, Greek, Roman, Islamic, and Asian art, the other to European—isn't large, but the quality is high. Add a stroll through the sculpture garden. (⇨ *Chapter 14.*)

Guggenheim Museum, Bilbao, Spain

(H) All swooping curves and rippling forms, this architecturally innovative museum was built on the site of the city's former shipyards and inspired by the shape of a ship's hull. The collection is pretty good as well, including such masters as Picasso and Miró. (⇨ *Chapter 15.*)

Gallerie dell'Accademia, Venice, Italy

The world's most extensive collection of Venetian painting is on display at this world-class museum. (⇨ *Chapter 12.*)

Museo del Prado, Madrid, Spain

Set in a magnificent neoclassical building on one of the capital's most elegant boulevards, the Prado is Spain's answer to the Louvre and a regal home to renowned Spanish masterpieces. Much of the collection dates back to the museum's inauguration in 1819. (⇨ *Chapter 17.*)

National Archaeological Museum, Athens, Greece

Many of the greatest achievements in ancient Greek sculpture and painting are housed here in the most important museum in Greece. (⇨ *Chapter 9.*)

TOP ATTRACTIONS: PICTURESQUE TOWNS

Brugge, Belgium

(A) Brugge is one of the most beautiful small cities in Europe. Stroll through the maze of winding, cobbled alleys, alongside the winding canals, and over the romantic bridges to see why UNESCO included it on the World Heritage list. (⇨ *Chapter 4.*)

Èze, the Riviera, France

(B) The most perfectly perched of the French Riviera's *villages perchés*, Èze has some of the most breathtaking views this side of a NASA space capsule. (⇨ *Chapter 7.*)

Bath, Great Britain

(C) Exquisitely preserved, this Georgian town's streets lined with Palladian buildings made of golden limestone, an ancient abbey, tea shops, boutiques, and ruined Roman baths combine to give Bath real character. (⇨ *Chapter 20.*)

Lucca, Tuscany, Italy

(D) This laid-back yet elegant town is surrounded by tree-bedecked 16th-century ramparts that are now a delightful promenade. With limited automobile traffic within the city walls, it's an ideal place for getting around by bike. (⇨ *Chapter 12.*)

Delft, The Netherlands

(E) Holland's most attractive town feels like a tiny Amsterdam, with canals, cobblestone streets, and the air of a simpler time. The quiet atmosphere pervades many of the paintings by Delft's most famous citizen, Johannes Vermeer. (⇨ *Chapter 13.*)

Sintra, Portugal

"A glorious Eden" is how Lord Byron described Sintra. It's a magical place studded with magnificent palaces, gardens, and luxury *quintas* (manor houses). UNESCO has deemed the entire town a Word Heritage Site in recognition of its splendid architecture. (⇨ *Chapter 14.*)

Mürren, Berner Oberland, Switzerland

A Noah's Ark village pasted 5,400 feet up a mountainside, Mürren offers a so-close-you-can-touch-it vista of the Jungfrau and the Eiger. This is the birthplace of downhill and slalom skiing. (⇨ *Chapter 18*.)

Giverny, Ile-de-France, France

(F) Replacing paint and canvas with earth and water, Claude Monet transformed his 5-acre garden into a veritable live-in Impressionist painting. Come to Giverny to see his lily pond, then peek around his charming home and stroll the time-warped streets to the ultrastylish American Art Museum. (⇨ *Chapter 7*.)

Ia, Santorini, Greece

(G) One of the world's most picturesque towns looks down onto the sunken caldera of a volcano that last erupted around 1600 BC. The views are a visual treat that makes the heart skip a beat or two. (⇨ *Chapter 9*.)

Hvar, Coratia

Popular with the jet set, Hvar is an island of chic, expensive boutique hotels, and beautiful (albeit rocky) beaches. (⇨ *Chapter 5*.)

Eger, Hungary

Surrounded by vineyards and filled with historical monuments, the picture-book baroque city of Eger is ripe for exploration. (⇨ *Chapter 10*.)

Ljubljana, Slovenia

Slovenia's small but exceedingly charming capital is immediately captivating and among the most beautiful urban areas in Europe. (⇨ *Chapter 16*.)

Talinn, Estonia

Talinn's picturesque Old Town is lined with romantic towers overlooking cobblestone streets. (⇨ *Chapter 15*.)

GREAT ITINERARIES

MAJOR CAPITALS IN 2 WEEKS

Happily, due to extremely efficient train and flight connections throughout Europe, it's possible to see the continent's major urban areas in a two-week trip. To get the most out of your short-but-sweet visits, just stick to a tightly planned itinerary like the one we recommend below.

2 Days: London

One of the great capitals of the world, London offers enough historical, cultural, and culinary enticements to fill a lifetime. But with just two days, we suggest focusing one day on the major museums that interest you—appealing choices include the Tate Modern, the British Museum, the Victoria and Albert, and so many others—with a break in one of London's famed parks, perhaps Hyde Park or St. James's Park. Cap off your first night with an early dinner and a show. Spend your second day sticking to one or two neighborhoods—Westminster and Royal London or Kensington and South Kensington, for example—walking, shopping, and soaking up the sights. ⇨ *Chapter 20, United Kingdom.*

Logistics: Buy an Oyster card to avoid ruinous single-trip Tube fares. Take the Eurostar from St. Pancras to Paris Gare du Nord in 2½ hours.

3 Days: Paris

After arriving via Eurostar, focus one of your days in the City of Light on the area between Notre-Dame (visit early to beat the crowds) and the Place de la Concorde, where you'll find some of Paris's most beautiful sights conveniently located along a single Métro line. Divide your other two days between strolling from the Eiffel Tower to the Arc de Triomphe, exploring the Marais to the Bastille, or seeing sights from Orsay to St-Germain-des-Prés. Be sure to fit in some much-needed downtime by relaxing in the lovely Luxembourg Gardens or strolling along the Seine. To maximize your sightseeing time, purchase tickets online in advance for major attractions like the Louvre, the Eiffel Tower, and the Musée d'Orsay. ⇨ *Chapter 7, France.*

Logistics: When moving on, Air France, Iberia, and Vueling fly direct from Paris to Florence in two hours for as little as €75.

2 Days: Florence

Take a two-hour flight to the birthplace of the Renaissance. Start with a visit to the wondrous gold mosaic–ceilinged Duomo and the bronze doors of the Battistero before spending the afternoon at the Galleria degli Uffizi, where you'll see masterpieces from Da Vinci, Raphael, and Botticelli (and to which you bought advance tickets online). On your second day, don't miss Michelangelo's David in the Galleria dell'Accademia (ditto the advance tickets or go an hour before closing) and the famous artworks inside Santa Croce. Wind down with a walk along the Arno River and across the famous Ponte Vecchio at sunset to truly appreciate the city's subtle beauty. ⇨ *Chapter 12, Italy.*

Logistics: You can get around Florence on foot for the most part. Moving on, a 90-minute train ride takes you to Rome.

3 Days: Rome

This open-air museum of a city can overwhelm with its sheer amount of historical treasures. To make the most of your visit, start with a half-day tour of the Vatican (arranged in advance), followed by a couple of hours exploring Navona and Campo, including the Pantheon and beautiful squares such as Piazza Navona. On

your second day, explore Rome's ancient sites, including the Colosseum and Roman Forum, before seeing the Trevi Fountain and shopping around the Spanish Steps. Spend your third day visiting the Galleria Borghese and San Clemente church and then strolling through the narrow streets of the Ghetto and medieval Trastevere, stopping at a lively café or *enoteca* (wine bar) to refuel and people-watch. ⇨ *Chapter 12, Italy.*

Logistics: Iberia, Ryanair, and Vueling fly direct from Rome to Barcelona in under two hours; fares can be found for under €70.

2 Days: Barcelona

Begin your visit to this edgy Mediterranean city with a stroll down La Rambla, Barcelona's colorful heart, with stops at the tempting Boqueria market and Gaudí's fanciful Palau Güell. Continue your walk into the medieval Barri Gòtic and shopping-centric El Born districts, popping into the Museu Picasso for a visit. Finish up with dinner near the beachfront in Barceloneta. Make your second day Gaudí-centric with stops at La Sagrada Familia and Park Güell, bookended by lunch and dinner at one of the city's many fabulous restaurants. ⇨ *Chapter 17, Spain.*

TIPS

■ Although you can reach all the cities on this itinerary by train, we recommend some flights to maximize your time.

■ Book as many major museum visits and all train tickets as far in advance as possible.

■ In Rome, consider a private Vatican tour; it's money well spent.

Logistics: The pleasant AVE train takes you to Madrid in three hours.

2 Days: Madrid

In the bustling Spanish capital, your short visit will be all about the art. Though the Prado (with works by Goya, Velázquez, and El Greco), Reina Sofía (home of Picasso's Guernica), and Thyssen-Bornemisza museums (with paintings from the 13th to 21st centuries) are all close together, we suggest spreading them out over your two days, alternating visits with a walk around the Royal Palace or a stop at a café or wine bar, to avoid museum fatigue. Tapas-bar hopping is another worthy endeavor during your stay. ⇨ *Chapter 17, Spain.*

GREAT ITINERARIES

CENTRAL EUROPE IN 2 WEEKS

This introduction to Central Europe takes you from the lively capital of Bavaria to the charming town of Salzburg, birthplace of Mozart, before exploring Vienna's captivating sights. The second half of the trip sees you sightseeing in the historic river towns of Prague, Budapest, and Ljubljana, wandering their lovely cobblestone streets and enjoying magnificent views.

2 Days: Munich

Begin your journey in the gateway to Central Europe, the atmospheric heart of Bavaria. Spend some time roaming the Old Town's pedestrian area, stopping by the glockenspiel of the Marienplatz and the Viktualienmarkt food stalls, before exploring the city's elegant museums and parks (we highly recommend viewing the European art masterpieces in the Alte Pinakothek; touring the halls and galleries of the fabulous Residenz, or Royal Palace; and relaxing in Germany's largest urban park, the Englischer Garten). Of course, no visit to Munich is complete without quenching your thirst at a beer hall—or two. ⇨ *Chapter 8, Germany.*

Logistics: Salzburg is an easy 90-minute train ride from Munich.

2 Days: Salzburg

This famed high baroque music town has much to delight even nonmusic fans, all in a compact and very walkable area. Start by touring the Fortress Hohensalzburg, the largest medieval fortress in Central Europe, before admiring the city views from the lovely Mirabellgarten. Baroque buffs shouldn't miss the 15th-century Residenz, onetime home to a prince-archbishop, and the Salzburg Museum, an archaeological collection housed in

the prince's other palace; music lovers will appreciate Mozart Wohnhaus (Mozart's family house) and Mozart Geburtshaus, where the great composer was born in 1756. ⇨ *Chapter 3, Austria.*

Logistics: Vienna is a three-hour train ride from Salzburg.

3 Days: Vienna

You'll reach the former home of the Austro-Hungarian Habsburg rulers, filled with impressive reminders of its Imperial past, by late morning. Spend a half day touring the gorgeous rococo-style Schönbrunn Palace, former home to Austro-Hungarian royalty. You'll also want to visit some of the renowned museums: there's the Kunsthistorisches, with its world-class art collection; the Albertina, home to wonderful old-master drawings; or the elegant baroque Belvedere Palace, which often contains modern art exhibits, to name a few. Taking a coffee-and-cake break at a historic coffeehouse or pastry shop, such as Demel, is a must, and, if you can, catch at least one musical performance at the Staatsoper (State Opera House) or Musikverein, home of the renowned Vienna Philharmonic. ⇨ *Chapter 3, Austria.*

Logistics: Consider flying round-trip to Ljubljana, or move this city to last in your itinerary and take a train from Budapest (eight hours, or 15 hours overnight with connections).

2 Days: Ljubljana

Explore Ljubljana's beautiful Old Town on foot, admiring the lovely baroque and neoclassical buildings. Take time to enjoy the view from the hilltop castle and check out some of the modern and historic museums (like the Modern Gallery or National Gallery) in this art-focused former Yugoslavian town. For a break, the

cafés along the riverfront have the perfect vantage point. ⇨ *Chapter 16, Slovenia.*

Logistics: Perhaps consider a late-evening connection through Vienna that will allow you to move directly on to Prague.

3 Days: Prague

Prague's charm lies in wandering through its 14th-century streets, admiring the historic architecture and elaborately decorated buildings before stopping for a Czech beer in Old Town Square. Focus your trip on the atmospheric Staré Mesto (Old Town), where you'll find the art-nouveau Municipal House and 14th-century Old Town Hall, and the picturesque Hradčany (Castle Area), home to the Gothic St. Vitus's Cathedral and brightly colored Golden Lane, where Kafka briefly lived. The Jewish Quarter, with its melancholy Old Jewish Cemetery, and Nové Mesto (New Town) are worth strolls, as well. Though beautiful during the day, Prague becomes even more magical at night with an unforgettable walk across the Charles Bridge. ⇨ *Chapter 6, Czech Republic.*

Logistics: Trains from Prague to Budapest run six times a day, take seven hours, and cost only €35 with advance purchase. There are direct 90-minute flights on Czech Airlines, but they tend to be pricey.

2 Days: Budapest

This striking city along the Danube is perfect for sightseeing from the historic Castle District, where you can explore the area's museums, cathedrals, and shops; admire the view from the Chain Bridge before riding the funicular up the hill for a great view. You'll also want to wander the Jewish District, where you'll find Dohány Street Synagogue, the largest in Europe. To break up all that walking, spend at least a half-day relaxing in one of the soothing thermal baths, such as Széchenyi or Gellért. Cap off your visit with a drink in one of Budapest's many outdoor bars, or with a taste of Hungarian wine at one of Budapest's many wine bars. ⇨ *Chapter 10, Hungary.*

GREAT ITINERARIES

FRANCE AND ITALY IN 2 WEEKS

This itinerary gives you the best of both worlds: the historic urban areas of France and northern Italy combined with jaunts through the beautiful French countryside. You'll start in one of Europe's cultural and food capitals, Paris, before heading west to Normandy's medieval Rouen and 12th-century Mont-St-Michel. Then you'll travel south to lovely Provence and the dramatic French Riviera, before making your way east into Italy, where the extraordinary art and scenery of Florence and Venice await.

3 Days: Paris

Thought by many to be the most beautiful city in the world, there's plenty to do in Paris. Beyond the can't-miss sights (the Louvre, Notre-Dame, and the Eiffel Tower), you're sure to find your own favorite corners of the city to people-watch, sip *un café,* and spend time enjoying the endless array of parks, museums, galleries, shops, and restaurants. If you feel like escaping the city, take a day trip to the Versailles, Monet's gardens at Giverny, or the Chartres cathedral. And if you can't see it all, don't worry—you'll be back. ⇨ *Chapter 7, France.*

Logistics: Rent a car and drive or hop an early-morning TGV train from Gare Montparnasse to Rennes followed by a bus (3½ hours total) to breathtaking Mont-St-Michel. If you drive to Normandy, consider taking a train out of Paris anyway.

2 Days: Normandy

Spend the day exploring Mont-St-Michel's monastery, museums, and shops, and then stay overnight to appreciate the site's peaceful serenity after the day-trippers

leave; if your timing is right and there's a full moon, you'll have the unforgettable experience of witnessing the high tides. Leave early the following morning by train or car for Rouen, the City of a Hundred Spires, including the highest spire in France, before making the 70-minute journey back to Paris to eat dinner and stay overnight. ⇨ *Chapter 7, France.*

Logistics: Having a car in Normandy is a major convenience. Drive south from Paris or take the TGV train from Gare de Lyon (2 hours, 40 minutes) to sophisticated Avignon. You'll be able to use a car in Provence, but you can visit most places easily by bus or train.

2 Days: Provence

After exploring Avignon's magnificent Papal Palace, take short trips by train, bus, or car to Arles (for the Romanesque Église-St-Trophime), Nîmes (to see the Roman amphitheater), and/or St-Rémy (onetime home of Van Gogh). End up in cosmopolitan Aix-en-Provence, visiting Cezanne's painting studio and wandering the elegant streets. Spend your second night here, ideally dining on a lovely outdoor terrace—and you may never want to leave. ⇨ *Chapter 7, France.*

Logistics: Drive or take the TGV train from Aix to Cannes (two hours).

3 Days: French Riviera

You'll want to spend at least half a day strolling the promenade and venturing into the historic Vieille Ville in Cannes (and star-gazing if you're here during the film festival in May). Then make your way up the coast to Nice (40 minutes from Cannes by train), from where you can explore the magnificent perched villages of St-Paul-de-Vence (and its wonderful art museum, the Fondation Maeght) and Èze. In Nice itself, be sure to wander

through the Old Town and then pop into a museum or two, like the Musée des Beaux-Arts Jules-Chéret, the Musée Matisse, or the Musée Chagall. ⇨ *Chapter 7, France.*

Logistics: From Nice, drive 4½ hours or take a six-hour bus to Florence.

2 Days: Florence

This amazingly preserved Renaissance city can overwhelm with the sheer amount of artistic treasures on offer, from Botticelli's Birth of Venus to Michelangelo's David. Reserve tickets for the Uffizi and Accademia galleries online in advance to avoid the queues. Other can't-miss sights include the beautiful Duomo, the Battistero's bronze doors, and Santa Croce church. Food lovers should swing by the Mercato Centrale food stalls, while fashionistas will swoon over Via Tornabuoni's elegant shops. ⇨ *Chapter 12, Italy.*

Logistics: Reserving tickets for the Uffizi is a must any time of the year, but you can sometimes drop into the Accademia an hour before closing if you just want to see the statue of David. The fast train from Florence to Venice takes just two hours.

2 Days: Venice

Venice's romantic scenery of endless canals and narrow, twisty streets always impresses. Besides making a visit to the

TIPS

■ This itinerary involves a mixture of trains, buses, and, if you choose, a car.

■ If possible, tackle this trip in the spring or fall when the crowds will be fewer and the weather less stifling.

■ Having a car will give you more flexibility, especially when traveling around France and into Italy; however, you'll also have the increased expense of the rental and gas. Ditch the car when you get into the urban areas.

unmissable Basilica di San Marco, wear comfy walking shoes to explore Venice's other *sestiere* (districts), including Dorsoduro, with its wonderful Venetian art collection at the Galleria dell'Accademia; San Polo and Santa Croce, home to the famous Rialto Bridge; and Castello and Cannaregio, where you'll find the gorgeous Ca' d'Oro palace and Jewish Ghetto. At sunset, nothing beats sipping an *Aperol spritz* in Piazza San Marco and watching the world go by. ⇨ *Chapter 12, Italy.*

Logistics: A *vaporetto* pass can be a money-saver in Venice if you want to minimize walking, but some walking is inevitable.

GREAT ITINERARIES

IBERIA IN 2 WEEKS

Food and art lovers will swoon over this itinerary, which hits most of the major sights of Spain and Portugal (barring each country's southern reaches, as both deserve their own separate trips). You'll start in Spain's fascinating capital of Madrid before a brief jaunt to Toledo, onetime home of painter El Greco. Next comes the architecturally rich Mediterranean port town of Barcelona and mouth-watering *pintxo* bars of once-industrial Bilbao. Finally, head even farther west to reach Portugal, exploring lively Lisbon and medieval Porto.

3 Days: Madrid

There's always something going on in Spain's capital, from art to music to nightlife. Hit Madrid's top museums to see the Prado's phenomenal classic artworks (the pieces from Goya, Velázquez, and El Greco are highlights), the Reina Sofía's modern pieces (including Picasso's *Guernica*) and the Thyssen's Renaissance to contemporary art. But also leave room to explore this vibrant city's charming backstreets between the 18th-century Royal Palace and Puerta del Sol. Break for tapas when you're weary, and make the evenings last at a bar or nightclub, mingling with the lively *madrileños*. ⇨ *Chapter 17, Spain.*

Logistics: Toledo makes a great day-trip from Madrid. Take the hourlong bus.

1 Day: Toledo

This Moorish-influenced town sits atop a rocky mount. Though the 10th-century Alcázar is the main attraction, you can while away a day wandering the twisty cobblestone streets, touring the chapels and synagogue, and viewing the paintings of El Greco, who spent much of his life in Toledo and captured some of the area's most enduring scenery. ⇨ *Chapter 17, Spain.*

Logistics: The high-speed AVE train will take you from Madrid to Barcelona in three hours.

3 Days: Barcelona

The stunning capital of Catalonia is a city made for strolling. From Barcelona's colorful main artery, the Rambla, to its moody Gothic Quarter and modernist Eixample district, this edgy city has tons of appeal. Architecture buffs can't miss Gaudí's fanciful La Sagrada Familia, Park Güell, and La Pedrera, plus the gorgeous Liceu Opera House and modernist Palau de la Música Catalana (Music Palace). Art aficionados will want to head to the inspiring Museu Picasso; Fundació Miró, devoted to the 20th-century art of Joan Miró; and the Catalonian National Museum of Art, built for the 1929 World's Fair. Finally, leave time to visit the tempting Boqueria food market and some of Barcelona's world-renowned restaurants and—if you're up for it—go-all-night parties. ⇨ *Chapter 17, Spain.*

Logistics: Travel from Barcelona to Bilbao by train (six hours) or, to save time, plane (Vueling, one hour).

2 Days: Bilbao

Though you'll be heading straight for the fabulous Frank Gehry–designed Museo Guggenheim Bilbao, don't neglect the fascinating Casco Viejo (Old Quarter) along the Nervión River, filled with enticing shops, bars, and restaurants. This area is also home to the amazing food market El Mercado de la Ribera and another often-overlooked yet world-class museum in its own right, the Museo de Bellas Artes (Museum of Fine Arts). Also keep in mind that Bilbao's wonderful

restaurants—many specializing in *pintxos,* or Basque "tapas"—are some of the finest in the country. ⇨ *Chapter 17, Spain.*

Logistics: Fly from Bilbao to Lisbon on easyJet or TAP (90 minutes).

3 Days: Lisbon

A bit gritty but never boring, Lisbon has a flavor unlike any other city in Europe. Take a historic street tram up the steep hills to Castelo de São Jorge and the 10th-century Romanesque cathedral (the Sé), surrounded by the atmospheric Moorish and later Jewish *bairro* of Alfama. Stroll the old streets of the Baixa, Chiado, and Bairro Alto neighborhoods, stopping at appealing shops and wine bars for a tipple, and head over to Belém to marvel at the 14th-century Jerónimos Monastery. Lisbon has many appealing museums, too, but one not to skip is the Museu Calouste Gulbenkian, with its stellar ancient art collection. If you're a fish fan, a lunch of traditional grilled sardines washed down with sangria or a tasty local wine hits the spot. Night owls should check out a *casa de fado* (fado house) to experience the sorrowful yet lovely native music. ⇨ *Chapter 14, Portugal.*

Logistics: A train from Lisbon to Porto takes only three hours.

TIPS

■ Much of Spain and Portugal is accessible by efficient trains and buses, while to get between the two countries your best bet is to fly.

■ Locals in Spain eat dinner quite late; do that as well to maximize touring time, but save time for a pre-dinner nap.

■ Driving in Portugal can be harrowing. We don't recommend it if you don't need to.

2 Days: Porto

You can easily fill an enjoyable day touring some of the 16 port wine lodges (appointments not necessary; tours start when they've gathered enough people) across the river in Vila Nova de Gaia. In Porto itself, the exciting Museu Nacional de Arte Contemporânea and its pretty gardens make a worthy stop, along with some of the many galleries in town. Try to catch a concert one night at the Rem Koolhaas–designed Casa da Música before you leave. ⇨ *Chapter 14, Portugal.*

GREAT ITINERARIES

THE BRITISH ISLES IN 2 WEEKS

This itinerary gives you a taste of the exciting mix of historic and modern found across Great Britain and Ireland. Ancient monuments? Check. Historic architecture? Check. Cutting-edge galleries and up-to-the-minute restaurants? Check those, too. First you'll explore Ireland, starting in old-but-new Dublin and continuing south to medieval Cashel and spirited Cork, before flying out to Scotland's magnificent capital of Edinburgh. A jaunt over to jam-packed London is followed by visits to the charming ancient spa town of Bath (with an excursion to Stonehenge) and a stay in the lively university city of Cambridge.

2 Days: Dublin

Ireland's capital city is more than just pubs (though they are undoubtedly a highlight of a visit) and Georgian townhouses. This revitalized and very walkable metropolis offers great shopping on Grafton Street and lively eateries in Temple Bar, plus masterworks in the National Gallery of Ireland and the imposing St. Patrick's Cathedral. Whatever you do, don't miss seeing the beautiful Book of Kells housed in Trinity College—and, if beer's your thing, visiting the iconic Guinness Brewery's museum before downing a pint. ⇨ *Chapter 11, Ireland.*

Logistics: The best way from Dublin to Cashel is a bus, which takes 2½ hours.

2 Days: Cashel and Cork

The awe-inspiring medieval Rock of Cashel is worth a day of exploring before continuing on a late-afternoon bus to Cork (90 minutes). Overnight in this vibrant university town before spending half a day wandering its charming streets; be sure to stop at the Crawford Art Gallery and English Market, perhaps lunching at one of the stalls. Make an afternoon excursion by bus (25 minutes) to kiss the Blarney Stone before catching a three-hour train back from Cork to Dublin to spend the night. ⇨ *Chapter 11, Ireland.*

Logistics: Dublin to Edinburgh is just a quick one-hour flight; Ryanair and Aer Lingus fly directly.

2 Days: Edinburgh

This striking city built on seven hills warrants a visit to see its majestic history-spanning architecture and lovely views. Start with a half-day exploration of Edinburgh Castle before walking the Royal Mile through the pre-18th-century Old Town to reach the Palace of Holyroodhouse (most famous as the home of Mary, Queen of Scots); the National Museum of Scotland's renowned collection is also worth a stop. Spend another day exploring the post-18th-century New Town, including the National Gallery of Scotland, with its Renaissance to postimpressionist paintings; if you have more time, a free bus connects the National Gallery to three other worthwhile galleries. ⇨ *Chapter 20, United Kingdom.*

Logistics: Hop on a 4½-hour train or 90-minute flight to reach London.

4 Days: London

One of the world's great urban areas is filled to the brim with historical sights, cultural happenings, dangerously good shopping, and culinary delights that reflect the multicultural makeup of the city. First-time visitors shouldn't miss the iconic sights: Big Ben, Westminster Abbey, the Tower of London, the National Gallery, the British Museum, and whatever other squares and museums personally appeal. Repeat visitors should check out

the latest exhibits at their favorites. You won't regret splurging on a first-rate theater, music, or opera performance and a memorable meal at one of the many fine restaurants. ⇨ *Chapter 20, United Kingdom.*

Logistics: Bath is a 90-minute train ride from London.

2 Days: Bath and Stonehenge

The stunning 18th-century architecture of Bath is reason enough to make this trip. Of course, the excavated Roman baths warrant a look, but you should also make time for strolling the evocative streets, catching a musical performance, and perhaps stopping for tea and a bun at the famous Sally Lunn's, dating from 1482. After an overnight stay (and maybe a relaxing dip in the Thermae Bath Spa), take a bus tour to mysterious prehistoric Stonehenge, 35 miles away, before spending a second night in Bath or back in London. ⇨ *Chapter 20, United Kingdom.*

Logistics: Cambridge is an hour from London by train.

2 Days: Cambridge

This exceedingly lovely university town is worth a visit if only to marvel at King's College Chapel, a sensational 13th-century Gothic masterpiece, and the art and antiquities at Fitzwilliam Museum.

TIPS

■ Though you'll need to fly to get between Ireland and Scotland, the rest of this trip can easily be done by train and bus.

■ If you don't want to spend the night in Bath, you can take a bus tour from London to see Bath, Stonehenge, and Salisbury.

■ London makes a great base for the short train rides to Bath and Cambridge; purchase your train tickets in advance on the busy London–Bath route to ensure seats and for better fares.

For the choicest views, set sail for a couple hours on the River Cam. If you want to tour any of the college buildings, plan ahead; public visiting hours vary between colleges, so check the Cambridge University website for opening times before you go, and consider taking a two-hour tour for the most access. ⇨ *Chapter 20, United Kingdom.*

GREAT ITINERARIES

SCANDINAVIAN AND BALTIC CAPITALS IN 2 WEEKS

You'll go by plane, boat, and bus to see the highlights of Scandinavia's four main capitals: Copenhagen's renowned museums, castles, and hip eateries; Oslo's watery views and magnificent Opera House; Stockholm's blend of medieval streets and trendy nightlife; and Helsinki's atmospheric churches and markets. Then it's on to two charming cities of the Baltic, Tallinn and Rīga, each with twisting streets and picturesque squares that will make you feel like you've stepped back in time. ⇨ *Chapter 15, Scandinavia.*

3 Days: Copenhagen

Start your trip in Denmark's cool yet cozy capital city. Spend some time strolling the huge pedestrian shopping street, Strøget, plus the side streets for lovely Danish design objects; tour the Christiansborg Slot castle; while away several hours at the National Museum; and explore some of the interesting neighborhoods, such as Christianshavn and Nyhavn. No matter what your age, if you visit in summer or around the winter holidays, the illuminated Tivoli park can be magical at night. And don't forget the food: even if you can't get into (or can't afford) famed eatery Noma, you can dine well at both the new-Nordic-cuisine restaurants and on the traditional *smørrebrød* open-face sandwiches.

Logistics: Fly from Copenhagen to Oslo in just one hour; Norwegian and SAS offer multiple daily flights.

2 Days: Oslo

Surrounded by natural beauty, the capital of Norway is also a top cultural destination. Don't miss seeing the Royal Palace; visiting the Rådhuset (City Hall), home of the Nobel Peace Prize; and hanging out at trendy Aker Brygge near the harbor, with its tempting selection of restaurants and shops. History buffs should take a ferry to Bygdøy to see the Vikingskiphuset (Viking Ship Museum), while modern art lovers will want to beeline to the Munch Museum. Before you leave, catch a performance at the modern and truly impressive Opera House.

Logistics: Either fly from Oslo to Stockholm (one hour; Norwegian and SAS) or, if you have time, take a beautiful six-hour train ride.

3 Days: Stockholm

Constructed on 14 small islands, historic Stockholm offers a medieval old town, pretty parks, and wonderful museums. Start with a trip to admire the views from the top of the 348-foot Stadhuset (City Hall) tower before heading to Gamla Stan and Skeppsholmen, the historic districts of your dreams, with twisting streets and quaint shops and cafés, as well as the stop-worthy Kungliga Slottet (Royal Palace). If the weather's nice, hang out or dine in the picture-perfect park Rosendals Trädgården.

Logistics: If you're a sailing fan, take an overnight 16-hour ferry from Stockholm to Helsinki (Silja or Viking Lines); if not, a one-hour flight's your best bet (Finnair, Norwegian, or SAS).

2 Days: Helsinki

It's easy to explore Helsinki's compact design-focused city center on foot. Clamber up to the green-domed Tuomiokirkko (Lutheran Cathedral) and gold onion domes of Uspenski Orthodox Cathedral, and stroll the chic shops of Esplanadi—plus don't miss the smoked fish and other delicacies on sale at Kauppatori (Market

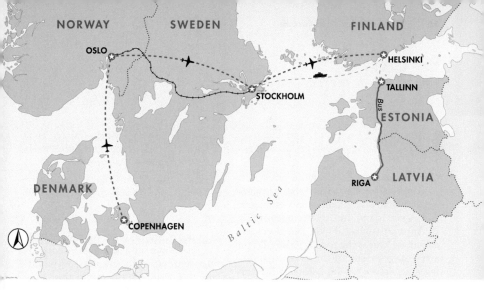

Square) and Vahna Kauppahalli (Old Market Hall). Spend an afternoon taking the 15-minute ferry over to Suomenlinna (Finland's Castle) for a scenic walk around the island fortress; when you return, go native and try a relaxing local sauna.

Logistics: The fast (90-minute) ferry from Helsinki deposits you a few minutes' walk from Talinn's charming old town.

2 Days: Tallinn

Talinn has one of the best-preserved medieval towns in Europe. Make your way through the cobblestone streets to visit some of its pretty churches, especially the Russian Orthodox Alexander Nevsky Cathedral and the 13th-century Holy Spirit Church, and seek out the marked view platforms for scenic overlooks out to the town's red tiled roofs. Be sure to relax with a drink or a meal as you people-watch in Town Hall Square.

Logistics: Rīga is about four hours by bus from Tallinn.

2 Days: Rīga

The appealing mishmash of medieval, art nouveau, and Soviet styles make the capital of Latvia an intriguing place to visit. The 13th-century Dome Cathedral has one of the largest organs in Europe, while the Rīga Art Nouveau Museum

TIPS

■ Though it's possible—and highly scenic—to travel within Scandinavia by boat, it's also slow. We recommend some time-saving options.

■ Scandinavia (especially Norway and Denmark) can be astoundingly expensive, but you can travel on a tighter budget if you plan carefully. The Baltic States are significantly cheaper.

■ It's possible to add St. Petersburg, Russia, onto this itinerary (it's an easy trip from Talinn), but you must get a visa in advance, which is not an easy process.

showcases objects from the late 19th and early 20th centuries. When you need a break, enjoy the cafés and restaurants in charming Town Hall Square, where you can admire the beautifully reconstructed House of Blackheads, originally built in 1334. If possible, make time for a show at the 18th-century National Opera House.

Logistics: When you're ready to leave, just hop on a flight to Helsinki or Stockholm to catch your plane back home.

GREAT ITINERARIES

BENELUX AND NORTHERN GERMANY IN 2 WEEKS

On this itinerary, you'll get a good mix of urban sophistication in Brussels, amazing artworks and quaint canals in Brugge and Amsterdam, and stunning shopping in Antwerp—plus, if you like beer and chocolate, this is the trip for you. Add on a few days in one of the most captivating cities in the world, Berlin—where an often-gritty history commingles with the dynamic art and culture of today—before wrapping up your trip in Hamburg, an often-overlooked harbor town on the Elbe River that has an appealing energy and must-see churches and museums.

2 Days: Brussels

Start in this cosmopolitan capital of the European Union, where cobbled lanes rub up against ultra-modern glass skyscrapers. You'll want to see the famed Manneken Pis, but also don't miss window-shopping in the Galeries St-Hubert and on the place du Grand Sablon, stopping to buy chocolate at one of the many tempting stores. Try to squeeze in a museum or two; you can't go wrong with the Musée d'Art Moderne and the Musée d'Art Ancien. ⇨ *Chapter 4, Belgium.*

Logistics: Hourlong trains run several times an hour between Brussels and Brugge.

2 Days: Brugge

With its adorable medieval streets, meandering canals, and perfectly preserved gabled houses, Brugge is lovely no matter what time of year you visit (and despite the persistent crowds). It's a city rich with museums, so fit in at least a few, such as the Groeninge and Memling, along with the Michelangelo sculpture in the Onze-Lieve-Vrouwekerk. The Begijnhof makes a peaceful retreat before you soak up the

scene in the Burg and Markt squares, ending with a well-deserved beer-and-mussels meal. ⇨ *Chapter 4, Belgium.*

Logistics: Trains from Brugge to Antwerp run about once an hour and take 90 minutes.

2 Days: Antwerp

Belgium's vibrant shopping capital, this old port town and diamond center is abuzz with trendy boutiques and world-class art. Besides shopping in the Oude Stad and Meir, you must see the MAS (Museum aan de Stroom), which relates the history of Antwerp; the painter Rubens's re-created house and studio at Rubenshuis; and the Bruegels at the Museum Mayer Van den Bergh. Cap it all off with a stroll along the river Scheldt and dinner at a hip eatery. ⇨ *Chapter 4, Belgium.*

Logistics: Trains from Antwerp to Amsterdam run about 10 times a day and take just over an hour.

3 Days: Amsterdam and Delft

Amsterdam's canals and often-crooked 17th-century houses never fail to charm. Besides the obligatory canal cruise and the Anne Frankhuis visit, you have your choice of top-tier museums, from the amazing Rijksmuseum to the comprehensive Van Gogh Museum to the contemporary Stedelijk Museum, while beer-lovers should beeline to the Heineken Experience. Then take your pick of churches (the 12th-century Oude Kerk and 14th-century Nieuwe Kerk are worth visits) and grab a pint and *bitterballen* in a historic brown café. If you can tear yourself away, take a day trip to Delft (one hour by train), the perfectly preserved 17th-century home of Vermeer. ⇨ *Chapter 13, Netherlands.*

Logistics: Hop a quick 90-minute flight from Amsterdam to Berlin. Buy your combined ticket for Museum Island at the less-visited Altes Museum to save time; the lines at the combined sales counter can be quite long.

3 Days: Berlin

The vibrant German capital is a fascinating blend of history and cutting-edge art, music, and design. You'll just get to scratch the surface of this spread-out city, so make sure you base yourself centrally, such as in Mitte, to more easily get around. Can't-misses include the Reichstag, Museum Island, the Kurfürstendamm shopping district, and just wandering the haunting memorials and lovely parks. Art mavens should check out the galleries of Mitte and Kreuzberg, while partiers will want to sample some of Berlin's legendary (and constantly evolving) nightlife. ⇨ *Chapter 8, Germany.*

Logistics: A 90-minute train ride takes you from Berlin to Hamburg.

2 Days: Hamburg

A 90-minute train takes you straight to Hamburg, home to Germany's biggest harbor, the Alster lakes, and the great Elbe River. Spend time wandering the 19th-century Altstadt (Old City); strolling along the down-and-dirty yet mesmerizing

TIPS

■ Fast, reliable trains connect the short distances between the cities of Belgium and the Netherlands, and between the cities of northern Germany. Buy tickets online in advance for the best prices.

■ It's possible to base yourself in Brussels, Amsterdam, and Berlin for this itinerary to maximize your time there and do some or all of the other destinations as day-trips since no place is more than two hours by train.

■ You must fly between Amsterdam and Berlin; otherwise, the train takes a full day.

Reeperbahn, packed with bars and sex clubs; admiring the expansive Freihafen Hamburg (Hamburg Freeport); and visiting St. Michaeliskirche (St. Michael's Church), with the largest tower clock in Germany and unparalleled city views. To get the best overview of this cosmopolitan city, be sure to fit in a boat tour on the Alster. ⇨ *Chapter 8, Germany.*

GREAT ITINERARIES

EASTERN EUROPE IN 2 WEEKS

This trip touches town in Turkey, Greece, and Croatia, taking you to some of Europe's most historic monuments, from the dazzling Blue Mosque in Istanbul to the unforgettable Acropolis in Athens, as well as some of the most stunning scenery, including the spectacular Aegean views from Santorini's volcanic caldera and the impressive panorama of Dubrovnik's red roofs. Add in stops to the lovely beaches of Mykonos and the historic town of Split, and you have the perfect combo of culture and relaxation for a satisfying vacation.

3 Days: Istanbul

A heady mix of old and new, East and West, Turkey's largest city definitely engages all the senses. You'll want to spend most of your time in the Old City (Sultanahmet), visiting the Ottoman and Byzantine monuments. The Blue Mosque, Aya Sofya mosque, and Topkapı Sarayı palace can't be missed, nor can the phenomenal Grand Bazaar. Also carve out time to stop by the sensational Byzantine frescos at Kariye Müzesi, the beautiful Süleymaniye Mosque, and the fascinating Istanbul Archaeology Museums. Finally, a trip to Istanbul isn't complete without a short cruise down the mighty Bosphorus and, if you have time, an invigorating scrub in a traditional hammam. ⇨ *Chapter 19, Turkey.*

Logistics: Turkish Airlines offers 90-minute flights from Istanbul to Athens several times daily; also check Aegean and Pegasus for sometimes very inexpensive flights.

3 Days: Athens

As you've no doubt heard, seeing the ancient Acropolis for the first time is an unforgettable sight. As for the rest of Athens, though . . . yes, it can be dirty and crowded, but it's also worth taking the time to seek out its magic. Spend time at the New Acropolis Museum and the National Archaeological Museum seeing the Acropolis treasures and other antiquities; wander past the whitewashed houses of Anafiotika; and explore the 19th-century streets of Plaka, stopping for a bite in one of the many *tavernas.* Plus, if you can squeeze it in, take a day trip to the mountainside ruins of Delphi, Greece's most sacred ancient site, showcasing equally dramatic views of the landscape below. ⇨ *Chapter 9, Greece.*

Logistics: Mykonos is just a 2½-hour ferry from Athens, or you can fly.

2 Days: Mykonos

Mykonos is often thought of as the party island. But it's also home to a fascinating old town with twisty streets, cubical whitewashed buildings, and tons of chic shops and (sometimes overpriced) restaurants from which to choose; unspoiled beaches inside scenic coves; and those famous blue-and-white windmills overlooking the Aegean. If you can tear yourself away, set aside a morning to take the 30-minute ferry over to ancient Delos, and try to catch a sunset at Little Venice, where bars perch right along the water's edge. ⇨ *Chapter 9, Greece.*

Logistics: Santorini is three hours by ferry from Mykonos.

2 Days: Santorini

This otherworldly island offers breathtaking views along the rim of its volcanic crater, or caldera, especially at sunset. Though you'll be tempted to spend all

your time staring at those mesmerizing views, be sure to walk the footpaths and steep stairs of Fira and Ia, exploring their shops and eateries; fit in a trip to the volcanic Black Beach and unique Red Beach; and if you're a wine aficionado, take a tour or rent a car to visit the island's wineries, renowned for their citrusy whites. *Chapter 9, Greece.*

Logistics: The only practical way to move on from Santorini is to fly; the ferry takes too long.

2 Days: Dubrovnik

You'll marvel at this stunning fortified city, renowned for its 13th-century walls and red roofs; climbing the walls to see the amazing views is the highlight of a visit here. All the main sights lie within pedestrian-only Stari Grad (Old Town), including the exquisite 15th-century Bishop's Palace; the 12th-century Franciscan Monastery, which includes the oldest pharmacy in Europe; and the 15th-century synagogue, Europe's second oldest. Be sure to spend one evening joining the *korzo,* a lively tradition of strolling the city, meeting in the outdoor cafés, and enjoying the open-air entertainment. ⇨ *Chapter 5, Croatia.*

Logistics: Take a bus (4½ hours) or drive (three hours) to Split; there is no train.

TIPS

■ Getting to Istanbul is relatively easy (if lengthy) from the U.S. After that, we recommend a combo of ferries, short flights, and buses or driving to reach the other destinations.

■ From Santorini, you'll need to return to Athens (45-minute flight) before flying on to Dubrovnik; during high season, Croatia Airlines offers direct 90-minute flights from Athens to Dubrovnik several times a week.

■ During the high season, you can fly directly from Split to most major European capitals.

---

2 Days: Split

Split's spectacular Old Town lives within the walls of Roman emperor Diocletian's Palace. Include a stop to admire the Cathedral of St. Dominius and the historic religious artifacts at the Museum of Croatian Archaeological Monuments. Also be sure to peruse the lively *pazar,* an open-air market that takes place every morning just outside the palace walls, and treat yourself to a seafood dinner prepared over a charcoal fire and served with the local Dalmatian wine. ⇨ *Chapter 5, Croatia.*

GREAT ITINERARIES

SWITZERLAND AND ITALY IN 2 WEEKS

This itinerary takes you to some of the most beautiful areas of Switzerland, from Lucerne's lovely lake and mountain views to Berner Oberland's iconic Swiss landscapes, with a dash of strolling, shopping, and museum hopping in elegant Zurich thrown in. Then it's off to two more world-class Italian beauties, the ravishing wine country of Tuscany and the unbeatable panoramas of the Amalfi Coast, with a second urban stop in alluring Naples and a touch of ancient history in Pompeii to balance things out.

2 Days: Zurich

The best way to see this grand city is simply to walk, following the banks of the Limmat River and admiring the medieval architecture of Zurich's Old Town and 13 guildhalls. Art mavens should hit the Kunsthaus, the Bührle's spectacular collection of impressionist and postimpressionist pieces, and Marc Chagall's lovely stained-glass windows in the Fraumünster church. Be sure to window shop along Bahnhofstrasse, Zurich's own Fifth Avenue, and spend at least one evening painting the town red in Zurich West, where factories have been transformed into hip restaurants, bars, and clubs. ⇨ *Chapter 18, Switzerland.*

Logistics: Trains run every half hour from Zurich to Luzern (45 minutes).

2 Days: Luzern

Medieval Luzern is one of the most charming towns in Europe. Stroll the lakeshore promenade for wondrous Alpine views, plus fit in a boat trip on Lake Lucerne to truly appreciate the stunning scenery. Head across Kapellbrücke, the oldest wooden bridge in Europe, and stop

---

TIPS

■ Take trains on the Switzerland portion of this trip to admire the gorgeous Alpine scenery; in Tuscany, you'll be better off with a car, but don't try to drive in Naples.

■ Your longest train ride will be from Interlaken to Florence; you'll need to switch trains in Spiez and Milan.

■ Some people will rent a car for the Amalfi Coast, but there are other options, including buses and ferries.

---

by Sammlung Rosengart to view fantastic paintings from late 19th- and 20th-century artists. In the evening, try to catch a show in the striking glass-and-steel concert hall, designed by renowned architect Jean Nouvel. ⇨ *Chapter 18, Switzerland.*

Logistics: The Luzern–Interlaken express train, with its panoramic windows, takes two hours.

2 Days: Berner Oberland

If you're seeking those amazing quintessential Swiss views—snowcapped mountaintops, lush waterfalls, and crystal-clear lakes—you've found the right place. Basing yourself in Interlaken, the main city, spend a day traveling to Lauterbrunnen Valley, home to more than 70 stunning waterfalls. For even more spectacular scenery, make your way to Mürren, birthplace of downhill and slalom skiing, with magnificent panoramic views, and to Jungfraujoch, home to Europe's highest railroad station. ⇨ *Chapter 18, Switzerland.*

Logistics: The train trip from Interlaken to Florence takes approximately five hours but requires two changes.

1

3 Days: Tuscany

After reaching Florence by train, rent a car and head straight into the Tuscan countryside. Settle into the Chianti region, from where you'll take day trips to the hill town of San Gimignano and medieval Siena (be sure to explore Siena's enchanting Piazza del Campo and Duomo). Spare a day to stop in Lucca, birthplace of Puccini, with its historic walled center and 99 churches, and Pisa for its famous leaning tower, Duomo, and Battistero. Make sure to leave time for wine tasting and for simply enjoying the gorgeous Tuscan scenery. ⇨ *Chapter 12, Italy.*

Logistics: If you keep your rental car, the drive from Florence to Naples takes about five hours, (and driving in Naples can be harrowing). The train takes three hours.

2 Days Naples and Pompeii

This most Italian of Italian cities has a lust for life, along with a splendid collection of churches and museums. Spend at least a couple hours at the legendary Museo Archeologico, with thousands of ancient items; leave the well-lit Museo di Capodimonte, with its stunning fine and decorative art collection, until late in the day. Take time to admire the royal apartments in the 15th-century Palazzo Reale; enjoy the views from the hilltop Certosa di San Martino; and stop by 12th-century Santa Chiara church to see its peaceful garden, before heading for pizza at Da Michele. If you've had enough of urban life, take an excursion to the famous preserved city of Pompeii; go late in the day to avoid the crowds. ⇨ *Chapter 12, Italy.*

Logistics: It can be convenient to have a car for the Amalfi Coast, but ferries run regularly in the high season. If you want the drive without driving, take a bus.

3 Days: Amalfi Coast

The unbelievably scenic cliffside villages of Positano, Amalfi, and Ravello lie just one hour's drive south of Naples. Base yourself in Positano or Ravello and explore the palazzos and gardens—if you can tear yourself away from the views. In Positano, stroll the seaside walkway all the way to Spiaggia di Fornillo beach. Leave a couple hours to drive or take a boat from Amalfi to the eerie green Grotta della Smeraldo. Amalfi, accessible by car or bus from Positano, has the Duomo and crypt to visit, and Ravello—which some say is the loveliest village in the world—has two Romanesque churches and lovely gardens. And those views . . . Alas, when you must go, bus it back to Naples or Rome to catch your flight home. ⇨ *Chapter 12, Italy.*

ON THE CALENDAR

From colorful winter carnivals and holiday markets to culture-packed summer music and arts festivals, Europe provides a treasure trove of events to plan your trip around. To increase your chances for fun, we've picked out the top happenings from countries throughout Europe; fitting any of them into your travels will make your memories just that much more special.

JANUARY

Hogmanay. Held in Edinburgh from December 30 to January 1, one of the world's largest New Year's celebrations starts off with a torchlight procession through the city, followed by traditional Scottish and international music, and capped off with an enormous fireworks display over Edinburgh Castle. ⊕ *www.edinburghshogmanay.org.*

Lux Helsinki. For five days in early January, Finnish and international artists light up Helsinki's dark winter sky with original light installations spread throughout the city, from the Olympic Stadium to Senate Square. ⊕ *www.luxhelsinki.fi.*

Tallinn Fire and Ice Festival. An old Estonian custom says that burning fir trees in mid-winter guarantees the return of the sun in spring. Today, in Tallinn, between January 4 and 20, Christmas trees are collected and made into sculptures that are then set afire, accompanied by drums and dancing. ⊕ *www.tallinnfireandice.ee.*

FEBRUARY

Carnevale Venezia. Celebrated in Venice since at least the 15th century, carnival-goers wear masks and elaborate costumes and attend balls throughout the city; the Grand Masked Ball, or Doge's Ball, is the main event. Carnevale runs from about February 15 to March 4 each year. ⊕ *www.carnevale. venezia.it.*

Nice Carnival. One of the largest carnivals in the world, the Nice Carnival takes place from February 14 to March 4 with colorful parades every night, including illuminated floats made from gigantic papier-mâché heads and real flowers, along with more than a thousand musicians and dancers. ⊕ *www.nicecarnaval.com.*

Wondercool Copenhagen. It's a full month of architectural city walks, cooking events, a fashion festival, concerts by Danish bands, and special art exhibitions throughout the Danish capital. ⊕ *www.wondercoolcopenhagen.com.*

1

MARCH

Budapest Spring Festival. During the last week of March and the first week of April, classical, opera, and jazz musicians from all over the world display their musical talents at this annual Budapest happening, the largest cultural event in Hungary. ⊕ *www.btf.hu.*

St. Patrick's Festival. This four-day event over St. Patrick's Day in Dublin is a taste of everything Irish, including an Irish Craft Beer Festival with brews and artisan nibbles, traditional Irish music, stand-up comedy shows, carnival rides, children's theater, Irish film screenings, and more. ⊕ *www. stpatricksfestival.ie.*

APRIL

Feria de Abril. The biggest festival in Andalusia, Seville's April Fair takes place the week before Easter Sunday and includes more than 1,000 brightly colored tents called *casetas*—most are private, but about 15 are open to the public—where you can drink sherry and dance flamenco. ⊕ *www.feriadesevilla. andalunet.com.*

Istanbul International Film Festival. Choose from more than 200 national and international films at this festival held for 16 days in April; screenings are held at venues throughout Istanbul. ⊕ *www.film.iksv.org.*

King's Day (Koningsdag). On April 27, the birthday of the Netherlands' king, deck yourself out in orange and join thousands of other revelers by drinking, eating, and making merry in Amsterdam's streets and on party boats floating down the canals. ⊕ *www.amsterdamkoningsdag.nl.*

MAY

Kunstenfestivaldesarts. For three weeks in May, more than 20 venues in Brussels showcase new and often avant-garde artistic works, from theater to opera to dance. Though many performances are in Flemish or French, keep an eye out for English-language shows. ⊕ *www.kfda.be.*

Prague Spring. The famed international music festival runs each year from May 12 to June 2, with a focus on classical music from both soloists and symphony orchestras, plus ballet and opera from the likes of the Bolshoi. ⊕ *www.festival.cz.*

Reykjavik Arts Festival. Starting in mid-May, this two-week-long arts festival presents theater, opera, dance, and concerts in both traditional and unconventional spaces—a recent highlight was a concert held totally in the dark—from more than 600 Icelandic and international artists. ⊕ *www.listahatid.is.*

JUNE	**Athens and Epidaurus Festival.** Between June and August, you can see ancient Greek tragedies—plus dance, theater, and film—in ancient venues. Festival locales include historic sites like the AD 160 Odeon of Herodes Atticus, on the slopes of the Acropolis, and the Ancient Theatre of Epidaurus, a two-hour bus ride from Athens. ⊕ *www.greekfestival.gr.*
	Bloomsday Festival. Named after Leopold Bloom of James Joyce's Ulysses, this weeklong Dublin festival runs annually from June 9 to 16 and includes literary walking and bus tours, a special Bloomsday Breakfast, and lectures on the famous Irish author. ⊕ *www.jamesjoyce.ie.*
	Wimbledon. The world's most famous tennis tournament usually runs from the last week of June into the first week of July. Either buy a tour package including tickets in advance, or get in the queue for the limited tickets made available each day. ⊕ *www.wimbledon.com.*
JULY	**Avignon Festival.** For three weeks each July, the 12th-century Popes' Palace, along with other historic venues, is the atmospheric setting for both classic and contemporary theater in the charming Provençal city of Avignon. ⊕ *www.festival-avignon.com.*
	Dubrovnik Summer Festival. From July 10 to August 25, the red-roofed Croatian capital's cobblestone streets, lively squares, historic churches, and elegant buildings play host to classical music, ballet, theater, and opera. ⊕ *www.dubrovnik-festival.hr.*
	Ljubljana Festival. Slovenia's main summer festival runs from early July to late August and highlights international ballet, opera, orchestras, and cinema, with most performances taking place outdoors. ⊕ *www.ljubljanafestival.si.*
	Salzburg Music Festival. For five weeks starting in late July, one of the world's most prestigious music festivals, featuring both classical and modern pieces, takes place surrounded by the lovely backdrop of Mozart's birthplace. ⊕ *www.salzburgerfestspiele.at.*
AUGUST	**Edinburgh International Festival and Edinburgh Festival Fringe.** Beginning in mid-August, the Scottish capital brings classical music, opera, theater, and dance to six major theaters and concert halls for three weeks. The Fringe, billed as the "largest arts festival in the world" and open to "anyone with

	a story to tell," takes place around the same time. ⊕ *www.eif. co.uk, www.edfringe.com.* **Stockholm Culture Festival.** This six-day festival in mid-August features more than 500 outdoor events in Stockholm's streets and squares ranging from music to street art to dance to visual art; everything's free of charge. ⊕ *www.kulturfestivalen. stockholm.se.* **Sziget Festival.** One of Europe's largest music festivals, Sziget takes place in Budapest, on an island in the Danube, and presents more than 100 live acts daily, from pop and rock to electronic, folk, jazz, and blues, over a week in mid-August. ⊕ *www.sziget.hu.*
SEPTEMBER	**Douro Film Harvest.** If you visit Portugal's Douro Valley during harvest time in mid-September, you can catch this weeklong food- and wine-focused film festival that also includes culinary discussions and tastings. ⊕ *www.dourofilmharvest.com.* **Oktoberfest.** Despite the name, the world's largest beer fair, held in Munich, starts in late September and runs for 16 days. Join thousands of beer drinkers in enormous tents, feasting on Bavarian food like sausages and pretzels and dancing to brass bands. ⊕ *www.oktoberfest.de.* **Zurich Film Festival.** A newer but increasingly important film event, this 10-day festival starting in late September screens more than 100 films from dozens of countries, featuring a mix of world premiers and classics, with a particular emphasis on German-speaking filmmakers. ⊕ *www.zff.com.*
OCTOBER	**Festival of Lights.** For 12 nights in October, Berlin hosts one of the world's largest light festivals, where monuments like the Brandenburg Gate and the Berlin Radio Tower are illuminated every night from 7 pm until midnight. ⊕ *www.festival-of-lights.de.* **Musica dei Popoli.** This truly international music festival, held the full month of October in Florence, focuses on ethnic and folk music and features more than 300 musicians from 80 countries. Here's your chance to hear music from Pakistan, Uzbek, Kashmir, and more. ⊕ *www.musicadeipopoli.com.*
NOVEMBER	**Lucerne Festival at the Piano.** World-renowned pianists strut their stuff in Jean Nouvel's famed concert hall for a week in mid-November. This is the third and final part of the Lucerne

Festival, following the classical music–focused festivals held for a week around Easter and a month in mid-August. ⊕ *www.lucernefestival.ch.*

Vienna Red Cross Ball. This baroque city's ball season, which runs through mid-February, kicks off with this charity ball held in the stunning Vienna City Hall. The ball is open to all with a donation; just don your finest duds and practice your waltz beforehand. ⊕ *www.wienerrotkreuzball.at.*

DECEMBER

Christmas Markets. Many European cities have their own Christmas markets, featuring stalls with local handicrafts, food, and drink—often mulled wine to help stave off the winter chill. Most begin in late November and continue until shortly before Christmas (though a few continue into early January). Some of the best are the markets in Barcelona, where hundreds of stalls sell handcrafted gifts; Dresden, whose Striezelmarkt is Germany's oldest; Brussels, which has not only market stalls but also an ice-skating rink and ferris wheel; Copenhagen, which has a bustling Christmas market inside Tivoli Park; Prague, whose lively Christmas markets are set up in Old Town Square and Wenceslas Square; and Vienna, where chestnuts, cookies, and mulled wine are highlights.

PLANNING A TRIP TO EUROPE

The more you know before you go, the better your trip will be. The purpose of this chapter is to help you plan a trip to Europe that lives up to your expectations. To that end, this chapter includes many websites, addresses, tips, and other useful pieces of information that have been amassed by Fodor's writers and editors in our 75-plus years of experience traveling on the Continent.

This chapter is divided into two parts. The first part gives you an overview of transportation to and around Europe. The second part is arranged alphabetically by topic and is filled with information on several important larger topics that will help you accomplish what you need to do in Europe. Much more country-specific information can be found in each chapter of this guide.

GETTING HERE AND AROUND

Except for those few Americans taking a trans-Atlantic crossing by sea, getting to Europe means flying. Whether you choose a U.S.-based or European-based carrier, you'll have a wide variety of airports from which to depart. Many European airlines fly out of New York's JFK International Airport, but increasingly, there is nonstop service from other major hubs, including Atlanta, Chicago, Dallas/Fort Worth, Seattle, and Los Angeles, among many others.

AIR TRAVEL

The main gateways to Europe from the United States are Amsterdam (AMS), Frankfurt (FRA), Paris–Charles de Gaulle (CDG), London–Heathrow (LHR), and Zürich (ZRH). From these airports it's easy to connect to almost any other destination on the Continent.

FLYING TIME
Flying time to London, the closest of these major gateways, is about 6½ hours from New York, 7½ hours from Chicago, 9 hours from Dallas, 10 hours from Los Angeles. Add an additional hour to Paris or Amsterdam; add an additional 90 minutes to Zürich or Frankfurt.

MAJOR GATEWAYS
AMSTERDAM
Located 17 km (11 miles) southeast of Amsterdam, Schiphol (pronounced "shh-kip-hole") is the main passenger airport for the Netherlands. With the annual number of passengers using Schiphol exceeding 50 million, it is ranked among the world's top five best-connected airports. Several hotels, a service to aid passengers with disabilities, train connections into Amsterdam and elsewhere in the Netherlands

and Europe, and a main office of the tourist board, Holland Tourist Information (in Arrivals 2 by Schiphol Plaza) can all prove most useful.

Contacts Amsterdam Schiphol Airport ⊠ *17 km (11 miles) southwest of Amsterdam, Amsterdam, Netherlands* ☎ *0900/0566 (€0.40 per min), 31/207940800 outside the Netherlands.* ⊕ *www.schiphol.nl.*

2

FRANKFURT

Frankfurt is Germany's primary air hub. The large airport has the convenience of its own long-distance train station, but if you're transferring between flights, don't dawdle or you could miss your connection. It's a big, confusing airport. Much simpler in layout and much more user-friendly is Munich, Germany's secondary air hub, which does have many services to North America and Asia but fewer ongoing connections to other European destinations. Assuming it finally opens, Berlin's new Brandenberg International Airport may become a major hub; until then, Tegel is handling Berlin's international air traffic.

Contacts Berlin Brandenburg *(BER).* ☎ *030/6091–1150 (€0.14 per min)* ⊕ *www.berlin-airport.de.* **Flughafen Frankfurt Main** *(FRA).* ☎ *01805/372–4636, 069/6900 outside Germany* ⊕ *www.frankfurt-airport.de.* **Flughafen München** *(MUC).* ☎ *089/97500* ⊕ *www.munich-airport.de.* **Tegel** *(TXL).* ☎ *030/000–186 (€0.14 per min)* ⊕ *www.berlin-airport.de.*

LONDON

Most international flights to London arrive at either Heathrow Airport (LHR), 15 miles west of London, or at Gatwick Airport (LGW), 27 miles south of the capital. Most flights from the United States go to Heathrow, with Terminals 3, 4, and 5 handling transatlantic flights (British Airways uses Terminal 5). Gatwick is London's second gateway, serving many U.S. destinations. A third, much smaller airport, Stansted (STN), is 40 miles northeast of the city. It handles mainly European and domestic traffic. Manchester (MAN) in northwest England handles some flights from the United States, as does Birmingham (BHX).

Airport Information Birmingham Airport ☎ *0871/222–0072* ⊕ *www. birminghamairport.co.uk.* **Gatwick Airport** ☎ *0844/892–0322* ⊕ *www. gatwickairport.com.* **Heathrow Airport** ☎ *0844/335–1801* ⊕ *www. heathrowairport.com.* **Manchester Airport** ☎ *0871/271–0711* ⊕ *www. manchesterairport.co.uk.* **Stansted Airport** ☎ *0844/355–1803* ⊕ *www. stanstedairport.com.*

PARIS

Charles de Gaulle (CDG) is France's major international gateway. At Charles de Gaulle, also known as Roissy, there's a TGV station at Terminal 2, where you can connect to trains going all over France. Travelers find CDG to be a confusing airport with poor services, so while it is convenient, it is not often a traveler's favorite. There is also nonstop service to Nice (NCE, the second-largest airport in France) from the U.S.

Contacts Aéroport Nice-Côte d'Azur ⊠ *France* ☎ *08–20–42–33–33* ⊕ *www. nice.aeroport.fr.* **Charles de Gaulle/Roissy** ☎ *39–50 in France (€.34 per min)* ⊕ *www.aeroportsdeparis.fr.*

ZÜRICH

The major gateway in Switzerland is the Zürich Airport (ZRH), but Geneva's Cointrin Airport (GVA) also has a fair number of international arrivals from the U.S. Most Swiss flights will fly via Zürich Airport, the airline's hub. In general allow yourself at least an hour to transfer to your connecting flight, but Swiss will often schedule flights with a much shorter connection time (and will sometimes hold flights for connecting passengers).

Contacts Cointrin Airport *(GVA)*. ☎ *022/7177105* ⊕ *www.gva.ch*. **Zürich Airport** *(ZRH)*. ☎ *043/8162211* ⊕ *www.zurich-airport.com*.

OTHER AIRPORTS

Many airports in Europe have nonstop service from the U.S., and many of those airports also offer wide-ranging connecting service to other destinations within Europe. These include Athens (ATH), Barcelona (BCN), Brussels (BRU), Budapest (BUD), Copenhagen-Kastrup (CPH), Dublin (DUB), Edinburgh (EDI), Helsinki-Vantaa (HEL), Istanbul-Atatürk (IST), Lisbon-Portela (LIS), Madrid-Barajas (MAD), Milan-Malpensa (MXP), Naples (NAP), Oslo-Gardermoen (OSL), Prague-Václav Havel (PRG), Reykjavik-Keflavik (KEF), Rome-Fiumicino (aka Leonardo da Vinci, FCO), Shannon (SNN), Stockholm-Arlanda (ARN), Venice-Marco Polo (VCE), and Vienna (VIE).

Contacts Aeroporto di Venezia *(VCE, also called Marco Polo)*. ⊠ *6 km (4 miles) north of Venice, Italy* ☎ *041/2609260* ⊕ *www.veniceairport.com*. **Aeroporto Fiumicino** *(FCO, also called Leonardo da Vinci)*. ⊠ *35 km [20 miles] southwest of Rome, Italy* ☎ *06/65951* ⊕ *www.adr.it*. **Aeroporto Internazionale di Napoli** *(NAP, also called Capodichino)*. ⊠ *7 km (4 miles) northeast of Naples, Italy* ☎ *081/7896111 weekdays 8–4, 848/888777 for flight info* ⊕ *www.naplesairport.com*. **Aeroporto Malpensa** *(MPX)*. ⊠ *45 km (28 miles) north of Milan, Italy* ☎ *02/232323* ⊕ *www.airportmalpensa.com*. **Aeroporto Portela** ⊠ *Lisbon, Portugal* ☎ *21/841–3500, 21/841–3700*. **Atatürk Airport** ☎ *212/463–3000* ⊕ *www.ataturkairport.com*. **Athens International Airport–Eleftherios Venizelos (ATH)** ⊠ *Spata, Greece* ☎ *210/353–0000 for flight info and customer service, 210/353–1335 for visitor services, 210/353–0515 for lost-and-found* ⊕ *www.aia.gr*. **Barcelona–El Prat de Llobregat** ☎ *902/404704* ⊕ *www.aena. es*. **Brussels Airport** ⊕ *www.brusselsairport.be*. **Copenhagen Airport, Kastrup** *(CPH)*. ☎ *(45) 32/31–32–31* ⊕ *www.cph.dk*. **Dublin Airport** ☎ *01/814–1111* ⊕ *www.dublinairport.com*. **Edinburgh Airport** ☎ *0844/444–8833* ⊕ *www. edinburghairport.com*. **Liszt Ferenc Airport** ☎ *1/296–7000 for customer service* ⊕ *www.bud.hu/english*. **Helsinki–Vantaa International Airport** ☎ *020/708–000* ⊕ *www.helsinki-vantaa.fi*. **Keflavík Airport** ⊠ *Reykjavík, Iceland* ☎ *425–6000* ⊕ *www.keflavikairport.com*. **Madrid–Barajas** ☎ *902/404704* ⊕ *www.aena.es*. **Oslo Airport Gardermoen** ☎ *06400 in Norway, 91–50–64–00 abroad* ⊕ *www.osl.no*. **Schwechat Airport (Vienna, VIE)** ☎ *01/70070* ⊕ *www. viennaairport.com*. **Shannon Airport** ☎ *061/712–000* ⊕ *www.shannonairport. com*. **Stockholm Arlanda Airport** ⊠ *Stockholm, Sweden* ☎ *10/109–10–00* ⊕ *www.swedavia.com*. **Václav Havel Airport** ⊠ *Czech Republic* ☎ *220–111–888* ⊕ *www.prg.aero*.

FLIGHTS

TO EUROPE

Major European destinations can often be reached on nonstop flights from many different airports throughout the U.S. Secondary destinations may require a change of planes in a European hub. But most destinations in Europe can be reached from New York with only one connection or less. Both European and American airlines fly to Europe, and virtually all the airlines that fly to major European gateways also offer connections to other European destinations themselves or as code-share flights with their partners.

Contacts Aer Lingus ☎ *800/474–7424, 353/818-365000* ⊕ *www.aerlingus. com.* **Air Berlin** ☎ *030/737–800, 866/266–5588 in U.S.* ⊕ *www.airberlin. com.* **Air Europa** ☎ *888/238–7672 in U.S., 902/401501 in Spain, 807/505050 in Spain* ⊕ *www.aireuropa.com.* **Air France** ☎ *04–95–29–45–45 Ajaccio, 01–45–46–90–00 Paris* ⊕ *www.airfrance.com.* **Alitalia** ☎ *800/223–5730 in U.S., 892/010 in Italy, 06/65640 for Rome office* ⊕ *www.alitalia.it.* **American Airlines** ☎ *800/433–7300, 0844/499–7300 in U.K.* ⊕ *www.aa.com.* **British Airways** ☎ *800/247–9297, 0844/493–0787 in U.K.* ⊕ *www.britishairways.com.* **Brussels Airlines** ☎ *516/296–9500 in U.S., 0905/609–5609 in U.K., 02/723–2345 in Belgium* ⊕ *www.brusselsairlines.com.* **Croatia Airlines** ✉ *Zagreb, Croatia* ☎ *01/481–9633 for info, 01/616-4581 for Zagreb airport* ⊕ *www.croatiaairlines. hr.* **Czech Airlines** (ČSA). ☎ *239–007–007 in Prague, 800/223–2365 in U.S.* ⊕ *www.csa.cz.* **Delta Airlines** ☎ *800/241–4141 for international reservations, 0871/221–1222 in U.K.* ⊕ *www.delta.com.* **Finnair** ☎ *0600/140–140, 800/950–5000 in the U.S.* ⊕ *www.finnair.com.* **Iberia** ☎ *870/609–0500* ⊕ *www.iberia. com.* **Icelandair** ☎ *0844/811–1190* ⊕ *www.icelandair.com.* **KLM Royal Dutch Airlines** ☎ *070/225–335 in Belgium, 0130/039–2192 in Australia, 020/474–7747 in the Netherlands, 09/921–6040 in New Zealand, 0871/231–0000 in U.K.* ☎ *800/618–0104 in U.S. and Canada* ⊕ *www.klm.com.* **Lufthansa** ☎ *800/645–3880* ⊕ *www.lufthansa.com.* **Norwegian Air Shuttle** ⊕ *www.norwegian.se.* **SAS** ⊕ *www.flysas.com.* **Swiss** ☎ *877/359–7947, 0848/700700 in Switzerland* ⊕ *www.swiss.com.* **TAP Air Portugal** ⊕ *www.flytap.com.* **THY/Turkish Airlines** ☎ *212/444-0849 in New York* ⊕ *www.turkishairlines.com.* **United Airlines** ☎ *800/864–8331 in U.S., 0845/607–6760 in U.K.* ⊕ *www.united.com.* **US Airways** ☎ *800/428–4322 for U.S. and Canada reservations, 0845/600–3300 in U.K.* ⊕ *www.usairways.com.* **Virgin Atlantic** ☎ *800/862–8621, 0800/874–7747 in U.K.* ⊕ *www.virgin-atlantic.com.*

WITHIN EUROPE

Flying can be the cheapest way to travel relatively long distances between destinations in Europe. Most intra-Europe flights are booked online and have stringent requirements regarding check-in and carry-on luggage. As in the U.S., flights are cheaper when booked in advance, carry myriad extra fees, and are usually nonrefundable; customer service may be difficult to contact directly and may be available only online. A few budget carriers in Europe require you to check-in online or pay a hefty penalty, something that may be less appealing when you are traveling without easy access to a printer—though some are starting to allow mobile boarding passes. Finally, some European discount carriers fly to distant airports. Paris-Beauvais, for example, is often used by European budget carriers but is 76 km (46 miles) north of Paris. Be sure you know the name and location of the airport to which you are flying. In many cases, the fares offered by these carriers—particularly when booked in advance—are far cheaper than what you will find from legacy carriers like Air France and British Airways. None of these carriers offers flights to the U.S.

Contacts **easyJet** ☎ *0871/244–2377* ⊕ *www.easyjet.com.* **Flybe** ⊕ *www.flybe. com.* **Germanwings** ☎ *0180/191–9100* ⊕ *www.germanwings.com.* **Jet2** ✉ *Ireland* ☎ *0871/226–1737* ⊕ *www.jet2.com.* **Ryanair** ☎ *0871/246–0000* ⊕ *www. ryanair.com.* **Smart Wings** ☎ *900–166–565 from Czech Republic (toll), 420/255– 700–827 outside Czech Republic* ⊕ *www.smartwings.net.* **TUIfly** ☎ *0180/1000– 2000* ⊕ *www.TUIfly.com.* **Transavia** ☎ *0900/0737 in the Netherlands* ⊕ *www. transavia.com.* **Vueling** ☎ *807/200100 (premium rate charged)* ⊕ *www.vueling. com.* **Wizz Air.** Wizz Air flies between Budapest, Barcelona (Girona), Brussels (Charleroi), London (Luton), Paris (Beauvais), Prague, Rome (Ciampino), and Stockholm (Skavsta). ☎ *90/181–181 in Hungary, 0906/959–0002 in the U.K.* ⊕ *www. wizzair.com.*

BOAT TRAVEL

Ferry routes for passengers and vehicles link the countries surrounding the North Sea, the Irish Sea, and the Baltic Sea; Italy with Greece and Croatia; and Spain, France, Italy, and Greece with their respective islands in the Mediterranean. Longer ferry routes—between, for instance, Britain and Spain or Scandinavia—can help you reduce the amount of driving and often save time. A number of modern ships offer improved comfort and entertainment ranging from slot machines to gourmet dining. See individual country chapters for more information on popular routes and ferry operators.

BUS TRAVEL

Buses can be a convenient and cost-effective way to move between smaller destinations in many European countries, but most longer bus journeys are less comfortable and not always cheaper than train trips. For information on specific worthwhile bus routes, see the individual country chapters.

CAR TRAVEL

The great attraction of renting is obviously that you become independent of public transport. Cost-wise, you should consider renting a car only if you are with at least one other person; single travelers pay a tremendous premium. Car rental costs vary from country to country; rates in Scandinavia are particularly high. If you're visiting a number of countries with varying rates, it makes sense to rent a vehicle in the cheapest country. For instance, if you plan to visit Normandy, the same company that rents you a car for a higher weekly rate in Paris will rent you one for less in Brussels, adding a few hours to your trip but at a significant savings.

Britain and Ireland in particular can be challenging places for most foreigners to drive, considering that people drive on the left side of the often disconcertingly narrow roads, many rental cars have standard transmissions, and the gearshift is on the wrong side entirely.

There may be some restrictions when taking a car from an EU country to a non-EU country, so always read the fine print on your rental documents carefully and inquire if there are any restrictions when arranging your rental. As Europe becomes more unified, these restrictions are less likely to cause you problems, but there are still some special requirements for renting or driving in some countries (mandatory extra insurance, for example), and these can add considerably to your costs.

Tolls are common, particularly in France, southern Europe, and Switzerland and can add considerably to your daily driving expenses, perhaps as much as €25 per day where they are charged.

CAR RENTAL

It is easy to rent a car in Europe but not always cheap. In most countries you must be 21 to rent a car. Rates with most major car-rental companies are based on a manual transmission car with unlimited mileage. You may have to pay considerably more for a car with an automatic transmission, and it may be a "full-size" as opposed to a regular-size vehicle.

Additional insurance is usually required in Ireland (Collision Damage Waiver, usually abbreviated "CDW") and Italy (theft and also CDW in some places) and may be required in other countries as well. Ask about additional required costs when making your initial rental reservation. Even in countries where it is not required, you may wish to carry some kind of insurance in addition to your own liability policy, and you should always double-check to make sure your personal auto insurance covers you when you rent a car abroad. Some people rent through a wholesaler to avoid having the sticker shock of extra charges since many of these companies include CDW and, where required, theft insurance in the original price quote.

If you're traveling with children, don't forget to ask for a car seat when you reserve. And ask about a GPS, which usually has an additional cost.

Depending on what you would like to see, you may or may not need a car for all or part of your stay. Since most parts of Europe are connected by reliable rail service, it might be a better plan to take a train to the region you plan to visit and rent a car only for side trips to out-of-the-way destinations.

DOCUMENTS

Though your driver's license will usually be recognized outside your home country, to be on the safe side, consider getting an international driving permit (IDP), available from AAA. These international permits, valid only in conjunction with your regular driver's license, are universally recognized; having one may save you a problem with local authorities.

Most border controls have been abolished within the EU (except in the U.K., Ireland, Scandinavia, and Greece), but it's important to realize that several countries in Europe (Switzerland most notably) are not EU members. Be sure to carry the documentation provided by your car-rental company when traveling between countries regardless of whether or not you expect to encounter border checkpoints.

GASOLINE

Gasoline is considerably more expensive in Europe than in the U.S. (about three or four times as expensive). Diesel is widely used and is often cheaper than regular gasoline, but be sure not to use it by mistake. Gas is often more expensive at stations on major motorways. Most of these large stations are open 24 hours a day, seven days a week. In rural areas, hours can vary, and most stations are closed on Sundays and at night. Most service stations accept major credit cards, and most are self-service; however—particularly on major motorways—some pumps may be automated and require a chip-and-pin card (⇨ *See Money for more information on these cards*). Regular U.S.-based swipe credit cards may not be accepted at these stations, especially outside of regular business hours.

PARKING

Parking regulations are strictly enforced throughout Europe, and fines are high. Many city streets have centralized "pay and display" machines, in which you deposit the required money and get a ticket allowing you to park for a set period of time. We cannot recommend renting a car if you are staying in a major European city. Instead, rent as you are planning to leave and explore the countryside.

RULES OF THE ROAD

Driving is on the left side of the road in Ireland and the U.K. In all other European countries, driving is on the right. Speed limits vary by jurisdiction and can be complicated, so it's always best to ask when you pick up your car. Seat belts are almost universally required, and in most countries it is illegal to talk on a handheld cell phone while driving. Drunk-driving laws are strictly enforced throughout Europe, and the limits on consumption are often much stricter than they are in the U.S.

Major Rental Agencies Avis ☎ *800/331–1212* ⊕ *www.avis.com.* **Budget** ☎ *800/472–3325* ⊕ *www.budget.com.* **Europecar** ⊕ *www.europecar.com.* **Hertz** ☎ *800/654–3001* ⊕ *www.hertz.com.*

Wholesalers Auto Europe ☎ *888/223–5555* ⊕ *www.autoeurope.com.* **Europe by Car** ☎ *212/581–3040 in New York, 800/223–1516* ⊕ *www.europebycar. com.* **Eurovacations** ☎ *877/471–3876* ⊕ *www.eurovacations.com.* **Kemwel** ☎ *877/820–0668* ⊕ *www.kemwel.com.*

TRAIN TRAVEL

PAYING

Cash and credit cards are accepted by all train ticket offices; credit cards are accepted over the phone and online. Just be aware that many auto-mated ticketing machines require a chip-and-pin credit card for purchases.

2

RESERVATIONS

Many high-speed trains require seat reservations, but in general reserving your ticket in advance is highly recommended. Even a reservation 24 hours in advance can provide a substantial discount. Look into cheap day returns if you plan to travel a round-trip in one day.

RAIL PASSES

If you're coming from the United States and are planning extensive train travel in Europe, check Rail Europe for Eurail passes. Whichever pass you choose, you must buy it before you leave for Europe. The Eurail Global Pass allows for travel in 24 European countries and includes unlimited first-class rail travel in all participating countries for the duration of the pass. The 24 participating countries include Austria, Belgium, Bulgaria, Croatia, Czech Republic, Denmark, Finland, France, Germany, Greece, Hungary, Ireland, Italy, Luxembourg, Netherlands, Norway, Portugal, Romania, Slovakia, Slovenia, Spain, Sweden, Switzerland, and Turkey. While Eurail passes are convenient, they are also expensive, so they may not be the most cost-effective way to travel. You should also explore whether a Select Pass (which allows you to travel for a certain number of days in three, four, or five countries) or a Regional Pass (which allows you to travel for a certain number of days in two or three—or in Scandinavia, four—nearby countries) or even a single-country pass might be the best option for you. Sometimes, advance-purchase individual rail fares can be a cheaper option.

Rail Pass Contacts BritRail ☎ *866/938–7245 in U.S.* ⊕ *www.britrail.com.* **Eurail** ⊕ *www.eurail.com.* **Rail Europe** ☎ *800/622–8600 in U.S., 800/361–7245 in Canada* ⊕ *www.raileurope.com.* **RailPass** ⊕ *www.railpass.com.*

Austria Train Contacts ÖBB *(Österreichische Bundesbahnen).* ⊕ *www.oebb.at.*

Belgium Train Contacts SNCB/NMBS ⊕ *www.b-rail.be.*

Croatia Train Contacts Hž Putnički Prijevoz *(Croatia Railways).* ✉ *Donji Grad, Zagreb, Croatia* ☎ *(385)1/3783–061* ⊕ *www.hzpp.hr.*

Czech Republic Train Contacts Czech Railways ✉ *Prague, Bohemia, Czech Republic* ⊕ *www.cd.cz.*

Estonia Train Contacts Edelaraudtee ⊕ *www.edel.ee.*

Europe Train Contacts Eurostar ☎ *0843/218–6186* ⊕ *www.eurostar.com.* **Thalys** ⊕ *www.thalys.com.*

France Train Contacts SNCF ☎ *36–35 in France (€0.34 per min)* ⊕ *www.sncf. com.*

Germany Train Contacts Deutsche Bahn *(German Rail).* ☎ *0800/150–7090 for automated schedule info, 11861 for 24-hr hotline 9€0.39 per min), 491805/996–633 outside Germany (€0.12 per min)* ⊕ *www.bahn.de.*

Hungary Train Contacts MAV Passenger Service ✉ *District V, József Attila utca 16, Budapest, Hungary* ☎ *06–40/49–49–49 for central infoline (local charge)* ⊕ *www.mav-start.hu.*

Ireland Train Contacts Irish Rail (*Iarnrod Éireann*). ☎ *01/836–6222* ⊕ *www. irishrail.ie.* Northern Ireland Railways ☎ *028/9066–6630* ⊕ *www.translink. co.uk/NI-Railways.*

Italy Train Contacts FS–Trenitalia ☎ *06/6847 5475 outside Italy (English), 892021 inside Italy* ⊕ *www.trenitalia.com.*

Latvia Train Contacts LDZ (*Latvia Railway*). ⊕ *travel.ldz.lv/en/ldz/ru-list.*

Netherlands Train Contacts NS–Nederlandse Spoorwegen/Dutch Railways ⊕ *www.ns.nl.*

Portugal Train Contacts CP ☎ *707/201280 outside Portugal, 808/208208* ⊕ *www.cp.pt.*

Scandinavia Train Contacts Scandinavia Rail ⊕ *www.scandinavianrail.com.*

Slovenia Train Contacts Slovenske železnice (*Slovenia Railways*). ☎ *(386) 1/29–13–391* ⊕ *www.slo-zeleznice.si.*

Spain Train Contacts RENFE ☎ *902/320320 for info, 902/109420 for tickets* ⊕ *www.renfe.es.*

Switzerland Train Contacts Swiss Federal Railways ☎ *0900/300300 (1.19 SF per min)* ⊕ *www.sbb.ch.*

Turkey Train Contacts Turkish State Railways (*Türkiye Cumhuriyeti Devlet Demiryolları*). ☎ *311–0602 (no area code required in Turkey)* ⊕ *www.tcdd.gov.tr.*

United Kingdom Train Contacts National Rail Enquiries ☎ *0845/748–4950, 020/7278–5240 outside U.K.* ⊕ *www.nationalrail.co.uk.* Trainline ☎ *0871/244– 1545* ⊕ *www.thetrainline.com.*

ESSENTIALS

ACCOMMODATIONS

Hotels, bed-and-breakfasts, rural inns, or holiday home or apartment rentals—there's a style and price to suit most travelers. Wherever you stay, it's a good idea to make reservations well in advance, particularly during the high season.

Most hotels and other lodgings require you to give your credit-card details before they will confirm your reservation. If you don't feel comfortable emailing this information, ask if you can fax it. However you book, get confirmation in writing and have a copy of it handy when you check in.

Be sure you understand the hotel's cancellation policy. Some places allow you to cancel without any kind of penalty—even if you prepaid to secure a discounted rate—provided you cancel at least 24 hours in advance. Others require you to cancel a week in advance or penalize you the cost of one night. Small inns and B&Bs are most likely to require you to cancel far in advance. Most hotels allow children under a certain age to stay in their parents' room at no extra charge, but others charge for them as extra adults; find out the cutoff age for discounts.

Our local writers vet every hotel to recommend the best overnights in each price category, from budget to expensive. Unless otherwise specified, you can expect private bath, phone, and TV in your room. *For expanded reviews, facilities, and current deals, visit Fodors.com.* Lodgings are indicated in the text by ⊡. Throughout Europe, lodging prices sometimes include breakfast.

2

APARTMENT AND HOUSE RENTALS

If you are staying in one destination, renting an apartment, where allowed, can be an affordable alternative to a hotel or B&B. Vacation apartments are especially popular in cities and resort areas. They range from simple rooms with just the basics to luxury apartments with all the trimmings. Some might offer full cleaning services and even include breakfast. The best way to find an apartment is through the local tourist office or the website of the town or village where you would like to stay.

Contacts At Home Abroad ☎ *212/421–9165* ⊕ *www.athomeabroadinc. com.* **Barclay International Group** ☎ *516/364–0064, 800/845–6636* ⊕ *www. barclayweb.com.* **Drawbridge to Europe** ☎ *541/482–7778, 888/268–1148* ⊕ *www.drawbridgetoeurope.com.* **Forgetaway** ⊕ *www.forgetaway.com.* **Home Away** ☎ *512/493–0382* ⊕ *www.homeaway.com.* **Interhome** ☎ *954/791–8282, 800/882–6864* ⊕ *www.interhome.us.* **Suzanne B. Cohen & Associates** ☎ *207/622–0743* ⊕ *www.villaeurope.com.* **Vacation Home Rentals Worldwide** ☎ *201/767–9393, 800/633–3284* ⊕ *www.vhrww.com.* **Villanet** ☎ *206/417– 3444, 800/964–1891* ⊕ *www.rentavilla.com.* **Villas & Apartments Abroad** ☎ *212/213–6435, 800/433–3020* ⊕ *www.vaanyc.com.* **Villas International** ☎ *415/499–9490, 800/221–2260* ⊕ *www.villasintl.com.* **Villas of Distinction** ☎ *707/778–1800, 800/289–0900* ⊕ *www.villasofdistinction.com.* **Wimco** ☎ *800/449–1553* ⊕ *www.wimco.com.*

BED-AND-BREAKFASTS

B&Bs can be a good budget option and will also help you meet the locals.

Reservation Services Bed & Breakfast.com ☎ *512/322–2710* ⊕ *www. bedandbreakfast.com.*

HOTELS

Most of the hotels we recommend have rooms with ensuite bathrooms, although some older ones may have only washbasins in the rooms; in this case, showers and toilets are usually down the hall. Throughout Europe, rooms and bathrooms may be smaller than those you find in the United States.

Many hotels in northern Europe do not have air-conditioning. This is particularly true of Germany, the Scandinavian countries and Baltic States, the U.K., and even parts of France. Hotels in warmer regions are more likely to have air-conditioning. Throughout Europe, twin rooms are more common than doubles, though both are offered throughout the region.

COMMUNICATIONS

INTERNET

If you're traveling with a laptop, carry a spare battery and adapter. So-called "hard" Internet connections (often called ethernet) are rarely available any longer. Wi-Fi, however, is available in almost all hotels, and wireless broadband coverage is widespread in cities. But it's not always free. This varies widely across the Continent. Estonia, for example, has almost universal, free Wi-Fi service, while large luxury hotels almost always charge a premium for any kind of connectivity. If you want to use Internet on your mobile outside of Wi-Fi areas, you can also buy a SIM card with Internet access (see Mobile Phones, below).

Contacts Cybercafes ⊕ *www.cybercafes.com.* **Wi-Fi Freespot** ⊕ *www. wififreespot.com.*

PHONES

Most calls (including local calls) made in Europe are charged by the length and time of day. Pay phones are becoming increasingly rare, and most require the use of prepaid telephone cards. Making a call from your hotel's room phone often results in a huge surcharge. For more information, see "Need to Know" in specific country chapters.

Access Codes AT&T Direct ☎ *0800/890–0011.* **MCI WorldPhone** ☎ *0800/279–5088.* **Sprint International Access** ☎ *817/698–4199.*

CALLING CARDS

Public card phones operate with special cards that you can buy from post offices, some newsstands, or on the Internet. To use a card phone, lift the receiver, insert your card, and dial the number. An indicator panel shows the number of units used. At the end of your call the card will be returned. Where credit cards are taken, slide the card in as indicated.

MOBILE PHONES

If you have a multiband phone (some countries use different frequencies from what's used in the United States) and your service provider uses the world-standard GSM network (as do T-Mobile, AT&T, and Verizon), you can probably use your phone abroad. But be warned: you will often be charged a high roaming fee, beginning at 99¢ per minute and going up to several dollars. These rates are becoming somewhat more reasonable, and T-Mobile in the U.S. recently announced that they will no longer add roaming charges for international data use and text messages (calls will still carry a small charge). Sending an international text message is usually a cheaper option on any U.S. mobile carrier, but be aware that fees abroad vary greatly (from 15¢ to 50¢ and up), and there's usually a charge for incoming messages.

You can purchase or rent a phone, or simply buy an international SIM from a company like Mobal or Cellular Abroad that you can use anywhere in the world, but these phones can be expensive.

If you just want to make local calls, consider buying a local SIM card in Europe (note that your provider may have to unlock your phone for you to use a different SIM card) or a cheap pay-as-you-go phone found at any post office or phone shop. You can then have a local number and make local calls at local rates. Many SIM cards also include data plans with Internet and texts. If your trip is extensive, you could also simply buy a new cell phone in your destination, as the initial cost will be offset over time.

■**TIP→** If you travel internationally frequently, save one of your old mobile phones or buy a cheap one online; ask your cell phone company to unlock it for you, and take it with you as a travel phone, buying a new SIM card with pay-as-you-go service in each destination.

SKYPE
Another option is to use Skype (⊕ *www.skype.com*), which allows you to make calls over the Internet. After downloading software, you can place no- or low-cost calls anywhere in the world with an Internet connection from your computer.

Contacts Cellular Abroad ☎ *800/287–5072* ⊕ *www.cellularabroad.com.* **Mobal** ☎ *888/888–9162* ⊕ *www.mobal.com.*

CUSTOMS AND DUTIES

You're always allowed to bring goods of a certain value back home without having to pay any duty or import tax. But there's a limit on the amount of tobacco and liquor you can bring back duty-free, and some countries have separate limits for perfumes; for exact figures, check with your customs department. The values of so-called duty-free goods are included in these amounts. When you shop abroad, save all your receipts, as customs inspectors may ask to see them as well as the items you purchased. If the total value of your goods is more than the duty-free limit, you'll have to pay a tax (most often a flat percentage) on the value of everything beyond that limit.

There are also restrictions on what you can carry to Europe and/or back into the United States. For the most part, these restrictions apply to food products (particularly meat and fresh fruits and vegetables but also some unpasteurized cheeses), controlled drugs, and firearms and ammunition. Some countries also have restrictions on pets; if you are traveling with your pet, be sure to contact the authorities in the country you are visiting far in advance to find out what those restrictions and requirements are.

U.S. Information U.S. Customs and Border Protection ☎ *877/228–5511 in U.S.* ⊕ *www.cbp.gov.*

EATING OUT

Most restaurants in Europe post their menus outside, so take a look before you enter. In many countries, restaurants offer two basic types of menu: à la carte and fixed-price (prix-fixe or *un menu*). The prix-fixe menu is usually the best value, though choices are more limited.

People in Europe—especially in major cities—often eat later than in the United States, though specific dining habits vary by country. See individual country chapters for more information on dining customs and cuisine.

PAYING

Credit cards are widely accepted in moderate to upscale restaurants but may not be as widely accepted in less expensive establishments and outside of major cities. Some restaurants may accept only chip-and-pin credit cards, which are not common in the U.S., for payment; in those cases, you'll need to use cash instead.

TAXES AND SERVICE

Most countries in Europe include all taxes in the menu prices, and many include service as well. Tipping is not as extensive as it is in the United States, but see individual country chapters for tipping information.

ELECTRICITY

The electrical current in Europe is generally 220–240 volts, 50 cycles alternating current (AC), but wall outlets differ regionally. Consider making a small investment in a universal adapter, which has several types of plugs in one lightweight, compact unit. Most laptops and mobile phone chargers are dual voltage (i.e., they operate equally well on 110 and 220 volts), so require only an adapter. These days the same may be true of small appliances such as hair dryers, but curling irons are much less likely to be dual voltage. Always check labels and manufacturer instructions. Don't use 110-volt outlets marked "For shavers only" for high-wattage appliances such as hair dryers. For more information, see "Need to Know" in specific country chapters.

Contacts Adaptelec. Adaptelec has information on electrical and telephone plugs around the world (search for "France" on the site for detailed info). ⊕ *www.adaptelec.com.*

HEALTH

If you take prescription drugs, keep a supply in your carry-on luggage and make a list of all your prescriptions to keep on file at home while you're abroad. You won't be able to renew a U.S. prescription at a pharmacy in Europe, but some drugs that are available only with a doctor's prescription in the U.S. can be prescribed directly by a pharmacist in Europe.

2

OVER-THE-COUNTER REMEDIES

Over-the-counter medications in Europe are similar to those in the United States, with a few significant differences. Medications are more often sold in boxes rather than bottles, and are sold in small amounts— usually no more than 24 pills. There may also be fewer brands and these are often different than in the U.S. Tylenol, for example, whose generic name is acetaminophen, is called paracetamol in Europe. More important, these medications are often sold only in pharmacies.

SHOTS AND MEDICATIONS

No special shots are required or suggested for any trip to Europe.

Health Warnings National Centers for Disease Control & Prevention (*CDC*). ☎ *800/232–4636 for travelers' health line* ⊕ *wwwnc.cdc.gov/travel.* **World Health Organization** (*WHO*). ⊕ *www.who.int.*

MAIL

Stamps can usually be purchased from post offices, from stamp machines outside post offices, and from newsagents. Some post offices are located within other stores, just as in the U.S. Allow seven days for a letter or postcard to reach the United States. Postal rates are generally higher in Europe than in the U.S.

SHIPPING PACKAGES

Most department stores and retail outlets can ship your goods home for a fee. Private delivery companies such as FedEx and DHL operate in Europe, but their services are expensive.

MONEY

Prices in Europe are often higher than in the U.S. because most countries include V.A.T. in their prices (a built-in value-added tax). Prices throughout this guide are given for adults. Substantially reduced fees are almost always available for children, students, and senior citizens.

ATMS AND BANKS

FEES

Your own bank may charge a fee for using ATMs abroad, and many banks in the U.S. charge an additional foreign-transaction fee of up to 3% on each withdrawal; the company processing the international transaction (most often the Cirrus or Plus system) generally charges a 1% fee of its own. Less often, the foreign bank you use may also charge a fee. Nevertheless, you always get a better rate of exchange at an ATM than you will at a currency-exchange office or even when changing money in a bank. And extracting funds as you need them is a safer option than carrying around a large amount of cash.

PIN NUMBERS

Readily found throughout Europe, ATMs offer the easiest and best way to get local currency.

Be aware that most ATMs in Europe are streetside and require you to insert your card; if the machine malfunctions or if you enter your PIN incorrectly and repeatedly, you'll have to go into the bank to retrieve it (this may mean returning during opening hours). Most ATMs in Europe accept cards from the Cirrus (which uses the Mastercard symbol) or PLUS (which uses the Visa symbol) system.

■ **TIP→** PINs with more than four digits are not recognized at ATMs in many countries. If yours has five or more, remember to change it before you leave.

USING DEBIT CARDS ABROAD

It may seem convenient to use your debit card for small purchases abroad. After all, that's what many Europeans do—at the grocery store, the coffee shop, and at the drugstore. They often do not use cash for small purchases, just as you do at home, but this is unwise when you are traveling. Although most banks limit your losses in cases of fraud and will eventually refund your money if your card is compromised, access to your funds may be limited for an extended period of time. It's best to use your ATM and/or debit card for cash withdrawals from bank ATMs only.

CREDIT CARDS

Major credit cards (MasterCard, Visa, and American Express) are accepted throughout Europe, though American Express may be accepted less often.

CHIP-AND-PIN CREDIT CARDS

Most credit cards issued in Europe are now so-called "chip-and-pin" credit cards that store user information on a computer chip embedded in the card instead of on a magnetic strip, which is the standard for cards issued in the U.S. Users are expected to know and use their pin number for all transactions rather than signing a charge slip, as is more often the case in the U.S. Chip-and-pin cards are not common in the U.S., though some companies issue them; more common are chip-and-signature cards, which can be processed through the same machines as chip-and-pin transactions but require a signature on the charge slip—but even these are not offered by all credit-card companies. While major credit-card companies in the U.S. will tell you that regular magnetic strip cards are still accepted throughout the world, you may find in practice that some places in Europe cannot or will not process your U.S. magnetic-strip credit card (this is most common away from major tourist areas). This is especially true in automated gas stations, in machines that sell train tickets, and in machines that process automated motorway tolls at unmanned booths. It's a good idea to carry enough cash to cover small purchases.

DYNAMIC CURRENCY CONVERSION

Dynamic currency conversion (DCC) programs are becoming increasingly widespread. Merchants who participate in them are supposed to ask whether you want to be charged in dollars or the local currency, but they don't always do so. And even if they do offer you a choice, they may well avoid mentioning the additional surcharges if you're charged in dollars. The good news is that you *do* have a choice. And if this practice really gets your goat, you can avoid it entirely thanks to American Express; with its cards, DCC simply isn't an option.

2

■ **TIP➜** Before you charge something, ask the merchant whether or not he or she plans to do a dynamic currency conversion (DCC). In such a transaction the credit-card processor (shop, restaurant, or hotel, not Visa or MasterCard) converts the currency and charges you in dollars. In most cases you'll pay the merchant an additional 3% fee for this service in addition to any credit-card company and issuing-bank foreign-transaction surcharges.

FEES

Although it's usually cheaper (and safer) to use a credit card abroad for large purchases (so you can cancel payments or be reimbursed if there's a problem), note that some credit-card companies *and* the banks that issue them add substantial percentages to all foreign transactions, whether they're in a foreign currency or not. Check on these fees before traveling.

PRECAUTIONS

Inform your credit-card company before you travel abroad. Otherwise, the credit-card company might put a hold on your card owing to unusual activity. Record all your credit-card numbers in a safe place. All major credit-card companies have general numbers you can call (collect if you're abroad) if your card is lost, but you're better off calling the number of your issuing bank; your bank's number is usually printed on your card.

Reporting Lost Cards American Express ☎ *336/393–1111 collect from abroad* ⊕ *www.americanexpress.com.* **Diners Club** ☎ *514/881–3735 collect from abroad* ⊕ *www.dinersclubus.com.* **MasterCard** ☎ *636/722–7111 collect from abroad* ⊕ *www.mastercard.com.* **Visa** ☎ *800/847–2911 collect from abroad* ⊕ *usa.visa.com.*

CURRENCY AND EXCHANGE

Most of the countries of Europe are members of the European Union, and many of those have adopted the euro, including Austria, Belgium, Croatia, Estonia, Finland, France, Germany, Greece, Ireland, Italy, Latvia, the Netherlands, Portugal, Slovenia, and Spain. However, several EU-member states have not joined the euro zone. These include Czech Republic (Czech koruna), Denmark (Danish krone), Hungary (Hungarian forint), Sweden (Swedish krona), and the United Kingdom (British pound sterling). Turkey (Turkish new lira), Switzerland (Swiss franc), Iceland (Icelandic krona), and Norway (Norwegian krone) are not EU members. Vatican City also uses the euro, though it's not a member of the EU. For more information, see "Need to Know" in specific country chapters.

Converting currency can usually be done at a bank or a currency-exchange booth, though often at rates less favorable than you would get from an ATM. Similarly, you can often convert your dollars into foreign currency before you leave home, though at a particularly unfavorable rate of exchange, even if your bank does not charge a separate fee. You can easily lose between 6% and 10% on each currency-exchange transaction, and this is usually much more than the typical foreign-transaction fee charged by a credit-card or debit-card transaction.

■ TIP→ Even if a currency-exchange booth has a sign promising no commission, rest assured that there's some kind of huge, hidden fee. And as for rates, you're almost always better off getting foreign currency at an ATM or exchanging money at a bank.

Currency Conversion Google ⊕ *www.google.com.* **Oanda.com** ⊕ *www. oanda.com.* **XE.com** ⊕ *www.xe.com.*

PACKING

Northern Europe can be cool, damp, and overcast, even in summer. You'll want a heavy coat for winter and a lightweight coat or warm jacket for summer. There's no time of year when a raincoat or umbrella won't come in handy. Southern Europe has more moderate temperatures in winter but can be extremely hot in the summer, though it can still be cold and wet in the winter. Particularly in cities, European men do not wear shorts as much as those in the U.S. unless they are hiking or in a resort destination. Europeans tend to dress up more than Americans, and in larger cities, dress can be very stylish, though this varies by the country; younger Europeans can be as casual in dress as Americans, however, so this difference may be decreasing. For travel to European cities, pack as you would for an American city: jackets and ties for men who plan to visit upscale places, casual clothes elsewhere; dresses and dressier shoes for women who plan to visit upscale places, casual clothes elsewhere. Always bring comfortable shoes for walking, since many European cities have charming yet uneven cobblestone streets. If you plan to stay in budget hotels, take your own soap and shampoo, though towels will be provided. Pack insect repellent if you plan to hike.

PASSPORTS AND VISAS

U.S. citizens need only a valid passport to enter most European destinations; for country-specific entry requirements, see the individual country chapters. (Turkey requires Americans to apply for a visa in advance of travel, but the whole process is electronic and can be done online.) If you're within six months of your passport's expiration date, renew it before you leave—nearly expired passports aren't strictly banned in most countries, but they make immigration officials anxious, and may cause you problems. Health certificates aren't required for any European destinations. For more information, see "Need to Know" in specific country chapters.

SAFETY

Most of Europe is considerably safer than the equivalent places in the U.S., but pickpocketing and petty theft (purse snatching and the like) is a persistent and growing problem in busier tourist areas.

Use common sense: when in a city center, if you're paying at a shop or a restaurant, never put your wallet down or let your bag out of your hand. When sitting on a chair in a public place, keep your purse or bag where you can see it. Don't flash fancy smart phones in crowded areas.

Since most ATMs are outside, be aware of your surroundings when withdrawing money. Store your passport in the hotel safe, and keep a copy with you. Don't leave anything of value in your car. Use licensed taxis in all destinations (ask your hotel if you have any doubt).

■ TIP→ It's fine to keep your cash, credit cards, and IDs in a purse or bag, just as the locals do, but be aware of your surroundings, and don't pull out a large amount of cash in public if you don't feel comfortable with your surroundings.

General Information and Warnings Transportation Security Administration (*TSA*). ☎ 866/289–9673 ⊕ *www.tsa.gov.* **U.K. Foreign & Commonwealth Office** ☎ 0207/008–1500 ⊕ *www.gov.uk/foreign-travel-advice.* **U.S. Department of State** ⊕ *www.travel.state.gov.*

TIME

England sets its clocks by Greenwich Mean Time, five hours ahead of the East Coast of the U.S. British summer time (GMT plus one hour) generally coincides with American daylight saving time adjustments. Most countries in western Europe are six hours ahead of the East Coast of the U.S. Countries in Eastern Europe are seven hours ahead. See "Need to Know" in specific country chapters.

Time Zones Timeanddate.com ⊕ *www.timeanddate.com.*

TIPPING

Tipping is done in most of Europe just as in the United States, but at a lower level than you would back home. Tipping at restaurants varies a bit more by country. For country-specific tipping information, see the individual country chapters.

V.A.T. REFUNDS

The prices for almost all goods and services in EU and non-EU countries in Europe include a Value Added Tax (or V.A.T.), which can be as high as 20% (more on some luxury goods).

When making a purchase, ask for a V.A.T. refund form and find out whether the merchant gives refunds—not all stores do, nor are they required to. If the store offers refunds, then you can claim a refund (less an administrative fee) for any goods purchased in the same store on a single day over a certain amount (which varies by country). Have the form stamped like any customs form by customs officials when you leave the country or, if you're visiting several European Union countries, when you leave the EU. After you're through passport control, take the form to a refund-service counter for an on-the-spot refund (which is usually the quickest and easiest option), or mail it to the address on the form (or the envelope with it) after you arrive home. You receive the total refund stated on the form, but the processing time can be long, especially if you request a credit-card adjustment, so most people opt for an on-the-spot refund even though the service fee can be a bit higher.

Be aware that you must usually show the receipt for your purchases and will sometimes be asked to show the purchases themselves.

V.A.T. Refunds Global Blue ⊕ *www.globalblue.com.*

VISITOR INFORMATION

For visitor information, see "Need to Know" in specific country chapters.

AUSTRIA

Vienna, Salzburg, Innsbruck

WHAT'S WHERE

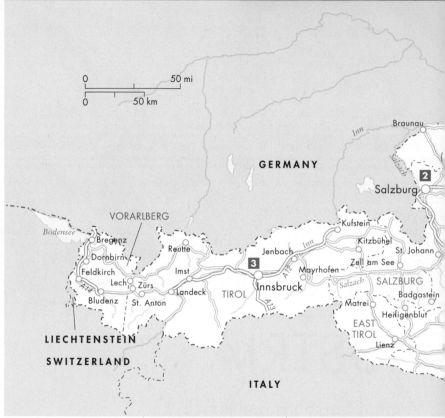

1 Vienna. In the country's northeast corner, Vienna intriguingly mixes old-world charm with elements of a modern metropolis. The city's neighborhoods offer a journey thick with history and architecture, peopled by the spirits of Empress Maria Theresa, Haydn, Beethoven, Mozart, and Klimt—but there is also space and renown for antitraditional structures like Friedensreich Hundertwasser's modernist Hundertwasserhaus. The famous coffeehouses are havens for the age-old coffee-drinking ritual.

2 Salzburg. Depending on who is describing this elegant city filled with gilded salons, palatial mansions, and Italianate churches, Salzburg is alternately known as the "Golden City of the High Baroque," the "Austrian Rome," or, thanks to its position astride the River Salzach,

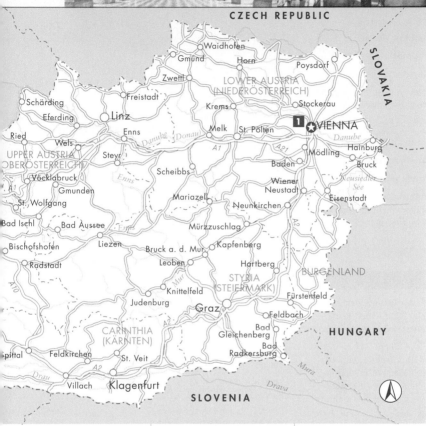

the "Florence of the North." What you choose to call this beloved city will depend on what brings you here, whether it be music, museums and architecture, the Trapp family, or simply the old-fashioned cafés, narrow medieval streets, and glorious fountains.

3 Innsbruck. The Tirol province is so different from the rest of Austria that you might think you've crossed a border, and in a way you have. The frontier between Salzburg and Tirol is defined by mountains; four passes routed over them are what make traffic possible. This is also where you'll find

the historic city Innsbruck: it's the Tirol's treasure house—historically, culturally, and commercially.

NEED TO KNOW

AT A GLANCE

Capital: Vienna

Population: 8,462,000

Currency: Euro

Money: ATMs are common; credit cards widely accepted

Language: German

Country Code: ☎ 43

Emergencies: ☎ 112

Driving: On the right

Electricity: 230v/50 cycles; electrical plugs have two round prongs

Time: Six hours ahead of New York

Documents: Up to 90 days with valid passport; Schengen rules apply

Mobile Phones: GSM (900 and 1800 bands)

Major Mobile Companies: A1, Hutchison Drei, T-Mobile

Vienna

AUSTRIA

WEBSITES

Austrian Tourist Office: ⊕ www.austria.info

Vacation Guide Austria: ⊕ www.tiscover.com

Vienna Tourist Information Guide: ⊕ www.wien. info/en

GETTING AROUND

✈ **Air Travel:** Vienna's Schwechat Airport is the largest, followed by Salzburg and Graz.

🚌 **Bus Travel:** Terminals are outside main railway stations. Buses are extensive, punctual, and clean.

🚗 **Car Travel:** In the countryside, a car rental is useful, but most major cities have traffic-free historic centers. Gas is expensive, and prepaid vignette-stickers are required for motorways.

🚆 **Train Travel:** Trains are fast and efficient, but Vienna's main station is under construction, so Westbahnhof and Meidling stations are filling in through December 2014.

PLAN YOUR BUDGET

	HOTEL ROOM	MEAL	ATTRACTIONS
Low Budget	€80	€15	Stairs to Cathedral Tower, €4
Mid Budget	€160	€25	Ticket to Kunsthistorisches Museum, €14
High Budget	€250	€120	Opera ticket, €185

WAYS TO SAVE

Eat at open-air markets. A huge variety of foods stalls offer inexpensive hot and cold dishes throughout the day. Sausage stands are a cheap and popular alternative too.

Book a rental apartment. For more spacious accommodations and a kitchen, consider a furnished rental—a great option for families or groups.

Travel with public transport. Buy daily or weekly passes. For cheaper, off-peak rail travel, see the Austrian railway website (⊕ www.oebb.at).

Look for concessions in museums. Seniors over 60 get reduced admission, and under-19s are usually free.

PLAN YOUR TIME

Hassle Factor	Low. Flights to Vienna are frequent, and Austria has great transport elsewhere.
3 days	You can see Vienna and take a half-day trip out to Abbey of Klosterneuburg and the northern Vienna Woods.
1 week	Combine a longer trip to Vienna with a one-day trip to the impressive Melk Abbey, the medieval town of Dürnstein and historic Krems, and another half-day trip to Mayerling, Heiligenkreuz, and the southern Vienna Woods.
2 weeks	You have time to spend in the provincial capitals, Vienna, Salzburg, and Innsbruck, and more time to discover "off the road" highlights, including trips to some of the most picturesque lakes and mountain valleys.

WHEN TO GO

High Season: May, June, and September are busy and expensive but offer major festivals and better weather. July and August are the hottest months in the east (less so to the west) but this is also when most Viennese take their own vacations.

Low Season: Late January and February are the best times for airfares and hotel deals—and to escape the crowds. But unless you are skiing, winter offers the least appealing weather. Snowfall, icy winds, and freezing temperatures can cause travel disruptions (more so in the mountainous west than in the dryer east).

Value Season: October is gorgeous, with temperate weather, good hotel deals, and lots of cultural events. By November temperatures start to drop. Late March and April are good months to visit, before the masses arrive but when snows are nearly gone and springtime activities are abuzz.

BIG EVENTS

April: Salzburg's Easter Festival offers great classical music off-season. ⊕ *www.osterfestspiele-salzburg.at*

May: Expect glamour at Vienna's fantastic Life Ball. ⊕ *www.lifeball.org*

December: Advent is magical; town squares are transformed into glittering fairytale scenes. ⊕ *www.austria. info.winter-holidays*

January–February: *Fasching* (carnival) offers glitzy balls in Vienna. ⊕ *www.ballkalender.cc*

READ THIS

■ *A Nervous Splendor,* Frederic Morton. Portrays significant moments in Austria's history.

■ *The Story of the Trapp Family Singers,* Maria Augusta Trapp. The *Sound of Music* memoir.

■ *The Hare with Amber Eyes,* Edmund De Waal. A memoir/detective story.

WATCH THIS

■ *Before Sunrise.* A couple meet on a train and have a brief romantic adventure in Vienna.

■ *Immortal Beloved.* After Beethoven dies, a romance is revealed.

■ *The Third Man.* Carol Reed's timeless spy thriller in postwar Vienna.

EAT THIS

■ **Tafelspitz:** boiled beef, served with apple and horseradish sauce

■ **Wienerschnitzel:** pan-fried, breaded veal cutlet

■ **Goulash:** paprika-spiced, beef stew

■ **Kaiserschmarrn:** dessert made of potato pancakes, with stewed plum sauce

■ **Salzburger Nockerln:** sweet, light, and fluffy soufflé dessert

■ **Käsespätzle:** macaroni-and-cheese mountain style

A "blast from the past" is how one recent visitor described her journey through Austria. It remains, she explained, a place where children laugh at marionette shows in the parks, couples linger for hours over pastries at gilt-ceiling cafés, and Lipizzan stallions dance to Mozart minuets—in other words, Austria is a country that has not forgotten the elegance of a time gone by.

In a way, this is true—but look beyond the postcard clichés of dancing white horses, the Vienna Boys Choir, and *The Sound of Music,* and you'll find a conservative-mannered yet modern country, one of Europe's richest, in which the juxtaposition of old and new often creates excitement. Vienna has its sumptuous palaces, but it is also home to an assemblage of UN organizations housed in a wholly modern complex. Salzburg may be known for its high-baroque architecture, but it also showcases avant-garde art in its Museum de Moderne. By no means is the country frozen in a time warp: rather, it is the contrast between the old and the new that makes Austria such a fascinating place to visit.

Where should you start? There's no question, really. Vienna's spectacular historical and artistic heritage—exemplified by the legacies of Beethoven, Freud, Klimt, and Mahler—remains to lure travelers. A fascinating mélange of Apfelstrudel and psychoanalysis, Schubert and sausages, Vienna possesses a definite old-world charm that natives would be the last to underplay. The sights here are not just the best in Austria, they're some of the most impressive in Europe. The grand Kunsthistorisches Museum holds one of the greatest art collections anywhere. The Staatsoper is one of the continent's finest opera houses. Schönbrunn Palace is indicative of the glories of Imperial Austria.

But as with most countries, the capital is only a small part of what Austria has to offer. A grand tour of the country reveals considerably more faces of Austria than the nine provinces would suggest. And no tour of Austria is complete without a visit to Salzburg, home every summer to one of the world's ritziest music festivals. As far as architecture goes, Salzburg's many fine buildings blend into a harmonious whole. Perhaps nowhere else in the world is there so cohesive a flowering of baroque splendor. You've seen many of these sights in *The Sound of Music,* but they are even more beautiful in person. Make sure, however, not to miss world-class art collections such as the Salzburg Museum.

As the hub of the Alps, Innsbruck beckons skiers to explore the resorts of Lech, St. Anton, and Kitzbuhel. The charming old-world aspect of Innsbruck has remained virtually intact, and includes ample evidence of its baroque lineage. The skyline encircling the center suffers somewhat from high-rises, but the heart—the Altstadt, or Old City—remains much as it was 400 years ago. The protective vaulted arcades along main thoroughfares, the tiny passageways giving way to noble

TOP REASONS TO GO

World of Music. Feel the spirit of 1,300 years of musical history as you listen to the music of Wolfgang Amadeus Mozart, the greatest composer who ever lived, in Salzburg's Mirabell Palace. Or delight your eyes and ears with a night out at Vienna's Staatsoper or Musikverein to experience what secured it the title "heart of the music world."

Ride the Ringstrasse. Hop on streetcar No. 1 or No. 2 and travel full circle along Vienna's best-known avenue. Those monumental buildings along it reflect the imperial splendor of yesteryear.

Kunsthistorisches Museum. In Vienna, enjoy the classic collection of fine art, including the best of Brueghel, Titian, Rembrandt, and Rubens, at Austria's leading museum.

Schönbrunn Palace. Rococo romantics and Habsburg acolytes should step back in time and spend a half day experiencing the Habsburgs' former summer home in Vienna.

An extended coffee break. Savor the true flavor of Vienna at some of its great café landmarks. Every afternoon around 4, the coffee-and-pastry ritual of *Kaffeejause* takes place from one end of the city to the other. For historical overtones, head for the Café Central, the opulent Café Landtmann, or elegant Café Sacher.

The view from Fortress Hohensalzburg: Go up to the fortress on the peak and see what visitors to Salzburg enjoy so much—the soul-stirring combination of gorgeous architecture in a stunning natural location.

Medieval city: After exploring the Salzburg's grand churches and squares, cross the river Salzach to take in the completely different atmosphere of the narrow 16th-century Steingasse, where working people once lived, and shops, galleries, and clubs now beckon.

Inviting Innsbruck. A city that preserves the charm of ancient times, Innsbruck has everything to offer: interesting culture, stellar restaurants, and trendy nightclubs.

3

squares, and the ornate restored houses all contribute to an unforgettable picture.

WHEN TO GO

Austria has two main tourist times: spring and early fall. The weather usually turns glorious around Easter and holds until about mid-October, sometimes later. Because much of the country remains "undiscovered," you'll usually find crowds only in the major cities and resorts. May and early June, September, and October are the most pleasant months for travel, when there is less demand for restaurant tables and hotel prices tend to be lower. A foreign invasion takes place between Christmas and New Year's Day and over the long Easter weekend, and hotel rooms in Vienna are then at a premium.

Austria has four distinct seasons, all fairly mild. But because of altitudes and the Alpine divide, temperatures and dampness vary considerably from one part of the country to another; for example, northern Austria's winter is often overcast and dreary, while the southern half of the country basks in sunshine. The eastern part of the country, especially Vienna and the areas near the Czech border, can become bitterly cold in winter. The *Föhn* is a wind that makes the country as a whole go haywire. It comes from the south, is warm, and announces itself by clear air, blue skies, and long wisps of cloud. Whatever the reason, the Alpine people (all the way to Vienna) begin acting up; some become obnoxiously aggressive, others depressive, many people have headaches, and (allegedly) accident rates rise. The Föhn breaks with clouds and rain.

GETTING HERE AND AROUND

AIR TRAVEL

Austria's major air gateway is Vienna's Schwechat Airport and the only one with nonstop service from the U.S. Salzburg Airport is Austria's second-largest airport. Two other airports you might consider, depending on where in Austria you intend to travel, are Bratislava's M. R. Stefanik international airport in neighboring Slovakia, and Munich's airport, not far from Salzburg. Bratislava is about 60 km (36 miles) east of Vienna and is the hub for RyanAir and Sky Europe, two budget carriers with connections to several European cities. Frequent buses can take you from Bratislava airport to Vienna in an hour. Consider Munich if your destination is Salzburg or Innsbruck.

Contacts M. R. Stefanik Airport (Bratislava, BTS) ☎ *421/233–0333–53 from outside of Slovakia.* **Munich Airport International (MUC)** ☎ *49/899–7500 from outside Germany.* **Salzburg Airport (SZG)** ☎ *0662/85800.* **Schwechat Airport (Vienna, VIE)** ☎ *01/70070* ⊕ *www.viennaairport.com.*

BUS TRAVEL

Austria has an extensive national network of buses run by the national postal and railroad services. Where Austrian trains don't go, buses do, and you'll find the railroad and post-office buses (bright yellow for easy recognition) in even remote regions carrying passengers as well as mail. You can get tickets on the bus, and in the off-season there is no problem getting a seat; on routes to favored ski areas, though, reservations are essential during holiday periods. Bookings can be handled at the ticket office (there's one in most towns with bus service) or by travel agents. In most communities bus routes begin and end at or near the railroad station, making transfers easy.

Contacts Post und Bahn ☎ *01/71101.*

CAR TRAVEL

If your plans are to see Vienna and one or two other urban destinations, you're better off saving yourself the hassles and added expense of driving, and take the train. Bear in mind the bumper-to-bumper traffic on most of the roads connecting the major cities and the constant headache of finding a place to park. But if your plan is a more leisurely tour of the country, including back roads and off-the-beaten-track destinations, then car rental is certainly an option. Roads in Austria are excellent and well maintained.

TRAIN TRAVEL

Austrian train service is excellent: it's fast and, for Western Europe, relatively inexpensive, particularly if you take advantage of discount fares. Austrian Federal Railways trains are identifiable by the letters that precede the train number on the timetables and posters. The IC (InterCity) or EC (EuroCity) trains are fastest.

Contacts ÖBB (Österreichische Bundesbahnen) ⊕ *www.oebb.at.*

HOTELS

You can live like a king in a real castle in Austria or get by on a modest budget. Starting at the lower end, you can find a room in a private house or on a farm. Next up the line come the simpler pensions, many of them identified as a *Frühstückspensionen* (bed-and-breakfasts). Then come *Gasthäuser,* the simpler country inns. Fancier pensions in cities can often cost as much as hotels; the difference lies in the services they offer. Most pensions, for example, do not staff the front desk around the clock. Among the hotels you can find accommodations ranging from the most modest, with a shower and toilet down the hall, to the most elegant, with every possible amenity. Increasingly, more and more hotels in the lower to middle price range include breakfast with the basic room charge, but check when booking. Room rates for hotels in the rural countryside often include breakfast and one other meal (in rare cases, all three meals are included).

RESTAURANTS

When dining out, you'll get the best value at simpler restaurants. Most post menus with prices outside. If you begin with the *Würstelstand* (sausage vendor) on the street, the next category would be the *Imbiss-Stube,* for simple, quick snacks. Many meat stores serve soups and a daily special at noon; a blackboard menu will be posted outside. A number of cafés also offer lunch, but watch the prices; some can turn out to be more expensive than restaurants. *Gasthäuser* are simple restaurants or country inns. Austrian hotels have some of the best restaurants in the country, often with outstanding chefs. With migration from Turkey and Northern Africa on the rise, thousands of small kebab restaurants have set up shop all over Austria, offering both Middle Eastern fare and sometimes pizza at a reasonable rate.

MEALS AND MEALTIMES

Besides the normal three meals—*Frühstück* (breakfast), *Mittagessen* (lunch), and *Abendessen* (dinner)—Austrians sometimes throw in a few snacks in between, or forego a meal for a snack. The typical day begins with an early continental breakfast of rolls and coffee. *Gabelfrühstück,* normally served a little later in the morning, is a slightly more substantial breakfast with eggs or cold meat. A main meal is usually served between noon and 2, and an afternoon *Jause* (coffee with cake) is taken at teatime. Unless you are dining out, a light supper ends the day, usually between 6 and 9, but tending toward the later hour. Many restaurant kitchens close in the afternoon, but some post a notice saying, "durchgehend warme Küche," meaning that hot food is available even between regular mealtimes. In Vienna some restaurants go on serving until 1 and 2 am, a tiny number also through the night. The rest of Austria is more conservative.

WINES, BEER, AND SPIRITS

Austrian wines range from unpretentious *Heurigen* whites to world-class varietals. Look for the light, fruity white *Grüner Veltliner*, intensely fragrant golden *Traminer*, full-bodied red *Blaufränkisch*, and the lighter red *Zweigelt*. Sparkling wine is called *Sekt*, some of the best coming from the Kamptal region northwest of Vienna. Some of the best sweet dessert wines in the world (*Spätlesen*) come from Burgenland. Austrian beer rivals that of Germany for quality. Each area has its own brewery and local beer that people are loyal to. A specialty unique to Austria is the dark, sweet *Dunkles* beer. Look for Kaiser Doppelmalz in Vienna. *Schnapps* is an after-dinner tradition in Austria; many restaurants offer several varieties to choose from.

HOTEL AND RESTAURANT PRICES

Prices in the restaurant reviews are the average cost of a main course at dinner or, if dinner is not served, at lunch; taxes and service charges are generally included. Prices in the hotel reviews are the lowest cost of a standard double room in high season, excluding taxes, service charges, and meal plans.

PLANNING YOUR TIME

If you're picking just one place in Austria to visit, there's no question that it should be Vienna. Austria's vibrant capital city has more than enough to captivate you for a week or more, but train service is so good here that you can take quick jaunts to almost anywhere else in the country with ease. On the other hand, if you're just looking to add a taste of Austria to a European adventure, you might find Vienna to be a little out of the way; if you happen to be in southern Germany, Salzburg makes a convenient side trip from Munich. (Many people use that city's airport when they are headed to Salzburg.) From Switzerland and Italy, Innsbruck can be a great excursion.

VIENNA

One of the great capitals of Europe, Vienna was for centuries the main stamping grounds for the Habsburg rulers of the Austro-Hungarian Empire. The empire is long gone, but many reminders of the city's imperial heyday remain, carefully preserved by the tradition-loving Viennese. When it comes to the arts, the glories of the past are particularly evergreen, thanks to the cultural legacy created by the many artistic geniuses nourished here.

PLANNING YOUR TIME

Culturally, high season in Vienna is May, June, and September, when festivals, marathons, concerts, and operas are in full swing. The ball season December to February offers everyone a chance to brush up on his or her footwork, and the many Christmas markets attract crowds from all over the world.

GETTING HERE AND AROUND

AIR TRAVEL

The City Airport Train (CAT) provides service from Schwechat to downtown Vienna for €8 (single ticket); the trip takes about 16 minutes. Travel into the city on the local S-bahn takes about 25 minutes and costs €4.50. Another cheap option is the fleet of buses operated by Vienna Airport Lines, which has separate routes to the city center at Schwedenplatz (20 minutes) and to the Westbahnhof (45 minutes). Buses operate every 30 minutes between 5 am and 12:30 am, and the fare is €8 each way. A taxi to the city center will charge between €33 and €37.

Contacts **CAT** ⊕ *www.cityairporttrain.com.* **S-bahn** ⊕ *www.schnellbahn-wien.at.*

BUS TRAVEL

International long-distance bus services arrive either at the Südbahnhof (south railway station) on the Gürtel or at the large Erdbergstrasse bus station. Most postal (local) and railroad buses arrive at either a railway station or the Wien Mitte-Landstrasse Bahnhof located behind the Hotel Hilton on Stadtpark.

Contacts **Vienna Bus** ⊕ *www.wienerlinien.at.*

CAR TRAVEL

On highways from points south or west or from Vienna's airport, "Zentrum" signs clearly mark the route to the center of Vienna. Traffic congestion within Vienna is not as bad as in some places, but driving to in-town destinations generally takes longer than public transportation does. In the city a car is a burden, and public transportation is always the better bet—it's clean, reliable, and easy to use.

PUBLIC TRANSIT TRAVEL

Vienna's public transportation system is fast, clean, safe, and easy to use. Five subway (U-bahn) lines, whose stations are prominently marked with blue "U" signs, crisscross the city. The most famous tram lines are No. 1, which travels the great Ringstrasse avenue clockwise, and No. 2, which travels it counterclockwise; each offers a cheap way to admire the glories of Vienna's 19th-century Ringstrasse monuments. Where streetcars don't run, buses (*Autobusse*) do. Buy single tickets for €2.20 from dispensers on the streetcar or bus; you'll need exact change for the former. The ticket machines (labeled "VOR-Fahrkarten") at subway stations give change. As with most transport systems in European cities, it is essential to validate your ticket. You'll find the validation machines on all buses, trams, and at the entrance of each U-bahn station.

Contacts **Wiener Linien** ☎ *01/790–9100* ⊕ *www.wienerlinien.at.*

TRAIN TRAVEL

Vienna's railway system is undergoing an extensive overhaul. By 2015, the former Südbahnhof will have been converted into the city's main railway station for national and international travel. In the meantime, trains from Germany, Switzerland, and western Austria arrive at the Westbahnhof (west station), located on Europaplatz. If you're coming

from Italy or Hungary, you'll generally arrive at the temporary Meidling Bahnhof. There are currently two stations for trains to and from Prague and Warsaw: Wien Praterstern Bahnhof and Franz-Josef Bahnhof.
Train Contacts Franz-Josef Bahnhof ⊠ *Julius-Tandler-Pl. 3, 9th District/ Alsergrund.* **Westbahnhof** ⊠ *Europapl. 2, 15th District/Fünfhaus.* **Wien-Mitte/ Landstrasse** ⊠ *Landstrasser Hauptstr. 1c, 3rd District/Landstrasse* ☎ *01/05711.* **Wien Praterstern Bahnhof** ⊠ *Lassallestr., 2nd District/Leopoldstadt.*

TOURS
When you're pressed for time, a good way to see the highlights of Vienna is via a sightseeing bus tour, which gives you a light once-over of the heart of the city and allows a closer look at Schönbrunn and Belvedere palaces. You can cover almost the same territory on your own by taking either tram No. 1 or 2 around the Ring and then walking through the heart of the city. For tours, there are a couple of reputable firms: Vienna Sightseeing Tours and Cityrama Sightseeing.
Contacts Cityrama Sightseeing ⊠ *Opernpassage, 1st District* ☎ *01/504–7500* ⊕ *www.cityrama.at.* **Vienna Sightseeing Tours** ⊠ *Weyringerg. 28A, 4th District/ Wieden* ☎ *01/712–4683–0* ⊕ *www.viennasightseeing.at.*

VISITOR INFORMATION
Contacts Vienna City Tourist Office ⊠ *Albertinapl., at Maysederg., 1st District* ☎ *01/24–555* ⊕ *www.wien.info.*

EXPLORING

Most of Vienna lies roughly within an arc of a circle with the straight line of the Danube Canal as its chord. The most prestigious address of city's 23 *Bezirke,* or districts, is its heart, the Innere Stadt ("Inner City"), or 1st District, bounded by the Ringstrasse (Ring Road). It's useful to note that the fabled 1st District holds the vast majority of sightseeing attractions and once encompassed the entire city.

The circular 1st District is bordered on its northeastern section by the Danube Canal and 2nd District, and clockwise from there along the Ringstrasse by the 3rd, 4th, 6th, 7th, 8th, and 9th districts. The 3rd District contains the Belvedere Palace. The 7th District has the celebrated Kunsthistorisches Museum and headline-making MuseumsQuartier, as well as the charming Spittelberg quarter. A little father out, the 13th District is home to the fabulous Schönbrunn Palace.

Albertina Museum. This not-to-be-missed collection is home to some of the greatest old-master drawings in Vienna—including Dürer's iconic *Praying Hands* and beloved *Alpine Hare.* The collection of nearly 65,000 drawings and almost a million prints was begun by the 18th-century Duke Albert of Saxony-Teschen. All the names are here, including Leonardo da Vinci, Michelangelo, Raphael, and Rembrandt. The Batliner Collection includes excellent examples of French and German impressionism and Russian avant-garde. The mansion's early-19th-century salons—all gilt boiserie and mirrors—provide a jewel-box setting. ⊠ *Augustinerstr. 1, 1st District* ☎ *01/534–830* ⊕ *www.albertina. at* ☑ *€9.50* ☉ *Thurs.–Tues. 10–6, Wed. 10–9* Ⓜ *Herrengasse (U-bahn).*

Fodor's Choice **Belvedere Palace.** One of the most splendid pieces of baroque architec-
★ ture anywhere, the Belvedere Palace—actually two imposing palaces
separated by a 17th-century French-style garden parterre—is one of the
masterpieces of architect Lucas von Hildebrandt. Built outside the city
fortifications between 1714 and 1722, the complex originally served
as the summer palace of Prince Eugene of Savoy; much later it became
the home of Archduke Franz Ferdinand, whose assassination in 1914
precipitated World War I. Though the lower palace is impressive in its
own right, it is the much larger upper palace, used for state receptions,
banquets, and balls, that is acknowledged as Hildebrandt's masterpiece. The upper palace displays a wealth of architectural invention
in its facade, avoiding the main design problems common to palaces:
monotony on the one hand and pomposity on the other.

Both the upper and lower palaces of the Belvedere are museums devoted
to Austrian painting. The Belvedere's main attraction is the collection
of 19th- and 20th-century Austrian paintings, centering on the work
of Vienna's three preeminent early-20th-century artists: Gustav Klimt,
Egon Schiele, and Oskar Kokoschka. Klimt was the oldest, and by the
time he helped found the Secession movement he had forged an idiosyncratic painting style that combined realistic and decorative elements
in a way that was revolutionary. *The Kiss*—his greatest painting—is
here on display. Schiele and Kokoschka went even further, rejecting the
decorative appeal of Klimt's glittering abstract designs and producing
works that ignored conventional ideas of beauty. ⊠ *Prinz-Eugen-Str. 27,
3rd District/Landstrasse* ☎ *01/795-57-134* ⊕ *www.belvedere.at* 🎟 *€16*
🕙 *Daily 10–6* Ⓜ *Karlsplatz (U-bahn), then Tram D or Tram No. 71.*

FAMILY **Haus der Musik** (*House of Music*). You could spend an entire day at
this ultra-high-tech museum housed on several floors of an early-19th-
century palace near Schwarzenbergplatz. Pride of place goes to the rooms
dedicated to each of the great Viennese composers—Haydn, Mozart,
Beethoven, Schubert, Strauss, and Mahler—complete with music samples and manuscripts. Other exhibits trace the evolution of sound (from
primitive noises to the music of the masters) and illustrate the mechanics
of the human ear (measure your own frequency threshold). There are
also dozens of interactive computer games. ⊠ *Seilerstätte 30, 1st District* ☎ *01/513-4850* ⊕ *www.hausdermusik.at/en/2.htm* 🎟 *€11* 🕙 *Daily
10–10* Ⓜ *Karlsplatz (U-bahn), then Tram D to Schwarzenbergplatz.*

Fodor's Choice **Hofbibliothek** (*formerly Court, now National, Library*). This is one of the
★ grandest Baroque libraries in the world, a cathedral of books. Its centerpiece is the spectacular Prunksaal—the Grand Hall—which probably
contains more book treasures than any comparable collection outside
the Vatican. ⊠ *Josefspl. 1, 1st District* ☎ *01/534-100* ⊕ *www.onb.ac.at*
🎟 *€7* 🕙 *Tues., Wed., and Fri.–Sun. 10–6, Thurs. 10–9* Ⓜ *Herrengasse
(U-bahn).*

Hofburgkapelle (*Chapel of the Imperial Palace*). Fittingly, this is the main
venue for the beloved Vienna Boys' Choir, since the group has its roots
in the Hofmusikkapelle choir founded by Emperor Maximilian I five
centuries ago (Haydn and Schubert were both participants as young
boys). The choir sings mass here at 9:15 on Sunday from mid-September

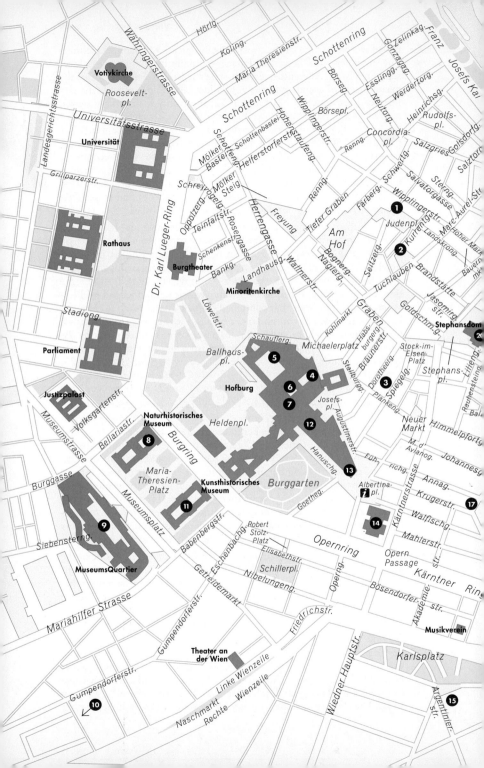

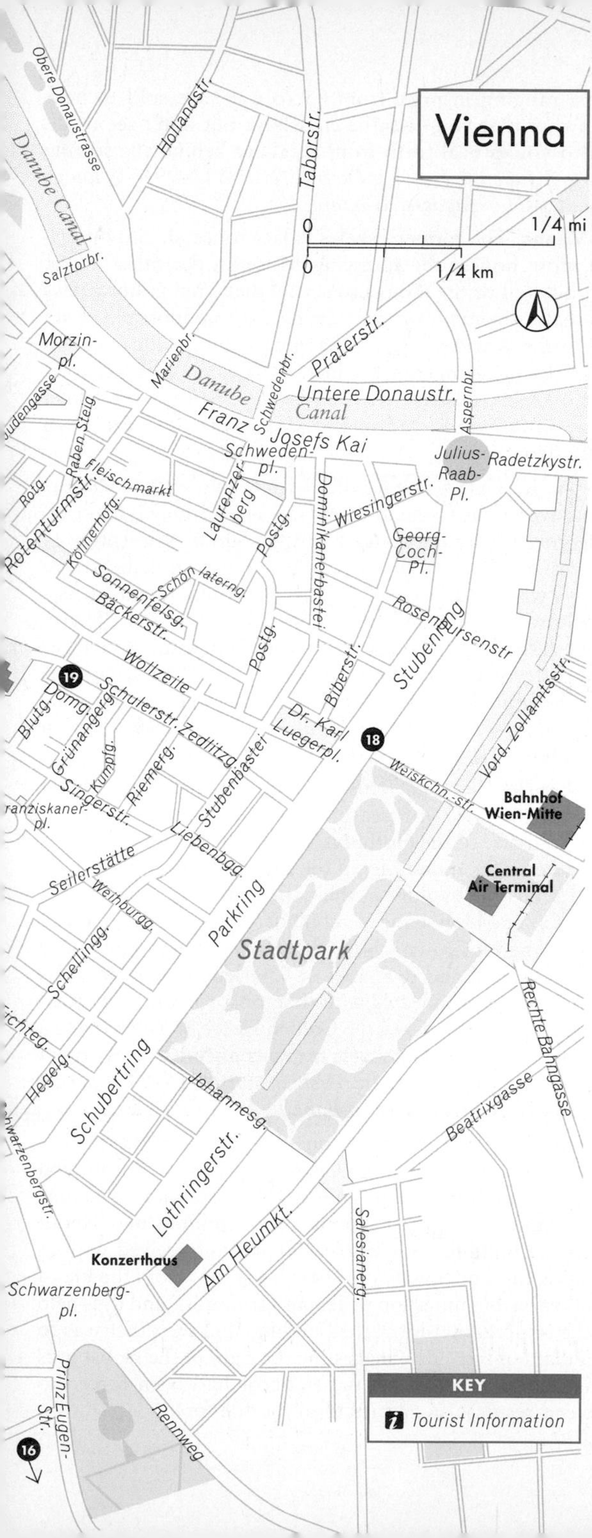

Vienna

0 _____ 1/4 mi

0 _____ 1/4 km

3

**Bahnhof
Wien-Mitte**

**Central
Air Terminal**

Stadtpark

Konzerthaus

*Schwarzenberg-
pl.*

KEY

🛈 *Tourist Information*

to June (tickets, ranging in price from €5 to €29, are sold to hear the choir). Be aware that you *hear* the choirboys but don't see them: soprano and alto voices peal forth from a gallery behind the seating area. ⊠ *Hofburg, Schweizer Hof, 1st District* ☎ *01/533–9927* ⊕ *www. hofburgkapelle.at* Ⓜ *Herrengasse (U-bahn).*

Jewish Museum Vienna. The former Eskeles Palace, once an elegant private residence, now houses the Jüdisches Museum der Stadt Wien. Permanent exhibits tell of the momentous role that Vienna-born Jews have played in realms from music to medicine, art to philosophy, both in Vienna and in the world at large. Changing exhibits add contemporary touches. The museum complex includes a café and bookstore. ⊠ *Dorotheerg. 11, 1st District* ☎ *01/535–0431* ⊕ *www.jmw.at/en* 🎟 *€10, includes admission to Judenplatz Museum* ☉ *Sun.–Fri. 10–6* Ⓜ *Stephansplatz (U-bahn).*

Judenplatz Museum. In what was once the old Jewish ghetto, construction workers discovered the fascinating remains of a 13th-century synagogue while digging for a new parking garage. Simon Wiesenthal (a former Vienna resident) helped to turn it into a museum dedicated to the Austrian Jews who died in World War II. Marking the outside is a concrete cube whose faces are casts of library shelves, signifying Jewish love of learning, designed by Rachel Whiteread. Downstairs are three exhibition rooms devoted to medieval Jewish life and the synagogue excavations. ⊠ *Judenpl. 8, 1st District* ☎ *01/535–0431* ⊕ *www.jmw. at/museum-judenplatz* 🎟 *€10, includes admission to Jewish Museum Vienna* ☉ *Sun.–Thurs. 10–6, Fri. 10–2.*

Fodor'sChoice
★

Kaiserliche Schatzkammer (*Imperial Treasury*). The entrance to the Schatzkammer, with its 1,000 years of treasures, is tucked away at ground level behind the staircase to the Hofburgkapelle. The elegant display is a welcome antidote to the monotony of the Imperial Apartments, and the crowns and relics fairly glow in their surroundings. Here you'll find such marvels as the Holy Lance—reputedly the lance that pierced Jesus's side—the Imperial Crown (a sacred symbol of sovereignty once stolen on Hitler's orders), and the Saber of Charlemagne. Don't miss the Burgundian Treasure, connected with that most romantic of medieval orders of chivalry, the Order of the Golden Fleece. ■ **TIP➜ The €18 combined ticket that includes admission to the Kunsthistorisches is a great deal.** ⊠ *Hofburg, Schweizer Hof, 1st District* ☎ *01/525–240* 🎟 *€12* ☉ *Wed.–Mon. 10–6* Ⓜ *Herrengasse (U-bahn).*

Karlskirche. Dominating the Karlsplatz is one of Vienna's greatest buildings, the Karlskirche, dedicated to St. Charles Borromeo. Before you is a giant Baroque church framed by enormous freestanding columns, mates to Rome's famous Trajan's Column. These columns may be out of keeping with the building as a whole, but were conceived with at least two functions in mind: one was to portray scenes from the life of the patron saint, carved in imitation of Trajan's triumphs, and thus help to emphasize the imperial nature of the building; and the other was to symbolize the Pillars of Hercules, suggesting the right of the Habsburgs to their Spanish dominions, which the emperor had been forced to renounce. The end result is an architectural tour de force.

If you are not afraid of heights take the panorama elevator up into the sphere of the dome and climb the top steps to enjoy an unrivalled view to the heart of the city. ✉ *Karlspl., 4th District/Wieden* ☎ *01/504–6187* ⊕ *www.karlskirche.at* 🖼 *€6* ⊙ *Daily 9–12:30 and 1–6, Sun. noon–5:45* Ⓜ *Karlsplatz (U-bahn).*

Fodor's Choice
★ **Kunsthistorisches Museum** (*Museum of Fine Art*). However short your stay in Vienna, you'll want to visit one of the greatest art collections in the world, that of the Kunsthistorisches Museum. This is no dry-as-dust museum illustrating the history of art, as its name implies. Rather, its collections of old-master paintings reveal the royal taste and style of many members of the mighty House of Habsburg, which during the 16th and 17th centuries ruled over the greater part of the Western world. Today you can enjoy what this great ruling house assiduously (and in most cases, selectively) brought together through the centuries. The collection stands in the same class with those of the Louvre, the Prado, and the Vatican.

The museum is most famous for the largest collection of paintings under one roof by the Netherlandish 16th-century master Pieter Brueghel the Elder—many art historians say that seeing his sublime *Hunters in the Snow* is worth a trip to Vienna. Brueghel's depictions of peasant scenes, often set in magnificent landscapes, distill the poetry and magic of the 16th century as few other paintings do. Room 10 is the Brueghel shrine—on its walls hang *Children's Games,* the *Tower of Babel,* the *Peasant Wedding,* the *Nest-Robber,* and eight other priceless canvases.

One of the best times to visit the Kunsthistorisches Museum is Thursday, when you can enjoy a sumptuous gourmet dinner (€39) in the cupola rotunda. Just across from the seating area, take a leisurely stroll through the almost-empty gallery chambers. Seating starts at 6:30 pm and the museum galleries close at 9 pm, so make sure you get your fill of art. ✉ *Maria-Theresien-Pl., 7th District/Neubau* ☎ *01/525–240* ⊕ *www.khm.at* 🖼 *€12* ⊙ *Tues., Wed., and Fri.–Sun. 10–6, Thurs. 10–9* Ⓜ *MuseumsQuartier (U-bahn), Volkstheater (U-bahn).*

Mozarthaus. This is Mozart's only still-existing abode in Vienna. Equipped with an excellent audio guide and starting out on the third floor of the building, you can hear about Mozart's time in Vienna: where he lived and performed, who his friends and supporters were, and his passion for expensive attire—he spent more money on clothes than most royals at that time. The second floor deals with Mozart's operatic works. The first floor focuses on the 2½ years that Mozart lived here, when he wrote dozens of piano concertos, as well as *The Marriage of Figaro* and the six quartets dedicated to Joseph Haydn. Save on the entrance fee by purchasing a combined ticket for Mozarthaus Vienna and Haus der Musik for €15. ✉ *Domg. 5, 1st District* ☎ *01/512–1791* ⊕ *www.mozarthausvienna.at* 🖼 *€10* ⊙ *Daily 10–7* Ⓜ *Stephansplatz (U-bahn).*

Museum für Angewandte Kunst (*Museum of Applied Arts*). This fascinating museum contains a large collection of Austrian furniture, porcelain, art objects, and priceless Oriental carpets. The Jugendstil display devoted to Josef Hoffman and his Secessionist followers at the Wiener Werkstätte is particularly fine. ⊠ *Stubenring 5, 1st District* ☎ *01/711–36–0* ⊕ *www. mak.at* ☜ *€7.90; free Sat.* ☉ *Tues. 10 am–midnight; Wed.–Sun. 10–6* Ⓜ *Stubentor (U-bahn).*

FAMILY **MuseumsQuartier** (*Museum Quarter*). One of the largest of its kind in the world, the MuseumsQuartier—or MQ, as many call it—is a sprawling collection of galleries housed in what was once the Imperial Court Stables, the 260-year-old baroque complex designed by Fischer von Erlach. Situated between the Kunsthistorisches Museum and the Spittelberg neighborhood, it's in one of Vienna's hippest enclaves. Where once 900 cavalry horses were housed, now thousands of masterworks of the 20th and 21st centuries are exhibited, all in a complex that is architecturally an expert and subtle blending of historic and cutting-edge: the original structure (adorned with pastry-white stuccoed ceilings and rococo flourishes) was retained, while ultramodern wings were added to house five museums, most of which showcase modern art at its best.

The Architekturzentrum, Kunsthalle, Leopold Museum, Museum Moderner Kunst Stiftung Ludwig, and the ZOOM Kinder Museum are all part of the MuseumsQuartier complex. In addition, the **Quartier21** showcases up-and-coming artists and musicians in the huge Fischer von Erlach wing facing the Museumsplatz. Modern-art lovers will find it easy to spend at least an entire day at MuseumsQuartier, and with several cafés, restaurants, gift shops, and bookstores, won't even need to venture outside. ⊠ *Museumspl. 1, 7th District/Neubau* ☎ *01/523–5881* ⊕ *www.mqw.at* ☜ *Combination tickets range from €17 to €25* ☉ *Daily 24 hrs* Ⓜ *MuseumsQuartier (U-bahn), Volkstheater (U-bahn).*

FAMILY **Naturhistorisches Museum** (*Natural History Museum*). The palatial 19th-century museum, twin of the celebrated Kunsthistorisches Museum, is the home of, among other artifacts, the *Venus of Willendorf*, a tiny statuette (actually, a replica—the original is in a vault) thought to be some 20,000 years old. This symbol of the Stone Age was originally unearthed in the Wachau Valley, not far from Melk. The reconstructed dinosaur skeletons draw the most attention, especially among kids. Tours are Friday at 4 and weekends at 3. ⊠ *Maria-Theresien-Pl., 7th District/Neubau* ☎ *01/52177* ☜ *€10* ☉ *Wed. 9–9, Thurs.–Mon. 9–6:30* Ⓜ *U2 or Volkstheater (U-bahn).*

Fodor'sChoice ★ **Schönbrunn Palace.** Originally designed by Johann Bernhard Fischer von Erlach in 1696 and altered considerably for Maria Theresa 40 years later, Schönbrunn Palace, the huge Habsburg summer residence, lies within the city limits, just a few subway stops west of Karlsplatz on the U4. Bus trips to Schönbrunn offered by the city's tour operators cost several times what you'd pay if you traveled by subway; the one advantage is that they get you there with a bit less effort. Go on your own if you want time to wander through the grounds, which are open dawn to dusk.

The most impressive approach to the palace and its gardens is through the front gate, set on Schönbrunner Schloss-Strasse halfway between the Schönbrunn and Hietzing subway stations. The vast main courtyard is ruled by a formal design of impeccable order and rigorous symmetry:

wing nods at wing, facade mirrors facade, and every part stylistically complements every other.

Of the 1,441 rooms, 40 are open to the public on the regular tour, of which two are of special note: the Hall of Mirrors, where the six-year-old Mozart performed for Empress Maria Theresa in 1762 (and where he met seven-year-old Marie Antoinette, developing a little crush on her), and the Grand Gallery, where the Congress of Vienna (1815) danced at night after carving up Napoléon's collapsed empire during the day. Ask about viewing the ground-floor living quarters (Berglzimmer), where the walls are painted with palm trees, exotic animals, and tropical views. ✉ *Schönbrunner-Schloss-Str., 13th District/Hietzing* ☎ *01/811–13–239* ⊕ *www.schoenbrunn.at* 🎟€*13.50, €15.50 for guided tour* ⊙ *Apr.–June, Sept., and Oct., daily 8:30–5; July and Aug., daily 8:30–6; Nov.–Mar., daily 8:30–4:30* Ⓜ *Schönbrunn (U-bahn).*

Silberkammer (*Museum of Court Silver and Tableware*). Fascinating for its behind-the-scenes views of state banquets and other elegant affairs, there are more than forks and finger bowls here. Stunning decorative pieces vie with glittering silver and gold for your attention. Highlights include Emperor Franz Josef's vermeil banqueting service, the jardinière given to Empress Elisabeth by Queen Victoria, and gifts from Marie-Antoinette to her brother Josef II. The fully set tables give you a view of court life. ✉ *Hofburg, Michaelertrakt, 1st District* ☎ *01/533–7570* 🎟€*10.50, includes admission to Kaiserappartements* ⊙ *Sept.–June, daily 9–5:30; July and Aug., daily 9–6* Ⓜ *Herrengasse (U-bahn).*

Spanische Reitschule (*Spanish Riding School*). Between Augustinerstrasse and the Josefsplatz is the world-famous Spanish Riding School, a favorite for centuries, and no wonder: who can resist the sight of the stark-white Lipizzaner horses going through their masterful paces? For the last 300 years they have been perfecting their haute école riding demonstrations to the sound of baroque music in a ballroom that seems to be a crystal-chandeliered stable. The interior of the riding school, the 1735 work of Fischer von Erlach the Younger, is makes it Europe's most elegant sports arena.

The performance schedule is fairly consistent throughout the year. From August to June, evening performances are held mostly on weekends and morning exercises with music are held mostly on weekdays. Booking months ahead is a good idea. If you do so, pick up tickets at the office under the Michaelerplatz rotunda dome. Otherwise tickets are available at the visitor center in Michaelerplatz, Tuesday–Saturday 9–4, and at Josefsplatz, on the day of the morning exercise, 9–5. ✉ *Michaelerpl. 1, 1st District* ☎ *01/533–9031* ⊕ *www.srs.at* 🎟€*23–€130, morning training €12* ⊙ *Aug.–June* Ⓜ *Herrengasse (U-bahn).*

Staatsoper (*State Opera House*). The Vienna Staatsoper vies with the cathedral for the honor of emotional heart of the city—it's a focus for Viennese life and one of the chief symbols of resurgence after World War II. Its directorship is one of the top jobs in Austria, almost as important as that of the president of the country, and one that draws even more public attention. The first of the Ringstrasse projects to be completed (in 1869), the opera house suffered disastrous bomb damage in the last days of World War II (only the outer walls, the front facade, and the main staircase survived). The auditorium is plain when compared to the red-and-gold eruptions of London's Covent Garden or some of the Italian opera houses, but it has an elegant individuality that shows to best advantage when the stage and auditorium are turned into a ballroom for the great Opera Ball.

Tours of the Opera House are given regularly, but starting times vary according to rehearsals; the current schedule is posted under the arcades on both sides of the building. Under the arcade on the Kärntnerstrasse side is an information office that also sells tickets to the main opera and the Volksoper. ⊠ *Opernring 2, 1st District* ☎ *01/514–44–2606* ⊕ *www.staatsoper.at* ⊠ *€5* ⊙ *Tours year-round* Ⓜ *Karlsplatz (U-bahn).*

Stephansdom (*St. Stephen's Cathedral*). Vienna's soaring centerpiece, this beloved cathedral enshrines the heart of the city—although when first built in the 12th century it stood outside the city walls. Vienna can thank a period of hard times for the Catholic Church for the cathedral's distinctive silhouette. Originally the structure was to have had matching 445-foot-high spires, a standard design of the era, but funds ran out, and the north tower to this day remains a happy reminder of what gloriously is not. The lack of symmetry creates an imbalance that makes the cathedral instantly identifiable from its profile alone. The cathedral, like the Staatsoper and some other major buildings, was very heavily damaged in World War II but has risen from the fires of destruction like a phoenix.

■ TIP→ **The wealth of decorative sculpture in St. Stephen's can be intimidating to the nonspecialist, so if you wish to explore the cathedral in detail, buy the admirably complete English-language description sold in the small room marked "Dom Shop."** One particularly masterly work should be seen by everyone: the stone pulpit attached to the second freestanding pier on the left of the central nave, carved by Anton Pilgram between 1510 and 1550. The bird's-eye views from the cathedral's beloved **Alter Steffl** (Old Stephen Tower) will be a highlight for some. The south tower is 450 feet high and was built between 1359 and 1433. The climb up the 343 steps is rewarded with vistas that extend to the rising slopes of the Wienerwald. The north steeple houses the big Pummerin bell and a lookout terrace (access by elevator). For a special treat, take the 90-minute Saturday-evening tour including a roof walk. ⊠ *Stephanspl., 1st District* ☎ *01/515–5237–67* ⊠ *Guided tour €4.50 (€10 on Sat.), catacombs €4.50, stairs to south tower €3.50, elevator to Pummerin bell €4.50; combined ticket €14.50* ⊙ *Mon.–Sat. 6 am–10 pm, Sun. 7 am–10 pm. English-language guided tour, Apr.–Oct. at 3:45; catacombs tour, Mon.–Sat. every half hr 10–11:30 and 1:30–4:30, Sun. every half hr 1:30–4:30; Pummerin bell, Apr.–June, Sept., and Oct., daily 8:30–5:30; July and Aug., daily 8:30–6; Nov.–Mar., daily 8:30–5; evening tours, June–Sept., Sat. at 7 pm* Ⓜ *Stephansplatz (U-bahn).*

Uhrenmuseum (*Clock Museum*). At the far end of Kurrentgasse, which is lined with appealing 18th-century houses, is the Uhrenmuseum (enter to the right on the Schulhof side of the building). The appealing museum's three floors display clocks and watches—more than 3,000 timepieces—dating from the 15th century to the present. The ruckus of bells and chimes pealing forth on any hour is impressive, but for the full cacophony try to be here at noon. ✉ *Schulhof 2, 1st District* ☎ *01/533–2265* 🎫 *€4* 🕐 *Tues.–Sun. 10–6* Ⓜ *Stephansplatz (U-bahn).*

WHERE TO EAT

$

BAKERY

Fodor'sChoice

★

✕ **Demel.** Vienna's best-known pastry shop, Demel offers a dizzying selection, so if you have a sweet tooth, a visit will be worth every euro. And in a city famous for its tortes, its almond-chocolate Senegaltorte takes the cake. Demel's shop windows have some of the most mouth-watering and inventive displays in Austria. ✉ *Kohlmarkt 14, 1st District* ☎ *01/535–17–170* 🌐 *www.demel.at* Ⓜ *Stephansplatz (U-bahn).*

$

AUSTRIAN

✕ **Figlmüller.** This Wiener schnitzel institution is known for breaded veal and pork cutlets so large they overflow the plate, and it's always packed. The cutlet is so large because it's been hammered (you can hear the mallets pounding from a block away). The schnitzel winds up wafer-thin but delicious, because the quality, as well as the size, is unrivaled (a quarter kilo for each). As the Viennese say, "Schnitzel should swim," so don't forget the lemon juice. If this location is full, try the one just around the corner on Bäckerstrasse 6. 💲 *Average main: €14* ✉ *Wollzeile 5, 1st District* ☎ *01/512–6177* 🌐 *www.figlmueller.at* Ⓜ *Stephansplatz (U-bahn).*

$

AUSTRIAN

✕ **Griechenbeisl.** Mozart, Beethoven, and Schubert all dined here—so how can you resist? Neatly tucked away in a quiet and quaint area of the Old City, this ancient inn goes back half a millennium. You can hear its age in the creaking floorboards when you walk through some of the small, dark-wood panel rooms. Yes, it's touristy, yet the food, including all the classic hearty dishes like goulash soup, Wiener schnitzel, and Apfelstrudel, is as good as in many other Beisln. The Mark Twain room has walls and ceiling covered with signatures of the famed who have been served here. 💲 *Average main: €17* ✉ *Fleischmarkt 11, 1st District* ☎ *01/533–1977* 🌐 *www.griechenbeisl.at* Ⓜ *Schwedenplatz (U-bahn).*

$$$

AUSTRIAN

Fodor'sChoice

★

✕ **Steirereck.** Considered one of the world's 50 best restaurants, this eatery is definitely the most raved-about place in Austria. It's in the former Milchhauspavilion, a grand Jugendstil-vintage dairy overlooking the Wienfluss promenade in the Stadtpark, the main city park on the Ringstrasse. Winning dishes include delicate smoked catfish, turbot in an avocado crust, or char in beeswax, yellow turnips, and cream. At the end of the meal, an outstanding selection of more than 120 cheeses await. If you don't want the gala Steirereck experience, opt for a bite in the more casual lower-floor Meierei, which is still stylish, with its hand-painted floor and furniture in shades of milky white. 💲 *Average main: €39* ✉ *Stadtpark, Am Heumarket 2A, 3rd District/Landstrasse* ☎ *01/713–3168* 🌐 *www.steirereck.at* ⚑ *Reservations essential* 🕐 *Closed weekends* Ⓜ *Stadtpark (U-bahn).*

$

CONTEMPORARY

✕ **Urania.** The year 1910 saw the inauguration of the Urania under the auspices of Emperor Franz Josef, and today this beautifully restored Jugendstil building is one of Vienna's trendiest locations. The interior design is cool, modern, and urban; its biggest boon besides the great food is the view from the terrace across the water. Chef Norbert

Fiedler's creations include fillet of trout on chanterelle risotto or spicy prawn linguine with a splash of lime, all brought to table by some of the handsomest waiters in town (rumor has it they are mostly models). Open times are an accommodating 9 am until 2 am, but the big event is Sunday brunch. The best deals are the two-course set lunches, served Tuesday to Friday and costing under €10. Ⓢ *Average main: €14* ⊠ *Uraniastr. 1, 1st District* ☎ *01/713–3066* ⊕ *www.barurania.com* ⌕ *Reservations essential* Ⓜ *Schwedenplatz (U-bahn).*

$$ ✗ **Vestibül.** Attached to the Burgtheater, this was once the carriage vesti-
ECLECTIC bule of the emperor's court theater. Today, the dining room with marble Corinthian columns, coffered arcades, and flickering candlelight adds romance, but don't expect high drama. An example of Ringstrasse architecture, the Burgtheater offers splendor at its most staid. Christian Domschitz, one of Austria's best chefs, took over the kitchen in 2010. The menu changes frequently, but often includes veal goulash, minced salmon in thyme oil, or the dish Domschitz is famed for, lobster with creamy cabbage. Ⓢ *Average main: €22* ⊠ *Burgtheater, Dr. Karl Lueger-Ring 2, 1st District* ☎ *01/532–4999* ⊕ *www.vestibuel.at* ⊘ *Closed Sun. and 3 wks in Aug. No lunch Sat.* Ⓜ *Tram No. 1 or 2.*

$$$$ ✗ **Zum Schwarzen Kameel.** Back when Beethoven dined at "the Black
AUSTRIAN Camel," it was already a foodie landmark. Since then, it has split into a
Fodor'sChoice *Delikatessen* and a restaurant. Try the former if you're in a hurry—fresh
★ sandwiches are served at the counter. If time is not an issue, dine in the elegant, intimate art-nouveau dining room. Let the headwaiter, the one with the Emperor Franz Josef mustache, rattle off the specials of the day in almost-perfect English; the *Beinschinken* (Viennese ham) is the specialty of the house and is renowned throughout Austria. Ⓢ *Average main: €30* ⊠ *Bognerg. 5, 1st District* ☎ *01/533–8125* ⊕ *www.kameel. at* ⌕ *Reservations essential* ⊘ *Closed Sun.* Ⓜ *Herrengasse (U-bahn).*

WHERE TO STAY

$$$ ⬚ **Astoria.** Built in 1912 and still retaining the outward charm of that
  era, the Astoria is one of the grand old Viennese hotels and enjoys a superb location on the Kärnterstrasse between the Opera House and St. Stephen's. **Pros:** location hard to beat; some specials available. **Cons:** no a/c, busy area at times noisy. Ⓢ *Rooms from: €258* ⊠ *Kärntnerstr. 32–34, 1st District* ☎ *01/51577* ⊕ *www.austria-trend.at/asw* ↗ *128 rooms* ⧖ *No meals.*

$$$$ ⬚ **Grand Hotel Wien.** With one of the great locations on the Ringstrasse,
HOTEL just across from the Musikverein and a minute on foot from the Sta-
Fodor'sChoice atsoper, the Grand Hotel Wien (the first luxury hotel in Vienna) has
★ risen to new splendor. **Pros:** two superb restaurants; good shopping next door. **Cons:** desk staff can seem haughty; check-in can be slow. Ⓢ *Rooms from: €410* ⊠ *Kärntnerring 9, 1st District* ☎ *01/515–800* ⊕ *www.grandhotelwien.com* ↗ *205 rooms* ⧖ *No meals.*

$$$$ ⬚ **Imperial.** One of the landmarks of the Ringstrasse, this hotel has
HOTEL exemplified the grandeur of imperial Vienna ever since it was built. **Pros:** discreet, unpretentious staff; excellent restaurant and café. **Cons:** pricey Internet access; some rooms are on the small side; bathrooms can be

tiny. $ *Rooms from: €415 ⊠ Kärntnerring 16, 1st District* ☎ *01/501–100* ⊕ *www.luxurycollection.com/imperial* ⤳ *138 rooms* ¶⦶¶ *Breakfast.*

$ 🖭 **Pension Zipser.** With an ornate facade and a gilt-trimmed coat of
HOTEL   arms, this 1904 house sits in the picturesque Josefstadt neighborhood
of small cafés, bars, and shops and is steps from the J tram line to
the city center. **Pros:** quiet area; some good bargains on select dates.
Cons: rather bare inside; far from the city center. $ *Rooms from: €109*
⊠ *Langeg. 49, 8th District/Josefstadt* ☎ *01/404–540* ⊕ *www.zipser.at*
⤳ *55 rooms* ¶⦶¶ *Breakfast.*

$$$$ 🖭 **The Ring.** Following the trend toward smaller boutique properties, this
HOTEL   luxury lodging takes its place alongside some of the Vienna's opulent
grand hotels. **Pros:** the best vodka bar in Vienna; good last-minute deals.
Cons: free Wi-Fi can be slow; trams frequently thunder around the
block. $ *Rooms from: €330 ⊠ Kärntner Ring 8, 1st District* ☎ *01/221–220* ⊕ *www.theringhotel.com* ⤳ *68 rooms* ¶⦶¶ *No meals.*

$$$ 🖭 **Radisson Blu Style Hotel.** Within the hotel's Art Nouveau facade, Lon-
HOTEL   don interior designer Maria Vafiadis has paid tribute to Viennese Art
Fodor's Choice   Deco, and the result is über-stylish yet comfortable. **Pros:** excellent rates
★   online; central location; quiet area of old city. **Cons:** small reception
area; reception desks oddly too low; not all room rates include break-
fast. $ *Rooms from: €259 ⊠ Herreng. 12, 1st District* ☎ *01/22–780–0*
⊕ *www.radissonblu.com/stylehotel-vienna* ⤳ *78 rooms* ¶⦶¶ *Breakfast.*

$$$ 🖭 **Wandl.** The restored facade identifies this 300-year-old house that has
been in family hands as a hotel since 1854. **Pros:** top location; quiet
square; helpful staff. **Cons:** rooms can get stuffy in summer. $ *Rooms
from: €210 ⊠ Peterspl. 9, 1st District* ☎ *01/534–55–0* ⊕ *www.hotel-wandl.com* ⤳ *138 rooms* ¶⦶¶ *Breakfast.*

THE ARTS

Konzerthaus. A three-minute walk from the Musikverein is the Konzerthaus, home to three performance halls: the Grosser Konzerthaussaal,
Mozartsaal, and Schubertsaal. The first is a room of magnificent size,
with red-velvet and gold accents. The calendar of Grosser Konzerthaussaal is packed with goodies, including the fabulous early-music
group Concentus Musicus Wien and concerts of the Wiener Philharmoniker and the Wiener Symphoniker. ⊠ *Lothringerstr. 20, 1st District*
☎ *01/242–002* ⊕ *www.konzerthaus.at.*

Musikverein. The city's most important concert halls are in the 1869
Gesellschaft der Musikfreunde, better known as the Musikverein. This
magnificent theater holds six performance spaces, but the one that
everyone knows is the venue for the annual New Year's Day Concert—
the Goldene Saal (Gold Hall). Possibly the world's most beautiful music
hall, it was designed by the Danish 19th-century architect Theophil
Hansen, a passionate admirer of ancient Greece who festooned it with
an army of gilded caryatids. In addition to being the main venue for the
Wiener Philharmoniker and the Wiener Symphoniker, the Musikverein
hosts many of the world's finest orchestras. ⊠ *Bösendorferstr. 12A, 1st
District* ☎ *01/505–8190* ⊕ *www.musikverein.at.*

Staatsoper (*State Opera House*). One of the world's great opera houses, the Staatsoper has been the scene of countless musical triumphs and a center of unending controversy over how it should be run and by whom. A performance takes place virtually every night from September to June, drawing on the vast repertoire of the house, with emphasis on Mozart, Verdi, and Wagner. Guided tours are given year-round. ⊠ *Opernring 2, 1st District* ☎ *01/514–440* ⊕ *www.wiener-staatsoper.at.*

SHOPPING

The **Kärntnerstrasse, Graben,** and **Kohlmarkt** pedestrian areas in the 1st District claim to have the best shops in Vienna, and for some items, like jewelry, they're probably some of the best anywhere, but prices are steep. The side streets in this area have developed their own character, with shops selling antiques, art, jewelry, and period furniture. The **Goldenes Quartier** (Golden Quarter) in the 1st District promises luxury shopping in a historic ambience. The area lies between Tuchlauben, Bognergasse, and Am Hof.

SALZBURG

Art lovers call Salzburg the "Golden City of High Baroque"; historians refer to it as the "Florence of the North" or the "German Rome"; and, of course, music lovers know it as the birthplace of one of the world's most beloved composers, Wolfgang Amadeus Mozart (1756–91).

PLANNING YOUR TIME

Salzburger Festspiele. The biggest event on the calendar—as it has been since it was first organized by composer Richard Strauss, producer Max Reinhardt, and playwright Hugo von Hofmannsthal in 1920—is the world-famous Salzburger Festspiele. The main summer festival is usually scheduled for the last week of July through the end of August. In addition, the festival presents two other major annual events: the Easter Festival (early April), and the Pentecost Baroque Festival (late May).

The most star-studded events—featuring the top opera stars and conductors such as Franz Welser-Möst and Nikolaus Harnoncourt—have tickets ranging from €22 to €340; for these glamorous events, first-nighters still pull out all the stops—summer furs, Dior dresses, and white ties stud the more expensive sections of the theaters. Other performances can run from €8 to €190, with still lesser prices for events outside the main festival halls, the **Grosses Festspielhaus** (Great Festival Hall) and the **Haus für Mozart** (House for Mozart), located shoulder to shoulder on the grand promenade of Hofstallgasse. This street, one of the most festive settings for a music festival, is especially dazzling at night, thanks to the floodlighted Fortress Hohensalzburg, which hovers on its hilltop above the theater promenade. Behind the court stables first constructed by Wolf-Dietrich in 1607, the Festspielhäser (festival halls) are modern constructions—the Grosses Haus was built in 1960 with 2,200 seats—but are actually "prehistoric," being dug out of the bedrock of the Mönchsberg mountain. There are glittering concerts and operas performed at many other theaters in the city. You can catch

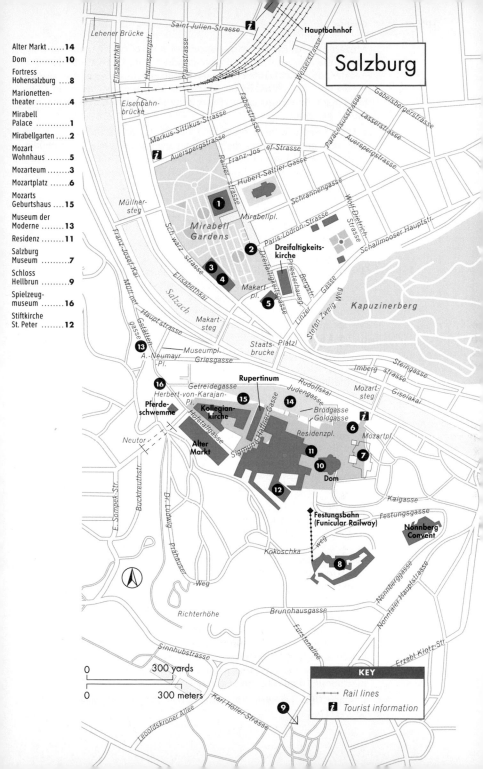

Salzburg

KEY

+—+—+ Rail lines

i Tourist information

0 | 300 yards

0 | 300 meters

Mozart concertos in the 18th-century splendor of two magnificent state rooms the composer himself once conducted in: the Rittersaal of the Residenz and the Marble Hall of the Mirabell Palace. Delightful Mozart productions are offered by the Salzburger Marionetten Theater. In addition, many important concerts are offered in the two auditoriums of the Mozarteum.

■**TIP**→ Since you must order your tickets as early as possible, make your decisions as soon as the program comes out (usually in the middle of November). Many major performances are sold out two or three months in advance, as hordes descend on the city to enjoy staged opera spectacles, symphony concerts by the Vienna Philharmonic and other great orchestras, recitals, church oratorios, and special evenings at the Mozarteum year after year. ⊠ *Hofstallg. 1* ☏ *0662/8045–500 for summer festival, 0662/8045–361 for Easter festival* ⊕ *www. salzburgfestival.at.*

GETTING HERE AND AROUND

A tourist map (available from tourist offices in Mozartplatz and the train station) shows all bus routes and stops; there's also a color-coded map of the public transport network, so you should have no problem getting around. Virtually all buses and trolleybuses (O-Bus) run via Mirabellplatz and/or Hanuschplatz. Single bus tickets bought from the driver cost €1.80.

AIR TRAVEL

Salzburg Airport, 4 km (2½ miles) west of the city center, is Austria's second-largest international airport. There are direct flights from London and other European cities to Salzburg, but not from the United States. From the United States you can fly to Munich and take the 90-minute train ride to Salzburg, or you can take a bus run by Salzburger Mietwagenservice. Taxis are the easiest way to get downtown from the Salzburg airport; the ride costs around €14–€15 and takes about 20 minutes. City Bus No. 2, which makes a stop by the airport every 15 minutes, runs down to Salzburg's train station (about 20 minutes). Bus No. 8 runs directly to the city center.

CAR TRAVEL

If driving, the fastest routes into Salzburg are the autobahns. From Vienna (320 km [198 miles]), take A1; from Munich (150 km [93 miles]), A8 (in Germany it's also E11); from Italy, A10. The only advantage to having a car in Salzburg itself is that you can get out of the city for short excursions. The Old City on both sides of the river is a pedestrian zone, and the rest of the city, with its narrow, one-way streets, is a driver's nightmare.

TRAIN TRAVEL

You can get to Salzburg by rail from most European cities. Salzburg Hauptbahnhof is a 20-minute walk from the center of town in the direction of Mirabellplatz. The bus station and the suburban railroad station are at the square in front. A taxi to the center of town should take about 10 minutes and cost €10.

Contacts ÖBB ⊕ *www.oebb.at.* **Salzburg Hauptbahnhof** ⊠ *Südtirolerpl.* ☏ *05/1717–4.*

TOURS

Several local companies conduct 1½- to 2-hour city tours. The tours are by minibus, since large buses can't enter the Old City. Tours briefly cover the major sights in Salzburg, including Mozart's Birthplace, the festival halls, the major squares, the churches, and the palaces at Hellbrunn and Leopoldskron. Bob's Special Tours is well known to American visitors—the company offers a 10% discount to Fodor's readers who book directly with them (not through their hotel). Salzburg Panorama Tours and Salzburg Sightseeing Tours offer similar tours.

> ### RIDING IN STYLE
>
> One of the most delightful ways to tour Salzburg is by horse-drawn carriage. Most of Salzburg's Fiaker are stationed in Residenzplatz, and cost €36 for 20 minutes, €72 for 50 minutes. During the Christmas season, large, decorated, horse-drawn carts take people around the Christmas markets.

Contacts Bob's Special Tours ⊠ *Rudolfskai 38* ☎ *0662/849–511* ⊕ *www. bobstours.com.* **Salzburg Panorama Tours** ⊠ *Schranneng. 2/2* ☎ *0662/883– 211* ⊕ *www.panoramatours.com.* **Salzburg Sightseeing Tours** ⊠ *Mirabellpl. 2* ☎ *0662/881–616* ⊕ *www.welcome-salzburg.at.*

VISITOR INFORMATION

Contacts Salzburg City Tourist Office ⊠ *Auerspergstr. 6* ☎ *0662/88987–0* ⊕ *www.salzburginfo.at.*

EXPLORING

Getting to know Salzburg is not too difficult, because most of its sights are within a comparatively small area. The Altstadt (Old City) is a compact area between the jutting outcrop of the Mönchsberg and the Salzach River. The rest of the Old City belonged to the wealthy burghers: the Getreidegasse, the Alter Markt (old market), the town hall, and the tall, plain burghers' houses (like Mozart's Birthplace).

Alter Markt (*Old Market*). Right in the heart of the Old City is the Alter Markt, the old marketplace and center of secular life in past centuries. The square is lined with 17th-century middle-class houses, colorfully hued in shades of pink, pale blue, and yellow ocher. Look in at the old royal pharmacy, the **Hofapotheke,** whose ornate black-and-gold Rococo interior was built in 1760. Inside, you'll sense a curious apothecarial smell, traced to the shelves lined with old pots and jars (labeled in Latin). These are not just for show: this pharmacy is still operating today. You can even have your blood pressure taken—but preferably not after drinking a *Doppelter Einspänner* (black coffee with whipped cream, served in a glass) in the famous Café Tomaselli just opposite. In warm weather the café's terrace provides a wonderful spot for watching the world go by as you sip a *Mélange* (another coffee specialty, served with frothy milk), or, during the summer months, rest your feet under the shade of the chestnut trees in the Tomaselli garden at the top end of the square. Next to the coffeehouse you'll find the **smallest house in Salzburg;** note the slanting roof decorated with a dragon gargoyle. In the center of the square, surrounded by flower stalls, is the marble **St. Florian's Fountain,** dedicated in 1734 to the patron saint of firefighters.

Dom (*Cathedral*). When you walk through the arches leading from Residenzplatz into **Domplatz,** it's easy to see why Max Reinhardt chose it in August of 1920 as the setting for what has become the annual summer production of Hugo von Hofmannsthal's *Jedermann* (*Everyman*). The plaza is one of Salzburg's most beautiful urban set pieces. In the center rises the Virgin's Column, and at one side is the cathedral, considered to be the first early Italian Baroque building north of the Alps. Its facade is of marble, its towers reach 250 feet into the air, and it holds 10,000 people. There has been a cathedral on this spot since the 8th century, but the present structure dates from the 17th century. The cathedral honors the patron saint of Salzburg, St. Rupert, who founded Nonnberg Abbey around 700, and also the Irish St. Virgil, the founder of the first cathedral consecrated in 774, whose relics lie buried beneath the altar. To see remains of the old cathedral, go down the steps from the left-side aisle into the crypt where the archbishops from 1600 on are buried. Mozart's parents, Leopold and Anna-Maria, were married here in 1747. Mozart was christened, the day after he was born, at the 14th-century font here, and he later served as organist from 1779 to 1781. Some of his compositions, such as the *Coronation Mass,* were written for the cathedral. ■TIP→ **On Sunday and all Catholic holidays, mass is sung at 10 am—the most glorious time to experience the cathedral's full splendor.** This is the only house of worship in the world with five independent fixed organs, which are sometimes played together during special church-music concerts. Many of the church's treasures are in a special museum on the premises. ✉ *Dompl. 1a* ☎ *0662/8047–1870* ⊕ *www.kirchen.net/dommuseum* ✉ *Museum €6* ☉ *Late May–late Oct., Mon.–Sat. 10–5, Sun. and holidays 11–6.*

FAMILY **Fortress Hohensalzburg.** Founded in 1077, the Hohensalzburg is Salzburg's acropolis and the largest preserved medieval fortress in Central Europe. Brooding over the city from atop the Festungsberg, it was originally founded by Salzburg's Archbishop Gebhard, who had supported the pope in the investiture controversy against the Holy Roman Emperor. Over the centuries the archbishops gradually enlarged the castle, using it originally only sometimes as a residence, then as a siege-proof haven against invaders and their own rebellious subjects. The exterior may look grim, but inside there are lavish state rooms, such as the glittering **Golden Room,** the **Burgmuseum**—a collection of medieval art—and the **Rainer's Museum,** with its brutish arms and armor. Politics and Church are in full force here: there's a torture chamber not far from the exquisite late-Gothic **St. George's Chapel** (although the implements on view came from another castle and were not used here). ■TIP→ **Climb up the 100 tiny steps to the Recturm, a grand lookout post with a sweeping view of Salzburg and the mountains.**

To reach the fortress, walk up the zigzag path that begins just beyond the Stieglkeller on Festungsgasse. Note that you don't need a ticket to walk the footpath. Visitor lines to the fortress can be long, so try to come early. ✉ *Fortress Hohensalzburg, Mönchsberg 34* ☎ *0662/620808–400*

⊕ *www.salzburgmuseum.at* ⊡ €7 ⊙ *Jan.–Apr. and Oct.–Dec., daily 9:30–5; May–Sept., daily 9–7.*

Festungsbahn (*Funicular railway*). The more-than-110-year-old Festungsbahn is the easy way up (advisable with young children). It's behind St. Peter's Cemetery. A round-trip pass including admission to all the museums in the fortress is €10.50, and a one-way ticket down is €2.40. Rides run every 10 minutes. ⊠ *Festungsg. 4* ☎ *0662/4480–9750* ⊕ *www.festungsbahn.at* ⊙ *Oct.–Apr., daily 9–5; May, June, and Sept., daily 9–8; July and Aug., daily 9 am–10 pm.*

FAMILY **Marionettentheater** (*Marionette Theater*). The Salzburger Marionettentheater is both the world's greatest marionette theater and—surprise!— a sublime theatrical experience. Many critics have noted that viewers quickly forget the strings controlling the puppets, which assume lifelike dimensions and provide a very real dramatic experience. The company is famous for its world tours, but is usually in Salzburg around Christmas, during the late-January Mozart Week, at Easter, and from May to September (schedule subject to change). ⊠ *Schwarzstr. 24* ☎ *0662/872– 406* ⊕ *www.marionetten.at* ⊡ *€18–€35* ⊙ *Salzburg season May–Sept., Christmas, Mozart Week (Jan.), Easter. Box office Mon.–Sat. 9–1 and 2 hrs before performance.*

FAMILY **Mirabellgarten** (*Mirabell Gardens*). While there are at least four entrances
Fodor'sChoice to the Mirabell Gardens—from the Makartplatz (framed by the statues
★ of Roman gods), the Schwarzstrasse, and Mirabell Square—you'll want to enter from the Rainerstrasse and head for the Rosenhügel (Rosebush Hill): you'll arrive at the top of the steps where Julie Andrews and her seven charges showed off their singing ability in *The Sound of Music*. This is also an ideal vantage point from which to admire the formal gardens and one of the best views of Salzburg, as it shows how harmoniously architects of the Baroque period laid out the city. The most famous part of the Mirabell Gardens is the **Zwerglgarten** (Dwarfs' Garden), which can be found opposite the Pegasus fountain. Here you'll find 12 statues of "Danubian" dwarves sculpted in marble—the real-life models for which were presented to the bishop by the landgrave of Göttweig. Prince-Archbishop Franz Anton von Harrach had the figures made for a kind of stone theater below. The **Heckentheater** (Hedge Theater) is an enchanting natural stage setting that dates from 1700. ⊙ *Daily 7 am–8 pm.*

Barockmuseum. Art lovers will make a beeline for the Barockmuseum, beside the Orangery of the Mirabell Gardens. It houses a collection of late-17th- and 18th-century paintings, sketches, and models illustrating the extravagant vision of life of the Baroque era—the signature style of Salzburg. Works by Giordano, Bernini, and Rottmayr are the collection's highlights. ⊠ *Orangeriegarten* ☎ *0662/877–432* ⊡ *€4.50* ⊙ *Wed.–Sun. 10–5; Christmas, Whitsun, and Jul.–Aug., Tues.–Sun. 10–5.*

Mirabell Palace. The "Taj Mahal of Salzburg," Schloss Mirabell was built in 1606 by the immensely wealthy and powerful Prince-Archbishop Wolf-Dietrich for his mistress, Salomé Alt, and their 15 children. It was originally called Altenau in her honor. Such was the palace's beauty that it was taken over by succeeding prince-archbishops, including Markus Sittikus (who renamed the estate), Paris Lodron, and finally, Franz Anton von Harrach, who brought in Lukas von Hildebrandt to give the place a Baroque facelift in 1727. A disastrous fire hit in 1818, but happily, three of the most spectacular set-pieces of the palace—the Chapel, the Marble Hall, and the Angel Staircase—survived. The Marble Hall is now used for civil wedding ceremonies, and is regarded as the most beautiful registry office in the world. Outdoor concerts are held at the palace and gardens May through August, Sunday mornings at 10:30 and Wednesday evenings at 8:30. ⊠ *Mirabelltpl.* ☎ *0662/889–87–330* 🖥 *Free* ⊙ *Weekdays 8–6.*

FAMILY **Mozart Wohnhaus** (*Mozart Residence*). The Mozart family moved from its cramped quarters in Getreidegasse to this house on the Hannibal Platz, as it was then known, in 1773. Wolfgang Amadeus Mozart lived here until 1780, his sister Nannerl stayed here until she married in 1784, and their father Leopold lived here until his death in 1787. The house is accordingly referred to as the Mozart Residence, signifying that it was not only Wolfgang who lived here. Besides an interesting collection of musical instruments (for example, his own pianoforte), among the exhibits on display are books from Leopold Mozart's library. Autographed manuscripts and letters can be viewed, by prior arrangement only, in the cellar vaults. ⊠ *Makartpl.* 8 ☎ *0662/874227–40* ⊕ *www. mozarteum.at* 🛒 *Mozart residence €7, combined ticket for Mozart residence and birthplace €12* ⊙ *Sept.–June, daily 9–5:30; July and Aug., daily 9–8.*

Mozarteum. Two institutions share the address in this building finished just before World War I—the International Foundation Mozarteum, set up in 1870, and the University of Music and Performing Arts, founded in 1880. Scholars come here to research in the **Bibliotheca Mozartiana,** the world's largest Mozart library (for research only and therefore not open to public). The Mozarteum also organizes the annual Mozart Week festival in January. Many important concerts are offered from October to June in its two recital halls, the Grosser Saal (Great Hall) and the Wiener Saal (Vienna Hall).

Behind the Mozarteum, sheltered by the trees of the Bastiongarten, is the famous **Zauberflötenhäuschen**—the little summerhouse where Mozart composed parts of *The Magic Flute,* with the encouragement of his frantic librettist, Emanuel Schikaneder, who finally wound up locking the composer inside to force him to complete his work. The house can generally be viewed only when concerts are offered in the adjacent Grosser Saal. ⊠ *Schwarzstr.* 26 ☎ *0662/88940–0* ⊕ *www.mozarteum. at* ⊙ *Summerhouse: only during Grosser Saal concerts.*

Mozartplatz (*Mozart Square*). In the center of the square stands the statue of Wolfgang Amadeus Mozart, a work by sculptor Ludwig Schwanthaler unveiled in 1842 in the presence of the composer's two surviving sons. It was the first sign of public recognition the great composer had received from his hometown since his death in Vienna in 1791. The statue, the first for a non-noble person in old Austria, shows a 19th-century stylized view of Mozart, draped in a mantle, holding a page of music and a copybook. A more appropriate bust of the composer, modeled by Viennese sculptor Edmund Heller, is found on the Kapuzinerberg.

Mozarts Geburtshaus (*Mozart's Birthplace*). As an adult, the great composer preferred Vienna to Salzburg, complaining that audiences in his native city were no more responsive than tables and chairs. Still, home is home, and this was Mozart's—when not on one of his frequent trips abroad—until the age of 17. Mozart was born on the third floor of this tall house on January 27, 1756, and his family lived here in the front apartment, when they were not on tour, from 1747 to 1773. As the child prodigy composed many of his first compositions in these rooms, it is fitting and touching to find Mozart's tiny first violin on display. ⊠ *Getreideg. 9* ☎ *0662/844–313* ⊕ *www.mozarteum.at* ✉ *€7, combined ticket for Mozart residence and birthplace €12* ⊗ *Sept.–June, daily 9–5:30; July and Aug., daily 9–8.*

Museum der Moderne. Enjoying one of Salzburg's most famous scenic spots, the dramatic museum of modern and contemporary art reposes atop the sheer cliff face of the Mönchsberg. The setting was immortalized in *The Sound of Music*—this is where Julie and the kids start warbling, "Doe, a deer, a female deer." Clad in minimalist white marble, the museum (2004) was designed by Friedrich Hoff Zwink of Munich. It has three exhibition levels, which bracket a restaurant with a large terrace—now, as always, the place to enjoy the most spectacular view over the city while sipping a coffee. Visit in the evening to see the city illuminated. ⊠ *Mönchsberg 32* ☎ *0662/842220–403* ⊕ *www. museumdermoderne.at* ✉ *€8* ⊗ *Tues.–Sun. 10–6, Wed. 10–8.*

Residenz. At the very heart of baroque Salzburg, the Residenz overlooks the spacious Residenzplatz and its famous fountain. The palace in its present form was built between 1600 and 1619 as the home of Wolf-Dietrich, the most powerful of Salzburg's prince-archbishops. The Kaisersaal (Imperial Hall) and the Rittersaal (Knight's Hall), one of the city's most regal concert halls, can be seen along with the rest of the magnificent **State Rooms** on a self-guided tour. Of particular note are the frescoes by Johann Michael Rottmayr and Martino Altomonte depicting the history of Alexander the Great. Upstairs on the third floor is the **Residenzgalerie,** a princely art collection specializing in 17th-century Dutch and Flemish art and 19th-century paintings of Salzburg. ⊠ *Residenzpl. 1* ☎ *0662/804–22–690, 0662/840–4510 for art collection* ⊕ *www.residenzgalerie.at* ✉ *€14.50 for both museums; €6 art collection only* ⊗ *Daily 10–5, except Easter wk and during the summer festival.*

Fodor's Choice
★

Salzburg Museum (*Neugebäude*). The biggest "gift" to Mozart was the opening, one day shy of his 250th birthday, on January 26, 2006, when Salzburg's mammoth 17th-century **Neue Residenz** (New Residence) welcomed visitors to an exhibition entitled "Viva! Mozart." The setting is splendid, as this building was Prince-Archbishop Wolf-Dietrich's "overflow" palace (he couldn't fit his entire archiepiscopal court into the main Residenz across the plaza). As such, it features 10 state reception rooms that were among the first attempts at a *stil Renaissance* in the North. Pride of place is given to the spectacular **Sattler Panorama,** one of the few remaining 360-degree paintings in the world, which shows the city of Salzburg in the early 19th century. Also here is the original composition of "Silent Night," composed by Franz Gruber in nearby Oberndorf in 1818. ✉ *Mozartpl. 1* ☏ *0662/620808–700* ⊕ *www.salzburgmuseum.at* 🎫 *€7* ⊗ *Tues., Wed., Fri.–Sun. 9–5, Thurs. 9–8.*

> **THE SALZBURG CARD**
>
> Consider purchasing the Salzburg Card. SalzburgKarten are good for 24, 48, or 72 hours for €25–€40, and allow no-charge entry to most museums and sights, use of public transportation, and special discount offers. Children under 15 pay half.

FAMILY

Fodor'sChoice

★

Schloss Hellbrunn (*Hellbrunn Palace*). Just 6½ km (4 miles) south of Salzburg, the Lustschloss Hellbrunn was the prince-archbishops' pleasure palace. It was built early in the 17th century by Santino Solari for Markus Sittikus, after the latter had imprisoned his uncle, Wolf-Dietrich, in the fortress. The castle has some fascinating rooms, including an octagonal music room and a banquet hall with a trompe-l'oeil ceiling. Hellbrunn Park became famous far and wide because of its **Wasserspiele,** or trick fountains. In the formal gardens (a beautiful example of the Mannerist style) owners added an outstanding mechanical theater that includes exotic and humorous fountains spurting water from strange places at unexpected times. The **Monatsschlösschen,** the old hunting lodge (built in one month), contains an excellent folklore museum. Following the path over the hill you find the **Steintheater** (Stone Theater), an old quarry made into the earliest open-air opera stage north of the Alps. The former palace deer park has become a **zoo** featuring free-flying vultures and Alpine animals that largely roam unhindered. You can get to Hellbrunn by Bus No. 25, by car on Route 159, or by bike or on foot along the beautiful Hellbrunner Allee past several 17th-century mansions. On the estate grounds is the little gazebo filmed in *The Sound of Music* ("I am 16, going on 17")—the doors are now locked because a person once tried to repeat the movie's dance steps, leaping from bench to bench, and managed to fall and break a hip. ✉ *Fürstenweg 37, Hellbrunn* ☏ *0662/820372–0* ⊕ *www.hellbrunn. at* 🎫 *Tour of palace and water gardens €9.50* ⊗ *Apr. and Oct., daily 9–4:30; May, June and Sept., daily 9–5:30; July and Aug., daily 9–6; evening tours July and Aug., daily at 7, 8 and 9.*

FAMILY

Spielzeugmuseum (*Toy Museum*). On a rainy day this is a delightful diversion for both young and old, with a collection of dolls, teddy bears, model trains, and wooden sailing ships. Special Punch and Judy–style puppet shows are presented. Performance days change, so call ahead. ✉ *Bürgerspitalpl. 2* ☏ *0662/620808–300* ⊕ *www.salzburgmuseum.at* 🎫 *€4* ⊗ *Tues.–Sun., daily 9–5.*

Stiftkirche St. Peter (*Collegiate Church of St. Peter*). The most sumptuous church in Salzburg, St. Peter's is where Mozart's famed *Great Mass in C Minor* premiered in 1783, with his wife, Constanze, singing the lead soprano role. Wolfgang directed the orchestra and choir and also played the organ. During every season of the city's summer music festival in

August, the work is performed here during a special church-music concert. The porch has beautiful Romanesque vaulted arches from the original structure built in the 12th century; the interior was decorated in the voluptuous late-Baroque style when additions were made in the 1770s. ⊠ *St. Peter Bezirk* ☎ *0662/844576–87* 🎫 *Free* ⊙ *Apr.–Sept., daily 6:30 am–7 pm; Oct.–Mar., daily 6:30–6.*

WHERE TO EAT

$ ✕ **Café Tomaselli.** This inn opened its doors in 1705 as an example of that
AUSTRIAN new-fangled thing, a *Wiener Kaffeehaus* (Vienna coffeehouse). It was
Fodor'sChoice an immediate hit. Enjoying its 11 types of coffee was none other than
★ Mozart's beloved, Constanze, who often dropped in, as her house was just next door. The Tomasellis set up shop here in 1850, becoming noted *Chocolatmachers*. Feast on the famous "Tomaselliums Café" (mocha, Mozart liqueur, and whipped cream) and the large selection of excellent homemade cakes, tarts, and strudels. Inside, the decor is marble, wood, and walls of 18th-century portraits. In summer the best seats are on the terrace and at the pretty "Tomaselli-Kiosk" on the square. $ *Average main: €10* ⊠ *Alter Markt 9* ☎ *0662/844488–0* ⊕ *www.tomaselli. at* ⊟ *No credit cards.*

$ ✕ **Mundenhamer.** Chef Ernst Breitschopf knows the repertoire of good
AUSTRIAN old Upper Austrian dishes inside and out: an *Innviertler* (raw ham with horseradish, dark bread, and butter); a garlic soup with bread croutons; a roast pork chop served in a pan with bread dumplings and warm bacon-cabbage salad; homemade spätzle with braised white cabbage and bacon; a Salzburger schnitzel (scallop of veal filled with minced mushrooms and ham) with buttered finger dumplings. Dessert? Nobody can resist the *Mohr im Hemd* (Moor-in-a-shirt), the warm chocolate cake garnished with fruits, chocolate sauce, vanilla ice cream, and whipped cream. $ *Average main: €15* ⊠ *Rainerstr. 2* ☎ *0662/875–693* ⊙ *Closed Sun.*

$$$$ ✕ **Pfefferschiff.** The "Pepper Ship" is one of the most acclaimed restau-
ECLECTIC rants in Salzburg—though it's 3 km (2 miles) northeast of the center. It's in a pretty, renovated rectory, dated 1640, adjacent to a pink-and-cream chapel. Klaus Fleishhaker, an award-winning chef, makes you feel pampered in the country-chic atmosphere, adorned with polished wooden floors, antique hutches, and tabletops laden with fine bone china and Paloma Picasso silverware. The menu changes seasonally. A taxi is the least stressful way of getting here, but if you have your own car, drive along the north edge of the Kapuzinerberg toward Hallwang and then Söllheim. $ *Average main: €30* ⊠ *Söllheim 3* ☎ *0662/661–242* ⌘ *Reservations essential.*

$$ ✕ **Stiftskeller St. Peter.** Legends swirl about the famous St. Peter's Beer
AUSTRIAN Cellar. Locals claim that Mephistopheles met Faust here, others say
Fodor'sChoice Charlemagne dined here, and some believe Columbus enjoyed a glass
★ of its famous Salzburg Stiegl beer just before he set sail for America in 1492. But there is no debating the fact that this place—first mentioned in a document dating back to 803—is Austria's oldest restaurant. It is also one of the most dazzling dining experiences in Salzburg. Choose between the fairly elegant, dark-wood-panel Prälatenzimmer (Prelates'

3

Room) or one of several less-formal banqueting rooms. Along with other Austrian standards, you can dine on fish caught in local rivers and lakes. [$] *Average main: €22* ✉ *St. Peter Bezirk 4* ☎ *0662/841268–0* 🌐 *www.haslauer.at.*

$ AUSTRIAN 🍴 **Zum Fidelen Affen.** The name means "At the Faithful Ape," which explains the monkey motifs in this popular Gasthaus dominated by a round copper-plated bar and stone pillars under a vaulted ceiling. Besides the beer on tap, the kitchen offers tasty Austrian dishes, such as *Schlutzkrapfen* (cheese ravioli with a light topping of chopped fresh tomatoes) or a big salad with strips of fried chicken. It's always crowded, so be sure to arrive early or book ahead. [$] *Average main: €10* ✉ *Priesterhausg. 8* ☎ *0662/877–361* ✍ *Reservations essential* ⏲ *Closed Sun. No lunch.*

WHERE TO STAY

$$ B&B/INN 🏨 **Boutiquehotel am Dom.** Tucked away on a tiny street near Residenzplatz, this small pension in a 14th-century building offers simply furnished rooms, some with oak-beam ceilings. **Pros:** rustic atmosphere; well-kept rooms. **Cons:** few amenities. [$] *Rooms from: €140* ✉ *Goldg. 17* ☎ *0662/842–765* 🌐 *www.amdom.at* 🛏 *15 rooms* ⏲ *Closed 2 wks in Feb.* 🍽 *Breakfast.*

$$$ HOTEL Fodor's Choice ★ 🏨 **Goldener Hirsch.** Celebrities from Picasso to Pavarotti have favored the "Golden Stag" for its legendary *Gemütlichkeit,* patrician pampering, and adorable decor. **Pros:** unbeatable location; top-notch dining; charm to spare. **Cons:** noisy neighborhood. [$] *Rooms from: €250* ✉ *Getreideg. 37/Herbert-von-Karajan-Pl. 5* ☎ *0662/80840* 🌐 *www.goldenerhirsch.com* 🛏 *64 rooms, 5 suites* 🍽 *No meals.*

$$$ HOTEL Fodor's Choice ★ 🏨 **Sacher Salzburg.** On the Salzach River, this mammoth hotel has attracted guests from the Beatles and the Rolling Stones to Hillary and Chelsea Clinton, but the owners, the Gürtler family, will make sure that even if you don't have a Vuitton steamer trunk you'll feel welcome. **Pros:** some great views; delicious buffet breakfast; plenty of dining options. **Cons:** gets overcrowded during festival. [$] *Rooms from: €234* ✉ *Schwarzstr. 5–7* ☎ *0662/88977* 🌐 *www.sacher.com* 🛏 *118 rooms* 🍽 *Breakfast.*

$$ HOTEL 🏨 **Weisse Taube.** In the heart of the pedestrian area of the Altstadt, the centuries-old "White Dove" is around the corner from Mozartplatz, the Salzburg Museum, and the Residenz. **Pros:** excellent location for walkers; friendly staff. **Cons:** noisy area at night. [$] *Rooms from: €135* ✉ *Kaig. 9* ☎ *0662/842–404* 🌐 *www.weissetaube.at* 🛏 *33 rooms* ⏲ *Closed 2 wks in Jan.* 🍽 *Breakfast.*

THE ARTS

MUSIC

Landestheater. The season at the Landestheater runs from September to June. Productions slated for 2012–2013 include *The Sound of Music* and a ballet of *Marie Antoinette.* You may place ticket orders by telephone Monday and Saturday 10–2, Tuesday–Friday 10–5. ✉ *Schwarzstr. 22* ☎ *0662/871–51–221* 🌐 *www.salzburger-landestheater.at.*

Salzburger Festungskonzerte. The Salzburger Festungskonzerte are presented in the grand Prince's Chamber at Festung Hohensalzburg. Concerts often include works by Mozart. A special candlelight dinner and concert-ticket combo is often offered. ⊠ *Fortress Hohensalzburg* ☎ *0662/825–858* ⊕ *www.mozartfestival.at* ⌨ *€33–€39.*

Fodor's Choice **Salzburger Schlosskonzerte.** The Salzburger Schlosskonzerte presents concerts in the legendary Marmorsaal (Marble Hall) at Mirabell Palace, where Mozart performed. ⊠ *Theaterg. 2* ☎ *0662/848–586* ⊕ *www. salzburger.schlosskonzerte.at* ⌨ *€29–€35.*

SHOPPING

The most fashionable specialty stores and gift shops are along Getreidegasse and Judengasse and around Residenzplatz. Linzergasse, across the river, is less crowded and good for more practical items. There are interesting antiques shops in the medieval buildings along Steingasse and Goldgasse.

INNSBRUCK

The charming old-world aspect of Innsbruck has remained virtually intact, and includes ample evidence of its baroque lineage. The skyline encircling the center suffers somewhat from high-rises, but the heart, the Altstadt, or Old City, remains much as it was 400 years ago. The protective vaulted arcades along main thoroughfares, the tiny passageways giving way to noble squares, and the ornate restored houses all contribute to an unforgettable picture.

GETTING HERE AND AROUND
AIR TRAVEL
All of Tirol uses the Innsbruck Flughafen, the airport 3 km (2 miles) west of the capital, which is served principally by Austrian Airlines. From Innsbruck Flughafen, take the F Line bus (Line F) into Innsbruck to the main train station (about 20 minutes). Get your ticket (€2) from the driver. Taxis into should take no more than 10 minutes, and the fare is about €10–€12.

Contacts **Innsbruck Flughafen Airport** (*INN*). ☎ *0512/22525 for flight information* ⊕ *www.innsbruck-airport.com.*

BUS TRAVEL
In Innsbruck, most bus and streetcar routes begin or end at Maria-Theresien-Strasse, nearby Bozner Platz, or the main train station (Hauptbahnhof). You can get single tickets costing €1.70 on the bus or streetcar. You can transfer to another line with the same ticket as long as you continue more or less in the same direction in a single journey.

TRAIN TRAVEL
Direct trains serve Innsbruck from Munich, Vienna, Rome, and Zürich, and all arrive at the railroad station Innsbruck Hauptbahnhof at Südtiroler Platz. The station is outfitted with restaurants, cafés, a supermarket, and even a post office.

3

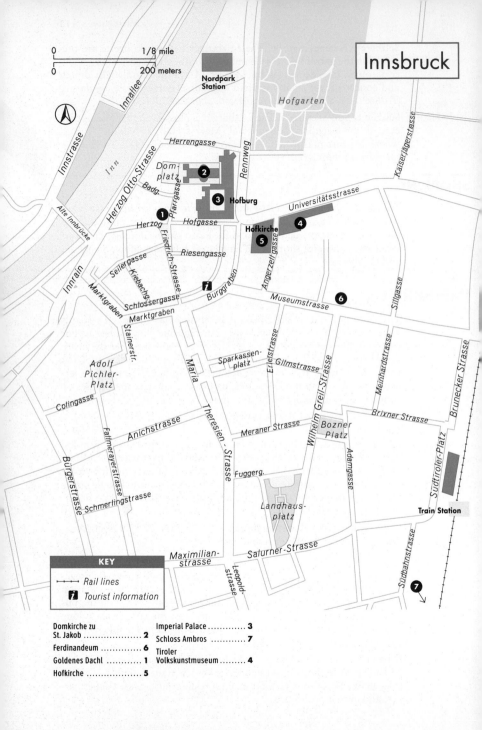

Innsbruck

0 _____ 1/8 mile
0 _____ 200 meters

Innallee

Innstrasse

Inn

Alte Innbrücke

Innrain

Herzog Otto-Strasse

Herrengasse

Dom-platz

Badg.

Pfarrgasse

Herzog

Hofgasse

2

1

3 Hofburg

Rennweg

Hofgarten

Nordpark Station

Kaiserjägerstrasse

Universitätsstrasse

4

Hofkirche

5

Angerzellgasse

Seilergasse

Kiebachg.

Friedrich-Strasse

Riesengasse

Schlossergasse

Stainerstr.

Marktgraben

Marktgraben

Burggraben

Museumstrasse

6

Stiftgasse

Adolf
Pichler-
Platz

Colingasse

Anichstrasse

Faltmeyerverstrasse

Bürgerstrasse

Schmerlingstrasse

Maria Theresien - Strasse

Sparkassen-platz

Erlerstrasse

Gilmstrasse

Meraner Strasse

Wilhelm Greil-Strasse

Bozner Platz

Adamgasse

Meinhardstrasse

Brixner Strasse

Brunecker Strasse

Südtiroler-Platz

Fuggerg.

Landhaus-platz

Maximilian-strasse

Leopold-strasse

Saturner-Strasse

Südbahnstrasse

Train Station

7

KEY

⊢—→ Rail lines

🛈 Tourist information

Train Information Innsbruck Hauptbahnhof ☒ *Südtiroler Pl.* ☎ *0512/930– 000.* **Österreichische Bundesbahn** ☎ *051–717 for information and reservations* ⊕ *www.oebb.at.*

TOURS

The red **Sightseer** bus, a service of the Innsbruck Tourist Office, is the best way to see the sights of Innsbruck without walking. It features a recorded commentary in several languages, including English. There are two routes, both beginning from Maria-Theresien-Strasse in the Old City, but you can catch the bus from any of the nine marked stops, and jump off and on the bus whenever you like. The ride is free with your Innsbruck Card, or you can buy your ticket from the driver or at the tourist office.

VISITOR INFORMATION

Contacts Innsbruck Tourist Office ☒ *Burggraben 3* ☎ *0512/59850* ⊕ *www. innsbruck.info.*

EXPLORING

Domkirche zu St. Jakob. The main attraction is the high-altar painting of the Madonna by Lucas Cranach the Elder, dating from about 1530. The cathedral was built in 1722. In the ornate Baroque interior, look in the north aisle for a monument from 1620 honoring Archduke Maximilian III. ☒ *Dompl. 6* ☎ *0512/5839–02* ☒ *Free* ☉ *Mon.–Sat. 10:15–6.30, Sun. 12:30–6:30 (except during worship).*

Ferdinandeum *(Tyrolean State Museum Ferdinandeum).* The Ferdinandeum houses Austria's largest collection of Gothic art, 19th- and 20th-century paintings, and medieval arms, along with special exhibitions. Here you'll find the original coats of arms from the Goldenes Dachl balcony. Chamber music concerts are offered throughout the year. ☒ *Museumstr. 5* ☎ *0512/59489* ⊕ *www.tiroler-landesmuseen.at* ☒ *€10 combined ticket with Zeughaus and Hofkirche* ☉ *Tues.–Sun. 9–5.*

Fodor's Choice
★ **Goldenes Dachl** *(Golden Roof).* Any walking tour of Innsbruck should start at the Goldenes Dachl, which made famous the late-Gothic mansion whose balcony it covers. In fact, the roof is capped with 2,600 gilded copper tiles, and its refurbishment is said to have taken nearly 31 pounds of gold. Legend has it that the house was built in the 1400s for Duke Friedrich (otherwise known as Friedl the Penniless), and that the indignant duke had the original roof covered with gold to counter the rumor that he was poor. In truth, the 15th-century house was owned by Maximilian I, who added a balcony in 1501 as a sort of "royal box" for watching street performances in the square below. The structure was altered and expanded at the beginning of the 18th century, and now only the loggia and the alcove are identifiable as original. Maximilian is pictured in the two central sculpted panels on the balcony. In the one on the left, he is with his first and second wives, Maria of Burgundy and Bianca Maria Sforza of Milan; on the right, he is pictured with an adviser and a court jester. The Golden Roof building houses the **Maximilianeum**, a small museum that headlines memorabilia and paintings from the life of Emperor Maximilian I. The

short video presentation about Maximilian is worth a look. ✉ *Herzog-Friedrich-Str. 15* ☎ *0512/5873–8029* 💲 *€4* ⊙ *Oct.–Apr., Tues.–Sun. 10–5; May–Sept., daily 10–5.*

Hofkirche (*Court Church*). Close by the Hofburg is the Hofkirche, built as a mausoleum for Maximilian I (although he is actually buried in Wiener Neustadt, south of Vienna). The emperor's ornate black-marble tomb is surrounded by 24 marble reliefs depicting his accomplishments, as well as 28 larger-than-life-size statues of his ancestors, including the legendary King Arthur of England. Andreas Hofer is also buried here. Don't miss the 16th-century **Silver Chapel,** up the stairs opposite the entrance, with its elaborate altar and silver Madonna. ✉ *Universitätsstr. 2* ☎ *0512/59489–511* ⊕ *www.hofkirche.at* 💲 *€5, €10 combined ticket with Zeughaus and Ferdinandeum* ⊙ *Mon.–Sat. 9–5, Sun. 12:30–5.*

Imperial Palace (*Hofburg*). One of Innsbruck's most historic attractions is the Hofburg, or Imperial Palace, which Maximilian I commissioned in the 15th century. Center stage is the **Giant's Hall**—designated a marvel of the 18th century as soon as it was topped off with its magnificent trompe-l'oeil ceiling painted by Franz Anton Maulpertsch in 1775. The Rococo decoration and the portraits of Habsburg ancestors in the ornate white-and-gold great reception hall were added in the 18th century by Maria Theresa. The booklet in English available at the ticket office will tell you more interesting tidbits about the palace than the tour guide. ✉ *Rennweg 1* ☎ *0512/587–186* 💲 *€8* ⊙ *Tours daily at 11 and 2.*

Schloss Ambras. When Archduke Ferdinand II wanted to marry a commoner for love, the court grudgingly allowed it, but the couple was forced to live outside the city limits. Ferdinand revamped a 10th-century castle for the bride, Philippine Welser, which was completed in 1556 and was every bit as luxe as what he had been accustomed to in town. Amid acres of gardens and woodland, it is an inviting castle with cheery red-and-white shutters on its many windows, and is, curiously, home to an oddball collection of armaments. The castle is 3 km (2 miles) southeast of the city. To reach it without a car, take Tram No. 3 or 6 to Ambras (a short walk from the castle) or Route 1 on the **Sightseer** from Maria-Theresien-Strasse. ✉ *Schloss Str. 20* ☎ *1/525–2448–02* ⊕ *www.khm.at/ambras* 💲 *€10* ⊙ *Sept., Oct., and Dec.–July, daily 10–5; Aug., daily 10–7.*

Tiroler Volkskunstmuseum (*Tyrolean Folk Art Museum*). In the same complex as the Hofkirche, this museum exhibits Christmas crèches, costumes, rustic furniture, and entire rooms from old farmhouses and inns, decorated in styles ranging from Gothic to rococo. Displays are somewhat static, and the information cards are in German. The small Christmas Manger Museum, on the other hand, is fascinating. ✉ *Universitätsstr. 2* ☎ *0512/594–89–511* ⊕ *www.tiroler-volkskunstmuseum. at* 💲 *€6* ⊙ *Mon.–Sat. 9–5, Sun. and holidays 10–5.*

WHERE TO EAT

$$$

AUSTRIAN

✕**Goldener Adler.** This restaurant is as popular with locals as it is with travelers. The traditional dining rooms on the arcaded ground floor and the summer-only terrace are popular places to sit. (We prefer the former, as they are more romantic and private.) Start with a glass of Sekt flavored with a dash of blackberry liqueur as you peruse the menu. The kitchen takes a modern approach to traditional dishes, so the pork medallions are topped with ham and Gorgonzola, and the veal steaks are ladled with a creamy herb sauce. $ *Average main: €20* ✉ *Herzog-Friedrich-Str. 6* ☎ *0512/5711.*

$ ✗ **Hofgarten.** This is *the* summer gathering place in Innsbruck, perhaps
AUSTRIAN   because it is so pleasant to eat and drink outdoors amid the beauty of the city's ancient and splendid park. Whether enjoying a beer and light meal on a sunny afternoon, or celebrating with friends after a show at the nearby Landestheater, this is a fine place for having fun. The place is popular with students, but on Tuesday they pack the place. $ *Average main: €12* ✉ *Rennweg 6a* ☎ *0512/588–871.*

$$ ✗ **Ottoburg.** This family-run restaurant offers excellent food and an
AUSTRIAN   extraordinary location. This ancient landmark, built in 1180 as city watchtower, conveys an abundance of historical charm. It's fun just to explore the rabbit warren of paneled rustic rooms named after emperors. Several of the bay-window alcoves in the shuttered house have great views of the main square, while others overlook the river. Try the *Tafelspitz,* a typical Viennese specialty of boiled beef served with vegetables and horseradish, or the *Pfandl,* a filet of pork and a steak served in an old-fashioned pan. On a sunny day come early to get a table outside $ *Average main: €16* ✉ *Herzog-Friedrich-Str. 1* ☎ *0512/584–338* ◷ *Closed Mon.*

$$$ ✗ **Schwarzer Adler.** This intimate, romantic restaurant on the ground
AUSTRIAN   floor of the Romantik Hotel Schwarzer Adler Hotel has lead-glass windows and rustic embellishments—and in summer, dining on the rooftop terrace—offering the perfect backdrop for a memorable meal. The innovative cooks present a new menu every couple of months based on regional seasonal specialties. The year-round classics, such as the garlic soup with croutons, or three kinds of local dumplings served with sauerkraut, are delicious. $ *Average main: €22* ✉ *Kaiserjägerstr. 2* ☎ *0512/587–109.*

$$ ✗ **Weisses Rössl.** In the authentically rustic dining rooms, an array of ant-
AUSTRIAN   lers adds to the charm. This is the right place for solid local standards, like *Tiroler Gröstl,* a tasty hash, and Wiener schnitzel, both of which taste even better on the outside terrace in summer. Ask about the specials that don't appear on the menu, such as wild game or freshly picked mushrooms. Because the place hosts regular local gatherings it can get quite lively here, but all you have to do is request a table in one of the smaller parlors. $ *Average main: €13* ✉ *Kiebachg. 8* ☎ *0512/583–057* ◷ *Closed Sun.*

WHERE TO STAY

$$$$ 🖼 **Grand Hotel Europa.** Opposite the train station, the Grand Hotel
HOTEL   Europa has provided lodging to the celebrated and wealthy in richly appointed, extremely comfortable rooms since it opened in 1869. **Pros:** spacious rooms; inviting restaurant Europa Stüberl. **Cons:** hotel caters to group travel. $ *Rooms from: €260* ✉ *Südtirolerpl. 2* ☎ *0512/5931*

🌐 *www.grandhoteleuropa.at* 🛏 *120 rooms, 10 suites* 🍴 *Multiple meal plans.*

$$ HOTEL 🏨 **Mondschein.** Among the city's oldest houses stands the pink Moonlight Hotel, a warm and welcoming family-run Best Western Hotel. **Pros:** very friendly staff; free parking; riverfront location. **Cons:** some rooms can be noisy; courtyard rooms are dark [$] *Rooms from: €135* ✉ *Mariahilfstr. 6* ☎ *0512/22784* 🌐 *www.mondschein.at* 🛏 *34 rooms* 🍴 *Breakfast.*

$$ HOTEL 🏨 **Weisses Kreuz.** You may fall in love at first sight with this hotel, set over stone arcades in the heart of the Old City. **Pros:** good value; family-friendly vibe; charming building. **Cons:** parking is a short walk from the hotel; noisy neighborhood; not all rooms have a/c. [$] *Rooms from: €110* ✉ *Herzog-Friedrich-Str. 31* ☎ *0512/59479* 🌐 *www.weisseskreuz.at* 🛏 *40 rooms, 9 rooms without bath* 🍴 *Breakfast.*

SHOPPING

The best shops are along the arcaded Herzog-Friedrich-Strasse in the heart of the Old City and along its extension, Maria-Theresien-Strasse, and the adjoining streets Meraner Strasse and Anichstrasse. Innsbruck is the place to buy native Tyrolean clothing, particularly lederhosen and loden.

BELGIUM

Brussels, Brugge, Antwerp

WHAT'S WHERE

1 Brussels. Not just the capital of Belgium, Brussels is also of the European Union. In many respects, it's a thoroughly modern city, with shining steel-and-glass office blocks jostling Gothic spires and art-nouveau town houses. It's the only place in the country that really exudes the "big city" feel, and as befits a capital, it's teeming with top-class museums and restaurants.

2 Brugge. Famed as the birthplace of Flemish painting, Brugge has museums displaying some of the finest masterpieces of Jan van Eyck, Memling, and Hieronymus Bosch. Just 60 miles from Brussels, you can contemplate its weathered beauty in the dark mirror of its peaceful canals. The medieval feel of the city center is so perfectly preserved you may feel you have slipped back in time to another era. The one drawback to this is that its beauty is no well-kept secret, and in the height of summer you will share your experience with hordes of others, creating long lines outside all the major attractions.

3 Antwerp. Vibrant Antwerp is a major port and diamond center 29 miles from Brussels. An unmistakably hip buzz permeates the entire city. While Antwerp is most famous for its diamond trade, these days fashionistas know it as a leader in avant-garde clothing design.

NETHERLANDS

Essen
Kalmthout
ANTWERP
Arendonk

Malle
Turnhout
Achel
Beveren
Antwerp
(Antwerpen)
Herentals
Lommel
Bree
Sint-
Niklaas
Lier
Geel
Peer
KEMPEN
EAST FLANDERS
Olen
Westerlo
LIMBURG
GERMANY
Gent
(Ghent)
Dendermonde
Mechelen
Aarschot
Diest
Aalst
Keerbergen
Hasselt
Genk
BRUSSELS
Leuven
BRABANT
Zoutleeuw
Oudenaarde
Gaasbeek
Tongeren
Geraards-
bergen
Beersel
Tienen
Sint
Truiden
nse
Halle
Hoegaarden
Enghien
Ronquières
Waterloo
Ath
Soignies
Nivelles
Liège
HAINAUT
Meuse

Namur
Huy
Spa
Malmedy
Mons
La Louvière
Gosselies
NAMUR
LIÈGE
Binche
Sambre
Charleroi
Yvoir
Durbuy
Houffalize
Thuin
Dinant
ARDENNES
Beaumont
Anhée
Rochefort
La Roche-
en-Ardenne
Wemperhaardt
Philippeville
Chimdy
Han-sur-Lesse
Bastogne
Notre Damede
Scourmant
LUXEMBOURG

Neufchâteau
Martelange
Romach
LUXEMBOURG
Bouillon
Florenville
Arlon
LUXEMBOURG
Orval
Virton
Pétange
Longwy

FRANCE

NEED TO KNOW

English Channel

Brussels ✪

BELGIUM

GETTING AROUND

✈ **Air Travel:** Brussels Airport (Zaventem) for international flights; Brussels South Charleroi, Antwerp Deurne, and Lieges for intra-Europe flights.

🚌 **Bus Travel:** Buses are reasonably priced for travel between (and within) urban areas, though the train is faster.

🚗 **Car Travel:** Distances between cities are short and there are no tolls, but traffic in and around Brussels and Antwerp is heavy.

🚆 **Train Travel:** Intercity in Belgium are excellent, linking most major towns and cities; regional trains stop in smaller towns and villages.

PLAN YOUR BUDGET

	HOTEL ROOM	MEAL	ATTRACTIONS
Low Budget	€120	€15	Manneken Pis, free
Mid Budget	€165	€22	Groeningemuseum, €8
High Budget	€295	€70	Opera ticket (Brussels), €122

WAYS TO SAVE

Make lunch your main meal. Good-value two- or three-course prix-fixe midday meals are common.

Weekend in Brussels or Antwerp. Brussels and Antwerp are major business centers, so hotels may offer appealing discounts on the weekends and in the summer.

Buy a multi-journey pass. Don't pay by the ride; purchase a pass that allows you unlimited travel for a day or longer or public transit in Brussels or Antwerp.

Plan your museum visits. Some Belgian museums are free, others have some free days or afternoons; check their websites before you visit for details. In Brugge, a museum pass lets you visit five museums for €20.

Hassle Factor	Low. Flights to Brussels are frequent, and transport within Belgium is great.
3 days	You can cover all the main sites of Brussels and spend a day in Brugge or Antwerp.
1 week	Spend a few days soaking up the culture in Brussels culture before heading to Brugge for two days of medieval charm. End your trip with some shopping and museum hopping in Antwerp.
2 weeks	You'll have plenty of time to explore Brussels, Brugge, and Antwerp at your leisure, and perhaps get out into the countryside or see the seashore.

WHEN TO GO

High Season: Brugge tends to be crowded all year long, though especially from June through August and over the December holiday season, when prices are also more expensive. Brussels and Antwerp see a steady influx of business travelers year-round outside of the summer months.

Low Season: December through March can be bitterly cold. Unless you're visiting the charming Christmas markets in Brugge or Brussels, a warmer time of year makes for a more pleasant visit.

Value Season: June through August is a good time to take a trip to Brussels or Antwerp; though some restaurants may be closed for vacation, you can usually get a good deal on hotel rooms and the crowds will be thinner. April, September, and October also see fewer tourists but usually pleasant weather.

BIG EVENTS

May: The three-week Kunstenfestivaldesarts in Brussels features opera, theater, dance, and more. ⊕ www.kfda.be

July: Belgium's National Day celebrations in Brussels include a military march, a huge outdoor feast, and spectacular fireworks.

October: The 12-day Film Fest Gent screens international feature and short films. ⊕ www.filmfestival.be

February: Try more than 300 beers at the weekend-long Brugge Beer Festival. ⊕ www.brugsbierfestival.be

READ THIS

■ *Flawless: Inside the Largest Diamond Heist in History,* Scott Andrew Selby and Greg Campbell. A true-crime thriller, set in Antwerp.

■ *Good Beer Guide Belgium,* Tim Webb. The definitive guide.

■ *Het Verdriet van Belgei (The Sorrow of Belgium),* Hugo Claus. A fictional coming-of-age story during WWII.

WATCH THIS

■ *In Bruges.* Black comedy about gangsters hiding out.

■ *La Promesse.* The tale of immigrants on the edge of Belgian society.

■ *Tout une Nuit.* A romantic look at one night in Brussels.

EAT THIS

■ **Beer:** endless varieties, from wheat to fruit

■ **Chocolate:** reputedly the best in the world

■ **Frites (French fries):** invented here, and always served with mayo

■ **Mussels:** tasty pots of shellfish, steamed with various sauces

■ **Waffles:** a delightful sweet treat, plain or with chocolate or fruit

■ **Waterzooi:** savory fish or chicken and vegetable stew

4

Belgium is a connoisseur's delight. Famous for its artistic inspiration, the land of Brueghel and Van Eyck, Rubens and Van Dyck, and Ensor and Magritte is where their best work can still be seen. Belgian culture was and remains that of a bourgeois, mercantile society. Feudal lords may have built Belgium's many castles, and the clergy its splendid churches, but merchants and craftsmen are responsible for the guild houses and sculpture-adorned town halls of Brussels, Antwerp, and Brugge.

Belgium packs nearly 6 million Flemish-speaking Flemings and just over 4 million French-speaking Walloons into a country the size of Vermont or Wales. The presence of two major language communities enriches its intellectual life but also creates constant political and social tension. The creation in the mid-1990s of three largely self-governing regions—Flanders, Wallonia, and the city of Brussels, which is bilingual—has only emphasized these divisions, and talks between the different factions often plunge the country into constitutional crisis.

Belgium's neutrality was violated during both world wars, when much of its architectural heritage was destroyed and great suffering was inflicted by the occupying forces. This may be why Belgium, home to most European Union (EU) institutions, staunchly supports the EU.

Belgium has attractions out of proportion to its diminutive size. The two largest, most cosmopolitan cities are Brussels (Brussel, Bruxelles), the lively capital, and Antwerp (Antwerpen, Anvers), a bustling port and high-fashion hotbed. The picture-book town of Brugge (Bruges) is a medieval gem with a staggering wealth of fine art. Beyond this the countryside contains the sites of some of the bloodiest stalemates of World War I, and—in perfect contrast to these somber memorials—a string of abbeys where brewing beer is the order of the day.

PLANNING

WHEN TO GO

The best times to visit this country are in the late spring—when the northern European days are long and the summer crowds have not yet filled the highways or the museums—and in fall. The stereotype of overcast Belgian skies is not unfounded, and early spring and fall do get quite a bit of rain, but the weather can change dramatically in the space of a few hours, and temperatures above 85°F (30°C) are also occasionally experienced at this time.

TOP REASONS TO GO

An Architectural Dream. The Grand'Place in Brussels is a spectacular fantasy of medieval architecture that will melt your heart and take your breath away.

Markets of All Varieties. Every day of the week guarantees at least one lively market where stalls sell everything from olives and fruit to antique furniture and dog-eared books.

Picturesque Brugge. The planning laws in picture-perfect Brugge have been very strict for many years, meaning there are few new buildings to spoil the illusion that you've waltzed back to another age.

Canals. The canals that cut though the centers of Brugge are among the most beautiful you will find anywhere. Take a boat trip and travel down them at a pace that befits their grandeur.

Belgium in Miniature. If you're looking to experience every cliché about Belgium in one tidy package, Brugge is the place to find it: chocolate, lace, waffles, fries, beer, and Flemish stepped gables—all within steps of one another.

Shopping. Antwerp is a sophisticated shopper's paradise, with a center that's crammed with trendy stores and designer boutiques showing off the latest creations by the region's top fashionistas.

Because Belgians take their vacations in July and August, these months are not ideal for visiting either countryside regions or Brugge, which is clogged with tourists. It is a very good time to be in Brussels or Antwerp, as you may be able to get a break on hotel prices; on the other hand, this is also vacation time for some restaurants.

You also may want to try to coincide a visit with one of Brussels' more spectacular festivals.

TOP FESTIVALS

Ommegang. The Ommegang takes over Brussels's Grand'Place on the first Thursday in July, and also the preceding Tuesday. It's a sumptuous and stately pageant reenacting a procession that honored Emperor Charles V in 1549. Book early if you want a room in town. ☎ *02/548–0454 ⊕ www.ommegang.be.*

Belgium's National Day. Belgium's National Day, July 21, is celebrated in Brussels with a military march, followed by a popular feast in the Parc de Bruxelles and brilliant fireworks.

GETTING HERE AND AROUND

AIR TRAVEL

The major international airport serving Belgium is Brussels Airport (Zaventem), 14 km (9 miles) northeast of Brussels. The airport has nonstop flights from the U.S. and Canada, and many destinations within Europe. Belgium's national airline, SN Brussels Airlines, has routes to the U.S., Africa, and all over Europe. Because of the country's size, there are no scheduled domestic flights within Belgium.

Trains run up to four times each hour from Brussels Airport to the city center, taking around 15 minutes. A one-way ticket costs €7.80. Direct services also run from the airport to several other cities. Bus connections to the city leave from Level 0. These cost about the same, but take longer. Taxis cost around €35 to the city center.

Brussels City Shuttle operates every half hour between Brussels South Charleroi Airport and Brussels Midi railway station. The journey takes one hour and costs €14 one-way, €28 return. Autocars l'Elan runs a similar service, with less frequency.

Contacts Autocars l'Elan ⊕ *www.voyages-lelan.be*. **Brussels Airport** ⊕ *www. brusselsairport.be*. **Brussels City Shuttle** ☏ *70/21–12–10 (€0.55 per min)* ⊕ *www.brussels-city-shuttle.com*.

BUS TRAVEL

Belgium has an extensive network of reasonably priced urban and intercity buses. STIB/MIVB covers service around the Brussels region. De Lijn runs buses in Flanders, including Antwerp and Brugge. Eurolines has up to three daily express services between Brussels and Amsterdam, Berlin, Frankfurt, Paris, and London, and offers student fares.

Contacts De Lijn ☏ *070/220–200 (€0.30 per min)* ⊕ *www.delijn.be*. **Eurolines** ☏ *02/274–1350* ⊕ *www.eurolines.com*. **STIB/MIVB** ☏ *070/232–000* ⊕ *www. stib.be*.

CAR TRAVEL

Belgium is a small country, and driving distances are not great. Most destinations are not more than two hours from Brussels. There are no tolls, but the major highways can get very congested. Driving within cities can be a nightmare if you're not used to Belgian roads. You may have to compete with trams or taxi drivers with a death wish. Brussels is 204 km (122 miles) from Amsterdam on E19; and 308 km (185 miles) from Paris on E19.

On highways in Belgium the speed limit is 120 kph (75 mph). The limit on other rural roads is 90 kph (55 mph), and 50 kph (30 mph) in urban areas. Use of seatbelts is compulsory, both in front and rear seats. Turning right on a red light is not permitted. Your car must carry a red warning triangle in case of breakdown. All cars rented in Belgium will already have these. Drinking and driving is prohibited.

FERRY TRAVEL

Transeuropa Ferries has services between Ramsgate, England, and Oostende, with four daily round-trips. P&O Ferries operates overnight ferry services once daily from Hull, England, to Zeebrugge. You can take your car.

Contacts P&O Ferries ✉ *In Holland Beneluxhaven, Havennummer 5805, Rotterdam/Europoort, Netherlands* ☏ *020/200–8333 in the Netherlands, 070/707–771 in Belgium* ⊕ *www.poferries.com*. **Transeuropa Ferries** ✉ *Slijkensesteenweg 2, Oostende, Belgium* ☏ *059/340–260 in Belgium, 01843/595–522 in U.K.* ⊕ *www. transeuropaferry.co.uk*.

TRAIN TRAVEL

The easiest mode of transportation within Belgium is the train. Belgian National Railways (SNCB/NMBS) maintains an extensive network of prompt and frequent services. Intercity trains have rapid connections between the major towns and cities, while local and regional trains stop at all smaller towns in between.

An expanding network of high-speed trains also puts Brussels within commuting distance of many European cities. Most of these services leave from Brussels's Gare du Midi.

Contacts Eurostar ⊕ *www.eurostar.com.* **SNCB/NMBS** ⊕ *www.b-rail.be.* **Thalys** ⊕ *www.thalys.com.*

4

HOTELS

Belgium offers a range of options, from the major international hotel chains and small, modern local hotels to family-run inns and historic houses. Prices in metropolitan areas are significantly higher than those in outlying towns and the countryside.

DISCOUNTS

Most hotels that cater to business travelers will offer substantial weekend discounts. These rates are often available during the week as well as in July and August, when business travelers are thin on the ground. Moreover, you can often qualify for a "corporate rate" when hotel occupancy is low. The rule is, always ask the best rate a hotel can offer before you book. Few hoteliers will give a lower rate unless you ask for it.

CLASSIFICATIONS

Hotels in Belgium are rated by the Benelux Hotel Classification System, an independent agency that inspects properties in Belgium, the Netherlands, and Luxembourg. The organization's star system is the accepted norm for these countries; one star indicates the most basic hotel and five stars indicates the most luxurious. Stars are based on detailed criteria—mainly facilities and amenities, such as private baths, specific items of furniture in guest rooms, and so on—not on "quality." That is, you can have a not-so-good five-star hotel just as you can have a wonderful one-star hotel. Rooms in one-star hotels are likely not to have a telephone or TV, and two-star hotels may not have air-conditioning or elevators. Four- and five-star hotels have conference facilities and offer amenities such as pools, tennis courts, saunas, private parking, dry-cleaning service, and room service. Three-, four-, and five-star hotels are usually equipped with hair dryers and coffeemakers. All hotels we recommend have private baths unless otherwise noted.

RESERVATIONS

It's wise to reserve your hotel in advance. Most hotels in Belgium offer online booking.

RESTAURANTS

Belgium's better restaurants are on a par with the most renowned in the world. Prices are similar to those in France and Britain. The Belgian emphasis on high-quality food filters down to more casual options as well, from main-square cafés to the street vendors you'll find in towns large and small.

Most restaurants are open for lunch and dinner only. A prix-fixe, three-course menu for lunch (*déjeuner* in French, *lunch* in Flemish) is offered in many restaurants. Dinner (*dîner* in French, *diner* in Flemish) menus are very similar to lunch menus. You can also order a quick sandwich lunch or a light one-course meal at cafés, pubs, cafeterias, and snack bars. Smoking in Belgian cafés and restaurants is prohibited. However, some bars above a certain size with adequate ventilation have an exemption.

MEALS AND MEAL TIMES

Belgian specialties include steamed mussels, served throughout the country. *Waterzooi is* a creamy stew made with chicken or fish. *Carbonnades* or *stoverij is* a beef stew cooked in beer, while *stoemp* is a filling mix of mashed potatoes and vegetables. Eel is served, most notably as *paling in 't groen* (Flemish) or *anguilles au vert* (French), with a green herb sauce. Belgian endive (*chicons* in French, *witloof* in Flemish) is usually cooked with ham, braised, and topped with a cheese gratin. Complete your meal with *frites* or *frieten* (french fries), which Belgians proudly claim to have invented. A favorite snack is the waffle (*gaufres* in French, *wafels* in Flemish), which you can buy at stands in cities. It would also be almost criminal to visit Belgium and not try a generous sampling of the country's world-famous chocolates.

Breakfast is served in hotels from about 7 to 10. Lunch is usually served from noon to 2, and dinner from about 7 to 9. Pubs and cafés often serve snacks until midnight.

PAYING

Major credit cards are widely accepted, but smaller establishments may take only cash. It is customary to round off the total of a restaurant bill, but tipping 15% is not customary or expected.

WINES, BEER, AND SPIRITS

Belgium is a beer-lover's paradise. Artisanal breweries produce around 800 types. Kriek, a fruit-flavored beer, and Duvel, a very strong blond beer, are favorites. Some Trappist monasteries still produce their own brews, such as Orval, Westmalle, Rochefort, and Chimay. Popular mass-produced brands are Stella Artois, Jupiler, and Maes. Keep in mind that many Belgian beers have a high alcohol content; 8% to 9% alcohol by volume (ABV) is not unusual.

Be sure to try locally produced *genièvre* or *jenever*, a strong, ginlike spirit taken neat. Sometimes its edge is taken off with sweeter fruit flavors like apple, lemon, and redcurrant.

Belgians tend not to drink their own tap water. It's perfectly safe to do so, but water aficionados don't like the taste. The locally produced Spa mineral water brands are an excellent and reasonably priced alternative.

HOTEL AND RESTAURANT PRICES

Prices in the restaurant reviews are the average cost of a main course at dinner or, if dinner is not served, at lunch; taxes and service charges are generally included. Prices in the hotel reviews are the lowest cost of a standard double room in high season, excluding taxes, service charges, and meal plans.

PLANNING YOUR TIME

The three cities listed in this chapter represent the essence of modern Belgium. How you divide your time between them depends on how much of it you have and where your main interests lie. But the beauty of this land's diminutive size is that you can comfortably base yourself in one place and trip out to the others. For a one- or two-day visit you would do best to concentrate on the one city that appeals to you most. With a week, you can get a taste of all three places mentioned here. All are worth spending a few nights getting to know if you can.

Brussels is the closest thing Belgium has to a metropolis, with great museums and restaurants and a definite cosmopolitan air. While there is enough to keep you happy here for many days, the noisy, traffic-clogged streets may leave you craving somewhere quieter after a while.

If that's the case, consider Brugge—known as an "Art City of Flanders," a phrase that immediately conjures up images of proud spires and medieval architecture. In the 15th century Brugge was among the richest cities in Europe, and the aura of that golden age still seems to emanate from its cloth halls, opulent merchants' homes, and cathedrals. While Brugge is thoroughly preserved—visiting there really does feel like stepping into another century—it's also extremely popular with tourists, all year long.

Antwerp merits at least a weekend for exploring its outstanding museums, lovely architecture, top fashion shopping, fabulous restaurants, and nonstop nightlife. While the city has grown and modernized apace, it preserves a great deal of yesterday's glories.

BRUSSELS

Brussels's vibrant, cosmopolitan atmosphere and multicultural beat make it much more than simply the administrative hub of Europe. For all its world-class restaurants, architecture, and art, though, the city keeps a relatively low profile, so you'll have the breathing room to relish its landmarks, cobbled streets, and beautiful parks.

Brussels started life as a village toward the end of the 10th century. Over the next eight centuries it grew as a center for trading and crafts, and was alternately ruled by everyone from local counts of Leuven, the Burgundians Philip the Good and Charles V, to the Spanish and later the Austrians. Despite its history of occupation, after 1815 the city resisted Dutch attempts to absorb it, and 1830 saw the uprising that finally gained Belgium its independence.

At the end of the 19th century Brussels was one of the liveliest cities in Europe, known for its splendid cafés and graceful art nouveau architecture. It later became the European Economic Community's headquarters, a precursor to its hosting of the EU's administrative and political arms. The city is technically bilingual, though French is the dominant language.

PLANNING YOUR TIME

Your first priority in Brussels should be to wander the narrow, cobbled lanes surrounding the main square and visit the graceful, arcaded Galeries St-Hubert, an elegant 19th-century shopping gallery. Head down rue de l'Etuve to see Manneken Pis, the famed statue. Walk to the place du Grand Sablon to window-shop at its many fine antiques stores and galleries. Have lunch in one of the cafés lining the perimeter, and don't forget to buy chocolates at one of the top chocolatiers on the square. Then head to the Musée d'Art Moderne and the Musée d'Art Ancien. End with dinner on the fashionable rue Antoine Dansaert or have a drink in one of Grand'Place's many cafés.

On your second day, start at the Musée des Instruments de Musique, which houses one of Europe's finest collections of musical instruments. Hop a tram to Avenue Louise in Ixelles for a little shopping and lunch. After lunch, visit architect Horta's own house, now the Musée Horta, on rue Américaine. For dinner head to place Ste-Catherine for a feast of Belgian seafood specialties. Later, check out the many cafés and bars around the Bourse.

GETTING HERE AND AROUND

CAR TRAVEL

Driving in Brussels can be an unnerving experience. Belgians weren't required to have driver's licenses until 1979; local driving habits are often slapdash, and roads can get very busy around peak hours.

PUBLIC TRANSPORTATION

The metro, trams, and buses operate as part of the same system run by the city's transport authority, STIB/MIVB. A single "Jump" ticket, which can be used on all three systems in an hour-long time frame, costs €2 (€2.50 on board). The best buy is a 10-trip ticket, which costs €13.50. Special tourist tickets are also a good value at €6.50 for a one-day unlimited travel card; €11 for three days; and €14 for five days (weekdays only). You can purchase these tickets in any metro station or at newsstands. Single tickets can be purchased on the bus or on the tram. You need to validate your ticket in the orange machines on the bus or tram; in the metro, validate your card at the orange machines in the station. Metro trains, buses, and trams run from around 5 am until midnight.

Contacts **STIB/MIVB** ☎ *070/232–000* ⊕ *www.stib.be.*

TAXI TRAVEL

You can catch a taxi at cab stands around town, indicated with yellow signs. All officially registered taxis have a yellow-and-blue sign on their roofs. A cab ride within the city center costs between €6 and €12. Tips are included in the fare.

Contacts **Taxis Oranges** ☎ *02/349–4343*. **Taxis Verts** ☎ *02/349–4949* ⊕ *www.taxisverts.be.*

VISITOR INFORMATION

Contacts **Tourist Information Brussels** (*TIB*). ✉ *Hôtel de Ville, Grand'Place, Lower Town* ☎ *02/513–8940* ⊕ *www.brusselsinternational.be.*

EXPLORING

LOWER TOWN

FAMILY

Fodor'sChoice

★

Centre Belge de la Bande Dessinée (*Belgian Center for Comic-Strip Art*). It fell to the land of Tintin, a cherished cartoon character, to create the world's first museum dedicated to the ninth art—comic strips. Despite its primary appeal to children, comic-strip art has been taken seriously in Belgium for decades, and in the Belgian Comic Strip Center it is wedded to another strongly Belgian art form: art nouveau. Based in an elegant 1903 Victor Horta–designed building, the museum is long on the history of the genre but sadly short on kid-friendly interaction and anglophone-friendly information (most is in French). Tintin, the cowlicked adventurer created in 1929 by the late, great Brussels native Hergé, became a worldwide favorite cartoon character. The collection includes more than 400 original plates by Hergé and his Belgian successors and 25,000 cartoon works. If you enjoy this, keep an eye out for the comic-strip murals dotted on walls around the city. ✉ *Rue des Sables 20, Lower Town* ☎ *02/219–1980* ⊕ *www.comicscenter.net* ✆ *€8* ⏱ *Tues.–Sun. 10–6* Ⓜ *Metro: Botanique.*

4

NEED A
BREAK?

A la Mort Subite. A Brussels institution named after a card game called "Sudden Death," A la Mort Subite is a 1920s café with high ceilings, wooden tables, and mirrored walls and remains a favorite of beer lovers from all over the world. It still brews its own traditional Brussels beers, Lambik, Gueuze, and Faro. These sour potent drafts may be an acquired taste, but, like singer Jacques Brel, who came here often, you'll find it hard to resist the bar's gruff charm. ✉ *Rue Montagne-aux-Herbes-Potagères 7, Lower Town* ☎ *02/513–1318.*

Fodor'sChoice

★

Grand'Place. This jewel box of a square is arguably Europe's most ornate and most theatrical. It's a vital part of the city—everyone passes through at some point. At night the burnished facades of the guild houses and their gilded statuary look especially dramatic: from April to September, the square is floodlighted after sundown with waves of changing colors, accompanied by music. Try to be here for the *Ommegang,* a magnificent historical pageant re-creating Emperor Charles V's reception in the city in 1549 (the first Tuesday and Thursday in July), or for the famed *Carpet of Flowers,* which fills the square with color for four days in mid-August in even-numbered years. You'll also find here a flower market, frequent jazz and classical concerts, and in December, under the majestic Christmas tree, a life-size crèche with sheep grazing around it. ✉ *Grand'Place* Ⓜ *Metro: De Brouckere, Gare Centrale. Tram: Bourse.*

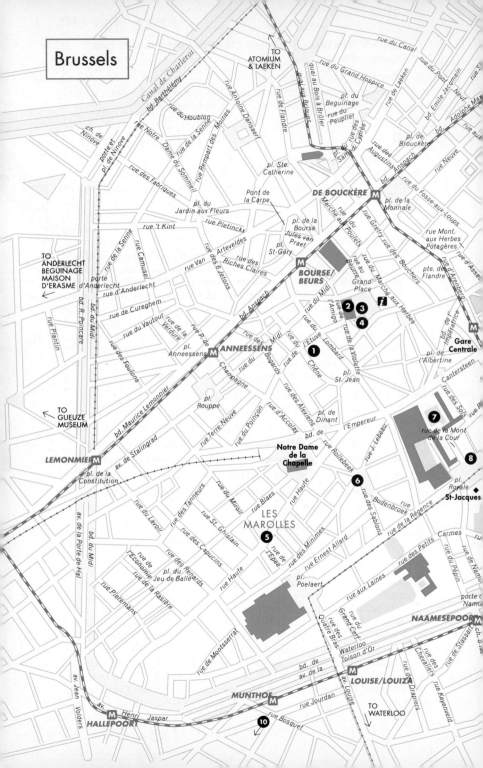

4

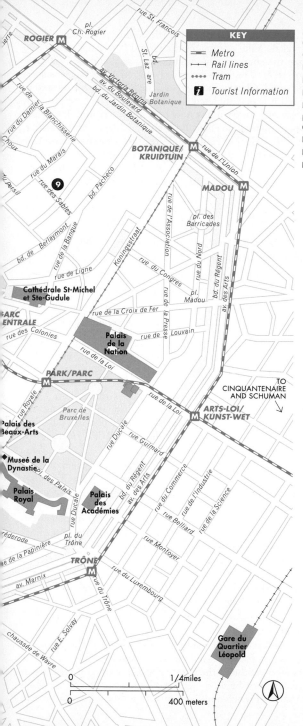

Fodor's Choice   **Hôtel de Ville.** Dating from the early 15th century, the magnificent
★   Gothic-era Hôtel de Ville dominates the Grand'Place. It's nearly 300
years older than the surrounding guild houses, as it survived the devastating fires of 1695. The left wing was begun in 1402 but was soon
found to be too small. Charles the Bold laid the first stone for the extension in 1444, and it was completed four years later. The extension left
the slender belfry off center; it has now been fully restored. Inside the
building are a number of excellent Brussels and Mechelen tapestries,
some of them in the Gothic Hall, where recitals and chamber-music
concerts are frequently held. Locals still get married in the town hall,
so keep an eye out for brides stepping gingerly over the cobbles on
summer mornings. ⊠ *Grand'Place, Lower Town* ☏ *02/548–0447* 🎟 *€5*
⊙ *Guided tours available in English on Wed. at 3 and Sun. at 10 and
2 (buy tickets at the tourist office in the right wing of the building)*
Ⓜ *Metro: De Brouckere, Gare Centrale. Tram: Bourse.*

**NEED A
BREAK?**   **Le Roy d'Espagne.** There are plenty of cafés to choose from on
Grand'Place. But Le Roy d'Espagne is by far the most popular. In the
summer, sit out on the terrace and soak up the beauty of the square; in
winter, snuggle up to the huge fire. You can expect to pay a few euros more
for coffees and beers in the Grand'Place area, but the view is worth it.
⊠ *Grand'Place 1, Lower Town* ☏ *02/513–0807* ⊕ *www.roydespagne.be.*

Maison de la Brasserie. On the same side of the Grand'Place as the Hôtel
de Ville, the Maison de la Brasserie was once the brewers' guild. The
building, also known as the *Arbre d'Or* (the "Golden Tree"), now
houses a modest brewery museum, the *Musée des Brasseurs Belges*,
appropriate enough in a country that still brews more than 1,100
different beers. There are audio guides in English. Happily enough,
the entrance ticket entitles you to a free beer at the end of your visit.
⊠ *Grand'Place 10, Lower Town* ☏ *02/511–4987* 🎟 *€6* ⊙ *Daily 10–5*
Ⓜ *Metro: De Brouckere, Gare Centrale. Tram: Bourse.*

Fodor's Choice   **Manneken Pis** (*"The Little Urinating Boy"*). This cocky emblem of Brus-
★   sels has drawn sightseers for centuries but after all the hype—after
all, this is an image that launched a thousand tchotchkes—you may
be underwhelmed by the minuscule statue of the peeing boy. The first
mention of the Manneken dates from 1377, and he's said to symbolize what Belgians think of the authorities, especially those of occupying forces. The present version was commissioned from noted sculptor
Jerome Duquesnoy in 1619. It is a copy; the original was seized by
French soldiers in 1747. In restitution, King Louis XV of France was
the first to present *Manneken Pis* with a gold-embroidered suit. ⊠ *Rue
de l'Etuve at Rue du Chêne, Lower Town* Ⓜ *Metro: Gare Centrale.
Bus: 34, 48, 95.*

UPPER TOWN

Les Marolles. If the Grand'Place stands for old money, the Marolles
neighborhood stands for old—and current—poverty. This was home
to the workers who produced the luxury goods for which Brussels was
famous. There may not be many left who still speak the old Brussels
dialect, which mixes French and Flemish with a bit of Spanish thrown

in, but the area still has some raffish charm. The Marolles has welcomed many waves of immigrants, the most recent from Spain, North Africa, and Turkey. Many come to the daily **Vieux Marché** (flea market) at place du Jeu de Balle (7–1), where old clothes are sold along with every kind of bric-a-brac, plain junk, and the occasional gem. For more browsing, hit the antiques shops on rue Haute and rue Blaes. This area can be sketchy at night, so you may want to leave by sunset, particularly if you're alone, though groups can enjoy some fun bars and restaurants. ✉ *Bordered by blvd. du Midi, blvd. de Waterloo heading southwest from Palais de Justice, and imaginary line running west from blvd. Maurice Lemonnier, Upper Town* Ⓜ *Metro: Louise/Gare du Midi.*

FAMILY
Fodor's Choice
★
Musée des Instruments de Musique (MIM). If you've ever been curious to know what a gamelan or Tibetan temple bell sounds like, here's your chance. In addition to seeing the more than 1,500 instruments on display, you can listen to them via infrared headphones, and you can hear musical extracts from almost every instrument as you stand in front of it. The more than 200 extracts range from ancient Greek tunes to mid-20th-century pieces. Paintings and ancient vases depicting the instruments being played throughout history enhance the experience. ✉ *Rue Montagne de la Cour 2, Upper Town* ☎ *02/545–0130* ⊕ *www.mim.be* ✉ *€5* ☉ *Tues.–Fri. 9:30–5, weekends 10–5, last entry 45 mins before closing* Ⓜ *Metro: Gare Centrale. Tram: 92, 94. Bus: 71.*

Fodor's Choice
★
Musée Magritte. After years sharing display space with his contemporaries in the neighboring Musée d'Art Moderne, Brussels's own surrealist genius René Magritte (1898–1967) was finally handed the honor of his own museum in 2009. You can reach it through an underground passage from the Musée d'Art Ancien, or enter via the separate entrance on place Royale where it is housed. Note: you must buy your tickets at the central desk in the Musée d'Art Ancien. The exhibition traces Magritte's life and work chronically, expanding key moments through letters, sculptures, films, and of course, a great many fine canvases. There are around 200 paintings on display, including such masterpieces as the haunting *The Empire of Light* and *The Domain of Arnheim.* ✉ *Entrance at pl. Royale 1; buy tickets at rue de la Régence 3, Upper Town* ☎ *02/508–3211* ⊕ *www.musee-magritte-museum.be* ✉ *€8, combo ticket for three museums €13* ☉ *Tues. and Thurs.–Sun. 10–5, Wed. 10–8* Ⓜ *Tram: 49.*

Place du Grand Sablon. "Sand Square" is where the people of Brussels come to see and be seen. Once, as the name implies, it was nothing more than a sandy hill. Today, it is an elegant square, surrounded by numerous restaurants, cafés, and antiques shops, some in intriguing alleys and arcades. Every weekend morning a lively antiques market of more than 100 stalls takes over the upper end of the square. It isn't for bargain hunters, though. For a little tranquility, pop into the beautiful Notre Dame du Sablon church or across the street to the lovely little Place du Petit Sablon garden. ✉ *Intersection of rue de Rollebeek, rue Lebeau, rue de la Paille, rue Ste-Anne, rue Boedenbroeck, rue des Sablons, petite rue des Minimes, rue des Minimes, and rue Joseph Stevens, Upper Town* Ⓜ *Metro: Louise. Tram: 92, 94.*

IXELLES

Fodor's Choice ★ **Musée Horta.** The house where Victor Horta (1861–1947), one of the major early exponents of art nouveau, lived and worked until 1919 is the best place to see his mesmerizing interiors and furniture. Horta's genius lay in his ability to create a sense of opulence, light, and spaciousness where little light or space existed. Inspired by the direction of the turn-of-the-20th-century British Arts and Crafts movement, he amplified such designs into an entire architectural scheme. He shaped iron and steel into fluid, organic curves; structural elements were revealed. The facade of his home and studio, built between 1898 and 1901 (with extensions a few years later), looks somewhat narrow, but once you reach the interior stairway you'll be struck by the impression of airiness. A glazed skylight filters light down the curling banisters, lamps hang like tendrils from the ceilings, and mirrored skylights evoke giant butterflies with multicolor wings of glass and steel. ✉ *Rue Américaine 25, Ixelles* ☎ *02/543–0490* 🌐 *www.hortamuseum.be* 🎟 *€7* ⏲ *Tues.–Sun. 2–5:30* [M] *Tram: 92, 81.*

WHERE TO EAT

$$ BELGIAN ✕ **Aux Armes de Bruxelles.** A reliable choice among the many tourist traps of the Ilôt Sacré, this kid-friendly restaurant attracts a largely local clientele with its slightly tarnished middle-class elegance and Belgian classics: turbot *waterzooi* (stew), a variety of steaks, and mussels prepared every conceivable way. The place is cheerful and light, and service is bustling but friendly. [$] *Average main: €20* ✉ *Rue des Bouchers 13, Lower Town* ☎ *02/511–5550* 🌐 *www.auxarmesdebruxelles.be* ⏲ *Closed for 4 wks around July* [M] *Metro: Gare Centrale.*

$$$$ FRENCH Fodor's Choice ★ ✕ **Comme Chez Soi.** Pierre Wynants, the perfectionist owner-chef of what some consider the best restaurant in the country, has decorated his bistro-size restaurant in art-nouveau style. The superb cuisine, excellent wines, and attentive service complement the warm décor. Wynants is ceaselessly inventive, and earlier creations are quickly relegated to the back page of the menu. One all-time favorite, filet of sole with a white-wine mousseline and shrimp, is, however, always available. Book weeks in advance to be sure of a table. [$] *Average main: €50* ✉ *Pl. Rouppe 23, Lower Town* ☎ *02/512–2921* 🌐 *www.commechezsoi.be* ✍ *Reservations essential* 👔 *Jacket and tie* ⏲ *Closed Sun., Mon., mid-July–mid-Aug., and Dec. 25–Jan. 10. No lunch Wed.* [M] *Metro: Anneessens.*

$$ BELGIAN Fodor's Choice ★ ✕ **In 't Spinnekopke.** True Brussels cooking flourishes in this charming restaurant. The low ceilings and benches around the walls remain from its days as a coach inn during the 18th century. Choose from among 100 artisanal beers, then tuck into dishes made with the tipple, such as *lapin à gueuze* (rabbit stewed in fruit beer). Go with an appetite, because portions are huge. The knowledgeable waiters can recommend beers to go with your food. [$] *Average main: €20* ✉ *Pl. du Jardin aux Fleurs 1, Lower Town* ☎ *02/511–8695* 🌐 *www.spinnekopke.be* ⏲ *Closed Sun. No lunch Sat.* [M] *Metro: De Brouckere. Tram: Bourse.*

$$$$ FRENCH ✕ **La Quincaillerie.** The name means "The Hardware Store," and that's precisely what this place used to be. It still looks the part, except now there are tables perched on the narrow balcony and there's an oyster

bar downstairs. It attracts a stylish, youngish clientele and offers good deals on business lunches. The menu consists mostly of brasserie standbys, but it's enlivened by such selections as honey-baked Barbary duck with lime and a glorious seafood platter. [$] *Average main: €31* ✉ *Rue du Page 45, Ixelles* ☎ *02/538–2553* ⏲ *No lunch weekends* [M] *Tram: 81.*

$$ BELGIAN Fodor's Choice ★ 🍴 **La Roue d'Or.** Bright orange and yellow murals pay humorous homage to the Surrealist René Magritte in this excellent art-nouveau brasserie. Bowler-hatted gentlemen ascend serenely to the ceiling, a blue sky inhabited by tropical birds. The good cuisine includes traditional Belgian fare—a generous fish waterzooi and homemade frites—as well as such brasserie staples as lamb's tongue vinaigrette with shallots, veal kidneys with tarragon and watercress cream, and foie gras. Menus in English are on hand. [$] *Average main: €17* ✉ *Rue des Chapeliers 26, Lower Town* ☎ *02/514–2554* ⏲ *Closed mid-July–mid-Aug.* [M] *Metro: Gare Centrale. Tram: Bourse.*

4

$$$ BELGIAN 🍴 **L'Idiot du Village.** Don't believe the modest name of this restaurant in the Marolles; its focus on smart, well-crafted food has fostered a loyal clientele. The decor is relaxed and intimate, kitschy rather than trendy. Dishes include bass with lemon confit, and warm escalope of foie gras with pepper and vanilla. [$] *Average main: €25* ✉ *Rue Notre-Seigneur 19, Upper Town* ☎ *02/502–5582* ⏲ *Closed weekends* [M] *Metro: Gare Centrale. Tram: 92, 94.*

$$ BELGIAN 🍴 **Taverne du Passage.** This art-deco brasserie in the famous shopping arcade has been here since 1928 and remains a benchmark of its kind, serving chicken waterzooi, sauerkraut, herring, and lobster from noon to midnight nonstop. Most fun of all, however, are the roasts, which are carved in front of you. The multilingual waiters are jolly, and the wine list is exceptional—not surprising in a restaurant owned by the president of the Belgian guild of sommeliers. [$] *Average main: €18* ✉ *Galerie de la Reine 30, Upper Town* ☎ *02/512–3731* ⏲ *Closed Wed. and Thurs., and June and July* [M] *Metro: Gare Centrale, De Brouckere.*

$ BELGIAN 🍴 **'t Kelderke.** Head down into this 17th-century vaulted cellar restaurant (watch out for the low door frame) for traditional Belgian cuisine served at plain wooden tables. Mussels are the house specialty, but the *stoemp et saucisses* (mashed potatoes and sausages) are equally tasty. It's a popular place with locals, as it's open from noon to 2 am. There are no reservations, so turn up early to be sure to snag a table. [$] *Average main: €14* ✉ *Grand'Place 15, Lower Town* ☎ *02/513–7344* 🌐 *www.restaurant-het-kelderke.be* [M] *Metro: De Brouckere. Tram: Bourse.*

WHERE TO STAY

$$$$ HOTEL 🏨 **Amigo.** A block from the Grand'Place, the Amigo pairs contemporary design and understated luxury with antiques and plush wall hangings. **Pros:** polished service; central location. **Cons:** some bathrooms are small; nearby streets can be noisy; very high rates. [$] *Rooms from: €660* ✉ *Rue d'Amigo 1–3, Lower Town* ☎ *02/547–4747* 🌐 *www.hotelamigo.com* 🛏 *174 rooms, 19 suites* 🍽 *Multiple meal plans* [M] *Metro: De Brouckere, Gare Centrale. Tram: Bourse.*

$ B&B/INN 🏨 **La Vieille Lanterne.** More bed-and-breakfast than hotel, this tiny, old place of six rooms is run by the family that owns the gift shops on the ground floor. **Pros:** good price for such a central location. **Cons:** its proximity to Manneken Pis makes it a noisy, hectic location; no on-site parking. $ *Rooms from: €75* ☒ *Rue des Grands Carmes 29, Lower Town* ☎ *02/512–7494* ➹ *6 rooms* ⦿ *Breakfast* Ⓜ *Metro: Bourse.*

$$$
HOTEL
Fodor'sChoice
★

⌗ **Le Dixseptième.** Here you can stay in what was once the residence of the Spanish ambassador. **Pros:** romantic setting; gorgeous rooms. **Cons:** no on-site parking. $ *Rooms from: €200* ☒ *Rue de la Madeleine 25, Lower Town* ☎ *02/517–1717* ⊕ *www.ledixseptieme.be* ➹ *22 rooms, 2 suites* ⦿ *Multiple meal plans* Ⓜ *Metro: De Brouckere.*

$
HOTEL

⌗ **Monty Hotel.** A stay here is like an overnight in a contemporary design showroom—with breakfast in the morning. **Pros:** great design; delicious breakfasts; fun atmosphere. **Cons:** a little off the beaten track; few parking spaces. $ *Rooms from: €85* ☒ *Blvd. Brand Whitlock 101, Laeken* ☎ *02/734–5636* ⊕ *www.monty-hotel.be* ➹ *18 rooms, 3 apartments* ⦿ *Breakfast* Ⓜ *Metro: Montgomery. Tram: 23.*

$
HOTEL

⌗ **NH Hotel du Grand Sablon.** Part of the Sablon square's lineup of antiques shops, cafés, and chocolate makers, this hotel offers discreet luxury behind an elegant white facade. **Pros:** lovely older building; shady courtyard; great value. **Cons:** front rooms can be noisy. $ *Rooms from: €90* ☒ *Rue Bodenbroeck 2–4, Upper Town* ☎ *02/518–1100* ⊕ *www.nh-hotels.be* ➹ *193 rooms, 6 suites* ⦿ *Breakfast* Ⓜ *Metro: Louise, Park.*

$$
HOTEL

⌗ **Stanhope.** This exclusive hotel was created out of three adjoining town houses and continues to expand. **Pros:** friendly staff, nice rooms. **Cons:** slightly farther from historic center than some hotels. $ *Rooms from: €130* ☒ *Rue du Commerce 9, Upper Town* ☎ *02/506–9111* ⊕ *www. summithotels.com* ➹ *108 rooms, 7 suites, 2 royal suites* ⦿ *Breakfast* Ⓜ *Metro: Trone.*

$$
HOTEL
FAMILY
Fodor'sChoice
★

⌗ **Welcome Hotel.** Among the many charms of the smallest hotel in Brussels are the incredibly friendly young owners, Michel and Sophie Smeesters. **Pros:** fantastic décor; lovely staff. **Cons:** rooms fill up quickly; some of them lack a/c. $ *Rooms from: €135* ☒ *Rue du Peuplier 5, Lower Town* ☎ *02/219–9546* ⊕ *www.hotelwelcome.com* ➹ *14 rooms, 3 suites* ⦿ *Breakfast* Ⓜ *Metro: Ste-Catherine.*

SHOPPING

There are galleries scattered across Brussels, but low rents have made **boulevard Barthélémy** the "in" place for avant-garde art. On the **place du Grand Sablon** and adjoining streets and alleys you'll find antiques dealers and smart art galleries. The **Galeries St-Hubert** is a rather stately shopping arcade lined with posh shops selling men's and women's clothing, books, and objets d'art. In the trendy **rue Antoine Dansaert** and **place du Nouveau Marché aux Grains,** near the Bourse, are a number of boutiques carrying fashions by young designers and interior design and art shops. **Avenue Louise** and its surrounding streets in Ixelles have a number of chic boutiques offering clothes new and vintage, jewelry, antiques, and housewares.

BRUGGE

Long thought of as a Sleeping Beauty reawakened, Brugge is an ancient village whose heritage has been well preserved. However, the contemporary comparison is sometimes closer to Beauty and the Beast—particularly in summer, when visitors flock here in overwhelming numbers. Still, in the quiet, colder seasons, the city offers a peaceful refuge, and you can feel the rhythm of life centuries ago. Brugge is compact, like a small island amid the winding waterways, and the twists and turns may lead you to unexpected pleasures.

PLANNING YOUR TIME
Must-see spots include the Begijnhof near Minnewater, as well as the great buildings around Burg and Markt squares. Soak up the artwork, including the Groeninge and Memling museums, and Michelangelo's sculpture in the Onze-Lieve-Vrouwekerk. You might take an afternoon canal ride—or, after dinner, when crowds have thinned, wander alongside the water.

GETTING HERE AND AROUND
BIKE TRAVEL
Considering the flat-as-a-pancake terrain, it's easy to travel on two wheels. You can rent bikes at rental shops or at the train station. A valid train ticket gets you a discounted rate. Quasimundo Bike Tours organizes a daily 2½-hour guided bike tour of Brugge for €25 per person.

Contacts Bauhaus Bike Rental ✉ *Langestraat 135* ☎ *050/34–10–93.* **Quasimundo Bike Tours** ☎ *050/33–07–75* ⊕ *www.quasimundo.com.*

BOAT TRAVEL
The waterways in the center of Brugge make for lovely sightseeing. Independent motor launches depart from four jetties along the Dijver and Katelijnestraat and by the Vismarkt as soon as they are reasonably full (every 15 minutes or so) daily from March through November and, depending on the weather, in December and February. The trips take half an hour and cost €7.60.

BUS TRAVEL
The De Lijn bus company provides bus services in Brugge. Most buses run every five minutes (less often on Sundays). Several lines take you from the station to the city center. Buy your tickets on board (€2) or from ticket machines (€1.30) at the terminus.

Contacts De Lijn ✉ *West Flanders* ☎ *059/56–52–11* ⊕ *www.delijn.be.*

CAR TRAVEL
Brugge is 5 km (3 miles) north of the E40 motorway, which links it to Brussels. It is 126 km (76 miles) from the Le Shuttle terminus at Calais. Access for cars into Brugge's center is severely restricted. The historic streets are narrow and often one-way. There are huge parking lots at the railway station and near the exits from the ring road, plus underground parking at 't Zand.

TRAIN TRAVEL
The Belgian national railway, **NMBS/SNCB,** sends two trains each hour to Brugge from Brussels (50 minutes).

VISITOR INFORMATION
Contacts In&Uit Brugge ⊠ 't Zand 34 ☎ 050/44–46–46 ⊕ www.brugge.be.

EXPLORING

Brugge has tangled streets, narrow canals, handsome squares, and old gabled buildings that were such a powerful magnet more than a century ago. Although often called Bruges, its French name, the city's official name is indeed Brugge (*bruhg*-guh), and you'll score points with the locals by using the Flemish title. You can buy a €20 combination ticket for entry into five municipal museums: the Museum voor Volkskunde, the Groeningemuseum, the Gruuthusemuseum, the Memling, and the Arentshuis. These tickets are available at all participating museums.

Begijnhof. This 13th-century *béguinage* is a pretty and serene cluster of small whitewashed houses, a pigeon tower, and a church surrounding a pleasant green at the edge of a canal. The Begijnhof was founded in 1245 by Margaret, Countess of Constantinople, to bring together the Beguines—girls and widows from all social backgrounds who devoted themselves to charitable work but who were not bound by religious vows. Led by a superintendent known as the Grand Mistress, the congregation flourished for 600 years. The last of the Beguines died about 50 years ago; today the site is occupied by the Benedictine nuns, who still wear the Beguine habit. You may join them, discreetly, for vespers in their small church of St. Elizabeth. ⊠ Oude Begijnhof, off Wijngaardstraat ☎ 050/33–00–11 ☜ Free, No. 1 house visit €2 ⊙ Begijnhof daily 6:30–6:30; house Mon.–Sat. 10–5, Sun. 2:30–5 Ⓜ Bus No. 12.

Fodor's Choice
★ **Burg.** A popular daytime meeting place and an enchanting, floodlighted scene after dark, the Burg is flanked by striking, centuries-old civic buildings. Named for the fortress built by Baldwin of the Iron Arm, the Burg was also the former site of the 10th-century Carolingian Cathedral of St. Donaas, which was destroyed by French Republicans in 1799. You can wander through the handsome, 18th-century law court, the Oude Gerechtshof, the Voormalige Civiele Griffie with its 15th-century front gable, the Stadhuis, and the Heilig Bloed Basiliek. The Burg is not all historic splendor, though—in sharp contrast to these buildings stands a modern construction by Japanese artist Toyo Ito, added in 2002. Public opinion is sharply divided over Ito's pavilion; you'll either love it or hate it. ⊠ Hoogstraat and Breidelstraat Ⓜ Bus No. 1 or 12.

Fodor's Choice
★ **Groeningemuseum.** The tremendous holdings of this gallery give you the makings for a crash course in the Flemish Primitives and their successors. Petrus Christus, Hugo Van der Goes, Hieronymus Bosch, Rogier van der Weyden, Gerard David, Pieter Bruegel (both Elder and Younger), Pieter Pourbus—all the greats are represented here. Here you can see Jan van Eyck's wonderfully realistic *Madonna with Canon Van der Paele,* in which van Eyck achieved texture and depth through multiple layers of oil and varnish. As if this weren't enough, the museum also encompasses a strong display of 15th- to 21st-century Dutch and Belgian works, sweeping through to Surrealist and contemporary art. The Groeninge is set back from the street in a pocket-size park behind a medieval gate. It isn't a huge museum; nonetheless, its riches warrant a full morning or

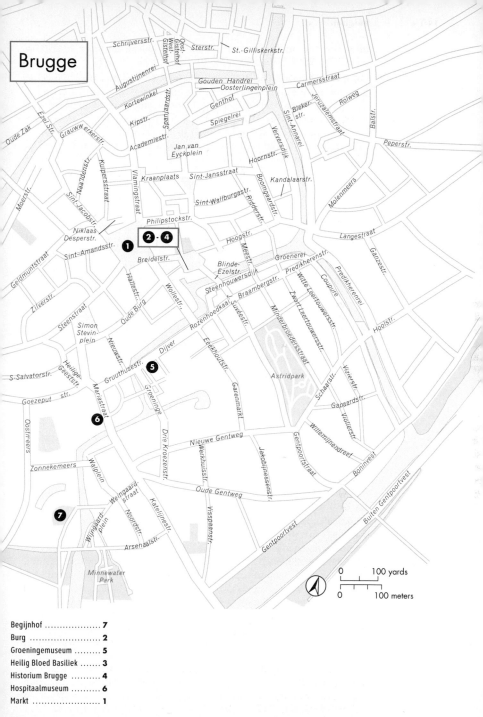

Brugge

afternoon. An audio guide is available in English. ⊠ *Dijver 12* 🕾 *050/ 44–87–11* 🖭 *€8* ⊙ *Tues.–Sun. 9:30–5* Ⓜ *Bus No. 1 or 12.*

Heilig Bloed Basiliek. The Basilica of the Holy Blood manages to include both the austere and the ornate under one roof—not to mention one of Europe's most precious relics. The 12th-century Lower Chapel retains a stern, Romanesque character. Look for the poignant, 14th-century Pietà and the carved statue of Christ in the crypt. The basilica's namesake treasure is a vial thought to contain a few drops of the blood of Christ, brought from Jerusalem to Brugge in 1149 by Derick of Alsace when he returned from the Second Crusade. It is exposed here every Friday in the Lower Chapel from 8:30 to 10 and in the Upper Chapel from 10 to 11 and from 3 to 4, and on other apparently random occasions for veneration: queue up to place your right hand on the vial and take a moment for quiet reflection. On Ascension Day, it becomes the centerpiece of the magnificent *De Heilig Bloedprocessie* (Procession of the Holy Blood), a major medieval-style pageant in which it is carried through the streets of Brugge. The small museum next to the basilica is the usual home of the basilica's namesake reliquary. ⊠ *Burg 13* ⊕ *www. holyblood.com* 🖭 *Museum, €2* ⊙ *Apr.–Sept., daily 9:30–noon and 2–5; Oct.–Mar., daily 10–noon and 2–4* Ⓜ *Bus No. 1 or 12.*

NEED A BREAK?

De Garre. In an alley off Breidelstraat you'll find the tiny, two-tier, brick-and-beam coffeehouse and pub De Garre. The menu lists more than 100 regional beers. A plate of cheese, such as Oude Brugge, is a good match with one of the heartier brews. De Garre is open from noon to midnight. No credit cards. ⊠ *De Garre 1* 🕾 *050/34–10–29.*

Historium Brugge. One of Brugge's newest attractions is a multimedia and multisensory journey through time. Visitors are transported back to 1435, as they walk through lifelike sets and are immersed in the sights, sounds, and even the smells of medieval Brugge. Visitors are immersed in a story of a young painter who works for Jan Van Eyck and experience what he goes through in a day. The whole experience takes about 90 minutes. ⊠ *Markt 1* 🕾 *050/27–03–11* ⊕ *www.historium.be* 🖭 *€11* ⊙ *Daily 10–6.*

Fodor'sChoice ★ **Hospitaalmuseum.** Home to the greatest collection of Hans Memling paintings in the world, the **Oud Sint-Janshospitaal** is one of the oldest surviving medieval hospitals in Europe. It was founded in the 12th century and remained in use until the early 20th century. Furniture, paintings, and hospital-related items are attractively displayed; the 13th-century middle ward, the oldest of three, was built in Romanesque style. Other fascinating 18th-century paintings show patients arriving by sedan chair and being fed and ministered to by sisters and clerics. Some of the actual sedan chairs that were used are also on display. But the highlights of the collection are the six major works (and plenty of minor ones) by Hans Memling (1440–94) that are of breathtaking quality and rank among the greatest—and certainly the most spiritual—of the Flemish Primitive school. There is a short guide to the museum in English, and the audio guide is in English, too. ⊠ *Mariastraat 38* 🕾 *050/44–87–11* 🖭 *€8* ⊙ *Tues.–Sun. 9:30–5* Ⓜ *Bus No. 1 or 12.*

Fodor's Choice ★ **Markt.** Used as a marketplace since 958, this square is still one of the liveliest places in Brugge. In the center stands a memorial to the city's medieval heroes, Jan Breydel and Pieter De Coninck, who led the commoners of Flanders to their short-lived victory over the aristocrats of France. On the east side of the Markt stand the provincial government house and the post office, an excellent pastiche of Burgundian Gothic. Old guild houses line the west and north sides of the square, their step-gabled facades overlooking the cafés spilling out onto the sidewalk. These buildings aren't always as old as they seem, though—often they're 19th-century reconstructions. The medieval **Belfort** (Belfry) on the south side of the Markt, however, is the genuine article. The tower dates to the 13th century, its crowning octagonal lantern to the 15th century. Altogether, it rises to a height of 270 feet, commanding the city and the surrounding countryside with more presence than grace. ✉ *Intersection of Steenstraat, St-Amandstraat, Vlamingstraat, Philipstockstraat, Breidelstraat, and Wollestraat* ☎ *050/44–87–11* 🎟 *Belfort €8, Salvador Dalí €10* ⏲ *Belfort daily 9:30–5, Salvador Dalí daily 10–6* [M] *Bus No. 1 or 12.*

A FAMILY BREW

De Halve Maan. This is the only family brewery left in Brugge. Their beers are called Brugse Zot (Fool of Brugge); it owes its name to Maximilian of Austria, who was welcomed to the city by a procession of fools and jesters. Work up a thirst by touring the brewery itself for €5, drink included. ✉ *Walplein, between Wijngaardstraat and Zonnkemeers* ☎ *050/33–26–97* ⏲ *Daily 10–6.*

4

WHERE TO EAT

$$$ FRENCH 🍴 **Chez Olivier.** Set above a quiet canal, with white swans gliding below, this French charmer is purely romantic. Chef Olivier Foucad uses impeccably fresh ingredients for "light food," such as scallops in ginger and herbs, duck in rosemary honey, and lightly marbled Charolais beef. Lunches are a bargain and the staff is flexible—if you want one main course or two starters instead of the full prix-fixe menu, just ask. For the best views, request a window seat next to the water. [$] *Average main: €28* ✉ *Meestraat 9* ☎ *050/33–36–59* 🌐 *www.chezolivier.be* ⏲ *Closed Thurs. and Sun. and 2 wks in July. No lunch Sat.* [M] *Bus No. 1.*

$$$$ FRENCH Fodor's Choice ★ 🍴 **De Karmeliet.** A world-renowned culinary landmark, De Karmeliet is set in a stately, 18th-century house. Owner-chef Geert Van Hecke's inventive kitchen changes the menu every two months, but during any season, the house style is an orgyization of ingredients, with on-top-of-on-top-of luxuries. The Hare Harlequin (rabbit), its legs stuffed with goose liver Royale, is one such example the Roasted Pheasant with black truffles and goose-liver Souvaroff parmentier is another. The waitstaff perfectly choreographs each course with a cool professionalism (remember to check out the wine list which plumbs the best international vintages) in keeping with the restaurant's formal ambience, set by the coved ceilings and gilt-framed paintings. But the showpiece is out back: an Italian-style garden replete with impressive topiaries and, all in all, one of the most stunningly graceful restaurant gardens

in Europe. $ *Average main: €70* ✉ *Langestraat 19* ☎ *050/33–82–59* 🌐 *www.dekarmeliet.be* ✍ *Reservations essential* 👔 *Jacket required* ⏲ *Closed Sun. and Mon., and 3 wks mid-June–mid-July* [M] *Bus No. 6.*

$$$$ SEAFOOD 🍴 **De Visscherie.** To find this popular seafood restaurant overlooking the Vismarkt, look for the modern sculpture of a fisherman and the large fish hanging from its balcony. Business at the busy outdoor terrace has been going strong for more than 25 years. Try one of the turbot variations, monkfish with Ganda ham and melon, or the langoustines with mozzarella, herbs, and sun-dried tomatoes. If you can't decide, order the restaurant's signature dish: waterzooi with saffron. $ *Average main: €35* ✉ *Vismarkt 8* ☎ *050/33–02–12* 🌐 *www.visscherie.be* ⏲ *Closed Tues.* [M] *Bus No. 6 or 16.*

$$$ BELGIAN Fodor's Choice ★ 🍴 **Le Mystique.** The Hotel Heritage, long established as a romantic hideaway close to the Markt square, now offers a romantic place to dine, too. The elegant dining room dates from 1869; its high ceilings, chandeliers, and linen tablecloths create a refined atmosphere, perfect for quiet conversation. Chef Koenraad Steenkiste creates exquisite modern French/Flemish cuisine using the freshest seasonal and local ingredients. There are some permanent à la carte choices, but the popular option is to let the chef decide for you and go for the monthly menu, available in four, five, or six courses, each one with a carefully matched wine. $ *Average main: €28* ✉ *Niklaas Desparsstraat 11* ☎ *050/44–44–44* ⏲ *Closed Sun. and Mon., and mid-July–mid-Aug.*

$$$$ BELGIAN 🍴 **'t Bourgoensch Hof.** Although its weathered timbers and sharp-raked roofs were rebuilt at the turn of the 20th century, this restaurant is housed in one of the most medieval-looking buildings in Brugge. It also has one of the city's most romantic, canal-side settings, with the light from the windows shedding kaleidoscopic reflections onto the water. The cuisine is as appealing as the setting, with selections including pan-fried langoustines with wild mushrooms, and turbot medallions with coriander and caramelized leeks. $ *Average main: €30* ✉ *Wollestraat 39* ☎ *050/33–16–45* 🌐 *www.bourgoensch-hof.be* ⏲ *Closed Tues. and Wed.* [M] *Bus No. 1 or 11.*

WHERE TO STAY

$ B&B/INN Fodor's Choice ★ 🏨 **De Pauw.** From the brick exterior covered with climbing roses to the fresh flowers and doilies in the breakfast parlor, this is a welcoming little family-run inn and restaurant, set in a square opposite Sint-Gillis church; for the price, this place really delivers if you're looking for charm. **Pros:** good value; very friendly; cozy atmosphere. **Cons:** far from sights; steep stairs. $ *Rooms from: €85* ✉ *Sint-Gilliskerkhof 8* ☎ *050/33–71–18* 🌐 *www.hoteldepauw.be* 🛏 *8 rooms* 🍴 *Breakfast* [M] *Bus No. 4 or 14.*

$$$ HOTEL Fodor's Choice ★ 🏨 **De Tuileriëen.** Magnificently beautiful, this canalside, 15th-century mansion is the ultimate in Brugian elegance and romantic charm, with parlors and guest rooms so suffused with patrician taste that they would be worthy of cover-photo status in *The World of Interiors*. **Pros:** the decor rivals the best hotels in Paris for sheer chic; turndown service includes chocolates; well-equipped spa; some room rates are bargains for what you get. **Cons:** some front rooms noisy. $ *Rooms from: €135*

4

✉ *Dijver 7* ☎ *050/34–36–91* 🌐 *www.hoteltuilerieen.com* 🛏 *22 rooms, 23 suites* 🍴 *Breakfast* [M] *Bus No. 1 or 12.*

$$ HOTEL Fodor's Choice ★ 🏨 **Egmond.** A gorgeous, gabled, yellow-hued 18th-century mansion near the Begijnhof, this is just the place to play lord of the manor, with an interior positively creaking with charm—thanks to any number of hearths and chimneypieces, beamed ceilings, and antiques—and an exterior so pretty you may not wish to leave the grounds. **Pros:** no-smoking hotel; pretty garden. **Cons:** rooms book up quickly. [$] *Rooms from: €98* ✉ *Minnewater 15* ☎ *050/34–14–45* 🌐 *www.egmond.be* 🛏 *8 rooms* 🍴 *Breakfast* [M] *Bus No. 3 or 12.*

$$$$ HOTEL Fodor's Choice ★ 🏨 **Hotel Heritage.** Once a private mansion, this 19th-century building has been converted into a lovely hotel. Old World–lovers should realize that the building has been so renovated that much of the patina is now missing. **Pros:** helpful staff; grand building; great location. **Cons:** some rooms are quite small for the price. [$] *Rooms from: €240* ✉ *Niklaas Desparsstraat 11* ☎ *050/44–44–44* 🌐 *www.hotel-heritage.com* 🛏 *20 rooms, 4 suites* 🍴 *Breakfast* [M] *Bus No. 2 or 12.*

$$$ HOTEL Fodor's Choice ★ 🏨 **Relais Bourgondisch Cruyce.** Situated in one of the most romantic corners of Brugge, this lovingly and stylishly restored historic pair of houses overlooks the Reien. **Pros:** a fairy-tale setting; great views of the water; lovely décor throughout. **Cons:** limited parking (reserve in advance); breakfast buffet is expensive. [$] *Rooms from: €185* ✉ *Wollestraat 41–47* ☎ *050/33–79–26* 🌐 *www.relaisbourgondischcruyce.be* 🛏 *16 rooms* 🍴 *No meals* [M] *Bus No. 1 or 11.*

ANTWERP

Antwerp is Europe's second-largest port, and has much of the zest often associated with a harbor town. But it also has an outsized influence in a very different realm: that of clothing design. Since the 1980s, Antwerp-trained fashion designers have become renowned for experimental styles paired with time-honored workmanship.

In its heyday, Antwerp (Antwerpen in Flemish, Anvers in French) played second fiddle only to Paris. Thanks to artists such as Rubens, Van Dyck, and Jordaens, it was one of Europe's leading art centers. Its printing presses produced missals for the farthest reaches of the Spanish empire. It became, and has remained, the diamond capital of the world. Its civic pride was such that the Antwerpen *Sinjoren* (patricians) considered themselves a cut above just about everybody else. They still do.

PLANNING YOUR TIME

If you're doing a day-trip, avoid Monday, when the museums are closed.

On your first day, wander the narrow streets of the Oude Stad, window-shopping and perhaps sampling some local beer along with a lunch of the ubiquitous mussels and French fries. Then head to Rubenshuis to see a faithful and rich re-creation of the famous painter's own house and studio. Afterward, walk along the river Scheldt, appreciating Antwerp's centuries-long tradition as a major European port, before stopping at MAS (Museum aan de Stroom) to marvel at the modern building and historic collections.

On a second day here, absorb a sense of the city's religious history by visiting some of its churches, including Sint-Pauluskerk and Sint-Jacobskerk, where Rubens is buried. Next make a trip to see the Bruegels at the Museum Mayer Van den Bergh before venturing to the Plantin-Moretus Museum, the home and printing plant of a publishing dynasty that spanned three centuries. Indulge your covetous streak with a trip to the Diamantwijk, and take advantage of Antwerp's ranking as a key European fashion center by window-shopping along the streets radiating off Meir.

GETTING HERE AND AROUND

CAR TRAVEL

Antwerp is 48 km (29 miles) north of Brussels on the E19. A car isn't necessary—and is often a burden—when exploring Antwerp's crowded central area. Street parking is rare, but there are several central parking lots, including lots near Grote Markt and Groenplaats.

BUS AND METRO TRAVEL

De Lijn operates Antwerp's city bus service; it's an easy system to use. Most lines begin outside Centraal Station on Koningin Astridplein. Antwerp's tram and metro public transit system is also extensive and reliable. The most useful subway line links Centraal Station (metro: Diamant) with the left bank (Linkeroever) via the Groenplaats (for the cathedral and Grote Markt). A €1.30 (€2 bought on board) ticket is good for one hour on all forms of public transport, including buses; a €5 (€7 on board) pass buys unlimited travel for one day. Tickets are available at De Lijn offices, the tourist office, and at the Diamant, Opera–Frankrijklei, and Groenplaats metro stops. Public transport runs from 6:30 am to midnight.

TRAIN TRAVEL

NMBS/SNCB, the national railway, connects Antwerp with all other major Belgian cities. There are four to five trains an hour between Antwerp and Brussels. Thalys trains also run seven times a day between Antwerp and Paris, and nearly every hour to and from Amsterdam.

TOURS

Touristram operates hour-long tram tours with cassette commentary in the Oude Stad and old harbor area. Tickets are sold on the tram, and tours leave on the hour. Departure is from Groenplaats. From mid-February to late-March and November to mid-December, tours run only on weekends 12–4; from mid-March to September they run daily 11–5; in October, daily 12–4.

Contacts Touristram ☎ 03/480–9388 ⊕ www.touristram.be.

VISITOR INFORMATION

Contacts Toerisme Antwerpen (*Antwerp City Tourist Office*). ✉ *Grote Markt 13, Oude Stad* ☎ *03/232–0103* ⊕ *www.antwerpen.be* ⊗ *Mon.–Sat. 9–5:45, Sun. 9–4:45.*

EXPLORING

Diamantwijk. Some 85% of the world's uncut diamonds pass through Antwerp, and the diamond trade has its own quarter, where the skills of cutting and polishing the gems have been handed down for generations by a tightly knit community. Multimillion-dollar deals are agreed upon with a handshake, and the Antwerp Diamond High Council was established in 1975 to further the industry. Twenty-five million carats are cut and traded here every year, more than anywhere else in the world. The district occupies a few nondescript city blocks west of Centraal Station. A large part of the community is Jewish, so you'll see shop signs in Hebrew and Hasidic men with traditional dark clothing and side curls. Below the elevated railway tracks, a long row of stalls and shops gleams with jewelry and gems.

Today the industry employs some 8,000 workers, including expert polishers and cutters, serving 1,800 dealers. Jewish establishments close on Saturday for the Sabbath, but there are still enough shops open in the neighborhood to have a good browse. ⊠ *Bounded by De Keyserlei, Pelikaanstraat, Lange Herentalsestraat, and Lange Kievitstraat, Diamantwijk* Ⓜ *Tram No. 2 or 15.*

Grote Markt. The heart of the Oude Stad is dominated by a huge fountain splashing water onto the paving stones. Atop the fountain stands the figure of the legendary Silvius Brabo, who has been poised to fling the hand of the giant Druon Antigon into the river Scheldt since the 19th century. Another famous monster-slayer, St. George, is perched on top of a 16th-century guild house at Grote Markt 5, while the dragon appears to be falling off the pediment.

Stadhuis. The triangular square is lined on two sides by guild houses and on the third by the Renaissance Stadhuis. Antwerp's town hall was built in the 1560s during the city's Golden Age, when Paris and Antwerp were the only European cities with more than 100,000 inhabitants. In its facade, the fanciful fretwork of the late-Gothic style has given way to the discipline and order of the Renaissance. The public rooms are suitably impressive, though the heavy hand of 19th-century restoration work is much in evidence. You can see the interior with a guided tour. City walks that include the Stadhuis take place (in English) on Sundays at 2 year-round and daily at 2 in July and August; tickets are €8 (€6 in advance) and can be purchased from the Tourist Office. ⊠ *Grote Markt, Oude Stad* ☎ *03/232–0103* Ⓜ *Tram No. 7, 10, or 11; Bus No. 30 or 34*

Fodor's Choice
★ **Museum aan de Stroom** (*MAS*). This ambitious museum in a striking red sandstone and glass building next to Antwerp's old dock area aims to place Antwerp's history into a world context. Five floors of exhibits explore themes such as trade and shipping, men and gods, here and elsewhere, and prestige and symbols, showcasing everything from pre-Columbian artifacts to gas masks from World War II. It's all capped off with a panoramic rooftop view and a 2-Michelin-star restaurant, 't Zilte. Note that most of the museum's documentation is not in English; for a translation, use your Smartphone to read the QR codes placed next to many exhibits, or borrow a MAS Smartphone from the information desk. ⊠ *Hanzestedenplaats 1, Oude Stad* ☎ *03/338–4434* ⊕ *www.*

Antwerp

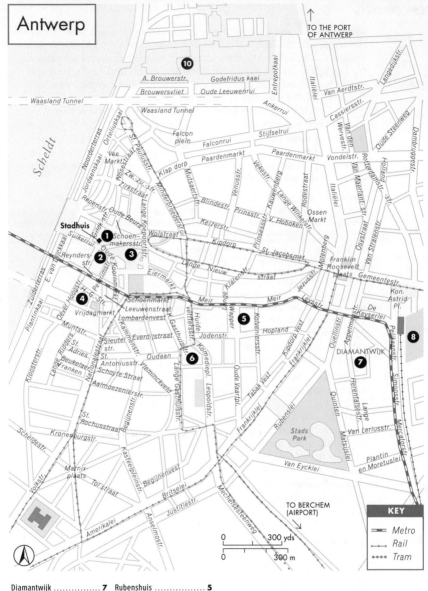

TO THE PORT
OF ANTWERP

KEY
〓〓 Metro
⊢⊣ Rail
•••• Tram

TO BERCHEM
(AIRPORT)

0 ____ 300 yds
0 ____ 300 m

mas.be ✉ *€10* ☉ *Tues.–Fri. 10–5, weekends 10–6; last tickets sold 1 hr before closing.*

Fodor'sChoice **Museum Mayer Van den Bergh.** Pieter Bruegel the Elder's arguably greatest
★ and most enigmatic painting, *Dulle Griet* (Room No. 9), is the show-
piece of the 4,000 works that passionate art connoisseur Mayer Van
den Bergh amassed in the 19th century. Often referred to in English as
"Mad Meg," the painting portrays an irate woman wearing helmet and
breastplate—a sword in one hand, and food and cooking utensils in the
other—striding across a field strewn with the ravages and insanity of
war. There is no consensus on how to read this painting. Some consider
it one of the most powerful antiwar statements ever made. Others claim
that it denounces the Inquisition. Either way, nothing could be further
from the Bruegelian villages than this nightmare world. ✉ *Lange Gas-
thuisstraat 19, Kruidtuin* ☎ *03/338–8188* ⊕ *www.mayervandenbergh.
be* ✉ *€8, combination ticket with Rubenshuis €10* ☉ *Tues.–Sun. 10–5;
free last Wed. of the month.* Ⓜ *Tram No. 7 or 8.*

Fodor'sChoice **Onze-Lieve-Vrouwekathedraal.** A miracle of soaring Gothic lightness, the
★ Cathedral of Our Lady contains some of Rubens's greatest paintings
and is topped by its 404-foot-high north spire—now restored to its original gleaming white and serving as a beacon that can be seen from far
away. Work began in 1352 and continued in fits and starts until 1521.
The monument is the work of a succession of remarkable architects,
including Peter Appelmans, Herman and Domien de Waghemakere, and
Rombout Keldermans the Younger. The tower holds a 49-bell carillon
played at various times throughout the year.

*De Hemelvaart van de Maagd Maria (The Assumption of the Virgin
Mary)*, painted for the high altar, shows the Virgin being carried upward
by massed ranks of cherubs toward the angel waiting to crown her
Queen of the Angels. *De Hemelvaart (The Assumption)* is skillfully displayed so that the rays of the sun illuminate it exactly at noon. ✉ *Hand-
schoenmarkt, Oude Stad* ☎ *03/213–9951* ⊕ *www.dekathedraal.be*
✉ *€5* ☉ *Weekdays 10–5, Sat. 10–3, Sun. 1–4* Ⓜ *Tram No. 2, 3, 4, 5,
8, 9, 10, 11, or 15.*

Plantin-Moretus Museum/Prentenkabinet. This was the home and printing plant of an extraordinary publishing dynasty. For three centuries,
beginning in 1576, the family printed innumerable bibles, breviaries,
and missals. Christophe Plantin's greatest technical achievement was the
Biblia Regia (Room No. 16): eight large volumes containing the Bible
in Latin, Greek, Hebrew, Syriac, and Aramaic, complete with notes,
glossaries, and grammars.

The first three rooms were the family quarters, furnished in 16th-
century luxury and containing several portraits by Rubens. Others
remain as they were when occupied by accountants, editors, and proof-
readers, while many contain Bibles and religious manuscripts dating
back to the 9th century, including one owned by King Wenceslas of
Bohemia. The workshops are filled with Plantin's 16 printing presses.
Two typefaces designed here, Plantin and Garamond, are still in use.
The presses are in working order—you can even purchase a copy of
Plantin's sonnet, *Le Bonheur de ce monde (An ode to contentment)*, in

any of seven European languages, printed on an original press. There's a free information brochure available in English. ⊠ *Vrijdagmarkt 22–23, Sint-Andrieskwartier* ☎ *03/221–1450* ⊕ *www.museumplantinmoretus. be* ⬚ *€8, free last Wed. of the month* ☉ *Tues.–Sun. 10–5; last ticket sold at 4:30* Ⓜ *Tram No. 3, 9, or 15. Bus No. 22, 25, or 26.*

Rubenshuis. A fabulous picture of Rubens as painter and patrician is presented here at his own house. Only the elaborate portico and temple, designed by Rubens in Italian Baroque style, were still standing three centuries after the house was built. Most of what's here is a reconstruction (completed in 1946) from the master's own design. It represents Rubens at the pinnacle of his fame, when he was appointed court painter to Archduke Albrecht and, with his wife, was sent on a diplomatic mission to Madrid, where he also painted some 40 portraits. The most evocative room in Rubens House is the huge studio, where drawings by Rubens and his pupils, as well as old prints, help to re-create the original atmosphere. A few Rubens works hang in the house, including a touching sketch in the studio of the Annunciation and a self-portrait in the dining room. Unfortunately, his young widow promptly sold off some 300 pieces after his death in 1640. ⊠ *Wapper 9, Meir* ☎ *03/201–1555* ⊕ *www.rubenshuis.be* ⬚ *€8, combination ticket with Museum Mayer Van den Bergh €10; free last Wed. of the month* ☉ *Tues.–Sun. 10–5; last ticket at 4:30* Ⓜ *Tram No. 2, 3, 5, or 15. Bus No. 22, 25, or 26.*

Fodor'sChoice
★

Vlaeykensgang. This quiet cobblestone lane in the center of Antwerp seems untouched by time. The mood and style of the 16th century are perfectly preserved here. There is no better time to linger than on a Monday night when the carillon concert is pealing from the cathedral. The alley ends in Pelgrimsstraat, where there is a great view of the cathedral spire.

FAMILY

Zoo Antwerpen. Antwerp's zoo houses its residents in style. Giraffes, ostriches, and African antelopes inhabit an Egyptian temple; a Moorish villa is home to the rhinoceroses; and a thriving okapi family grazes around an Indian temple. In part, this reflects the public's taste when the zoo was created 170 years ago. Today animals are allowed maximum space, and much research is devoted to endangered species. The zoo also has sea lions, an aquarium, and a house for nocturnal animals. ⊠ *Koningin Astridplein 26, Centraal Station* ☎ *03/202–4540* ⊕ *www. zooantwerpen.be* ⬚ *€2* ☉ *Jan., Feb., Nov., and Dec., daily 10–4:45; Mar., Apr., and Oct., daily 10–5:30; May, June, and Sept. daily 10–6; July and Aug. daily 10–7. Ticket office closes 1 hr before zoo.* Ⓜ *Tram No. 2, 3, 5, 6, 10, 11, 12, or 24.*

WHERE TO EAT

$$$$
FRENCH
Fodor'sChoice
★

✕ **Dôme.** Architecture and food aficionados will appreciate the classic French cuisine and somber decor in this splendid art-nouveau building. This former teahouse, sewing school, and police office maintains its original mosaic floor, and the whitewashed walls and domed roof parallel its haute cuisine. French chef Julien Burlat and wife Sophie Verbeke, former stylist for Dries Van Noten, set up this restaurant (and its marine version, Dôme sur Mer, just a stone's throw away) in the upscale Zurenborg neighborhood. Choose from the *Carte Blanche* for €79 or seasonal dishes like pigeon rubbed with spices, fresh peas, broad beans, and sage. For a quicker bite, pop into their latest addition, bakery Domestic. $ *Average main: €39* ✉ *Grote Hondstraat 2, Zurenborg* ☎ *03/239–9003* ⊕ *www.domeweb.be* ⚓ *Reservations essential* ⊘ *Closed Sun. and Mon. No lunch Sat.*

$$$$ ✕ **Het Nieuwe Palinghuis.** The name means The New Eelhouse, and sweet-
SEAFOOD fleshed eel, prepared in a variety of ways, is the house specialty, along with grilled turbot, sole, scallops, and a myriad of other crustaceans, including lobster and mussels (in season). Fittingly for an Antwerp landmark, the restaurant has dark wood and a comfortable, deep-rooted air. $ *Average main: €32* ✉ *St-Jansvliet 14, Oude Stad* ☎ *03/231–7445* ⊕ *www.hetnieuwepalinghuis.be* ⊘ *Closed Mon. and Tues.*

$$$ ✕ **Horta.** The iron framework of the 19th-century Maison du Peuple, a
CONTEMPORARY building designed by famed art-nouveau architect Victor Horta, sup-
FAMILY ports this brasserie. It siphons a hip crowd from trendy Hopland Street and keeps a sunny feel with large mustard-yellow industrial beams and windows all around. The kitchen sends out brasserie favorites like Aberdeen Angus ribeye frites as well as tempting contemporary dishes, with lighter wraps, bagels, and salad options for lunch. $ *Average main: €24* ✉ *Hopland 2, Oude Stad* ☎ *03/203–5660* ⊕ *www.grandcafehorta. be* Ⓜ *Tram No. 4, 7, 8, 10, or 11.*

$$$ ✕ **In de Schaduw van de Kathedraal.** Cozier and more traditional than
BELGIAN the wave of contemporary restaurants dominating the scene, this little place makes good on its name: it has a dining room facing the cathedral square and a terrace where you can take your meal in the cathedral's shadow. Try the delicious North Sea crab gratinée. $ *Average main: €28* ✉ *Handschoenmarkt 17–21, Oude Stad* ☎ *03/232–4014* ⊕ *www. indeschaduwvandekathedraal.be* ⊘ *Closed Tues.* Ⓜ *Tram No. 10 or 11. Bus No. 30 or 34.*

$$ ✕ **'t Hofke.** It's worth visiting here for the location alone, in the
BELGIAN Vlaeykensgang alley, where time seems to have stood still. The cozy dining room has the look and feel of a private home. The lunch menu includes a large selection of salads and omelets, as well as more substantial fare in the evening. Try for a table in the courtyard. $ *Average main: €17* ✉ *Vlaeykensgang, Oude Koornmarkt 16, Oude Stad* ☎ *03/233–8606* ⊕ *www.thofke.com* Ⓜ *Tram No. 2, 3, 4, 5, 8, or 15.*

WHERE TO STAY

$$$$ ▦ **De Witte Lelie.** Three step-gabled 17th-century houses have been
HOTEL combined to create Antwerp's most exclusive hotel. **Pros:** large rooms;
Fodor'sChoice friendly, attentive service; complimentary minibars. **Cons:** some rooms
★ have no elevator access; breakfast not included in room rate. $ *Rooms from: €295* ✉ *Keizerstraat 16–18, Stadswaag* ☎ *03/226–1966* ⊕ *www. dewittelelie.be* ➴ *5 rooms, 6 suites* ⏀ *No meals* Ⓜ *Tram No. 10 or 11.*

$$$ ▦ **Hilton Antwerp.** This five-story complex incorporates the fin-de-siè-
HOTEL cle facade of what was once the Grand Bazar department store. **Pros:** luxurious, large rooms; centrally located; 24-hour gym. **Cons:** Extra charge for Wi-Fi in rooms and public areas. $ *Rooms from: €199*

✉ *Groenplaats 32, Oude Stad* ☎ *03/204–1212* ⊕ *www.hilton.com* ⇆ *193 rooms, 18 suites* ❍ *No meals* Ⓜ *Tram No. 2, 3, 4, 5, 8, 9, or 15.*

$$
HOTEL

⬚ Hotel Les Nuits. These modern surroundings (with furnishings from the Flamant design shop just next door) come with convenience to Antwerp's main shopping streets. **Pros:** quiet location; a/c; room service from hotel restaurant. **Cons:** no real lobby; no minibar; no on-site parking (though public parking nearby). Ⓢ *Rooms from: €145* ✉ *Lange Gasthuisstraat 12, Kruidtuin* ☎ *03/225–0204* ⊕ *www.hotellesnuits.be* ⇆ *24 rooms* ❍ *No meals* Ⓜ *Tram No. 4, 7, or 8.*

$$
HOTEL

⬚ Hotel Rubens. A peaked tower, said to be the oldest in Antwerp and part of the original city walls, makes this small, colorful hotel directly behind the Grote Markt stand out. **Pros:** friendly staff; great location; quiet courtyard garden. **Cons:** limited parking. Ⓢ *Rooms from: €150* ✉ *Oude Beurs 29, Oude Stad* ☎ *03/222–4848* ⊕ *www.hotelrubensantwerp.be* ⇆ *36 rooms* ❍ *Breakfast* Ⓜ *Tram No. 10 or 11.*

$$
HOTEL

⬚ Radisson Blu Astrid Hotel. Directly across from Antwerp's Centraal Station and convenient to many public transportation options, this business-oriented hotel with friendly service provides easy access to the Diamond District and shopping on the Meir. **Pros:** near train station; 24-hour fitness center; free Wi-Fi in rooms. **Cons:** bit of a walk to Cathedral and Grote Markt; somewhat generic feel. Ⓢ *Rooms from: €119* ✉ *Koningin Astridplein 7, Centraal Station* ☎ *03/203–1234* ⊕ *www.radissonblu.com/astridhotel-antwerp* ⇆ *247 rooms* ❍ *No meals* Ⓜ *Tram No. 2, 3, 5, 6, 10, 11, 12, or 24. Bus No. 19, 23, 31, or 68.*

SHOPPING

The elegant **Meir,** together with its extension to the east, **De Keyserlei,** and at the opposite end, **Huidevettersstraat,** is where you will find high-street standbys and long-established names. Shopping galleries branch off from all three streets—**Century Center** and **Antwerp Tower** from De Keyserlei, **Meir Square** from Meir, and **Nieuwe Gaanderij** from Huidevettersstraat. The area in and around the glamorous **Horta Complex,** on Hopland, the street parallel to the Meir between Centraal Station and the Oude Stad, is also a popular shopping hub. For more avant-garde tastes, the best-known area is **De Wilde Zee,** which straddles the Meir and Oude Stad, consisting of Groendalstraat, Lombardenstraat, Wiegstraat, and Korte Gasthuisstraat. The nearby Schuttershofstraat, Kammenstraat, and Nationalestraat are also fizzing with new spots.

CROATIA

Split, Hvar, Dubrovnik

WHAT'S WHERE

1 Split. The port town of Split centers on Diocletian's Palace, a splendid Roman structure and UNESCO World Heritage Site. The palace's south facade faces directly onto the seafront promenade, overlooking the Adriatic Sea.

2 Hvar. Hvar Town lies in a sheltered bay on the south-west coast of the island of Hvar. The car-free Old Town centers on a large paved piazza, and the entire scene is presided over by a hilltop fortress.

3 Dubrovnik. Croatia's most popular tourist destination, Dubrovnik's pedestrian-only Old Town is protected by sturdy medieval walls. The southern walls overlook the Adriatic, while north of the complex rise the rocky heights of Mount Srdj.

AUSTRIA

SLOVEN

ITALY

Portorož   Opatija

Rijeka

ISTRIA

Krk   S

Pula   Cres

KVARNER

Rab

Lošinj   Pa

Adriatic

D
O

Sea

ITALY

HUNGARY

Varaždin

ZAGREB

Virovitica

Danube

Karlovac   *Sava*   Daruvar   Osijek

CROATIA   SLAVONIA

Una   Sl. Brod   *Sava*

SERBIA

NORTHERN
DALMATIA

BOSNIA AND HERCEGOVINA

Zadar

Knin

CENTRAL
DALMATIA

Sibenik

Split **1**

Makarska

Brač

Hvar

2 SOUTHERN
DALMATIA

Korčula   *Pelješac*

Mljet   **3**

Dubrovnik

Herceg-Novi

MONTENEGRO

ALBANIA

NEED TO KNOW

AT A GLANCE

Capital: Zagreb

Population: 4,284,889

Currency: Kuna (Kn.)

Money: ATMs are common; cash is preferred at cheaper places

Language: Croatian

Country Code: ☎ 385

Emergencies: ☎ 112

Driving: On the right

Electricity: 200v/50 cycles; electrical plugs have two round prongs

Time: Six hours ahead of New York

Documents: Up to 90 days with valid passport; Schengen rules apply

Mobile Phones: GSM (900 and 1800 bands)

Major Mobile Companies: T-Mobile, Vipnet, Tele2

WEB SITES

Croatia: ⊕ www.croatia.hr

Dubrovnik: ⊕ www.tzdubrovnik.hr

Hvar Town: ⊕ www.tzhvar.hr

GETTING AROUND

✈ **Air Travel:** The major airports are Zagreb, Dubrovnik, and Split.

🚌 **Boat Travel:** Frequent ferries link Split to Hvar, and a (rather slow) twice-weekly coastal ferry runs between Split and Dubrovnik.

🚗 **Car Travel:** You might rent a car to drive down the coast from Split to Dubrovnik or to explore the interior of the island of Hvar, but in Split and Dubrovnik themselves, a car is unnecessary.

🚆 **Train Travel:** Daily trains link Zagreb with Split, but there is no rail service south of Split to Dubrovnik.

PLAN YOUR BUDGET

	HOTEL ROOM	MEAL	ATTRACTIONS
Low Budget	€100	60 Kn.	War Photo Limited, Dubrovnik, 60 Kn.
Mid Budget	€160	120 Kn.	City Walls, Dubrovnik, 90 Kn.
High Budget	€400	150 Kn.	Dubrovnik Summer Festival ticket, 150 Kn.–350 Kn.

WAYS TO SAVE

Eat lunch picnic-style. Shop for fresh bread, cheese, and seasonal fruit, and eat by the sea.

Book a rental apartment. Dalmatia has plenty of comfortable self-catering apartments, offering more space and a kitchen, that are cheaper than hotels.

Use public transport. Bus travel between Dubrovnik and Split is easier than driving. Hvar has good bus service.

Night of the Museums. On the last Friday in January, more than 100 Croatian museums and galleries offer free entry from 6 pm to 1 am.

Hassle Factor	Medium. There are no nonstop flights from the U.S. to Croatia, but in summer numerous airlines offer air connections via Europe to Dubrovnik and Split.
3 days	You can visit both Dubrovnik and Split for a brief taste of what Dalmatia has to offer.
1 week	Combine the magnificent coastal cities of Dubrovnik and Split with a few days' chilling out on the island of Hvar.
2 weeks	You have time both to move around and to see the highlights, including several days in both Dubrovnik and Split, plus excursions to the islands, most notably Hvar, and adventure sports such as sailing, scuba diving, and sea kayaking.

WHEN TO GO

High Season: July through August is the most expensive and popular time to visit Dalmatia. August is especially crowded. The weather is hot and sunny, ideal for the beach.

Low Season: Winter offers the least appealing weather, though it's the best time for hotel deals and seeing Dalmatia without the tourists. However, some hotels and many restaurants close completely, and museums have restricted opening hours.

Value Season: May through June and September through October offer warm, sunny weather, though you should be prepared for occasional rain, at times torrential, as the seasons change in May and October. As it's not too hot or crowded, these months are ideal for sightseeing. Hotel prices tend to be more reasonable and restaurants less busy.

BIG EVENTS

February: Dubrovnik's Carnival week culminates with a masked ball before Lent. ⊕ www.karnevalfest.hr

July/August: Dubrovnik Summer Festival sees world-renowned musicians and actors performing at open-air venues in the Old Town. ⊕ www.dubrovnik-festival.hr

July/August: The Split Summer Festival brings opera, classical music, dance, and theater. ⊕ www.splitsko-ljeto.hr

August: The Hvar Half Marathon draws competitors on a run from Stari Grad (Old Town) to Hvar Town. ⊕ www.hvarmarathon.com

READ THIS

■ *Black Lamb and Grey Falcon,* Rebecca West. A journey through pre-WWII Yugoslavia.

■ *Croatia: A Nation Forged by War,* Marcus Tanner. How Croatia won its independence.

■ *Café Europa: Life after Communism,* Slavenka Drakulić. Yugoslavia after the fall of Communism.

WATCH THIS

■ *Game of Thrones.* Filming locations in both Dubrovnik and Split.

■ *Casanova.* This BBC mini-series was partly filmed in Dubrovnik.

■ *Bridget's Sexiest Beaches.* The Travel Channel series (Season 1, Ep. 2) visited Dubrovnik and Hvar.

EAT THIS

■ **Salata od hobotnice:** a flavorsome octopus salad

■ **Crni rižot:** black risotto, made from cuttlefish ink

■ **Škampi na buzaru:** shrimps sautéed with olive oil, garlic, and white wine

■ **Pršut:** Dalmatian smoked, dried ham, similar to Italian prosciutto

■ **Pašticada:** beef stewed in wine and prunes, served with gnocchi

■ **Palačinke:** crêpes, filled with walnut cream, chocolate, or apricot jam

5

By Jane Foster   With 1,778 km (1,111 miles) of coastline and more than a thousand islands (66 of which are inhabited), Croatia is one of Europe's most beautiful seaside destinations. In south Croatia, backed by dramatic mountains, Dalmatia's sapphire-blue waters are scattered with pine-scented islands and presided over by finely preserved, walled medieval towns, packed with Venetian monuments. But Dalmatia's calm sea belies a checkered past. Like its Balkan neighbors, Croatia has a history shadowed by conflict and political strife.

The region's earliest inhabitants were the Illyrians, and the principal tribe, the Delmata, gave their name to Dalmatia. The coastal region was colonized by Greece and later Rome.

Dalmatia (excluding Dubrovnik, which remained an independent republic) then came under the rule of Venice. Lying on the trade route to the Orient, port towns such as Split and Hvar flourished, and many of the region's finest buildings date from this period. However, after Venice fell in 1797, all of Croatia was under Austro-Hungarian rule by the 19th century.

After Germany declared war on Yugoslavia in 1941, Ante Pavelić set up the Independent State of Croatia (NDH), notorious for the mass murder of Jews, Serbs, and Gypsies. Simultaneously, Josip Broz Tito founded the Partizan movement, aimed at pushing Fascist forces out of Yugoslavia. When the war ended, Tito created the Socialist Federal Republic of Yugoslavia with Croatia as one of six constituent republics. The Tito years saw a period of peace and prosperity, and during the 1960s Croatia became a popular international tourist destination.

Following Tito's death in 1980, an economic crisis set in, and relations between Croatia and the Serb-dominated Yugoslav government deteriorated. In 1989 Franjo Tudjman founded the Croatian Democratic Union (HDZ), calling for an independent Croatia, while in Serbia the nationalist leader Slobodan Milošević rose to power. In 1991 Croatia declared independence, and the events that followed led to a horrendous civil war in which some 20,000 people were killed and hundreds of thousands displaced.

After the war, a decade of political and economic isolation ensued, due to the international community's preoccupation with Croatia's poor human rights record. Gradually the country made amends, notably by arresting war criminals and announcing that all refugees should be allowed to return to their homes.

TOP REASONS TO GO

■ **Diocletian's Palace.** Explore this massive 3rd-century AD Roman edifice that now shelters Split's pedestrian-only Old Town within its walls. This is a must-do if you are traveling to Split.

■ **Hvar's beaches.** Beaches in Dalmatia tend to be pebbly and rocky, and sand is extremely rare. Hvar Town compensates for this with several chic beach clubs, with wooden decks built into the rocks, offering easy access into the sea.

■ **Dubrovnik's Old Town.** Walk the entire circuit of Dubrovnik's sturdy medieval city walls—which date back to the 13th century—for splendid views over the terra-cotta rooftops of Old Town and out to sea.

■ **Kayaking.** Head out from Dubrovnik in a sea kayak to the scattered Elafiti islands, or from Hvar to the pine-scented Pakleni islets.

■ **Sailing.** Dalmatia, with its myriad islands and clear blue sea, is a sailor's paradise. Numerous charter companies hire out yachts (with skipper); most boats rent only by the week, but several companies also offer one-day sailing trips.

5

On July 1, 2013, Croatia became a member of the European Union. While Croats themselves continue to struggle against problems of severe unemployment, low wages, and high living costs, visitors to Dalmatia can expect more than comfortable accommodations, excellent restaurants serving fresh seasonal produce, and a truly stunning coastline, as beautiful as it ever was.

PLANNING

WHEN TO GO

High season runs from July through August, when the region is inundated with foreign tourists, predominantly Italians. During this period prices rise significantly; it's difficult to find a place to sleep if you haven't reserved in advance; restaurant staff are overworked; and beaches are crowded. On top of everything, it can be very hot. On the positive side, some museums and churches have extended opening hours, the season's open-air bars and clubs bring nightlife to the fore, and there are several cultural festivals with performances starring international musicians, dancers, and actors.

GETTING HERE AND AROUND

AIR TRAVEL

Through summer, various budget airlines, including EasyJet, Jet2.com, and Wizz Air, operate flights to Split, while EasyJet, Jet2.com, and Monarch operate flights to Dubrovnik from several European countries. Croatian Airlines offers flights from Zagreb to both destinations year-round. During the winter low season, these flights are reduced. There are no nonstop flights from the U.S. to Croatia.

Contacts **Croatia Airlines** ✉ *Obala Hrvatskog Narodnog Preporoda 9, Grad, Split* ☎ *021/362-997* ⊕ *www.croatiaairlines.com.* **EasyJet** ⊕ *www.easyjet.com.* **Jet2.com** ⊕ *www.jet2.com.* **Monarch** ⊕ *www.monarch.co.uk.* **Wizzair** ⊕ *www. wizzair.com.*

BOAT TRAVEL

Through summer, Jadrolinija operates a coastal route, departing from Rijeka twice weekly in the evening to arrive in Dubrovnik early the following evening. From Dubrovnik the ferries depart early in the morning to arrive in Rijeka early the following morning (approximately 23 hours in either direction). Coming and going, these ferries stop at both Stari Grad (island of Hvar) and Split. Jadrolinija and Blue Line also both offer regular service to Ancona (Italy) from Split. And from mid-June to mid-September the Italian company SNAV runs Croazia Jet, a daily catamaran service between Ancona (Italy) and Split. All ferry service is reduced in the off-season.

Contacts **Blue Line** ☎ *021/352-533* ⊕ *www.blueline-ferries.com.* **Jadrolinija** ✉ *Split ferry port, Gat Sv.Duje bb* ☎ *021/338-333* ⊕ *www.jadrolinija.hr.* **SNAV** ☎ *021/322-252* ⊕ *www.snav.it.*

BUS TRAVEL

There are good bus connections between Dubrovnik and Split (about 12 buses daily).

Contacts **Dubrovnik Bus Station** ✉ *Obala Pape Ivana Pavla II 44A, Gruž, Dubrovnik* ☎ *060/305-070* ⊕ *libertasdubrovnik.hr.* **Split Bus Station** ✉ *Obala Kneza Domogoja 12, Split* ☎ *060/327-777* ⊕ *www.ak-split.hr.*

CAR TRAVEL

While visiting Split, Hvar, and Dubrovnik, you are certainly better off without a car. If you want to explore the countryside, then it can be useful to have one.

TRAIN TRAVEL

There are three day trains and two night trains (with sleeping cars) daily between Split and Zagreb (5½ hours daytime; 8½ hours nighttime). There is no train service to Dubrovnik.

Contacts **Split Train Station** ✉ *Obala Kneza Domogoja 9, Split* ☎ *060/333-444* ⊕ *www.hznet.hr.*

HOTELS

Croatia offers a wide choice of lodgings: hotels, apartments, rooms in private homes, campsites, and agrotourism (working farms offering accommodation). Hotel prices tend to be on a par with those in Western Europe and are most expensive in Dubrovnik and in Hvar Town on the island of Hvar. While you can find some excellent low-season offers, prices skyrocket through July and August, when there is an influx of German and Italian visitors.

BOOKING

Advance reservations are an absolute requirement in summer. In winter, it's not nearly as difficult to find a hotel room, but some places, especially on the islands, close seasonally.

SAVING MONEY

Visitors to Dalmatia can save money by booking a private apartment rental, which is generally cheaper than a comparable hotel room and offers cooking facilities. Tourist agencies can also help you find rooms in private homes (*sobe*), which can be even cheaper. Standards are high, en-suite bathrooms and self-catering facilities being the norm. Host families are generally friendly and hospitable, and many visitors find a place they like, then return year after year.

RESTAURANTS

SAVING MONEY

In restaurants, be aware that fresh fish is priced by the kilogram, so prices vary dramatically depending on how big your fish is. Blue fish (tuna, sardines, etc.) are far less expensive than white fish (sea bass, sea bream, etc.), but do not always feature on the menu. Likewise, house wine, served by the carafe, is cheaper than bottled wine, and is often quite acceptable—ask to taste a little first if you are unsure.

MEALS AND MEAL TIMES

Seafood predominates throughout the region. Restaurants in Dubrovnik are the most expensive, and tend to cater to upmarket international tastes, with expensive white fish topping most menus and multilingual waiters pampering diners.

Lunch is generally eaten between 12:30 and 3, dinner between 7 and 10, though on hot summer nights diners might linger till midnight. Most restaurants close between lunch and dinner, where as a *konoba* (tavern) might stay open all day and serve meals right through the afternoon. Also worth a mention, *merenda* is a set-menu "fisherman's brunch," unique to Dalmatia and served from 10 to noon at some informal eateries frequented by locals.

PAYING

Most restaurants now accept credit cards, though some cheaper places may still accept only cash, particularly beyond the major tourist areas.

RESERVATIONS AND DRESS

In peak season (July and August), the more popular restaurants get very busy, and reservations are recommended. Casual dress is acceptable, but Dalmatians are quite style-conscious, so scruffy clothes should be avoided.

TIPPING

A 10% tip (left on the table, in cash) is much appreciated if you are satisfied with the service.

WINE, BEER, AND SPIRITS

Traditionally, Dalmatians drink wine with their meals, favoring white wine with seafood and red with meat. Local quality wines to look out for are the white Pošip (from the island of Korčula), and the reds Dingač (from the Pelješac peninsula) and Plavac (from the island of Hvar). Most restaurants also serve house wine by the carafe, while bars serve wine by the glass. Croatian beers include Karlovačko, Ožujsko, Zlatorog, and Pan, which are all light-colored lagers served by the bottle, well-chilled. Regarding spirits, potent *rakija* (made from distilled grapes) is drunk throughout Croatia, generally as an aperitif.

HOTEL AND RESTAURANT PRICES

Prices in the restaurant reviews are the average cost of a main course at dinner or, if dinner is not served, at lunch; taxes and service charges are generally included. Prices in the hotel reviews are the lowest cost of a standard double room in high season, excluding taxes, service charges, and meal plans (except at all-inclusives). Prices for rentals are the lowest per-night cost for a one-bedroom unit in high season.

VISITOR INFORMATION

Contacts **Dubrovnik & Neretva County Tourist Board** ✉ *Cvijete Zuzorić 1/1, Stari Grad, Dubrovnik* ☎ *020/324–999* ⊕ *www.visitdubrovnik.hr.* **Split & Dalmatia County Tourist Board** ✉ *Prilaz brace Kaliterna 10/I, Split* ☎ *021/490–032* ⊕ *www.dalmatia.hr.* **Hvar Town Tourist Information Center** ✉ *Trg Sv Stjepana bb, Hvar Town* ☎ *021/741–059* ⊕ *www.tzhvar.hr.*

SPLIT

Split's ancient core is so spectacular and unusual that a visit is more than worth your time. The heart of the city lies within the walls of Roman emperor Diocletian's retirement palace, which was built in the 3rd century AD. Diocletian, born in the nearby Roman settlement of Salona in AD 245, achieved a brilliant career as a soldier and became emperor at the age of 40. In 295 he ordered this vast palace to be built in his native Dalmatia, and when it was completed he stepped down from the throne and retired to his beloved homeland. Upon his death, he was laid to rest in an octagonal mausoleum, around which Split's magnificent cathedral was built.

In 615, when Salona was sacked by barbarian tribes, those fortunate enough to escape found refuge within the stout palace walls and divided up the vast imperial apartments into more modest living quarters. Thus, the palace developed into an urban center, and by the 11th century the settlement had expanded beyond the ancient walls.

Under the rule of Venice (1420–1797), Split—as a gateway to the Balkan interior—became one of the Adriatic's main trading ports, and the city's splendid Renaissance palaces bear witness to the affluence of those times. When the Habsburgs took control during the 19th century, an overland connection to Central Europe was established by the construction of the Split–Zagreb–Vienna railway line.

After World War II, the Tito years saw a period of rapid urban expansion: industrialization accelerated and the suburbs extended to accommodate high-rise apartment blocks. Today the historic center of Split is included on UNESCO's list of World Heritage Sites.

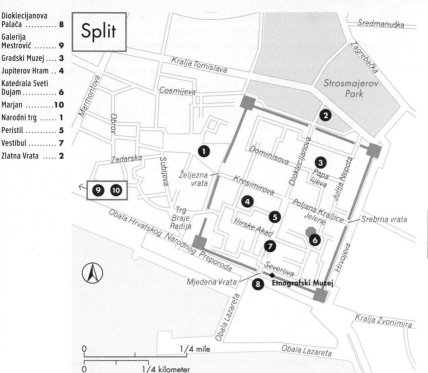

GETTING HERE AND AROUND
AIRPORT TRANSFERS
Contacts **Split airport bus** ☏ *021/203–119* ⊕ *www.plesoprijevoz.hr.*

TAXIS
Contacts **Radio Taxi** ☏ *021/475–343 in Split.*

TOURS
Contacts **Split Excursions** ⊕ *www.split-excursions.com.*

EXPLORING

The Old Town (often referred to as the Grad), where most of the architectural monuments are found, lies within the walls of Diocletian's Palace, which fronts on the seafront promenade, known to locals as the Riva. West of the center, Varoš is a conglomeration of stone fishermen's cottages built into a hillside, behind which rises Marjan, a 3½-km-long (2-mile-long) peninsula covered with pinewoods. Southeast of the center, the ferry port, bus station, and train station are grouped close together on Obala Kneza Domagoja.

Dioklecijanova Palača (*Diocletian's Palace*). The original palace was a combination of a luxurious villa and a Roman garrison, based on the ground plan of an irregular rectangle. Each of the four walls bore a main gate, the largest and most important being the northern Zlatna Vrata (Golden Gate), opening onto the road to the Roman settlement of Salona. The entrance from the western wall was the Željezna Vrata (Iron Gate), and the entrance through the east wall was the Srebrena Vrata (Silver Gate). The Mjedna Vrata (Bronze Gate) in the south wall faced directly onto the sea, and during Roman times boats would have docked here. The city celebrated the palace's 1,700th birthday in 2005. ⊠ *Obala Hrvatskog Narodnog Preporoda, Grad.*

Galerija Meštrović (*Meštrović Gallery*). A modern villa surrounded by extensive gardens, this building designed by Ivan Meštrović was his summer residence during the 1920s and '30s. Some 200 of his sculptural works in wood, marble, stone, and bronze are on display, both indoors and out. There is a small open-air café in the garden with a lovely sea view. ⊠ *Šetalište Ivana Meštrovicá 46, Meje* ☎ *021/340–800* ⊕ *www. mdc.hr* 🖃 *30 Kn* ⊘ *May–Sept., Tues.–Sun. 9–7; Oct.–Apr., Tues.–Sat. 9–4, Sun. 10–3.*

Kaštelet. Entrance to the Galerija Meštrović is also valid for the nearby Kaštelet, housing a chapel containing a cycle of New Testament bas-relief wood carvings that many consider Meštrović's finest work. ⊠ *Šetalište Ivana Meštrovicá 39, Meje*

Gradski Muzej (*City Museum*). Split's city museum is worth a quick look both to marvel at the collection of medieval weaponry and to see the interior of this splendid 15th-century town house. The dining room, on the first floor, is furnished just as it would have been when the Papalić family owned the house, giving some idea of how the aristocracy of that time lived. ⊠ *Papaličeva 1, Grad* ☎ *021/360–171* ⊕ *www.mgst. net* 🖃 *20 Kn* ⊘ *May.–Oct, Tues.–Fri. 9–9, Sat.–Mon. 9–4; Nov.–Apr., Tues.–Fri. 10–4, Sat. 9–1, Sun. 10–1.*

Jupiterov Hram (*Jupiter's Temple*). This Roman temple was converted into a baptistery during the Middle Ages. The entrance is guarded by the mate (unfortunately damaged) of the black-granite sphinx that stands in front of the cathedral. Inside, beneath the coffered barrel vault and ornamented cornice, the 11th-century baptismal font is adorned with a stone relief showing a medieval Croatian king on his throne. Directly behind it, the bronze statue of St. John the Baptist is the work of Meštrović. ⊠ *Kraj Sv Ivana, Grad* 🖃 *15 Kn* ⊘ *May–Oct., daily 8–7.*

Katedrala Sveti Dujam (*Cathedral of St. Dominius*). The main body of the cathedral is the 3rd-century octagonal mausoleum designed as a shrine to Emperor Diocletian. During the 7th century, refugees from Salona converted it into an early Christian church, ironically dedicating it to Sv Duje (St. Domnius), after Bishop Domnius of Salona, one of the many Christians martyred during the late emperor's persecution campaign. The cathedral's monumental main door is ornamented with magnificent carved wooden reliefs, the work of Andrija Buvina of Split, portraying 28 scenes from the life of Christ and dated 1214. Inside, the hexagonal Romanesque stone pulpit, with richly carved decoration, is from the 13th century. The high altar, surmounted by a late-Gothic canopy, was executed by Bonino of Milan in 1427. Nearby is the 15th-century canopied Gothic altar of Anastasius by Juraj Dalmatinac. The elegant 200-foot Romanesque-Gothic bell tower was constructed in stages between the 12th and 16th centuries; the tower is sometimes closed in winter during bad weather. ✉ *3 Ul. Kraj Sv. Duje, Grad* ✉ *Cathedral 25 Kn (including crypt), bell tower 15 Kn* ⊘ *Nov.–Apr., daily 8–6; May–Oct., daily 8–7.*

Marjan (*Marjan Hill*). Situated on a hilly peninsula, this much-loved park is planted with pine trees and Mediterranean shrubs and has been a protected nature reserve since 1964. A network of paths crisscrosses the grounds, offering stunning views over the sea and islands. ✉ *Marjan.*

Narodni trg (*People's Square*). A pedestrianized expanse paved with gleaming white marble, and rimmed by open-air cafés, this is contemporary Split's main square. Although religious activity has to this day centered on Peristil, Narodni trg became the focus of civic life during the 14th century. In the 15th century the Venetians constructed several important public buildings here: the Town Hall (housing a contemporary art gallery, with erratic opening hours), plus the Rector's Palace and a theater, the latter two sadly demolished by the Habsburgs in the 19th century. The Austrians, for their part, added a Secessionist building at the west end of the square. ✉ *Grad.*

Peristil (*Peristyle*). From Roman times up to the present day, the main public meeting place within the palace walls, this spacious central courtyard is flanked by marble columns topped with Corinthian capitals and richly ornamented cornices linked by arches. There are six columns on both the east and west sides, and four more at the south end, which mark the monumental entrance to the Vestibul. During summer, occasional live concerts are held here. ✉ *Grad.*

Vestibul. The cupola of this domed space would once have been decorated with marble and mosaics. Today there's only a round hole in the top of the dome, but it produces a stunning effect: the dark interior, the blue sky above, and the tip of the cathedral's bell tower framed in the opening. ✉ *Peristil, Grad.*

Zlatna Vrata (*Golden Gate*). Formerly the main entrance into the palace, Zlatna Vrata, on the north side of the palace, is the most monumental of the four gates—two guards in Roman costume stand here through summer. Just outside stands Meštrović's gigantic bronze **statue of Grgur Ninski** (Bishop Gregory of Nin). During the 9th century, the bishop campaigned for the use of the Slav language in the Croatian Church, as opposed to Latin, thus infuriating Rome. This statue was created in 1929 and placed on Peristil to mark the 1,000th anniversary of the Split Synod, then moved here in 1957. Note the big toe on the left foot, which is considered by locals to be a good luck charm and has been worn gold through constant touching. ✉ *Dioklecijanova, Grad.*

WHERE TO EAT

Split does have some good restaurants, though they're not always easy to find. As in any city of fishermen and sailors, seafood predominates here. In most restaurants, fresh fish is normally prepared over a charcoal fire and served with *blitva sa krumpirom* (Swiss chard and potato with garlic and olive oil). For a cheaper option, bear in mind that the pizza in Split is almost as good as (and sometimes even better than) that in Italy. Last but not least, complement your meal with a bottle of Dalmatian wine.

$$ MEDITERRANEAN 🍴 **Apetit.** On the second floor of a 15th-century palazzo, just off the main square, Apetit serves traditional local dishes with a twist. Look out for favorites such as *tuna ala pašticada* (fresh tuna cooked in wine and served with gnocchi), or the house specialty, *rezanci Apetit* (homemade tagliatelle with shrimp, salmon, and zucchini). The dining room combines medieval stonework with minimalist black and white furniture and several big bold modern oil paintings. [$] *Average main: 90 Kn* ✉ *Šubićeva 5, Grad* ☎ *021/332–549* 🌐 *www.apetit-split.hr.*

$ EASTERN EUROPEAN 🍴 **Fife.** With a small terrace out front overlooking the wooden fishing boats of Matejuška harbor, Fife has long been a favorite with local fishermen. Come summer, it's also incredibly popular with tourists, who come here for the reasonably priced, down-to-earth Dalmatian cooking. Although they now have two dining rooms plus outdoor tables on the front terrace, you'll probably have to queue for a table, and may well be asked to share a table with other guests—but that's part of the fun. [$] *Average main: 55 Kn* ✉ *Trubičeva Obala 11, Matejuška* ☎ *021/345–223* 💳 *No credit cards.*

$$$ EASTERN EUROPEAN 🍴 **Kod Jose.** This typical Dalmatian *konoba* is relaxed and romantic, with exposed stone walls and heavy wooden furniture set off by candlelight. The waiters are wonderfully discreet, and the *rižot frutta di mare* (seafood risotto) delicious. You'll find it just outside the palace walls, a five-minute walk from Zlatna Vrata (Golden Gate)—it's slightly hidden away, so many tourists miss it. There are also tables outside on a small open-air terrace if you come here in summer. [$] *Average main: 120 Kn* ✉ *Sredmanuška 4, Manuš* ☎ *021/347–397.*

$$$ EASTERN EUROPEAN 🍴 **Konoba Varoš.** The dining-room walls are hung with seascapes and fishing nets, and the waiters wear traditional Dalmatian waistcoats. The place can seem a little dour at lunchtime, but mellows when the candles are lighted during the evening. The fresh fish and *pržene lignje* (fried squid) are excellent, and there's also a reasonable choice of Croatian meat dishes. It's a five-minute walk west of the center, at the bottom of Varoš, and has a couple of tables outside by the entrance. [$] *Average main: 120 Kn* ✉ *Ban Mladenova 7, Varoš* ☎ *021/396–138.*

$$ PIZZA 🍴 **Pizzeria Galija.** The best pizzas in town, as well as delicious pasta dishes and a range of colorful salads, good draft beer and wine sold by the glass, are to be found in this centrally located pizzeria, which is close to the fish market. A favorite with locals, its dining room is bustling and informal, with heavy wooden tables and benches. There's also a terrace for open-air dining out front. Note that service can be rather slow when it is busy. The owner, Željko Jerkov, is a retired Olympic-gold-medal-

winning basketball player. $ *Average main: 65 Kn* ☒ *Tončićeva 12, Grad* ☎ *021/347–932* ⊟ *No credit cards.*

WHERE TO STAY

In the past, Split was overlooked as a sightseeing destination and considered a mere transit point to the islands. As a result, it still suffers from a shortage of good places to stay. However, there is now a handful of recommendable hotels within the palace walls, plus several pleasant, reasonably priced hotels within walking distance from Old Town.

$$$
HOTEL

Hotel Luxe. A five-minute walk from the old town, above the ferry port, this slick modern hotel opened in summer 2010. **Pros:** central location close to ferry port; light and airy rooms; funky contemporary interior design; friendly professional staff. **Cons:** busy main road out front and an unappealing facade; no restaurant (just a breakfast room). $ *Rooms from: €200* ☒ *K. Zvonimira 6* ☎ *021/314–444* ⊕ *www. hotelluxesplit.com* ↗ *27 rooms, 3 suites* ❢❍❢ *Breakfast.*

$$$$
HOTEL

Hotel Marmont. In a 15th-century stone building in Split's Old Town, this stylish hotel combines a peaceful historic location with chic contemporary design. **Pros:** central old town location; stylish interior; friendly professional staff. **Cons:** parking near hotel an issue; no restaurant (just a breakfast room). $ *Rooms from: €350* ☒ *Zadarska 1, Grad* ☎ *021/308–060* ⊕ *www.marmonthotel.com* ↗ *21 rooms, 1 suite* ❢❍❢ *Breakfast.*

$$
HOTEL

Hotel Peristil. One of only a handful of hotels within the palace walls, Hotel Peristil lies behind the cathedral, just inside Srebrena Vrata, the city gate leading to the open-air market. **Pros:** inside the palace walls; small (so guests receive individual attention); lovely open-air restaurant terrace. **Cons:** small and often fully booked; nearby parking difficult; limited facilities. $ *Rooms from: €162* ☒ *Poljana Kraljice Jelena 5, Grad* ☎ *021/329–070* ⊕ *www.hotelperistil.com* ↗ *12 rooms* ❢❍❢ *Breakfast.*

$$$$
B&B/INN
Fodor'sChoice
★

Hotel Vestibul Palace. Three palaces from different eras have been combined to form this intimate Old Town standout with interiors that have been carefully renovated to expose Roman stone- and brickwork, along with more modern, minimalist designer details. **Pros:** history and standout architecture; inside the palace walls; beautiful interior; small and intimate; individual attention. **Cons:** expensive for most of the season; often fully booked; no sports facilities. $ *Rooms from: €328* ☒ *Iza Vestibula 4, Grad* ☎ *021/329–329* ⊕ *www.vestibulpalace.com* ↗ *7 rooms, 4 suites* ❢❍❢ *Breakfast.*

$$$
RESORT

Le Meridien Lav. A world unto its own, this vast, self-contained complex lies 8 km (5 miles) south of Split. **Pros:** beautifully designed modern interior; excellent sports facilities; luxurious spa. **Cons:** far from the center of Split; expensive; large (so the hotel can seem somewhat impersonal). $ *Rooms from: €230* ☒ *Grljevačka 2A, Podstrana* ☎ *021/500–500* ⊕ *www.lemeridienlavsplit.com* ↗ *364 rooms, 17 suites* ❢❍❢ *Breakfast.*

5

NIGHTLIFE AND THE ARTS

Split is much more lively at night during the summer season, when bars stay open late, discos hold open-air parties by the sea, and the Split Summer Festival offers a respectable program of opera and classical music concerts.

NIGHTLIFE

Through summer, many bars have extended licenses and stay open until 2 am. In August, rock musicians from Croatia and the other countries of the former Yugoslavia perform open-air concerts. There's no particular source of information about what's on, but you'll see posters around town if anything special is planned.

Galerija Plavca. In a narrow side street off Trg Braće Radića (better known to locals as Voćni trg), Galerija Plavca is a laid-back café-bar with outdoor seating in a pleasant courtyard, plus occasional art and photography exhibitions. ⊠ *Kaštelanova 12, Grad.*

Ghetto Klub. With a colorful, bohemian interior and a courtyard garden lit with flaming torches, Ghetto Klub pulls in the cool, young, artsy crowd and hosts occasional exhibitions and concerts. ⊠ *Dosud 10, Grad.*

Teak. Close to Zlatna Vrata, Teak is a small café with an exposed-stonework-and-wood interior plus tables outside through summer. It's popular with highbrow locals, who come here to leaf through the piles of international newspapers and magazines. ⊠ *Majstora Jurja 11, Grad.*

THE ARTS

Split Summer Festival. Running from mid-July to mid-August, the Split Summer Festival includes a variety of open-air opera, classical-music concerts, dance and theatrical performances, the highlight being opera on Prokurative (Republic Square). ■TIP→ **Tickets can be purchased online or from the theater box office.** ⊠ *Croatian National Theater, Trg Gaje Bulata 1, Grad* ☎ *021/306–908* ⊕ *www.splitsko-ljeto.hr.*

SPORTS AND THE OUTDOORS

BEACHES

Uvala Bačvica (*Bačvice Bay*). This is the area's best beach and it's a 10-minute walk east of the Old Town. It does get very busy in summer, but if you don't mind the crowds, you can rent beach chairs and umbrellas, and there's a string of cafés and bars along this stretch of coast. **Amenities:** food and drink; showers. **Best for:** partiers; swimming. ⊠ *Šetalište Petra Preradovića, Bačvica.*

SAILING

Well connected to the rest of Europe by plane and ferry—and within just a few hours' sailing of several of the Adriatic's most beautiful islands—Split is the center of the yacht-charter business in Dalmatia.

ACI marina. The 355-berth ACI marina is southwest of the city center. It stays open all year, and is a base for dozens of charter companies organizing sailing on the Adriatic. ⊠ *Uvala Baluni 8, Zvončac* ☎ *021/398–599* ⊕ *www.aci-club.hr.*

SHOPPING

Dalmatian women—and those from Split in particular—are renowned for their elegant sense of style. Despite a poor local economy, you'll find countless exclusive little boutiques selling women's clothes, some representing the new generation of young Croatian designers, and shoes imported from Italy. However, the city's most memorable shopping venue remains the *pazar*, the colorful open-air market held each morning just outside the palace walls. When looking for gifts, bear in mind that Dalmatia produces some excellent wines, which you can buy either in Split or while visiting the islands.

Croata. Overlooking Trg Brace Radića, close to the seafront, Croata specializes in "original Croatian ties" in presentation boxes. ✉ *Mihovilova Širina 7, Grad* ☎ *021/346–336.*

Vinoteka Terra. Vinoteka Terra is a stone cellar close to Bačvice bay, where you can taste Croatian regional wines, accompanied by savory appetizers, before purchasing bottles. It also stocks truffle products and olive oils. ✉ *Prilaz Braće Kaliterna 6, Bačvice* ☎ *021/314–800* ⊕ *vinoteka.hr.*

HVAR

Fodor's Choice
★ The island of Hvar bills itself as the "sunniest island in the Adriatic." Not only does it have the figures to back up this claim—an annual average of 2,724 hours of sunshine with a maximum of two foggy days a year—but it also makes visitors a sporting proposition, offering them a money-back guarantee if there are seven consecutive days of snow (snow has been known to fall here, the last time being February 2012).

GETTING HERE AND AROUND

From Split, Jadrolinija runs regular car ferries (seven times daily during the summer; two hours one-way) to and from Stari Grad on Hvar, though you then need to take a bus or drive from Stari Grad to Hvar Town. Alternatively, the same company runs faster passenger-only catamarans (twice daily during the summer; one hour one-way) from Split direct to Hvar Town.

EXPLORING

Hvar is both the name of the island and the name of the capital, near the island's western tip. Little **Hvar Town** rises like an amphitheater from its harbor, backed by a hilltop fortress and protected from the open sea by a scattering of small islands known as Pakleni Otoci. Along the palm-lined quay, a string of cafés and restaurants is shaded by colorful awnings and umbrellas. A few steps away, the magnificent main square, **Trg Sveti Stjepan,** the largest piazza in Dalmatia, is backed by the 16th-century **Katedrala Sveti Stjepan** (Cathedral of St. Stephen). Other notable sights include the *kazalište* (a theater) and the Franjevački Samostan (Franciscan Monastery). Hvar Town is currently a very "in" spot, so expect it to be crowded and expensive through peak season.

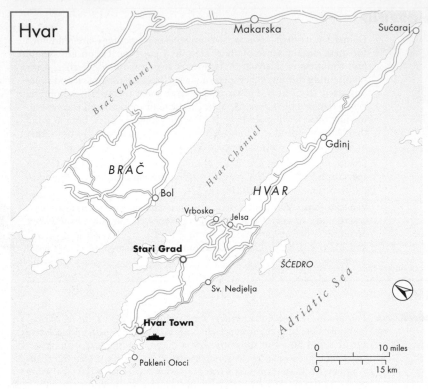

Recent visitors have included Tom Cruise, Beyoncé, Italian clothing entrepreneur Luciano Benetton, and local tennis champion Goran Ivanišević. The easiest way to reach Hvar Town is to catch a midafternoon Jadrolinija catamaran from Split, which stops at Hvar Town (23 nautical miles) before continuing to the South Dalmatian islands of Korčula and Lastovo. Alternatively, take an early-morning Jadrolinija ferry from Split to Stari Grad (23 nautical miles) and then catch a local bus across the island.

Franjevački samostan (*Franciscan monastery*). East of town, along the quay past the Arsenal, lies the Franjevački samostan. Within its walls, a pretty 15th-century Renaissance cloister leads to the former refectory, now housing a small museum with several notable artworks. ⊠ *Križa bb* ⊡ *25 Kn* ☉ *May–Oct., daily 9–1 and 5–7.*

Stari Grad. The site of the original Greek settlement on Hvar, called Pharos by the Greeks, Stari Grad is a conglomeration of smaller communities; it's also the entry-point to the island for bus transportation from the mainland, as well as passenger ferries. The town is 10 km (6 miles) east of Hvar Town. ⊠ *Hvar* ⊕ *www.stari-grad-faros.hr.*

Tvrdalj. The main sight is the Tvrdalj, the fortified Renaissance villa of the 16th-century poet Petar Hektorović. The home has been renovated twice over the centuries, first in the 18th-century baroque style; a partial restoration was also done in the 19th century. Hektorović attempted to create a "model universe" to be embodied in his home. To that end, a large fish pond is stocked with gray mullet, as they were in the poet's own time, representing the sea; above the fish pond in a tower is a dovecote, representing the air. Ivy was allowed to cover the walls to tie the home to the land. Quotations from his poetry are inscribed on many walls. ✉ *8 Ul. Molo Njiva, Stari Grad, Hvar* ☎ *021/765–068* 🎟 *15 Kn* ⏲ *May–June and Oct., daily 10–1; July–Sept., daily 10–1 and 6–8.*

WHERE TO EAT

$$ MEDITERRANEAN FAMILY 🍴 **Konoba Menego.** On the steps between the main square and the castle, this authentic stone-walled konoba has candlelit tables and whole *pršut* (prosciutto) hanging from the wooden beamed ceiling. Come here to snack on small platters of locally produced, cold Dalmatian specialties such as *kožji sir* (goat cheese), pršut, *salata od hobotnice* (octopus salad) and *masline* (olives), accompanied by a carafe of homemade wine. They also do a special Children's Plate. Before leaving, round off your meal with *pijane smokve* (figs marinated in brandy), and be sure to check out the world atlas where guests sign on the pages of their home towns. [$] *Average main: 80 Kn* ✉ *Groda bb* ☎ *021/742–036* 🌐 *www.menego.hr* 💳 *No credit cards* ⏲ *Closed Dec.–Mar.*

$$$ SEAFOOD Fodor's Choice ★ 🍴 **Macondo.** This superb fish restaurant lies hidden away on a narrow, cobbled street between the main square and the fortress—to find it, follow the signs from Trg Sv Stjepana. The dining room is simply furnished with wooden tables, discreet modern art, and a large open fire. The food and service are practically faultless. Begin with the delicate scampi pâté, followed by a mixed seafood platter, and round off with a glass of homemade *orahovica* (walnut rakija). [$] *Average main: 120 Kn* ✉ *2 blocks north of Trg Sv Stjepana* ☎ *021/742–850* ⏲ *Closed Dec.–Mar.*

$$$ SEAFOOD 🍴 **Restoran Palmižana.** On the tiny island of Sveti Klement, a 20-minute taxi-boat ride from Hvar Town, this terrace restaurant is backed by a romantic wilderness of Mediterranean flora and offers stunning views over the open sea. The walls are decorated with contemporary Croatian art, and there are classical-music recitals on Sunday morning. Besides fresh seafood, goodies include *kožji sir sa rukolom* (goat cheese with arugula), and *pašticada* (beef stewed in sweet wine and prunes). [$] *Average main: 120 Kn* ✉ *Vinogradišće Uvala, Sveti Klement, Hvar* ☎ *021/717–270* ⏲ *Closed Nov.–Mar.*

WHERE TO STAY

$$$$ HOTEL 🏨 **Hotel Adriana.** On the seafront, looking across the busy harbor toward the Old Town, the Adriana reopened in June 2007 after total renovation. **Pros:** prime location on seafront promenade; beautifully designed interior; luxurious spa. **Cons:** very expensive; most bathrooms have a big shower but no tub; some guests complain that breakfast is sub-par for a hotel of this price range. [$] *Rooms from: €407* ✉ *Fabrika bb* ☎ *021/750–200* 🌐 *www.suncanihvar.hr* 🛏 *50 rooms, 9 suites* 🍽 *Breakfast.*

5

$$$$ HOTEL FAMILY
🏨 **Hotel Amfora.** This colossal white, modern structure sits in its own bay, backed by pinewoods, a pleasant 10-minute walk along the coastal path from the center of town. **Pros:** location in newly landscaped grounds overlooking the sea; chic modern design; private beach cabins. **Cons:** vast 1970s building lacks charm even after renovation; large and somewhat impersonal; poor signage within the complex (some guests complain they get lost). [$] *Rooms from: €364* ✉ *Majerovića bb* ☎ *021/750–300* 🌐 *www.suncanihvar.hr* 🛏 *246 rooms, 78 suites* 🍴 *Breakfast.*

$$$$ HOTEL
🏨 **Hotel Riva.** Occupying a 100-year-old stone building on the palm-lined waterfront, opposite the ferry landing station, the Riva is considered one of Hvar's hippest hideaways. **Pros:** prime location on seafront promenade; beautifully designed interior; excellent bar and restaurant. **Cons:** very expensive; rooms in front can be noisy at night (bars) and in the early morning (ferry); rooms are rather small. [$] *Rooms from: €380* ✉ *Riva bb* ☎ *021/750–100* 🌐 *www.suncanihvar.hr* 🛏 *46 rooms, 8 suites* 🍴 *Breakfast.*

$$$ HOTEL
🏨 **Podstine.** This peaceful, family-run hotel lies on the coast, a 20-minute walk west of the town center. **Pros:** peaceful seafront location; beautiful gardens; small beach out front with sun beds and umbrellas. **Cons:** far from Old Town; absolutely no nightlife nearby (the hotel's bar shuts at 11 pm even in summer); standard rooms are rather dark and gloomy and have no views. [$] *Rooms from: €219* ✉ *Podstine bb* ☎ *021/740–400* 🌐 *www.podstine.com* 🛏 *40 rooms* 🕒 *Closed Nov.–Mar.* 🍴 *Breakfast.*

NIGHTLIFE AND THE ARTS

Croatia is generally not a hot spot for nightlife, but the island of Hvar may be starting a renaissance on the party front. Several stylish cocktail bars and open-air clubs have opened in the past few years to cater to the annual influx of summer visitors.

Carpe Diem Bar. A harborside cocktail bar with a summer terrace decked out with Oriental furniture and potted plants and two burly bouncers at the gate, this is Hvar's most talked-about nightlife venue. Besides the glamorous see-and-be-seen crowd, it's also popular with twentysomething backpackers looking for a late-night party, and has contributed to Hvar's reputation as the next Ibiza. ✉ *Riva* ☎ *021/742–369* 🌐 *www.carpe-diem-hvar.com.*

Veneranda. Veneranda offers open-air drinking and dancing by a pool in the grounds of a former Greek Orthodox monastery. Most evenings begin with a film projection after dusk: the crowds arrive after midnight. It is a 10-minute walk west of town. Follow the seafront promenade, then head for the lights in the pine woods. ✉ *Sv Veneranda, Gornja cesta bb* ☎ *095/454–5705* 🌐 *www.veneranda.hr.*

SPORTS AND THE OUTDOORS

BEACHES

Although there are several decent beaches within walking distance of town—the best-equipped being the Hotel Amfora's Bonj Les Bain beach, 10 minutes west of the main square—sun worshippers in the know head for the nearby Pakleni Otoci (Pakleni Islands), which can be reached by taxi boats that depart regularly (in peak season, every hour from 8 to 8) from in front of the Arsenal in the town harbor. The best known and best served are **Sveti Jerolim** (on the island of the same name, predominantly a nudist beach), Carpe Diem beach club (in Stipanska bay on the island of Marinkovac), and **Palmižana** (on the island of Sveti Klement). Another popular swimming area is on the rocks around the trendy Hula Hula beach bar, a 20-minute walk west of town, past Bonj Les Bain.

Carpe Diem Beach. Doubling as a daytime beach club and an after-dark party venue, Carpe Diem Beach lies on the tiny pine-scented island of Stipanska, a 10-minute taxi boat ride from Hvar Town's harbor. It has two pebble beaches complete with wooden sun-beds and big parasols, an outdoor pool and an open-air massage pavilion. There's also a lounge-bar and restaurant, and from mid-July to mid-August it hosts international DJs playing till sunrise. **Amenities:** food and drink; showers; toilets. **Best for:** partiers; swimming. ⊠ *Stipanska, Hvar* ⊕ *www. carpe-diem-beach.com.*

DIVING

Diving Center Viking. Those with a taste for underwater adventure might have a go at scuba diving. The seabed is scattered with pieces of broken Greek amphorae, while the area's biggest underwater attraction is the Stambedar seawall, home to red and violet gorgonians (a type of coral), which is close to the Pakleni Islands. For courses at all levels, try Diving Center Viking. ⊠ *Hotel Podstine, Podstine bb* ☎ *021/742–529* ⊕ *www. viking-diving.com.*

SAILING

Hvar Town is a popular port of call for those sailing on the Adriatic; the town harbor is packed with flashy yachts through peak season.

ACI Marina. Located in Palmižana Bay on the island of Sveti Klement, one of the Pakleni Otoci, ACI Marina lies just 2.4 nautical miles from Hvar Town. This 211-berth marina is open from April through October, and is served by regular taxi boats from Hvar Town through peak season. ⊠ *Palmižana Bay, Sveti Klement, Hvar* ☎ *021/744–995* ⊕ *www. aci-club.hr.*

5

DUBROVNIK

Lying 216 km (135 miles) southeast of Split and commanding a splendid coastal location, Dubrovnik is one of the world's most beautiful fortified cities. Its massive stone ramparts and splendid fortress towers curve around a tiny harbor, enclosing graduated ridges of sun-bleached orange-tiled roofs, copper domes, and elegant bell towers.

In the 7th century AD, residents of the Roman city Epidaurum (now Cavtat) fled the Avars and Slavs of the north and founded a new settlement on a small rocky island, which they named Laus, and later Ragusa. On the mainland hillside opposite the island, the Slav settlement called Dubrovnik grew up. In the 12th century the narrow channel separating the two settlements was filled in, and Ragusa and Dubrovnik became one. The city was surrounded by defensive walls during the 13th century, and these were reinforced with towers and bastions in the late 15th century.

From 1358 to 1808 the city thrived as a powerful and remarkably sophisticated independent republic, reaching its golden age during the 16th century. In 1667 many of its splendid Gothic and Renaissance buildings were destroyed by an earthquake. The defensive walls survived the disaster, and the city was rebuilt in baroque style.

Dubrovnik lost its independence to Napoléon in 1808, and in 1815 passed to Austria-Hungary. During the 20th century, as part of Yugoslavia, the city became a popular tourist destination, and in 1979 it was listed as a UNESCO World Heritage Site. During the war for independence, it came under heavy siege, though thanks to careful restoration work few traces of damage remain. Today Dubrovnik is once again a fashionable, high-class destination, drawing not a few celebrities.

GETTING HERE AND AROUND
AIRPORT TRANSFERS
Contacts Airport bus ☎ *020/442–222* ⊕ *www.atlas-croatia.com.*

TAXIS
Contacts Taxi Station Gruž ☎ *0800/0970.* **Taxi Station Pile** ☎ *0800/0970.*
Taxi Station Ploče ☎ *0800/0970.*

TOURS
Atlas organizes one-day excursions from Dubrovnik to Ston and Korčula, as well as day trips to neighboring countries (passports required), including Mostar, Bosnia-Herzegovina, with its Turkish-inspired Old Town and reconstructed bridge; and the Bay of Kotor, Budva, and the jet-setters' retreat of Sveti Stefan, Montenegro.

Contacts Atlas ⊠ *Vukovarska 19* ☎ *020/442–222* ⊕ *www.atlas-croatia.com.*

EXPLORING

All of the main sites lie in Stari Grad (Old Town) within the city walls, an area which is compact and car-free.

Dominikanski samostan (*Dominican monastery*). With a splendid, late-15th-century floral Gothic cloister as its centerpiece, the monastery is

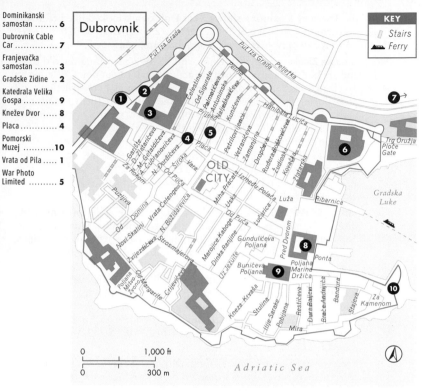

best known for its museum, which houses a rich collection of religious paintings by the so-called Dubrovnik School from the 15th and 16th centuries. Look out for works by Božidarević, Hamzić, and Dobričević, as well as gold and silver ecclesiastical artifacts crafted by local goldsmiths. ⊠ *Sv Domina 4, Stari Grad* ☎ *020/321–423* 🎫 *30 Kn* 🕒 *May–Oct., daily 9–6; Nov.–Apr., daily 9–5.*

FAMILY **Dubrovnik Cable Car.** Reopened in July 2010, the ultra-modern cable car has two light and airy carriages with a capacity of 30 persons each. You take a three-minute scenic ride to the top of Mt. Srdj (405 meters), for spectacular views down onto the Old Town and the islands. Facilities at the top include two viewing terraces with binoculars, a restaurant, snack bar, and souvenir shop. ⊠ *Lower station, Frana Supila 35a* ☎ *020/325–393* ⊕ *www.dubrovnikcablecar.com* 🎫 *50 kn (one-way); 94 kn (return)* 🕒 *June–Aug., daily 9 am–midnight; Sept., daily 9 am–10 pm; Oct. and Apr. and May, daily 9–8; Nov. and Feb.–Mar., daily 9–5; Dec. and Jan., daily 9–4.*

Franjevačka samostan (*Franciscan monastery*). The monastery's chief claim to fame is its pharmacy, which was founded in 1318 and is still in existence today; it's said to be the oldest in Europe. There's also a delightful cloistered garden, framed by Romanesque arcades supported by double columns, each crowned with a set of grotesque figures. In the Treasury a painting shows what Dubrovnik looked like before the disastrous earthquake of 1667. ⊠ *Placa 2, Stari Grad* ☎ *020/321–410* 🖾 *30 Kn* ☉ *May–Oct., daily 9–6; Nov.–Apr., daily 9–5.*

Fodor's Choice **Gradske Zidine** (*city walls*). Dubrovnik's city walls define the old town
★ and are both a popular tourist attraction and lookout point, offering an excellent view of the Adriatic. Most of the original construction took place during the 13th century, though the walls were further reinforced with towers and bastions over the following 400 years. On average they are 80 feet high and up to 10 feet thick on the seaward side, 20 feet thick on the inland side. They may look familiar to viewers of *Game of Thrones* since they are regularly featured as the walls of King's Landing. ⊠ *Placa, Stari Grad* ☎ *020/324–641* 🖾 *90 Kn* ☉ *June and July, daily 8–7:30; Aug.–mid-Sept., daily 8–7; May and mid-Sept.–Oct., daily 8–6; Nov.–Apr., daily 10–3.*

Katedrala Velika Gospa (*Cathedral of Our Lady*). The present structure was built in baroque style after the original was destroyed in the 1667 earthquake. The interior contains a number of notable paintings, including a large polyptych above the main altar depicting the *Assumption of Our Lady*, attributed to Titian. The Treasury displays 138 gold and silver reliquaries, including the skull of St. Blaise in the form of a bejeweled Byzantine crown and also an arm and a leg of the saint, likewise encased in decorated gold plating. ⊠ *Držićeva Poljana, Stari Grad* ☎ *020/323–459* 🖾 *Cathedral free, treasury 15 Kn* ☉ *May–Oct., Mon.–Sat. 9–5, Sun. 11:30–5; Nov.–Apr., Mon.–Sat. 10–12 and 3–5, Sun. 11–12 and 3–5.*

Knežev Dvor (*Bishop's Palace*). Originally created in the 15th century but reconstructed several times through the following years, this exquisite building with an arcaded loggia and an internal courtyard shows a combination of late-Gothic and early Renaissance styles. On the ground floor there are large rooms where, in the days of the republic, the Great Council and Senate held their meetings. Over the entrance to the meeting halls a plaque reads, "Obliti privatorum publica curate" ("Forget private affairs, and get on with public matters"). Upstairs, the rector's living quarters now accommodate the Cultural History Museum, containing exhibits that give a picture of life in Dubrovnik from early days until the fall of the republic. Visitors buy a combination ticket, which is valid for four museums, including the Maritime Museum, the Ethnographic Museum, and the Archaeology Museum (all in separate locations). ⊠ *Pred Dvorom 3, Stari Grad* ☎ *020/321–497* ⊕ *www.dumus.hr* 🖾 *70 Kn (includes all 4 Dubrovnik city museums)* ☉ *May–Oct., daily 9–6; Nov.–Apr., daily 9–4.*

Placa (*Stradun*). This was once the shallow sea channel separating the island of Laus from the mainland. Although it was filled in during the 12th century, it continued to divide the city socially for several centuries, the nobility living in the area south of Placa and the commoners living on the hillside to the north. Today it forms the venue for the *korzo*, an evening promenade where locals meet to chat, maybe have a drink at one of the numerous open-air cafés, and generally size one another up. ⊠ *Stari Grad.*

Pomorski Muzej (*Maritime Museum*). Above the aquarium, on the first floor of St. John's Fortress, this museum's exhibits illustrate how rich and powerful Dubrovnik became one of the world's most important seafaring nations. On display are intricately detailed models of ships as well as engine-room equipment, sailors' uniforms, paintings, and maps. Visitors buy a combination ticket, which is valid for four museums, including the Bishop's Palace. ✉ *Damjana Jude 2, Stari Grad* ☎ *020/323–904* ✄ *70 Kn (includes all 4 Dubrovnik city museums)* ⊙ *May–Oct., Tues.–Sun. 9–6; Nov.–Apr., Tues.–Sun. 9–4.*

Vrata od Pila (*Pile Gate*). Built in 1537 and combining a Renaissance arch with a wooden drawbridge on chains, this has always been the main entrance to the city walls. A niche above the portal contains a statue of Sveti Vlah (St. Blaise), the city's patron saint, holding a replica of Dubrovnik in his left hand. From May to October, guards in deep-red period-costume uniforms stand vigilant by the gate through daylight hours, just as they would have done when the city was a republic. ✉ *Pile, Stari Grad.*

Fodor's Choice ★ **War Photo Limited.** Shocking but impressive, this modern gallery devotes two entire floors to war photojournalism. Past exhibitions include images from conflicts in Afghanistan, Iraq, the former Yugoslavia, Israel, Palestine, and Lebanon. Refreshingly impartial by Croatian standards, the message—that war is physically and emotionally destructive whichever side you are on—comes through loudly and clearly. You'll find it in a narrow side street running between Placa and Prijeko. ✉ *Antuninska 6, Stari Grad* ☎ *020/322–166* ⊕ *www.warphotoltd.com* ✄ *30 Kn* ⊙ *May and Oct., Tues.–Sun. 10–4; June–Sept., daily 10–10.*

WHERE TO EAT

As elsewhere along the coast, seafood dominates restaurant menus. The narrow, cobbled street Prijeko, which runs parallel to Placa, is packed with touristy restaurants and waiters touting for customers. Less commercial and infinitely more agreeable eateries are scattered throughout the town.

$$$
SUSHI
✗ **Bota Šare Oyster & Sushi Bar.** For a change from standard Croatian fare, this chic eatery offers friendly professional service and beautifully presented sushi, served at tall white tables on a small terrace with views onto Dubrovnik's cathedral. They do a delightful shrimp tempura and a fine tuna tartare, as well as platters of mixed sushi, including salmon maki and amberjack nigiri. Alternatively, opt for fresh oysters (from nearby Ston) and champagne. The restaurant now accepts credit cards. 💲 *Average main: 120 Kn* ✉ *Od Pustijerne bb, Stari Grad* ☎ *020/324–034* ⊕ *www.bota-sare.hr* ⊙ *Closed Jan. and Feb.*

$$
SEAFOOD
Fodor's Choice
★
✗ **Lokanda Peškarija.** Just outside the town walls—and affording unforgettable views over the old harbor—this seafood restaurant is a particularly good value. The seafood on offer is guaranteed fresh each day, not least because the restaurant stands next door to Dubrovnik's covered fish market. It has a beautifully designed, split-level interior with exposed stone walls and wooden beams, plus romantic outdoor candlelit tables by the water. Service can be slow when it is crowded.

■ TIP→ Definitely not only for tourists, locals love eating here as well, so reservations are recommended, especially for dinner. $ *Average main: 90 Kn* ⊠ *Na Ponti, Stari Grad* ☎ *020/324–750* ⊕ *www.mea-culpa.hr* ☉ *Closed Jan.–Mar.*

$$ ✕ **Nishta.** Specializing in vegetarian and vegan fare, this friendly eatery
VEGETARIAN in the old town has just a dozen tables and is deservedly extremely
FAMILY popular. You might start with the excellent gazpacho, followed by either the Grah (a spicy bean ragout served with grilled polenta alla parmigiana) or the Indiastic (a platter of yellow dahl, palak paneer, and a vegetable curry, served with rice and naan bread). There's also a salad bar, plus a limited choice of indulgent desserts. ■ TIP→ **Reservations recommended, especially for dinner.** $ *Average main: 70 Kn* ⊠ *Prijeko bb* ☎ *020/322–088* ⊕ *www.nishtarestaurant.com* ☉ *Closed Sun.*

$$$$ ✕ **Proto.** A reliable choice for dinner, Proto is on a side street off Stra-
SEAFOOD dun, with tables arranged on a vine-covered, upper-level, open-air terrace. The menu features a good selection of traditional Dalmatian seafood dishes—including oysters from nearby Ston—and barbecued meats, notably succulent steaks. The restaurant dates back to 1886. Recent celebrity guests have included actor Richard Gere and Bono. ■ TIP→ **Reservations are recommended.** $ *Average main: 150 Kn* ⊠ *Široka 1, Stari Grad* ☎ *020/323–234* ⊕ *www.esculaprestaurants.com.*

$$$ ✕ **Taverna Otto.** Away from the crowded Old Town, you'll find Tav-
MEDITERRANEAN erna Otto in a lovely old stone building overlooking the harbor, just a 10-minute walk from Gruž port, where the cruise ships moor up. The menu is short, ensuring all the dishes are freshly prepared that day, and includes treats such as Caesar salad with chicken, rump steak in a green pepper sauce served with homemade fries, and a delicious chocolate soufflé. There's a good wine list and the staff are welcoming and professional. $ *Average main: 105 Kn* ⊠ *Nikole Tesle 8, Gruž* ☎ *020/358–633* ⊕ *www.tavernaotto.com* ☉ *Closed Sun., and Dec.–Feb.*

WHERE TO STAY

There are only two small but extremely desirable hotels within the city walls. The most exclusive establishments line the coastal road east of the center, offering stunning views of Old Town and the sea, whereas modern hotels with cheaper rooms and decent sports facilities can be found in Lapad, 3 km (2 miles) west of the center. The only way to save money in Dubrovnik is to rent a private room, and there are several excellent options in Old Town, but, like the hotels, even these can be up to double the price of those elsewhere in Croatia.

$ ⚏ **Amoret Apartments.** In the heart of the Old Town, these delightful
RENTAL two-person studio apartments occupy three carefully restored 16th-century stone buildings, one on Restićeva (a narrow street behind the cathedral), one on Dinka Ranjine (a narrow street behind the Church of St. Blaise) and the third on Ilije Šarake 4 (also behind the cathedral). **Pros:** located in Old Town; homey and atmospheric rooms with antique furniture; inexpensive by Dubrovnik standards. **Cons:** often fully booked; rooms can be noisy at night (nearby restaurants and neighbors). $ *Rooms from: €100* ⊠ *Restićeva 2, Stari Grad* ☎ *020/324–005*

🌐 *www.dubrovnik-amoret.com* 🛏 *15 apartments* 💳 *No credit cards* 🍴 *No meals.*

$$$ HOTEL 🏨 **Hotel Bellevue.** Built into a spectacular rocky cliff overlooking the sea, this design hotel lies between the Old Town and Gruž harbor. **Pros:** clifftop location overlooking the sea; chic interiors; luxurious spa; beach. **Cons:** expensive; not in Old Town; service rather impersonal and sometimes indifferent. [$] *Rooms from: €225* ✉ *Pera Čingrije 7* ☎ *020/430–830* 🌐 *www.alh.hr* 🛏 *91 rooms, 14 suites* 🍴 *Breakfast.*

$$ HOTEL 🏨 **Hotel Berkeley.** One block back from Gruž harbor, close to the cruise terminal, this welcoming three-star hotel is run by a Croatian-Australian family. **Pros:** friendly atmosphere; proximity to port; good value for money; outdoor pool, excellent cooked-to-order breakfast. **Cons:** distance from Old Town; no restaurant. [$] *Rooms from: €150* ✉ *Andrije Hebranga 116A, Gruž* ☎ *020/494–160* 🌐 *www.berkeleyhotel.hr* 🛏 *13 rooms, 7 studios, 4 apartments.*

$$$$ HOTEL Fodor's Choice ★ 🏨 **Pučić Palace.** In the heart of the Old Town, occupying a beautifully restored 18th-century baroque palace, this small luxury boutique hotel offers the sort of aristocratic delights that its location suggests: rooms with dark oak parquet floors and wood-beam ceilings, antique furnishings, and Italian mosaic-tile bathrooms supplied with Bulgari toiletries. **Pros:** located in Old Town; beautifully furnished interior; small enough that guests receive individual attention from staff. **Cons:** very expensive; lacks many facilities; in Old Town so no parking nearby. [$] *Rooms from: €465* ✉ *Ul od Puča 1, Stari Grad* ☎ *020/326–200* 🌐 *www.thepucicpalace.com* 🛏 *19 rooms* 🍴 *Breakfast.*

$$$$ HOTEL 🏨 **Villa Dubrovnik.** Reopened in summer 2010 following a complete renovation, this romantic retreat lies a 20-minute walk east of the center and comprises a white modernist structure built into the rocks, as well as a series of terraces and a garden coming down to a hideaway cove with a small beach. **Pros:** hillside location with a view of the Old Town; chic design; sophisticated restaurants and rooftop lounge. **Cons:** very expensive; 20-minute walk from Old Town. [$] *Rooms from: €480* ✉ *V Bukovca 6, Ploče* ☎ *020/500–301* 🌐 *www.villa-dubrovnik.hr* 🛏 *50 rooms, 6 suites* 🍴 *Some meals.*

NIGHTLIFE AND THE ARTS

Restrained through winter, aristocratic Dubrovnik wakes up with a vengeance come summer. Most nightlife takes place under the stars, as bars set up outdoor seating, discos take place by the sea, and even the cinema is open-air. The world-renowned Dubrovnik Summer Festival offers quality theatrical performances and classical-music concerts with international performers. An after-dinner drink at an outdoor table in Old Town makes a romantic way to round out the evening. Those in search of more lively pursuits should visit one of several chic nightclubs with music and open-air bars, which cater to the city's tanned and glamorous summer visitors.

NIGHTLIFE
BARS
Buža. With tables arranged on a series of terraces built into the rocks, Buža overlooks the sea just outside the south-facing city walls. The informal bar makes a romantic venue for an evening drink. Don't expect high style—drinks are served in plastic cups—but the mellow music, crashing waves, and nighttime candles make it a memorable experience. Open throughout summer, daily until 2 am. ⊠ *Od Margarite bb, Stari Grad* ☎ *091/589–4936.*

D'Vino Wine Bar. Tucked away in narrow side street just off Placa, this cozy little wine bar has a stonewall interior and mellow candlelight. The owners are friendly, knowledgeable and enthusiastic, and have amassed an impressive selection of regional Croatian wines, served both by the glass and by the bottle. They also offer wine-tasting flights, so you can try several different types, accompanied by platters of cheese. ⊠ *Palmatićeva 4a, Stari Grad* ☎ *020/321–130* ⊕ *www.dvino.net.*

Hard Jazz Cafe Troubadour. This is a long-standing Dubrovnik institution with occasional impromptu jazz concerts. Well-worn antiques and memorabilia fill the cozy, candlelit interior. In summer, tables spill outside onto the piazza with a small wooden stage. ⊠ *Bunićeva Poljana 2, Stari Grad* ☎ *020/323–476.*

Nonenina. Nonenina is a see-and-be-seen cocktail bar with outdoor tables and cushioned wicker chairs, opposite the Rector's Palace, perfect for people-watching. ⊠ *Pred Dvoram 4, Stari Grad* ☎ *091/333–0601* ⊕ *www.nonenina.com.*

DANCE CLUBS
Eastwest Beach Club. This is one of several chic establishments where you might spot well-known actors and sports celebrities. Eastwest combines a daytime café overlooking a well-equipped beach and a nighttime restaurant with a creative Mediterranean menu and a cocktail bar and rooftop VIP open-air lounge open until 4 am. You'll find it a five-minute walk east of the Old Town. ⊠ *Frana Supila, Banje Beach* ☎ *020/412–220* ⊕ *www.ew-dubrovnik.com.*

THE ARTS
Dubrovnik Summer Festival. Dubrovnik's cultural highlight is the annual Dubrovnik Summer Festival, which runs from mid-July to late August. The world-renowned festival includes a variety of open-air classical concerts and theatrical performances at various venues within the city walls. Summer 2012 saw the Choir of King's College Cambridge and the Venice Baroque Orchestra perform here. ☎ *020/326–100* ⊕ *www. dubrovnik-festival.hr.*

SPORTS AND THE OUTDOORS

BEACHES
The more upmarket hotels, such as the Excelsior and Villa Dubrovnik, have their own beaches that are exclusively for the use of hotel guests. The most natural and peaceful beaches lie on the tiny island of **Lokrum**, a short distance south of Old Town. Through high season boats leave

from the Old Harbor, ferrying visitors back and forth from morning to early evening. Boats run every half hour from 9 to 7:30. Round-trip tickets cost 50 Kn. It used to be possible to take a sea-kayaking trip to Lokrum, but these have now been suspended due to the number of motorboats in the sea channel. However, sea-kayaking trips are still possible elsewhere in the vicinity of Dubrovnik.

Eastwest Beach. Eastwest Beach Club is on Banje beach, just a short distance from Ploče Gate, with views across the sea to the tiny island of Lokrum. It's a fashionable spot, with a curving stretch of golden sand, complete with chaise longues and parasols for rent, and a chic bar-restaurant. **Amenities:** food and drink; showers; toilets. **Best for:** partiers; swimming. ⊠ *Frana Supila, Banje Beach* ☎ *020/412–220.*

Lokrum. Some of Dubrovnik's most natural and peaceful beaches lie on the tiny island of Lokrum, a short distance southeast of the Old Town. Lush and fertile, this tiny island is also home to the ruins of an abandoned 11th-century monastery, set in exotic gardens. From here, a network of footpaths lead down to the rocky shoreline, where it's possible to swim. There's also a small stretch of coast reserved for nudists. To reach Lokrum, take a taxi-boat from the old harbor; they run every half hour from 9 to 7:30 during the summer. Round-trip tickets cost 50 Kn. **Amenities:** food and drink. **Best for:** walking; nudists. ⊠ *A 15-min boat ride from Dubrovnik's old harbor, Island of Lokrum* ⊕ *www.lokrum.hr.*

SAILING
ACI marina. The 425-berth ACI marina is 2 nautical miles from Gruž harbor and 6 km (3½ miles) from the city walls. The marina is open year-round, and a number of charter companies are based there. ⊠ *Mokošica* ☎ *020/455–020.*

SEA KAYAKING
Fodor's Choice ★ **Adriatic Kayak Tours.** Besides introductory half-day sea-kayaking tours around Zaton bay (with transfer from Dubrovnik included), Adriatic Kayak Tours offers a one-week island-hopping itinerary by kayak around the Elafiti Islands, as well as cycling and snorkeling trips. ⊠ *Zrinsko Frankopanska 6, Ploče* ☎ *020/312–770* ⊕ *www.adriatickayaktours. com.*

SHOPPING
Despite its role as an important tourist destination, Dubrovnik offers little in the way of shopping or souvenir hunting. If you're in search of gifts, your best bet is a bottle of good Dalmatian wine or rakija.

Croata. This small boutique close to the Rector's Palace in the Old Town specializes in "original Croatian ties" in presentation boxes. ⊠ *Pred dvorom 2, Stari Grad* ☎ *020/638–330* ⊕ *www.croata.hr.*

Dubrovačka Kuća. Tastefully decorated, the wine shop stocks a fine selection of regional Croatian wines, rakija, olive oil, and truffle products, plus works of art by contemporary local artists on the upper two levels; it's close to Ploče Gate. ⊠ *Svetog Dominika bb, Stari Grad* ☎ *020/322–092.*

Ronchi. A long-standing Dubrovnik institution, this delightful hat shop dates back to 1858, when the present owner's great-great-grandfather arrived here from Milan, Italy. Expect an amusing array of stylish (if somewhat eccentric) reasonably priced handmade bonnets. ⊠ *Lučarica 2, Stari Grad* ☎ *020/323–699.*

CZECH REPUBLIC

Prague, Kutná Hora, Konopiště, Český Krumlov

WHAT'S WHERE

GERMANY

Děčín
Liberec
Teplice Ústí
Jablonec
Česká Lípa
Most
Litoměřice
Chomutov
Mladá
Boleslav
Náchod
Louny
Karlovy
Vary
E48
Hradec
Králové
Cheb
Mariánské
Lázně
Kladno
☆PRAGUE
🔲1
Kolín
Pardubic
Beroun
Kutná
Hora
🔲2
Chrudim
Plzeň E60
BOHEMIA
Příbram 🔲3
Kámek
Konopiští
Havlíčkův
Brod
Milevsko
Klatovy
Tábor
Jihlava
Strakonice
Písek
Telč
Třeboň
Znojmo
🔲4
České
Budějovice
GERMANY
Český
Krumlov

Donau (Danub

🔲1 **Prague.** Praha, "Golden Prague," the "City of One Hundred Spires," the "Beer Drinking Capital of Europe": the Czech capital goes by many names . . . and has many neighborhoods, each of which boasts a distinct personality: Old Town is Prague's historic heart. This is also "tourist central," jam-packed with people marveling at the architectural mélange while waiting for a 15th-century astronomical clock to strike the hour. There's also the original Jewish Quarter, where the past is still apparent in the tilting headstones of the Old Jewish Cemetery and in the synagogues. The "Lesser Quarter" is filled with winding (and hilly!) cobblestone streets edged with baroque buildings. The high point of this city—quite literally—is Prague Castle, looming above Prague since the 10th century. Proving that "new" is a relative term in these parts, Prague's "New Town" was laid out in the 14th century. Its focal point is Wenceslas Square: a grand commercial boulevard lined with shops, restaurants, and hotels.

POLAND

Opava

Svitavy

MORAVIA

Ostrava

Karviná

Český Tesín

Nový Jicín

Frydek-Místek

Olomouc

Prostejov

Přerov

Vsetín

Brno

Otrokovice

Zlín

Uherské Hradiste

Mikulov

Břeclav

SLOVAKIA

2 Kutná Hora. Kutná Hora makes for a popular excursion from the capital, both to see the faded remains of a once-glorious 16th-century mining town and the spooky "bone church," a nearby monastery whose interior is constructed exclusively from human skeletons. A sight you're not soon to forget.

3 Konopištì. For castle and history buffs, a trip to Konopištì offers a real treat. Parts of this impressive turreted castle date back to the 13th century. It was also the main residence—and hunting lodge—of Archduke Franz Ferdinand d'Este, the Austrian Habsburg nobleman whose tragic assassination in Sarajevo in 1914 was the spark that started World War I.

4 Český Krumlov. If you can see only one castle in the Czech Republic, make it Hrad Krumlov. Perched above popular Český Krumlov (a UNESCO World Heritage Site), it comes complete with a tower, moat, and dungeon, and in the Czech Republic it is second only to Pražský Hrad in Prague in terms of size.

NEED TO KNOW

AT A GLANCE
Capital: Prague
Population: 10,500,000
Currency: Koruna (Kč)
Money: ATMs are common
Language: Czech
Country Code: ☎ 420
Emergencies: ☎ 112
Driving: On the right
Electricity: 200v/50 cycles; electrical plugs have two round prongs

Prague
CZECH REPUBLIC

Time: Six hours ahead of New York

Documents: Up to 90 days with valid passport; Schengen rules apply

Mobile Phones: GSM (900 and 1800 bands)

Major Mobile Companies: Vodafone, O2, T-Mobile

WEBSITES
Official Prague Tourist Information: ⊕ www.praguewelcome.cz

Czech Republic Tourism: ⊕ www.praguetourism.cz

My Czech Republic: ⊕ www.myczechrepublic.com

GETTING AROUND

✈ **Air Travel:** Prague is the main airport, but some budget carriers fly to Brno.

🚌 **Bus Travel:** Good for travel within regions or for some destinations, such as Karlovy Vary, that do not have direct train connections to Prague.

🚗 **Car Travel:** Rent a car to explore at your own pace, but never in Prague because of all the tiny, one-way streets.

🚂 **Train Travel:** Best for longer connections between major cities, though prices tend to be a bit higher than for buses.

PLAN YOUR BUDGET

	HOTEL ROOM	MEAL	ATTRACTIONS
Low Budget	2,000 Kč	200 Kč	National Gallery Museum, 150 Kč
Mid Budget	3,000 Kč	500 Kč	Prague Castle admission, 250 Kč
High Budget	5,000 Kč	1,000 Kč	Concert ticket, 800 Kč

WAYS TO SAVE

Eat lunch picnic-style. Take advantage of the multitude of bakeries, sandwich shops, and grocers to pack a picnic lunch.

Book a rental apartment. If you want more spacious accommodations and a kitchen, consider a furnished rental—a good bet for families.

Have your main meal at lunch. Many restaurants offer daily lunch specials for half the dinner price.

Skip the admission for Prague Castle or the Jewish Museum. Both are relatively expensive and not necessarily worth it; soak up the atmosphere for free.

PLAN YOUR TIME

Hassle Factor	Low. Flights to Prague from the U.S. and Europe are frequent, and the Czech Republic has great transport elsewhere.
3 days	You can see most of the major sites of Prague and perhaps take a half-day trip to Kutná Hora or Konopišti.
1 week	You have plenty of time to see Prague at leisure, plus work in a day-trip to Kutná Hora and a longer trip to stunning Český Krumlov.
2 weeks	You have the luxury of taking in the country's best. Spend five days in Prague and then explore parts of Bohemia and Moravia. Don't miss Moravia's wine region and the city of Olomouc.

WHEN TO GO

High Season: The Christmas, New Year, and Easter holidays are traditionally the busiest and most expensive times to visit. July and August are also very busy and expensive, though you can normally expect warm temps and sunny skies.

Low Season: Unless you are skiing, December through March offer the least appealing weather, though it's the best time for airfares and hotel deals—and to escape the crowds. Prague can get lots of snow but the Charles Bridge looks great in white.

Value Season: Spring (outside of Easter) and fall are still technically considered "high" season by the tourist office, but the crowds tend to be thinner, and the weather is a little cooler than summer (but still reliably sunny most years). By mid-October there's an undeniable chill in the air, and winter gets going in earnest by November.

BIG EVENTS

May: The annual Prague Spring classical music festival kicks off summer in style. ⊕ www.festival.cz

March: Film lovers will want to catch Febiofest, the largest film festival in Central Europe ⊕ www.febiofest.cz

July: The action shifts to Èeský Krumlov for the acclaimed International Music Festival of opera, classical, and contemporary music. ⊕ www.festivalkrumlov.cz

December: You'll find traditional Christmas markets in many cities; the best is Prague's Old Town Square.

READ THIS

■ **The Unbearable Lightness of Being,** Milan Kundera. Witty tale of love and drama in 1968 Prague.

■ **Prague in Danger,** Peter Demetz. Prague under the Nazis.

■ **The Good Soldier Švejk,** Jaroslav Hašek. Classic comedy about a WW I–era slacker named Švejk.

WATCH THIS

■ **Amadeus.** The Mozart drama was filmed in Prague.

■ **Closely Watched Trains.** "Czech New Wave" comedy from the 1960s.

■ **Czech Dream.** "Mockumentary" about the arrival of capitalism.

EAT THIS

■ **Knedliky:** bread or potato dumplings

■ **Duck:** served with dumplings and sweetish sauerkraut

■ **Palačinky:** dessert pancakes topped with chocolate sauce or stuffed with fruit

■ **Pork:** Czech staple usually served roasted or in a bowl of goulash (Guláš)

■ **Svíčková na smetanì:** braised sirloin in gravy with whipped cream and cranberry sauce

■ **Kulajda:** a soup featuring sour cream, dill, and egg

6

The experience of visiting the Czech Republic still involves stepping back in time. Even in Prague, now deluged by tourists two-thirds of the year, the sense of history—stretching back through centuries of wars, empires, and monuments to everyday life—remains uncluttered by the trappings of modernity. The peculiar melancholy of Central Europe still lurks in narrow streets and forgotten corners. Crumbling facades, dilapidated palaces, and treacherous cobbled streets both shock and enchant the visitor used to a world where what remains of history has been spruced up for tourists' eyes.

Outside the capital, for those willing to forego Prague's modern amenities and conveniences, the sense of rediscovering a neglected world is even stronger. And the range is startling: from imperial spas, with their graceful colonnades and dilapidated villas, to the many arcaded town squares, modestly displaying the passing of time with each splendid layer of once-contemporary style. Gothic towers, Renaissance facades, baroque interiors, and aging modern supermarkets merge. Between the man-made sights, you are rewarded with glorious mountain ranges and fertile rolling countryside laced with carp ponds and forests.

PLANNING

WHEN TO GO

Prague is beautiful year-round, but in summer and during the Christmas and Easter holidays the city is overrun with tourists. Spring and fall generally combine good weather with a more bearable level of tourism. In winter you'll encounter fewer tourists and have the opportunity to see Prague breathtakingly covered in snow, but it can get very cold. In much of the rest of Bohemia and Moravia, even in midsummer, the number of visitors is far smaller than in Prague. The Giant Mountains of Bohemia come into their own in winter. January and February generally bring the best skiing—and great difficulty in finding a room. If you're not a skier, try visiting the mountains in late spring (May or June) or fall, when the colors are dazzling and you'll have the hotels and restaurants nearly to yourself. The off-season keeps shrinking as people discover the pleasures of touring the country in every season. Castles and museums now frequently stay open 9, 10, or even 12 months of the year. In midwinter, however, you may well come across attractions that are closed for the season.

GETTING HERE AND AROUND

AIR TRAVEL

Almost all international flights go into Prague (PRG), with a few budget flights now landing in Brno (BRQ). Czech Airlines, the main carrier in the country, also flies to Ostrava and Brno.

ČSA (Czech Airlines), the Czech national carrier, offers nonstop flights from the United States (from New York–JFK) to Prague (daily flights during the busiest season); Delta offers nonstop flights from Atlanta (ATL). It's also possible to connect through a major European airport and continue to Prague. The flight from New York to Prague takes about 8 hours; from the West Coast, including a stopover, 12 to 16 hours. Wizz Air, easyJet, and others offer discount flights to Prague via London. Connections through Berlin, Frankfurt, and Vienna are also convenient.

BUS TRAVEL

Several bus companies run direct services between major Western European cities and Prague. The Czech Republic's extremely comprehensive state-run bus service, ČSAD, is usually much quicker than the normal trains and more frequent than express trains, unless you're going to the major cities. Prices are quite low—essentially the same as those for second-class rail tickets. Buy your tickets from the ticket window at the bus station or directly from the driver on the bus. Buses can be full to bursting. On long-distance trips it's a good idea to buy advance tickets when available (indicated by an "R" in a circle on timetables); get them at the local station or at some travel agencies. The only drawback to traveling by bus is figuring out the timetables. They are easy to read, but beware of the small letters denoting exceptions to the times given. If in doubt, inquire at the information window or ask someone for assistance.

Contacts ČSAD ✉ *Florenc station, Křižíkova 4, Karlín* ☎ *900–144–444* ⊕ *www. idos.cz* Ⓜ *Line B or C: Florenc.* **Eurolines** ☎ *224–218–680* ⊕ *www.eurolines.com.*

CAR TRAVEL

There are no special requirements for renting a car in the Czech Republic, but be sure to shop around, as prices can differ greatly. A surcharge of 5% to 12% applies to rental cars picked up at Prague's Ruzynì Airport.

The Prague city center is mostly a snarl of traffic, one-way streets, and tram lines. If you plan to drive outside the capital, there are few four-lane highways, but most of the roads are in reasonably good shape, and traffic is usually light. Roads can be poorly marked, however, so before you start out, buy a multilingual driving atlas at any bookstore, or bring along your car's portable GPS device, such as a Garmin. Czech roads are well covered by satellite navigation, but be sure to download the right map set (Europe or Central Europe) for your device.

TRAIN TRAVEL

You can take a direct train from Paris via Frankfurt to Prague (daily) or from Berlin via Dresden to Prague (five times a day). Vienna is a good starting point for Prague, Brno, or Bratislava. There are at least three trains a day from Vienna's Südbahnhof (South Station) to Prague (five hours). Southern Moravia and southern Bohemia are served by trains from Vienna and Linz.

The state-run rail system is called České dráhy (ČD). On longer runs, it's not really worth taking anything less than an express (*rychlík*) train, marked in red on the timetable. Tickets are still very inexpensive. First-class is considerably more spacious and comfortable and well worth the cost (50% more than a standard ticket). A 40 Kč–60 Kč supplement is charged for the excellent international expresses, EuroCity (EC) and InterCity (IC), and for domestic SuperCity (SC) schedules. A 20 Kč supplement applies to reserved seats on domestic journeys. If you haven't bought a ticket in advance at the station (mandatory for seat reservations), you can buy one aboard the train from the conductor. On timetables, departures (*odjezd*) appear on a yellow background; arrivals (*příjezd*) are on white. It is possible to book sleepers (*lůžkový*) or the less roomy couchettes (*lehátkový*) on most overnight trains.

Contacts Czech Railways ⊕ *www.cd.cz.*

HOTELS

The number of hotels and pensions has increased dramatically throughout the Czech Republic, in step with the influx of tourists. Finding a room should not be a problem, although it is highly recommended that you book ahead during the peak tourist season (nationwide, July and August; in Prague, April through October and the Christmas, New Year, and Easter holidays). Hotel prices, in general, remain high.

Most of the old-fashioned hotels away from the major tourist centers, invariably situated on a town's main square, have been modernized and now provide private bathrooms in most or all rooms and a higher comfort level throughout. Newer hotels, often impersonal concrete boxes, tend to be found on the outskirts of towns; charming, older buildings in the center of town—newly transformed into hotels and pensions—are often the best choice. Bare-bones hostels are a popular means of circumventing Prague's summer lodging crunch; many now stay open all year.

At certain times, such as Easter and during festivals, prices can jump 15% to 25%. As a rule, always ask the price before taking a room. Unless otherwise noted, breakfast is included in the rate.

RESTAURANTS

The quality of restaurant cuisine and service in the Czech Republic has improved dramatically in recent years. In Prague you can expect sophisticated cuisine on the level of that of any other European capital. Outside of Prague dining can be uneven, but delicious meals can be found. You'll still find that the traditional dishes—roast pork or duck with dumplings, or broiled meat with sauce—can be quite tasty when well prepared. Grilled trout appears on many menus and is often the best item available. You should discreetly check the bill, since a few unscrupulous proprietors still overcharge foreigners.

TOP REASONS TO GO

Karlův Most. Paris has the Eiffel Tower and Prague has this beautiful Gothic bridge. Dotted with statues, both romantic and frightful, the bridge is packed with crowds taking in the riverside views.

Stunning City Skyline. Walking next to the Vltava River, stop to admire the Prague skyline, one of the most striking collections of architecture in Europe.

Castles and Châteaux. More than 2,000 castles, manor houses, and châteaux form a precious and not-to-be-missed part of the country's cultural and historical heritage. Grim ruins glower from craggy hilltops, and fantastical Gothic castles guard ancient trade routes.

Beer. Czechs drink more beer per capita than any other nation on earth; small wonder, as many connoisseurs rank Bohemian lagers among the best in the world. This cool, crisp brew was invented in Plzeò in 1842, although older varieties of Czech beer had been brewed for centuries.

Hiking. The Czech Republic has 40,000 km (25,000 miles) of well-kept, -marked, and -signposted trails both in the mountainous regions and leading from town to town through beautiful countryside. The most scenic areas are the Beskydy range in northern Moravia and the Krkonoše ("Giant Mountains") range in northern Bohemia.

Shopping. In Prague and elsewhere in Bohemia, look for elegant and unusual crystal and porcelain. Bohemia is also renowned for the quality and deep-red color of its garnets; keep an eye out for beautiful rings and brooches.

6

Lunch, usually eaten between noon and 2, is the main meal for Czechs and the best deal. Many restaurants put out a special lunch menu (*denní lístek*), with more appetizing selections at better prices. Dinner is usually served from 5 until 9 or 10, but don't wait too long to eat. Restaurant cooks frequently leave early on slow nights, and the later you arrive, the more likely it is that the kitchen will be closed. In general, dinner menus do not differ substantially from lunch offerings, with the exception of prices, which are higher.

HOTEL AND RESTAURANT PRICES

Prices in the restaurant reviews are the average cost of a main course at dinner or, if dinner is not served, at lunch; taxes and service charges are generally included. Prices in the hotel reviews are the lowest cost of a standard double room in high season, excluding taxes, service charges, and meal plans.

PLANNING YOUR TIME

Many visitors to the Czech Republic concentrate on Prague alone, but that's a pity. It's easy to travel around various parts of the Bohemian countryside, and you'll get a more realistic view of daily life outside the touristy capital. Both the bus system and the train system make traveling from town to town a single-day effort. Some excursions, like Kutná Hora, can even be done as day-trips from Prague.

PRAGUE

A stunning backdrop of towering churches and centuries-old bridges and alleyways makes this European capital flat-out beautiful. Prague achieved much of its present glory in the 14th century, during the long reign of Charles IV, king of Bohemia and Holy Roman Emperor. It was Charles who established a university in the city and laid out the New Town, charting Prague's growth.

Amid Prague's cobblestone streets and gold-tipped spires, new galleries, cafés, and clubs teem with young Czechs and members of the city's colony of "expatriates." New shops and—perhaps most noticeably—scads of new restaurants have opened, expanding the city's culinary reach far beyond the traditional roast pork and dumplings. Many have something to learn in the way of presentation and service, but Praguers still marvel at a variety that was unthinkable not so many years ago.

PLANNING YOUR TIME

Most of Prague's top sights are crowded near one another and could be connected together in a long one-day stroll. However, just because they're near each other doesn't mean you can comfortably do all these sights in a day. Prague Castle could take a full day, depending on how much you explore the courtyards and other spaces. If you have a limited amount of time focus on the Old Town and the Castle Area (crossing the Charles Bridge between them), and with more time take in the Lesser Quarter and the New Town. Remember to build in some time for getting lost on the winding side streets.

GETTING HERE AND AROUND

AIR TRAVEL

Prague's Václav Havel Airport is 20 km (12 miles) northwest of the downtown area. It's small but easily negotiated. An expanded main terminal has eased traffic flow.

Contacts **Václav Havel Airport** ☎ 220–111–888 ⊕ www.prg.aero.

PUBLIC TRANSPORTATION

Prague's subway system, the Metro, is clean and reliable; the stations are marked with an inconspicuous "M" sign. Validate your ticket at an orange machine before descending the escalator. Prague's extensive bus and streetcar network allows for fast, efficient travel throughout the city. Tickets (*jízdenky*) are the same as those used for the metro, although you validate them at machines inside the bus or tram. They can be bought at some hotels, newsstands, and from dispensing machines in the metro stations.

Contacts **Dopravní Podnik** ⊕ www.dpp.cz.

CAR TRAVEL

If your visit is restricted to the Czech capital, you'll do better not to rent a car. The capital is congested, and you'll save yourself a lot of hassle if you rely on public transportation. If you are planning to take excursions into the country, then a car can be useful, but don't pick it up until you are ready to depart. If you are arriving by car, you'll find that Prague is well served by major roads and highways from anywhere in the country. On arriving in the city, simply follow the signs to "Centrum" ("city center").

TAXI TRAVEL

Though far less common than before, dishonest taxi drivers remain a problem. Luckily, you probably won't need to rely on taxis for trips within the city center (it's usually easier to walk or take the subway). To minimize the chances of getting ripped off, avoid taxi stands in Wenceslas Square, Old Town Square, and other heavily touristed areas. The best alternative is to phone for a taxi in advance. Many radio-taxi firms have English-speaking operators.

TRAIN TRAVEL

International trains arrive at and depart from either of two stations: the main station, Hlavní nádraží, is about 500 yards east of Wenceslas Square on Opletalova or Washingtonova Street. Then there's the suburban Nádraží Holešovice, about 2 km (1 mile) north of the city center. Always make certain you know which station your train is using.

VISITOR INFORMATION

Contacts Czech Tourist Authority ⊕ www.czechtourism.com. Prague Information Service (PIS). ⊠ Staroměstská radnice (Old Town Hall), Staré Město ⊕ www.pis.cz ⊠ Hlavní nádraží, lower hall, Staré Město ⊠ Malostranská mostecká věž, Malá Strana.

6

STARÉ MĚSTO (OLD TOWN)

Prague's Old Town was spared from bombing during World War II, leaving it with one of the best-preserved centers of any major city in Europe. On any sunny summer weekend Old Town Square is rush hour, packed with revelers. The 15th-century astronomical clock, which is on the side of the town hall, has a procession of 12 apostles that make their rounds when certain hours strike. From another side, the Church of Our Lady before Týn's Gothic spires and the solid gold effigy of the Virgin Mary keep watch over onlookers. You will find the streets most subdued on early weekday mornings.

EXPLORING

Jan Hus monument. Few memorials in Prague elicited as much controversy as this one, dedicated in July 1915, exactly 500 years after Hus was burned at the stake in Constance, Germany. Some maintain that the monument's Secessionist style (the inscription seems to come right from turn-of-the-20th-century Vienna) clashes with the Gothic and baroque style of the square. Others dispute the romantic depiction of Hus, who appears here as tall and bearded in flowing garb, whereas the real Hus, as historians maintain, was short and had a baby face. Either way, the fiery preacher's influence is not in dispute. His ability to transform doctrinal disagreements, both literally and metaphorically, into the language of the common man made him into a religious and national symbol for the Czechs. ⊠ Staroměstské nám., Staré Město Ⓜ Line A: Staroměstská.

Kostel Matky Boží před Týnem (*Church of Our Lady Before Týn*). The twin-spired Týn Church is an Old Town Square landmark and one

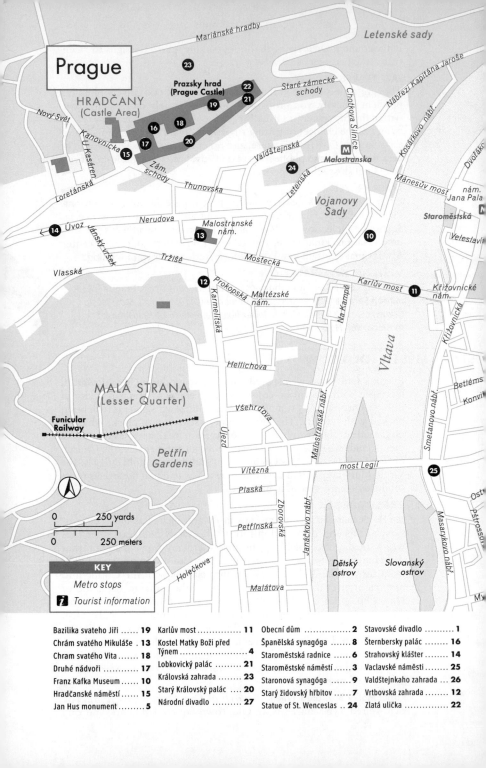

Prague

HRADČANY
(Castle Area)

Mariánské hradby

Letenské sady

Nový Svět

Kanovnická

U Kasáren

Loretánská

**Prazsky hrad
(Prague Castle)**

Staré zámecké
schody

Chotkova Silnice

Nábřezí Kapitána Jaroše

Kosárkovo nábř.

Dvořáko...

Zám.
schody

Thunovska

Valdštejnská

Ⓜ Malostranska

Mánesův most

nám.
Jana Pala

Ⓜ

Úvoz

Jánský vršek

Nerudova

Malostranské
nám.

Letenská

Vojanovy
Sady

Staroměstská

Ⓜ

Veleslaví

Vlasská

Tržiště

Prokopská

Mostecká

Karmelitská

Maltézské
nám.

Na Kampě

Karlův most

Křižovnické
nám.

Křižovnická

Vltava

Betléms...

MALÁ STRANA
(Lesser Quarter)

Hellichova

Všehrdova

Újezd

Malostranské nábř.

Smetanovo nábř.

Konvi...

**Funicular
Railway**

Petřín
Gardens

Vítězná

Plaská

most Legií

Ⓜ

Ost...

Pštross...

0 — 250 yards
0 — 250 meters

Petřínská

Zborovská

Janáčkovo nábř.

Masarykovo nábř.

Dětský
ostrov

Slovanský
ostrov

My...

KEY

Metro stops

🛈 *Tourist information*

Holečkova

Malátova

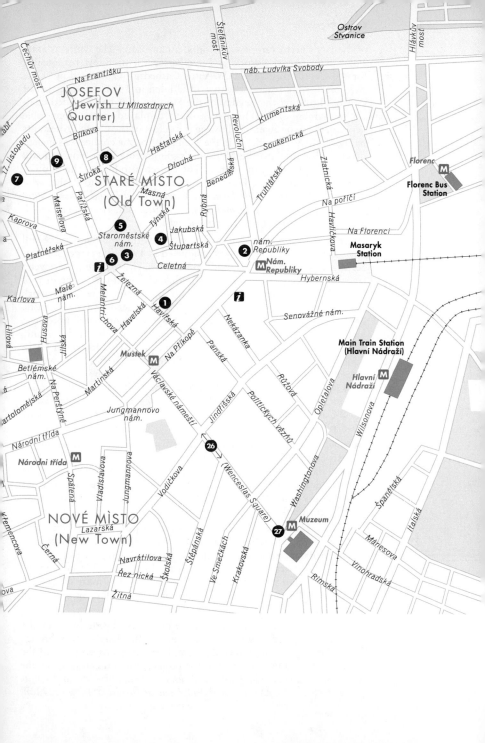

of the city's best examples of Gothic architecture. The church's exterior was in part the work of Peter Parler, the architect responsible for the Charles Bridge and St. Vitus Cathedral. Construction of the twin black-spire towers began a little later, in 1461, by King Jiří of Poděbrad, during the heyday of the Hussites. Jiří had a gilded chalice, the symbol of the Hussites, proudly displayed on the front gable between the two towers. Following the defeat of the Czech Protestants by the Catholic Hapsburgs in the 17th century, the chalice was melted down and made into the Madonna's glimmering halo (you can still see it resting between the spires). The church also houses the tomb of renowned Danish (and Prague court) astronomer Tycho Brahe, who died in 1601. ⊠ *Staroměstské nám., between Celetná and Týnská, Staré Město* ☎ *222–318–186* ⊕ *www.tyn.cz* ⊙ *Tues.–Sat. 10–noon and 1–3, Sun. 10:30–noon* Ⓜ *Line A: Staroměstská.*

Obecní dům (*Municipal House*). The city's art-nouveau showpiece still fills the role it had when it was completed in 1911 as a center for concerts, rotating art exhibits, and café society. The mature art-nouveau style echoes the lengths the Czech middle class went to at the turn of the 20th century to imitate Paris. Much of the interior bears the work of Alfons Mucha, Max Švabinský, and other leading Czech artists. Mucha decorated the Hall of the Lord Mayor upstairs with impressive, magical frescoes depicting Czech history; unfortunately it's visible only as part of a guided tour. The beautiful Smetanova síň (Smetana Hall), which hosts concerts by the Prague Symphony Orchestra as well as international players, is on the second floor. Tours are normally held at two-hour intervals in the afternoons; check the website for details. ⊠ *Nám. Republiky 5, Staré Město* ☎ *222–002–100* ⊕ *www.obecnidum. cz* ⊠ *Guided tours 290 Kč* ⊙ *Information center and box office daily 10–8* Ⓜ *Line B: Náměstí Republiky.*

Fodor's Choice **Staroměstská radnice** (*Old Town Hall*). This is a center of Prague life for
★ tourists and locals alike. Hundreds of visitors gravitate here throughout the day to see the hour struck by the mechanical figures of the **astronomical clock**. This theatrical spectacle doesn't reveal the way this 15th-century marvel indicates the time—by the season, the zodiac sign, and the positions of the sun and moon.

Old Town Hall served as the center of administration for Old Town beginning in 1338, when King John of Luxembourg first granted the city council the right to a permanent location. The impressive 200-foot **Town Hall Tower**, where the clock is mounted, was first built in the 14th century. For a rare view of the Old Town and its maze of crooked streets and alleyways, climb the ramp or ride the elevator to the top of the tower.

Tours of the interiors depart from the main desk inside (most guides speak English, and English texts are on hand). There's also a branch of the tourist information office, here. Previously unseen parts of the tower have now been opened to the public, and you can now see the inside of the famous clock. ⊠ *Staroměstské nám., Staré Město* ⊕ *www. praguewelcome.cz* ⊠ *Interiors 100 Kč, tower 100 Kč* ⊙ *Interiors Mon.*

11–6, Tues.–Sun. 9–6; tower Mon. 11–10, Tues.–Sun. 9 am–10 pm
Ⓜ *Line A: Staroměstská.*

Fodor's Choice **Staroměstské náměstí** (*Old Town Square*). The hype about Old Town
★ Square is completely justified. Picture a perimeter of colorful baroque
houses contrasting with the sweeping old-Gothic style of the Týn church
in the background. The unexpectedly large size gives it a majestic presence as it opens up from feeder alleyways. As the heart of Old Town,
the square grew to its present proportions when Prague's original marketplace moved away from the river in the 12th century. Its shape
and appearance have changed little since that time (the monument to
religious reformer Jan Hus, at the center of the square, was erected in
the early-20th century). During the day the square pulses with activity,
as musicians vie for the attention of visitors milling about. In summer
the square's south end is dominated by sprawling outdoor restaurants.
During the Easter and Christmas seasons it fills with wooden booths of
vendors selling everything from simple wooden toys to fine glassware
and mulled wine. At night the brightly lighted towers of the Týn church
rise gloriously over the glowing baroque facades. ⊠ *Staroměstské nám.,
Staré Město* Ⓜ *Line A: Staroměstská.*

U Minuty. One of the most interesting houses on Old Town Square
juts out into the small extension leading into Malé náměstí. Trimmed
with elegant cream-color 16th-century Renaissance *sgraffiti* of biblical
and classical motifs, the house, called U Minuty, was the young Franz
Kafka's home in the 1890s. ⊠ *2 Staroměstské nám., Staré Město* Ⓜ *Line
A: Staroměstská.*

Stavovské divadlo (*Estates Theater*). It's impossible to visit Prague
without knowing that Mozart conducted the world premiere of *Don
Giovanni* on this stage way back in 1787. Fittingly, the interior was used
for scenes in Miloš Forman's movie *Amadeus.* It's stylish and refined
without being distracting. This is a branch of the National Theater,
and high-quality productions of Mozart are usually in the repertoire
together with other classic operas, plays and the occasional smaller
ballet. ⊠ *Ovocný trh 6, Nové Město* ☎ *224–901–448* ⊕ *www.narodni-
divadlo.cz* Ⓜ *Line A or B: Můstek.*

JOSEFOV (JEWISH QUARTER)

Prague's Jews survived centuries of discrimination, but two unrelated
events of modern times have left their historic ghetto little more than a
collection of museums. Around 1900, city officials decided for hygienic
purposes to raze the minuscule neighborhood—at this time the majority
of its residents were actually poor Gentiles—and pave over its crooked
streets. Only some of the synagogues, the town hall, and the cemetery
survived this early attempt at urban renewal. The second event was the
Holocaust. Under Nazi occupation, a staggering percentage of the city's
Jews were deported or murdered in concentration camps. Of the 35,000
Jews living in Prague before World War II, only about 1,200 returned
to resettle the city after the war.

6

EXPLORING

Španělská synagóga (*Spanish Synagogue*). This domed, Moorish-style synagogue was built in 1868 on the site of an older synagogue, the Altschul. Here the historical exposition that begins in the Maisel Synagogue continues to the post–World War II period. The displays are not very compelling, but the building's painstakingly restored interior definitely is. ⊠ *Vězeňská 1, Josefov* ☏ *222–317–191* ⊕ *www. jewishmuseum.cz* ✉ *Combined ticket to museums 300 Kč (480 Kč with Old-New Synagogue)* ⊘ *Apr.–Oct., Sun.–Fri. 9–6; Nov.–Mar., Sun.–Fri. 9–4:30, closed during Jewish holidays.*

Staronová synagóga (*Old-New Synagogue, or Altneuschul*). Dating from the mid-13th century, this is the oldest functioning synagogue in Europe and one of the most important works of early Gothic in Prague. The name refers to the legend that the synagogue was built on the site of an ancient Jewish temple, and the temple's stones were used to build the present structure. Amazingly, the synagogue has survived fires, the razing of the ghetto, and the Nazi occupation intact; it's still in use. The entrance, with its vault supported by two pillars, is the oldest part of the synagogue. Note that men are required to cover their heads inside, and during services men and women sit apart. ⊠ *Červená 2, Josefov* ☏ *222–317–191* ⊕ *www.jewishmuseum.cz* ✉ *200 Kč, combined ticket to Old-New Synagogue and museums 480 Kč* ⊘ *Apr.–Oct., Sun.–Fri. 9–6; Nov.–Mar., Sun.–Fri. 9–4:30, closed during Jewish holidays.* Ⓜ *Line A: Staroměstská.*

Fodor's Choice ★   **Starý židovský hřbitov** (*Old Jewish Cemetery*). An unforgettable sight, this cemetery is where all Jews living in Prague from the 15th century to 1787 were laid to rest. The lack of any space in the tiny ghetto forced graves to be piled on top of one another. Tilted at crazy angles, the 12,000 visible tombstones are but a fraction of countless thousands more buried below. Walk the path amid the gravestones; the relief symbols you see represent the names and professions of the deceased. ⊠ *Široká 3, enter through Pinkasova synagóga, Josefov* ☏ *222–317–191* ⊕ *www.jewishmuseum.cz* ✉ *Combined ticket to museums 300 Kč (480 Kč with Old-New Synagogue)* ⊘ *Apr.–Oct., Sun.–Fri. 9–6; Nov.–Mar., Sun.–Fri. 9–4:30, closed during Jewish holidays.* Ⓜ *Line A: Staroměstská.*

KARLŮV MOST (CHARLES BRIDGE) AND MALÁ STRANA (LESSER QUARTER)

One of Prague's most exquisite neighborhoods, the Lesser Quarter (or Little Town) was established in 1257 and for years was where the merchants and craftsmen who served the royal court lived. The Lesser Quarter is not for the methodical traveler. Its charm lies in the tiny lanes, the sudden blasts of bombastic architecture, and the soul-stirring views that emerge for a second before disappearing behind the sloping roofs.

EXPLORING

Chrám svatého Mikuláše (*Church of St. Nicholas*). With its dynamic curves, this church is arguably the purest and most ambitious example of high baroque in Prague. The celebrated architect Christoph

Dientzenhofer began the Jesuit church in 1704 on the site of one of the more active Hussite churches of 15th-century Prague. Work on the building was taken over by his son Kilian Ignaz Dientzenhofer, who built the dome and presbytery. Anselmo Lurago completed the whole thing in 1755 by adding the bell tower. The juxtaposition of the broad, full-bodied dome with the slender bell tower is one of the many striking architectural contrasts that mark the Prague skyline. ⊠ *Malostranské nám., Malá Strana* ☎ *257–534–215* ⊕ *www.stnicholas.cz* ☎ *Tower 75 Kč, concerts 490 Kč* ☉ *Daily 9–4:30 for sightseeing, tower daily 9–8* Ⓜ *Line A: Malostranská, then Tram No. 12, 20, or 22.*

Franz Kafka Museum. The great early-20th-century Jewish author Kafka wasn't Czech and he wrote in German, but he lived in Prague nearly his entire short, anguished life, so it's fitting that he's finally gotten the shrine he deserves here. Because the museum's designers believed in channeling Kafka's darkly paranoid and paradoxical work, they created exhibits true to this spirit. And even if the results are often goofy, they get an "A" for effort. Facsimiles of manuscripts, documents, first editions, photographs, and newspaper obits are displayed in glass vitrines, which in turn are situated in "Kafkaesque" settings: huge open filing cabinets, stone gardens, piles of coal. The basement level of the museum gets even freakier, with expressionistic representations of Kafka's work itself, including a model of the horrible torture machine from the "Penal Colony" story. Not a place for young children, or even lovers on a first date, but fascinating to anyone familiar with Kafka's work. ⊠ *Hergetova Cihelna, Cihelna 2b, Malá Strana* ☎ *257–535–507* ⊕ *www. kafkamuseum.cz* ☎ *180 Kč* ☉ *Daily 10–6* Ⓜ *Line A: Malostranská.*

Fodor's Choice
★

Karlův most (*Charles Bridge*). This is Prague's signature monument, and worth the denomination. The view from the foot of the bridge on the Old Town side, encompassing the towers and domes of the Lesser Quarter and the soaring spires of St. Vitus's Cathedral, is nothing short of breathtaking. This heavenly vista subtly changes in perspective as you walk across the bridge, attended by a host of baroque saints that decorate the bridge's peaceful Gothic stones. At night its drama is spellbinding: St. Vitus's Cathedral lit in a ghostly green, the Castle in monumental yellow, and the Church of St. Nicholas in a voluptuous pink, all viewed through the menacing silhouettes of the bowed statues and the Gothic towers. Night is the best time to visit the bridge, which is choked with visitors, vendors, and beggars by day. The later the hour, the thinner the crowds—though the bridge is never truly empty, even at daybreak. Tourists with flash cameras are there all hours of the night, and as dawn is breaking, revelers from the dance clubs at the east end of the bridge weave their way homeward, singing loudly and debating where to go for breakfast.

Staroměstská mostecká věž (Old Town Bridge Tower), at the bridge entrance on the Old Town side, is where Peter Parler, the architect of the Charles Bridge, began his bridge building. The carved facades he designed for the sides of the tower were destroyed by Swedish soldiers in 1648, at the end of the Thirty Years' War. The sculptures facing the Old Town, however, are still intact (although some are recent copies). They depict an old and gout-ridden Charles IV with his son, who became

Wenceslas IV. Above them are two of Bohemia's patron saints, Adalbert of Prague and Sigismund. The top of the tower offers a spectacular view of the city for 70 Kč; it's open daily from 10 to 10, year-round. ⊠ *Staré Město* Ⓜ *Line A: Staroměstská.*

Valdštejnska Zahrada (*Wallenstein Palace Gardens*). With its idiosyncratic high-walled gardens and superb, vaulted Renaissance *sala terrena* (room opening onto a garden), this palace displays superbly elegant grounds. Walking around the formal paths, you come across numerous fountains and statues depicting figures from classical mythology or warriors dispatching a variety of beasts. However, nothing beats the trippy "Grotto," a huge dripstone wall packed with imaginative rock formations, like little faces and animals hidden in the charcoal-colored landscape, and what's billed as "illusory hints of secret corridors." Here, truly, staring at the wall is a form of entertainment. Most of the palace itself now serves the Czech Senate as meeting chamber and offices. The palace's cavernous former *Jízdárna*, or riding school, now hosts occasional art exhibitions. ⊠ *Letenská 10, Malá Strana* ⊕ *www.senat. cz* ⊠ *Free* ☾ *Apr.–May and Oct., weekdays 7:30–6, weekends 10–6; June–Sept., weekdays 7:30–7, weekends 10–7.* Ⓜ *Line A: Malostranská.*

Vrtbovská zahrada (*Vrtba Garden*). An unobtrusive door on noisy Karmelitská hides the entranceway to a fascinating sanctuary with one of the best views of the Lesser Quarter. The street door opens onto the intimate courtyard of the Vrtbovský palác (Vrtba Palace). Two Renaissance wings flank the courtyard; the left one was built in 1575, the right one in 1591. Built in five levels rising behind the courtyard in a wave of statuary-bedecked staircases and formal terraces reaching toward a seashell-decorated pavilion at the top, it's a popular spot for weddings, receptions, and occasional concerts. (The fenced-off garden immediately behind and above belongs to the U.S. Embassy—hence the U.S. flag that often flies there.) ⊠ *Karmelitská 25, Malá Strana* ☏ *272–088–350* ⊕ *www.vrtbovska.cz* ⊠ *60 Kč* ☾ *Apr.–Oct., daily 10–6* Ⓜ *Line A: Malostranská, then Tram No. 12, 20 or 22.*

HRADČANY (CASTLE AREA)

To the west of Prague Castle is the residential Hradčany (Castle Area), the town that during the early 14th century emerged out of a collection of monasteries and churches. The concentration of history packed into Prague Castle and Hradčany challenges those not versed in the ups and downs of Bohemian kings, religious uprisings, wars, and oppression. The picturesque area surrounding Prague Castle, with its breathtaking vistas of the Old Town and the Lesser Quarter, is ideal for just wandering. But the castle itself, with its convoluted history and architecture, is difficult to appreciate fully without investing a little more time.

EXPLORING

Hradčanské náměstí (*Hradčany Square*). With its fabulous mixture of baroque and Renaissance houses, topped by the Castle itself, this square had a prominent role in the film *Amadeus* (as a substitute for Vienna). Czech director Miloš Forman used the house at No. 7 for Mozart's residence, where the composer was haunted by the masked figure he thought was his father. The flamboyant rococo Arcibiskupský palác (Archbishop's Palace), on the left as you face the Castle, was the Viennese archbishop's palace. Sadly, the plush interior shown off in the film is rarely open to the public. For a brief time after World War II, No. 11 was home to a little girl named Marie Jana Korbelová, better known as former U.S. Secretary of State Madeleine Albright. ⊠ *Hradčanské náměstí, Hradčany* Ⓜ *Line A: Malostranská, then Tram No. 22.*

Šternberský palác (*Sternberg Palace*). The 18th-century Šternberský palác houses the National Gallery's collection of paintings by European masters from the 15th to the 18th centuries. The holdings include impressive works by El Greco, Rubens, and Rembrandt, as well as many other household names in European art. ⊠ *Hradčanské nám. 15, Hradčany* ☏ *233–090–570* ⊕ *www.ngprague.cz* 🖼 *150 Kč* ⊙ *Tues.–Sun. 10–6* Ⓜ *Line A: Malostranská, then Tram No. 22.*

Strahovský klášter (*Strahov Monastery*). Founded by the Premonstratensian order in 1140, the monastery remained theirs until 1952, when the communists suppressed all religious orders and turned the entire complex into the **Památník národního písemnictví** (Museum of National Literature). The major building of interest is the **Strahov Library**, with its collection of early Czech manuscripts, the 10th-century Strahov New Testament, and the collected works of famed Danish astronomer Tycho Brahe. ⊠ *Strahovské nádvoří 1/132, Hradčany* ☏ *233–107–718* ⊕ *www.strahovskyklaster.cz* 🖼 *80 Kč library* ⊙ *Gallery daily 9–noon and 12:30–5; library daily 9–noon and 1–5* Ⓜ *Line A: Malostranská, then Tram No. 22 to Pohořelec.*

PRAŽSKÝ HRAD (PRAGUE CASTLE)

Despite its monolithic presence, the Prague Castle is not a single structure but rather a collection of buildings dating from the 10th to the 20th century, all linked by internal courtyards. The most important structures are **Chrám svatého Víta,** clearly visible soaring above the castle walls, and the **Starý královský palác,** the official residence of kings and presidents and still the center of political power in the Czech Republic. The castle is compact and easy to navigate.

EXPLORING

Bazilika svatého Jiří (*St. George's Basilica*). Inside, this church looks more or less as it did in the 12th century; it's the best-preserved Romanesque relic in the country. The effect is at once barnlike and peaceful, as the warm golden yellow of the stone walls and the small arched windows exude a sense of enduring harmony. Prince Vratislav I originally built it in the 10th century, though only the foundations remain from that time. The father of Prince Wenceslas (of Christmas carol fame) dedicated it to St. George (of dragon fame), a figure supposedly more agreeable to the still largely pagan people. The outside was remodeled during early baroque times, although the striking rusty-red color is in keeping with the look of the Romanesque edifice. The painted, house-shape tomb at the front of the church holds Vratislav's remains. ⊠ *Nám. U sv. Jiří, Pražský Hrad* ☏ *224–372–434* ⊕ *www.hrad.cz* 🖼 *250 Kč–350 Kč for*

6

2-day castle ticket ⊙ *Apr.–Oct., daily 9–5; Nov.–Mar., daily 9–4* Ⓜ *Line A: Malostranská, then Tram No. 22 to Pražský Hrad.*

Fodor's Choice **Chrám svatého Víta** (*St. Vitus's Cathedral*). With its graceful, soaring tow-
★ ers, this Gothic cathedral—among the most beautiful in Europe—is the spiritual heart of Prague Castle and of the Czech Republic itself. The cathedral has a long and complicated history, beginning in the 10th century and continuing to its completion in 1929. Note that it's no longer free to enter the cathedral; entry is included in the combined ticket to see the main castle sights. It's perfectly okay just to wander around inside and gawk at the splendor, but you'll get much more out of the visit with the audio guide, which is available at the castle information centers.

Once you enter the cathedral, pause to take in the vast but delicate beauty of the Gothic and neo-Gothic interior. Colorful light filters through the brilliant stained-glass windows. This western third of the structure, including the facade and the two towers you can see from outside, was not completed until 1929, following the initiative of the Union for the Completion of the Cathedral. Don't let the neo-Gothic illusion keep you from examining this new section. The six stained-glass windows to your left and right and the large rose window behind are modern masterpieces.

A key element of the cathedral's teeming, rich exterior decoration is the **Last Judgment mosaic** above the ceremonial entrance, called the Golden Portal, on the south side. The use of mosaic is quite rare in countries north of the Alps; this work, constructed from 1 million glass and stone tesserae, dates from the 1370s. The once-clouded glass now sparkles again, thanks to many years of restoration funded by the Getty Conservation Institute. ⊠ *Hrad III. nádvoří 48/2, Pražský Hrad* ☎ *224–372–434* ⊕ *www.katedralasvatehovita.cz* 🎫 *250 Kč –350 Kč for 2-day castle ticket* ⊙ *Apr.–Oct., Mon.–Sat. 9–5, Sun. noon–5; Nov.–Mar., Mon.–Sat. 9–4, Sun. noon–4* Ⓜ *Line A: Malostranská, then Tram No. 22 to Pražský Hrad.*

Druhé nádvoří (*Second Courtyard*). Except for the view of the spires of St. Vitus's Cathedral, the exterior courtyard offers little for the eye to feast on. Empress Maria Theresa's court architect, Nicolò Pacassi, received imperial approval to remake the castle in the 1760s, as it was badly damaged by Prussian shelling during the Seven Years' War in 1757. The Second Courtyard was the main victim of Pacassi's attempts at imparting classical grandeur to what had been a picturesque collection of Gothic and Renaissance styles. This courtyard also houses the rather gaudy **Kaple svatého Kříže** (Chapel of the Holy Cross), with decorations from the 18th and 19th centuries, which now serves as a souvenir and ticket stand. ⊠ *Obrazárna, Pražský Hrad* ☎ *224–372–434* ⊕ *www. hrad.cz* 🎫 *Courtyard free; gallery 150 Kč (included with 250 Kč –350 Kč for 2-day castle ticket), free Mon. 4–6* ⊙ *Gallery Apr.–Oct., daily 9–6; Jan.–Mar., Nov. and Dec., daily 9–4.* Ⓜ *Line A: Malostranská, then Tram No. 22 to Pražský Hrad.*

Královská zahrada (*Royal Garden*). This peaceful swath of greenery affords lovely views of St. Vitus's Cathedral and the Castle's walls and bastions. Originally laid out in the 16th century, it endured devastation in war, neglect in times of peace, and many redesigns, reaching its present parklike form early in the 20th century. Luckily, its Renaissance treasures survived. One of these is the long, narrow **Míčovna** (Ball Game Hall), built by Bonifaz Wohlmut in 1568, its garden front completely covered by a dense tangle of allegorical sgraffiti.

The **Královský letohrádek** (Royal Summer Palace, aka the Belvedere), at the garden's eastern end, deserves its unusual reputation as one of the most beautiful Renaissance structures north of the Alps. Italian architects began it; Wohlmut finished it off in the 1560s with a copper roof like an upturned boat's keel riding above the graceful arcades of the ground floor. During the 18th and 19th centuries military engineers tested artillery in the interior, which had already lost its rich furnishings to Swedish soldiers during their siege of the city in 1648. The Renaissance-style *giardinetto* (little garden) adjoining the summer palace centers on another masterwork, the Italian-designed, Czech-produced Singing Fountain, which resonates from the sound of falling water. ⊠ *U Prašného mostu ulice and Mariánské hradby ulice near Chotkovy Park, Pražský Hrad* ☎ *224–372–434* ⊕ *www.hrad.cz* ☉ *Apr. and Oct., daily 10–6; May and Sept., daily 10–7; June and July, daily 10–9; Aug., daily 10–8.* Ⓜ *Line A: Malostranská, then Tram No. 22 to Pražský Hrad.*

Lobkovický palác (*Lobkowicz Palace*). Greatly benefiting from a recent renovation, this palace is a showcase for baroque and rococo styling. Exhibits trace the ancestry of the Lobkowicz family, who were great patrons of the arts in their heyday. (Beethoven was one of the artists who received their funding.) The audio tour adds a personal touch: it's narrated by William Lobwicz, the family scion who spearheaded the property's restitution and rehabilitation, and includes quite a few anecdotes about the family through the years. Although inside Prague Castle, this museum has a separate admission. ⊠ *Jiřská 3, Pražský Hrad* ☎ *233–312–925* ⊕ *www.lobkowicz.cz* 💰 *275 Kč* ☉ *Daily 10–6* Ⓜ *Line A: Malostranská, then Tram No. 22 to Pražský Hrad.*

Starý královský palác (*Old Royal Palace*). A jumble of styles and add-ons from different eras are gathered in this palace. The best way to grasp its size is from within the **Vladislavský sál** (Vladislav Hall), the largest secular Gothic interior space in Central Europe. Benedikt Ried completed the hall in 1493. In its heyday, the hall held jousting tournaments, festive markets, banquets, and coronations. In more recent times, it has been used to inaugurate presidents, from the communist leader Klement Gottwald (in 1948) to modern-day leaders like Václav Havel and current president Miloš Zeman.

From the front of the hall, turn right into the rooms of the **Česká kancelář** (Bohemian Chancellery). This wing was built by Benedikt Ried only 10 years after the hall was completed, but it shows a much stronger Renaissance influence. Pass through the portal into the last chamber of the chancellery. In 1618 this room was the site of the second defenestration of Prague, an event that marked the beginning of the Bohemian rebellion and, ultimately, the Thirty Years' War throughout Europe. The square window used in this protest is on the left as you enter the room. ⊠ *Hrad III. nádvoří, Pražský Hrad* ☎ *224–372–434* ⊕ *www.*

hrad.cz 🖥 *250 Kč–350 Kč for 2-day castle ticket* ⊘ *Apr.–Oct., daily 9–5; Nov.–Mar., daily 9–4* Ⓜ *Line A: Malostranská, then Tram No. 22 to Pražský Hrad.*

Zlatá ulička (*Golden Lane*). A jumbled collection of tiny, ancient, brightly colored houses crouched under the fortification wall look remarkably like a set for *Snow White and the Seven Dwarfs*. Purportedly, these were the lodgings for an international group of alchemists whom Rudolf II brought to the court to produce gold. But the truth is a little less romantic: The houses were built during the 16th century for the castle guards. By the early 20th century Golden Lane had become the home of poor artists and writers. Franz Kafka, who lived at No. 22 in 1916 and 1917, described the house on first sight as "so small, so dirty, impossible to live in, and lacking everything necessary." But he soon came to love the place. The lane now holds tiny stores selling books, music, and crafts, and has become so popular that an admission fee is charged. The houses are cute, but crowds can be uncomfortable, and the fact remains that you are paying money for the privilege of shopping in jammed little stores. ✉ *Zlatá ulička, Pražský Hrad* ☎ *224–372–434* ⊕ *www.hrad.cz* 🖥 *250 Kč–350 Kč for 2-day castle ticket* ⊘ *Apr.–Oct., daily 9–5; Nov.–Mar., daily 9–4* Ⓜ *Line A: Malostranská, then Tram No. 22 to Pražský Hrad.*

NOVÉ MĚSTO (NEW TOWN)

To this day, Charles IV's most extensive scheme, the New Town, is still such a lively, vibrant area that you may hardly realize that its streets, Gothic churches, and squares were planned as far back as 1348. With Prague fast outstripping its Old Town parameters, Charles IV extended the city's fortifications. A high wall surrounded the newly developed 2½-square-km (1½-square-mile) area south and east of the Old Town, tripling the walled territory on the Vltava's right bank. The wall extended south to link with the fortifications of the citadel called Vyšehrad. In the mid-19th century, new building in the New Town boomed in a welter of Romantic and neo-Renaissance styles, particularly on Wenceslas Square and avenues such as Vodičkova, Na Poříčí, and Spálená. One of the most important structures was the Národní divadlo (National Theater), meant to symbolize in stone the revival of the Czechs' history, language, and sense of national pride.

EXPLORING

Národní divadlo (*National Theater*). Statues representing Drama and Opera rise above the riverfront side entrances to this theater, and two gigantic chariots flank figures of Apollo and the nine Muses above the main facade. The performance space lacks restraint as well—it's filled with gilding, voluptuous plaster figures, and plush upholstery. The idea for a Czech national theater began during the revolutionary decade of the 1840s. In a telling display of national pride, donations to fund the plan poured in from all over the country, from people of every socioeconomic stratum. The cornerstone was laid in 1868, and the "National Theater generation" who built the neo-Renaissance structure became the architectural and artistic establishment for decades to come. Today, it's still the country's leading dramatic stage. **■TIP→ Guided tours in English can be arranged by phone in advance.** ✉ *Národní třída 2, Nové Město* ☎ *224–901–506 for box office* 🌐 *www.narodni-divadlo.cz* 🎟 *Tours 200 Kč* [M] *Line A: Staroměstská.*

Statue of St. Wenceslas. Josef Václav Myslbek's impressive equestrian representation of St. Wenceslas with other Czech patron saints around him has been a traditional meeting place for locals for years ("Let's meet at the horse," as the expression goes). In 1939, Czechs gathered here to oppose Hitler's annexation of Bohemia and Moravia. In 1969, student Jan Palach set himself on fire near here to protest the Soviet-led invasion of the country a year earlier. And in 1989, many thousands successfully gathered here and all along the square to demand the end of the communist government. ✉ *Václavské nám., Nové Město* [M] *Line A or C: Muzeum.*

Václavské náměstí (*Wenceslas Square*). This "square"—more of a rectangle, actually—was first laid out by Charles IV in 1348, and began its existence as a horse market at the center of the New Town. Today, it functions as the commercial heart of the city center and is far brasher and more modern than the Old Town Square. Throughout much of Czech history, Wenceslas Square has served as the focal point for public demonstrations and celebrations. It was here in the heady days of November 1989 that some 500,000 people gathered to protest the policies of the then-communist regime. After a week of demonstrations, the government capitulated without a shot fired or the loss of a single life. After that, the first democratic government in 40 years (under playwright-president Václav Havel) was swept into office. This peaceful transfer of power is referred to as the "Velvet Revolution" (the subsequent "Velvet Divorce" from Slovakia took effect in 1993). ✉ *Václavské náměstí, Nové Město* [M] *Line A: Muzeum, Line A or B: Můstek.*

WHERE TO EAT

STARÉ MĚSTO (OLD TOWN)

$$ CAFÉ

🍴 **Kavárna Slavia.** Easily the city's best-known café, Slavia serves good coffee, drinks, and light snacks, as well as the greatest hits of Czech cuisine: roast duck with potato dumplings and sauerkraut, beef goulash, and roast smoked pork with white cabbage and potato pancakes. Plus, the café offers rich views of the National Theater and Prague Castle. The spectacular location has a historic air that reaches back to the days of Viktor Oliva's painting *The Absinthe Drinker* (which hangs in the main room) and through the 1970s and '80s when the late Václav Havel was a regular. [$] *Average main: 180 Kč* ✉ *Smetanovo nábř. 1012/2, Staré Město* ☎ *224–218–493* 🌐 *www.cafeslavia.cz* [M] *Line A: Staroměstská.*

$$ EASTERN EUROPEAN

🍴 **Kolkovna.** For Czechs, this chainlet remains one of the most popular spots to take visitors for a taste of local cuisine without the stress of tourist rip-offs. And it's a solid choice. The wood-and-copper decor gives off an appropriate air of a brewery taproom, and you can wash down traditional meals—such as *svíčková* (beef tenderloin in cream sauce), roast duck, and fried pork cutlets, or upgrades of traditional food, such as turkey steak with Roquefort sauce and walnuts—with a mug of unpasteurized Pilsner Urquell. $ *Average main: 220 Kč* ✉ *V Kolkovně, V Kolkovně 8, Staré Město* ☎ *224-818-701* ⊕ *www. vkolkovne.cz* Ⓜ *Line A: Staroměstská.*

$$$
ITALIAN
Fodor'sChoice
★
✕ **La Finestra in Cucina.** One of Prague's hottest tables, La Finestra is the meaty counterpart to its sister restaurant Aromi, right down to the wooden tables and brick walls. Catering to local gourmands and boldface names, this restaurant lives up to the hype. As at Aromi, waiters display an array of freshly caught fish for the day's specials, but here they also do the same with meat, including dry-aged cuts flown in from Italy. Complimenting this array of protein are fried chickpeas and fresh focaccia to nibble on and expertly crafted, al dente pastas like oxtail agnolotti and spaghetti with sea urchin. $ *Average main: 500 Kč* ✉ *Platnéřská 13, Staré Město* ☎ *222-325-325* ⊕ *www.lafinestra.cz* ⌕ *Reservations essential* Ⓜ *Line A: Staroměstská.*

$$
CZECH
Fodor'sChoice
★
✕ **Lokál.** Sleek and relatively sophisticated, Lokál takes the Czech pub concept to a new level with fresh, local ingredients, perfectly poured beers, and friendly, efficient service. It makes for an idealized version of a corner restaurant out of another era, right down to the stark white walls, waiters in vests, and bathrooms wallpapered with old pinups and airplane posters. Many of the dishes have a modern twist: schnitzel is made from pork neck and served atop buttery whipped potatoes, while the Czech classic of svíčková is tangy and fresh, not often the case at most pubs. $ *Average main: 150 Kč* ✉ *Dlouhá 33, Staré Město* ☎ *222-316-265* ⊕ *www.ambi.cz* ⌕ *Reservations essential* Ⓜ *Line B: Náměstí Republiky.*

$$$$
SEAFOOD
Fodor'sChoice
★
✕ **Zdenek's Oyster Bar.** In the few short years since it's been open, Zdenek's Oyster Bar has established itself as the city's best seafood bar. Aside from the namesake oysters (more than a dozen different varieties), head chef Jiří Nosek has developed creative entrées around mussels, shrimp, crab, lobster, and various types of fish. The restaurant occupies a quiet corner in the middle of the Old Town. The interior is classy but relaxed, and while the prices here can be high, you get what you pay for and there's never any pretension or attitude. $ *Average main: 600 Kč* ✉ *Malá Štupartská 5, Staré Město* ☎ *725-946-250* ⊕ *www.oysterbar. cz* ⌕ *Reservations essential* Ⓜ *Line A: Staroměstská.*

MALÁ STRANA (LESSER QUARTER)

$$
CAFÉ
Fodor'sChoice
★
✕ **Cukrkávalimonáda.** An excellent pit stop while exploring Malá Strana, this warm, inviting cafe and bakery serves freshly made soups, salads, sandwiches, and pasta dishes, making it a convenient stop for lunch. Or just rest your feet with a coffee and a slice of pie or cake. The light-wood booths and exposed-beam ceilings give Cukrkávalimonáda a country-farmhouse feel. Lunchtime can be overcrowded, so try to book a spot in advance; at other times, you can normally find a seat. Note: the café closes daily at 7 pm. $ *Average main: 180 Kč* ✉ *Lázeňská 7, Malá Strana* ☎ *257-225-396* ⊕ *www.cukrkavalimonada.com* ▭ *No credit cards* Ⓜ *Line A: Malostranská.*

$$$$
EUROPEAN
✕ **Kampa Park.** The zenith of riverside dining is offered at this legendary restaurant just off Charles Bridge, known almost as much for its chic decor and celebrity guests as it is for its elegant continental cuisine and

great wines—it's the kind of place where European royals and heads of state mingle with their head-of-studio counterparts from Hollywood. But the real star power arrives on the plate, with dishes like butter-poached lobster with avocado puree, or venison loin served with green lentils. The only drawback: the food and views command some of the highest prices in town. $\boxed{\text{\$}}$ *Average main: 800 Kč* ✉ *Na Kampě 8/b, Malá Strana* ☎ *257–532–685* ⊕ *www.kampagroup.com* ⌖ *Reservations essential* Ⓜ *Line A: Malostranská.*

$$
THAI
Fodor's Choice
★

✕ **Noi.** A lounge-y spot on a well-trafficked stretch of Újezd, Noi delivers on the promise of its Zen interior by cooking excellent Thai classics. The lithe staff is quick to accommodate its hip clientele at low tables surrounded by Buddha statues. And the kitchen excels at standards like a citrusy pad thai and addictive fried shrimp cakes. Curries, which run from tingly to tear-inducing hot, are cut by the creaminess of coconut milk and jasmine rice. There's an excellent selection of wines and special teas. $\boxed{\text{\$}}$ *Average main: 220 Kč* ✉ *Újezd 19, Malá Strana* ☎ *257–311–411* ⊕ *www.noirestaurant.cz* Ⓜ *Line A: Malostranská.*

$$$
CZECH
Fodor's Choice
★

✕ **U Modré kachničky.** This old-fashioned tavern puts on airs, but if you're looking for the perfect Czech venue for a special occasion, it's hard to beat the "Blue Duckling." Dusty portraits hanging on the walls and lavish curtains and table settings impart a certain slightly frilly 19th-century look. The menu, filled with succulent duck and game choices, brings things down to earth a notch. There's dining on two levels, but the upper floor's intimacy, with secluded tables in each nook and cranny and soft piano music wafting through the air, is preferable. $\boxed{\text{\$}}$ *Average main: 500 Kč* ✉ *Nebovidská 6, Malá Strana* ☎ *257–320–308* ⊕ *www.umodrekachnicky.cz* ⌖ *Reservations essential* Ⓜ *Line A: Malostranská.*

NOVÉ MĚSTO (NEW TOWN)

$$$
ASIAN FUSION
Fodor's Choice
★

✕ **Sansho.** When Sansho opened in 2011, it radically redefined the local dining scene. Head chef Paul Day introduced many novel concepts to Prague's foodies, like pairing a simple, unadorned interior with highly intricate Asian-fusion cuisine, leaving the full focus on the plate. The public was initially skeptical but once they gathered around the long, communal tables, they were won over by the quality of the cooking. (Not surprising as Day learned his craft at London's Michelin-starred Nobu.) Diners are encouraged to order a six-course tasting menu, featuring duck, pork belly, and soft-shell crab among other delicacies. Desserts, especially the sticky toffee pudding, can reflect a little of the London background. $\boxed{\text{\$}}$ *Average main: 500 Kč* ✉ *Petrská 4, Nové Město* ☎ *222–317–425* ⊕ *www.sansho.cz* ⌖ *Reservations essential* ⊘ *Closed Sun. and Mon.* Ⓜ *Line B, C: Florenc.*

VINOHRADY

$
CAFÉ
Fodor's Choice
★

✕ **Bio Zahrada.** A cheerful little spot, this beautiful café and organic bakery, full of blond wood and clean white walls, has a relaxed, peaceful garden out back. Choose from a counter of delicious, homemade baked goods, or opt for one of the daily luncheon specials (usually something simple but satisfying, like a rice curry or steamed vegetables). Or just come for a cup of coffee, easily the best in the area. $\boxed{\text{\$}}$ *Aver-*

age main: 100 Kč ⊠ *Belgická 33, Vinohrady* ☎ *222–518–698* ⊕ *www. bio-zahrada.cz* ⊗ *Closed Sun.* Ⓜ *Line A: Náměstí Miru.*

$$
BURGER
FodorsChoice
★

✕ **The Tavern.** A hopping burger bar on the fringe of Riegrovy Sady park in Vinohrady, the Tavern arguably serves the city's best hamburgers and cheeseburgers. The restaurant began as the dream of an American couple to use classic American burger combinations, like bacon-cheddar or blue cheese and caramelized onion, and then pair them with locally sourced beef and toppings. The result? It's been packed since the 2012 opening and shows no signs of slowing down. They also do veggie burgers, along with American-style diner food, and pies, cocktails, and craft beers. ■TIP→ **The opening hours are irregular, so check the website before heading out here. Reservations only by email; there's no phone.** Ⓢ *Average main: 160 Kč* ⊠ *Chopinova 26, Vinohrady* ⊕ *www.thetavern.cz* ⌖ *Reservations essential* ⊗ *Closed Sun. and Mon. No lunch Tues.* Ⓜ *Line A: Jiřího z Poděbrad.*

WHERE TO STAY

STARÉ MĚSTO (OLD TOWN)

$$
HOTEL

🖭 **Hotel U Zlatého Jelena.** Authentically austere, what U Zlatého Jelena lacks in personality and amenities it makes up for with a killer location off Old Town Square. **Pros:** excellent location; large rooms. **Cons:** no a/c; street noise in non-courtyard rooms. Ⓢ *Rooms from: 2500 Kč* ⊠ *Celetná 11, Staré Město* ☎ *257–531–925* ⊕ *www.goldendeer.cz* ⌖ *19 rooms* ⦿ *Breakfast* Ⓜ *Line A: Staroměstská.*

$$$$
HOTEL
FodorsChoice
★

🖭 **Mamaison Suite Hotel Pachtuv Palace.** Made from four structures— a baroque palace, two medieval houses, and a neoclassical building from 1836—the Pachtuv Palace can't really be matched for authenticity. **Pros:** friendly service; giant rooms. **Cons:** meager breakfast doesn't match the surroundings; some street noise. Ⓢ *Rooms from: 7500 Kč* ⊠ *Karolíny Světlé 34, Staré Město* ☎ *234–705–111* ⊕ *www.mamaison. com/pachtuvpalace* ⌖ *7 rooms, 43 suites* ⦿ *Breakfast* Ⓜ *Line A: Staroměstská.*

MALÁ STRANA (LESSER QUARTER)

$$$$
HOTEL
FodorsChoice
★

🖭 **Alchymist Grand Hotel and Spa.** A baroque fever-dream of Prague masterminded by an Italian developer, the Alchymist doesn't go the understated route. **Pros:** unique design; high-quality spa. **Cons:** steep uphill walk from the tram; loud a/c. Ⓢ *Rooms from: 6200 Kč* ⊠ *Tržiště 19, Malá Strana* ☎ *257–286–011* ⊕ *www.alchymisthotel.com* ⌖ *26 rooms, 20 suites* ⦿ *Breakfast* Ⓜ *Line A: Malostranská.*

$$$$
HOTEL
FodorsChoice
★

🖭 **The Augustine.** There's plenty of competition in Prague's high-end hotel market, but the Augustine has vaulted to the top. **Pros:** impeccable service; clever design; impressive spa. **Cons:** high Wi-Fi fees; noisy wood floors. Ⓢ *Rooms from: 7500 Kč* ⊠ *Letenská 12, Malá Strana* ☎ *266–112–233* ⊕ *www.theaugustine.com* ⌖ *101 rooms, 16 suites* ⦿ *No meals* Ⓜ *Line A: Malostranská.*

$$$$
HOTEL
FodorsChoice
★

🖭 **Golden Well.** Consistently rated one of Prague's best boutique hotels, the Golden Well is hidden away at the top of a narrow side street in Malá Strana. **Pros:** great views; friendly service; spacious rooms. **Cons:** outlet shortage; far from subway and tram stops. Ⓢ *Rooms from: 5000 Kč*

⌂ *U Zlate Studne 4, Malá Strana* ☎ *257–011–213* ⊕ *www.goldenwell. cz* ⟿ *17 rooms, 2 suites* ¶◎¶ *No meals* Ⓜ *Line A: Malostranská.*

$$
B&B/INN
Fodor's Choice
★

⌂ **Lokál Inn.** The 18th-century Lokál Inn offers an unbeatable combination of location, ambience, and convenience. **Pros:** central location; historic surroundings; modern amenities. **Cons:** rooms get a bit of noise from restaurant at night. Ⓢ *Rooms from: 3200 Kč* ⊠ *Míšeňská 12, Malá Strana* ☎ *257–014–800* ⊕ *www.lokalinn.cz* ⟿ *8 rooms, 4 suites* Ⓜ *Line A: Malostranská.*

$$$
HOTEL
Fodor's Choice
★

⌂ **Mandarin Oriental Prague.** Architects wisely chose to retain many of this restored Dominican monastery's original flourishes, creating a peaceful, inspired backdrop for the Mandarin Oriental's luxurious offerings, including a celebrated spa and the renowned restaurant, Essensia. **Pros:** historic building; lovely setting; boffo spa; attentive, personalized service; luxurious beds. **Cons:** some rooms are small; Wi-Fi and breakfast can cost extra depending on your reservation. Ⓢ *Rooms from: 9000 Kč* ⊠ *Nebovidská 1, Malá Strana* ☎ *233–088–888* ⊕ *www. mandarinoriental.com* ⟿ *77 rooms, 22 suites* ¶◎¶ *No meals* Ⓜ *Line A: Malostranská.*

$$
HOTEL

⌂ **U Tří Pštrosů.** This historic inn has taken a couple of licks—first it was flooded, then burned to the ground, and then rebuilt, only to be taken by the communists, and finally restituted to the family owners. **Pros:** location, location, location. **Cons:** small rooms up top; no elevator or a/c. Ⓢ *Rooms from: 2600 Kč* ⊠ *Dražického nám. 12, Malá Strana* ☎ *257–288–888* ⊕ *www.utripstrosu.cz* ⟿ *14 rooms, 4 suites* ¶◎¶ *Breakfast* Ⓜ *Line A: Malostranská.*

NOVÉ MĚSTO (NEW TOWN)

$$$
HOTEL
Fodor's Choice
★

⌂ **Icon Hotel & Lounge.** From the fashionable staff to its plush, all-natural bedding, this hotel is dressed to impress. **Pros:** youthful, exuberant staff; all-day breakfast spread; good metro and tram connections. **Cons:** small spa; busy, urban location will not appeal to everyone. Ⓢ *Rooms from: 3800 Kč* ⊠ *V jámě 6, Nové Město* ☎ *221–634–100* ⊕ *www.iconhotel. eu* ⟿ *29 rooms, 2 suites* ¶◎¶ *No meals* Ⓜ *Line A and B: Můstek.*

VINOHRADY

$$$$
HOTEL
Fodor's Choice
★

⌂ **Hotel Le Palais.** This venerable 19th-century mansion served as the home and shop of Prague's main butcher (one of the front rooms was even used to produce and sell sausage until 1991). **Pros:** gorgeous hotel; helpful, courteous staff. **Cons:** nice neighborhood but requires public transit to get anywhere; pricey Internet; small beds in basic rooms. Ⓢ *Rooms from: 5000 Kč* ⊠ *U Zvonařky 1* ☎ *234–634–111* ⊕ *www. vi-hotels.com* ⟿ *60 rooms, 12 suites* ¶◎¶ *Breakfast* Ⓜ *Line C: I. P. Pavlova.*

NIGHTLIFE AND THE ARTS

PERFORMING ARTS

Classical concerts are held all over the city throughout the year. In addition to Prague's two major professional orchestras, classical ensembles are the most common finds, and the standard of performance ranges from adequate to superb, though the programs tend to take few risks. Serious fans of baroque music may have the opportunity to hear works of little-known Bohemian composers at these concerts. Some of the best chamber ensembles are the Prague Chamber Philharmonic (aka the Prague Philharmonia; ⊕ *www.pkf.cz*), the Wihan Quartet 9 ⊕ *www.wihanquartet.com*), the Collegium Marianum (⊕ *www.collegiummarianum.cz*), and the Agon contemporary music group (⊕ *www.petrkofron.com*).

Performances are held regularly at many of the city's palaces and churches, including the Gardens Below Prague Castle (where the music comes with a view); both Churches of St. Nicholas; the Church of Sts. Simon and Jude on Dušní in the Old Town; the Church of St. James on Malá Štupartská, near Old Town Square; the Zrcadlová kaple (Mirror Chapel) in the Klementinum on Mariánské námìstí in the Old Town; and the Lobkowicz Palace at Prague Castle. If you're an organ-music buff, you'll most likely have your pick of recitals held in Prague's historic halls and churches. Popular programs are offered at the Church of St. Nicholas in the Lesser Quarter and the Church of St. James, where the organ plays amid a complement of baroque statuary.

NIGHTLIFE
For details of cultural and nightlife events, check out popular online sites like ⊕ *www.expats.cz* or Prague TV (⊕ *prague.tv*).

Most social life of the drinking variety takes place in pubs (*pivnice* or *hospody*), which are liberally sprinkled throughout the city's neighborhoods. Tourists are welcome to join in the evening ritual of sitting around large tables and talking, smoking, and drinking beer. Before venturing in, however, it's best to familiarize yourself with a few points of pub etiquette: always ask if a chair is free before sitting down (*Je tu volno?*). To order a beer (*pivo*), do not wave the waiter down or shout across the room; he will usually assume you want beer—most pubs serve just one or two brands—and bring it over to you without asking. He will also bring subsequent rounds to the table without asking. To refuse, just shake your head or say no, thanks (*ne, dìkuju*).

SHOPPING

Bohemian crystal and porcelain deservedly enjoy a worldwide reputation for quality, and plenty of shops offer excellent bargains. The local market for antiques and art is still relatively undeveloped, although dozens of antiquarian bookstores harbor some excellent finds, particularly German and Czech books and graphics.

SHOPPING DISTRICTS
The major shopping areas are **Na Příkopì**, which runs from the foot of Wenceslas Square to námìstí Republiky (Republic Square), and the area around **Old Town Square.** The Old Town **Pařížská ulice** and **Karlova ulice** are streets dotted with boutiques and antiques shops. In the Lesser Quarter, try **Nerudova ulice,** the street that runs up to Hradčany.

Southern Bohemia

GERMANY

AUSTRIA

20 miles

30 km

6

SIDE TRIPS FROM PRAGUE

With Prague at its heart and Germany and the former Austro-Hungarian Empire on its mountainous borders, the kingdom of Bohemia was for centuries buffeted by religious and national conflicts, invasions, and wars. But its position also meant that Bohemia benefited from the cultural wealth and diversity of Central Europe. The result is a glorious array of history-laden castles, walled cities, and spa towns set in a gentle, rolling landscape.

Southern Bohemia (separate sections on the northern and western areas follow) is particularly famous for its involvement in the Hussite religious wars of the 15th century. But the area also has more than its fair share of well-preserved and stunning walled towns, built up by generations of noble families, who left behind layers of Gothic, Renaissance, and baroque architecture (particularly notable in Český Krumlov). Farther north and an easy drive (or bus or train trip) east of Prague is the old silver-mining town of Kutná Hora, once a rival to Prague for the royal residence.

Český Krumlov offers some of the best accommodations in the Czech Republic outside the capital.

GETTING HERE AND AROUND

BUS TRAVEL

All the major destinations in the region are reachable from Prague and České Budìjovice on the ČSAD bus network.

CAR TRAVEL

A rental car affords the greatest ease and flexibility in this region. The main artery through the region, the two-lane E55 from Prague south to Tábor and České Budìjovice, though often crowded, is in relatively good shape. If you are driving from Vienna, take the E49 toward Gmünd.

TRAIN TRAVEL

Benešov (Konopištì), Tábor, and České Budìjovice lie along the major southern line in the direction of Linz, and train service to these cities from Prague is frequent and comfortable. Most Vienna–Prague trains travel through Moravia, but a few stop at Třeboò and Tábor (with a change at Gmünd).

KUTNÁ HORA

The approach to Kutná Hora looks much as it has for centuries. The town owes its illustrious past to silver, discovered here during the 12th century. For some 400 years the mines were worked with consummate efficiency. As the silver began to run out during the 16th and 17th centuries, however, Kutná Hora's importance faded. Since the early 1990s the town has beautified itself to a degree, but despite a significant tourist industry, modern Kutná Hora is dwarfed by the splendors of the Middle Ages. The city became a UNESCO World Heritage Site in 1995.

GETTING HERE

You can either take the train or bus to Kutná Hora; each trip takes about an hour. The train actually stops in the neighboring town of Sedlec, which gives you a chance to see the "Bone Church," but means a long walk of over a mile into town. By car, Highway 333 goes all the way to Kutná Hora.

VISITOR INFORMATION

Contacts Info-Centre Kutná Hora ✉ *Palackého nám. 377* ☎ *327–512–378* ⊕ *www.kutnahora.cz.*

EXPLORING

České Muzeum Stříbra (*Czech Museum of Silver*). Silver mines are a bit more romantic than a run-of-the-mill coal mine, and this silver museum combines all manner of medieval mining and minting equipment with the real deal: the chance to tour a medieval silver mine. It's fun, but if you're claustrophobic it's worth noting that the tunnel is a bit tight, and you're underground for about 30 minutes. The city boasted some of the deepest mines in the world back in the 16th century, and the trek nowadays will probably make you glad you weren't a miner. ✉ *Barborská ul. 28* ☎ *327–512–159* ⊕ *www.cms-kh.cz* 🖃 *90 Kč –140 Kč, 20 Kč for foreign-language explanation* ☉ *Apr. and Oct., Tues.–Sun. 9–5; May, June, and Sept., Tues.–Sun. 9–6; July and Aug., Tues.–Sun. 10–6; Nov., Tues.–Sun. 10–4. Last admission 90 mins before closing. Tours start every half-hr. Mine can close in bad weather.*

Fodor's Choice ★ **Chrám svaté Barbory** (*St. Barbara's Cathedral*). Getting to this beautiful cathedral is nearly as pleasurable as a visit to the Gothic church itself. It's about a 10-minute walk from the main Palackého náměstí along a road lined with baroque statues where you can gaze at the surrounding countryside and watch the massive shape of the cathedral come closer. From afar, the church resembles a grand circus tent more than a religious center. As the jewel in Kutná Hora's crown, it's a highpoint of Gothic style, although through the centuries there have been alterations and improvements. Upon entering, look up. The soaring ceiling is one of the church's most impressive features. It was added in 1558, and replaced and restored in the late 1800s. If you walk to the western façade, you'll see a lovely view over the town and the visibly leaning tower of St. James's Church. Do explore the whole of the church—gazing down at the splendor below from the elevated sections is particularly lovely. ✉ *Barborská ul.* ☎ *775–363–938 for parish* 🌐 *www.khfarnost.cz* 🎫 *60 Kč* 🕒 *Apr.–Oct., daily 9–6; Nov.–Mar., daily 10–4.*

Fodor's Choice ★ **Kostnice** (*ossuary*). This is the reason many people outside the Czech Republic have heard of, and make the trip to, Kutná Hora. Forget all that beautiful baroque architecture and descend into the darkness with some bones. Bones from about 40,000 people have been lovingly arranged in the Kaple Všech svatých (All Saints Chapel), more commonly called the Bone Church. Built in the 16th century, this church forced the movement of a nearby graveyard. Monks from the nearby Sedlec Monastery decided to use the displaced cemetery bones to decorate the church with beautiful, weird, and haunting results. ■ **TIP→ Check out the chandelier as it's made with every bone in the human body. It's downright spooky.** ✉ *Zámecká 127, Sedlec* ☎ *326–551–049* 🌐 *www.kostnice.cz* 🎫 *90 Kč, 110 Kč for ossuary and church* 🕒 *Nov.–Feb., daily 9–4; Apr.–Sept., daily 8–6, Sun. daily 9–6; Oct.–Mar. daily 9–5.*

Vlašský dvůr (*Italian Court*). Coins were first minted here in 1300, made by Italian artisans brought in from Florence—hence the mint's odd name. The Italian Court was where the Prague groschen, one of the most widely circulated coins of the Middle Ages, was minted until 1726. There's a **coin museum**, where you can see the small, silvery groschen being struck and buy replicas. ✉ *Havlíčkovo nám. 552* ☎ *327–512–873* 🌐 *www.vlassky-dvur.cz* 🎫 *105 Kč* 🕒 *Apr.–Sept., daily 9–6; Oct. and Mar., daily 10–5; Nov.–Feb., daily 10–4. Last admission 30 mins before closing.*

WHERE TO EAT

$$ CZECH 🍴 **Harmonia.** A charming spot just off Komenského náměstí near St. James's, Harmonia serves good food at good prices. The small back patio is relatively secluded and the perfect place for an espresso and quiet conversation. Food, like chicken cutlets and steaks, is simple and hearty. ■ **TIP→ It's also no-smoking, which is rare in this part of the world.** [$] *Average main: 150 Kč* ✉ *Husova 104* ☎ *327–512–275* 🌐 *www.harmonia.wz.cz.*

6

KONOPIŠTĚ

History buffs of World War I take note: Konopiště Castle could be the highlight of your trip. It was the home of none other than Franz Ferdinand d'Este, the ill-fated heir to the Austrian throne whose assassination in Sarajevo in 1914 is credited with unleashing the "Great War" that same year. Franz Ferdinand's castle and surrounding gardens, lakes, and woodland paths make for a blissfully peaceful half-day excursion from Prague. The neo-Gothic castle dates from the 14th century and was passed down through several noble families before the Habsburg heir made it his residence in the late 19th century.

GETTING HERE

If you're driving, Konopiště is an easy hour or so south of the city, starting out along the D1 highway in the direction of Brno and following the signs to the proper turnoff. By train, the nearest station is Benešov, from where you can walk (about 45 minutes) or take a taxi. There are also infrequent buses.

EXPLORING

Zámek Konopiště (*Konopiště Castle*). Set in a huge, beautiful park, Konopiště Castle dates from the 14th century and is best known as the hunting lodge of Archduke Franz Ferdinand. He no doubt had a whale of a time hunting in the grounds before he met his untimely end, and now visitors can wander the forests, gaze at the lake, and even watch plays in summer, as well as musing on the Archduke's global significance. In a suitably historic touch, there's also bear who lives in the castle moat; he's a bit shy so you might not see him.

The castle itself is also worth a look, with a carefully preserved interior including many original furnishings from Ferdinand's time. The rooms reflect his incredible opulence as well as his fondness for hunting—there are animal trophies and weapons everywhere. For a properly immersive experience, you can even stay inside the castle walls at a little pension.

Getting to the castle usually involves a ⅓-mile walk through the woods. It can only be seen on a guided tour; book in advance for an English-speaking guide. If one isn't available, ask for an English text to accompany the tour. ✉ *Zámek Konopiště, Benešov* ☎ *317–721–366 for castle information, 224–497–492 for reservations* 🌐 *www.zamek-konopiste.cz* 🎫 *Tours 220 Kč–320 Kč* 🕒 *Apr.–May and Sept., Tues.–Sun. 10–4; Jun.–Aug., Tues.–Sun. 10–5; Oct.–Nov., weekends, 10–3.*

WHERE TO STAY

$ HOTEL 🏨 **Amber Hotel Konopiště.** Konopiště is so close to Prague that it's easy to do in a day trip, but if you're looking for a sporty weekend with a bit of relaxation at the end, Amber Hotel should satisfy. **Pros:** many sport facilities and gorgeous woodlands to walk in. **Cons:** remote location may be too isolated for some. [$] *Rooms from: 1300 Kč* ✉ *Benešov* ☎ *739–246–726* 🌐 *www.amberhotels.cz* 🛏 *44 rooms, 1 apartment* 🍴 *Breakfast.*

ČESKÝ KRUMLOV

Fodor's Choice ★ Český Krumlov, the official residence of the Rosenbergs for some 300 years, is an eye-opener. None of the surrounding towns or villages, with their open squares and mixtures of old and new buildings, will prepare you for the beauty of the Old Town. Here the Vltava works its wonders as nowhere else but in Prague itself, swirling in a nearly complete circle around the town. Across the river stands the proud castle, rivaling any in the country in size and splendor.

For the moment, Český Krumlov's beauty is still intact, even as the once-dilapidated but still-charming buildings that lend the town its unique atmosphere are rapidly being converted into boutiques and pensions. Visitor facilities are improving but can become overburdened during peak months. Overlook any minor inconveniences, however, and enjoy a rare, unspoiled trip in time back to the Bohemian Renaissance. Greenways cycling paths lead to and from the town; for details, contact the tourist office.

While it's technically possible to do this as a day-trip, you really should spend the night.

GETTING HERE

A direct bus connects Prague to Český Krumlov. The trip takes about three to four hours. There is no direct train, but you can reach the town by connecting trains. By car, follow signs for České Budějovice and then continue following signs for Český Krumlov.

VISITOR INFORMATION

Contacts Český Krumlov Tourist Information ✉ *Nám. Svornosti 2* ☎ *380–704–622* ⊕ *www.ckrumlov.cz.*

EXPLORING

Egon Schiele Center. A large and rambling former brewery now showcases the work of Schiele along with other modern and contemporary Czech and European artists. The Renaissance building, built in three phases in the early 1600s, is a wonder, with soaring ceilings in some places and wooden-beamed rooms in others. Schiele often painted landscapes of Český Krumlov from the castle's bridge. The museum does close unexpectedly on occasion in winter, but is one of the only sites in town normally opened year-round. ✉ *Široká 71* ☎ *380–704–011* ⊕ *www. schieleartcentrum.cz* 🕿 *120 Kč* ☉ *Daily 10–6.*

FAMILY **Hrad Krumlov** (*Krumlov Castle*). Like any good protective fortress, the castle is visible from a distance, but you may wonder how to get there. From the main square, take Radniční Street across the river and head up the staircase on your left from Latrán Street. (Alternatively, you can continue on Latrán and enter via the main gateway; also on your left.) You'll first come across the oldest part of the castle, a round 13th-century **tower** renovated in the 16th century to look something like a minaret, with its delicately arcaded Renaissance balcony. Part of the old border fortifications, the tower guarded Bohemian frontiers from the threat of Austrian incursion. It's now repainted with an educated guess of its Renaissance appearance, since the original designs have long been lost. From dungeon to bells, its inner secrets can be seen climbing the

6

interior staircase. Go ahead and climb to the top, you'll be rewarded with a view of the castle grounds and across the countryside.

Next up is the moat, fearlessly protected by a pair of brown bears—truthfully not really much help in defending the castle; their moods range from playful to lethargic. But bears have been residents of this moat since 1707. In season, the castle rooms are open to the public. Crossing the bridge, you enter the second courtyard, which contains the ticket office. ✉ *Zámek 59* ☎ *380–704–711* 🌐 *www.castle.ckrumlov.cz* 🎫 *Garden free, castle tours (English) 240 Kč–250 Kč, tower 50 Kč, theater tours (English) 380 Kč. Combination discounts available; included on Český Krumlov Card.* 🕒 *Garden Apr.–Oct., Tues.–Sun. dawn–dusk. Castle interior Apr., May, Sept., and Oct., Tues.–Sun. 8:45–4; June–Aug., Tues.–Sun. 8:45–5. Tower Apr., May, Sept., and Oct., Tues.–Sun. 8:45–4; June–Aug., Tues.–Sun. 8:45–5. Theater May–Oct., Tues.–Sun. 10–4.*

Kostel svatého Víta (*St. Vitus's Church*). This neo-Gothic church with its octagonal tower provides a nice contrast with the castle's older tower across the river. Step inside to see the elaborate baptismal font and frescoes. Much reconstruction took place in the 17th and 18th centuries, however the Gothic entrance portal dates from 1410. ✉ *Kostelní ul.* 🌐 *www.farnostck.bcb.cz.*

Náměstí Svornosti (*Unity Square*). A little odd-shape, yes, but a "square" nonetheless; Unity Square should be home base for your explorations. Pick a street and head off into the tiny alleys that fan out in all directions. There's no real sense in "planning" your route, simply choose a direction and go—you'll end up where you started eventually. Each turn seems to bring a new charming vista, and cute buildings and shops will amuse and keep shutterbugs busy. Don't forget to look up in the direction of the castle every once in a while; it pokes through in some amazing places. The actual square has a couple of notable buildings, including the Town Hall with its Renaissance friezes and Gothic arcades.

WHERE TO EAT

$ CZECH Fodor's Choice ★

🍴 **Na Louži.** Czech comfort food is served up every night at Na Louži. Lovingly preserved wood furniture and paneling lend a traditional touch to this warm, inviting, family-run pub. The food is unfussy yet satisfying. Look for the roast pork with dumplings and cabbage, or the grilled carp with garlic and potatoes. (The 10 country-style rooms upstairs [$] are basic and cheap, perfect for a one-night stay; breakfast is included.) [$] *Average main: 156 Kč* ✉ *Kájovská 66* ☎ *380–711–280* 🌐 *www.hospodanalouzi.cz* ✍ *Reservations essential* 💳 *No credit cards.*

WHERE TO STAY

$$$ HOTEL Fodor's Choice ★

🏨 **Hotel Růže.** Converted from a Jesuit school, this excellent centrally located hotel with spacious rooms is a two-minute walk from the main square. **Pros:** central location; great views; quality restaurant. **Cons:** inconsistent room layouts; baroque decorations are a bit overdone; pricey. [$] *Rooms from: 5500 Kč* ✉ *Horní 154* ☎ *380–772–100* 🌐 *www.hotelruze.cz* 🛏 *71 rooms* 🍽 *Breakfast.*

FRANCE

Paris, Île de France, Normandy,
Provence, the French Riviera

WHAT'S WHERE

1 Paris. A quayside vista that takes in the Seine, a passing boat, Notre-Dame, the Eiffel Tower, and mansard roofs all in one generous sweep is enough to convince you that Paris is indeed the most beautiful city on Earth.

2 Île-de-France. Appearing like all France in miniature, the Île-de-France region is the nation's heartland and easily accessible to Paris as day trips. Here Louis XIV built vainglorious Versailles, Chartres brings the faithful to their knees, and Monet's Giverny enchants all.

3 Normandy. Sculpted with cliff-lined coasts, Normandy has been home to saints and sculptors, with a dramatic past marked by Mont-St-Michel's majestic abbey, Rouen's towering cathedral, and the D-Day beaches.

4 Provence. Famed for its Lavender Route, the honey-gold hill towns of the Luberon, and vibrant cities like Aix and Marseilles, this region was dazzlingly abstracted into geometric daubs of paint by Van Gogh and Cézanne.

5 French Riviera. From glamorous St-Tropez through beauteous Antibes to sophisticated Nice, this sprawl of pebble beaches and zillion-dollar houses has always captivated sun-lovers and socialites.

0 ___ 50 miles
0 ___ 75 km

La Manche
(English Channel)

Roscoff
Brest
Morlaix
St-Malo
St-Brieuc
BRITTANY
Quimper
Rennes
Lorient
Vannes
Nantes

Les Sables
d'Olonne

La Roche

Royc

Bayonne
Biarritz

SPAIN

NORTH

Calais
Boulogne
Lille
Arras
Dieppe
PICARDY
Amiens
Cambrai
St. Quentin
Beauvais
Rouen
Reims
CHAMPAGNE
ARDENNES
Le Havre
Caen
PARIS
ÎLE-DE-
FRANCE
Metz
Châlons-en-
Champagne
Nancy
Strasbourg
NORMANDY
Chartres
Sens
Troyes
Colmar
Le Mans
Orléans
Mulhouse
Angers
Tours
Blois
Auxerre
ALSACE
Belfort
PAYS-DE-
LOIRE
LOIRE
VALLEY
Bourges
Dijon
Besançon
Niort
Poitiers
Nevers
Beaune
BURGUNDY
FRANCHE-
COMTÉ
POITOU-
CHARENTES
Vichy
Mâcon
Bourg-en-
Bresse
SWITZERLAND
Saintes
Limoges
Angoulême
LIMOUSIN
Clermont-
Ferrand
Lyon
ALPES
Périgueux
AUVERGNE
Chambéry
Bordeaux
Brive-la-
Gaillarde
Aurillac
Le Puy
RHÔNE
VALLEY
Grenoble
ITALY
Langon
Cahors
Rodez
Montélimar
Gap
UITAINE
Montauban
Millau
PROVENCE
Sisteron
Albi
Nîmes
Avignon
FRENCH
RIVIERA
Monte
Carlo
MIDI-
PYRÉNÉES
Toulouse
LANGUEDOC
ROUSSILLON
Montpellier
Aix-en-
Provence
Nice
Antibes
Cannes
Tarbes
Carcassonne
Narbonne
Marseille
St-Tropez
ANDORRA
Perpignan
Mediterranean
Sea
Toulon

BELGIUM
LUXEMBOURG
LORRAINE

7

NEED TO KNOW

Paris ✪

FRANCE

Mediterranean Sea

CORSICA

AT A GLANCE
Capital: Paris

Population: 63,460,000

Currency: Euro

Money: ATMs are common; credit cards widely accepted

Language: French

Country Code: ☎ 33

Emergencies: ☎ 112

Driving: On the right

Electricity: 220v/50 cycles; electrical plugs have two round prongs

Time: Six hours ahead of New York

Documents: Up to 90 days with valid passport; Schengen rules apply

Mobile Phones: GSM (900 and 1800 bands)

Major Mobile Companies: Bouygues, Orange, Free, SFR

WEBSITES
France: ⊕ *us.franceguide.com*

Paris City Hall: ⊕ *paris.fr/english*

Paris Tourism: ⊕ *parisinfo.com*

GETTING AROUND

✈ **Air Travel:** The major airports are Paris, Lyons, Nice, and Marseille.

🚌 **Bus Travel:** Good for smaller regional towns and the only direct public transit to Giverny from Paris.

🚗 **Car Travel:** Renting a car is the best way to explore at your own pace, but never in Paris, and beware of unmanned gas stations and toll booths on major highways. Gas is very expensive.

🚆 **Train Travel:** Fast TGV trains link Paris with major cities like Rouen, Avignon, and Nice; switch to local trains for smaller places.

PLAN YOUR BUDGET

	HOTEL ROOM	MEAL	ATTRACTIONS
Low Budget	€105	€17	Stairs to Eiffel Tower, Level 2, €5
Mid Budget	€160	€30	Louvre ticket with temp. exhibitions, €16
High Budget	€300	€120	Opera ticket: €135

WAYS TO SAVE

Eat lunch picnic-style. Take advantage of France's wonderful outdoor markets and shops, then eat picnic-style indoors or out.

Book a rental apartment. For more space and a kitchen, consider a furnished rental—a good bet for families.

Book rail tickets in advance. For the cheapest rail fares, book online 90 days before travel at the website for the French railway. *www.sncf.com*.

Look for free museum days. Most museums are free on the first Sunday of the month, and often one afternoon or evening a week.

Hassle Factor	Low. Flights to Paris are frequent, and France has great transport elsewhere.
3 days	You can see some of the magic of Paris and perhaps take a half-day trip out to Versailles or Chartres.
1 week	Combine a short trip to Paris with at least one day trip to Normandy or Giverny, as well as an additional day or two in a place within easy reach by high-speed train (TGV) like Lyons or Marseille.
2 weeks	You have time to move around and for the highlights, including a stop in Paris, excursions to Normandy, and a trip to take in the highlights of atmospheric Provence and the ritzy French Riviera.

WHEN TO GO

High Season: June through August is the most expensive and popular time to visit France. June and July in Paris are especially crowded; August is quieter in Paris but is the busiest month in the south. Famously fickle weather means you never know what to expect in the north.

Low Season: Unless you are skiing, winter offers the least appealing weather, though it's the best time for airfares and hotel deals—and to escape the crowds. Particularly in the south, the famous *mistral* winds make travel uncomfortable.

Value Season: September is gorgeous, with temperate weather, saner airfares, and cultural events. October still has great weather, though temperatures start to drop by late November. Late April or May is a great time to visit, before the masses arrive but when cafés are abuzz. March and early April weather can be changeable and wet.

BIG EVENTS

May: The French Open kicks off the last week of May in Paris. ⊕ *www.rolandgarros.com*

July: Every town celebrates *le quatorze juillet* (Bastille Day). ⊕ *www.14-juilletcityvox.com*

September: The Journée du Patrimoine opens France's most beautiful buildings on the third Sunday. ⊕ *www.journeesdupatrimoine.culture.fr*

February: The Carnaval de Nice rocks Lent for three weeks. ⊕ *www.nicecarnaval.com*

READ THIS

■ ***A Food Lover's Guide to France,*** Patricia Wells. For all lovers of food and wine.

■ ***A Year in Provence,*** Peter Mayle. Satirical introduction to French country life.

■ ***France Today,*** John Ardagh. The best introduction to modern France.

WATCH THIS

■ ***Amelie.*** A quirky and romantic view of Paris.

■ ***The Untouchables.*** A touching tale of an unlikely friendship.

■ ***Jean de Florette.*** A view of rural Provençal life.

EAT THIS

■ **Boeuf bourgignon:** the famous French stew

■ **Confit de canard:** tender and delicious duck leg

■ **Crêpes:** savory or sweet, streetside or in a café

■ **Croissant or pain au chocolat:** from a café or boulangerie

■ **Fromage:** French cheese comes in seemingly endless varieties.

■ **Salade Niçoise:** a classic French Riviera lunch (with a glass of rosé, of course)

It is a fabled land of unmatched food and delicious wine that has inspired many to gasp in satisfied contentment, "We all have two countries—our own, and France!" But it is not just a country for those who worship at the altar of gastronomy. The sheer beauty of the rose-colored rooftops, the immaculately restored farm houses, architecture, cultivated scenery, and historic hearts give justice to the sentiment. Not to mention those glorious hidden landscapes that only those lucky few in the know ever discover.

Who can resist the allure of Paris? Even the grumpy waiters have a certain charm. Especially if you can try a little bit of French—a simple *Bonjour* or *Parlez-vous anglais?* will take you a long way, and you'll find out how quickly a surly waiter will melt if you say hello.

But if you want to visit France at its most French, and have already visited Paris—at least for the first time—head to the Îleȋle-de-France, just south and north of Paris. Here, at the heart of the country, you'll find French culture at its most elegant, pure and refined—even the language here is fabled for its refined beauty and grace. Farther afield this "Frenchiness" becomes mixed (delightfully so) with other cultures.

If you go west to solidly Norse Normandy, you'll find D-Day landings, with the dramatic Mont-St-Michel overlooking La Manche (the English Channel). In Provence and Cote d'Azur you'll learn the most important thing in France—to slow down—and you can easily linger over a bottle of wonderful local vintage and watch the sun go down over the magnificent bay and make your visit all the more authentic and satisfying.

PLANNING

WHEN TO GO

Summer is the most popular (and expensive) season. July in Paris is crowded and hot, although the Paris Plage, the "beach" on the banks of the Seine, is very popular with locals and tourists alike. The Riviera sparkles in August—but the notorious *embouteillages* (traffic jams) on the drive south can make you'd wish you stayed home. Famously fickle weather means you never know what to expect in Normandy and Brittany, where picture-postcard villages and languorous sandy beaches are never jam-packed.

TOP REASONS TO GO

Paris: There is no other town like it in the world. Trip the light fantastic at the Eiffel Tower's nightly show, or shine your best half-smile on Mona in the Louvre, and then, when you are ready for some serious fun, paint the town *rouge* at Au Lapin Agile, Picasso's hangout.

Cathédrale Notre-Dame, Chartes: This 13th-century masterpiece is the pinnacle of Gothic achievement, with peerless stained glass and a hilltop silhouette visible for miles around.

Giverny: Come to Giverny to see his lily pond—a half-acre "Monet"—then peek around his charming home and stroll the time-warped streets to the superb Musée des Impressionnismes.

Mont-St-Michel: The spire-topped silhouette of this mighty offshore mound, dubbed the Marvel of the Occident, is one of the greatest sights in Europe. Get there at high tide, when the water races across the endless sands.

Cours Mirabeau, Aix-en-Provence: It's considered to be the Champs-Élysees of Provence: a tree-lined boulevard laced with cafés in which a lengthy roster of famous literati have lounged about.

Nice: With its candy-striped palaces, crystal-blue Bay of Angels and time-less (and time-stained) Old Town, this is one of France's most colorful cities.

GETTING HERE AND AROUND

AIR TRAVEL

There are two major gateway airports to France just outside the capital: Orly, 16 km (10 miles) south of Paris, and Charles de Gaulle, 26 km (16 miles) northeast of the city. At Charles de Gaulle, also known as Roissy, there's a TGV (*train à grande vitesse*) station at Terminal 2, where you can connect to high-speed trains going all over the country.

TRAIN TRAVEL

Once in France, the best way to travel is by train, either high-speed TGV or regional train. A France Rail Pass allows three days of unlimited train travel in a one-month period. With train service efficient and enjoyable, long-distance bus service is rarely used, though there are some regional buses that cover areas where train service is spotty.

CAR TRAVEL

If you're traveling by car, there are excellent links between Paris and most French cities, but less so to the provinces. For the fastest route between two points, look for roads marked "A" for *autoroute*. A *péage* (toll) must be paid on most expressways: the rate varies, but can be steep. Note that gas prices are also much more expensive than they are in the U.S.

Although renting a car is about twice as expensive as in the United States, it's the best way to see remote corners of the lovely French countryside. To get the best rate, book a rental car at home, and well in advance if you're planning a trip in summer and early fall. If you want automatic transmission, which is more expensive, be sure to ask for it when you reserve. If you are traveling from Paris but ending your trip in, say, Nice, be sure to use a larger rental company like Avis or Hertz so that you can pick up at one location and drop off at another.

Another good tip: If you're traveling from Paris, a practical option is to take the TGV to another large city, such as Marseille or Nice, and pick up your rental car there.

HOTELS

If your France fantasy involves staying in a historic hotel with the smell of fresh-baked croissants gently rousing you in the morning, here's some good news: you need not be Ritz-rich to realize it. Throughout the country, you'll find stylish lodging options—from charming hotels and intimate bed-and-breakfasts to regal apartments and grand country houses—in all price ranges. Rates are always by room, not per person. Sometimes a hotel in a certain price category will have a few less expensive rooms; it's worth asking about. In the off-season—usually November to Easter (except for southern France)—tariffs may be lower.

APARTMENT AND HOUSE RENTALS

If you want more spacious accommodations with cooking facilities, consider a furnished rental. These can save you money, especially if you're traveling with a group. Renting a *gîte rural* (furnished house in the country) for a week or month can also save you money. Gîtes are nearly always maintained by on-site owners, who greet you on your arrival and provide information on groceries, doctors, and nearby attractions.

RESTAURANTS

Forget the Louvre—the real reason for a visit to France is to dine at its famous temples of gastronomy. Once you dive into Taillevent's lobster soufflé, you'll quickly realize that food in France is far more than fuel. The French regard gastronomy as essential to the art of living, so don't feel guilty if your meal at Paris's Grand Véfour takes as long as your visit to the Musée d'Orsay: two hours for a three-course menu is par, and you may, after relaxing into the routine, feel pressured at less than three.

MEALS AND MEAL TIMES

Restaurants follow French mealtimes, serving lunch from noon to 2 or 2:30 and dinner from 7:30 or 8 on. Some cafés in larger cities serve food all day long.

RESERVATIONS

Always reserve a table for dinner, as top restaurants book up weeks or even months in advance. You must ask for the check (it's considered rude to bring it unbidden) except in cafés, where a register slip often comes with your order.

MONEY-SAVING TIPS

To save money on food, take advantage of France's wonderful outdoor markets and chain supermarkets. Just about every town has its own market once or a couple of times a week. For supermarkets, the largest chains are Monoprix and Carrefour. Some of the bigger stores have cafés where you can sit down and eat whatever you buy.

HOTEL AND RESTAURANT PRICES

Prices in the restaurant reviews are the average cost of a main course at dinner or, if dinner is not served, at lunch; taxes and service charges are generally included. Prices in the hotel reviews are the lowest cost of a standard double room in high season, excluding taxes, service charges, and meal plans (except at all-inclusives). Prices for rentals are the lowest per-night cost for a one-bedroom unit in high season.

PLANNING YOUR TIME

Every trip to France should start in Paris. It is one of the most magical cities in the world and the easiest to travel to and from. It is *très facile* to spend your whole trip here—the city alone would take months to explore properly. But let's assume that you've at least seen Paris, and you're ready to venture into the peerless French countryside. Here are some ideas to help you plan your time exploring France to maximum effect, no matter where your interests lie.

Normandy can be explored, if only on the surface, as a day trip from Paris, though an overnight stay will give you more options and will let you get farther from the capital. A few hours south of Paris by train takes you deep into the heart of Provence. Arles is the atmospheric, sun-drenched southern town that inspired Van Gogh and Gauguin. Make a day trip into grand old Avignon, home to the 14th-century rebel popes, to view their imposing palace. And make a pilgrimage to the Pont du Gard, the famous triple-tiered Roman aqueduct west of Avignon. From here, two hours' drive will bring you to the glittering Côte d'Azur.

7

PARIS

If there's a problem with a trip to Paris, it's the embarrassment of riches that faces you. No matter which aspect of Paris you choose—touristy, historic, fashion-conscious, pretentious-bourgeois, thrifty, or the legendary bohemian arty Paris of undying attraction—one thing is certain: you will carve out your own Paris, one that is vivid, exciting, ultimately unforgettable.

Veterans know that Paris is a city of vast, noble perspectives and intimate, ramshackle streets, of formal *espaces vertes* (green open spaces) and quiet squares. This combination of the pompous and the private is one of the secrets of its perennial pull. Another is its size: Paris is relatively small as capitals go, with distances between many of its major sights and museums easily walkable.

For the first-timer there will always be several must-dos at the top of the list, but getting to know Paris will never be quite as simple as a quick look at Notre-Dame, the Louvre, and the Eiffel Tower. You'll discover that around every corner, down every *ruelle* (little street) lies a resonance-in-waiting. If this is your first trip, you may want to take a guided tour of the city—a good introduction that will help you get your bearings and provide you with a general impression before you return to explore the sights that particularly interest you.

PLANNING YOUR TIME

Paris is one of the world's most-visited cities—with crowds to prove it, so it pays to be prepared. Buy tickets online when you can. Investigate alternate entrances at popular sites (there are three at the Louvre) and check when rates are reduced, often during once-a-week late openings. Also, most major museums—including the Louvre and the Musée d'Orsay—are free the first Sunday of each month. Museums are also closed one day a week (usually Tuesday), and most stay open late at least one night each week, which is also the least crowded time to visit.

A Paris Museum Pass can save you money if you're planning serious sightseeing, but better yet, it allows you to bypass the lines. It's sold at the destinations it covers and at airports, major métro stations, and the tourism office in the Carrousel du Louvre (two-, four- or six-day passes are €39, €54, and €69, respectively; ⊕ *www.parismuseumpass.com*).

If you plan to take public transport everywhere, consider getting a one-day or multi-day Paris Visite, which also gives discounts at some museums (€10.55 for one day up to €33.70 for five days.).

GETTING HERE AND AROUND

AIR TRAVEL

Paris is served by two international airports, Orly and Charles de Gaulle (also called Roissy). Orly has two terminals: Orly Ouest (domestic flights) and Orly Sud (international, regular, and charter flights).

RER trains travel between Paris and the suburbs. When they go through Paris, they act as a sort of supersonic métro—they connect with the métro network at several points—and can be great time-savers. From Charles de Gaulle, take the RER-B into Paris; the journey takes 30 minutes. Additionally, the Roissybus runs directly between Roissy and rue Scribe by the Opéra. The RER-C line goes into Paris from Orly Airport; the train journey takes about 35 minutes. There's also the Orlybus between Orly and the Denfert-Rochereau métro station. In addition, Paris has five international train stations: Gare du Nord; Gare St-Lazare; Gare de l'Est; Gare de Lyon; and Gare d'Austerlitz.

Contacts Charles de Gaulle (*CDG*). ☎ *0033/1–70–36–39–50 outside of France* ⊕ *www.adp.fr.* **RATP (including Roissybus, Orlybus, Orlyval)** ☎ *3246 (€0.34 per min)* ⊕ *www.ratp.com.*

CAR TRAVEL

If you're driving into Paris, which is not advisable, the major ring road encircling the city is called the *périférique,* with the *périférique intérieur* going counterclockwise around the city, and the *périférique extérieur,* or the outside ring, going clockwise. Up to five lanes wide, the périférique is a major highway from which *portes* (gates) connect Paris to the major highways of France.

MÉTRO TRAVEL

The *métro* (subway) goes just about everywhere you're going for €1.70 a ride (a *carnet,* or "pack" of 10 tickets is €13.30); tickets are good for buses and trams, too.

EXPLORING

In the center of Paris, nestled in the River Seine are the two celebrated islands, the Île de la Cité, where you'll find Notre-Dame, and the Île St-Louis. Nearby is the immense Louvre, and beyond it lie the graceful Tuileries Gardens, the grand place de la Concorde—the very hub of the city—and the Belle Époque splendor of the Grand Palais and the Pont Alexandre III. All in all, this area comprises some of the most historic and beautiful sights to see in Paris.

FROM NOTRE-DAME TO THE PLACE DE LA CONCORDE

Paris is divided into 20 *arrondissements* (neighborhoods) spiraling out from the center of the city. The numbers reveal the neighborhood's location and its age, the 1st arrondissement at the city's heart being the oldest. The arrondissements in central Paris—the 1st to 8th—are the most-visited, but the 9th and 12th are up-and-coming, with plenty of chic boutiques and restaurants.

Grand Palais. With its curved-glass roof and gorgeously restored Belle Époque ornamentation, you can't miss the Grand Palais whether you're approaching from the Seine or the Champs-Élysées. It forms an elegant duo with the Petit Palais across Avenue Winston Churchill: both stone buildings, adorned with mosaics and sculpted friezes, were built for the 1900 World's Fair, and, like the Eiffel Tower, were not intended to be permanent. The exquisite main exhibition space called le Nef (or nave) plays host to large-scale shows that might focus on anything from jewelry to cars. To skip the long lines, it pays to book an advance ticket online, which will cost you an extra euro. ⊠ *Av. Winston Churchill, Champs-Élysées* ☎ *01–44–13–17–17* ⊕ *www.grandpalais.fr, www.rmn. fr for reservations* 🎫€12 *(can vary)* ⊘ *Wed.–Mon. 10–8 or 10–10, depending on the exhibit* Ⓜ *Champs-Élysées–Clemenceau.*

FAMILY
Fodor'sChoice
★

Jardin des Tuileries. The quintessential French garden, with its verdant lawns, manicured rows of trees, and gravel paths, was designed by André Le Nôtre for Louis XIV. After the king moved his court to Versailles, in 1682, the Tuileries became *the* place for stylish Parisians to stroll. (Ironically, the name derives from the decidedly unstylish factories which once occupied this area: they produced *tuiles,* or roof tiles, fired in kilns called *tuileries.*) Monet and Renoir captured the garden with paint and brush, and it's no wonder the Impressionists loved it— the gray, austere light of Paris's famously overcast days make the green trees appear even greener.

The garden still serves as a setting for one of Paris's loveliest walks. Laid out before you is a vista of must-see monuments, with the Louvre at one end and the place de la Concorde at the other. The Tour Eiffel is on the Seine side, along with the Musée d'Orsay, reachable across a footbridge in the center of the garden.

■ TIP→ Garden buffs will enjoy the small bookstore at the place de la Concorde entrance, open 10 to 7. Aside from volumes on gardening and plants (including some titles in English), it has gift items, knickknacks, and toys for the junior gardener.

7

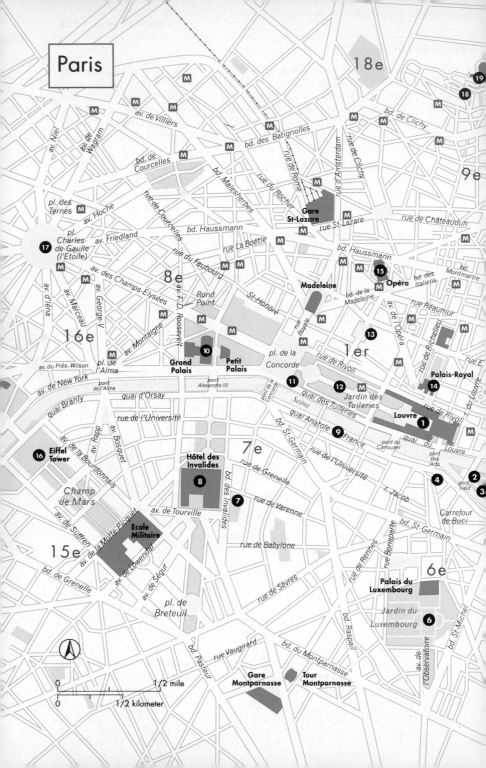

7

The Tuileries is one of the best places in Paris to take kids if they're itching to run around. There's a carrousel (€2.50), trampolines (€2) and, in summer, an amusement park. ⊠ *Bordered by Quai des Tuileries, pl. de la Concorde, and rue de Rivoli, Louvre/Tuileries* ☎ *01–40–20–90–43* ☜ *Free* ☉ *June, July, and Aug., daily 7 am–11 pm; Apr., May, and Sept., daily 7:30 am–9 pm; Oct.–Mar., daily 7:30–7:30* Ⓜ *Tuileries or Concorde.*

Fodor'sChoice
★

The Louvre. The most recognized symbol of Paris is the Tour Eiffel, but the ultimate traveler's prize is the Louvre. This is the world's greatest art museum—and the largest, with 675,000 square feet of works from almost every civilization on earth. The three most popular pieces here are, of course, the *Mona Lisa,* the *Venus de Milo,* and *Winged Victory.* Beyond these must-sees, your best bet is to focus on whatever interests you the most—and don't despair about getting lost, for you're bound to stumble on something memorable. Pick up an excellent color-coded map at the information desk. There are slick Nintendo 3DS multimedia guides at the entrance to each wing; for €5 you get four self-guided tours and details about 250 works of art, plus a function to help you find your bearings. There are 90-minute guided tours (€9) in English daily at 11 and 2. Thematic leaflets (including some for kids) and Louvre guided tours are available from the front desk.

Don't skip the coat checks on the ground floor of the Denon or Richelieu wings—much of the museum is hot and stuffy.

To save time, avoid the main entrance at the Pyramide and head for the entrance in the underground mall, Carrousel du Louvre, which has automatic ticket machines, or to the Porte de Lions entrance (closed Friday) on the southwestern corner. Ticket-holders can come and go through the Porte Richelieu on the rue de Rivoli side.

The shortest lines tend to be around 9:30 am and 1 pm. Crowds are also thinner on Wednesday and Friday nights, when the museum is open late. Remember that the Louvre is closed Tuesday. ⊠ *Palais du Louvre, Louvre/Tuileries* ☎ *01–40–20–53–17 for information* ⊕ *www.louvre. fr* ☜ *€12; €13 for Napoléon Hall exhibitions; €16 with all temporary exhibits and same-day entry to Musée Eugène Delacroix. Free 1st Sun. of month* ☉ *Mon., Thurs., and weekends 9–6, Wed. and Fri. 9 am–9:30 pm* Ⓜ *Palais-Royal–Musée du Louvre.*

Musée de l'Orangerie. The lines can be long to see Claude Monet's huge, meditative *Water Lilies (Nymphéas),* displayed in two curved galleries designed in 1914 by the master himself. But they are well worth the wait. These works are the highlight of the Orangerie Museum's small but excellent collection, which includes early-20th-century paintings by Renoir, Cézanne, and Matisse. Many hail from the private holdings of art dealer Paul Guillaume (1891–1934), including Guillaume's portrait by Modigliani entitled *Novo Pilota (New Pilot),* signaling Guillaume's status as an important presence in the arts world. Built in 1852 to shelter orange trees, the museum reopened in 2006 after a long renovation that unearthed a portion of the city's 16th-century wall (you can see remnants on the lower floor). ⊠ *Jardin des Tuileries at pl. de la Concorde, Louvre/ Tuileries* ☎ *01–44–77–80–07* ⊕ *www.musee-orangerie.fr* ☜ *€7.50, €14 joint ticket with Musée d'Orsay* ☉ *Wed.–Mon. 9–6* Ⓜ *Concorde.*

Fodor'sChoice **Notre-Dame.** Looming above place du Parvis on the Île de la Cité is the
★ iconic Cathédrale de Notre-Dame. Begun in 1163, completed in 1345,
badly damaged during the Revolution, and restored by architect Eugène
Viollet-le-Duc in the 19th century, Notre-Dame may not be France's
oldest or largest cathedral, but in beauty and architectural harmony it
has few peers—as you can see by studying the facade from the square
in front. The ornate doors seem like hands joined in prayer, the sculpted
kings above them form a noble procession, and the west (front) rose
window gleams with what seems like divine light. The most dramatic
approach to Notre-Dame is from the Rive Gauche, crossing at the Pont
au Double from Quai de Montebello, at the St-Michel métro or RER
stop. This bridge will take you to the large square, place du Parvis, in
front of the cathedral, which serves as *kilomètre zéro*—the spot from
which all distances to and from the city are officially measured. A polished brass circle set in the ground, about 20 yards from the cathedral's
main entrance, marks the exact spot.

A separate entrance, to the left of the front facade if you're facing it,
leads to the 387 stone steps of the south tower. Looking out from the
tower, you can see how Paris—like the trunk of a tree developing new
rings—has grown outward from the Île de la Cité. To the north is Montmartre; to the west is the Arc de Triomphe, at the top of the Champs-
Elysées; and to the south are the towers of St-Sulpice and the Panthéon.

■ **TIP→** Lines to climb the tower are shortest on weekday mornings.

The best time to visit is early in the morning, when the cathedral is at
its brightest and least crowded.

Down the stairs in front of the cathedral is the **Crypte Archéologique,**
an archaeological museum. It offers a fascinating subterranean view
of this busy area from the 1st century when Paris was a Roman city
called Lutetia (note the ruins of houses, baths and even a quay) through
medieval times when the former rue Neuve-Notre-Dame that passed
through here was packed with houses and shops. A renovation in late
2012 cleaned the remains and added 3-D video touch-screen panels that
bring the ruins to life. ✉ *Pl. du Parvis, Île de la Cité* ☎ *01–42–34–56–10*
⊕ *www.notredamedeparis.fr* ✉ *Cathedral free, towers €8.50, crypt €5,
treasury €3* ⊙ *Cathedral: weekdays 8–6:45, weekends 8–7:15. Towers:
Apr.–June and Sept., daily 10–6:30; July and Aug., weekdays 10–6:30,
weekends 10 am–11 pm; Oct.–Mar., daily 10–5:30; note towers close
early when overcrowded. Treasury weekdays 9:30–6, Sat. 9:30–6:30,
Sun. 1:30–6:30. Crypt Tues.–Sun. 10–6* Ⓜ *Cité.*

Pont Neuf *(New Bridge).* Crossing the Île de la Cité, just behind Square
du Vert-Galant, is the oldest bridge in Paris, confusingly called the New
Bridge—the name was given when it was completed in 1607, and it
stuck. It was the first bridge in the city to be built without houses lining
either side, allegedly because Henri IV wanted a clear view of Notre-
Dame from his windows at the Louvre. ✉ *Ile de la Cité* Ⓜ *Pont-Neuf.*

Fodor'sChoice **Sainte-Chapelle.** Built by the obsessively pious Louis IX (1226–70), this
★ Gothic jewel is home to the oldest stained-glass windows in Paris. The
chapel was constructed over three years, at phenomenal expense, to
house the king's collection of relics acquired from the impoverished

emperor of Constantinople. These included Christ's Crown of Thorns, fragments of the Cross, and drops of Christ's blood—though even in Louis's time these were considered of questionable authenticity. Some of the relics have survived and can be seen in the treasury of Notre-Dame, but most were lost during the Revolution.

■ TIP→ Sunset is the optimal time to see the rose window; however, to avoid waiting in killer lines, plan your visit for a weekday morning, the earlier the better.

Sights aside, the chapel makes a divine setting for classical concerts; check the schedule at ⊕ *www.infoconcert.com*. ✉ *4 bd. du Palais, Île de la Cité* ☎ *01–53–40–60–97* ⊕ *www.sainte-chapelle.monuments-nationaux.fr* 🎫 *€8.50; joint ticket with Conciergerie €12.50* ⊘ *Mar.– Oct., daily 9:30–6; Nov.–Feb., daily 9–5* Ⓜ *Cité.*

FROM THE EIFFEL TOWER TO THE ARC DE TRIOMPHE

The Eiffel Tower (or Tour Eiffel, to use the French) lords over southwest Paris, and from nearly wherever you are on this walk you can see its jutting needle. Water is the second highlight in this area: fountains playing beneath place du Trocadéro and boat tours along the Seine on a Bateau Mouche. Museums are the third; the area around Trocadéro is full of them. Style is the fourth, and not just because the buildings here are overwhelmingly elegant—but because this is also the center of haute couture, with the top names in fashion all congregated around Avenue Montaigne, only a brief walk from the Champs-Élysées, to the north.

Fodor'sChoice   **Arc de Triomphe.** Inspired by Rome's Arch of Titus, this colossal, 164-
★   foot triumphal arch was ordered by Napoléon—who liked to consider himself the heir to Roman emperors—to celebrate his military successes. Unfortunately, Napoléon's strategic and architectural visions were not entirely on the same plane, and the Arc de Triomphe proved something of an embarrassment. Although the emperor wanted the monument completed in time for an 1810 parade in honor of his new bride, Marie-Louise, it was still only a few feet high, and a dummy arch of painted canvas was strung up to save face. Empires come and go, but Napoléon's had been gone for more than 20 years before the Arc was finally finished in 1836. A small museum halfway up recounts its history.

■ TIP→ France's Unknown Soldier is buried beneath the arch, and a commemorative flame is rekindled every evening at 6:30. That's the most atmospheric time to visit, but, to beat the crowds, come early in the morning or buy your ticket online.

Be wary of the traffic circle that surrounds the arch. It's infamous for accidents—including one several years ago that involved the French transport minister. Use the underground passage from the northeast corner of the Avenue des Champs-Élysées. ✉ *Pl. Charles-de-Gaulle, Champs-Élysées* ☎ *01–55–37–73–77* ⊕ *arc-de-triomphe.monuments-nationaux.fr* 🎫 *€9.50* ⊘ *Apr.–Sept., daily 10 am–11 pm; Oct.–Mar., daily 10 am–10:30 pm* Ⓜ *Métro or RER: Étoile.*

Fodor'sChoice   **Eiffel Tower** (*Tour Eiffel*). The Eiffel Tower is to Paris what the Statue of
★   Liberty is to New York and what Big Ben is London: the ultimate civic emblem. French engineer Gustave Eiffel—already famous for building

viaducts and bridges—spent two years working to erect this monument for the World Exhibition of 1889.

Because its colossal bulk exudes a feeling of mighty permanence, you may have trouble believing that it nearly became 7,000 tons of scrap metal (the 1,063-foot *tour* contains 12,000 pieces of metal and 2,500,000 rivets) when its concession expired in 1909. Gradually, though, the Tour Eiffel became part of the Parisian landscape, entering the hearts and souls of Parisians and visitors alike. Today it is most breathtaking at night, when every girder is highlighted in a sparkling display originally conceived to celebrate the turn of the millennium. The tower does its electric shimmy for five minutes every hour on the hour until 1 am.

You can stride up the stairs as far as the third floor, but if you want to go to the top you'll have to take the elevator. (Be sure to take a close look at the fantastic ironwork.) Although the view of the flat sweep of Paris at 1,000 feet may not beat the one from the Tour Montparnasse skyscraper, the setting makes it considerably more romantic—especially if you come in the late evening, after the crowds have dispersed. ■TIP➜ Beat the crushing lines by reserving your ticket online. You can also book a guided tour. ⊠ *Quai Branly, Trocadéro/Tour Eiffel* ☎ *01–44–11–23–23* ⊕ *www.toureiffel.fr* ⌨ *By elevator: 1st and 2nd levels €8.50, top €14. By stairs: 1st and 2nd levels €5.* ☉ *June–late Aug., daily 9 am–12:45 am (11 pm for summit); late Aug.–June, daily 9:30 am–11 pm. Stairs close at 6 pm in winter* Ⓜ *Bir-Hakeim, Trocadéro, École Militaire; RER: Champ de Mars.*

RUE ST-HONORÉ

Fashions change, but the rue St-Honoré, just north of the Champs-Élysées and the Tuileries, has been unfailingly chic since the early 1700s. The streets of this walk include some of the oldest in Paris. The centerpiece of the area is the stately place Vendôme; on this ritzy square, famous jewelers sit side by side with famous banks—but then elegance and finance have never been an unusual combination.

Fodor's Choice
★

Palais-Royal. The quietest, most romantic Parisian garden is enclosed within the former home of Cardinal Richelieu (1585–1642). It's an ideal spot to while away an afternoon, cuddling with your sweetheart on a bench under the trees, soaking up the sunshine beside the fountain, or browsing the 400-year-old arcades that are now home to boutiques ranging from retro quirky (picture toy soldiers and music boxes) to modern chic (think Stella McCartney and Marc Jacobs). One of the city's oldest restaurants is here, the haute-cuisine Le Grand Véfour, where brass plaques recall regulars like Napoléon and Victor Hugo. ⊠ *Pl. du Palais-Royal, Louvre/Palais-Royal* Ⓜ *Palais-Royal.*

Place Vendôme. Jules-Hardouin Mansart, an architect of Versailles Palace, designed this perfectly proportioned octagonal plaza near the Tuileries in 1702; and, to maintain a uniform appearance, he gave the surrounding *hôtels particuliers* (private mansions) identical facades. It was originally called place des Conquêtes to extoll the military conquests of Louis XIV, whose statue on horseback graced the center until Revolutionaries destroyed it in 1792. Later, Napoléon ordered his likeness erected atop a 144-foot column modestly modeled after Rome's

Trajan Column. But that, too, was toppled in 1871 by painter Gustave Courbet and his band of radicals. The Third Republic raised a new column and sent Courbet the bill, though he died in exile before paying it. Chopin lived and died at No. 12, which is also where Napoléon III enjoyed trysts with his mistress; since 1902 it has been home to the high-end jeweler Chaumet. The Hotel Ritz at No. 15 and its famous Hemingway Bar closed in 2012 for a top-to-bottom renovation; reopening is set for summer 2014. ⊠ *Louvre/Tuileries* Ⓜ *Tuileries.*

GRANDS BOULEVARDS

The makeup of the neighborhoods along the Grand Boulevards changes steadily as you head east from the posh 8e arrondissement toward working-class east Paris. The *grands magasins* (department stores) centralize fashionable Paris shopping and stand on Boulevard Haussmann. The opulent Opéra Garnier, just past the grands magasins, is the architectural showpiece of the period.

Fodor's Choice
★
Opéra Garnier. Haunt of the Phantom of the Opera and the real-life inspiration for Edgar Degas's dancer paintings, the gorgeous Opéra Garnier is one of two homes of the National Opera of Paris. The building, the Palais Garnier, was begun in 1860 by then-unknown architect Charles Garnier, who finished his masterwork 15 long years later, way over budget. Festooned with (real) gold leaf, colored marble, paintings, and sculpture from the top artists of the day, the opera house was about as subtle as Versailles and sparked controversy in post-Revolutionary France. The sweeping marble staircase, in particular, drew criticism from a public skeptical of its extravagance. But Garnier, determined to make a landmark that would last forever, spared no expense. The magnificent grand foyer, restored in 2004, is one of the most exquisite salons in France.

The Opéra Garnier plays host to the Paris Ballet as well as a few operas each season (most are performed at the Opéra Bastille). If you're planning to see a performance, reserve two months in advance, when tickets go on sale (€5–€180), or try your luck at the last minute at the box office. ■ TIP➔ To learn about the building's history, and get a taste of aristocratic life during the Second Empire, take the entertaining guided tour in English. The ticket also allows entry to the auditorium. ⊠ *Pl. de l'Opéra, Opéra/Grands Boulevards* ☎ *08–92–89–90–90* ⊕ *www.operadeparis. fr* ☒ *€9, €12.50 for guided tour* ☉ *Daily 10–5, summer until 6; guided tours Wed. and weekends at 11:30 and 3:30* Ⓜ *Opéra.*

THE MARAIS AND THE BASTILLE

The Marais is one of the city's most historic and sought-after residential districts. Except for the architecturally whimsical Pompidou Center, the tone here is set by the gracious architecture of the 17th and 18th centuries. Many hôtels particuliers have been restored; many are now museums, including the noted Musée Picasso and Musée Carnavalet. There are hyper-trendy boutiques and cafés among the kosher shops in what used to be a predominantly Jewish neighborhood around rue des Rosiers. Also here is the gorgeous place des Vosges, a definite don't-miss.

FAMILY
Fodor's Choice
★
Centre Pompidou. Love it or hate it, the Pompidou is certainly the city's most unique-looking building. Most Parisians have warmed to the industrial, Lego-like exterior that caused a scandal when it opened in

1977. Named after French president Georges Pompidou (1911–74), it was designed by then-unknowns Renzo Piano and Richard Rogers. The architects' claim to fame was putting the building's guts on the outside and color-coding them: water pipes are green, air ducts are blue, electrics are yellow, and things like elevators and escalators are red. Art from the 20th century to the present day is what you can find inside.

■ TIP→ The Pompidou's permanent collection takes up a relatively small amount of the space when you consider this massive building's other features: temporary exhibition galleries, with a special wing for design and architecture; a highly regarded free reference library (there's often a queue of university students on rue Renard waiting to get in); and the basement, which includes two cinemas, a theater, a dance space, and a small, free exhibition space. ⊠ *Pl. Georges-Pompidou, Beaubourg/Les Halles* ☎ *01–44–78–12–33* ⊕ *www.centrepompidou.fr* ⊠ *€11; €13 during temporary exhibitions* ۞ *Wed.–Mon. 11–9, Thurs. 11–11 during temporary exhibitions; Atelier Brancusi Wed.–Mon. 2–6* Ⓜ *Rambuteau.*

Fodor's Choice
★ **Cimitère du Père-Lachaise.** Bring a red rose for "the Little Sparrow" Edith Piaf when you visit the cobblestone avenues and towering trees that make this 118-acre oasis of green perhaps the world's most famous cemetery. Named for Père François de la Chaise, Louis XIV's confessor, Père-Lachaise is more than just a who's who of celebrities. The Paris Commune's final battle took place here on May 28, 1871, when 147 rebels were lined up and shot against the Mur des Fédérés (Federalists' Wall) in the southeast corner.

Two of the biggest draws are Jim Morrison's grave (with its own guard to keep Doors fans under control) and the life-size bronze figure of French journalist Victor Noir, whose alleged fertility-enhancing power accounts for the patches rubbed smooth by hopeful hands. Other significant grave sites include those of 12th-century French philosopher Pierre Abélard and his lover Héloïse; French writers Colette, Honoré de Balzac, and Marcel Proust; American writers Richard Wright, Gertrude Stein, and Alice B. Toklas; Irish writer Oscar Wilde; the French playwright and actor Molière; and French singer Edith Piaf.

■ TIP→ Pinpoint grave sites on the website before you come, but buy a map anyway outside the entrances—you'll still get lost, but that's part of the fun. ⊠ *Entrances on rue des Rondeaux, Bd. de Ménilmontant, and rue de la Réunion, Père Lachaise* ☎ *01–55–25–82–10* ⊕ *www.pere-lachaise.com* ۞ *Daily 8–6, 5:30 in winter (opens 8:30 Sat. and 9 Sun.)* Ⓜ *Gambetta, Philippe-Auguste, Père-Lachaise.*

Fodor's Choice
★ **Musée Picasso.** To the chagrin of Picasso fans everywhere, this immensely popular museum closed in August 2009 for a top-to-bottom overhaul. Delays have pushed back the reopening until summer 2014. (About 200 works from the permanent collection have been on the road in the United States and elsewhere during the renovation.) The $70 million face-lift will thoroughly transform the Picasso, more than quadrupling the museum's size to 75,000 square feet with new galleries and a performance space. A new 4,800-square-foot building in the back garden, dedicated to temporary exhibitions and other programs, will open when the final stage of the renovations is completed.

7

■TIP→ The most recent projected reopening date is mid 2014 but check the website for updates or call before you go in case of further delays. ⊠ *5 rue de Thorigny, Marais* ☎ *01–42–71–25–21* ⊕ *www.musee-picasso.fr* ☑ *Admission to be determined when opened* ⊙ *No information until opening* Ⓜ *St-Sébastien.*

FAMILY

Fodor's Choice

★

Place des Vosges. The oldest square in Paris and—dare we say it?—the most beautiful, the place des Vosges is one of Europe's oldest stabs at urban planning. The precise proportions offer a placid symmetry, but things weren't always so calm here. Four centuries ago this was the site of the Palais des Tournelles, home to King Henry II and Queen Catherine de Medici. The couple staged regular jousting tournaments, and during one of them, in 1559, Henry was fatally lanced in the eye. Catherine fled for the Louvre, abandoning her palace and ordering it destroyed. In 1612 it became the place Royal on the occasion of Louis XIII's engagement to Anne of Austria. Napoléon renamed it place des Vosges to honor the northeast region of Vosges, the first in the country to pony up taxes to the Revolutionary government. ⊠ *Off rue des Francs Bourgeois, near rue de Turenne, Marais* ☑ *Free* ⊙ *Year-round* Ⓜ *Bastille, St-Paul.*

ILE ST-LOUIS AND THE LATIN QUARTER

Set behind the Île de la Cité is one of the most romantic spots in Paris, tiny Île St-Louis. Of the two islands in the Seine—the Île de la Cité is just to the west—the St-Louis best retains the romance and loveliness of *le Paris traditionnel.* South of the Île St-Louis on the Left Bank of the Seine is the bohemian Quartier Latin (Latin Quarter), with its warren of steep, sloping streets, populated largely by Sorbonne students and academics.

NEED A
BREAK?

Berthillon. The king of Parisian ice cream is served at cafés all over town, but it's worth making a pilgrimage to the mothership to understand what all the fuss is about. The family-owned Berthillon shop features more than 30 flavors that change with the seasons, from mouth-puckering *cassis* (black currant) in summer to nutty *marron glacé* (candied chestnut) in winter. Expect to wait in a lengthy line for a tiny scoop. Note, too, the quirky hours. Though open most months from Wednesday through Sunday 10–8, it closes during peak season from mid-July to early September—a fact *Le Parisien* newspaper once denounced with a single word: *sacrilège!* ⊠ *31 rue St-Louis-en-l'Île, Île St-Louis* ☎ *01-43-54-31-61* Ⓜ *Pont-Marie.*

Fodor's Choice

★

Musée National du Moyen-Age (*National Museum of the Middle Ages, also called the Musée Cluny*). Built on the ruins of Roman baths, the Hôtel de Cluny has been a museum since medievalist Alexandre Du Sommerard established his collection here in 1844. The ornate 15th-century mansion was created for the abbot of Cluny, leader of the mightiest monastery in France. Symbols of the abbot's power surround the building, from the crenellated walls that proclaimed his independence from the king, to the carved Burgundian grapes twining up the entrance that symbolize his valuable vineyards. The highlight of the museum's collection is the world-famous *Dame à la Licorne* (*Lady and the Unicorn*) tapestry series, woven in the 16th century, probably in Belgium. The vermillion tapestries (Room No. 13) are an allegorical representation of the five senses. In each, a unicorn and a lion surround an elegant young woman against an elaborate *millefleur* (literally, "1,000 flowers") background. The *frigidarium* (Room No. 9) is a stunning reminder of the city's cold-water Roman baths; the soaring space, painstakingly renovated in 2009, houses temporary exhibits. Also notable is the pocket-size chapel (Room No. 20) with its elaborate Gothic ceiling. Outside, in the place Paul Painlevé, is a charming medieval-style garden with flora depicted in the unicorn tapestries. ■TIP→ The free audioguide in English is highly recommended. ⊠ *6 pl. Paul-Painlevé, Latin Quarter* ☎ *01–53–73–78–00* ⊕ *www.musee-moyenage.fr* ⊠ *€8.50 (includes English audio guide). Free 1st Sun. of month* ☉ *Wed.–Mon. 9:15–5:45* Ⓜ *Cluny–La Sorbonne.*

FROM ORSAY TO ST-GERMAIN-DES-PRÉS

This area covers the Left Bank, from the Musée d'Orsay in the stately 7e arrondissement to the chic and colorful area around St-Germain-des-Prés in the 6e. To the east, away from the splendor of the 7e, the Boulevard St-Michel slices the Left Bank in two: on one side, the Latin Quarter; on the other, the Faubourg St-Germain, named for St-Germain-des-Prés, the oldest church in Paris. In the southern part of this district is the city's most colorful park, the Jardin du Luxembourg.

Fodor'sChoice
★ **Hôtel des Invalides.** The Baroque complex known as Les Invalides (pronounced *lehz-ahn-vah-leed*) is the eternal home of Napoléon Bonaparte (1769–1821) or, more precisely, the little dictator's remains, which lie entombed under the towering golden dome.

If you see only a single sight, make it the Église du Dome (one of Les Invalides' two churches) at the back of the complex. Napoléon's tomb was moved here in 1840 from the island of Saint Helena, where he died in forced exile. The emperor's body is protected by a series of no fewer than six coffins—one set inside the next, sort of like a Russian nesting doll—which is then encased in a sarcophagus of red quartzite. The bombastic tribute is ringed by statues symbolizing Napoléon's campaigns of conquest. ⊠ *Pl. des Invalides, Tour Eiffel* ☎ *01–44–42–38–77* ⊕ *www. invalides.org* ⊠ *€9.50* ☉ *Église du Dôme and museums Apr.–Oct., daily 10–6; Nov.–Mar., daily 10–5. Closed 1st Mon. of every month Oct–June* Ⓜ *La Tour-Maubourg/Invalides.*

FAMILY
Fodor'sChoice
★ **Jardin du Luxembourg.** The Luxembourg Gardens has all that is charming, unique, and befuddling about Parisian parks: cookie-cutter trees, ironed-and-pressed walkways, sculpted flower beds, and immaculate emerald lawns meant for admiring, not for lounging. The tree- and bench-lined paths are, however, a marvelous reprieve from the bustle of the two neighborhoods it borders: the Quartier Latin and St-Germain-des-Prés. Beautifully austere during the winter months, the garden grows intoxicating as spring brings blooming beds of daffodils, tulips, and hyacinths, and the circular pools teem with boats nudged along by children. The park's northern boundary is dominated by the Palais du Luxembourg and the Sénat (Senate), which is one of two chambers that make up the Parliament.

7

If you're looking for a familiar face, one of the original (miniature) casts of the Statue of Liberty was installed in the gardens in 1906. ⊠ *Bordered by Bd. St-Michel and rues de Vaugirard, de Medicis, Guynemer, and Auguste-Comte, St-Germain-des-Prés* ⊕ *guignolduluxembourg. monsite-orange.fr for Les Marionettes du Théâtre du Luxembourg* ⊠ *Free* ☉ *Daily 7:30–dusk (hrs vary depending on season)* Ⓜ *Odéon; RER: B Luxembourg.*

Fodor's Choice
★ **Musée d'Orsay.** Opened in 1986, this gorgeously renovated Belle Époque train station displays a world-famous collection of Impressionist and Postimpressionist paintings on three floors. To visit the exhibits in a roughly chronologic manner, start on the first floor, take the escalators to the top, and end on the second. If you came to see the biggest names here, head straight for the top floor and work your way down. English audio guides and free color-coded museum maps (both available just past the ticket booths) will help you plot your route. Note, though, that renovations will be ongoing until 2015, so expect some gallery closings.

■ TIP→ Lines here are among the worst in Paris. Book ahead online or buy a Museum Pass; then go directly to entrance C. Otherwise, go early. Thursday evening the museum is open until 9:45 pm and less crowded.

The d'Orsay is closed Monday, unlike the Pompidou and the Louvre, which are closed Tuesday. ⊠ *1 rue de la Légion d'Honneur, St-Germain-des-Prés* ☎ *01–40–49–48–14* ⊕ *www.musee-orsay.fr* ⊠ *€12 (€9 without special exhibit); €9.50 (€6.50 without special exhibit) after 4:30 (Thurs. after 6)* ☉ *Tues.–Sun. 9:30–6; Thurs. 9:30 am–9:45 pm* Ⓜ *Solférino; RER: Musée d'Orsay.*

Musée Rodin. Auguste Rodin (1840–1917) briefly made his home and studio in the Hôtel Biron, a grand 18th-century mansion that now houses a museum dedicated to his work. He died rich and famous, but many of the sculptures that earned him a place in art history were originally greeted with contempt by the general public, which was unprepared for his powerful brand of sexuality and raw physicality. During a much-needed, multiyear renovation that has closed parts of the Hôtel Biron (it's set to finish in late 2014), the museum is showcasing a pared-down, "greatest hits" selection of Rodin's works. Most of his best-known sculptures are in the gardens.

An English audioguide (€6) is available for the permanent collection and for temporary exhibitions. Skip the line by buying a ticket online. ⊠ *79 rue de Varenne, Trocadéro/Tour Eiffel* ☎ *01–44–18–61–10* ⊕ *www. musee-rodin.fr* ⊠ *€9, €1 gardens only; free 1st Sun. of month* ☉ *Tues., Thurs.–Sun. 10–5:45, Wed. 10–8:45* Ⓜ *Varenne.*

MONTMARTRE

On a dramatic rise above the city is Montmartre, site of the Sacré-Coeur Basilica and home to a once-thriving artist community. This was the quartier that Toulouse-Lautrec and Renoir immortalized with a flash of their brush and a tube of their paint. Although the great painters are long departed, and the fabled nightlife of Old Montmartre has fizzled down to some glitzy nightclubs and skin shows, Montmartre still exudes history and Gallic charm.

Moulin Rouge. When this world-famous cabaret opened in 1889, aristo-crats, professionals, and the working classes all flocked in to ogle the scandalous performers (the cancan was considerably more kinky in Toulouse-Lautrec's day, when girls kicked off their knickers). There's not much to see from the outside except for tourist buses and sex shops, but this square, called place Blanche, takes its name from the chalky haze once churned up by carts carrying plaster of Paris down from the quarries. Souvenir seekers should check out the Moulin Rouge gift shop (around the corner at 11 rue Lepic), which sells better-quality official merchandise, from jewelry to sculpture, by reputable French makers. ✉ *82 bd. de Clichy, Montmartre* ☎ *01–53–09–82–82* ⊕ *www. moulinrouge.fr* Ⓜ *Blanche.*

Fodor'sChoice
★
Sacré-Coeur. It's hard to not feel as though you're climbing up to heaven when you visit Sacred Heart Basilica, the white castle in the sky, perched atop Montmartre. The French government commissioned it in 1873 to symbolize the return of self-confidence after the devastating years of the Commune and Franco-Prussian War; and architect Paul Abadie employed elements from Romanesque and Byzantine styles when design-ing it—a mélange many critics dismissed as gaudy. Construction lasted until World War I, and the church was finally consecrated in 1919.

■ TIP➔ **The best time to visit Sacré-Coeur is early morning or early evening, and preferably not on a Sunday, when the crowds are thick. If you're coming to worship, there are daily masses.**

To avoid the steps, take the funicular, which costs one métro ticket each way. ✉ *Pl. du Parvis-du-Sacré-Coeur, Montmartre* ☎ *01–53–41–89–00* ⊕ *www.sacre-coeur-montmartre.com* ✉ *Basilica free, dome €6, crypt €3, combined ticket €8* ⊙ *Basilica daily 6 am–11 pm; dome and crypt Oct.–Mar., daily 9–6; Apr.–Sept., daily 9–7* Ⓜ *Anvers, plus funicular; Jules Joffrin plus Montmartrobus.*

WHERE TO EAT

A new wave of culinary confidence is running through one of the world's great food cities and spilling over both banks of the Seine. Whether cooking up *Grand-mère's* roast chicken and *riz au lait* or plac-ing a whimsical hat of cotton candy atop wild-strawberry-and-rose ice cream, Paris chefs are breaking free from the tyranny of tradition and following their passions.

But self-expression is not the only driving force behind the changes. A traditional high-end restaurant can be prohibitively expensive to oper-ate. As a result, more casual bistros and cafés have become attractive businesses for even top chefs, making the cooking of geniuses such as Joël Robuchon and Pierre Gagnaire more accessible to all (even if these star chefs rarely cook in their lower-priced restaurants).

1ER ARRONDISSEMENT (LOUVRE/LES HALLES/OPÉRA)

$$$
BISTRO
Fodor'sChoice
★
✕**L'Ardoise.** A minuscule storefront, decorated with enlargements of old sepia postcards of Paris, L'Ardoise is a model of the kind of con-temporary bistros making waves in Paris. Chef Pierre Jay's first-rate three-course dinner menu for €36 tempts with such original dishes as

mushroom-and-foie-gras ravioli with smoked duck; farmer's pork with porcini mushrooms; and red mullet with creole sauce (you can also order à la carte, but it's less of a bargain). Just as enticing are the desserts, such as a superb *feuillantine au citron*—caramelized pastry leaves filled with lemon cream and lemon slices—and a boozy baba au rhum. With friendly waiters and a small but well-chosen wine list, L'Ardoise would be perfect if it weren't so popular (meaning noisy and crowded). [$] *Average main: €27* ⊠ *28 rue du Mont Thabor, 1er, Louvre/Tuileries* ☎ *01–42–96–28–18* ⊕ *www.lardoise-paris.com* ⚠ *Reservations essential* ⊙ *Closed Sun. No lunch* [M] *Concorde.*

$$
MODERN FRENCH
Fodor's Choice
★

✕ **La Régalade St. Honoré.** When Bruno Doucet bought the original La Régalade from bistro-wizard Yves Camdeborde, some feared the end of an era. How wrong they were. While Doucet kept some of what made the old dining room so popular (country terrine, wine values, convivial atmosphere), he had a few tricks under his toque, creating a brilliantly successful haute-cuisine-meets-comfort-food destination with dishes like earthy morel mushrooms in a frothy cream for a starter, followed by the chef's signature succulent caramelized pork belly over tender Puy lentils, and a perfectly cooked fillet of cod, crispy on the outside and buttery within, served in a rich shrimp bouillon. For dessert, don't skip the updated take on *grand-mère*'s creamy rice pudding or the house Grand Marnier soufflé. With an excellent price-to-value ratio (€35 prix-fixe menu at lunch and dinner), this chic bistro and its elder sister in the 14th have evolved into staples for Paris gastronomes. [$] *Average main: €24* ⊠ *123 rue Saint-Honoré, 1er, Faubourg St-Honoré* ☎ *01–42–21–92–40* ⚠ *Reservations essential* ⊙ *Closed weekends, Aug., and 1 wk at Christmas* [M] *Louvre-Rivoli.*

$$$$
MODERN FRENCH

✕ **Le Grand Véfour.** Victor Hugo could stride in and still recognize this restaurant, which was in his day, as now, a contender for the title of most beautiful restaurant in Paris. Originally built in 1784, it has welcomed everyone from Napoléon to Colette to Jean Cocteau under its mirrored ceiling, and amid the early-19th-century glass paintings of goddesses and muses that create an air of restrained seduction. The rich and fashionable gather here to enjoy chef Guy Martin's unique blend of sophistication and rusticity, as seen in dishes such as frogs' legs with sorrel sauce, and oxtail *parmentier* (a kind of shepherd's pie) with truffles. There's an outstanding cheese trolley, and for dessert try the house specialty, *palet aux noisettes* (meringue cake with chocolate mousse, hazelnuts, and salted caramel ice cream). Prices are as extravagant as the decor, but there is a €98 lunch menu. [$] *Average main: €120* ⊠ *17 rue de Beaujolais, 1er, Louvre/Tuileries* ☎ *01–42–96–56–27* ⊕ *www. grand-vefour.com* ⚠ *Reservations essential* ⊙ *Closed weekends, Aug., and Christmas holidays. No dinner Fri.* [M] *Palais-Royal.*

2E ARRONDISSEMENT (OPÉRA/GRANDS BOULEVARDS/LES HALLES)

$$
MODERN FRENCH
FAMILY

✕ **Drouant.** Best known for the literary prizes awarded here since 1914, Drouant has shed its dusty image to become a forward-thinking restaurant. The man behind the transformation is Alsatian chef Antoine Westermann, who runs the hit bistro Mon Vieil Ami on Île St-Louis. At Drouant the menu is more playful, revisiting the French hors d'oeuvres tradition with starters that come as a series of four plates. Diners can pick from themes such as French classics (like a deconstructed leek salad) or convincing mini-takes on Thai and Moroccan dishes. Main courses similarly encourage grazing, with accompaniments in little cast-iron pots and white porcelain dishes. Even desserts take the form of several tasting plates. Pace yourself, since portions are generous and the cost of a meal quickly adds up. This is the place to bring adventurous young eaters, thanks to the €15 children's menu, and there's a special post-theater prix fixe (€42 for two courses, €54 for three) from 10:30 pm to midnight. The revamped dining room is bright and cheery, though the designer has gone slightly overboard with the custard-yellow paint and fabrics. [$] *Average main: €18* ✉ *16–18 pl. Gaillon, 2e, Opéra/Les Halles* ☎ *01–42–65–15–16* 🌐 *www.drouant.com* 🕓 *Daily* [M] *Pyramides.*

3E ARRONDISSEMENT (BEAUBOURG/ MARAIS/RÉPUBLIQUE)

$ BISTRO

🍴 **Café des Musées.** Warm and authentic, this bustling little bistro offers a convivial slice of Parisian life—and excellent value. Here traditional French bistro fare is adapted to a modern audience, and the best choices are the old tried-and-trues: hand-cut tartare de boeuf; rare entrecôte served with a side of golden-crisp frites and homemade Béarnaise; and the classic parmentier with pheasant instead of the usual ground beef. Portions are ample, but save room for dessert: old-style favorites like *diplomate aux cherises,* a rum-soaked, cherry-laden sponge cake, or the terrine de chocolate with crème Anglaise are not to be missed. Fixed-price menus are a bargain at €14 for lunch. [$] *Average main: €17* ✉ *49 rue de Turenne, 3e, Marais* ☎ *01–42–72–96–17* ✍ *Reservations essential* 🕓 *Closed Aug. and 1 wk in Jan.* [M] *St-Paul.*

7

4E ARRONDISSEMENT (MARIS/ILE ST-LOUIS)

$ MIDDLE EASTERN FAMILY

🍴 **L'As du Fallafel.** Look no further than the fantastic falafel stands on thc pedestrian rue de Rosiers for some of the cheapest and tastiest meals in Paris. L'As (the Ace) is widely considered the best of the bunch, which accounts for the lunchtime line that extends down the street, despite the recent expansion of the dining room from 70 to 115 seats. A falafel sandwich costs €5 to go, €7.50 in the dining room, and comes heaped with grilled eggplant, cabbage, hummus, tahini, and hot sauce. The *shawarma* (grilled, skewered meat) sandwich, made with chicken or lamb, is also one of the finest in town. Though takeout is popular, it can be more fun (and not as messy) to eat off a plastic plate in one of the two frenzied dining rooms. Fresh lemonade is the falafel's best match. [$] *Average main: €10* ✉ *34 rue des Rosiers, 4e, Marais* ☎ *01–48–87–63–60* 🕓 *Closed Sat. No dinner Fri.* [M] *St-Paul.*

$$$ MODERN FRENCH

🍴 **Le Georges.** One of those rooftop show-stopping venues so popular in Paris, Le Georges preens atop the Centre Georges Pompidou, accessed by its own entrance to the left of the main doors. The staff is as streamlined and angular as the furniture, and about as responsive. Come snappily dressed or you may be relegated to something resembling a dentist's waiting room. Part of the Costes brothers' empire, the establishment trots out fashionable dishes such as sesame-crusted tuna and coriander-spiced beef filet flambéed with cognac. It's all considerably less dazzling than the view, except for the suitably decadent desserts (indulge in the Cracker's cheesecake with yogurt sorbet). [$] *Average main: €28* ✉ *Centre Pompidou, 6th fl., 19 rue Beaubourg, 4e, Les Halles* ☎ *01–44–78–47–99* ✍ *Reservations essential* ⏲ *Closed Tues.* [M] *Rambuteau.*

5E ARRONDISSEMENT (LATIN QUARTER/ST-GERMAIN)

$$ MODERN FRENCH 🍴 **Le Pré Verre.** Chef Philippe Delacourcelle knows his cassia bark from his cinnamon thanks to a long stint in Asia. He opened this lively bistro with its purple-gray walls and photos of jazz musicians to showcase his culinary style, rejuvenating archetypal French dishes with Asian and Mediterranean spices. So popular has it proved, especially with Japanese visitors, that the restaurant opened a branch in Tokyo in late 2007. His bargain prix-fixe menus (€13.90 at lunch for a main dish, glass of wine, and coffee; €30.90 for three courses at dinner) change constantly, but his trademark spiced suckling pig with crisp cabbage is always a winner, as is his rhubarb compote with gingered white-chocolate mousse. Ask for advice in selecting wine from a list that highlights small producers. [$] *Average main: €18* ✉ *8 rue Thénard, 5e, Latin Quarter* ☎ *01–43–54–59–47* 🌐 *www.lepreverre.com* ✍ *Reservations essential* ⏲ *Closed Sun. and Mon.* [M] *Maubert-Mutualité.*

$$ WINE BAR 🍴 **Les Papilles.** Part wineshop and épicerie, part restaurant, Les Papilles has a winning formula—pick any bottle off the well-stocked shelf and pay a €7 corkage fee to drink it with your meal; or savor one of several superb wines by the glass at your table or around the classic zinc bar. The superb no-choice menu—made with top-notch, seasonal ingredients—usually begins with a luscious *velouté,* a velvety soup served from a large tureen, and proceeds with a hearty-yet-tender meat dish alongside perfectly cooked vegetables—well worth spending a little extra time for lunch or dinner. [$] *Average main: €18* ✉ *30 rue Gay-Lussac, 5e, Latin Quarter* ☎ *01–43–25–20–79* 🌐 *www.lespapillesparis.fr* ✍ *Reservations essential* ⏲ *Closed Sun., Mon., last wk of July and 2 wks in Aug.* [M] *Cluny–La Sorbonne.*

6E ARRONDISSEMENT (ST-GERMAIN/LATIN QUARTER)

$$$$ MODERN FRENCH 🍴 **Hélène Darroze.** The most celebrated female chef in Paris is now cooking at the Connaught in London, but her St-Germain dining room is an exclusive setting for her sophisticated take on southwestern French food. Darroze's intriguingly modern touch comes through in such dishes as a sublime duck foie-gras confit served with an exotic-fruit chutney, or a blowout of roast wild duck stuffed with foie gras and truffles. If the food, at its best, lives up to the very high prices, the service sometimes struggles to reach the same level. For a more affordable taste, try the relatively casual Salon d'Hélène downstairs, which serves a reasonable €35 seven-course tapas lunch that includes a glass of wine. [$] *Average main: €85* ✉ *4 rue d'Assas, 6e, St-Germain-des-Prés* ☎ *01–42–22–00–11* 🌐 *www.helenedarroze.com* ✍ *Reservations essential* ⏲ *Closed Sun. and Mon.* [M] *Sèvres-Babylone.*

$$ BISTRO 🍴 **Le Comptoir du Relais Saint-Germain.** Run by legendary bistro chef Yves Camdeborde, this tiny art-deco hotel restaurant is booked up well in advance for the single dinner sitting that comprises a five-course, €65 set menu of haute-cuisine food. On weekends from noon to 10 pm and before 6 pm during the week a brasserie menu is served and reservations

are not accepted, resulting in long lines and brisk, sometimes shockingly rude, service. Start with charcuterie or pâté, then choose from open-faced sandwiches like a smoked-salmon-and-comté cheese croque-monsieur, gourmet salads, and a variety of hot dishes such as braised beef cheek, roast tuna, and Camdeborde's famed deboned and breaded pig's trotter. If you don't mind bus fumes, sidewalk tables make for prime people-watching in summer. Le Comptoir also runs Avant Comptoir next door; a miniscule stand-up zinc bar with hanging hams and sausages, where you can score a superb plate of charcuterie, a couple warm dishes, and an inky glass of Morgon. Quality crêpes and sandwiches are still served from the window out front. [$] *Average main: €22* ✉ *9 carrefour de l'Odéon, 6e, St-Germain-des-Prés* ☎ *01–44–27–07–50* [M] *Odéon.*

7E ARRONDISSEMENT (TOUR EIFFEL/ TROCADÉRO/INVALIDES)

$$$$ FRENCH FUSION

🍴 **Il Vino.** It might seem audacious to present hungry diners with nothing more than a wine list, but the gamble is paying off for Enrico Bernardo at his wine-centric restaurant with a branch in Courchevel, in the French Alps. This charismatic Italian left the George V to oversee a dining room where food plays second fiddle (in status, not quality). The hip decor—plum-color banquettes, body-hugging white chairs, a few high tables—attracts a mostly young clientele that's happy to play the game by ordering one of the blind, multicourse tasting menus. The €98 menu, with four dishes and four wines, is a good compromise that might bring you a white Mâcon with saffron risotto, crisp Malvasia with crabmeat and black radish, a full-bodied red from Puglia with Provençal-style lamb, sherrylike *vin jaune* d'Arbois with aged Comté cheese, and sweet Jurançon with berry crumble. You can also order individual wine-food combinations à la carte or pick a bottle straight from the cellar and ask for a meal to match. [$] *Average main: €40* ✉ *13 bd. de la Tour-Maubourg, 7e, Invalides* ☎ *01–44–11–72–00* 🌐 *www.ilvinobyenricobernardo.com* 🕓 *Closed Sun.* [M] *Invalides.*

$$$$ MODERN FRENCH

🍴 **L'Atelier de Joël Robuchon.** Worldwide phenomenon Joël Robuchon retired from the restaurant business for several years before opening this red-and-black-lacquer space with a bento-box-meets-tapas aesthetic. High seats surround two U-shape bars, and this novel plan encourages neighbors to share recommendations and opinions. Robuchon's devoted kitchen staff whip up small plates for grazing (€19–€75) as well as full portions, which can turn out to be the better bargain. Highlights from the oft-changing menu have included an intense tomato jelly topped with avocado puree and the thin-crusted mackerel tart, although his inauthentic (but who's complaining?) take on carbonara with cream and Alsatian bacon, and the *merlan* Colbert (fried herb butter) remain signature dishes. Reservations are taken for the first sittings only at lunch and dinner. [$] *Average main: €36* ✉ *5 rue Montalembert, 7e, St-Germain-des-Prés* ☎ *01–42–22–56–56* 🌐 *joel-robuchon.net* [M] *Rue du Bac.*

$$$ MODERN FRENCH

🍴 **Le Violon d'Ingres.** Following in the footsteps of Joël Robuchon and Alain Senderens, Christian Constant gave up the Michelin star chase in favor of relatively accessible prices and a packed dining room (book at least a week ahead). And with Jérémie Tourdjman in charge of the kitchen here, Constant can dash among his four restaurants on this street, making sure the hordes are happy. Why wouldn't they be? The food is sophisticated and the atmosphere is lively; you can even find signature dishes like the almond-crusted sea bass with rémoulade sauce (a buttery caper sauce), alongside game and scallops (in season), and comforting desserts like *pots de crème* and chocolate tart. The food is still heavy on the butter, but with wines starting at around €25 (and a €48 lunch menu on weekdays) this is a wonderful place for a classic yet informal French meal. [$] *Average main: €34* ✉ *135 rue St-Dominique, 7e, Around the Eiffel Tower* ☎ *01–45–55–15–05* 🌐 *www.leviolondingres.com* ✍ *Reservations essential* [M] *École Militaire.*

8E ARRONDISSEMENT (CHAMPS-ÉLYSÉES)

$$$ BISTRO

🍴 **Chez Savy.** Just off the glitzy Avenue Montaigne, Chez Savy occupies its own circa-1930s dimension, oblivious to the area's fashionization. The art-deco cream-and-burgundy interior is blissfully intact (avoid the back room unless you're in a large group), and the waiters show not a trace of attitude. Fill up on rib-sticking specialties from the Aveyron region of central France—lentil salad with bacon, foie gras (prepared on the premises), perfectly charred lamb with feather-light shoestring frites, and pedigreed Charolais beef. Order a celebratory bottle of Mercurey with your meal and feel smug that you've found this place. À la carte prices are high, but there is a set menu for €31.60. [$] *Average main: €29* ✉ *23 rue Bayard, 8e, Champs-Élysées* ☎ *01–47–23–46–98* 🕒 *Closed weekends and Aug.* [M] *Franklin-D.-Roosevelt.*

$$$$ MODERN FRENCH

🍴 **Taillevent.** Perhaps the most traditional—for many diners this is only high praise—of all Paris luxury restaurants, this grande dame basks in renewed freshness under brilliant chef Alain Solivérès, who draws inspiration from the Basque country, Bordeaux, and Languedoc for his daily-changing menu. Traditional dishes such as scallops *meunière* (with butter and lemon) are matched with contemporary choices like a splendid spelt risotto with truffles and frogs' legs or panfried duck liver with caramelized fruits and vegetables. One of the 19th-century paneled salons has been turned into a winter garden, and contemporary paintings adorn the walls. The service is flawless, and the exemplary wine list is well priced. All in all, a meal here comes as close to the classic haute-cuisine experience as you can find in Paris. There's an €82 lunch menu and special wine "degustation" evenings, pairing food with exceptional wines from their legendary cave for €180. [$] *Average main: €110* ✉ *15 rue Lamennais, 8e, Champs-Élysées* ☎ *01–44–95–15–01* 🌐 *www.taillevent.com* ✍ *Reservations essential* 👔 *Jacket and tie* 🕒 *Closed weekends and Aug.* [M] *Charles-de-Gaulle–Étoile.*

11E ARRONDISSEMENT (BASTILLE/RÉPUBLIQUE)

$$ BISTRO Fodor's Choice ★

🍴 **Le Bistrot Paul Bert.** Faded 1930s decor: check. Boisterous crowd: check. Thick steak with real frites: check. Good value: check. The Paul Bert delivers everything you could want from a traditional Paris bistro, so it's no wonder its two dining rooms fill every night with a cosmopolitan crowd. Some are from the neighborhood, others have done their bistro research, but they've all come for the balance of ingredients that makes for a feel-good experience every time. The impressively stocked wine cellar helps, as does the cheese cart, the laid-back yet efficient staff, and hearty dishes such as monkfish with white beans and duck with pears. The reasonable prix fixe is three courses for €36, or you can order à la carte. If you're looking for an inexpensive wine, choose from the chalkboard rather than the wine list. [$] *Average main: €22* ✉ *18 rue Paul Bert, 11e, Bastille/Nation* ☎ *01–43–72–24–01* ✍ *Reservations essential* 🕑 *Closed Sun., Mon., and Aug.* [M] *Rue des Boulets.*

CAFÉS AND SALONS DE THÉ

Along with air, water, and wine (Parisians eat fewer and fewer three-course meals), the café remains one of the basic necessities of life in Paris; following is a small selection of cafés and *salons de thé* (tearooms) to whet your appetite.

Jacques Genin. Pared down to the essentials, Genin offers the essence of great chocolate: not too sweet, with handpicked seasonal ingredients for the velvety ganaches. ✉ *133 rue de Turenne, 3e, Marais* ☎ *01–45–77–29–01* [M] *Oberkampf.*

Ladurée. Founded in 1862, Ladurée oozes period atmosphere—even at the new, large Champs-Élysées branch—but nothing beats the original tearoom on rue Royale, with its pint-size tables and frescoed ceiling. Ladurée claims a familial link to the invention of the macaron, and appropriately there's a fabulous selection of these cookies: classics like pistachio, salted caramel, and coffee, and, seasonally, violet–black currant, chestnut, and lime-basil. ✉ *16 rue Royale, 8e, Louvre/Tuileries* ☎ *01–42–60–21–79* [M] *Madeleine* ✉ *75 av. des Champs-Élysées, 8e, Champs-Élysées* ☎ *01–40–75–08–75* [M] *George V* ✉ *21 rue Bonaparte, 6e, Latin Quarter* ☎ *01–44–07–64–87* [M] *Odéon.*

les éditeurs. A trendy café favored by the Parisian publishing set, les éditeurs is a perfect place to sip a kir (white wine with black currant syrup) from a perch on the skinny sidewalk or at an inside table shadowed by book-lined walls. The menu offers a modern twist on French classics. ✉ *4 carrefour de l'Odéon, St-Germain-des-Prés* ☎ *01–43–26–67–76* 🌐 *www.lesediteurs.fr.* [M] *Odéon.*

Mariage Frères. Mariage Frères, with its colonial *charme* and wooden counters, has 100-plus years of tea purveying behind it. Choose from more than 450 blends from 32 countries, not to mention teapots, teacups, books, and tea-flavor biscuits and candies. Both tearooms serve high tea and a light lunch, although the St. Germain location is considerably less frenzied. ✉ *30 rue du Bourg-Tibourg, 4e, Marais* ☎ *01–42–72–28–11* [M] *Hôtel de Ville* ✉ *13 rue des Grands-Augustins, 6e, St-Germain-des-Prés* ☎ *01–40–51–82–50* [M] *Mabillon, St-Michel.*

WHERE TO STAY

Winding staircases, flower-filled window boxes, concierges who seem to have stepped out of a 19th-century novel—all of these can still be found in Paris hotels, and despite the scales' being tipped in favor of the well-heeled, overall there's good news for travelers of all budgets. Increased competition means that the bar for service and amenities has been raised everywhere. Now it's not uncommon for mid-range hotels to have a no-smoking floor, for inexpensive hotels to offer air-conditioning and buffet breakfast service, and even for budget places to have wireless Internet or an Internet terminal in their little lobbies. So, whatever price you're looking for, compared to most other cities Paris is a paradise for the weary traveler tired of dreary, out-of-date, or cookie-cutter rooms.

1ER ARRONDISSEMENT (LOUVRE/LES HALLES)

$ HOTEL **Hôtel Henri IV.** This 17th-century building, which once housed King Henri IV's printing presses on the Île de la Cité, offers few comforts or amenities, but you'll be hard-pressed to find a more central hotel for this price. **Pros:** very quiet; top rooms have balconies; basic breakfast included. **Cons:** steep stairs in poor condition and no elevator; few services or amenities; reservations by phone only. [$] *Rooms from: €78* ✉ *25 pl. Dauphine, 1er* ☎ *01–43–54–44–53* 🌐 *www.henri4hotel.fr* 🛏 *15 rooms, 14 with bath* 🍴 *Breakfast* [M] *Cité, St-Michel, Pont Neuf.*

$$$ HOTEL **Hôtel Londres St-Honoré.** Across from a historic 17th century church smack-dab in the center of Paris, this no-frills inexpensive hotel is comfortable and clean. **Pros:** within walking distance of major sites; free Wi-Fi; friendly service. **Cons:** small beds with worn décor; tiny elevator that doesn't go to ground floor; extremely narrow staircase. [$] *Rooms from: €147* ✉ *13 rue St-Roch, 1er, Louvre/Tuileries* ☎ *01–42–60–15–62* 🌐 *www.hotellondressthonore-paris.com* 🛏 *24 rooms, 4 suites* 🍴 *Breakfast* [M] *Pyramides.*

$$$$ HOTEL FAMILY Fodor's Choice ★ **Hôtel Meurice.** Since 1835, the Meurice has welcomed royalty and celebrities from the Duchess of Windsor to Salvador Dalí—who both resided in the grande-dame establishment—and Paris' first palace hotel continues to please with service, style, and views. **Pros:** classic Parisian history; stunning art and architecture; views over the Tuileries gardens; central location convenient to métro and major sites; trendy public spaces. **Cons:** popularity makes the public areas not very discreet; inconsistent front desk service at times unattentive; tres expensive. [$] *Rooms from: €720* ✉ *228 rue de Rivoli, 1er, Louvre/Tuileries* ☎ *01–44–58–10–09* 🌐 *www.lemeurice.com* 🛏 *118 rooms, 42 suites* [M] *Tuileries, Concorde.*

$$$$ HOTEL Fodor's Choice ★ **Park Hyatt Paris Vendôme.** Understated luxury with a contemporary Zen vibe differentiates this Hyatt from its more classic neighbors between the place Vendôme and Opéra Garnier. **Pros:** the latest hotel technology and stylish urban chic design; spa suites; gastronomic restaurants. **Cons:** as part of the Hyatt chain, it can feel anonymous; many corporate events held on site; expensive room rates. [$] *Rooms from: €730* ✉ *3–5 rue de la Paix, 2e, Opéra/Grands Boulevards* ☎ *01–58–71–12–34* 🌐 *www.paris.vendome.hyatt.com* 🛏 *132 rooms, 36 suites* 🍴 *Breakfast* [M] *Concorde, Opéra.*

3E ARRONDISSEMENT (BEAUBOURG/MARAIS)

$$$$ HOTEL **Pavillon de la Reine.** This enchanting countrylike château is hidden off the regal place des Vosges behind a stunning garden courtyard. **Pros:** Parisian historic character; proximity to place des Vosges without the noise; Carita spa treatments. **Cons:** expensive for the Marais and the size of the rooms; the nearest métro is a few blocks away; no uniform theme in interior design. [$] *Rooms from: €410* ✉ *28 pl. des Vosges, 3e, Marais* ☎ *01–40–29–19–19, 800/447–7462 in U.S.* 🌐 *www.pavillon-de-la-reine.com* 🛏 *31 rooms, 23 suites* 🍴 *Breakfast* [M] *Bastille, St-Paul.*

4^E ARRONDISSEMENT (MARAIS/ILE ST-LOUIS)

$$$ HOTEL [H] **Hôtel Caron de Beaumarchais.** For that traditional French feeling, book a room at this intimate, romantic hotel with 19 affordable rooms—the theme is the work of former next-door neighbor Pierre-Augustin Caron de Beaumarchais, supplier of military aid to American revolutionaries and playwright who penned *The Marriage of Figaro* and *The Barber of Seville*. **Pros:** cozy Parisian decor of yesteryear; breakfast in bed (served until noon); excellent location in easy walking distance to major monuments. **Cons:** small rooms with no major facilities; busy street of bars and cafés can be noisy; historic charm may feel old-fashioned and outdated for younger crowd. [$] *Rooms from: €165* ✉ *12 rue Vieille-du-Temple, 4e, Marais* ☎ *01–42–72–34–12* 🌐 *www.carondebeaumarchais.com* 🛏 *19 rooms* 🍴 *Breakfast* [M] *Hôtel de Ville.*

$$ HOTEL [H] **Hôtel Jeanne-d'Arc.** You can get your money's worth at this hotel for its unbeatable location off the tranquil place du Marché Ste-Catherine, one of the city's lesser-known pedestrian squares. **Pros:** charming street close to major sites; good value for the Marais; lots of drinking and dining options nearby. **Cons:** garbage trucks and late-night revelers on the square after midnight can be noisy; minimal amenities; rooms are small with dreary decor and not air-conditioned. [$] *Rooms from: €96* ✉ *3 rue de Jarente, 4e, Marais* ☎ *01–48–87–62–11* 🌐 *www.hoteljeannedarc.com* 🛏 *35 rooms* [M] *St-Paul.*

5^E ARRONDISSEMENT (LATIN QUARTER)

7

$$ HOTEL FAMILY [H] **Hôtel Marignan.** Not to be confused with the hotel of the same name near the Champs-Élysées, this Latin Quarter Marignan lies squarely between budget-basic and youth hostel (no TVs or elevator) and offers lots of communal conveniences—a fully stocked kitchen, free laundry machines, and copious tourist information. **Pros:** great value for the location; free kitchen, breakfast, and laundry facilities; free Wi-Fi. **Cons:** no elevator; room phones take only incoming calls; has a youth-hostel atmosphere. [$] *Rooms from: €115* ✉ *13 rue du Sommerard, 5e, Latin Quarter* ☎ *01–43–54–63–81* 🌐 *www.hotel-marignan.com* 🛏 *30 rooms, 12 with bath* 🍴 *Breakfast* [M] *Maubert-Mutualité.*

$$$ HOTEL [H] **Hôtel Saint Jacques.** Nearly every wall in this bargain Latin Quarter hotel is bedecked with faux-marble and trompe-l'oeil murals. **Pros:** unique Parisian decor; close to Latin Quarter sights; free Wi-Fi. **Cons:** very busy street makes it too noisy to open windows in summer; thin walls between rooms; rooms need refurbishment. [$] *Rooms from: €168* ✉ *35 rue des Écoles, 5e, Latin Quarter* ☎ *01–44–07–45–45* 🌐 *www.hotel-saintjacques.com* 🛏 *38 rooms* [M] *Maubert-Mutualité.*

$$$ HOTEL [H] **Les Jardins du Luxembourg.** Blessed with a personable staff and a warm ambience, this hotel on a calm cul-de-sac a block away from the Jardin du Luxembourg is an oasis for contemplation. **Pros:** on a quiet street close to major sites and transport; sauna; hot buffet breakfast. **Cons:** extra charge to use Wi-Fi; some very small rooms; a/c not very strong. [$] *Rooms from: €190* ✉ *5 impasse Royer-Collard, 5e, Latin Quarter* ☎ *01–40–46–08–88* 🌐 *www.les-jardins-du-luxembourg.com* 🛏 *26 rooms* 🍴 *Breakfast* [M] *RER: Luxembourg.*

6ᴱ ARRONDISSEMENT (ST-GERMAIN)

$$ ⚃ **Hôtel de Nesle.** This one-of-a-kind budget hotel has no elevator,
HOTEL phones, or breakfast, and some rooms share baths, but the quirky,
enchanting dollhouse rooms are cleverly decorated by theme. **Pros:**
unique, fun decor; good value for chic location; small garden. **Cons:**
no amenities or services; reservations by phone only; decor and bath-
rooms in need of renovation. Ⓢ *Rooms from: €100* ✉ *7 rue de Nesle,
6e, St-Germain-des-Prés* ☎ *01–43–54–62–41* ⊕ *www.hoteldenesleparis.
com* ⟿ *20 rooms, 9 with bath* Ⓜ *Odéon.*

$$$$ ⚃ **Hôtel Relais Saint-Sulpice.** Sandwiched between St-Sulpice and the Jardin
HOTEL du Luxembourg, this little hotel wins for location. **Pros:** chic location;
close to two métro stations; bright breakfast room and courtyard. **Cons:**
smallish rooms in the lower category; noise from the street on weekend
evenings; poorly designed lighting and interior aesthetics may be unsatis-
factory to discerning clientele. Ⓢ *Rooms from: €200* ✉ *3 rue Garancière,
6e, St-Germain-des-Prés* ☎ *01–46–33–99–00* ⊕ *www.relais-saint-sulpice.
com* ⟿ *26 rooms* ⑩ *Breakfast* Ⓜ *St-Germain-des-Prés, St-Sulpice.*

$$$$ ⚃ **Relais Christine.** On a quiet street on the Left Bank, this exquisite *hotel
HOTEL de charme* property dates back to the 13th century as a former abbey of
the Grands-Augustins and has an impressive stone courtyard and interior
garden. **Pros:** quiet location while still close to the Latin Quarter action;
historic character; Carita spa. **Cons:** thin walls in some rooms; no on-site
restaurant; a bit touristy. Ⓢ *Rooms from: €398* ✉ *3 rue Christine, 6e, St-
Germain-des-Prés* ☎ *01–40–51–60–80, 800/525–4800 in U.S.* ⊕ *www.
relais-christine.com* ⟿ *33 rooms, 18 suites* ⑩ *Breakfast* Ⓜ *Odéon.*

7ᴱ ARRONDISSEMENT (TOUR EIFFEL/INVALIDES)

$$$$ ⚃ **Hôtel Le Tourville.** One of six boutique Parisian hotels operated by
HOTEL the Inwood Collection, this cozy, contemporary haven near the Eiffel
Tower, Champs de Mars, and Invalides is a comfortable, quiet base for
exploring Paris. **Pros:** convenient location near métro; friendly service;
soundproofed windows. **Cons:** Standard rooms are small; a/c works
only during summer months; no restaurant. Ⓢ *Rooms from: €295*
✉ *16 av. de Tourville, 7e, Around the Eiffel Tower* ☎ *01–47–05–62–
62* ⊕ *www.hoteltourville.com* ⟿ *27 rooms, 3 suites* Ⓜ *École Militaire.*

$$$$ ⚃ **Le Bellechasse.** If you like eclectic modern interior design with no
HOTEL central theme, a tiny boutique hotel right around the corner from the
popular Musée d'Orsay, in Saint-Germain, may be a good choice for
its convenient location to major sites. **Pros:** central location near top
Paris museums; one-of-a-kind style with complimentary WiFi; friendly,
helpful 24-hour staff. **Cons:** small rooms; street-facing rooms can be
noisy; open bathrooms lack privacy. Ⓢ *Rooms from: €360* ✉ *8 rue de
Bellechasse, 7e, Around the Eiffel Tower* ☎ *01–45–50–22–31* ⊕ *www.
lebellechasse.com* ⟿ *33 rooms, 1 suite* ⑩ *Breakfast* Ⓜ *Solferino.*

8ᴱ ARRONDISSEMENT (CHAMPS-ÉLYSÉES)

$$$$ ⚃ **Four Seasons Hôtel George V Paris.** The George V is as poised and pol-
HOTEL ished as the day it opened in 1928—the original plaster detailing and
FAMILY 17th-century tapestries have been restored, the bas-reliefs regilded, and
Fodor's Choice the marble-floor mosaics rebuilt tile by tile—yet the guest rooms are
★ technologically updated with TVs integrated into bathroom mirrors and

DVD/CD players. **Pros:** privileged address near couture shopping district; courtyard dining in summer; guest-only indoor swimming pool. **Cons:** several blocks from the nearest métro; slow dial-up internet in rooms (extra €28 for wireless connection); lacks the personal intimacy of smaller boutique hotels with service catering more to VIPs and wealthy clientele. [$] *Rooms from: €815* ✉ *31 av. George V, 8e, Champs-Élysées* ☎ *01-49-52-70-00, 800/332-3442 in U.S.* 🌐 *www.fourseasons.com/paris* 🛏 *184 rooms, 60 suites* 🍴 *Breakfast* [M] *George V.*

$$$$ HOTEL FAMILY Fodor's Choice ★

🏨 **Hôtel Plaza Athénée.** Superlative: the word sums up the overall impression of this glamorous landmark hotel on one of the most expensive avenues in Paris with luxury shops. **Pros:** Eiffel Tower views; special attention to children; Dior Institute spa. **Cons:** vast difference in style of rooms; easy to feel anonymous in such a large hotel and if not a VIP; very expensive prices. [$] *Rooms from: €995* ✉ *25 av. Montaigne, 8e, Champs-Élysées* ☎ *01-53-67-66-65, 866/732-1106 in U.S.* 🌐 *www.plaza-athenee-paris.com* 🛏 *194 rooms, 46 suites* 🍴 *Breakfast* [M] *Alma-Marceau.*

9E ARRONDISSEMENT (OPÉRA)

$$$ HOTEL

🏨 **Hôtel George Sand.** This family-run boutique hotel where the 19th-century writer George Sand once lived is fresh and modern, while preserving some original architectural details. **Pros:** next door to two famous department stores; historic atmosphere; clean rooms. **Cons:** noisy street; can hear métro rumble on lower floors; some rooms are quite small. [$] *Rooms from: €250* ✉ *26 rue des Mathurins, 9e, Opéra/Grands Boulevards* ☎ *01-47-42-63-47* 🌐 *www.hotelgeorgesand.com* 🛏 *20 rooms* 🍴 *Breakfast* [M] *Havre Caumartin.*

NIGHTLIFE AND THE ARTS

Detailed entertainment listings can be found in the weekly magazines *Pariscope* (🌐 *www.pariscope.fr)* and *L'Officiel des Spectacles.* Also look for the online *Paris Voice* (🌐 *www.parisvoice.com*), and *Figaroscope,* the weekend supplements to the newspapers *Le Monde* and *Le Figaro,* respectively. The 24-hour hotline and the website of the **Paris Tourist Office** (☎ *08-92-68-30-00 in English [€0.34 per min]* 🌐 *www.parisinfo.com*) are other good sources of information.

NIGHTLIFE

For those who prefer clinking glasses with the A-list set, check out the Champs-Élysées area, where the posh surroundings are met with expensive drinks and surly bouncers. More laid-back, bohemian-chic revelers can be found in the northeastern districts like Canal St. Martin and Belleville. Students tend to infiltrate the Bastille and Latin Quarter, and fun-loving types can find a wild party nearly every night in the Marais. The Grands Boulevards and rue Montorgueil, just north of Les Halles, are quickly turning into party central for young professionals and the fashion crowd, and the Pigalle/Montmartre area is increasingly lively with plenty of theaters, cabarets, bars, and concert venues. In warm weather, head to the Seine, where floating clubs and bars are moored from Bercy to the Eiffel Tower.

Fodor's Choice **Au Lapin Agile.** An authentic survivor from the 19th century, Au Lapin
★ Agile considers itself the doyen of cabarets. Founded in 1860, it inhabits
the same modest house that was a favorite subject of painter Maurice
Utrillo. It became the home-away-from-home for Braque, Modigliani,
Apollinaire, and Picasso—who once paid for a meal with one of his
paintings, then promptly exited and painted another that he named
after this place. There are no topless dancers; this is a genuine French
cabaret with songs, poetry, and humor (in French) in a publike setting.
Entry €24. ✉ *22 rue des Saules, 18e, Montmartre* ☎ *01–46–06–85–87*
⊕ *www.au-lapin-agile.com* Ⓜ *Lamarck Caulaincourt.*

Closerie des Lilas. La Closerie's swank "American-style" bar lets you
drink in the swirling action of the adjacent restaurant and brasserie at
a piano bar adorned with plaques honoring former habitués like Man
Ray, Jean-Paul Sartre, Samuel Beckett, and Ernest Hemingway, who
talks of "the Lilas" in *A Moveable Feast.* ✉ *171 bd. du Montparnasse,
6e, Montparnasse* ☎ *01–40–51–34–50* Ⓜ *Montparnasse.*

Fodor's Choice **Delaville Café.** With its huge, heated sidewalk terrace, Belle Époque
★ mosaic-tile bar, graffiti'd walls, and swishy lounge, Delaville Café boasts
a funky Baroque ambience. Hot Paris DJs ignite the scene Thursday
to Saturday, so arrive early on weekends if you want a seat. ✉ *34 bd.
Bonne Nouvelle, 10e, Opéra/Grands Boulevards* ☎ *01–48–24–48–09*
Ⓜ *Bonne Nouvelle, Grands Boulevards.*

SHOPPING

Window shopping is one of this city's greatest spectator sports; the
French call it *lèche-vitrine*—literally, "licking the windows"—which
is fitting because many of the displays look good enough to eat. The
capital of style, Paris has an endless panoply of delights to tempt shop-
'til-you-droppers, from grand couturiers like Dior to the funkiest flea
markets. Most stores—excepting department stores and flea markets—
stay open until 6 or 7, but some take a lunch break sometime between
noon and 2. Most shops traditionally close on Sunday.

SHOPPING BY NEIGHBORHOOD
AVENUE MONTAIGNE
Shopping doesn't come much more chic than on Avenue Montaigne,
with its graceful town mansions housing some of the top names in inter-
national fashion: **Chanel, Dior, Céline, Valentino, Krizia, Ungaro, Prada, Dolce
& Gabbana,** and many more. Neighboring rue François 1er and Avenue
George-V are also lined with many designer boutiques: **Versace, Fendi,
Givenchy,** and **Balenciaga.**

CHAMPS-ÉLYSÉES
Cafés and movie theaters keep the once-chic Champs-Élysées active 24
hours a day, but the invasion of exchange banks, car showrooms, and
fast-food chains has lowered the tone. Four glitzy 20th-century arcade
malls—**Galerie du Lido, Le Rond-Point, Le Claridge,** and **Élysées 26**—capture most of the retail action, not to mention the **Gap** and **Abercrombie
& Fitch.** Some of the big luxe chain stores—also found in cities around
the globe—are here. **Guerlain** has reintroduced a touch of elegance, and

the mothership **Louis Vuitton** (on the Champs-Élysées proper) has kept the cool factor soaring.

THE FAUBOURG ST-HONORÉ AND THE RUE ST-HONORÉ

This chic shopping and residential area is also quite a political hub. It's home to the Élysée Palace as well as the official residences of the American and British ambassadors. The Paris branches of **Sotheby's** and **Christie's** and renowned antiques galleries such as **Didier Aaron** add artistic flavor. Boutiques include **Hermès, Lanvin, Gucci, Chloé,** and **Christian Lacroix.**

LEFT BANK

For an array of bedazzling boutiques with hyper-picturesque goods—high-end interior-decor boutiques, books on gardening—and the most fascinating antiques stores in town, be sure to head to the area around rue Jacob, lined almost completely with *antiquaires,* and the streets around super-posh place Furstenberg. After decades of clustering on the Right Bank's venerable shopping avenues, the high-fashion houses have stormed the Rive Gauche. The first to arrive were **Sonia Rykiel** and **Yves St Laurent** in the late 1960s. Some of the more recent arrivals include **Christian Dior, Giorgio Armani,** and **Louis Vuitton.** Rue des St-Pères and rue de Grenelle are lined with designer names.

LOUVRE–PALAIS ROYAL

The elegant and eclectic shops clustered in the 18th-century arcades of the Palais-Royal sell such items as antiques, gloves, music boxes, perfume, scarves, and some of the world's most exclusive designer stores, including **Stella McCartney, Marc Jacobs, Rick Owens,** and **Pierre Hardy.**

LE MARAIS

The Marais is a mixture of many moods and many influences; its lovely, impossibly narrow cobblestone streets are filled with some of the most original small name, nonglobal goods to be had—a true haven for the original gift—including the outposts of **Jamin Puech, Zadig et Voltaire,** and **Sentou Galerie.** Avant-garde designer **Tsumori Chisato** and haute-couture **Azzedine Alaïa** have boutiques within a few blocks of stately place des Vosges and the Picasso and Carnavalet museums. The Marais is also one of the few neighborhoods that has a lively Sunday-afternoon shopping scene (usually from 1).

OPÉRA TO LA MADELEINE

Two major department stores—**Printemps** and **Galeries Lafayette**—dominate Boulevard Haussmann, behind Paris's ornate 19th-century Opéra Garnier. Place de la Madeleine tempts many with its two luxurious food stores, **Fauchon** and **Hédiard.**

PLACE DES VICTOIRES AND RUE ÉTIENNE MARCEL

The graceful, circular place des Victoires, near the Palais-Royal, is the playground of fashion icons such as **Kenzo,** while **agnès b** and **Yohji Yamamoto** line rue Étienne Marcel. In the nearby oh-so-charming Galerie Vivienne shopping arcade, **Jean-Paul Gaultier** has a shop that has been renovated by Philippe Starck, and is definitely worth a stop.

PLACE VENDÔME AND RUE DE LA PAIX

The magnificent 17th-century place Vendôme, home of the Ritz Hotel, and rue de la Paix, leading north from Vendôme, are where you can find the world's most elegant jewelers: **Cartier, Boucheron, Bulgari,** and **Van Cleef & Arpels.** The most exclusive, however, is the discreet **Jar's.**

RUE ST-HONORÉ

A fashionable set makes its way to rue St-Honoré to shop at Paris's trendiest boutique, **Colette.** The street is lined with numerous designer names, while on nearby rue Cambon you can find the wonderfully elegant **Chloé** and the main **Chanel** boutique.

ÎLE-DE-FRANCE

Paris may be small as capital cities go, with just under 2 million inhabitants, but Île-de-France, the region around Paris, contains more than 10 million people—a sixth of France's entire population. That's why on closer inspection the once-rustic villages of Île-de-France reveal cosseted gardens, stylishly gentrified cottages, and extraordinary country restaurants no peasant farmer could afford to frequent.

Ile-de-France offers a rich and varied mini-sampling of everything you expect from France—cathedrals, painters' villages, lavish palaces, along with the bubblegum-pink turrets of Disneyland Paris—and all delightfully set within easy day trips from Paris.

PLANNING YOUR TIME

With so many legendary sights in the Île-de-France—many of which are gratifying human experiences rather than just guidebook necessities—you could spend weeks visiting the region. For a stimulating mix of pomp, nature, and spirituality, we suggest your three priorities should be Versailles, Giverny, and Chartres. You definitely need a day for Versailles, the world's grandest palace. For that sublime treat of medieval art and architecture, the cathedral of Chartres, you need at least half a day. Ditto for Monet's ravishing home and garden at Giverny. You can easily see Fontainebleau and Vaux-le-Vicomte in a day. As for Disneyland Paris, it all depends on your priorities.

GETTING HERE AND AROUND

A comprehensive rail network ensures that most towns in Île-de-France can make comfortable day trips from Paris, but make sure you know the right station to head out from (Gare de Lyon for Fontainebleau and Gare Montparnasse for Chartres). RER (commuter) trains tunnel through central Paris en route to Versailles and Disneyland.

A handful of venues need other means of access. To reach Giverny, rail it to Vernon, then take a taxi or local bus (or bike). To reach Vaux-le-Vicomte, head first for Melun, then take a taxi or local bus (in summer a shuttle service). Note that Fontainebleau station is in neighboring Avon, and getting to the château means a 10-minute bus ride.

A13 links Paris (from the Porte d'Auteuil) to Versailles. You can get to Chartres on A10 from Paris (Porte d'Orléans). For Fontainebleau, take A6 from Paris (Porte d'Orléans), or for a more attractive although slower route through the Forest of Sénart and the northern part of the

Forest of Fontainebleau, take N6 from Paris (Porte de Charenton) via Melun. A4 runs from Paris (Porte de Bercy) to Disneyland. The only way to crisscross the region without returning to the capital is by car. There's no shortage of expressways or fast highways, but be prepared for delays close to Paris and during the morning and evening rush hours.

Contacts Gare SNCF Fontainebleau ⊠ *1 pl. François-Mitterrand* ☎ *03–80–43–16–34.* **Gare SNCF Versailles** ⊠ *Cour de la Gare* ☎ *03–80–43–16–34.* **SNCF** ☎ *36–35 in France (€0.34 per min)* ⊕ *www.sncf.com.*

VISITOR INFORMATION

Contacts Chartres Tourist Office ⊠ *Pl. de la Cathédrale, Chartres* ☎ *02–37–18–26–26* ⊕ *www.chartres-tourisme.com.* **Disneyland Paris reservations office** ☎ *01–60–30–60–90, 407/939–7675 in U.S.* ⊕ *www.disneylandparis.com.* **Espace du Tourisme d'Ile-de-France** ⊠ *Carrousel du Louvre, 99 rue de Rivoli* ☎ *08–26–16–66–66.* **Versailles Tourist Office** ⊠ *2 bis, av. de Paris, Versailles* ☎ *01–39–24–88–88* ⊕ *www.versailles-tourisme.com.*

VERSAILLES

16 km (10 miles) west of Paris via A13.

GETTING HERE

Versailles has three train stations, all reached from different stations in Paris (journey time 25–40 mins). The handiest is Versailles Rive Gauche, reached by the RER-C5 line (main stations at Paris's Gare d'Austerlitz, St-Michel, Invalides, and Champ-de-Mars). The round-trip fare is €6. There are also regional SNCF trains from Gare Montparnasse to Versailles Chantiers, and from Gare St-Lazare to Versailles Rive Droite. Versailles Chantiers (about a 20-min walk from Versailles's front gates, although a municipal bus runs between the two) connects Versailles with several other towns in the Île-de-France, notably Chartres (with about three trains every two hours for the 50-minute trip). The other two stations in Versailles are about a 10-minute walk from the château, although the municipal Bus B or a summertime shuttle service (use métro ticket or pay small fee in coins) can also deposit you at the front gates.

EXPLORING

Fodor's Choice ★ **Château de Versailles.** Today the château seems monstrously big, but it wasn't large enough for the army of 20,000 noblemen, servants, and hangers-on who moved in with Louis. A new city—a new capital, in fact—had to be constructed from scratch to accommodate them. Tough-thinking town planners promptly dreamed up vast mansions and avenues broader than the Champs-Élysées—all in bicep-flexing baroque.

It was hardly surprising that Louis XIV's successors rapidly felt out of sync with their architectural inheritance. Louis XV and Louis XVI preferred to cower in small retreats in the gardens, well out of the mighty château's shadow. The two most famous of these structures are the Petit Trianon, a model of classical harmony and proportion built for Louis XV, and the Hameau, where Marie-Antoinette could play at being a shepherdess amid the ersatz rusticity of her Potemkin hamlet. The contrast between the majestic and the domesticated is an important part of Versailles's appeal. But pomp and bombast tend to prevail, and you

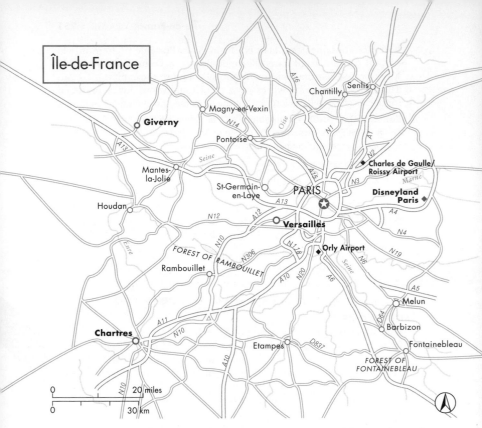

Île-de-France

won't need reminding that you're in the world's grandest palace—or one of France's most popular tourist attractions. The park and gardens outside are a great place to stretch your legs while taking in details of formal landscaping.

One of the highlights of the tour is the dazzling **Galerie des Glaces** (Hall of Mirrors). Lavish balls were once held here, as was a later event with much greater world impact: the signing of the Treaty of Versailles, which put an end to World War I on June 28, 1919.

Despite its sprawl, the palace of Versailles can get stiflingly crowded, especially as visitors are funneled through one narrow side of most of the rooms, with the furniture and objets d'art roped off. You may be able to avoid the crowds (and lines for tours) if you arrive here at 9 am. The main entrance is near the top of the courtyard to the right; there are different lines depending on tour, physical ability, and group status. Frequent guided tours in English visit the private royal apartments. More detailed hour-long tours explore the opera house or Marie Antoinette's private parlors. You can go through the grandest rooms—including the Hall of Mirrors and Marie Antoinette's stunningly opulent bedchamber—without a group tour. To figure out the system, pick up a brochure at the information office or ticket counter, or visit the site online in English. ⊠ *Pl. d'Armes* ☎ *01–30–83–78–00* ⊕ *www.chateauversailles.*

fr 🎟 *€18 general admission; €25 all-attractions pass; €10 Marie-Antoinette's Domain; park free (weekend fountain show €9, Apr.–Oct.). On 1st Sun. of month Nov.–Mar. all palace tours are free* 🕒 *Palace Apr.–Oct., Tues.–Sun. 9–6:30; Nov.–Mar., Tues.–Sun. 9–5:30. Trianons Apr.–Oct., Tues.–Sun. noon–6:30; Nov.–Mar., Tues.–Sun. 12–5:30. Garden Apr.–Oct., daily 8 am–8:30 pm; Nov.–Mar., Tues.–Sun. 8–6. Park Apr.–Oct., daily 7 am–8:30 pm; Nov.–Mar., Tues.–Sun. 8–6.*

WHERE TO EAT

$$$$ MODERN FRENCH Fodor's Choice ★

🍴 **Gordon Ramsay au Trianon.** Although he cut his culinary teeth in the kitchens of master chefs Guy Savoy and Joël Robuchon, this is Gordon Ramsay's first eatery on French soil. The delicious results—overseen by his longstanding London number two, Simone Zanoni—are predictably conversation-worthy: raviolo of langoustines and lobster cooked in a riesling bisque with Petrossian caviar and lime consommé; or the Périgord foie gras done "2 ways," roasted with a beetroot tart and pressed with green apple and Sauternes, are two top main dishes. Desserts are marvels, too, with chocolate meringue with vanilla ice cream, candied pear, and black currant vying for top honors with the raspberry soufflé with chocolate and tarragon ice cream. The Trianon's more casual, 60-seat Véranda restaurant is now also under Ramsay's sway, and in its black-and-white contemporary setting you can opt for Ramsay's "light, modern take" on such bistro novelties as radicchio and parmesan risotto with chorizo oil or the filet of sole in a parsley crust, cèpes, and sautéed artichokes. Teatime provides a delightful (and reasonable) restorative for weary château-goers, with a French take on high tea: scones, madeleines, and heavenly macaroons. [$] *Average main: €150* ✉ *1 bd. de la Reine* ☎ *01–30–84–55–55* 🌐 *www.gordonramsay.com/grautrianon* ✍ *Reservations essential* 👔 *Jacket required* 🕒 *Closed Sun. and Mon. No lunch Tues.–Thurs.*

$$$ MODERN FRENCH Fodor's Choice ★

🍴 **L'Angelique.** After the stellar success of his first Michelin-starred restaurant, L'Escarbille (in Meudon), chef Régis Douysset's newest venture confirms his commitment to refined-yet-unfussy French cuisine. The dining room, in a restored 17th-century town house, is serene and comfortable, with white walls, wood-beam ceilings, dark wood paneling, and tasteful artwork—a handsome setting in which to relax into one of the best meals in town. The seasonally changing menu offers a good balance of seafood, game, and meat: a delicate perch filet with spaghetti *de mer* (in a shellfish bouillon) or the venison shoulder with grilled turnips and a spätzle of girolle mushrooms. Desserts are not to be missed—the tart *feuilletée,* with candied peaches, cardamom, and peach sorbet is ethereal. Having earned a Michelin star, this spot is justifiably popular, so reserve well in advance. [$] *Average main: €28* ✉ *27 av. de Saint-Cloud* ☎ *01–30–84–98–85* 🌐 *www.langelique.fr* 🕒 *Closed Sun. and Mon.*

CHARTRES

39 km (24 miles) southwest of Rambouillet via N10 and A11, 88 km (55 miles) southwest of Paris.

All the descriptive prose and poetry that have been lavished on this supreme cathedral can only begin to suggest the glory of its 12th- and

13th-century statuary and stained glass, somehow suffused with burning mysticism and a strange sense of the numinous. Chartres is more than a church—it's a nondenominational spiritual experience. If you arrive in summer from Maintenon across the edge of the Beauce, the richest agrarian plain in France, you can see Chartres's spires rising up from oceans of wheat. The whole town—with its old houses and picturesque streets—is worth a leisurely exploration.

GETTING HERE

Both regional and main-line (Le Mans–bound) trains leave Paris's Gare Montparnasse for Chartres (50–70 mins); ticket price is around €25 round-trip. Chartres's train station on place Pierre-Sémard puts you within walking distance of the cathedral.

EXPLORING

Fodor'sChoice **Cathédrale Notre-Dame.** Worship on the site of the Cathédrale Notre-
★ Dame, better known as Chartres Cathedral, goes back to before the Gallo-Roman period—the crypt contains a well that was the focus of druid ceremonies. In the late ninth century Charles II (known as "the Bald") presented Chartres with what was believed to be the tunic of the Virgin Mary, a precious relic that went on to attract hordes of pilgrims. The current cathedral, the sixth church on the spot, dates mainly from the 12th and 13th centuries and was erected after the previous building, dating from the 11th century, burned down in 1194. A well-chronicled outburst of religious fervor followed the discovery that the Virgin Mary's relic had miraculously survived unsinged. Princes and paupers, barons and bourgeoisie gave their money and their labor to build the new cathedral. Ladies of the manor came to help monks and peasants on the scaffolding in a tremendous resurgence of religious faith that followed the Second Crusade. Just 25 years were needed for Chartres Cathedral to rise again, and it has remained substantially unchanged since.

Your eyes will need time to adjust to the somber interior. The reward is seeing the gemlike richness of the stained glass, with the famous deep Chartres blue predominating. The oldest window is arguably the most beautiful: **Notre-Dame de la Belle Verrière** (Our Lady of the Lovely Window), in the south choir. The cathedral's windows are gradually being cleaned—a lengthy, painstaking process—and the contrast with those still covered in the grime of centuries is staggering. ■TIP→ It's worth taking a pair of binoculars along with you to pick out the details. If you wish to know more about stained-glass techniques and the motifs used, visit the small exhibit in the gallery opposite the north porch. Since 2008, the cathedral has been undergoing an ambitious renovation—to the tune of a staggering €270 million (about $350 million)—that will continue through 2015. To date, two major chapels (the chapels of the Martyrs and the Apostles) have been completely restored, as have the two bays of the nave and the lower choir and the transept windows.

For even more detail, try to arrange a tour (in English) with local institution Malcolm Miller, whose knowledge of the cathedral's history is formidable. (He leads tours twice daily Monday through Saturday, April–October, once daily Monday through Saturday,

November–March, at noon. You can reach him at the telephone number below, or at ✉ *millerchartres@aol.com.*) ✉ *16 cloître Notre-Dame* ☎ *02–37–21–75–02* 🌐 *www.chartres-tourisme.com* 🎫 *Crypt €2.70, tours €7.50* ⏲ *Cathedral daily 8:30–7:30; guided tours of crypt Apr.–Oct., daily at 11, 2:15, 3:30, and 4:30; Nov.–Mar., daily at 11 and 4:15.*

WHERE TO EAT

$$ FRENCH 🍴 **Moulin de Ponceau.** Ask for a table with a view of the River Eure, with the cathedral looming above, at this 16th-century converted water mill. Better still, on sunny days you can eat outside, beneath a parasol on the stone terrace by the water's edge—an idyllic setting. Choose from a regularly changing menu of French stalwarts such as rabbit terrine, trout with almonds, and tarte tatin, or splurge on "la trilogie" of scallops, foie gras, and langoustine. [$] *Average main: €21* ✉ *21 rue de la Tannerie* ☎ *02–37–35–30–05* 🌐 *www.moulindeponceau.fr* ⏲ *Closed Mon. No dinner Sun.*

GIVERNY

8 km (5 miles) west of La Roche-Guyon on D5, 45 km (27 miles) northwest of Thoiry via D11 and D147, 70 km (44 miles) northwest of Paris.

The small village of Giverny (pronounced "jee-vair-nee"), just beyond the Epte River, which marks the boundary of Île-de-France, has become a place of pilgrimage for art lovers. It was here that Claude Monet lived for 43 years, until his death at the age of 86 in 1926. Although his house is now prized by connoisseurs of 19th-century interior decoration, it's his garden, with its Japanese-inspired water-lily pond and its bridge, that remains the high point for many—a 5-acre, three-dimensional Impressionist painting you can stroll around at leisure.

7

GETTING HERE

Take a main-line train (departures every couple of hours) from Paris's Gare St-Lazare to Vernon (50 minutes) on the Rouen–Le Havre line, then a taxi, bus, or bike (which you can hire at the café opposite Vernon station—head down to the river and take the cycle path once you've crossed the Seine) to Giverny, 6 miles away. Buses, which run April through October only, meet the trains daily and whisk you away to Giverny for €6 more.

EXPLORING

Fodor's Choice ★ **Maison et Jardin Claude Monet** (*Monet's House and Garden*). The Maison et Jardin Claude Monet has been lovingly restored. Monet was brought up in Normandy and, like many of the Impressionists, was captivated by the soft light of the Seine Valley. After several years in Argenteuil, just north of Paris, he moved downriver to Giverny in 1883 along with his two sons, his mistress, Alice Hoschedé (whom he later married), and her six children. By 1890 a prospering Monet was able to buy the house outright. With its pretty pink walls and green shutters, the house has a warm feeling that may come as a welcome change after the stateliness of the French châteaux. Rooms have been restored to Monet's original designs: the kitchen with its blue tiles, the buttercup-yellow dining room, and Monet's bedroom on the second floor. The house was fully and glamorously restored only in the 1970s, thanks to the millions contributed by fans and patrons (who were often Americans). Reproductions of his works, and some of the Japanese prints he avidly collected, crowd its walls. During this era, French culture had come under the spell of Orientalism, and these framed prints were often gifts from visiting Japanese diplomats whom Monet had befriended in Paris.

The garden is a place of wonder, filled with butterflies, roosters, nearly 100,000 plants bedded every year, and more than 100,000 perennials. No matter that nearly 500,000 visitors troop through it each year; they fade into the background thanks to all the beautiful roses, purple carnations, lady's slipper, aubrieta, tulips, bearded irises, hollyhocks, poppies, daises, nasturtiums, lambs' ears, larkspur, and azaleas, to mention just a few of the blooms (note that the water lilies flower during the latter part of July and the first two weeks of August). Even so, during the height of spring, when the gardens are particularly popular, try to visit during midweek. If you want to pay your respects, Monet is buried in the family vault in Giverny's village church. ⊠ *84 rue Claude Monet, Giverny* ☎ *02–32–51–28–21* ⊕ *www.fondation-monet.com* ⊠ *Gardens and home €9.50* ☉ *Apr.–Oct., daily 9:30–6.*

WHERE TO EAT

$$
BRASSERIE
Fodor'sChoice
★

✕ **Hôtel Baudy.** Back in Monet's day, this pretty-in-pink villa, originally an *épicerie-buvette* (café-cum-grocer's-store), was the hotel of the American painters' colony. Today, the rustic dining room and flowery patio have been overshadowed by all the hubbub at the museums down the road but be sure to detour here as this remains one of the most charming spots in the Île-de-France, as you'll discover in the stage-set dining room (renovated to appear as in Monet's day) and the extraordinarily pretty rose garden out back, whose embowered paths lead to the adorable studio that Cézanne once used. The surroundings retain more historic charm than the simple cuisine (mainly warm and cold salads, large enough to count as a main course in their own right, or straightforward warm dishes, like an omelet or gigot d'agneau) or the busloads of tour groups (luckily channeled upstairs). A decent three-course prix-fixe lunch or dinner is also available. $ *Average main: €18* ⊠ *81 rue Claude-Monet, Giverny* ☎ *02–32–21–10–03* ☉ *Closed Nov.–Mar.*

DISNEYLAND PARIS

68 km (40 miles) southwest of Pierrefonds via D335, D136, N330, and A4, 38 km (24 miles) east of Paris via A4.

GETTING HERE

Take the RER from central Paris (stations at Étoile, Auber, Les Halles, Gare de Lyon, and Nation) to Marne-la-Vallée–Chessy, 100 yards from the Disneyland entrance. Journey time is around 40 minutes, and trains operate every 10–30 minutes, depending on the time of day. Note that a TGV station links Disneyland to Lille, Lyon, Brussels, and London (via Lille and the Channel Tunnel). Disneyland's hotel complex offers a shuttle-bus service to Orly and Charles de Gaulle airports for a little as €16.

EXPLORING

FAMILY
Fodor's Choice
★

Disneyland Paris. A slightly downsized version of its United States counterpart, Disneyland Paris is nevertheless a spectacular sight, created with an acute attention to detail. Disney never had quite the following here as it did Stateside, so when it opened, few turned up. Today, however, the place is jammed with crowds with families from around the world reveling in the many splendors of the Disney universe.

Some of the rides can be a bit scary for little kids, but tots adore Alice's Maze, Peter Pan's Flight, and especially the whirling Mad Hatter's Teacups. Also getting high marks are the afternoon parades, which feature music and introductions in five languages and huge floats swarming with all of Disney's most beloved characters—just make sure to stake your place along Main Street in advance for a good spot (check for posted times). There's a lot here, so pace yourself: kids can easily feel overwhelmed with the barrage of stimuli or frustrated by extra-long waits at the rides. (Also be aware that there are size restrictions for some rides.) The older the child, the more they will enjoy Walt Disney Studios, a cinematically driven area, where many of the newer Disney character-themed rides can be found.

Disneyland Park, as the original theme park is styled, consists of five "lands": Main Street U.S.A., Frontierland, Adventureland, Fantasyland, and Discoveryland. The central theme of each land is relentlessly echoed in every detail, from attractions to restaurant menus to souvenirs. The park is circled by a railroad, which stops three times along the perimeter. **Main Street U.S.A.** goes under the railroad and past shops and restaurants toward the main plaza; Disney parades are held here every afternoon and, during holiday periods, every evening.

Walt Disney Studios opened next to the Disneyland Park in 2002. The theme park is divided into four "production zones." Beneath imposing entrance gates and a 100-foot water tower inspired by the one erected in 1939 at Disney Studios in Burbank, California, **Front Lot** contains shops, a restaurant, and a studio re-creating the atmosphere of Sunset Boulevard. In **Animation Courtyard,** Disney artists demonstrate the various phases of character animation; Animagique brings to life scenes from *Pinocchio* and *The Lion King,* while the Genie from *Aladdin* pilots Flying Carpets over Agrabah. **Production Courtyard** hosts the Walt Disney Television Studios; Cinémagique, a special-effects tribute to U.S. and European cinema; and a behind-the-scenes Studio Tram tour of location sites, movie props, studio interiors, and costuming, ending with a visit to Catastrophe Canyon in the heart of a film shoot. **Back Lot** majors in stunts. At Armageddon Special Effects you can confront a flaming meteor shower aboard the Mir space station, then complete your visit at the giant outdoor arena with a Stunt Show Spectacular involving cars, motorbikes, and Jet Skis. ☎ 01–60–30–60–90 ⊕ *www.disneylandparis.com* ✉ *€79, or €160 for 3-day Passport; includes admission to all individual attractions within Disneyland or Walt Disney Studios. Tickets for Walt Disney Studios are also valid for admission to Disneyland during last 3 opening hrs of same day* ⊙ *Disneyland mid-June–mid-Sept., daily 9 am–10 pm; mid-Sept.–Dec.*

7

19 and Jan. 5–mid-June, weekdays 10–8, weekends 9–8; Dec. 20–Jan. 4, daily 9–8. Walt Disney Studios daily 10–6.

WHERE TO STAY

$$$$ HOTEL **Sequoia Lodge.** Ranging from superluxe to still-a-pretty-penny, Disneyland Paris has 5,000 rooms in five hotels, but your best bet on all counts may be the Sequoia Lodge, just a few minutes' walk from the theme park, where the mood—a grand recreation of an American mountain lodge—is quite different from the other, glitzier big hotels here. **Pros:** package deals include admission to theme park; cozy, secluded feel; great pools. **Cons:** restaurants a bit ho-hum; many rooms do not have lake view; room rates are €400 and up (and this is considered "mid-range" in Disneyland). [$] *Rooms from: €400* ☎ *01–60–30–60–90, 407/939–7675 in U.S.* 🌐 *www.disneylandparis.com* 🍴 *All meals.*

NORMANDY

For generations England and Normandy vacillated and blurred, merged, and diverged. Today you can still feel the strong flow of English culture over the Channel, from the Deauville horse races frequented by high-born ladies in gloves to silver spoons mounded high with teatime cream; from the bowfront, slope-roof shops along the harbor at Honfleur to the black-and-white row houses of Rouen, which would seem just as much at home in the setting of *David Copperfield* as they are in *Madame Bovary.*

And just as in the British Isles, no matter how you concentrate on history and culture, sooner or later you'll find yourself beguiled by the countryside, by Normandy's rolling green hills dotted with dairy cows and half-timber farmhouses. Like the locals, you'll be tempted by seafood fresh off the boat, by sauces rich with crème fraîche, by cheeses redolent of farm and pasture. And perhaps with cheeks pink from the apple-scented country air, you'll eventually succumb to the local antidote to northern damp and chill: a mug of tangy hard cider sipped by a crackling fire, and the bracing tonic of Normandy's famous apple brandy, Calvados.

PLANNING YOUR TIME

You won't want to miss medieval Rouen, seaside Honfleur, or magnificent Mont-St-Michel. But if you get away from these popular spots you can lose yourself along the cliff-lined coast and in the green spaces inland, where the closest thing to a crowd is a farmer with his herd of brown-and-white cows. From Rouen to the coast—the area known as Upper Normandy—medieval castles and abbeys stand guard above rolling countryside, while resort and fishing towns line the white cliffs of the Côte d'Alabâtre. Popular seaside resorts and the D-Day landing sites occupy the sandy beaches along the Côte Fleurie; apple orchards and dairy farms sprinkle the countryside of the area known as Lower Normandy. The Cotentin Peninsula to the west juts out into the English Channel. Central Normandy encompasses the peaceful, hilly region of La Suisse Normande, along the scenic Orne River.

Normandy

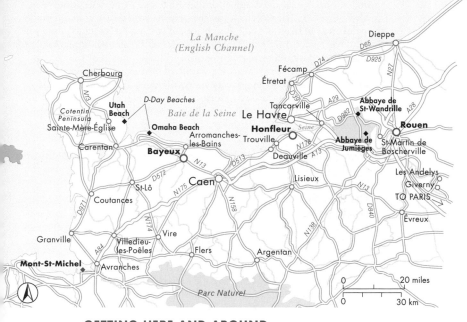

GETTING HERE AND AROUND

If driving, the A13 expressway is the gateway from Paris, running north-west to Rouen and then to Caen. From there the A84 takes you almost all the way to Mont-St-Michel.

Although this is one of the few areas of France with no high-speed rail service—perhaps because it's so close to Paris, or because it's not on a lucrative route to a neighboring country—Normandy's regional rail network is surprisingly good, meaning that most towns can be reached by train. Rouen is the hub for Upper Normandy, Caen for Lower Normandy. For Mont-St-Michel, a combination of train and bus is required. To visit the D-Day beaches, a guided minibus tour, leaving from Caen is your best bet.

Contacts Gare SNCF Rouen ⊠ *Rue Jeanne d'Arc* ☎ *36–35* ⊕ *www.ter-sncf.com.*

VISITOR INFORMATION

Contacts Caen Tourist Office ⊠ *Pl. du Canada, Caen* ☎ *02–31–27–90–30* ⊕ *www.tourisme.caen.fr.* **Honfleur Tourist Office** ⊠ *Quai Lepaulmier, Honfleur* ☎ *02–31–89–23–30* ⊕ *en.ot-honfleur.fr.* **Mont-St-Michel Tourist Office** ⊠ *Corps de Garde, Bd. Avancée, Le Mont-St-Michel* ☎ *02–33–60–14–30* ⊕ *www. ot-montsaintmichel.com.* **Rouen Tourist Office** ⊠ *25 pl. de la Cathédrale, Rouen* ☎ *02–32–08–32–40* ⊕ *www.rouentourisme.com.*

ROUEN

32 km (20 miles) north of Louviers, 130 km (80 miles) northwest of Paris, 86 km (53 miles) east of Le Havre.

"O Rouen, art thou then to be my final abode!" was the agonized cry of Joan of Arc as the English dragged her out to be burned alive on May 30, 1431. The exact spot of the pyre is marked by a concrete-and-metal cross in front of the Église Jeanne-d'Arc, an eye-catching modern church on place du Vieux-Marché, just one of the many landmarks that make Rouen a fascinating destination. Although much of the city was destroyed during World War II, a wealth of medieval half-timber houses still lines the cobblestone streets, many of which are pedestrian only—most famously rue du Gros-Horloge between place du Vieux-Marché and the cathedral, suitably embellished halfway along with a giant Renaissance clock. Rouen is also a busy port—the fifth largest in France.

GETTING HERE

Trains from Paris (Gare St-Lazare) leave for Rouen every two hours or so (€15–€23); the 85-mile trip takes 70 minutes. Change in Rouen for Dieppe (2 hrs from Paris, €30).

EXPLORING

Abbaye St-Ouen. Next to the imposing Neoclassical City Hall, this stupendous example of high Gothic architecture is noted for its stained-glass windows, dating from the 14th to the 16th century. They are the most spectacular grace notes of the spare interior along with the 19th-century pipe organ, among the finest in France. ⊠ *Pl. du Général-de-Gaulle, Hôtel de Ville* ☎ *02–32–08–32–40* ⊘ *Apr.–Oct., Wed.–Mon. 10–12 and 2–6; Nov.–Mar., Tues.–Thurs. and weekends 10–12 and 2–7.*

Cathédrale Notre-Dame. Lording it over Rouen's "Hundred Spires" this cathedral is crowned with the highest spire in France, erected in 1876, a cast-iron tour-de-force rising 490 feet above the crossing. The original 12th-century construction was replaced after a devastating fire in 1200; only the left-hand spire, the **Tour St-Romain** (St. Romanus Tower), survived the flames. Construction on the imposing 250-foot steeple on the right, known as the **Tour de Beurre** (Butter Tower), was begun in the 15th century and completed in the 17th, when a group of wealthy citizens donated large sums of money for the privilege of continuing to eat butter during Lent. Interior highlights include the 13th-century choir, with its pointed arcades; vibrant stained glass depicting the crucified Christ (restored after heavy damage during World War II); and massive stone columns topped by some intriguing carved faces. The first flight of the famous **Escalier de la Librairie** (Library Stairway), attributed to Guillaume Pontifs (also responsible for most of the 15th-century work seen in the cathedral), rises from a tiny balcony just to the left of the transept. ⊠ *Pl. de la Cathédrale, St-Maclou* ☎ *02–32–08–32–40* ⊘ *Daily 8–6.*

Église Jeanne d'Arc (*Joan of Arc Church*). Dedicated to Joan of Arc, this church was built in the 1970s on the spot where she was burned to death in 1431. The aesthetic merit of its odd cement-and-wood design is debatable—the shape of the roof is *supposed* to evoke the flames of

Joan's fire. Not all is new, however: the church showcases some remarkable 16th-century stained-glass windows taken from the former Église St-Vincent, bombed out in 1944. The adjacent **Musée Jeanne-d'Arc** relates Joan's history with waxworks and documents. ✉ *Pl. du Vieux-Marché, Vieux-Marché* ☎ *02–32–08–32–40* 🌐 *www.jeanne-darc.com* 🎟 *free* 🕒 *Mon.–Thurs. 10–12, Fri.–Sun. 2–6.*

Musée des Beaux-Arts (*Fine Arts Museum*). One of Rouen's cultural mainstays, this museum is famed for its scintillating collection of paintings and sculptures from the 16th to the 20th century, including works by native son Géricault as well as by David, Rubens, Caravaggio, Velasquez, Poussin, Delacroix, Chassériau, Degas, and Modigliani. Most popular of all, however, is the impressive Impressionist gallery, with Monet, Renoir, and Sisley, and the Postimpressionist School of Rouen headed by Albert Lebourg and Gustave Loiseau. ✉ *Square Verdrel, Gare* ☎ *02–35–71–28–40* 🌐 *www.rouen-musees.com* 🎟 *€5 (free first Sun. of month), €8 includes Musée Le Secq des Tournelles and Musée de la Céramique* 🕒 *Wed.–Mon. 10–6.*

Musée Le Secq des Tournelles (*Wrought-Iron Museum*). Not far from the Musée des Beaux-Arts, this museum claims to have the world's finest collection of wrought iron, with exhibits spanning the 4th through the 19th century. The displays, imaginatively housed in a converted medieval church, include the professional instruments of surgeons, barbers, carpenters, clockmakers, and gardeners. ✉ *2 rue Jacques-Villon, Gare* ☎ *02–35–88–42–92* 🎟 *€3, €8 includes Musée des Beaux-Arts and Musée de la Céramique* 🕒 *Wed.–Mon. 10–1 and 2–6.*

7

WHERE TO STAY

$ HOTEL

🏨 **Cathédrale.** There are enough half-timber walls and beams here to fill a super-luxe hotel, but the happy news is that this is a budget option—even better, this 17th-century building is found on a narrow pedestrian street just behind Rouen's cathedral. **Pros:** storybook surroundings; can't-be-beat location. **Cons:** small rooms; no car access. [$] *Rooms from: €79* ✉ *12 rue St-Romain, St-Maclou* ☎ *02–35–71–57–95* 🌐 *www.hotel-de-la-cathedrale.fr* 🛏 *26 rooms.*

$$$$ MODERN FRENCH Fodor's Choice ★

🍴 **La Couronne.** If P. T. Barnum, Florenz Ziegfeld, and Cecil B. DeMille had put together a spot distilling all the charm and glamour of Normandy, this would be it. Behind a half-timber facade gushing geraniums, the "oldest inn in France," dating from 1345, is a sometimes-ersatz extravaganza crammed with stained leaded glass, sculpted wood beams, marble Norman chimneys, leather-upholstered chairs, and damask curtains. The Salon Jeanne d'Arc is the largest room and has a wonderful wall-wide sash window and quaint paintings, but the only place to sit is the adorably cozy, wood-lined Salon des Rôtisseurs, an antiquarian's delight. The star attractions on Vincent Taillefer's menu—lobster stew with chestnut, sheeps' feet, duck in blood sauce—make few modern concessions. Dine at La Couronne and you'll be adding your name to a list that includes Sophia Loren, John Wayne, Jean-Paul Sartre, Salvador Dalí, and Princess Grace of Monaco. [$] *Average main: €35* ✉ *31 pl. du Vieux-Marché, Vieux-Marché* ☎ *02–35–71–40–90* 🌐 *www.lacouronne.com.fr.*

HONFLEUR

Fodor's Choice ★ *24 km (15 miles) southeast of Le Havre via A131 and the Pont de Normandie, 27 km (17 miles) northwest of Pont-Audemer, 80 km (50 miles) west of Rouen.*

The colorful port town of Honfleur has become increasingly crowded since the opening of the elegant Pont de Normandie, providing a direct link with Le Havre and Upper Normandy. (The world's largest cable-stayed bridge, it's supported by two concrete pylons taller than the Eiffel Tower and is designed to resist winds of 160 mph.) Honfleur, full of half-timber houses and cobbled streets, was once an important departure point for maritime expeditions, including the first voyages to Canada in the 15th and 16th centuries. The 17th-century harbor is fronted on one side by two-story stone houses with low, sloping roofs and on the other by tall, narrow houses whose wooden facades are topped by slate roofs. Note that parking can be a problem. Your best bet is the parking lot just beyond the Vieux-Bassin (old harbor) on the left as you approach from the land side.

GETTING HERE

To get to Honfleur, take the bus from Deauville (30 minutes, €2); from Caen (1 hour 45 minutes, €7); or from Le Havre (30 minutes, €4). Buses run every two hours or so and are operated by **Bus Verts du Calvados** (☎ *08–10–21–42–14* 🌐 *www.busverts.fr*).

EXPLORING

Ste-Catherine. Soak up the seafaring atmosphere by strolling around the old harbor and paying a visit to the ravishing wooden church of Ste-Catherine, which dominates a tumbling square. The church and the ramshackle belfry across the way—note the many touches of marine engineering in their architecture—were built by townspeople to show their gratitude for the departure of the English at the end of the Hundred Years' War, in 1453. ✉ *Rue des Logettes* ☎ *02–31–89–11–83.*

WHERE TO STAY

$$$$ HOTEL 🏨 **Ferme St-Siméon.** The story goes that this 19th-century manor house was the famed birthplace of Impressionism, and that its park inspired Monet and Sisley—neither of whom would have dismissed the welcoming rich mix of 19th-century elegance and down-home Norman delights inside, where rich fabrics, grand paintings, and Louis Seize chairs are married with rustic antiques, ancient beams, and half-timbered walls; the result casts a deliciously cozy spell. **Pros:** famed historic charm. **Cons:** expensive; bland annex rooms. [$] *Rooms from: €400* ✉ *Rue Adolphe-Marais, on D513 to Trouville* ☎ *02–31–81–78–00* 🌐 *www.fermesaintsimeon.fr* 🛏 *34 rooms, 3 suites* 🍴 *Some meals.*

$$$ HOTEL 🏨 **L'Absinthe.** A 16th-century presbytery with stone walls and beamed ceilings houses a small and charming hotel and the acclaimed restaurant of the same name; guest rooms are comfortable and stylish but small, except for the attic suite, which has a private living room, and four rooms and one suite have harbor views. **Pros:** enchanting building; superb restaurant. **Cons:** small rooms; gawky blend of old and modern furnishings. [$] *Rooms from: €160* ✉ *10 quai de la Quarantaine*

☎ *02–31–89–23–23* 🌐 *www.absinthe.fr* 🛏 *9 rooms, 2 suites* ⏰ *Closed mid-Nov.–mid-Dec.* 🍴 *Some meals.*

$$$ HOTEL 🏨 **Le Manoir des Impressionnistes.** An archetypal fin-de-siècle villa, perched on top of a small wooded hill 200 yards from the sea, this gorgeous half-timber, dormer-roof manor welcomes you with a pretty green-and-white facade in the Anglo-Norman style and guest rooms that have sweeping views; all are traditionally and tastefully furnished, and have modern marble bathrooms, and the room on the first floor has a four-poster bed and its own balcony. **Pros:** exquisitely decorated and furnished; sea views; stylish bathrooms. **Cons:** away from town center; no elevator. [$] *Rooms from: €190* ✉ *Phare du Butin* ☎ *02–31–81–63–00* 🌐 *www.manoirdesimpressionnistes.eu* 🛏 *10 rooms* ⏰ *Closed Jan.* 🍴 *Some meals.*

BAYEUX

28 km (17 miles) northwest of Caen.

Bayeux, the first town to be liberated during the Battle of Normandy, was already steeped in history—as home to a Norman Gothic cathedral and the world's most celebrated piece of needlework: the Bayeux Tapestry. Bayeux's medieval backcloth makes it a popular base, especially among British travelers, for day trips to other towns in Normandy. Since Bayeux had nothing strategically useful like factories or military bases, it was never bombed by either side, leaving its beautiful cathedral and Old Town intact. The Old World mood is at its most boisterous during the Fêtes Médiévales, a market-cum-carnival held in the streets around the cathedral on the first weekend of July. A more traditional market is held every Saturday morning. The town is a good starting point for visits to the World War II sites; there are many custom tour guides, but Taxis du Bessin (☎ *02–31–92–92–40*) is one of the best.

EXPLORING

Fodor's Choice ★ **Bayeux Tapestry.** Really a 225-foot-long embroidered scroll stitched in 1067, the Bayeux Tapestry, known in French as the *Tapisserie de la Reine Mathilde* (*Queen Matilda's Tapestry*), depicts, in 58 comic strip–type scenes, the epic story of William of Normandy's conquest of England in 1066, narrating Will's trials and victory over his cousin Harold, culminating in the Battle of Hastings on October 14, 1066. The tapestry was probably commissioned from Saxon embroiderers by the count of Kent—who was also the bishop of Bayeux—to be displayed in his newly built cathedral, the Cathédrale Notre-Dame. Despite its age, the tapestry is in remarkably good condition; the extremely detailed, often homey scenes provide an unequaled record of the clothes, weapons, ships, and lifestyles of the day. It's showcased in the **Musée de la Tapisserie** (Tapestry Museum; free audioguides let you listen to an English commentary about the tapestry). ✉ *Centre Guillaume-le-Conquérant, 13 bis rue de Nesmond* ☎ *02–31–51–25–50* 🌐 *www.tapisserie-bayeux.fr* 🎟 *€9* ⏰ *Mid-Mar–mid-Nov., daily 9–5:45 (until 6:15 in summer); mid-Nov.–mid-Mar., daily 9:30–11:45 and 2–5:15.*

Cathédrale Notre-Dame. Bayeux's mightiest edifice, the Cathédrale Notre-Dame, is a harmonious mixture of Norman and Gothic architecture.

Note the portal on the south side of the transept that depicts the assassination of English archbishop Thomas à Becket in Canterbury Cathedral in 1170, following his courageous opposition to King Henry II's attempts to control the church. ✉ *Rue du Bienvenu* ☎ *02–31–92–01–85* ⏲ *Daily 9–12 and 2–6.*

WHERE TO STAY

$$$$ HOTEL 🏨 **Château d'Audrieu.** Princely opulence, overstuffed chairs, wall sconces, antiques—this family-owned château with an elegant 18th-century facade and grand restaurant fulfills a Hollywood notion of a palatial property. Guest rooms 50 and 51 have peaked ceilings with exposed wood beams, and the enchanting restaurant (closed Monday; no lunch weekdays)—white wainscoting, crystal chandeliers, gilt accents—has an extensive wine list. **Pros:** grandiose building; magnificent gardens. **Cons:** out of the way; bland interiors in some rooms. [$] *Rooms from: €330* ✉ *13 km (8 miles) southeast of Bayeux off N13, Audrieu* ☎ *02–31–80–21–52* 🌐 *www.chateaudaudrieu.com* 🛏 *25 rooms, 4 suites* ⏲ *Closed Dec. and Jan.* 🍴 *Some meals.*

$ HOTEL 🏨 **Grand Hôtel du Luxembourg.** The Luxembourg has small but adequate guest rooms, fully renovated with bland modern furniture but with chic color schemes (all but two face a courtyard garden), and one of the best restaurants in town. **Pros:** quiet; central; fine restaurant. **Cons:** unprepossessing lobby; some rooms are on the dark side. [$] *Rooms from: €100* ✉ *25 rue des Bouchers* ☎ *02–31–92–00–04* 🌐 *www.hotel-luxembourg-bayeux.com* 🛏 *25 rooms, 3 suites* 🍴 *Some meals.*

THE D-DAY BEACHES

History focused its sights along the coasts of Normandy at 6:30 am on June 6, 1944, as the 135,000 men and 20,000 vehicles of the Allied troops made land in their first incursion in Europe in World War II. The entire operation on this "Longest Day" was called Operation Overlord—the code name for the invasion of Normandy. Five beachheads (dubbed Utah, Omaha, Gold, Juno, and Sword) were established along the coast to either side of Arromanches. Preparations started in mid-1943, and British shipyards worked furiously through the following winter and spring building two artificial harbors (called "mulberries"), boats, and landing equipment. The British and Canadian troops that landed on Sword, Juno, and Gold on June 6, 1944, quickly pushed inland and joined with parachute regiments previously dropped behind German lines, before encountering fierce resistance at Caen, which did not fall until July 9. Today the best way to tour this region is by car. Or—since public buses from Bayeux are infrequent—opt for one of the guided bus tours leaving from Caen.

EXPLORING

Omaha Beach. You won't be disappointed by the rugged terrain and windswept sand of Omaha Beach, 16 km (10 miles) northwest of Bayeux. Here you can find the **Monument du Débarquement** (Monument to the Normandy Landings) and the **Musée-Mémorial d'Omaha Beach,** a large shedlike structure packed with tanks, dioramas, and archival photographs that stand silent witness to "Bloody Omaha." Nearby, in

Vierville-sur-Mer, is the **U.S. National Guard Monument.** Throughout June 6, Allied forces battled a hailstorm of German bullets and bombs, but by the end of the day they had taken the Omaha Beach sector, although they had suffered grievous losses. In Colleville-sur-Mer, overlooking Omaha Beach, is the hilltop **American Cemetery and Memorial,** designed by landscape architect Markley Stevenson. You can look out to sea across the landing beach from a platform on the north side of the cemetery. ✉ *Musée-Mémorial d'Omaha Beach, Les Moulins, av. de la Libération, Saint-Laurent-sur-Mer* ☎ *02–31–21–97–44* ⊕ *www. musee-memorial-omaha.com* 🖳 *€6* ⊙ *Feb. 15–Mar. 15, daily 10–12:30 and 2:30–6; Mar. 16–May 15, daily 9:30–6:30; May 16–Sept. 15, daily 9:30–7; Sept. 16–Nov. 15, daily 9:30–6:30.*

Pointe du Hoc. The most spectacular scenery along the coast is at the Pointe du Hoc, 13 km (8 miles) west of St-Laurent. Wildly undulating grassland leads past ruined blockhouses to a cliff-top observatory and a German machine-gun post whose intimidating mass of reinforced concrete merits chilly exploration. Despite Spielberg's cinematic genius, it remains hard to imagine just how Colonel Rudder and his 225 Rangers—only 90 survived—managed to scale the jagged cliffs with rope ladders and capture the German defenses in one of the most heroic and dramatic episodes of the war. A granite memorial pillar now stands on top of a concrete bunker, but the site otherwise remains as the Rangers left it—look down through the barbed wire at the jutting cliffs the troops ascended and see the huge craters left by exploded shells.

Sainte-Mère Église. Head west on N13, pause in the town of **Carentan** to admire its modern marina and the mighty octagonal spire of the Église Notre-Dame, and continue northwest to Sainte-Mère Église. At 2:30 am on June 6, 1944, the 82nd Airborne Division was dropped over Ste-Mère, heralding the start of D-Day operations. After securing their position at Ste-Mère, U.S. forces pushed north, then west, cutting off the Cotentin Peninsula on June 18 and taking Cherbourg on June 26. German defenses proved fiercer farther south, and St-Lô was not liberated until July 19. Ste-Mère's symbolic importance as the first French village to be liberated from the Nazis is commemorated by the Borne 0 (Zero) outside the town hall—a large dome milestone marking the start of the Voie de la Liberté (Freedom Way), charting the Allies' progress across France. ✉ *Ste-Mère Eglise.*

Utah Beach. Head east on D67 from Ste-Mère to Utah Beach, which, being sheltered from the Atlantic winds by the Cotentin Peninsula and surveyed by lowly sand dunes rather than rocky cliffs, proved easier to attack than Omaha. Allied troops stormed the beach at dawn, and just a few hours later had managed to conquer the German defenses, heading inland to join up with the airborne troops.

Musee d'Utah Beach. In La Madeleine inspect the newly renovated, sleek, and modern **Utah Beach Landing Museum** (✉ *Ste-Marie du Mont* ☎ *02–33–71–53–35*), whose exhibits include a W5 Utah scale model detailing the German defenses. It's open June–September, daily 9:30–7; April, May, and October, daily 10–6; February, March, and November, daily 10–6; closed December and January. Continue north to the **Dunes**

de Varreville, set with a monument to French hero General Leclerc, who landed here. Offshore you can see the fortified Îles **St-Marcouf.** Continue to **Quinéville,** at the far end of Utah Beach, with its **museum** (✉ *Memorial de la Liberte, rue de la Plage* ☎ *02–33–95–95–95*) evoking life during the German Occupation. The museum is open March 22 through mid-November, daily 10–7. ✉ *Plage de La Madeleine, Ste Marie du Mont* ☎ *02–33–71–53–35* 🌐 *www.utah-beach.com* 🎫 *€7.50.*

WHERE TO STAY

$ HOTEL 🏨 **Hotel du Casino.** You can't get closer to the action than this—the handsome, postwar, triangular-gabled stone hotel, run by the same family since it was built in the 1950s, looks directly onto Omaha Beach. **Pros:** calm; right by the beach. **Cons:** small bathrooms; slow service in restaurant. [$] *Rooms from: €88* ✉ *Rue de la Percée, Vierville-sur-Mer* ☎ *02–31–22–41–02* 🌐 *www.logis-de-france.fr* 🛏 *13 rooms* 🕒 *Closed mid-Nov.–mid-Mar.* 🍴 *Some meals.*

$$$$ HOTEL 🏨 **La Chenevière.** Topped by an impressive mansard roof, occupying an elegant 18th-century château mansion, and surrounded by cheerful gardens, this is a true oasis of peace a few kilometers down the road—and yet a million miles away—from World War II sites like Omaha Beach; inland from Port-en-Bessin, the hotel allures with super-stylish guest rooms, which comprise a fetching mix of Louis Seize chairs, gilded ormolu objects, modern photographs, and very chic fabrics. **Pros:** magnificent architecture; luxurious rooms. **Cons:** three different buildings; no a/c in the château. [$] *Rooms from: €300* ✉ *Les Escures, Commes* ☎ *02–31–51–25–25* 🌐 *www.lacheneviere.com* 🛏 *26 rooms, 3 suites* 🕒 *Closed Dec.– Mar.* 🍴 *Some meals.*

MONT-ST-MICHEL

Fodor'sChoice ★ *44 km (27 miles) south of Granville via D973, N175, and D43; 123 km (77 miles) southwest of Caen; 67 km (42 miles) north of Rennes; 325 km (202 miles) west of Paris.*

That marvel of French architecture, Mont-St-Michel, is the most-visited sight in France after the Eiffel Tower and the Louvre. This beached mass of granite, rising some 400 feet, was begun in 709 and is crowned with the "Marvel," or great monastery, that was built during the 13th century. Fortifications were added 200 years later to withstand attacks from the English.

GETTING HERE

There are two routes to Mont-St-Michel, depending on whether you arrive from Caen or from Paris. From Caen you can take either an early-morning or an afternoon train to Pontorson (2 hrs, €27.30), the nearest station; then it's another 15 minutes to the foot of the abbey by bus or taxi. (Both leave from in front of the station.) From Paris, take the TGV from Gare Montparnasse to Rennes, then take a Keolis bus (☎ *02–99–19–70–70*). The total journey takes 3 hours, 20 minutes (about €40 if booked in advance). There are three trains daily, but the only one that allows you a full day on the Mont leaves at 7:04 am and arrives at 10:08 am. The other options are 10:08 (arriving 3:13 pm) and 2:05 pm (arriving 6:00).

EXPLORING

Abbaye du Mont-St-Michel. Wrought by nature and centuries of tireless human toil, this sea-surrounded mass of granite adorned with the soul-lifting silhouette of the Abbaye du Mont-St-Michel may well be your most lasting image of Normandy. The abbey is perched on a 264-foot-high rock a few hundred yards off the coast: it's surrounded by water during the year's highest tides and by desolate sand flats the rest of the time. Be warned: tides in the bay are dangerously unpredictable. The sea can rise up to 45 feet at high tide and rushes in at incredible speed—more than a few ill-prepared tourists over the years have drowned. Also, be warned that there are patches of dangerous quicksand. A causeway—to be replaced in time by a bridge, allowing the bay waters to circulate freely—links Mont-St-Michel to the mainland. Leave your car in the parking lot (€4) along the causeway, outside the main gate. Just inside you can find the tourist office, to the left, and a pair of old cannons (with cannonballs) to the right. If you're staying the night on Mont-St-Michel, take what you need in a small suitcase; you cannot gain access to your hotel by car and the parking lot is unguarded at night. The Mont's tourist office is in the Corps de Garde des Bourgeois, just to the left of the island gates.

All year long, the hour-long guided tour in English (two a day and night in high season) and French (up to two an hour) takes you through the impressive Romanesque and Gothic abbey and the spectacular **Église Abbatiale,** the abbey church, which crowns the rock, as well as the **Merveille,** a 13th-century, three-story collection of rooms and passageways. La Merveille was built by King Philippe Auguste around and on top of the monastery; on its second floor is the Mont's grandest chamber, the **Salle des Chevaliers.** Another tour, which also includes the celebrated **Escalier de Dentelle** (Lace Staircase), and the pre-Roman and exquisitely evocative **Notre-Dame-sous-Terre** is longer, has a higher ticket price, and is only given in French. Invest in at least one tour while you are here—some of them get you on top of or into things you can't see alone. If you do go it alone, stop halfway up Grande-Rue at the medieval parish church of St-Pierre to admire the richly carved side chapel with its dramatic statue of St. Michael slaying the dragon. The **Grand Degré,** a steep, narrow staircase, leads to the abbey entrance, from which a wider flight of stone steps climbs to the **Saut Gautier Terrace** (named after a prisoner who jumped to his death from it) outside the sober, dignified church. After visiting the arcaded cloisters alongside, which offer vertiginous views of the bay, you can wander at leisure, and probably get lost, among the maze of rooms, staircases, and vaulted halls. Scattered throughout the mount are four minimuseums (closed January), which cost €8 individually or €16 together. The island village, with its steep, narrow streets, is best visited out of season, from September to June. In summer the hordes of tourists and souvenir sellers can be stifling. Give yourself at least half a day here, and follow your nose. The mount is full of nooks, crannies, little gardens, and echoing views from the ramparts. The Mont is spectacularly illuminated every night from dusk to midnight. ⊠ *Le Mont-St-Michel* ☎ *02–33–89–80–00* ⊕ *www.mont-*

7

saint-michel.monuments-nationaux.fr 🖼 *€9, €13.50 with audio guide*
⊗ *May–Aug., daily 9–6; Sept.–Apr., daily 9:30–5.*

PROVENCE

As you approach Provence there's a magical moment when you finally leave the north behind: cypresses and red-tile roofs appear; you hear the screech of cicadas and breathe the scent of wild thyme and lavender. Along the highway, oleanders bloom on the center strip against a backdrop of austere, sun-filled landscapes, the very same that inspired the Postimpressionists.

This is Provence, a disarming culture of *pastis* (an anise-based aperitif), *pétanque* (lawn bowling), and shady plane trees, where dawdling is a way of life. You may seat yourself at a sidewalk café, wander aimlessly down narrow cobbled alleyways, heft melons in the morning marketplace and, after a three-hour lunch, take an afternoon snooze in the cool shade of a 500-year-old olive tree.

Plus, there are plenty of sights to see: some of the finest Roman ruins in Europe, from the Pont du Gard to the arenas at Arles and Nîmes; the pristine Romanesque abbeys of Senanque and de Montmajour; bijou chapels and weathered *mas* (farmhouses); the monolithic Papal Palace in old Avignon; and everywhere vineyards, pleasure ports, and sophisticated city museums. Between sights, allow yourself time to feel the rhythm of modern Provençal life, to listen to the pulsing *breet* of the insects, smell the *parfum* of a tiny country path, and feel the air of a summer night on your skin.

PLANNING YOUR TIME

Provence is about lazy afternoons and spending "just one more day," and Avignon is a good place to have a practice run: it's cosmopolitan enough to keep the most energetic visitor occupied, while old and wise enough to teach the value of time. From here you can access every part of Provence easily, either by train, by bus, or by car.

You'll eat late in the south, rarely before 1 for lunch, usually after 9 at night. In summer, shops and museums may shut down until 3 or 4, as much to accommodate lazy lunches as for the crowds taking sun on the beach.

GETTING HERE AND AROUND

Public transport is well organized in Provence, with most towns accessible by train or by bus. It's best to plan on combining the two—often smaller Provençal towns won't have their own train station, but a local bus connection to the train station at the nearest town over.

BUS TRAVEL

If you plan to explore Provence by bus, Avignon, Marseille, Aix-en-Provence, and Arles are good bases. Avignon is also the starting point for excursion-bus tours and boat trips down the Rhône. In most cases, you can buy bus tickets on the bus itself.

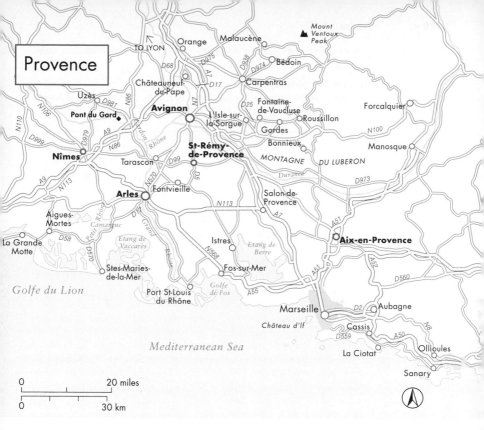

Provence

TO LYON
Orange
Malaucène
Mount Ventoux Peak
Châteauneuf-du-Pape
Bédoin
Carpentras
Uzès
Avignon
Fontaine-de-Vaucluse
Forcalquier
Pont du Gard
L'Isle-sur-la-Sorgue
Roussillon
Gordes
St-Rémy-de-Provence
Bonnieux
Manosque
Nîmes
Tarascon
MONTAGNE DU LUBERON
Durance
Arles
Fontvieille
Salon-de-Provence
Aigues-Mortes
Camargue
Istres
Etang de Berre
Aix-en-Provence
La Grande Motte
Etang de Vaccarès
Fos-sur-Mer
Golfe de Fos
Marseille
Aubagne
Stes-Maries-de-la-Mer
Port St-Louis du Rhône
Château d'If
Cassis
Ollioules
Golfe du Lion
Mediterranean Sea
La Ciotat
Sanary

0   20 miles
0   30 km

Contacts Aix-en-Provence Gare Routière ✉ *Av. de la Europe* ☎ *04–42–91–26–80.* **Avignon Gare Routière** ✉ *58 bd. St-Roch* ☎ *04–90–82–07–35.* **Marseille Gare Routière** ✉ *3 pl. Victor Hugo, Saint Charles, Marseille* ☎ *3635.*

CAR TAVEL

Driving is also a good option, although for the first-time visitor driving on the highways in Provence can be a scary experience. It is fast . . . regardless of the speed limit. A6–A7 (a toll road) from Paris, known as the Autoroute du Soleil—the Highway of the Sun—takes you straight to Provence, where it divides at Orange, 659 km (412 miles) from Paris; the trip can be done in a fast five or so hours.

TRAIN TRAVEL

The high-speed *Méditerranée* line ushered in a new era in Trains à Grande Vitesse travel in France; the route means that you can travel from Paris's Gare de Lyon to Avignon (first-class, one-way tickets cost between €25 and €190, depending on when you book your ticket) in 2 hours, 40 minutes, with a mere three-hour trip to Nîmes, Aix-en-Provence, and Marseille. Not only is the idea of Provence as a day trip now possible (though, of course, not advisable), you can even whisk yourself there directly upon arrival at Paris's Charles de Gaulle airport.

Train Contacts Aix-en-Provence *Gare SNCF* ✉ *Av. Victor Hugo* ☎ *36–35.* **Marseille** *Gare St-Charles* ☎ *04–91–08–16–40.* **SNCF** ☎ *36–35 (€0.34 per min)*

⊕ *www.voyages-sncf.com.* **TGV** ☎ *36–35 (€0.34 per min)* ⊕ *www.tgv.com.* **www. beyond.fr** ⊕ *www.beyond.fr.*

VISITOR INFORMATION
Contacts Comité Regional du Tourisme de Provence-Alpes-Côte d'Azur
✉ *61 La Canebière, Marseille* ☎ *04–91–56–47–00* ⊕ *www.tourismepaca.fr.*

ARLES

36 km (22 miles) southwest of Avignon, 31 km (19 miles) east of Nîmes, 92 km (57 miles) northwest of Marseille, 720 km (430 miles) south of Paris.

If you were obliged to choose just one city to visit in Provence, lovely little Arles would give Avignon and Aix a run for their money. It's too chic to become museumlike, yet has a wealth of classical antiquities and Romanesque stonework, quarried-stone edifices and shuttered town houses, and graceful, shady Vieille Ville streets and squares. Throughout the year there are pageantry, festivals, and cutting-edge arts events. Its panoply of restaurants and small hotels makes it the ideal headquarters for forays into the Alpilles and the Camargue.

The remains of this golden age are reason enough to visit Arles today, yet its character nowadays is as gracious and low-key as it once was cutting-edge. Seated in the shade of the plane trees on place du Forum or strolling the rampart walkway along the sparkling Rhône, you can see what enchanted Gauguin and drove Van Gogh frantic with inspiration.

If you plan to visit many of the monuments and museums in Arles, buy a *visite generale* ticket for €13.50. This covers the entry fee to the Musée de l'Arles et de la Provence Antiques and any and all of the other museums and monuments (except the independent Museon Arlaten, which charges €4). The ticket is good for the length of your stay.

GETTING HERE
If you're arriving by plane, note that Arles is roughly 20 km (12 miles) from the Nîmes-Arles-Camargue airport (☎ *04–66–70–49–49*). The easiest way from the landing strip to Arles is by taxi (about €30). Buses run between Nîmes and Arles three times daily on weekdays and twice on Saturday (not at all on Sunday), and four buses weekdays between Arles and Stes-Maries-de-la-Mer, through Cars de Camargue (☎ *04–90–52–20–85*). The SNCF (☎ *08–92–33–53–35*) runs three buses Monday–Saturday from Avignon to Arles, and Cartreize (☎ *08–00–19–94–13* ⊕ *www.lepilote.com*) runs a service between Marseille and Arles. Arles is along the main coastal train route, and you can take the TGV to Avignon from Paris and jump on the local connection to Arles. For all train information, check out ⊕ *www.voyages-sncf.com,* or call.

EXPLORING
Église St-Trophime. Classed as a world treasure by UNESCO, this extraordinary Romanesque church alone would justify a visit to Arles. The side aisles date from the 11th century and the nave from the 12th; the church's austere symmetry and ancient artworks (including a stunning early Christian sarcophagus) are fascinating. But it's the church's superbly preserved Romanesque sculpture on the 12th-century

portal—the recently renovated entry facade—that earns international respect. Particularly remarkable is the frieze of the Last Judgment, with souls being dragged off to Hell in chains or, on the contrary, being lovingly delivered into the hands of the saints. Christ is flanked by his chroniclers, the evangelists: the eagle (John), the bull (Luke), the angel (Matthew), and the lion (Mark). ✉ *Pl. de la République* 🌐 *www.arlestourisme.com* 🎟 *Free* 🕒 *Not open to the public between noon and 2 pm.*

Musée Départemental Arles Antiques (*Museum of Ancient Arles*). Though it's a hike from the center, this state-of-the-art museum is a good place to set the tone and context for your exploration of Arles. You can learn all about the city in its Roman heyday, from the development of its monuments to details of daily life. The bold, modern triangular structure (designed by Henri Ciriani) lies on the site of an enormous Roman *cirque* (chariot-racing stadium), and the permanent collection includes jewelry, mosaics, town plans, and carved fourth-century sarcophagi. **■ TIP→ A new wing features a rare intact barge dating from AD 50 and a fascinating display illustrating how the boat was meticulously dredged from the nearby Rhône**. The quantity of these treasures gives an idea of the extent of Arles's importance. Seven superb floor mosaics can be viewed from an elevated platform, and you exit via a hall packed tight with magnificently detailed paleo-Christian sarcophagi. As you leave you will see the belt of St-Césaire, the last bishop of Arles, who died in AD 542 when the countryside was overwhelmed by the Franks and the Roman era met its end. Ask for an English-language guidebook. ✉ *Ave de la 1ère Division Française Libre, Presqu'île du Cirque Romain* ☎ *04–13–31–51–03* 🌐 *www.arles-antique.cg13.fr* 🎟 *€8, free first Sun. of the month* 🕒 *Wed.–Mon. 10–6.*

7

WHERE TO EAT

$$
FRENCH

🍴 **Brasserie Nord-Pinus.** With its tile-and-ironwork interior straight out of a design magazine and its place du Forum terrace packed with all the right people, this cozy-chic retro brasserie highlights light, simple, and purely Provençal cooking in dishes such as roast rack of lamb au jus and pan-fried fillet of beef in a morel-and-cream sauce. The fois-gras cocotte is simply delicious. Discreet service and a nicely balanced wine list only add to its charm. And wasn't that Christian Lacroix (or Kate Moss or Juliette Binoche) under those Ray-Bans? [$] *Average main: €24* ✉ *Pl. du Forum* ☎ *04–90–93–58–43* 🌐 *www.nord-pinus.com* ✍ *Reservations essential* 🕒 *Closed Sun. and Mon.*

$$$$
FRENCH
Fodor's Choice ★

🍴 **La Chassagnette.** Reputedly the original registered "organic" restaurant in Provence, this sophisticated yet down-home comfortable spot—located 12 km (7½ miles) south of Arles—is fetchingly designed and has a dining area that extends outdoors, where large family-style picnic tables await under a wooden-slate canopy overlooking the extensive gardens. Using ingredients that are grown right on the property, innovative master chef Armand Arnal (who has been awarded a Michelin star) serves prix-fixe menus that are a refreshing, though not inexpensive, mix of modern and classic French-country cuisine—you can expect to pay €85–€125 per person. The à la carte options are equally admirable and much more affordable: picture a filet of wild sole with roasted asparagus and bottarga for €35. Environmentally conscious oenophiles can wash it all down with a glass of eco-certified wine. [$] *Average main: €37* ✉ *Rte. du Sambuc, D36* ☎ *04–90–97–26–96* 🌐 *www.chassagnette.fr* ✍ *Reservations essential* ⏲ *Closed Feb., Tues. and Wed. Closed May–Oct.; Mon.–Wed. Nov.–Apr.*

WHERE TO STAY

$$$ HOTEL Fodor's Choice ★ 🏨 **Grand Hotel Nord-Pinus.** A richly atmospheric stage-set for literati (or literary poseurs), decor-magazine shoots, and people who prize ambience, this scruffy-chic landmark is not for everyone—but if Picasso once felt at home here, perhaps you will too. **Pros:** unique atmosphere transports you to a less complicated time, when bullfighting was not part of the political arena, and people still dressed for dinner; free mineral water in rooms. **Cons:** rooms at front of hotel can be noisy, especially in summer. [$] *Rooms from: €185* ✉ *Pl. du Forum* ☎ *04–90–93–44–44* 🌐 *www.nord-pinus.com* 🛏 *25 rooms, 1 apartment* 🍴 *No meals.*

$$$$ HOTEL Fodor's Choice ★ 🏨 **L'Hôtel Particulier.** Once owned by the Baron of Chartrouse, this extraordinary 18th-century *hôtel particulier* (mansion) is delightfully intimate and decorated in sophisticated yet charming style, with gold-framed mirrors, white-brocade chairs, marble writing desks, artfully hung curtains, and hand-painted wallpaper. **Pros:** quiet and secluded but only a short walk to town; combines historical ambiance with modern high-tech conveniences. **Cons:** a 50% non-refundable deposit is required when booking; the pool is small, which can be difficult in summer when every guest wants to be in the water; optional breakfast is steep (€23). [$] *Rooms from: €309* ✉ *4 rue de la Monnaie* ☎ *04–90–52–51–40* 🌐 *www.hotel-particulier.com* 🛏 *18 rooms* 🍴 *No meals.*

$ HOTEL 🏨 **Muette.** This Old Town option has 12th-century exposed stone walls, a 15th-century spiral staircase, and weathered wood, plus Provençal prints and fresh sunflowers in every room to add just the right homey touch. **Pros:** excellent value; enthusiastic welcome; generous buffet breakfast (extra). **Cons:** some rooms can be very noisy, especially in the summer; parking can be tricky. [$] *Rooms from: €70* ✉ *15 rue des Suisses* ☎ *04–90–96–15–39* 🌐 *www.hotel-muette.com* 🛏 *18 rooms* ⏲ *Closed mid-Nov.–Feb.* 🍴 *No meals.*

NÎMES

35 km (20 miles) north of Aigues-Mortes, 43 km (26 miles) south of Avignon, 121 km (74 miles) west of Marseille.

If you've come to the south seeking Roman treasures, you need look no farther than Nîmes (pronounced *neem*): the Arènes and Maison Carrée are among continental Europe's best-preserved antiquities. But if you've come in search of a more modern mythology—of lazy, graceful Provence—give Nîmes a wide berth. It's a feisty, run-down rat race of a town, with jalopies and Vespas roaring irreverently around the ancient temple. Its medieval Vieille Ville has none of the gentrified grace of those in Arles or St-Rémy. Yet its rumpled and rebellious ways trace directly back to its Roman incarnation, when its population swelled with newly victorious soldiers flaunting arrogant behavior after their conquest of Egypt in 31 BC.

Already anchoring a fiefdom of pre-Roman *oppida* (elevated fortresses) before ceding to the empire in the 1st century BC, this ancient city grew to formidable proportions under the Pax Romana. Its next golden age bloomed under the Protestants, who established an anti-Catholic stronghold here and wreaked havoc on iconic architectural treasures— not to mention the papist minority. Their massacre of some 200 Catholic citizens in 1567 is remembered as the Michelade; many of those murdered were priests sheltered in the *évêché* (bishop's house), now the Museum of Old Nîmes.

GETTING HERE

On the Paris-Avignon-Montpellier train line, Nîmes has a direct rail link to and from Paris (about a three-hour ride). For TGV and train information go to ⊕ *www.voyages-sncf.com,* or call ☎ *08–36–35–35–35.* The Nîmes *gare routière* (bus station) is just behind the train station. Cars de Camargue (☎ *04–90–52–20–85*) runs several buses to and from Arles (four daily Mon.–Sat., two on Sun.). Edard (☎ *08–10–33–42–73*) has several buses (daily except Sun.) between Avignon and Nîmes and Uzès and Nîmes. Some Uzès buses stop at Remoulins for the Pont du Gard and a few continue on to St-Quentin-la-Poterie. Note that although all the sites in Nîmes are walkable, the useful Tango bus (⊕ *www.tangobus. fr*) runs a good loop from the station and passes by many of the principal sites along the way for €1.

EXPLORING

Fodor'sChoice
★

Arènes. The best-preserved Roman amphitheater in the world is a miniature of the Colosseum in Rome (note the small carvings of Romulus and Remus—the wrestling gladiators—on the exterior and the intricate bulls' heads etched into the stone over the entrance on the north side). More than 435 feet long and 330 feet wide, it had a seating capacity of 24,000 in its day. Bloody gladiator battles, criminals being thrown to animals, and theatrical wild-boar chases drew crowds to its bleachers—and the vomitoria beneath them. Nowadays the *corrida* (bullfight) transforms the arena (and all of Nîmes) into a sangria-flushed homage to Spain. Concerts are held here year-round, thanks to a high-tech glass-and-steel structure that covers the arena for winter use. ✉ *Bd. des Arènes* ☎ *04–66–21–82–56, 04–66–02–80–80 for feria box office* ⊕ *www.arenes-nimes.com* ✆ *€8.50, joint ticket with Tour Magne and Maison Carrée €11* ☉ *Mar. and Oct, daily 9–6; Apr., May, and Sept., daily 9–6:30; June, daily 9–7; July and Aug., daily 9–8; Nov.–Feb., daily 9:30–5.*

Temple de Diane (*Temple of Diana*). This shattered Roman ruin dates from the second century BC. The temple's function is unknown, though it's thought to have been part of a larger Roman complex that is still unexcavated. In the Middle Ages Benedictine nuns occupied the building before it was converted into a church. Destruction came during the Wars of Religion. ✉ *Jardins de la Fontaine.*

Tour Magne (*Magne Tower*). At the far end of the Jardins de la Fontaine, you'll find the remains of a tower the emperor Augustus had built on Gallic foundations; it was probably used as a lookout post. Despite losing 30 feet in height over the course of time, the tower still provides fine views of Nîmes for anyone energetic enough to climb the 140 steps. ✉ *Jardins de la Fontaine, Pl. Guillaume-Apollinaire* ☎ *04–66–21–82–56* 🎟 *€3, joint ticket with Arènes and Maison Carrée €11* ⏲ *Nov.–Feb., daily 9:30–1 and 2–4:30; Mar. and Oct., daily 9:30–1 and 2–6; Apr., May, and Sept., daily 9:30–6:30; June, daily 9–7; July and Aug., daily 9–8.*

WHERE TO EAT AND STAY

$$$$ MODERN FRENCH

🍴 **Alexandre.** Chef Michel Kayser adds a personal touch to local specialties at this à la mode modern restaurant. The menu changes according to the season and the chef's creative whimsy. Golden zucchini flowers with frothy truffle mousseline followed by a rich bull steak, roasted in its own juice and served with pan-roasted potatoes, may not leave room for dessert. The decor is elegantly spare, with stone walls and large bay windows; but the gardens are extensive, and often apricots and peaches plucked from the overhanging branches will appear on your plate, magically transformed into some delicious creation. [$] *Average main: €50* ✉ *2 rue Xavier Tronc, Rte. de l'Aeroport* ☎ *04–66–70–08–99* 🌐 *www.michelkayser.com* ✍ *Reservations essential* ⏲ *Closed Mon. and Tues. Sept.–June, and Sun. and Mon. July–Aug. Closed 2 weeks end of Feb. and Aug. No dinner Sun.*

$$ FRENCH

🍴 **Le Jardin d'Hadrien.** This chic enclave, with its quarried white stone, ancient plank-and-beam ceiling, and open fireplace, would be a culinary haven even without its lovely hidden garden, a shady retreat for summer meals. Chef Christophe Adlin changes menus monthly to bring the freshest seasonal combinations to your palate, so you might be treated to fresh cod and zucchini flowers filled with *brandade* (the creamy, light paste of salt cod and olive oil) or, in winter, sautéed veal and crayfish with saffron potatoes. Two prix-fixe menus served year-round—gourmand and saveur—change every other month. [$] *Average main: €21* ✉ *11 rue Enclos Rey* ☎ *04–66–21–86–65* 🌐 *www.lejardindhadrien.fr* ✍ *Reservations essential* ⏲ *No lunch Mon.–Thurs.; no dinner Sun.*

$$$ B&B/INN

🏨 **La Maison de Sophie.** Far from the hustle of town and yet just five minutes from the arena, this luxurious hôtel particulier has all the charm—especially in its elegant and tranquil guest rooms—that the city itself often lacks. **Pros:** big-city elegance mixes nicely with country charm and quiet nights; warm welcome. **Cons:** often fully booked long in advance; pool is quite small. [$] *Rooms from: €190* ✉ *31 av. Carnot* ☎ *04–66–70–96–10* 🌐 *www.hotel-nimes-gard.com* 🛏 *5 rooms, 2 suites* 🍽 *No meals.*

ST-RÉMY-DE-PROVENCE

8 km (5 miles) north of Les Baux, 24 km (15 miles) northeast of Arles, 19 km (12 miles) south of Avignon.

There are other towns as pretty as St-Rémy-de-Provence, and others in more dramatic or picturesque settings. Ruins can be found throughout the south, and so can authentic village life. Yet something felicitous has happened in this market town in the heart of the Alpilles—a steady infusion of style, of art, of imagination—all brought by people with a respect for local traditions and a love of Provençal ways. Here, more than anywhere, you can meditate quietly on antiquity, browse redolent markets with basket in hand, peer down the very row of plane trees you remember from a Van Gogh, and also enjoy urbane galleries, cosmopolitan shops, and specialty food boutiques. An abundance of chic choices in restaurants, mas, and even châteaux awaits you; the almond and olive groves conceal dozens of stone-and-terra-cotta gîtes, many with pools. In short, St-Rémy has been gentrified through and through, and is now a sort of arid, southern Martha's Vineyard or, perhaps, the Hamptons of Provence.

EXPLORING

FAMILY **Glanum.** A slick visitor center prepares you for entry into the ancient village of Glanum, with scale models of the site in its various heydays. A good map and an English brochure guide you stone by stone through the maze of foundations, walls, towers, and columns that spread across a broad field; helpfully, Greek sites are noted by numbers, Roman ones by letters. Glanum is across the street from Les Antiques and set back from the D5, and the only parking is in a dusty roadside lot on the D5 south of town (in the direction of Les Baux). ✉ *Rte. des Baux de Provence, off D5, direction Les Baux* ☎ *04–90–92–23–70* 🌐 *www.glanum.monuments-nationaux.fr* 🎟 *€7.50* 🕒 *Apr.–Aug., daily 10–6:30; Sept., Tues.–Sun. 10–6:30; Oct.–Mar., Tues.–Sun. 10–5.*

Les Antiques. Two of the most miraculously preserved classical monuments in France are simply called Les Antiques. Dating from 30 BC, the **Mausolée** (mausoleum), a wedding-cake stack of arches and columns, lacks nothing but a finial on top, and is dedicated to a Julian, probably Caesar Augustus. A few yards away stands another marvel: the **Arc Triomphal,** dating from AD 20.

7

WHERE TO EAT

$$$$ FRENCH ✕ **La Maison Jaune.** This 18th-century retreat with a Michelin star in the Vieille Ville draws crowds of summer people to its pretty roof terrace, with accents of sober stone and lively contemporary furniture both indoors and out. The look reflects the cuisine: with vivid flavors and a cool, contained touch, chef François Perraud prepares fresh Mediterranean sea bream, bouillabaisse, grilled lamb from Provence, and other specialties on his seasonally changing menus. [$] *Average main: €36* ✉ *15 rue Carnot* ☎ *04–90–92–56–14* 🌐 *www.lamaisonjaune.info* ✍ *Reservations essential* 🕒 *Closed Sun. and Mon. Mar.–June and Sept.–Feb.*

AVIGNON

82 km (51 miles) northwest of Aix-en-Provence, 95 km (59 miles) northwest of Marseille, 224 km (140 miles) south of Lyon.

Avignon is anything but a museum; it surges with modern ideas and energy and thrives within its ramparts as it did in the heyday of the popes—and, like those radical church lords, it's sensual, cultivated, and cosmopolitan, with a taste for worldly pleasures. Avignon remained papal property until 1791, and elegant mansions bear witness to the town's 18th-century prosperity. From its famous Palais des Papes (Papal Palace), where seven exiled popes camped between 1309 and 1377 after fleeing from the corruption and civil strife of Rome, to the long, low bridge of childhood-song fame stretching over the river, you can beam yourself briefly into 14th-century Avignon, so complete is the context, so evocative the setting. Note that the free Avignon PASSion (available at all major sights and museums) gives 10% to 50% reductions on most museums and sights after you buy the first ticket.

GETTING HERE

Taxi Avignon (✉ *Pl. Pie* ☎ *04–90–82–20–20*) is the easiest way to get into town. The main bus station is on Avenue Monteclar (☎ *04–90–82–07–35*) next to the train station. Town buses and services to the TGV station are run by TCRA (☎ *04–32–74–18–32* ⊕ *www.tcra.fr*). Avignon is at the junction of the Paris–Marseille and Paris–Montpellier lines. The Gare Centre Ville has frequent links to Arles, Nîmes, Orange, Toulon, and Carcassonne. The Gare TGV (☎ *08–92–33–53–35* ⊕ *www. tgv.com*) is 4 km (2½ miles) south of Avignon. Train information can be found at ⊕ *www.voyages-sncf.com,* or call ☎ *08–92–33–53–35.* A bus service leaves from the station at the arrival of each train and takes passengers to the Centre Ville station, and leaves from the Centre Ville station to the TGV station every 15 minutes.

EXPLORING

Le Musée du Petit Palais. This residence of bishops and cardinals before Pope Benedict built his majestic palace houses a large collection of old-master paintings, the majority of which are Italian works from the early-Renaissance schools of Siena, Florence, and Venice—styles with which the Avignon popes would have been familiar. Later works here include Sandro Botticelli's *Virgin and Child,* and Venetian paintings by Vittore Carpaccio and Giovanni Bellini. ✉ *Pl. du Palais* ☎ *04–90–86–44–58* ⊕ *www.petit-palais.org* 🎫 *€6* ⊙ *Wed.–Mon. 10–1 and 2–6.*

Palais des Papes. This colossal palace creates a disconcertingly fortress-like impression, underlined by the austerity of its interior. Most of the original furnishings were returned to Rome with the papacy; others were lost during the French Revolution. Some imagination is required to picture the palace's medieval splendor, awash with color and with worldly clerics enjoying what the 14th-century Italian poet Petrarch called "licentious banquets." On close inspection, two different styles of building emerge at the palace: the severe **Palais Vieux** (Old Palace), built between 1334 and 1342 by Pope Benedict XII, a member of the Cistercian order, which frowned on frivolity, and the more decorative **Palais Nouveau** (New Palace), built in the following decade by the artsy, lavish-living Pope Clement VI. The Great Court, entryway to the complex, links the two. ✉ *Pl. du Palais, 6 rue Pente Rapide* ☎ *04–32–74–32–74* ⊕ *www.palais-des-papes.com* 🎫 *€11 (€13.50, includes tour of Pont St-Bénéze); audio guide €2 for the palace, free for the bridge.* ⊙ *Mar., daily 9–6:30; Apr.–June and Sept.–Oct., daily 9–7; July, daily 9–8; Aug., daily 9–8:30; Nov.–Feb., daily 9:30–5:45.*

Bouteillerie. For wine lovers, there's a wine cellar devoted to Côtes du Rhônes at the Bouteillerie of the Popes' Palace, where you can sample and buy regional wines. The selection changes every year. Although it's in the palais, you don't need to pay admission to go to the store.

✉ *Pl. du Palais* ☎ *04–90–27–50–85* ⏲ *Daily, with the mid-day closure from 1–2.*

Pont St-Bénézet (*St. Bénézet Bridge*). This bridge is the subject of the famous children's song: "*Sur le pont d'Avignon on y danse, on y danse. . .*" ("On the bridge of Avignon one dances, one dances . . ."). Unlike London Bridge, which fell down in another nursery ditty, Pont St-Bénézet still stretches its arches across the river, but only partway: half was washed away in the 17th century. Its first stones allegedly laid with the miraculous strength granted St-Bénézet in the 12th century, it once reached all the way to Villeneuve. ✉ *Port du Rochre* 🌐 *www.palais-des-papes.com* 🎟 *€4.50 includes new tactile PDA audio guide; €13 includes entry to Palais des Papes* ⏲ *Mar., daily 9–6:30; Apr.–June and Sept.–Oct., daily 9–7; July, daily 9–8; Aug., daily 9–8:30; Nov.–Feb., daily 9:30–5:45.*

Fodor's Choice ★ **Rocher des Doms** (*Rock of the Domes*). Set on bluff above town, this lush hilltop garden has grand Mediterranean pines, a man-made lake (complete with camera-ready swans), plus glorious views of the palace, the rooftops of Old Avignon, the Pont St-Bénézet, and formidable Villeneuve across the Rhône. On the horizon loom Mont Ventoux, the Luberon, and Les Alpilles. The garden has lots of history as well: Often called the "cradle of Avignon," its rocky grottoes were among the first human habitations in the area. ✉ *Montée du Moulin off pl. du Palais* ☎ *04–32–74–32–74* 🌐 *www.avignon-tourisme.com* ⏲ *Dec.–Jan., daily 7–5:30; Feb. and Nov., daily 7:30–6; Mar., daily 7:30–7; Apr.–May, and Sept., daily 7:30–8; June–Aug., daily 7:30–9; Oct., daily 7:30–6:30.*

WHERE TO EAT

$$ FRENCH Fodor's Choice ★ 🍴 **La Fourchette.** The food here is some of the best in town, as the bevy of locals clamoring to get in proves. It all smells so good that you may be tempted to rip one of the decorative forks off the wall and attack your neighbor's plate. Service is prompt and friendly, and you can dig in to heaping portions of escalope of salmon, chicken cilantro à l'orange, or what is likely the best Provençal daube (served with macaroni gratin) in France. [$] *Average main: €20* ✉ *17 rue Racine* ☎ *04–90–85–20–93* 🌐 *www.la-fourchette.net* ✍ *Reservations essential* ⏲ *Closed Sat.–Sun. and first 3 wks of Aug.*

$$ BISTRO 🍴 **Le 26.** The Piedoie, as this place was formerly known, built a die-hard following of locals by providing excellent cuisine at fair prices. New chef-owner Joël Laurent and his wife Laurence have kept the crowds coming with set menus that include a starter, main dish, and dessert, with four choices for each course (they change every two months to reflect what the markets are selling). If you like to try a little of this and a little of that, the *gourmande* lunch menu (only €15) serves all four starters—and for an extra euro, they'll add dessert. If you are traveling *avec enfants,* a children's menu is available as well. [$] *Average main: €22* ✉ *26 rue des Trois Faucons* ☎ *04–90–86–51–53* 🌐 *www.le26avignon.fr* ✍ *Reservations essential* ⏲ *Closed Mon. No dinner Wed.; no lunch Sat.*

7

WHERE TO STAY

$$$$ HOTEL Fodor's Choice ★ **Hôtel de la Mirande.** A designer's dream of a hotel, this *petit palais* permits you to step into 18th-century Avignon—enjoy painted coffered ceilings, sumptuous antiques, extraordinary handmade wall coverings, and other superb *grand siècle* touches (those rough sisal mats on the floors were the height of chic back in the baroque era). **Pros:** spectacular setting of the hotel; free bottled water from minibar during your stay. **Cons:** rooms can be a little stuffy; breakfast is expensive. [$] *Rooms from: €450* ✉ *Pl. de la Mirande* ☎ *04–90–14–20–20* 🌐 *www.la-mirande.fr* 🛏 *25 rooms, 1 suite, 1 apartment* 🍴 *No meals.*

$$$ B&B/INN **La Banasterie.** Hidden away on a side street by the Palais des Papes, this little inn offers luxuriously decorated bedrooms and a sweet welcome—both literally and figuratively. **Pros:** on a quiet side street in the center of town; very comfortable rooms; breakfast included; computer available for guests. **Cons:** can be hard to find. [$] *Rooms from: €190* ✉ *11 rue de la Banasterie* ☎ *04–32–76–30–78* 🌐 *www.labanasterie.com* 🛏 *2 rooms, 3 suites* 🍴 *Breakfast.*

AIX-EN-PROVENCE

Fodor's Choice ★ *48 km (29 miles) southeast of Bonnieux, 82 km (51 miles) southeast of Avignon, 176 km (109 miles) west of Nice, 759 km (474 miles) south of Paris.*

Gracious, posh, cultivated, and made all the more cosmopolitan by the presence of some 30,000 international university students, the lovely old town of Aix (pronounced *ex*) was once the capital of Provence. The vestiges of that influence and power—fine art, noble architecture, and graceful urban design—remain beautifully preserved today. That and its thriving market, vibrant café life, and world-class music festival make Aix vie with Arles and Avignon as one of the towns in Provence that shouldn't be missed.

Romans were first drawn here by mild thermal baths, naming the town Aquae Sextiae (Waters of Sextius) in honor of the consul who founded a camp near the source in 123 BC. Just 20 years later some 200,000 Germanic invaders besieged Aix, but the great Roman general Marius pinned them against the mountain known ever since as Ste-Victoire. Marius remains a popular local first name to this day. Under the wise and generous guidance of Roi René (King René) in the 15th century, Aix became a center of Renaissance arts and letters. At the height of its political, judicial, and ecclesiastic power in the 17th and 18th centuries, Aix profited from a surge of private building, each grand hôtel particulier vying to outdo its neighbor. Its signature *cours* (courtyards) and *places* (squares), punctuated by grand fountains and intriguing passageways, date from this time.

GETTING HERE

The center of Aix is best explored on foot, but there's a municipal bus service that serves the entire town and the outlying suburbs. Most leave from La Rotonde in front of the tourism office (☎ *04–42–16–11–61* 🌐 *www.aixenprovencetourism.com*), where you can also buy tickets (€1 one-way) and ask for a bus route map. The Aix TGV station is 10 km

(6 miles) west of the city and is served by regular shuttle buses. The old Aix station is on the slow Marseille–Sisteron line, with trains arriving roughly every hour from Marseille St-Charles.

EXPLORING

Atelier Cézanne (*Cézanne's Studio*). Just north of the Vieille Ville loop you'll find Cézanne's studio. After the death of his mother forced the sale of the painter's beloved country retreat, Jas de Bouffan, he had this atelier built and some of his finest works, including *Les Grandes Baigneuses* (*The Large Bathers*), were created in the upstairs workspace. But what is most striking is the collection of simple objects that once featured prominently in his portraits and still lifes—redingote, bowler hat, ginger jar—all displayed as if awaiting his return. The atelier is behind an obscure garden gate on the left as you climb the avenue Paul-Cézanne. ■ **TIP→ After-dark shows that take place in July and August include movie screenings in the garden.** ✉ *9 av. Paul-Cézanne* ☎ *04–42–21–06–53* 🌐 *www.atelier-cezanne.com* 🎟 *€5.50* 🕒 *Apr.–June and Sept., daily 10–noon and 2–6; July and Aug., daily 10–6; Oct.–Mar., daily 10–noon and 2–5. Closed Sun. Dec.–Feb.*

Cathédrale St-Sauveur. Many eras of architectural history are clearly delineated and preserved here. The cathedral has a double nave—Romanesque and Gothic side by side—and a Merovingian (5th-century) **baptistery,** its colonnade mostly recovered from Roman temples built to honor pagan deities. The deep bath on the floor is a remnant of total-immersion baptism. Shutters hide the ornate 16th-century carvings on the **portals,** opened by a guide on request. The guide can also lead you into the tranquil Romanesque **cloister** next door, with carved pillars and slender columns. ✉ *Pl. des Martyrs de la Résistance* ☎ *04–42–23–45–65* 🌐 *www.cathedrale-aix.net.*

7

Fodor's Choice ★ **Pavillon de Vendôme.** This extravagant baroque villa was built in 1665 as a country house for the Duke of Vendome; its position just outside the city's inner circle allowed the duke to commute discreetly from his official home on the Cours Mirabeau to this retreat, where his mistress, La Belle du Canet, was comfortably installed. The villa was expanded and heightened in the 18th century to draw attention to the classical orders—Ionic, Doric, and Corinthian—on parade in the row of neo-Grecian columns. Inside the cool, broad chambers you can find a collection of Provençal furniture and artwork. Note the curious two giant Atlantes that hold up the interior balcony. ✉ *32 rue Celony* ☎ *04–42–91–88–75* 🌐 *www.aixenprovence.fr* 🎟 *€3.50* 🕒 *Mid-Oct.–mid-Apr., Wed.–Mon. 1:30–5; mid-Apr.–mid-Oct., Wed.–Mon. 10–6. Closed Jan.*

WHERE TO EAT

$$ FRENCH 🍴 **Brasserie Les Deux Garçons.** As you revel in the exquisite gold-ivory decor, which dates from the restaurant's founding in 1792, it's not hard to picture the greats—Churchill, Sartre, Picasso, Delon, Belmondo, and Cocteau among them—enjoying a drink under these mirrors. The food is not memorable, but 365 days a year you can savor the linen-decked sidewalk tables that look out to the Cours Mirabeau. [$] *Average main: €24* ✉ *53 cours Mirabeau* ☎ *04–42–26–00–51* 🌐 *www.les2garcons.fr.*

WHERE TO STAY

$$$$ HOTEL Fodor's Choice ★ **Le Pigonnet.** Cézanne painted Ste-Victoire from what is now the large flower-filled terrace of this enchanting abode, and you can easily imagine former guests Princess Caroline, Iggy Pop, and Clint Eastwood swanning their way through the magnificent, pool-adorned, topiary-accented garden or relaxing in the spacious, light-filled guest rooms, each a marvel of decoration—and renovated in 2013. **Pros:** unique garden setting in the center of Aix; welcome is friendly; rooms all have large French windows. **Cons:** reception area has been called stuffy and old-fashioned; some of the antiques are a little threadbare; breakfast is extra (€25). [$] *Rooms from: €360* ✉ *5 av. du Pigonnet* ☎ *04–42–59–02–90* 🌐 *www.hotelpigonnet.com* *40 rooms, 4 suites* 🍴 *No meals.*

$ HOTEL **Quatre Dauphins.** A noble hôtel particulier in the quiet, soigné, and chic Mazarin quarter offers modest but impeccable lodging, with pretty, comfortable little rooms that have been spruced up with *boutis* (Provençal quilts), Les Olivades fabrics, quarry tiles, jute carpets, and hand-painted furniture. **Pros:** ideal center-of-town location; friendly staff; rooms with showers are cheaper than ones with a bath. **Cons:** rooms are small; in summer it is impossible to get a room; breakfast is extra. [$] *Rooms from: €80* ✉ *54 rue Roux-Alphéran* ☎ *04–42–38–16–39* 🌐 *www.lesquatredauphins.fr* *13 rooms* 🍴 *No meals.*

THE FRENCH RIVIERA

Veterans of the area know that the beauty of the French Riviera coastline is only skin deep, a thin veneer of coddled glamour that hugs the water and hides a more ascetic region up in the hills. These low-lying mountains and deep gorges are known as the *arriére-pays* (backcountry) for good cause: they are as aloof and isolated as the waterfront resorts are in the swim. Medieval stone villages cap rocky hills and play out scenes of Provençal life—the game of boules, the slowly savored pastis (the anise-and-licorice-flavored spirit mixed slowly with water), the farmers' market—as if the ocean were a hundred miles away. Some of them—Èze, St-Paul, Vence—have become virtual Provençal theme parks, catering to busloads of tourists day-tripping from the coast. But just behind them, dozens of hill towns stand virtually untouched, and you can lose yourself in a cobblestone maze.

PLANNING YOUR TIME

If you're settling into one town and making day trips, it's best to divide your time by visiting west and then east of Nice. Parallel roads along the Corniches allow for access into towns with different personalities. Main autoroute A8 (keep spare change at the ready, as it costs €2.90 to use this road between Cannes and Nice), as well as the coastal train, makes zipping up and down from Monaco to Fréjus-St-Raphael a breeze.

Visit different resort towns, but make sure you tear yourself away from the coastal *plages* (beaches) to visit the perched villages that the region is famed for. Venturing farther north to reach these villages, east or west, either by the Route Napoléon (RN98), the D995, or on the Corniche roads, plan on at least one overnight.

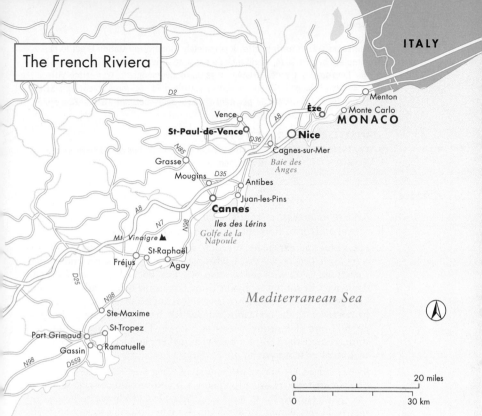

The French Riviera

ITALY

Menton
Monte Carlo
MONACO

Èze

Vence

St-Paul-de-Vence

Nice

Cagnes-sur-Mer

Grasse

Mougins

Antibes

Baie des
Anges

Juan-les-Pins

Cannes

Iles des Lérins

Mt. Vinaigre ▲

Golfe de la
Napoule

St-Raphaël

Fréjus

Agay

Mediterranean Sea

Ste-Maxime

St-Tropez

Port Grimaud

Gassin

Ramatuelle

0   20 miles

0   30 km

And unless you enjoy jacked-up prices, traffic jams, and sardine-style beach crowds, avoid the coast like the plague in July and August. Many of the better restaurants simply shut down to avoid the coconut-oil crowd, and the Estérel is closed to hikers during this flash-fire season. Cannes books up early for the film festival in May, so aim for another month (April, June, September, or October). Between Cannes and Menton, the Côte d'Azur's gentle microclimate usually provides moderate winters; it's protected by the Estérel from the mistral wind that razors through places like Fréjus and St-Raphaèl.

GETTING HERE AND AROUND

The less-budget-conscious can consider jetting around by helicopter (heliports in Monaco, Nice, Cannes, St-Tropez, and some of the hill towns) or speedboat (access to all resort towns), but affordable public transport along the Riviera boils down to the train, the bus, or renting a car. The train accesses all major coastal towns, and most of the gares are in town centers. Note that only a handful of hill towns have train stations. The bus network between towns is fantastic. Renting a car is a good option, and the network of roads here is well marked and divided nicely into slow and very curvy (Bord de Mer Coast Road), faster and curvy (Route National 98), and fast and almost straight (Autoroute A8). Make sure you leave extra time if you're driving or taking the bus, as traffic is always heavy.

Contacts **Gare Cannes Ville**. A completely modernized station is set to be complete by mid 2014; it will include separate arrival and departure points. ✉ *1 rue Jean-Jaurès, Cannes* ⊕ *www.gares-en-mouvement.com.* **Gare Nice Ville** ✉ *Av. Thiers, Nice* ☎ *08–36–35–35–35* ⊕ *www.gares-en-mouvement.com.* **SNCF** ☎ *08–36–35–35–35 (€0.34 per min)* ⊕ *en.voyages-sncf.com.* **TGV** ☎ *284–8633 (€0.34 per min)* ⊕ *www.tgv.com/en.*

VISITOR INFORMATION

Contacts **Côte d'Azur Tourisme** ✉ *455 promenade des Anglais—Horizon, Nice* ☎ *04–93–37–78–78* ⊕ *www.cotedazur-tourisme.com.*

CANNES

6 km (4 miles) east of Mandelieu-La Napoule, 73 km (45 miles) northeast of St-Tropez, 33 km (20 miles) southwest of Nice.

A tasteful and expensive breeding ground for the upscale, Cannes is a sybaritic heaven for those who believe that life is short and sin has something to do with the absence of a tan. Backed by gentle hills and flanked to the southwest by the Estérel, warmed by dependable sun but kept bearable in summer by the cool Mediterranean breeze, Cannes is pampered with the luxurious climate that has made it one of the most popular and glamorous resorts in Europe. The cynosure of sun worshippers since the 1860s, it has been further glamorized by the modern success of its film festival.

Its bay served as nothing more than a fishing port until 1834, when an English aristocrat, Lord Brougham, fell in love with the site during an emergency stopover with a sick daughter. He had a home built here and returned every winter for a sun cure—a ritual quickly picked up by his peers. With the democratization of modern travel, Cannes has become a tourist and convention town; there are now 20 compact Twingos for every Rolls-Royce. But glamour—and the perception of glamour—is self-perpetuating, and as long as Cannes enjoys its ravishing climate and setting, it will maintain its incomparable panache. If you're a lover of noncelluloid art, however, you should look elsewhere—there are only two museums here: one is devoted to history, the other to a collection of dolls. Still, as his lordship instantly understood, this is a great place to pass the winter.

GETTING HERE

Cannes has one central train station, the Gare SNCF (✉ *Rue Jean Jaures* ⊕ *www.voyages-sncf.com*). All major trains pass through here—check out the SNCF website for times and prices—but many of the trains run the St-Raphaël–Ventimiglia route. You can also take the TGV directly from Paris (5 hours). Cannes's main bus station, which is on place de l'Hôtel-de-Ville by the port, serves all coastal destinations. Rapides Côtes d'Azur runs most of the routes out of the central bus station on place Bernard Gentille, including Nice (1½ hours), Mougins (20 minutes), Grasse (45 minutes), and Vallauris (30 minutes), all for a one-way price of €1.50.

Within Cannes, Bus Azur runs the routes, with a ticket costing €1.50 (a weekly ticket is available). The bus line RCA (☎ *08–00–06–01–06*

🌐 *www.rca.tm.fr*) goes to Nice along the coast road, stopping in all villages along the way, and to the Nice airport, every 30 minutes, Monday–Saturday, for a maximum ticket price of €20 round-trip. From the Gare SNCF, RCA goes to Grasse every 30 minutes Monday–Saturday and every hour Sunday, via Mougins. The other option is any of the Transport Alpes Maritimes (TAM) buses (☎ *08–10–06–10–06* 🌐 *www.lignedazur.com*), which service the same destinations and are now cheaper thanks to a government initiative toward communal transport and are a bargain-basement €1.50 to all destinations along the coast (but, be patient, you may not get a seat).

EXPLORING

Le Suquet. Climb up rue St-Antoine into the picturesque vieille ville neighborhood known as Le Suquet, on the site of the original Roman *castrum*. Shops proffer Provençal goods, and the atmospheric cafés provide a place to catch your breath; the pretty pastel shutters, Gothic stonework, and narrow passageways are lovely distractions. ✉ *Rue St-Antoine.*

Musée de la Castre. The hill is topped by an 11th-century château, housing the Musée de la Castre, with its mismatched collection of weaponry, ethnic artifacts, and ceramics amassed by a 19th century aristocrat. The imposing four-sided **Tour du Suquet** (Suquet Tower) was built in 1385 as a lookout against Saracen-led invasions. ✉ *Pl. de la Castre, Le Suquet* ☎ *04–93–38–55–26* 🎟 *€6* 🕐 *Oct.–Mar., Tues.–Sun. 10–1 and 2–5; Apr. and May, Tues.–Sun. 10–1 and 2–6; June and Sept., Tues. and Thurs.–Sun. 10–1 and 2–6, Wed. 10–1 and 2–9; July and Aug., Thurs.–Tues. 10–7, Wed. 10–9.*

7

WHERE TO EAT

$$$$ SEAFOOD 🍴 **Astoux et Cie Brun.** This beacon to all fish lovers since 1953 is deserving of its reputation for impeccably fresh *fruits de mer*. Well-trained staff negotiate cramped quarters to lay down heaping seafood platters, shrimp casseroles, and piles of oysters shucked to order. Open 365 days a year, Astoux is noisy, cheerful, and always busy, so arrive early (noon for lunch, 6 pm for dinner) to get a table and avoid the line—they do not accept reservations. [$] *Average main: €35* ✉ *27 rue Felix Faure, La Croisette* ☎ *04–93–39–21–87* 🌐 *www.astouxbrun.com* ✍ *Reservations not accepted.*

$ BISTRO 🍴 **La Sousta.** There are some restaurants you just don't want to share for fear of never being able to get a table. One of them is La Sousta, neatly tucked away from the touristy side of the Croisette in Cannes's old quarter, Le Suquet. The selective Provençal menu is scribbled on the blackboard, yet the kitchen is very willing to adapt orders—something almost unheard-of in France. Whatever is market fresh is what you'll find on your plate. You may have to fight some locals for a seat, but just say "merci" and all will be forgiven. [$] *Average main: €13* ✉ *11 rue du Pré, Le Suquet* ☎ *04–93–39–19–18* 🕐 *No dinner Sun.–Thurs. Oct.–Film Festival.*

WHERE TO STAY

$ ⬛ **Hotel Colette.** Facing the train station, this four-star boutique hotel
HOTEL is incredibly affordable—not just for Cannes, but for any luxurious
lodging near the beach. **Pros:** close to the Palais de Festival; interior
courtyard; L'Occitane toiletries provided. **Cons:** walls may be a little
thin but no street noise; local parking could be expensive. $ *Rooms
from: €67* ⊠ *5 pl. de la Gare* ☎ *04–93–39–01–17* ⊕ *www.hotelcolette.
com* ⟿ *45 rooms.*

$$$ ⬛ **Le Cavendish Boutique Hotel.** Lovingly restored by friendly owners
HOTEL Christine and Guy Welter, the giddily opulent former residence of Lord
Cavendish is a true delight, playing up both contemporary décor and
19th-century elegance. **Pros:** genuine welcome is a refreshing change
from the notoriously frosty reception at other Cannes palace hotels; bar
has complimentary drinks and snacks for guests each evening from 6 to
9. **Cons:** even though rooms all have double-pane windows, the hotel
is on the busiest street in Cannes, which means an inevitable amount
of noise. $ *Rooms from: €195* ⊠ *11 bd. Carnot* ☎ *04–97–06–26–00*
⊕ *www.cavendish-cannes.com* ⟿ *34 rooms* ⊙ *Closed mid-Dec.–mid-
Mar.* ¶⊙¶ *Breakfast.*

ST-PAUL-DE-VENCE

Fodor's Choice *4 km (2½ miles) south of Vence, 18 km (11 miles) northwest of Nice.*
★ The famous medieval village of St-Paul-de-Vence can be seen from
afar, standing out like its companion, Vence, against the skyline. In the
Middle Ages St-Paul was basically a city-state, and it controlled its own
political destiny for centuries. But by the early 20th century St-Paul had
faded to oblivion, overshadowed by the growth of Vence and Cagnes—
until it was rediscovered in the 1920s when a few penniless artists began
paying for their drinks at the local auberge with paintings. Those art-
ists turned out to be Signac, Modigliani, and Bonnard, who met at the
Auberge de la Colombe d'Or, now a sumptuous inn, where the walls
are still covered with their ink sketches and daubs. Nowadays art of
a sort still dominates in the myriad tourist traps that take your eyes
off the beauty of St-Paul's old stone houses and its rampart views. The
most commercially developed of Provence's hilltop villages, St-Paul is
nonetheless a magical place when the tourist crowds are thin. Artists are
still drawn to St-Paul's light, its pure air, its wraparound views, and its
honey-color stone walls, soothingly cool on a hot Provençal afternoon.
Film stars continue to love its lazy yet genteel ways, lingering on the
garden-bower terrace of the Colombe d'Or and challenging the locals
to a game of pétanque under the shade of the plane trees. Even so, you
have to work hard to find the timeless aura of St-Paul; get here early
in the day to get a jump on the cars and tour buses, which can clog the
main D36 highway here by noon, or plan on a stay-over. Either way,
do consider a luncheon or dinner beneath the Picassos at the Colombe
d'Or, even if the menu prices seem almost as fabulous as the collection.

EXPLORING

Fondation Maeght. Many people come to St-Paul just to visit the Fondation Maeght, founded in 1964 by art dealer Aimé Maeght. High above the medieval town, the small modern art museum attracts 200,000 visitors a year. It's an extraordinary marriage of the arc-and-plane architecture of Josep Sert; the looming sculptures of Miró, Moore, and Giacometti; the mural mosaics of Chagall; and the humbling hilltop setting, complete with pines, vines, and flowing planes of water. On display is an intriguing and ever-varying parade—one of the most important in Europe—of works by modern masters, including Chagall's wise and funny late-life masterpiece *La Vie* (*Life*). On the extensive grounds, fountains and impressive vistas help to beguile even those who aren't into modern art. Café F, should you need time to reflect, is open year round. ✉ *623 Chem. des Gardettes* ☎ *04–93–32–81–63* 🌐 *www.fondation-maeght.com* 🎟 *€15* 🕐 *Oct.–June., daily 10–6; July–Sept., daily 10–7.*

WHERE TO STAY

In addition to being a wonderful place to stay, La Colombe d'Or has a highly regarded restaurant.

$$$$ B&B/INN Fodor's Choice ★ 🏨 **La Colombe d'Or.** Often called the most beautiful inn in France, "the golden dove" occupies a rose-stone Renaissance mansion just outside the walls of St-Paul and is so perfect overall that some contend you haven't really been to the French Riviera until you've stayed or dined here. **Pros:** where else can you have an aperitif under a real Picasso? Where else can you wander in the garden, glass of wine in hand, and stare at a real Rodin? **Cons:** some rooms in the adjoining villa have blocked views; menu often outshone by the art; service not always a work of art. [$] *Rooms from: €310* ✉ *Pl. Général-de-Gaulle* ☎ *04–93–32–80–02* 🌐 *www.la-colombe-dor.com* 🛏 *13 rooms, 12 suites* 🕐 *Closed Nov.–Christmas* 🍴 *Breakfast.*

NICE

As the fifth-largest city in France, this distended urban tangle is sometimes avoided, but that decision is one to be rued: Nice's waterfront, paralleled by the famous Promenade des Anglais and lined by grand hotels, is one of the noblest in France. It's capped by a dramatic hilltop château, below which the slopes plunge almost into the sea and at whose base a bewitching warren of ancient Mediterranean streets unfolds.

It was in this old quarter, now Vieux Nice, that the Greeks established a market-port in the 4th century BC and named it Nikaia. After falling to the Saracen invasions, Nice regained power and developed into an important port in the early Middle Ages. In 1388, under Louis d'Anjou, Nice, along with the hill towns behind, effectively seceded from the county of Provence and allied itself with Savoie as the Comté de Nice (Nice County). It was a relationship that lasted some 500 years, and added rich Italian flavor to the city's culture, architecture, and dialect.

Nowadays Nice strikes an engaging balance between historic Provençal grace, port-town exotica, urban energy, whimsy, and high culture. You could easily spend your vacation here, attuned to Nice's quirks, its rhythms, its very multicultural population, and its Mediterranean tides.

The high point of the year falls in mid-February, when the city hosts one of the most spectacular Carnival celebrations in France (⊕ *www. nicecarnaval.com*).

GETTING HERE

Nice is the main point of entry into the French Riviera region. It's home to the second-largest airport in France, which sits on a peninsula between Antibes and Nice, the Aéroport Nice-Côte d'Azur (☎ *08–20– 42–33–33* ⊕ *www.nice.aeroport.fr)*), which is 7 km (4 miles) south of the city. From the airport, you can take a bus to almost anywhere. Lignes d'Azur (☎ *08–10–16–10–06* ⊕ *www.lignesdazur.com*) covers Nice and 46 towns and villages on the Côte d'Azur; the Transport Alpes Maritimes (TAM) is an intercity network of buses (☎ *08–10–06–10–06* ⊕ *www.lignedazur.com* ✉ *€1.50*). If you plan on heading on via train, take the No. 99 bus from the airport (✉*€6*), which will take you to the main SNCF train station (✉ *Av. Thiers* ☎ *08–92–33–53–35*). From here you can access all major coastal cities by train.

EXPLORING

Cathédrale Ste-Réparate. An ensemble of columns, cupolas, and symmetrical ornaments dominates the Vieille Ville, flanked by an 18th-century bell tower and glossy ceramic-tile dome. The cathedral's interior, restored to a bright palette of ocher, golds, and rusts, has elaborate plasterwork and decorative frescoes on every surface. Note that it's usually closed between noon and 2, and also Monday. ✉ *3 pl. Rossetti, Vieux Nice* ⊕ *cathedrale-nice.com.*

Cours Saleya. This long pedestrian thoroughfare—half street, half square—is the nerve center of Old Nice, the heart of the Vieille Ville, and the stage-set for the daily dramas of marketplace and café life. Framed with 18th-century houses and shaded by plane trees, the narrow square bursts into a fireworks-show of color Tuesday through Sunday until 1 pm, when flower-market vendors roll armloads of mimosas, roses, and orange blossoms into *cornets* (paper cones) and thrust them into the arms of shoppers, who then awkwardly continue forward to discover a mix of local farmers and stallholders selling produce (try the fresh figs), spices, olives, and little gift soaps. Cafés and restaurants, all more or less touristy (don't expect friendly service) fill outdoor tables with onlookers who bask in the sun. At the far east end, antiques and *brocantes* (collectibles) draw avid junk-hounds every Monday morning. At this end you can also find place Charles Félix. From 1921 to 1938, Matisse lived in the imposing yellow stone building at Number 1, and you don't really need to visit the local museum that bears his name to understand this great artist: simply stand in the doorway of his former home and study the place de l'Ancien Senat 10 feet away—the scene is a classic Matisse.

Musée des Beaux-Arts (*Jules-Chéret Fine Arts Museum*). Originally built for a member of Nice's Old Russian community, the Princess Kotschoubey, this Italianate mansion is a Belle Époque wedding cake, replete with one of the grandest staircases on the coast. After the *richissime* American James Thompson took over and the last glittering ball was held here, the villa was bought by the municipality as a museum in the 1920s. Unfortunately, much of the period decor was sold; but in its place are paintings by Degas, Boudin, Monet, Sisley, Dufy, and Jules Chéret, whose posters of winking *damselles* distill all the *joie* of the Belle Époque. From the Negresco Hotel area the museum is about a 15-minute walk up a gentle hill. ⊠ *33 av. des Baumettes, Centre Ville* ☎ *04–92–15–28–28* ⊕ *www.musee-beaux-arts-nice.org* ⊠ *Free; guided tours €5 (in French only; reservations required)* ۞ *Tues.–Sun., 10–6; tours Wed. and Thurs. at 3.*

Musée Masséna (*Masséna Palace*). This spectacular Belle Époque villa houses the **Musée d'Art et d'Histoire** (Museum of Art and History), where familiar paintings from French, Italian, and Dutch masters line the walls. A visit to the palace gardens set with towering palm trees, a marble bust of the handsome General Masséna, and backdropped by the ornate trim of the Hôtel Negresco, is a delight; this is one of Nice's most imposing oases. ⊠ *Entrance at 65 rue de France, Centre Ville* ☎ *04–93–91–19–10* ⊠ *Free* ۞ *Wed.–Mon. 10–6.*

ÈZE

Fodor's Choice
★ *2 km (1 miles) east of Beaulieu, 12 km (7 miles) east of Nice, 7 km (4½ miles) west of Monte Carlo.*

Towering like an eagle's nest above the coast and crowned with ramparts and the ruins of a medieval château, preposterously beautiful Èze (pronounced *ehz*) is unfortunately the most accessible of all the perched villages—this means crowds, many of whom head here to shop in the boutique-lined staircase-streets (happily most shops here are quite stylish, and there's a nice preponderance of bric-a-brac and vintage fabric dealers). But most come here to drink in the views, for no one can deny that this is the most spectacularly sited of all coastal promontories; if you can manage to shake the crowds and duck off to a quiet overlook, the village commands splendid views up and down the coast, one of the draws that once lured fabled visitors—lots of crowned heads, Georges Sand, Friedrich Nietzsche—and residents: Consuelo Vanderbilt, when she was tired of being duchess of Marlborough, traded in Blenheim Palace for a custom-built house here.

GETTING HERE

Èze is one of the most-visited perched villages in France and is fairly easy to access via public transporation. Take the train from Nice's Gare SNCF (⊠ *Av. Thiers* ☎ *08–92–33–53–35* ⊕ *www.voyages-sncf.com*) to the village by the sea, Èze-bord-de-Mer. From the station there, take Bus No. 112 run by Lignes d'Azur bus (☎ *08–10–06–10–06* ⊕ *www.lignedazur.com*) for a shuttle (frequent departures) between the station and the sky-high village of Èze, which runs about every hour year-round and costs €1.50. Note that if you're rushing to make a train connection, this shuttle trip has many switchbacks up the steep mountainside and takes a full 15 minutes. If you want to avoid the train entirely and are traveling on a budget, from the Nice Gare Routière (⊠ *5 bd. Jean Jaures* ⊕ *www.rca.tm.fr*) you can take the Transport Alpes Maritimes's 100 TAM bus (☎ *04–93–85–61–81* ⊕ *www.cg06.fr/transport/transports-tam.html*), which costs €1.50 and will take you directly to

7

Èze-bord-de-Mer along the lower Corniche, where you can then transfer to the No. 83 shuttle listed above. Otherwise, you can take the RCA Bus No. 112 at Nice's Gare Routière, which goes from Nice to Beausoleil and stops at Èze Village. By car, you should arrive using the Moyenne Corniche, which deposits you near the gateway to Èze Village; buses (from Nice and Monaco) also use this highway.

EXPLORING

Jardin Exotique de Monaco (*Tropical Garden*). Six hundred varieties of cacti and succulents cling to a sheer rock face at Monaco's magnificent Tropical Garden, a brisk half-hour walk west from the palace. The garden traces its roots to days when Monaco's near-tropical climate nurtured unheard-of exotica, amazing visitors from the northlands as much as any zoo. The plants are of less interest today, especially to Americans familiar with southwestern flora. The views over the Rock and coastline, however, are spectacular. Also on the grounds, or actually under them, are the **Grottes de l'Observatoire**—spectacular grottoes and caves adrip with stalagmites and spotlit with fairy lights. The **Musée d'Anthropologie** showcases two rooms: Albert I covers general prehistory while Ranier III unearths regional palaeolithic discoveries. ✉ *62 bd. du Jardin Exotique, Monaco* 🌐 *www.jardin-exotique.mc* 🎫 *€7.20* ⏲ *Nov.–Jan., daily 9–5; Feb.–Apr. and Oct., daily 9–6; May–Sept., daily 9–7.*

WHERE TO STAY

$$$$ HOTEL Fodor's Choice ★

🏨 **Château de la Chèvre d'Or.** The "Château of the Golden Goat" is actually an entire stretch of the village, streets and all, bordered by gardens that hang from the mountainside in nearly Babylonian style, and offering some of the most breathtaking Mediterranean views—at a price. **Pros:** unique setting; fabulous infinity pool; faultless service. **Cons:** one-night deposit required for all bookings; no elevator; bit of cobblestone walking involved to reach hotel. [$] *Rooms from: €400* ✉ *Rue du Barri* ☎ *04–92–10–66–66* 🌐 *www.chevredor.com* 🛏 *30 rooms, 8 suites* ⏲ *Closed Dec.–Feb.* 🍴 *No meals.*

$$$ B&B/INN

🏨 **La Bastide aux Camelias.** There are only four bedrooms and one suite in this lovely B&B, each individually decorated with softly draped fabrics and polished antiques. **Pros:** heartwarming welcome is genuine; breakfast is scrumptious; perfect place to get away from it all. **Cons:** walking distance from the village is significant; you need a car (free parking) to tour the coast from here. [$] *Rooms from: €140* ✉ *Rte. de l'Adret* ☎ *04–93–41–13–68* 🌐 *www.bastideauxcamelias.com* 🛏 *4 rooms, 1 suite* 🍴 *Breakfast.*

GERMANY

Munich, Neuschwanstein, Dachau,
the Bavarian Alps, Heidelberg,
Hamburg, Berlin, Saxony

WHAT'S WHERE

1 Munich. If Germany has a second capital, it must be Munich. Munich boasts wonderful opera, theater, museums, and churches, but the main appeal is its laid-back attitude, appreciated best in its parks, cafés, and beer gardens.

2 Side Trips from Munich. Munich is within easy reach of soaring castles, medieval villages, and imposing churches. Two of the highlights are Schloss Neuschwanstein, King Ludwig II's fantastical castle, and nearby Hohenschwangau, where the king spent most of his youth. Dachau, also nearby, is a sobering reminder of the tragedy of World War II-era Germany.

3 The Bavarian Alps. Majestic peaks, lush green pastures, and frescoed houses brightened by flowers make for Germany's most photogenic region. Quaint villages like Garmisch-Partenkirchen and Berchtesgaden have preserved their charming historic architecture, but nature is the prime attraction here.

4 Heidelberg. This medieval town is quintessential Germany, full of cobblestone alleys, half-timber houses, vineyards, castles, wine pubs, and Germany's oldest university—all of which attract crowds of camera-carrying vacationers. Still, if you're looking for a fairy-tale town, Heidelberg is it.

5 Hamburg. Hamburg loves to be snobbish, and the Hanseaten can be a little stiff, but the city, dominated by lakes, canals, the river Elbe, and Germany's biggest harbor, is undeniably beautiful. World-class museums of modern art, the Reeperbahn, and a new warehouse quarter make Hamburg worth the visit.

6 Berlin. No trip to Germany is complete without a visit to Berlin—Europe's hippest city. Berlin has an intensity that makes it a unique laboratory for new trends and ideas. Check out the cutting-edge art exhibits, stage dramas, musicals, rock bands, and two cities' worth of world-class museums and historical sights.

7 Saxony. Saxony is the pearl of eastern Germany: the countryside is dotted with beautifully renovated castles and fortresses, and the people are charming and full of energy. (They also speak in an almost incomprehensible local dialect.) Dresden and Leipzig are cosmopolitan centers that combine the energy of the avant-garde with a distinct respect for tradition.

DENMARK

BALTIC SEA

Flensburg

SCHLESWIG-
HOLSTEIN   Kiel
            Neustadt
    Lübeck   Rostock   MECKLENBURG-
                                VORPOMMERN

Bremerhaven   5 HAMBURG
                  Hamburg   E26   24
Oldenburg   E55
    Bremen FORMER BORDER   POLAND
BREMEN BETWEEN EAST AND
        WEST GERMANY   Neuruppin   Oranienburg
LOWER SAXONY   10
                                      6   10
            E45   Wolfsburg   BERLIN   Frankfurt-an-der-Oder
abrück. E30   2   Brandenburg   10 E30   Oder
    Minden Braunschweig   E49
Bielefeld   Magdeburg   51   Lübben
                                      Cottbus
            SAXONY-   E36   15
            ANHALT   Bitterfeld   13
    Göttingen   E55
                        Leipzig
    Kassel   14   Görlitz
            E45   SAXONY   7   Dresden
    Eisenach Weimar Gera E441
HESSEN Alsfeld   E40 4   Chemnitz
Giessen Fulda   THURINGIA   72
baden   7   Plauen
         E45
    OFrankfurt-am-Main   9 Münchberg
Jainz   3   Würzburg   Bayreuth   THE CZECH
Darmstadt E42   E51   REPUBLIC
5   E45   3
Mannheim 81
    Heidelberg   Nürnberg
4
    E50   E45   E56
Karlsruhe Heilbronn 6   BAVARIA   Regensburg
    E41   3   Deggendorf
aden-Baden   Passau
         8   Danube   Danube
81   Ulm   8 Augsburg   Isar
BADEN-   Neu-Ulm   1
WÜRTTEMBERG E41   E52 Munich   Inn   AUSTRIA
    A7   2
    Memmingen   8
    18   Bad Reichenhall   Berchtesgaden
                                0   100 miles
Bodensee   3
                                0   150 km
ITZERLAND

NEED TO KNOW

Berlin ✪

GERMANY

North Sea

AT A GLANCE

Capital: Berlin

Population: 80,500,000

Currency: Euro

Money: ATMs common; credit cards not widely accepted

Language: German

Country Code: ☎ 49

Emergencies: ☎ 110

Driving: On the right

Electricity: 220–240v/50 cycles; plugs have two round prongs

Time: Six hours ahead of New York

Documents: Up to 90 days with valid passport; Schengen rules apply

Mobile Phones: GSM (900 and 1800 bands)

Major Mobile Companies: Telekom, Vodafone, o2, E-Plus

WEBSITES

Germany: ⊕ www.germany.travel

Berlin: ⊕ www.visitberlin.de

Bavaria: ⊕ www.bavaria.us

GETTING AROUND

✈ **Air Travel:** The major airports are Frankfurt, Munich, Düsseldorf, and Berlin.

🚌 **Bus Travel:** Buses cover all major routes at much cheaper prices than trains or planes.

🚗 **Car Travel:** Renting a car is easy in any major or minor city. Gas is very expensive.

🚆 **Train Travel:** Germany has an excellent train network. Regional trains stop frequently, while InterCity Express (ICE) trains connect major cities. However, train travel can be more expensive than air travel, especially last-minute bookings.

PLAN YOUR BUDGET

	HOTEL ROOM	MEAL	ATTRACTIONS
Low Budget	€90	€12	Bier & Oktoberfest Museum, €4
Mid Budget	€160	€25	Neuschwanstein/Hohenschwangau admission, €17
High Budget	€220	€80	Ticket to Berlin's Staatsoper, €86

WAYS TO SAVE

Eat lunch picnic-style. Germany has wonderful outdoor markets and shops, so eat picnic-style. In winter, old market halls have good indoor alternatives.

Book a rental apartment. Get more space and a kitchen with a furnished rental. This is especially good for a family or group.

Book rail tickets in advance. For the cheapest rail fares, book online up to 90 before travel (www.bahn.de).

Look for free museum days. Most museums are free at least one day a week, and many historical sights are free.

PLAN YOUR TIME

Hassle Factor	Low. Flights to Germany are frequent, and it has a fantastic network of trains, buses, and cheap domestic flights.
3 days	Visit one major city, like Berlin or Munich, and venture out on a half- or full-day trip out of town.
1 week	Combine two major destinations, visiting Hamburg, Dresden, or Leipzig along with Berlin, or the Bavarian Alps along with Munich. Enjoy a boat cruise along a scenic German river, like the Rhine, the Elbe, or the Mosel.
2 weeks	Pick a region and really dig deep, combining stops in major cities with a long weekend at the Baltic Sea's beaches and islands or a hiking trip through the legendary Black Forest.

WHEN TO GO

High Season: June through August is the most expensive and popular time to visit Germany. June weather can be unpredictable, and in July and August, many Germans head to the beach (in the north) or the mountains and lakes (in the south). December brings flocks with its charming Christmas markets.

Low Season: January to March can be cold and uncomfortable, and locals may be in the sour mood that only perpetual grayness brings. Consequently, there are deals on lodging and airfare.

Value Season: September is gorgeous, with temperate weather and saner airfares. October has great weather, though temperatures start to drop by late November. Late April and May is a great time to visit, before crowds arrive but when the trees are in bloom and the locals are starting to venture outdoors, though the weather can be changeable and wet.

BIG EVENTS

May: May Day (May 1) brings street music and festivals followed by workers' rallies and left-wing protests.

June: Daylong music festival Fête de la Musique marks the summer solstice. ⊕ www.fetedelamusique.de

September: Oktoberfest, the world's most famous beer festival, actually begins in September. ⊕ www.oktoberfest.de

February: Cologne rings in the Carnival (Fasching) season on Rose Monday. ⊕ www.koelnerkarneval.de

READ THIS

■ **Five Germanys I Have Known,** Fritz Stern. 20th-century German history from a scholar who lived it.

■ **Stasiland,** Anna Funder. A moving collection of East German stories.

■ **Germania,** Simon Winder. A personal, satirical account of Germany, its history, and its people.

WATCH THIS

■ **The Lives of Others.** East German artists and the man who spies on them.

■ **Wings of Desire.** Angels watch over a divided Berlin.

■ **Cabaret.** A thousand clichés later, it remains an iconic look at Weimar Germany.

EAT THIS

■ **Currywurst:** curry-ketchup-covered curried sausage—typical Berlin fare

■ **Schweinshaxe:** Bavarian crispy pork knuckle

■ **Käsespätzle:** Swabian noodles made from special cheese dough.

■ **Weisser Spargel:** sweet white asparagus (April–May)

■ **Federweisser mit Zwiebelkuchen:** an onion tart served with sparkling wine popular in the fall

■ **Germknödel:** dumplings, sometimes stuffed with plums or apricots, with vanilla sauce and poppy seeds

8

Germany is a land of half-timber towns, of pastoral land-scapes with castles, churches, and hillside vineyards. It is filled with a strong sense of cultural heritage, where men still don Lederhosen and women Dirndls, at least in southern regions like Bavaria. There is beer by the stein under the shade of old chestnut trees. No matter what part of Germany you visit, there are thick layers of history: from Roman relics to medieval castles and from baroque palaces to Communist-era apartment blocks.

But, for all the tradition, Germany is a modern country. High-speed autobahns and clean, comfortable trains link its cities. It's a leader in avant-garde fashion, culture, and art, which is reflected in its many museums and the vibrant Berlin art scene.

Germans take their leisure seriously. The great outdoors has always been an important escape, with great beaches in the north, Alpine skiing in the south, and world-class hiking almost anywhere. Big-city party neighborhoods like Hamburg's seedy Reeperbahn and just about anywhere in Berlin help shake things up.

Each season has its own festivities: Fasching (Carnival) heralds the end of winter, beer gardens open up with the first warm rays of sunshine, fall is celebrated with Munich's Oktoberfest, and Advent brings the colorful Christmas markets.

PLANNING

WHEN TO GO

The tourist season in most of Germany runs from May through October, when the weather is at its best. Prices are generally higher in summer, so consider visiting during the off-season to save money (but be aware that the weather is often cold and some attractions are closed or have shorter hours in winter). Munich's Oktoberfest comes late in the tourist season, in late September and early October. The Christmas markets, held in just about every city during the month leading up to Christmas, are another off-season draw. The riotous Fasching season takes place during the weeks before Ash Wednesday in February or March.

It's wise to avoid cities at times of major trade fairs, when attendees commandeer all hotel rooms and prices soar. You can check trade-fair schedules with the German National Tourist Office.

TOP REASONS TO GO

Munich's Oktoberfest: For 12 days at the end of September and into early October, Munich hosts the world's largest beer bonanza, one that now welcomes over 6 million visitors and serves more than 5 million liters of beer.

Herrenchiemsee Castle: Take the old steam-driven ferry to the island in Chiemsee in the Bavarian Alps to visit the last and most glorious castle of "Mad" King Ludwig II.

Neuschwanstein Castle: Look familiar? Walt Disney modeled the castle in *Sleeping Beauty* and later the Disneyland castle itself on Neuschwanstein. Its position at the end of the Romantic Road only adds to its fairy-tale quality.

Heidelberg Castle: The architectural highlight of the region's most beautiful castle is the Renaissance courtyard—harmonious, graceful, and ornate.

Harbor Cruises: Take a bumpy harbor tour through Hamburg's Freihafen, absorb the grand scenery of the city, and gaze at the seafaring steel hulks ready to ply the oceans of the world.

Berlin's Museum Island: The architectural monuments and art treasures here will take you from an ancient Greek altar to a Roman market town to 18th-century Berlin and back in a day.

Christmas Markets: You can catch the spirit of the season throughout December when just about every German city sets up its outdoor Christmas market.

GETTING HERE AND AROUND

8

AIR TRAVEL

Most flights into Germany arrive at Frankfurt's Flughafen Frankfurt Main (FRA) or Munich's Flughafen München (MUC). Flying time to Frankfurt is 1½ hours from London, and 7½ hours from New York.

Domestic air travel can be cheaper than the train. Air Berlin, German-Wings, and Lufthansa offer very low fares on inter-German routes, and a number of airlines, notably Ryanair, offer cheap flights into Germany from secondary European airports.

Contacts Flughafen Frankfurt Main (*FRA*). ☎ *01805/372–4636, 069/6900 from outside Germany* ⊕ *www.frankfurt-airport.de.* **Flughafen München** (*MUC*). ☎ *089/97500* ⊕ *www.munich-airport.de.***Hamburg International Airport** (*HAM*). ☎ *040/50750* ⊕ *www.ham.airport.de.* **Schönefeld** (*SXF*). ☎ *030/000–186 (€0.14 per min)* ⊕ *www.berlin-airport.de.* **Tegel** (*TXL*). ☎ *030/000–186 (€0.14 per min)* ⊕ *www.berlin-airport.de.*

BUS TRAVEL

Deutsche Touring, a subsidiary of the Deutsche Bahn (German Railroad), travels from Germany to other European countries, and offers one-day tours along the Castle Road and the Romantic Road. Towns of every size have local buses, which often link up with trams (streetcars), electric railway (S-bahn), and subway (U-bahn) services. Fares sometimes vary according to distance, but a ticket usually allows you to transfer freely between the various forms of transportation. Most cities issue day tickets at special rates.

Contacts Deutsche Touring ☎ *069/790–3501* ⊕ *www.touring.de.*

CAR TRAVEL

Entry formalities for motorists are few: all you need is proof of insurance, an international car-registration document, and a U.S., Canadian, Australian, or New Zealand driver's license. All major car-rental companies are represented in Germany. Gasoline is very expensive (about $8.50 per gallon), and parking in major cities can be difficult. Nevertheless, a car gives you the flexibility to explore on your own. The marvelous autobahn network enables you to get wherever you want to go in a hurry, and entirely toll-free. ■ TIP→ **Most cars in Germany have manual transmission, and more and more cities are banning environmentally unfriendly cars from their city centers.**

TRAIN TRAVEL

Travel by train is the most relaxing and often fastest way to go. The super-fast InterCity Express (ICE) trains of the Deutsche Bahn (DB, or German Railroad) are frequent, fast, and comfortable. They serve all the large cities, and there are plenty of local trains to get you to small towns as well. Tickets are always less expensive online or from ticket machines than from ticket agents, and tickets with flexible schedules cost more. The DB's website will tell you everything you want to know, in English, about trains, departures, connections, and prices.

There are a number of ways the savvy traveler can save. Ask about the "Sparpreis 50" and "Sparpreis 25" tickets, which get you, respectively, half or a fourth off the ticket price under certain conditions. There's also the "Nice Weekend Ticket" providing unlimited travel for up to five persons on local trains. Eurail and German Rail passes get you unlimited train travel, but you must order them before you leave for Europe.

Contacts Deutsche Bahn (*German Rail*). ☎ *0800/150–7090 for automated schedule info, 11861 for 24-hr hotline (€0.39 per min), 491805/996–633 from outside Germany (€0.12 per min)* ⊕ *www.bahn.de.* **Eurail** ⊕ *www.eurail.com.*

HOTELS

The standards of German hotels are very high. You can nearly always expect courteous and polite service and clean and comfortable rooms. Most hotels in Germany do not have air-conditioning, nor do they need it.

BED-AND-BREAKFASTS

Bed-and-breakfasts remain one of the most popular options. They are often inexpensive, although the price depends on the amenities. For breakfast, expect some muesli, cheese, cold cuts, jam, butter, and hard-boiled eggs at the very least. Some B&Bs also supply lunch baskets if you intend to go hiking, or arrange an evening meal for a very affordable price.

BOOKING

Tourist offices will help you make bookings for a nominal fee, but they may have difficulty doing so after 4 pm in high season and on weekends. Most hotels and other lodgings require you to give your credit-card details before they will confirm your reservation. Get confirmation in writing and have a copy of your confirmation handy when you check in. Most hotels allow children under a certain age to stay in their parents' room at no extra charge, but others charge for them as extra adults; find out the cutoff age ahead of time.

RESTAURANTS

MEALS AND MEAL TIMES

In most restaurants it is not customary to wait to be seated. Simply walk in and take any unreserved space. When in doubt, ask. German restaurants do not automatically serve water. If you order water, you will be served mineral water and be expected to pay for it. If you are already ordering a paid drink, be it alcoholic or non, it is more acceptable to ask for tap water (*Leitungswasser*) as well. Try to order it as your only beverage, however, and you'll probably be met with some gruffness.

Most hotels serve a buffet-style breakfast (*Frühstück*), which is often included in the price of a room. By American standards, a cup (*Tasse*) of coffee in Germany is very petite. Order a pot, or *Kännchen,* if you want a larger portion. For lunch (*Mittagessen*) many fine restaurants have special, affordable lunch menus. Dinner (*Abendessen*) is usually accompanied by a potato or spätzle side dish. A salad sometimes comes with the main dish.

Gaststätten (restaurants) normally serve hot meals from 11:30 to 9; many places stop serving hot meals between 2 and 6, although you can still order cold dishes. Once most restaurants have closed, your options are limited. Take-out pizza parlors and Turkish eateries often stay open later. Failing that, your best option is a train station or a gas station with a convenience store. Many bars serve snacks.

PAYING

German waitstaff are more than happy to split the check so that everyone can pay individually. Credit cards are generally accepted only in moderate to expensive restaurants, so check before sitting down. You will need to ask for the bill (*die Rechnung*), and when you get it pay the waiter directly rather than leaving any money or tip on the table. When you get the check, round up to the next even euro. Add a euro if the total is more than €20. For larger amounts, rounding up and adding 5% is appropriate. Don't leave a tip on the table.

RESERVATIONS AND DRESS

It's a good idea to make reservations ahead of time. Very few restaurants nowadays require gentlemen to wear a jacket and tie, but even when Germans dress casually, their look is generally crisp and neat.

HOTEL AND RESTAURANT PRICES

Prices in the restaurant reviews are the average cost of a main course at dinner or, if dinner is not served, at lunch; taxes and service charges are generally included. Prices in the hotel reviews are the lowest cost of a standard double room in high season, excluding taxes, service charges, and meal plans (except at all-inclusives).

PLANNING YOUR TIME

If the romance of castles, cobblestone streets, half-timber houses, and quaint towns entices, head to Heidelberg or the Bavarian Alps. Must-sees include two of King Ludwig's castles, Neuschwanstein and Schloss Herrenchiemsee. It's a good idea to get an early start at major attractions like Heidelberg's castle, Rothenburg-ob-der-Tauber, and Neuschwanstein.

If fashion, culture, and art are your dish, head to one of the four big cities: Munich, Hamburg, or Berlin. Check out the museums by day, like the Kunsthalle and the Deichtorhallen in Hamburg or Museum Island in Berlin. Then indulge in the rich nightlife of Hamburg's titillating Reeperbahn, Munich's beer gardens, or Berlin's hip bar scene.

VISITOR INFORMATION

Contacts **German National Tourist Office** ☎ *212/661-7200* ⊕ *www.germany. travel.*

MUNICH

Munich represents what the rest of the world sees as "typical Germany," embodied in the world-famous Oktoberfest, traditional *Lederhosen* (leather pants), busty Bavarian waitresses in *Dirndls* (traditional dresses), beer steins, and sausages. There are myriad local brews to say *Prost* (cheers) with, either in one of the cavernous beer halls or a smaller *Kneipe,* a bar where all types get together to eat and drink. When the first rays of spring sun begin warming the air, follow the locals to their beloved beer gardens, shaded by massive chestnut trees.

Respect for the fine arts is another Munich hallmark. The city's appreciation of the arts began under the kings and dukes of the Wittelsbach Dynasty, which ruled Bavaria for more than 750 years until 1918. The Wittelsbach legacy is alive and well in the city's fabulous museums, the Opera House, the Philharmonic, and of course, the Residenz, the city's royal palace.

PLANNING YOUR TIME

Set aside at least a whole day for the Old Town, hitting Marienplatz when the Glockenspiel plays at 11 am or noon before a crowd of spectators. The pedestrian zone can get maddeningly full between noon and 2, when everyone in town seems to be taking a quick shopping break. If you've already seen the Glockenspiel, try to avoid the area at that time. Avoid the museum crowds in Schwabing and Maxvorstadt by visiting as early in the day as possible. All Munich seems to discover an interest in art on Sunday, when most municipal and state-funded museums are free; you might want to take this day off from culture and have a late breakfast or brunch at the Elisabethmarkt. Some beer gardens and taverns have Sunday-morning jazz concerts. Many Schwabing bars have happy hours between 6 and 8—a relaxing way to end your day.

GETTING HERE AND AROUND

AIR TRAVEL

Munich's International Airport is 28 km (17 miles) northeast of the city center and has excellent air service from all corners of the world. An excellent train service links the airport with downtown. The bus service is slower than the S-bahn link and more expensive. A taxi from the airport costs around €50.

Contacts **Flughafen München** ☎ *089/97500* ⊕ *www.munich-airport.de.*

BUS TRAVEL

Touring Eurolines buses arrive at and depart from Arnulfstrasse, north of the main train station in the adjoining Starnberger Bahnhof. Check their excellent website for trips to Neuschwanstein and the Romantic Road.

Contacts **Touring Eurolines** ✉ *DTG-Ticket-Center München, Hackerbrücke 4, ZOB, Ludwigvorstadt* ☎ *089/8898–9513* ⊕ *www.eurolines.de.*

CAR TRAVEL

From the north (Nürnberg or Frankfurt), leave the autobahn at the Schwabing exit. From Stuttgart and the west, the autobahn ends at Obermenzing, Munich's most westerly suburb. The autobahns from Salzburg and the east, Garmisch and the south, and Lindau and the southwest all join the Mittlerer Ring (city beltway). When leaving any autobahn, follow the signs reading "Stadtmitte" for downtown Munich.

PUBLIC TRANSIT TRANSIT

Munich has an efficient and well-integrated public-transportation system, consisting of the U-bahn (subway), the S-bahn (suburban railway), the Strassenbahn (streetcars), and buses. Marienplatz forms the heart of the U-bahn and S-bahn network.

TAXI TRAVEL

Munich's cream-color taxis are numerous. Hail them in the street or phone for one. A novel way of seeing the city is to hop on one of the bike-rickshaws. The bike-powered two-seater cabs operate between Marienplatz and the Chinesischer Turm in the Englischer Garten.

Contacts **Taxi München** ☎ *089/21610, 089/19410* ⊕ *www.taxi-muenchen.com.*

TRAIN TRAVEL

All long-distance rail services arrive at and depart from the Hauptbahnhof. For travel information at the main train station, go to the DB counter at the center of the main departures hall. With more complex questions, go to the EurAide office, which serves English-speaking train travelers.

VISITOR INFORMATION

Contacts **Munich Tourist Office—Hauptbahnhof** ✉ *Bahnhofpl. 2, Ludwigvorstadt* ☎ *089/2339–6500* ⊕ *www.muenchen.de/tam.* **Munich Tourist Office—Rathaus** ✉ *Marienpl. 2, City Center* ☎ *089/2339–6500.*

EXPLORING

Munich is a wealthy city—and it shows. At times this affluence may come across as conservatism. But what makes Munich so unique is that it's a new city superimposed on the old. Hip neighborhoods are riddled with traditional locales, and flashy materialism thrives together with a love of the outdoors.

CITY CENTER

FAMILY

Fodor's Choice

★

Deutsches Museum (*German Museum*). Aircraft, vehicles, cutting-edge technology, historic machinery, and even a mine fill a monumental building on an island in the Isar River, which comprises one of the best science and technology museums in the world. The collection is spread out over 47,000 square meters, six floors of exhibits, and about 50 exhibition areas. The Centre for New Technologies includes interactive exhibitions, such as nanotechnology, biotechnology, and robotics. It could change the way you think about science forever. Children have their own area, the Kinderreich, where they can learn about modern technology and science through numerous interactive displays (parents must accompany their children). One of the most technically advanced planetariums in Europe has four shows daily. The Internet café on the third floor is open daily 9–3, other cafés until 4. ■TIP→ **To arrange for a two-hour tour in English, call at least six weeks in advance.** ✉ *Museum-sinsel 1, Ludwigvorstadt* ☎ *089/21791* ⊕ *www.deutsches-museum.de* 🎫 *Museum €8.50* 🕙 *Daily 9–5* Ⓜ *Isartor (S-bahn).*

Frauenkirche (*Church of Our Lady*). Munich's *Dom* (cathedral) is a distinctive late-Gothic brick structure with two huge towers. Each is 99 meters high, an important figure today because, in a nonbinding referendum, Münchners narrowly voted to restrict all new buildings to below this height within the city's middle ring road. The main body of the cathedral was completed in 20 years (1468–88)—a record time in those days, and the distinctive onion dome–like cupolas were added by 1525. The twin towers are easily the most recognized feature of the city skyline and a Munich trademark. In 1944–45, the building suffered severe damage during Allied bombing raids, and was restored between 1947 and 1957. Inside, the church combines most of von Halspach's plans, with a stark, clean modernity and simplicity of line, emphasized by slender, white octagonal pillars that sweep up through the nave to the tracery ceiling. As you enter the church, look on the stone floor for the dark imprint of a large foot—the *Teufelstritt* (Devil's Footprint). According to lore, the devil challenged von Halspach to build a church without windows. The architect accepted the challenge. When he completed the job, he led the devil to a spot in the bright church from which the 66-foot-high windows could not be seen. The devil triumphantly stomped his foot and left the Teufelstritt, only to be enraged when he ventured further inside and realized that windows had been included. ✉ *Frauenpl. 2, City Center* ☎ *089/290–0820* 🎫 *Cathedral free, tower €3* 🕙 *Tower closed until at least 2015 for renovation* Ⓜ *Marienplatz (U-bahn and S-bahn).*

Marienplatz. Bordered by the Neues Rathaus, shops, and cafés, this square is named after the gilded statue of the Virgin Mary that has watched over it for more than three centuries. It was erected in 1638 at the behest of Elector Maximilian I as an act of thanksgiving for the city's survival of the Thirty Years War, the cataclysmic, partly religious struggle that devastated vast regions of Germany. When the statue was taken down from its marble column for cleaning in 1960, workmen

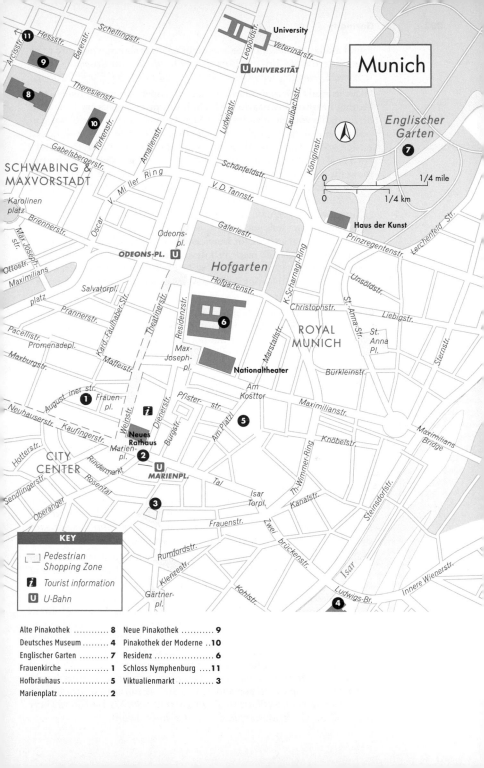

Munich

Englischer Garten

Haus der Kunst

Hofgarten

ROYAL MUNICH

Nationaltheater

SCHWABING & MAXVORSTADT

CITY CENTER

Neues Rathaus

University

UNIVERSITÄT

ODEONS-PL.

MARIENPL.

0 — 1/4 mile
0 — 1/4 km

KEY

- Pedestrian Shopping Zone
- **i** Tourist information
- **U** U-Bahn

found a small casket in the base containing a splinter of wood said to be from the cross of Christ. ⊠ *Bounded by Kaufingerstr., Rosenstr., Weinstr., and Dienerstr., City Center* Ⓜ *Marienplatz (U-bahn and S-bahn).*

Viktualienmarkt (*Victuals Market*). The city's open-air market really is the beating heart of downtown Munich. It has just about every fresh fruit or vegetable you can imagine, as well as German and international specialties. All kinds of people come here for a quick bite, from well-heeled businesspeople and casual tourists to mortar- and paint-covered workers. It's also the realm of the garrulous, sturdy market women who run the stalls with dictatorial authority. ■ **TIP→ Whether here, or at a bakery, do not try to select your pickings by hand. Ask, and let it be served to you.** There's also a great beer garden (open pretty much whenever the sun is shining), where you can enjoy your snacks with cold local beer. A sign above the counter tells you what's on tap. The choice rotates throughout the year among the six major Munich breweries, which are displayed on the maypole. These are also the only six breweries officially allowed to serve their wares at the Oktoberfest. ⊠ *15 Viktualienmarkt, City Center* ☉ *Weekdays 10–6; Sat. 10–3* Ⓜ *Marienplatz (U-bahn and S-bahn).*

ROYAL MUNICH

Englischer Garten (*English Garden*). Bigger than New York's Central Park and London's Hyde Park, this seemingly endless green space blends into the open countryside at the north of the city. Today's park covers more than 1,000 acres and has 78 km (48 miles) of paths, 8.5 km (5.2 miles) of streams, and more than 100 foot- and other bridges. The open, informal landscaping—reminiscent of the rolling parklands with which English aristocrats of the 18th century liked to surround their country homes—gave the park its name. It has a boating lake, four beer gardens, and a series of curious decorative and monumental constructions. In the center of the park's most popular beer garden is a Chinese pagoda, erected in 1790. It was destroyed during the war and then reconstructed. ■ **TIP→ The Chinese Tower beer garden is hugely popular, but the park has prettier places for sipping a beer: the Aumeister, for example, along the northern perimeter, is in an early-19th-century hunting lodge.** At the Seehaus, on the shore of the Kleinhesseloher *See* (lake), choose between a smart restaurant or a cozy *Bierstube* (beer tavern) in addition to the beer garden right on the lake. ⊠ *Main entrances at various points on Prinzregentenstr. and Königinstr., City Center/Schwabing.*

Hofbräuhaus. Duke Wilhelm V founded Munich's most famous brewery in 1589; it's been at its present location since 1808. As beer and restaurants became major players in the city's economy, it needed to be completely rebuilt and modernized in 1897. The last major work was its reconstruction in 1950 after its destruction in the war. Hofbräu means "court brewery," and the golden beer is poured in pitcher-size liter mugs. If the cavernous ground-floor hall is too noisy for you, there is a quieter restaurant upstairs. In this legendary establishment Americans, Australians, and Italians often far outnumber locals, who regard it as too much of a tourist trap. The brass band that performs here most days adds modern pop and American folk music to the traditional German numbers. ⊠ *Platzl 9, City Center* ☎ *089/2913–6100* ☉ *Daily 9 am–11:30 pm* Ⓜ *Marienplatz (U-bahn and S-bahn).*

Residenz (*Royal Palace*). One of Germany's true treasures, Munich's royal Residenz began in 1363 as the modest **Neuveste** (New Fortress) on the northeastern city boundary. By the time the Bavarian monarchy fell, in 1918, the palace could compare favorably with the best in Europe. With the Residenz's central location, it was pretty much inevitable that the Allied bombing of 1944–45 would cause immense damage, and susbequent reconstruction took decades. For tourists today, however, it really is a treasure chamber of delight. To wander around the Residenz can last anywhere from three hours to all day. The 16th-century, 70-meter-long arched **Antiquarium**, built for Duke Albrecht V's collection of antiques and library, is recognized as one of the most impressive Renaissance creations outside Italy (today it's used chiefly for state receptions). ■ **TIP→ All the different rooms, halls, galleries, chapels, and museums within the Residenzmuseum, as well as the Cuvilliés-Theater and Treasury, can be visited with a combination ticket that costs €13.** ✉ *Max-Joseph-Pl. 3, City Center* ☎ *089/290–671* ⊕ *www.residenz-muenchen. de* ☾ *Residenz Museum and Treasury mid-Apr.–mid-Oct., daily 9–6; mid-Oct.–mid-Mar., daily 10–5* Ⓜ *Odeonsplatz (U-bahn).*

Schatzkammer (*Treasury*). The Schatzkammer comprises many hundreds of masterworks, including a host of treasures from the Wittelsbach royal crown jewels. A highlight is the crown belonging to Bavaria's first king, Maximilian I, created in Paris in 1806–07. The Schatzkammer collection has a staggering centerpiece—a renowned 50-cm-high Renaissance statue of St. George studded with diamonds, pearls, and rubies. ✉ *1a Residenzstr.* ▦ *€7, combined ticket with Residenzmuseum €11* ☾ *Mid-Apr.–mid-Oct., daily 9–6; mid-Oct.–mid-Mar., daily 10–5.*

Residenzmuseum. The Residenzmuseum comprises everything in the Residenz apart from the Schatzkammer (Treasury) and the Cuvilliés-Theater. Paintings, tapestries, furniture, and porcelain are housed in various rooms and halls. Look out for the **Grüne Galerie** (Green Gallery), named after its green silk decoration, and the great and the good of the Wittelsbach royal family in the **Ahnengalerie** (Ancestral Gallery). ✉ *Max-Joseph-Pl.* ▦ *€7, combined ticket with Schatzkammer €11* ☾ *Mid-Apr.–mid-Oct., daily 9–6; mid-Oct.–mid-Mar., daily 10–5.*

Cuvilliés-Theater (*Bavarian State Opera*). This stunning example of a rococo theater was originally built by court architect François Cuvilliés between 1751 and 1753 and it soon became the most famous in Germany. In 1781 it premiered Mozart's *Idomeneo*, commissioned by the Elector of Bavaria, Karl Theodor. After extensive restoration work, it reopened in 2008 with a performance of *Idomeneo*. It's home to the hugely respected Bavarian State Opera, led by American conductor Kent Nagano. ✉ *Max-Joseph-Pl. 2* ✛ *Enter via Residenzstr. 1* ⊕ *www. bayerische.staatsoper.de for opera tickets* ▦ *€3.50 to view the theater, combined ticket with Residenzmuseum and Schatzkammer €11* ☾ *Closed during rehearsals.*

MAXVORSTADT AND OUTER MUNICH

Fodor's Choice
★
Alte Pinakothek. With numerous Old Master paintings from the Netherlands, Italy, France, and Germany, the long redbrick Alte Pinakothek holds one of the most significant art collections in the world. Among

the European masterpieces on view are paintings by Dürer, Titian, Rembrandt, da Vinci, Rubens (the museum has one of the world's largest Rubens collections), and two celebrated Murillos. Most of the picture captions are in German only, so it is best to rent an English audio guide, although the audio tour does not cover every painting. ∎TIP→ To save money, get a Tageskarte (day ticket), which provides entry to all these museums (plus the Schack Gallery, in Lehel) for just €12. ✉ *Barerstr. 27 (entrance facing Theresienstr.), Maxvorstadt* ☎ *089/2380–5216* ⊕ *www.alte-pinakothek.de* ☜ *€9, €3 Sun.* ☉ *Wed.–Sun. 10–6, Tues. 10–8* Ⓜ *Königsplatz (U-bahn).*

Fodor'sChoice
★
Neue Pinakothek. Another museum packed with masters, the fabulous Neue Pinakothek reopened in 1981 to house the royal collection of modern art left homeless and scattered after its original building was destroyed in the war. The exterior of the modern building mimics an older one with Italianate influences. The interior offers a magnificent environment for picture gazing, partly owing to the natural light flooding in from skylights. French impressionists—Monet, Degas, Manet—are all well represented, while the comprehensive collection also includes great Romantic landscape painters Turner and Caspar David Friedrich, and other artists of the caliber of Van Gogh, Cezanne, and Monet. This is another must-see. ✉ *Barerstr. 29, Maxvorstadt* ☎ *089/2380–5195* ⊕ *www.neue-pinakothek.de* ☜ *€7, €1 Sun.* ☉ *Wed. 10–8, Thurs.–Mon. 10–6* Ⓜ *Königsplatz (U-bahn), Pinakotheken (Tram).*

Pinakothek der Moderne. Opened to much fanfare in 2002, this fascinating, light-filled building is home to four outstanding museums under one cupola-topped roof: art, graphic art, architecture, and design. The striking 12,000-meter-square glass-and-concrete complex by Stefan Braunfels has permanent and temporary exhibitions throughout the year in each of the four categories. The design museum is particularly popular, showing permanent exhibitions in vehicle design, computer culture, and design ideas. ✉ *Barerstr. 40, Maxvorstadt* ☎ *089/2380–5360* ⊕ *www.pinakothek.de* ☜ *€10, €1 Sun.* ☉ *Tues., Wed., Fri.–Sun. 10–6, Thurs. 10–8* Ⓜ *Königsplatz (U-bahn), Pinakotheken (Tram).*

Schloss Nymphenburg. This glorious baroque and rococo palace, the largest of its kind in Germany, draws around 500,000 visitors a year; only the Deustches Museum is more popular in Munich. Within the original building, now the central axis of the palace complex, is the magnificent **Steinerner Saal** (Great hall). It extends over two floors and is richly decorated with stucco and grandiose frescoes by masters such as Francois Cuvilliés the Elder and Johann Baptist Zimmermann. In summer, chamber-music concerts are given here. One of the surrounding royal chambers houses Ludwig I's famous **Schönheitsgalerie** (Gallery of Beauties). The walls are hung from floor to ceiling with portraits of women who caught the roving eye of Ludwig, among them a shoemaker's daughter and Lady Jane Ellenborough, the scandal-thriving English aristocrat.

The palace is in a park laid out in formal French style, with low hedges and gravel walks extending into woodland. Among the ancient tree stands are three fascinating pavilions. The **Amalienburg** hunting lodge is

OKTOBERFEST

Not even the wildest Bavarians can be held wholly responsible for the staggering consumption of beer and food at the annual Oktoberfest, which starts at the end of September and ends in early October. On average, around 1,183,000 gallons of beer along with 750,000 roasted chickens and 650,000 sausages are put away by revelers from around the world. To partake, book lodging by April, and if you're traveling with a group, also reserve bench space within one of the 14 tents. See Munich's website, ⊕ *www.muenchen-tourist.de*, for beer-tent contacts. The best time to arrive at the grounds is lunchtime, when it's easier to find a seat—by 4 it's packed and they'll close the doors. Take advantage of an hour or two of sobriety to tour the fairground rides, which are an integral part of Oktoberfest. Under no circumstances attempt any rides—all of which claim to be the world's most dangerous—after a couple of beers.

a rococo gem built by François Cuvilliés. The **Pagodenburg** was built for slightly informal royal tea parties. Its elegant French exterior disguises an Asian-influenced interior, in which exotic teas from India and China were served. Take Tram No. 17 or Bus No. 51 from the city center to the Schloss Nymphenburg stop. ⊠ *Schloss Nymphenburg, Nymphenburg* ☎ *089/179–080* ⊕ *www.schloss-nymphenburg.de* ⊠ *€11.50 Apr.–mid-Oct., €8.50 mid-Oct.–Mar. (includes Marstallmuseum and Museum Nymphenburger Porzellan)* ; ⊙ *Apr.–mid-Oct., daily 9–6; mid-Oct.–Mar., daily 10–4.*

Marstallmuseum & Porzellan Manufaktur Nymphenburg (*Museum of Royal Carriages & Porcelain Manufacturer Nymphenburg*). Nymphenburg contains so much of interest that a day hardly provides enough time. Don't leave without visiting the former royal stables, now the Marstallmuseum. It houses a fleet of vehicles, including an elaborately decorated sleigh in which King Ludwig II once glided through the Bavarian twilight, flaming torches lighting the way. Also exhibited in the Marstallmuseum are examples of the world-renowned Nymphenburg porcelain, which has been produced on the palace grounds since 1761. ⊠ *208 Schloss Nymphenburg* ☎ *089/179–080 for Schloss Nymphenburg* ⊠ *€4.50* ⊙ *Apr.–mid-Oct., daily 9–6; mid-Oct.–Mar., daily 10–4.*

Museum Mensch und Natur (*Museum of Man and Nature*). This museum concentrates on three areas of interest: the variety of life on Earth, the history of humankind, and our place in the environment. Main exhibits include a huge representation of the human brain and a chunk of Alpine crystal weighing half a ton. ⊠ *Schloss Nymphenburg* ☎ *089/179–5890* ⊕ *www.musmn.de* ⊠ *€3, Sun. €1* ⊙ *Tues., Wed., and Fri. 9–5, Thurs. 9–8, weekends 10–6.*

8

WHERE TO EAT

CITY CENTER

$
GERMAN
✕ **Bier- und Oktoberfest Museum.** In one of the oldest buildings in Munich, dating to the 14th century, the museum takes an imaginative look at the history of this popular elixir, the monasteries that produced it, the purity laws that govern it, and Munich's own long tradition with it. The rustic Museumsstüberl restaurant, consisting of a few heavy wooden tables, accompanies the museum. It serves traditional *Brotzeit* (breads, cheeses, and cold meats) during the day and hot Bavarian dishes from 6 pm. ■TIP→ You can visit the Museumsstüberl restaurant without paying the museum's admission fee and try beer from one of Munich's oldest breweries, the Augustiner Bräu. Ⓢ *Average main: €8* ⊠ *Sterneckerstr. 2, City Center* ☎ *089/2424–3941* ⊕ *www.bier-und-oktoberfestmuseum. de* 🏛 *Museum €4* ⊙ *Museum Tues.–Sat. 1–6; restaurant Mon. 6 pm–midnight, Tues.–Sat. 1 pm–midnight* Ⓜ *Isartor (U-bahn and S-bahn).*

$$$$
ECLECTIC
✕ **Königshof.** Don't be fooled as you cross the threshold of the dour and unremarkable-looking postwar Hotel Königshof. The contrast with the opulent interior is remarkable. From a window table in this elegant and luxurious restaurant in one of Munich's grand hotels, you can watch the hustle and bustle of Munich's busiest square, Karlsplatz, below. You'll forget the outside world, however, when you taste the outstanding French- and Japanese-influenced dishes created by Michelin-starred chef Martin Fauster, former sous-chef at Tantris. Ingredients are fresh and menus change often, but you might see lobster with fennel and candied ginger, or venison with goose liver and celery, and for dessert, flambéed peach with champagne ice cream. Service is expert and personal; let the sommelier help you choose from the fantastic wine selection. Ⓢ *Average main: €45* ⊠ *Karlspl. 25, City Center* ☎ *089/551–360* ⊕ *www.koenigshof-hotel.de* ⚠ *Reservations essential* 🛈 *Jacket and tie* ⊙ *Closed 1st wk in Aug.–1st wk in Sept.; closed Sun. and Mon. Jan.–Sept.* Ⓜ *Karlsplatz (U-bahn and S-bahn).*

$
GERMAN
✕ **Nürnberger Bratwurst Glöckl am Dom.** One of Munich's most popular beer taverns is dedicated to the delicious *Nürnberger Bratwürste* (finger-size sausages), a specialty from the rival Bavarian city of Nürnberg. They're served by a busy team of friendly waitresses dressed in Bavarian dirndls who flit between the crowded tables with remarkable agility. There are other options available as well. In warmer months, tables are placed outside, partly under a large awning, beneath the towering Frauenkirche. In winter the mellow dark-panel dining rooms provide relief from the cold. ■TIP→ For a quick, cheaper beer go to the side door where, just inside, there is a little window serving fresh Augustiner from a wooden barrel. You can stand around with the regulars or enjoy the small courtyard if the weather is nice. Ⓢ *Average main: €10* ⊠ *Frauenpl. 9, City Center* ☎ *089/291–9450* ⊕ *www.bratwurst-gloeckl.de* Ⓜ *Marienplatz (U-bahn and S-bahn).*

LEOPOLDVORSTADT AND SCHWABING

$
GERMAN
✕ **Augustiner Keller.** This flagship beer restaurant of one of Munich's oldest breweries originated about 1812. It is also the location of the unbeatable Augustiner beer garden, which should be at the top of any visitor's beer garden list. The menu offers Bavarian specialties, including

half a duck with a good slab of roast suckling pig, dumpling, and blue cabbage. If you're up for it, end your meal with a *Dampfnudel* (yeast dumpling served with custard), though you probably won't feel hungry again for quite a while. $ *Average main: €14* ⊠ *Arnulfstr. 52, Maxvorstadt* ☎ *089/594–393* ⊕ *www.augustinerkeller.de* Ⓜ *Hauptbahnhof (U-bahn and S-bahn).*

$$$$
EUROPEAN
Fodor's Choice
★

✗ **Tantris.** Despite the slightly dramatic exterior, which is adorned by three concrete animals, few restaurants in Germany can match the Michelin-starred Tantris. Select the menu of the day and accept the suggestions of the sommelier or choose from the à la carte options and you'll be in for a treat, for example: variation of char with marinated white asparagus and orange hollandaise, followed by roast lamb filets with spinach, beans and fennel-curry puree, superbly complemented by stuffed semolina dumpling with raspberries and cheese-curd ice cream. It surprises few that head chef Hans Haas has kept his restaurant at the top of the critics' charts in Munich for so long. ■ **TIP→ Look out for the Tantris Standl, a small outlet at the city-centre Schrannenhalle, selling spirits, wines, coffees, chutneys, and sweets.** $ *Average main: €100* ⊠ *Johann-Fichte-Str. 7, Schwabing* ☎ *089/361–9590* ⊕ *www.tantris. de* ⚘ *Reservations essential* 🏛 *Jacket and tie* ☉ *Closed Sun., Mon., and bank holidays* Ⓜ *Münchener Freiheit (U-bahn).*

WHERE TO STAY

CITY CENTER

$$$$
HOTEL
Fodor's Choice
★

🖵 **Bayerischer Hof.** There's the Michelin-starred restaurant, the swanky suites, the roof-top Blue Spa and Lounge with panoramic city views, fitness studio, pool, private cinema, and to top it all suites in Palais Montgelas, the adjoining early 19th-century palace. **Pros:** superb public rooms with valuable oil paintings; the roof garden restaurant has an impressive view of the Frauenkirche two blocks away; Atelier restaurant has again been awarded a Michelin star. **Cons:** expensive; Wi-Fi is extra. $ *Rooms from: €360* ⊠ *Promenadepl. 2–6, City Center* ☎ *089/21200* ⊕ *www.bayerischerhof.de* ⇆ *340 rooms, 65 suites* ⎧⎹ *Breakfast* Ⓜ *Karlsplatz (U-bahn and S-bahn), Marienplatz (U-bahn and S-bahn).*

$
HOTEL

🖵 **Hotel am Markt.** You can literally stumble out the door of this hotel onto the Viktualienmarkt. **Pros:** excellent location; friendly and helpful staff; free Wi-Fi; decent restaurant. **Cons:** rooms are simple; some spots could use fresh paint; no credit cards. $ *Rooms from: €77* ⊠ *Heiliggeiststr. 6, City Center* ☎ *089/225–014* ⊕ *www.hotel-am-markt.eu* ⇆ *22 rooms* ⎧⎹ *Breakfast* Ⓜ *Marienplatz (U-bahn and S-bahn).*

$$$
HOTEL

🖵 **Platzl Hotel.** The privately owned Platzl has won awards and wide recognition for its ecologically aware management, which uses heat recyclers in the kitchen, environmentally friendly detergents, recyclable materials, waste separation, and other eco-friendly practices. **Pros:** good restaurant; progressive environmental credentials; around the corner from the Hofbräuhaus; free Wi-Fi throughout. **Cons:** rooms facing the Hofbräuhaus get more noise; some rooms are on the small side. $ *Rooms from: €212* ⊠ *Sparkassenstr. 10, City Center* ☎ *089/2370–3722* ⊕ *www.platzl.de* ⇆ *167 rooms* ⎧⎹ *Breakfast* Ⓜ *Marienplatz (U-bahn and S-bahn).*

8

HAUPTBANHOF AND ISARVORSTADT

$$$ HOTEL Fodor's Choice ★ **Admiral.** The small, privately owned, tradition-rich Admiral enjoys a quiet side-street location and its own garden, close to the river Isar, minutes from the Deutsches Museum. **Pros:** attention to detail; quiet; excellent service. **Cons:** no restaurant. [$] *Rooms from: €199* ✉ *Kohlstr. 9, Isarvorstadt* ☎ *089/216–350* 🌐 *www.hotel-admiral.de* 🛏 *33 rooms* 🍴 *Breakfast* [M] *Isartor (S-bahn).*

$$ HOTEL **Hotel Mirabell.** This family-run hotel is used to American tourists who appreciate the friendly service, central location (between the main railway station and the Oktoberfest fairgrounds), and reasonable room rates. **Pros:** Wi-Fi free throughout; family-run; personalized service. **Cons:** no restaurant; this area of the Hauptbahnhof is not the most salubrious. [$] *Rooms from: €115* ✉ *Landwehrstr. 42, entrance on Goethestr., Hauptbahnhof* ☎ *089/5491740* 🌐 *www.hotelmirabell.de* 🛏 *65 rooms, 3 apartments* 🍴 *Breakfast* [M] *Hauptbahnhof (U-bahn and S-bahn).*

BOGENHAUSEN AND LUDWIGVORSTADT

$ HOTEL Fodor's Choice ★ **Hotel Uhland.** This stately villa is a landmark building and is additionally special in that the owner and host was born here and will make you feel at home, too. **Pros:** a real family atmosphere; care is given to details; free Wi-Fi. **Cons:** no restaurant or bar. [$] *Rooms from: €95* ✉ *Uhlandstr. 1, Ludwigvorstadt* ☎ *089/543–350* 🌐 *www.hotel-uhland.de* 🛏 *27 rooms* 🍴 *Breakfast.*

$ HOTEL **Westin Grand München.** The building itself, with 22 floors, may raise a few eyebrows as it stands on a slight elevation and is not the shapeliest of the Munich skyline. **Pros:** luxurious lobby and restaurant; rooms facing west toward the city have a fabulous view. **Cons:** it's not possible to reserve west-facing rooms; hotel is difficult to reach via public transportation; at €27, breakfast is expensive; high-speed Wi-Fi costs extra. [$] *Rooms from: €100* ✉ *Arabellastr. 6, Bogenhausen* ☎ *089/92640* 🌐 *www.westin.com/munich* 🛏 *627 rooms, 28 suites* 🍴 *Breakfast* [M] *Arabellapark (U-bahn).*

NIGHTLIFE

Munich has a lively nocturnal scene ranging from beer halls to bars to chic, see-and-be-seen clubs. The fun neighborhoods for a night out are City Center, Isarvorstadt (around Gärtnerplatz), and Schwabing around Schellingstrasse and Münchener Freiheit. Regardless of their size or style, many bars, especially around Gärtnerplatz, have DJs spinning either mellow background sounds or funky beats. The city's eclectic taste in music is quite commendable.

BARS

CITY CENTER

Atomic Café. Near the Hofbräuhaus, this club/lounge has excellent DJs nightly, playing everything from '60s Brit pop to '60s/'70s funk and soul. Atomic also has great live acts on a regular basis. ✉ *Neuturmstr. 5, City Center* ☎ *089/228–3053* 🌐 *www.atomic.de.*

Bar Centrale. Around the corner from the Hofbräuhaus, Bar Centrale is very Italian—the waiters don't seem to speak any other language.

The coffee is excellent; small fine meals are served as well. They have a retro-looking back room with leather sofas. ✉ *Ledererstr. 23, City Center* ☎ *089/223–762* ⊕ *www.bar-centrale.com.*

Eisbach. Eisbach occupies a corner of the Max Planck Institute building opposite the Bavarian Parliament. The bar is among Munich's biggest and is overlooked by a mezzanine restaurant area where you can choose from a limited but ambitious menu. Outdoor tables nestle in the expansive shade of huge parasols. The nearby Eisbach brook, which gives the bar its name, tinkles away, lending a relaxed air. ✉ *Marstallpl. 3, City Center* ☎ *089/2280–1680* ⊕ *www.eisbach.eu.*

Hotel Vier Jahreszeiten Kempinski. The hotel offers piano music until 9 pm, and then dancing to recorded music or a small combo. ✉ *Maximilianstr. 17, City Center* ☎ *089/2125–2799* ⊕ *www.kempinski.com/de/munich.*

Night Club Bar. The Bayerischer Hof's Night Club Bar has live music, most famously international stars from the jazz scene, but also reggae to hip-hop and everything in between. ✉ *Promenadepl. 2–6, City Center* ☎ *089/212–0994 for table reservations* ⊕ *www.bayerischerhof. de/en/bars.*

Pusser's Bar Munich. At the American-inspired, nautical-style Pusser's Bar, great cocktails and Irish-German black-and-tans (Guinness and strong German beer) are made to the sounds of live jazz. Try the "Pain Killer," a specialty of the house. ✉ *Falkenturmstr. 9, City Center* ☎ *089/220–500* ⊕ *www.pussersbar.de.*

Schumann's. At Schumann's, Munich's most famous bar, the bartenders are busy shaking cocktails after the curtain comes down at the nearby opera house. ✉ *Odeonspl. 6–7, City Center* ☎ *089/229–060* ⊕ *www. schumanns.de.*

Trader Vic's. Exotic cocktails are the specialty at Trader Vic's, a smart cellar bar in the Hotel Bayerischer Hof that's as popular among out-of-town visitors as it is locals. It's open till 3 in the morning. ✉ *Promenadenpl. 2–6, City Center* ☎ *089/212–0995* ⊕ *www.bayerischerhof. de/en/bars.*

SCHWABING

Alter Simpl. Media types drink Weissbier, Helles, as well as Guinness and Kilkenny, at the square bar at Alter Simpl. More than 100 years old, this establishment serves German food until 2 am (weekends till 3 am). ✉ *Türkenstr. 57, Maxvorstadt* ☎ *089/272–3083* ⊕ *www.eggerlokale.de.*

Schall und Rauch. Up on Schellingstrasse, this legendary student hangout, whose name literally means "Noise and Smoke," has great music and food. ✉ *Schellingstr. 22, Schwabing* ☎ *089/2880–9577.*

Schelling Salon. Another absolute cornerstone in the neighborhood is the Schelling Salon. On the corner of Barerstrasse, this sizeable bar has several pool tables and even a secret ping-pong room in the basement with an intercom for placing beer orders. The food's not bad and pretty inexpensive. It's closed Tuesday and Wednesday. ✉ *Schellingstr. 54, Schwabing* ☎ *089/272–0788* ⊕ *www.schelling-salon.de.*

8

Türkenhof. Across the street is the Türkenhof, another solid local joint that serves Augustiner and good food. ⊠ *Türkenstr. 78, Schwabing* ☎ *089/280–0235* ⊕ *www.augustiner-braeu.de.*

BEER GARDENS

Aside from one notable example in the City Center, the rest of Munich's beer gardens are a bit farther afield and can be reached handily by bike or S- and U-bahn.

CITY CENTER

Biergarten am Viktualienmarkt. The only true beer garden in the city center, and therefore the easiest to find, is the one at the Viktualienmarkt. The beer on tap rotates every six weeks among the six Munich breweries to keep everyone happy throughout the year. ⊠ *Viktualienmarkt* ☎ *089/2916–5993* ⊕ *www.biergarten-viktualienmarkt.com.*

ENGLISCHER GARTEN

Biergarten am Chinesischen Turm. This famous Biergarten is at the five-story Chinese Tower in the Englischer Garten. Enjoy your beer to the strains of oompah music played by traditionally dressed musicians. ⊠ *Englischer Garten 3* ☎ *089/383–8730* ⊕ *www.chinaturm.de.*

Hirschau. Pleasantly located in the Englischer Garten, the Hirschau has room for 2,500 guests, and it's about 10 minutes north of the Kleinhesselohersee. ⊠ *Gysslingstr. 15, Englischer Garten* ☎ *089/3609–0490* ⊕ *www.hirschau-muenchen.de.*

Seehaus im Englischen Garten. The Seehaus is on the banks of the artificial lake Kleinhesseloher See, where all of Munich converges on hot summer days. Take Bus No. 44 and exit at Osterwaldstrasse, or U-bahn No. 3 or 6 and stroll through the park. ⊠ *Kleinhesselohe 3, Englischer Garten* ☎ *089/381–6130* ⊕ *www.kuffler-gastronomie.de/de/muenchen/seehaus.*

HAUPTBAHNHOF

Augustiner Keller Biergarten. The Augustiner Keller is one of the more authentic of the beer gardens, with excellent food, beautiful chestnut shade trees, a mixed local crowd, and Munich Augustiner beer. It's a few minutes from the Hauptbahnhof and Hackerbrucke. ⊠ *Arnulfstr. 52, Ludwigvorstadt* ☎ *089/594–393* ⊕ *www.augustinerkeller.de.*

SIDE TRIPS FROM MUNICH

When the city bustle gets a bit overwhelming, it's time to head out of town for the day. Of course, since this is Germany, the natural, mountainous beauty surrounding Munich is tempered with fabled castles, legendary lakes, and a sobering dose of Holocaust history.

DACHAU

20 km (12 miles) northwest of Munich.

Dachau is infamous worldwide as the site of the first Nazi concentration camp, which was built just outside it. Dachau preserves the memory of the camp and the horrors perpetrated there with deep contrition while trying to signal that the town has other points of interest.

GETTING HERE AND AROUND

By public transport take the S-2 from Marienplatz or Hauptbahnhof in the direction of Petershausen, and get off at Dachau. From there, take the clearly marked bus from right outside the Dachau S-bahn station (it leaves about every 20 minutes). If you are driving from Munich, take the autobahn toward Stuttgart, get off at Dachau, and follow the signs.

VISITOR INFORMATION

Contacts Tourist-Information Dachau ⊠ *Konrad-Adenauer-Str. 1, Dachau* ☎ *08131/75286* ⊕ *www.dachau.de.*

EXPLORING

Dachau Concentration Camp Memorial Site. The site of the infamous camp, now the KZ-Gedenkstätte Dachau, is just outside town. Photographs, contemporary documents, the few cell blocks, and the grim crematorium create a somber and moving picture of the camp, where more than 41,000 of the 200,000-plus prisoners lost their lives. A documentary film in English is shown daily at 11:30 and 3:30. The former camp has become more than just a grisly memorial: it's now a place where people of all nations meet to reflect upon the past and on the present. Several religious shrines and memorials have been built to honor the dead, who came from Germany and nations around the world. ⊠ *Alte Römerstr. 75, Dachau* ☎ *08131/669–970* ⊕ *www.kz-gedenkstaette-dachau.de* ⊠ *Free* ☉ *Tues.–Sun. 9–5. Tours in English Tues.–Sun. at 11 and 1.*

NEUSCHWANSTEIN AND HOHENSCHWANGAU

93 km (60 miles) south of Augsburg, 105 km (65 miles) southwest of Munich.

8

These two famous castles belonging to the Wittelsbachs, one historic and the other nearly "make-believe," are 1 km (½ mile) across a valley from each other, near the town of Schwangau. Bavaria's King Ludwig II (1845–86) spent much of his youth at Schloss Hohenschwangau (Hohenschwangau Castle). It's said that its neo-Gothic atmosphere provided the primary influences that shaped his wildly romantic Schloss Neuschwanstein (Neuschwanstein Castle), the fairy-tale castle he built after he became king, which has since become one of Germany's most recognized sights.

GETTING HERE AND AROUND

From Schwangau (5 km [3 miles] north of Füssen, 91 km [59 miles] south of Augsburg, 103 km [64 miles] southwest of Munich), follow the road signs marked "Königschlösser" (Royal Castles). After 3 km (2 miles) you come to Hohenschwangau, a small village consisting of a few houses, some good hotels, and five spacious parking lots (parking €4.50). You have to park in one of them and then walk to the ticket center serving both castles. The main street of the small village of Hohenschwangau is lined with restaurants and quick eateries of all categories.

TICKETS

Contacts Ticket Center ⊠ *Alpseestr. 12, Hohenschwangau* ☎ *08362/930–830* ⊕ *www.hohenschwangau.de.*

EXPLORING

FodorśChoice **Neuschwanstein.** It's hard to believe that this over-the-top creation that
★   soars from its mountainside is real—it's no surprise that Walt Disney
took it as the model for his castle in the movie *Sleeping Beauty* and later
for the Disneyland castle itself. The life of this spectacular castle's king
reads like one of the great Gothic mysteries of the 19th century, and
the castle symbolizes that life. Yet during the 17 years from the start
of Schloss Neuschwanstein's construction until King Ludwig's death,
the king spent less than six months here, and the interior was never
finished. The Byzantine-style throne room is without a throne; Ludwig
died before one could be installed. There are also some spectacular
walks around the castle. The delicate **Marienbrücke** (Mary's Bridge) is
spun like a medieval maiden's hair across a deep, narrow gorge. From
this vantage point there are giddy views of the castle and the great
Upper Bavarian Plain beyond. ■TIP→ Tickets need to be purchased at
the ticket center in the village of Hohenschwangau, so be sure to stop there
first. To reach Neuschwanstein from the ticket center below, take one of
the clearly marked paths (about a 40-minute uphill walk) or one of the
horse-drawn carriages that leave from Hotel Müller (uphill €6, downhill
€3). A shuttle bus leaves from the Hotel Lisl (uphill €1.80, downhill €1)
and takes you halfway up the hill past an outlook called Aussichtspunkt
Jugend to a spot just above the castle. ⚠ From there it's a steep 10-minute
downhill walk to the castle (not recommended for those with mobility problems) or a 5-minute uphill walk to the Marienbrücke. ⊠ *Neuschwanstein-*
str. 20, Hohenschwangau ☎ *08362/930–830* ⊕ *www.neuschwanstein.*
de ⊠*€12, includes guided tour; combined ticket for Neuschwanstein*
and Hohenschwangau €23 ⊘ *Mid-Mar.–mid-Oct. daily 8–5:30; mid-*
Oct.–mid-Mar., daily 9–3:30.

Schloss Hohenschwangau. Built by the knights of Schwangau in the 12th
century, this castle was remodeled later by King Ludwig II's father,
the Bavarian crown prince and future king Maximilian, between
1832 and 1836. Unlike Ludwig's more famous castle across the valley,
Neuschwanstein, the mustard-yellow Schloss Hohenschwangau actually feels like a noble home, where comforts would be valued as much
as outward splendor. Ludwig spent his childhood summers surrounded
by the castle's murals, depicting ancient Germanic legends. It was here
that the young prince met the composer Richard Wagner. Their friendship shaped and deepened the future king's interest in theater, music,
and German mythology—the mythology Wagner drew upon for his
Ring cycle of operas.

After obtaining your ticket at the ticket center in the village, you can
take a 25-minute walk up either of two clearly marked paths to the
castle, or board one of the horse-drawn carriages that leave from the
ticket center (uphill €4, downhill €2) or the Hotel Müller (uphill €6,
downhill €3). ⊠ *Alpseestr. 12, Hohenschwangau* ☎ *08362/930–830*
⊕ *www.hohenschwangau.de* ⊠*€12, includes guided tour; combined*
ticket for Hohenschwangau and Neuschwanstein €23 ⊘ *Mid-Mar.–mid-*
Oct. daily 8–5:30; mid-Oct.–mid-Mar., daily 9–3:30.

CLOSE UP

The Fairy-Tale King

King Ludwig II (1845–86), the enigmatic presence indelibly associated with Bavaria, was one of the last rulers of the Wittelsbach dynasty, which ruled Bavaria from 1180 to 1918. Though his family had created grandiose architecture in Munich, Ludwig II disliked the city and preferred isolation in the countryside, where he constructed monumental edifices born of fanciful imagination and spent most of the royal purse on his endeavors. Although he was also a great lover of literature, theater, and opera (he was Richard Wagner's great patron), it is his fairy-tale-like castles that are his legacy.

Ludwig II reigned from 1864 to 1886, all the while avoiding political duties whenever possible. By 1878 he had completed his Schloss Linderhof retreat and immediately began Schloss Herrenchiemsee, a tribute to Versailles and Louis XIV. The grandest of his extravagant projects is Neuschwanstein, one of Germany's top attractions and concrete proof of the king's eccentricity. In 1886, before Neuschwanstein was finished, members of the government became convinced that Ludwig had taken leave of his senses. A medical commission declared the king insane and forced him to abdicate. Within two days of incarceration in the Berg Castle, on Starnbergersee, Ludwig and his doctor were found drowned in the lake's shallow waters. Their deaths are still a mystery.

WHERE TO STAY

$$ HOTEL 🏨 **Hotel Müller.** With a convenient location between the two Schwangau castles, the Müller fits beautifully into the stunning landscape, its creamy Bavarian baroque facade a contrast to the mountain forest. **Pros:** view of the castles; personalized service; variety of rooms. **Cons:** crowds during the day; expensive in season. [$] *Rooms from: €150* ✉ *Alpseestr. 16, Hohenschwangau* ☎ *08362/81990* 🌐 *www.hotel-mueller.de* 🛏 *39 rooms, 4 suites* 🕒 *Closed Nov. and early Jan.–late Mar.* 🍴 *Breakfast.*

8

THE BAVARIAN ALPS

Fir-clad mountains, rocky peaks, lederhosen, and geranium-covered houses make for Germany's most photogenic region. Quaint towns full of frescoed half-timber houses covered in snow pop up among the mountain peaks and shimmering hidden lakes, as do the creations of "Mad" King Ludwig II. The entire area has sporting opportunities galore, regardless of the season, including the country's finest skiing in Garmisch-Partenkirchen.

Each region of the Bavarian Alps has its die-hard fans. The constants, however, are the incredible scenery, clean air, and a sense of Bavarian *Gemütlichkeit* (coziness) omnipresent in every Hütte, Gasthof, and beer garden. The focus here is on the outdoors; the area almost completely lacks the high-culture institutions that dominate German urban life.

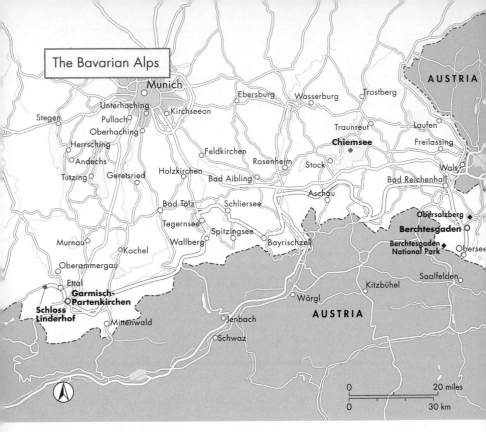

The Bavarian Alps

PLANNING YOUR TIME

The Alps are spread along Germany's southern border, but are fairly compact and easy to explore. Choose a central base and fan out from there. Garmisch-Partenkirchen and Berchtesgaden are the largest towns with the most convenient transportation connections. Smaller destinations like Ettal are quieter and make for pleasant overnight stays.

GETTING HERE AND AROUND

CAR TRAVEL

The Bavarian Alps are well connected to Munich by train, and an extensive network of buses links even the most remote villages. But the best way to visit the area is by car. Three autobahns reach into the Bavarian Alps: A-7, A-95, and A-8. It is a good idea to pick a town like Garmisch-Partenkirchen as a base and explore the area from there.

TRAIN TRAVEL

Most Alpine resorts are connected with Munich by regular express and slower service trains. With some careful planning—see ⊕ *www.bahn.de* for schedules and to buy tickets—you can visit this region without a car.

VISITOR INFORMATION

Contacts Tourismusverband München Oberbayern ✉ *Radolfzeller Str. 15, Munich* ☎ *089/829–2180* ⊕ *www.oberbayern-tourismus.de.*

GARMISCH-PARTENKIRCHEN

90 km (55 miles) southwest of Munich.

Garmisch, as it's more commonly known, is a bustling, year-round resort and spa town and is the undisputed capital of Alpine Bavaria. Winter sports rank high on the agenda here. There are more than 99 km (62 miles) of downhill ski runs, 40 ski lifts and cable cars, and 180 km (112 miles) of *Loipen* (cross-country ski trails). You can usually count on good skiing from December through April (and into May on the Zugspitze).

GETTING HERE AND AROUND

Garmisch-Partenkirchen is the cultural and transportation hub of the Werdenfelser Land. The autobahn A-95 links Garmisch directly to Munich. Regional German Rail trains head directly to Munich (90 minutes). Garmisch is a walkable city, and you probably won't need to use its frequent city-bus services.

The Garmisch mountain railway company, the Bayerische Zugspitzbahn, offers special excursions to the top of the Zugspitze, Germany's highest mountain, by cog rail and cable car.

Contacts Bayerische Zugspitzbahn ☎ *08821/7970* ⊕ *www.zugspitze.de.*

VISITOR INFORMATION

Contacts Garmisch-Partenkirchen ✉ *Richard-Strauss-Pl. 2, Garmisch-Partenkirchen* ☎ *08821/180–700* ⊕ *www.gapa.de* ☉ *Mid-Oct.–mid-Dec. and mid-Mar.–mid-May, weekdays 9–5, Sat. 9–3; mid-Dec.–mid-Mar. and mid-May–mid-Oct., weekdays 9–6, Sun. 10–noon.*

EXPLORING

The number one attraction in Garmisch is the **Zugspitze,** the highest mountain in Germany at 2,966 meters (9,731 feet). There are two ways up the mountain: a leisurely 75-minute ride on a cog railway from the train station in the town center, combined with a cable-car ride up the last stretch; or a 10-minute hoist by cable car, which begins its giddy ascent from the Eibsee, 10 km (6 miles) outside town on the road to Austria. There are two restaurants with sunny terraces at the summit and another at the top of the cog railway.

St. Martin Church. Garmisch-Partenkirchen isn't all sports and cars, however. In Garmisch, some beautiful examples of Upper Bavarian houses line Frühlingstrasse, and a pedestrian zone begins at Richard-Strauss-Platz. Off Marienplatz, at one end of the car-free zone, is the 18th-century parish church. It contains some significant stuccowork by the Wessobrunn artist Joseph Schmutzer and rococo work by Matthäus Günther. ✉ *Marienpl., Garmisch* ⊕ *www.erzbistum-muenchen. de/Pfarrei/Page007033.aspx.*

Werdenfelser Museum. Objects and exhibitions on the region's history can be found in this excellent museum, which is itself housed in a building dating back to around 1200. The museum is spread over 19 rooms and five floors, and explores every aspect of life in the Werdenfelser region, which was an independent state for more than 700 years (until 1802). ✉ *Ludwigstr. 47, Partenkirchen* ☎ *08821/751–710* ⊕ *www.werdenfels-museum.de* 🎫 *€2.50* ☉ *Tues.–Sun. 10–5.*

8

Richard Strauss Institut. On the eastern edge of Garmisch, at the end of Zöppritzstrasse, stands the home of composer Richard Strauss, who lived here until his death in 1949. It's not open to visitors but across town the Richard Strauss Institut is the center of activity during the Richard-Strauss-Tage, an annual music festival held in mid-June that features concerts and lectures on the town's most famous son. Other concerts are given year-round and there is also a Strauss exhibition (€3.50). ✉ *Schnitzschulstr. 19, Garmisch* 🌐 *www.richard-strauss-institut.de.*

WHERE TO EAT

$ GERMAN 🍴 **See-Hotel Riessersee.** On the shore of a small, blue-green, tranquil lake—a leisurely 3-km (2-mile) walk from town—this café-restaurant is an ideal spot for lunch or afternoon tea (on summer weekends there's live zither music from 3 to 5). House specialties are fresh trout and seasonal local game (which fetches the higher prices on the menu). [$] *Average main: €13* ✉ *Riess 5, Garmisch-Partenkirchen* ☎ *08821/758–123* 🌐 *www.riessersee.de* 🕓 *Closed Mon. and Dec. 1–15.*

WHERE TO STAY

$$ HOTEL 🏨 **Reindl's Partenkirchner Hof.** Karl Reindl ranked among the world's top hoteliers, and his daughter Marianne Holzinger has maintained high standards since taking over this hotel. **Pros:** ample-size rooms; great views. **Cons:** front rooms are on a busy street. [$] *Rooms from: €130* ✉ *Bahnhofstr. 15, Garmisch-Partenkirchen* ☎ *08821/943–870* 🌐 *www.reindls.de* 🛏 *35 rooms, 17 suites* 🍽 *Breakfast.*

SPORTS AND THE OUTDOORS

HIKING AND WALKING

There are innumerable spectacular walks on 300 km (186 miles) of marked trails through the lower slopes' pinewoods and upland meadows. If you have the time and good walking shoes, try one of the two trails that lead to striking gorges (*Klammen*).

Deutscher Alpenverein (*German Alpine Association*). Call here for details on hiking and on staying in the mountain huts. ✉ *Von-Kahr-Str. 2–4, Munich* ☎ *089/140–030* 🌐 *www.alpenverein.de.*

Höllentalklamm. The Höllentalklamm route starts in the town and ends at the mountaintop (you'll want to turn back before reaching the summit unless you have mountaineering experience). You can park in the villages of Hammersbach and Grainau, and start your tour. ✉ *Garmisch-Partenkirchen* ☎ *08821/8895* 🌐 *www.hoellentalklamm-info.de* 🕓 *May–Oct., depending on weather.*

Zugspitze Mountain railway terminal. Zugspitze Mountain railway terminal ✉ *Olympiastr. 27, Garmisch-Partenkirchen.*

Partnachklamm. The Partnachklamm route is quite challenging, and takes you through a spectacular, tunneled water gorge (entrance fee), past a pretty little mountain lake, and far up the Zugspitze; to do all of it, you'll have to stay overnight in one of the huts along the way. Ride part of the way up in the **Eckbauer cable car**, which sets out from the Skistadion off Mittenwalderstrasse. The older, more scenic **Graseckbahn** takes you right over the dramatic gorges. Day cards for the cable car cost €23 (cheaper depending on how far you want to ride and time of year). There's a handy inn at the top, where you can gather strength for the hourlong walk back down to the Graseckbahn station. ⊠ *Olympia-Skistadion, Garmisch-Partenkirchen* ⊕ *www.eckbauerbahn.de.*

Lohnkutschevereinigung. Horse-drawn carriages also cover the first section of the route in summer; in winter you can skim along it in a sleigh. The carriages wait near the Skistadion. Or you can call the local coaching society, the Lohnkutschevereinigung, for information. ⊠ *Olympia Skistadion, Garmisch-Partenkirchen* ☎ *0172/860–4105* ⊕ *www.kutschenfahrten-garmisch.de*

SKIING AND SNOWBOARDING

Garmisch-Partenkirchen was the site of the 1936 Winter Olympics, and remains Germany's premier winter-sports resort. The upper slopes of the Zugspitze and surrounding mountains challenge the best ski buffs and snowboarders, and there are also plenty of runs for intermediate skiers and families. The area is divided into two basic regions. The **Riffelriss** with the **Zugspitzplatt** is Germany's highest skiing area, with snow guaranteed from November to May. Access is via the **Zugspitzbahn** funicular. Cost is €34.50 for a day pass, €75 for a 2½-day pass (valid from noon on the first day). The **CLASSIC-Gebiet**, or classical area, has 17 lifts in the **Alpspitz, Kreuzeck,** and **Hausberg** region. Day passes cost €29.50, a two-day pass €53. The town has a number of ski schools and tour organizers.

Alpine Auskunftstelle. The best place for information for all your snow-sports needs is the Alpine office at the Garmisch tourist-information office. ⊠ *Richard-Strauss-Pl. 2, Garmisch* ☎ *08821/180–700* ⊕ *www. gapa.de* ☺ *Mid-Oct.–mid-Dec. and mid-Mar.–mid-May, weekdays 9–5, Sat. 9–3; mid-Dec.–mid-Mar. and mid-May–mid-Oct., weekdays 9–6, Sun. 10–noon.*

Erste Skilanglaufschule Garmisch-Partenkirchen. Cross-country skiers should check with the Erste Skilanglaufschule Garmisch-Partenkirchen at the eastern entrance of the Olympic stadium in Garmisch. ⊠ *Olympia-Skistadion, Garmisch-Partenkirchen* ☎ *08821/1516* ⊕ *www.ski-langlauf-schule.de.*

Skischule Alpin. Skiers looking for instruction can try the Skischule Alpin. ⊠ *Reintalstr. 8, Garmisch* ☎ *08821/945–676* ⊕ *www.alpin-skischule.de.*

SCHLOSS LINDERHOF

95 km (59 miles) south of Munich.

Set in sylvan seclusion in Graswang Valley, high in the Alps, the royal palace of Linderhof was built by King Ludwig II on the site of his father's hunting lodge. This was the first of Ludwig's big building projects and the only one completed during his lifetime.

GETTING HERE AND AROUND

The easiest way to reach this isolated castle is by regional Deutsche Bahn train from Munich Hauptbahnhof to Oberammergau. Buy the Bayern Ticket, which allows for a full day of travel (for up to 5 people), including the bus fare (Bus No. 9622) to Linderhof from the Oberammergau

8

train station. Or you can take an organized bus tour, but no tours at this writing visit only Linderhof; most also go to Neuschwanstein.

EXPLORING

Schloss Linderhof. Built between 1870 and 1879 on the spectacular grounds of his father's hunting lodge, Schloss Linderhof was the smallest of this ill-fated king's castles, but his favorite country retreat among the various palaces at his disposal. ■TIP➜ **If you plan on visiting more of Ludwig's castles, purchase the Kombiticket Königsschlösser. The ticket costs €24 and allows the holder to visit Neuschwanstein, Linderhof, and Herrenchiemsee, one time each, within six months.** Set in sylvan seclusion, between a reflecting pool and the green slopes of a gentle mountain, the charming, French-style rococo confection is said to have been inspired by the Petit Trianon at Versailles. From an architectural standpoint it's a whimsical combination of conflicting styles, lavish on the outside, somewhat overly decorated on the inside. Ludwig's bedroom is filled with brilliantly colored and gilded ornaments, the Hall of Mirrors is a shimmering dream world, and the dining room has a clever piece of 19th-century engineering—a table that rises from and descends to the kitchens below.

The formal gardens contain still more whimsical touches. There's a Moorish pavilion—bought wholesale from the 1867 Paris Universal Exposition—and a huge artificial grotto in which Ludwig had scenes from Wagner operas performed, with full lighting effects. ⊠ *Schloss- und Gartenverwaltung Linderhof, Linderhof 12, Linderhof* ☎ *08822/92030* ⊕ *www.schlosslinderhof.de* ◫ *€8.50 in summer, €7.50 in winter (palace by guided tour only); €5 palace grounds (summer only)* ⊗ *Apr.–Oct., daily 9–6; Oct.–Mar., daily 10–4; pavilion and grotto closed in winter.*

CHIEMSEE

80 km (50 miles) southeast of Munich, 120 km (75 miles) northeast of Garmisch-Partenkirchen.

Chiemsee is north of the Deutsche Alpenstrasse, but it demands a detour, if only to visit King Ludwig's huge palace on one of its idyllic islands. It's the largest Bavarian lake, and although it's surrounded by reedy flatlands, the nearby mountains provide a majestic backdrop. The town of **Prien** is the lake's principal resort. ■TIP➜ **The tourist offices of Prien and Aschau offer a €19 transportation package covering a boat trip, a round-trip rail ticket between the two resorts, and a round-trip ride by cable car to the top of Kampen Mountain, above Aschau.**

GETTING HERE AND AROUND

Prien is the jumping-off point for exploring the Chiemsee. Frequent trains connect Prien with Munich and Salzburg. The only way to reach the Herreninsel is by boat.

VISITOR INFORMATION

Contacts Chiemsee Infocenter ⊠ *Felden 10, Bernau am Chiemsee* ☎ *08051/96555–0* ⊕ *www.chiemsee-alpenland.de.*

EXPLORING

Fodor's Choice ★ **Schloss Herrenchiemsee.** Despite its distance from Munich, the beautiful Chiemsee drew Bavarian royalty to its shores. Its dreamlike, melancholy air caught the imagination of King Ludwig II, and it was on one of the lake's three islands that he built Schloss Herrenchiemsee, his third and last castle. As with most of Ludwig's projects, the building was never completed, and Ludwig spent only nine days in the castle. Nonetheless, what remains is impressive—and ostentatious. Regular ferries out to the island depart from Stock, Prien's harbor.

Most spectacular is the Hall of Mirrors, a dazzling gallery where candlelit concerts are held in summer. Also of interest are the ornate bedrooms Ludwig planned, the "self-rising" table that ascended from the kitchen quarters, the elaborately painted bathroom with a small pool for a tub, and the formal gardens. The south wing houses a **museum** containing Ludwig's christening robe and death mask, as well as other artifacts of his life. ✉ *Schloss Herrenchiemsee, Herrenchiemsee, Chiemsee* ☎ *08051/68870 for palace* 🌐 *www.herren-chiemsee.de* 🎫 *€8, includes Museum im Alten Schloss* ⏲ *Apr.–late Oct., daily 9–6; late Oct.–Mar., daily 10–4:45; English-language palace tours daily, once per hr.*

WHERE TO STAY

$ HOTEL 🏨 **Hotel Luitpold am See.** Boats to the Chiemsee islands tie up right outside your window at this handsome old Prien hotel, which organizes shipboard disco evenings as part of its entertainment program. **Pros:** directly on the lake (though the sister property is 328 feet away); "limousine service" offers pick-up from Munich airport for €100. **Cons:** near a busy boat dock. [$] *Rooms from: €82* ✉ *Seestrasse 110, Prien am Chiemsee* ☎ *08051/609–100* 🌐 *www.luitpold-am-see.de* 🛏 *54 rooms* 🍴 *Breakfast.*

8

BERCHTESGADEN

20 km (12 miles) south of Salzburg, Austria.

Berchtesgaden's reputation is unjustly rooted in its brief association with Adolf Hitler, who dreamed of his "1,000-year Reich" from the mountaintop where millions of tourists before and after him drank in only the superb beauty of the Alpine panorama. The historic old market town and mountain resort has great charm. In winter it's a fine place for skiing and snowboarding; in summer it becomes one of the region's most popular (and crowded) resorts. An ornate palace and working salt mine make up some of the diversions in this heavenly setting.

GETTING HERE AND AROUND

The easiest way to reach Berchtesgaden is with the hourly train connection via Bad Reichenhall from Salzburg Hbf. Trains to Munich require a change in Freilassing. Hamburg and Dortmund are both served with one direct train per day. Frequent local bus service makes it easy to explore the town and to reach the Königssee. The Schwaiger bus company runs tours of the area and across the Austrian border as far as Salzburg. An American couple runs Eagle's Nest Historical Tours out of the local tourist office, opposite the railroad station.

VISITOR INFORMATION

Contacts Berchtesgadener Land Tourismus ⊠ *Bahnhofpl. 4* ☎ *08652/656–5050* ⊕ *www.berchtesgadener-land.com.* **Eagle's Nest Historical Tours** ⊠ *Königseer Str. 2* ☎ *08652/64971* ⊕ *www.eagles-nest-tours.com.* **Schwaiger** ☎ *08652/2525* ⊕ *www.bus-schwaiger.de/en.*

EXPLORING

The Obersalzberg. The site of Hitler's luxurious mountain retreat is part of the north slope of the Hoher Goll, high above Berchtesgaden. It was a remote mountain community of farmers and foresters before Hitler's deputy, Martin Bormann, selected the site for a complex of Alpine homes for top Nazi leaders. Hitler's chalet, the Berghof, and all the others were destroyed in 1945, with the exception of a hotel that had been taken over by the Nazis, the Hotel zum Türken. The round-trip from Berchtesgaden's post office by bus and elevator costs €16.10 per person. The bus runs mid-May through September, daily from 9 to 4:50. By car you can travel only as far as the Obersalzberg bus station. The full round trip takes one hour. ■ **TIP→ To get the most out of your visit to the Kehlsteinhaus, consider taking one of the informative tours offered by David Harper. Reserve in advance at** ☎ *08652/64971* **or** ⊕ *www.eagles-nest-historical-tours.com.* **Tours meet across from the train station and cost €50.** ⊠ *Königseer Str. 2* ⊕ *www.eagles-nest-tours.com.*

Bunkers. Beneath the hotel is a section of the labyrinth of tunnels built as a last retreat for Hitler and his cronies; the macabre, murky bunkers can be visited. ⊠ *Hintereck 2* ☎ *08652/2428* ⊕ *www.hotel-zum-tuerken.de/hotel.html* ☜ *€3* ◷ *Apr.–Oct., daily 10–5; by appointment in winter.*

Dokumentation Obersalzberg. Nearby, the Dokumentation Obersalzberg documents the notorious history of the Third Reich, and a special focus on Obersalzberg, with some surprisingly rare archive material. ⊠ *Salzbergstr. 41* ☎ *08652/947–960* ⊕ *www.obersalzberg.de* ☜ *€3* ◷ *Apr.–Oct., daily 9–5; Nov.–Mar., Tues.–Sun. 10–3.*

Kehlsteinhaus. Beyond Obersalzberg, the hairpin bends of Germany's highest road come to the base of the 6,000-foot peak on which sits the Kehlsteinhaus, also known as the Adlerhorst (Eagle's Nest), Hitler's personal retreat and his official guesthouse. It was Martin Bormann's gift to the führer on Hitler's 50th birthday. The road leading to it, built in 1937–39, climbs more than 2,000 dizzying feet in less than 6 km (4 miles). A tunnel in the mountain will bring you to an elevator that whisks you up to what appears to be the top of the world (you can walk up in about half an hour). There are refreshment rooms and a restaurant. ⊠ *Kehlstein Busabfahrt, Hintereck* ☎ *08652/2969* ⊕ *www.kehlsteinhaus.de*

The Salzbergwerk. This salt mine is one of the chief attractions of the region. In the days when the mine was owned by Berchtesgaden's princely rulers, only select guests were allowed to see how the source of the city's wealth was extracted from the earth. Today, during a 90-minute tour, you can sit astride a miniature train that transports you nearly 1 km (½ mile) into the mountain to an enormous chamber where the salt is mined. Included in the tour are rides down the wooden chutes used by miners to get from one level to another and a boat ride on an underground saline lake the size of a football field. Although the tours take about an hour, plan an extra 45–60 minutes for purchasing the tickets and changing into and out of miners clothing. You may wish to partake in the special four-hour **brine dinners** down in the mines (€90). These are very popular, so be sure to book early. ⊠ *Bergwerkstr. 83, 2 km (1 mile) from center of Berchtesgaden on B-305 (Salzburg Rd.)* ☎ *08652/600–220* ⊕ *www.salzzeitreise.de* ⊠ *€15.50, combined ticket with Bad Reichenhall's saline museum €18.50* ⊙ *May–Oct., daily 9–5; Nov.–Apr., Mon.–Sat. 11–3.*

WHERE TO STAY

$$
HOTEL

⊡ **Hotel zum Türken.** The view alone is worth the 10-minute journey from Berchtesgaden to this hotel. **Pros:** great location; sense of history; Frau Schafenberg can cook! **Cons:** not all rooms have attached bathrooms. $ *Rooms from: €90* ⊠ *Hintereck 2, Obersalzberg-Berchtesgaden* ☎ *08652/2428* ⊕ *www.hotel-zum-tuerken.de* ⤴ *17 rooms (12 with bath or shower)* ⊙ *Closed Nov.–Dec. 20* ⦿ *Breakfast.*

HEIDELBERG

The natural beauty of Heidelberg is created by the embrace of mountains, forests, vineyards, and the Neckar River—all crowned by the famous ruined castle. If any city in Germany encapsulates the spirit of the country, it is Heidelberg. Scores of poets and composers—virtually the entire 19th-century German Romantic movement—have sung its praises. Goethe and Mark Twain both fell in love here: the German writer with a beautiful young woman, the American author with the city itself. Sigmund Romberg set his operetta *The Student Prince* in the city; Carl Maria von Weber wrote his lushly Romantic opera *Der Freischütz* here. Composer Robert Schumann was a student at the university. The campaign these artists waged on behalf of the town has been astoundingly successful. Heidelberg's fame is out of all proportion to its size (population 140,000); more than 3½ million visitors crowd its streets every year.

Above all, Heidelberg is a university town, with students making up a large part of its population. And a youthful spirit is felt in the lively restaurants and pubs of the Altstadt. Modern Heidelberg has changed as U.S. army barracks and industrial development stretched into the suburbs, but the old heart of the city remains intact, exuding the spirit of romantic Germany.

PLANNING YOUR TIME

To fully appreciate Heidelberg, try to be up and about before the tour buses arrive. After the day-trippers have gone and most shops have closed, the good restaurants and the nightspots open up. Walking the length of Heidelberg's Hauptstrasse (main street) will take an hour— longer if you are easily sidetracked by the shopping opportunities. Strolling through the Old Town and across the bridge to look at the castle will take you at least another half hour, not counting the time you spend visiting the sites.

GETTING HERE AND AROUND
TRAIN TRAVEL
Heidelberg is 15 minutes away from Mannheim, where four InterCity Express (ICE) trains and five Autobahn routes meet. Everything in town may be reached on foot. A funicular takes you up to the castle and Heidelberg's Königstuhl mountain, and a streetcar takes you from the center of the city to the main station.

Contacts **TLS** ☎ *06221/770–077* ⊕ *www.tls-heidelberg.de.*

VISITOR INFORMATION
Contacts **Heidelberg Tourist Information** ✉ *Rathaus, Marktpl.* ☎ *06221/58444* . **Heidelberg Tourist Information** ✉ *Hauptbahnhof, Willy-Brandt-Pl. 1* ☎ *06221/19433* ⊕ *www.heidelberg-marketing.de.*

EXPLORING

Alte Brücke (*Old Bridge*). Framed by two *Spitzhelm* towers (so called for their resemblance to old German helmets), this bridge was part of Heidelberg's medieval fortifications. In the west tower are three dank dungeons that once held common criminals. Above the portcullis you'll see a memorial plaque that pays warm tribute to the Austrian forces that helped Heidelberg beat back a French attempt to capture the bridge in 1799. As you enter the bridge from the Old Town, you'll also notice a statue of an animal that appears somewhat catlike. It's actually a monkey holding a mirror. Legend has it the statue was erected to symbolize the need for both city-dwellers and those who lived on the other side of the bridge to take a look over their shoulders as they cross—that neither group was more elite than the other. The pedestrian-only bridge is at the end of Steingasse, not far from the Marktplatz. ✉ *End of Steing.*

Alte Universität (*Old University*). The three-story baroque structure was built between 1712 and 1735 at the behest of the elector Johann Wilhelm, although Heidelberg's Ruprecht Karl University was originally founded in 1386. Today it houses the **University Museum**, with exhibits that chronicle the history of Germany's oldest university. The present-day Universitätsplatz (University Square) was built over the remains of an Augustinian monastery that was destroyed by the French in 1693. ✉ *Grabeng. 1–3* ☎ *06221/542–152* 🎫 *€3* ⊙ *Apr.–Sept., Tues.–Sun. 10–6; Oct., Tues.–Sun. 10–4; Nov.–Mar., Tues.–Sat. 10–4.*

Königstuhl (*King's Throne*). The second-highest hill in the Odenwald range—1,800 feet above Heidelberg—is only a hop, skip, and funicular ride from Heidelberg. On a clear day you can see as far as the Black Forest to the south and west to the Vosges Mountains of France. The hill is at the center of a close-knit network of hiking trails. Signs and colored arrows from the top lead hikers through the woods of the Odenwald.

Königstuhl Bergbahn (*Funicular*). Hoisting visitors to the summit of the Königstuhl in 17 minutes, the funicular stops on the way at the ruined Heidelberg Schloss and Molkenkur. A modern funicular usually leaves every 10 minutes, and a historical train comes every 20 minutes. ✉ *Kornmarkt* ⊕ *www.bergbahn-heidelberg.de* 🎫 *Königstuhl*

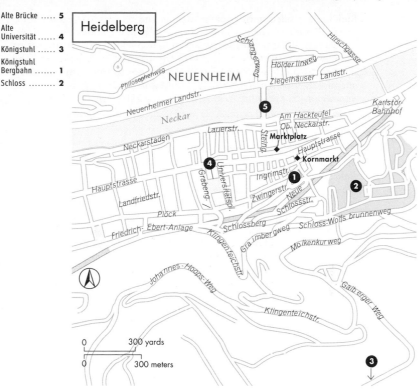

€12 round-trip, Schloss €6.50 round-trip ⊗ Mid-Apr.–mid-Oct., daily 9–8:25; mid-Oct.–mid-Apr., daily 9–5:45.

Fodor's Choice
★

Schloss (*Castle*). What's most striking is the architectural variety of this great complex. The oldest parts still standing date from the 15th century, though most of the castle was built during the Renaissance in the baroque styles of the 16th and 17th centuries, when the castle was the seat of the Palatinate electors. There's an "English wing," built in 1612 by the elector Friedrich V for his teenage Scottish bride, Elizabeth Stuart; its plain, square-window facade is positively foreign compared to the castle's more opulent styles. The architectural highlight remains the Renaissance courtyard—harmonious, graceful, and ornate.

Even if you have to wait, make a point of seeing the *Grosses Fass* (Great Cask) in the cellar, possibly the world's largest wine barrel, made from 130 oak trees and capable of holding 58,500 gallons. ■TIP➙ **Take the Königstuhl Bergbahn, or funicular (€6.50 round-trip), faster and less tiring than hiking to the castle on the Burgweg. Audioguides are available in seven languages.** ⊠ *Schlosshof* ☎ *06221/538–431* ⊕ *www.heidelberg-schloss.de* ⊡*€6, audio guide €4* ⊗ *Daily 8–5; tours in English daily 11:15–3:15, when demand is sufficient.*

Deutsches Apotheken–Museum (*German Apothecary Museum*). This museum, on the lower floor of the Ottheinrichsbau (Otto Heinrich

Building), is filled with ancient flagons and receptacles (each with a carefully painted enamel label), beautifully made scales, little drawers, shelves, dried beetles and toads, and marvelous reconstructions of six apothecary shops from the 17th through the 20th centuries. The museum also offers young visitors the chance to smell various herbs and mix their own teas. ☎ *06221/25880* ⊕ *www.deutsches-apotheken-museum.de* ⊙ *Apr.–Oct., daily 10–6, Nov.–Mar., daily 10–5:30.*

WHERE TO EAT

$$$$
GERMAN

✕ **Scharff's Schlossweinstube.** Elegant, romantic and expensive, this baroque dining room inside the famous Heidelberg castle specializes in *Ente von Heidelberg* (roast duck), but there's always something new on the seasonal menu. Whatever you order, pair it with a bottle from the extensive selection of international wines. Less pricey is the adjacent Bistro Backhaus, which has rustic furnishings and a nearly 50-foot-high *Backkamin* (baking oven). Light fare as well as coffee and cake are served indoors and on the shaded terrace. You can sample rare wines (Eiswein, Beerenauslese) by the glass in the shared wine cellar, or pick up a bottle with a designer label depicting Heidelberg. Reservations are essential for terrace seating in summer. $ *Average main: €100* ✉ *Schlosshof, on castle grounds* ☎ *06221/872–7010* ⊕ *www.heidelberger-schloss-gastronomie.de* ⊙ *Closed Wed. and late Dec.–Jan. No lunch.*

$$$
MEDITERRANEAN

✕ **Simplicissimus.** Olive oil and herbs of Provence accentuate many of the chef's culinary delights. Saddle of lamb and sautéed liver in honey-pepper sauce are specialties, as are season specialties with asparagus and mushrooms. The *Dessertteller,* a sweet sampler, is a crowning finish to any meal. The wine list focuses on old-world estates, particularly clarets. The elegant art-nouveau interior is done in shades of red with dark-wood accents, and a quiet courtyard offers alfresco dining in summer. $ *Average main: €25* ✉ *Ingrimstr. 16* ☎ *06221/183–336* ⊕ *www.restaurant-simplicissimus.de* ⊙ *Closed Mon. No lunch.*

$$$
EUROPEAN

✕ **Zur Herrenmühle.** A 17th-century grain mill has been transformed into this romantic restaurant in the heart of the Altstadt (Old Town). The old beams add to the warm atmosphere. In summer, try to arrive early to get a table in the idyllic courtyard. Fish, lamb, and homemade pasta are specialties. Or opt for the three- or four-course prix-fixe menu. $ *Average main: €21* ✉ *Near Karlstor, Hauptstr. 239* ☎ *06221/602–909* ⊕ *www.herrenmuehle-heidelberg.de* ⊙ *Closed Sun. No lunch.*

$
GERMAN
Fodor's Choice
★

✕ **Zum Roten Ochsen.** Many of the rough-hewn oak tables here have initials carved into them, a legacy of the thousands who have visited Heidelberg's most famous old tavern. Mark Twain, Marilyn Monroe, and John Wayne may have left their mark—they all ate here, and Twain's photo is on one of the memorabilia-covered walls. Wash down simple fare, such as goulash soup and bratwurst, or heartier dishes like *Tellerfleisch* (boiled beef) or Swabian *Maultaschen* (meat filled raviolis) with regional German wines or local Heidelberg beer. The "Red Ox" has been run by the Spengel family for more than 170 years. Come early to get a good seat, and stay late for the piano player and *Gemütlichkeit* (easy-going friendliness). $ *Average main: €12* ✉ *Haupt-*

str. 217 ☎ *06221/20977* 🌐 *www.roterochsen.de* 🕒 *Closed Sun. and mid-Dec.–mid-Jan. No lunch Nov.–Mar.*

WHERE TO STAY

$$ HOTEL Fodor's Choice ★ 🏨 **Der Europäische Hof–Hotel Europa.** On secluded grounds next to the Old Town, this most luxurious of Heidelberg hotels has been welcoming guests since 1865. **Pros:** indoor pool; castle views from the two-story fitness and spa center. **Cons:** restaurant closed in July and August. [$] *Rooms from: €170* ✉ *Friedrich-Ebert-Anlage 1* ☎ *06221/5150* 🌐 *www.europaeischerhof.com* 🛏 *100 rooms, 14 suites, 3 apartments, 1 penthouse* 🍴 *Breakfast.*

$$$ HOTEL Fodor's Choice ★ 🏨 **Hotel Die Hirschgasse.** A stunning castle view, fine restaurants, a literary connection, and a touch of romance distinguish this historic inn (1472) across the river from the Old Town, opposite Karlstor. **Pros:** terrific view; very good food in both restaurants; close to "museum row." **Cons:** limited parking; 15-minute walk to the Old Town. [$] *Rooms from: €205* ✉ *Hirschg. 3* ☎ *06221/4540* 🌐 *www.hirschgasse.de* 🛏 *20 suites* 🕒 *Le Gourmet closed Sun. and Mon., 2 wks in early Jan., and 2 wks in early Aug.; Mensurstube closed Sun. No lunch at either restaurant* 🍴 *Multiple meal plans.*

$$ HOTEL 🏨 **NH Heidelberg.** The glass-covered entrance hall of this primarily business hotel is spacious—not surprising, as it was the courtyard of a former brewery. **Pros:** good food; reasonably priced; free Wi-fi. **Cons:** lacks charm; located about 1 km (½ mile) from the Old Town; parking expensive. [$] *Rooms from: €120* ✉ *Bergheimerstr. 91* ☎ *06221/13270* 🌐 *www.nh-hotels.com* 🛏 *156 rooms, 18 suites* 🍴 *Breakfast.*

$$ HOTEL Fodor's Choice ★ 🏨 **Hotel zum Ritter.** If this is your first visit to Germany, try to stay here—it's the only Renaissance building in Heidelberg (1592), built as the private home of a wealthy merchant, and has an unbeatable location opposite the market square in the heart of the Altstadt. **Pros:** charm and elegance; nice views; spacious rooms. **Cons:** off-site parking, rooms facing the square can be noisy. [$] *Rooms from: €118* ✉ *Hauptstr. 178* ☎ *06221/1350* 🌐 *www.ritter-heidelberg.de* 🛏 *36 rooms, 1 suite* 🍴 *No meals.*

NIGHTLIFE

Heidelberg nightlife is concentrated in the area around the Heiliggeistkirche (Church of the Holy Ghost), in the Old Town. Don't miss a visit to one of the old student taverns that have been in business for ages. Today's students, however, are more likely to hang out in one of the dozen or more bars on **Untere Strasse,** which runs parallel to and between Hauptstrasse and the Neckar River, starting from the market square.

HAMBURG

Water—in the form of the Alster Lakes and the Elbe River—is Hamburg's defining feature and the key to the city's success. A harbor city with an international appeal, Hamburg is one of the most open-minded of German cities. But for most Europeans the port city invariably triggers thoughts of the gaudy Reeperbahn underworld, that sleazy strip of clip joints, sex shows, and wholesale prostitution that helped earn Hamburg its reputation as "Sin City." Today the infamous red-light district is just as much a hip meeting place for young Hamburgers and tourist crowds, who flirt with the bright lights and chic haunts of the not-so-sinful Reeperbahn, especially on warm summer nights.

The distinguishing feature of downtown Hamburg is the artificial lake known as the Alster. It's lined with stately hotels, department stores, fine shops, and cafés and by parks and gardens against a backdrop of private mansions. The city is at the mouth of the Elbe, one of Europe's great rivers and the 97-km (60-mile) umbilical cord that ties the harbor to the North Sea.

PLANNING YOUR TIME

The downtown area features most of Hamburg's must-see attractions, such as the grand, historic churches and most museums. Take a stroll along the two major boulevards in the area, the Jungfernstieg along the Alster and the Mönckebergstrasse, and venture out to the many side streets and canalside walks. Any visit to Hamburg should include a walk along the Reeperbahn in St. Pauli, as well as a closer inspection of the Altstadt with its 19th-century warehouses and cobblestone alleys. Boat tours of the massive harbor and the cosmopolitan Alster Lake are very good ways to get to know the city.

GETTING HERE AND AROUND

AIR TRAVEL

Hamburg's international airport, Fuhlsbüttel, is 11 km (7 miles) north-west of the city. The Airport-City-Bus runs nonstop between the airport and Hamburg's main train station daily at 15- to 30-minute intervals.

Contacts Hamburg Airport. ✉ *Flughafenstr. 1–3* ☎ *040/50750* ⊕ *www. airport.de.*

BUS AND SUBWAY TRAVEL

Hamburg's bus station, the Zentral-Omnibus-Bahnhof, is directly behind the main train station. The HVV, Hamburg's public transportation system, includes the U-bahn, the S-bahn, and buses. Tickets are available on all buses and at automatic machines in all stations and at most bus stops. You must validate your ticket at a machine at the start of your journey. If you are found without a validated ticket, the fine is €40.

Contacts HVV (*Hamburg Transportation Association*). ✉ *Johanniswall 2, Altstadt* ☎ *040/19449* ⊕ *www.hvv.de.* **Zentral-Omnibus-Bahnhof** (*ZOB*). ✉ *Adenauerallee 78, St. Georg* ☎ *040/247–576* ⊕ *www.zob-hamburg.de.*

CAR TRAVEL

Hamburg is easier to handle by car than many other German cities, and traffic is relatively uncongested. During rush hour, however, there can be gridlock. Several autobahns (A-1, A-7, A-23, A-24, and A-250) connect with Hamburg's three beltways, which then easily take you to the downtown area.

TAXI TRAVEL

Taxi meters start at €2.40, then add €1.68 per km thereafter. You can hail taxis on the street or at stands, or order one by phone.

Contacts **Taxi** ☎ *040/211–211* ⊕ *www.taxi211211.de.*

TRAIN TRAVEL

There are two principal stations: the central Hauptbahnhof (Main Train Station) and Hamburg-Altona, west of the downtown area. EuroCity and InterCity (IC) trains connect Hamburg with all German cities and many major European ones. InterCity Express (ICE) "supertrain" lines link Hamburg with Berlin, Frankfurt, and Munich.

Contacts **Deutsche Bahn** ☎ *0180/699–6633* ⊕ *www.bahn.de.*

VISITOR INFORMATION

Contacts **Hamburg Tourismus** ⊠ *Steinstr. 7, Altstadt* ☎ *040/3005–1300 for hotline* ⊕ *www.hamburg-travel.com.*

EXPLORING

Hamburg's most important attractions stretch between the Alster Lakes to the north and the harbor and Elbe River to the south. This area consists of four distinct quarters. St. Georg is the business district around the Hauptbahnhof. The historic Altstadt (Old City) clusters near the harbor and surrounds the Rathaus (Town Hall). West of the Altstadt is Neustadt (New City). The shabby but thrilling district of St. Pauli includes the Reeperbahn, a strip of sex clubs and bars.

DOWNTOWN

Jungfernstieg. This wide promenade looking out over the Alster lakes is the beginning of the city's premier shopping district. Laid out in 1665, it used to be part of a muddy millrace that channeled water into the Elbe. Hidden from view behind the sedate facade of Jungfernstieg is a network of several small shopping centers that together account for almost a mile of shops selling everything from souvenirs to haute couture. Many of these passages have sprung up in the past two decades, but some have been here since the 19th century; the first glass-covered arcade, called Sillem's Bazaar, was built in 1845. ⊠ *Neustadt* Ⓜ *Jungfernstieg (U-bahn).*

Fodor's Choice **Rathaus** *(Town Hall).* To most Hamburgers this impressive neo-Renais-
★ sance building is the symbolic heart of the city. The seat of the city's Senate (State Government) and Bürgerschaft (Parliament), it was constructed between 1886 and 1897, with 647 rooms and an imposing clock tower. Along with much of the city center, the Rathaus was heavily damaged during World War II, but was faithfully restored to its original beauty in the postwar years, and it's now one of the most photographed sights in Hamburg. The forty-minute tours of the building begin in the ground floor Rathausdiele, a vast pillared hall. Although visitors are only shown the state rooms, their tapestries, glittering chandeliers, coffered ceilings, and grand portraits give you a sense of the city's great wealth in the 19th century and the Town Hall's status as an object of civic pride. ⊠ *Rathausmarkt, Altstadt* ☎ *040/42831–2064* ⊕ *www.*

8

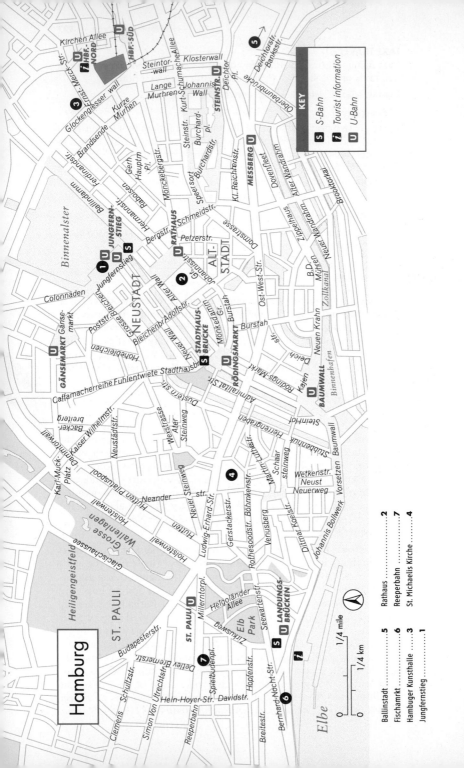

Hamburg

KEY
S S-Bahn
i Tourist information
U U-Bahn

Ballinstadt **5**
Fischamrkt **6**
Hamburger Kunsthalle **3**
Jungfernstieg **1**

Rathaus **2**
Reeperbahn **7**
St. Michaelis Kirche **4**

1/4 mile
1/4 km

ST. PAULI

Elbe

Binnenalster

NEUSTADT

ALT-STADT

GÄNSEMARKT

HBF.-SÜD
HBF.-NORD

MESSBERG

BAUMWALL

LANDUNGS-BRÜCKEN

ST. PAULI

STADTHAUS-BRÜCKE

RÖDINGSMARKT

JUNGFERN-STIEG

RATHAUS

STEINSTR.

hamburgische-buergerschaft.de 🎫 €4 ⊙ *Daily tours in English hrly from 10:15* Ⓜ *Rathaus (U-bahn), Jungfernstieg (U-bahn and S-bahn).*

THE HARBOR AND HISTORIC HAMBURG

Hamburger Kunsthalle (*Art Gallery*). One of the most important art museums in Germany, the Kunsthalle has 3,500 paintings, 650 sculptures, and a coin and medal collection that dates from the ancient Roman era. In the postmodern, cube-shaped building designed by Berlin architect O. M. Ungers, the **Galerie der Gegenwart** has housed a collection of international modern art since 1960, including works by Andy Warhol, Joseph Beuys, Georg Baselitz, and David Hockney. With 1,200 drawings and other works, graphic art is well represented, including works by Pablo Picasso and Horst Janssen, a Hamburg artist famous for his satirical worldview. The outstanding collection of German Romantic paintings includes pieces by Caspar David Friedrich. ✉ *Glockengiesserwall, Altstadt* 📞 *040/4281–31200* ⊕ *www.hamburger-kunsthalle.de* 🎫 *€12* ⊙ *Tues., Wed., and Fri.–Sun. 10–6, Thurs. 10–9.* Ⓜ *Hauptbahnhof (U-bahn and S-bahn).*

Fodor's Choice **St. Michaelis Kirche** (*St. Michael's Church*). The Michel, as it's called
★ locally, is Hamburg's principal church and northern Germany's finest baroque-style ecclesiastical building. Its first incarnation, built between 1649 and 1661 (the tower followed in 1669), was razed after lightning struck almost a century later. It was rebuilt between 1750 and 1786 in the decorative Nordic baroque style, but was gutted by a terrible fire in 1906. The replica, completed in 1912, was demolished during World War II. The present church is a reconstruction.

The distinctive 436-foot brick-and-iron tower bears the largest tower clock in Germany, 26 feet in diameter. Just above the clock is a viewing platform (accessible by elevator or stairs) that affords a magnificent panorama of the city, the Elbe River, and the Alster lakes. ■ **TIP→ Twice a day, at 10 am and 9 pm (Sunday at noon), a watchman plays a trumpet solo from the tower platform.**

For a great view of Hamburg's skyline, head to the clock tower at night. In the evenings you can sip a complimentary soft drink while listening to classical music in a room just below the tower. This is usually held from 5:30 to 11:00: check ⊕ *www.nachtmichel.de* to confirm times. ✉ *Englische Planke 1, Neustadt* 📞 *040/376–780* ⊕ *www.st-michaelis.de* 🎫 *Tower €5; crypt and movie €4; show, tower, and crypt €7* ⊙ *May–Oct., daily 9–7:30; Nov.–Apr., daily 10–5:30* Ⓜ *Rödingsmarkt (U-bahn), Stadthausbrücke (S-bahn).*

ST. PAULI AND THE REEPERBAHN

BallinStadt. This museum and family-research center tells the story of European emigration to the United States and elsewhere. The complex on the peninsula here, completed in 1901, was built by the HAPAG shipping line for its passengers, which came from all across Europe to sail across the Atlantic.

During the first 34 years of the 20th century, about 1.7 million people passed through emigration halls. Processing this many people took a long time, and Hamburg officials did not want foreigners roaming the city. To accommodate visitors for several days or months, the shipping

8

company built a town, complete with a hospital, church, music hall, housing, and hotels. The emigrant experience comes to life with artifacts; interactive displays; detailed reproductions of the buildings (all but one was demolished); and firsthand accounts of oppression in Europe, life in the "city," conditions during the 60-day ocean crossing, and life in their new home.

As compelling as the exhibits are, the main draw is the research booths, where you can search the complete passenger lists of all ships that left the harbor. ■TIP➔ **Research assistants are available to help locate and track your ancestors.** From St. Pauli, the museum can be reached by S-bahn or Maritime Circle Line at St. Pauli Landungsbrücken No. 10. ✉ *Veddeler Bogen 2, Veddel* ☎ *040/3197–9160* ⊕ *www.ballinstadt.de* 🖃 *€12.50* ⊙ *Apr.–Oct., daily 10–6; Nov.–Mar., daily 10–4:30* Ⓜ *Veddel (S-bahn).*

Fischmarkt (*Fish Market*). A trip to the Altona Fischmarkt is definitely worth getting out of bed early—or staying up all night—for. The Sunday markets hark back to the 18th century, when fishermen sold their catch before church services. Today, freshly caught fish sold by salty auctioneers to the locals from little stalls is only a part of the scene. You can find almost anything here: live parrots and palm trees, armloads of flowers and bananas, valuable antiques, and fourth-hand junk. Those keen to continue partying from the night before can get down to live bands rocking the historic Fischauktionshalle. ✉ *Grosse Elbestr. 9, St. Pauli* ⊙ *Apr.–Oct., Sun. 5 am–9:30 am; Nov.–Mar., Sun. 7 am–9:30 am* Ⓜ *Landungsbrücken (U-bahn and S-Bahn), Fischmarkt (Bus No. 112).*

Fodor'sChoice
★

Reeperbahn. The hottest nightspots in town are concentrated on and around St. Pauli's pulsating thoroughfare, the Reeperbahn, and a buzzing little side street known as Grosse Freiheit ("Great Freedom"). It was there, in the early 1960s, that a then-obscure band called the Beatles polished their live act. It has long been famed for its music halls and drinking holes, but also for its strip clubs, sex shops, and brothels.

The Kiez is about more than just its red-light activities, however, and the Reeperbahn swells on evenings and weekends with bar hoppers and nightclubbers, concert- and theatergoers, and locals and out-of-towners out for dinner and a few drinks. And maybe a walk on or at least through the wild side afterward. ✉ *Reeperbahn, St. Pauli* Ⓜ *St. Pauli (U-bahn), Reeperbahn (S-bahn).*

WHERE TO EAT

DOWNTOWN AND HISTORIC HAMBURG

$$$
GERMAN
Fodor'sChoice
★

✗**Fillet of Soul.** The art of fine dining is celebrated in the open show kitchen of this hip, fairly casual restaurant set among the modern art exhibits of the Deichtorhallen. The chefs prepare straightforward, light German dishes with an emphasis on fresh fish. The minimalist dining room, highlighted only by an orange wall, might not be to everyone's liking, but the buzzing atmosphere, artsy clientele, fragrant food, and great personal attention from the waitstaff make this a top choice. ■TIP➔ **Although it's not as sophisticated as the evening's offerings, the lunch menu here is still very good. And with most dishes hovering around** ten euros, it's also a good deal. $ *Average main: €21* ⊠ *Deichtorstr. 2, Altstadt* ☎ *040/7070–5800* ⊕ *www.fillet-of-soul.de* ⊙ *No dinner Sun. and Mon.* Ⓜ *Steinstrasse (U-bahn).*

ST. PAULI

$$$ ✕ **Mess.** This is one of the most popular restaurants in the hip Karolinen-
GERMAN viertel (called "Karo-Viertel" by Hamburgers). It serves wild flavors
Fodor'sChoice like *Thunfisch-Mangostapel mit Grüne Tomatenmarmelade, Pak Choi*
★ *und Jasminreis* (a tower of tuna and mango with green-tomato chutney served with bok choy and jasmine rice) along with more traditional German fare such as Wiener schnitzel and *Bratkartoffeln* (fried potatoes). For lunch, order the two-course lunch menu (€20) or the pasta special for €9. ■TIP➔ **In summer, try to get a table in the small garden under the pergola and sample vintages from the restaurant's own wine store.** $ *Average main: €25* ⊠ *Turnerstr. 9, Schanzenviertel* ☎ *040/4325–0152* ⊕ *www.mess.de* ⊙ *Closed Sun. No lunch Sat.* Ⓜ *Feldstrasse (U-bahn).*

$$$ ✕ **River-Kasematten.** There is no other restaurant in town that better
ECLECTIC embodies Hamburg's international spirit and its lust for style, entertainment, and good seafood. This former jazz club, now elegantly decorated with black oak floors, leather seats, and redbrick walls, hosts a mix of hip guests. New Zealand lamb, Angus steak, spiced-up regional fish dishes, and exotic soups are the order of the day. $ *Average main: €21* ⊠ *Fischmarkt 28–32, St. Pauli* ☎ *040/892–760* ⊕ *www.river-kasematten.de* ⏘ *Reservations essential* ⊙ *Closed Mon.–Wed. No lunch Thurs.–Sat.* Ⓜ *Fischmarkt (Bus No. 112), Reeperbahn (S-bahn).*

ST. GEORG

$$ ✕ **Doria.** At the end of 2010, Doria started drawing adventurous food-
MODERN lovers to the seedy Hansaplatz. Ignoring the prostitutes and junkies
EUROPEAN outside, they came for the modern European cuisine that the convivial
Fodor'sChoice owner Hasko Sadrina expertly prepared—and for Doria's softly lit,
★ rustic ambience. These days the square isn't quite as sketchy, but the food and service is just as good. You still might have to sidestep the occasional streetwalker, but you'll be rewarded with expertly prepared dishes that include poached salmon with asparagus and wild venison with cranberry sorbet. $ *Average main: €20* ⊠ *Hansapl. 14, St. Georg* ☎ *040/3867–2848* ⊕ *www.doria14.de* ⊙ *Closed Mon.* Ⓜ *Hauptbahnhof (U-bahn).*

WHERE TO STAY

DOWNTOWN AND HISTORIC HAMBURG

$ 🖼 **Hotel Village.** Near the central train station and once a thriving
HOTEL brothel, this hotel and its red-and-black carpets, glossy wallpaper, and dinky chandeliers still exudes lasciviousness. **Pros:** in the heart of downtown; individually designed rooms; fun decor; free coffee at reception. **Cons:** sometimes casual service; although it's slowly being gentrified, the neighborhood remains a little seedy. $ *Rooms from: €85* ⊠ *Steindamm 4, St. Georg* ☎ *040/480–6490* ⊕ *www.hotel-village.de* ⮌ *20 rooms, 3 suites, 4 apartments* 🍴 *No meals* Ⓜ *Hauptbahnhof (U-bahn and S-bahn).*

8

$$ HOTEL — **SIDE.** Futuristic, minimalistic—call it what you like, but this hip five-star hotel has been a byword for inner city cool since its opening in 2001. **Pros:** Nespresso pod coffeemakers in rooms; convenient but quiet location. **Cons:** some might find decor sterile; most guest rooms lack views. [$] *Rooms from: €160* ✉ *Drehbahn 49, Neustadt* ☎ *040/309–990* 🌐 *www.side-hamburg.de* 🛏 *168 rooms, 10 suites* 🍴 *No meals* [M] *Gänsemarkt (U-bahn).*

ALTONA AND ELSEWHERE

$$ HOTEL — **Gastwerk Hotel Hamburg.** Proudly dubbing itself Hamburg's first design hotel, the Gastwerk, named after the 100-year-old gasworks housed inside, is certainly one of the most stylish places to stay in town. **Pros:** large and well-equipped health club; free use of a MINI car. **Cons:** removed from downtown area and most sightseeing spots; breakfast room, bar and other public spaces can get crowded. [$] *Rooms from: €160* ✉ *Beim Alten Gaswerk 3, Altona* ☎ *040/890–620* 🌐 *www.gastwerk.com* 🛏 *127 rooms, 14 suites* 🍴 *No meals* [M] *Bahrenfeld (S-bahn).*

$$$ HOTEL Fodor's Choice ★ — **Le Royal Méridien Hamburg.** This luxury hotel along the Alster offers you beauty inside and outside its walls. **Pros:** great location with views of the Alster; smartly designed, large rooms; outstanding pool area; Wi-Fi free in lobby. **Cons:** pricey Wi-Fi; top-floor bar and restaurant can be crowded. [$] *Rooms from: €189* ✉ *An der Alster 52–56, St. Georg* ☎ *040/21000* 🌐 *www.leroyalmeridienhamburg.com* 🛏 *265 rooms, 19 suites* 🍴 *No meals* [M] *Hauptbahnhof (U-bahn and S-bahn).*

$ HOTEL — **YoHo.** Housed in a historic villa that's an easy walk from the Schanzenviertel, this friendly, modern little hotel was originally designed and priced to attract a young, cosmopolitan crowd, but lots of others head here, too. **Pros:** quiet neighborhood; free Wi-Fi throughout hotel; free parking. **Cons:** sometimes noisy due to young travelers; removed from all major sightseeing sights. [$] *Rooms from: €99* ✉ *Moorkamp 5, Eimsbüttel* ☎ *040/284–1910* 🌐 *www.yoho-hamburg.de* 🛏 *30 rooms* 🍴 *No meals* [M] *Christuskirche (U-bahn), Schlump (U-bahn).*

NIGHTLIFE

Whether you think it sordid or sexy, the Reeperbahn, in the St. Pauli district, is as central to the Hamburg scene as the classy shops along Jungfernstieg. A walk down **Herbertstrasse** (men only, no women or children permitted), just two blocks south of the Reeperbahn, can be quite an eye-opener. Here prostitutes sit displayed in windows as they await customers—nevertheless, it's the women choosing their clients, as these are the highest-paid prostitutes in the city. On nearby **Grosse Freiheit** you'll find a number of the better-known sex-show or table-dance clubs: **Colibri,** at No. 34; **Safari,** at No. 24; and **Dollhouse,** at No. 11. They cater to the package-tour trade as well as those on the prowl by themselves. Prices are high. Not much happens here before 10 pm.

Schmidts Theater and Schmidts Tivoli. The quirky Schmidt Theater and Schmidts Tivoli has become Germany's most popular variety theater, presenting a classy repertoire of live music, vaudeville, and cabaret. ✉ *Spielbudenpl. 24–28, St. Pauli* ☎ *040/3177–8899* 🌐 *www.tivoli.de.*

BARS

Christiansen's Fine Drinks & Cocktails. This cozy bar, a short distance from the Fischmarkt, mixes some of the best cocktails in town. ⊠ *Pinnasberg 60, St. Pauli* ☎ *040/317–2863* ⊕ *www.christiansens.de.*

Mandalay. This is one of several upscale, sleek bars catering to thirty-somethings that are in and around St. Pauli and Sternschanze. ⊠ *Neuer Pferdemarkt 13, Schanzenviertel* ☎ *040/4321–4922* ⊕ *www.mandalay.tv.*

BERLIN

Since the fall of the Iron Curtain, no city in Europe has seen more development and change than Berlin. In the scar of barren borderland between the two parts of the city sprang up government and commercial centers that have become the glossy spreads of travel guides and architecture journals. The city's particular charm lies in its spaciousness, its trees and greenery, and its anything-goes atmosphere. The city embraces its future as an international center for avant-garde fashion, culture, art, and media, with a zeal rarely found in other cities. The really stunning parts of the prewar capital are in the historic eastern part of town, which has grand avenues, monumental architecture, and museums that house world treasures.

Berlin began prospering in the 1300s, thanks to its location at the intersection of important trade routes. Later, Frederick the Great (1712–86) made Berlin and nearby Potsdam his glorious centers of the enlightened yet autocratic Prussian monarchy. In 1871 Prussia, ruled by the "Iron Chancellor" Count Otto von Bismarck, unified the many independent German states into the German Empire and made Berlin the capital. World War I ended the German monarchy. But it also brought an end to Prussian autocracy, resulting in Berlin's golden years during the Roaring '20s. The city, the energetic, modern, and sinful counterpart to Paris, became a center for the cultural avant-garde.

The golden era came to an end with the Depression and the rise of Hitler, who also made Berlin his capital. By World War II's end, 70% of the city lay in ruins. Berlin was partitioned and finally divided by the Berlin Wall, with Soviet-controlled East Berlin as the capital of its new communist puppet state, the German Democratic Republic (GDR), and West Berlin an outpost of Western democracy completely surrounded by the communist GDR.

PLANNING YOUR TIME

As one of Europe's biggest cities and certainly one of the world's top capitals, with very distinctive individual neighborhoods and sights, Berlin is difficult to tackle in just one or two days. Any visit should include a walk on the Kurfürstendamm, the city's premier shopping boulevard. For culture buffs, great antique, medieval, Renaissance, and modern art can be found at the Kulturforum south of Tiergarten, and on Museum Island in Mitte—both cultural centers are a must, and either will occupy at least a half-day. Most of the historic sights of German and Prussian history line the city's other grand boulevard, Unter den Linden, in eastern Berlin, which can be strolled in a leisurely two hours, with stops. Avail yourself of the efficient transportation options and you'll see more. Note that shops are closed on Sunday.

GETTING HERE AND AROUND

AIR TRAVEL

Major airlines continue to serve western Berlin's Tegel Airport (TXL) after a first stop at a major European hub (such as Frankfurt) since eastern Berlin's Schönefeld Airport, about 24 km (15 miles) outside the center, has experienced major delays in its expansion into Berlin-Brandenburg International (BBI), the international airport of the capital region. Schönefeld is used principally by charter and low-budget airlines. Massive Tempelhof Airport closed in late 2008. The Berlin airports share a central phone number.

Contacts Central airport service ☎ *030/500–0186* ⊕ *www.berlin-airport.de.*

BUS TRAVEL

BerlinLinien Bus is the only intra-Germany company serving Berlin. Gullivers Reisen serves foreign destinations. Make reservations at ZOB-Reisebüro, or buy your ticket at its office at the central bus terminal, the Omnibusbahnhof.

Contacts ZOB-Reisebüro ✉ *Zentrale Omnibusbahnhof, Masurenallee 4–6, at Messedamm, Charlottenburg* ☎ *030/301–0380 for reservations* ⊕ *www. zob-reisebuero.de* ⊙ *Weekdays 6 am–9 pm, weekends 6 am–8 pm.*

CAR TRAVEL

Rush hour is relatively mild in Berlin, but the public transit system is so efficient here that it's best to leave your car at the hotel. As of 2008 cars entering downtown Berlin inside the S-bahn ring need to have an environmental certificate. Daily parking fees at hotels can run up to €18 per day. Vending machines in the city center dispense timed tickets to display on your dashboard. Thirty minutes cost €0.50.

PUBLIC TRANSPORTATION

The city has one of the most efficient public-transportation systems in Europe, a smoothly integrated network of subway (U-bahn) and suburban (S-bahn) train lines, buses, and trams (in eastern Berlin only). Get a map from any information booth.

Most visitor destinations are in the broad reach of the fare zones A and B. Tickets are available from vending machines at U-bahn and S-bahn stations. After you purchase a ticket, you are responsible for validating it when you board the train or bus. If you're caught without a ticket or with an unvalidated one, the fine is €40.

Contacts Berliner Verkehrsbetriebe *(BVG).* ☎ *030/19449* ⊕ *www.bvg.de.* **S-Bahn Berlin GmbH** ☎ *030/2974–3333* ⊕ *www.s-bahn-berlin.de.* **VBB** ☎ *030/2541–4141 for info* ⊕ *www.vbbonline.de* ⊙ *Weekdays 8–8, weekends 9–6.*

TAXI TRAVEL

The base rate is €3, after which prices vary according to a complex tariff system. Figure on paying around €8 for a ride the length of the Kurfürstendamm. You can hail cabs on the street, get them at taxi stands or order them by calling.

Contacts Taxis ☎ *030/210–101, 030/443–322, 030/261–026.*

TRAIN TRAVEL

All long-distance trains stop at the huge and modern central station, Hauptbahnhof, which lies at the north edge of the government district in former West Berlin. Regional trains also stop at the two former "main" stations of the past years: Bahnhof Zoo, short for Zoologischer Garten (in the West) and Ostbahnhof (in the East). Regional trains also stop at the central eastern stations Friedrichstrasse and Alexanderplatz.

VISITOR INFORMATION

Contacts **Visit Berlin** (*Berlin Tourist Info*). ✉ *Kurfürstendamm 22, in the Neues Kranzler Eck, Charlottenburg* ☎ *030/250–025* ⊕ *www.visitberlin.de* ☉ *Mon.–Sat. 9:30–8, Sun. 10–6.* **Museumsinformation Berlin** ☎ *030/2474–9888* ☉ *Weekdays 9–4, weekends 9–1.*

EXPLORING

Berlin is a large city with several downtown centers that evolved during the 30 years of separation. Of Berlin's 12 boroughs, the most interesting are Charlottenburg-Wilmersdorf in the west; Tiergarten (a district of the Mitte borough) and Kreuzberg-Friedrichshain in the center; Mitte, the historic core of the city in the eastern part of town; and Prenzlauer Berg in the northeast. Southwest Berlin has lovely escapes in the secluded forests and lakes of the Grunewald area.

KURFÜRSTENDAMM AND CHARLOTTENBURG

Kaiser-Wilhelm-Gedächtnis-Kirche (*Kaiser Wilhelm Memorial Church*). A dramatic reminder of World War II's destruction, the ruined bell tower is all that remains of this once massive church, which was completed in 1895 and dedicated to the emperor, Kaiser Wilhelm I. The Hohenzollern dynasty is depicted inside in a gilded mosaic, whose damage, like that of the building, will not be repaired. The exhibition revisits World War II's devastation throughout Europe. On the hour, the tower chimes out a melody composed by the last emperor's great-grandson, the late Prince Louis Ferdinand von Hohenzollern. In stark contrast to the old bell tower (dubbed the "Hollow Tooth"), which is in sore need of restoration now, are the adjoining Memorial Church and Tower, designed by the noted German architect Egon Eiermann and finished in 1961. ✉ *Breitscheidpl., Charlottenburg* ☎ *030/218–5023* ⊕ *www. gedaechtniskirche-berlin.de* ☞ *Free* ☉ *Memorial Church daily 9–7* Ⓜ *Zoologischer Garten (U-bahn and S-bahn).*

Kurfürstendamm. This busy thoroughfare began as a riding path in the 16th century. The elector Joachim II of Brandenburg used it to travel between his palace on the Spree River and his hunting lodge in the Grunewald. The Kurfürstendamm (Elector's Causeway) was transformed into a major route in the late 19th century, thanks to the initiative of Bismarck, Prussia's Iron Chancellor.

Even in the 1920s, the Ku'damm was still relatively new and by no means elegant; it was fairly far removed from the old heart of the city, Unter den Linden in Mitte. The Ku'damm's prewar fame was due mainly to its rowdy bars and dance halls, as well as the cafés where the cultural avant-garde of Europe gathered. Almost half of its 245

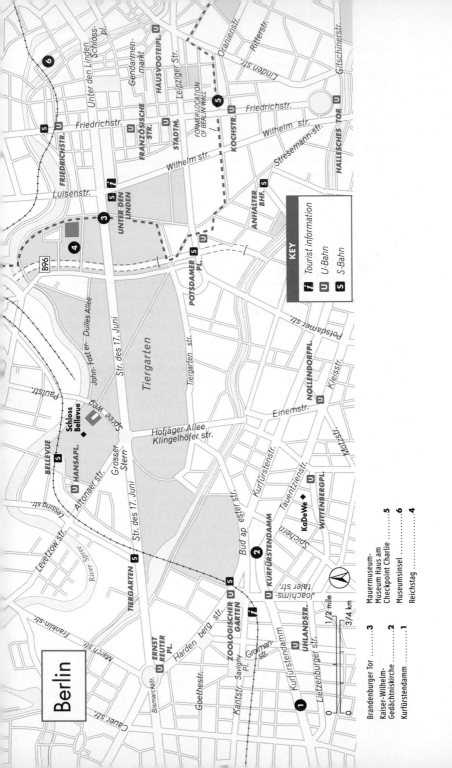

Berlin

KEY

- 🛈 Tourist information
- Ⓤ U-Bahn
- Ⓢ S-Bahn

Brandenburger Tor 3
Kaiser-Wilhelm-
Gedächtniskirche 2
Kurfürstendamm 1

Mauermuseum-
Museum Haus am
Checkpoint Charlie 5
Museumsinsel 6
Reichstag 4

Schloss Bellevue

Tiergarten

1/2 mile
3/4 km

late-19th-century buildings were completely destroyed in the 1940s, and the remaining buildings were damaged to varying degrees. As in most of western Berlin, what you see today is either restored or newly constructed.

TIERGARTEN AND THE GOVERNMENT DISTRICT

Fodor's Choice
★

Brandenburger Tor (*Brandenburg Gate*). Once the pride of Prussian Berlin and the city's premier landmark, the Brandenburger Tor was left in a desolate no-man's-land when the Wall was built. Since the Wall's dismantling, the sandstone gateway has become the scene of the city's Unification Day and New Year's Eve parties. This is the sole remaining gate of 14 built by Carl Langhans in 1788–91, designed as a triumphal arch for King Frederick Wilhelm II. Its virile classical style pays tribute to Athens's Acropolis. The quadriga, a chariot drawn by four horses and driven by the Goddess of Victory, was added in 1794. Troops paraded through the gate after successful campaigns—the last time in 1945, when victorious Red Army troops took Berlin. The upper part of the gate, together with its chariot and Goddess of Victory, was destroyed in the war. In 1957 the original molds were discovered in West Berlin, and a new quadriga was cast in copper and presented as a gift to the people of East Berlin. A tourist-information center is in the south part of the gate. ⊠ *Pariser Pl., Mitte* Ⓜ *Unter den Linden (S-bahn).*

Fodor's Choice
★

Reichstag (*Parliament Building*). After last meeting here in 1933, the Bundestag, Germany's federal parliament, returned to its traditional seat in the spring of 1999. British architect Sir Norman Foster lightened up the gray monolith with a glass dome, which quickly became one of the city's main attractions: you can circle up a gently rising ramp while taking in the rooftops of Berlin and the parliamentary chamber below. At the base of the dome is an exhibit on the Reichstag's history, in German and English. Completed in 1894, the Reichstag housed the imperial German parliament and later served a similar function during the ill-fated Weimar Republic. On the night of February 27, 1933, the Reichstag burned down in an act of arson, a pivotal event in Third Reich history. The fire led to state protection laws that gave the Nazis a pretext to arrest their political opponents. The Reichstag was rebuilt but again badly damaged in 1945. The graffiti of the victorious Russian soldiers can still be seen on some of the walls in the hallways. After terrorism warnings at the end of 2010, the Reichstag tightened its door policy, asking all visitors to register their names and birthdates in advance and reserve a place on a guided tour. Since then, the crowds that used to snake around the outside of the building have subsided, and a visit is worth the planning. As always, a reservation at the pricey rooftop Käfer restaurant (☎ *030/2262–9933*) will also get you in. A riverwalk with great views of the government buildings begins behind the Reichstag. ⊠ *Pl. der Republik 1, Tiergarten* ☎ *030/2273–2152 for Reichstag* ⊕ *www.bundestag.de* 🖙 *Free with prior registration* ☉ *Daily 8 am–11 pm* Ⓜ *Unter den Linden (S-bahn), Bundestag (U-bahn).*

8

KREUZBERG AND MITTE

Mauermuseum–Museum Haus am Checkpoint Charlie. Just steps from the famous crossing point between the two Berlins, the Wall Museum–House at Checkpoint Charlie presents visitors with the story of the Wall and, even more riveting, the stories of those who escaped through, under, and over it. An infamous hot spot during the Cold War, this border crossing for non-Germans was manned by the Soviet military in East Berlin's Mitte district and, several yards south, by the U.S. military in West Berlin's Kreuzberg district. Today the touristy intersection consists of a replica of an American guardhouse and signage, plus cobblestones that mark the old border.

This homespun museum reviews the events leading up to the Wall's construction and, with original tools and devices, plus recordings and photographs, shows how East Germans escaped to the West (one of the most ingenious contraptions was a miniature submarine). Exhibits about human rights and paintings interpreting the Wall round out the experience. ■TIP→ **Come early or late in the day to avoid the multitudes dropped off by tour buses.** Monday can be particularly crowded because the state museums are closed. ✉ *Friedrichstr. 43–45, Kreuzberg* ☎ *030/253-7250* ⊕ *www.mauermuseum.com* ✆ *€12.50* ☉ *Daily 9 am–10 pm* Ⓜ *Kochstrasse (U-bahn).*

Fodor's Choice **Museumsinsel** (*Museum Island*). On the site of one of Berlin's two origi-
★   nal settlements, this unique complex of five state museums—a UNESCO World Heritage Site—is an absolute must.

The **Alte Nationalgalerie** (Old National Gallery, entrance on Bodestrasse) houses an outstanding collection of 18th-, 19th-, and early 20th-century paintings and sculptures. Works by Cézanne, Rodin, Degas, and one of Germany's most famous portrait artists, Max Liebermann, are part of the permanent exhibition. The **Altes Museum** (Old Museum), a red-marble, neoclassical building abutting the green Lustgarten, was Prussia's first structure purpose-built to serve as a museum. Etruscan art is its highlight, and there are a few examples of Roman art. At the northern tip of Museum Island is the **Bode-Museum,** a somber-looking gray edifice graced with elegant columns. The museum presents the state museums' stunning collection of German and Italian sculptures since the Middle Ages, the Museum of Byzantine Art, and a huge coin collection. Even if you think you aren't interested in the ancient world, make an exception for the **Pergamonmuseum** (entrance on Kupfergraben), one of the world's greatest museums. The museum's name is derived from its principal display, the Pergamon Altar, a monumental Greek temple discovered in what is now Turkey and dating from 180 BC. Museum Island's new shining star, however, is the **Neues Museum** (New Museum), which reopened in 2009. Originally designed by Friedrich August Stüler in 1843–55, the building was badly damaged in World War II and has only now been elaborately redeveloped by British star architect David Chipperfield, who has been overseeing the complete restoration of Museum Island. Instead of completely restoring the Neues Museum, the architect decided to integrate modern elements into the historic landmark, while leaving many of its heavily bombed and dilapidated areas untouched. The result is a stunning experience, considered by many to be one of the world's greatest museums. Home to the Egyptian Museum, including the famous bust of Nefertiti (who, after some 70 years, has returned to her first museum location in Berlin). ⊠ *Museumsinsel, Mitte* ☎ *030/2664–24242* ⊕ *www.smb.museum* 🎫 *All Museum Island museums: €18* ⊙ *Pergamonmuseum: Fri.–Wed. 10–6, Thurs. 10–8. Alte Nationalgalerie: Tues., Wed., and Fri.–Sun. 10–6; Thurs. 10–8. Altes Museum: Tues., Wed., and Fri.–Sun. 10–6; Thurs. 10–8. Neues Museum: Fri.–Wed. 10–6, Thurs. 10–8. Bode-Museum: Tues., Wed., and Fri.–Sun. 10–6; Thurs. 10–8* Ⓜ *Hackescher Markt (S-bahn).*

WHERE TO EAT

CHARLOTTENBURG

$ ✕ **Lubitsch.** One of the few traditional, artsy restaurants left in bohe-
GERMAN mian Charlottenburg, the Lubitsch—named after the famous Berlin film director Ernst Lubitsch—exudes an air of faded elegance and serves hearty local fare (and lighter international options) that's hard to find these days. Dishes like *Königsberger Klopse* (cooked dumplings in a creamy caper sauce) and *Kassler Nacken mit Sauerkraut* (salted, boiled pork knuckle) are examples of home-style German cooking. The local clientele don't mind the dingy seating or good-humored, but sometimes cheeky service. In summer the outdoor tables are perfect for people-watching on one of Berlin's most beautiful streets. The three-course lunch is a great bargain at €10. $ *Average main: €13* ⊠ *Bleibtreustr. 47, Charlottenburg* ☎ *030/882–3756* ⊕ *www.restaurant-lubitsch.de* ⊙ *No lunch Sun.* Ⓜ *Savignyplatz (S-bahn).*

$ ✕ **Sasaya.** In a city that still sometimes struggles to get sushi right,
JAPANESE Sasaya's concept can seem groundbreaking: simple, authentic Japanese food in an equally comfortable, no-fuss atmosphere. Don't expect sushi rolls to be the center of the menu, though—the focus is on reasonably priced small plates made for sharing. Pickled vegetables, seaweed salad, crispy pork belly, raw octopus, and a number of soups served with the traditional Japanese dashi (fish and seaweed) broth are highlights. Dessert favorites include green tea ice cream and satisfyingly chewy balls of mochi. ■TIP→ **Reservations are essential; call early enough and you might score one of the low tables by the windows, where long, low couches mean you can recline languidly during your meal.** $ *Average main: €12* ⊠ *Lychenerstr. 50, Prenzlauer Berg* ☎ *030/4471–7721* ⊕ *www.sasaya-berlin-en.tumblr.com* ⚄ *Reservations essential* ▤ *No credit cards* ⊙ *Closed Tues. and Wed.* Ⓜ *Eberswalder Strasse (U-bahn).*

MITTE

$$$ ✕ **Lutter & Wegner.** One of the city's oldest vintners (*Sekt*, German cham-
GERMAN pagne, was first conceived here in 1811 by actor Ludwig Devrient), Lutter & Wegner has returned to its historic location across from Gendarmenmarkt. The dark-wood-panel walls, parquet floor, and multiple rooms take diners back to 19th-century Vienna, and the food, too, is mostly Austrian, with superb game dishes in winter and, of course, the classic Wiener schnitzel with potato salad. The *Sauerbraten* (marinated pot roast) with red cabbage is a national prizewinner. ■TIP→ **In the**

8

Weinstube, a cozy room lined with wine shelves meat and cheese plates are served until 3 am. There are several other locations around Berlin but this one is widely considered the best. [$] *Average main: €23* ✉ *Charlottenstr. 56, Mitte: Unter den Linden* ☎ *030/2029–5417* 🌐 *www.l-w-berlin.de* [M] *Französische Strasse and Stadtmitte (U-bahn).*

$$$$ GERMAN Fodor's Choice ★ 🍴 **Pauly Saal.** A new meeting point for the hip Mitte set, Pauly Saal is in the newly renovated and converted Ehemalige Jüdische Mädchenschule (Old Jewish Girls' School), a worthy destination in its own right due to its beautifully restored interior and several noteworthy galleries. With indoor seating in what used to be the school gym, and outdoor tables taking over the building's expansive courtyard, the setting alone is a draw, but the food is also some of the most exquisite in this part of Mitte. The focus is on artful presentation and local ingredients, like meat sourced directly from Brandenburg. ■ **TIP→ the lunch prix-fixe (€28) is a great way to sample the restaurant's best dishes.** [$] *Average main: €34* ✉ *Auguststr. 11–13, Ehemalige Jüdische Mädchenschule, Mitte: Scheunenviertel* ☎ *030/3300–6070* 🌐 *www.paulysaal.com* ⏲ *Closed Sun.* [M] *Tucholskystrasse (S-bahn).*

TIERGARTEN

$$$$ ECLECTIC Fodor's Choice ★ 🍴 **Facil.** One of Germany's top restaurants, Facil is also one of the more relaxed of its class. The elegant, minimalist setting—it's in the fifth-floor courtyard of the Mandala Hotel, with exquisite wall panels and a glass roof that opens in summer—and impeccable service give the place an oasislike feel. Diners can count on a careful combination of German classics and Asian inspiration; the options are to choose from the four- to eight-course set meals, or order à la carte. Seasonal dishes include goose liver with celery and hazelnuts, char with an elderflower emulsion sauce, or roasted regional squab. The wine list is extensive but the staff can provide helpful advice. [$] *Average main: €40* ✉ *Mandala Hotel, Potsdamerstr. 3, Tiergarten* ☎ *030/5900–51234* 🌐 *www.facil.de* ⏲ *Closed weekends* [M] *Potsdamer Platz (U-bahn and S-bahn).*

WHERE TO STAY

CHARLOTTENBURG

$$ B&B/INN 🏨 **Hotel Art Nouveau.** The English-speaking owners' discerning taste in antiques, color combinations, and even televisions (a few designed by Philippe Starck) makes this B&B-like pension a great place to stay. **Pros:** stylish ambience; friendly and personal service; great B&B feeling, despite being a hotel. **Cons:** front rooms can be noisy due to heavy traffic on Leibnizstrasse; few amenities for a hotel of this price category; downtown location, yet longer walks to all major sights in the area. [$] *Rooms from: €126* ✉ *Leibnizstr. 59, Charlottenburg* ☎ *030/327–7440* 🌐 *www.hotelartnouveau.de* 🛏 *16 rooms, 6 suites* 🍽 *Breakfast* [M] *Adenauerplatz (U-bahn).*

CHARLOTTENBURG

$$ B&B/INN 🏨 **Hotel-Pension Dittberner.** For traditional Berlin accommodations, this third-floor pension (with wooden elevator) run by Frau Lange since 1958 is the place to go. **Pros:** personal touch and feel of a B&B;

unusually large rooms; good location on quiet Ku'damm side street. **Cons:** unexciting breakfast; some rooms and furniture in need of update; staff sometimes not up to task. $ *Rooms from: €115* ✉ *Wielandstr. 26, Charlottenburg* ☎ *030/884–6950* 🌐 *www.hotel-dittberner.de* 🛏 *21 rooms, 1 suite* 🍴 *Breakfast* [M] *Adenauerplatz (U-bahn).*

MITTE

$$ HOTEL Fodor's Choice ★ 🏨 **Arte Luise Kunsthotel.** The Luise is one of Berlin's most original boutique hotels, with each fantastically creative room in the 1825 building or 2003 built-on wing—facing the Reichstag—styled by a different artist. **Pros:** central location; historic flair; individually designed rooms. **Cons:** simple rooms with limited amenities and hotel facilities; can be noisy because of the nearby rail station. $ *Rooms from: €110* ✉ *Luisenstr. 19, Mitte: Unter den Linden* ☎ *030/284–480* 🌐 *www.luise-berlin.com* 🛏 *54 rooms (36 with bath)* 🍴 *No meals* [M] *Friedrichstrasse (U-bahn and S-bahn).*

$$$$ HOTEL Fodor's Choice ★ 🏨 **Hotel Adlon Kempinski Berlin.** The first Adlon was considered Europe's ultimate luxury resort until it was destroyed in the war and the new version, built in 1997, has a nostalgic aesthetic, and the elegant rooms are furnished with turn-of-the-century photos of the original hotel, along with cherrywood trim, mahogany furnishings, and brocade silk bedspreads. **Pros:** top-notch luxury hotel; surprisingly large rooms; excellent in-house restaurants. **Cons:** sometimes stiff service with an attitude; rooms off Linden are noisy with the windows open; inviting lobby often crowded. $ *Rooms from: €260* ✉ *Unter den Linden 77, Mitte: Unter den Linden* ☎ *030/22610* 🌐 *www.kempinski.com/adlon* 🛏 *304 rooms, 78 suites* 🍴 *No meals* [M] *Brandenburger Tor (U-bahn and S-bahn).*

$$ HOTEL 🏨 **Lux Eleven.** This designer apartment hotel is coveted for its discreet service and great minimalist design. **Pros:** great location in northern Mitte; extremely stylish yet comfortable rooms; friendly, knowledgeable service. **Cons:** immediate neighborhood may be noisy; not a good choice for families. $ *Rooms from: €119* ✉ *Rosa-Luxemburg-Str. 9–13, Mitte: Alexanderplatz* ☎ *030/936–2800* 🌐 *www.lux-eleven.com* 🛏 *72 rooms, 1 suite* 🍴 *No meals* [M] *Weinmeisterstrasse (U-bahn).*

NIGHTLIFE

Today's Berlin has a tough time living up to the reputation it gained from the film *Cabaret.* Political gaffes are now the prime comic material for Berlin's cabarets, so your German will have to be up to snuff to understand them. Berlin's nightspots are open to the wee hours of the morning. Clubs often switch the music they play nightly, so their crowds and popularity can vary widely. Clubs and bars in downtown western Berlin as well as in Mitte tend to be dressier and more conservative; the scene in Kreuzberg, Prenzlauer Berg, the Scheunenviertel, and Friedrichshain is laid-back, alternative, and grungy. Dance clubs don't get going until about 12:30 am, but parties labeled "after-work" start as early as 8 pm for professionals looking to socialize during the week.

BARS AND LOUNGES

In Germany the term *Kneipen* is used for down-to-earth bars that are comparable to English pubs. These places are pretty simple and laid-back; you probably shouldn't try to order a three-ingredient cocktail at one unless you spot a lengthy drink menu. The most elegant bars and lounges are in Charlottenburg, and though not frequented by Berliners, Berlin's five-star hotels provide stylish, seductive settings.

TIERGARTEN

Victoria Bar. The elegant Victoria Bar is a stylish homage to 1960s and '70s jet-setters, and the cocktails are mixed with care. It usually attracts a middle-age, affluent, and artsy crowd. ✉ *Potsdamerstr. 102, Tiergarten* ☎ *030/2575–9977* ⊕ *www.victoriabar.de.*

SCHÖNEBERG

Green Door. A grown-up crowd focused on conversation and appreciating outstanding cocktails heads to Green Door, a Schöneberg classic. The decor is 1960s retro style, with gingham walls and stand-alone lamps. ■**TIP**➔ **Although the expertly crafted drinks are not cheap by Berlin standards, happy hour (6–8) means you can order them at nearly half price.** ✉ *Winterfeldstr. 50, Schöneberg* ☎ *030/215–2515* ⊕ *www.greendoor.de.*

MITTE

Newton Bar. This posh bar in Mitte has been around for ages. Helmut Newton's larger-than-life photos of nude women decorate the walls. ✉ *Charlottenstr. 57, Mitte* ☎ *030/2029–5421* ⊕ *www.newton-bar.de.*

Redwood. Run by a California native, this simple, solid cocktail bar serves near-perfect concoctions that belie the bare wood surroundings. If loud crowds and smoky rooms aren't your thing, this is the place for you—the cocktails are excellent and you'll be able to carry on a conversation in a normal voice. The menu is helpfully arranged according to "dry" or "sweet and sour" but if you're still unsure whether to go for a Dark-and-Stormy or a Blood-and-Sand, ask the friendly young bartenders—everyone speaks English here. ✉ *Bergstr. 25, Mitte: Scheunenviertel* ☎ *030/7024–8813* ⊕ *www.redwoodbar.de* ☉ *Closed Sun. and Mon.* Ⓜ *Nordbahhof (S-bahn).*

KREUZBERG

Freischwimmer. When it's warm out, the canalside deck chairs at Freischwimmer are the perfect place to be, though heat lamps and an enclosed area make this a cozy setting for cool nights, too. To get here, walk five minutes east of the elevated Schlesisches Tor U-bahn station and turn left down a path after the 1920s Aral gas station, the oldest in Berlin. ✉ *Vor dem Schlesischen Tor 2a, Kreuzberg* ☎ *030/6107–4309* ⊕ *www.freischwimmer-berlin.com.*

Würgeengel. Named after a 1962 surrealist film by Luis Buñuel ("The Exterminating Angel" in English), this classy joint has offered an elaborate cocktail menu in a well-designed space off Kottbusser Tor since 1992—long before this part of Kreuzberg was hip, or even safe. Today, the bar's loyal fans spill out onto the streets on busy nights, and an evening tapas menu comes from the neighboring restaurant **Gorgonzola Club**. The team behind the restaurant **Renger-Patzsch** run Würgeengel and the Gorgonzola Club. ✉ *Dresdenerstr. 122, Kreuzberg* ✛ *Dresdener*

Str. is reachable through passageway under buildings at Kottbusser Tor, next to Adalbertstr. ☏ *030/615–5560* ⊕ *www.wuergeengel.de* ☺ *Open 7–late.*

SAXONY

The people of Saxony identify themselves more as Saxon than German. Their hardworking and rustic attitudes, their somewhat peripheral location on the border with the Czech Republic and Poland, and their almost incomprehensible dialect, are the targets of endless jokes and puns. However, Saxon pride rebuilt three cities magnificently: Dresden, Leipzig—the showcase cities of eastern Germany—and the smaller town of Görlitz, on the Neisse River. All of these can be visited as day-trips from Berlin. Each requires between two and three hours of travel, so it's possible to leave in the morning and return in time for a late dinner; however, an overnight stay is also easy to arrange.

LEIPZIG

184 km (114 miles) southwest of Berlin.

Leipzig is, in a word, cool—but not so cool as to be pretentious. With its world-renowned links to Bach, Schubert, Mendelssohn, Martin Luther, Goethe, Schiller, and the fantastic Neue-Leipziger-Schule art movement, Leipzig is one of the great German cultural centers. It has impressive art-nouveau architecture, an incredibly clean city center, meandering narrow streets, and the temptations of coffee and cake on every corner. In *Faust,* Goethe describes Leipzig as "a little Paris"; in reality it's more reminiscent of Vienna, while remaining a distinctly energetic Saxon town.

Leipzig's musical past includes Johann Sebastian Bach (1685–1750), who was organist and choir director at Leipzeig's Thomaskirche, and the 19th-century composer Richard Wagner, who was born in the city in 1813. Today's Leipzig continues the cultural focus with extraordinary offerings of music, theater, and opera, not to mention fantastic nightlife.

Wartime bombs destroyed much of Leipzig's city center, but reconstruction efforts have uncovered one of Europe's most vibrant cities. Leipzig's art-nouveau flair is best discovered by exploring the countless alleys, covered courtyards, and passageways. Many unattractive buildings from the postwar period remain, but only reinforce Leipzig's position on the line between modernity and antiquity.

With a population of about 523,000, Leipzig is the second-largest city in eastern Germany (after Berlin) and has long been a center of printing and bookselling. Astride major trade routes, it was an important market town in the Middle Ages, and it continues to be a trading center, thanks to the *Leipziger Messe* (trade and fair shows) throughout the year that bring together buyers from East and West.

Unfortunately, Leipzig has a tendency to underwhelm first-time visitors. If you take Leipzig slow and have some cake, its subtle, hidden charms may surprise you.

8

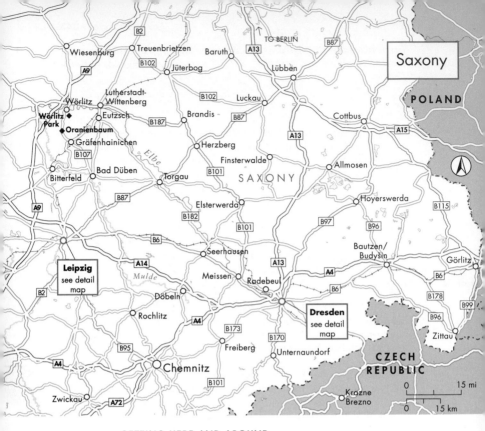

GETTING HERE AND AROUND

Leipzig is an hour from Berlin by train. Leipzig-Halle airport serves many European destinations, but no North American ones.

TIMING

Leipzig can easily be explored in one day; it's possible to walk around the downtown area in just about three hours. The churches can be inspected in less than 20 minutes each. But if you're interested in German history and art, plan for two full days, so you can spend one day just visiting the museums and go to the symphony. The Völkerschlachtdenkmal, a magnificent, bombastic monument to commemorate the defeat of Napoleon in the 1813 Battle of Leipzig, is perfect for a three-hour side trip.

VISITOR INFORMATION

Contacts Leipzig Tourismus und Marketing ⊠ *Augustuspl. 9* ☎ *0341/710–4260* ⊕ *www.leipzig.de.*

EXPLORING

Grassimuseum. British star architect David Chipperfield restored and modernized this fine example of German art deco in 2003–05. The building, dating to 1925–29, houses three important museums. ⊠ *Johannispl. 5–11* ⊕ *www.grassimuseum.de* ☺ *Tues.–Sun. 10–6.*

Museum für Angewandte Kunst (*Museum of Applied Art*). This museum showcases 2,000 years of works from Leipzig's and eastern Germany's proud tradition of handicrafts, such as exquisite porcelain, fine tapestry art, and modern Bauhaus design. ⊠ *Johannispl. 5–11* ☎ *0341/222–9100* ⊕ *www.grassimuseum.de* 🖳 *€5* 🕓 *Tues.–Sun. 10–6.*

Museum für Musikinstrumente (*Musical Instruments Museum*). Historical musical instruments, mostly from the Renaissance, include the world's oldest clavichord, constructed in 1543 in Italy. There are also spinets, flutes, and lutes. Recordings of the instruments can be heard at the exhibits. ⊠ *Johannispl. 5–11* ☎ *0341/973–0750* 🖳 *€5* 🕓 *Tues.– Sun. 10–6.*

Museum für Völkerkunde (*Ethnological Museum*). Presenting arts and crafts from all continents and various eras, this museum includes a thrilling collection of Southeast Asian antique art and the world's only Kurile Ainu feather costume, in the Northeast Asia collection. ⊠ *Johannispl. 5–11* ☎ *0341/973–1300* ⊕ *www.grassimuseum.de* 🖳 *€6* 🕓 *Tues.–Sun. 10–6.*

Mädlerpassage (*Mädler Mall*). The ghost of Goethe's Faust lurks in every marble corner of Leipzig's finest shopping arcade. One of the scenes in *Faust* is set in the famous Auerbachs Keller restaurant, at No. 2. A bronze group of characters from the play, sculpted in 1913, beckons you down the stone staircase to the restaurant. ■**TIP➔** **Touching the statues' feet is said to bring good luck.** A few yards away is a delightful art nouveau bar called Mephisto. ⊠ *Grimmaische Str.*

Markt. Leipzig's showpiece is its huge, old market square. One side is completely occupied by the Renaissance town hall, the **Altes Rathaus.**

Stadtgeschichtliches Museum. Inside the Altes Rathaus, this museum documents Leipzig's past. The entrance is behind the Rathaus. The museum is expanding its exhibition space behind the Museum for Applied Arts. ⊠ *Böttchergässchen 3* ☎ *0341/965–130* ⊕ *www. stadtgeschichtliches-museum-leipzig.de* 🖳 *€6* 🕓 *Tues.–Sun. 10–6.*

Museum der Bildenden Künste (*Museum of Fine Arts*). The city's leading art gallery is minimalism incarnate, set in a huge concrete cube encased in green glass in the middle of Sachsenplatz Square. The museum's collection of more than 2,700 paintings and sculptures represents everything from the German Middle Ages to the modern Neue Leipziger Schule. Especially notable are the collections focusing on Lucas Cranach the Elder and Caspar David Friedrich. ■**TIP➔** **Be sure to start at the top and work your way down. Don't miss Max Klinger's Beethoven as Zeus statue.** ⊠ *Katharinenstr. 10* ☎ *0341/216–990* ⊕ *www.mdbk.de* 🖳 *€5, €6–€8 for special exhibits* 🕓 *Tues. and Thurs.–Sun. 10–6, Wed. noon–8.*

Museum in der Runden Ecke (*Museum in the Round Corner*). This building once served as the headquarters of the city's detachment of the Communist secret police, the dreaded *Staatssicherheitsdienst.* The exhibition *Stasi—Macht und Banalität* (Stasi—Power and Banality) presents not only the Stasi's offices and surveillance work, but also hundreds of documents revealing the magnitude of its interests in citizens' private lives. Though the material is in German, the items and atmosphere convey an impression of what life under the regime might have been like.

8

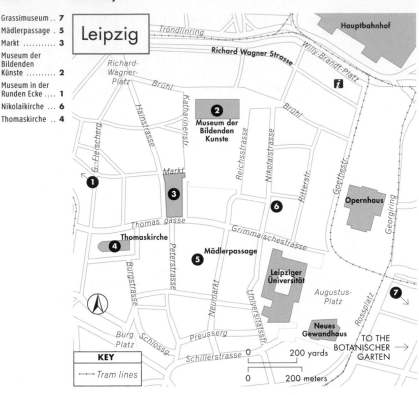

The exhibit about the death penalty in the GDR is particularly chilling. ✉ *Dittrichring 24* ☎ *0341/961–2443* ⊕ *www.runde-ecke-leipzig.de* 🎫 *Free, €4 tour in English (by appointment)* ⊙ *Daily 10–6.*

Nikolaikirche (*St. Nicholas Church*). This church with its undistinguished facade was center stage during the demonstrations that helped bring down the Communist regime. Every Monday for months before the government collapsed, thousands of citizens gathered in front of the church chanting, *Wir sind das Volk* ("We are the people"). Inside are a soaring Gothic choir and nave. Note the unusual patterned ceiling supported by classical pillars that end in palm-tree-like flourishes. Martin Luther is said to have preached from the ornate 16th-century pulpit. ■TIP→ **The prayers for peace that began the revolution in 1989 are still held on Monday at 5 pm.** ✉ *Nikolaikirchhof* ☎ *0341/960–5270* 🎫 *Free* ⊙ *Mon.–Sat. 10–6, Sun. services at 9:30, 11:15, and 5.*

Fodor's Choice **Thomaskirche** (*St. Thomas's Church*). Bach was choirmaster at this Gothic
★ church for 27 years, and Martin Luther preached here on Whitsunday 1539, signaling the arrival of Protestantism in Leipzig. Originally the center of a 13th-century monastery, the tall church (rebuilt in the 15th century) now stands by itself. Bach wrote most of his cantatas for the church's famous boys' choir, the Thomanerchor, which was founded in

the 13th century; the church continues as the choir's home as well as a center of Bach tradition.

■ **TIP→ You can listen to the famous boys' choir during the Motette, a service with a special emphasis on choral music.** ✉ *Thomaskirchhof* ☎ *0341/222–240* ⊕ *www.thomaskirche.org* 🔁 *Free, Motette €2* ◔ *Daily 9–6; Motette Fri. at 6 pm, Sat. at 3; no Motette during Saxony summer vacation (usually mid-July to end of Aug.).*

WHERE TO EAT

$
GERMAN
Fodor'sChoice
★
✕ **Auerbachs Keller.** The most famous of Leipzig's restaurants is actually two restaurants: one that's upscale, international, and gourmet (down the stairs to the right) and a rowdy beer cellar (to the, left) specializing in hearty Saxon fare, mostly roasted meat dishes. The fine dining section's five-course menus (€110) are worth a splurge, and it also has a good wine list. The beer cellar has been around since 1530, making it one of the oldest continually running restaurants on the continent. Goethe immortalized one of the vaulted historic rooms in his *Faust*, and Bach was a regular here because of the location halfway between the Thomaskirche and the Nikolaikirche. Ⓢ *Average main: €15* ✉ *Mädlerpassage, Grimmaische Str. 2–4* ☎ *0341/216–100* ⚒ *Reservations essential* ◔ *Closed Mon.*

$
GERMAN
✕ **Gasthaus & Gosebrauerei Bayrischer Bahnhof.** Hidden on the far southeast edge of the city center, the Bayrischer Bahnhof was the terminus of the first rail link between Saxony and Bavaria. The brewery here is the heart of a cultural renaissance, and is the only place currently brewing Gose in Leipzig. The restaurant is well worth a visit for its solid Saxon and German cuisine. Brewery accents surface in dishes such as rump steak with black-beer sauce, and the onion rings can't be beat. If the Gose is too sour for your tastes, order it with one of the sweet syrups—raspberry is the best. Groups of four or more can try dinner prepared in a *Römertopf* (a terra-cotta baking dish; the first was brought to Germany by the Romans, centuries ago). ■ **TIP→ In summer the beer garden is a pleasant place to get away from the bustle of the city center.** Ⓢ *Average main: €11* ✉ *Bayrischer Pl. 1* ☎ *0341/124–5760* ⊕ *www.bayrischer-bahnhof.de* ⊟ *No credit cards.*

WHERE TO STAY

$$
HOTEL
Fodor'sChoice
★
🖿 **Hotel Fürstenhof Leipzig.** The city's grandest hotel—part of Starwood's Luxury Collection—is inside the renowned Löhr-Haus, a revered old mansion 500 meters from the main train station on the ring road surrounding the city center. **Pros:** an elegant full-service hotel with stunning rooms; safes big enough for a laptop are a nice touch. **Cons:** the ring road can be noisy at night, especially on Friday and Satur-

8

day. $\boxed{\$}$ *Rooms from: €149* ✉ *Tröndlinring 8* ☎ *0341/140–370* ⊕ *www. luxurycollection.com* ⌁ *80 rooms, 12 suites.*

SHOPPING

Small streets leading off the Markt attest to Leipzig's rich trading past. Tucked in among them are glass-roof arcades of surprising beauty and elegance, including the wonderfully restored **Specks Hof, Barthels Hof, Jägerhof,** and the **Passage zum Sachsenplatz.** Invent a headache and step into the *Apotheke* (pharmacy) at Hainstrasse 9—it is spectacularly art nouveau, with finely etched and stained glass and rich mahogany. For more glimpses into the past, check out the antiquarian bookstores of the nearby **Neumarkt Passage.**

Hauptbahnhof. Leipzig's main train station has more than 150 shops, restaurants, and cafés, all open Monday through Saturday 9:30 am–10 pm; many are also open on Sunday, at the same hours. ✉ *Willy-Brandt-Pl.*

DRESDEN

25 km (16 miles) southeast of Meissen, 140 km (87 miles) southeast of Leipzig, 193 km (120 miles) south of Berlin.

Saxony's capital city sits in baroque splendor on a wide sweep of the Elbe River, and its proponents have worked with German thoroughness to recapture the city's old reputation as "the Florence on the Elbe." Its yellow and pale-green facades are enormously appealing, and their mere presence is even more overwhelming when you compare what you see today with photographs of Dresden from February 1945, after an Allied bombing raid destroyed the city overnight. Dresden was the capital of Saxony as early as the 15th century, although most of its architectural masterpieces date from the 18th century and the reigns of Augustus the Strong and his son, Frederick Augustus II.

Although some parts of the city center still look as if they're stuck halfway between demolition and construction, the present city is an enormous tribute to the Dresdeners' skills and dedication. The resemblance of today's riverside to Dresden cityscapes painted by Canaletto in the mid-1700s is remarkable. Unfortunately, the war-inflicted gaps in the urban landscape in other parts of the city are too big to be closed anytime soon.

GETTING HERE AND AROUND

Dresden is two hours from Berlin on the Hamburg-Berlin-Prague-Vienna train line. The city's international airport serves mostly European destinations with budget airlines. The newly completed Norman Foster train station is a short walk along the Prager Strasse from the city center. Streetcars are cheap and efficient.

Dresden bus tours (in German and English, run by the Dresdner Verkehrsbetriebe) leave from Postplatz daily at 10, 11:30, and 3. The Stadtrundfahrt Dresden bus tours (also in German and English) leave from Theaterplatz/Augustusbrücke (April–October, daily 9:30–5, every 30 minutes; November–March, daily 10–3, every hour) and stop at most sights.

TIMING

A long full day is sufficient for a quick tour of historic Dresden with a brief visit to one of the museums. The focus of your day should be a visit to the Grünes Gewölbe. If you plan to explore any of the museums at length, such as the Zwinger, or take a guided tour of the Semperoper, you'll need more time. One of the best ways to see Dresden is as a stop between Berlin and Prague.

TOURS

Contacts Dresdner Verkehrsbetriebe AG ⊠ *Service Center, Postpl. 1* ☎ *0351/857–2201.* **Stadtrundfahrt Dresden** ⊠ *Theaterpl.* ☎ *0351/899–5650.*

Contacts Dresden Tourist ⊠ *Schlossstr. 1, inside the Kulturpalast* ☎ *0351/491–920* ⊕ *www.dresden.de.*

GOSE

Bismarck once remarked that "Gose isn't a beer, it is a way of viewing the world." Gose, which originated in Goslar, is an obscure, top-fermented wheat beer flavored by adding coriander and salt to the wort. Gose came to Leipzig in 1738, and was so popular that, by the end of the 1800s, it was considered the local brewing style. It's extremely difficult to make, and after beer production stopped during the war (due to grain shortages), the tradition seemed lost. Today, through the efforts of Lothar Goldhahn at the Bayrischer Bahnhof, Gose production has returned to Leipzig.

EXPLORING

Fodor's Choice ★ **Frauenkirche** (*Church of Our Lady*). This masterpiece of baroque church architecture was completed in 1743. On February 15, 1945, two days after the bombing of Dresden, the burned-out shell of the magnificent Stone Bell collapsed. For the following five decades the remains of the church, a pile of rubble, remained a gripping memorial to the horrors of war. In a move shocking to the East German authorities, who organized all public demonstrations, a group of young people spontaneously met here on February 13, 1982, for a candlelight vigil for peace.

Although the will to rebuild the church was strong, the political and economic situation in the GDR prevented it. It wasn't until the reunification of Germany that Dresden began to seriously consider reconstruction. In the early 1990s a citizens' initiative, joined by the Lutheran Church of Saxony and the city of Dresden, decided to rebuild the church using the original stones. The goal of completing the church by 2006, Dresden's 800th anniversary, seemed insurmountable. Money soon started pouring in from around the globe, however, and work began.

On Sunday, October 30, 2005 (almost a year ahead of schedule), Dresden's skyline became a little more complete with the consecration of the Frauenkirche. ⊠ *An der Frauenkirche* ☎ *0351/498–1131* ⊕ *www. frauenkirche-dresden.org* 🎫 *Free, cupola and tower €8, audio guides in English €2.50* ⏱ *Weekdays 10–noon and 1–6; cupola and tower daily 10–6.*

Residenzschloss (*Royal Palace*). Restoration work is still under way behind the Renaissance facade of this former royal palace, much of which was built between 1709 and 1722. Some of the finished rooms in the **Georgenbau** (Count George Wing) hold historical exhibits, among them an excellent one on the reconstruction of the palace itself. The palace's main gateway, the Georgentor, has an enormous statue of the fully armed Saxon count George. ■TIP➔ From April through October, the palace's old Hausmannsturm (Hausmann Tower) offers a wonderful view of the city and the Elbe River. The main attraction in the Royal Palace, though, is the world-famous **Historisches Grünes Gewölbe** (Historic Green Vault). Named after a green room in the palace of Augustus the Strong, the collection is divided into two sections.

The palace also houses the **Münzkabinett** (Coin Museum) and the **Kupferstichkabinett** (Museum of Prints and Drawings), with more than 500,000 pieces of art spanning several centuries. Changing exhibits at the Kupferstichkabinett have presented masterworks by Albrecht Dürer, Peter Paul Rubens, and Jan van Eyck; 20th-century art by Otto Dix, Edvard Munch, and Ernst Ludwig Kirchner; East European art; and some Southeast Asian prints. The **Türckische Cammer** (Turkish Chamber) comprises a huge number of Ottoman artifacts collected by Saxon dukes over centuries. It's worth going just to see the six carved Arabian horses, bedecked with jeweled armor. ✉ *Schlosspl.* ☎ *0351/491–4619* ⊕ *www.skd.museum* ✎ *All museums and collections except Historic Green Vault €10; Historic Green Vault €14* ☽ *Wed.–Mon. 10–6; Historic Green Vault by appointment.*

Historisches Grünes Gewölbe (*Historic Green Vault*). This section of the castle most reflects Augustus the Strong's obsession with art as a symbol of power. The intricately restored baroque interior is an integral part of the presentation, highlighting the objects in the collection. The last section of the museum houses the Jewel Room, which displays the ceremonial crown jewels of Augustus the Strong and his son. Access to the Historic Green Vault is limited to 100 visitors per hour by appointment only, reserved by phone or online. ✉ *Taschenberg 2* ☎ *0351/4919–2285 for tours* ⊕ *www.skd.museum* ✎ *€14* ☽ *By appointment.*

Neues Grünes Gewölbe (*New Green Vault*). The exquisite collection here consists of objets d'art fashioned from gold, silver, ivory, amber, and other precious and semiprecious materials. Among the crown jewels are the world's largest "green" diamond, 41 carats in weight, and a dazzling group of tiny gem-studded figures called *Hofstaat zu Delhi am Geburtstag des Grossmoguls Aureng-Zeb* (the Court at Delhi during the Birthday of the Great Mogul Aureng-Zeb). ✉ *Taschenberg 2* ⊕ *www.skd.museum.*

Semperoper (*Semper Opera House*). One of Germany's best-known and most popular theaters, this magnificent opera house saw the premieres of Richard Wagner's *Rienzi, Der Fliegende Holländer,* and *Tannhäuser* and Richard Strauss's *Salome, Elektra,* and *Der Rosenkavalier.* The Dresden architect Gottfried Semper built the house in 1838–41 in Italian Renaissance style, then saw his work destroyed in a fire caused by a careless lamplighter. Semper had to flee Dresden after participating in a democratic uprising, but his son Manfred rebuilt the theater in the neo-Renaissance style you see today, though even Manfred Semper's version had to be rebuilt after the devastating bombing raid of February 1945. On the 40th anniversary of that raid—February 13, 1985—the

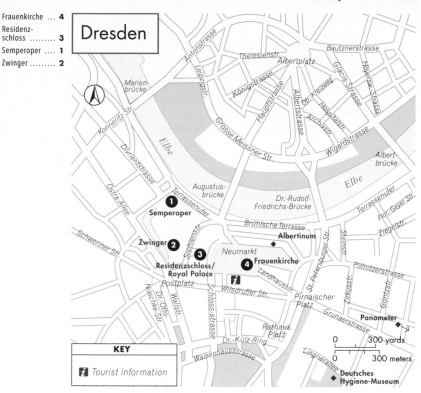

Dresden

KEY

7 *Tourist information*

0   300 yards

0   300 meters

8

Semperoper reopened with a performance of *Der Freischütz,* by Carl Maria von Weber, the last opera performed in the building before its destruction. ⊠ *Theaterpl. 2* ☎ *0351/491–1496* ⊕ *www.semperoper-erleben.de* ☞ *Tour €9.*

Fodor's Choice
★
Zwinger (*Bailey*). Dresden's magnificent baroque showpiece is entered by way of the mighty Kronentor (Crown Gate), off Ostra-Allee. Augustus the Strong hired a small army of artists and artisans to create a "pleasure ground" worthy of the Saxon court on the site of the former bailey, part of the city fortifications.

The Zwinger is quite a scene—a riot of garlands, nymphs, and other baroque ornamentation and sculpture. Wide staircases beckon to galleried walks and to the romantic Nymphenbad, a coyly hidden courtyard where statues of nude women perch in alcoves to protect themselves from a fountain that spits unexpectedly. The Zwinger once had an open view of the riverbank, but the Semper Opera House now occupies that side. Stand in the center of this quiet oasis, where the city's roar is kept at bay by the outer wings of the structure, and imagine the court festivities once held here. ⊠ *Entrance on Ostra–Allee* ⊕ *www.skd.museum* ⊙ *Tues.–Sun. 10–6.*

Gemäldegalerie Alte Meister (*Gallery of Old Masters*). This museum, in the northwestern corner of the complex, was built to house portions of the royal art collections. Among the priceless paintings are works by Dürer, Holbein, Jan van Eyck, Rembrandt, Rubens, van Dyck, Hals, Vermeer, Raphael, Titian, Giorgione, Veronese, Velázquez, Murillo, Canaletto, and Watteau. The highlight of the collection is Raphael's *Sistine Madonna,* whose mournful look is slightly less famous than the two cherubs who were added by Raphael after the painting was completed, in order to fill an empty space at the bottom. ☎ *0351/4914–2000* 🎫 *€12* 🕒 *Tues.–Sun. 10–6.*

Porzellansammlung (*Porcelain Collection*). Stretching from the curved gallery that adjoins the Glockenspielpavillon to the long gallery on the east side, this collection is considered one of the best of its kind in the world. The focus, naturally, is on Dresden and Meissen china, but there are also outstanding examples of Japanese, Chinese, and Korean porcelain. ☎ *0351/4914–2000* 🎫 *€6* 🕒 *Tues.–Sun. 10–6.*

Rüstkammer (*Armory*). Holding medieval and Renaissance suits of armor and weapons, the Rüstkammer is in two parts: the main exhibit in the Semperbau and the Türckische Cammer in the Residenzschloss. ☎ *0351/4914–2000* 🎫 *€10* 🕒 *Tues.–Sun. 10–6.*

WHERE TO EAT

$$ GERMAN 🍴 **Alte Meister.** Set in the historic mansion of the architect who rebuilt the Zwinger, and named after the school of medieval painters that includes Dürer, Holbein, and Rembrandt, the Alte Meister has a sophisticated Old World flair that charms locals and tourists alike. The food is very current, despite the decor, and the light German nouvelle cuisine with careful touches of Asian spices and ingredients has earned chef Dirk Wende critical praise. In summer this is one of the city's premier dining spots, offering a grand view of the Semperoper from a shaded terrace. [$] *Average main: €18* ✉ *Theaterpl. 1a* ☎ *0351/481–0426.*

WHERE TO STAY

$$ HOTEL 🏨 **Hotel Bülow-Residenz.** One of the most intimate first-class hotels in eastern Germany, the Bülow-Residenz is in a baroque palace built in 1730 by a wealthy Dresden city official. **Pros:** extremely helpful staff. **Cons:** a/c can be noisy; hotel is located in Neustadt, a 10-minute walk across the river to the city center. [$] *Rooms from: €159* ✉ *Rähnitzg. 19* ☎ *0351/80030* 🌐 *www.buelow-residenz.de* 🛏 *25 rooms, 5 suites.*

$$$ HOTEL 🏨 **Kempinski Hotel Taschenbergpalais Dresden.** Rebuilt after wartime bombing, the historic Taschenberg Palace—the work of Zwinger architect Matthäus Daniel Pöppelmann—is Dresden's premier address and the last word in luxury, as befits the former residence of the Saxon crown princes. **Pros:** ice-skating in the courtyard in winter; concierge knows absolutely everything about Dresden. **Cons:** expensive extra charges for breakfast and Internet. [$] *Rooms from: €199* ✉ *Taschenberg 3* ☎ *0351/49120* 🌐 *www.kempinski-dresden.de* 🛏 *188 rooms, 25 suites.*

GREECE

Athens, Delphi, Mykonos, Santorini

WHAT'S WHERE

1 Athens. The capital is greeting visitors with new swaths of parkland, a rich cultural life, regenerated neighborhoods, a sleek subway, and other spiffy and long-overdue municipal makeovers. But for five million Athenians and their 15 million annual visitors, it's still the tried and true pleasures that put the spin on urban life here: sitting in an endless parade of cafés (mostly talking about the ongoing economic crisis), strolling the streets of the Plaka and other old neighborhoods, and most of all, admiring the glorious remnants of one the greatest civilizations the West ever produced, such as the Acropolis, the Agora, and the Theater of Herod Atticus.

2 Delphi and the Apollo Coast. Attica, the southeastern tip of Central Greece, is much more than the home of Athens—it is also a fertile land, with sandy beaches to the south, serene mountains like Parnassus to the north, and beautiful Byzantine monasteries in between. Amazing archaeology abounds. Just a few hours from Athens lies Delphi, the center of the universe for the ancients. Southward along the coast lies the spectacular Temple of Poseidon. Hovering between sea and sky atop its cliff, it is the hero of a 1,001 travel posters.

3 Mykonos. These Cyclades compose a quintessential Mediterranean archipelago, with ancient sites, droves of vineyards and olive trees, and stark whitewashed cubist houses, all seemingly crystallized in a backdrop of lapis lazuli. On lively, liberated Mykonos, the rich arrive by private yacht, the middle class by plane, the backpackers by boat—but everyone is out to enjoy the golden sands and Dionysian nightlife. Happily, the old ways of life continue in fishing ports and along mazelike town streets.

4 Santorini. Volcanic, spectacular Santorini is possibly the last remnant of the "lost continent" of Atlantis—the living here is as high as the towns' cliff-top perches. There's no shortage of worldly pleasures on this most southerly of the islands, from shopping to yachting, but pastimes need be no more fancy than climbing up a snakelike staircase to the top of the 1,000-foot cliffs encircling the famed flooded caldera or simply gazing out to sea across the blindingly white cubes of Cycladic architecture.

NEED TO KNOW

GREECE

Athens

RODHES

CRETE

Mediterranean Sea

Black Sea

Caspian Sea

AT A GLANCE

Capital: Athens

Population: 10,815,197

Currency: Euro

Money: ATMs are common; some smaller places don't take credit cards

Language: Greek

Country Code: ☎ 30

Emergencies: ☎ 166

Driving: On the right

Electricity: 200v/50 cycles; electrical plugs have two round prongs

Time: Six hours ahead of New York,

Documents: Up to 90 days with valid passport; Schengen rules apply

Mobile Phones: GSM (900 and 1800 bands)

Major Mobile Companies: Cosmote, Vodafone, Wind

WEBSITES

Greece: ⊕ *visitgreece.gr*

Athens: ⊕ *www. thisisathens.org*

Ministry of Culture: ⊕ *www.culture.gr*

GETTING AROUND

✈ **Air Travel:** Most flights are to Athens (or Thessaloniki). Crete, Mykonos, and Santorini also have international airports.

🚌 **Bus Travel:** There is an extensive network of inexpensive, orange KTEL buses that are fairly modern and depart from Athens for major sites such as Sounion, Delphi, and Olympia.

🚗 **Car Travel:** If you want to explore at your own pace on the mainland or islands, a car is a good idea.

🚃 **Train Travel:** Except for the Athens metro, trains in Greece are limited and unreliable.

PLAN YOUR BUDGET

	HOTEL ROOM	MEAL	ATTRACTIONS
Low Budget	€80	€10	90-minute Athens metro ticket, €1.40
Mid Budget	€120	€25	Ticket for the Athens Concert Hall (Megaron Mousikis), €25
High Budget	€400	€120	Night out at a Greek music club (*bouzoukia*), €100

WAYS TO SAVE

Share a platter of *mezedes*. Typical small plates with a bit of wine make a great meal.

Visit the local farmers' market. Weekly farmers' markets sell fresh ingredients for a home-cooked Greek meal.

Take advantage of air ticket offers. Even with the merger of Aegean and Olympic Air, there are still frequent sales on domestic flights.

Unification of Archaeological Sites ticket. The combined ticket (€12) includes a week of access to major sights in Athens.

Hassle Factor	Medium. Flights to Athens are frequent, but most require a change in Europe; in the summer, cheaper charter flights go directly to the islands.
3 days	Visit Athens and venture out to watch the sun set over the Temple of Poseidon at Sounion, or you can do a short island escape.
1 week	Combine a short trip to Athens with an island stay and perhaps an overnight at Delphi.
2 weeks	You can visit Mykonos and Santorini to take in the beauty of whitewashed cubic houses perched on the cliffs, before heading back to Athens to visit the Acropolis and its museum.

WHEN TO GO

High Season: June through August is the most expensive and popular time to visit Greece. Athens is fairly empty in August, except for the mobs of tourists.

Low Season: Most island hotels are closed in the low season, from mid-October to the end of April, although this is the perfect time to discover the mountainous regions of the mainland, including the ski resorts not too far from Delphi. Athens is cold and humid.

Value Season: May and September offer the best combination of mild Mediterranean weather and value. The Aegean may still be too cold for swimming in May, but things get better in early June, when you are still beating the crowds. Some island hotels are open until the start of November, others close in early October. An Athenian city break is a good, affordable option all year round.

BIG EVENTS

April/May: Greek Easter is a movable feast: a traditional highlight is lamb roasting on the spit.

August: The Assumption of Mary on August the 15 marks summer vacation for Greeks.

November: Run in the Athens Classic Marathon. ⊕ www.athensclassicmarathon.com

May to October: The Athens and Epidavros Festival invites global artists to perform in magnificent surroundings. ⊕ www.greekfestival.gr

READ THIS

■ *Eurydice Stree: A Place in Athens,* Sofka Zinovieff. The author adapts to life in Athens.

■ *Murder in Mykonos,* Jeffrey Siger. Big-time detective from Athens needs to prove himself fast.

■ *Sunlight in the Wine,* Robert Leigh. An Englishman moves to the island of Andros for a simpler life.

WATCH THIS

■ *Mamma Mia!* A feel-good Abba musical.

■ *Captain Corelli's Mandolin.* A WWII Italian officer falls in love on Cephallonia.

■ *Zorba the Greek.* Anthony Quinn brings the Greek spirit to life.

EAT THIS

■ **Feta cheese:** crumbly aged sheep or goat cheese

■ **Greek salad:** country salad with feta and seasoning

■ **Moussaka:** layered eggplant, potato, and ground meat, topped with béchamel

■ **Fava:** a traditional Santorini dip made of puréed yellow split peas

■ **Pita me gyro:** spit-roasted meat, wrapped in pita with tomatoes, onions, and tzatziki

■ **Lamb kleftiko:** slow-roasted leg of lamb wrapped in baking paper

9

The sight greets you time and again in Greece—a line of solid, sun-bleached masonry silhouetted against a clear blue sky. If you're lucky, a cypress waves gently to one side. What makes the scene all the more fulfilling is the realization that a kindred spirit looked up and saw the same temple or theater some 2,000 or more years ago.

Temples, theaters, statues, a stray Doric column or two, the fragment of a Corinthian capital: these traces of the ancients are thick on the ground in Greece. Perhaps this is one reason why it can be disorienting—especially for visitors conditioned by textbooks, college Greek, and Keats's Grecian Urn—to arrive in Athens and find the natives roaring around in sports cars and talking about the latest nouvelle restaurant. Shouldn't they look like the truncated statues in the British Museum and have brows habitually crowned with wild olive? Incongruous as it may seem, most Greeks have two arms and two legs attached to the torso in the normal places. And these days a goodly number of them are talking about the hottest new nightspot.

From its recently opened museums to its hipsterish island hangouts, Greece is more than ever a dazzling paradox—the word is Greek—of old and new, ancient and modern. Despite its recent economic woes, the country is alive with vibrant trends and styles. It seems that the mammoth 2004 Olympic Games held in Athens did well to catapult the country into the 21st century. "European" Greece dazzles with boutique hotels, postmodern eateries, and elegant resorts that dramatically challenge the old Zorba-era conceptions of the Spartan Aegean.

Thankfully, Greece still remains an agelessly impressive land. Western poetry, music, architecture, politics, medicine, law—all had their birth centuries ago here. The Greek countryside itself remains a stunning presence, dotted with cypress groves, vineyards, and olive trees; carved into gentle bays or dramatic coves bordered with startling white sand; or articulated into rolling hills and rugged mountain ranges that plunge into the sea. In Greece, indeed, you cannot travel far across the land without encountering the sea, or far across the sea without encountering one of its roughly 2,000 islands. Approximately equal in size to New York State, Greece has 15,019 km (9,312 miles) of coastline, more than any other country of its size. The sea is everywhere, not on three sides only but at every turn, reaching into the shoreline like a probing hand.

Wherever you head, you should explore this fascinating country with open eyes. Chances are you'll enjoy it in all its forms: its slumbering cafés and buzzing tavernas, its elaborate religious rituals, and its stark, bright beauty. As the lucky traveler soon learns, although their countryside may be bleached and stony, the Greeks themselves provide the vibrant color that has long since vanished from classical monuments once saturated with blue, gold, and vermilion pigment under the eye-searing Aegean sun.

TOP REASONS TO GO

Athens's Acropolis: The great emblem of Classical Greece has loomed above Athens (whose harbor of Piraeus is the gateway to all the Greek Islands) for 2,500 years. Even from afar, the sight of the Parthenon—the great marble temple that the 5th-century BC statesmen Pericles conceived to crown the site—stirs strong feelings about the achievements and failings of Western Civilization.

Delphi: Set in a spectacular vale, this was the ancient site of the most venerated and consulted Greek oracle. The site is breathtaking, and the remnant artworks, such as the fabled *Charioteer*, even more so.

Mykonos: Backbackers and jet-setters alike share the beautiful beaches and the Dionysian nightlife—this island is not called the St-Tropez of the Aegean without reason—but the old ways of life continue undisturbed in fishing ports and along mazelike town streets. Not only are the hotels and cafés picture-perfect, the famous windmills actually seem to be posing for your camera.

Delos: Just a short boat ride away from sybaritic, this-worldly Mykonos is ruin-strewn Delos, a proudly *other-worldly* and sacred island. Windswept and uninhabited, this islet was revered as the sacred birthplace of Apollo. Ponder the evidence of past glory: the sprawling site was once the religious and commercial center of the entire eastern Mediterranean.

Santorini: One of the world's most picturesque islands cradles the sunken caldera of a volcano that last erupted in 1650 BC. To merely link the phenomenon to the Atlantis myth and the Minoan collapse misses the point—what matters is the ravishing sight of the multicolored cliffs rising 1,100 feet out of sparkling blue waters, a visual treat that makes the heart miss a beat or two. The main town of Ia is a white cubist stage set for sunsets that make the knees go weak.

9

PLANNING

WHEN TO GO

The best times to visit Greece are late spring and early fall. In May and June the days are warm, even hot, but dry, and the seawater has been warmed by the sun. For sightseeing or hitting the beach, this is the time. Greece is relatively tourist-free in spring, so if beaches and swimming don't top your agenda, April and early May are good; the local wildflowers are at their loveliest, too. Carnival, usually in February just before Lent, and Greek Easter are seasonal highlights. July and August (most locals vacation in August) are always busy—especially on the islands. If you visit during this peak, plan well ahead and be prepared to fight the crowds. September and October are a good alternative to spring and early summer, especially in the cities where bars and cultural institutions stay open. Elsewhere, things begin to shut down in November. Transportation to the islands is limited in winter, and many hotels outside large cities are closed until April.

GETTING HERE AND AROUND

AIR TRAVEL

There are many direct flights to Athens from Europe but relative few nonstops from the U.S., and most of those are seasonal. It is essential to book well in advance for summer or for festivals and holidays, especially on three-day weekends. Domestic flights are a good deal for many destinations. There are flights most days between Athens and both Santorini and Mykonos. The option of flying to them is a good choice, especially if you're on a tight schedule: unlike ferries, flights are rarely affected by the weather. In late 2013, it was announced that Aegean Airlines would purchase Olympic Air, and this will no doubt have some effect on flight schedules and offerings, and perhaps prices.

Contacts Athens International Airport-Eleftherios Venizelos (ATH)
⊠ *Spata* ☎ *210/353-0000 for flight info and customer service, 210/353-1335 for visitor services, 210/353-0515 for lost and found* ⊕ *www.aia.gr.*

BOAT AND FERRY TRAVEL

Ferries, catamarans, and hydrofoils make up an essential part of the national transport system of Greece. With so many private companies operating, so many islands to choose from, and complicated timetables with departures changing not just by season but also by day of the week, the most sensible way to arrange island hopping is to select the islands you would like to see, then visit a travel agent to ask how your journey can be put together. Greece's largest and busiest port is Piraeus, which lies 10 km (6 miles) south of downtown Athens. Athens's second port is Rafina, with regular daily ferry crossings to the Cycladic islands of Mykonos and Santorini during the summer months. You can also travel to Greece's ports of Igoumenitsa and Patras by boat directly from Italy, and from Turkey to various Aegean islands.

Contacts Blue Star Ferries ⊠ *123-125 Syngrou Ave. and Torva 3, Athens* ☎ *210/891-9800, 18130 within Greece, 210/891-9810 for customer service* ⊕ *www.bluestarferries.gr.* **Hellenic Seaways** ⊠ *Astigos 6, Plateia Karaiskaki, Piraeus* ☎ *210/419-9000 for ticket info, 210/419-9100 for administration* ⊕ *www.hellenicseaways.gr.* **Seajets** ⊠ *Dim. Gounari 2, 2nd floor, Piraeus* ☎ *210/412-0001, 210/412-1901* ⊕ *www.seajets.gr.* **Superfast Ferries** ⊠ *123-125 Syngrou Ave. and Torva 30, Athens* ☎ *210/891-9130* ⊕ *www.superfast.com.*

BUS TRAVEL

Organized bus tours can be booked together with hotel reservations by your travel agent. Many tour operators have offices in and around Syntagma and Omonia squares in central Athens. It is easy to get around Greece on buses, and it is the preferred mode of arriving at Delphi, the great ancient site in Attica. The price of public transportation in Greece has risen steeply since the 2004 Olympic year, but it is still cheaper than in other Western European cities. Greece has an extensive and reliable regional bus system (KTEL) made up of local operators—buses often reach even the most far-flung villages.

Contacts Downtown Athens KTEL terminal ⊠ *Aigyptou Sq., Mavromateon and Leoforos Alexandras, near Pedion Areos park, Athens* ☎ *210/880-8080, 210/818-0221* ⊕ *www.ktel.org, www.ktelattikis.gr.*

CAR TRAVEL

Road conditions in Greece have improved significantly since the 1990s, yet driving in Greece still presents certain challenges. If you are traveling by ferry, taking along a car increases ticket costs substantially and limits your ease in hopping on any ferry. International driving permits (IDPs) are required for drivers who are not citizens of an EU country. These international permits, valid only in conjunction with your regular driver's license, are universally recognized; having one may save you a problem with local authorities.

TRAIN TRAVEL

Greece is not particularly geared to rail travel, so traveling around Greece by train can be laborious, since the trains are sluggish and often late. Moreover, at this writing, there is no international train travel into Greece.

Contacts Greek Railway Organization (*OSE*). ✉ *Karolou 1, Omonia Sq., Athens* ☎ *210/529–7006 for Central Office, 210/529–7007* ⊕ *www.ose.gr* ✉ *Sina 6, Athens* ☎ *210/362–4402, 210/362–4405.*

HOTELS

The days of the bare cottage, the creaky apartment, and the shabby motel have come and gone. So accommodations now vary from super-luxurious island xanadus bedecked with latest in-room high-tech amenities to simple yet charming traditional settlements incorporating local style to inexpensive basic rented rooms peddled at the harbor. Apartments with kitchens are available as well in most resort areas. Most areas have pensions—usually clean, bright, and recently built. On islands in summer owners still wait for tourists at the harbor, and signs in English throughout villages indicate available "rooms to rent." Look for the words *Domatia* (rooms) or *Pansions* (pensions). The quality of these rooms has improved a great deal in recent years, with many featuring air-conditioning, a TV, and a refrigerator. One rule remains: look before you commit.

PRICES AND MAKING RESERVATIONS

Often you can reduce the price by eliminating breakfast, by bargaining when it's off-season, or by going through a local travel agency for the larger hotels on major islands and in Athens. A 6.5% government tax (5% outside the major cities) and 0.5% municipality tax are added to all hotel bills. Though the rate quoted usually includes the tax, be sure to ask. If your room rate covers meals, another 2% tax may be added. It is probably wise to book at least one month in advance for the months of June, July, and September, and ideally even two to three months in advance for the high season, from late July to the end of August, especially in high-profile destinations like Mykonos and Santorini.

RESTAURANTS

Restaurants in Greece range from the classic taverna—where the chef is often a grandma who's following her grandma's recipes—to luxurious nouvelle temples of gastronomy that have made Athens into a culinary hotspot. There are many kinds of eateries here. You'll often find fine tablecloths, carefully placed silverware, candles, and multipage menus at an *estiatorio,* or restaurant. Now enjoying a retro resurgence, the simple *oinomageirio* is often packed with blue-collar workers filling up on casseroles and listening to *rembetika,* Greece's version of the blues. A *taverna* is vintage Greece—a family-style eatery noted for great spreads of grilled meat "tis oras" (of the hour), all shared around a big table. A *psarotaverna* is every bit like a regular taverna, except the star of the menu is fresh fish (remember that fish usually comes whole; if you want it fileted, ask, Mporo na exo fileto?). *Mezedopoleia* are the Greek version of tapas bars, where you can graze on a limited menu of dips, salads, and hot and cold mezedes. An *ouzeri* serves up the potent liquor known as ouzo, along with plates of mezedes. Coffee rules at the *kafeneio* (café), along with light menus of food. Finish up a dinner at a *zacharoplasteio* (patisserie).

HOURS
Breakfast is available from 7 to 10:30 at most hotels and until early afternoon in relaxed beach resorts. Lunch is between 12:30 and 4:00, and dinner is served from about 8:30 to midnight, later in the big cities and resort islands. Most Greeks dine late, around 10 or 11 pm. In the early evening, they can often be found sipping frappé in a busy café, preparing for the long night ahead. Tips are included in restaurant bills, but most people add more money if service was good.

MEALS AND FAVORITE DISHES
Greeks eat their main meal at either lunch or dinner, and this can be a traditional dish like *ladero,* or oil-based home-cooked style foods such as meat with potatoes or rice, vegetables, pulses, or short pasta. Simpler, faster options include cheese, spinach, or other pies from chain-stores such as Everest or Grigoris, where the customer can compose the perfect sandwich from a broad variety of ingredients, or fast-food chains such as Goodys. Appetizers at tavernas include bread accompaniments such as *taramosalata* (made from fish roe), *melitzanosalata* (made from smoked eggplant, lemon, oil, and garlic), *tyrokafteri* (spicy feta cheese), and the well-known yogurt, cucumber, and garlic dip *tzatziki* as well as, of course, the classic *horiatiki* or Greek salad, made with tomato, feta cheese, cucumber, onion, olives, and oregano. In most places, the menu is broken down into appetizers (*orektika*) and main courses (*kiria piata*)—mainly grilled meats—with additional headings for salads (this includes dips like tzatziki) and vegetable side plates. Often the food arrives all at the same time, or as soon as it's prepared. Locals prefer the cheaper yet sometimes highly qualitative *hima* (house) wine, served in jugs and often drunk with a small splash of soda water or ice for extra zing.

HOTEL AND RESTAURANT PRICES
Prices in the restaurant reviews are the average cost of a main course at dinner or, if dinner is not served, at lunch; taxes and service charges are generally included. Prices in the hotel reviews are the lowest cost of a standard double room in high season, excluding taxes, service charges, and meal plans.

PLANNING YOUR TIME

Greece offers two main experiences, the mainland and the islands. Both have wooed and wowed travelers for many centuries. Many people recommend that you visit Athens first when you arrive in Greece. *Don't.* Instead, the first leg of the journey should be the islands. Only when you've enjoyed several idyllic days on Mykonos and Santorini will be you well rested enough to enjoy the mighty bustle and sophistication of Athens. So, hard as it may be, arrive at Athens's airport only to use it as a transfer point to a flight (or opt for a ferry from Piraeus) heading to the islands. The most admired are Santorini (4–9 hours from Piraeus depending on type of boat) and Mykonos (3–6 hours). Take note that ferry schedules change frequently, and it can be tricky to coordinate island-hopping excursions in advance, so if tight on time it is best to fly—both islands have airports. If that is the case, remember to book well in advance.

ATHENS

It's no wonder that all roads lead to the fascinating yet maddening metropolis of Athens. Lift your eyes 200 feet above the city to the Parthenon, its honey-colored marble columns rising from a massive limestone base, and you behold architectural perfection that has not been surpassed in 2,500 years. But today this shrine of classical form, this symbol of Western civilization and political thought, dominates a 21st-century boomtown. Athens is now home to 4.5 million souls, many of whom spend the day discussing the economic crisis and the city's faults: the murky pollution cloud known as the *nefos,* the overcrowding, the traffic jams with their hellish din, the rising numbers of the homeless, and the characterless cement apartment blocks. Romantic travelers, nurtured on the truth and beauty of Keats's Grecian Urn, are dismayed to find that much of Athens has succumbed to that red tubular glare that owes only its name—neon—to the Greeks.

To experience Athens—Athìna in Greek—fully is to understand the essence of Greece: ancient monuments surviving in a sea of cement, startling beauty amid the squalor, tradition juxtaposed with modernity—a smartly dressed lawyer chatting on her cell phone as she maneuvers around a priest in flowing robes heading for the ultramodern metro. Locals depend upon humor and flexibility to deal with the chaos; you should do the same. The rewards are immense if you take the time to catch the purple glow of sundown on Mt. Hymettus, light a candle in a Byzantine church beside black-shrouded grandmas while teens outside argue vociferously about soccer, or breathe in the tangy sea air while sipping a Greek coffee after a night at the coastal clubs.

WHEN TO GO

Athens has a typical Mediterranean climate: hot, dry summers and cool, wet winters. Snow is not uncommon in Athens, and many places are not well heated. Spring and fall are the best times to go, with warm days and balmy evenings. In midsummer, the hot winds from Africa

9

make overheated (and overpolluted) Athens a hellish challenge, so try to head here in the "shoulder seasons."

GETTING HERE AND AROUND
AIR TRAVEL
The best way to get to the sleek Eleftherios Venizelos International Airport from downtown Athens is by metro or light rail. Single tickets cost €8 and include transfers (don't forget to validate the ticket again) to bus, trolley, or tram. Also, in Athens four reliable express buses connect the airport with the metro (Dafni metro station and Ethniki Amyna station among others), Syntagma Square, KTEL terminal station on Kifisos Aveue, and Piraeus. Bus X93 takes you to the KTEL regional bus terminal on Kifisos Avenue, where buses depart for Delphi and other northern Greece destinations. Bus X95 will take you to Syntagma Square (Amalias Avenue), also stopping at the Ethniki Amyna metro stop (Line 3), which will get you into Syntagma within 10 minutes. Bus X96 takes the Vari–Koropiou road inland and links with the coastal road, passing through Voula, Glyfada, and Alimos; it then goes on to Piraeus (opposite Karaiskaki Square). Finally, Bus X97 follows the Vari-Koropiou inland road, and continues inland towards the southwest, finishing at the Dafni metro station. Bus tickets to and from the airport cost €5 one-way. Taxis are readily available at the airport; they cost an average of €35 to get to the city in the daytime while the nighttime rate rises to €50 (between midnight and 5).

BUS TRAVEL
Athens and its suburbs are covered by a good network of buses and trams, with express buses running between central Athens and major neighborhoods, including nearby beaches. During the day buses tend to run every 15–30 minutes, with reduced service at night and on weekends. Buses run from about 5 am to midnight. Main bus stations are at Akadimias and Sina and at Kaningos Square. Bus tickets cost €1.40 and can be used for all public transport transfers for 90 minutes, including the metro. A three-day tourist ticket costs €20 and allows unlimited access to urban mass transport (buses, metro, tram, light railway), including a one-way journey to or from El.Venizelos international airport. A tram link between downtown Athens and the coastal suburbs features three main lines. Line A runs from Syntagma to Voula, ending by the Asklipeion hospital. Line B runs from Syntagma to the Peace and Friendship Stadium on the outskirts of Piraeus. Line C traces the shoreline from Asklipeion Voulas hospital to the Peace and Friendship Stadium.

Contacts City tram ⊕ *www.stasy.gr.* **KTEL** 🕿 *210/821–0872, 14505, 210/880–8080* ⊕ *www.ktel.org.*

METRO TRAVEL
The best magic carpet ride in town is the metro. It's fast, cheap, and convenient, and the three lines go to all the major spots in Athens. Just be aware of pickpockets and bag theft; if you keep your belongings close to you and in hand, you should have few problems. Line 1, or the Green Line, is often called the *elektrikos,* or the electrical train and runs from Piraeus to the northern suburb of Kifissia, with several downtown

stops. Downtown stations on Line 1 most handy to tourists include Victorias Square, near the National Archaeological Museum; Omonia Square; Monastiraki, in the old Turkish bazaar; and Thission, near the ancient Agora and the nightlife districts of Psirri and Thission. Line 2, or the Red Line, starts from Syntagma Square and includes stops at Panepistimiou (near Numismatic Museum), Omonia Square, Stathmos Larissis (next to train station), and the Acropolis. Line 3, or the Blue Line, heads to Gazi and Monastiraki districts. Tickets are €1.40 and are valid for 90 minutes and for all means of urban transport. Validate all tickets in machines before you board.

You can buy a day pass covering the metro, buses, trolleys, and trams for €4; a weekly pass for €25; or, at the beginning of each month, a monthly pass for €45.

Contacts Athens Metro ⊕ *www.ametro.gr.*

TAXI TRAVEL
Most drivers in Athens speak basic English. Although you can find an empty taxi on the street, it's often faster to call out your destination to one carrying passengers; if the taxi is going in that direction, the driver will pick you up. Likewise, don't be alarmed if your driver picks up other passengers (although he should ask your permission first, and he should never pick up another fare if you are a woman traveling alone at night). Each passenger pays full fare for the distance he or she has traveled. Neither tipping nor bargaining is generally practiced; if your driver has gone out of the way for you, a small gratuity (10% or less) is appreciated. The leading taxi companies are Athina I, Kosmos, Ermis, Hellas, and Parthenon—ask your hotel concierge for contact information.

TOUR OPTIONS
One way to get an overview of Athens is to opt for a ride on a hop-on/hop-off bus from City Sightseeing that stops at all the city's main sights. These privately owned buses run every 30 minutes; tickets cost €18 per adult for Athens; a 48-hour ticket that includes Piraeus costs €20.50. The Athens tour takes 90 minutes, but you can enter or exit as you please in one of the 18 stops (including Syntagma Square) throughout the day; an audio guide is available in 11 languages.

There are also full-day (and nighttime) tours by bus, often including a guided tour of the New Acropolis Museum (the museum is closed on Mondays). Morning tours usually begin around 8:45. Reservations can be made through most hotels. The tours run daily, year-round, and cost around €68. Two top bus-tour companies are CHAT Tours and Key Tours.

Contacts CHAT Tours ✉ *Xenofontos 9, Syntagma* ☎ *210/322–3137* ⊕ *www. chatours.gr.* **City Sightseeing** ☎ *210/921–4174* ⊕ *www.city-sightseeing.com.* **Key Tours** ☎ *210/923–3166* ⊕ *www.keytours.gr.*

VISITOR INFORMATION
The main office of the Greek National Tourism Organization (GNTO; EOT in Greece) is on Tsocha Street, in the Ambelokipi district, near the Megaron Mousikis concert hall, in the heart of Athens. Their offices

9

are generally open between 8 and 3. The city of Athens maintains an informative and lively English-speaking website on Athenian life and cultural events (⊕ *www.breathtakingathens.gr*).

Contacts **Greek National Tourism Organization (EOT)** ✉ *Tsoha 7, near Megaron Mousikis, Ambelokipi* ☏ *210/870–7000* ⊕ *www.visitgreece.gr.* ✉ *EOT Information desk, Dionysiou Areopageitou 10, Plaka* ☏ *210/331–0392, 210/331–0716*

EXPLORING

Although Athens covers a huge area, the major landmarks of the ancient Greek, Roman, and Byzantine periods are close to the modern city center. The center of the city is small, stretching from the Acropolis in the southwest to Mt. Lycabettus in the northeast. The layout is simple: three parallel streets—Stadiou, Eleftheriou Venizelou (familiarly known as Panepistimiou), and Akadimias—link two main squares, Syntagma (Constitution) and Omonia (Concord). As you explore, you will discover that Athens may seem like one huge city but it is really a conglomeration of neighborhoods with distinctive characters. The Eastern influences that prevailed during the 400-year rule of the Ottoman Empire are still evident in Monastiraki, the bazaar area near the foot of the Acropolis. On the northern slope of the Acropolis, stroll through Plaka, an area of tranquil streets lined with renovated mansions, to get the flavor of the 19th-century's gracious lifestyle. The narrow lanes of Anafiotika, a section of Plaka, thread past tiny churches and small, color-washed houses with wooden upper stories, recalling a Cycladic island village.

Formerly run-down old quarters, such as Thission, Gazi, Kerameikos, and Psirri, popular nightlife areas filled with bars and *mezedopoleia* (similar to tapas bars), are being gentrified, although they still retain much of their original charm. The area around Syntagma Square, the tourist hub, and Omonia Square, the commercial heart of the city about 1 km (½ mile) northwest, is distinctly European, having been designed by the court architects of King Otho, a Bavarian, in the 19th century. To the east, the chic shops and bistros of ritzy Kolonaki nestle at the foot of Mt. Lycabettus, Athens's highest hill (909 feet), and the best place for a bird's-eye view of all Athens.

WEST ATHENS: THE ACROPOLIS, PLAKA, ANAFIOTIKA, AND MONASTIRAKI
(ΑΚΡΟΠΟΛΗ, ΠΛΑΚΑ, ΑΝΑΦΙΩΤΙΚΑ, & ΜΟΝΑΣΤΗΡΑΚΙ)
Towering over the modern metropolis of 4.5 million as it once stood over the ancient capital of 50,000, the ancient Acropolis has remained Athens's most spectacular attraction ever since its first settlement around 5000 BC. After viewing the Parthenon, all will at first seem to be an anticlimax. But there is still much that is well worth seeing on the citadel's periphery, including the neoclassic buildings lining its main pedestrianized street, Dionyssiou Areopagitou, and the great centuries-old Odeon of Herodes Atticus.

Fanning north from the slopes of the Acropolis, the relentlessly pictur-esque Plaka is the last corner of 19th-century Athens. Set with Byzantine accents provided by churches, the "Old Town" district extends north to Ermou Street and eastward to Amalias Avenue. At night merrymakers crowd the old tavernas, which feature traditional music and dancing; many have rooftops facing the Acropolis. If you keep off the main tour-ist shopping streets of Kidathineon and Adrianou, you will be amazed at how peaceful the area can be, even in summer.

Above Plaka is Anafiotika, built on winding lanes that climb up the slopes of the Acropolis, its upper reaches resembling a tranquil village.

To the west of Anafiotika lies Athens's fabled ancient Agora, once the focal point of urban life and site of the Hephaistion, the best-preserved Doric temple in Greece.

Just to the north of the Agora, you can still experience the sights and sounds of the marketplace in Monastiraki, the former Turkish bazaar area, which retains vestiges of the 400-year period when Greece was subject to the Ottoman Empire. On the opposite side of the Agora is another meeting place of sorts: Thission, one of the most sought-after residential neighborhoods since about 1990 and a vibrant nightlife district.

Fodor'sChoice
★

Acropolis. You don't have to look far in Athens to encounter perfection. Towering above all—both physically and spiritually—is the Acropolis, the ancient city of upper Athens. The Greek term Akropolis means "High City," and today's traveler who climbs this table-like hill is pay-ing tribute to the prime source of Western civilization.

Most of the notable structures on this flat-top limestone outcrop, 512 feet high, were built from 461 to 429 BC, when the intellectual and artistic life of Athens flowered under the influence of the Athenian statesman Pericles. Since then, the buildings of the Acropolis have undergone transformations into, at various times, a Florentine palace, an Islamic mosque, and a Turkish harem. They have also weathered the hazards of wars, right up to 1944, when British paratroopers posi-tioned their bazookas between the Parthenon's columns. Today, the Erechtheion temple has been completely restored, and conservation work on the Parthenon, the Temple of Athena Nike, and the Propy-laea is due for completion by the end of 2012. With most of the major restoration work now completed, a visit to the Acropolis evokes the spirit of the ancient heroes and gods who were once worshiped here. The sight of the Parthenon—the Panathenaic temple at the crest of this *ieros vrachos* (sacred rock)—has the power to stir the heart as few other ancient relics do.

The walk through the Acropolis takes about four hours, depending on the crowds, including an hour spent in the Acropolis Museum. In general, the earlier you start out the better—in summer the heat is blis-tering by noon and the light's reflection off the rock and marble ruins is almost blinding. Remember to bring water, sunscreen, and a hat to protect yourself from the sun. An alternative, in summer, is to visit after 5 pm, when the light is best for taking photographs. The two hours before sunset, when the fabled violet light occasionally spreads from

the crest of Mt. Hymettus and embraces the Acropolis, is an ideal time to visit in any season. After dark the hill is spectacularly floodlighted, creating a scene visible from many parts of the capital.

Most people take the metro to the Acropolis station, where the Acropolis Museum is just across the main exit; it was inaugurated in the summer of 2009. They then follow the Dionyssiou Aeropagitou, the pedestrianized street which traces the foothill of the Acropolis to its entrance at the Beulé Gate. Another entrance is along the rock's northern face via the Peripatos, a paved path from the Plaka district. The summit of the Acropolis can also now be reached by people with disabilities via an elevator.

Don't throw away your Acropolis ticket after your tour. It will get you into all the other sites in the Unification of Archaeological Sites for seven days—and for free.

Guides to the Acropolis are quite informative and will also help kids understand the site better. ⊠ *Dionyssiou Areopagitou, Acropolis* ☎ *210/321–4172, 210/321–0219* ⊕ *www.culture.gr* ⌑ *€12 Unification of Archaeological Sites ticket (includes Ancient Agora and Tower of the Winds)* ☽ *Daily 8–6:30 (last entry)* Ⓜ *Acropolis.*

Fodor'sChoice   **Acropolis Museum.** Designed by the celebrated Swiss architect Bernard
★   Tschumi in collaboration with Greek architect Michalis Fotiadis, the Acropolis Museum made world headlines when it opened in June 2009. If some buildings define an entire city in a particular era, Athens's newest museum boldly sets the tone of Greece's modern era. Occupying a large plot of the city's most prized real estate, the Acropolis Museum nods to the fabled ancient hill above it but speaks—thanks to a spectacular building—in a contemporary architectural language.

The museum drew 90,000 visitors in its first month and proved it is spacious enough to accommodate such crowds (happily, as a whopping 5,503,677 visitors had entered the doors of the ingenious, airy structure by June 2013). Unlike its crammed, dusty predecessor, there is lots of elbow room, from the museum's olive tree–dotted grounds to its prized, top-floor Parthenon Gallery. The terrace restaurant with an eagle eye's view of the Acropolis, right next to the large gift shop, has also been an instant hit.

Regal glass walkways, very high ceilings, and panoramic views are all part of the experience. In the five-level museum, every shade of marble is on display and bathed in abundant, UV-safe natural light. Visitors pass into the museum through a broad entrance and move ever upwards. Delicate ancient craftsmanship is contrasted throughout with industrial modern accents (massive columns and symmetrical wall apertures); abundant glass on floors and balcony spaces allow the exhibition levels to gracefully communicate with each other.

Museum politics are unavoidable here. This gallery was designed—as Greek officials have made obvious—to hold the Parthenon Marbles in their *entirety*. This includes the sculptures Lord Elgin brought to London two centuries ago. Currently, 50 meters of the frieze are in Athens, 80 meters in London's British Museum, and another 30 meters scattered in museums around the world. The spectacular and sumptuous new museum challenges the British claim that there is no suitable home for the Parthenon treasures in Greece. Pointedly, the museum avoids replicas, as the top-floor gallery makes a point of highlighting the abundant missing original pieces. ✉ *Dionyssiou Areopagitou 15, Acropolis* ☎ *210/900–0900* ⊕ *www.theacropolismuseum.gr* ▣ *€5* ☉ *Apr.–Oct., Tues.–Sun. 8–8, Fri. 8–10; Nov.–Mar., Tues.–Thurs. 9–5, Fri. 9–10, weekends 9–8* Ⓜ *Acropolis.*

FAMILY
Fodor's Choice
★

Anafiotika. Set in the shadow of the Acropolis and often compared to the whitewashed villages of rural Greek islands, the Anafiotika quarter is populated by many descendants of the Anafi stonemasons who arrived from that small island in the 19th century to work in the expanding capital. It remains an enchanting area of simple stone houses, many nestled right into the bedrock, most little changed over the years, others stunningly restored. Cascades of bougainvillea and pots of geraniums and marigolds enliven the balconies and rooftops, and the prevailing serenity is in blissful contrast to the cacophony of modern Athens. In classical times, this district was abandoned because the Delphic Oracle claimed it as sacred ground. The buildings here were constructed by masons from Anafi island, who came to find work in the rapidly expanding Athens of the 1840s and 1850s. They took over this area, whose rocky terrain was similar to Anafi's, hastily erecting homes overnight and taking advantage of an Ottoman law that decreed that if you could put up a structure between sunset and sunrise, the property was yours. Ethiopians, imported as slaves by the Turks during the Ottoman period, stayed on after independence and lived higher up, in caves, on the northern slopes of the Acropolis. ✉ *On northeast slope of Acropolis rock, Plaka* Ⓜ *Acropolis.*

Fodor's Choice
★

Ancient Agora. The commercial hub of ancient Athens, the Agora was once lined with statues and expensive shops, the favorite strolling ground of fashionable Athenians as well as a mecca for merchants and students. The long colonnades offered shade in summer and protection from rain in winter to the throng of people who transacted the day-to-day business of the city, and, under their arches, Socrates discussed matters with Plato and Zeno expounded the philosophy of the Stoics (whose name comes from the six *stoa*, or colonnades of the Agora).

The Agora's showpiece was the **Stoa of Attalos II,** where Socrates once lectured and incited the youth of Athens to adopt his progressive ideas on mortality and morality. Today the Museum of Agora Excavations, this two-story building was first designed as a retail complex and erected in the 2nd century BC by Attalos, a king of Pergamum. The reconstruction in 1953–56 used Pendelic marble and creamy limestone from the original structure. The colonnade, designed for promenades, is protected from the blistering sun and cooled by breezes. The most notable sculptures, of historical and mythological figures from the 3rd and 4th centuries BC, are at ground level outside the museum.

On the low hill called Kolonos Agoraios in the Agora's northwest corner stands the best-preserved Doric temple in all Greece, the **Hephaistion,** sometimes called the Thission because of its friezes showing the exploits of Theseus. Like the other monuments, it is roped off, but you can walk

9

around it to admire its preservation. A little older than the Parthenon, it is surrounded by 34 columns and is 104 feet in length, and was once filled with sculptures (the only remnant of which is the mutilated frieze, once brightly colored). It never quite makes the impact of the Parthenon, in large part due to the fact that it lacks a noble site and can never be seen from below, its sun-matured columns towering heavenward. ✉ *3 entrances: from Monastiraki on Adrianou; from Thission on Apostolou Pavlou; and descending from Acropolis on Ayioi Apostoloi, Monastiraki* ☎ *210/321–0185* ⊕ *www.culture.gr* ✉ *€4; €12 Unification of Archaeological Sites ticket (includes Acropolis and Tower of the Winds)* ⊙ *Daily 8–3; museum Mon. 11–3, Tues.–Sun. 8–3* Ⓜ *Thiseio.*

Odeon of Herodes Atticus. Hauntingly beautiful, this ancient theater was built in AD 160 by the affluent Herodes Atticus in memory of his wife, Regilla. Known as the Irodion by Athenians, it is nestled Greek-style into the hillside, but with typically Roman arches in its three-story stage building and barrel-vaulted entrances. The circular orchestra has now become a semicircle, and the long-vanished cedar roof probably covered only the stage and dressing rooms, not the 34 rows of seats. The theater, which holds 5,000, was restored and reopened in 1955 for the Athens and Epidaurus Festival. To enter you must hold a ticket to one of the summer performances, which range from the Royal Ballet to ancient tragedies and Attic comedies usually performed in modern Greek. Contact the Festival's box office for ticket information. Children under 6 are not allowed except at some special performances. ✉ *Dionyssiou Areopagitou, near Propylaion, Acropolis* ☎ *210/324–1807* ⊕ *www. greekfestival.gr* ⊙ *Performances only* Ⓜ *Acropolis.*

Fodor's Choice
★
Tower of the Winds (*Aerides*). Surrounded by a cluster of old houses on the western slope of the Acropolis, the world-famous Tower of the Winds (Aerides), located inside the Roman Agora, is the most appealing and well preserved of the Roman monuments of Athens, keeping time since the 1st century BC. It was originally a sundial, water clock, and weather vane topped by a bronze Triton with a metal rod in his hand, which followed the direction of the wind. Its eight sides face the direction of the eight winds into which the compass was divided; expressive reliefs around the tower personify these eight winds, called *I Aerides* (the Windy Ones) by Athenians. Note the north wind, Boreas, blowing on a conch, and the beneficent west wind, Zephyros, scattering blossoms. ✉ *Roman Agora* ☎ *210/324–5220* ✉ *€2; €12 Unification of Archaeological Sites ticket (includes Acropolis and Ancient Agora).*

NEED A BREAK?
Vyzantino. Directly on Plaka's main square, Vyzantino is great for a good, reasonably priced bite to eat in the center of all the action. Try the *lahanodolmades* (stuffed cabbage leaves in egg and lemon sauce), the roast potatoes, or the stuffed oven chicken. ✉ *Kidathineon 18, Plaka* ☎ *210/322–7368* ⊕ *www.vyzantinorestaurant.gr* Ⓜ *Acropolis.*

O Glikis. Traditional-looking Glikis and its shady, far-from-the-madding-crowd courtyard are perfect for a Greek coffee or ouzo and a *mikri pikilia* (a small plate of appetizers, including cheese, sausage, olives, and dips). ⊠ *Aggelou Geronta 2, Plaka* ☎ *210/322–3925* ⊘ *10 am–1:30 am.*

FROM CENTRAL ATHENS TO NATIONAL ARCHAEOLOGICAL MUSEUM

ΑΘΗΝΑ (ΚΕΝΤΡΟ) ΤΟ ΕΘΝΙΚΟ ΑΡΧΑΙΟΛΟΓΙΚΟ ΜΟΥΣΕΙΟ

Sooner or later, everyone passes through the heart of modern Athens: spacious Syntagma Square (Constitution Square), which is surrounded by sights that span Athens's history from the days of the Roman emperors to King Otho's reign after the 1821 War of Independence, whose former palace is now the national Parliament. It is here, on this square, that the Evzone guards, dressed in their *foustanella* (pleated skirts), stand on duty at the Tomb of the Unknown Soldier. In many places in downtown Athens, the grand rubs elbows with the squalid. The cavernous, chaotic Central Market sits cheek-by-jowl with incense-scented, 12th-century Byzantine churches; they, in turn, are shadowed by hideous 1970s apartment blocks. The mix has become more heady as artists and fashionistas move to the neighborhoods of Kerameikos, Psirri, and Gazi and transform long-neglected warehouses into galleries, nightclubs, and ultrachic restaurants.

Head a good 10 blocks directly north of the Old University complex to find the glorious National Archaeological Museum. One of the most exciting collections of Greek antiquities in the world, this is a must-do for any travelers to Athens, nay, Greece. Here are the sensational finds made by Heinrich Schliemann, discoverer of Troy and father of modern archaeology, in the course of his excavations of the royal tombs on the Homeric site of Mycenae in the 1870s. Here, too, are world-famous bronzes such as the *Jockey of Artemision* and a bronze of Poseidon throwing a trident—or is it Zeus hurling a thunderbolt? Neighboring Kolonaki—the chic shopping district and one of the most fashionable residential areas—occupies the lower slopes of Mt. Lycabettus. Take the funicular ride to the top of the peak, three times the height of the Acropolis, as the view—pollution permitting—reveals that this center-city sector is packed with marvels and wonders.

9

FodorsChoice **Benaki Museum.** Greece's oldest private museum received a spectacular
★ face-lift in 2004, just before the Athens Olympics, with the addition of a hyper-modern wing that looks like it was airlifted in from New York City. Located on the gentrifying Pireos Street, this construction is all the more striking when compared to the main museum, set in an imposing neoclassic mansion in the posh Kolonaki neighborhood. Established in 1926 by an illustrious Athenian family, the Benaki was one of the first to place emphasis on Greece's later heritage at a time when many archaeologists were destroying Byzantine artifacts to access ancient objects. The permanent collection (more than 20,000 items are on display in 36 rooms, and that's only a sample of the holdings) moves chronologically from the ground floor upward, from prehistory to the formation of the modern Greek state.

The eye-popping new Benaki museum wing is located at 138 Pireos Street, one of the busiest and most industrially developed city axis. The minimalistic exterior is covered in smooth pink stone—a kind of beacon of modernity, clean lines, and creativity on the dusty, loud avenue. Inside, all is high-ceilinged atriums, walkway ascents, and multiple levels, a dramatic setting for the museum's temporary exhibitions (many of which are more avant-garde in character than the ones housed in the main building). ⊠ *Koumbari 1, Kolonaki* ☎ *210/367–1000* ⊕ *www. benaki.gr* ▧ *€7 (free Thurs.)* ⊙ *Wed. and Fri. 9–5, Thurs. and Sat. 9 am–midnight, Sun. 9–3* Ⓜ *Syntagma or Evangelismos.*

FAMILY
Fodor's Choice
★

Mt. Lycabettus. Myth claims that Athens's highest hill came into existence when Athena removed a piece of Mt. Pendeli, intending to boost the height of her temple on the Acropolis. While she was en route, a crone brought her bad tidings, and the flustered goddess dropped the rock in the middle of the city. Kids love the ride up the steeply inclined *teleferique* (funicular) to the summit (every 30 minutes), crowned by whitewashed **Ayios Georgios** chapel with a bell tower donated by Queen Olga. On a clear day, you can see Aegina island, with or without the aid of coin-operated telescopes. Built into a cave on the side of the hill, near the spot where the I Prasini Tenta café used to be, is a small shrine to **Ayios Isidoros.** ⊠ *Kolonaki* ⚓ *The base is a 15-min walk northeast of Syntagma Sq.; funicular runs every 30 mins (every 10 mins during rush hour) from corner of Ploutarchou and Aristippou (take Minibus No. 060 from Kanari or Kolonaki Sq.)* ☎ *210/721–0701 for funicular info* ▧ *Funicular €7 round-trip* ⊙ *Funicular daily 9 am–2:30 am.*

FAMILY
Fodor's Choice
★

Museum of Cycladic Art. Also known as the Nicholas P. and Dolly Goulandris Foundation, and funded by one of Greece's richest families, this museum has an outstanding collection of 350 Cycladic artifacts dating from the Bronze Age, including many of the enigmatic marble figurines whose slender shapes fascinated such artists as Picasso, Modigliani, and Brancusi. The main building is an imposing glass-and-steel design dating from 1985 and built to convey "the sense of austerity and the diffusion of refracted light that predominate in the Cycladic landscape," as the museum puts it. Along with Cycladic masterpieces, a wide array from other eras is also on view, ranging from the Bronze Age through the 6th century AD. The third floor is devoted to Cypriot art while the fourth floor showcases a fascinating exhibition on "scenes from daily life in antiquity." To handle the overflow, a new wing opened in 2005. A glass corridor connects the main building to the gorgeous 19th-century neoclassic Stathatos Mansion, where temporary exhibits are mounted. There is also a lovely skylit café in a courtyard centered around a Cycladic-inspired fountain, a charming art shop, and many children-oriented activities all year round. ⊠ *Neofitou Douka 4, Kolonaki* ☎ *210/722–8321 through 210/722–8323* ⊕ *www.cycladic. gr* ▧ *€7 (half-price Mon.)* ⊙ *Mon., Wed., Fri., Sat. 10–5, Thurs. 10–8, Sun. 11–5* Ⓜ *Evangelismos.*

Fodor's Choice
★

National Archaeological Museum. Many of the greatest achievements in ancient Greek sculpture and painting are housed here in the most important museum in Greece. Artistic highlights from every period of its ancient civilization, from Neolithic to Roman times, make this a treasure trove beyond compare. With a massive renovation completed, works (more than 11,000 of them) that have languished in storage for decades are now on view, reorganized displays are accompanied by enriched English-language information, and the panoply of ancient Greek art appears more spectacular than ever.

While the classic culture that was the grandeur of the Greek world no longer exists—it died, for civilizations are mortal—it left indelible markers in all domains, most particularly in art, and many of its masterpieces are on show here. The museum's most celebrated display is the **Mycenaean Antiquities.** Here are the stunning gold treasures from Heinrich Schliemann's 1876 excavations of Mycenae's royal tombs: the funeral mask of a bearded king, once thought to be the image of Agamemnon but now believed to be much older, from about the 15th century BC; a splendid silver bull's-head libation cup;

> ## FULL FRONTAL FASHION
>
> Near the Parliament, you can watch the changing of the Evzones guards at the Tomb of the Unknown Soldier—in front of Parliament on a lower level—which takes place at intervals throughout the day. On Sunday the honor guard of tall young men don a dress costume—a short white *foustanella* (kilt) with 400 neat pleats, one for each year of the Ottoman occupation, and red shoes with pompons—and still manage to look brawny rather than silly. A band accompanies them: they all arrive by 11:15 am in front of Parliament.

and the 15th-century BC Vaphio Goblets, masterworks in embossed gold. Mycenaeans were famed for their carving in miniature, and an exquisite example is the ivory statuette of two curvaceous mother goddesses, each with a child nestled on her lap.

Withheld from the public since they were damaged in the 1999 earthquakes, but not to be missed, are the beautifully restored **frescoes from Santorini,** delightful murals depicting daily life in Minoan Santorini. Along with the treasures from Mycenae, these wall paintings are part of the museum's Prehistoric Collection. ⊠ *28 Oktovriou (Patission) 44, Exarchia* ☎ *213/214–4800, 213/214–4891* ⊕ *www.namuseum.gr* 🖂 *€7* ☽ *Mon. 1–8, Tues.–Sat. 8–8, Sun. 8–3* Ⓜ *Victoria, then 10-min walk.*

Fodor's Choice ★ **Numismatic Museum Iliou Melathron.** Even those uninterested in coins might want to visit this museum for a glimpse of the former home of Heinrich Schliemann, who famously excavated Troy and Mycenae in the 19th century. Built by the Bavarian architect Ernst Ziller for the archaeologist's family and baptized the "Iliou Melanthron" (or Palace of Troy), it flaunts an imposing neo-Venetian facade. Inside are some spectacular rooms, including the vast and floridly decorated Hesperides Hall, ashimmer with colored marbles and neo-Pompeian wall paintings. Today, in this exquisite neoclassic mansion, seemingly haunted by the spirit of the great historian, you can see more than 600,000 coins; displays range from the archaeologist's own coin collection to 4th-century BC measures employed against forgers to coins grouped according to what they depict—animals, plants, myths, and famous buildings like the Lighthouse of Alexandria. ⊠ *Panepistimiou 12, Syntagma Sq.* ☎ *210/363–2057, 210/361–2834* ⊕ *www.nma.gr* 🖂 *€3* ☽ *Tues.–Sun. 8–5, Mon. 1–8* Ⓜ *Syntagma or Panepistimiou.*

9

Syntagma (Constitution) Square. At the top of the city's main square stands the Greek **Parliament,** formerly King Otto's (Othon's in Greek) royal palace, completed in 1838 for the new monarchy. It seems a bit austere and heavy for a southern landscape, but it was proof of progress, the symbol of the new ruling power. The building's saving grace is the stone's magical change of color from off-white to gold to rosy mauve as the day progresses. Here you can watch the **Changing of the Evzone Guards** at the **Tomb of the Unknown Soldier**—in front of Parliament on a lower level—which takes place at intervals throughout the day. On a wall behind the Tomb of the Unknown Soldier, the bas-relief of a dying soldier is modeled after a sculpture on the Temple of Aphaia in Aegina; the text is from the funeral oration said to have been given by Pericles. In recent years the square has become the new frontline of mass protests against harsh austerity measures and the ongoing economic crisis in Greece, as well as the base for the citizen movement of the "Indignants." ⊠ *Vasilissis Amalias and Vasilissis Sofias, Syntagma Sq.* Ⓜ *Syntagma.*

NEED A BREAK?

Ethnikon. Lovely cafés like Ethnikon have opened in the square as a result of the city's 2004 Olympic remodeling. This café-brasserie is shady, atmospheric, and has an excellent selection of desserts, including chocolate cake and homemade spoon sweets, or *glyka tou koutaliou.* ⊠ *Vas. Georgiou 2, Syntagma Sq.* ☎ *210/331–0676.*

Temple of Olympian Zeus. Begun in the 6th century BC, this gigantic temple was completed in AD 132 by Hadrian, who also commissioned a huge gold-and-ivory statue of Zeus for the inner chamber and another, only slightly smaller, of himself. Only 15 of the original Corinthian columns remain, but standing next to them may inspire a sense of awe at their bulk, which is softened by the graceful carving on the acanthus-leaf capitals. The clearly defined segments of a column blown down in 1852 give you an idea of the method used in its construction. The site is floodlighted on summer evenings, creating a majestic scene when you round the bend from Syngrou Ave. On the outskirts of the site to the north are remains of Roman houses, the city walls, and a Roman bath. Hellenic "neopagans" also use the site for ceremonies. Hadrian's Arch lies just outside the enclosed archaeological site. ⊠ *Vasilissis Olgas 1, National Garden* ☎ *210/922–6330* 🎟 *€2; €12 Unification of Archaeological Sites* ticket (includes Acropolis, Ancient Agora, and Tower of the Winds) ☉ *Tues.–Sun. 8:30–3* Ⓜ *Acropolis.*

WHERE TO EAT

Whether you sample octopus and ouzo in a 100-year-old taverna or cutting-edge cuisine in a trendy restaurant, dining in the city is just as relaxing as it is elsewhere in Greece. Athens's dining scene is experiencing a renaissance, with a particular focus on the intense flavors of regional Greek cooking. International options such as classic Italian and French still abound—and a recent Greek fascination with all things Japanese means that sushi is served in every happening bar in town—but today traditional and nouvelle Greek are the leading contenders for the Athenian palate. Traditional restaurants serve cuisine a little closer to what a Greek grandmother would make. Just follow your nose to find the classic authentic Athenian taverna—the one where wicker chairs inevitably pinch your bottom, checkered tablecloths are covered with butcher paper, wobbly tables need coins under one leg, and wine is drawn from the barrel.

$$
MODERN GREEK

🍴 **Aegli Zappiou.** The lush Zappeion Gardens have always been a tranquil green oasis for stressed-out Athenians, who head here to gaze at the distant views of the Parthenon and Temple of Olympian Zeus, catch an open-air cinema showing, or chill out at the landmark café Aegli Zappiou. Sharing the same premises as the café, this chic restaurant is luring fashionables, business people, and even families. It is a must during summer with its beautiful garden—shady in daytime, beautifully lighted at night. The food has a modern Greek touch, and it offers excellent value for money. Try the take on traditional local dishes as the Greek salad, fried zucchini balls, or the kebabs. The meat platter is another excellent choice. After dinner, have a drink and listen to the latest grooves at the Aegli bar. Reservations are recommended for dinner in the summer. [$] *Average main: €35* ✉ *Zappion Gardens, National Garden* ☎ *210/336–9364* 🌐 *www.aeglizappiou.gr.*

$$$$
CONTEMPORARY
Fodor's Choice ★

🍴 **Balthazar.** With its airy neoclassic mansion and leafy minimalist courtyard—paved with original painted tiles, canopied by huge date palms, and illuminated by colored lanterns—Balthazar truly feels like an summer oasis in the middle of Athens. The crowd is fun and hip, moneyed, cosmopolitan, and beautiful, so you might wish to come for dinner, then stay to mingle and taste the cocktails (like the passion fruit martini) as the DJ picks up the beat. Chef Christos Manousopoulos keeps the quality and flavor high on the up-to-the-minute Mediterranean menu, or you can try the Japanese creations of sushi chef Osakazu Yoshida. Opt for any of the creative appetizers (especially the "trilogy" of marinated tuna, salmon, and shrimp), the tasty main dishes (such as the sea bream with cherry tomatoes and capers sauce, as well as the various risottos), and the homemade desserts, especially the Napoleon Pavlova with fresh strawberries or the various sorbets and ice creams. Though it's been around for a decade, the place has miraculously managed to remain as fresh and trendy today as when it first opened. [$] *Average main: €40* ✉ *Tsoha 27, at Vournazou, Ambelokipi* ☎ *210/644–1215* 🌐 *www.balthazar.gr* ✍ *Reservations essential* ⏲ *No lunch.*

$$$
MEDITERRANEAN
Fodor's Choice ★

🍴 **Dionysos Zonars.** "Location, location, location" used to be the catchphrase that best summed up the raison d'être of this famously historic restaurant. It just happened to be the spot where movies were always filmed (those window views!), political treaties were signed, and tourists rested their feet after their heated Acropolis climbs. But a change of management and renovation work have lifted this legendary high-end restaurant up another notch. It now serves high-quality, traditional Greek and international dishes with a creative twist, such as *arnaki ambelourgou* (lamb wrapped in vine leaves, with melted cheese and vegetables) and *kritharoto me garides* (Greek pasta in tomato sauce with shrimp). The traditional syrupy *baklava* dessert is also exceptional. Extending all the good vibes, the adjoining café now serves breakfast and stays open until after midnight. $ *Average main: €30* ☒ *Robertou Galli 43, Makriyianni* ☎ *210/923–3182* ⊕ *www.dionysoszonars. gr* ⚑ *Reservations essential.*

$ ✕**Diporto.** It's the savvy local's treasured secret. Through the years,
GREEK everyone wandering around Omonia Square has come here for lunch—
butchers from the Central Market, suit-clad businessmen and lawyers,
artists, migrants, and even bejeweled ladies who lunch (and they're
often sitting at the same tables when it gets crowded). Owner-chef
Barba Mitsos keeps everyone happy with his handful of simple, delicious, and dirt-cheap homemade dishes. There's always an exceptional
horiatiki, sometimes studded with fiery-hot green pepperoncini; other
favorites are his buttery *gigantes* (large, buttery white beans cooked in
tomato sauce), *vrasto* (boiled goat, pork, or beef with vegetables), and
fried finger-size fish. Wine is drawn directly from the barrels lining the
walls. As for decor, the feeling is authentic '50s Athens. There is no sign
on the door: just walk down the staircase of this corner neoclassical
building. $ *Average main: €10* ☒ *Socratous 9, Platia Theatrou, Central
Market* ☎ *210/321–1463* ⊟ *No credit cards* ⊙ *Closed Sun. No dinner.*

$$ ✕**I Palia Taverna tou Psarra.** Founded way back in 1898, this is one of
SEAFOOD the few remaining Plaka tavernas serving reliably good food as well as
having the obligatory mulberry-shaded terrace (with live music every
day except Tuesday). The previous owners (the taverna is now run by
a well-known family of Greek restaurateurs) claimed to have served
Brigitte Bardot and Laurence Olivier, but it's the number of Greeks
who come here that testifies to Psarra's (aka the Fisherman's Tavern)
appeal. Oil-oregano marinated octopus and *gavros* (a small fish) are
good appetizers. Simple, tasty entrées include rooster in wine, *arnaki
pilino* (lamb baked in clay pots), and pork chops with ouzo. Can't make
up your mind? Try the *ouzokatastasi* ("ouzo situation"), a plate of tidbits to nibble while you decide. A bit hard to find, it's definitely worth
the effort. $ *Average main: €20* ☒ *Erechtheos 16 and Erotokritou 12,
Plaka* ☎ *210/321–8733* ⊕ *www.psaras-taverna.gr.*

$$ ✕**Kuzina.** Sleek, dazzlingly decorated, and moodily lit, this bistro
GREEK FUSION attracts many style-conscious Athenians. But Kuzina isn't just a pretty
Fodor's Choice face. The food—especially the inventive seafood and pasta dishes con-
★ cocted by chef Aris Tsanaklides—is among the best in Athens, standing
out on touristy Adrianou. Happily, the decor is almost as attractive as
the two three-course prix-fixe menus. Past an outdoor table setting,
the main room soars skyward, glittering with birdcage chandeliers and
factory ducts, with a vast lemon-yellow bar set below a spotlighted
wall lined with hundreds of wine bottles. The menu showcases new-
fangled Greek as well as old faves, including tuna tataki with caper
leaves, krittamo and wamake seaweed; yellow split-pea puree from
Santorini with caper leaves and tomato; and slow-roasted pork sea-
soned with lime, green apple, and cucumber. Whether you sit outside
on the street, in the spectacular main dining room, or opt for a table
on the roof (the *Tarazza* offers a fantastic view of the Acropolis and
some tasty cocktails), finish your meal off with a delicious dessert such
as the white-chocolate mousse with strawberries and rose meringue.

Greek Fast Food

The *souvlaki* is the original Greek fast food: spit-roasted or grilled meat, tomatoes, onions, and garlicky tzatziki wrapped in a pita to go. You can try it in some of its best variations at the bottom of Mitropoleos Street, in the center of Athens. Greeks on the go have always eaten street food such as the endless variations of cheese pie, *koulouri* (sesame-covered bread rings), roasted chestnuts or ears of corn, and palm-size paper bags of nuts. But modern lifestyles and the arrival of foreign pizza and burger chains have cultivated a taste for fast food—and spawned several local brands definitely worth checking out. Goody's serves burgers and spaghetti as well as some salads and sandwiches. Items like baguettes with grilled vegetables or seafood salads are seasonal additions to the menu. Everest is tops when it comes to "tost"–oval-shape sandwich buns with any combination of fillings, from omelets and smoked turkey breast to fries, roasted red peppers, and various spreads. It also sells sweet and savory pies, salads, ice cream, and desserts. Its main rival is Grigoris, a chain of sandwich and pie shops where you can also have a quick coffee on the go. If you want to sit down while you eat your food, look for a Flocafe Espresso Bar. Along with espresso, frappé, *filtro* (drip), and cappuccino, they also serve a selection of pastries and sandwiches, including brioche with mozzarella and pesto.

ⓢ *Average main: €25* ✉ *Adrianou 9, Thission* ☎ *210/324–0133* ⊕ *www. kuzina.gr* ♨ *Reservations essential.*

$$$
SEAFOOD ✕ **Orizontes Lycabettus.** Have a seat on the terrace atop Mt. Lycabettus: the Acropolis glitters below, and beyond, Athens unfolds like a map out to the Saronic Gulf. It's tough for the dining experience to compete with such a view, although this mostly seafood restaurant has a decent kitchen and better-than-decent service. Best bets include the chicken with artichokes and mushrooms in a lime sauce, or the grouper cheeks with risotto in a lemon sauce. For dessert, try the Greek version of walnut pie, *karydopita*. Remember that no road goes this high: the restaurant is reached by cable car (the ticket price of €7 is deductible from your restaurant bill). ⓢ *Average main: €35* ✉ *Mt. Lycabettus, Kolonaki* ☎ *210/722–7065* ⊕ *www.orizonteslycabettus.gr* ♨ *Reservations essential.*

$$
GREEK
Fodor's Choice
★
✕ **Strofi.** Walls lined with autographed photos of actors from the nearby Odeon of Herodes Atticus attest to Strofi's success with the after-the-ater crowd that flocks to the Greek festival. Despite the strong following among tourists, the renovated rooftop garden with dramatic views of the lighted Acropolis still attracts locals who have been coming here for decades. In fact, the amazing views come close to stealing the show, although the cuisine comes a very close second. Start with some mezedes, including the smoked eggplant salad or a velvety tzatziki, which perfectly complements the baked zucchini. Another good appetizer is fava, a puree of yellow split peas. For the main course, choose roast lamb wrapped in grape leaves and stuffed with cheese, the rooster

9

in wine sauce served with Greek pasta, perch filet à la Spetsiota, or a variety platter of specially grilled meats. Reservations are essential for the rooftop garden with the famed Acropolis view. $ *Average main: €20* ✉ *Rovertou Galli 25, Makriyianni* ☎ *210/921–4130* ⊕ *www.strofi. gr* ⚲ *Reservations essential* ⊙ *Closed Mon.*

$$ ✗ **Taverna Filippou.** This unassuming urban taverna is hardly the sort
GREEK of place you'd expect to find in chic Kolonaki, yet its devotees (since 1932) have included cabinet ministers, diplomats, actresses, and film directors. The appeal is simple, well-prepared Greek classics, mostly *ladera* (vegetable or meat casseroles cooked in an olive-oil-and-tomato sauce), *moussaka* (a baked dish of sliced eggplant layered with ground beef and smothered in a thin white sauce), and *pastitsio* (baked pasta with minced meat and a béchamel topping). Everything's home-cooked, so the menu adapts to what's fresh at the open-air produce market. In summer and on balmy spring or autumn evenings, choose a table on the pavement under the ivy; in winter, seating is in a cozy dining room a few steps below street level. $ *Average main: €20* ✉ *Xenokratous 19, Kolonaki* ☎ *210/721–6390* ⊙ *Closed Sun. and mid-Aug. No dinner Sat.*

$$$$ ✗ **To Varoulko.** Not one to rest on his Michelin star, acclaimed chef
SEAFOOD Lefteris Lazarou is constantly trying to outdo himself with magnificent
Fodor's Choice results. Rather than ordering from a menu, you can simply give him an
★ idea of what you like and let him create your seafood dish from what he found that day at the market. Among his most fabulous compilations are the orzo with crayfish flavored with Limnio wine, smoked red chili, and Parmesan; the white grouper with cherry tomatoes, sour apple, and smoked mashed potatoes; and the sea bream with red bell pepper sauce and ratatouille. Some dishes fuse traditional peasant fare like the flowers of courgettes with unusual flavors like framboise. In the summer, dinner is served on a rooftop terrace with a wonderful Acropolis view. $ *Average main: €150* ✉ *Pireos 80, Gazi* ☎ *210/522–8400* ⊕ *www.varoulko. gr* ⚲ *Reservations essential* ⊙ *Closed Sun. No lunch.*

WHERE TO STAY

Along with higher quality have come higher hotel prices: room rates in Athens are not much less than in many European cities. Still, there are bargains to be had. Paradoxically, you may get up to a 20% discount if you book the hotel through a local travel agent; it's also a good idea to bargain in person at smaller hotels, especially off-season. When negotiating a rate, bear in mind that the longer the stay, the lower the nightly rate.

$ ⊡ **Acropolis Select.** For only €10 more than many basic budget options,
HOTEL you get to stay in a slick-looking hotel with a lobby full of designer fur-
Fodor's Choice niture in the residential neighborhood of Koukaki, south of Filopappou
★ Hill, a 10-minute walk from the Acropolis, so not quite in the center of things. **Pros:** comfortable rooms; friendly staff; located in a pretty, low-key neighborhood; great value for money. **Cons:** no free Wi-Fi in the rooms; small elevator. $ *Rooms from: €70* ✉ *Falirou 37–39, Koukaki* ☎ *210/921–1610* ⊕ *www.acropoliselect.gr* ⤶ *72 rooms* ⊙| *Multiple meal plans.*

$$$$ HOTEL Fodor's Choice ★ 🏨 **Electra Palace.** If you want simple elegance, excellent service, and a great location, this is the hotel for you—rooms from the fifth floor up have a view of the Acropolis and in summer you can bask in the sunshine at the outdoor swimming pool as you take in the view of Athens's greatest monument or catch the sunset from the rooftop garden. **Pros:** gorgeous rooms; great location; outstanding service: early check-in available. **Cons:** pricey! [$] *Rooms from: €330* ✉ *Nikodimou 18–20, Plaka* ☎ *210/337–0000* 🌐 *www.electrahotels.gr* 🛏 *135 rooms, 20 suites* 🍴 *Breakfast.*

$$$$ HOTEL Fodor's Choice ★ 🏨 **Grande Bretagne.** With a guest list that includes more than a century's worth of royals, rock stars, and heads of state, the landmark Grande Bretagne remains the most exclusive hotel in Athens but as you marvel at one of the most eye-knocking views of the Acropolis from the terrace restaurant, or rest on custom-made silk ottomans in the lobby, or call your personal butler 24 hours a day from your room, you may very well think it is the very best. **Pros:** all-out luxury; beautiful rooms; excellent café, spa and pool lounge; central location. **Cons:** pricey, no free Wi-Fi. [$] *Rooms from: €320* ✉ *Vasileos Georgiou A'1 at Syntagma Sq., Syntagma Sq.* ☎ *210/333–0000, 210/331–5555 through 210/331–5559 for reservations* 🌐 *www.grandebretagne.gr* 🛏 *321 rooms, 56 suites* 🍴 *No meals.*

$ HOTEL 🏨 **Jason Inn.** Though it's on a run-down, seemingly out-of-the-way little corner, the modern Jason Inn is steps away from the buzzing nightlife districts of Psirri and Thission, not to mention the ancient Agora. **Pros:** strategic location; reasonable price. **Cons:** run-down neighborhood; rooms feel dated. [$] *Rooms from: €95* ✉ *Ayion Assomaton 12, Thission* ☎ *210/520–2491, 210/523–4721* 🌐 *www.douros-hotels.com* 🛏 *57 rooms* 🍴 *Breakfast.*

$$$$ HOTEL Fodor's Choice ★ 🏨 **King George Palace.** One of the most historic and luxurious hotels in Athens, the King George Palace has reopened its doors after an extensive renovation. **Pros:** beautiful design; high-luxe, opulent rooms; attentive service; outstanding food; 24-hour business center. **Cons:** slow elevators; thin walls in rooms. [$] *Rooms from: €235* ✉ *2 Vasileos Georgiou A, Syntagma Sq.* ☎ *210/322–2210* 🌐 *www.kinggeorgepalace.com* 🛏 *77 rooms, 25 suites* 🍴 *No meals.*

$$ HOTEL Fodor's Choice ★ 🏨 **The New Hotel.** Years in the making, the New Hotel was heralded as an aesthetic triumph in the inner city's ever-changing landscape when it opened in 2011, thanks to its five-star reviews and cutting-edge design. **Pros:** that "Dakis" touch; sleek design; helpful staff; free Wi-Fi in public areas; sumptuous breakfasts; central location. **Cons:** pricey pay-per-view TV; front-facing rooms can be noisy. [$] *Rooms from: €160* ✉ *Filellinon 16, Syntagma Sq.* ☎ *210/628–4800* 🌐 *www.yeshotels.gr* 🛏 *79 rooms and suites* 🍴 *Multiple meal plans.*

$$ HOTEL Fodor's Choice ★ 🏨 **Periscope.** This sleek concept hotel combines minimalist urban-chic design, amenity-filled rooms, and exceptional service for a truly relaxing experience—business travelers and urbane globe-trotters love the efficient service, spotless rooms, and the old-money, chic neighborhood of Kolonaki. **Pros:** great locale; eatery (PBox) created by award-winning chef; great breakfast; outstanding service. **Cons:** rooms are a bit on the small side and have limited views; only suites have balconies. [$] *Rooms*

from: €150 ✉ *Haritos 22, Kolonaki* ☎ *210/729–7200* 🌐 *www.periscope.gr* 🛏 *17 rooms, 4 suites* 🍴 *No meals.*

$$ HOTEL 🏨 **Plaka Hotel.** Comfortable, with deep-blue velvet curtains that match the upholstery on the wood-arm easy chairs, the guest rooms in this charming, central hotel are a comfortable place to rest while in the heart of old Athens. **Pros:** excellent location; diligent staff; good breakfast and lounge areas. **Cons:** small and sometimes stuffy rooms; no pets allowed. [$] *Rooms from: €125* ✉ *Kapnikareas 7 and Mitropoleos, Plaka* ☎ *210/322–2706* 🌐 *www.plakahotel.gr* 🛏 *67 rooms* 🍴 *Breakfast.*

NIGHTLIFE AND THE ARTS

From ancient Greek tragedies in quarried amphitheaters to the chicest disco clubs, Athens rocks at night. Several of the former industrial districts are enjoying a renaissance, most notably Gazi, a neighborhood surrounding Technopolis, a former 19th-century foundry-turned-arts complex. Today Gazi is synonymous with the hippest restaurants, edgiest galleries, and trendiest nightclubs in town, providing one-stop shopping for an evening's entertainment.

For all listings, consult the Greek pocket-size weekly *Athinorama* for current performances, gallery openings, and films, along with the monthly magazine *Athens Insider* and daily *Kathimerini,* inserted in the *International Herald Tribune,* available Monday through Saturday.

NIGHTLIFE

Athens's heady nightlife starts late. Most bars and clubs don't get hopping until midnight, and they stay open at the very least until 3 am. Often there is a cover charge on weekends at the most popular clubs, which also have bouncers. In summer many major downtown bars and clubs close their in-town location and move to the seaside. Ask your hotel for recommendations and summer closings. Few bars take credit cards for drinks.

BARS

Fodor's Choice ★ **Aliarman.** Hidden in one of the tiny backstreets of the popular district of Gazi is this cozy treasure. The converted workers' house has a fairytale vibe, with impressive floor mosaics, floral frescoes, and atmospheric lighting. Colorful cocktails include the apple martini, strawberry daiquiri, and mai tai—and you can also grab a bite to eat in the shabby-chic garden. ✉ *Sofroniou 2, Gazi* ☎ *210/342–6322* 🌐 *www.aliarman.gr.*

Stavlos. All ages feel comfortable at the bar in what used to be the Royal Stables. Sit in the courtyard or in the brick-wall restaurant for a snack like Cretan *kaltsounia* (similar to a calzone), or dance in the long bar. Stavlos often hosts art and jewelry exhibits, film screenings, miniconcerts, and other "happenings," as the Greeks call them, throughout the week. ✉ *Irakleidon 10, Thission* ☎ *210/345–2502, 210/346–7206* 🌐 *www.stavlos.gr.*

BOUZOUKIA

Many tourists think Greek social life centers on large clubs where live bouzouki music plays while patrons smash up the plates. Plate-smashing is now prohibited, but plates of flowers are sold for scattering over the performer or your companions when they take to the dance floor. Be aware that bouzoukia food is overpriced and often second-rate. There is normally a per-person minimum (€30) or a prix-fixe menu. For those who choose to stand at the bar, a drink runs about €15 to €20 at a good bouzoukia place.

Fever. One of Athens's most popular bouzoukia clubs showcases the biggest singers of the day, including Yiannis Parios, Sakis Rouvas, and Stamatis Gonidis. It's open Friday and Saturday, from September to June. ⊠ *Syngrou Ave. and Lagoumitzi 25, near Fix, Neos Kosmos* ☎ *210/921–7331* ⊕ *www.fever.gr.*

Iera Odos. Local pop and bouzouki stars regularly appear at this popular nightspot delivering all the joyous frenzy expected of a Greek-style night out. The club (open Thursday to Sunday) is packed on weekends as Athenians flock there to sing along with popular and traditional Greek music hits as well as some international tunes. ⊠ *Iera Odos 18–20, Gazi* ☎ *210/342–8272* ⊕ *www.ieraodos.gr.*

REMBETIKA

The Greek equivalent of the urban blues, rembetika is rooted in the traditions of Asia Minor and was brought to Greece by refugees from Smyrna in the 1920s and still enthralls clubgoers today. At these thriving clubs you can even join the dances. The two most common dances are the *zeimbekikos,* in which the man improvises in circular movements that become ever more complicated, and the belly-dance-like *tsifteteli.* Most of the clubs are closed in summer; call in advance. Food is often expensive and unexceptional; it's wisest to order a fruit platter or a bottle of wine.

Stoa Athanaton. "Arcade of the Immortals" has been around since 1930, housed in a converted warehouse in the meat-market area. Not much has changed since then. The music is enhanced by an infectious, devil-may-care mood and the enthusiastic participation of the audience, especially during the best-of rembetika afternoons (3:30–7:30). The small dance floor is always jammed. Food here is delicious and reasonably priced, but liquor is expensive. Make reservations for evening performances, when the orchestra is led by old-time rembetika greats. Open Saturday and Sunday (rembetika afternoons are held on Friday, Saturday, and Sunday). This landmark is closed in summer. ⊠ *Sofokleous 19, Central Market* ☎ *210/321–4362* ⊕ *www.rebetadiko-stoaathanaton.gr.*

Taximi. At one time or other, most of Greece's greatest rembetika musicians have played at this old-time live venue housed in an elegant neoclassical building (closed in summer); many of their black-and-white portraits and photos are on the smoke-stained walls. Not to be missed: the *Smyrnaika* music night every Tuesday, with old rembetika songs from Asia Minor. ⊠ *Isavron 29, at Harilaou Trikoupi, Exarchia* ☎ *210/363–9919.*

TAVERNAS WITH MUSIC

Kapnikarea. The ideal refreshing lunchtime spot to relax at after shopping on busy Ermou Street, Kapnikarea is named after the sunken Byzantine church that's next to it. Take in live rembetika music as you sip ouzo and savor traditional specialties and ethnic dishes inspired from owner Dimitris's world travels. ⊠ *Hristopoulou 2 and Ermou 57* ☎ *210/322–7394.*

Stamatopoulos Palia Taverna. This taverna has everything: good food, barrel wine, an acoustic band with three guitars, and bouzouki troupes playing old Athenian songs in an 1882 house. In summer the show moves to the garden. Whatever the season, Greeks will often get up and dance, beckoning you to join them (don't be shy). Live music starts at about 8:30 pm and goes on until 1 am. ⊠ *Lysiou 26, Plaka* ☎ *210/322–8722* ⊕ *www.stamatopoulostavern.gr.*

THE ARTS
CONCERTS, DANCE, AND OPERA

Fodor'sChoice **Dora Stratou Theater.** The country's leading folk dance company performs
★ exhilarating and sublime Greek folk dances (from all regions), as well as from Cyprus, in eye-catching authentic costumes in programs that change every two weeks. Performances are held Wednesday through Sunday from the end of May through September. Show times are at 9:30 pm, with shows on Saturday and Sunday at 8:15 pm. Tickets cost €15 and they can be purchased at the box office before the show (each performance lasts 90 minutes, with no intermission). ⊠ *Arakinthou and Voutie, Filopappou* ☎ *210/921–4650 for theater, 210/324–4395 for troupe's office* ⊕ *www.grdance.org.*

FESTIVALS

Fodor'sChoice **The Athens and Epidavros Festival.** The city's primary artistic event (for-
★ merly known as the Hellenic Festival) runs from June through August at a dozen venues, including the ancient Odeon of Herodes Atticus. The festival has showcased performers such as Norah Jones, Dame Kiri Te Kanawa, Luciano Pavarotti, and Diana Ross; such dance troupes as the Royal London Ballet, the Joaquin Cortes Ballet, and Maurice Béjart; symphony orchestras; and local groups performing ancient Greek drama. Usually a major world premier is staged during the festival. Starting in 2006, creative director Yiorgos Loukos rejuvenated the festival, adding more youthful venues and bringing a wider gamut of performances, including world musicians, modern dance, and multimedia artists. Prices range from €20 to as high as €120 for the big names; student and youth discounts are available. ⊠ *Odeon of Herodes Atticus, Dionyssiou Areopagitou, Acropolis* ☎ *210/928–2900 for info* ⊕ *www. greekfestival.gr* ⊠ *Festival box office, Panepistimiou 39, Syntagma Sq.* ☎ *210/928–2900 for info, 210/928–2952 for box office, 210/327–2000 for telephone bookings* ⊕ *www.greekfestival.gr.*

SHOPPING

For serious retail therapy, most natives head to the shopping streets that branch off central Syntagma and Kolonaki squares. Syntagma is the starting point for popular Ermou, a pedestrian zone where large, international brands like Zara, Esprit, and Marks & Spencer's have edged out small, independent retailers. You'll find local shops on streets parallel and perpendicular to Ermou: Mitropoleos, Voulis, Nikis, Perikleous, and Praxitelous among them. Much ritzier is the Kolonaki quarter, with boutiques and designer shops on fashionable streets like Anagnostopoulou, Tsakalof, Skoufa, Solonos, and Kanari.

Fodor'sChoice **Center of Hellenic Tradition.** The Center is an outlet for quality handi-
★ crafts—ceramics, weavings, sheep bells, wood carvings, prints, and old paintings. Take a break from shopping in the center's quiet and quaint I Oraia Ellas café, to enjoy a salad or mezedes in clear view of the Parthenon. Upstairs is an art gallery hosting temporary exhibitions of Greek art. ✉ *Mitropoleos 59 and Pandrossou 36, Monastiraki* ☎ *210/321–3023, 210/321–3842 for café* ⊕ *www.kelp.gr.*

Fodor'sChoice **Diplous Pelekys.** A large variety of handwoven articles, genuine folk art,
★ ceramics from all over Greece, and traditional and modern jewelry all on show here make excellent and affordable gifts. The cozy and tasteful shop is run by third-generation weavers and is the oldest folk art shop in Athens (established 1925). ✉ *Voulis 7 and Kolokotroni 3, inside Bolani Arcade, Syntagma Sq.* ☎ *210/322–3783* ⊕ *www.diplouspelekys.gr.*

Fodor'sChoice **Lalaounis.** This world-famous Greek jewelry house experiments with
★ its designs, taking ideas from nature, biology, African art, and ancient Greek pieces—the last are sometimes so close to the original that they're mistaken for museum artifacts. The pieces are mainly in gold, some in silver—look out for the decorative objects inspired by ancient Greek houseware. The famed tradition here started with Ilias Lalaounis (also founder of the Lalaounis Jewelry Museum) and is now proudly continued by his four daughters and grandchildren. ✉ *Panepistimiou 6 and Voukourestiou, Syntagma Sq.* ☎ *210/361–1371* ⊕ *www.lalaounis.gr* ✉ *Papadiamandi 7, Kifissia* ☎ *210/623–9000.*

Fodor'sChoice **Martinos.** Antiques collectors should head here to look for items such
★ as exquisite dowry chests, old swords, precious fabrics, and Venetian glass. You will certainly discover something you like in the four floors of this renovated antique shop that has been an Athens landmark over the past 100 years. ✉ *Pandrossou 5, Monastiraki* ☎ *210/321–3110* ⊕ *www. martinosart.gr* ✉ *Pindarou 24, Kolonaki* ☎ *210/360–9449* ⊕ *www. martinosart.gr.*

9

DELPHI AND THE APOLLO COAST ΔΕΛΦΟΙ

Athens is set between two of the most magnificent ancient sites in Greece. Masses of Athenians engulf the Apollo Coast—the stretch of shoreline that runs about 40 miles southeast of the city—to commune with the sea, frolic at lavish resorts like Glyfada and Vouliagmeni, and visit the fabled Temple of Poseidon. Perched atop a cliff at Sounion, this is a coastal site where thousands of travelers have come to "ooh" and "ahh" (including Lord Byron, who in a fit of ego, carved his name on one of the temple's columns). Heading westward from Athens for about 120 miles brings you to spectacular Delphi, the center of the universe for the ancients and one of the most beautiful and revered sites for lovers of antiquity. Heading out from Athens, bus excursion companies specialize in ferrying travelers to these sights, two great trophies for any sightseer to bag on their trip to Greece.

PLANNING YOUR TIME

The trip out to Sounion is the most famous day-trip of all from Athens, but if you want to overnight there is a wide array of hotels here. Below the temple is one of Greece's most famous beaches, so allot some hours for sun worshipping if you so desire. As for Delphi, stunning mountain scenery, a world-famous archaeological site, and an excellent museum can easily add up to two full days. If you day-trip it, get an early start from Athens, as the trip can last as long as four hours by car. Numerous bus companies run day-trip excursions to the site, but to truly savor the spectacle opt for an overnight.

GETTING HERE AND AROUND

Orange KTEL buses (2-hour trip) leave for Sounion from the Mavro-mateon terminal (28 Oktovriou, at Platía Aigyptou) and Platía Klafth-monos (on Odos Stadiou, between Syntagma and Omonia squares). Take a *paraliakó* (coastal) rather than a *mesoyiakó* (inland) bus, as they're faster and more scenic. Other than the private bus excursion companies offering day trips to Delphi—CHAT and Key Tours are among the most popular—take a KTEL bus (3 hours, about €16), which serves western Attica from Terminal B in Athens (to get to Terminal B from downtown Athens, catch Bus No. 24 on Amalias in front of the National Garden; tickets for these buses are sold only at this terminal, so book seats well in advance during high season). The bus stops at the site, but if you want to ensure a seat on the bus, walk the 2 km (1 mile) back from the ruins to the "bus station" (a table in a taverna) on the far side of modern Delphi.

Contacts Athens Terminal B ✉ *Liossion 260, Kato Patissia* ☎ *210/831–7096 for Delphi, 210/831–7173 for Livadia (Osios Loukas via Distomo).* **KTEL Delphi and Arachova** ✉ *260 Liossion Ave., Peristeri* ☎ *210/831–7096, 6936/648–239 for agent's mobile* ⊕ *www.ktel-fokidas.gr.* **KTEL Sounion** ✉ *Mavromateon St. at Egyptou Sq., Pedion Areos* ☎ *210/880–8081, 210/880–8080 for info* ⊕ *www.ktelattikis.gr.*

TOURS

CHAT and Key Tours have the best service and guides, plus comfortable air-conditioned buses. Taking a half-day trip to the breathtaking Temple of Poseidon at Sounion (€43) avoids the hassle of dealing with the crowded public buses or paying a great deal more for a taxi. A one-day tour to Delphi with lunch costs €101, but the two-day tour (€132) gives you more time to explore this wonder.

Contacts CHAT ✉ *Xenofontos 9, Syntagma* ☎ *210/322–3137* ⊕ *www.chatours.gr.* **Key Tours** ☎ *210/923–3166* ⊕ *www.keytours.gr.*

DELPHI ΔΕΛΦΟΙ

10 km (6 miles) west of Arachova, 189 km (118 miles) northwest of Athens.

Nestled in the mountain cliffs, modern Delphi is perched dramatically on the edge of a grove leading to the sea, west of an extraordinary ancient site. Ancient Delphi, the home of a famous oracle in antiquity, can be seen from the town's hotels or terraced village houses. It's easily reached from almost any point in the central town, at most a 5- to 10-minute walk. When the archaeological site is first seen from the road, it would appear that there is hardly anything left to attest to the existence of the ancient religious city. Only the Treasury of the Athenians and a few other columns are left standing, but once you are within the precincts, the plan becomes clearer and the layout is revealed in such detail that it is not impossible to conjure up a vision of what the scene must have once been when Delphi was the holiest place in all Greece.

According to Plutarch, who was a priest of Apollo at Delphi, the famous oracle was discovered by chance, when a shepherd noticed that his flock went into a frenzy when it came near a certain chasm in the rock. When he approached, he also came under a spell and began to utter prophecies, as did his fellow villagers. Eventually a *Pythia,* an anointed woman over 50 who lived in seclusion, was the one who sat on the three-footed stool and interpreted the prophecy. During the 8th and 7th centuries BC, the oracle's advice played a significant role in the colonization of southern Italy and Sicily (Magna Graecia) by Greece's Amphictyonic League. Increasingly an international center, Delphi attracted supplicants from beyond the Greek mainland, including such valued clients as King Midas and King Croesus, both hailing from Asia Minor. During this period of prosperity many cities built treasure houses at Delphi.

Fodor's Choice **Ancient Delphi.** After a square surrounded by late-Roman porticoes, pass
★ through the main gate to Ancient Delphi and continue on to the **Sacred Way,** the approach to the Altar of Apollo. Walk between building foundations and bases for votive dedications, stripped now of ornament and statue, mere scraps of what was one of the richest collections of art and treasures in antiquity. Thanks to the 2nd-century AD writings of Pausanias, archaeologists have identified treasuries built by the Thebans, the Corinthians, the Syracusans, and others—a roster of 6th- and 5th-century BC powers. The **Treasury of the Athenians,** on your left as you turn right, was built with money from the victory over the Persians at Marathon. The **Stoa of the Athenians,** northeast of the treasury, housed, among other objects, an immense cable with which the Persian king Xerxes roped together a pontoon bridge for his army to cross the Hellespont from Asia to Europe.

The **Temple of Apollo** visible today (there were three successive temples built on the site) is from the 4th century BC. Although ancient sources speak of a chasm within, there is no trace of that opening in the earth from which emanated trance-inducing vapors. Above the temple is the well-preserved **theater,** which seated 5,000. It was built in the 4th century BC, restored in about 160 BC, and later was restored again by the Romans. From a sun-warmed seat on the last tier, you see a panoramic bird's-eye view of the sanctuary and the convulsed landscape that encloses it. Also worth the climb is the view from the **stadium** still farther up the mountain, at the highest point of the ancient town. Built and restored in various periods and cut partially from the living rock, the stadium underwent a final transformation under Herodes Atticus, the Athenian benefactor of the 2nd century AD. It lies cradled in a grove of pine trees, a quiet refuge removed from the sanctuary below and backed by the sheer, majestic rise of the mountain. Markers for the

9

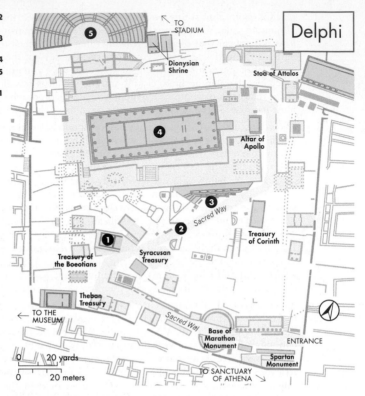

starting line inspire many to race the length of the stadium. ✉ *Road to Arachova, immediately east of modern Delphi* ☎ *22650/82312* ⊕ *www.culture.gr* 🎫 *€6; €9 combination ticket (includes museum, and Sanctuary of Athena)* ⊙ *Daily 9–4 (last entry at 3:40).*

Fodor'sChoice
★ **Delphi Museum.** Visiting this museum is essential to understanding the site and sanctuary's importance to the ancient Greek world, which considered Delphi its center (literally—look for the copy of the *omphalos*, or Earth's navel, a sacred stone from the adytum of Apollo's temple.) The museum is home to a wonderful collection of art and architectural sculpture, principally from the Sanctuaries of Apollo and Athena Pronoia. Curators have used an additional 15,000 square feet of museum space, opened in 2004, to create contextual, cohesive exhibits. You can now view all the pediments from Apollo's temple together and new exhibits include a fascinating collection of 5th-century BC votives.

One of the greatest surviving ancient bronzes on display commands a prime position in a spacious hall, set off to advantage by special lighting: the *Charioteer* is a sculpture so delicate in size (but said to be scaled to life) it is surprising when you see it in person for the first time. Created in about 470 BC, the human figure is believed to have stood on a terrace wall above the Temple of Apollo, near which it was found in 1896. It was part of a larger piece, which included a four-horse chariot. ✉ *East of Ancient Delphi* ☎ *22650/82313* 🌐 *www.culture.gr* 🎟 *€6; €9 combination ticket (includes Ancient Delphi site and Sanctuary of Athena)* 🕒 *Daily 9–4 (last entry at 3:40).*

Sanctuary of Athena. Start your tour of the old Delphi in the same way the ancients did, with a visit to the Sanctuary of Athena. Pilgrims who arrived on the shores of the bay of Itea proceeded up to the sanctuary, where they paused before going on to the Ancient Delphi site. The most notable among the numerous remains on this terrace is the **Tholos** (Round Building), a graceful 4th-century BC ruin of Pendelic marble, the purpose and dedication of which are unknown, although round templelike buildings were almost always dedicated to a goddess. By the 2nd millennium BC, the site was already a place of worship of the earth goddess Gaia and her daughter Themis, one of the Titans. The gods expressed themselves through the murmuring of water flooding from the fault, from the rustle of leaves, and from the booming of earth tremors. The Tholos remains one of the purest and most exquisite monuments of antiquity. Theodoros, its architect, wrote a treatise on his work: an indication in itself of the exceptional architectural quality of the monument. Beneath the Phaedriades, in the cleft between the rocks, a path leads to the **Castalian Fountain,** a spring where pilgrims bathed to purify themselves before continuing. (Access to the font is prohibited because of the danger of falling rocks.) On the main road, beyond the Castalian Fountain, is the modern entrance to the sanctuary. ✉ *Below road to Arachova, before Phaedriades* 🎟 *€6; €9 combination ticket (includes Ancient Delphi site and museum)* 🕒 *Daily 9–4 (last entry at 3:40).*

WHERE TO EAT

$$ GREEK

🍴 **Taverna Vakchos.** Owner Ilias Theorodakis, his wife, and their two sons keep a watchful eye on the kitchen and on the happiness of their customers. Choose to eat in the spacious dining room or out on the large sheltered veranda with vines growing across the balcony rail, a Bacchus-theme wall painting, and a stunning valley view. The menu is heavy on meat dishes, either grilled, boiled, or simmered in the oven, but vegetarians can put together a small feast from boiled greens and other homemade meatless Greek classics, like sweet peas in tomato sauce. Seasonal dishes in the winter season include game such as hare and, if you're really lucky, venison. Service is especially efficient and friendly, as are prices. [$] *Average main: €16* ✉ *Apollonos 31* ☎ *22650/83186* 🌐 *www.vakhos.com.*

WHERE TO STAY

$$ HOTEL Fodor's Choice ★

🏨 **Amalia Hotel Delphi.** Clean-cut retro chic predominates at this 1965 landmark built by well-known Greek architect Nikos Valsamakis as a part of one of the country's oldest hotel chains—one look reveals the sleek, modern, low-lying hotel blending seamlessly with 35 acres of hotel gardens which spread down the mountainside to the olive groves and pines of surrounding Delphi with, in the distance, a breathtaking vista of Itea port and the Corinthian bay. **Pros:** great vintage architecture and decoration; charming gardens and public areas; nice variety of breakfast buffet options; free Wi-Fi in the lobby. **Cons:** a bit off-center of town compared to other hotels; caters mostly to tour groups; slightly impersonal service. [$] *Rooms from: €100* ✉ *Apollonos 1 and Osiou Louka 47* ☎ *22650/82101, 210/607–2000 in Athens* 🌐 *www.amaliahoteldelphi.gr* 🛏 *184 rooms* 🍴 *Breakfast.*

$ B&B/INN 🏨 **Fedriades.** This hotel in the center of Delphi was purchased by the family that all runs the hotels Epikouros and Acropole, and their renovation work has created a simple, functional look accented by warm colors and a touch of Greek mountain style, while avoiding the "ancient kitsch" of other nearby hotels. **Pros:** spic-and-span cleanliness; convenient location for sightseeing. **Cons:** smallish rooms; can be noisy due to traffic on the main street; somewhat dated furniture. [$] *Rooms from: €70* ✉ *Karamanli 46* ☎ *22650/82370* 🌐 *www.fedriades.com* 🛏 *21 rooms, 3 suites* 🍴 *Breakfast.*

SOUNION ΣΟΥΝΙΟ

70 km (44 miles) southeast of Athens.

Poised at the edge of a rugged 195-foot cliff, the Temple of Poseidon hovers between sea and sky, its "marble steep, where nothing save the waves and I may hear mutual murmurs sweep" unchanged in the centuries since Lord Byron penned these lines. Today the archaeological site at Sounion is one of the most photographed in Greece. There is a tourist café-restaurant by the temple, and a few minimarts are on the road, but no village proper. Arrange your visit so that you enjoy the panorama of sea and islands from this airy platform either early in the morning, before the summer haze clouds visibility and the tour groups arrive, or at dusk, when the promontory has one of the most spectacular sunset vantage points in Attica. The Cape of Sounion was called the "sacred headland" by Homer. From here Aegeus, legendary king of Athens, threw himself off the cliff when he saw his son's ship approaching flying a black flag. Theseus, in fact, had forgotten to change his ship's sails from black to white—the signal that his mission had succeeded. To honor Aegeus, the Greeks named their sea, the Aegean, after him.

Fodor's Choice ★ **Temple of Poseidon.** Although the columns at the Temple of Poseidon appear to be gleaming white from a distance in the full sun, when you get closer you can see that they are made of gray-veined marble, quarried from the Agrileza valley 2 km (1 mile) north of the cape, and have 16 flutings rather than the usual 20. Climb the rocky path that roughly follows the ancient route, and beyond the scanty remains of an ancient *propylon* (gateway), you enter the temple compound. On your left is the *temenos* (precinct) of Poseidon, on your right, a *stoa* (arcade) and rooms. The temple itself (now roped off) was commissioned by Pericles, the famous leader of Greece's golden age. It was probably designed by Ictinus, the same architect who helped design the Temple of Hephaistos in the ancient Agora of Athens, and was built between 444 and 440 BC. The people here were considered Athenian citizens, the sanctuary was Athenian, and Poseidon occupied a position second only to Athena herself. The badly preserved frieze on the temple's east side is thought to have depicted the fight between the two gods to become patron of Athens.

The temple was built on the site of an earlier cult to Poseidon; two colossal statues of youths, carved more than a century before the temple's construction (perhaps votives to the god), were discovered in early excavations. Both now reside at the National Archaeological Museum in Athens. The 15 Doric columns that remain stand sentinel over the Aegean, visible from miles away. Lord Byron had a penchant for carving his name on ancient monuments, and you can see it and other graffiti on the right corner pillar of the portico. The view from the summit is breathtaking. In the slanting light of the late-afternoon sun, the landmasses to the west stand out in sharp profile: the bulk of Aegina backed by the mountains of the Peloponnese. To the east, on a clear day, one can spot the Cycladic islands of Kea, Kythnos, and Serifos. On the land side, the slopes of the acropolis retain traces of the fortification walls. ⊠ *Cape Sounion* ☎ *22920/39363* ⊕ *www.culture.gr* 🖃 *€4* ☾ *Daily 9:30 am–dusk.*

MYKONOS ΜΥΚΟΝΟΣ

The magical words "Greek Islands" conjure up beguiling images. If for you they suggest blazing sun and sea, bare rock and mountains, olive trees and vineyards, white rustic architecture and ancient ruins, fresh fish and fruity oils, the Cyclades are isles of quintessential plenty, the ultimate Mediterranean archipelago. Set in the heart of the Grecian Mediterranean, the nearly 2,000 islands and islets are scattered like a ring (*Cyclades* is the Greek word for "circling ones") around the sacred isle of Delos, birthplace of the god Apollo. Closer to Athens than Santorini, Mykonos is one of the most famous and beloved Greek islands. In a magnificent fusion of sunlight, stone, and sparkling aqua sea, it offers both culture and hedonism: ancient sites, Byzantine castles and museums, lively nightlife, shopping, dining, and beaches plain and fancy. Many people start off their island adventure in the famed town of Mykonos, where whitewashed houses huddle together against the *meltemi* winds and backpackers rub elbows with millionaires in the glorious mazelike white marble streets. Beaches on Mykonos are generally better than those on Santorini as well.

PLANNING YOUR TIME

The experience of Mykonos is radically different in summer than in winter. In summer all services are operating on overload, the beaches are crowded, the clubs noisy, the restaurants packed, and the scene swinging. Walkers, nature lovers, and devotees of classical and Byzantine Greece would do better to come in spring and fall, ideally in late April–June or September and October, when temperatures are lower and tourists are fewer. But off-season travel means less frequent boat service; in winter many shops, hotels, and restaurants are closed, and the open cafés are full of locals recuperating from summer's intensities. While it is true that feverish partying can overwhelm the young in summer, other seasons allow for temptations that are fewer, gentler, and more profound.

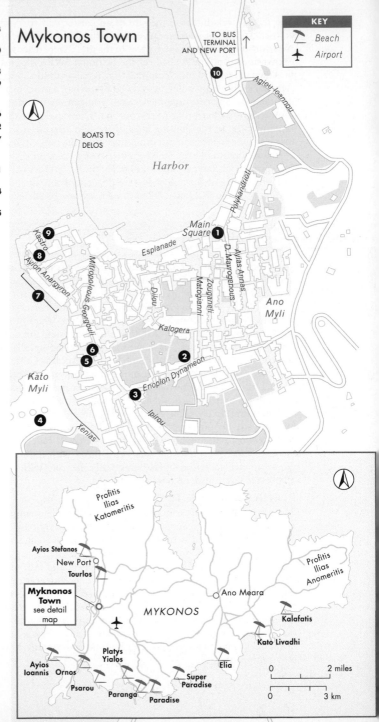

Mykonos Town

KEY

Beach

Airport

TO BUS TERMINAL AND NEW PORT

Harbor

BOATS TO DELOS

Main Square 1

Esplanade

Ano Myli

Kastro 9

Ayion Anargyron 8

7

Mitropoleous Georgouli

Diliou

Kalogera

Polikandrioti

Agiou Ioannou

Ayias Annas

D. Mavrogenous

Zouganeli

Matogianni

6
5

2

3 Enoplon Dynameon

Ipirou

Xenias

Kato Myli

4

10

Profitis Ilias Katomeritis

Ayios Stefanos

New Port

Tourlos

Myknonos Town see detail map

Ano Meara

Profitis Ilias Anomeritis

Kalafatis

Kato Livadhi

MYKONOS

Ayios Ioannis

Ornos

Platys Yialos

Psarou

Paranga

Paradise

Super Paradise

Elia

0   2 miles

0   3 km

GETTING HERE AND AROUND

AIR TRAVEL

Olympic Airways has six flights daily to Mykonos (10 daily during peak tourist season). During the summer months (July to mid-September) Olympic Airways also has three 25-minute-long flights per week connecting Mykonos and Santorini. The Olympic Airways offices in Mykonos are at the port and at the airport. Aegean Airlines has three daily flights to Mykonos.

Contacts Aegean Airlines ☎ *210/626–1000 from a mobile phone or abroad, 801/11–20000 within Greece* ⊕ *www.aegeanair.com.* **Olympic Airways** ✉ *Port, Mykonos Town* ☎ *22890/22490, 22890/22495* ⊕ *www.olympicair.com* ✉ *Ayia Athanassiou, Santorini, Fira* ☎ *22860/22493, 22860/22793.* **Mykonos Airport** ✉ *4 km (2½ miles) southeast of Mykonos town* ☎ *22890/79000.*

FERRY TRAVEL

In summer there are two to three ferries daily to Mykonos from Piraeus port in Athens, as well as the faster speed ferries. There are daily departures via ferry and the faster sea jets to Santorini. Check which dock they leave from, as there are both new and old docks. For complete information, consult travel agencies in town and in Athens.

BUS TRAVEL

On Mykonos itself, the main bus station is at Ayios Loukas in the Fabrica quarter at the south end of town.

Contacts Mykonos KTEL Buses ✉ *Ayios Loukas, Fabrica, Mykonos Town* ☎ *22890/23360, 22890/26797.*

TOURS

Windmills Travel takes a group every morning for a day tour of the sacred isle of Delos (€43). The company also has half-day guided tours of the Mykonos beach towns, with a stop in Ano Mera for the Panayia Tourliani Monastery (€28). Windmills arranges private tours of Delos and Mykonos and off-road jeep trips (cost varies according to number of participants).

Contacts Windmills Travel ✉ *Main Square, Mykonos Town* ☎ *22890/26555, 22890/23877* ⊕ *www.windmillstravel.com.*

MYKONOS TOWN ΜΥΚΟΝΟΣ (ΧΩΡΑ)

Put firmly on the map by Jackie O in the 1960s, Mykonos Town—called Hora by the locals—remains the St-Tropez of the Greek islands. The scenery is memorable, with its whitewashed streets, Little Venice, the Kato Myli ridge of windmills, and Kastro, the town's medieval quarter. Its cubical two- or three-story houses and churches, with their red or blue doors and domes and wooden balconies, have been long celebrated as some of the best examples of classic Cycladic architecture. Luckily, the Greek Archaeological Service decided to preserve the town, even when the Mykonians would have preferred to rebuild, and so the authentic Old Town has been impressively preserved. Pink oleander, scarlet hibiscus, and trailing green pepper trees form a contrast amid the dazzling whiteness, whose frequent renewal with whitewash is required by law.

EXPLORING

Aegean Maritime Museum. The charming Aegean Maritime Museum contains a collection of model ships, navigational instruments, old maps, prints, coins, and nautical memorabilia. The backyard garden displays some old anchors and ship wheels and a reconstructed 1890 lighthouse, once lighted by oil. ⊠ *10 Enoplon Dynameon* ☎ *22890/22700* ⊡ *€4* ⊙ *Daily 10:30–1 and 6:30–9.*

Archaeological Museum. Before setting out on the mandatory boat excursion to the isle of Delos, check out the Archaeological Museum, set at the northern edge of town. It affords insight into the intriguing history of its ancient shrines. The museum houses Delian funerary sculptures, many with scenes of mourning; most were moved to Rhenea when the Athenians cleansed Delos in the 6th century, during the sixth year of the Peloponnesian war, and, under instruction from the Delphic Oracle, the entire island was purged of all dead bodies. The most significant work from Mykonos is a 7th-century BC *pithos* (storage jar), showing the Greeks in the Trojan horse and the sack of the city. ⊠ *Ayios Stefanos between boat dock and town* ☎ *22890/22325* ⊡ *€2* ⊙ *April–Oct., Tues.–Sun. 8–3.*

Fodor's Choice ★ **Church of Paraportiani** (*Our Lady of the Postern Gate*). Mykonians claim that exactly 365 churches and chapels dot their landscape, one for each day of the year. The most famous of these is the Church of Paraportiani. The sloping, whitewashed conglomeration of four chapels, mixing Byzantine and vernacular idioms, looks fantastic. It is solid and ultimately sober, and its position on a promontory facing the sea sets off the unique architecture. ⊠ *Ayion Anargyron near folk museum.*

Fodor's Choice ★ **Delos.** Arrive at the mythical, magical, and magnificent site of Delos (6 nautical miles southwest of Mykonos) and you might wonder how this barren islet, which has virtually no natural resources, became the religious and political center of the Aegean. One answer is that Dhílos (to use the Modern Greek transliteration) provided the safest anchorage for vessels sailing between the mainland and the shores of Asia; another answer is that it had no other use. A third is provided if you climb Mt. Kynthos to see that the isle (which is not more than 5 km long and 1 km wide) is shielded on three sides by other islands. Indeed, this is how the Cyclades—the word means "circling ones"—got their name: they circle around the sacred island.

By 1000 BC the Ionians, who inhabited the Cyclades, had made Delos their religious capital. Homeric Hymn 3 tells of the cult of Apollo in

---

THE PRANCE OF THE PELICAN

By the time morning's open-air fish market picks up steam in Mykonos Town, Petros the Pelican—the town mascot—preens and cadges eats. In the 1950s a group of migrating pelicans passed over Mykonos, leaving behind a single exhausted bird; the fisherman Vassilis nursed it back to health, and locals say that the pelican in the harbor is the original Petros (though there are several, and pelicans generally live a maximum of 25 years).

the 7th century BC. One can imagine the elegant Ionians, whose central festival was here, enjoying the choruses of temple girls—"Delian *korai,* who serve the Far-Shooter"—singing and dancing their hymn and displaying their graceful tunics and jewelry. But a difficult period began for the Delians when Athens rose to power and assumed Ionian leadership. In 543 BC an oracle at Delphi conveniently decreed that the Athenians purify the island by removing all the graves to Rhenea, a dictate designed to alienate the Delians from their past.

After the defeat of the Persians in 478 BC, the Athenians organized the Delian League, with its treasury and headquarters at Delos (in 454 BC the funds were transferred to the Acropolis in Athens). Delos had its most prosperous period in late Hellenistic and Roman times, when it was declared a free port and quickly became the financial center of the Mediterranean, the focal point of trade, where 10,000 slaves were sold daily. Foreigners from as far as Rome, Syria, and Egypt lived in this cosmopolitan port, in complete tolerance of one another's religious beliefs, and each group built its various shrines. But in 88 BC Mithridates, the king of Pontus, in a revolt against Roman rule, ordered an attack on the unfortified island. The entire population of 20,000 was killed or sold into slavery. Delos never fully recovered, and later Roman attempts to revive the island failed because of pirate raids. After a second attack in 69 BC, Delos was gradually abandoned.

In 1872, the French School of Archaeology began excavating on Delos—a massive project, considering that much of the island's 4 square km (1½ square mile) is covered in ruins. The work continues today. Delos remains dry and shadeless; off-season, the snack bar is often closed and most guards leave on the last boat to Mykonos in the early afternoon. But if on the way to Mykonos you see dolphins leaping (it often happens), you'll know Apollo is about and approves.

The **Sacred Way,** east of the agora, was the route, during the holy Delian festival, of the procession to the Sanctuary of Apollo. The **Propylaea,** at the end of the Sacred Way, were once a monumental white marble gateway with three portals framed by four Doric columns. Beyond the Propylaea is the Sanctuary of Apollo; though little remains today, when the Propylaea were built in the mid-2nd century BC, the sanctuary was crowded with altars, statues, and temples—three of them to Apollo. Inside the sanctuary and to the right is the **House of the Naxians,** a 7th- to 6th-century BC structure with a central colonnade. Dedications to Apollo were stored in this shrine. Outside the north wall a massive rectangular **pedestal** once supported a colossal statue of Apollo (one of the hands is in Delos's Archaeological Museum, and a piece of a foot is in the British Museum).

Southeast of the Sanctuary of Apollo are the ruins of the **Sanctuary of the Bulls,** an extremely long and narrow structure built, it is thought, to display a trireme, an ancient boat with three banks of oars, dedicated to Apollo by a Hellenistic leader thankful for a naval victory. Maritime symbols were found in the decorative relief of the main halls, and the head and shoulders of a pair of bulls were part of the design of an interior entrance. A short distance north of the Sanctuary of the Bulls is an oval indentation in the earth where the **Sacred Lake** once sparkled. It is surrounded by a stone wall that reveals the original periphery. According to islanders, the lake was fed by the river Inopos from its source high on Mt. Kynthos until 1925, when the water stopped flowing and the lake dried up. One of the most evocative sights of Delos is the 164-foot-long **avenue of the Lions.** These are replicas; the originals are in the museum. The five Naxian marble beasts crouch on their haunches, their forelegs stiffly upright, vigilant guardians of the Sacred Lake. They are the survivors of a line of at least nine lions, erected in the second half of the 7th century BC by the Naxians. One, removed in the 17th century, now guards the Arsenal of Venice (though with a later head). Northeast of the palaestras is the **gymnasium,** a square courtyard nearly 131 feet long on each side. A road south from the gymnasium leads to the **tourist pavilion,** which has a meager restaurant and bar. The **Archaeological Museum** is also on the road south of the gymnasium; it contains most of the antiquities found in excavations on the island: monumental statues of young men and women, stelae, reliefs, masks, and ancient jewelry.

Immediately to the right of the museum is a small **Sanctuary of Dionysus,** erected about 300 BC. Outside it is one of the more-boggling sights of ancient Greece: several monuments dedicated to Apollo by the winners of the choral competitions of the Delian festivals, each decorated with a huge phallus, emblematic of the orgiastic rites that took place during the Dionysian festivals. Around the base of one of them is carved a lighthearted representation of a bride being carried to her new husband's home. A marble phallic bird, symbol of the body's immortality, also adorns this corner of the sanctuary. Floor mosaics of snakes, panthers, birds, dolphins, and Dionysus channeled rainwater into cisterns below; the best-preserved can be seen in the **House of the Dolphins,** the **House of the Masks,** and the **House of the Trident.** A flight of steps goes up 368 feet to the summit of **Mt. Kynthos** (after which all Cynthias are named), on whose slope Apollo was born.

⚠ **The island has no shade, so don't forget to bring a hat, your sunscreen, and plenty of water.** ✉ *Accessible only by boat from Mykonos Town, Delos* ☎ *22890/22259 for archaelogical museum, 22890/22218 for departures info* ⊕ *www.culture.gr* 💶 *€5* ⊗ *Tues.–Sun. 8–3.*

Folk Museum. Housed in an 18th-century house originally built for Captain Nikolaos Malouchos, this museum exhibits a bedroom furnished and decorated in the fashion of that period. On display are looms and lace-making devices, Cycladic costumes, old photographs, and Mykoniot musical instruments that are still played at festivals. ✉ *South of boat dock near Paraportiani church, Kastro* ☎ *22890/22591* 💶 *Free* ⊗ *Mon.–Sat. 4–8, Sun. 5:30–8.*

Greek Orthodox Cathedral of Mykonos. This cathedral is dedicated to Virgin Mary the Great (as locals know it by) and is noted for its number of old icons of the post-Byzantine period. ✉ *Alefkandra Sq., at the intersection of Anargyron and Odos Mitropolis.*

Lena's House. Take a peek into Lena's House, an annex of the local Folk Museum, and experience an accurate restoration of a middle-class Mykonos house from the 19th century. ✉ *Enoplon Dynameon* ☎ *22890/22390* ✉ *Free* ☉ *Apr.–Oct., Mon.–Sat. 6:30 pm– 9:30 pm.*

Fodor'sChoice
★
Little Venice. Many of the early ships' captains built distinguished houses directly on the sea here, with wooden balconies overlooking the water. Today this neighborhood, at the southwest end of the port, is called Little Venice. This area, architecturally unique and one of the most attractive in all the islands, is so called because its handsome houses, which once belonged to shipowners and aristocrats, rise from the edge of the sea, and their elaborate buttressed wooden balconies hang over the water—these are no Venetian marble palazzi reflected in still canals. Many of these fine old houses are now elegant bars specializing in sunset drinks, or cabarets, or shops, and crowds head to the cafés and clubs, many found a block inland from Little Venice. These are sometimes soundproofed. Little Venice is waiting to be discovered and presents countless photo ops, especially at sunset. ✉ *Mitropoleos Georgouli.*

Mando Mavrogenous Square. Start a tour of Mykonos Town on the main square, Mando Mavrogenous Square (sometimes called Taxi Square). Pride of place goes to a bust of Mando Mavrogenous, the island heroine, standing on a pedestal. In the 1821 War of Independence the Mykonians, known for their seafaring skills, volunteered an armada of 24 ships, and in 1822, when the Ottomans landed a force on the island, Mando and her soldiers forced them back to their ships. After independence, a scandalous love affair caused the heroine's exile to Paros, where she died. An aristocratic beauty who becomes a great revolutionary war leader and then dies for love may seem unbelievably Hollywoodish, but it is true. ✉ *Mando Mavrogenous Square.*

Mykonos windmills. Across the water from Little Venice, set on a high hill, are the famous Mykonos windmills, echoes of a time when wind power was used to grind the island's grain. The area from Little Venice to the windmills is called **Alefkandra,** which means "whitening": women once hung their laundry here. A little farther toward the windmills the bars chockablock on shoreside decks are barely above sea level, and when the north wind is up (often) surf splashes the tables. Farther on, the shore spreads into an unprepossessing beach, and tables are placed on sand or pebbles. After dinner (there are plenty of little tavernas here), the bars turn up their music, and knowing the beat thumps into the night, older tourists seek solace elsewhere. ✉ *Alefkandra Sq..*

Roman Catholic Cathedral. Next to the Greek Orthodox Cathedral is the Roman Catholic Cathedral, the Virgin of St. Rosary, from the Venetian period. The name and coat of arms of the Ghisi family, which took over Mykonos in 1207, are inscribed in the entrance hall. ✉ *Alefkandra Sq., at the intersection of Anargyron and Odos Mitropolis.*

BEACHES

There is a beach for every taste in Mykonos. Beaches near Mykonos town, within walking distance, are **Tourlos** and **Ayios Ioannis. Ayios Stefanos,** about a 45-minute walk from Mykonos town, has a minigolf course, water sports, restaurants, and umbrellas and lounge chairs for rent. The south coast's **Psarou,** protected from wind by hills and

9

surrounded by restaurants, offers a wide selection of water sports and is often called the finest beach. Nearby **Platys Yialos,** popular with families, is also lined with restaurants and dotted with umbrellas for rent. **Ornos** is also perfect for families; boats leave from here for more distant beaches, and there is lively nightlife patronized by locals as well as visitors. **Paranga, Paradise, Super Paradise,** and **Elia** are all on the southern coast of the island, and are famously nude, though getting less so; one corner of Elia is gay. **Super Paradise** is half gay, half straight, and swings at night. The scene at Paradise's bars throbs till dawn. All have tavernas on the beach.

WHERE TO EAT

$$ ✕ **Avra.** Nikos Iliopoulos' Avra restaurant recently moved to a spacious,
GREEK shady garden in the center of town. The hospitable service, Greek-Mediterranean menu, and quiet ambience make it the perfect place to go with friends, which is why locals eat here. A good starter would be fried feta in pastry topped with sesame seeds, grapes, and rose petal jelly. For a main dish, try the stuffed lamb (it is not on the menu, but usually available). Then again, you could always have tortilla shells filled with veal, pork, or chicken. For dessert, the orange pie is famous. To find it, look for the sign for the cross street off Matogianni. $ *Average main: €22* ✉ *Kalogera 27* ☎ *22890/22298* ⊕ *www.avra-mykonos.com* ⟐ *Reservations essential* ◷ *Closed Nov.–Apr.*

$$$ ✕ **Caprice Sea Satin Market.** If the wind is up, the waves sing at this magi-
SEAFOOD cal spot, set on a far tip of land below the famous windmills of Mykonos. The preferred place for Greek shipowners, Caprice the restaurant (as opposed to the bar by the same name, which is nearby) sprawls out onto a seaside terrace and even onto the sand of the beach bordering Little Venice. When it comes to fish, prices vary according to weight. Shellfish is a specialty, and everything is beautifully presented. In summer, live music and dancing add to the liveliness. $ *Average main: €35* ✉ *On seaside under windmills, Little Venice* ☎ *22890/24676* ⊕ *www.caprice.gr* ⟐ *Reservations essential.*

$$ ✕ **Nammos.** This beach restaurant has become the in spot for well-to-do
MODERN GREEK Athenians and for Mykonians who want to be strut a bit on fashionable Psarou Beach. All open-air, white wood, stone, bamboo, and palm trees, it serves up Mediterranean fusion cuisine (their words) and is especially popular for a late lunch. For appetizer try *louza* (Mykonian sun-dried pork filet), or eggplant millefeuille with feta and shrimp. Sea sounds will tempt you to order fresh fish or sushi, or dive into the great seared tuna tartare with white sauce or the homemade pasta with sea urchins. A non-svelte dessert is the chunky chocolate crème "guanajo" with blackberries and praline. $ *Average main: €30* ✉ *Psarou Beach, Psarou* ☎ *22890/22440* ⊕ *www.nammos.gr.*

WHERE TO STAY

$$$$ 🏠 **Belvedere.** You may feel compelled to book a trip to Greece immedi-
HOTEL ately upon viewing the "movie" presentation on this hotel's web site—it is almost as relaxing, blue-and-white, and high-style as this hotel—but not quite. **Pros:** this is Mykonos town's most "in" hotel. **Cons:** you can pay plenty for a small room with no view. $ *Rooms from: €350*

✉ *Lakka Rohari, School of Fine Arts district* ☎ *22890/25122* 🌐 *www.belvederehotel.com* 🛏 *35 rooms, 8 suites, 1 villa* 🍴 *Breakfast.*

$ B&B/INN 🏨 **Philippi.** Of the inexpensive hotels scattered throughout town, this is the most attractive. **Pros:** very inexpensive; central; cleanliness; free Wi-fi. **Cons:** if you want to get away from it all, go elsewhere; no transfers; smallish basic rooms in need of some updating. [$] *Rooms from: €90* ✉ *Kalogera 25* ☎ *22890/22294* 🌐 *www.philippihotel.com* 🛏 *13 rooms* 🕓 *Closed Nov.–Mar.*

NIGHTLIFE AND THE ARTS

Whether it's bouzouki music, break beat, or techno, Mykonos's nightlife beats to an obsessive rhythm until undetermined hours—little wonder Europe's gilded youth come here *just* to enjoy the night scene. After midnight, they often head to the techno bars along the Paradise and Super Paradise beaches. Some of Little Venice's nightclubs become gay in more than one sense of the word, while in the Kastro, convivial bars welcome all for tequila-*sambukas* at sunset. What is "the" place of the moment? The scene is ever-changing—so you'll need to track the buzz once you arrive.

BARS AND DISCOS

Galleraki. Little Venice is a good place to begin an evening, and Damianos Griparis's Galleraki is one of the best cocktail bars in town; it's so close to the water you may get wet when a boat passes. Upstairs in the old mansion (Delos's first archaeologists lived here), you'll find an art gallery—a handy sanctum for drinks on windy nights. ✉ *Little Venice, Skarpa* ☎ *22890/27118* 🌐 *www.galleraki.gr.*

Kastro Bar. Kostas Karatzas's long-standing Kastro Bar, with heavy beamed ceilings and island furnishings, creates an intimate environment for enjoying the evening sunset over the bay to classical music. ✉ *Little Venice, Paraportiani* ☎ *22890/23072* 🌐 *www.kastrobar.com (under construction).*

Montparnasse. This lively spot hangs paintings by local artists. Its superb sunset view precedes nights of live cabaret and musicals. ✉ *Ayion Anargyron 24, Little Venice* ☎ *22890/23719* 🌐 *www.thepianobar.com.*

Skandinavian Bar. Toward the end of Mykonos town's main market street is the Skandinavian Bar, which spreads over two buildings, two floors (one for pub chats, one for dancing), and an outside seating area. The music in the three bars ranges from classic rock to pop to dance. ✉ *K. Georgouli St.* ☎ *22890/22669* 🌐 *www.skandinavianbar.com.*

SHOPPING

The main shopping street, Matoyanni, which is perpendicular to the harbor, is lined with jewelry stores, clothing boutiques, chic cafés, and candy shops. Owing to the many cruise ships that disgorge thousands of shoppers daily in season, the rents here rival Fifth Avenue's, and the more interesting shops have skedaddled to less prominent side streets.

Anna Gelou. Anna Gelou's eponymous shop, started by her mother 50 years ago, carries authentic copies of traditional handmade embroideries, all using white Greek cotton, in clothing, tablecloths, curtains, and such. ✉ *Ayion Anargyron 16, Little Venice* ☎ *22890/26825.*

Galatis. Designer Yiannis Galatis has outfitted such famous women as Elizabeth Taylor, Ingrid Bergman, and Jackie Onassis. He will probably greet you personally and show you some of his costumes and hostess gowns. His memoirs capture the old days on Mykonos, when Jackie O. was a customer. His new art gallery is adjacent. ⊠ *Mando Mavrogenous Sq., opposite Lalaounis* ☎ *22890/22255.*

Nikoletta. Mykonos used to be a weaver's island, where 500 looms clacked away. Only two active weavers remain today and Nikoletta Xidakis is one of them. She sells her skirts, shawls, and bedspreads made of local wool, as she has for 50 years. ⊠ *Little Venice, Skarpa* ☎ *22890/27503.*

Parthenis. Opened by Dimitris Parthenis in 1978, Parthenis now features designs by his daughter Orsalia, all showcased in a large Mykonian-style building on the up side of Alefkandra Square in Little Venice. The collection of cotton and silk garments (mostly in neutral colors) is very popular for their soft draping and clinging wrap effect. ⊠ *Alefkandra Sq.* ☎ *22890/23080* ⊕ *www.orsalia-parthenis.gr.*

SANTORINI (THIRA) ΣΑΝΤΟΡΙΝΗ (ΘΗΡΑ)

Undoubtedly the most extraordinary island in the Aegean, crescent-shape Santorini remains a mandatory stop on the Cycladic tourist route—even if it 's necessary to enjoy the sensational sunsets from Ia, the fascinating excavations, and the dazzling white towns with a million other travelers. Called Kállisti (the "Loveliest") when first settled, the island has now reverted to its subsequent name of Thira, after the 9th-century BC Dorian colonizer Thiras. The place is better known, however, these days as Santorini, a name derived from its patroness, St. Irene of Thessaloniki, the Byzantine empress who restored icons to Orthodoxy and died in AD 802.

Fly to Santorini if you need to save time, but a boat trip around the caldera is a must—a spectacular, almost mandatory introduction to the unforgettable volcanic crater, one of the world's truly breathtaking sights: a demilune of cliffs rising 1,100 feet, with the white clusters of the white-on-white towns of Fira and Ia perched along the top. Santorini and its four neighboring islets are the fragmentary remains of a larger landmass that exploded about 1600 BC: the volcano's core blew sky high, and the sea rushed into the abyss to create the great bay. There has been much speculation about the identification of Santorini with the mythical Atlantis, and if the island is known as the "Greek Pompeii," it is because of the archaeological site of ancient Akrotiri, near the tip of the southern horn of the island. In July and August, of course, the masses arrive and you will have a pushy time walking down Fira's main street. Nevertheless, there's plenty of unforgettable Greek splendor if you know where to look for it.

PLANNING YOUR TIME

Crowds in Fira and Ia towns in the peak season months of July and August resemble the running of the bulls in Pamplona, so try to visit in May, June, or September instead. And slow down to savor it all: if you

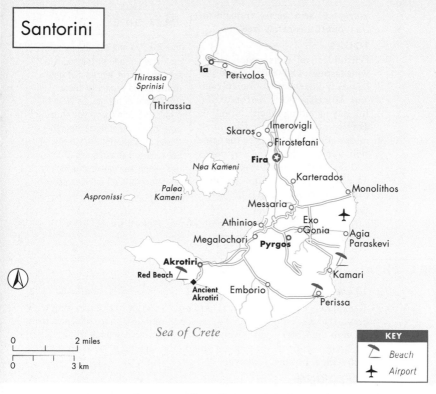

Santorini

Thirassia
Sprinisi

Thirassia

Ia

Perivolos

Skaros

Imerovigli

Firostefani

Fira

Nea Kameni

Karterados

Monolithos

Palea
Kameni

Aspronissi

Messaria

Athinios

Exo
Gonia

Agia
Paraskevi

Megalochori

Pyrgos

Akrotiri

Red Beach

Ancient
Akrotiri

Emborio

Kamari

Perissa

Sea of Crete

| 0 | 2 miles |
| 0 | 3 km |

KEY	
⌇	*Beach*
✈	*Airport*

move too fast, you will see little, and the beauty here is in the general impression of sea, sky, mountain, and village.

GETTING HERE AND AROUND

AIR TRAVEL

Olympic has three daily flights to Santorini Airport from Athens in peak season. Aegean Airlines has four daily flights to Santorini in summer, but their schedules are often subject to change.

Contacts Aegean Airlines ☎ 210/626–1000 ⊕ www.aegeanair.com. **Olympic Airways** ✉ Port, Mykonos Town ☎ 22890/22490 ⊕ www.olympicair.com. **Santorini Airport** ✉ On east coast, 6 km (3½ miles) from Fira, Monolithos ☎ 22860/28400 ⊕ www.santoriniairport.com.

BUS TRAVEL

On Santorini buses leave from the main station in central Fira (Deorgala) for Ia and other villages.

FERRY TRAVEL

Fast ferries connect Mykonos and Santorini, and these are busy routes. Some travelers prefer to take a ferry to Santorini from Athens, but since it's twice as far as Mykonos, others prefer not to spend so much time in transit. The ferry port for Santorini is fairly isolated, so once you step off the boat, you'll need to take a taxi up the cliffs to your hotel. Some hotels will arrange for transportation, but this is rarely free.

TOURS

Pelican Travel runs coach tours, wine tastings, and visits to Ia; it also has daily boat trips to the volcano and Thirassia (€19 half-day, €50 full-day including lunch). Nomikos Travel—also a top place for tourist information—has tours to the same sights and to the island's wineries and the Monastery of Profitis Ilias. This is the place to sign up for a caldera submarine trip (€65).

> ### WALK ON BY
>
> Tourist touts still like to promote mules as a mode of transport to take you up the zigzag cliff path to the island capital of Thera. But animal-rights groups would prefer you didn't. And you should be aware of another reason: the mules on Santorini are piously believed to contain souls of the dead, who are thus doing their purgatory. It is an arduous ascent.

Contacts Nomikos Travel
✉ *Fira* ☎ *22860/23660* ⊕ *www.nomikosvillas.gr.* **Pelican Travel** ✉ *Fira* ☎ *22860/22220* ⊕ *www.pelican.gr.*

FIRA ΦHPA

10 km (6 miles) west of the airport, 14 km (8½ miles) southeast of Ia.

To experience life here as it was until only a couple of decades ago, walk down the much-photographed, winding staircase that descends from town to the water's edge. Walk or take the cable car back up, avoiding the drivers who will try to plant you on the sagging back of one of their bedraggled-looking donkeys.

EXPLORING

Archaeological Museum. This fascinating squint into the island's millenia of history offers displays of pottery, statues, and grave artifacts found at excavations mostly from ancient Thira and Akrotiri, from the Minoan through the Byzantine periods. ✉ *Stavrou and Nomikos, Mitropoleos, behind big church* ☎ *22860/22217* ⊕ *www.culture.gr* 🖭*€3* ☉ *Nov.–Mar., Tues.–Sun. 8–4; Apr.–Oct., Mon and Wed.–Sun. 9–4.*

Eikostis Pemptis Martiou (*25th of March street*). Along Eikostis Pemptis Martiou Street, you'll find inexpensive restaurants and accommodations. ✉ *East of Panayia Ypapantis, Eikostis Pemptis Martiou.*

Panayia Ypapantis. The modern Greek Orthodox cathedral of Panayia Ypapantis is a major landmark; you'll quickly note how the local priests, with somber faces, long beards, and black robes, look strangely out of place in summertime, tourist-jammed Fira. ✉ *Southern part of town.*

Kato Fira (*Lower Fira*). The blocked-off Ypapantis street (west of Panayia Ypapantis) leads to Kato Fira, built into the cliff side overlooking the caldera, where prices are higher and the vista wonderful. For centuries the people of the island have been digging themselves rooms-with-a-view right in the cliff face—many bars and hotel rooms now occupy the caves.

Museum of Prehistoric Thera. This is the treasure house that displays pots and frescoes from the famed excavations at Akrotiri. Note the fresco fragments with the painted swallows (who flocked here because they loved the cliffs) and the women in Minoan dresses. The swallows, which still come in spring, remain the island's favorite design motif. The fossilized olive leaves from 60,000 BC prove the olive to be indigenous. ✉ *Mitropoleos, behind big church* ☎ *22860/23217, 22860/25405* 🌐 *www.culture.gr* 🎟 *€3* 🕓 *Nov.–Mar., Tues.–Sun. 8–3; Apr.–Oct., Mon., Wed.–Sun. 9–4.*

WHERE TO EAT

$ GREEK 🍴 **Nicholas.** This is Santorini's oldest taverna, where you'll find the natives camped out in winter. Island dishes are prepared well and served in a simple, attractive room. Try the local fava bean puree, an island specialty, and the lamb fricassee *(stifado)* with an egg-lemon sauce. During high season, reservations are strongly recommended; in the off-season, you can get a table almost anytime. [$] *Average main: €12* ✉ *2 streets in from cliffside on Erythrou Stavrou* ☎ *22860/24550* 💳 *No credit cards.*

WHERE TO STAY

$$$$ RENTAL Fodor's Choice ★ 🏨 **Aigialos.** For a taste of old aristocratic Santorini, venture to Aigialos ("seashore"), comprising a cluster of buildings from the 18th and 19th centuries, and discover the most comfortable and discreetly luxurious—as well as the most poetic and serenely quiet—array of one- and two-bedroom villas to stay in Fira. **Pros:** not a phony set-up for tourists; quiet elegance; friendly, discreet service. **Cons:** the usual endless steps; the pool is tiny. [$] *Rooms from: €290* ✉ *South end of cliffside walkway* ☎ *22860/25191 through 22860/25195* 🌐 *www.aigialos.gr* 🛏 *17 villas* 🕓 *Closed Nov.–Mar.* 🍽 *Breakfast.*

$ B&B/INN 🏨 **Costa Marina Villas.** Set in a tranquil neighborhood, surrounded by a garden, vaulted and shimmering-white in archetypal Cycladic fashion, this is a nifty option (built in 2002) and one that is open all year. **Pros:** great value for the money; superb service and hospitality; guests get discount in nearby family restaurant. **Cons:** a 15-minute hike from the caldera. [$] *Rooms from: €94* ✉ *Along road leading to campgrounds* ☎ *22860/28923* 🌐 *www.costamarina.gr* 🛏 *15 rooms* 🍽 *Breakfast.*

SHOPPING

Costas Dimitrokalis. With purchases that can be mailed anywhere, Costas Dimitrokalis and Matthew Dimitrokalis sell locally made embroideries of Greek linen and Egyptian cotton, rugs, pillowcases in hand-crocheted wool with local designs, and more. ✉ *1 block from cable car* ☎ *22860/22957.*

Phenomenon. Christoforos Asimis studied painting at Athens University, and has had many exhibitions there and abroad. The nearby cathedral's murals are his. His paintings specialize in the light and landscape of his home island. His wife, Eleni Kollaitou, who also studied in Athens, creates some of Santorini's most elegant jewelry, bronze sculptures, and ceramics. ✉ *Ypapantis walkway, Palia Fabrika* ☎ *22860/23041* 🌐 *www.ak-galleries.com.*

IA OIA

14 km (8½ miles) northwest of Fira.

At the tip of the northern horn of the island sits Ia (or Oia), Santorini's second-largest town and the Aegean's most photographed village. Ia is more tasteful than Fira (for one thing, no establishment here is allowed to play music that can be heard on the street), and the town's cubical white houses (some vaulted against earthquakes) stand out against the green-, brown-, and rust-color layers of rock, earth, and solid volcanic ash that rise from the sea. Every summer evening, travelers from all over the world congregate at the caldera's rim—sitting on whitewashed fences, staircases, beneath the town's windmill, on the old **kastro**—each looking out to sea in anticipation of the performance: the Ia sunset. The three-hour rim-edge walk from Ia to Thera at this hour is magnificent.

Although Thera, also damaged in the 1956 earthquake, rebuilt rapidly, Ia proceeded slowly, sticking to the traditional architectural style. The perfect example of that style is the Restaurant 1800, a renovated ship-captain's villa. Ia is set up like the other three towns—Thera, Firostefani, and Imerovigli—that adorn the caldera's sinuous rim. There is a car road, which is new, and a cliffside walkway (Nikolaos Nomikou), which is old. Shops and restaurants are all on the walkway, and hotel entrances mostly descend from it—something to check carefully if you cannot negotiate stairs easily. Although it is not as crowded as Thera, where the tour boats deposit their thousands of hasty shoppers, relentless publicity about Ia's beauty and tastefulness, accurate enough, are making it impassable in August. The sunset in Ia may not really be much more spectacular than in Thera, but there is something tribally satisfying at the sight of so many people gathering in one spot to celebrate pure beauty.

WHERE TO EAT

$$$
GREEK FUSION
Fodor's Choice
★

✕ **1800.** Clearly, some of Santorini's old sea captains lived graciously, as you'll note when dining at one of the Cyclades's most famous restaurants, 1800 (the name refers to the date when the house was built). Owner, architect, and restaurateur John Zagelidis has lovingly restored this magnificent old captain's house with original colors (white, olive green, and gray) and furnishings, including antique sofas, wooden travel chests, and a hand-painted Venetian bed. To top it all off, a superlative roof terrace was constructed, with a vista framed by Ia's most-spectacular church cupolas—a perfect perch on hot nights for taking in the famous Ia sunset.

The eclectic menu offers a blend of Greek fusion and molecular cuisine and will appeal especially to the most adventurous palates. For starters try octopus and chickpea salad on baby spinach with feta and Florina red peppercorns; or the scallops with an aromatic cauliflower tartare and tandoori cream. Entrées include black angus veal with cannelloni stuffed with broccoli and arugula with graviera foam and mushroom sauce; and cod with herb ash, black-eyed beans, beetroot salad, and fish roe with cuttlefish ink. Ivoire chocolate with pineapple carpaccio and white-chocolate powder is a fine dessert. The wine list is large and nicely tops off a fine dining experience. This restaurant is a tad pricey perhaps, but provides a unique dining experience in Ia. $ *Average main: €35* ✉ *Main St.* ☎ *22860/71485* ⊕ *www.oia-1800.com* ⊘ *Closed Nov.–Apr.*

$$ ✕**Kastro.** Spyros Dimitroulis's restaurant is primarily patronized for its
GREEK view of the famous Ia sunset, and at the magical hour it is always filled. Happily, the food makes a fitting accompaniment. A good starter is olives stuffed with cream cheese dipped in beer dough and fried, served on arugula with a balsamic sauce. For a main dish try mussels with oil-pepper sauce. Lunch is popular. In the evening, table 2 has the best unobstructed view of the sunset. $ *Average main: €20* ✉ *Near Venetian castle* ☎ *22860/71045* ⊕ *www.kastro-ia.gr* ⌂ *Reservations essential.*

WHERE TO STAY

$$$$ ⊡**Katikies.** Sumptuously appointed, this immaculate white cliff-side complex layered on terraces offers ultimate luxury and sleek modern design, including Andy Warhol wall prints, stunning fabrics, and handsome furniture—chic as the surroundings are, the barrel-vaulted ceilings and other architectural details also lend a traditional air to the place. **Pros:** cliff-side infinity pool; all luxuries. **Cons:** many stairs; rather impersonal; pricey. $ *Rooms from: €540* ✉ *Ia cliff face, edge of main town* ☎ *22860/71401* ⊕ *www.katikies.com* ⊅ *5 rooms, 22 suites* ⊘ *Closed Nov.–Mar.* ⦿ *Breakfast.*

PYRGOS ΠΥΡΓΟΣ

5½ km (3½ miles) south of Fira.

Fodor's Choice Though today Pyrgos has only 500 inhabitants, until the early 1800s
★ it was the capital of the island. Stop here to see its medieval houses, stacked on top of one another and back to back for protection against pirates. The beautiful neoclassic building on the way up is a luxury hotel. The view from the ruined Venetian castle is panoramic. And reward yourself for the climb up the picturesque streets, which follow the shape of the hill, with a stop at the panoramic terrace of the Café Kastelli, for Greek coffee and homemade sweets. In Pyrgos you are really in old Santorini—hardly anything has changed.

WHERE TO EAT

$$$ ✕**Selene.** Always a great restaurant, Selene is now probably the best in
GREEK the Cyclades, with a beautiful location, elegant setting and service, and
Fodor's Choice a deep love of island cuisine with local ingredients. The terrace of the
★ old aristocratic house has two sea-views—south and caldera sunset— and overlooks vineyards spreading to the Aegean. Excellent starters include squid with smoked fava and cuttlefish ink flakes, or smoked quail *kouskousela* on crispy potatoes. Among the creative entrées are Aegean codfish with garlic-scented Jerusalem artichoke velouté and the lamb with vine shoots and lemon-scented potato croquette foam. Desserts are not neglected: the chocolate *mandolato* and the baklava with local pistachios are both supreme. The Greek wine list is extensive. On Selene's lower level there is a café-restaurant where you can sample Selene's dishes or even have a sandwich. Next to it is Selene's agricultural museum in an old winery. Georgia Tsara, the maîtresse d', oversees all with grace, efficiency, and knowledge. In summer, owner George

9

Hatziyianakis and his chefs give daylong cooking classes (be sure to check the website for details). [$] *Average main: €30* ☎ *22860/22249* 🌐 *www.selene.gr* ✍ *Reservations essential* 🕒 *Closed Nov.–Mar.*

AKROTIRI ΑΚΡΩΤΗΡΙ

7 km (4½ miles) west of Pyrgos, 13 km (8 miles) south of Fira.

Fodor's Choice ★ **Ancient Akrotiri.** If Santorini is known as the "Greek Pompeii" and is claimant to the title of the lost Atlantis, it is because of the archaeological site of ancient Akrotiri, near the tip of the southern horn of the island. The site re-opened in April 2012 after undergoing lengthy structural repairs of the protective roof spanning the entire enclosed site, which is in fact a whole ancient city buried under the volcanic ashes and still waiting to be unearthed—almost intact.

In the 1860s, in the course of quarrying volcanic ash for use in the Suez Canal, workmen discovered the remains of an ancient town. The town was frozen in time by ash from an eruption 3,600 years ago, long before Pompeii's disaster. In 1967 Spyridon Marinatos of the University of Athens began excavations, which occasionally continue. It is thought that the 40 buildings that have been uncovered are only one-thirtieth of the huge site and that excavating the rest will probably take a century.

Culturally an outpost of Minoan Crete, Akrotiri was settled as early as 3000 BC and reached its peak after 2000 BC, when it developed trade and agriculture and settled the present town. The inhabitants cultivated olive trees and grain, and their advanced architecture—three-story frescoed houses faced with masonry (some with balconies) and public buildings of sophisticated construction—is evidence of an elaborate lifestyle. ✉ *South of modern Akrotiri, near tip of southern horn* ☎ *22860/81939* 🌐 *www.culture.gr* 🎫 *€5* 🕒 *Tues.–Sun. 8–8.*

HUNGARY

Budapest, the Danube Bend, Eger

WHAT'S WHERE

1 Budapest. Hungary's main geographical region begins with the capital city and thriving urban heart of Budapest. Divided by the river Danube into Buda and Pest, the city has much to offer in terms of natural beauty, architecture, and culture. Distinctly Hungarian—yet also international—this gateway between East and West is loaded with attractions, the foremost being the city itself.

2 Danube Bend. Just north of Budapest, the Danube forms a gentle, heart-shaped curve along which lie the romantic and historic towns of the region called the Danube Bend. Easily accessible by public transportation and trains that depart from Budapest, the towns of the Danube Bend offer a rustic hospitality that bustling capital sometimes overlooks. The most attractive day trips here include Szentendre and Visegrád.

3 Eger. The more rural and gently mountainous stretch of northern Hungary includes the handsome, vibrant town of Eger. A diverse range of sights easily seen by foot and excellent restaurants characterize this nontouristy, typically Hungarian town. For wine lovers, the cellars of Szépassonyvölgy (Valley of the Maidens) can provide a full day of tasting fun.

AUSTRIA

Hegyeshalom
Mosonmagyaróvár
Neusiedler See
Sopron   85   Győr
Kapuvár

Kőszeg   Sárvár   Pápa
Szombathely   Z
Körmend   Vasvár   Ajka
Zala   Tapolca
Zalaegerszeg   Keszthely
Fenékpuszta   Boglár
Lenti   Marca
E71
Nagykanizsa
61
Kaposv
Nagyatád
Szige
Barcs

SLOVENIA

CROATIA

POLAND

SLOVAKIA

UKRAINE

Aggtelek
Sátoraljaújhely
Sárospatak
Kisvárda
Vásárosnamény

Kazinbarcika
Tokaj
Miskolc
37
Mátészalka
Nyíregyháza
41

Balassagyarmat
Salgótarján
Eger
3
Tiszaújváros
Nyírbátor

Ipoly
22

Visegrád
Mezįkövesd

Esztergom
2 Vác
Gyöngyös
Tisza
Hajdúböszörmény

Komárom
Dorog
Hatvan
Heves
Tiszafüred
Debrecen

E60
Szentendre
31
Kiskörei
Reservoir
Hortobágy

M1
Gödöllį
Jászberény

abánya
1 BUDAPEST
Karcag
Hajdúszoboszló

Lake
Velence
M5
Cegléd
Törökszentmiklós
Kisújszállás

Székesfehérvár
5
Szolnok
Türkeve

Várpalota
Nagykįrös
Kecskemét
Körös
Szarvas

szprém
Dunaújváros
52
Kiskunfélegyháza
Csongrád
Békés

alatonfüred
Dunaföldvár

tok
Paks
Kiskįrås
Szentes
Békéscsaba

mási
53
Orosháza
Gyula

Kalocsa
Kiskunhalas
Hódmezįvásárhely
ROMANIA

Dombóvár
Szeged
Makó

Szekszárd
55
E68

Komló
Baja

écs Bátaszék

Mohács

SERBIA

Danube
Sió
Sió
E71
E71
E75
Tisza
Tisza

0   50 mi

0   50 km

10

NEED TO KNOW

AT A GLANCE

Capital: Budapest

Population: 9,944,000

Currency: Forint (HUF)

Money: ATMs are common; euros sometimes accepted.

Language: Hungarian

Country Code: ☎ 36

Emergencies: ☎ 104

Driving: On the right

Electricity: 200v/50 cycles; electrical plugs have two round prongs

Budapest

HUNGARY

Time: Six hours ahead of New York

Documents: Up to 90 days with valid passport; Schengen rules apply

Mobile Phones: GSM (900 and 1800 bands)

Major Mobile Companies: Vodafone, T-Mobile, Telenor

WEBSITES

Hungarian Government Tourist Office: ⊕ www.visit-hungary.com

Budapest Tourist Office: ⊕ www.budapest.com

Hungarian Ministry of Tourism: ⊕ www.gotohungary.com

GETTING AROUND

✈ **Air Travel:** The closest major airports are Budapest and Vienna.

🚌 **Bus Travel:** Good for smaller regional towns.

🚗 **Car Travel:** Rent a car to explore at your own pace, but be aware of aggressive drivers and frequent police drunk-driving checks. Be sure to have appropriate papers on you. Gas is very expensive.

🚃 **Train Travel:** You can find both new, modern trains and old, creaky trains that link you to cities like Eger, Sopron, and Pécs. Train service in Hungary is wide-reaching and reliable.

PLAN YOUR BUDGET

	HOTEL ROOM	MEAL	ATTRACTIONS
Low Budget	€60	2750 HUF	Funicular ride, 1000 HUF
Mid Budget	€80	5400 HUF	Széchenyi baths, 4100 HUF
High Budget	€200	1,240 HUF	Opera tickets, 21000 HUF

WAYS TO SAVE

Eat at the market halls. Farmers' market halls have cheap lunch-only canteens that serve hot, fresh local cuisine.

Book a rental apartment. Excellent values for central apartments or rooms can be found on sights like airbnb.com and through rental agencies. **Get a Budapest Card.** Good for public transport, free admission to a bath house, and free city tours—plus some restaurant discountss—the Budapest card is an amazing value. ⊕ www.budapest-card.com.

Take public transport. Budapest has fantastic and cheap options. Trams are a great way to see Budapest, particularly the 4/6 and the number 2 tram.

PLAN YOUR TIME	
Hassle Factor	Medium. There are few nonstop flights from the U.S. to Hungary and only one international airport in the country.
3 days	You can see quite a bit of Budapest in just three days, and still get in an afternoon at nearby Szentendre, Visegrád, or Etyek.
1 week	Spend half the week in Budapest, then set off north to see Eger and Tokaj, or head south for Pécs and Villany.
2 weeks	You can get a good sense of Budapest and still find time to make your way up to the beautiful Danube Bend. Take overnight excursions to the Austrian-flavored Sopron, the wine-loving Tokaj, and the Alföld (the Hungarian plain).

WHEN TO GO

High Season: Budapest is very busy from June through August. This is also when many of the major music and culinary festivals take place, not to mention the emergence of popular outdoor *rom kerts* (beer gardens). Hotels are at full capacity and charge their most expensive rates.

Low Season: Winters are dark and long in Hungary, and Hungarians are notoriously grumpy in these months. With little skiing and few winter sports, businesses tend to close over the holiday season. Many hotels lower their prices, and availability rises sharply, so keep your eye open for winter specials.

Value Season: You can catch the tail end of the wine festival and the Jewish festival in September, after the stream of backpackers diminishes. The weather in Hungary is gorgeous in September, just right to sample a sweet wine from Tokaj or sit in an outdoor mineral bath.

BIG EVENTS

August: The Sziget Festival is the biggest music festival in Europe. ⊕ *www.sziget.hu/fesztival*

March/April: Classical music lovers come from all corners for the Budapest Spring Festival. ⊕ *www.btf.hu*

October: The Contemporary Arts Festival has an emphasis on jazz. ⊕ *www.cafebudapestfest.hu/2013*

January: Budapesters celebrate pre–New Year's festivities at the horse races. ⊕ *www.magyarturf.hu*

READ THIS

■ *Budapest 1900,* John Lukacs. A view of Budapest's "golden age."

■ *Prague,* Arthur Philips. Novel about ex-pat life in postcommunist Budapest.

■ *The Hungarians: 1,000 Years of Victory in Defeat,* Paul Lendvai. A great overview.

WATCH THIS

■ *Kontroll.* A quirky, poignant look at the lives of Budapest metro ticket-checkers.

■ *Sunshine.* Story of a Jewish Budapest family around WWII.

■ *A Tanú (The Witness).* Hilarious send-up of communist Hungary.

EAT THIS

■ **Gulyás:** the traditional spicy Hungarian soup

■ **Csirke paprikás:** a creamy chicken stew in paprika sauce

■ **Hortobágyi palacsinta:** meat-filled crêpes with a sour cream/paprika sauce

■ **Sólet:** a traditionally Jewish, slow-cooked bean stew

■ **Kolbász:** dry sausage that comes in many varieties

■ **Libamáj:** good liver, either in pâté, fried, or in a mousse

10

Budapest, an old-world city with a throbbing urban pulse, is a must-stop on any trip to Central Europe. Szentendre and Eger have their own charms, including majestic hilltop castles and cobblestone streets winding among lovely baroque buildings. All this, and the generosity of the Magyar soul, sustains visitors to this land of vital spirit and beauty.

Hungary sits at the crossroads of Central Europe, having retained its own identity by absorbing countless invasions and foreign occupations. Its industrious, resilient people have a history of brave but unfortunate uprisings: against the Turks in the 17th century, the Hapsburgs in 1848, and the Soviet Union in 1956. With the withdrawal of the last Soviet soldiers from Hungarian soil in 1991, Hungary embarked on a decade of sweeping changes. The adjustment to a free-market economy has not all been easy sailing, but Hungary at long last has regained self-determination and a chance to rebuild an economy devastated by years of communist misrule.

Hungary joined NATO in 1999, and the country joined the European Union (EU) in May 2004. In 2002, then 39-year-old Prime Minister Viktor Orbán was the subject of gentle mockery when he suggested that the Hungarian economy was like a guided missile that had taken off and which could not be shot down. Orbán's increasingly right-wing FIDESZ party won the 2010 parliamentary elections, achieving a super-majority, and the party has since redrawn the Hungarian constitution.

Two rivers cross the country: the famous Duna (Danube) flows from the west through Budapest on its way to the southern frontier, and the smaller Tisza flows from the northeast across the Nagyalföld (Great Plain). What Hungary lacks in size it makes up for in beauty and charm. Hungarians are known for their hospitality. Although their unusual and difficult language is anything but a quick study, English is fast becoming the second language of Hungary, even superseding German. But what all Hungarians share is a deep love of music, and the calendar is studded with it, from Budapest's famous opera to its annual spring music festival. And at many restaurants Gypsy violinists serenade you during your evening meal.

PLANNING

WHEN TO GO

The ideal times to visit Hungary are in the spring (May–June) and end of summer and early fall (late August–September). July and August, peak vacation season for Hungarians as well as foreign tourists, can be extremely hot and humid; Budapest is stuffy and crowded, and other vacation destinations are overrun with vacationers. Many of Hungary's major fairs and festivals take place during the spring and fall, including the Spring Festival (in many cities and towns) from late March to early April and the myriad wine-harvest festivals in late summer and early fall. Summer holds the unforgettable and quintessentially Hungarian sights of sweeping fields of swaying golden sunflowers and giant white storks summering in their bushy nests built on chimney tops.

GETTING HERE AND AROUND

AIR TRAVEL

There are no nonstop flights to Hungary from the U.S., so travelers generally connect in another European airport and get a nonstop flight to Budapest's Liszt Ferenc Airport. Several airlines offer connecting service from North America, including Air Berlin (via Berlin), Air France (via Paris CDG), Austrian Airlines (via Vienna), British Airways (via London LHR), Czech Airlines (via Prague), Finnair (via Helsinki), KLM (via Amsterdam), and Lufthansa (via Frankfurt or Munich).

Many hotels offer their guests car or minibus transportation to and from Liszt Ferenc, but all of them charge for the service. You should arrange for a pickup in advance. If you're taking a taxi, allow anywhere between just 25 minutes during nonpeak hours and at least an hour during rush hours (7 am–9 am from the airport, 4 pm–6 pm from the city).

Contacts Liszt Ferenc Airport ☎ *1/296–7000 for customer service* ⊕ *www. bud.hu/english.*

BOAT TRAVEL

From late July through early September, two swift hydrofoils leave Vienna daily at 8 am and 1 pm (once-a-day trips are scheduled mid-April–late July and September–late October). After a 5½-hour journey downriver, with a stop in the Slovak capital, Bratislava, and views of Hungary's largest church, the cathedral in Esztergom, the boats head into Budapest via its main artery, the Danube. The upriver journey takes about an hour longer.

CAR TRAVEL

10

The main routes into Budapest are the M1 from Vienna (via Győr), the M3 from near Gyöngyös, the M5 from Kecskemét, and the M7 from the Balaton; the M3 and M5 are being upgraded and extended to Hungary's borders with Slovakia and Yugoslavia, respectively. Budapest, like any Western city, is plagued by traffic jams during the day, but motorists should have no problem later in the evening. Motorists not accustomed to sharing the city streets with trams should pay extra attention. You should be prepared to be flagged down numerous times by police conducting routine checks for drunk driving and stolen cars. Be sure all of your papers are in order and readily accessible; unfortunately, the police have been known to give foreigners a hard time. Don't rent a car on arrival if your sole destination is Budapest, but it may be worthwhile to have one if you want to explore the countryside.

TRAIN TRAVEL

International trains—and there is a steady stream of them, from all directions—are routed to two stations in Budapest. Keleti Pályaudvar (East Station) receives most international rail traffic coming in from the west, including Vienna. Nyugati Pályaudvar (West Station) handles a combination of international and domestic trains. Déli handles trains to the Lake Balaton region and to Pécs. Within Hungary, there is frequent and convenient rail service to many smaller cities and towns on the many routes that radiate in all directions from Budapest.

Contacts Keleti Pályaudvar (*East Railway Station*). ⊠ *District VIII, Baross tér, Budapest.* **Nyugati Pályaudvar** (*West Railway Station*). The iron-laced glass hall of the West Railway Station is in complete contrast to—and much more modern than—the newer East Railway Station. Built in the 1870s, it was designed by a team of architects from Gustav Eiffel's office in Paris. ⊠ *District XIII, Teréz körút, Around Nyugati Train Station, Budapest* Ⓜ *M3: Nyugati Train Station.*

HOTELS

Budapest has a wide range of hotels in all price categories, with several very good luxury options at (for Europe at least) relatively moderate prices.

BOOKING

Advance reservations are an absolute requirement in summer, especially at the smaller, lower-priced hotels and during the week in August that Formula I racing descends upon Budapest. In winter it's not anywhere near as difficult to find a hotel room, even at the last minute, and prices are usually reduced by 20% to 30%.

SAVING MONEY

Visitors to Budapest can save money by booking a private apartment rental, which is generally cheaper than a comparable hotel room and offers cooking facilities.

RESTAURANTS

SAVING MONEY

Although prices are steadily increasing, there are plenty of good, affordable restaurants offering Hungarian and international dishes. Even in Budapest, eating out can provide you with some of the best value for the money of any European capital. In almost all restaurants, an inexpensive prix-fixe lunch called a *menü* is available, usually for as little as 1,000 HUF. It includes soup or salad, a main course, and a dessert. The days of charging customers for each slice of bread taken from the bread basket and of embellishing tourists' bills are, happily, fast receding.

MEALS AND MEAL TIMES

Breakfast normally consists of eggs; bread smeared with lard, red onion, and paprika; and perhaps whatever fruit is in season. Hungarians eat early—you still risk offhand service and cold food if you arrive at some traditional Hungarian restaurants after 9 pm. Lunch, the main meal for many, is served from noon to 2.

PAYING

Most *étkezdes* (lunch canteens) operate on a cash-only basis. There are still a number of more formal restaurants that don't take cards either, so it is always advisable to check when making reservations. Restaurants are required to give an itemized receipt. We recommend you check it for accuracy.

RESERVATIONS AND DRESS

Reservations for dinner are necessary in most of the nicer restaurants in Budapest but are usually unnecessary at lunch. A day or two in advance is usually time. Dress is casual but neat at most moderately priced and expensive restaurants. Jackets are rarely required.

TIPPING

At a restaurant, give your server at least a 10% tip (customarily done by telling them the total, but it's fine to do subsequently). Increasingly the bill will arrive with a 10%–12% tip already added. It will be listed as *tip, szerviz,* or *borravaló.*

WINE, BEER, AND SPIRITS

Hungarian wines make up the bulk of the offerings on most Budapest wine lists. While not cheap, most wines are affordable and nearly all are quite drinkable. Some visitors to Hungary find the local wines very good indeed. *Tokaj aszú,* Hungary's unique dessert wine, excites enthusiasts, and you shouldn't miss the chance to taste at least one glass while you're in Hungary.

HOTEL AND RESTAURANT PRICES

Prices in the restaurant reviews are the average cost of a main course at dinner or, if dinner is not served, at lunch; taxes and service charges are generally included. Prices in the hotel reviews are the lowest cost of a standard double room in high season, excluding taxes, service charges, and meal plans (except at all-inclusives). Prices for rentals are the lowest per-night cost for a one-bedroom unit in high season.

VISITOR INFORMATION

Contacts Budapest.com ⊕ *www.budapest.com.* **Visit Hungary** ⊕ *www. visithungary.com.*

10

BUDAPEST

Situated on both banks of the Danube, Budapest unites the colorful hills of Buda and the wide, businesslike boulevards of Pest. Though it was the site of a Roman outpost during the 1st century, the city was not officially created until 1873, when the towns of Óbuda, Pest, and Buda united. Since then, Budapest has been the cultural, political, intellectual, and commercial heart of Hungary; for the 20% of the nation's population who live in the capital, anywhere else is simply *vidék* ("the country").

Budapest has suffered many ravages in the course of its long history. It was totally destroyed by the Mongols in 1241, captured by the Turks in 1541, and nearly destroyed again by Soviet troops in 1945. But this

TOP REASONS TO GO

Great Value. Historical architecture, bustling neighborhoods, and attractions cost less than you would spend elsewhere in Europe

Great Food. Hungarian is one of Europe's most distinct and underrated cuisines, loaded with spicy paprika and farm-fresh produce.

Thermal Baths. The bathhouses of Budapest were designed for Turkish emperors. You could go to one a day for a week and still not see them all.

Neighborhoods for Strolling. Budapest is highly accessible on foot. Set off in any direction for an instant create-your-own walking tour.

Live Music. Be it the opera, the Jewish festival, or the Sziget festival, Budapest has live music events to fit all tastes, year-round.

bustling industrial and cultural center survived as the capital of the People's Republic of Hungary after the war—and then, as the 1980s drew to a close, it became renowned for "goulash socialism," a phrase used to describe the state's tolerance of an irrepressible entrepreneurial spirit. Budapest has undergone a radical makeover since the free elections of 1990. Change is still in the air. As more and more restaurants, bars, shops, and boutiques open their doors—and with fashion-conscious youths parading the streets—almost all traces of communism may seem to have disappeared. But then look again: the elderly ladies selling flowers at the train station are a poignant reminder that some Hungarians have been left behind in this brave new world of competition.

Much of the charm of a visit to Budapest lies in unexpected glimpses into shadowy courtyards and in long vistas down sunlit cobbled streets. Although some 30,000 buildings were destroyed during World War II and in the 1956 Revolution, the past lingers on in the often crumbling architectural details of the antique structures that remain.

The principal sights of the city fall roughly into three areas, each of which can be comfortably covered on foot. The Budapest hills are best explored by public transportation. Note that, by tradition, the district number—a Roman numeral designating one of Budapest's 22 districts—precedes each address. For the sake of clarity, in this book, the word "District" precedes the number. Districts V, VI, and VII are in downtown Pest; District I includes Castle Hill, the main tourist district of Buda.

PLANNING

PLANNING YOUR TIME

If you are in Hungary for a few days, you can still see plenty of Budapest. A stroll down Andrássy Avenue is in order to see the heart of classical Budapest, taking you past the gorgeous Magyar Állami Operaház (Opera House). Spend the afternoon at one of the thermal baths: the two must-see ones are Széchenyi in Pest and the Buda-side Gellért. Evenings are ripe for concerts, be it at the Liszt Ferenc Music Academy, the opera, or in a *rom kért* (beer garden). Mornings are perfect for taking in the view from the Chain Bridge, then riding the funicular up to Budapest's historic Castle District, which offers museums, cathedrals, and breathtaking views of the entire city. An afternoon in the Jewish district (District VII) will not disappoint. The Dohány Street Synagogue is the largest in Europe, and the more humble Rumbach Synagogue is right around the corner, as is the Dob Street Synagogue. A trip to the central Market Hall and walk down Vaci Street will fill you up with food and souvenirs. If you have time, take a day trip to the Danube Bend or Eger.

GETTING HERE AND AROUND
BUS AND TRAM TRAVEL
Trams and buses are abundant and convenient for travel within Budapest. A single-fare ticket is valid for only one ride in one direction. Tickets are widely available in metro stations and newsstands and must be validated on board by inserting them downward facing you into the little devices provided for that purpose, then pulling the knob. Alternatively, you can purchase a one-day ticket or three-day tourist ticket, which allows unlimited travel on all services within the city limits. Hold on to whatever ticket you have; spot checks by aggressive officials (look for the red armbands) are numerous and often targeted at tourists. Trolley-bus stops are marked with red, rectangular signs that list the route stops; regular bus stops are marked with similar light blue signs. (The trolley buses and regular buses themselves are red and blue, respectively.) Tram stops are marked by light blue or yellow signs. Most lines run from 5 am and stop operating at 11 pm, but there is all-night service on certain key routes. Consult the separate night-bus map posted in most metro stations for all-night service.

SUBWAY TRAVEL
Service on Budapest's subways is cheap, fast, and frequent; stations are easily located on maps and streets by the big letter "M" (for metro). Tickets—valid on all forms of mass transportation—can be bought at hotels, metro stations, newsstands, and kiosks. They are valid for one ride only; you can't change lines or direction. Tickets must be validated in the time-clock machines in station entrances and should be kept until the end of the journey, as there are frequent checks by undercover inspectors; a fine for traveling without a ticket is 2,500 HUF. Other options include a one-day ticket, a three-day "tourist ticket," and a seven-day ticket (passport photo required); all allow unlimited subway travel within city limits.

10

TAXI TRAVEL
There are plenty of honest taxi drivers in Budapest and a few too many dishonest ones. Fortunately, the reliable ones are easy to spot: they will have a company logo and phone number and a working meter. If one is hailed on the street, the base fare is generally 200 HUF, then 200 HUF each kilometer thereafter. When ordering a taxi by phone (and all the companies here have English-speaking operators), the rate begins around 450 HUF base fare, then 250 HUF–280 HUF per kilometer.

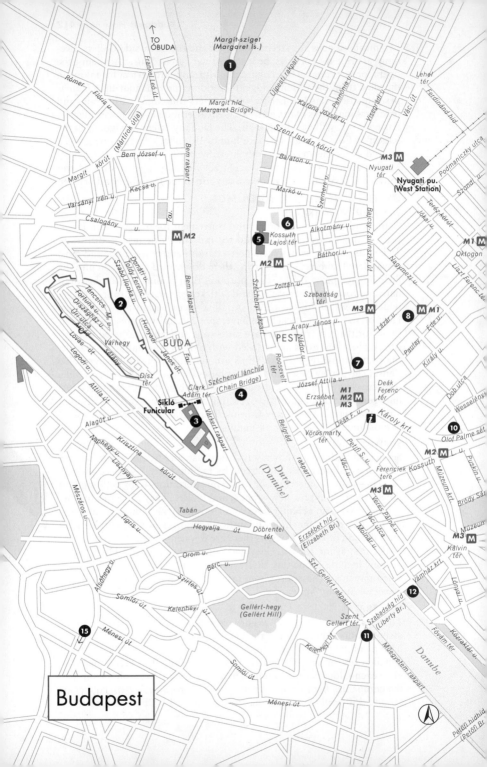

KEY

- **M** Metro stops
- **𝑖** Tourist information
- Rail lines

0 — 500 yards

0 — 500 meters

10

Contacts City Taxi ☎ 1/211–1111 ⊕ www.citytaxi.hu. Taxi 2000 ☎ 2/000–000 ⊕ taxi2000.hu.

TOURS

Context Travel. Context is a trusted international brand, and the company's Budapest tours are known to be well curated and well informed. Specializing in walking tours that are focused on historical and architectural topics including the Jewish Quarter, Belle Époque Budapest, and Communist Budapest, the tours are led by local scholars and get high marks for the quality of their local guides. ☎ 800/691–6036 in the U.S. ⊕ www.contexttravel.com/city/budapest.

Taste Hungary. Taste Hungary is quickly becoming the most respected boutique company for walking tours in Budapest and day trips around Hungary. The company started out in wine tourism, and their expert tours of nearby wine regions like Etyek and Eger are a great way to see some of the countryside. Budapest options include specialized walking tours focusing on such varied subjects as the culinary scene, Jewish Budapest, or craft beers. Owned by a Hungarian and American couple, Taste Hungary has a lot to offer. ☎ 36/30–551–9932 ⊕ www.tastehungary.com.

EXPLORING

VÁRHEGY (CASTLE HILL)

Fodor's Choice
★ **Halászbástya** (*Fishermen's Bastion*). The wondrous porch overlooking the Danube and Pest is the neo-Romanesque Fishermen's Bastion, a merry cluster of white stone towers, arches, and columns above a modern bronze statue of St. Stephen, Hungary's first king. Although you must pay to wander over most of it during the day over much of the year (as has been the practice since 2000), the price is reasonable. Medieval fishwives once peddled their wares here, but now you see merchants selling souvenirs and crafts, musicians, and—less visible but always present—pickpockets. Buy your tickets at the tiny office beside the Tourinform by the adjacent park. ⊠ District I, east of Szentháromság tér, Castle Hill ☎ 600 HUF Mar.–Oct., free Nov.–Feb. ☉ Daily 24 hrs Ⓜ Várbusz (4th stop from M2: Széll Kálmán tér).

Fodor's Choice
★ **Magyar Nemzeti Galéria** (*Hungarian National Gallery*). The Magyar Nemzeti Galéria, which comprises the immense center block of the Royal Palace (Wings B, C, and D), exhibits Hungarian fine art, from medieval ecclesiastical paintings and statues through Gothic, Renaissance, and baroque art, to a rich collection of 19th- and 20th-century works. Especially notable are the works of the romantic painter Mihály Munkácsy, the impressionist Pál Szinyei Merse, and the surrealist Mihály Tivadar Kosztka Csontváry, whom Picasso much admired. There is also a large collection of modern Hungarian sculpture. Labels and commentary for both permanent and temporary exhibits are in English. Note that there's a charge to take pictures (1,600 HUF) or film video (2,100 HUF) inside the museum. ⊠ District I, Királyi Palota (entrance in Wing C), Dísz tér 17, Castle Hill ☎ 06–20/439–7325, 06–20/439–7331 ⊕ www.mng.hu ☜ 1,400 HUF, special exhibits 3,200 HUF ☉ Tues.–Sun. 10–6 Ⓜ Várbusz (5th stop from M2: Széll Kálmán tér).

TABÁN AND GELLÉRT-HEGY (TABÁN AND GELLÉRT HILL)
Gellért Szálloda és Thermál Fürdő (*Gellért Hotel & Thermal Baths*). At the foot of Gellért Hill the beautiful art-nouveau Danubius Hotel Gellért is the oldest spa hotel in Hungary, with hot springs that have supplied curative baths for nearly 2,000 years. Its baths are the most popular among tourists, both because you don't need reservations, as you do at most other hotel-based thermal spas, and also because there's a wealth of treatments—including chamomile steam baths, salt-vapor inhalations, and hot mud packs. Many of these treatments require a doctor's prescription; prescriptions from foreign doctors are accepted. Most staff speak English. Men and women have separate steam and sauna rooms; both the indoor pool and the outdoor wave pool are coed. ⊠ *District XI, Gellért tér 1, at the foot of the hill, Gellért-hegy and Tabán* ☎ *1/466–6166 for baths* ⊠ *4,900 HUF weekdays, 5,300 HUF weekends. Private cabins 400 HUF extra.* ☉ *Baths 6 am–8 pm; tickets sold until 5 pm* Ⓜ *M3: Kálvin tér, then Tram No. 47 or 49 (2nd stop across the Danube).*

Szobor Park (*Statue Park*). After the collapse of the Iron Curtain, Hungarians were understandably keen to rid Budapest of the symbols of Soviet domination. The communist statues and memorials that once dotted Budapest's streets and squares have been moved to this open-air "Disneyland of Communism." As well as the huge figures of Lenin and Marx, there are statues of the Hungarian worker shaking hands with his Soviet army comrade, and Hungarian puppet prime minister János Kádár. Somewhat tacky but amusing souvenirs are for sale, and songs from the Hungarian and Russian workers' movements play on a tinny speaker system.

To get there, first go to Etele tér in Buda via either a red Bus No. 7 or Bus No. 173 from Ferenciek tere, Tram No. 49 from Deák tér, or Tram No. 19 from Batthyány tér; then catch the yellow Volán bus from Platform 2 (but ask here to be sure). ■ **TIP→ The park also has a tour package, picking you up from Deak ter daily at 11.** ⊠ *District XXII, Balatoni út, corner of Szabadkai út, South Buda* ☎ *1/424–7500* ⊕ *www.szoborpark. hu* ⊠ *1,500 HUF, guided tours 1,200 HUF* ☉ *Daily 10–dusk.*

10

NORTH BUDA AND MARGARET ISLAND

FAMILY **Margit-sziget** (*Margaret Island*). More than 2½ km (1½ miles) long and
Fodor'sChoice covering nearly 200 acres, this island was first mentioned almost 2,000
★ years ago as the summer residence of the commander of the Roman garrison at nearby Aquincum. Later known as Rabbit Island (Insula Leporum), it was a royal hunting ground during the Árpád dynasty. King Imre, who reigned from 1196 to 1204, held court here, and several convents and monasteries were built here during the Middle Ages. (During a walk round the island, you'll see the ruins of a few of these buildings.) It's current name is taken from St. Margaret (1242–71), the pious daughter of King Béla IV, who at the ripe old age of 10 retired to a Dominican nunnery situated here from the 13th to the 16th centuries.

Today, it's an island park that's ideal for strolling, jogging, sunbathing, or just loafing. In good weather it draws a multitudinous cross section of the city's population out to its gardens and sporting facilities. The outdoor pool complex of the Palatinus Strand, built in 1921, can attract tens of thousands of people on a summer day. Nearby are a tennis stadium, a youth athletic center, boathouses, sports grounds, and, most impressive of all, the Nemzeti Sportuszoda (National Sports Swimming Pool), designed by the architect Alfred Hajós (while still in his teens, Hajós won two gold medals in swimming at the first modern Olympic Games, held in Athens in 1896).

The island's natural curative hot springs have given rise to the Danubius Grand and Danubius Health Spa Resort spa hotels on the northern end of the island. Waters from here are also piped into two spa hotels on the mainland, the Aquincum on the Buda bank and the Danubius Hélia on the Pest side.

On weekdays you'll share the island only with joggers and children playing hooky from school. ■**TIP→ To experience Margaret Island's role in Budapest life fully, go on a Saturday or, even better, a Sunday afternoon to join and/or watch people whiling away the day.**

At the northern end of the island is a copy of the water-powered Marosvásárhelyi zenélő kút (Marosvásárhely Musical Fountain), which plays songs and chimes. The original was designed more than 150 years ago by a Transylvanian named Péter Bodor. It stands near a serene, artificial rock garden with Japanese dwarf trees and lily ponds. The stream coursing through it never freezes, for it comes from a natural hot spring, causing it instead to give off thick steam in winter that enshrouds the garden in a mystical cloud. ⊠ *Margit-sziget* ⊕ *www.margitsziget.info* Ⓜ *M3: Árpád híd.*

DOWNTOWN PEST AND THE KIS KÖRÚT (LITTLE RING ROAD)

Fodor'sChoice **Néprajzi Múzeum** (*Museum of Ethnography*). The 1890s neoclassical
★ temple formerly housed the Supreme Court. Now an impressive permanent exhibition, "The Folk Culture of the Hungarian People," explains all aspects of peasant life from the end of the 18th century until World War I; explanatory texts are provided in both English and Hungarian. Besides embroideries, pottery, and carvings—the authentic pieces you can't see at touristy folk shops—there are farming tools, furniture, and traditional costumes. The central room of the building alone is worth the entrance fee: a majestic hall with ornate marble staircases and pillars, and towering stained-glass windows. ⊠ *District V, Kossuth tér 12, Parliament* ☎ *1/473–2400* ⊕ *www.neprajz.hu* ▣ *1,400 HUF* ☉ *Tues.– Sun. 10–6* Ⓜ *M2: Kossuth tér.*

Országház (*Parliament*). The most visible symbol of Budapest's left bank is the huge neo-Gothic Parliament, mirrored in the Danube much the way Britain's Parliament is reflected in the Thames. It was designed by the Hungarian architect Imre Steindl and built by a thousand workers between 1885 and 1902. The grace and dignity of its long facade and 24 slender towers, with spacious arcades and high windows balancing its vast central dome, lend this living landmark a refreshingly baroque spatial effect. The exterior is lined with 90 statues of great figures from Hungarian history; the corbels are ornamented by 242 allegorical statues. Inside are 691 rooms, 10 courtyards, and 29 staircases; some 88 pounds of gold were used for the staircases and halls. These halls are also a gallery of late-19th-century Hungarian art, with frescoes and canvases depicting Hungarian history, starting with Mihály Munkácsy's large painting of the Magyar Conquest of 896.

Parliament's most sacred treasure isn't the Hungarian legislature but rather the Szent Korona (Holy Crown), which reposes with other royal relics under the cupola. The crown sits like a golden soufflé above a Byzantine band of holy scenes in enamel and pearls and other gems. Known as the Crown of St. Stephen, it has been regarded—even by communist governments—as the legal symbol of Hungarian sovereignty and unbroken statehood.

The only way you can visit the Parliament and see the crown is on one of the daily tours. Lines may be long, so it's best to call in advance for reservations. Note that the building is closed to the public during ceremonial events and when the legislature is in session (usually Monday and Tuesday from late summer to spring). ⊠ *District V, Kossuth tér, Parliament* ☎ *1/441–4412, 1/441–4415, 1/441–4904 for info and tour reservations* ⊕ *www.mkogy.hu* ☑ *3,400 HUF (EU citizens free)* ۞ *Mon. 8 am–11 am, Tues.–Fri. 8–6, Sat. 8–4, Sun. 8–2. Daily tours in English at 10, noon and 2, starting from Gate No. 10, just right of main stairs* Ⓜ *M2: Kossuth tér.*

Széchenyi Lánchíd (*Chain Bridge*). This is the oldest and most beautiful of the seven road bridges that span the Danube in Budapest. When lit up at night, it captures Budapest's radiance as do few other scenes. It was constructed at the initiative of the great Hungarian reformer and philanthropist Count István Széchenyi, using an 1839 design by the English civil engineer William Tierney Clark. This classical, almost poetically graceful and symmetrical suspension bridge was finished by the Scotsman Adam Clark (no relation to William Tierney Clark), who also built the 383-yard tunnel under Castle Hill, thus connecting the Danube quay with the rest of Buda.

After it was destroyed by the Nazis, the bridge was rebuilt in its original form (though widened for traffic) and was reopened in 1949, on the centenary of its inauguration. ∎TIP➔ **At the Buda end of the Chain Bridge is Clark Ádám tér (Adam Clark Square), where you can zip up to Castle Hill on the Sikló funicular.** ⊠ *District I, linking Clark Ádám tér with Roosevelt tér, around Váci utca* ☑ *Funicular 1,000 HUF one-way* ۞ *Funicular daily 7:30 am–10 pm* Ⓜ *M2: Batthyány tér, M1, M2, or M3: Deák Ferenc tér.*

Fodor's Choice ★ **Szent István Bazilika** (*St. Stephen's Basilica*). Handsome and massive, this is one of the chief landmarks of Pest and the city's largest church—it can hold 8,500 people. Its very Holy Roman front porch greets you with a tympanum bustling with statuary. The basilica's dome and the dome of Parliament are by far the most visible in the Pest skyline, and this is no accident: with the Magyar Millennium of 1896 in mind (the lavishly celebrated thousandth anniversary of the settling of the Carpathian Basin in 896), both domes were planned to be 315 feet high.

The millennium was not yet in sight when architect József Hild began building the basilica in neoclassical style in 1851, two years after the

10

revolution was suppressed. After Hild's death, the project was taken over in 1867 by Miklós Ybl, the architect who did the most to transform modern Pest into a monumental metropolis. Ybl died in 1891, five years before the 1,000-year celebration, and the basilica was completed in neo-Renaissance style by József Kauser—but not until 1905.

Below the cupola is a rich collection of late-19th-century Hungarian art: mosaics, altarpieces, and statuary (what heady days the Magyar Millennium must have meant for local talents). There are 150 kinds of marble, all from Hungary except for the Carrara in the sanctuary's centerpiece: a white statue of King (St.) Stephen I, Hungary's first king and patron saint. Stephen's mummified right hand is preserved as a relic in the Szent Jobb Kápolna (Holy Right Chapel); press a button and it will be illuminated for two minutes. You can also climb the 364 stairs (or take the elevator) to the top of the cupola for a spectacular view of the city. Guided tours (available in English) cost 2,000 HUF and leave five times a day on weekdays (the first at 9:30) and twice on Saturdays (at 9:30 and 11). ⊠ *District V, Szt. István tér, Szent István Bazilika* ☎ *1/338–2151* ⊕ *en.bazilika.biz* ☎ *Church and Szt. Jobb Chapel free, cupola 500 HUF* ☉ *Church: Mon.–Sat. 9–5:30, Sun. 1–5:30. Szt. Jobb Chapel: Apr.–Oct., Mon.–Sat. 9–5, Sun. 1–5; Nov.–Mar., Mon.–Sat. 10–4, Sun. 1–4. Cupola: Apr. and Sept.–Oct., daily 10–5; May–Aug., daily 9–6* Ⓜ *M1, M2, or M3: Deák Ferenc tér, M3: Arany János utca.*

Vásárcsarnok (*Central Market Hall*). The magnificent hall, a 19th-century iron-frame construction, was reopened in late 1994 after years of renovation (and disputes over who would foot the bill). Even during the leanest years of communist shortages, the abundance of food came as a revelation to shoppers from East and West. Today the cavernous, three-story market, which is near the southern end of Váci utca and at the head of the Szabadsag Bridge, once again teems with people browsing among stalls packed with salamis and red-paprika chains. Upstairs you can buy folk embroideries and souvenirs and have your fill of Hungarian-style fast food. Also not to be missed are the inexpensive Hungarian lunch options on the upstrairs right side corridor, not to mention the kiosks that sell samplings of local *pálinka* (fruit brandy). ⊠ *District IX, Vámház körút 1–3, around Fővam tér* ☎ *1/366–3497* ☉ *Mon. 6 am–5 pm, Tues.–Fri. 6–6, Sat. 6–3* Ⓜ *M3: Kálvin tér, Tram No. 2: Fővám tér.*

Zsidó Múzeum (*Jewish Museum*). The four-room museum, around the corner from the Great Synagogue, has displays explaining the effect of the Holocaust on Hungarian and Transylvanian Jews. (There are labels in English.) In late 1993 burglars ransacked the museum and got away with approximately 80% of its priceless collection; several months later, the stolen objects were found in Romania and returned to their rightful home. Keep an eye out for the photographs of the World War II–era Jewish ghetto in Budapest: they represent the only images of horror and conditions Hungarian Jews were subjected to during that time. ⊠ *District VII, Dohány utca 2, around Astoria* ☎ *1/343–6756* ⊕ *www. zsidomuzeum.hu* ☎ *2,250 HUF* ☉ *Mar. 1–Nov. 1, Mon.–Thurs. 10–6, Fri. and Sun. 10–4; Nov. 2–Apr. 28, Mon.–Thurs. 10–4, Fri. and Sun. 10–2* Ⓜ *M2: Astoria.*

ANDRÁSSY ÚT

Hősök tere. Andrássy út ends in grandeur at Heroes' Square, with Budapest's answer to Berlin's Brandenburg Gate. Cleaned and refurbished in 1996 for the millecentenary (1100th anniversary), the Millenniumi Emlékmű (Millennial Monument) is a semicircular twin colonnade with statues of Hungary's kings and leaders between its pillars. Set back in its open center, a 118-foot stone column is crowned by a dynamic statue of the archangel Gabriel, his outstretched arms bearing the ancient emblems of Hungary. At its base ride seven bronze horsemen: the Magyar chieftains, led by Árpád, whose tribes conquered the land in 896.

Before the column lies a simple marble slab, the Nemzeti Háborús Emlék Tábla (National War Memorial), the nation's altar, at which every visiting foreign dignitary lays a ceremonial wreath. It appeared in the film *Evita* (set in Argentina, not Hungary), and was featured in a Michael Jackson music video. ⊠ *District VI, Høsök tere, Városliget* Ⓜ *M1: Høsök tere.*

Magyar Állami Operaház (*Hungarian State Opera House*). Miklós Ybl's crowning achievement is the neo-Renaissance Opera House, built between 1875 and 1884. Badly damaged during the siege of 1944–45, it was restored for its 1984 centenary. Two buxom marble sphinxes guard the driveway; the main entrance is flanked by Alajos Strobl's "romantic-realist" limestone statues of Liszt and of another 19th-century Hungarian composer, Ferenc Erkel, the father of Hungarian opera (his patriotic opera *Bánk bán* is still performed for national celebrations).

Inside, the spectacle begins even before the performance does. You glide up grand staircases and through wood-paneled corridors and gilt lime-green salons into a glittering jewel box of an auditorium. Its four tiers of boxes are held up by helmeted sphinxes beneath a frescoed ceiling by Károly Lotz. Lower down there are frescoes everywhere, with intertwined motifs of Apollo and Dionysus. In its early years the Budapest Opera was conducted by Gustav Mahler (1888–91), and after World War II by Otto Klemperer (1947–50).

The best way to experience the Opera House's interior is to see a ballet or opera; and while performance quality varies, tickets are relatively affordable and easy to come by, at least for tourists. There are no performances in summer, except for the weeklong BudaFest international opera and ballet festival in mid-August. You cannot view the interior on your own, but 45-minute tours in English are usually conducted daily; buy tickets in the Opera Shop, by the sphinx at the Hajós utca entrance. ⊠ *District VI, Andrássy út 22, around Andrássy út* ☎ *1/331–2550 for tours, 1/353–0170 for box office* ⊕ *www.opera.hu* ⊠ *Tours 2,900 HUF* ☉ *Tours daily at 3 and 4* Ⓜ *M1: Opera.*

Széchenyi Fürdő (*Széchenyi Baths*).The largest medicinal bathing complex in Europe, Széchenyi Fürdő is housed in a beautiful neo-baroque building in the middle of City Park. There are several thermal pools indoors as well as two outdoor pools, which remain open even in winter, when dense steam hangs thick over the hot water's surface—you can just barely make out the figures of elderly men, submerged shoulder deep, crowded around waterproof chessboards. To use the baths,

10

you pay a standard price (unless you get a doctor's prescription, in which case it's free), plus a small surcharge if you prefer having a private changing cabin instead of a locker. Facilities include medical and underwater massage treatments, carbonated bath treatments, and mud wraps. A great way to sweat away last night's *pálinka* (fruit brandy). ⊠ *District XIV, Városliget, Állatkerti körút 11* ☎ *1/363–3210* ⊕ *www. szechenyifurdo.hu* ⊒ *Weekdays 4,100 HUF, weekends 4,300 HUF; cabin 500 HUF extra* ⊙ *Daily 6 am–10 pm.*

Terror Háza (*Terror House*). The most controversial museum in post-communist Hungary was established at great cost, with the support of the center-right government in power from 1998 to 2002. Some critics alleged that its exhibits are less than objective—sensational attacks on those even loosely associated with the communist-era dictatorship—and place less emphasis on the terrors of the fascist era and the Holocaust in particular. The museum director replied that the collection is dedicated to the victims of both regimes (fascist and communist)—noting that there is an exhibit on the atrocities against Jews before and during World War II—and that it was painstakingly researched and designed by experts.

The building itself has a terrible history. Starting in 1939 it was headquarters of the Arrow Cross. From 1945 to 1956 the notorious communist state security police, the ÁVO (later succeeded by the ÁVH), used it as its headquarters and as its interrogation-cum-torture center. A powerful visual and sensual experience, this state-of-the-art, multimedia museum features everything from videos of sobbing victims telling their stories to a full-size Soviet tank. An English-language audio guide is available; groups needing them for each member should call several days or more in advance to reserve, as the number of units is limited. ⊠ *District VI, Andrássy út 60, Around Andrássy út* ☎ *1/374– 2600* ⊕ *www.terrorhaza.hu* ⊒ *2,000 HUF, audio guide 1,300 HUF* ⊙ *Tues.–Sun. 10–6* Ⓜ *M1: Vörösmarty utca.*

EASTERN PEST AND THE NAGY KÖRÚT (GREAT RING ROAD)

Fodor's Choice
★ **Művészetek Palotája** (*Palace of the Arts*). In southern Pest, at the foot of the Lágymányosi Bridge, right beside the similarly grand National Theater (which opened five years earlier), this monumental (750,000-square-foot) venue is not just a place where the capital's nouveau riche can spend their forints on a wide array of musical, theatrical, and dance performances in addition to dining in style. As per the title of a brochure advertising its splendors, it is also an "experience in every sense"—much of which is accessible free of charge to anyone who wants to wander around inside. Of course, you first have to make your way to Boráros tér and take the HÉV commuter train one stop—a bit of a bother, but worth it, if you have several days in Budapest. On the outside the place does indeed look palatial, in a very modern sense. The inside, as spacious and as sparkling as it is, contains plenty of intimate, well-cushioned little nooks on all floors on both sides of its National Concert Hall—which occupies its center—where you can take a seat and ponder life and/or art. ⊠ *District IX, Komor Marcell*

utca 1, around Boráros tér ☎ *1/555–3000* 🌐 *www.mupa.hu* 🎟 *Free (performance prices vary)* [M] *M3: Ülløi út.*

WHERE TO EAT

DOWNTOWN PEST AND THE SMALL RING ROAD

$$$$ INTERNATIONAL Fodor's Choice ★

🍴 **Borkonyha.** The "Wine Kitchen" is the best place in Budapest for carefully assembled, fresh, and innovative Hungarian-French fusion cuisine. Crispy duck liver, tuna tartare, daily seafood specials, bacon from *mangalica* (the Hungarian wonder pig), and pan-fried duck are standouts on the small but excellent menu. Specials on the chalkboards will be explained in English. Ask your server for wine-pairing recommendations, as one of the owners was a prime mover with the Hungarian Wine Society. This very friendly, romantic, upscale restaurant has risen quickly to become a favorite of many local foodies. [$] *Average main: 4,700 HUF* ✉ *District V, Sas Utca 3, Szent István Bazilika* ☎ *1/266–0835* 🌐 *www.borkonyha.hu* ✍ *Reservations essential* 🕒 *Closed Sun.*

$$$ CAFÉ Fodor's Choice ★

🍴 **Centrál Kávéház.** A classic turn-of-the-20th-century gathering spot for Hungarian writers of the *Nyugat* (*West*) magazine, this coffeehouse has endured two wars and a communist closure. For 19th-century grandeur in 21st-century comfort, this popular café can't be beat. Coffees are served on silver trays with glasses of mineral water just as in the old days, but these days they are enjoyed in an air-conditioned, no-smoking room. The menu includes substantial dishes like *hortobágyi palacsinta* (meat pancakes with paprika sauce) and *borjú paprikás* (paprika veal stew) all day. Don't miss the excellent cakes and pastries, on view in a glass display case. [$] *Average main: 3,500 HUF* ✉ *District V, Károlyi Mihály utca 9, around Váci utca* ☎ *1/266–2110* 🌐 *www.centralkavehaz.hu* [M] *M3: Ferenciek tere.*

$$ HUNGARIAN Fodor's Choice ★

🍴 **Kádár Étkezde.** Known to locals as Kádár bácsi's (Uncle Kadar's place), this home-style family restaurant has been around for a while—long enough to have more than one generation of fans. The walls are decorated with photos of celebrities from years gone by and the tables are topped with old-fashioned spritzer bottles from which you serve yourself water. Good old-fashioned Hungarian Jewish cooking is the thing here (not kosher, though); think stuffed kohlrabi, *káposztás kocka* (cabbage pasta), and lots of boiled beef. On Saturdays you can get *sólet* (cholent), a meat and barley stew traditionally served on the sabbath that is especially good topped with goose meat. Everyone orders the tasty raspberry *(málna)* drink. Tell the cashier what you ate including how many slices of bread, and pay at the door. It's only open from 11:30 to 3:30. [$] *Average main: 2,000 HUF* ✉ *District VII, Klauzá tér 9, Around Király utca* ☎ *1/321–3622* ✍ *Reservations not accepted* 💳 *No credit cards* 🕒 *Closed Sun. and Mon. No dinner* [M] *M2: Blaha Lujza tér.*

$$$ HUNGARIAN

🍴 **Kispiac Bisztró.** Kispiac Bisztró is a tiny gem of a restaurant (its name means "little market") that specializes in huge portions of fresh roasted meat, which come straight from the nearby District V market hall. Delicious pork belly, beef ribs, ham hock, or roast duck are the way to go, along with a plate of homemade pickles. Eating here is a bit like being invited home for dinner by the local butcher. No more than 18

10

HOW TO SPA IN BUDAPEST

Visiting one or more of the thermal baths in Budapest is one of the city's best experiences. Knowing a bit about the etiquette (and knowing what to expect) will help you enjoy your steam.

ARRIVING

The entrance procedure to *gyógyfürdők* (thermal baths) in Budapest can be baffling to visitors. Some baths post prices and treatments in English, but it remains unclear what kind of ticket you need and what you're actually getting. Sadly, in most of the state-run baths there's not much help from the staff. Much of the information on the price list pertains to medical treatments offered at the spa for patients with prescriptions from their doctors. There's also a lengthy explanation of the refund policy, which entitles you to a refund of the ticket price if you stay no more than around three hours. In general, buy a *belépő jegy* (entrance ticket), then choose a locker or cabin (cabins are slightly more expensive). An entrance ticket allows you to use both the thermal baths and the swimming pools. Most places issue small bits of paper as tickets. Hold on to these because you'll need them for the refund you can receive at the cashier's desk upon leaving.

GETTING READY

Once you've paid, follow the directions to the locker room, where you will change. Once you have changed into your swimsuit—or disrobed completely if you're in a single-sex spa—a locker attendant will lock your cabin and give you a key. You might have to go looking for him or her, so keep an eye on your belongings meanwhile. Make sure to tie this key around your wrist or attach it to your swimsuit. With the exception of the Király, where swimsuits are now required all the time, in the single-sex places you'll be given a sheet, or a cotton frock of some kind to wear when you walk between the locker room and the thermal bath. Signs posted in all thermal baths instruct you to shower before entering the water.

WHAT TO BRING

As a rule, bring shower shoes to all thermal baths and a towel to all but the big wellness hotels. Swimsuits are required in mixed company (at wellness hotels; at the Lukács, the Rudas, and the Széchenyi thermal baths; and at the swimming pool at the Gellért), and a bathing cap is required in most swimming pools. Keep some small change (100 HUF–200 HUF) with you to tip locker attendants on your way out and in case you want a beverage in between soaks (another 200 HUF–400 HUF). Check all your other valuables in a locker, which you can ask for when you buy your ticket. It's useful to bring your own shampoo, body lotion, and a comb for showering afterward, but most thermal baths have hair dryers.

diners fit in the small room at once, so making reservations at Kispiac is a must. $ *Average main: 3,000 HUF* ✉ *District V, Hold utca 13, around Parliament* ☎ *1/269–4231* ⊕ *www.kispiac.eu* ⚐ *Reservations essential* ⊗ *Closed Sun.*

$$$$
HUNGARIAN

✘ **Onyx.** Onyx distinguishes itself by being one of only two Budapest restaurants to earn a Michelin star, yet at the same time it remains somewhat affordable by offering an inexpensive prix-fixe lunch menu. Dinner is another story, when exotic dishes like wild sea bass and outstanding local game fill the menu. Try the six-course Hungarian Evolution tasting menu, which is loaded with modern takes on Hungarian specialties like *gulyas* (goulash soup) and goose liver. Dinner will get inevitably pricey, but Onyx is still a good value for the quality of the experience. It's a modern, chic room, and you'll fit right in if you dress smartly. $ *Average main: 10,500 HUF* ✉ *Vörösmarty tér 7–8, around Vörösmarty tér* ☎ *36–0/30–508–0622* ⊕ *www.onyxrestaurant.hu* ⚐ *Reservations essential* ⊗ *Closed Sun. and Mon.*

NEAR ST. STEPHEN'S BASILICA

$$$
EUROPEAN

✘ **Café Kör.** The wrought-iron tables, vaulted ceilings, and crisp white tablecloths give this chic bistro a decidedly downtown feel. In the heart of the busy District V, Café Kör is ideal for lunch or dinner when touring nearby St. Stephen's Basilica, although it's best to go early, since the place enjoys a loyal local following. True to bistro aspirations, the daily specials are scribbled on the wall, in both Hungarian and English. Let the friendly waitstaff guide you—even if steamed leg of veal sounds a bit less than tempting, it's heavenly. Grilled ewe-cheese salad is a favorite with regulars. $ *Average main: 3,300 HUF* ✉ *District V, Sas utca 17, St. Stephen's Basilica* ☎ *1/311–0053* ⊕ *www.cafekor.com* ⚐ *Reservations essential* ▭ *No credit cards* ⊗ *Closed Sun.* Ⓜ *M3: Arany János utca.*

$
ISRAELI
Fodor's Choice
★

✘ **Hummus Bar.** A favorite go-to place for students and tourists who want a break from heavy Hungarian cuisine, Hummus Bar is cheap, healthy, and loaded with Middle Eastern vegetarian options. It goes without saying that the hummus is fantastic, but elsewhere on the menu you can find wonderful dishes like a tomato bomb called *shakshouka*, a spicy vegetable couscous, and the best falafel in the city. Meat eaters will find plenty to love in the grilled chicken and liver dishes. Adventurous diners should try the "Jerusalem Mix," which has both chicken liver and chicken heart. It's all served up with some serious Middle Eastern spice and a complimentary glass of mint tea. $ *Average main: 1,350 HUF* ✉ *Október 6 utca 19, around St. Stephen's Basilica* ☎ *1/354–0108* ⊕ *www.hummusbar.hu.*

ANDRÁSSY ÚT

$$$
EASTERN
EUROPEAN
Fodor's Choice
★

✘ **Menza.** Somebody's clever vision of a 1970s-style communist-era cafeteria right in the heart of trendy Liszt Ferenc tér is a big hit. Details like retro table settings, orange and olive green Formica, and the very worst in communist lighting design miraculously come together to give this place a cool hipster vibe. Quirky dishes like homemade Hungarian soups served with cereal croutons get a giggle from most diners, and greasy childhood treats like *langós* (fried dough) get reinvented and stuffed with chicken and mushrooms. In spite of the grooviness, there's

10

good old-fashioned Hungarian comfort food here and pretty attentive, non-communist-era service. Check out the Kádár-era soft-drink list at the bar, and try *meggy marka*, a surprisingly refreshing sour cherry soda. $ *Average main: 3,000 HUF* ⊠ *District VI, Liszt Ferenc tér 2, around Andrássy út* ☎ *1/413–1482* ⊕ *www.menzaetterem.hu* ⚞ *Reservations essential* Ⓜ *M1: Oktogon.*

NORTH BUDA

$$$

EUROPEAN

✕**Csalogány 26.** Perennially on the Michelin radar, Csalogány 26 is one of the few truly great restaurants on the Buda side, and it's an ideal place to dine after or before taking in the Castle District. It also offers one of the best prix-fixe lunches in the city, for a fraction of the cost of dinner. For dinner, you can order à la carte or create your own tasting menu from entrées like goat cheese brûlée, suckling pig, veal liver, and Norwegian salmon. The dining room is a small, simple—some say drab—room, but the restaurant is still very popular and worth the trip to inner Buda. $ *Average main: 3,000 HUF* ⊠ *District I, Csalogány 26, North Buda* ☎ *1/201–7892* ⊕ *www.csalogany26.hu* ⚞ *Reservations essential* ⊘ *Closed Sun. and Mon.*

ÓBUDA

$$$

EASTERN
EUROPEAN
Fodor's Choice
★

✕**Kisbuda Gyöngye.** Considered by many the finest restaurant in Óbuda, this intimate place is filled with antique furniture and decorated with an eclectic but elegant patchwork of carved wooden cupboard doors and panels. The mood is set by the veteran pianist, who can serenade guests in a dozen languages, but who is at his best with Hungarian ballads. Meat and game dishes stand out here. Try the tarragon ragout of game, or sample the goose wedding feast, a richly flavorful dish that includes a crispy goose leg with braised red cabbage, grilled goose liver, and lightly fried goose cracklings. The excellent Serbian fish dishes are also worth a taste. $ *Average main: 3,000 HUF* ⊠ *District III, Kenyeres utca 34, Óbuda* ☎ *1/368–6402, 1/368–9246* ⊕ *www.remiz.hu* ⚞ *Reservations essential* ⊘ *Closed Sun.*

WHERE TO STAY

All room rates given are based on double occupancy in high season. For luxury hotels, VAT of 12% and sometimes breakfast and a tourist tax of 3% will not be included in the room rate. Assume they are included unless there is a note to the contrary.

APARTMENT RENTALS

Apartments, available for short- and long-term rental, are often an economical alternative to staying in a hotel, with an increasing number of options available, as Hungarian entrepreneurs find uses for old family homes and inherited apartments. A short-term rental in Budapest will probably cost anywhere from 6800 HUF to 14000 HUF a day.

Budapest Vacation Rentals. Private apartments in historical buildings are the specialty of Budapest Vacation Rentals. Take your pick from many different but central Budapest districts at many different price levels. The apartments accommodate solo travelers as well as families. The owner is American, so communication in English won't be a problem.

Note: the company prefers to be contacted via email. ■ **TIP→ Apartment Max overlooks one of Budapest's best kept parks, Károly Kert. It's about the best location possible in downtown Pest.** ☎ *29/945–1679* ✉ *john@budapestvacationrentals.eu* 🌐 *budapestvacationrentals.com.*

IBUSZ Private Accommodation Service. With offices throughout the city, IBUSZ rents out apartments in downtown Budapest, most consisting of two rooms plus a fully equipped kitchen and bathroom. Private rooms are also available. The main office is open weekdays 9–6:30, but you can explore the options 24/7 on the website. ✉ *District V, József Attila utca 20, around Deák tér* ☎ *1/501–4910* 🌐 *www.ibusz.hu.*

VÁRHEGY (CASTLE HILL)

$$$ HOTEL FAMILY

🏨 **Budapest Hilton.** The exterior certainly betrays the hotel's 1970s origins, but the modern and tasteful rooms and great views from Castle Hill will soothe the most delicate of aesthetic sensibilities. You'll have to decide for yourself if this hotel, built in 1977 around the remains of a 17th-century Gothic chapel and adjacent to the Matthias Church, is a successful integration or not. **Pros:** great views, 24-hour business center, free airport shuttle. **Cons:** minimal fitness facilities. [$] *Rooms from: 56,700 HUF* ✉ *District I, Hess András tér 1–3, Castle Hill* ☎ *1/889–6600, 800/445–8667 in the U.S. and Canada* 🌐 *www.budapest.hilton.com* 🛏 *322 rooms, 25 suites* 🍴 *No meals* [M] *M2: Széll Kálmán tér, then Várbusz.*

GELLÉRT HILL AND SOUTH BUDA

$$$ HOTEL

🏨 **Danubius Hotel Gellért.** Budapest's most renowned art nouveau hotel underwent an overhaul that restored the original Jugendstil style popular when it was built during World War I. [$] *Rooms from: 51,000 HUF* ✉ *District XI, Szent Gellért tér 1, Gellért-hegy and Tabán* ☎ *1/889–5500* 🌐 *www.danubiusgroup.com* 🛏 *234 rooms, 10 suites* 🍴 *Breakfast* [M] *Tram No. 18, 19, 47, or 49 to Szent Gellért tér.*

$ B&B/INN Fodor's Choice ★

🏨 **Kalmár Bed & Breakfast.** This elegant stone mansion, dating from 1900, is on the lower slopes of Gellért Hill, right behind the Hotel Gellért. **Pros:** friendly staff; authentic ambience; breakfast served on delicate matching porcelain. **Cons:** no real amenities; some baths only have shower stalls (no tubs); lots of stairs and no elevator. [$] *Rooms from: 20,700 HUF* ✉ *District XI, Kelenhegyi út 7–9, Gellért-hegy and Tabán* ☎ *1/372–7530, 1/271–9312 for English-speakers, 06–30/271–9312* 🌐 *www.kalmarpension.net* 🛏 *10 rooms, 2 suites, 1 apartment* 🍴 *Breakfast* [M] *Tram No. 18, 19, 47, or 49 to Szent Gellért tér.*

AROUND DEÁK FERENC TÉR

$$$$ HOTEL Fodor's Choice ★

🏨 **Four Seasons Hotel Gresham Palace Budapest.** It doesn't get much better than this: a centrally located, super-deluxe hotel in a museum-quality landmark with the prettiest views in town. **Pros:** luxurious; lots of amenities. **Cons:** no real deals to be had here. [$] *Rooms from: 85,500 HUF* ✉ *District V, Roosevelt tér 5–6, around Váci utca* ☎ *1/268–6000* 🌐 *www.fourseasons.com/budapest* 🛏 *179 rooms, 17 suites* 🍴 *Breakfast* [M] *M1: Vörösmarty tér.*

10

AROUND ANDRÁSSY ÚT AND KIRÁLY UTCA

$$ HOTEL Fodor's Choice ★ **Mamaison Hotel Andrássy Budapest.** Budapest's best boutique hotel is housed in a Bauhaus-style structure built in 1937 and once used as an orphanage. **Pros:** free Wi-Fi throughout; free access to a nearby fitness center. **Cons:** a surcharge applies to children staying with their parents. [$] *Rooms from: 22,750 HUF ✉ District VI, Andrássy út 111, around Andrássy út ☎ 1/462–2118 🌐 www.andrassyhotel.com 🛏 68 rooms, 7 suites [M] M1: Bajza utca.*

AROUND KÁLVIN TÉR

$$ B&B/INN **Brody House.** Brody House is a hip-as-you-like guesthouse, where each of the rooms is named after the local artist whose work adorns the walls; it also offers a few apartments. **Pros:** romantic; well located; hip, sceney place. **Cons:** no exercise facilities; no meal plans offered; may be a bit too hip for some. [$] *Rooms from: 21,000 HUF ✉ 10 Bródy Sándor utca, Around Kálvin tér ☎ 1/266–1211 🌐 www.brodyhouse.com 🛏 11 rooms.*

$$$ HOTEL **Hotel Palazzo Zichy Budapest.** For an elegant, chic hotel stay, with flavors of old and modern Budapest, it is hard to beat this boutique conversion of the former palace of Hungarian Count Nándor Zichy. **Pros:** gorgeous building; great breakfast; on-site exercise facility; newly renovated. **Cons:** smallish rooms; not exactly the most central location; room service comes from a nearby pub, not an in-house restaurant. [$] *Rooms from: 25,000 HUF ✉ Lørinc Pap tér 2, around Kálvin tér ☎ 1/235–4000 🌐 www.hotel-palazzo-zichy.hu 🛏 80 rooms 🍴 Breakfast.*

AROUND NYUGATI TRAIN STATION

$$ B&B/INN **Kapital Inn.** Kapital Inn is a small but well-appointed B&B owned by a former chef (and friendly host) who returned home to Hungary after working in England and the U.S; needless to say, breakfast is a highlight. **Pros:** spacious rooftop terrace; guest office; friendly and professional host; great breakfast. **Cons:** no elevator; no exercise facility. [$] *Rooms from: 27,000 HUF ✉ Kapital Inn, Aradi utca 30, around Nyugati Train Station ☎ 36/30–915–2029 🌐 kapitalinn.com 🛏 4 rooms 🍴 Breakfast.*

AROUND BLAHA LUJZA TÉR AND FRERENC KÖRÚT

$$$ HOTEL **Boscolo Budapest.** This refurbished belle-époque grande dame, once known as the New York Palace and now part of the Italian Boscolo chain, is a pleasing mix of traditional and contemporary. **Pros:** great combination of old and new; deals to be had. **Cons:** some rooms have only shower stalls (no tubs); reviews on the service are mixed. [$] *Rooms from: 48,000 HUF ✉ District VII, Erzsébet körút 9–11, around Blaha Lujza tér ☎ 1/886–6111 🌐 www.budapest.boscolohotels.com 🛏 185 rooms, 29 suites 🍴 No meals [M] M2: Blaha Lujza tér.*

$$$ HOTEL Fodor's Choice ★ **Corinthia Hotel Budapest.** The Corinthia first opened as the luxurious Grand Royal Hotel in time for the Magyar Millennium in 1896, and, despite being destroyed during Hungary's 1956 revolution, it's just as luxurious today. **Pros:** opulent setting without a break-the-bank price; amazing spa and spa package deals; great restaurants in the hotel. **Cons:** may be too big and too formal for some; non-spa packages don't offer the same value for money. [$] *Rooms from: 42,600 HUF ✉ District VII,*

*Erzsébet körút 43–49, Around Blaha Lujza tér ☎ 1/479–4000 ⊕ www.
corinthia.com ⇆ 414 rooms, 34 suites, 26 apartments ⦿ No meals
Ⓜ M2: Blaha Lujza tér.*

NIGHTLIFE AND THE ARTS

THE ARTS

For the latest on arts events, consult the entertainment listings of the
English-language press. Their entertainment calendars map out all that's
happening in Budapest's arts and culture world—from thrash bands
in wild clubs to performances at the Opera House. Hotels and tourist
offices will provide you with a copy of the monthly publication *Pro-
gramme,* which contains details of all cultural events.

Tickets can be bought at the venues themselves, but many ticket offices
sell them without an extra charge. Prices are still very low, so mark-ups
of even 30% shouldn't dent your wallet if you book through your hotel.
Inquire at Tourinform if you're not sure where to go. Ticket availability
depends on the performance and season—it's usually possible to get
tickets a few days before a show, but performances by major international artists sell out early. Tickets to Budapest Festival Orchestra
concerts and festival events also go particularly quickly.

NIGHTLIFE

Budapest is filled with *sörözős* (beer bars), but the way to go is to head
for one of the *rom kerts* ("ruin bars," which are housed in the courtyards of abandoned buildings. There you will meet a cross section of
artists, professionals, students, and tourists enjoying a DJ or Hungarian
microbrew. If wine is more your thing, don't miss spending a few hours
in a wine bar (more upscale than the divey *borozós*). Wine bars have
lengthy wine lists comprising excellent Hungarian wines, and most serv-
ers speak reasonable enough English to recommend a wine and explain
what you are getting.

SHOPPING

10

Strictly speaking, Budapest is not a shopping town. There are interesting things to buy, of course, but a weekend in Budapest doesn't promise
the same shopping thrill that, say, a weekend in Istanbul or Paris does.
Major European and American retailers have outposts here and show
the latest fashions, but prices are generally about the same as anywhere
else in Europe and the selections can be limited.

Shops are generally open until 5 or 6 on weekdays and until 1 on Saturday (only shops in the malls are open on Sunday, for the most part).

MAJOR SHOPPING NEIGHBORHOODS

You'll find plenty of expensive boutiques, folk-art and souvenir shops,
foreign-language bookstores, and classical-record shops on or around
touristy **Váci utca,** Budapest's famous, upscale pedestrian-only promenade in District V. While a stroll along Váci utca is integral to a Budapest
visit, browsing among some of the smaller, less touristy, more typically
Hungarian shops in Pest—on the **Kis körút** (Small Ring Road) and **Nagy
körút** (Great Ring Road)—may prove more interesting and less pricey.

Lots of arty boutiques are springing up in the section of District V **south of Ferenciek tere** and **toward the Danube,** and around **Kálvin tér.** **Falk Miksa utca,** also in District V, running south from Szent István körút, is one of the city's best antiques districts, lined on both sides with atmospheric little shops and galleries.

THE DANUBE BEND

About 40 km (25 miles) north of Budapest, the Danube abandons its eastward course and turns abruptly south toward the capital, cutting through the Börzsöny and Visegrád hills. This area is called the Danube Bend and includes the baroque town of Szentendre as well as the hilltop castle ruins and town of Visegrád, both on the Danube's west bank. The most scenically varied part of Hungary, the region is best known for a chain of riverside spas and beaches, bare volcanic mountains, and limestone hills. Here, in the heartland, are the traces of the country's history—the remains of the Roman Empire's frontier, the battlefields of the Middle Ages, and the relics of the Hungarian Renaissance.

GETTING HERE AND AROUND

CAR TRAVEL

The district can be covered by car in one day, the total round trip no more than 112 km (70 miles), although this affords only a cursory look around. A day trip to Szentendre from Budapest plus another for Visegrád, with a night in Eger, would be best.

BOAT AND FERRY TRAVEL

From April 1 to September 30, the most interesting way to get to either Szentendre or Visegrád is by ferry. The Visegrád trip leaves from a dock off Budapest's Vigadó Square at 9:30 am. It is an hour-long trip up the Danube, returning at 5:30 pm; tickets cost 6,000 HUF. The ride to Szentendre departs from the same place at 10 am, arriving 90 minutes later. More information can be found at ⊕ *www.mahartpassnave.hu.*

TRAIN TRAVEL

Szentendre is easy to get to on local commuter trains (HÉV) that leave from a platform in Batthyány Tér underground, adjoining the metro stop. Buy tickets at the window next to the track and validate them on the train. Since this trip is outside of Budapest, any daily or weekly transit pass you are using will need to be supplemented with a ticket. There are three to five trains leaving every hour, so you'll have no need to rush to catch one. It's about a 40-minute trip (without air-conditioning, or much by way of comfort, mind you).

Visegrád can also be reached by train from Budapest. Take a train to Nagymaros-Visegrád station from Nyugati Station, where trains depart at seven minutes past the hour (towards Szob); the trip takes 41 minutes. After getting off the train in Nagymaros, you walk down to the hourly car ferry that takes you across the river to Visegrád.

Train timetables can be found at ⊕ *elvira.mav-start.hu.*

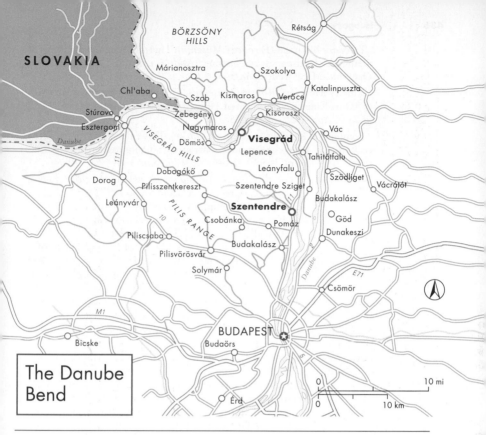

The Danube Bend

SZENTENDRE

21 km (13 miles) north of Budapest.

A romantic, lively little town with a flourishing artists' colony, this is the highlight of the Danube Bend. With its profusion of enchanting church steeples, colorful baroque houses, and winding, narrow cobblestone streets, it's no wonder Szentendre attracts swarms of visitors, tripling its population in peak season.

Szentendre was first settled by Serbs and Greeks fleeing the advancing Turks in the 16th and 17th centuries. They built houses and churches in their own style—rich in reds and blues seldom seen elsewhere in Hungary. To truly savor Szentendre, duck into any and every cobblestone side street that appeals to you. Baroque houses with shingle roofs (often with an arched eye-of-God upstairs window) and colorful stone walls will enchant your eye and pique your curiosity.

EXPLORING

Fø tér. Szentendre's main square, the centerpiece of Fø tér is an ornate **Memorial Cross** erected by Serbs in gratitude because the town was spared from a plague. The cross has a crucifixion painted on it and stands atop a triangular pillar adorned with a dozen icon paintings. Every house on Fø tér is a designated landmark. ⊠ *Fø tér.*

Ferenczy Múzeum (*Ferenczy Museum*). This museum has paintings of Szentendre landscapes. ✉ *Fő tér 6* ⏲ *Mid-Mar.–Sept., Tues.–Sun. 10–6; Oct.–mid-Mar., Wed.–Sun. 9–5.*

Kmetty Múzeum (*Kmetty Museum*). This museum displays the work of János Kmetty, a pioneer of Hungarian avant-garde painting. ✉ *Fő út 21* ⏲ *Apr.–Oct., daily 1–5.*

Szentendrei Képtár (*Municipal Gallery*). This gallery has an excellent collection of local contemporary art and changing exhibits of international art. ✉ *Fő út 2–5* ⏲ *Apr.–Oct., Wed.–Sun. 9–5.*

Görög templom (*Greek Church, or Blagovestenska Church*). Gracing the corner of Görög utca (Greek Street) and Szentendre's main square, Fø tér, the so-called Görög templom is actually a Serbian Orthodox church that takes its name from the Greek inscription on a red-marble gravestone set in its wall. This elegant edifice was built between 1752 and 1754 by a rococo master, Andreas Mayerhoffer, on the site of a wooden church dating to the Great Serbian Migration (around AD 690). Its greatest glory—a symmetrical floor-to-ceiling panoply of stunning icons—was painted between 1802 and 1804 by Mihailo Zivkovic, a Serbian painter from Buda. ✉ *Görög utca, at Fø tér* ☎ *26/313–917* 🌐 *www.templom.hu* 🎟 *300 HUF* ⏲ *Mar.–Oct., Tues.–Sun. 10–5.*

Kovács Margit Múzeum. If you have time for only one of Szentendre's myriad museums, don't miss the Kovács Margit Múzeum, which displays the collected works of Budapest ceramics artist Margit Kovács, who died in 1977. She left behind a wealth of richly textured work that ranges from ceramics to life-size sculptures. Admission to the museum is limited to 15 persons at a time, so it is wise to line up early or at lunchtime, when the herds of tour groups are occupied elsewhere. ✉ *Vastagh György utca 1, off Görög utca* ☎ *26/310–244* 🌐 *www.pmmi.hu* 🎟 *1,000 HUF* ⏲ *Tues.–Sun. 10–6.*

WHERE TO EAT

$$$ EASTERN EUROPEAN Fodor's Choice ★

🍴 **Aranysárkány.** A favorite of early-20th-century Hungarian writer Frigyes Karinthy, the Golden Dragon has seen more recent high-profile guests including Laura Bush (who visited Hungary years before her husband dropped by in June 2006). The food is all prepared in an open kitchen. Since there are only eight tables, be prepared to share on a busy night. Begin with *sárkány erø leves* (dragon's bouillon) with quail eggs. Main-course specialties include trout filets steamed in Campari, and venison steak in an almond crust. If you can still accommodate dessert, try the poppy-seed-spiked "opium" pudding or the cottage-cheese pudding with cranberries. A wine list with 60 varieties will tempt the inquisitive palate. Reservations are a must in the summer. [$] *Average main: 3,200 HUF* ✉ *Alkotmány utca 1/a* ☎ *26/301–479, 26/311–670* 🌐 *www.aranysarkany.hu* ⏲ *Closed mid-Dec.–mid-Jan.*

$$$ EASTERN EUROPEAN

🍴 **Régimódi.** This restaurant which has an excellent wine list and specializes in fish and game dishes is practically on Fø tér. Lace curtains, antique knickknacks, and lovely old paintings give the small upstairs dining room—which is air-conditioned and no-smoking—a homey intimacy; and, perhaps, the restaurant its name: Old-Fashioned (in the best sense, mind you). The downstairs dining room also has a certain antiques-induced charm to it, while the comparatively colorless seating out front carries only the advantage of allowing you to people-watch. The summer terrace, likewise upstairs, is a delightful place to dine alfresco and look out over the red-tile rooftops. $ *Average main: 2,900 HUF* ✉ *Dumtsa Jenő utca 2* ☎ *26/311–105* ⊕ *www.regimodirestaurant.hu.*

BICYCLING
The waterfront and streets beyond Szentendre's main square are perfect for a bike ride—free of jostling cobblestones and relatively calm and quiet. Check with Tourinform for local rental outfits. Rentals are possible in Budapest; bicycles are permitted in a designated car of each HÉV suburban railway train. Many people make the trip between Budapest and Szentendre on bicycle along the designated bike path, which runs on busy roads in some places, but is pleasant and separate from the road for the stretch between Békásmegyer and Szentendre.

SHOPPING
Flooded with tourists in summer, Szentendre is saturated with the requisite souvenir shops. Among the attractive but overpriced goods sold in every store are dolls dressed in traditional folk costumes, wooden trinkets, pottery, and colorful hand-embroidered tablecloths, doilies, and blouses. The best bargains are the hand-embroidered blankets and bags sold by dozens of elderly women in traditional folk attire, who stand for hours on the town's crowded streets. (Because of high weekend traffic, most Szentendre stores stay open all day on weekends, unlike those in Budapest. Galleries, closed Monday, accept major credit cards, although other stores may not.)

VISEGRÁD

23 km (14 miles) north of Szentendre.

Visegrád was the seat of the Hungarian kings during the 14th century, when a fortress built here by the Angevin kings became the royal residence. Today, the imposing fortress at the top of the hill towers over the peaceful little town of quiet, tree-lined streets and solid old houses. The forested hills rising just behind the town offer popular hiking possibilities. For a taste of Visegrád's best, climb to the Fellegvár, and then wander and take in the views of the Danube curving through the countryside; but make time to stroll around the village center a bit—on Fő utca and other streets that pique your interest.

10

EXPLORING
Fellegvár (*Citadel*). Crowning the top of a 1,148-foot hill, the dramatic Fellegvár was built in the 13th century and served as the seat of Hungarian kings in the early 14th century. In the Middle Ages the citadel was where the Holy Crown and other royal regalia were kept, until they were stolen by a dishonorable maid of honor in 1440; 23 years later King Matthias had to pay 80,000 HUF to retrieve them from Austria. (For the foreseeable future, the crown is safe in the Parliament building in Budapest.) A *panoptikum* (akin to slide projection) show portraying the era of the kings is included with admission. The

breathtaking views of the Danube Bend below are ample reward for the strenuous 40-minute hike up. Then again, you can always drive up the hill from the center of Visegrád in five minutes. ✉ *Fellegvár Nagyvillám* ☎ *26/398–101* 🎫 *Fellegvár 1,400 HUF (1,700 HUF with panoptikum)* 🕒 *Jan.–Oct., daily 10–5; Nov.–Dec. daily 9–3.*

Mátyás Király Múzeum (*King Matthias Museum*). In the 15th century, King Matthias Corvinus had a separate palace built on the bank of the Danube below the citadel. It was eventually razed by the Turks, and not until 1934 were the ruins finally excavated. Nowadays you can see the disheveled remnants of the Királyi palota (Royal Palace) and its Salamon torony (Salamon Tower), which are part of the Mátyás Király Múzeum. The Salamon Tower has two small exhibits displaying ancient statues and well structures from the age of King Matthias. Especially worth seeing is the red-marble well, built by a 15th-century Italian architect. Above a ceremonial courtyard rise the palace's various halls; on the left you can still see a few fine original carvings, which give an idea of how magnificent the palace must once have been. Inside the palace is a small exhibit on its history, as well as a collection of gravestones dating from Roman times to the 19th century. Friday in May, the museum hosts medieval crafts demonstrations. ✉ *Fő utca 29* ☎ *26/398–026* 🌐 *www.visegrad.hu/muzeum* 🎫 *1,100 HUF castle, 700 HUF Solamon Tower* 🕒 *Royal Palace Tues.–Sun. 9–5. Salomon Tower May–Sept., Tues.–Sun. 9–5.*

WHERE TO EAT

$$$ EASTERN EUROPEAN

🍴 **Sirály Restaurant.** With low lighting and funky, colorful, illuminated marsh scenes by your table mitigating its overall tourist-trap nature, this big but cramped restaurant opposite the ferry landing—which operates jointly with the Hotel Visegrád's adjacent Renaissance Restaurant—specializes in wild game while also offering traditional fare and some well-intended vegetarian dishes (e.g., fried soy steak in mayonnaise sauce with vegetables). In summer, when cooking is often done on the terrace overlooking the Danube, expect barbecued meats and stews, soups, and gulyás served in old-fashioned pots. [$] *Average main: 2,900 HUF* ✉ *Rév utca 15* ☎ *26/398–376* 🌐 *www.siralyvisegrad.hu.*

SPORTS AND THE OUTDOORS

HIKING

Visegrád makes a great base for exploring the trails of the Visegrád and Pilis hills. A hiking map is posted on the corner of Fő utca and Rév utca, just above the pale-green Roman Catholic Parish Church. A well-trodden, well-marked hiking trail (posted with red signs) leads from the edge of Visegrád to the town of Pilisszentlászló, a wonderful 8½-km (5-mile) journey that takes about three hours, through the oak and beech forests of the Visegrád Hills into the Pilis conservation region. Deer, wild boars, and mouflons roam freely here, and there are fields of yellow-blooming spring pheasant's eye and black pulsatilla.

TOBOGGAN SLIDE

FAMILY

Wiegand Toboggan Run. Winding through the trees on Nagy-Villám Hill is the Wiegand Toboggan Run, one of the longest slides you've ever seen. You ride on a small cart that is pulled uphill by trolley, then careen down the slope in a small, steel trough that resembles a bobsled run. ⊠ *Panoráma út, ½ km (¼ mile) from Fellegvár* 🕾 *26/397–397* ⊕ *www. bobozas.hu* 🖘 *400 HUF, 2,100 HUF for 6 runs* 🕙 *Weekends 10–5, weekdays 10–6.*

EGER

40 km (25 miles) east of Gyöngyös.

With vineyard surroundings and more than 175 of Hungary's historic monuments—a figure surpassed only by Budapest and Sopron—the picture-book baroque city of Eger is ripe for exploration. The city, which lies in a fertile valley between the Mátra Mountains and their eastern neighbor, the Bükk range, has borne witness to much history, heartbreak, and glory. It was settled quite early in the Hungarian conquest of the land, and it was one of five bishoprics created by King Stephen I when he Christianized the country almost a millennium ago.

In 1552 the city was attacked by the Turks, but the commander, István Dobó, and fewer than 2,000 men and women held out for 38 days against 80,000 Turkish soldiers and drove them away. One of Hungary's great legends tells of the women of Eger pouring hot pitch onto the heads of the Turks as they attempted to scale the castle walls (the event is depicted in a famous painting now in the National Gallery in Budapest). Despite such heroism, however, Eger fell to the Turks in 1596 and became one of the most important northern outposts of Muslim power until its reconquest in 1687.

Today, restored baroque and rococo buildings line Eger's cobblestone streets, making for excellent strolling and sightseeing. Wherever you wander, make a point of peeking into open courtyards, where you may happen upon otherwise hidden architectural gems.

GETTING HERE AND AROUND

The easiest way to get to Eger from Budapest is by train, which leaves at least once an hour (every 30 minutes, during peak hours) from Keleti Station. The trip lasts just under two hours. Tickets can be purchased in the underground just inside the entrance to Keleti. The last train back from Eger is at 7:30 in the evening, so perhaps go easy on the wine. Check train schedules at ⊕ *www.mav-start.hu.*

10

EXPLORING

Bazilika. The grand, neoclassical Bazilika, the second-largest cathedral in Hungary, was built in the center of town early in the 19th century. It is approached by a stunning stairway flanked by statues of Sts. Stephen, László, Peter, and Paul—the work of Italian sculptor Marco Casagrande, who also carved 22 biblical reliefs inside and outside the building. Ironically, perhaps, a few yards to the left of the main steps leading up to the Bazilika—on what appears to be its property—is a popular wine bar built into the high brick wall that flanks each side of the steps. From May 15 through October 15, organ recitals are held Monday through Saturday at 11:30 am and Sunday at 12:45 pm. It's

best to visit when no masses are taking place—from 9 until 6. ⊠ *Esz-terházy tér* ☎ *36/515–725* ⊕ *www.eger-bazilika.plebania.hu* ⊠ *Free* ⊙ *Daily 8–7:30.*

FAMILY **Eger Vár** (*Eger Castle*). Eger Vár was built after the devastating Tatar
Fodor'sChoice invasion of 1241–42. When Béla IV returned from exile in Italy, he
★ ordered the erection of mighty fortresses like those he had seen in the West. Within the castle walls an imposing Romanesque cathedral was built and then, during the 15th century, rebuilt in Gothic style; today only its foundations remain. Inside the foundation area, a statue of Szent István (St. Stephen), erected in 1900, looks out benignly over the city. Nearby are catacombs that were built in the second half of the 16th century by Italian engineers. By racing back and forth through this labyrinth of underground tunnels and appearing at various ends of the castle, the hundreds of defenders tricked the attacking Turks into thinking there were thousands of them. The Gothic-style **Püspök Ház** (Bishop's House) contains the castle history museum and, in the basement, a numismatics museum where coins can be minted and certified (in English). Also here are an art gallery displaying Italian and Dutch Renaissance works; a prison exhibit, near the main entrance; and a wax museum, depicting characters from the Hungarian historical novel *Eclipse of the Crescent Moon*, about Hungary's final expulsion of

the Turks. ■ **TIP→ Videotaping and picture-taking are not allowed inside the museums, but are OK (at no charge) on the castle grounds.** ✉ *Dózsa György tér* ☎ *36/312–744* 🌐 *www.egrivar.hu* 🎫 *Castle and museums 1,400 HUF, numismatics museum 800 HUF* 🕒 *Castle grounds: Mar. and Oct., daily 8–6; May–Aug. daily 8–8; Nov.–Feb. daily 8–5; Apr. and Sept., daily 8–7. Museums: Nov.–May, daily 10–4; Apr.–Oct. daily 10–5. Prison exhibit and catacombs May–Oct., daily 10–4. Wax museum daily 9–6.*

FAMILY **Kisvonat.** The Kisvonat, a miniature train that actually runs on wheels, leaves from Dobó tér every hour on the hour for an approximately 40-minute tour of Eger's historical sights. ✉ *Dobó tér* ☎ *34/487–381, 20/388–6241* 🎫 *500 HUF* 🕒 *Apr.–Oct. and late Dec.–early Jan., daily 9–5.*

Szépasszony-völgy. Eger wine is renowned beyond Hungary. The best-known variety is *Egri Bikavér* (Bull's Blood of Eger), a full-bodied red wine. Other outstanding vintages are the Medoc Noir, a dark red dessert wine; Leányka, a delightful dry white; and the sweeter white Muskotály. The place to sample them is the Szépasszony-völgy, a vineyard area on the southwestern edge of Eger's city limits. More than 200 small wine cellars (some of them literally holes-in-the-wall) stand open and inviting in warm weather, and a few are open in winter, too. You may be given a tour of the cellar, and wines will be tapped from the barrel into your glass by the vintners themselves at the tiniest cost (but it's prudent to inquire politely how much it will cost before imbibing). ✉ *Szépasszpny Völgy* 🌐 *www.szepasszony-volgy.hu.*

WHERE TO EAT

$$$ EASTERN EUROPEAN 🍴 **Fehér Szarvas.** The name of this homey rustic cellar, a longtime Eger dining landmark, means "white stag," and game is the uncontested specialty. Favorites include venison filet served in a pan sizzling with goose liver and herbed butter; wild boar with juniper berries in red-wine sauce; rabbit (presumably not wild) spiced with thyme; and knuckle of lamb (no, not wild either) with mushroom-bacon sweetbreads. The many antlers, skulls, skins, and mounted birds hanging from rafters and walls—not to mention the two little stuffed goats by the entrance—make the inn look like Archduke Franz Ferdinand's trophy room. [$] *Average main: 3,300 HUF* ✉ *Klapka György utca 8* ☎ *36/411–129* 🌐 *www.feherszarvasetterem.hu.*

$$ EUROPEAN 🍴 **HBH Bajor Sörház.** For substantial Hungarian (and, it seems, Bavarian) fare, it's impossible to beat the popular HBH Bavarian Beer Tavern, which has a great location on Dobó tér. The cuisine ranges from traditional Hungarian fare such as veal paprikash to Bavarian-style knuckle of ham. Any of these will go down smoothly with a glass of Bull's Blood—or perhaps a Munich Hofbräuhaus, the beer that gives the restaurant its initials. [$] *Average main: 2,250 HUF* ✉ *Bajcsy Zsilinszky utca 19, at Dobó tér* ☎ *36/515–516* 🌐 *www.hbh-eger.hu.*

$$$ HUNGARIAN 🍴 **Macok.** The restaurant in the Imola Udvarház offers perhaps the best dining experience in Eger. The spacious room is a bit formal for backpackers, but welcoming nonetheless. As this is Eger, wine plays

an important part on the menu, which features upscale comfort food like whole trout with garlic sauce, roast mangalica pig, and rosemary lamb with buckwheat. Wines are culled from the best Eger has to offer. Order a St. Andrea Hangács Bikavér if you want to sample the heady red wine Eger is best known for. [$] *Average main: 3,200 HUF* ✉ *Imola Udvarház, Dózsa György tér 4* ☎ *36/414–825* 🌐 *imolaudvarhaz.hu/en/* 🕓 *Closed Mon.*

$$ EASTERN EUROPEAN 🍴 **Palacsinta Vár Étterem.** The Palacsinta Castle Restaurant is *the* place to have your fill, and how, of Hungary's famous rolled-up pancake, the *palacsinta*. In this hip little cellar establishment (pleasantly cool on a hot summer day), adorned with funky wall art from Dalí prints to a display of cigarette packs to a stamp collection (and an aquarium full of live fish), you can choose from any of more than two dozen varieties, from the "Boss's Favorite"—a potato-flour palacsinta filled with (pork) knuckle ragout, beans, cabbage, and sour cream—to vegetarian (indeed, egg-free) sorts including the "Spring Pancake" (ewe cheese with dill and chives), to traditional, sweet, jam-filled palacsintas. Servings are lavish, prices quite reasonable. ■ **TIP→ If you order a meat- or vegetable-filled palacsinta, you might ask them to take it easy on the salt.** [$] *Average main: 2,000 HUF* ✉ *Dobó utca 9* ☎ *36/413–980* 🌐 *www.palacsintavar.hu.*

IRELAND

Dublin, Cashel and County Cork,
the Ring of Kerry, Belfast

WHAT'S WHERE

1 Dublin. A transformed city since the days of O'Casey and Joyce, Ireland's capital may have replaced its legendary tenements with modern high-rises but its essential spirit remains intact. Despite the recent economic downturn, Dublin remains a colossally entertaining city, all the more astonishing considering its intimate size. It has art, culture, Georgian architecture, an army of booksellers, and, of course, hundreds of pubs where conversation and vocal dexterity continue to flourish within its increasingly multicultural mix.

2 Cashel and County Cork. Heading south from Dublin you enter the Southeast, Ireland's sunniest corner, where blue skies will hopefully be shining over the medieval, magical, and magnificent Rock of Cashel (buses directly connect the town of Cashel with Dublin). As you explore Ireland's most impressive medieval monument—once fabled home to the Kings of Munster—you'll be following in the footsteps of St. Patrick himself. Continue southwest to County Cork, where Cork city is a Venice-like port city of canals and bridges, a bustling mercantile center that remains one of Ireland's

liveliest. Nearby, don't forget to kiss the Blarney Stone.

3 The Ring of Kerry. Ever since Killarney and the Ring of Kerry were discovered by travelers in the late 18th century, visitors have come away searching for superlatives to describe the vistas afforded by its heather-clad sandstone mountains, deep blue island-studded lakes, long sandy beaches, wild rocky headlands, and sheltered wooded coves. Combining mountainous splendour with a spectacularly varied coastline, the Ring of Kerry is a 176-km (110-mile) drive that can be accessed at a number of places, although most people start out from the town of Killarney. If you don't mind sharing the road with half of Ireland—this is one of the country's most popular tourist destinations—you can glory in Ireland's most beautiful rugged countryside.

4 Belfast. Belfast's location is striking, nestled on the coast, buffered by green water on one side and by heath-covered hills on the other. Once you tour the Victorian city, head to its outskirts to visit three marvels: Belfast Castle, the Mount Stewart estate, and the Ulster Folk and Transport Museum.

ATLANTIC OCEAN

Achill Island

Clare Island

Inishturk

Inishbofin

Oileáin Árainn
(Aran Islands

Mouth of
the Shannon

Corca Dhuib
(Dingle Penins

Blasket
Islands

Dingle Bay

KER

Iveragh
Peninsula

Skellig
Rocks

Kenmare Bay

Bea
Penin

Bantry

Mizen Head

Malin Head

Toraigh
(Tory Island)

Rathlin Island

Lough Foyle

Portrush

Coleraine

SCOTLAND
(UNITED KINGDOM)

North Channel

Ariann Mhor
(Aranmore Island)

Derry City

DERRY

Letterkenny

DONEGAL

Strabane

NORTHERN
IRELAND
(UNITED KINGDOM)

Ballymena

Larne

ANTRIM

Island Magee

BELFAST

Belfast Lough

Gweebarra
Bay

Donegal
Town

Omagh

Cookstown

Lough
Neagh

Newtownards

Donegal
Bay

Ballyshannon

Lower
Lough Erne

TYRONE

Dungannon

DOWN

Sligo
Bay

FERMANACH

Upper
Lough Erne

Armagh City

Killala
Bay

LEITRIM

Monaghan
City

ARMAGH

Newcastle

Ballina

Sligo Town

SLIGO

MONAGHAN

Newry

AYO

Lough
Conn

Dundalk

Castlebar

ROSCOMMON

CAVAN

Cavan

Dundalk Bay

Knock

Longford

LOUTH

Lough
Mask

LONGFORD

MEATH

Drogheda

Lough
Corrib

GALWAY

Athlone

WESTMEATH

Mullingar

DUBLIN

Galway
City

Ballinasloe

OFFALY

Naas

DUBLIN

Dún Laoghaire

Galway Bay

Birr

KILDARE

Bray

Irish Sea

REPUBLIC OF IRELAND

Portlaoise

Athy

WICKLOW

Wicklow

Ennis

Nenagh

Roscrea

LAOIS

CLARE

Shannon

TIPPERARY

Kilkenny
City

CARLOW

Arklow

Kilrush

Limerick

Thurles

Gorey

LIMERICK City

Cashel

KILKENNY

Newcastle
West

Tipperary
Town

WEXFORD

istowel

Clonmel

Carrick-on-Suir

Wexford Town

lee

Farahy

WATERFORD

Waterford

illarney

Mallow

CORK

Youghal

Midleton

Cork City

Cobh

Kinsale

St. George's Channel

Skibbereen

0   50 mi

0   50 km

NEED TO KNOW

Atlantic Ocean

IRELAND

Dublin

Irish Sea

AT A GLANCE
Capital: Dublin

Population: 4,487,000

Currency: Euro

Money: ATMs are common

Language: English and Irish

Country Code: ☎ 353

Emergencies: ☎ 999

Driving: On the left

Electricity: 230v/50 cycles; electrical plugs have three prongs

Time: Five hours ahead of New York

Documents: Up to 90 days with valid passport; Schengen rules apply

Mobile Phones: GSM (900 and 1800 bands)

Major Mobile Companies: Vodafone, O2, Meteor

WEBSITES
Ireland: ⊕ www.discoverireland.ie

Irish Country Houses: ⊕ www.irelands-blue-book.ie

Dublin: ⊕ www.visitdublin.com

GETTING AROUND

✈ **Air Travel:** The major international airports are in Dublin and Shannon, and there's good service from the U.S. Two major airports for intra-Europe flights are Cork and Belfast.

🚌 **Bus Travel:** A good network operates to and from bigger towns and cities, but service is more sporadic elsewhere.

🚗 **Car Travel:** Driving on major roads is easy, though on the left. Smaller roads are narrow and winding. Gas is very expensive.

🚆 **Train Travel:** The good intercity service can be a little pricey, and there's no rail service to the smaller towns.

PLAN YOUR BUDGET

	HOTEL ROOM	MEAL	ATTRACTIONS
Low Budget	€90	€14	Chester Beatty Library, free
Mid Budget	€150	€25	Guinness Storehouse Ticket with free pint, €16.50
High Budget	€250	€55	Private Table at Galway Races, €225

WAYS TO SAVE

Order from pretheater menus. Some top restaurants have early bird specials (before 7 pm).

Book a rental apartment. Furnished rentals—good for families and groups—offer more space and a kitchen.

Book rail tickets online. Huge discounts for advance online bookings include up to 50% off on some routes. Look for specials online (⊕ www.irishrail.ie).

Hit the free cultural sights first. Most of the major national museums and parks are free of charge, and there are enough of them to satisfy the most ardent culture junkie.

PLAN YOUR TIME

Hassle Factor	Low. Flights to Dublin are frequent, and distances for driving are very short.
3 days	Dip your toe into the culture of Dublin and perhaps take half-day trips out to Wicklow and Newgrange.
1 week	Combine a few days in Dublin with trip along the spectacular west coast, staying in Galway and Kerry.
2 weeks	This is enough time to really see the whole of Ireland at your own pace. You can do Dublin, the West, and even venture into the undiscovered midlands. A trip to Northern Ireland should also be in the cards. The sunny southeast is a good stop on your way back to Dublin.

WHEN TO GO

High Season: June through August is the most expensive and popular time to visit, and the major tourist spots can be quite crowded then. Famously fickle weather means you should always have a light rain jacket handy.

Low Season: The post-Christmas months of January and February are the quietest, but they are vibrant times in the cities with new theater season openings. There are also the prime months for cheap hotels (be prepared to haggle for a killer price). But expect rain, and plenty of it.

Value Season: September is actually the driest month in Ireland. Saner airfares and a host of cultural events also make it a very attractive time to visit. Late April and May is another great shoulder season, before the masses arrive but when cafés are abuzz and the students are still in town.

BIG EVENTS

March: St. Patrick's celebrations last a week. ⊕ *www.stpatricksfestival.ie*

June: Bloomsday is now a weeklong Dublin festival. ⊕ *www.jamesjoyce.ie*

September: The All Ireland hurling and football finals are the climax of the Gaelic sporting calendar. ⊕ *www.gaa.ie*

October: The Wexford Opera festival has become one of Ireland's must-see glamour events. ⊕ *www.wexfordopera.com*

READ THIS

- *Slow Dublin,* Anto Howard. Written for the locals, it's full of city secrets.

- *Round Ireland with a Fridge,* Tony Hawk. Hilarious and warm travelogue.

- *Oxford Guide to Literary Britain and Ireland,* Daniel Hahn and Nicholas Robins. Ireland's literary greats.

WATCH THIS

- *Michael Collins.* A great primer to modern Irish history.

- *The Quiet Man.* Romantic and silly but brings the countryside alive.

- *The Commitments.* A view of the Dublin few tourists see.

EAT THIS

- **Irish Spring Lamb:** when it's fresh, there is none to equal its flavor

- **West Cork Cheese:** a host of varieties from tiny, artisan cheese makers

- **Oatmeal:** topped with local fruit and honey

- **New Irish Potatoes:** a summer staple; melt-in-your-mouth perfect

- **Fish Stew:** best in the west, fresh and meaty

- **Toasted sandwich with a pint of Guinness:** the go-to meal in the old-school Dublin pubs

If you fly into Ireland, your descent will probably be shrouded by gray clouds. As your plane breaks through the mists, you'll see the land for which the Emerald Isle was named: a lovely patchwork of rolling green fields speckled with farmhouses, cows, and sheep. Shimmering lakes, meandering rivers, narrow roads, and stone walls add to the impression that rolled out before you is a luxurious welcome carpet, one knit of the legendary "forty shades of green." This age-old view of misty Ireland may be exactly what you imagined. But don't expect to still find Eire the land of leprechauns, shillelaghs, shamrocks, and mist. The only known specimens of leprechauns or shillelaghs these days are those in souvenir shop windows; shamrock only blooms on St. Patrick's Day or around the borders of Irish linen handkerchiefs and tablecloths; and the mists—in reality a soft, apologetic rain—can envelop the entire country, in a matter of minutes.

Today's Ireland is two-faced, like the Janus stones and sheela-na-gigs of its pre-Christian past. It's a complex place where the mystic lyricism of the great poet W. B. Yeats, the hard Rabelaisian passions of James Joyce, and the spare, aloof dissections of Samuel Beckett grew not only from a rich and ancient culture but also from 20th-century upheavals, few of which have been as dramatic as the transformation that has changed Ireland since the 1990s. Until it hit a recent speed-bump, Ireland's economy—christened the "Celtic Tiger"—was one of the fastest-growing in the industrialized world. And since 2000, galleries, art-house cinemas, elegant shops, and a stunning variety of restaurants have transformed Dublin from a provincial capital that once suffocated Joyce into a city almost as cosmopolitan as the Paris to which he fled. Irish culture also has boomed, thanks to Bono and U2, Daniel Day-Lewis, *Riverdance* (18 million people and more than $1 billion in box office receipts at last count), and Conor McPherson's plays.

Thankfully, the pace of life outside Dublin is more relaxed. Indeed, the farther you travel from the metropolis, the more you'll be inclined to linger. And once you take a deep breath of some of the best air in the western world and look around, you'll find some dazzling sights: the fabled Rock of Cashel, the fun and foodie-friendly hub of Cork city, and the spectacularly majestic Ring of Kerry. In one of the little villages on this peninsula of Ireland's extreme southwest, you'll hopefully be able to venture down a back road, find an old pub, and savor the *craic,* the Irish term for a rousing good time. Undoubtedly, you'll be on first-name terms in no time.

PLANNING

WHEN TO GO

In summer the weather is pleasant, the days are long (daylight lasts until after 10 pm in late June and July), and the countryside is green. But there are crowds in popular holiday spots, and prices for accommodations are at their peak. As British and Irish school vacations overlap from late June to mid-September, vacationers descend on popular coastal resorts in the south, west, and east. Unless you're determined to enjoy the short (July and August) swimming season, it's best to visit Ireland outside peak travel months. Fall and spring are good times to travel (late September can be dry and warm, although the weather can be unpredictable). Seasonal hotels and restaurants close from early or mid-November until mid-March or Easter. During this off-season, prices are lower than in summer, but your selection is limited, and many minor attractions close. St. Patrick's Week gives a focal point to a spring visit, but some Americans may find the saint's-day celebrations a bit less enthusiastic than the ones back home.

GETTING HERE AND AROUND

AIR TRAVEL

Flying time to Ireland is 6½ hours from New York, 7½ hours from Chicago, 10 hours from Los Angeles, and 1 hour from London. The major gateways to Ireland are Dublin Airport (DUB) on the east coast, 10 km (6 miles) north of the city center, and Shannon Airport (SNN) on the west coast, 25 km (16 miles) west of Limerick. Belfast (BFS) has its own busy airport, though there is only one nonstop from the U.S. (a United flight from EWR).

Contacts Belfast International Airport at Aldergrove ☎ *028/9448–4848* ⊕ *www.belfastairport.com.* **Dublin Airport** ☎ *01/814–1111* ⊕ *www.dublinairport. com.* **Shannon Airport** ☎ *061/712–000* ⊕ *www.shannonairport.com.*

BOAT TRAVEL

The ferry is a convenient way to travel between Ireland and elsewhere in Europe, particularly the United Kingdom. There are six main ferry ports to Ireland; three in the republic at Dublin Port, Dun Laoghaire, and Rosslare. Irish Ferries operates the *Ulysses,* the world's largest car ferry, on its Dublin to Holyhead, Wales, route (3 hours, 15 minutes); there's also an express service (1 hour, 50 minutes) between these two ports. Stena Line sails several times a day between Dublin and Holyhead (3 hours, 15 minutes). Norfolk Line sails from Dublin to Liverpool service, while P&O Irish Sea vessels run between Larne and Troon,

TOP REASONS TO GO

Dublin's Book of Kells: If you visit only one attraction in Dublin, let it be this extraordinary creation housed in Trinity College. Often called "the most beautiful book in the world," the manuscript dates to the eighth or ninth century and remains a marvel of intricacy and creativity, thanks to its elaborate interlaces, abstractions, and "carpet-pages."

Blarney Stone: One of the country's most enduring, and some would say ludicrous, myths, wherein kissing a stone high upon the battlements of a ruined Cork castle bestows a magical eloquence on the visitor. Grasped by the ankles and hanging perilously upside down to pucker upon ancient rock, you'll certainly have a tall tale to tell the folks back home.

Rock of Cashel: The center of tribal and religious power for over a thousand years, this medieval and mountainous settlement became the seat of the Munster kings in the 5th century. Handed over to the early Christian Church in 1101, the medieval abbey perched on a limestone mount in Tipperary contains rare Romanesque carvings celebrating St. Patrick's visit there in 450.

Cork City: Long called "The Rebel County," Cork is a Venice-like port city of canals and bridges. It was once home to writers Sean O'Faolain and Frank O'Connor, and is famed for its hip university, its fabulous food markets, and its passion for hurling, that fast and furious ancient game that makes soccer look like kick-the-can.

Ballymaloe House: The breeding ground for the new Irish gastronomy, this old Georgian farm estate was where Myrtle Allen created her everything-old-is-new-again-but-better take on Irish cookery. Long before organic became a buzzword, she made freshness her mantra. Today Darina Allen—the Martha Stewart of Ireland—runs the place.

Ring of Kerry: Just to the north of Cork, travelers have been thrilling to the Ring of Kerry's natural beauty for centuries, as they've gazed down from the heights of Killarney or been awed by spectacular natural wonders like the shoreline's Skellig Islands. Diverse and brazenly scenic, this is Ireland's most celebrated coastal drive.

Belfast, Gateway City. As the locals put it, "Despite what you've probably heard, Belfast is not what you expect"—so get ready to love this bustling city that bristles with Victorian shop fronts, hip restaurants, and the Titanic Belfast Visitor Centre.

Scotland. Bear in mind, too, that flying can be cheaper, so look into all types of transportation before booking.

Contacts Irish Ferries ☎ 0818/300–400 in Ireland, 0871/730-0400 in U.K. ⊕ www.irishferries.com. **P&O Ferries** ☎ 01/407–3434 in Ireland, 0871/702–3477 in U.K. ⊕ www.poferries.com. **Stena Line** ☎ 01/204–7777 in Ireland, 028/9074–7747 in Northern Ireland, 0844/770–7070 in U.K. ⊕ www.stenaline.co.uk.

BUS TRAVEL

In the Republic of Ireland, long-distance bus services are operated by Bus Éireann, which also provides local service in Cork, Galway, Limerick, and Waterford. Outside of the peak season, schedules can be limited. There's often only one trip a day on express routes, and one a week to some remote villages. To ensure that a bus journey is feasible, buy a copy of Bus Éireann's timetable—€6 from any bus terminal—or check online. Many of the destination indicators are in Irish (Gaelic), so make sure you get on the right bus. Check with the bus office to see if reservations are accepted for your route; if not, show up early to get a seat. A round trip from Dublin to Cork costs €18.

Contacts Bus Éireann ☎ *01/836–6111 in Ireland* ⊕ *www.buseireann.ie.*

CAR TRAVEL

The Irish, like the British, drive on the left-hand side of the road. Safety belts must be worn by the driver and all passengers, and children under 12 must travel in the back unless riding in a car seat. Despite the relatively light traffic, parking in towns can be a problem. Signs with the letter *P* indicate that parking is permitted; a stroke through the *P* warns you to stay away or you'll be liable for a fine of €20–€65. If your car gets towed away, the fine is around €180. Note that Ireland has the highest auto-accident fatality rate in Europe. Road signs in the republic are generally in both Irish and English. U.S. driver's licenses are recognized in Ireland.

On the new green signposts distances are in kilometers; on the old white signposts they're in miles. Speed limits are generally 100 to 120 kph (60 to 75 mph) on motorways, 80 kph (50 mph) on other roads, and 50 kph (30 mph) in towns. Roads are classified as *M, N,* or *R*: those designated with an *M* for "motorway" are double-lane divided highways with paved shoulders; *N*, or national, routes are generally undivided highways with shoulders; and *R*, or regional, roads tend to be narrow and twisty.

TRAIN TRAVEL

The republic's Irish Rail trains are generally reliable, reasonably priced, and comfortable. You can easily reach all the principal towns from Dublin, though routes between provincial cities can be circuitous. To get to Cork City from Wexford, for example, you have to go via Limerick Junction. It's often quicker, though perhaps less comfortable, to take a bus. Most mainline trains have one standard class. Round-trip tickets are usually cheapest. You should plan to be at the train station at least 30 minutes before your train departs to ensure you'll get a seat. It's not uncommon on busier routes to find that you have to stand, since all seats have been sold and taken. Train schedules are easy to obtain and available in a variety of formats, including online, by Irish Rail. Sample fare? A round-trip ticket from Dublin to Cork will cost around €60.

Contacts Irish Rail (*Iarnrod Éireann*). ☎ *01/836–6222* ⊕ *www.irishrail.ie.* **Northern Ireland Railways** ☎ *028/9066–6630* ⊕ *www.translink.co.uk/ NI-Railways.*

HOTELS

Dublin is famous for its elegant boutique hotels that occupy former Georgian town houses on both sides of the Liffey, but there are plenty of new, full-scale luxury options also available. Thankfully, the city also has a decent selection of inexpensive accommodations, including many moderately priced hotels with basic but agreeable rooms. Outside Dublin, manors and castles offer a unique combination of luxury and history. Less impressive, but equally charming, are the provincial inns and country hotels with simple but adequate facilities. B&Bs are classified by Faílte Ireland as either town homes, country homes, or farmhouses. A legacy of the Celtic Tiger years, hotel choices and quality have expanded exponentially, but so have prices. So it's more important than ever to get the best deal for your dollar. Most hotels and other lodgings require you to give your credit-card details before they will confirm your reservation.

RESTAURANTS

Restaurants range from inexpensive ethnic eateries to luxurious outposts of Cuisine Irelandaise (Irish food accented with a French touch), from classic "carveries" to traditional pubs. In fact, the next time you wander into a pub bent on downing a platter of steak, bland potatoes, and mushy peas, don't be surprised if you end up with a meal of skewered John Dory in Clonmel Cider Sauce and a finale of Cooleeney Camembert ganache with lavender jelly. For the last decade and more, the New Irish Cuisine has remade the old beige, boiled, and boring menu of yore. Today haute-hungry foodies packing chubby wallets are all abuzz over discovering emerging culinary wizards; artisanal producers of farmhouse cheeses; organic beef and smoked fish; and some of the best farmers' markets and provisioners around.

FAVORITE DISHES

The abundant high-quality produce the country is famous for is finally receiving the care and attention of world-class chefs in the capital city's restaurants, so don't be surprised to find your Irish stew is spiced and topped with a tangy avocado salsa. Even the humble potato is being shaped and transformed into *boxty* (potato-and-flour pancake) and *colcannon*—a traditional Irish dish with bacon and cabbage—is getting a nouvelle spin. Besides excellent Irish beef, pork, ham, and lamb, look for the rich seafood harvests of fresh and smoked salmon, oysters, mussels, and shellfish in many guises. Ireland is famed for its excellent dairy products, so leave room for the mature cheddars and luscious blue cheeses, the slightly sweet Dubliner, St. Tola goat's cheese from Clare, and Carrigburne brie from Wexford. Indulge at least once in the traditional Irish breakfast, which is often served all day. It includes rashers (bacon), sausages, black-and-white pudding (other types of sausage), mushrooms, tomatoes, and a fried egg—with lots of traditional homemade brown and soda breads and the famous Irish creamery butter. This "breakfast" is often the biggest meal of the day. But portions in Ireland can be huge for any meal, and this can happily mean shared dishes—another way to beat the euro.

HOURS

The Irish dine later than Americans. They stay up later, too, and reservations are usually not booked before 6:30 or 7 pm (watch for those "Early Bird" specials) and up to around 10 pm. Lunch is generally served from 12:30 to 2:30. Pubs often serve food through the day until 8:30 or 9 pm. Most pubs are family-friendly and welcome children until 7 pm.

HOTEL AND RESTAURANT PRICES

Prices in the restaurant reviews are the average cost of a main course at dinner or, if dinner is not served, at lunch; taxes and service charges are generally included. Prices in the hotel reviews are the lowest cost of a standard double room in high season, excluding taxes, service charges, and meal plans (except at all-inclusives).

PLANNING YOUR TIME

There are two contrasting aspects to Ireland: its go-ahead, cosmopolitan capital city, glowing with energy and confidence, and the quieter, timeless charm of its unspoiled countryside. Any first-time, weeklong tour of Ireland should focus on both sides of the coin: the friendly people found in Dublin and Cork and the beautiful rural landscape, often gloriously framed by Ireland's time-burnished villages and medieval sites. We assume you'll arrive in the capital city and then fly back out from Shannon (on the West coast) to save time on a short tour. If you have a couple of extra days to spare, an excursion to Belfast will also add to your experience. The city is small enough to see in a short amount of time; just don't miss the must-see Titanic Experience.

Plan on using a mix of cars, buses, and trains. Opt for public transportation on the longer hauls (Dublin/Cork), then rent cars from where you're based (or research if bus lines can get you around: start with ⊕ *www.irishrail.ie* and ⊕ *www.buseireann.ie*). Remember that Irish roads can be twisty and signposting nonexistent, while public transportation allows you to plan the next destination, not spend a white-knuckled day dodging speeding traffic.

DUBLIN

Although it has hit an economic speed bump, Europe's most intimate capital became a full-fledged boomtown since 1990. Despite the dramatic economic slowdown since 2008, the old city has been forever transformed by the explosion of construction, confidence, and money that dominated those crazy years. Indeed, if the town's most famous homeboy—the noted 20th-century author James Joyce—were to return to his once genteel town today and take a quasi-Homeric odyssey through the city (as Leopold Bloom so famously does in *Ulysses*), would he even recognize Dublin as his "Dear Dirty Dumpling, foostherfather of fingalls and dotthergills"?

For instance, what would he make of Temple Bar—the city's erstwhile down-at-the-heels neighborhood, now crammed with restaurants and trendy hotels and suffused with a nonstop, international-party atmosphere? Or the old market area of Smithfield, whose Cinderella transformation has changed it into an impressive plaza and winter ice-skating venue? The truth is that local skeptics await the outcome of "Dublin: The Sequel." Can the "new Dublin" get beyond the rage stage without losing its very essence? Their greatest fear is the possibility that the tattered old lady on the Liffey is becoming like everywhere else. Oh ye of little faith: the rare aul' gem that is Dublin is far from buried. The fundamentals—the Georgian elegance of Merrion Square, the Norman drama of Christ Church Cathedral, the foamy pint at an atmospheric pub—are still on hand to gratify and enchant.

PLANNING YOUR TIME

Dublin is delightfully compact—nearly all main sights are within walking distance of the entrance to famed Trinity College. That noted, attempting to explore the city will require the wisdom of Solomon, as the Liffey River neatly splits Dublin into the Southside and the Northside. The Southside is the logical place to begin: many of the top sights are there, set among graceful squares and terraces dating from the city's elegant Georgian heyday. The Northside is still the place to soak up the pure, unadulterated city. It's here that Dublin's literary heart beats strongest. How long will this highlights tour take? If you're moving at speed reader's pace, a frantic day, but you'll want to slow down and pace yourself over two days—even three—to truly savor the Irish Oz.

GETTING AROUND

Central Dublin is compact, so walking is the first choice for getting around. Main thoroughfares can become crowded with pedestrians, especially at rush hour, so plan routes along side streets with less bustle. When your feet need a break, turn to public transit.

There's an extensive network of buses, most of which are green double-deckers. Some bus services run on cross-city routes, including the smaller "Imp" buses, but most buses start in the city center. Another regular bus route connects the two main provincial railway stations, Connolly and Heuston. If the destination board indicates "an lár," that means that the bus is going to the city center. In the city, fares begin at €1.05 and are paid to the driver, who will accept inexact fares but will not give change (you'll have to go to the central office in Dublin to pick up your change as marked on your ticket). The pleasant LUAS tram system also has two lines running through the city center. There are taxi stands beside the central bus station, and at train stations, O'Connell Bridge, St. Stephen's Green, College Green, and near major hotels; the Dublin telephone directory has a complete list. The initial charge is €4.10, with an additional charge of about €1 per km thereafter. Navigating the city on your own in a rental car is an expensive headache.

Contacts **Heuston Station** ⊠ *End of Victoria Quay, Dublin West.* **Irish Rail–Iarnod Éireann** ☎ *01/836-6222* ⊕ *www.irishrail.ie.*

DISCOUNTS AND DEALS

Like many tourist capitals around the world, Dublin now features a special pass to help travelers save on admission prices. In conjunction with Dublin Tourism, the Dublin Pass is issued for one, two, three, or six days, and allows free (or, rather, reduced, since the cards do cost something) admission to 30 sights, including the Guinness Brewery, the Dublin Zoo, the Dublin Writers Museum, and Christ Church Cathedral. Prices are €35 for one day; €55 for two days; €65 for three days; and €95 for six days; children's prices are much lower. You can buy your card online and have it waiting for you at one of Dublin's tourist information offices when you arrive.

TOURS

Dublin Bus has three- and four-hour "City Tours" of the city center that include Trinity College, the Royal Hospital Kilmainham, and Phoenix Park. The one-hour City Tour, with hourly departures, allows you to hop on and off at any of the main sights. Tickets are available from the driver or Dublin Bus. There's also a continuous guided open-top bus tour (€14), run by Dublin Bus, which allows you to hop on and off the bus as often as you wish and visit some 15 sights along its route. Gray Line Tours runs city-center tours that cover the same sights as the Dublin Bus itineraries.

Contacts Dublin Bus ✉ *59 Upper O'Connell St., Northside* ☎ *01/873–4222* ⊕ *www.dublinbus.ie.*

VISITOR INFORMATION

Contacts Dublin Discover Ireland Centre ✉ *Suffolk St. off Grafton St., Southside* ☎ *1850/230330* ⊕ *www.visitdublin.com.*

EXPLORING

The River Liffey provides a useful aid of orientation, flowing as it does through the direct middle of Dublin. If you ask a native Dubliner for directions—from under an umbrella, as it will probably be raining in the approved Irish manner—he or she will most likely reply in terms of "up" or "down," up meaning away from the river, and down toward it.

SOUTHSIDE

Until recently, Dublin's center of gravity was O'Connell Bridge. But Dublin's heart now beats loudest southward across the Liffey, due in part to a large-scale refurbishment and pedestrianization of Grafton Street, which made this already upscale shopping address the main street on which to shop, stop, and be seen. At the foot of Grafton Street is the city's most famous and recognizable landmark, Trinity College; at the top of it is Dublin's most popular strolling retreat, St. Stephen's Green, a 27-acre landscaped park.

Eastward lies Dublin's elegant Georgian quarter. If there's one travel poster that signifies "Dublin" more than any other, it's the one that depicts 50 or so Georgian doorways—door after colorful door, all graced with lovely fanlights upheld by columns. A building boom began in Dublin in the early 18th century as the Protestant Ascendancy constructed terraced town houses for themselves, and civic structures for their city, in the style that came to be known as Georgian, after the four successive British Georges who ruled from 1714 through 1830. But Georgian splendor is just the icing on the cake hereabouts, for there are also three of the most fascinating museums in Ireland, conveniently

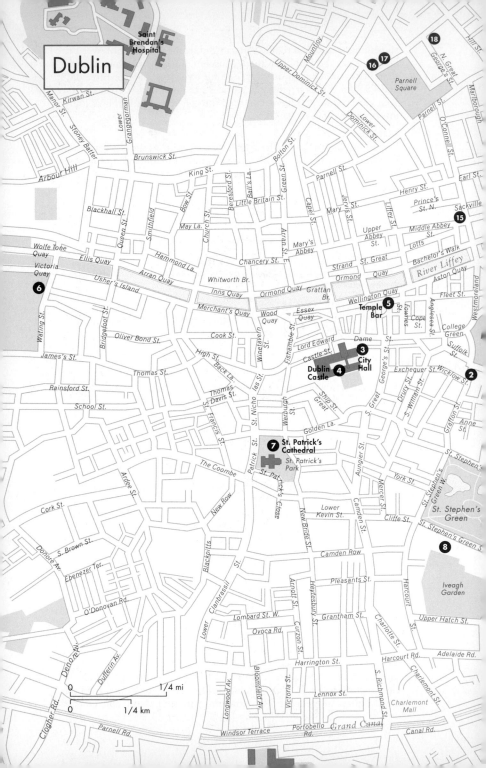

Summerhill

Sean McDermott St.

Killarney St.

Railway St.

Amiens St.

Seville Pl.

Gardiner St.

Foley St.

Connolly Station

Talbot St.

St. N

Lower Sheriff St.

Pl.

Inner Dock

Lower Abbey St.

Custom House
14

Georges Dock

Commons St.

Eden Quay

Custom

Butt Br.

Talbot Mem. Br.

House Quay

River Liffey

Burgh Quay

George's Quay

Poolbeg St.

Tara St. Station

City Quay

Doller St.

Gloucester St.

Townsend St.

College St.

Pearse St.

Lombard St. E.

Magennis Pl.

Pearse Station

Trinity College
1

Nassau St.

Leinster St.

Lincoln Place

Clare St.

Westland Row

Pearse St.

Hogan Pl.

Macken St.

St.

Duke St.

Frederick La. S.

Fenian St.

Molesworth St.

Dawson

Kildare St.

11

12

Merrion Sq. West

Merrion Sq. N.

Natural Gallery of Ireland

Natural Museum of Archaeology & History
10

13

Upper Merrion St.

Merrion

Merrion Square

Green N.

Merrion Row

Fitzwilliam La.

Lower Merrion St.

Lower Mount St.

9

Lower

Upper Fitzwilliam St.

Upper Mount St.

James's Pl.

Pembroke St.

Baggot St.

Herbert St.

Herbert Pl.

Percy Pl.

Upper Fitzwilliam St.

Lad La.

Haddington Rd.

Earlsfort Ter.

St.

Lower Hatch

Lower Leeson St.

Wilton Terrace

Mespil Rd.

Upper Baggot St.

Pembroke Lane

Charlemont Pl.

Grand Parade

Dartmouth Sq. North

Burleigh Ct.

Burlington Rd.

Waterloo Rd.

Waterloo Lane

Dartmouth Sq. South

Sussex Rd.

Upper Leeson St.

Lower Leeson St.

Heytsbury Lane

sitting cheek by jowl: the National Gallery of Ireland, the National Library, and the National Museum of Archaeology and History.

City Hall. Facing the Liffey from Cork Hill at the top of Parliament Street, this grand Georgian municipal building (1769–79), once the Royal Exchange, marks the southwest corner of Temple Bar. Today it's the seat of Dublin Corporation, the elected body that governs the city. Thomas Cooley designed the building with 12 columns that encircle the domed central rotunda, which has a fine mosaic floor and 12 frescoes depicting Dublin legends and ancient Irish historical scenes. The 20-foot-high sculpture to the right is of Daniel O'Connell, "The Liberator." He looks like he's about to begin the famous speech he gave here in 1800. The building houses a multimedia exhibition—with artifacts, kiosks, graphics, and audiovisual presentations—tracing the evolution of Ireland's 1,000-year-old capital. ⊠ *Dame St., Dublin West* 🕾 *01/222–2204* ⊕ *www.dublincity.ie/RecreationandCulture* 🖾 *€4* ☉ *Mon.–Sat. 10–5:15.*

Dublin Castle. As seat and symbol of the British rule of Ireland for more than seven centuries, Dublin Castle figured largely in Ireland's turbulent history early in the 20th century. It's now mainly used for Irish and EU governmental purposes. The sprawling Great Courtyard is the reputed site of the Black Pool (Dubh Linn, pronounced *dove*-lin) from which Dublin got its name. In the Lower Castle Yard, the Record Tower, the earliest of several towers on the site, is the largest remaining relic of the original Norman buildings, built by King John between 1208 and 1220. The clock-tower building houses the fabulous Chester Beatty Library. The State Apartments (on the southern side of the Upper Castle Yard)—formerly the residence of the English viceroys and now used by the president of Ireland to host visiting heads of state and EU ministers—are lavishly furnished with rich Donegal carpets and illuminated by Waterford glass chandeliers. The largest and most impressive of these chambers, St. Patrick's Hall, with its gilt pillars and painted ceiling, is used for the inauguration of Irish presidents.

Enter the castle through the Cork Hill Gate, just west of City Hall. One-hour guided tours are available every half hour, but the rooms are closed when in official use, so call ahead. The Castle Vaults hold an elegant little patisserie and bistro. ⊠ *Castle St., Dublin West* 🕾 *01/645–8813* ⊕ *www.dublincastle.ie* 🖾 *State Apartments €4.50, includes tour* ☉ *Mon.–Sat. 10–4:45, Sun. 2–4:45.*

Grafton Street. It's no more than 200 yards long and about 20 feet wide, but brick-lined Grafton Street, open only to pedestrians, can claim to be the most humming street in the city, if not in all of Ireland. It's one of Dublin's vital spines: the most direct route between the front door of Trinity College and St. Stephen's Green, and the city's premier shopping street, with Dublin's most distinguished department store, Brown Thomas, as well as tried and trusted Marks & Spencer. Grafton Street and the smaller alleyways that radiate off it offer dozens of independent stores, a dozen or so colorful flower sellers, and some of the Southside's most popular watering holes. In summer, buskers from all over the world line both sides of the street, pouring out the sounds of drum, whistle, pipe, and string.

NEED A
BREAK?

Bewley's Oriental Café. The granddaddy of the capital's cafés, and an essential part of the character of Grafton Street, Bewley's Oriental Café, came within a heartbeat of extinction a few years back, after having served coffee and sticky buns to Dubliners since its founding by the Quakers in 1840. Fortunately, the old dame was saved and turned into a combination café, pizza, and pasta joint. Best of all, a revamp brought back some of the old grandeur associated with Bewley's, including the exotic picture wallpaper and trademark stained-glass windows, designed by the distinguished early-20th-century artist Harry Clarke. ✉ *78 Grafton St., Southside* ☎ *01/672–7700* ⊕ *bewleys.com/bewleys-grafton-street-cafe.*

Fodor'sChoice
★ **Guinness Storehouse.** Ireland's all-dominating brewery—founded by Arthur Guinness in 1759 and at one time the largest stout-producing brewery in the world—spans a 60-acre spread west of Christ Church Cathedral. Not surprisingly, it's the most popular tourist destination in town—after all, the Irish national drink is Guinness stout, a dark brew made with roasted malt. The brewery itself is closed to the public, but the Guinness Storehouse is a spectacular attraction, designed to woo—some might say brainwash—you with the wonders of the "dark stuff." In a 1904 cast-iron-and-brick warehouse, the museum display covers six floors built around a huge, central glass atrium which is shaped like a giant pint glass. Beneath the glass floor of the lobby you can see Arthur Guinness's original lease on the site, for a whopping 9,000 years. The exhibition elucidates the brewing process and its history, with antique presses and vats, a look at bottle and can design through the ages, a history of the Guinness family, a fascinating archive of Guinness advertisements, and a chance to pull your own perfect pint. The star attraction is undoubtedly the top-floor **Gravity Bar,** with 360-degree floor-to-ceiling glass walls that offer a nonpareil view out over the city at sunset while you sip your free pint. One of the bar's first clients was one William Jefferson Clinton. You'll find the Guinness logo on everything from piggy banks to underpants in the Guinness Store on the ground floor. ✉ *St. James' Gate, Dublin West* ☎ *01/408–4800* ⊕ *www.guinness-storehouse.com* 🎫 *€16.50* ⊙ *July and Aug., daily 9:30–7; Sept.–June, daily 9:30–5.*

Fodor'sChoice
★ **Merrion Square.** Created between 1762 and 1764, this tranquil square a few blocks east of St. Stephen's Green is lined on three sides by some of Dublin's best-preserved Georgian town houses, many of which have brightly painted front doors crowned by intricate fanlights. Leinster House, the National Museum of Natural History, and the National Gallery line the west side of the square. It's on the other sides, however, that the Georgian terrace streetscape comes into its own—the finest houses are on the north border. Even when the flower gardens here are not in bloom, the vibrant, mostly evergreen grounds, dotted with sculpture and threaded with meandering paths, are worth strolling through. Several distinguished Dubliners have lived on the square, including

Oscar Wilde's parents, Sir William and "Speranza" Wilde (No. 1); Irish national leader Daniel O'Connell (No. 58); and authors W. B. Yeats (Nos. 52 and 82) and Sheridan LeFanu (No. 70). ⊠ *Georgian Dublin* ⊕ *www.merrionsquareart.com* ☉ *Daily sunrise–sunset.*

Fodor's Choice **National Gallery of Ireland.** Caravaggio's *The Taking of Christ* (1602), ★ Van Gogh's *Rooftops of Paris* (1886), Vermeer's *Lady Writing a Letter with Her Maid* (circa 1670)—you get the picture, or rather, you'll *find* the picture here. Established in 1864, and designed by Francis Fowke (who also designed London's Victoria & Albert Museum), the National Gallery of Ireland is one of Europe's finest smaller art museums, with "smaller" being a relative term: the collection holds more than 2,500 paintings and some 10,000 other works. But unlike Europe's largest art museums, the National Gallery can be thoroughly covered in a morning or afternoon without inducing exhaustion.

A highlight of the museum is the major collection of paintings by Irish artists from the 17th through 20th centuries, including works by Roderic O'Conor (1860–1940), Sir William Orpen (1878–1931), and William Leech (1881–1968). The Yeats Museum section contains works by members of the Yeats family, including Jack B. Yeats (1871–1957), the brother of writer W. B. Yeats, and by far the best-known Irish painter of the 20th century. ⊠ *Merrion Sq. W, Georgian Dublin* ☎ *01/661–5133* ⊕ *www.nationalgallery.ie* ⊠ *Free, special exhibits €10* ☉ *Mon.–Wed., Fri., and Sat. 9:30–5:30, Thurs. 9:30–8:30, Sun. noon–5:30.*

QUICK BITES **The Silk Road Cafe.** A great-value, Middle Eastern delight hidden away in the Chester Beatty Library, the Silk Road Café has a buffet-style menu always full of exotic surprises. The light-filled room (☉ Tues.-Fri. 10–4:30, Sat. 11–4:30, and Sun. 1–4:30) and serene atmosphere make you want to linger longer than you should. ⊠ *Chester Beatty Library, Castle St., Dublin West* ☎ *01/407-0770* ⊕ *www.silkroadcafe.ie.*

National Library. Along with works by W. B. Yeats (1923), George Bernard Shaw (1925), Samuel Beckett (1969), and Seamus Heaney (1995), the National Library contains first editions of every major Irish writer, including books by Jonathan Swift, Oliver Goldsmith, and James Joyce (who used the library as the scene of the great literary debate in *Ulysses*). In addition, almost every book ever published in Ireland is kept here, along with an unequaled selection of old maps and an extensive collection of Irish newspapers and magazines—more than 5 million items in all.

The library is housed in a rather stiff neoclassical building with colonnaded porticoes and an excess of ornamentation—it's not one of Dublin's architectural showpieces. But inside, the main Reading Room, opened in 1890 to house the collections of the Royal Dublin Society, has a dramatic dome ceiling, beneath which countless authors have researched and written. The personal papers of greats such as W. B. Yeats are also on display. ⊠ *Kildare St., Georgian Dublin* ☎ *01/603-0200* ⊕ *www.nli.ie* ⊠ *Free* ☉ *Mon.–Wed. 9:30–9, Thurs. and Fri. 9:30–5, Sat. 9:30–4:30.*

11

Fodor's Choice
★

National Museum of Archaeology. Just south of Leinster House is Ireland's National Museum of Archaeology, one of four branches of The National Museum of Ireland, and home to a fabled collection of Irish artifacts dating from 7000 BC to the present. Organized around a grand rotunda, the museum is elaborately decorated, with mosaic floors, marble columns, balustrades, and fancy ironwork. It has the largest collection of Celtic antiquities in the world, including gold jewelry, carved stones, bronze tools, and weapons.

The Treasury collection, including some of the museum's most renowned pieces, is open on a permanent basis. The "*Or*: Ireland's Gold" exhibition gathers together the most impressive pieces of surprisingly delicate and intricate prehistoric goldwork—including sun disks and the late Bronze Age gold collar known as the Gleninsheen Gorget—that range in dates from 2200 to 500 BC. The newest attraction is an exhibition entitled "Kinship and Sacrifice," centering on a number of Iron Age "bog bodies" found along with other objects in Ireland's peat bogs. ⊠ *Kildare St. Annex, 7–9 Merrion Row, Georgian Dublin* ☎ *01/677–7444* ⊕ *www.museum.ie* ☒ *Free* ☉ *Tues.–Sat. 10–5, Sun. 2–5.*

Newman House. One of the finest examples of Georgian Dublin, Newman House is actually two imposing town houses joined together. The earlier of the two, No. 85 St. Stephen's Green (1738), has two landmarks of Irish Georgian style: the Apollo Room, decorated with stuccowork depicting the sun god and his muses; and the magnificent Saloon, crowned with an exuberant ceiling aswirl with cupids and gods, created by the Brothers Lafranchini–the finest *stuccadores* (plaster-workers) of 18th-century Dublin. Next door at No. 86 (1765), the staircase, set against pastel walls, is one of the city's most beautiful Rococo examples—with floral swags and musical instruments picked out in cake-frosting white. To explore the rich history and architecture of the houses you must join a guided tour. At the back of Newman House hides Dublin's "secret garden." ⊠ *85–86 St. Stephen's Green, Georgian Dublin* ☎ *01/475–7255* ⊕ *www.ucd.ie/campusdevelopment/developmentprojects* ☒ *House and garden €5* ☉ *Tours June–Aug., Tues.–Fri. at 2, 3, and 4.*

Fodor's Choice
★

St. Patrick's Cathedral. The largest cathedral in Dublin and also the national cathedral of the Church of Ireland, St. Patrick's was built in honor of Ireland's patron saint, who—according to legend—baptized many converts at a well on this site in the 5th century. The original building, dedicated in 1192 and early English Gothic in style, was an unsuccessful attempt to assert supremacy over the capital's other Protestant cathedral, Christ Church Cathedral. At 305 feet, this is the longest church in the country, a fact Oliver Cromwell's troops found useful as they made the church's nave into their stable in the 17th century. Make sure you see the gloriously heraldic Choir of St. Patrick's, hung with colorful medieval banners, and find the tomb of the most famous of St. Patrick's many illustrious deans, Jonathan Swift, immortal author of *Gulliver's Travels,* who held office from 1713 to 1745. Swift's tomb is in the south aisle, not far from that of his beloved "Stella," Mrs. Esther Johnson. Swift's epitaph is inscribed over the robing-room door. ⊠ *Patrick St., Dublin West* ☎ *01/453–9472* ⊕ *www.*

stpatrickscathedral.ie ☜ €5.50 ⊘ *Mar.–Oct., weekdays 9–5, Sat. 9–6, Sun. 9–10:30, 12:30–2:30, and 4:30–6; Nov.–Feb., Mon.–Sat. 9–5, Sun. 9–10:30 and 12:30–2:30.*

Fodor's Choice
★ **St. Stephen's Green.** Dubliners call it simply Stephen's Green, and green it is (year-round)—a verdant, 27-acre Southside square that was used for the public punishment of criminals until 1664. After a long period of decline, it became a private park in 1814—the first time in its history that it was closed to the public. Its fortunes changed again in 1880, when Sir Arthur Guinness paid for it to be laid out anew. Flower gardens, formal lawns, a Victorian bandstand, and an ornamental lake with lots of waterfowl are all within the park's borders, connected by paths guaranteeing that strolling here or just passing through will offer up unexpected delights (such as palm trees). Among the park's many statues are a memorial to W. B. Yeats and another to Joyce by Henry Moore. In the 18th century the walk on the north side of the green was referred to as the Beaux Walk because most of Dublin's gentlemen's clubs were in town houses here. Today it's dominated by the legendary Shelbourne hotel. On the south side is the alluring Georgian Newman House. ⊠ *Southside* ☜ *Free* ⊘ *Daily sunrise–sunset.*

Temple Bar. Locals sometimes say the place has the feel of a "Dublin Theme Park," but a visit to modern Dublin wouldn't be complete without spending some time in the city's most vibrant area. The area, which takes its name from one of the streets of its central spine, took off in the 1990s as Dublin's version of New York's SoHo, Paris's Bastille, or London's Notting Hill—a thriving mix of high and alternative culture. Dotting the area's narrow cobblestone streets and pedestrian alleyways are new apartment buildings, vintage-clothing stores, postage-stamp-size boutiques selling €250 sunglasses and other expensive gewgaws, art galleries, the Clarence (a hotel resuscitated by U2), hip restaurants, pubs, clubs, European-style cafés, a Wall of Fame (devoted to Irish rockers), and a smattering of cultural venues, including the Irish Film Institute. ⊠ *Bordered by Dame St., the Liffey, Fishamble St., and Westmoreland St.*

Fodor's Choice
★ **Trinity College Dublin.** Founded in 1592 by Queen Elizabeth I to "civilize" (Her Majesty's word) Dublin, Trinity is Ireland's oldest and most famous college. The memorably atmospheric campus is a must; here you can track the shadows of some of the noted alumni, such as Jonathan Swift (1667–1745), Oscar Wilde (1854–1900), Bram Stoker (1847–1912), and Samuel Beckett (1906–89). Trinity College, Dublin (familiarly known as TCD), was founded on the site of the confiscated Priory of All Hallows. For centuries Trinity was the preserve of the Protestant Church; a free education was offered to Catholics—provided that they accepted the Protestant faith. As a legacy of this condition, until 1966 Catholics who wished to study at Trinity had to obtain a dispensation from their bishop or face excommunication.

Trinity's grounds cover 40 acres. Most of its buildings were constructed in the 18th and early 19th centuries. The extensive **West Front,** with a classical pedimented portico in the Corinthian style, faces College Green and is directly across from the Bank of Ireland; it was built between 1755 and 1759, and is possibly the work of Theodore Jacobsen, architect of London's Foundling Hospital. On the right side of the cobblestone quadrangle of **Parliament Square** (commonly known as Front Square) is Sir William Chambers's theater, or Examination Hall, dating from the mid-1780s, which contains the college's most splendid Adamesque interior, designed by Michael Stapleton. The looming campanile, or bell tower, is the symbolic heart of the college; erected in 1853, it dominates the center of the square. ☎ *01/896–1000* ⊕ *www. tcd.ie.*

The Douglas Hyde Gallery. Trinity College's starkly modern Arts and Social Sciences Building, with an entrance on Nassau Street, houses the **Douglas Hyde Gallery of Modern Art,** which concentrates on contemporary art exhibitions and has its own bookstore. Also in the building, down some steps from the gallery, is a snack bar serving coffee, tea, and sandwiches, where students willing to chat about life in the old college frequently gather. ✉ *Nassau St., Southside* ☎ *18/96111* ⊕ *www. douglashydegallery.com* ▣ *Free* ⊙ *Mon.–Wed. and Fri. 11–6, Thurs. 11–7, Sat. 11–4:45.*

NORTHSIDE

Faded stereotypes about the Northside being Dublin's poorer and more deprived half have been washed away by the economic boom of Celtic Tiger development. Locals and visitors alike are discovering the no-nonsense, laid-back charm of the Northside's revamped Georgian wonders, understated cultural gems, high-quality restaurants, and buzzing ethnic diversity. Here you can begin a pilgrimage into James Joyce country, along the way savoring the captivating sights of Dublin's Northside, a mix of densely thronged shopping streets and genteelly refurbished homes. Once-derelict swaths of houses, especially on and near the Liffey, have been rehabilitated, and large shopping centers have opened on Mary and Jervis streets. The high-rise Docklands area, east of the Custom House, is the new hot place to live. O'Connell Street itself has been partially pedestrianized, and most impressive of all is the Spire, the street's new 395-foot-high stainless-steel monument.

Custom House. Seen at its best when reflected in the waters of the Liffey during the short interval when the high tide is on the turn, the Custom House is the city's most spectacular Georgian building. Extending 375 feet on the north side of the river, this is the work of James Gandon, an English architect who arrived in Ireland in 1781, when the building's construction commenced (it continued for 10 years). Note the exquisitely carved lions and unicorns supporting the arms of Ireland at the far ends of the facade. After Republicans set fire to the building in 1921, it was completely restored and reconstructed to house government offices. A visitor center traces the building's history and significance, and the life of Gandon. ✉ *Custom House Quay, Northside* ☎ *01/874–2961* ⊕ *www.visitdublin.com* ▣ *€1* ⊙ *Mid-Mar.–Oct., weekdays 10–12:30, weekends 2–5; Nov.–mid-Mar., Wed.–Fri. 10–12:30, Sun. 2–5.*

Dublin City Gallery, The Hugh Lane. The Francis Bacon studio, reconstructed here exactly as the artist left it on his death (including his diary, books, walls, floors, ceiling, and even dust!), makes this already impressive gallery a must-see for art lovers and fans of the renowned British artist. Built as a town house for the Earl of Charlemont in 1762, this residence was so grand that the Parnell Square street on which it sits was nicknamed "Palace Row" in its honor. His home is now a gallery, named after Sir Hugh Lane, a nephew of Lady Gregory (W. B. Yeats's aristocratic patron). Irish artists represented include Roderic O'Conor, well known for his views of the west of Ireland; William Leech, including his *Girl with a Tinsel Scarf* and *The Cigarette*; and the most famous of the group, Jack B. Yeats. The museum has a dozen of his paintings, including *Ball Alley* and *There Is No Night.* The mystically serene Sean Scully Gallery displays seven giant canvasses by Ireland's renowned abstract modernist. They also host free classical concerts every Sunday. ⊠ *Parnell Sq. N, Northside* ☎ *01/222–5550* ⊕ *www.hughlane.ie* ⊠ *Free* ☉ *Tues.–Thurs. 10–6, Fri. and Sat. 10–5, Sun. 11–5.*

Dublin Writers Museum. "If you would know Ireland—body and soul—you must read its poems and stories," wrote W. B. Yeats in 1891. Further investigation into the Irish way with words can be found at this unique museum, in a magnificently restored 18th-century town house on the north side of Parnell Square. The mansion, once the home of John Jameson, of the Irish whiskey family, centers on the Gallery of Writers, an enormous drawing room gorgeously decorated with paintings, Adamesque plasterwork, and a deep Edwardian lincrusta frieze. Rare manuscripts, diaries, posters, letters, limited and first editions, photographs, and other mementos commemorate the lives and works of the nation's greatest writers—and there are many of them, so leave plenty of time—including Joyce, Shaw, J. M. Synge, Lady Gregory, W. B. Yeats, Beckett, and others. On display are an 1804 edition of Swift's *Gulliver's Travels,* an 1899 first edition of Bram Stoker's *Dracula,* and an 1899 edition of Wilde's *Ballad of Reading Gaol.* There's a "Teller of Tales" exhibit showcasing Behan, O'Flaherty, and O'Faoláin. Readings are periodically held, and there's a room dedicated to children's literature. The bookshop and café make this an ideal place to spend a rainy afternoon. ⊠ *18 Parnell Sq. N, Northside* ☎ *01/872–2077* ⊕ *www.writersmuseum.com* ⊠ *€7.50* ☉ *Mon.–Sat. 10–5, Sun. 11–5.*

James Joyce Centre. Few may have read him, but everyone in Ireland has at least heard of James Joyce (1882–1941)—especially since owning a copy of his censored and suppressed *Ulysses* was one of the top status symbols of the early 20th century. Joyce is of course now acknowledged as one of the greatest modern authors, and his *Dubliners, Finnegan's Wake,* and *A Portrait of the Artist as a Young Man* can even be read as quirky "travel guides" to Dublin. Open to the public, this restored 18th-century Georgian town house, once the dancing academy of Professor Denis J. Maginni (which many will recognize from a reading of *Ulysses*), is a center for Joycean studies and events related to the author. It has an extensive library and archives, exhibition rooms, a bookstore, and a café. The collection includes letters from Beckett, Joyce's guitar and cane, and a celebrated edition of *Ulysses* illustrated by Matisse. The interactive "James Joyce and Ulysses" exhibition allows you to delve into the mysteries and controversies of the novel. The center is the main organizer of "Bloomstime," which marks the week leading up to the Bloomsday celebrations. (Bloomsday, June 16, is the single day *Ulysses* chronicles, as Leopold Bloom winds his way around Dublin in 1904.) ✉ *35 N. Great George's St., Northside* ☎ *01/878–8547* 🌐 *www.jamesjoyce.ie* 🎫 *€5, guided tour €10* 🕓 *April–Sept., Mon.–Sat. 10–5, Sun. 12–5; Oct.– Mar., Tues.–Sat. 10–5, Sun. noon–5.*

O'Connell Street. Dublin's most famous thoroughfare, which is 150 feet wide, was previously known as Sackville Street, but its name was changed in 1924, two years after the founding of the Irish Free State. After the devastation of the 1916 Easter Rising, the Northside street had to be almost entirely reconstructed, a task that took until the end of the 1920s. At one time the main attraction of the street was Nelson's Pillar, a Doric column towering over the city center and a marvelous vantage point, but it was blown up in 1966, on the Rising's 50th anniversary. A major cleanup and repaving have returned the street to some of its old glory. The large monument at the south end of the street is dedicated to Daniel O'Connell (1775–1847), "The Liberator," and was erected in 1854 as a tribute to the orator's achievement in securing Catholic Emancipation in 1829. Look closely and you'll notice that O'Connell is wearing a glove on one hand, as he did for much of his adult life, a self-imposed penance for shooting a man in a duel. But even the great man himself is dwarfed by the newest addition to O'Connell Street: the 395-foot-high Spire was built in Nelson's Pillar's place in 2003, and today this gigantic, stainless-steel monument dominates the street.

WHERE TO EAT

$
CAFÉ
Fodor's Choice ★

🍴 **Cake Café.** When the former head of the Slow Food Dublin movement opens a café, expectations are going to be high. Michelle Darmody's dreamy little Cake Café fulfills every one of them. As it is in a plant-filled courtyard at the back of the restored Daintree building, try to snag an outside table if the weather is decent. Then chill out and chow down on simple savory and sweet delights, all made with a loving, homey touch. Local, organic, and seasonal are the words to live by here and the terrine of Cashel Blue cheese with hazelnut is a typically delicious lunch dish. Save room for the delicate tarts and moist sugar-dusted sponges. This is also the perfect summer spot for a cheeky daytime glass of prosecco with a few nibbles in the courtyard. And don't forget their fun cookery classes: they are the talk of the town. [$] *Average main: €11* ✉ *The Daintree Building, Pleasants Pl., Southside* ☎ *01/478–9394* 🌐 *www.thecakecafe.ie* 🕓 *Closed Sun. No dinner Mon. and Sat.*

$$$$
MODERN IRISH
Fodor's Choice ★

🍴 **Chapter One.** This wonderful, culture-vulture favorite gets its name from its location, downstairs in the vaulted, stone-wall basement of the Dublin Writers Museum; the natural stone-and-wood setting makes it cozily cavelike. The contemporary French eatery is currently the culinary king of the Northside, thanks to chef-proprietor Ross Lewis's way with such dishes as a feta cheese mousse with organic beetroot essence, pear purée, spiced apple, and pumpkin oil. Yeats himself would have loved the halibut cooked in aromatic oil with fried eggplant and green-olive anchoiade, while Synge probably would have fancied the Dublin version of Proust's madeleine: rich bread-and-butter pudding, a favorite of working-class Irish mothers for generations, here turned into an outrageously filling work of art. [$] *Average main: €33* ✉ *18–19 Parnell Sq., Northside* ☎ *01/873–2266* 🌐 *www.chapteronerestaurant.com* ✍ *Reservations essential* ⏲ *Closed Sun. and Mon. No lunch Sat.*

$ ITALIAN Fodor's Choice ★ 🍴 **Dunne and Crescenzi.** Nothing succeeds like success. So popular is this classy little Italian joint just off Nassau Street that they've expanded into the premises two doors down. Pity the poor little coffee shop in between trying to compete with the unpretentious brilliance of this brother-and-sister restaurant and deli. The menu is extensive but simple: panini, a horde of antipasti choices, a few choice pasta specials, and some evening meat dishes and desserts. The all-Italian kitchen staff work wonders with high-quality imported ingredients. The tagliere della casa—a selection of typical Italian salami and farmhouse cheeses garnished with preserves and served on warm bread—makes a great light lunch. A couple of long tables make it perfect for a group, and the hundreds of bottles of wine on shelves cover every inch of the walls. They have opened a second café in nearby Sandymount. [$] *Average main: €14* ✉ *14 S. Fredrick St., Southside* ☎ *01/677–3815* 🌐 *www.dunneandcrescenzi.com.*

$$ FRENCH Fodor's Choice ★ 🍴 **L'Gueuleton.** Dubliners don't do waiting, but you'll see hungry crowds doing just that outside this no-reservations-accepted, exceptional eatery just off George's Street. L'Gueuleton lost a little of its intimacy when it expanded, but the crowds still come for authentic French food at a fair price. Start with the duck-egg mayonnaise with celery, salt, and watercress. For a main course, the sautéed rabbit with red wine, sage, and Barolo tagliatelle somehow manages to be hearty and adventurous at the same time. Desserts have a devilishly childish touch to them—passion-fruit cake with white chocolate sauce is a typical example. Although you can't phone in a reservation, you can go there early in the evening and put your name and phone number down for a table, and then pop next door to Hogan's bar while you're waiting. [$] *Average main: €22* ✉ *1 Fade St., Southside* ☎ *01/675–3708* 🌐 *www.lgueuleton.com.*

$$$ MODERN IRISH Fodor's Choice ★ 🍴 **One Pico.** Chef-owner Eamonn O'Reilly cuts quite a dash, but it's his sophisticated, daring, contemporary cuisine that tends to seduce visitors to his little restaurant tucked away in a quiet lane only a few minutes from Stephen's Green. Try the incredible langoustine risotto with prawns, truffle, bisque, and sorrel to start. Dishes such as roast rump of veal with fricassee of girolles, pearl onion, and truffle, and *pomme sarladaise* (a southern French version of mashed potatoes) demonstrate a savvy use of native ingredients. Follow this with the mango cheesecake with mango and lime foam. As is usual with Dublin's luxe eateries, the fixed-price lunch and pretheater menus offer great value. [$] *Average main: €31* ✉ *5–6 Molesworth Pl., off Schoolhouse La., Southside* ☎ *01/676–0300* 🌐 *www.onepico.com* ✍ *Reservations essential.*

$$$$ FRENCH Fodor's Choice ★ 🍴 **Restaurant Patrick Guilbaud.** Also known as "Dublin's finest restaurant," this do-be-impressed place on the ground floor of the Merrion Hotel boasts a menu described as French, but chef Guillaume Lebrun's genius lies in his occasional daring use of traditional Irish ingredients—so often taken for granted—to create the unexpected. The best dishes are flawless: Clogher Head lobster ravioli, veal sweetbreads, and licorice, or the slow-cooked pork with pomme purée, lemon star anise,

and licorice. Follow that, if you can, with the *assiette au chocolat* (a tray of five hot and cold chocolate desserts). The ambience is just as delicious—if you're into lofty, minimalist dining rooms and Irish modern art (the Roderic O'Conors and Louis le Brocquys are all from the owner's private collection). Nearly as impressive is the 70-page wine list, the view of the Merrion's manicured gardens, and the two-course lunch special for €38. Soaring white vaults and white walls won't make you feel warm and cozy, but you can always go somewhere else for that. $ *Average main: €55* ✉ *21 Upper Merrion St., Georgian Dublin* ☎ *01/676–4192* ⊕ *www.restaurantpatrickguilbaud.ie* ⌫ *Reservations essential* ☉ *Closed Sun. and Mon.*

$$

MODERN IRISH

✕ **The Tea Room.** In the Clarence Hotel, you can sit around all day and hope that Bono and the boys of U2—they own the joint, after all—might turn up for a quick snack. Other stars of stage and screen often stay at the hotel and stop in at the Tea Room. Minimalistically hued in golden oak, eggshell white, and light yellows, the high-ceilinged room is a perfect stage for off-duty celebs. The contrast between this vaulted cocoon and busy Essex Street—whose madding crowds can be glimpsed through the double-height windows—could not be more dramatic. The menu has been slimmed down in recent times with a focus on a smaller number of dramatic dishes, such as duck with Parmesan tuiles and red-wine sauce, or the panfried gnocchi with wild mushrooms and caramelized onions. $ *Average main: €19* ✉ *Clarence Hotel, 6–8 Wellington Quay, Temple Bar* ☎ *01/407–0813* ⊕ *www.theclarence.ie* ⌫ *Reservations essential.*

$$

IRISH

✕ **The Winding Stair.** Once Dublin's favorite secondhand bookshop–café, the Winding Stair now houses an atmospheric, buzzing little restaurant, replete with old wooden floors, simple decor, a downstairs bookshop, and grand views of the Ha'penny Bridge and the river Liffey. Upstairs, former habitués will enjoy seeing the old bookcases around the walls (some of which are now stacked with wine). Hearty portions of upmarket traditional Irish food best describes the terrific menu, which is greatly helped by locally sourced ingredients, and reads like a list of small, artisan Irish producers. The wild venison cushion with colcannon bake, buttered kale, and wild mushrooms is a standout, as is the flatbread with Irish ricotta, whipped artichoke, and tomato sauce. An inventive wine list and a wonderful Irish farmhouse-cheese selection are two more treats on offer. Your sweet tooth insists that you try the bread-and-butter pudding for dessert. $ *Average main: €24* ✉ *40 Ormond Quay, Northside* ☎ *01/872–7320* ⊕ *www.winding-stair.com.*

WHERE TO STAY

$$

HOTEL

Fodor'sChoice

★

🎦 **Central Hotel Dublin.** Every city center needs its little oasis, and the Central's book-and-armchair-filled Library Bar—warmed by a Victorian fireplace—nicely fits the bill. **Pros:** delightful Library Bar; original 1887 facade; old-fashioned feel. **Cons:** rooms a bit snug; street noise in some rooms; you have to prepay up front! $ *Rooms from: €159* ✉ *1–5 Exchequer St., Southside* ☎ *01/679–7302* ⊕ *www.centralhotel.ie* ⤴ *67 rooms, 3 suites* ❘◉❘ *Breakfast.*

$$ HOTEL **The Clarence.** Temple Bar's most prestigious hotel, and occasional home to your potential new best friends/elevator buddies, co-owners Bono and the Edge of U2, this renovated 1852 grand old hotel is the place to be to sample Temple Bar's nightlife, even if your pals are too busy rocking to hang. **Pros:** stylish Octagon Bar; the owners might be on-premises; Tea Room restaurant. **Cons:** rooms a bit small; some rooms suffer from street noise; paying a premium for "cool." [$] *Rooms from: €189* ✉ *6–8 Wellington Quay, Temple Bar* ☎ *01/407–0800* 🌐 *www.theclarence.ie* 🛏 *44 rooms, 5 suites* 🍴 *No meals.*

$ HOTEL Fodor's Choice ★ **Kellys Hotel Dublin.** With buzzing Hogan's bar and the classy L'Gueuleton restaurant right downstairs, this cool little hotel is already at the epicenter of trendy Dublin living. **Pros:** killer city-center location; cool vibe; one of the city's best restaurants downstairs; great spot to bump into interesting Dubliners. **Cons:** some rooms are cramped; can suffer from street noise; no elevator. [$] *Rooms from: €89* ✉ *36 S. Great Georges St., Southside* ☎ *01/648–0010* 🌐 *www.kellysdublin.com* 🛏 *15 rooms, 1 suite* 🍴 *Breakfast.*

$ B&B/INN **Kilronan House Hotel.** Just a five minute walk from St. Stephen's Green, this mid-19th-century terraced guesthouse, with its elegant white facade and cozy sitting-room fire, will welcome you home at the end of a long day's sightseeing. **Pros:** great price for location; beautiful, calming facade; cozy sitting room. **Cons:** public areas a bit worn; uncreative room furnishings; no Internet in rooms; no elevator. [$] *Rooms from: €119* ✉ *70 Adelaide Rd., Georgian Dublin* ☎ *01/475–5266* 🌐 *www.kilronanhouse.com* 🛏 *12 rooms* 🍴 *Breakfast.*

$ B&B/INN **Marian Guest House.** A veritable Everest of fine Irish meats, the Marian's mighty Irish breakfast, with black pudding and smoked bacon, is reason enough to stay at this family-run redbrick guesthouse just off beautiful Mountjoy Square. **Pros:** excellent breakfast; family-owned and -run; small. **Cons:** located in a slightly run-down part of the city; gets some street noise; fairly basic rooms. [$] *Rooms from: €70* ✉ *21 Upper Gardiner St., Northside* ☎ *01/874–4129* 🌐 *www.marianguesthouse.ie* 🛏 *6 rooms* 🍴 *Breakfast.*

$$$ HOTEL Fodor's Choice ★ **Merrion Hotel.** Stately and spiffy, and splendidly situated directly across from Government Buildings between Stephen's Green and Merrion Square, this luxurious hotel actually comprises four exactingly restored Georgian town houses. **Pros:** Patrick Guilbaud restaurant; infinity pool; city-center location; attentive staff. **Cons:** you'll pay extra for a room in the original house; some rooms are overdecorated. [$] *Rooms from: €250* ✉ *Upper Merrion St., Georgian Dublin* ☎ *01/603–0600* 🌐 *www.merrionhotel.com* 🛏 *123 rooms, 19 suites* 🍴 *No meals.*

$$$ B&B/INN Fodor's Choice ★ **Number 31.** Whether your lodging style is sublime Georgian elegance or serene cool modern, this one-in-a-million guesthouse, a short walk from St. Stephen's Green, serves up both—as well as the best made-to-order breakfast in town. **Pros:** the king and queen of guesthouse hosts; serene decor and art; best breakfast in the city. **Cons:** a few rooms can be a little noisy; no elevator; minimum two-night stay on summer weekends. [$] *Rooms from: €220* ✉ *31 Leeson Close, Georgian Dublin* ☎ *01/676–5011* 🌐 *www.number31.ie* 🛏 *21 rooms* 🍴 *Breakfast.*

$$$ HOTEL Fodor's Choice ★ 🏨 **The Shelbourne Dublin, Renaissance.** Paris has the Ritz, New York has the Pierre, and Dublin has the Shelbourne—today, newly resplendent in its broad, ornamented, pink-and-white, mid-Victorian facade after a no-expense-spared renovation by the big Marriott chain. **Pros:** afternoon tea in Lord Mayor's Lounge; Irish art worth gazing at; new spa and wellness center; all-around luxury. **Cons:** some noise in front rooms; pricey; feels a little stuffy at times. [$] *Rooms from: €220* ✉ *27 St. Stephen's Green, Southside* ☎ *01/663–4500, 800/543–4300 in U.S.* 🌐 *www.marriott.co.uk/hotels/travel/dubbr-the-shelbourne-dublin-a-renaissance-hotel* 🛏 *246 rooms, 19 suites* 🍴 *No meals.*

NIGHTLIFE AND THE ARTS

Check the following newspapers for informative listings: the *Irish Times* publishes a daily guide to what's happening in Dublin and the rest of the country, and has complete film and theater schedules. The *Evening Herald* lists theaters, cinemas, and pubs with live entertainment. The *Big Issue* is a weekly guide to film, theater, and musical events around the city. The *Event Guide,* a weekly free paper that lists music, cinema, theater, art shows, and dance clubs, is available in pubs and cafés around the city.

NIGHTLIFE

Some wag once asked if it was possible to cross Dublin without passing a single pub along the way. The answer was "Yes, but only if you go into every one."

NORTHSIDE

The Academy. A music mecca with four floors of entertainment of every kind, the Academy is anchored by big-name local and international DJs and gigs. It attracts a young, dance-crazy crowd who like to party until the wee hours. ✉ *57 Middle Abbey St., Northside* ☎ *01/877–9999* 🌐 *www.theacademydublin.com.*

The Flowing Tide. Directly across from the Abbey Theatre, the Flowing Tide draws a lively pre- and post-theater crowd. No TVs, quality pub talk, and a great pint of Guinness make it a worthwhile visit (although the decor won't win any prizes). ✉ *Lower Abbey St., Northside* ☎ *01/874–0842.*

SOUTHSIDE

ALT. Once a bastion of experimental theatre, Andrew's Lane Theatre has been reborn as ALT, a cozy club with regular live indie gigs. ✉ *Andrews Lane, Southside* ☎ *01/478–0766* 🌐 *andrewslanetheatre.wordpress.com.*

Bewley's Café Theatre. With its intimate nights in this small, Victorian venue, Bewley's Café Theatre has become the atmospheric cabaret hot spot in Dublin. Set in the Oriental Room on the second floor above the glorious, stained-glass jewel that is the Grafton Street restaurant, the unique lunchtime performances here—a one-act play by O'Casey or Wilde with a bowl of soup and soda bread—are also noteworthy. ✉ *78/79 Grafton St., 2nd fl., Southside* ☎ *086/878–4001* 🌐 *www.bewleyscafetheatre.com.*

Davy Byrne's. A noted pilgrimage stop for Joyceans, Davy Byrne's is where Leopold Bloom stops in for a glass of Burgundy and a Gorgonzola-cheese sandwich in *Ulysses* (and ruminates before helping a blind man cross the road). Unfortunately, the decor—quite an eyeful, with its gaudily painted ceiling, stained glass cupola, and blush pastels—is greatly changed from Joyce's day ("He entered Davy Byrnes. Moral pub."), but it still serves some fine pub grub. ⊠ *21 Duke St., Southside* ☎ *167/75217* ⊕ *www.davybyrnes.com.*

Fodor's Choice ★ **Grogan's.** Also known as the Castle Lounge, Grogan's is a small place packed with creative folk. Owner Tommy Grogan is known as a patron of local artists, and his walls are covered with their work. ⊠ *15 S. William St., Southside* ☎ *01/677–9320.*

Fodor's Choice ★ **Horseshoe Bar.** A recent massive face-lift, along with the rest of the Shelbourne hotel, made the Horseshoe Bar the hottest ticket in town. There's comparatively little space for drinkers around the famous semicircular bar—but this does wonders for making friends quickly. ⊠ *Shelbourne, 27 St. Stephen's Green, Southside* ☎ *01/676–6471* ⊕ *www.marriott. co.uk.*

Fodor's Choice ★ **Lillie's Bordello.** Once the hot spot for celebs, Lillie's Bordello is now more for regular Joes: a popular hangout for a young late-night crowd. Hot or not, the decor remains a knock-out: Victorian brocaded velvets and gilded frames plus pink and purple neon lasers. Take a rest from the dance floor in the gorgeous Library room. ⊠ *Grafton St., Southside* ☎ *01/679–9204* ⊕ *www.lilliesbordello.ie.*

The Long Hall. One of Dublin's most ornate traditional taverns, the Long Hall has Victorian lamps, a mahogany bar, mirrors, chandeliers, and plasterwork ceilings, all more than 100 years old. The pub serves sandwiches and an excellent pint of Guinness. ⊠ *51 S. Great George's St., Southside* ☎ *01/475–1590.*

Neary's. With an exotic, Victorian-style interior, Neary's was once the haunt of music-hall artists and a certain literary set, including Brendan Behan. Join the actors from the adjacent Gaiety Theatre for a good pub lunch. ⊠ *1 Chatham St., Southside* ☎ *01/677–7371.*

Fodor's Choice ★ **Stag's Head.** A Victorian beaut, the Stag's Head dates from 1770 and was rebuilt in 1895. Theater people from the nearby Olympia, journalists, and Trinity students gather around the unusual Connemara red-marble bar, study their reflections in the many mirrors, and drink in all the oak carvings. ⊠ *1 Dame Ct., Southside* ☎ *01/679–3701.*

Toner's. Though billed as a Victorian bar, Toner's actually goes back 200 years, with an original flagstone floor to prove its antiquity, as well as wooden drawers running up to the ceiling—a relic of the days when bars doubled as grocery shops. Oliver St. John Gogarty, who was the model for Buck Mulligan in James Joyce's *Ulysses,* accompanied W. B. Yeats here, in what was purportedly the latter's only visit to a pub. ⊠ *139 Lower Baggot St., Georgian Dublin* ☎ *01/676–3090* ⊕ *www. tonerspub.ie.*

11

TEMPLE BAR

Button Factory. A happening music venue, the Button mixes top DJs and up-and-coming live acts. ⊠ *Curved St., Temple Bar* ☎ *01/670–9202* ⊕ *www.buttonfactory.ie.*

Oliver St John Gogarty. A lively bar that attracts all ages and nationalities, the Oliver St. John Gogarty overflows with patrons in summer. On most nights there's traditional Irish music upstairs. ⊠ *57 Fleet St., Temple Bar* ☎ *01/671–1822* ⊕ *www.gogartys.ie.*

The Workman's Club. This no-frills, hip spot specializes in Indie club nights and attracts an artistic and hipster crowd. It has three floors of music and live gigs. Check the website for upcoming nights. ⊠ *10 Wellington Quay, Temple Bar* ☎ *01/670–6692* ⊕ *www.theworkmansclub.com.*

DUBLIN WEST

Brazen Head. Reputedly Dublin's oldest pub (the site has been licensed since 1198), the Brazen Head doesn't have much of a time-burnished decor—except for one big exception: an enchanting stone courtyard that is intimate, charming, and delightful. The front is a faux one-story castle, complete with flambeaux, while the interior looks modern day (except for the very low ceilings). People love to jam the place not for its history but for its traditional-music performances and lively sing-along sessions on Sunday evenings. On the south side of the Liffey quays, it's a little difficult to find—turn down Lower Bridge Street and make a right onto the old lane. ⊠ *20 Lower Bridge St., Dublin West* ☎ *01/677–9549* ⊕ *www.brazenhead.com.*

Fodor'sChoice
★ **Ryan's Pub.** One of Dublin's last genuine, late-Victorian-era pubs, Ryan's has changed little since its last (1896) remodeling. ⊠ *28 Parkgate St., Dublin West* ☎ *01/677–6097.*

THE ARTS

CLASSICAL MUSIC AND OPERA

The National Concert Hall. Just off St. Stephen's Green, the National Concert Hall is Dublin's main theater for classical music of all kinds, from symphonies to chamber groups. The slightly austere neoclassical building was transformed in 1981 into one of Europe's finest medium-size concert halls. ⊠ *Earlsfort Terr., Georgian Dublin* ☎ *01/417–0000* ⊕ *www.nch.ie.*

ROCK AND CONTEMPORARY MUSIC

Whelan's. It might look a bit shabby around the edges, but Whelan's is one of the city's best—and most popular—music venues. Well-known performers play everything from rock to folk to traditional music. ⊠ *25 Wexford St., Southside* ☎ *01/478–0766* ⊕ *www.whelanslive.com.*

THEATER

Fodor'sChoice
★ **Abbey Theatre.** One of the most fabled theaters in the world, the Abbey is the home of Ireland's national theater company. In 1904 W. B. Yeats and his patron, Lady Gregory, opened the theater, which became a major center for the Irish literary renaissance—the place that first staged works by J. M. Synge and Sean O'Casey, among many others. Plays by recent Irish drama heavyweights like Brian Friel, Tom Murphy, Hugh Leonard, and John B. Keane have all premiered here, and memorable productions of international greats like Mamet, Ibsen, and Shakespeare

have also been performed. You should not, however, arrive expecting 19th-century grandeur: the original structure burned down in 1951. A starkly modernist auditorium was built in its place—but what it may lack in esthetics it makes up for in space and acoustics. Some say the repertoire is overly reverential and mainstream, but such chestnuts as Dion Boucicault's *The Shaughran* wind up being applauded by many. Happily, the Abbey's second stage offers more experimental drama. But the Abbey will always be relevant since much of the theatergoing public still looks to it as a barometer of Irish culture. ⊠ *Lower Abbey St., Northside* ☎ *01/878–7222* ⊕ *www.abbeytheatre.ie.*

Gate Theatre. An intimate 371-seat theater in a jewellike Georgian assembly hall, the Gate produces the classics and contemporary plays by leading Irish writers, including Beckett, Wilde (the production of *Salome* was a worldwide hit), Shaw, and the younger generation of dramatists, such as Conor McPherson. ⊠ *Cavendish Row, Parnell Square, Northside* ☎ *01/874–4045* ⊕ *www.gate-theatre.ie.*

SHOPPING

Dublin has a tremendous variety of stores, many of which are quite sophisticated—as a walk through Dublin's central shopping area, from O'Connell to Grafton Street, will prove. Most large shops and department stores are open Monday to Saturday 9 to 6, with late hours on Thursday until 9.

NORTHSIDE

The city's main thoroughfare, O'Connell Street is more downscale than Southside city streets (such as Grafton Street), but it is still worth a walk. One of Dublin's largest department stores, Clery's, is here, across from the GPO. On the same side of the street as the post office is Eason's, a large book, magazine, and stationery store.

Trinity Crafts. Your one-stop shop for everything kitschy Irish, head to Trinity Crafts for such trashy treasures as "the leprechauns made me do it" mugs and Guinness-logo underwear. ⊠ *27 Nassau St., Southside* ☎ *01/672–5663* ⊕ *www.thesweatershop.ie.*

SOUTHSIDE

Dublin's bustling pedestrian-only main shopping street, Grafton Street has two department stores: down-to-earth Marks & Spencer and *trés* chic Brown Thomas. The rest of the street is taken up by shops, many of them branches of international chains, such as the Body Shop and Bally, and many British chains. This is also the spot to buy fresh flowers, available at reasonable prices from outdoor stands. On the smaller streets off Grafton Street—especially Duke Street, South Anne Street, and Chatham Street—are worthwhile crafts, clothing, and designer housewares shops.

SHOPPING CENTERS

Powerscourt Centre. Once the regal former town home of Lord Powerscourt (built in 1771), this was largely gutted two decades ago to make room for an interior roofed-over courtyard and a space shared by a mix of restaurants, cafés, antiques stores, and boutiques of original

Irish fashions by young designers. A pianist often plays on the dais at ground-floor level. ⊠ *59 S. William St., Southside* ☎ *01/679–4144* ⊕ *www.powerscourtcentre.com.*

Fodor's Choice
★
St. Stephen's Green Centre. Dublin's city center's largest and most ambitious shopping complex, St. Stephen's Green Centre resembles a giant greenhouse, with Victorian-style ironwork. On three floors overlooked by a giant clock, the 100 mostly small shops sell crafts, fashions, and household goods. ⊠ *NW corner of St. Stephen's Green, Southside* ☎ *01/478–0888* ⊕ *www.stephensgreen.com.*

RECOMMENDED STORES

Avoca. A beautiful store with an eclectic collection of knitwear, jewelry, ceramics, and housewares from contemporary Irish designers. ⊠ *11–13 Suffolk St., Southside* ☎ *01/274–6900* ⊕ *www.avoca.ie.*

Fodor's Choice
★
Costume. A classy boutique where Dubliners with fashion sense and money like to shop for colorful, stylish clothes. Costume showcases local designers include Leigh, Helen James, and Helen Steele; Temperley and Preen are among the international designers featured. ⊠ *10 Castel Market, Southside* ☎ *01/679–4188* ⊕ *www.costumedublin.ie.*

Gael Linn. A specialist in traditional Irish music and Irish-language recordings, Gael Linn is where the aficionados go. ⊠ *35 Dame St., Southside* ☎ *01/675–1200* ⊕ *www.gael-linn.ie.*

Fodor's Choice
★
Hodges Figgis. Dublin's leading independent bookstore, Hodges Figgis stocks 1½ million books on three floors. Once considered Ireland's oldest, its "independent" claim is a bit bogus, as a giant chain bought it some years ago. That noted, it has a stock, staff, look, and even aroma of an independent bookstore, and might even still please James Joyce (who alludes to it in his *Ulysses*). ⊠ *56–58 Dawson St., Southeast Dublin* ☎ *01/677–4754.*

Indigo and Cloth. This has quickly become the place where Irish men with a bit of taste come for quality, slightly edgy clothing. Designers like Oliver Spencer and Velour dominate, and they also have a small, but classy, women's section. ⊠ *Basement 27, S. William St., Southside* ☎ *01/670–6403* ⊕ *www.indigoandcloth.com.*

Fodor's Choice
★
Kevin and Howlin. A quintessential Irish store, Kevin and Howlin stocks spiffing fashions, with lots of stylish handwoven tweed men's jackets, suits, and hats, along with an array of treasures woven from tweedy fabrics. All in all, a fabulous, one-stop shop for traditional clothes with flair. Wait until you see the whole wall devoted to headgear—eat your heart out, Ralph Lauren! ⊠ *31 Nassau St., Southside* ☎ *01/677–0257* ⊕ *www.kevinandhowlin.com.*

Kilkenny Shop. Specializing in contemporary Irish-made ceramics, pottery, and silver jewelry, Kilkenny Shop regularly holds exhibits of exciting new work by Irish craftspeople and has a wide array of gifts fashioned by Orla Kiely and other top Irish designers. ⊠ *6–15 Nassau St., Southside* ☎ *01/677–7066* ⊕ *www.kilkennyshop.com.*

Fodor's Choice
★
Stokes Books. A gem of an antique bookstore, Stokes has a great used-book section and specializes in Irish history and literature. While on the small side, Stokes is a treasure trove that will turn on most

book-lovers. ✉ *George's Street Arcade, Southside* ☎ *01/671–3584* ⊕ *www.georgesstreetarcade.ie/stokes-books/index.php.*

Weir & Sons. Dublin's most prestigious jeweler, Weir & Sons sells not only jewelry and watches, but also china, glass, lamps, silver, and leather. Founded in 1869, its flatiron building has long been a landmark on Grafton Street. ✉ *96 Grafton St., Southside* ☎ *01/677–9678* ⊕ *www.weirandsons.ie.*

CASHEL AND COUNTY CORK

Nobody ever came twice to Ireland looking for a tan. But if they did, they would head to the country's Southeast region, which has the mildest, sunniest, and also driest weather in Ireland. Other than the cities of Kilkenny and Waterford, the leading sight of the region is the spectacular Rock of Cashel, one of Ireland's greatest medieval sites and a must-see for many. A further 160 km (100 miles) southwest lies Cork City, Ireland's second-biggest city and one of its most vibrant. A great base for touring the countryside, it's not too far from the Blarney Stone, where you can supposedly get "the gift of the gab" at beautiful Blarney Castle.

PLANNING YOUR TIME

Providing you catch a morning bus from Dublin, you'll be able to enjoy a full afternoon at the Rock of Cashel. However, an overnight is suggested in the town of Cashel (especially if you don't want to hand over your luggage to the attendants at the Rock for storage—unfortunately, they don't have an official cloakroom); note that while Cashel has few hotels it does have many guesthouses—inquire at the tourist office. Or you can opt to forge on that day and catch a bus around sunset heading to Cork. A full day is needed for this large city, plus an extra day for the excursion west to Blarney Castle.

GETTING HERE

The only public transportation that goes directly to the Rock of Cashel is the Dublin–Cork bus, run by Bus Éireann; departures are usually every two hours and the bus ride lasts about 2½ hours. Aircoach is a private line that also runs between Dublin and Cork and passes through Cashel. Alternatively, there are trains from Dublin to Thurles, a village 15 minutes away from Cashel (connect via tax or infrequent buses). Bus Éireann's Dublin-Cork bus then connects Cashel with Cork. By car, Cashel is on the big N8 highway connecting north and south. There are numerous trains every day from Dublin to Cork (3 hours). To get to Blarney Castle from Cork, catch buses from the Parnell Place station.

Bus Contacts Aircoach ☎ *01/844–7118* ⊕ *www.aircoach.ie.* **Bus Éireann** ☎ *01/836–6111* ⊕ *www.buseireann.ie.*

Train Contacts Irish Rail *(Iarnrod Éireann).* ☎ *01/836–6222* ⊕ *www.irishrail.ie.*

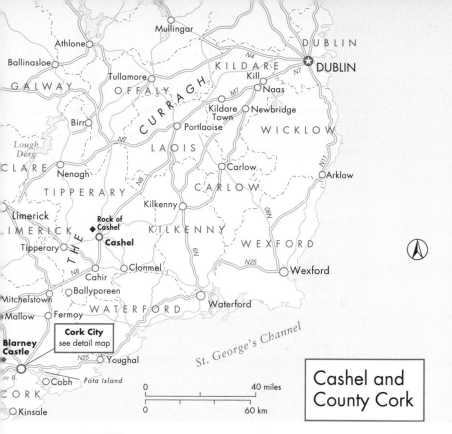

Cashel and
County Cork

TOURS

Bus Éireann offers a range of daylong and half-day guided tours of the region around Cork from June to September. A full-day tour costs about €30, half-day €15. Bus Éireann also offers open-top bus tours of Cork City on Tuesday and Saturday in July and August for €6.

Contacts Bus Éireann Tours and Trips ☎ *021/450–8188 in Cork* ⊕ *www. buseireann.ie/inner.php?id=273.*

ROCK OF CASHEL

160 km (100 miles) southwest of Dublin on the N8.

Cashel Heritage Centre. In the same building as the tourism office, the Cashel Heritage Centre explains the historic relationship between the town and the Rock and includes a scale model of Cashel as it looked during the 1600s. ⊠ *City Hall, Main St.* ☎ *062/62511* ⊕ *www.cashel.ie* ✉ *Free* ⊗ *Mar.–Oct., daily 9:30–5:50; Nov.–Feb., weekdays 9:30–5:30.*

Fodor's Choice **The Rock of Cashel.** Seat of the Kings of Munster and the hallowed spot ★ where St. Patrick first plucked a shamrock to explain the mystery of the Trinity, the Rock of Cashel is Ireland's greatest group of ecclesiastical ruins. Standing in the middle of a sloped, treeless valley, the Rock's titanic grandeur and majesty creates what one ancient scribe called "a fingerpost to Heaven." Today, the great limestone mass still rises 300 feet to command a panorama over all it surveys—fittingly, the name derives from the Irish *caiseal,* meaning "stone fort," and this gives a good idea of its strategic importance in days of yore.

For centuries, Cashel was known as the "city of the kings"—from the 5th century, the lords of Munster ruled over much of southern Ireland from here. In 1101, however, they handed Cashel over to the Christian fathers, and the rock soon became the center of the reform movement that reshaped the Irish Church. Along the way, the church fathers embarked on a centuries-long building campaign that resulted in the magnificent group of chapels, round towers, and walls you see at Cashel today.

The real showpiece of Cashel is **Cormac's Chapel,** built in 1127 by Cormac McCarthy, King of Desmond and Bishop of Cashel. It is the finest example of Hiberno-Romanesque architecture. Preserved within the chapel is a splendid but broken sarcophagus, once believed to be Cormac's final resting place. At the opposite end of the chapel is the nave, where you can look for wonderful medieval paintings now showing through old plasterwork.

With thick walls that attest to its origin as a fortress, the now roofless **St. Patrick's Cathedral** is the largest building on the site. In the Choir, look for the noted Tomb of Myler McGrath. Note the tombs in the North Transept, whose carvings—of the apostles, other saints, and the Beasts of the Apocalypse—are remarkably detailed. The octagonal staircase turret that ascends the cathedral's central tower leads to a series of defensive passages built into the thick walls—from the top of the tower, you'll have wonderful views.

As the oldest building on the Rock, the **Round Tower** rises 92 feet to command a panoramic view of the entire Vale of Tipperary. A constant lookout was posted here to warn of any advancing armies. ✉ *Rock of Cashel* ☎ *062/61437* 🌐 *www.heritageireland.ie* 🎟 *€6* 🕒 *Mid-Mar.–early June, daily 9:30–5:30; early June–mid-Sept., daily 9–7; mid-Sept.–mid-Oct., daily 9–5:30; mid-Oct.–mid-Mar., daily 9–4:30.*

WHERE TO STAY

$$ HOTEL Fodor's Choice ★ 🏨 **Cashel Palace Hotel.** This grand house is a palace in every sense: red-pine paneling, barley-sugar staircases, Corinthian columns, and a surfeit of cosseting antiques all create an air of Georgian volupté, while outside the majestic manse is gorgeously offset by parkland with fountains and centuries-old trees. **Pros:** glorious period main house; great strolling gardens; good restaurant. **Cons:** expensive for this region; popular for weddings; few in-room facilities. [$] *Rooms from: €170* ✉ *Main St.* ☎ *062/62707* 🌐 *www.cashel-palace.ie* 🛏 *21 rooms* 🍴 *Breakfast.*

CORK CITY

77 km (48 miles) west of Cashel, 254 km (158 miles) south of Dublin.

The major metropolis of the south, Cork is Ireland's second-largest city—but you have to put this in perspective. It actually runs a distant second, with a population of 123,000, roughly one-tenth the size of

Dublin. Cork is a spirited place, with a formidable pub culture, a lively traditional-music scene, a respected and progressive university, attractive art galleries, and offbeat cafés. The city's major sights are spread out a bit, but still the best way to see the city is on foot. Patrick Street is the city center's main thoroughfare. You can tour the center of the city in a morning or an afternoon, depending on how much you plan to shop along the way. To really see everything, however, allow a full day, with a break for lunch at the Farmgate Café in the English Market. Also note that the Crawford Gallery and the English Market are closed on Sunday.

Cork Vision Centre. In the renovated St. Peter's Church, an 18th-century building in what was the bustling heart of medieval Cork, this historical society provides an excellent introduction to the city's history and geography. The highlight is a detailed 1:500-scale model of the city, showing how it has changed over the ages. ☒ *N. Main St., Washington Village* ☎ *021/427–9925* ⊕ *www.corkvisioncentre.com* ✉ *Free* ⊙ *Tues.–Sat. 10–5.*

Fodor'sChoice
★ **Crawford Art Gallery.** The large redbrick building was built in 1724 as the customs house and is now home to Ireland's leading provincial art gallery. An imaginative expansion has added gallery space for visiting exhibitions and adventurous shows of modern Irish artists. The permanent collection includes landscape paintings depicting Cork in the 18th and 19th centuries. Take special note of works by Irish painters William Leech (1881–1968), Daniel Maclise (1806–70), James Barry (1741–1806), and Nathaniel Grogan (1740–1807). The café, run by the Allen family of Ballymaloe, is a good place for a light lunch or a homemade sweet. ☒ *Emmet Pl., City Center South* ☎ *021/480–5042* ⊕ *www.crawfordartgallery.ie* ✉ *Free* ⊙ *Mon.–Wed., Fri. and Sat. 10–5, Thurs. 10–8.*

Fodor'sChoice
★ **English Market.** Food lovers (and, who, pray, isn't?): be sure to make a beeline for one of the misleadingly small entrances to this large and famous mecca for foodies. Fetchingly housed in an elaborate, brick-and-cast-iron Victorian building, such is the fame of the English Market that Her Majesty Queen Elizabeth insisted on an impromptu walk-about here on her historic first visit to Ireland in May 2011. Among the 140 stalls, keep an eye out for the Alternative Bread Co., which produces more than 40 varieties of handmade bread every day. Iago, Sean Calder-Potts's deli, has fresh pasta, lots of cheeses, and charcuterie. The Olive Stall sells olive oil, olive-oil soap, and olives from Greece, Spain, France, and Italy. Kay O'Connell's Fish Stall, in the legendary fresh-fish alley, purveys local smoked salmon. O'Reilly's Tripe and Drisheen is the last existing retailer of a Cork specialty, tripe (cow's stomach), and *drisheen* (blood sausage). Upstairs is the Farmgate, an excellent café. ☒ *Entrances on Grand Parade and Princes St., City Center South* ⊕ *www.corkenglishmarket.ie* ⊙ *Mon.–Sat. 9:30–5:30.*

Patrick Street. Extending from Grand Parade in the south to Patrick's Bridge in the north, Panna (as it's known locally) is Cork's main shopping thoroughfare. It has been designed as a pedestrian-priority area with wide walks and special streetlights. A mainstream mix of

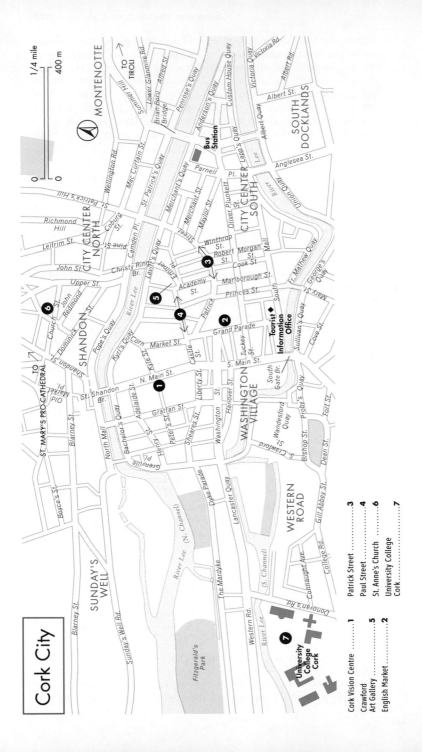

Cork City

MONTENOTTE

CITY CENTER NORTH

SHANDON

CITY CENTER SOUTH

SOUTH DOCKLANDS

WASHINGTON VILLAGE

SUNDAY'S WELL

WESTERN ROAD

Fitzgerald's Park

University College Cork

Bus Station

Tourist Information Office

TO TIVOLI →

TO ST. MARY'S PRO-CATHEDRAL →

1/4 mile

400 m

Cork Vision Centre 1
Crawford
Art Gallery 5
English Market 2

Patrick Street 3
Paul Street 4
St. Anne's Church 6
University College
Cork 7

department stores, boutiques, pharmacies, and bookshops lines the way.
■**TIP→ If you look above some of the plate-glass storefronts, you can see
examples of the bowfront Georgian windows that are emblematic of old
Cork.** The street saw some of the city's worst fighting during the War of
Independence. ⊠ *City Center South.*

Paul Street. A narrow stretch between the River Lee and Patrick Street
and parallel to both, Paul Street is the backbone of the trendy shopping
district that now occupies Cork's old French Quarter. The area was first
settled by Huguenots fleeing religious persecution in France. Musicians
and other street performers often entertain passersby in the Rory Gal-
lagher Piazza, named for the late rock guitarist, whose family was from
Cork. The shops here offer the best in modern Irish design—from local
fashions to hand-blown glass. ⊠ *City Center South.*

St. Anne's Church. The church's pepper-pot Shandon steeple, which has
a four-sided clock and is topped with a golden, salmon-shaped weather
vane, is visible from throughout the city and is the chief reason why
St. Anne's is so frequently visited. The Bells of Shandon were immortalized in an atrocious but popular 19th-century ballad of that name.
Your reward for climbing the 120-foot-tall tower is the chance to ring
the bells, with the assistance of sheet tune cards, out over Cork. Beside
the church, **Firkin Crane**, Cork's 18th-century butter market, houses
two small performing spaces. Adjacent is the **Shandon Craft Market.** ⊠ *Church St., Shandon* ☎ *021/450–5906* ⊕ *www.shandonbells.ie*
☒ *Church free, tower €5* ☉ *Mar.–May and Oct., Mon.–Sat. 10–4, Sun.
11:30–4:30; June–Sept., Mon.–Sat. 10–5, Sun. 11:30–4:30; Nov.–Feb.,
Mon.–Sat. 11–3.*

Fodor's Choice
★

University College Cork. The Doric, porticoed gates of UCC stand about
2 km (1 mile) from the city center. The college, which has a student
body of roughly 10,000, is a constituent of the National University of
Ireland. The main quadrangle is a fine example of 19th-century university architecture in the Tudor-Gothic style, reminiscent of many Oxford
and Cambridge colleges. Several ancient ogham stones are on display
in the North Quadrangle (near the visitor center), and the renovated
Crawford Observatory's 1860 telescope can be visited. The Honan Collegiate Chapel, east of the quadrangle, was built in 1916 and modeled
on the 12th-century, Hiberno-Romanesque style, best exemplified by
the remains of Cormac's Chapel at Cashel. The UCC chapel's stained-
glass windows, as well as its collection of art and crafts, altar furnishings, and textiles in the Celtic Revival style, are noteworthy. ⊠ *College
Rd., Western Road* ☎ *021/490–1876* ⊕ *www.ucc.ie* ☒ *Free* ☉ *Visitor
center weekdays 9–5; call for hrs Easter wk, July, Aug., and mid-Dec.–
mid-Jan.; guided tours by appointment.*

WHERE TO EAT

$
IRISH

✕**Farmgate Café.** One of the best—and busiest—informal lunch spots
in town is on a terraced gallery above the fountain at the Princes Street
entrance to the atmospheric English Market. All ingredients used at the
café are purchased in the market below. One side of the gallery opens
onto the market and is self-service; the other side is glassed in and has
table service (reservations advised). Tripe and drisheen is one dish that

is always on the menu; daily specials include less challenging but no less traditional dishes, such as corned beef with *colcannon* (potatoes and cabbage mashed with butter and seasonings) and loin of smoked bacon with *champ* (potatoes mashed with scallions or leeks). $ *Average main: €14* ⊠ *English Market, City Center South* ☎ *021/427–8134* ⊕ *www.corkenglishmarket.ie* ⊘ *Closed Sun. No dinner.*

$$ ✕ **Greenes.** Tucked away on a cobbled patio accessible only on foot, this

EUROPEAN   surprising haven is part of a Victorian warehouse conversion that also

Fodor'sChoice   contains Hotel Isaacs. The stone and redbrick walls are the backdrop for

★   a minimalist modern interior with tall-back green rattan chairs and small tables with linen place mats. The real surprise is out back where a gigantic rock wall waterfall makes a stunning backdrop to a dining terrace. The ambitious French chef, Federic Desormeaux, has created a menu featuring classic French and Mediterranean cuisine. Highlights include the 10-ounce ribeye steak with a brandy pepper sauce and dauphinoise potatoes and the king scallops on a pea and ham-hock potato cake. Classic desserts with a twist include fresh raspberry crème brûlée, and chocolate charlotte with pistachio anglaise. $ *Average main: €24* ⊠ *Hotel Isaacs, 48 MacCurtain St., City Center North* ☎ *021/455–2279* ⊕ *www.greenesrestaurant.com* ⊘ *Closed Sun. except a few holidays. No lunch Sat.–Mon.*

$$$$ ✕ **Ivory Tower.** Don't be put off by the seedy-looking street entrance to

CONTEMPORARY   this second-floor restaurant: Seamus O'Connell, the American-born owner-chef here, is one of the stars of the Irish culinary scene. He describes his approach as "trans-ethnic fusion." He has cooked in Mexico and Japan, so his accomplished menu has such quirky, eclectic dishes as wild duck with vanilla, sherry, and jalapeños or pheasant tamale. His mastery of Japanese cooking is impressive, and he also works wonders with Irish staples: combining monkfish cheeks with pearl barley risotto, and in early spring serving a memorable nettle-and-wild-garlic soup. Imaginative presentation, including a surprise taster to set the mood, compensates for the bare wooden floors and stark decor of the corner dining room, as does the house tradition that the maestro himself often serves the dishes he has created. The eight-course tasting menu (€60) is a great introduction to O'Connell's inimitable style. $ *Average main: €60* ⊠ *35 Princes St., Washington Village* ☎ *021/427–4665* ⊕ *www. ivorytower.ie* ⊟ *No credit cards* ⊘ *Closed Sun.–Wed. No lunch.*

WHERE TO STAY

$ ⊡ **Garnish House.** A pair of large Victorian town houses near the uni-

B&B/INN   versity are run by owner-manager Johanna Lucey, who will be offering you tea and homemade chocolate cake before you have even crossed the threshold of her home—the kind of old-fashioned hospitality that is fast disappearing in modern Ireland. **Pros:** a friendly welcome; a genuine Irish experience. **Cons:** seriously unhip; located on a busy main road; rooms book up well in advance. $ *Rooms from: €88* ⊠ *Western Rd., Washington Village* ☎ *021/427–5111* ⊕ *www.garnish.ie* ⚲ *21 rooms* ⏀⏀ *Breakfast.*

$$ ⊡ **Hayfield Manor.** Ruddy with red brick and brightened by white-

HOTEL   sash windows, Hayfield Manor's exterior hints at the comfy luxury

Fodor'sChoice   within—beyond a splendid, carved-wood double staircase, lies a draw-

★   ing room that's a symphony of gilded silk, with a white-marble fireplace,

a 19th-century chandelier, and chic armchairs, a surprisingly soigné modern homage to the country-house style. **Pros:** stylish and chic; good value for luxury accommodation. **Cons:** a taxi or car ride to city center or a dull 15-minute walk; lack of scenic views. [$] *Rooms from: €179* ✉ *College Rd. and Perrott Ave., Western Road* ☎ *021/484–5900* 🌐 *www.hayfieldmanor.ie* 🛏 *88 rooms* 🍴 *Breakfast.*

NIGHTLIFE AND THE ARTS

See the *Examiner* or the *Evening Echo* for details about movies, theater, and live music performances.

Bierhaus. The huge worldwide beer selection, poker on Tuesday, and a DJ on Saturday lure a young hip crowd here. ✉ *Pope's Quay, Shandon* ☎ *021/455–1648* 🌐 *www.thebierhauscork.com.*

The Savoy. The major venue for night owls, the Savoy operates Thursday to Saturday from 11 until late. Live acts from Ireland and elsewhere are on offer in the main room, and in the foyer there are comedy acts and DJ sets, which can vary from the Electric Dream 80s Club to Detroit techno. ✉ *Patrick St., City Center South* ☎ *021/427–4299* 🌐 *www.savoytheatre.ie* ⏲ *Closed Sun.–Wed.*

BLARNEY CASTLE

8 km (5 miles) northwest of Cork City on R617.

On Galway sands they kiss your hands, they kiss your lips at Carney, but by the Lee they drink strong tea, and kiss the stone at Blarney. This famous rhyme celebrates one of Ireland's most noted icons—the Blarney Stone, which is the main reason most people journey to this small community built around a village green. It's best seen as a day trip from Cork.

Fodor's Choice ★ **Blarney Castle.** In the center of Blarney is Blarney Castle, or what remains of it: the ruined central keep is all that's left of this mid-15th-century stronghold. The castle contains the famed **Blarney Stone**. Kissing the stone, it's said, endows the kisser with the fabled "gift of the gab." It's 127 steep steps to the battlements. To kiss the stone, you must lie down on the battlements, hold on to a guardrail, and lean your head way back. It's good fun and not at all dangerous. Expect a line from mid-June to early September; while you wait, you can admire the views of the wooded River Lee valley and chuckle over how the word "blarney" came to mean what it does. As the story goes, Queen Elizabeth I wanted Cormac MacCarthy, Lord of Blarney, to will his castle to the Crown, but he refused her requests with eloquent excuses and soothing compliments. Exhausted by his comments, the queen reportedly exclaimed, "This is all Blarney. What he says he rarely means."

You can take pleasant walks around the castle grounds; Rock Close contains oddly shaped limestone rocks landscaped in the 18th century, and a grove of ancient yew trees that is said to have been a site of Druid worship. In early March there's a wonderful display of naturalized daffodils. ✉ *Village Green, Blarney* ☎ *021/438–5252* 🌐 *www.blarneycastle.ie* 🎟 *€12* ⏲ *May and Sept., Mon.–Sat. 9–6:30, Sun.*

9–5:30; June–Aug., Mon.–Sat. 9–7, Sun. 9–5:30; Oct.–Apr., Mon.–Sat. 9–sunset, Sun. 9–5 or sunset.

THE RING OF KERRY

If writers like Sir Walter Scott and William Thackeray had to struggle finding the superlatives to describe the lakes of Killarney and mountains framing the Ring of Kerry, it is not surprising that they remain among the most celebrated attractions in Ireland. As well as among the most popular: on a sunny day, it seems like half the nation's visitors are traveling along this two-lane road. The Ring of Kerry, which follows the shoreline of the Iveragh Peninsula, offers incredibly stunning mountain and coastal views—replete with sandy beaches, stone villages, and rocky coves—around almost every turn. The road is narrow and curvy, and the local sheep think nothing of using it for a nap; take it slowly. And because rain blocks views across the water to the Beara Peninsula in the east and the Dingle Peninsula in the west, hope for sunshine. It makes all the difference. Gateway to the Ring of Kerry is the famous town of Killarney, where all tour buses depart.

PLANNING YOUR TIME

Arrive in Killarney from Cork via train. Overrun with touristy hotels, the town will just be a place to park yourself at night in order to spend the next unforgettable day touring the Ring of Kerry. You can rent a car or see the area by bike or by foot, but the most popular option is still an escorted bus tour. Bear in mind that most of these buses leave Killarney between 9 and 10 am. The trip covers 176 km (110 miles) on N70 (and briefly R562) if you start and finish in Killarney; the journey will be 40 km (25 miles) shorter if you venture only between Kenmare and Killorglin.

GETTING HERE

Take the daily Irish Rail train from Cork to the Killarney Railway Station. Head out to tour the Ring of Kerry using the regular public Bus Éireann service between mid-June and mid-September; note there are only two buses a day, leaving Killarney at 8:45 am or 1:45 pm. The trip takes more than four hours. As for escorted bus tours of the Ring, they tend to start in Killarney and ply the Ring counterclockwise (to get the best views). On your last morning, connect by train from Killarney to Limerick and then transfer to a bus to get to Shannon Airport.

Bus Contacts Bus Éireann ☎ *01/836–6111 in Ireland* ⊕ *www.buseireann.ie.*

Train Contacts Irish Rail *(Iarnrod Éireann).* ☎ *01/836–6222* ⊕ *www.irishrail.ie.*

TOURS

Dero's Tours and Corcoran's Tours organize full-day and half-day trips by coach or taxi around Killarney and the Ring of Kerry. Bus Éireann also offers a range of daylong and half-day guided tours of the region.

Contacts Bus Éireann ☎ *061/313–333 in Limerick, 066/716–4700 in Tralee* ⊕ *www.buseireann.ie.*

KILLARNEY

102 km (65 miles) west of Cork City.

You may want to limit time spent in Killarney itself if discos, Irish cabarets, and singing pubs aren't your thing. But the surrounding countryside is glorious and everybody catches the Ring of Kerry tour buses in this town.

Aghadoe Heights. Here's an outstanding place to get a feel for what Killarney is all about: lake and mountain scenery. Stand beside Aghadoe's 12th-century ruined church and round tower, and watch the shadows creep gloriously across Lower Lake, with Innisfallen Island in the distance and the Gap of Dunloe to the west. ✉ *R562, 5 km (3 miles) west of Killarney on Beaufort–Killorglin Rd.*

FAMILY Fodor's Choice ★ **Muckross House.** Hero of a 1,001 travel posters, the ivy-covered 19th-century Elizabethan-style manor known as Muckross House now houses the Kerry Folklife Centre. Downstairs, bookbinders, potters, and weavers demonstrate their crafts. Upstairs, elegantly furnished rooms portray the lifestyle of the landed gentry in the 1800s; in the basement you can experience the conditions of servants employed in the house. Next door you'll find the Killarney National Park Visitor Centre. The informal grounds are noted for their rhododendrons and azaleas, the water garden, and the outstanding limestone rock garden. In the park beside the house, the Muckross Traditional Farms comprise reconstructed farm buildings and outbuildings, a blacksmith's forge, a carpenter's workshop, and a selection of farm animals. It's a reminder of the way things were done on the farm before electricity and the mechanization of farming. Meet and chat with the farmers and their wives as they go about their work. The visitor center has a shop and a restaurant. ✉ *Killarney National Park, Muckross Park, Muckross Rd. (N71), 6½ km (4 miles) south of Killarney* ☎ *064/667–0144* 🌐 *www.muckross-house.ie* 🎟 *House €7, farms €7.50, farms and house €12, visitor center free* 🕒 *House and visitor center: Sept.–June, daily 9–5:30; July and Aug., daily 9–7. Farms: mid-Mar.–Apr. and Oct., weekends 1–6; May and Sept., daily 1–6; June–Aug., daily 1–7.*

WHERE TO EAT

$$$$ SEAFOOD 🍴 **Gaby's Seafood.** Expect the best seafood in Killarney from Belgian owner-chef Gert Maes. Inside the rustic exterior is a little bar beside an open fire; steps lead up to the main dining area, where ornate wooden stick-back chairs sit atop a plush gold and navy carpet. They match a huge wooden dresser that has adorned the room since the restaurant opened in 1978. In summer you can sip an aperitif in the small garden. Try the seafood platter (seven or eight kinds of fish in a cream-and-wine sauce) or lobster Gaby (shelled, simmered in a cream-and-cognac sauce, and served back in the shell). Turbot, salmon, and sole are also regular menu items. There is also a selection of filet and sirloin steaks, au poivre or with garlic butter, and herb-scented rack of lamb. [$] *Average main: €32* ✉ *27 High St.* ☎ *064/663–2519* 🕒 *Closed Sun.–Wed. Jan.–mid-Mar. No lunch.*

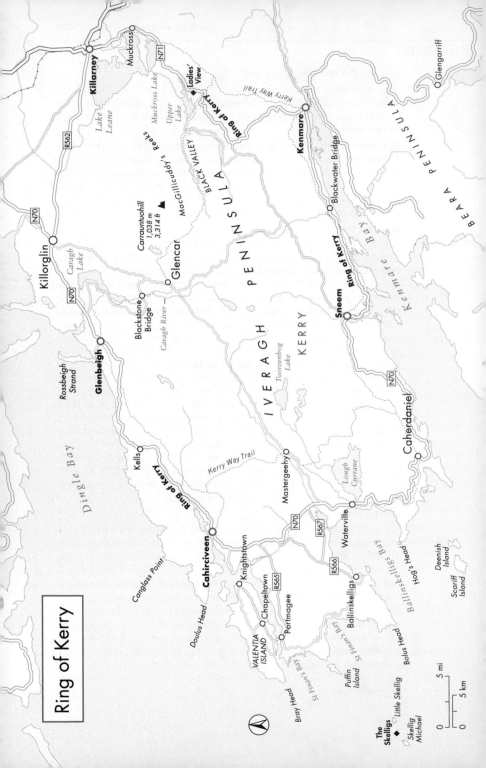

Ring of Kerry

BEARA PENINSULA

Glengarriff

Killarney
Muckross

N71

Ladies' View
Ring of Kerry
Kerry Way Trail

Kenmare

Lake Leane

R552

Muckross Lake
Upper Lake

BLACK VALLEY

Blackwater Bridge

Carrauntuohill
1,038 m
3,314 ft
MacGillicuddy's Reeks

P E N I N S U L A

Sneem
Ring of Kerry

Kenmare Bay

N70

Killorglin

Caragh Lake

Glencar

Caragh River

Blackstone Bridge

N70

I V E R A G H

Toorenbog Lake

K E R R Y

N70

Caherdaniel

Glenbeigh

Rossbeigh Strand

Kells

Ring of Kerry

Kerry Way Trail

Mastergeehy

Lough Currane

Dingle Bay

Caunglass Point

Cahirciveen

Knightstown

N70

R567

Waterville

R566

Ballinskelligs Bay

Deenish Island

Scariff Island

Doulus Head

Chapeltown

R565

Portmagee

Ballinskelligs

Hog's Head

Bolus Head

VALENTIA ISLAND

Bray Head

St Finan's Bay

Puffin Island

The Skelligs
Little Skellig
Skellig Michael

5 mi

5 km

WHERE TO STAY

$$

HOTEL

Fodor's Choice

★

Cahernane House Hotel. Get a glimpse of the Killarney that attracted discerning 19th-century visitors at this imposing gray-stone house—clearly, if you need a refuge from the touristy buzz of Killarney town, this is the place. **Pros:** great old-world atmosphere; very luxe; fantastic views. **Cons:** standard rooms are disappointingly plain; lots of weddings. $ *Rooms from: €190* ✉ *Muckross Rd.* ☎ *064/663–1895* ⊕ *www. cahernane.com* ↪ *36 rooms, 2 suites* ☉ *Closed Dec. 23–mid-Mar.* ❣️ *Breakfast.*

$

B&B/INN

Earls Court House. In a quiet suburb within walking distance of Killarney's center, this spacious guesthouse is furnished with interesting antiques collected by Emer Moynihan, who likes to greet her guests by offering home-baked goods in front of the open fire. **Pros:** quiet location; plenty of parking; warm welcome. **Cons:** long walk or taxi ride to town; bland suburban location. $ *Rooms from: €110* ✉ *Woodlawn Junct., Muckross Rd.* ☎ *064/663–4009* ⊕ *www.killarney-earlscourt. ie* ↪ *24 rooms, 6 suites* ☉ *Closed mid-Nov.–mid-Mar.* ❣️ *Breakfast.*

GLENBEIGH

27 km (17 miles) northeast of Cahirciveen on N70.

The road from Glenbeigh to Cahirciveen is one of the Ring's highlights. To the north are Dingle Bay and the jagged peaks of the Dingle Peninsula, which will, in all probability, be shrouded in mist. If they aren't, the gods have indeed blessed your journey. The road runs close to the water here, and around the small village of Kells it climbs high above the bay, hugging the steep side of Drung Hill as it makes its descent to Glenbeigh. Note how different the stark character of this stretch of the Ring is from the gentle, woody Kenmare Bay side. On a boggy plateau by the sea, the blocklong town of Glenbeigh is a popular holiday base—there's excellent hiking in the Glenbeigh Horseshoe, as the surrounding mountains are known, and exceptionally good trout fishing in Lough Coomasaharn. The area south of Glenbeigh and west of Carrantouhill Mountain, around the shores of the Caragh River and the village of Glencar, is known as the Kerry Highlands. The scenery is wild and rough but strangely appealing. A series of circular walks have been signposted, and parts of the Kerry Way pass through here.

Caragh Lake. A signpost to the right outside Glenbeigh points to Caragh Lake, a tempting excursion south to a beautiful expanse of water set among gorse- and heather-covered hills and majestic mountains. The road hugs the shoreline much of the way.

FAMILY

Kerry Bog Village Museum. Worth a quick look, this museum is a cluster of reconstructed, fully furnished cottages that vividly portray the daily life of the region's working class in the early 1800s. The adjacent pub is famous for its Irish coffee. ✉ *Beside Red Fox Bar* ☎ *066/976–9184* ⊕ *www.kerrybogvillage.ie* 💰 *€6* ☉ *Daily 9–6.*

WHERE TO STAY

$$ HOTEL Fodor's Choice ★ [H] **Carrig Country House.** A rambling two-story Victorian house covered in flowering creepers and set on 4 acres of lush gardens along a secluded lakeshore, this comes pretty close to most people's dream rural retreat. **Pros:** lovely secluded location; real country-house atmosphere; affable owner-managers. **Cons:** tricky to find first time (see website for directions). [$] *Rooms from: €190* ✉ *Caragh Lake, Ring of Kerry, Killorglin* ☎ *066/976–9100* 🌐 *www.carrighouse.com* 🛏 *17 rooms* 🕒 *Closed Nov.–early Mar.* 🍴 *Breakfast.*

CAHIRCIVEEN

18 km (11 miles) north of Waterville on N70.

Cahirciveen (pronounced cah-her-sigh-*veen*), at the foot of Bentee Mountain, is the gateway to the eastern side of the Ring of Kerry and the main market town for southern Kerry. Following the tradition in this part of the world, the modest, terraced houses are each painted in different colors (sometimes two or three)—the brighter the better.

Caherciveen Parish Daniel O'Connell Memorial Church. This large, elaborate, neo-Gothic structure dominates the main street. It was built in 1888 of Newry granite and black limestone to honor the local hero Daniel O'Connell—the only church in Ireland named after a layman. ☎ *066/947–2210* 🌐 *www.caherciveenparish.com.*

Old Barracks Heritage Centre. The converted former barracks of the Royal Irish Constabulary, an imposing, castlelike structure (built after the Fenian Rising of 1867 to suppress further revolts) now houses this museum. Well-designed displays depict scenes from times of famine, the life of Daniel O'Connell, and the restoration of this fine building from a blackened ruin. ✉ *The Barracks* ☎ *066/947–2777* 🌐 *www.theoldbarracks.com* 🎟 *€4* 🕒 *Weekdays 10–4:30, Sat. 11:30–4:30, Sun. 1–5.*

THE SKELLIGS

21 km (13 miles) northwest of Waterville.

Skellig Experience. Located across the bridge to Valentia Island, the Skellig Experience offers an alternative for the less adventurous traveler. This center contains exhibits on local birdlife, the history of the lighthouse and keepers, and the life and work of the early Christian monks. There's also a 15-minute audiovisual show that allows you to "tour" the Skelligs without leaving dry land. The center also offers a 90-minute non-landing cruise around the islands. But if you're up for it, don't miss the boat ride from Portmagee that lets you land on the rocks; Skellig Michael is something you won't soon forget. ✉ *Valentia Island* ☎ *066/947–6306* 🌐 *www.skelligexperience.com* 🎟 *€5, cruise €27.50* 🕒 *Mar.–June and Sept., daily 10–6; July and Aug., daily 10–7; Oct. and Nov., daily 10–6.*

Fodor's Choice ★ **The Skellig Islands.** In the far northwestern corner of the Ring of Kerry, across Portmagee Channel, lies **Valentia Island**, which is reachable by a bridge erected in 1971. Visible from Valentia, and on a clear day from other points along the coast, are the Skelligs, one of the most spectacular sights in Ireland. Sculpted as if by the hand of God, the islands of **Little Skellig, Great Skellig,** and the **Washerwoman's Rock** are distinctively cone-shaped, surrounded by blue swirling seas. The largest island, the Great Skellig, or Skellig Michael, distinguished by its twin peaks, rises 700 feet from the Atlantic. It has the remains of a settlement of early Christian monks, reached by climbing 600 increasingly precipitous steps. In spite of a thousand years of battering by Atlantic storms, the church, oratory, and beehive-shaped living cells are surprisingly well preserved.

During the journey to these islands you'll pass Little Skellig, the breeding ground of more than 22,000 pairs of gannets. Puffin Island, to the north, has a large population of shearwaters and storm petrel. Puffins nest in sand burrows on the Great Skellig in the month of May. But the masterpiece is the phenomenal Skellig Michael, home to that amazing 7th- to 12th-century village of monastic beehive dwellings, and offering vertigo-inducing views.

WHERE TO STAY

$ B&B/INN 🏨 **Shealane Country House Bed & Breakfast.** A large, modern detached house set on Valentia Island, located beside the bridge to the mainland, Shealane is easily reached but also affords views of cows grazing in the adjoining field and a breakfast room with ocean views. **Pros:** friendly welcome from local family; quiet rural location. **Cons:** outside the village; rooms book far in advance for July and August. [$] *Rooms from: €80* ✉ *Corha-Mor, Valentia Island* ☎ *066/947–6354* 🌐 *www.valentiaskelligs.com* 🛏 *5 rooms* 🕒 *Closed Nov.–mid-Mar.* 🍴 *Breakfast.*

SNEEM

27 km (17 miles) southwest of Kenmare on N70.

The pretty village of Sneem (from the Irish for "knot") is settled around an English-style green on the Ardsheelaun River estuary, and its streets are filled with houses washed in different colors. The effect has been somewhat diminished by a cluster of developments on the southern approach. Beside the parish church are the "pyramids," as they're known locally. These 12-foot-tall, traditional stone structures with stained-glass insets look as though they've been here forever. In fact, the sculpture park was completed in 1990 to the design of the Kerry-born artist James Scanlon, who has won international awards for his work in stained glass.

Staigue Fort. The approximately 2,500-year-old, stone Staigue Fort, signposted 4 km (2 miles) inland at Castlecove, is almost circular and about 75 feet in diameter with a single south-side entrance. From the Iron Age (from 500 BC to the 5th century AD) and early Christian times (6th century AD), such "forts" were, in fact, the fortified homesteads for several families of one clan and their cattle. The walls at Staigue Fort are almost 13 feet wide at the base and 7 feet wide at the top; they still stand 18 feet high on the north and west sides. Within them, stairs lead to narrow platforms on which the lookouts stood. (Private land must be crossed to reach the fort, and a "compensation for trespass" of €1 is often requested by the landowner.)

WHERE TO STAY

$$$
RESORT
FAMILY
Fodor's Choice
★

🏨 **Parknasilla Resort.** For over a century Parknasilla, a towering, gray-stone mansion set on a stunningly beautiful inlet of the Kenmare estuary, has been synonymous with old-style resort luxury, attracting guests like George Bernard Shaw, Princess Grace, and Charles de Gaulle. **Pros:** excellent sports facilities and spa; sheltered coastal location; great family destination. **Cons:** grounds and hotel big enough to get lost in; hugely popular with families in July and August. $ *Rooms from: €209* 🖷 *064/667–5600* ⊕ *www.parknasillahotel.ie* ⤶ *11 suites, 72 rooms* ⊙ *Closed Jan.–mid-Mar.* ◐◠ *Breakfast.*

KENMARE

21 km (13 miles) north of Glengarriff on N71, 34 km (21 miles) south of Killarney.

A lively touring base, this market town is set at the head of the sheltered Kenmare River estuary. It's currently a matter of lively debate as to whether Kenmare has displaced Kinsale as the culinary capital of Ireland. Kenmare offers an amazing number of stylish little restaurants for a town its size. The town was founded in 1670 by Sir William Petty (Oliver Cromwell's surveyor general, a multitasking entrepreneur), and most of its buildings date from the 19th century, when it was part of the enormous Lansdowne Estate—itself assembled by Petty.

Kenmare Heritage Centre. Come to this center in the Tourist Office to learn about the town's history. They can outline a walking route to Kenmare's places of interest. ⊠ *The Square* 🖷 *064/664–1233* ⊕ *www. discoverireland.ie/Heritage/kenmare-heritage-centre* 🖾 *Free* ⊙ *Easter–Oct., Mon.–Sat. 9:30–5:30.*

WHERE TO EAT

$$$
EUROPEAN

✕ **Lime Tree.** An open fire, stone walls, and a minstrel's gallery on a large balcony above the main room lend considerable character to this restaurant. Built in 1823 as a schoolhouse, it is located in its own leafy gardens at the top of town near the Park Hotel (where many of its staff trained). Tables are set with Irish linen napery, and in the long summer evenings light streams in from tall windows. Try one of the imaginative vegetarian options, such as hummus and blue cheese strudel, or go for roast loin of Kerry lamb with a red-onion-and-sun-dried-tomato tarte tatin. Leave room for the blackberry and pear fruit crumble. Advance booking is advisable. $ *Average main: €25* ⊠ *Shelburne St.* 🖷 *064/664–1225* ⊕ *www.limetreerestaurant.com* ⊙ *Closed Nov.–mid-Feb., and weekdays in late Feb., Mar., and Oct. No lunch.*

WHERE TO STAY

$
B&B/INN

🏨 **Sea Shore Farm.** Mary Patricia O'Sullivan offers a warm but professional welcome to her spacious farmhouse on Kenmare Bay. **Pros:** quiet rural spot with views of calm estuary; personal attention from owner-manager. **Cons:** on a working cattle farm; a mile out of town; no bar or restaurant. $ *Rooms from: €90* ⊠ *Tubrid* 🖷 *064/664–1270*

⊕ *www.seashorekenmare.com* ⇆ *6 rooms* ⊘ *Closed Nov.–mid-Mar.* ᵀ◎ᵀ *Breakfast.*

11

SPORTS AND THE OUTDOORS

FAMILY **Seafari Seal and Eagle Watching Cruises.** With complimentary tea and coffee for adults, plus lollipops for the kids, Seafari features fun two-hour ecotours with regular sightings of seals and white-tailed sea eagles. Cruises cost €20 per adult, with special family rates. Reservations are essential. ⊠ *Kenmare Pier, 3 Pier Rd.* ☎ *064/664–2059* ⊕ *www. seafariireland.com* ⊘ *Closed Dec.–Mar.*

BELFAST

The city of Belfast was a great Victorian success story, an industrial boomtown whose prosperity was built on trade—especially linen and shipbuilding. Famously (or infamously), the *Titanic* was built here, giving Belfast, for a time, the nickname "Titanic Town."

For many years it wasn't talked about, but in 2012 the city commemorated the 100th anniversary of the liner's sinking on April 15, 1912, by opening a dazzling Titanic Belfast exhibition center. With nine galleries spread over six floors, the enormous multiprow-shaped building—about the same height as *Titanic* and twice the size of City Hall—the center certainly has the wow factor. It has generated international interest, bringing in much-needed revenue and creating jobs at a difficult economic time.

Tourist numbers have increased as never before, and this dramatically transformed city is enjoying an unparalleled renaissance. The record-breaking number of visitors speaks for itself: Titanic Belfast exceeded all expectations, welcoming more than 750,000 people in its first year; the Metropolitan Arts Centre, which opened in 2012, doubled its attendance expectations in the first 12 months; and the Ulster Museum, which was revamped in 2011, has enjoyed record numbers through its doors.

This is all a welcome change from the period when news about Belfast meant reports about "the Troubles." Since the 1994 ceasefire, Northern Ireland's capital city has benefited from major hotel investment, gentrified quaysides (or strands), a sophisticated new performing arts center, and major initiatives to boost tourism. Although the 1996 bombing of offices at Canary Wharf in London disrupted the 1994 peace agreement, the ceasefire was officially reestablished on July 20, 1997, and this embattled city began its quest for a newfound identity.

Since 2008, the city has restored all its major public buildings such as museums, churches, theaters, City Hall, Ulster Hall—and even the glorious Crown Bar—spending millions of pounds on its built heritage. A jail that at the height of the Troubles held some of the most notorious murderers involved in paramilitary violence is now a major visitor attraction.

Belfast's city center is made up of three roughly contiguous areas that are easy to navigate on foot. From the south end to the north it's about an hour's leisurely walk.

PLANNING YOUR TIME

Belfast is small enough that you can see the highlights in a couple of days. A good guided tour can help you see a lot in a little time. Whatever you do, don't miss the Titanic Belfast Visitor Centre.

GETTING HERE AND AROUND

BUS TRAVEL

Pink-and-white Metro buses are the best way to get around. Fares range from £1.40 to £2, depending on the zone. If you're staying a few days, buy a Smartlink Travel Card for more than five journeys, which is a 30% saving; a weekly card is £14.50, plus £1.50 for the card. A Metro day ticket costs £3.80 (£3.20 between 9:30 am and 3 pm) and takes you anywhere on the network. Most bus routes start from Donegall Square or adjoining streets, where the Metro Kiosk, on Donegall Square West, has details and timetables.

Contacts Belfast Metro Service ✉ *Donegall Square W* ☎ *028/9066–6630* ⊕ *www.translink.co.uk/metro.*

CAR TRAVEL

Belfast is 167 km (104 miles) north of Dublin. Motorways, or dual carriageways, lead into Belfast's city center from the main airports and seaports, and the fast N1/A1 motorway links the city with Dublin. The trip takes about two hours. The drive from Derry takes 90 minutes. The main arterial routes into central Belfast are busy only at peak commuter times, between 8 and 9 am and 5 and 6 pm.

Street parking costs between 80p and £1.20 per hour for a pay-and-display ticket from a meter. The maximum parking time is two hours for such street spaces. Be careful not to overstay, as zealous clamping wardens operate. Multistory car park garages are at the Victoria Square and Castle Court shopping centers. Some, but not all, hotels have car parking. If you'll need parking, ask a hotel or inn prior to booking.

TRAIN TRAVEL

As the capital city of Northern Ireland, Belfast is well served by an efficient train network. Most trains arrive and leave from Central Station, a 15-minute walk from the city center.

Contacts Central Rail Station ✉ *E. Bridge St.* ☎ *028/9089–9400.*

TOURS

Bespoke Tours offers historical walking and driving tours that come with tales of myths and legends. The company also runs excursions outside Belfast to some of Northern Ireland's major tourist attractions. The owner tailors his tours to suit individual interests and requirements.

Belfast City Sightseeing runs the most comprehensive open-top tour through Belfast. The Belfast City Tour covers the City Hall, University Quarter, Shipyard, Titanic Quarter, Stormont, Shankill Road, peace line, and Falls Road, and goes past the Grand Opera House on Great Victoria Street. You can hop off and hop on as you please at any of

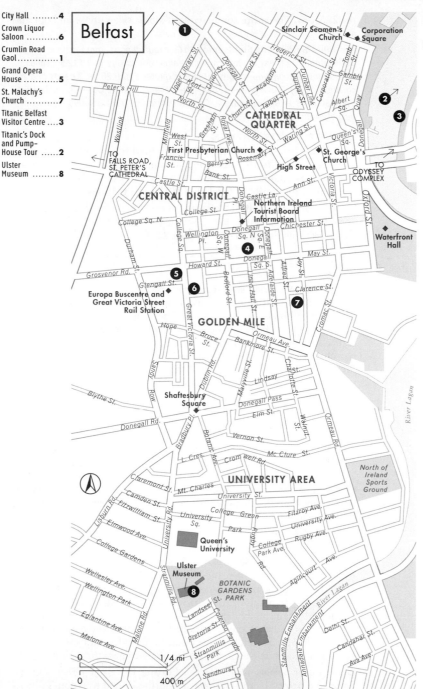

the 22 stops. The entire route, without stops, takes about an hour and a half.

Bus Tours Belfast City Sightseeing ⊠ *City Tour departs from Castle Pl. (opposite McDonald's)* ⊕ *www.belfastcitysightseeing.com* ✉ *City Tour £12.50, valid 48 hrs on a hop-on, hop-off basis; Titanic Explorer £10 (£28 for 2 adults and 2 children)* ⊙ *City Tour Mar.–Sept., daily 10–4 every 15 mins; Oct.–Feb., daily 10–4 every 30 mins.* **Bespoke Tours** ⊠ *Central District* ☎ *079/1229–0935* ⊕ *www. bespoke-tours.com.*

VISITOR INFORMATION

The Belfast Visitor pass is good for unlimited travel within a specified zone, as well as for discounts on tours and entrance to major attractions such as Titanic Belfast Visitor Centre, the Ulster Folk & Transport Museum, Crumlin Road Gaol, and W5 at the Odyssey.

Visitor Information Belfast Welcome Centre ⊠ *8–10 Donegall Square N, Central District* ☎ *028/9024–6609* ⊕ *www.gotobelfast.com* ⊙ *Oct.–May, Mon.– Sat. 9–5:30; June–Sept., Mon.–Sat. 9–7, Sun. 11–4.*

EXPLORING

Magnificent Victorian structures still line the streets of the city center, but instead of housing linen mills or cigarette factories, they are home to chic new hotels and fashionable bars. Smart restaurants abound, and the people of Belfast, who for years would not venture out of their districts, appear to be making up for lost time. Each area of the city has changed considerably in the new peaceful era, but perhaps none more than the docklands around the Harland and Wolff shipyards, whose historic and enormous cranes, known to the locals as Samson and Goliath, still dominate the city's skyline. New developments—such as the Titanic Quarter—are springing up all around deserted shipyards, ranging from luxury hotels to modern office blocks. And in the center of the city, Victoria Square is a gigantic shopping and residential complex, replete with a geodesic dome, floors of glossy shops, and renovated Victorian row houses. In the west of the city, the physical scars of the Troubles are still evident, from the peace line that divides Catholic and Protestant West Belfast to the murals on every gable wall. Visitors are discovering that it's safe to venture beyond the city center, and taxi tours of these once-troubled areas are very popular.

GOLDEN MILE

The arrowhead-shape district extending from Howard Street in the north to Shaftesbury Square at the southern tip, and bordered on the west by Great Victoria Street and on the east by Bedford Street and Dublin Road, is a great area from which to begin an exploration of Belfast. Although it doesn't glow quite the way the name suggests, the bustling Golden Mile and its immediate environs harbor noteworthy historic buildings. In addition, the area is filled with hotels and major civic and office buildings, as well as some restaurants, cafés, and shops. Even if you don't end up staying here, you're likely to pass through it often.

FodorsChoice
★

Crown Liquor Saloon. Opposite the Europa Hotel on Great Victoria Street and owned by the National Trust (the United Kingdom's official conservation organization), the Crown is one of Belfast's glories. It began life in 1826 as the Railway Tavern; in 1885 the owner asked Italian craftsmen working on churches in Ireland to moonlight on rebuilding it, and its place in Irish architectural pub history was assured. The bar has richly carved woodwork around cozy snugs (cubicles—known to regulars as "confessional boxes"), leather seats, color tile work, and an abundance of mirrors. An ostentatious box of delights, it has been immaculately preserved—it is still lighted by gas. The pièce de résistance is the embossed ceiling with its swirling arabesques and rosettes of burnished primrose, amber, and gold, as dazzling again now as the day it was installed. The Crown claims to serve the perfect pint of Guinness—so no need to ask what anyone's drinking—and you can order a great plateful of warming Irish stew. ⊠ *46 Great Victoria St., Golden Mile* ☎ *028/9024–3187* ⊕ *www.crownbar.com* ⊘ *Mon.–Wed. 11:30–11, Thurs.–Sat 11:30–midnight, Sun. 12:30–10.*

FAMILY
Fodor'sChoice
★

Crumlin Road Gaol. Since opening full-time in 2012, Crumlin Road Gaol has become one of Belfast's hot tourist tickets. Designed by Charles Lanyon in 1841, the gaol originally opened in 1846 and at its height held more than 500 prisoners. Throughout its 150-year lifetime, around 25,000 convicts passed through its doors. During the worst years of the Troubles, between 1969 and 1996 (when the prison closed), it held some of the North's most notorious murderers, including many involved in paramilitary violence. The building has undergone a £10 million restoration, and, with its cream-walled corridors and black railings, has been transformed to reflect the way it looked in Victorian days. The engrossing 75-minute tour takes in the holding, punishment, and condemned cells—the latter where the prisoners were held before being taken to the gallows for execution. The highlight is the execution chamber, hidden behind a moving bookcase where the guide explains the gory details of how the long-drop method was used to break the prisoner's neck. ⊠ *53–55 Crumlin Rd., North Belfast* ☎ *028/9074–1500* ⊕ *www. crumlinroadgaol.com* ⊠ *£7.50* ⊘ *10–6; last tour at 4:30.*

Grand Opera House. Belfast's opera house exemplifies the Victorians' fascination with ornamentation, opulent gilt moldings, and intricate plasterwork. The renowned theater architect Frank Matcham beautifully designed the building in 1894. Since 2005, the theater has undergone a massive extension program that has almost doubled its size, thanks to a new foyer bar, café, restaurant, and party room. Contemporary Irish artist Cherith McKinstry's exquisite angel-and-cherub-laden fresco floats over the auditorium ceiling. You can take a one-hour behind-the-scenes tour, but by far the best way to see and enjoy the place is to attend a show. The theater regularly hosts musicals, operas, plays, and concerts. ⊠ *2 Great Victoria St., Golden Mile* ☎ *028/9024–1919* ⊕ *www.goh.co.uk* ⊠ *£4* ⊘ *Tours Thurs. and Sat. at 11 am.*

St. Malachy's Church. Opened in 1844, St. Malachy's Church is one of the most impressive redbrick Tudor Revival churches in Ireland. One of the interior highlights is the densely patterned fan-vaulted ceiling, a delightfully swirling masterpiece of plasterwork—whose inspiration was taken from the chapel of Henry VII at Westminster Abbey in London—tastefully repainted in cream. The high altarpiece featuring Pugin's *Journey* *to Calvary* was originally carried out by the portraitist Felix Piccioni whose family were refugees to Belfast from Austrian Italy. In 1868 the largest bell in Belfast was added to the church but after complaints that its deafening noise was interfering with the maturing of whiskey in the nearby Dunville distillery, it was wrapped in felt to soften its peal and vibration. ⊠ *Alfred St., Golden Mile* ☎ *028/9032–1713* ⊕ *www. saintmalachys.ie* 🖾 *Free.*

CENTRAL DISTRICT

Belfast's Central District, immediately north of the Golden Mile, extends from Donegall Square north to St. Anne's Cathedral. It's not geographically the center of the city, but it's the old heart of Belfast. It's a frenetic place—the equivalent of Dublin's Grafton and Henry streets in one—where both locals and visitors shop. Cafés, pubs, offices, and shops of all kinds, from department stores to the Gap and Waterstones (there's even a Disney store), occupy the redbrick, white Portland-stone, and modern buildings that line its narrow streets. Many streets are pedestrian only, so it's a good place to take a leisurely stroll, browse, and see some sights to boot. It's easy to get waylaid shopping and investigating sights along the river when taking this walk, so give yourself at least two hours to cover the area comfortably.

Fodor's Choice ★ **City Hall.** Built of Portland stone between 1898 and 1906 and modeled on St. Paul's Cathedral in London, this Renaissance Revival–style edifice—the cynosure of central Belfast—was designed by Brumwell Thomas (who was knighted but had to sue to get his fee). Before you enter, take a stroll around Donegall Square to see statues of Queen Victoria and a column honoring the U.S. Expeditionary Force, which landed in the city on January 26, 1942—the first contingent of the U.S. Army to arrive in Europe during World War II. A monument commemorating the *Titanic* stands in the grounds, and in 2012 a granite memorial was unveiled in a newly opened *Titanic* memorial garden for the 100th anniversary of the ship's sinking. With its complicated series of arches and openings, stained-glass windows, Italian-marble inlays, decorative plasterwork, and paintings, this is Belfast's most ornate public space—a veritable homage to the might of the British Empire. After an £11 million restoration, the modernized building has been brought into the 21st century and is now home to the Bobbin café and the "Waking a Giant" exhibition, in which historic photographs tell the story of Belfast's industrial development. Another permanent exhibition, "No Mean City," an interactive and photographic display, celebrates 68 inspirational people of the last 100 years, including Thomas Andrews (the designer of the *Titanic*), singer Van Morrison, and footballer George Best. ⊠ *Donegall Sq., Central District* ☎ *028/9027–0456* ⊕ *www.belfastcity.gov.uk* 🖾 *Tours free* ☉ *Tours weekdays at 11, 2, and 3, Sat. at 2 and 3.*

FAMILY **Fodor's**Choice ★ **Titanic Belfast Visitor Centre.** This world-class attraction headlines a Titanic Experience exhibition along with showcasing nine linked interpretative galleries that outline the *Titanic*'s dramatic story as well as the wider theme of Belfast's seafaring and industrial heritage. The stunning bow-shaped facade of the six-story building reflects the lines of the great ship, the shard-like appearance created from 3,000 different-shape panels each folded from silver anodized aluminum sheets into asymmetrical geometries. The ultimate, startling effect is of light caught by a cut diamond. As you wander through Titanic Belfast you will learn about the thriving boomtown at the turn of the century; the ride through the reconstruction of the shipyards echoes with the sounds and sensations of 100 years ago. In one of the galleries, the ship's saga is brought up to the present with the discovery of the wreck and into the future with live links to contemporary undersea exploration. Also on site is a movie theater designed by the *Titanic* explorer Robert Ballard (he discovered the wreck in 1985), which shows films about the ship. ■**TIP→ Tickets can be bought online (5% cheaper); the least crowded time to go is on Sunday morning.** ⊠ *Titanic House, 6 Queen's Rd., Titanic Quarter, East Belfast* ⊕ *www.titanicbelfast.com* ⊠ *£14.75* ⊙ *Apr.–Sept., daily 9–7; Oct.–Mar., Tues.–Sun. 10–5.*

Fodor's Choice
★

Titanic's Dock and Pump-House Tour. The atmospheric 900-foot-long dock where *Titanic* was built—in its time the biggest in the world—is open to the public and ranks as one of *the* great attractions in Northern Ireland. Since 2012, and the events held for the 100th anniversary, *Titanic's* Dock—officially known as the Thompson Dry Dock—has been accessible to visitors. Steps lead deep down 44 feet (13½ meters) to the floor of the dock, and for the first time in history you can bask in the evocative spirit of this remarkable place well below sea level. In its heyday in the early 20th century, the dock could hold 21 million gallons of water. Today it is Belfast's outstanding relic of *Titanic's* legacy and strikingly represents the ship's physical footprint. To access the dock and pumphouse you must join one of Colin Cobb's fascinating, fact-filled walks that help visitors—through visual aids of the *Titanic*—imagine, relive, and reflect on both a singular marvel of engineering and the importance of shipbuilding in Belfast's heritage. Taking Metro Bus No. 26, 26b, or 26c from City Hall is the easiest way to get to the Dock and Pump-House; you can take a train to the new Titanic Quarter halt or opt for a 20-minute walk from Belfast city center to Queen's Road (home to the Odyssey Arena and W5 science center). ⊠ *Queen's Rd., Titanic Quarter* ☎ *028/9073–7813* ⊕ *www.titanicsdock.com* ⊠ *£7* ⊙ *Tours Mar.–Oct., daily on the hour 11–3.*

UNIVERSITY AREA

At Belfast's southern end, the part of the city around Queen's University is dotted with parks, botanical gardens, and leafy streets with fine, intact, two- and three-story 19th-century buildings. The area evokes an older, more leisurely pace of life. The many pubs and excellent restaurants make this area the hub of the city's nightlife. However, remember that Belfast is a student town and this is the main university area—the pace of life here can be fast (and sometimes a little furious) during school-term weekends.

FAMILY
Fodor's Choice
★

Ulster Museum. Set in an impressive edifice at the southwest corner of the Botanic Gardens, the rejuvenated Ulster Museum, with its spacious light-filled atrium and polished steel is a big hit with visitors. The museum's forte is the history and prehistory of Ireland using exhibitions to colorfully trace the rise of Belfast's crafts, trade, and industry, and offering a reflective photographic archive of the Troubles. In addition, the museum has a large natural history section, with famed skeleton of the extinct Irish giant deer, and a trove of jewelry and gold ornaments recovered from the Spanish Armada vessel *Girona,* which sank off the Antrim coast in 1588. Take time to seek out the *Girona*'s stunning gold salamander studded with rubies and still dazzling after 400 years in the Atlantic. ✉ *Stranmillis Rd., University Area* ☎ *028/9044–0000* 🌐 *www.nmni.com/um* 🎟 *Free* 🕒 *Tues.–Sun. 10–5. Closed Mon., except for Northern Irish holidays.*

WHERE TO EAT

GOLDEN MILE

$$ EUROPEAN Fodor's Choice ★

🍴 **The Ginger Bistro.** Chef-owner Simon McCance's modern Irish classics with an international twist attract foodies to this gem just off Great Victoria Street. A short but perfectly balanced menu emphasizes locally sourced seafood and lean meats. Fishy dinner highlights include filet of hake or sea bass; pan-roasted breast of duck or the braised-then-roasted belly of pork with fennel are also highly recommended. The flavorsome fried squid far outsells anything else on the menu, however, and don't forget the parsnip chips to go with it. For lunchgoers in a hurry there is an excellent-value menu offering haddock-and-chips, fish pie, and ribeye steak. The wines are outstanding, or try malt-flavored hand-crafted Belfast ales or lagers from the Mourne Mountains. Chalked-up blackboards warn: "Can't have any pudding if you don't eat your greens." For those who do, the desserts include the delectable crème brûlée with raspberry compote, the soft-centered chocolate cake with berries, pears and cream with champagne jelly, and the unforgettable sticky-toffee pudding. [$] *Average main: £16* ✉ *7–8 Hope St., Golden Mile* ☎ *028/9024–4421* 🌐 *www.gingerbistro.com* 🕒 *Closed Sun. No lunch Mon.*

CENTRAL DISTRICT

$$$ EUROPEAN Fodor's Choice ★

🍴 **Deanes Restaurant.** Belfast's dining elite love feasting in Deanes, a classy experience offering food served with artistry and style. Delights such as slow-braised veal shin with creamed polenta and gremolata and roast monkfish with *pommes mousseline* (fancy mashed potatoes), pancetta, and a bourguignon garnish are available in the main restaurant. Steak, lamb, chicken, and venison dishes are all menu staples. For fabulously fresh fish, head to the informal 20-seater all-white Seafood Bar, where the feel is strictly Cape Cod: coral curtains, shells, and nautical memorabilia are complemented by two large and boldly stylized Graham Knuttel paintings and his colorful wooden sculpture of a mackerel. The food is equally distinctive: highlights include salt-and-chili squid, fish cakes, or fish pie. The Linen Lunch is £10; if you want to spend less in the Seafood Bar, for £6.50 you can have a filling bowl of chowder or mushroom risotto with crab mayo. The Deanes empire also includes Deanes Deli Bistro and, in the leafy University Area, Deanes at Queens (also open on Sunday; see website for details). [$] *Average main: £19* ✉ *36–40 Howard St., Central District* ☎ *028/9033–1134* 🌐 *www.michaeldeane.co.uk* 🕒 *Closed Sun.*

$$$$ EUROPEAN **Fodor's Choice** ★ 🍴 **The Great Room.** Inside the swank and lavish Merchant Hotel, beneath the grand dome of this former bank's great hall and Ireland's biggest chandelier, you'll find the perfect setting for a memorable dinner of adventurous European fare. Exceptional offerings from the kitchen include Dover sole niçoise, rib of Kettyle beef, or, for vegetarians, pappardelle pasta with black truffles and olive oil. The wonderful extravaganza of profiterole swans swimming delicately in a small lake of chocolate sauce is just one delight found on the dessert trolley. First-class service in truly opulent surroundings makes this restaurant worth a detour. The set dinner menu (£22.50 per person) Monday through Thursday (until 6:30; £26.50 thereafter) is great value; on the weekend it increases to between £80 and £100 for two, with a bottle of wine included. [$] *Average main: £23* ✉ *35 Waring St., Cathedral Quartert* ☎ *028/9023–4888* 🌐 *www.themerchanthotel.com.*

$ IRISH 🍴 **Long's.** During 2014 Long's will be celebrating 100 years of serving fish-and-chips in its completely basic Athol Street premises, close to the city center. Garbage collectors, millionaires, schoolboys from the nearby Royal Belfast Academical Institution, and patrons from every sector in between flock here for the secret-batter-recipe fish, served with chips, bread and butter, and a mug of tea. Long's closes at 6:30 pm. [$] *Average main: £7* ✉ *39 Athol St., Golden Mile* ☎ *028/9032–1848* 💳 *No credit cards* 🕒 *Closed Sun. No dinner.*

$$$ SEAFOOD 🍴 **Mourne Seafood Bar.** This seafood bar hidden down a side street has established itself as a firm favorite on the Belfast dining scene. Cofounder Bob McCoubrey was originally a marine biologist and has teamed up with experienced head chef Andy Rae to create a restaurant that has helped to reinvigorate the city's gastronomic scene. Daily specials might include seafood dumplings or seared king scallops with butternut squash risotto and crispy sage. The salmon, cod, hake, and sea bream are all done to perfection, but the standout dish for many is the gurnard, a whole fish served with bacon and clam velouté. The upstairs Oyster Bar, a cheaper alternative to the main dining room, offers small and big plates. Small plates (they're brimful) cost £4, and include Indian-spiced mackerel with focaccia crisps and Thai seafood dumplings with chili jam. The big plates average £9, for which you get a filling portion of mussels, squid, fish fingers, prawn linguine, or the cold seafood platter with wheaten bread—a big hit with a glass of the oyster stout (don't ask for Guinness here) made by the Whitewater brewery in Kilkeel. [$] *Average main: £13* ✉ *34–36 Bank St., Central District* ☎ *028/9024–8544* 🌐 *www.mourneseafood.com* 🕒 *No dinner Sun.*

WHERE TO STAY

CENTRAL DISTRICT

$$ HOTEL 🏨 **Benedict's of Belfast.** Friendly, lively, and convenient, Benedict's looms large on Bradbury Place—guest rooms on the second floor are bright and colorful, and have wooden floors; the carpeted rooms on the third floor are darker, with an Asian influence, simple but comfortable. **Pros:** rooms plain, but functional and clean; great-value dining. **Cons:** guests have experienced late check-in due to rooms not being ready; some

parts of hotel show wear and tear. [$] *Rooms from: £75* ✉ *7–21 Bradbury Pl., Golden Mile* ☎ *028/9059–1999* 🌐 *www.benedictshotel.co.uk* 🛏 *32 rooms* 🍴 *Breakfast.*

$$$$ HOTEL Fodor's Choice ★ 🏨 **The Merchant Hotel.** A mix of Victorian grandeur and art-deco-inspired modernity, this hotel—regarded by some as Ireland's most spectacular—was built as the headquarters of Ulster Bank in the mid-19th century and since opening in 2006 has led the way in style and sophistication. **Pros:** opulent place with attentive reception and friendly bar staff; deep King Koil mattresses leave a mellow afterglow; history and architecture buffs will love it. **Cons:** revelers from pubs and clubs in the surrounding streets detract from the internal serenity; at £15, breakfast room service is for high rollers only. [$] *Rooms from: £190* ✉ *16 Skipper St., Cathedral Quarter* ☎ *028/9023–4888* 🌐 *www.themerchanthotel.com* 🛏 *63 rooms, 5 suites* 🍴 *No meals.*

$$$ HOTEL 🏨 **Ten Square.** You don't get much more downtown or contemporary than this fashionable boutique hotel right behind City Hall. **Pros:** luxurious surroundings; attention to detail in the attractive rooms; super-king beds; convivial feel to the Grill Room. **Cons:** the noisy bar can be sweaty; sit outside, but only if you don't mind the traffic fumes. [$] *Rooms from: £129* ✉ *10 Donegall Sq. S* ☎ *028/9024–1001* 🌐 *www.tensquare.co.uk* 🛏 *22 rooms* 🍴 *Multiple meal plans.*

UNIVERSITY AREA

$$ HOTEL 🏨 **Dukes at Queens.** This handsome hotel brings a hint of trendiness to Botanic Avenue, an area that's about as bohemian as Belfast gets; although retaining its distinguished redbrick Victorian facade, the inside has been revamped in a cool contemporary style. **Pros:** stylish hotel offering excellent service; good value for the money; convenient location. **Cons:** area is thronged at lunchtime with office workers and even busier at night—noise is an ever-present reality. [$] *Rooms from: £65* ✉ *65–67 University St., University Area* ☎ *028/9023–6666* 🌐 *www.dukesatqueens.com* 🛏 *32 rooms* 🍴 *Breakfast.*

BELFAST ENVIRONS

$$ B&B/INN Fodor's Choice ★ 🏨 **The Old Inn.** Set in the village of Crawfordsburn, this 1614 coach inn, reputedly Ireland's oldest, certainly looks the part: it's pure 17th century with a sculpted thatch roof, half doors, and leaded-glass windows. **Pros:** a proverbial step back in time; lots of character; comfortable rooms. **Cons:** slow service; breakfasts not always up to snuff. [$] *Rooms from: £80* ✉ *15 Main St., 16 km (10 miles) east of Belfast on A2, Crawfordsburn* ☎ *028/9185–3255* 🌐 *www.theoldinn.com* 🛏 *31 rooms, 8 suites* 🍴 *Breakfast.*

NIGHTLIFE

Belfast has dozens of pubs packed with relics of the Victorian and Edwardian periods. Although pubs typically close around 11:30 pm, many Central District–Golden Mile nightclubs stay open until 1 am.

11

GOLDEN MILE

The glorious Crown Liquor Saloon is far from being the only old pub in the Golden Mile area—some, but by no means all of Belfast's evening life, takes place in bars and restaurants here. At several replicated Victorian bars, more locals and fewer visitors gather.

CENTRAL DISTRICT

The John Hewitt Bar. A must for every traveler's hit list, this bar named after one of Ulster's most famous poets (who ironically wasn't a big drinker) is traditional in style with a marble counter, waist-high wooden paneling, high ceilings, and open fire. It channels Hewitt's socialist sensibility, as it's owned by the Belfast Unemployed Centre (which it helps fund with its profits)—top pub grub is served at lunch and live music is featured most nights, including the excellent Panama Jazz Band on Friday (except the first Friday of each month). ✉ *51 Donegall St., Central District* ☎ *028/9023–3768* ⊕ *www.thejohnhewitt.com.*

UNIVERSITY AREA

Fodor's Choice ★ **Belfast Empire Music Hall.** Inside a deconsecrated church, the Music Hall is the city's leading music venue. Most nights are devoted to concerts from groups such as local heroes Snow Patrol. Stand-up comedy nights are usually on Tuesdays—Patrick Kielty was a regular until he hit the big time in London. The Rab McCullough blues nights on Thursdays are popular, as are Friday Glamaramas, devoted to Queen, Bowie, and the like. ✉ *42 Botanic Ave., University Area* ☎ *028/9024–9276* ⊕ *www.thebelfastempire.com.*

THE ARTS

Cultúrlann McAdam Ó Fiaich. A £2 million renovation and extension in 2011 to mark its 20th anniversary breathed new life into this venue. Celebrating Gaeilge (Irish language) and culture, this cosmopolitan arts center hosts exhibitions, book launches, concerts, theater, and poetry readings. Two choirs—one from a children's drama school and the other from resident theater company Aisling Ghéar—are based here. For travelers interested in the Gaeltacht experience, this is a great place to start. On the ground floor, the Dillon Gallery, named after the Falls Road artist Gerard Dillon, who spent much time painting in Connemara in the west of Ireland, mounts shows by top local and international artists. A shop sells Irish-language and English books as well as crafts and the all-important West Belfast Mural Map. Also here are a tourist information point, Wi-Fi access, and a café. The center's staff can arrange regional tours and book accommodation. ■ **TIP→ At the time of going to press, plans are underway to create a 2½-mile walking route, The Gaeltacht Way, due for completion in 2014. Check with the staff for details.** ✉ *216 Falls Rd., West Belfast* ☎ *028/9096–4180* ⊕ *www.culturlann.ie* ☉ *Daily 9–9.*

SHOPPING

Belfast's main shopping streets include High Street, Donegall Place, Royal Avenue, and several of the smaller streets connecting them. Except for buses and delivery vehicles, the area is mostly traffic-free. The long thoroughfare of Donegall Pass, running from Shaftesbury Square at the point of the Golden Mile east to Ormeau Road, contains a mix of biker shops, ethnic restaurants, and antiques arcades. Another retail haven is Lisburn Road, jam-packed with nearly a hundred trendy designer shops, lifestyle emporia, galleries, and antiques stores. The Lisburn Road Business Association (LRBA) has special offers on its website (⊕ *www.visitlisburnroad.com*). For a break from shopping, let the Victorian-style Maryville House Tea Rooms (⊕ *www.maryvillehouse. co.uk*), just off Lisburn Road, transport you back to another era, starting with the foyer's 1792 map of Ireland dedicated to His Majesty King George III. The 20 different house teas range from a zesty rooibos citrus to lemongrass with ginger twist.

St. George's Market. For an authentic blast of Belfast life make your way to the renovated St. George's Market, an enormous indoor market on Friday, Saturday, and Sunday mornings. When it opened in the 1890s, this historic market sold butter, eggs, poultry, and fruit. In those days Belfast was known as the "City of Seven Smells": they came from such fixtures as gasworks, slaughterhouses, and soap factories. Today the market is a vibrant place with 150 traders selling everything from apples to zippers and antiques to shark meat. The Friday Variety Market starts at 6 am and runs until 2 pm; the Saturday City Food and Garden Market is from 9–3, and the Sunday Food, Craft and Antique market is 10–4. ⊠ *May St., Central District* ☎ *028/9043–5704* ⊕ *www.belfastcity. gov.uk/stgeorgesmarket.*

ITALY

Rome, Florence, Tuscany, Naples,
Pompeii, the Amalfi Coast, Venice

WHAT'S WHERE

1 Rome. Italy's capital is one of the great cities of Europe. It's a large, busy metropolis that lives in the here and now, yet there's no other place on earth where you'll encounter such powerful evocations of a long and spectacular past, from the Colosseum to the dome of St. Peter's. For 2,500 years, emperors, popes, and common citizens have left their mark on the city.

2 Florence. It's hard to think of a place that's more closely linked to one specific historical period than Florence. The 15th-century Renaissance changed the way people see the world. Five hundred years later it remains the reason people see Florence—the abundance of treasures is mind-boggling. Present-day Florentines pride themselves on living well, and that means you'll find exceptional restaurants and first-rate shopping to go with all that amazing art.

3 Tuscany. Nature outdid herself in Tuscany, the central Italian region that has Florence as its principal city. The hills, draped with woods, vineyards, and olive groves, may not have the drama of mountain peaks or waves crashing on the shore, yet there's an undeniable magic about them. Its greatest appeal lies in the smaller towns, often perched on hilltops and not significantly altered since the Middle Ages.

4 Naples. Italy's third-largest city is densely packed with people, cafés, pizzerias, and an amazing number of Norman and baroque churches.

5 Pompeii. The famous town shows you through its excavated ruins how ancient Romans lived the good life—until, one day in AD 79, Mt. Vesuvius buried them in volcanic ash and lava.

6 The Amalfi Coast. The most shockingly beautiful coastal drive in the world links together Positano, Amalfi, and Ravello, all magically set against a bluer-than-blue sea and sky.

7 Venice. One of the world's most novel cities, Venice has canals where the streets should be and an atmosphere of faded splendor that practically defines the word decadent. It was once one of the world's great sea-trading powers, which explains its rich history and its exotic, East-meets-West architecture.

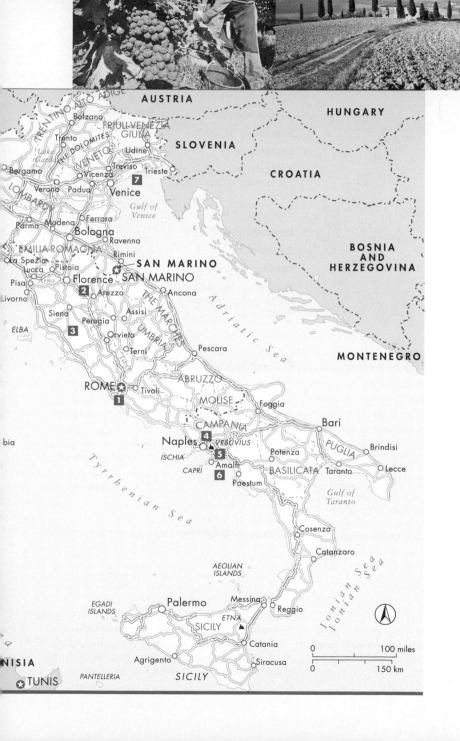

AUSTRIA

HUNGARY

SLOVENIA

Bolzano

TRENTINO-ALTO ADIGE

FRIULI-VENEZIA GIULIA

Trento

THE DOLOMITES

Lake Garda

VENETO

Udine

Bergamo

Verona

Vicenza

Treviso

Trieste

Padua

7 Venice

LOMBARDY

Gulf of Venice

Parma

Modena

Ferrara

Bologna

Ravenna

CROATIA

EMILIA-ROMAGNA

Rimini

La Spezia

Pistoia

SAN MARINO

BOSNIA AND HERZEGOVINA

Lucca

Pisa

Arno

2 Florence

SAN MARINO

Livorno

Arezzo

Ancona

Siena

THE MARCHES

ELBA

3

Perugia

Assisi

UMBRIA

Orvieto

Terni

Pescara

Adriatic Sea

MONTENEGRO

ROME

Tivoli

ABRUZZO

1

MOLISE

Foggia

bia

CAMPANIA

Bari

Naples

4

VESUVIUS

5

PUGLIA

Brindisi

ISCHIA

Potenza

CAPRI

Amalfi

6

Paestum

BASILICATA

Taranto

Lecce

Gulf of Taranto

Tyrrhenian Sea

Cosenza

Catanzaro

AEOLIAN ISLANDS

Ionian Sea

Palermo

Messina

Reggio

EGADI ISLANDS

ETNA

SICILY

Catania

NISIA

Agrigento

SICILY

Siracusa

PANTELLERIA

TUNIS

0   100 miles

0   150 km

NEED TO KNOW

ITALY

Rome

SARDINIA

SICILY

Mediterranean Sea

AT A GLANCE
Capital: Rome

Population: 60,920,000

Currency: Euro

Money: ATMs are common; cash is more common than credit.

Language: Italian

Country Code: ☎ 29

Emergencies: ☎ 112

Driving: On the right

Electricity: 200v/50 cycles; electrical plugs have two round prongs

Time: Six hours ahead of New York

Documents: Up to 90 days with valid passport; Schengen rules apply

Mobile Phones: GSM (900 and 1800 bands)

Major Mobile Companies: Vodafone, TIM, Wind, Tre

WEBSITES
Italy: ⊕ www.italia.it

Farmstays: ⊕ www.agriturismo.it

Culture: ⊕ www.beniculturali.it

GETTING AROUND

✈ **Air Travel:** The major airports are Rome, Milan, Bergamo, and Venice.

🚌 **Bus Travel:** Good for smaller towns and the best way to travel the Amalfi coast.

🚗 **Car Travel:** Rent a car to explore at your own pace, but never to use in the cities themselves (including Rome and Florence). Always rent a GPS along with the car, as Italy's roads can be confounding. Gas is very expensive.

🚆 **Train Travel:** Excellent and fast between major cities. The slower, regional trains connect many smaller towns, as well.

PLAN YOUR BUDGET

	HOTEL ROOM	MEAL	ATTRACTIONS
Low Budget	€140	€25	Visiting Florence's Duomo, free
Mid Budget	€290	€45	Ticket to the Vatican and the Sistine Chapel, €16
High Budget	€350	€60	Evening gondola ride in Venice, €150

WAYS TO SAVE

Stay at an *agriturismo*. Farm-stays are Italy's best-kept secret. In beautiful settings, they sometimes include meals and are often for half the price of a hotel.

Drink from the free fountains. No need to buy bottled water; fill up at the free public fountains, especially in Rome.

Book rail tickets in advance. Book online at least a week in advance for half the price. ⊕ www.trenitalia.com.

Enjoy aperitivo. This northern Italian tradition entails getting a drink and access to a buffet—which can be light or heavy—for about €8 to €10.

PLAN YOUR TIME

Hassle Factor	Low. Flights to Rome, Milan, and Venice are frequent, and Italy has great transport elsewhere.
3 days	You can see some of the magic of Rome and perhaps take a day trip to Pompeii or Florence.
1 week	Spend time in Rome with a one-day trip to Pompeii, Umbria, or the Amalfi coast, as well as an additional day or two in Florence. Alternatively, tour the main cities with three days in Rome, two in Florence, and one in Venice.
2 weeks	You have time to move around and for the highlights, including stops in Rome, Florence, and Venice, excursions to Pompeii, Naples, and the Amalfi coast, and a trip to beautiful Tuscany or Umbria.

WHEN TO GO

High Season: June through September expensive and busy. In August, most Italians take their own summer holidays; cities are less crowded, but many shops and restaurants close. July and August can be uncomfortably hot.

Low Season: Unless you are skiing, winter offers the least appealing weather, though it's the best time for airfares and hotel deals—and to escape the crowds. Especially in the south, temperatures are still mild.

Value Season: By late September, temperate weather, saner airfares, and more cultural events can make for a happier trip. October is also great, but November is often rainy and (hence) quiet. From late April to early May, the masses have not yet arrived but cafés are already abuzz. March and early April can be changeable and wet.

BIG EVENTS

February: Carnevale kicks off across Venice and around Italy. ⊕ www.carnevaleitaliano.it

April: Religious processions commemorate Easter. On Easter Monday, *Pasquetta*, most Italians picnic.

June: The *Festa della Repubblica* commemorates Italy's 1946 vote for the republic. ⊕ www.festadellarepubblica.it

October: Alba's *Fiera del Tartufo* is devoted to the area's white truffles. ⊕ www.fieradeltartufo.org

READ THIS

■ *Delizia! The Epic History of the Italians and Their Food,* John Dickie. A great book.

■ *Under the Tuscan Sun,* Frances Mayes. The memoir that launched a thousand Tuscan trips.

■ *La Bella Figura,* Beppe Severgnini. A humorous introduction to modern Italy.

WATCH THIS

■ *Roman Holiday.* The 1953 classic starring Audrey Hepburn—and, of course, Rome.

■ *La Dolce Vita.* Fellini's famous study of glitzy 1950s Italy.

■ *Il Postino.* Romance in an Italian fishing village.

EAT THIS

■ **Mozzarella di bufala:** a specialty of Campania and the south

■ **Prosciutto crudo:** tender, dry-cured ham, especially from Parma and San Daniele.

■ **Pasta carbonara:** a Roman dish of eggs, cured pork jowl (*guanciale*), cheese, and pepper

■ **Bistecca fiorentina:** the classic Tuscan T-bone

■ **Wine:** from Barolo to Chianti

■ **Sfogliatelle:** a layered and filled southern Italy pastry

Where else in Europe can you find the blend of great art, delicious food and wine, and human warmth and welcome that awaits you in Italy? This Mediterranean country has made a profound contribution to Western civilization, producing some of the world's greatest thinkers, writers, politicians, saints, and artists. Impressive traces of their lives and works can still be seen in Italy's great buildings and enchanting countryside.

The whole of Italy is one vast attraction, but the triangle of its most-visited cities—Rome (Roma), Florence (Firenze), and Venice (Venezia)—represents the great variety found here. In Rome, especially, you can feel the uninterrupted flow of the ages, from the classical era of the ancient Romans to the bustle and throb of contemporary life being lived in centuries-old settings. Florence is the jewel of the Italian Renaissance, which is evident in the formal grandeur of its palaces and piazzas and the sumptuous villas in the surrounding countryside. Venice, by contrast, seems suspended in time, the same today as it was when it held sway over the eastern Mediterranean. Each of these cities reveals a different aspect of the Italian character: the baroque exuberance of Rome, Florence's Renaissance harmony, and the dreamy sensuality of Venice.

PLANNING

WHEN TO GO

The main tourist season runs from April to mid-October. The so-called low season from fall to early spring may be cooler and rainier, but it has its rewards: less time waiting in line and more time for unhurried views of what you want to see.

Tourists crowd the major art cities at Easter, when Italians flock to resorts and to the country. From March through May, busloads of schoolchildren take cities of artistic and historical interest by storm.

The best months for sightseeing are April, May, June, September, and October, when the weather is mild. The hottest months, July and August, can be unpleasant. Winters are relatively mild in most places on the main tourist circuit but always include some rainy spells.

GETTING HERE AND AROUND

AIR TRAVEL

The major gateways to Italy are Rome's Aeroporto Leonardo da Vinci (FCO), better known as Fiumicino, and Milan's Aeroporto Malpensa (MAL). There are some direct flights to Venice, Naples, and Pisa, but

TOP REASONS TO GO

The Vatican. The home of the Catholic Church, a tiny independent state tucked within central Rome, holds some of the city's most spectacular sights, including St. Peter's Basilica, the Vatican Museums, and Michelangelo's Sistine ceiling.

Ancient Rome. The Colosseum and the Roman Forum are remarkable ruins from Rome's ancient past. Sitting above it all is the Campidoglio, with a piazza designed by Michelangelo and museums containing Rome's finest collection of ancient art.

Pompeii. The excavated ruins of Pompeii offer a unique, occasionally spooky glimpse into everyday life—and sudden death—in Roman times.

Venice's Grand Canal. A trip down Venice's "Main Street," whether by water bus or gondola, is a signature Italian experience.

Galleria degli Uffizi, Florence. The Uffizi—Renaissance art's hall of fame—contains masterpieces by Leonardo, Michelangelo, Raphael, Botticelli, Caravaggio, and dozens of other luminaries.

Duomo, Florence. The massive dome of Florence's Cathedral of Santa Maria del Fiore (aka the Duomo) is one of the world's great feats of engineering.

Ravello. High above the Amalfi Coast, this place is a contender for the title of most beautiful village in the world.

Piazza del Campo, Siena. Siena is Tuscany's classic medieval hill town, and its heart is the Piazza del Campo, the beautiful, one-of-a-kind town square.

12

to fly into most other Italian cities you need to make connections at Fiumicino and Malpensa or another European airport. You can also take the FS airport train to Rome's Termini station or a bus to Milan's central train station (Centrale) and catch a train to any other location in Italy. It will take a half hour to get from Fiumicino, or an hour from Malpensa, to the appropriate train station.

Italy's major airports are not known for being new, fun, or efficient. Airports in Italy have also been ramping up security measures, which include random baggage inspection and bomb-sniffing dogs. All of the airports have restaurants and snack bars, and there is Internet access. Each airport has at least one nearby hotel. In the case of Florence and Pisa, the city centers are only a 15-minute taxi ride away—so if you encounter a long delay, spend it in town.

BUS TRAVEL

Italy's regional bus network, much of it operated by private companies, is extensive, but buses are usually not as attractive an option as comparatively cheap, convenient train travel. Schedules are often drawn up with commuters and students in mind and may be sketchy on weekends. Occasionally, though, buses can be faster and more direct than local trains, so it's a good idea to compare bus and train schedules. Most of the major cities in Italy have urban bus services. These buses are inexpensive, but they can become jammed, particularly at rush hours.

Contacts **Lazzi** ✉ *Via Mercadante 2, Florence* ☎ *0573/1937900* ⊕ *www.lazzi.
it.* **SITA** ✉ *Varco Immacolata, inside Molo Beverello port, Naples* ☎ *089/405145*
⊕ *www.sitasudtrasporti.it.*

CAR TRAVEL

Italy has an extensive network of *autostrade* (toll highways), complemented by equally well-maintained but free *superstrade* (expressways).
Save the ticket you are issued at an autostrada entrance, as you need
it to exit; on some shorter autostrade you pay the toll when you enter.
Viacards, on sale for €25 at many autostrada locations, allow you to
pay for tolls in advance. At special lanes you simply slip the card into
a designated slot.

An *uscita* is an "exit." A *raccordo* is a ring road surrounding a city.
Strade regionale and *strade provinciale* (regional and provincial highways, denoted by *S, SS, SR,* or *SP* numbers) may be two-lane roads, as
are all secondary roads; directions and turnoffs aren't always clearly
marked.

TRAIN TRAVEL

In Italy traveling by train is simple and efficient. Service between major
cities is frequent, and trains usually arrive on schedule.

Trains are operated by the **Ferrovie dello Stato** (FS; ☎ *892021 in Italy*
⊕ *www.trenitalia.com*), the Italian State Railways. Although you can
buy Eurostar Italia tickets at the station, more popular routes sometimes sell out, so it's advisable to book in advance. The next-fastest
trains are the Intercity (IC) trains. *Diretto* and *interregionale* trains
make more stops and are a little slower. *Regionale* and *locale* trains
are the slowest; many serve commuters. There is also a new option,
Italy's first private high-speed rail network, called Italotreno, which has
competitive prices on popular routes; check ⊕ *www.italotreno.com* for
schedules and fares.

Most Italian trains have first and second classes. On local trains a first-
class fare gets you little more than a clean doily on your headrest, but
on long-distance trains you get wider seats, more legroom, and better
ventilation and lighting.

Some cities—Milan, Florence, and Rome included—have more than one
train station, so be sure you get off at the right place. Always purchase
tickets before boarding the train, as you cannot purchase one from a
conductor. ■ TIP→ **You must validate your ticket before boarding the train
by punching it at a yellow box located in the waiting area of smaller train
stations or at the end of the track in larger stations.**

HOTELS

Italy has a varied and abundant number of hotels, bed-and-breakfasts,
agriturismi (farm stays), and rental properties. Throughout the cities
and the countryside you can find very sophisticated, luxurious palaces
and villas as well as rustic farmhouses and small hotels. Six-hundred-
year-old palazzi and converted monasteries have been restored as luxurious hotels, while retaining the original atmosphere. At the other end
of the spectrum, boutique hotels inhabit historic buildings using chic

Italian design for the interiors. Increasingly, the famed Italian wineries are creating rooms and apartments for three-day to weeklong stays.

Hotels in Italy are usually well maintained (especially if they've earned our recommendation in this book), but in some respects they won't match what you find at comparably priced U.S. lodgings. Keep the following points in mind as you set your expectations and you're likely to have a good experience:

First and foremost, rooms are usually smaller, particularly in cities. If you're truly cramped, ask for another room, but don't expect things to be spacious.

A "double bed" is commonly two singles pushed together. In the bathroom, tubs are not a given—request one if it's essential. In budget places, showers sometimes use a drain in the middle of the bathroom floor. And washcloths are a rarity.

Most hotels have satellite TV, but there are fewer channels than in the United States, and only one or two will be in English. Don't expect wall-to-wall carpeting. Particularly outside the cities, tile floors are the norm.

RESTAURANTS

Italian cuisine is still largely regional, so wherever you are, ask what the local specialties are. Although most restaurants in Italy serve traditional local cuisine, you can find Asian and Middle Eastern alternatives in Rome, Venice, and other cities.

DINING CUSTOMS
A meal in Italy has traditionally consisted of five courses, and every menu you encounter will still be organized along this five-course plan:

First up is the antipasto (appetizer), often consisting of cured meats or marinated vegetables. Next to appear is the primo, usually pasta or soup, and after that the secondo, a meat or fish course with, perhaps, a contorno (vegetable dish) on the side. A simple dolce (dessert) rounds out the meal.

This, you've probably noticed, is a lot of food. Italians have noticed as well—a full, five-course meal is an indulgence usually reserved for special occasions. Instead, restaurant meals are a mix-and-match affair: you might order a primo and a secondo, or an antipasto and a primo, or a secondo and a contorno.

The crucial rule of restaurant dining is that you should order at least two courses. It's a common mistake for tourists to order only a secondo, thinking they're getting a "main course" complete with side dishes. What they wind up with is one lonely piece of meat.

HOTEL AND RESTAURANT PRICES
Prices in the restaurant reviews are the average cost of a main course at dinner or, if dinner is not served, at lunch; taxes and service charges are generally included. Prices in the hotel reviews are the lowest cost of a standard double room in high season, excluding taxes, service charges, and meal plans (except at all-inclusives).

PLANNING YOUR TIME

It is not difficult to see two or three diverse parts of Italy in a one-week visit because of the ease of travel by car on the fast freeway system, via the comprehensive railway with the speedy Eurostar trains, and lastly, by air from the two major airports in Milan and Rome to the smaller airports serving Venice, Florence, and Pisa. On the other hand, while you are planning your itinerary, remember that Italy is a long, narrow country and that you don't want to spend your entire vacation in transit. When traveling by car along the smaller country roads or by train on local lines that stop at every station, it will probably take you longer than you think to get from place to place.

Trying to soak up Italy's rich artistic heritage poses a challenge. The country's many museums and churches draw hordes of visitors, all wanting to see the same thing at the same time. From May through September the Sistine Chapel, Michelangelo's *David*, Piazza San Marco, and other key sights are more often than not swamped by tourists. Try to see the highlights at off-peak times. If they are open during lunch, this is often a good time. Seeing some attractions—such as the gleaming facades of Rome's glorious baroque churches and fountains—does not require waiting in long lines.

Making the most of your time in Italy doesn't mean rushing through it. To gain a rich appreciation for the country, don't try to see everything at once. Practice the Italian-perfected *il dolce far niente*—the sweet art of idleness. Skip a museum to sit at a table in a pretty café and enjoy the sunshine and a cappuccino. Art—and life—is to be enjoyed, and the Italians can show you how.

ROME

The timeless city to which all roads lead, Rome enthralls visitors today as she has since time immemorial. More than Florence, more than Venice, this is Italy's treasure storehouse. Here, the ancient Romans made us heirs-in-law to what we call Western Civilization; where centuries later Michelangelo painted in the Sistine Chapel; where Gian Lorenzo Bernini's baroque nymphs and naiads still dance in their marble fountains; and where, at Cinecittà Studios, Fellini filmed *La Dolce Vita* and *8½*. Today the city remains a veritable Grand Canyon of culture: Ancient Rome rubs shoulders with the medieval, the modern runs into the Renaissance, and the result is like nothing so much as an open-air museum.

PLANNING YOUR TIME

Roma, non basta una vita ("Rome, a lifetime is not enough"): this famous saying should be stamped on the passport of every first-time visitor to the Eternal City. On the other hand, it's a warning: Rome is so packed with sights that it is impossible to take them all in. It's easy to run yourself ragged trying to check off the items on your must-see list. At the same time, the saying is a celebration of the city's abundance. There's so much here, you're bound to make discoveries you hadn't anticipated. To conquer Rome, strike a balance between visits to major sights and leisurely neighborhood strolls.

In the first category, the Vatican and the remains of ancient Rome loom the largest. Both require at least half a day; a good strategy is to devote your first morning to one and your second to the other. Leave the afternoons for exploring the neighborhoods that comprise "baroque Rome" and the shopping district around the Spanish Steps and Via Condotti. If you have more days at your disposal, continue with the same approach. Among the sights, Galleria Borghese and the multilayered church of San Clemente are particularly worthwhile, and the neighborhoods of Trastevere and the Ghetto make for great roaming.

Since there's a lot of ground to cover in Rome, it's wise to plan your busy sightseeing schedule with possible savings in mind, and purchasing the Roma Pass (⊕ *www.romapass.it*) allows you to do just that. The three-day pass costs €34 and is good for unlimited use of buses, trams and the metro. It includes free admission to two of more than 40 participating museums or archaeological sites, including the Colosseum (and bumps you to the head of the long line there, to boot), the Ara Pacis museum, the Musei Capitolini, and Galleria Borghese, plus discounted tickets to many other museums. The Roma Pass can be purchased at tourist information booths across the city, at Termini Station, or at Terminal C of the International Arrivals section of Fiumicino Airport.

GETTING HERE

Rome's principal airport is Leonardo da Vinci Airport/Fiumicino (☎ *06/65951* ⊕ *www.adr.it*), commonly known by the name of its location, Fiumicino (FCO). It's 30 km (19 miles) southwest of the city but has a direct train link with downtown Rome. Rome's other airport, with no direct train link, is Ciampino (CIA; ☎ *06/794941* ⊕ *www.adr.it*), 15 km (9 miles) south of downtown and used mostly by low-cost airlines.

By car, the main access routes from the north are A1 (Autostrada del Sole) from Milan and Florence and the A12–E80 highway from Genoa. All highways connect with the Grande Raccordo Anulare Ring Road (GRA), which channels traffic into the city center. For driving directions, check out ⊕ *www.tuttocitta.it*. Note: Parking in Rome can be a nightmare—private cars are not allowed access to the entire historic center during the day (weekdays 8–6; Saturday 2–6), except for residents.

The main train stations in Rome are Termini, Tiburtina, Ostiense, and Trastevere. On long-distance routes (to Florence and Venice, for instance), you can either travel by the cheap, but slow, diretto trains, or the fast, but more expensive, Intercity or the Eurostar.

GETTING AROUND

Rome's integrated transportation system, ATAC (☎ *06/4695–2027 or 800/431–784* ⊕ *www.atac.roma.it*), includes the Metropolitana subway, city buses, and trams. A ticket (BIT) valid for 110 minutes on any combination of buses and trams and one entrance to the metro costs €1.50. Day passes can be purchased for €6, and weekly passes for €24. Tickets (singly or in quantity—it's a good idea to have a few extra tickets handy) are sold at tobacconists, newsstands, some coffee bars, automatic ticket machines in metro stations, some bus stops, and ATAC and COTRAL ticket booths. Time-stamp tickets at metro turnstiles and in little yellow machines on buses and trams when boarding the first vehicle.

Taxis in Rome do not normally cruise for fares, but if free they will stop if you flag them down. They wait at stands and can also be called by phone (☎ 06/6645, 06/3570, 06/4994, 06/5551, or 06/4157). Use only licensed cabs, which are white and have lettering on the side identifying them as official. Flat rates are set by the city for fares between the airports to the *centro storico* (the historic center), which includes the Vatican, Piazza Navona, Spanish Steps, and Colosseum areas; the cost is €48 from Leonardo da Vinci–Fiumicino or €30 from Ciampino, including all baggage and up to four passengers. Travelers should avoid taking a taxi from Ciampino, however, as the taxis there are known for price-gouging (legal rates aside).

VISITOR INFORMATION

Rome's main APT (Azienda Per Turismo) Tourist Information Office is at Via Parigi 5–11 (☎ 06/488991 ⊕ *www.romaturismo.it*), near the main Termini rail station. In addition, green APT information kiosks with multilingual personnel are near the most important sights and squares, as well as at Termini Station and Leonardo da Vinci Airport.

EXPLORING

ANCIENT ROME

If you ever wanted to feel like the Caesars—with all of ancient Rome (literally) at your feet—simply head to Michelangelo's famed Piazza del Campidoglio. There, make a beeline for the terrace flanking the side of the center building, the Palazzo Senatorio, Rome's ceremonial city hall.

From this balcony atop the Capitoline Hill (or from the Tabularium arcade, situated right below in the Musei Capitolini complex), you can take in a panorama that seems like a remnant of a Cecil B. DeMille movie spectacular. For looming before you is the entire Roman Forum, the *"caput mundi"*—the center of the known world for centuries.

Before the Christian era, before the emperors, before the powerful Republic that ruled the ancient seas, Rome was founded on seven hills, and two of them—the Capitoline and the Palatine—surround the Roman Forum, where the Romans of the later Republic and Imperial ages worshiped deities, debated politics, and wheeled and dealed. It's all history now, but this remains one of the world's most striking and significant concentrations of ancient remains—an emphatic reminder of the genius and power that made Rome the fountainhead of the Western world.

The Campidoglio. Spectacularly transformed by Michelangelo's late-Renaissance designs, the Campidoglio was once the epicenter of the Roman Empire, the place where the city's first shrines stood, including its most sacred, the Temple of Jupiter.

Originally, the Capitoline Hill consisted of two peaks: the Capitolium and the Arx (where Santa Maria in Aracoeli now stands). The hollow between them was known as the Asylum. Here, prospective settlers once came to seek the protection of Romulus, legendary first king of Rome—hence the term "asylum." Later, during the Republic, in 78 BC, the Tabularium, or Hall of Records, was erected here.

By the Middle Ages, however, the Capitoline had become an unkempt hill strewn with ancient rubble. In preparation for the impending visit of Charles V in 1536, triumphant after the empire's victory over the Moors, his host, Pope Paul III Farnese, decided that the Holy Roman Emperor should follow the route of the emperors, climaxing at the Campidoglio.

But the pope was embarrassed by the decrepit goat pasture the hill had become and commanded Michelangelo to restore the site to glory; he added a third palace along with Renaissance-style facades and a grand paved piazza. ⊠ *Piazza dei Campidoglio, incorporating the Palazzo Senatorio and the two Capitoline Museums, the Palazzo Nuovo, and the Palazzo dei Conservatori.*

The Colosseum. The most spectacular extant edifice of ancient Rome, the Colosseo has a history that is half gore, half glory. Here, before 50,000 spectators, gladiators would salute the emperor and cry, *Ave, imperator, morituri te salutant* ("Hail, emperor, men soon to die salute thee"); it is said that when one day they heard the emperor Claudius respond, "Or maybe not," they became so offended that they called a strike.

Once inside, take the steep stairs or elevator up to the second floor, where you can get a birds'-eye view of the hypogeum: the subterranean passageways that were the architectural engine rooms that made the slaughter above proceed like clockwork. In a scene prefiguring something from Dante's *Inferno,* hundreds of beasts would wait to be eventually launched via a series of slave-powered hoists and lifts into the bloodthirsty sand of the arena above. The newly restored hypogeum, along with the third level of the Colosseum, reopened to much acclaim in fall 2010 (visitable only via a prebooked, guided tour). Since then, however, it's open and shut, depending on the season and recent rains. Check the Pierreci website for its current state.

Are there ways to beat the big ticket lines at the Colosseum? Yes and no. First off, if you go to the Roman Forum, a couple of hundred yards down Via dei Fori Imperiali on your left, or to the Palatine, down Via di San Gregorio, the €12 ticket you purchase there includes admission to the Colosseum and, even better, lets you jump to the head of the *loooooooong* line. Another way is to buy the Romapass (⊕ *www. romapass.it*) ticket; the Colosseo is covered and you get booted to the front of the line. Or you can book a ticket in advance through ⊕ *www. pierreci.it* (small surcharge), the main ticket reservation service for many Italian cultural sights. Finally, you can book another tour online with a company (do your research to make sure it's reputable) that lets you "skip the line."

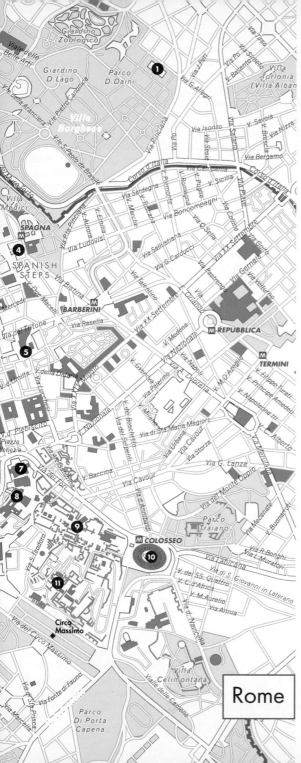

12

No matter what, however, avoid the tours that are being sold on-the-spot right around the Colosseum, including on the piazza and just outside of the metro. ⊠ *Piazza del Colosseo* ☎ *06/3996–7700* ⊕ *www.pierreci.it* 🖱 *€12 combined ticket with the Roman Forum, Palatine Hill, and Imperial Forums (if used within 2 days)* ⊘ *Daily 8:30–1 hr before sunset* Ⓜ *Colosseo; Bus No. 117, 87, 186, 85, or 850.*

FodorsChoice
★
Musei Capitolini. Surpassed in size and richness only by the Musei Vaticani, this immense collection was the first public museum in the world. A greatest-hits collection of Roman art through the ages, from the ancients to the baroque, it is housed in the twin Museo Capitolino and Palazzo dei Conservatori that bookend Michelangelo's famous piazza. Here, you'll find some of antiquity's most famous sculptures, such as the poignant *Dying Gaul,* the regal *Capitoline Venus,* the *Esquiline Venus* (identified as possibly another Mediterranean beauty, Cleopatra herself), and the *Lupa Capitolina,* the symbol of Rome. Although some pieces in the collection—which was first assembled by Sixtus IV (1414–84), one of the earliest of the Renaissance popes—may excite only archaeologists and art historians, others are unforgettable, including the original bronze statue of Marcus Aurelius whose copy sits in the piazza.

The heart of the museum, however, is the Exedra of Marcus Aurelius (Sala Marco Aurelio), a large, airy room with skylights and high windows, which showcases the spectacular original bronze statue of the Roman emperor whose copy sits in the piazza below. Created in the 2nd century AD, the statue should have been melted down like so many other bronze statues of emperors after the decline of Rome, but this one is thought to have survived because it was mistaken for the Christian emperor Constantine.

Inside the Palazzo Nuovo on the stairs you find yourself immediately dwarfed by Mars in full military rig and lion-topped sandals. Upstairs is the noted Sala degli Imperatori, lined with busts of Roman emperors, along with the Sala dei Filosofi, where busts of philosophers sit in judgment—a fascinating who's who of the ancient world, and a must-see of the museum. ⊠ *Piazza del Campidoglio, Campidoglio* ☎ *06/0608* ⊕ *www.museicapitolini.org* 🖱 *€12; audio guide €5* ⊘ *Tues.–Sun. 9–8* Ⓜ *Bus No. 44, 63, 64, 81, 95, 85, or 492.*

Palatine Hill. Just beyond the Arch of Titus, the Clivus Palatinus gently rises to the heights of the **Colle Palatino** (Palatine Hill)—the oldest inhabited site in Rome. Despite its location overlooking the Forum's traffic and attendant noise, the Palatine was the most coveted address for ancient Rome's rich and famous. More than a few of the Twelve Caesars called the Palatine home, including Caligula, who was murdered in the still-standing and unnerving (even today) tunnel, the Cryptoporticus. The palace of Tiberius was the first to be built here; others followed, notably the gigantic extravaganza constructed for Emperor Domitian. But perhaps the most famous lodging goes back to Rome's very beginning. Once upon a time, skeptics thought Romulus was a myth. Then, about a century ago, Rome's greatest archaeologist, Rodolfo Lanciani, excavated a site on the hill and uncovered the remains of an Iron Age settlement dating back to the 9th century BC, supporting the belief that Romulus, founder of Rome, lived here. In fall 2007, archaeologists unearthed a sacred sanctuary dedicated to Romulus and Remus set beneath the House of Augustus near the Palatine Hill. This sanctuary is now being renovated. ⊠ *Entrances at Piazza del Colosseo and Via di San Gregorio 30, Roman Forum* ☎ *06/39967700* ⊕ *www.pierreci.it* 🎫 *€12 (combined ticket with the Colosseum and Roman Forum, if used within 2 days)* ⊙ *Daily 8:30 am–one hour before sunset* Ⓜ *Colosseo.*

The Roman Forum. From the entrance on Via dei Fori Imperiali, descend into the extraordinary archaeological complex that is the Foro Romano. Before the 1st century, when the Roman Republic gave over to hedonistic imperial Rome, this was the heart of the empire. The Forum began life as a marshy valley between the Capitoline and Palatine hills—a valley crossed by a mud track and used as a cemetery by Iron Age settlers. Over the years a market center and some huts were established here, and after the land was drained in the 6th century BC, the site eventually became a political, religious, and commercial center: the Forum.

Hundreds of years of plunder reduced the Forum to its current desolate state. But this enormous area was once Rome's pulsating heart, filled with stately and extravagant temples, palaces, and shops, and crowded with people from all corners of the empire. Adding to today's confusion is the fact that the Forum developed over many centuries; what you see today are not the ruins from just one period but from a span of almost 900 years, from about 500 BC to AD 400. Nonetheless, the enduring romance of the place, with its lonely columns and great broken fragments of sculpted marble and stone, makes for a quintessential Roman experience. ⊠ *Entrance at Via dei Fori Imperiali, Roman Forum* ☎ *06/3996–7700* ⊕ *www.pierreci.it* 🎫 *€12 combined ticket with the Colosseum and Palatine Hill (if used within 2 days); audio guide €5 Forum, €7 Forum and Palatine* ⊙ *Jan.–Feb. 15, daily 8:30–4:30; Feb. 16–Mar. 15, daily 8:30–5; Mar. 16–last Sat. in Mar., daily 8:30–5:30; last Sun. in Mar.–Aug., daily 8:30–7:15; Sept., daily 8:30–7; Oct. 1–last Sat. in Oct., daily 8:30–6:30; last Sun. in Oct.–Dec., daily 8:30–4:30* Ⓜ *Colosseo.*

PIAZZA NAVONA AND CAMPO DE' FIORI

This time-burnished district is the city's most beautiful neighborhood. Set between the Via del Corso and the Tiber's bend, it is filled with narrow streets bearing curious names, airy piazzas, and half-hidden courtyards. Some of Rome's most coveted residential addresses are nestled here. So, too, are the ancient Pantheon and the medieval square of Campo de' Fiori, but the spectacular, over-the-top baroque monuments of the 16th and 17th centuries predominate.

The hub of the district is the queen of squares, Piazza Navona—a cityscape adorned with the most eye-knocking fountain by Gian Lorenzo Bernini, father of the baroque. Streets running off the square lead to many historic must-sees, including noble churches by Borromini and Caravaggio's greatest paintings at San Luigi dei Francesi. This district has been an integral part of the city since ancient times, and its position between the Vatican and Lateran palaces, both seats of papal rule, put it in the mainstream of Rome's development from the Middle Ages onward. Craftsmen, shopkeepers, and famed artists toiled in the shadow of the huge palaces built to consolidate the power of leading figures in the papal court. Artisans and artists still live here, but their numbers are diminishing as the district becomes increasingly posh and—so critics say—"Disneyfied." But three of the liveliest piazzas in Rome, Piazza Navona, Piazza del

Pantheon, and the Campo de' Fiori, are lodestars in a constellation of some of Rome's most authentic cafés, stores, and wine bars.

Campo de' Fiori. A bustling marketplace in the morning (Mon.–Sat. 8–1) and a trendy meeting place the rest of the day (and night), this piazza has plenty of earthy charm. By sunset, all the fish, fruit, and flower vendors disappear and this so-called *piazza trasformista* takes on another identity, becoming a circus of bars particularly favored by study-abroads, tourists, and young expats. Brooding over the piazza is a hooded statue of the philosopher Giordano Bruno, who was burned at the stake here in 1600 for heresy. His was the first of the executions that drew Roman crowds to Campo de' Fiori in the 17th century. ⊠ *Intersection of Via dei Baullari, Via Giubbonari, Via del Pellegrino, and Piazza della Cancelleria, Campo.*

Fodor's Choice
★

Pantheon. One of the wonders of the ancient world, this onetime pagan temple, a marvel of architectural harmony and proportion, is the best-preserved ancient building in Rome. It was entirely rebuilt by the emperor Hadrian around AD 120 on the site of an earlier pantheon (from the Greek *pan*—all—and *theon*—gods) erected in 27 BC by Augustus's general Agrippa.

The most striking thing about the Pantheon is not its size, immense though it is (until 1960 the dome was the largest ever built), nor even the phenomenal technical difficulties posed by so vast a construction; rather, it's the remarkable unity of the building. You don't have to look far to find the reason for this harmony: the diameter described by the dome is exactly equal to its height. It's the use of such simple mathematical balance that gives classical architecture its characteristic sense of proportion and its nobility and why some call it the world's only architecturally perfect building. The great opening at the apex of the dome, the oculus, is nearly 30 feet in diameter and was the temple's only source of light. It was intended to symbolize the "all-seeing eye of heaven."

Although little is known for sure about the Pantheon's origins or purpose, it's worth noting that the five levels of trapezoidal coffers represent the course of the five then-known planets and their concentric spheres. Then, ruling over them, comes the sun represented symbolically and literally by the 30-foot-wide eye at the top.

CLOSE UP

Going Baroque

Flagrantly emotional, heavily expressive, and visually sensuous, the 17th-century artistic movement known as the baroque was born in Rome. It was the creation of three geniuses: the sculptor and architect Gianlorenzo Bernini (1598–1680), the painter and architect Pietro da Cortona (1596–1669), and the architect and sculptor Francesco Borromini (1599–1667). From the drama found in the artists' paintings to the jewel-laden, gold-on-gold detail of 17th-century Roman palaces, baroque style was intended both to shock and delight by upsetting the placid, "correct" rules of proportion and scale in the Renaissance. If a building looks theatrical—like a stage or a theater, especially with curtains being drawn back—it is usually baroque. Look for over-the-top, curvaceous marble work, trompe l'oeil, allusions to other art, and high drama to identify the style. Baroque's appeal to the emotions made it a powerful weapon in the hands of the Counter-Reformation.

The Pantheon is by far the best preserved of the major monuments of imperial Rome, a condition that is the result of it being consecrated as a church in AD 608. (It's still a working, Mass-holding church today, and it's the church name, the Basilica of Saint Mary and the Martyrs, that you'll see on the official signs.)

One-hour tours (€10) are run regularly in English; check at the information desk on your right as you enter. ⊠ *Piazza della Rotonda, Navona* ☎ *06/6830–0230* ⊕ *www.pantheonroma.com* ✉ *Free; audio guides €5* ⏱ *Mon.–Sat. 9–7:30, Sun. 9–6, public holidays during the wk 9–1* Ⓜ *Closest bus hub: Argentina (Bus No. 40, 85, 53, 46, 64, 87, or 571, Tram No. 8).*

Piazza Navona. Here, everything that makes Rome unique is compressed into one beautiful baroque piazza. Always camera-ready, Piazza Navona has Bernini sculptures, three gorgeous fountains, a magnificently baroque church (Sant'Agnese in Agone), and, best of all, the excitement of so many people strolling, admiring the fountains, and enjoying the view.

At center stage is the Fontana dei Quattro Fiumi, created for Innocent X by Bernini in 1651. Bernini's powerful figures of the four rivers represent the four corners of the world: the Nile; the Ganges; the Danube; and the Plata, with its hand raised.

Fodor's Choice ★ **San Luigi dei Francesi.** A pilgrimage spot for art lovers everywhere, San Luigi's Contarelli Chapel is adorned with three stunningly dramatic works by Caravaggio (1571–1610), the baroque master of the heightened approach to light and dark. At the altar end of the left nave, they were commissioned for San Luigi, the official church of Rome's French colony (San Luigi is St. Louis, patron of France). The inevitable coin machine will light up his *Calling of St. Matthew, Matthew and the Angel,* and *Matthew's Martyrdom,* seen from left to right, and Caravaggio's mastery of light takes it from there. When painted, they caused considerable consternation to the clergy of San Luigi, who thought the artist's dramatically realistic approach was scandalously disrespectful. A first version of the altarpiece was rejected; the priests were not particularly happy with the other two, either. Time has fully vindicated Caravaggio's patron, Cardinal Francesco del Monte, who secured the commission for these works and stoutly defended them. They're now recognized to be among the world's greatest paintings. ⊠ *Piazza San Luigi dei Francesi, Navona* ☎ *06/688271* ☉ *Fri.–Wed. 10–12:30 and 3–7, Thurs. 10–12:30.*

PIAZZA VENEZIA TO THE SPANISH STEPS

In spirit, and in fact, this section of the city is its most grandiose. The overblown Vittoriano monument, the labyrinthine treasure-chest palaces of Rome's surviving aristocracy, even the diamond-draped denizens of Via Condotti's shops—all embody the exuberant ego of a city at the center of its own universe. Here's where you'll see ladies in furs gobbling pastries at café tables, and walk through a thousand snapshots as you climb the famous Spanish Steps, admired by generations from Byron to Versace. Cultural treasures abound around here: gilded 17th-century churches, glittering palaces, and the greatest example of portraiture in Rome: Velázquez's incomparable *Innocent X* at the Galleria Doria Pamphilj. Have your camera ready—along with a coin or two—for that most beloved of Rome's landmarks, the Trevi Fountain.

Monumento a Vittorio Emanuele II, or Altare della Patria (*Victor Emmanuel Monument, or Altar of the Nation*). The huge white mass of the "Vittoriano" is an inescapable landmark—Romans say you can avoid its image only if you're actually standing on it. Some have likened it to a huge wedding cake; others, to an immense typewriter. Though not held in the highest esteem by present-day citizens, it was the source of great civic pride at the time of its construction, at the turn of the 20th century. Built to honor the unification of Italy and the nation's first king, Victor Emmanuel II, it also shelters the eternal flame at the tomb of Italy's Unknown Soldier killed during World War I. The flame is guarded day and night by sentinels, while inside the building there is the (rather dry) Institute of the History of the Risorgimento.

The views from the top are some of Rome's most panoramic. The only way up is by elevator (located to the right as you face the monument); stop at the museum entrances (to the left and right of the structure) to get a pamphlet identifying the sculpture groups on the monument itself and the landmarks you will be able to see once at the top. ⊠ *Entrance at Piazza Ara Coeli, next to Piazza Venezia, around Via del Corso* ☎ *06/0608* ⊕ *www.060608.it* 🎟 *Free, elevator €7* ☉ *Elevator Mon.–Thurs. 9:30–5:45, Fri. and weekends 9:30–6:45; stairs winter 9:30–4:30, summer 9:30–5:30.*

Fodor's Choice
★ **Palazzo Doria Pamphilj.** Along with the Palazzo Colonna and the Galleria Borghese, this spectacular family palace provides the best glimpse of aristocratic Rome. Here, the main attractions are the legendary Old Master paintings, including treasures by Velázquez and Caravaggio, the splendor of the main galleries, and a unique suite of private family apartments. The beauty of the graceful 18th-century facade of this

12

patrician palace may escape you unless you take time to step to the opposite side of the street for a good view; it was designed by Gabriele Valvassori in 1730. The foundations of the immense complex of buildings probably date from classical times. The current building dates from the 15th century, with the exception of the facade. It passed through several hands before it became the property of the famous seafaring Doria family of Genoa, who had married into the Roman Pamphilj (also spelled Pamphili) clan. As in most of Rome's older patrician residences, the family still lives in part of the palace. ✉ *Via del Corso 305* ☎ *06/679–7323* ⊕ *www.doriapamphilj.it* ✆ *€11* ☉ *Daily 9–7.*

FAMILY

Fodor'sChoice

★

The Spanish Steps. That icon of postcard Rome, the Spanish Steps (often called simply *la scalinata*—"the staircase"—by Italians) and the Piazza di Spagna from which they ascend both get their names from the Spanish Embassy to the Vatican on the piazza—even though the staircase was built with French funds in 1723. In honor of a diplomatic visit by the king of Spain, the hillside was transformed by architect Francesco de Sanctis to link the church of Trinità dei Monti at the top with the Via dei Condotti below. In an allusion to the church, the staircase is divided by three landings (beautifully banked with azaleas from mid-April to mid-May). For centuries, the scalinata and its neighborhood have welcomed tourists, dukes, and writers in search of inspiration—among them Stendhal, Honoré de Balzac, William Makepeace Thackeray, and Byron, along with today's enthusiastic hordes. Bookending the bottom of the steps are two monuments to the 18th-century days when the English colonized the area: to the right, the Keats-Shelley House, to the left, Babington's Tea Rooms, both beautifully redolent of the Grand Tour era. For weary sightseers, there is an elevator at Vicolo del Bottino 8 (next to the adjacent Metro entrance). ✉ *Intersection of vias Condotti, del Babuino, and Due Macelli, Spagna* Ⓜ *Spagna.*

Fodor'sChoice

★

Trevi Fountain. Alive with rushing waters commanded by an imperious Oceanus, the Fontana di Trevi (Trevi Fountain) earned full-fledged iconic status in 1954 when it starred in 20th Century Fox's *Three Coins in the Fountain.* As the first color film in Cinemascope to be produced on location, it caused practically half of America to pack their bags for the Eternal City.

From the very start, however, the Trevi has been all about theatrical effects. An aquatic marvel in a city filled with them, the fountain's unique drama is largely due to the site: its vast basin is squeezed into the tight meeting of three little streets (the "tre vie," which may give the fountain its name) with cascades emerging as if from the wall of Palazzo Poli.

Everyone knows the famous legend that if you throw a coin into the Trevi Fountain you will ensure a return trip to the Eternal City. But not everyone knows how to do it the right way: You must toss a coin with your right hand over your left shoulder, with your back to the fountain. One coin means you'll return to Rome; two, you'll return *and* fall in love; three, you'll return, find love, and marry. The fountain grosses some €600,000 a year, and aside from incidences of opportunists fishing coins from the water, all of the money goes to charity. ⊠ *Piazza di Trevi* Ⓜ *Barberini–Fontana di Trevi.*

VILLA BORGHESE AND PIAZZA DEL POPOLO

Touring Rome's artistic masterpieces while staying clear of its hustle and bustle can be, quite literally, a walk in the park. Some of the city's finest sights are tucked away in or next to green lawns and pedestrian piazzas, offering a breath of fresh air for weary sightseers, especially in the Villa Borghese park. One of Rome's largest, this park can alleviate gallery gout by offering an oasis in which to cool off under the ilex, oak, and umbrella pine trees. If you feel like a picnic, have an *alimentare* (food shop) make you some panini before you go; food carts within the park are overpriced.

Fodor's Choice
★

Ara Pacis Augustae *(Altar of Augustan Peace).* This vibrant monument of the imperial age has been housed in one of Rome's newest architectural landmarks: a gleaming, rectangular glass-and-travertine structure designed by American architect Richard Meier. Overlooking the Tiber on one side and the ruins of the marble-clad **Mausoleo di Augusto** (Mausoleum of Augustus), on the other, the result is a serene, luminous oasis right in Rome's center. Opened in 2006, after a decade of bitter controversy over the monument's relocation, the altar itself dates back to 13 BC; it was commissioned to celebrate the Pax Romana, the era of peace ushered in by Augustus's military victories. It is covered with spectacular and moving relief sculptures. ⊠ *Lungotevere in Augusta, around Via del Corso* ☎ *06/0608* ⊕ *www.arapacis.it* ⊡ *€8.50* ☾ *Tues.–Sun. 9–7 (last admission 1 hr before closing)* Ⓜ *Flaminio (Piazza del Popolo).*

Fodor's Choice
★

Galleria Borghese. It's a real toss-up as to which is more magnificent: the villa built for Cardinal Scipione Borghese in 1612, or the art that lies within. Despite its beauty, the villa never was used as a residence. Instead, the luxury-loving cardinal built it as a showcase for his fabulous collection of both antiquities and more "modern" works, including those he commissioned from the masters Caravaggio and Bernini. Today, it's a monument to Roman interior decoration at its most extravagant. With the passage of time, however, the building has become less celebrated than the collections housed within, including one of the finest collections of Baroque sculpture anywhere in the world.

Admission to the Museo is by reservation only. Visitors are admitted in two-hour shifts 9 am to 5 pm. Prime-time slots can sell out days in advance, so in high season reserve by phone or directly through the Borghese's website. You need to collect your reserved ticket at the museum ticket office a half hour before your entrance. However, when it's not busy you can purchase your ticket at the museum for the next entrance appointment. ⊠ *Piazza Scipione Borghese 5, off Via Pinciana, Villa Borghese* ☎ *06/32810 for reservations, 06/8413979 for info* ⊕ *www. galleriaborghese.it* ⊡ *€11 (including €2 reservation fee), audio guide €5, English tour €5* ☾ *Tues.–Sun. 8:30–7:30, with sessions at 9, 11, 1, 3, and 5* Ⓜ *Bus No. 910 from Piazza della Repubblica, or Tram No. 19 or Bus No. 3 from Policlinico.*

Piazza del Popolo. With its obelisk and twin churches, this immense square is a famed Rome landmark. It owes its current appearance to architect Giuseppe Valadier, who designed it about 1820, also laying out the terraced approach to the Pincio and the Pincio's gardens. It marks what was for centuries the northern entrance to the city, where all roads from the north converge and where visitors, many of them pilgrims, would get their first impression of the Eternal City. The desire to make this entrance to Rome something special had been a pet project of popes and their architects for more than three centuries. The piazza takes its name from the 15th-century church of Santa Maria del Popolo, huddled on the right side of the Porta del Popolo, or city gate. ⊠ *Piazza del Popolo* Ⓜ *Flaminio.*

THE VATICAN

Capital of the Catholic Church, this tiny walled city-state is a place where some people go to find a work of art—Michelangelo's frescoes, rare ancient Roman marbles, or Bernini's statues. Others go to find their soul. Whatever the reason, thanks to being the seat of world Catholicism and also address to the most overwhelming architectural achievement of the Renaissance—St. Peter's Basilica—the Vatican attracts millions of travelers every year. In addition, the Vatican Museums are famed for magnificent rooms decorated by Raphael, sculptures such as the *Apollo Belvedere* and the *Laocoön,* frescoes by Fra Angelico, paintings by Giotto and Leonardo, and the celebrated ceiling of the Sistine Chapel. The Church power that emerged as the Rome of the emperors declined gave impetus to a profusion of artistic expression and shaped the destiny of the city for a thousand years. Allow yourself an hour to see St. Peter's Basilica, two hours for the museums, an hour for Castel Sant'Angelo, and an hour to climb to the top of the dome. Note that ushers at the entrance of St. Peter's Basilica and the Vatican Museums bar entry to people with "inappropriate" clothing—which means no bare knees or shoulders.

Fodor'sChoice
★
Basilica di San Pietro. The world's largest church, built over the tomb of St. Peter, is the most imposing and breathtaking architectural achievement of the Renaissance (although much of the lavish interior dates to the baroque). The physical statistics are impressive: it covers 18,000 square yards, runs 212 yards in length, and is surmounted by a dome that rises 435 feet and measures 138 feet across its base. Its history is equally impressive. No fewer than five of Italy's greatest artists—Bramante, Raphael, Peruzzi, Antonio Sangallo the Younger, and Michelangelo—died while striving to erect this new St. Peter's.

The history of the original St. Peter's goes back to AD 349, when the emperor Constantine completed a basilica over the site of the tomb of St. Peter, the Church's first pope. The original church stood for more than 1,000 years, undergoing a number of restorations and alterations, until, toward the middle of the 15th century, it was verging on collapse. In 1452 a reconstruction job began but was quickly abandoned for lack of money. In 1503, Pope Julius II instructed the architect Bramante to raze all the existing buildings and to build a new basilica, one that would surpass even Constantine's for grandeur. It wasn't until 1626 that the basilica was completed and consecrated.

As you climb the shallow steps up to the great church, flanked by the statues of Sts. Peter and Paul, you'll see the **Loggia delle Benedizioni** (Benediction Loggia) over the central portal. This is the balcony where newly elected popes are proclaimed, and where they stand to give their apostolic blessing on solemn feast days. The vault of the vestibule is encrusted with rich stuccowork, and the mosaic above the central entrance to the portico is a much-restored work by the 14th-century painter Giotto that was in the original basilica. The bronze doors of the main entrance also were salvaged from the old basilica. The sculptor Filarete worked on them for 12 years; they show scenes from the martyrdom of St. Peter and St. Paul, and the life of Pope Eugene IV (1431–47), Filarete's patron.

With advance notice you can take a 1¼-hour guided tour in English of the **Vatican Necropolis** (☎ *06/6988–5318* ✆ *€12* ☉ *Ufficio Scavi weekdays 9–6, Sat. 9–5, visits 9–3:30*), under the basilica, which gives a rare glimpse of Early Christian Roman burial customs and a closer look at the tomb of St. Peter. Apply by fax or email (✐ *scavi@fsp.va*) at least 2–3 weeks in advance, specifying the number of people in the group (all must be age 15 or older), preferred language, preferred time, available dates, and your contact information in Rome.

Under the Pope Pius V monument, the entrance to the sacristy also leads to the **Museo Storico-Artistico e Tesoro** (*Historical-Artistic Museum and Treasury;* ☎ *06/6988–1840* ✆ *€10, includes audio guide* ☉ *Apr.– Sept., daily 8–7; Oct.–Mar., daily 8–6:20*), a small collection of Vatican treasures. They range from the massive and beautifully sculptured 15th-century tomb of Pope Sixtus IV by Pollaiuolo, which you can view from above, to a jeweled cross dating from the 6th century and a marble tabernacle by Donatello.

Proceed to the right side of the Basilica's vestibule; from here, you can either take the elevator or climb the long flight of shallow stairs to the roof (☎ *06/6988–3462* ✆ *Elevator €7, stairs €5* ☉ *Apr.–Sept., daily 8–6; Oct.–Mar., daily 8–4; Papal Audience Wed. opens around noon [after audience]; closed during ceremonies in piazza*). From here, you'll see a surreal landscape of vast, sloping terraces, punctuated by domes. The roof affords unusual perspectives both on the dome above and the piazza below. The terrace is equipped with the inevitable souvenir shop and restrooms. A short flight of stairs leads to the entrance of the *tamburo* (drum)—the base of the dome—where, appropriately enough, there's a bust of Michelangelo, the dome's principal designer.

Only if you're of stout heart and strong lungs should you then make the taxing climb from the drum of the dome up to the *lanterna* (lantern) at the dome's very apex. A narrow, seemingly interminable staircase follows the curve of the dome between inner and outer shells, finally releasing you into the cramped space of the lantern balcony for an absolutely gorgeous panorama of Rome and the countryside on a clear day. There's also a nearly complete view of the palaces, courtyards, and gardens of the Vatican. Be aware, however, that it's a tiring, slightly claustrophobic climb. There's one stairway for going up and a different one for coming down, so you can't change your mind halfway and turn back.

The entrance to the **Grotte Vaticane** (*Vatican Grottoes;* ⌨ *Free* ☉ *Weekdays and Sat. 9–4, Sun. 1:30–3:30; Papal Audience Wed. opens around noon [after audience]*) is to the right of the Basilica's main entrance. The crypt, lined with marble-faced chapels and tombs occupying the area of Constantine's basilica, stands over what is believed to be the tomb

12

of St. Peter himself, flanked by two angels and visible through glass. Among the most beautiful tombs leading up to it are that of Borgia pope Calixtus III with its carving of the Risen Christ, and the tomb of Paul II featuring angels carved by Renaissance great Mino da Fiesole. ⊠ *Piazza di San Pietro* ☉ *Apr.–Sept., daily 7–7; Oct.–Mar., daily 7–6; Papal Audience Wed. opens around noon (after audience)* Ⓜ *Ottaviano–San Pietro.*

FAMILY **Castel Sant'Angelo.** Standing between the Tiber and the Vatican, this circular and medieval "castle" has long been one of Rome's most distinctive landmarks. Opera-lovers know it well as the setting for the final scene of Puccini's *Tosca*; at the opera's end, the tempestuous diva throws herself from the rampart on the upper terrace. In fact, the structure began life many centuries before as a mausoleum for the emperor Hadrian. Started in AD 135, it was completed by the emperor's successor, Antoninus Pius, about five years later. It initially consisted of a great square base topped by a marble-clad cylinder on which was planted a ring of cypress trees. Above them towered a gigantic statue of Hadrian. From the mid-6th century the building became a fortress, a place of refuge for popes during wars and sieges. Its name dates from 590, when Pope Gregory the Great, during a procession to plead for the end of a plague, saw an angel standing on the summit of the castle, sheathing his sword. Taking this as a sign that the plague was at an end, the pope built a small chapel at the top, placing a statue next to it to celebrate his vision—thus the name, Castel Sant'Angelo. ⊠ *Lungotevere Castello 50* ☎ *06/681–9111 for central line, 06/689–6003 tickets* ⊕ *www. castelsantangelo.com* ⌨ *€8.50* ☉ *Tues.–Sun. 9–7:30 (ticket office closes 6:30)* Ⓜ *Lepanto.*

Fodor'sChoice **Musei Vaticani** (*Vatican Museums*). Other than the pope and his papal
★ court, the occupants of the Vatican are some of the most famous artworks in the world. The museums that contain them are part of the **Vatican Palace,** residence of the popes since 1377. The palace consists of an estimated 1,400 rooms, chapels, and galleries. The pope and his household occupy only a small part of the palace; most of the rest is given over to the Vatican Library and Museums. Beyond the glories of the Sistine Chapel, the collection is so extraordinarily rich you may just wish to skim the surface, but few will want to miss out on the great

antique sculptures, Raphael Rooms, and the Old Master paintings, such as Leonardo da Vinci's *St. Jerome.*

Among the collections on the way to the chapel, the **Egyptian Museum** (in which Room II reproduces an underground chamber tomb of the Valley of Kings) is well worth a stop. The **Chiaramonti Museum** was organized by the Neoclassical sculptor Canova and contains almost 1,000 copies of classical sculpture. The gems of the Vatican's sculpture collection are in the **Pio-Clementino Museum,** however. Just off the hall in Room X, you can find the *Apoxyomenos (Scraper),* a beautiful 1st-century-AD copy of the famous bronze statue of an athlete. There are other even more famous pieces in the **Octagonal Courtyard,** where Pope Julius II installed the pick of his private collection.

Rivaling the Sistine Chapel for artistic interest—and for the number of visitors—are the recently-restored **Stanze di Raffaello** (Raphael Rooms). Pope Julius II moved into this suite in 1507, four years after his election. Reluctant to continue living in the Borgia apartments downstairs, with their memories of his ill-famed predecessor Alexander VI, he called in Raphael to decorate his new quarters. When people talk about the Italian High Renaissance—thought to be the very pinnacle of Western art—it's probably Raphael's frescoes they're thinking about.

The first "Raphael Room" is the **Hall of Constantine**—actually decorated by Giulio Romano and Raphael's other assistants after the master's untimely death in 1520. The frescoes represent various scenes from the life of Emperor Constantine, including the epic-sized *Battle of the Milvian Bridge.* Guided by three low-flying angels, Constantine charges to victory as his rival Maxentius drowns in the river below.

The **Room of Heliodorus** is a private antechamber. Working on the theme of Divine Providence's miraculous intervention in defense of the faith, Raphael depicted Leo the Great's encounter with Attila; it's on the wall in front of you as you enter.

After the Room of the Signature, the last room is the **Room of the Borgo Fire.** The final room painted in Raphael's lifetime, it was executed mainly by Giulio Romano, who worked from Raphael's drawings for the new pope, Leo X. It was used for the meetings of the Segnatura Gratiae et Iustitiae, the Holy See's highest court. The frescoes depict stories of previous popes called Leo, the best of them showing the great fire in the Borgo.

In the frescoed exhibition halls, the **Vatican Library** displays precious illuminated manuscripts and documents from its vast collections. The **Aldobrandini Marriage Room** contains beautiful ancient frescoes of a Roman nuptial rite, named for their subsequent owner, Cardinal Aldo-brandini. The **Braccio Nuovo** (New Wing) holds an additional collection of ancient Greek and Roman statues, the most famous of which is the *Augustus of Prima Porta.*

Equally celebrated are the works on view in the **Pinacoteca** (Picture Gallery). These often world-famous paintings, almost exclusively of religious subjects, are arranged in chronological order, beginning with works of the 12th and 13th centuries. A fitting finale to your Vatican visit can be found in the **Museo Pio Cristiano** (Museum of Christian

Antiquities), where the most famous piece is the 3rd-century AD statue called the *Good Shepherd,* much reproduced as a devotional image.

To avoid the line into the museums, which can be three hours long in the high season, consider booking your ticket in advance online (⊕ *biglietteriamusei.vatican.va*); there is a €4 surcharge. For those interested in guided visits to the Vatican Museums, tours are €31 to €36, including entrance tickets, and can also be booked online. Other offerings include a regular two-hour guided tour of the Vatican gardens and the semiregular Friday night openings, allowing visitors to the museums until 11 pm; call to confirm. For more information, call ☎ *06/6988–4676* or go to ⊕ *mv.vatican.va.* For information on tours, call ☎ *06/6988–3145* or ☎ *06/6988–4676*; visually impaired visitors can arrange tactile tours by calling *06/6988–4947.* Wheelchairs are available (free) and can be booked in advance by emailing ✑ *accoglienza.musei@ scv.va* or by request at the "Special Permits" desk in the entrance hall.

Note: Ushers at the entrance of St. Peter's and sometimes the Vatican Museums will bar entry to people with bare knees or bare shoulders. ✉ *Viale Vaticano, near intersection with Via Leone IV* ⊕ *www. mv.vatican.va* ✑ *€1 (free last Sun. of month)* ☽ *Mon.–Sat. 9–6 (last entrance at 4), last Sun. of month 9–12:30. Closed Jan. 1 and 6, Feb. 11, Mar. 19, Easter and Easter Monday, May 1, June 29, Aug. 14 and 15, Nov. 1, and Dec. 8, 25, and 26* Ⓜ *Cipro–Musei Vaticani or Ottaviano–San Pietro. Bus No. 64 or 40.*

Piazza di San Pietro. Mostly enclosed within high walls that recall the papacy's stormy history, the Vatican opens the spectacular arms of Bernini's colonnade to embrace the world only at St. Peter's Square, scene of the pope's public appearances. One of Bernini's most spectacular masterpieces, the elliptical Piazza di San Pietro was completed in 1667 after only 11 years' work and holds 400,000 people.

Surrounded by a pair of quadruple colonnades, it is gloriously studded with 140 statues of saints and martyrs. Look for the two disks set into the piazza's pavement on either side of the central obelisk. If you stand on either disk, a trick of perspective makes the colonnades look like a single row of columns.

Officially called Informazioni per Turisti e Pellegrini, the Main Information Office is just left of the basilica as you face it, a couple of doors down from the Braccio di Carlo Magno bookshop. On the south side of the Piazza Pio XII you'll find another Vatican bookshop, which contains the Libreria Benedetto XVI. As for the famous Vatican post offices (known for fast handling of outgoing mail), they can be found on both sides of St. Peter's Square and inside the Vatican Museums complex. You can also buy Vatican stamps and coins at the shop annexed to the information office. Although postage rates are the same at the Vatican as elsewhere in Italy, the stamps are not interchangeable, so any material stamped with Vatican stamps must be placed into a blue or yellow Posta Vaticana box. Public toilets are near the Information Office, under the colonnade, and outside the exit of the crypt. ✉ *West end of Via della Conciliazione* ☎ *06/6988–1662* ☽ *Daily 6:30 am–11 pm (midnight during Christmas)* Ⓜ *Cipro–Musei Vaticani or Ottaviano–San Pietro.*

THE JEWISH GHETTO, TIBER ISLAND, AND TRASTEVERE

Each staunchly resisting the tides of change, these three areas are hard to beat for the authentic atmosphere of Old Rome. You begin in the Ghetto, a warren of twisting, narrow streets, where Rome's Jewish community was once confined, then deported, and now, barely, persists. Ancient bridges, the Ponte Fabricio and Ponte Cestio, link the Ghetto to Tiber Island, the tiny island that is one of Rome's most picturesque sights. On the opposite side of the Tiber lies Trastevere—"across the Tiber"—long cherished as Rome's Greenwich Village and now subject to rampant gentrification. In spite of this, Trastevere remains about the most tightly knit community in the city, the Trasteverini proudly proclaiming their descent from the ancient Romans. This area is Rome's enchanting, medieval heart.

Jewish Ghetto. Rome has had a Jewish community since the 2nd century BC, and from that time until the present its living conditions have varied widely according to its relations with the city's rulers. In 1555 Pope Paul IV Carafa established Rome's Ghetto Ebraico in the neighborhood marked off by the Portico d'Ottavia, the Tiber, and the Piazza dei Cenci. It measured only 200 yards by 250 yards. Jews were obligated to live there by law and the area quickly became Rome's most densely populated and least healthy. The laws were rescinded when Italy was unified in 1870 and the pope lost his political authority, but German troops tragically occupied Rome during World War II and in 1943 wrought havoc here. Today there are a few Judaica shops and kosher groceries, bakeries, and restaurants (especially on Via di Portico d'Ottavia), but the neighborhood mansions are now being renovated and much coveted by rich and stylish expats. The Museo Ebraico arranges tours of the Ghetto. The museum has exhibits detailing the millennial history of Rome's Jewish community.

FAMILY **Piazza Santa Maria in Trastevere.** At the very heart of the Trastevere *rione* (district) lies this beautiful piazza, with its elegant raised fountain and sidewalk café. The showpiece is the 12th-century church of Santa Maria in Trastevere. The striking mosaics on the church's facade—which add light and color to the piazza, particularly when they're spotlighted at night—are believed to represent the Wise and Foolish Virgins. Through innumerable generations, this piazza has seen the comings and goings of tourists and travelers, intellectuals and artists, who lounge on the steps of the fountain or eat lunch at an outdoor table at Sabatini's. At night, it's the center of Trastevere's action, with street festivals, musicians, and gamboling dogs vying for attention from the throngs of people taking the evening air. ⊠ *Via della Lungaretta, Via della Paglia, and Via San Cosimato, Trastevere.*

WHERE TO EAT

Rome has been known since ancient times for its great feasts and banquets, and, though the days of the triclinium and the Saturnalia are long past, dining out is still the Romans' favorite pastime. The city is distinguished more by its good attitude toward eating out than by a multitude of world-class restaurants; simple, traditional cuisine reigns, although things are slowly changing as talented young chefs explore new culinary frontiers. Many of the city's restaurants cater to a clientele of regulars, and atmosphere and attitude are usually friendly and informal. The flip side is that in Rome the customer is not always right—the chef and waiters are in charge, and no one will beg forgiveness if you wanted *skim* milk in that cappuccino. Be flexible and you're sure to *mangiar bene* (eat well). Lunch is served from approximately 12:30 to 2:30 and dinner from 8 until about 11, though some restaurants stay open later, especially in summer, when patrons linger at sidewalk tables to enjoy the parade of people and the *ponentino* (evening breeze).

PANTHEON, NAVONA, TREVI, AND QUIRINALE

$$ WINE BAR Fodor's Choice ★

🍴 **Cul de Sac.** This popular wine bar near Piazza Navona is among the city's oldest enoteche and offers a book-length selection of wines from Italy, France, the Americas, and elsewhere. Food is eclectic, ranging from a huge assortment of Italian meats and cheeses (try the delicious *lonza,* cured pork loin, or *speck,* a northern Italian smoked prosciutto) to various Mediterranean dishes, including delicious *baba ghanoush,* a tasty Greek salad, and a spectacular wild boar pâté. Outside tables get crowded fast, so arrive early, or come late—they serve until about 12:30 am. [$] *Average main: €35* ✉ *Pasquino 73, Piazza Navona* ☎ *06/6880–1094* 🌐 *www.enotecaculdesac.com* ✍ *Reservations not accepted.*

$ PIZZA

🍴 **Da Baffetto.** Down a cobblestone street not far from Piazza Navona, this is one of Rome's most popular pizzerias and a summer favorite for street-side dining. The debate is constant whether or not this spot is massively overrated, but as with all the "great" pizzerias in Rome, it's hard to argue with the line that forms outside here on weekends (the wait can be up to an hour). Happily, outdoor tables—enclosed and heated in winter—provide much-needed additional seating and turnover is fast—and lingering not encouraged. (Baffetto 2, at Piazza del Teatro di Pompeo 18, also offer pasta and secondi, and doesn't suffer from the same overcrowding—plus you can reserve a table, an option not available at the original location.) [$] *Average main: €22* ✉ *Via del Governo Vecchio 114, Navona* ☎ *06/686–1617* 💳 *No credit cards* 🕒 *Closed Tues. and Aug. No lunch weekdays.*

$$$$ MODERN ITALIAN Fodor's Choice ★

🍴 **Il Convivio.** In a tiny, nondescript vicolo north of Piazza Navona, the three Troiani brothers—Angelo in the kitchen, and brothers Giuseppe and Massimo presiding over the dining room and wine cellar—have quietly been redefining the experience of Italian eclectic *alta cucina* (haute cuisine) for many years. Antipasti include a selection of ultra-fresh raw seafood preparations in the mixed *crudi,* while a "carbomare" pasta is a riff on tradition, substituting pancetta with fresh fish roe and house-cured *bottarga* (salted fish roe). Or opt for one of the famed signature dishes, including a fabulous version of a cold-weather pigeon main course prepared four different ways. Service is attentive without being overbearing, and the wine list is exceptional. It is definitely a splurge spot. [$] *Average main: €110* ✉ *Vicolo dei Soldati 31, Navona* ☎ *06/686–9432* ✍ *Reservations essential* 🕒 *Closed Sun. and 2 wks in Aug. No lunch.*

$$$ ITALIAN

🍴 **Obikà.** If you've ever wanted to take in a "mozzarella bar," here's your chance. Mozzarella is featured here much like sushi bars showcase fresh fish—even the decor is modern Japanese minimalism–meets–ancient Roman grandeur. The cheese, in all its varieties, is the focus of the dishes: there's the familiar cow's milk, the delectable water buffalo milk varieties from the Campagnia region, and the sinfully rich *burrata* from Puglia (a fresh cow's milk mozzarella encasing a creamy center of unspun mozzarella curds and fresh cream). They're all served with various accompanying cured meats, vegetables, sauces, and breads. An outdoor deck is a great spot for dining alfresco. Also visit the new, super-central smaller location in Campo de'Fiori (✉ Corner of Via dei Baullari ☎ 06/6880–2366) and the one in posh Parioli (✉ Via Guido d'Arezzo 49 ☎ 06/6853–44184). Indeed, the concept has been such a success that other locations recently opened in cities from Florence and Istanbul to midtown Manhattan and L.A. [$] *Average main: €45* ✉ *Piazza di Firenze 26, Navona* ☎ *06/683–2630* 🌐 *www.obika.it.*

CAMPO DE' FIORI

$ ITALIAN Fodor's Choice ★

🍴 **Filetti di Baccalà.** For years, Dar Filettaro a Santa Barbara (to use its official name) has been serving just that—battered, deep-fried filets of salt cod—and not much else. You'll find no-frills starters such as *bruschette al pomodoro* (garlic-rubbed toast topped with fresh tomatoes and olive oil), sautéed zucchini, and, in winter months, the cod is served alongside *puntarelle,* (chicory stems tossed with a delicious anchovy-garlic-lemon vinaigrette). The location, down the street from Campo de' Fiori in a little piazza in front of the beautiful Santa Barbara church, begs you to eat at one of the outdoor tables, weather permitting. Long operating hours allow those still on U.S. time to eat as early (how gauche!) as 5 pm. [$] *Average main: €18* ✉ *Largo dei Librari 88* ☎ *06/686–4018* 💳 *No credit cards* 🕒 *Closed Sun. and Aug. No lunch.*

TERMINI AND SAN LORENZO

$$$$ MODERN ITALIAN Fodor's Choice ★

🍴 **Agata e Romeo.** For the perfect marriage of fine dining, creative cuisine, and rustic Roman tradition, the husband-and-wife team of Agata Parisella and Romeo Caraccio is the top. Romeo presides over the dining room and delights in the selection of wine-food pairings. And Chef Agata was perhaps the first in the capital to put a gourmet spin on Roman ingredients and preparations, elevating dishes of the common folk to new levels. Staples like *cacio e pepe* (a traditional Roman dish: pasta tossed in pecorino romano cheese and fresh black pepper) are transformed with the addition of even richer Sicilian aged cheese and saffron; "*baccala'* 5 ways" showcases salt cod of the highest quality; and many dishes are the best versions of classics you can get. Prices are steep, but for those who appreciate extremely high-quality ingredients, an incredible wine cellar, and warm service, dining here is a real treat. [$] *Average main: €100* ✉ *Via Carlo Alberto 45, Termini* ☎ *06/446–6115* 🌐 *www.agataeromeo.it* ✍ *Reservations essential* 🕒 *Closed Sun. and 2 wks in Aug. No lunch Sat. and Mon.* [M] *Vittorio Emanuele.*

$$$ SOUTHERN ITALIAN Fodor's Choice ★

🍴 **Tram Tram.** The name refers to its proximity to the tram tracks, but could also describe its size, as it's narrow-narrow and often stuffed to the rafters-rafters (in warmer weather, happily, there's a "side car" of tables enclosed along the sidewalk). The cuisine is derived from cook's hometown region of Puglia. You'll find an emphasis on seafood and vegetables—maybe prawns with saffron-kissed sautéed vegetables—as well as pastas of very particular shapes. Try the homemade *orecchiette*, ear-shaped pasta, made here with clams and broccoli. Meats tend towards the traditional Roman offerings. No matter where you sit, you'll soon understand why Tram Tram is so snugly packed with satisfied Romans. [$] *Average main: €40* ⊠ *Via dei Reti 44/46, San Lorenzo* ☎ *06/490–416* ⊕ *www. ristorantetramtramroma.com* ⌂ *Reservations essential* ☾ *Closed Mon. and 1 wk mid-Aug.*

12

$$$
ITALIAN
Fodor'sChoice
★

✕ **Trattoria Monti.** Not far from Santa Maria Maggiore, Trattoria Monti is one of the most dependable, moderately priced trattorias in the city, featuring the cuisine of Le Marche, an area to the northeast of Rome. There are surprisingly few places specializing in this humble fare considering there are more people hailing from Le Marche in Rome than currently living in that whole region. Served up by the Camerucci family, it's hearty and simple, represented by various roasted meats and game, and a selection of generally vegetarian timbales and soufflés that change seasonally. The region's rabbit dishes are much loved, and here the *timballo di coniglio con patate* (rabbit casserole with potatoes) is no exception. [$] *Average main: €45* ⊠ *Via di San Vito 13a, Monti* ☎ *06/446–6573* ⌂ *Reservations essential* ☾ *Closed Aug., 1 wk at Easter, and 10 days at Christmas* Ⓜ *Vittorio Emanuele.*

VATICAN

$$$$
MODERN ITALIAN

✕ **Taverna Angelica.** The area surrounding St. Peter's Basilica isn't known for culinary excellence, but this is an exception. Its tiny size allows the chef to concentrate on each individual dish, and the menu is creative without being pretentious. Dishes such as warm scampi with artichokes and tomatoes are more about taste than presentation. The breast of duck with honey and rye bread brings hunter's cuisine to a new level, and spaghetti with crunchy pancetta and leeks is what the Brits call "more-ish" (meaning you want *more* of it). Fresh sliced tuna in a pistachio crust with orange sauce is light and delicious. It may be difficult to find, on a section of the street that's set back and almost subterranean, but Taverna Angelica is worth seeking out. [$] *Average main: €55* ⊠ *Piazza A. Capponi 6, Borgo* ☎ *06/687–4514* ⊕ *www.tavernaangelica.it* ⌂ *Reservations essential* ☾ *No lunch Mon.–Sat.* Ⓜ *Ottaviano.*

TRASTEVERE

$$
ROMAN
FAMILY

✕ **Alle Fratte di Trastevere.** Here you can find staple Roman trattoria fare as well as dishes with a southern slant. This means that *spaghetti alla carbonara* (with pancetta, eggs, and cheese) shares the menu with the likes of penne *alla Sorrentina* (with tomato, basil, and fresh mozzarella). For starters, the bruschette here are exemplary, as is the pressed octopus carpaccio on a bed of arugula. As for secondi, you can again look south and to the sea for a mixed seafood pasta or a grilled sea bass with oven-roasted potatoes, or go for the meat with a filet *al pepe verde* (green peppercorns in a brandy cream sauce). Service is always with a smile, as owner Francesco and his trusted staff make you feel at home. [$] *Average main: €35* ✉ *Via delle Fratte di Trastevere 49–50* ☎ *06/583–5775* 🌐 *www.allefratteditrastevere.com* 🕓 *Closed Wed. and 2 wks in Aug.*

$ PIZZA 🍴 **Dar Poeta.** Romans drive across town for great pizza from this neighborhood institution on a small street in Trastevere. Maybe it's the dough—it's made from a secret blend of flours that's reputed to be easier to digest than the competition. They offer both thin-crust pizza and a thick-crust (*alta*) Neapolitan-style pizza with any of the given toppings. For dessert, there's a ridiculously good calzone with Nutella chocolate-hazelnut spread and ricotta cheese, so save some room. Service from the owners and friendly waitstaff is smile-inducing. [$] *Average main: €22* ✉ *Vicolo del Bologna 45, Trastevere* ☎ *06/588–0516* 🌐 *www.darpoeta.com.*

WHERE TO STAY

When planning your Roman holiday, you may be surprised to learn that you really will have to *do* as the Romans do, meaning that unless you're coveting a luxury suite at the Eden, you'll probably find yourself in a tiny room. The air-conditioning may be weak and the customer service will likely be indifferent. Naturally, there are exceptions, but the Eternal City simply doesn't offer the cushy standards that most Americans are accustomed to, though standards in general are improving.

If you're looking for luxury, you're most likely to find it around Via Veneto and the Spanish Steps area. Meanwhile, many of the city's cheapest accommodations are located near Stazione Termini. Regardless of which area you pick, try to stay in the centro storico, which is anything within the ancient Aurelian walls that surround the city's heart.

PANTHEON

$$$ HOTEL Fodor's Choice ★ 🏨 **Albergo Santa Chiara.** If you're looking for a good location (right behind the Pantheon) and top-notch service—not to mention comfortable beds and a quiet stay—look no further. **Pros:** great location in the historical center; staff is polite and helpful; lovely terrace/sitting area in front, overlooking the piazza. **Cons:** the rooms are small and could use some restyling; some rooms don't have a window. [$] *Rooms from: €250* ✉ *Via Santa Chiara 21* ☎ *06/687–2979* 🌐 *www.albergosantachiara.com* 🛏 *96 rooms, 3 suites, 3 apartments* 🍽 *Breakfast.*

$$$$ HOTEL 🏨 **Pantheon.** A superb little hotel right next to the monument itself, the Pantheon has a typically Roman lobby—warm and cozy yet opulent—and equally welcoming staff that exemplifies true Italian hospitality. **Pros:** proximity to the Pantheon; big, clean bathrooms; friendly staff. **Cons:** rooms are in need of some upgrading; the lighting is low and the rooms can feel a bit stuffy. [$] *Rooms from: €320* ✉ *Via dei Pastini 131* ☎ *06/678–7746* 🌐 *www.hotelpantheon.com* 🛏 *12 rooms, 1 suite* 🍽 *Breakfast.*

12

CAMPO DE' FIORI AND GHETTO

$ HOTEL **Arenula.** A hefty bargain by Rome standards, with an almost unbeatable location (in the Ghetto just across the river from Trastevere), the Arenula has an imposingly elegant stone exterior, and simple but comfortable rooms. **Pros:** a real bargain; conveniently located, close to Campo de' Fiori and Trastevere; spotless. **Cons:** totally no-frills accommodations; no elevator; can still be a bit noisy despite the double-glazed windows. [$] *Rooms from: €133* ✉ *Via Santa Maria dei Calderari 47, off Via Arenula, Ghetto* ☎ *06/687–9454* 🌐 *www.hotelarenula.com* 🛏 *50 rooms* 🍴 *Breakfast.*

WORD OF MOUTH

"I've stayed both in the area of the Spanish Steps and also close to Piazza Navona. The latter is more centrally located, and I think better for someone who is coming to Rome for the first time. From my hotel just north of Piazza Navona, I was able to walk quite easily to the Vatican, the Pantheon, Campo de' Fiori, Trastevere, and to the Spanish Steps."
—wanderful

$$$$ HOTEL **Hotel Campo de' Fiori.** Each room in this ivy-draped hotel, perhaps one of Rome's most handsome, is entirely unique in its colors, furnishings, and refined feel, and the views of Roman rooftops from the terrace certainly don't disappoint. **Pros:** modern amenities such as flat-screen LCD TV with satellite, individual a/c, and free Wi-Fi; rooftop terrace; 5% discount if you pay in cash. **Cons:** some of the rooms are very small; the staff isn't as hospitable as most Italians. [$] *Rooms from: €300* ✉ *Via del Biscione 6, Campo de' Fiori* ☎ *06/6880–6865* 🌐 *www.hotelcampodefiori.it* 🛏 *23 rooms* 🍴 *Breakfast.*

VENETO, BORGHESE AND SPAGNA

$$$$ HOTEL Fodor's Choice ★ **Eden.** One of Rome's top luxury lodgings, once a favorite haunt of Hemingway, Ingrid Bergman, and Fellini, this superlative hotel combines dashing elegance, exquisitely lush interiors, and stunning vistas with true Italian hospitality. **Pros:** gorgeous mirrored roof terrace restaurant; you could be rubbing elbows with the stars; 24-hour room service. **Cons:** expensive (unless money is no object); Wi-Fi costs €15 per day; some say the staff can be hit-or-miss. [$] *Rooms from: €440* ✉ *Via Ludovisi 49, Veneto* ☎ *06/478–121* 🌐 *www.lemeridien.com/eden* 🛏 *121 rooms, 13 suites* 🍴 *No meals* [M] *Spagna.*

$$$$ HOTEL Fodor's Choice ★ **The Hassler.** When it comes to million-dollar views, this exclusive hotel atop the Spanish Steps has the best seats in the house, so it's no surprise that generations of fans, many rich and famous (Tom Cruise and Jennifer Lopez included), are willing to pay top dollar to stay here. **Pros:** charming Old World feel; prime location and panoramic views; near some of the best shopping in the world. **Cons:** VIP prices; many think the staff is too standoffish; spa facilities are far from 5-star material. [$] *Rooms from: €780* ✉ *Piazza Trinità dei Monti 6, Spagna* ☎ *06/6993–4755, 800/223–6800 toll-free from the U.S.* 🌐 *www.hotelhasslerroma.com* 🛏 *82 rooms, 14 suites* 🍴 *No meals* [M] *Spagna.*

$$ 🖭 **San Carlo.** Decidedly classical and refined, this renovated 17th-cen-
HOTEL   tury-mansion-turned-hotel with modern comforts at reasonable prices—
right around the corner from the best shopping district in Rome—has
bright and comfortable rooms, some with their own terraces overlook-
ing the city's rooftops. **Pros:** rooms with terraces and views of historic
Rome; rooftop garden; attentive staff. **Cons:** breakfast is basic Italian
fare (great coffee but otherwise just *cornetti* [Italian croissants], cereal,
and yogurt); rooms can be noisy. $ *Rooms from: €195* ✉ *Via delle Car-
rozze 92–93, Spagna* ☎ *06/678–4548* ⊕ *www.hotelsancarloroma.com*
🛏 *50 rooms, 2 suites* ⍾⃝ *Breakfast.*

REPUBBLICA AND SAN LORENZO

$ 🖭 **The Beehive.** Living the American dream in Italy is exactly what one
B&B/INN   Los Angeles couple did in 1999, when they opened the Beehive, a hip,
Fodor's Choice   alternative budget hotel near Termini station where you can go organic
★   in the on-site café, or lounge the afternoon away in the lovely garden
or reading lounge. **Pros:** massage and other therapies offered on site;
organic weekend brunches and dinners on Wednesday and weekends.
Cons: some rooms share bathrooms; in classic rooms, no TV or a/c;
breakfast is not included in the room rate. $ *Rooms from: €80* ✉ *Via
Marghera 8, San Lorenzo* ☎ *06/4470–4553* ⊕ *www.the-beehive.com*
🛏 *8 rooms, 1 dormitory, 3 apartments* ⍾⃝ *No meals.*

$ 🖭 **Italia.** Just a block from bustling Via Nazionale, this friendly, family-
HOTEL   run hotel feels like a classic pensione: low budget with a lot of heart,
inexpensive rooms with big windows, and a generous buffet breakfast.
Pros: free Wi-Fi throughout the hotel; Internet point for guests traveling
without a laptop; great price; individual attention and personal care.
Cons: can be a bit noisy; a/c is an extra €10. $ *Rooms from: €135* ✉ *Via
Venezia 18, Monti* ☎ *06/482–8355* ⊕ *www.hotelitaliaroma.com* 🛏 *35
rooms, 1 apartment* ⍾⃝ *Breakfast* Ⓜ *Repubblica.*

$ 🖭 **Yes Hotel.** This chic hotel may fool you into thinking these digs are
HOTEL   expensive, but the contemporary coolness comes at a budget price,
Fodor's Choice   and its location near Termini Station makes it a great base for sight-
★   seeing. **Pros:** flat-screen TVs with satellite TV; around the corner from
Termini Station; doesn't have the feel of a budget hotel; discount if
you pay cash; great value. **Cons:** rooms are small; charge for Wi-Fi.
$ *Rooms from: €100* ✉ *Via Magenta 15, Termini* ☎ *06/4436–3836*
⊕ *www.yeshotelrome.com* 🛏 *38 rooms, 2 suites* ⍾⃝ *Breakfast* Ⓜ *Ter-
mini, Castro Pretorio.*

VATICAN

$$ 🖭 **Alimandi.** A stone's throw away from the Vatican Museums, this
HOTEL   family-run hotel offering good service and good prices comes with
all sorts of perks: great location, a spiffy lobby, spacious lounges, a
tavern, a roof-top terrace, and roof gardens; and while the hotel is a
bit out of the center, two nearby metro stops help you move about.
Pros: nice family-owned hotel with a friendly staff; a rooftop terrace; a
gym; near reasonably priced restaurants and shops. **Cons:** breakfast is
a good spread but it goes quickly; rooms are small; not close to much
of interest other than the Vatican. $ *Rooms from: €180* ✉ *Via Tunisi 8*
☎ *06/3972–3948* ⊕ *www.alimandi.it* 🛏 *35 rooms* ⍾⃝ *Breakfast.*

$ HOTEL Fodor's Choice ★ **Hotel San Pietrino.** The San Pietrino is one secret we just can't keep to ourselves: a cute, simple hotel on the third floor of a 19th-century palazzo a five-minute walk from the Vatican that continues to offer rock-bottom prices even in tough economic times. **Pros:** heavenly prices near the Vatican; TVs with DVD players; high-speed Internet; close to Rome's famous farmers' market, Mercato Trionfale. **Cons:** a couple of metro stops away from the center of Rome; no breakfast; no bar. [$] *Rooms from: €100* ✉ *Via Giovanni Bettolo 43, Prati* ☎ *06/370–0132* 🌐 *www.sanpietrino.it* 🛏 *12 rooms* 🍴 *No meals.*

TRASTEVERE

$$$ HOTEL Fodor's Choice ★ **Hotel Santa Maria.** A Trastevere treasure with a pedigree going back four centuries, this ivy-covered, mansard-roofed, rosy-brick-red, erstwhile Renaissance-era convent is just steps away from the glorious Santa Maria in Trastevere church and a few blocks from the Tiber. **Pros:** a quaint and pretty oasis in a central location; relaxing courtyard; stocked wine bar. **Cons:** it might be tricky to find; some of the showers drain slowly; finding a cab is not always easy in Trastevere. [$] *Rooms from: €230* ✉ *Vicolo del Piede 2* ☎ *06/589–4626* 🌐 *www.htlsantamaria.com* 🛏 *20 rooms* 🍴 *Breakfast.*

$ HOTEL **Hotel Trastevere.** This tiny hotel captures the villagelike charm of the Trastevere district with its exposed medieval brickwork, a scattering of antiques, and a lively food market on the piazza outside. **Pros:** cheap with a good location; convenient to transportation; free Wi-Fi; friendly staff. **Cons:** no frills; few amenities. [$] *Rooms from: €105* ✉ *Via Luciano Manara 24–25* ☎ *06/581–4713* 🌐 *www.hoteltrastevere.net* 🛏 *18 rooms* 🍴 *Breakfast.*

NIGHTLIFE AND THE ARTS

THE ARTS

Cultural events are publicized well in advance through the city's website (🌐 *www.coopculture.it*). Weekly events listings can be found in the Cronaca and Cultura sections of Italian newspapers, as well in *Metro* (the free newspaper). The most comprehensive listings are in the weekly *roma c'è* booklet, which comes out every Wednesday, or the English-language magazine *Romeing,* which also has a website (🌐 *www.romeing.it*). On the web, also check out 🌐 *www.inromenow.com,* an events site written exclusively for the English-speaking community and updated monthly, as well as the site for *Time Out Roma* (🌐 *www.timeout.com*). Two monthly English-language periodicals (with accompanying websites), *Wanted in Rome* (🌐 *www.wantedinrome.com*) and *The American* (🌐 *www.theamericanmag.com*), available at many newsstands, have good coverage of arts events. Events and concert listings can also be found in both English and Italian at 🌐 *www.musicguide.it.*

NIGHTLIFE

Rome's nightlife is decidedly more happening for locals and insiders who know whose palms to grease and when to go where. The "flavor of the month" factor is at work here, and many places fade into oblivion after their 15 minutes of fame. Smoking has been banned in all public areas in Italy (yes, it actually happened); Roman aversion to clean air has meant a decrease in crowds at bars and clubs. The best sources for an up-to-date list of nightspots are the *roma c'è* and *Time Out Roma* magazines. Trastevere and the area around Piazza Navona are both filled with bars, restaurants, and, after dark, people. In summer, discos and many bars close to beat the heat (although many relocate to the Tiber river and others to the beach, where many Romans spend their summer nights). The city-sponsored Estate Romana (Rome Summer) festival takes over, lighting up hot city nights with open-air concerts, bars, and discos. Pick up the event guide at newsstands.

First and foremost among the bar scene is the wine bar, found (often with outdoor seating) in almost every piazza and on side streets throughout the city. These *enoteche* are mostly small in size, offering a smattering of antipasti to accompany a variety of wines.

SHOPPING

They say when in Rome to do as the Romans do—and the Romans love to shop. Stores are generally open from 9 or 9:30 to 1 and from 3:30 or 4 to 7 or 7:30. There's a tendency for shops in central districts to stay open all day, and hours are becoming more flexible throughout the city. Many places close Sunday, though this is changing, too, especially in the city center. With the exception of food stores, many stores also close Monday morning from September to mid-June and Saturday afternoon from mid-June through August. Stores selling food are usually closed Thursday afternoon.

You can stretch your euros by taking advantage of the "Tax-Free for Tourists" V.A.T. tax refunds, available at most large stores for purchases over €155. Or hit Rome in January and early February or in late July, when stores clean house with the justly famous biannual sales. There are so many hole-in-the-wall boutiques selling top-quality merchandise in Rome's center that even just wandering you're sure to find something that catches your eye.

SHOPPING DISTRICTS

The city's most famous shopping district, **Piazza di Spagna,** is conveniently compact, fanning out at the foot of the Spanish Steps in a galaxy of boutiques selling gorgeous wares with glamorous labels. Here you can ricochet from Gucci to Prada to Valentino to Versace with less effort than it takes to pull out your credit card. If your budget is designed for lower altitudes, you also can find great clothes and accessories at less extravagant prices. But here buying is not necessarily the point—window displays can be works of art, and dreaming may be satisfaction enough. Via Condotti is the neighborhood's central axis, but there are shops on every street in the area bordered by Piazza di Spagna on the east, Via del Corso on the west, between Piazza San Silvestro and Via della Croce, and extending along Via del Babuino to Piazza del Popolo. Shops along **Via Campo Marzio,** and adjoining Piazza San Lorenzo in Lucina, stock eclectic, high-quality clothes and accessories—both big names (Bottega Veneta, Louis Vuitton) and unknowns—at slightly lower prices. Running from Piazza Venezia to Piazza del Popolo lies **Via**

del Corso, a main shopping avenue that has more than a mile of clothing, shoes, leather goods, and home furnishings from classic to cutting-edge, although mostly brand-name stores you can find easily elsewhere. Running west from Piazza Navona, **Via del Governo Vecchio** has numerous women's boutiques and secondhand-clothing stores. **Via Cola di Rienzo,** across the Tiber from Piazza del Popolo, is block after block of boutiques, shoe stores, department stores, and midlevel chain shops, as well as street stalls and upscale food shops. **Via dei Coronari,** across the Tiber from Castel Sant'Angelo, has quirky antiques and home furnishings. **Monti,** the small *rione* next to the Forum, is a favorite shopping area for locals, who are attracted to the neighborhood's well-priced boutiques and artisans. Via Giulia and other surrounding streets are good bets for decorative arts. The **Termini** train station has become a good one-stop place for many shopping needs. Its 60-plus shops are open until 10 pm and include a Nike store, the Body Shop, Sephora, Mango (women's clothes), a UPIM department store, and a grocery store.

FLORENCE

Florence, the city of the lily, gave birth to the Renaissance and changed the way we see the world. For centuries it has captured the imagination of travelers, who have come seeking rooms with views and phenomenal art. Florence's is a subtle beauty—its staid, unprepossessing palaces built in local stone are not showy. They take on a certain magnificence when day breaks and when the sun sets; their muted colors glow in this light. A walk along the Arno offers views that don't quit and haven't much changed in 700 years; navigating Piazza Signoria, almost always packed with tourists and locals alike, requires patience. There's a reason why everyone seems to be here, however. It's the heart of the city, and home to the Uffizi—arguably the world's finest repository of Renaissance art.

Florence was "discovered" in the 1700s by upper-class northerners making the grand tour. It became a mecca for travelers, particularly the Romantics, who were inspired by the elegance of its palazzi and its artistic wealth. Today millions of modern visitors follow in their footsteps. When the sun sets over the Arno and, as Mark Twain described it, "overwhelms Florence with tides of color that make all the sharp lines dim and faint and turn the solid city to a city of dreams," it's hard not to fall under the city's spell.

PLANNING YOUR TIME

With some planning you can see Florence's most famous sights in a couple of days. Start at the city's most awe-inspiring work of architecture, the Duomo, climbing to the top of the dome if you have the stamina. On the same piazza, check out Ghiberti's bronze doors at the Battistero. (They're actually high-quality copies; the Museo dell'Opera del Duomo has the originals.) Set aside the afternoon for the Galleria degli Uffizi, making sure to reserve tickets in advance.

On Day 2, visit Michelangelo's David in the Galleria dell'Accademia— reserve tickets here, too. Linger in the Piazza della Signoria, Florence's central square, where a copy of David stands in the spot the original occupied for centuries, then head east a couple of blocks to Santa Croce, the city's most artistically rich church. Double back and walk across Florence's landmark bridge, the Ponte Vecchio.

Do all that, and you'll have seen some great art, but you've just scratched the surface. If you have more time, put the Bargello, the Museo di San Marco, and the Cappelle Medicee at the top of your list. When you're ready for an art break, stroll through the Boboli Gardens or explore Florence's lively shopping scene, from the food stalls of the Mercato Centrale to the chic boutiques of the Via Tornabuoni.

GETTING HERE

To get into the city center from the airport by car, take the autostrada A11. Tickets for the local bus service into Florence are sold at the airport's second-floor bar—Bus No. 62 runs once an hour directly to the train station at Santa Maria Novella. The airport's bus shelter is beyond the parking lot.

Florence is on the principal Italian train route between most European capitals and Rome, and within Italy it is served frequently from Milan, Venice, and Rome by Intercity (IC) and nonstop Eurostar trains.

Florence is connected to the north and south of Italy by the Autostrada del Sole (A1). It takes about 1½ hours of driving on scenic roads to get to Bologna (although heavy truck traffic over the Apennines often makes for slower going), about 3 hours to Rome, and 3 to 3½ hours to Milan. The Tyrrhenian Coast is an hour west on the A11.

Aeroporto A. Vespucci. Florence's small Aeroporto A. Vespucci, commonly called Peretola, is just outside of town, and receives flights from Milan, Rome, London, and Paris. ✉ *10 km (6 miles) northwest of Florence* ☎ *055/30615* ⊕ *www.aeroporto.firenze.it.*

Aeroporto Galileo Galilei. Pisa's Aeroporto Galileo Galilei is the closest landing point with significant international service, including a few direct flights from New York each week on Delta. Sadly, the flight is seasonal and shuts down when it's cold outside. It's a straight shot down the SS67 to Florence. A train service, which used to connect Pisa's airport station with Santa Maria Novella, has as of press time been temporarily suspended. It's possible to take a bus to the train station at Pisa Centrale, and then go on to Florence Santa Maria Novella. ✉ *12 km (7 miles) south of Pisa and 80 km (50 miles) west of Florence* ☎ *050/849–300* ⊕ *www.pisa-airport.com.*

Stazione Centrale di Santa Maria Novella. Florence's main train station is in the center of town. ☎ *892021* ⊕ *www.trenitalia.com.*

GETTING AROUND

Florence's flat, compact city center is made for walking, but when your feet get weary, you can use the efficient bus system, which includes small electric buses making the rounds in the center. Buses also climb to Piazzale Michelangelo and San Miniato south of the Arno.

Maps and timetables for local bus service are available for a small fee at the ATAF (Azienda Trasporti Area Fiorentina) booth next to the train station, or for free at visitor information offices. Tickets must be bought in advance from tobacco shops, newsstands, automatic ticket machines near main stops, or ATAF booths. The ticket must be canceled in the small validation machine immediately upon boarding.

Taxis usually wait at stands throughout the city (in front of the train station and in Piazza della Repubblica, for example), or you can call for one (☎ *055/4390, 055/4798*). The meter starts at €3.30, with a €5 minimum and extra charges at night, on Sunday, and for radio dispatch.

An automobile in Florence is a major liability. If your itinerary includes parts of Italy where you'll want a car (such as Tuscany), pick the vehicle up on your way out of town.

VISITOR INFORMATION

The Florence tourist office, known as the **APT** (☎ *055/290832* ⊕ *www. comune.firenze.it*), has locations next to the Palazzo Medici-Riccardi, in the main train station, and around the corner from the Basilica di Santa Croce. The offices are generally open from 9 in the morning until 7 in the evening. The multilingual staff will give you directions (but usually not free maps) and the latest on happenings in the city. It's particularly worth a stop if you're interested in finding out about performing-arts events. The APT website is in Italian only.

EXPLORING

THE DUOMO TO THE PONTE VECCHIO

The heart of Florence, stretching from the Piazza del Duomo south to the Arno, is as dense with artistic treasures as any single place in the world. The churches, medieval towers, Renaissance palaces, and world-class museums and galleries contain some of the most outstanding aesthetic achievements of Western history.

Much of the centro storico is closed to automobile traffic, but you still must dodge mopeds, cyclists, and masses of fellow tourists as you walk the narrow streets, especially in the area bounded by the Duomo, Piazza della Signoria, Galleria degli Uffizi, and Ponte Vecchio.

Bargello. This building started out as the headquarters for the Capitano del Popolo (captain of the people) during the Middle Ages, and was later used as a prison. The exterior served as a "most wanted" billboard: effigies of notorious criminals and Medici enemies were painted on its walls. Today it houses the **Museo Nazionale,** home to what is probably the finest collection of Renaissance sculpture in Italy. The concentration of masterworks by Michelangelo (1475–1564), Donatello (circa 1386–1466), and Benvenuto Cellini (1500–71) is remarkable; the works are distributed among an eclectic collection of arms, ceramics, and miniature bronzes, among other things. For Renaissance art lovers, the Bargello is to sculpture what the Uffizi is to painting. ⊠ *Via del Proconsolo 4, Bargello* ☎ *055/294–883* ⊕ *www.polomuseale.firenze.it* ☞ *€4* ⊙ *Daily 8:15–5; closed 2nd and 4th Mon. of month.*

Battistero (*Baptistery*). The octagonal Baptistery is one of the supreme monuments of the Italian Romanesque style and one of Florence's oldest structures. Local legend has it that it was once a Roman temple dedicated to Mars, and modern excavations suggest that its foundations

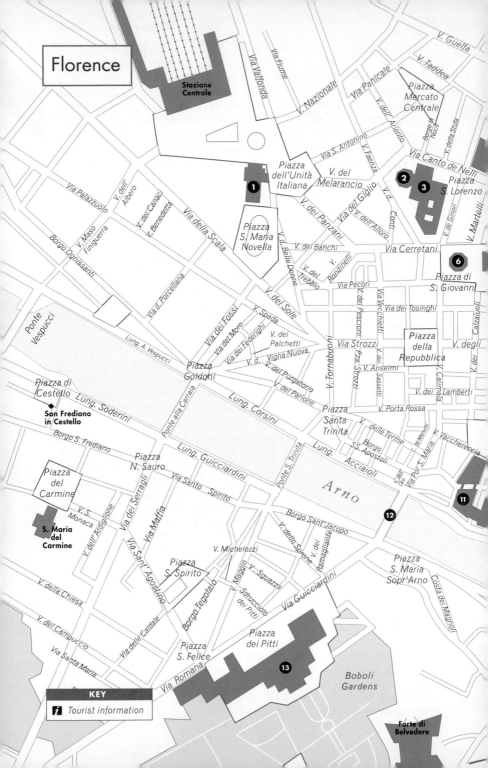

12

V. S. Gallo

Santissima Annunziata

V. Gino Capponi

V. Laura

Piazza SS. Annunziata

V. Colonna

V. Cavour

V. Ricasoli

Palazzo Medici-Riccardi

V. dei Servi

V. degli Alfani

Via de' Pucci

V. del Castellaccio

Via Bufalini

V. Nuova dei Caccini

V. della Pergola

Piazza del Duomo

Borgo Pinti

V. di Mezzo

V. dell'Oriuolo

Via S. Egidio

Via Fiesolana

V. S. Studio

V. Proconsolo

Piazza San Pier Maggiore

Piazza Salvemini

Speziali

V. del

Borgo degli Albizi

V. Matteo Palmieri

V. San Pier Maggiore

V. dell' Ulivo

V. D. Alighieri

V. del Pandolfini

V. dell'Agnolo

V. del Cimatori

V. Ghibellina

V. della Condotta

V. della Vigna Vecchia

Piazza S. Firenze

V. d. Acqua

V. d. Burella

V. Verrazzano

V. Ghibellina

Piazza della Signoria

Via Torta

V. San Cristofano

V. della Pinzochere

Palazzo Vecchio

Borgo dei Greci

Piazza Santa Croce

V. di S. Giuseppe

V. Leoni

V. d. Corno

Via Vinegia

V. d. Pepi

V. d. Magalotti

V. de' Rustici

V. de' Benci

V. Antonio Magliabechi

V. dei Castellani

V. dei Neri

V. d. Pandolfini

Borgo S. Croce

Via d. Vagelli

Via V. Malenchini

Corso Tintori

Lung. Diaz

V. Tripoli

Lung. d. Grazie

Ponte alle Grazie

Lung. Torrigiani

V. dei Bardi

Piazza dei Mozzi

Lung. Serristori

V. dei Renai

Via V. di S. Niccolò

Via S. Miniato

0   1/4 mile

0   400 meters

date from the 1st century AD. The round Romanesque arches on the exterior date from the 11th century, and the interior dome mosaics from the beginning of the mid-13th century are justly renowned, but—glittering beauties though they are—they could never outshine the building's famed bronze Renaissance doors decorated with panels crafted by Lorenzo Ghiberti. These doors—or at least copies of them—on which Ghiberti worked most of his adult life (1403–52) are on the north and east sides of the Baptistery, and the Gothic panels on the south door were designed by Andrea Pisano (circa 1290–1348) in 1330. Ghiberti's original doors were removed to protect them from the effects of pollution and acid rain and have been beautifully restored; they are now on display in the Museo dell'Opera del Duomo. Ghiberti's north doors depict scenes from the life of Christ; his later east doors (dating from 1425–52), facing the Duomo facade, render scenes from the Old Testament. ⊠ *Piazza del Duomo* ☎ *055/230–2885* ⊕ *www.operaduomo. firenze.it* ☜ *€10* ⊙ *Mon.–Sat. 11:15–7; Sun. 8:30–2, 1st Sat. of month 8:30–2.*

Fodor's Choice **Duomo** (*Cattedrale di Santa Maria del Fiore*). In 1296 Arnolfo di Cam-
★ bio (circa 1245–circa 1310) was commissioned to build "the loftiest, most sumptuous edifice human invention could devise" in the Romanesque style on the site of the old church of Santa Reparata. The immense Duomo was not completed until 1436, the year it was consecrated. The imposing facade dates only from the 19th century; its neo-Gothic style somewhat complements Giotto's genuine Gothic 14th-century campanile. The real glory of the Duomo, however, is Filippo Brunelleschi's dome, presiding over the cathedral with a dignity and grace that few domes to this day can match. Brunelleschi's **cupola** was an ingenious engineering feat. The space to be enclosed by the dome was so large and so high above the ground that traditional methods of dome construction—wooden centering and scaffolding—were of no use whatsoever. So Brunelleschi developed entirely new building methods, which he implemented with equipment of his own design (including a novel scaffolding method). Beginning work in 1420, he built not one dome but two, one inside the other, and connected them with common ribbing that stretched across the intervening empty space, thereby considerably lessening the crushing weight of the structure. He also employed a new method of bricklaying, based on an ancient Roman herringbone pattern, interlocking each course of bricks with the course below in a way that made the growing structure self-supporting. The result was one of the great engineering breakthroughs of all time, and today the Duomo has come to symbolize Florence in the same way that the Eiffel Tower symbolizes Paris. The **climb to the top of the dome** (463 steps) is not for the faint of heart, but the view is superb. ⊠ *Piazza del Duomo* ☎ *055/230–2885* ⊕ *www.operaduomo.firenze.it* ☜ *Church free, €10combination ticket including Baptistery, Crypt, Museo, Campanile, cupola* ⊙ *Duomo only: May and Oct., Thurs.–Sat. 10–4:45, Sun. 1:30–4:45; July–Sept., Sat. 10–4:45, Sun. 1:30–4:45; Jan.–Apr. and Nov.–Dec., Thurs. 10–4:30, Sat. 10–4:45, Sun. 1:30–4:45. Crypt Mon.–Wed. and Fri. 10–5, Thurs. 10–4:30, Sat. 10–4:45. Cupola weekdays 8:30–7, Sat. 8:30–5:40.*

Fodor's Choice **Galleria degli Uffizi.** The vener-
★ able Uffizi Gallery occupies two
floors of the U-shaped **Palazzo
degli Uffizi,** designed by Giorgio
Vasari (1511–74) in 1560 to hold
the *uffizi* (administrative offices)
of the Medici grand duke Cosimo
I (1519–74). Later, the Medici
installed their art collections here,
creating what was Europe's first
modern museum, open to the pub-
lic (at first only by request) since 1591.

Among the highlights are Paolo Uccello's *Battle of San Romano,* its
brutal chaos of lances one of the finest visual metaphors for warfare
ever captured in paint (in returned from a glorious restoration in the
summer of 2012); the *Madonna and Child with Two Angels,* by Fra
Filippo Lippi (1406–69), in which the impudent eye contact established
by the angel would have been unthinkable prior to the Renaissance; the
Birth of Venus and *Primavera* by Sandro Botticelli (1445–1510), the
goddess of the former seeming to float on air and the fairy-tale charm
of the latter exhibiting the painter's idiosyncratic genius at its zenith; the
portraits of the Renaissance duke Federico da Montefeltro and his wife
Battista Sforza, by Piero della Francesca (circa 1420–92); the *Madonna
of the Goldfinch* by Raphael (1483–1520), which underwent a stunning
years-long restoration, completed in 2009 (check out the brilliant blues
that decorate the sky, as well as the eye contact between mother and
child, both clearly anticipating the painful future; Michelangelo's *Doni
Tondo*; the *Venus of Urbino* by Titian (circa 1488/90–1576); and the
splendid *Bacchus* by Caravaggio (circa 1571/72–1610).

Late in the afternoon is the least crowded time to visit. For a €4 fee,
advance tickets can be reserved by phone, online, or, once in Florence, at the Uffizi reservation booth (⊠ *Consorzio ITA, Piazza Pitti
1* ☎ *055/294–883)* at least one day in advance of your visit. Keep the
confirmation number and take it with you to the door at the museum
marked "Reservations." ⊠ *Piazzale degli Uffizi 6, Piazza della Signoria* ☎ *055/23885* ⊕ *www.uffizi.firenze.it, www.polomuseale.firenze.it*
for *reservations* ⊠ *€11 during special exhibitions, reservation fee €4*
⊗ *Tues.–Sun. 8:15–6:50.*

Piazza della Signoria. This is by far the most striking square in Florence.
It was here, in 1497, that the famous "bonfire of the vanities" took
place, when the fanatical friar Savonarola induced his followers to hurl
their worldly goods into the flames; it was also here, a year later, that
he was hanged as a heretic and, ironically, burned. A bronze plaque in
the piazza pavement marks the exact spot of his execution.

The statues in the square and in the 14th-century **Loggia dei Lanzi** on
the south side vary in quality. Cellini's famous bronze *Perseus* holding
the severed head of Medusa is certainly the most important sculpture in
the loggia. Other works here include *The Rape of the Sabine* and *Hercules and the Centaur,* both late-16th-century works by Giambologna

(1529–1608), and in the back, a row of sober matrons dating from Roman times.

In the square, the Neptune Fountain, created between 1550 and 1575, takes something of a booby prize. It was created by Bartolomeo Ammannati, who considered it a failure himself. The Florentines call it il Biancone, which may be translated as "the big white man" or "the big white lump."

Ponte Vecchio (*Old Bridge*). This charmingly simple bridge was built in 1345 to replace an earlier bridge swept away by flood. Its shops first housed butchers, then grocers, blacksmiths, and other merchants. But in 1593 the Medici grand duke Ferdinand I (1549–1609), whose private corridor linking the Medici palace (Palazzo Pitti) with the Medici offices (the Uffizi) crossed the bridge atop the shops, decided that all this plebeian commerce under his feet was unseemly. So he threw out the butchers and blacksmiths and installed 41 goldsmiths and eight jewelers. The bridge has been devoted solely to these two trades ever since.

The **Corridoio Vasariano** (⊠ *Piazzale degli Uffizi 6, Piazza della Signoria* ☎ *055/23885, 055/294–883*), the private Medici elevated passageway, was built by Vasari in 1565. Though the ostensible reason for its construction was one of security, it was more likely designed so that the Medici family wouldn't have to walk amid the commoners. The corridor is notoriously fickle with its operating hours; at this writing, it is temporarily open but only to groups. It can sometimes be visited by prior special arrangement. Call for the most up-to-date details.

SAN LORENZO TO THE ACCADEMIA

A sculptor, painter, architect, and even a poet, Florentine native son Michelangelo was a consummate genius, and some of his finest creations remain in his hometown. The Biblioteca Medicea Laurenziana is perhaps his most fanciful work of architecture. A key to understanding Michelangelo's genius can be found in the magnificent Cappelle Medicee, where both his sculptural and architectural prowess can be clearly seen. Planned frescoes were never completed, sadly, for they would have shown in one space the artistic triple threat that he certainly was. The towering yet graceful *David,* his most famous work, resides in the Galleria dell'Accademia.

After visiting San Lorenzo, resist the temptation to explore the market that surrounds the church. You can always come back later, after the churches and museums have closed; the market is open until 7. Note that the Museo di San Marco closes at 1:50 on weekdays.

Cappelle Medicee (*Medici Chapels*). This magnificent complex includes the **Cappella dei Principi,** the Medici chapel and mausoleum that was begun in 1605 and kept marble workers busy for several hundred years, and the **Sagrestia Nuova** (New Sacristy), designed by Michelangelo.

The result was a tour de force of architecture and sculpture. Architecturally, Michelangelo was as original and inventive here as ever, but it is, quite properly, the powerfully sculpted tombs that dominate the room. The scheme is allegorical: on the tomb on the right are figures representing Day and Night, and on the tomb to the left are figures representing

Dawn and Dusk; above them are idealized sculptures of the two men, usually interpreted to represent the active life and the contemplative life. But the allegorical meanings are secondary; what is most important is the intense presence of the sculptural figures and the force with which they hit the viewer. Ticket prices jump to €9 when special exhibitions are on—which is frequently. ✉ *Piazza di Madonna degli Aldobrandini, San Lorenzo* ☎ *055/294–883 for reservations* 🎫 *€6; €9 during special exhibits* ☉ *Daily 8:15–1:50. Closed 1st, 3rd, and 5th Mon. and 2nd and 4th Sun. of month.*

FAMILY **Galleria dell'Accademia** (*Accademia Gallery*). The collection of Florentine paintings, dating from the 13th to the 18th centuries, is largely unremarkable, but the sculptures by Michelangelo are worth the price of admission. The unfinished *Slaves*, fighting their way out of their marble prisons, were meant for the tomb of Michelangelo's overly demanding patron Pope Julius II (1443–1513). But the focal point is the original *David*, moved here from Piazza della Signoria in 1873. *David* was commissioned in 1501 by the Opera del Duomo (Cathedral Works Committee), which gave the 26-year-old sculptor a leftover block of marble that had been ruined forty years earlier by two other sculptors. Michelangelo's success with the block was so dramatic that the city showered him with honors, and the Opera del Duomo voted to build him a house and a studio in which to live and work.

Today *David* is beset not by Goliath but by tourists, and seeing the statue at all—much less really studying it—can be a trial. Save yourself a long wait in line by reserving tickets in advance. A Plexiglas barrier surrounds the sculpture, following a 1991 attack on it by a self-proclaimed hammer-wielding art anarchist who, luckily, inflicted only a few minor nicks on the toes. The statue is not quite what it seems. It is so poised and graceful and alert—so miraculously alive—that it is often considered the definitive sculptural embodiment of High Renaissance perfection.

Music lovers might want to check out the Museo degli Instrumenti Musicali contained within the Accademia; its Stradivarius is the main attraction. ✉ *Via Ricasoli 60, San Marco* ☎ *055/294–883 for reservations, 055/238–8609 for gallery* ⊕ *www.galleriaaccademia.org* 🎫 *€11, reservation fee €4* ☉ *Tues.–Sun. 8:15–6:50.*

Museo di San Marco. A Dominican convent adjacent to the church of San Marco now houses this museum, which contains many stunning works by Fra Angelico (circa 1400–55), the Dominican friar famous for his piety as well as for his painting. When the friars' cells were restructured between 1439 and 1444, he decorated many of them with frescoes meant to spur religious contemplation. His unostentatious and direct paintings exalt the simple beauties of the contemplative life. Fra Angelico's works are everywhere, from the friars' cells to the superb panel paintings on view in the museum. Don't miss the famous *Annunciation,* on the upper floor, and the works in the gallery off the cloister as you enter. Here you can see his beautiful *Last Judgment*; as usual, the tortures of the damned are far more inventive and interesting than the pleasures of the redeemed. ✉ *Piazza San Marco 1* ☎ *055/238–8608*

📖 €4 ⊘ *Weekdays 8:15–1:50, weekends 8:15–6:50. Closed 1st, 3rd, and 5th Sun., and 2nd and 4th Mon. of month.*

San Lorenzo. Filippo Brunelleschi designed this basilica, as well as that of Santo Spirito in the Oltrarno, in the 15th century. He never lived to see either finished. The two interiors are similar in design and effect. San Lorenzo, however, has a grid of dark, inlaid marble lines on the floor, which considerably heightens the dramatic effect. The grid makes the rigorous geometry of the interior immediately visible, and is an illuminating lesson on the laws of perspective. If you stand in the middle of the nave at the church entrance, on the line that stretches to the high altar, every element in the church—the grid, the nave columns, the side aisles, the coffered nave ceiling—seems to march inexorably toward a hypothetical vanishing point beyond the high altar, exactly as in a single-point-perspective painting. Brunelleschi's **Sagrestia Vecchia** (Old Sacristy) has stucco decorations by Donatello; it's at the end of the left transept. ⊠ *Piazza San Lorenzo* ☎ *055/264–5144* 📖 *€4.50* ⊘ *Nov.– Feb., Mon.–Sat. 10–5; Mar.–Oct., Mon.–Sat. 10–5, Sun. 1:30–5.*

SANTA MARIA NOVELLA TO THE ARNO

Piazza Santa Maria Novella, near the train station, suffers a degree of squalor, especially at night. Nevertheless, the streets in and around the piazza have their share of architectural treasures, including some of Florence's most tasteful palaces. Between Santa Maria Novella and the Arno is Via Tornabuoni, Florence's finest shopping street.

Santa Maria Novella. The facade of this church looks distinctly clumsy by later Renaissance standards, and with good reason: it is an architectural hybrid. The lower half was completed mostly in the 14th century; its pointed-arch niches and decorative marble patterns reflect the Gothic style of the day. About 100 years later (around 1456), architect Leon Battista Alberti was called in to complete the job. The marble decoration of his upper story clearly defers to the already existing work below, but the architectural motifs he added evince an entirely different style. Alberti's most important addition—the S-curve scrolls (called volutes) surmounting the decorative circles on either side of the upper story— had no precedent whatsoever in antiquity.

Exploration is essential, however, because the church's store of art treasures is remarkable. Highlights include the 14th-century stained-glass rose window depicting the *Coronation of the Virgin* (above the central entrance); the Cappella Filippo Strozzi (to the right of the altar), containing late-15th-century frescoes and stained glass by Filippino Lippi; the *cappella maggiore* (the area around the high altar), displaying frescoes by Ghirlandaio; and the Cappella Gondi (to the left of the altar), containing Filippo Brunelleschi's famous wood crucifix, carved around 1410 and said to have so stunned the great Donatello when he first saw it that he dropped a basket of eggs.

Of special interest for its great historical importance and beauty is Masaccio's *Trinity,* on the left-hand wall, almost halfway down the nave. Painted around 1426–27 (at the same time he was working on his frescoes in Santa Maria del Carmine), it unequivocally announced the arrival of the Renaissance. ⊠ *Piazza Santa Maria*

Novella 19 ☎ *055/210–113, 055/282–187 for museum* ⊕ *www. museicivicifiorentini.it* 📧 €5 ⊘ *Mon.–Thurs. 9–5:30, Fri. 11–5:30, Sat. 9–5, Sun. 12–5 (1–5 Oct.–June).*

SANTA CROCE

The Santa Croce quarter, on the southeast fringe of the historic center, was built up in the Middle Ages outside the second set of medieval city walls. The centerpiece of the neighborhood was the basilica of Santa Croce, which could hold great numbers of worshippers; the vast piazza could accommodate any overflow and also served as a fairground and, allegedly, since the middle of the 16th century, as a playing field for no-holds-barred soccer games. A center of leatherworking since the Middle Ages, the neighborhood is still packed with leatherworkers and leather shops.

Fodor'sChoice
★ **Santa Croce.** Like the Duomo, this church is Gothic, but, also like the Duomo, its facade dates from the 19th century. As a burial place, the church probably contains more skeletons of Renaissance celebrities than any other in Italy. The tomb of Michelangelo is on the right at the front of the basilica; he is said to have chosen this spot so that the first thing he would see on Judgment Day, when the graves of the dead fly open, would be Brunelleschi's dome through Santa Croce's open doors. The tomb of Galileo Galilei (1564–1642) is on the left wall; he was not granted a Christian burial until 100 years after his death because of his controversial contention that Earth was not the center of the universe. The tomb of Niccolò Machiavelli (1469–1527), the political theoretician whose brutally pragmatic philosophy so influenced the Medicis, is halfway down the nave on the right. The grave of Lorenzo Ghiberti, creator of the Baptistery doors, is halfway down the nave on the left.

The collection of art within the complex is by far the most important of any church in Florence. The most famous works are probably the Giotto frescoes in the two chapels immediately to the right of the high altar. They illustrate scenes from the lives of St. John the Evangelist and St. John the Baptist (in the right-hand chapel) and scenes from the life of St. Francis (in the left-hand chapel). ✉ *Piazza Santa Croce 16* ☎ *055/246–6105* ⊕ *www.santacroceopera.it* 📧 €6 *combined admission to church and museum,* €8.50 *combined ticket with Casa Buonarroti* ⊘ *Mon.–Sat. 9:30–5:30, Sun. 1–5.*

THE OLTRARNO

A walk through the Oltrarno (literally "the other side of the Arno") takes in two very different aspects of Florence: the splendor of the Medici, manifest in the riches of the mammoth Palazzo Pitti and the gracious Giardino di Boboli; and the charm of the Oltrarno, a slightly gentrified but still fiercely proud working-class neighborhood with artisans' and antiques shops.

Farther east across the Arno, a series of ramps and stairs climbs to Piazzale Michelangelo, where the city lies before you in all its glory (skip this trip if it's a hazy day). More stairs (behind La Loggia restaurant) lead to the church of San Miniato al Monte. You can avoid the long walk by taking Bus No. 12 or 13 at the west end of Ponte alle Grazie and getting off at Piazzale Michelangelo; you still have to climb the monumental stairs to and from San Miniato, but you can then take the bus from Piazzale Michelangelo back to the center of town. If you decide to take a bus, remember to buy your ticket before you board.

Palazzo Pitti. This enormous palace is one of Florence's largest architectural set pieces. The original palazzo, built for the Pitti family around 1460, comprised only the main entrance and the three windows on either side. In 1549 the property was sold to the Medici, and Bartolomeo Ammannati was called in to make substantial additions. Although he apparently operated on the principle that more is better, he succeeded only in producing proof that more is just that: more.

Today the palace houses several museums. The **Museo degli Argenti** displays a vast collection of Medici treasures, including exquisite antique vases belonging to Lorenzo the Magnificent. The **Galleria del Costume** showcases fashions from the past 300 years. The **Galleria d'Arte Moderna** holds a collection of 19th- and 20th-century paintings, mostly Tuscan. Most famous of the Pitti galleries is the **Galleria Palatina,** which contains a broad collection of paintings from the 15th to 17th centuries. The rooms of the Galleria Palatina remain much as the Lorena, the rulers who took over after the last Medici died in 1737, left them. Their floor-to-ceiling paintings are considered by some to be Italy's most egregious exercise in conspicuous consumption, aesthetic overkill, and trumpery. Still, the collection possesses high points, including a number of portraits by Titian and an unparalleled collection of paintings by Raphael, notably the double portraits of Angelo Doni and his wife, the sullen Maddalena Strozzi. The price of admission to the Galleria Palatina also allows you to explore the former **Appartamenti Reali,** containing furnishings from a remodeling done in the 19th century. ✉ *Piazza Pitti* ☎ *055/210–323* 🖥 *€9.50 combined ticket for Galleria Palatina and Galleria d'Arte Moderna; €10 combined ticket for Galleria del Costume, Giardino Bardini, Giardino di Boboli, Museo degli Argenti, and Museo Porcelleane* ⊙ *Tues.–Sun. 8:15–6:50.*

WHERE TO EAT

Florence's popularity with tourists means that, unfortunately, there's a higher percentage of mediocre restaurants here than you'll find in most Italian towns. Some restaurant owners cut corners and let standards slip, knowing that a customer today is unlikely to return tomorrow, regardless of the quality of the meal. So, if you're looking to eat well, it pays to do some research, starting with the recommendations here—we promise there's not a tourist trap in the bunch.

Dining hours start at around 1 for lunch and 8 for dinner. Many of Florence's restaurants are small, so reservations are a must. You can sample such specialties as creamy *fegatini* (a chicken-liver spread) and *ribollita* (minestrone thickened with bread and beans and swirled with extra-virgin olive oil) in a bustling, convivial trattoria, where you share long wooden tables set with paper place mats, or in an upscale *ristorante* with linen tablecloths and napkins.

THE DUOMO TO THE PONTE VECCHIO

$$

TUSCAN

✗**Frescobaldi Wine Bar.** The Frescobaldi family has run a vineyard for more than 700 years, and this swanky establishment offers tasty and sumptuous fare to accompany the seriously fine wines. Warm terracotta-color walls with trompe-l'oeil tapestries provide a soothing atmosphere. The menu is typically Tuscan, but turned up a notch or two: the *faraona in umido con l'uva* (stewed guinea fowl with grapes) comes with a side of feather-light mashed potatoes. Save room for dessert, as well as one of the dessert wines. A separate, lovely little wine bar called Frescobaldino has a shorter—but equally good—menu and a delightful, multilingual barman called Primo. $ *Average main: €35* ✉ *Via de' Magazzini 2–4/r, Piazza della Signoria* ☎ *055/284–724* ⊘ *Closed Sun. No lunch Mon.*

SAN LORENZO

$

TUSCAN

Fodor'sChoice

★

✗**Mario.** Florentines flock to this narrow family-run trattoria near San Lorenzo to feast on Tuscan favorites served at simple tables under a wooden ceiling dating from 1536. A distinct cafeteria feel and genuine Florentine hospitality prevail: you'll be seated wherever there's room, which often means with strangers. Yes, there's a bit of extra oil in most dishes, which imparts calories as well as taste, but aren't you on vacation in Italy? Worth the splurge is *riso al ragù* (rice with ground beef and tomatoes). $ *Average main: €20* ✉ *Via Rosina 2/r, corner of Piazza del Mercato Centrale* ☎ *055/218–550* ⚎ *Reservations not accepted* ⊘ *Closed Sun. and Aug. No dinner.*

$$$

TUSCAN

Fodor'sChoice

★

✗**Taverna del Bronzino.** Want to have a sophisticated meal in a 16th-century Renaissance artist's studio? The former studio of Santi di Tito, a student of Bronzino's, has a simple, formal decor, with white tablecloths and place settings. The classic, elegantly presented Tuscan food is superb, and the solid, affordable wine list rounds out the menu—especially because Stefano, the sommelier, really knows his stuff. The service is outstanding. Reservations are advised, especially for eating at the wine cellar's only table. $ *Average main: €45* ✉ *Via delle Ruote 25/r, San Marco* ☎ *055/495–220* ⊘ *Closed Sun. and 3 wks in Aug.*

SANTA MARIA NOVELLA TO THE ARNO

$

TUSCAN

✗**Il Latini.** It may be the noisiest, most crowded trattoria in Florence, but it's also one of the most fun. The genial host, Torello ("little bull") Latini, presides over his four big dining rooms, and somehow it feels as if you're dining in his home. Ample portions of ribollita prepare the palate for the hearty meat dishes that follow. Both Florentines and tourists alike tuck into the *agnello fritto* (fried lamb) with aplomb. There's almost always a wait, even with a reservation. $ *Average main: €15* ✉ *Via dei Palchetti 6/r* ☎ *055/210–916* ⊘ *Closed Mon. and 15 days at Christmas.*

SANTA CROCE

$

DELI

✗**All'Antico Vinaio.** Florentines liked to grab a quick bite to eat at this narrow little sandwich shop near the Uffizi and now, too, does everyone else: word is out, the lines are long, and clog the street. A handful of stools offer places to perch while devouring one of their very fine sandwiches; most folks, however, simply grab a sandwich, pour themselves a glass of inexpensive wine in a paper cup (more serious wines can be poured into glasses), and mingle on the pedestrians-only street in front. If *porchetta* (a very rich, deliciously fatty roasted pork) is on offer, don't miss it. They also offer first-rate primi, which change daily. [$] *Average main: €8* ✉ *Via de' Neri 65* 💳 *No credit cards.*

$ ITALIAN 🍴 **Baldovino.** David and Catherine Gardner, expat Scots, have created this lively, brightly colored restaurant down the street from the church of Santa Croce. From its humble beginnings as a pizzeria, it has evolved into something more. It's a happy thing that pizza is still on the menu, but now it shares billing with sophisticated primi and secondi. The menu changes monthly, and has such treats as *filetto di manzo alla Bernaise* (filet mignon with light béarnaise sauce). Baldovino also serves pasta dishes and grilled meat until the wee hours. [$] *Average main: €12* ✉ *Via San Giuseppe 22/r* ☎ *055/241–773.*

$$ TUSCAN Fodor's Choice ★ 🍴 **Cibrèo.** The food at this upscale trattoria is fantastic, from the creamy crostini *di fegatini* (a savory chicken-liver spread) to the melt-in-your-mouth desserts. Many Florentines hail this as the city's best restaurant, and Fodor's readers tend to agree—though some take issue with the prices and complain of long waits for a table (even with a reservation). If you thought you'd never try tripe—let alone like it—this is the place to lay any doubts to rest: the *trippa in insalata* (cold tripe salad) with parsley and garlic is an epiphany. The food is traditionally Tuscan, impeccably served by a staff that's multilingual—which is a good thing, because there are no written menus. [$] *Average main: €30* ✉ *Via A. del Verrocchio 8/r* ☎ *055/234–1100* ✍ *Reservations essential* 🕒 *Closed Sun. and Mon. and July 25–Sept. 5.*

$ TUSCAN 🍴 **da Rocco.** At one of Florence's biggest markets you can grab lunch to go, or you could cram yourself into one of the booths and pour from the straw-cloaked flask (wine here is *da consumo,* which means they charge you for how much you drink). Food is abundant, Tuscan, and fast; locals pack in. The ample menu changes daily (nine secondi are the norm), and the prices are great. [$] *Average main: €10* ✉ *In Mercato Sant'Ambrogio, Piazza Ghiberti* ✍ *Reservations not accepted* 💳 *No credit cards* 🕒 *Closed Sun. No dinner.*

$$ ITALIAN 🍴 **La Giostra.** This clubby spot, whose name means "carousel" in Italian, was created by the late Prince Dimitri Kunz d'Asburgo Lorena, and is now expertly run by his handsome twin sons. In perfect English they will describe favorite dishes, such as the *taglierini con tartufo bianco,* a decadently rich pasta with white truffles. The constantly changing menu has terrific vegetarian and vegan options, and any meal that does not include truffles is significantly less expensive than those that do. For dessert, this might be the only show in town with a sublime tiramisù *and* a wonderfully gooey Sacher torte. [$] *Average main: €30* ✉ *Borgo Pinti 12/r* ☎ *055/241–341* 🌐 *www.ristorantelagiostra.com* ✍ *Reservations essential* 🕒 *No lunch weekends.*

$ ITALIAN Fodor's Choice ★ 🍴 **Osteria de'Benci.** A few minutes from Santa Croce, this charming osteria serves some of the most eclectic food in Florence. Try the spaghetti *degli eretici* (in tomato sauce with fresh herbs). The grilled meats are justifiably famous; the *carbonata* is a succulent piece of grilled beef served rare. Weekly specials complement what's happening in the market, and all of the food pairs beautifully with their wine list, which is heavy on things Tuscan. When it's warm, you can dine outside with a view of the 13th-century tower belonging to the prestigious Alberti family. $ *Average main: €15 ✉ Via de' Benci 11–13/r ☎ 055/234–4923 ⚲ Reservations essential ⊙ Closed 2 wks in Aug.*

$ ✕**Simon Boccanegra.** Florentine epicures flock to this place named for
ITALIAN   a *condottiere* (mercenary) hero in a Verdi opera. Under high ceilings, candles on every table cast a rosy glow; the fine wine list and superb service make a meal here a true pleasure. The chef has a deft hand with fish dishes, as well as an inventiveness when it comes to reinterpreting such classics as risotto with chicken liver—he adds leek and saffron to give it a lift. A less expensive, less formal wine bar serving a basic Tuscan menu is also on the premises. $ *Average main: €20 ✉ Via Ghibellina 124/r ☎ 055/200–1098 ⚲ Reservations essential ⊙ Closed Sun. No lunch.*

THE OLTRARNO

$ ✕**La Casalinga.** *Casalinga* means "housewife," and this place has the
TUSCAN   nostalgic charm of a 1950s kitchen with Tuscan comfort food to match. If you eat ribollita anywhere in Florence, eat it here—it couldn't be more authentic. Mediocre paintings clutter the semipaneled walls, tables are set close together, and the place is usually jammed. The menu is long, portions are plentiful, and service is prompt and friendly. For dessert, the lemon sorbet perfectly caps off the meal. $ *Average main: €13 ✉ Via Michelozzi 9/r, Santo Spirito ☎ 055/218–624 ⊙ Closed Sun., 1 wk at Christmas, and 3 wks in Aug.*

$ ✕**Osteria Antica Mescita San Niccolò.** It's always crowded, always good,
TUSCAN   and always inexpensive. The osteria is next to the church of San Niccolò, and if you sit in the lower part you'll find yourself in what was once a chapel dating from the 11th century. The subtle but dramatic background is a nice complement to the food, which is simple Tuscan at its best. The *pollo con limone* is tasty pieces of chicken in a lemon-scented broth. In winter, try the *spezzatino di cinghiale con aromi* (wild boar stew with herbs). Reservations are advised. $ *Average main: €7 ✉ Via San Niccolò 60/r, San Niccolò ☎ 055/234–2836 ⊙ Closed Sun. and Aug.*

WHERE TO STAY

No stranger to visitors, Florence is equipped with hotels for all budgets; for instance, you can find both budget and luxury hotels in the centro storico and along the Arno. Florence has so many famous landmarks that it's not hard to find lodging with a panoramic vista. The equivalent of the genteel *pensioni* of yesteryear still exist, though they are now officially classified as hotels. Generally small and intimate, they often have a quaint appeal that usually doesn't preclude modern plumbing.

Florence's importance not only as a tourist city but as a convention center and the site of the Pitti fashion collections guarantees a variety of accommodations. The high demand also means that, except in winter, reservations are a must. If you find yourself in Florence with no reservations, go to **Consorzio ITA** (✉ *Stazione Centrale, Santa Maria Novella* ☎ *055/282893*). You must go there in person to make a booking.

THE DUOMO TO THE ARNO

$$$$ HOTEL Fodor's Choice ★ 🏨 **Hotel Helvetia and Bristol.** From the cozy yet sophisticated lobby with its stone columns to the guest rooms decorated with prints, you might feel as if you're a guest in a sophisticated manor house. **Pros:** central location; superb staff. **Cons:** rooms facing the street get some noise. [$] *Rooms from: €390* ✉ *Via dei Pescioni 2, Piazza della Repubblica* ☎ *055/26651* 🌐 *www.hbf.royaldemeure.com* 🛏 *54 rooms, 13 suites* 🍴 *No meals.*

$$$ B&B/INN Fodor's Choice ★ 🏨 **In Piazza della Signoria.** A cozy feeling permeates these charming rooms, all of which are uniquely decorated and lovingly furnished; some have damask curtains, others fanciful frescoes in the bathroom. **Pros:** marvelous staff; tasty breakfast with a view of Piazza della Signoria. **Cons:** short flight of stairs to reach elevator. [$] *Rooms from: €250* ✉ *Via dei Magazzini 2, near Piazza della Signoria* ☎ *055/239–9546* 🌐 *www.inpiazzadellasignoria.com* 🛏 *10 rooms, 3 apartments* 🍴 *Breakfast.*

SAN LORENZO

$ B&B/INN 🏨 **Residenza Johanna I.** Savvy travelers and those on a budget should look no further, as this residenza is a tremendous value for quality and location. **Pros:** great value. **Cons:** staff goes home at 7; no credit cards. [$] *Rooms from: €93* ✉ *Via Bonifacio Lupi 14, San Marco* ☎ *055/481–896* 🌐 *www.johanna.it* 🛏 *11 rooms* 💳 *No credit cards* 🍴 *No meals.*

SANTA MARIA NOVELLA TO THE ARNO

$$ B&B/INN 🏨 **Alessandra.** An aura of grandeur pervades this clean, ample rooms a block from the Ponte Vecchio. **Pros:** several rooms have views of the Arno; the spacious suite is a bargain. **Cons:** stairs to elevator; some rooms share bath. [$] *Rooms from: €150* ✉ *Borgo Santi Apostoli 17, Santa Maria Novella* ☎ *055/283–438* 🌐 *www.hotelalessandra.com* 🛏 *26 rooms (19 with bath), 1 suite, 1 apartment* ⏲ *Closed Dec. 10–26* 🍴 *Breakfast.*

$$ HOTEL 🏨 **Beacci Tornabuoni.** Florentine pensioni don't get any classier than this: old-fashioned style, enough modern comfort to keep you happy, and a 14th-century palazzo. **Pros:** multilingual staff; flower-filled terrace. **Cons:** hall noise can sometimes be a problem. [$] *Rooms from: €200* ✉ *Via Tornabuoni 3, Santa Maria Novella* ☎ *055/212–645* 🌐 *www.tornabuonihotels.com* 🛏 *37 rooms, 16 suites* 🍴 *Breakfast.*

$$$$ HOTEL Fodor's Choice ★ 🏨 **JK Place.** Hard to spot from the street, these sumptuous appointments provide all the comforts of a luxe home away from home—expect soothing earth tones in the guest rooms, free minibars, crisp linens, and a room service menu with organic dishes. **Pros:** private, intimate feel; stellar staff; free minibar; organic meal choices. **Cons:** breakfast at a shared table (which can be easily gotten around with room service). [$] *Rooms from: €380* ✉ *Piazza Santa Maria Novella 7* ☎ *055/264–5181* 🌐 *www.jkplace.com* 🛏 *14 doubles, 6 suites* 🍴 *Breakfast.*

$$ B&B/INN 🏨 **Torre Guelfa.** If you want a taste of medieval Florence, try one of these character-filled guest rooms—some with canopied beds, some with balconies—housed within a 13th-century tower. **Pros:** rooftop terrace with tremendous views; wonderful staff; some family-friendly triple and

quadruple rooms. **Cons:** 72 steps to get to the terrace. $ *Rooms from: €190* ⊠ *Borgo Santi Apostoli 8, Santa Maria Novella* ☎ *055/239–6338* ⊕ *www.hoteltorreguelfa.com* ⊷ *28 rooms, 3 suites* ⦿ *Breakfast.*

SANTA CROCE

$
B&B/INN
⌂ **Istituto Oblate dell'Assunzione.** Seven nuns run this convent, minutes from the Duomo, with spotlessly clean, simple rooms; some have views of the cupola, and others look out onto a carefully tended garden where you are welcome to relax. **Pros:** bargain price; great location; quiet rooms; garden. **Cons:** curfew; no credit cards. $ *Rooms from: €90* ⊠ *Borgo Pinti 15* ☎ *055/2480582* ⊕ *www.sanctuarybbfirenze.com* ⊷ *28 rooms (22 with bath)* ▤ *No credit cards* ⦿ *No meals.*

$$$
HOTEL
Fodor's Choice
★
⌂ **Monna Lisa.** Though some rooms are small, they are tasteful, and best of all, housed in a 15th-century palazzo that retains some of its wood-coffered ceilings from the 1500s, as well as its original staircase. **Pros:** lavish buffet breakfast; cheerful staff; garden. **Cons:** rooms in annex are less charming than those in palazzo; street noise in some rooms. $ *Rooms from: €259* ⊠ *Borgo Pinti 27* ☎ *055/247–9751* ⊕ *www. monnalisa.it* ⊷ *45 rooms* ⦿ *Breakfast.*

$$
B&B/INN
⌂ **Morandi alla Crocetta.** You're made to feel like privileged friends of the family at this charming and distinguished residence, furnished comfortably in the classic style of a gracious Florentine home . **Pros:** interesting, offbeat location near the sights; terrific staff; great value. **Cons:** two flights of stairs to reach reception and rooms. $ *Rooms from: €150* ⊠ *Via Laura 50, Santissima Annunziata* ☎ *055/234–4747* ⊕ *www. hotelmorandi.it* ⊷ *10 rooms* ⦿ *Breakfast.*

SHOPPING

Window-shopping in Florence is like visiting an enormous contemporary-art gallery. Many of today's greatest Italian artists are fashion designers, and most keep shops in Florence. Discerning shoppers may find bargains in the street markets. ∎ **TIP→ Do not buy any knockoff goods from any of the hawkers plying their fake Prada (or any other high-end designer) on the streets. It's illegal, and fines are astronomical if the police happen to catch you. (You pay the fine, not the vendor.)**

Shops are generally open 9 to 1 and 3:30 to 7:30 and are closed Sunday and Monday mornings most of the year. Summer (June to September) hours are usually 9 to 1 and 4 to 8, and some shops close Saturday afternoon instead of Monday morning.

SHOPPING DISTRICTS

Florence's most fashionable shops are concentrated in the center of town. The fanciest designer shops are mainly on **Via Tornabuoni** and **Via della Vigna Nuova.** The city's largest concentrations of antiques shops are on **Borgo Ognissanti** and the Oltrarno's **Via Maggio.** The **Ponte Vecchio** houses reputable but very expensive jewelry shops, as it has since the 16th century. The area near **Santa Croce** is the heart of the leather merchants' district.

TUSCANY

Midway down the Italian peninsula, Tuscany (Toscana in Italian) is distinguished by rolling hills, snowcapped mountains, dramatic cypress trees, and miles of coastline on the Tyrrhenian Sea—which all adds up to gorgeous views at practically every turn. The beauty of the landscape proves a perfect foil for the region's abundance of superlative art and architecture. It also produces some of Italy's finest wines and olive oils. The combination of unforgettable art, sumptuous views, and eminently drinkable wines that pair beautifully with its simple food makes a trip to Tuscany something beyond special.

Many of Tuscany's cities and towns have retained the same fundamental character over the past 500 years. Civic rivalries that led to bloody battles centuries ago have given way to soccer rivalries. Renaissance pomp lives on in the celebration of local feast days and centuries-old traditions such as the Palio in Siena and the Giostra del Saracino (Joust of the Saracen) in Arezzo. Often, present-day Tuscans look as though they might have served as models for paintings produced hundreds of years ago. In many ways, the Renaissance still lives on in Tuscany.

PLANNING YOUR TIME

Tuscany isn't the place for a jam-packed itinerary. One of the greatest pleasures here is indulging in rustic hedonism, marked by long lunches and show-stopping sunsets. Whether by car, bike, or foot, you'll want to get out into the glorious landscape, but it's smart to keep your plans modest. Set a church or a hill town as your destination, knowing that half the pleasure is in getting there—admiring as you go the stately palaces, the tidy geometry of row upon row of grape vines, the fields vibrant with red poppies, sunflowers, and yellow broom.

You'll need to devise a Siena strategy. The place shouldn't be missed; it's compact enough that you can see the major sights on a day trip, and that's what many people do. Spend the night, and you'll get to see the town breathe a sigh and relax upon the day-trippers' departure. The flip side is, your favorite Tuscan hotel isn't likely to be in Siena.

You face similar issues with Pisa and Lucca in the northwest. Pisa's famous tower is worth seeing, but ultimately Lucca has greater charms, making it a better choice for an overnight.

GETTING HERE AND AROUND

Driving is the only way (other than hiking or biking) to get to many of Tuscany's small towns and vineyards. The cities west of Florence are easily reached by the A11, which leads to Lucca and then to the sea. Florence and Siena are connected by a superstrada and also the panoramic SS222, which threads through Chianti.

The Florence–Siena Superstrada (no number) is a four-lane, divided road with exits onto smaller country roads. The Via Cassia (SR2) winds its way south from Florence to Siena, along the western edge of the Chianti region. The superstrada is more direct, but much less scenic, than the SR2, and it can have a lot of traffic, especially on Sunday evenings. The Strada Chiantigiana (SR222) cuts through the center of Chianti, to the east of the superstrada, in a curvaceous path past vineyards and countryside.

Trains on Italy's main north–south rail line stop in Florence. Another major line connects Florence with Pisa, and the coastal line between Rome and Genoa passes through Pisa as well. There's regular, nearly hourly service from Florence to Lucca, and several trips a day between Florence and Siena. Siena's train station is 2 km (1 mile) north of the centro storico, but cabs and city buses are readily available.

For other parts of Tuscany—Chianti, for example—you are better off going by car. Stations, when they exist, are far from the historic centers (although local buses usually are scheduled to connect passengers from incoming trains with the nearby town), and service is infrequent.

VISITOR INFORMATION
The tourist information office in Greve is an excellent source for general information about the Chianti wine region and its hilltop towns. In Siena the centrally located tourist office, in Piazza del Campo, has information about Siena and its province. Both offices book hotel rooms for a nominal fee. Offices in smaller towns can also be a good place to check if you need last-minute accommodations. Tourist bureaus in larger towns are typically open from 8:30 to 1 and 3:30 to 6 or 7; bureaus in villages are generally open from Easter until early November, but usually remain closed on Saturday afternoon and Sunday.

LUCCA

51 km (31 miles) southwest of Florence.

Ramparts built in the 16th and 17th centuries enclose a charming town filled with churches (99 of them), terra-cotta-roof buildings, and narrow cobblestone streets, along which local ladies maneuver bikes to do their daily shopping. Here Caesar, Pompey, and Crassus agreed to rule Rome as a triumvirate in 56 BC. Lucca was later the first Tuscan town to accept Christianity, and it still has a mind of its own: when most of Tuscany was voting communist as a matter of course, Lucca's citizens rarely followed suit. The famous composer Giacomo Puccini (1858–1924) was born here; his work forms the nucleus of the summer Opera Theater and Music Festival of Lucca. The ramparts circling the center city are the perfect place to take a stroll, ride a bicycle, kick a ball, or just stand and look down upon Lucca.

GETTING HERE
You can reach Lucca easily by train from Florence; the historic center is a short walk from the station. If you're driving, take the A11/E76.

VISITOR INFORMATION
Lucca Tourism Office ✉ *Piazza Santa Maria* ☎ *0583/91991* ⊕ *www. luccaturismo.it.*

EXPLORING
The historic center of Lucca is walled, and motorized traffic is restricted. Walking and biking are the most efficient and most enjoyable ways to get around. You can rent bicycles, and the flat center makes biking

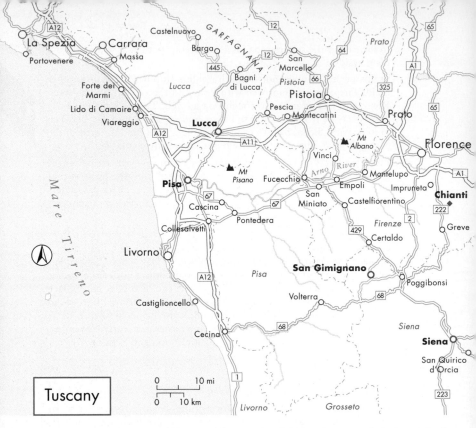

Tuscany

easy. A combination ticket costing €6.50 gains you admission to both the Museo Nazionale di Villa Guinigi and the Pinacoteca Nazionale di Palazzo Mansi.

Duomo. The blind arches on the cathedral's facade are a fine example of the rigorously ordered Pisan Romanesque style, in this case happily enlivened by an extremely varied collection of small, carved columns. Take a closer look at the decoration of the facade and that of the portico below; they make this one of the most entertaining church exteriors in Tuscany. The Gothic interior contains a moving Byzantine crucifix—called the Volto Santo, or Holy Face—brought here, according to legend, in the 8th century (though it probably dates from between the 11th and early 13th centuries). The masterpiece of the Sienese sculptor Jacopo della Quercia (circa 1371–1438) is the marble *Tomb of Ilaria del Carretto* (1407–08). ⊠ *Piazza del Duomo* ☎ *0583/490–530* ⊕ *www. museocattedralelucca.it* ☞ *Church free, tomb €3* ☉ *Duomo: Nov. 3–Mar. 14, weekdays 9:30–4:45, Sat. 9:30–6:45, Sun. 9:30–10:45 and noon–5; Mar. 15–Nov. 2, weekdays 9:30–5:45, Sat. 9–6:45, Sun. 9:30–10:45 and 11:30–6.*

Passeggiata delle Mura. Any time of day when the weather is nice, you can find the citizens of Lucca cycling, jogging, strolling, or kicking a soccer ball in this green, beautiful, and very large park—neither inside nor outside the city but rather right atop and around the ring of ramparts that defines Lucca. Sunlight streams through two rows of tall plane trees to dapple the *passeggiata delle mura* (walk on the walls), which is 4.2 km (2½ miles) in length. Ten bulwarks are topped with lawns, many with picnic tables and some with play equipment for children. Be aware at all times of where the edge is—there are no railings, and the drop to the ground outside the city is a precipitous 40 feet. 🌐 *www.lemuradilucca.it.*

WORD OF MOUTH

"For history and charm the small walled city of Lucca is, I think, absolutely magical. The food in Lucca also eclipses most all of Tuscany too!"

—hanabilly

12

FAMILY **Torre Guinigi.** The tower of the medieval Palazzo Guinigi contains one of the city's most curious sights: a grove of ilex trees has grown at the top of the tower, and their roots have pushed their way into the room below. From the top you have a magnificent view of the city and the surrounding countryside. (Only the tower is open to the public, not the palazzo.) ✉ *Palazzo Guinigi, Via Sant'Andrea* ☎ *0583/583–086* 🌐 *www.lemuradilucca.it* 🎫 *€4* 🕓 *Nov.–Feb., daily 9:30–4:30; Mar. and Oct, daily 9:30–5:30; Apr.–Sept., daily 9:30–7:30.*

WHERE TO EAT

$ TUSCAN Fodor's Choice ★ 🍴 **Buca di Sant'Antonio.** The staying power of Buca di Sant'Antonio—it's been around since 1782—is the result of superlative Tuscan food brought to the table by waitstaff who doesn't miss a beat. The menu includes the simple but blissful, like *tortelli lucchesi al sugo* (meat-stuffed pasta with a tomato-and-meat sauce), and more daring dishes such as roast *capretto* (kid) with herbs. A white-wall interior hung with copper pots and brass musical instruments creates a classy but comfortable dining space. [$] *Average main: €15* ✉ *Via della Cervia 3* ☎ *0583/55881* 🕓 *Closed Mon., 1 wk in Jan., and 1 wk in July. No dinner Sun.*

$ ITALIAN 🍴 **Trattoria da Leo.** A few short turns away from the facade of San Michele, this noisy, informal, traditional trattoria delivers *cucina alla casalinga* (home cooking) in the best sense. Try the typical minestra di farro to start or just go straight to secondi; in addition to the usual roast meats, there's excellent chicken with olives and a good cold dish of boiled meats served with a sauce of parsley and pine nuts. Save some room for a dessert, such as the rich, sweet, fig-and-walnut torte or the lemon sorbet brilliantly dotted with bits of sage, which tastes almost like mint, and is indescribably delicious. So, too, is the chestnut ice cream. [$] *Average main: €9* ✉ *Via Tegrimi 1, at corner of Via degli Asili* ☎ *0583/492–236* 💳 *No credit cards* 🕓 *Closed Sun. Nov.–Mar. No lunch Sun.*

WHERE TO STAY

$ HOTEL 🏨 **Hotel Ilaria.** The former stables of the Villa Bottini have been transformed into a modern hotel with stylish rooms done in a warm wood veneer with blue-and-white fittings. **Pros:** a Fodor's reader sums it up as a "nice, modern small hotel"; free bicycles. **Cons:** though in the city center, it's a little removed from main attractions. $ *Rooms from:* €138 ✉ *Via del Fosso 26* ☎ *0583/47615* ⊕ *www.hotelilaria.com* 💬 *36 rooms, 5 suites* ⍟ *Breakfast.*

$ ⊡ **Piccolo Hotel Puccini.** Steps away from the busy square and church
HOTEL of San Michele, this little hotel is quiet and calm—and a great deal. **Pros:** cheery, English-speaking staff. **Cons:** breakfast costs extra; some rooms are on the dark side. $ *Rooms from:* €80 ✉ *Via di Poggio 9* ☎ *0583/55421* ⊕ *www.hotelpuccini.com* 💬 *14 rooms* ⍟ *No meals.*

PISA

84 km (52 miles) west of Florence.

When you think Pisa, you think Leaning Tower. Its position as one of Italy's most famous landmarks is a heavy reputation to bear, and it comes accompanied by abundant crowds and kitschy souvenirs. But the building *is* interesting and novel, and even if it doesn't captivate you, Pisa has other treasures that make a visit worthwhile. Taken as a whole, the Campo dei Miracoli (Field of Miracles), where the Leaning Tower, Duomo, and Baptistery are located, is among the most dramatic architectural complexes in Italy.

GETTING HERE

Pisa is an easy hour train ride from Florence. By car it's a straight shot on the Fi-Pi-Li autostrada. The Pisa–Lucca train runs frequently and takes about 30 minutes.

VISITOR INFORMATION

Pisa Tourism Office ✉ *Piazza Vittorio Emanuele II* ☎ *050/42291* ⊕ *www. pisaunicaterre.it.*

EXPLORING

Like many other Italian cities, Pisa is best seen on foot. The views along the Arno are particularly grand and shouldn't be missed—there's a sense of spaciousness here that the Arno in Florence lacks. You should weigh the different options for combination tickets to sights on the Piazza del Duomo when you begin your visit. Combination tickets are sold at the ticket office behind the Duomo opposite the Leaning Tower; one monument costs €5, two monuments €7, up to €9 for all the main sights, excluding the Leaning Tower.

Battistero. This lovely Gothic baptistery, which stands across from the Duomo's facade, is best known for the pulpit carved by Nicola Pisano (circa 1220–84; father of Giovanni Pisano) in 1260. Every half hour, an employee will dramatically close the doors, then intone and chant, thereby demonstrating how remarkable the acoustics are in the place. ✉ *Piazza del Duomo* ☎ *050/835–011* ⊕ *www.opapisa.it* 💲 *€5, discounts available if bought in combination with tickets for other monuments* ⊘ *Nov.–Feb., daily 10–5; Mar., daily 9–6; Apr.–Sept., daily 8–8; Oct., daily 9–7.*

Duomo. Pisa's cathedral brilliantly utilizes the horizontal marble-stripe motif (borrowed from Moorish architecture) that became common to Tuscan cathedrals. It is famous for the Romanesque panels on the transept door facing the tower that depict scenes from the life of Christ. The beautifully carved 14th-century pulpit is by Giovanni Pisano (son of Nicola). ⊠ *Piazza del Duomo* 🕾 *050/835–011* ⊕ *www.opapisa.it* 🖃 *€5* ⊙ *Nov.–Feb., daily 10–12:45 and 2–5; Mar., daily 10–6; Apr.–Sept., daily 10–8; Oct., daily 10–7.*

Fodor'sChoice **Leaning Tower (Torre Pendente).** Legend holds that Galileo conducted an
★ experiment on the nature of gravity by dropping metal balls from the top of the 187-foot-high Leaning Tower of Pisa. Historians, however, say this legend has no basis in fact—which isn't quite to say that it's false. Work on this tower, built as a campanile for the Duomo, started in 1173: the lopsided settling began when construction reached the third story. The tower's architects attempted to compensate through such methods as making the remaining floors slightly taller on the leaning side, but the extra weight only made the problem worse. The settling continued, and by the late 20th century it had accelerated to such a point that many feared the tower would simply topple over, despite all efforts to prop it up. The structure has since been firmly anchored to the earth. The final phase to restore the tower to its original tilt of 300 years ago was launched in early 2000 and finished two years later. Reservations, which are essential, can be made online or by calling the Museo dell'Opera del Duomo; it's also possible to arrive at the ticket office and book for the same day. Note that children under eight years of age are not allowed to climb. ⊠ *Piazza del Duomo* 🕾 *050/835–011* ⊕ *www. opapisa.it* 🖃 *€18* ⊙ *Dec. and Jan., daily 10–5; Nov. and Feb., daily 9:40–5:40; Mar., daily 9–6; Apr.–Sept., daily 8:30–8; Oct., daily 9–7.*

12

WHERE TO EAT

$ ✕ **Osteria dei Cavalieri.** This charming white-wall restaurant, a few steps
ITALIAN from Piazza dei Cavalieri, is reason enough to come to Pisa. They can do it all here—serve up exquisitely grilled fish dishes, please vegetarians, and prepare *tagliata* (thin slivers of rare beef) for meat lovers. Three set menus, from the sea, garden, and earth, are available, or you can order à la carte. For dinner there's an early seating (around 7:30) and a later one (around 9); opt for the later one if you want time to linger over your meal. $ *Average main: €14* ⊠ *Via San Frediano 16* 🕾 *050/580–858* ⚭ *Reservations essential* ⊙ *Closed Sun., 2 wks in Aug., and Dec. 29–Jan. 7. No lunch Sat.*

WHERE TO STAY

$ 🎞 **Royal Victoria.** In a pleasant palazzo facing the Arno, a 10-minute
HOTEL walk from the Campo dei Miracoli, room styles range from the 1800s, complete with frescoes, to the 1920s; the most charming are in the old tower. **Pros:** friendly staff; lovely views of the Arno from many rooms. **Cons:** rooms vary significantly in size; all are a little worn. $ *Rooms from: €78* ⊠ *Lungarno Pacinotti 12* 🕾 *050/940–111* ⊕ *www. royalvictoria.it* ↴ *48 rooms (40 with bath)* ⦿ *Breakfast.*

CHIANTI

76 km (47 miles) south of Florence.

Chianti, directly south of Florence, is one of Italy's most famous wine-producing areas; its hill towns, olive groves, and vineyards are quintessential Tuscany. Many British and northern Europeans have relocated here, drawn by the unhurried life, balmy climate, and charming villages; there are so many Britons, in fact, that the area has been nicknamed Chiantishire. Still, it remains strongly Tuscan in character, with drop-dead views of vine-quilted hills and elegantly elongated cypress trees.

The sinuous SS222 highway, known as the Strada Chiantigiana, runs from Florence through the heart of Chianti. Its most scenic section connects Strada in Chianti, 16 km (10 miles) south of Florence, and **Greve in Chianti.** If there's an unofficial capital of Chianti, it's Greve, a friendly market town with no shortage of cafés, *enoteche* (wine bars), and craft shops lining its main square. The gently sloping, asymmetrical Piazza Matteotti is an attractive arcade whose center holds a statue of the discoverer of New York harbor, Giovanni da Verrazano (circa 1480–1527). Check out the lively market held here on Saturday morning.

South of Greve on the SR222, **Radda in Chianti** sits on a hill separating two valleys, Val di Pesa and Val d'Arbia. It's one of many tiny Chianti villages that invite you to stroll their steep streets; follow the signs pointing you toward the *camminamento,* a covered medieval passageway circling part of the city inside the walls.

EXPLORING

Fodor's Choice ★ **Castello di Brolio.** If you have time for only one castle in Tuscany, this is it. At the end of the 12th century, when Florence conquered southern Chianti, Brolio became Florence's southernmost outpost, and it was often said, "When Brolio growls, all Siena trembles." Brolio was built about AD 1000 and owned by the monks of the Badia Fiorentina; the "new" owners, the Ricasoli family, have been in possession since 1141. Bettino Ricasoli (1809–80), the so-called Iron Baron, was one of the founders of modern Italy, and is said to have invented the original formula for Chianti wine. Brolio, one of Chianti's best-known labels, is still justifiably famous. Its cellars may be toured by appointment. The grounds are worth visiting, even though the 19th-century manor house is not open to the public. A small museum, where the Ricasoli Collection is housed in a 12th-century tower, displays objects that relate the long history of the family and the origins of Chianti wine. There are two apartments here available for rent by the week. ✉ *Località Brolio, 2 km (1 mile) southeast of Gaiole, Gaiole in Chianti* ☎ *0577/730–280* 🌐 *www.ricasoli.it* 🎟 *€5 gardens, €8 gardens and museum, €10 guided tours* 🕒 *Apr.–Oct., daily 10–7 (ticket sales until 6).*

WHERE TO EAT

$ TUSCAN 🍴 **Enoteca Fuoripiazza.** Detour off Greve's flower-strewn main square for food that relies heavily on local ingredients (like cheese and salami produced nearby). The lengthy wine list provides a bewildering array of choices to pair with *affettati misti* (a plate of cured meats) or one of their primi—the *pici* (a thick, short noodle) is deftly prepared here. All the dishes are made with great care. [$] *Average main: €12* ✉ *Via I Maggio, Greve in Chianti* ☎ *055/854–6313* 🕒 *Closed Mon.*

$$ ITALIAN 🍴 **Osteria di Passignano.** In an ancient wine cellar owned by the Antinori family—who also happen to own much of what you see in these

parts—is a sophisticated restaurant ably run by chef Marcello Crini and his attentive staff. The menu changes seasonally; traditional Tuscan cuisine is given a delightful twist through the use of unexpected herbs. When porcini mushrooms are in season, a particularly tantalizing treat is the *filetto di vitello in panura di funghi secchi e noci al sedano rapa e porcini* (veal sirloin in a crust of dried mushrooms, walnuts, celeriac, and fresh porcini). The extensive wine list includes local vintages as well as numerous international labels. Day-long cooking courses are also available. [$] *Average main: €35* ✉ *Via Passignano 33, Passignano* ☎ *055/807–1278* 🌐 *www.osteriadipassignano.com* 🕒 *Closed Sun., 3 wks in Jan., and 1 wk in Aug.*

$ TUSCAN Fodor's Choice ★ 🍴 **Osteria Le Panzanelle.** Silvia Bonechi's experience in the kitchen—with the help of a few precious recipes handed down from her grandmother—is one of the reasons for the success of this small restaurant. The other is the front-room hospitality of Nada Michelassi. These two *panzanelle* (women from Panzano) serve a short menu of tasty and authentic dishes at what the locals refer to as *il prezzo giusto* (the right price). Both the *pappa al pomodoro* (tomato soup) and the *peposo* (peppery beef stew) are exceptional. Whether you are eating inside or under large umbrellas on the terrace near a tiny stream, the experience is always congenial. "The best food we had in Tuscany," writes one user of fodors.com. Reservations are essential in July and August. [$] *Average main: €15* ✉ *Località Lucarelli 29, 8 km (5 miles) northwest of Radda on the road to Panzano, Radda in Chianti* ☎ *0577/733–511* 🌐 *www.osteria.lepanzanelle.it* 🕒 *Closed Mon. and Jan. and Feb.*

WHERE TO STAY

$ B&B/INN 🏨 **La Bottega di Giovannino.** This is a fantastic place for the budget-conscious traveler, as rooms are immaculate and most have a stunning view of the surrounding hills. **Pros:** great location in the center of town; close to restaurants and shops; super value. **Cons:** some rooms are small; some bathrooms are down the hall; basic decor. [$] *Rooms from: €70* ✉ *Via Roma 6–8, Radda in Chianti* ☎ *0577/738–056* 🌐 *www.labottegadigiovannino.it* 🛏 *9 rooms, 1 apartment* 🍽 *No meals.*

$$ B&B/INN 🏨 **Relais Fattoria Vignale.** A refined and comfortable country house offers numerous sitting rooms with terra-cotta floors and attractive stonework and wood-beamed guest rooms filled with simple wooden furnishings and handwoven rugs. **Pros:** intimate public spaces; excellent restaurant; helpful and friendly staff; nice grounds and pool. **Cons:** north-facing rooms blocked by tall cypress trees; single rooms are small; annex across a busy road. [$] *Rooms from: €185* ✉ *Via Pianigiani 9, Radda in Chianti* ☎ *0577/738–300 for hotel, 0577/738–094 for restaurant* 🌐 *www.vignale.it* 🛏 *42 rooms, 5 suites* 🕒 *Closed Nov.–Mar. 15* 🍽 *Breakfast.*

SAN GIMIGNANO

57 km (35 miles) southwest of Florence.

GETTING HERE

You can reach San Gimignano by car from the Florence–Siena Superstrada. Exit at Poggibonsi Nord and follow signs for San Gimignano. Although it involves changing buses in Poggibonsi, getting to San

Gimignano by bus is a relatively straightforward affair. SITA operates the service between Siena or Florence and Poggibonsi, while Tra-In takes care of the Poggibonsi to San Gimignano route. You cannot reach San Gimignano by train.

VISITOR INFORMATION

San Gimignano Tourism Office ✉ *Piazza Duomo 1* ☎ *0577/940–008* 🌐 *www.sangimignano.com.*

EXPLORING

When you're on a hilltop surrounded by soaring medieval towers silhouetted against the sky, it's difficult not to fall under the spell of San Gimignano—despite the serious tour-bus crowds. Its tall walls and narrow streets are typical of Tuscan hill towns, but it's the medieval "skyscrapers" that set the town apart from its neighbors. Today 14 towers remain, but at the height of the Guelph–Ghibelline conflict there was a forest of more than 70, and it was possible to cross the town by rooftop rather than by road. The towers were built partly for defensive purposes—they were a safe refuge and useful for pouring boiling oil on attacking enemies—and partly for bolstering the egos of their owners, who competed with deadly seriousness to build the highest tower in town.

Today San Gimignano isn't much more than a gentrified walled city. If you can, stay overnight; tour groups tend to arrive early and clog the wine-tasting rooms—San Gimignano is famous for its light white Vernaccia—and art galleries for much of the day. But most sights stay open through late afternoon, when most have departed, and in the evening, it's still possible to experience the village in relative tranquility.

WHERE TO EAT

$ TUSCAN 🍴 **La Mangiatoia.** Multicolor gingham tablecloths provide an interesting juxtaposition with rib-vaulted ceilings dating from the 13th century. The lighthearted touch might be explained by the influence of chef Susi Cuomo, who has been presiding over the kitchen for more than 20 years. The menu is seasonal—in autumn, don't miss her *tonnarelli cacio e pepe* (thick spaghetti with cheese and pepper). In summer, eat lighter fare on the intimate, flower-bedecked terrace in the back. [$] *Average main: €18* ✉ *Via Mainardi 5* ☎ *0577/941–528* 🌐 *www.ristorantelamangiatoia.it* 🕒 *Closed Tues., 3 wks in Nov., and 1 wk in Jan.*

WHERE TO STAY

$ B&B/INN 🏨 **Pescille.** A rambling farmhouse has been transformed into a handsome hotel with understated contemporary furniture in the bedrooms and country-classic motifs such as farm implements hanging on the walls in the bar. **Pros:** splendid views; quiet atmosphere; 10-minute walk to town. **Cons:** furnishings a bit austere; there's an elevator for luggage but not for guests. [$] *Rooms from: €95* ✉ *Località Pescille, 4 km (2½ miles) south of San Gimignano* ☎ *0577/940–186* 🌐 *www.pescille.it* 🛏 *38 rooms, 12 suites* 🕒 *Closed Nov.–Mar.* 🍽 *Breakfast.*

SIENA

51 km (32 miles) south of Florence.

With its narrow streets and steep alleys, a stunning Gothic Duomo, a bounty of early Renaissance art, and the glorious Palazzo Pubblico overlooking its magnificent Campo, Siena is often described as Italy's best-preserved medieval city. Victory over Florence in 1260 at Montaperti marked the beginning of Siena's golden age. During the following decades Siena erected its greatest buildings (including the Duomo); established a model city government presided over by the Council of Nine; and became a great art, textile, and trade center. Siena succumbed to Florentine rule in the mid-16th century, when a yearlong siege virtually eliminated the native population. Ironically, it was precisely this decline that, along with the steadfast pride of the Sienese, prevented further development, to which we owe the city's marvelous medieval condition today.

GETTING HERE

From Florence, the quickest way to Siena is via the Florence–Siena Superstrada. Otherwise, take the Via Cassia (SR2), for a scenic route. Coming from Rome, leave the A1 at Valdichiana, and follow the Siena–Bettole Superstrada. SITA provides excellent bus service between Florence and Siena. Because buses are direct and speedy, they are preferable over the train, which sometimes involves a change in Empoli.

VISITOR INFORMATION

Siena Tourism Office ⊠ *Piazza del Campo 56* ☎ *0577/28–0551* ⊕ *www. terresiena.it.*

EXPLORING

If you come by car, you're better off leaving it in one of the parking lots around the perimeter of town. Driving is difficult or impossible in most parts of the city center. Practically unchanged since medieval times, Siena is laid out in a "Y" over the slopes of several hills, dividing the city into *terzi* (thirds). Although the most interesting sites are in a fairly compact area around the Campo at the center of town in the neighborhoods of Città, Camollìa, and San Martino, be sure to leave some time to wander into the narrow streets that rise and fall steeply from the main thoroughfares, giving yourself at least two days to really explore the town. At the top on the list of things to see is the Piazza del Campo, considered by many to be the finest public square in Italy. The Palazzo Pubblico sits at the lower end of the square and is well worth a visit. The Duomo is a must-see, as is the nearby Cripta.

Fodor's Choice ★ **Cripta.** After it had lain unseen for possibly 700 years, a crypt was rediscovered under the grand *pavimento* (floor) of the Duomo during routine excavation work and was opened to the public in 2003. An unknown master executed the breathtaking frescoes here sometime between 1270 and 1280; they retain their original colors and pack an emotional punch even with sporadic damage. The *Deposition/Lamentation* gives strong evidence that the Sienese school could paint emotion just as well as the Florentine school—and did it some 20 years before Giotto. Guided tours in English take place more or less every half hour and are limited to no more than 35 persons. ✉ *Piazza del Duomo, entrance on the right side of the cathedral, Città* ☎ *0577/286–300* ⊕ *www.operaduomo.siena.it* 💻 *€6; €12 combined ticket includes the Duomo, Battistero, and Museo dell'Opera Metropolitana* ☾ *Mar.–Oct., daily 10:30–7; Nov.–Feb., daily 10:30–5:30.*

Fodor's Choice ★   **Duomo.** Siena's cathedral is beyond question one of the finest Gothic churches in Italy. The multicolored marbles and painted decoration are typical of the Italian approach to Gothic architecture—lighter and much less austere than the French. The amazingly detailed facade has few rivals in the region. It was completed in two brief phases at the end of the 13th and 14th centuries. The statues and decorative work were designed by Nicola Pisano and his son Giovanni, although most of what we see today are copies, the originals having been removed to the nearby Museo dell'Opera Metropolitana. The gold mosaics are 18th-century restorations. The campanile (no entry) is among central Italy's finest, the number of windows increasing with each level, a beautiful and ingenious way of reducing the weight of the structure as it climbs to the heavens.

The Duomo is most famous for its unique and magnificent inlaid-marble floors, which took almost 200 years to complete; more than 40 artists contributed to the work, made up of 56 separate compositions depicting biblical scenes, allegories, religious symbols, and civic emblems. The floors are covered for most of the year for conservation purposes, but are unveiled during September and October. In striking contrast to all the Gothic decoration in the nave are the magnificent Renaissance frescoes in the **Biblioteca Piccolomini,** off the left aisle. Painted by Pinturicchio (circa 1454–1513) and completed in 1509, they are in excellent condition, and have a freshness rarely seen in work so old.

✉ *Piazza del Duomo, Città* ☎ *0577/286–300* 💻 *€4 Nov.–Aug., €7 Sept. and Oct.; €12 combined ticket includes the Cripta, Battistero, and Museo dell'Opera Metropolitana* ☾ *Mar.–Oct., Mon.–Sat. 10:30–7, Sun. 1:30–6; Nov.–Feb., Mon.–Sat. 10:30–5:30, Sun. 1:30–5:30.*

Palazzo Pubblico. The Gothic Palazzo Pubblico, the focal point of the Piazza del Campo, has served as Siena's town hall since the 1300s. It now also contains the Museo Civico, with walls covered in early Renaissance frescoes. The nine governors of Siena once met in the Sala della Pace, famous for Ambrogio Lorenzetti's frescoes called Allegories of Good and Bad Government, painted in the late 1330s to demonstrate the dangers of tyranny. The good-government side depicts utopia, showing first the virtuous ruling council surrounded by angels and then scenes of a perfectly running city and countryside. Conversely, the bad government fresco tells a tale straight out of Dante. The evil ruler and his advisers have horns and fondle strange animals, and the town scene depicts the seven mortal sins in action. Interestingly, the bad government fresco is severely damaged, and the good government fresco is in terrific condition. The **Torre del Mangia,** the palazzo's famous bell tower, is named after one of its first bell ringers, Giovanni di Duccio (called Mangiaguadagni, or earnings eater). The climb up to the top is long and steep, but the view makes it worth every step. ✉ *Piazza del Campo 1, Città* ☎ *0577/292232* 🎫 *Museum €8, tower €8, combined ticket €13* 🕒 *Museum: Nov.–Mar. 15, daily 10–6; Mar. 16–Oct., daily 10–7. Tower: Nov.–Mar. 15, daily 10–4; Mar. 16–Oct., daily 10–7.*

12

Fodor's Choice ★ **Piazza del Campo.** The fan-shaped Piazza del Campo, known simply as il Campo (The Field), is one of the finest squares in Italy. Constructed toward the end of the 12th century on a market area unclaimed by any contrada, it's still the heart of town. The bricks of the Campo are patterned in nine different sections—representing each member of the medieval Government of Nine. At the top of the Campo is a copy of the early 15th-century **Fonte Gaia** by Siena's greatest sculptor, Jacopo della Quercia. The 13 sculpted reliefs of biblical events and virtues that line the fountain are 19th-century copies; the originals are in the museum of the Spedale di Santa Maria della Scala. On Palio horse-race days (July 2 and August 16), the Campo and all its surrounding buildings are packed with cheering, frenzied locals and tourists craning their necks to take it all in. ✉ *Piazza del Campo, Città.*

WHERE TO EAT

$$ TUSCAN Fodor's Choice ★

🍴 **Le Logge.** Bright flowers provide a dash of color at this classic Tuscan dining room, and stenciled designs on the ceilings add some whimsy. The wooden cupboards (now filled with wine bottles) lining the walls recall its past as a turn-of-the-19th-century grocery store. The menu, with four or five primi and secondi, changes regularly, but almost always includes their classic *malfatti all'osteria* (ricotta and spinach dumplings in a cream sauce). Desserts such as *coni con mousse al cioccolato e gelato allo zafferano* (two diminutive ice-cream cones with chocolate mousse and saffron ice cream) provide an inventive ending to the meal. When not vying for one of the outdoor tables, make sure to ask for one in the main downstairs room. [$] *Average main: €25* ✉ *Via del Porrione 33, San Martino* ☎ *0577/48013* 🌐 *www.osterialelogge.it* ✍ *Reservations essential* 🕒 *Closed Sun. and 3 wks in Jan.*

WHERE TO STAY

$$ HOTEL Fodor's Choice ★

🏨 **Palazzo Ravizza.** This romantic palazzo exudes a sense of genteel shabbiness, and lovely guest rooms have high ceilings, antique furnishings, and bathrooms decorated with hand-painted tiles. **Pros:** 10-minute walk to the center of town; pleasant garden with a view beyond the city walls; professional staff. **Cons:** not all rooms have views; some rooms are a little cramped. [$] *Rooms from: €180* ✉ *Pian dei Mantellini 34, Città* ☎ *0577/280–462* 🌐 *www.palazzoravizza.it* 🛏 *38 rooms, 4 suites* 🍽 *Breakfast.*

NAPLES

Before the Italian unification in 1860, Naples rivaled Paris as a cultural capital and the ultimate Grand Tour destination. Today, Naples can be difficult to warm to: noise and air pollution levels are high (but improving—much of the center is now pedestrianized) and graffiti unsightly. Yet it has an energy unmatched by almost any other Italian city, not to mention some of the finest gems of art and architecture in all of Europe.

It's said that northern Italians vacation here to remind themselves of the time when Italy was *molto Italiana*—really Italian. In this respect, Naples—Napoli in Italian—doesn't disappoint: Neapolitan rainbows of laundry wave in the wind over alleyways open-windowed with friendliness; mothers caress children; men break out into impromptu arias at sidewalk cafés; and street scenes offer Fellini-esque slices of life. Nowhere is this more apparent than along the Spaccanapoli (the street that "cuts Napoli" in two), everywhere contrasting elements of faded gilt and romance, rust and calamity, grandeur and squalor form a pageant of pure *Italianità*—Italy at its most Italian. In most of the city you need a good sense of humor and a firm grip on your pocketbook and camera.

PLANNING YOUR TIME

To get a feel for Naples, you should give it a couple of days at a minimum. The train station makes a harsh first impression (a recent overhaul softens the blow), but the city grows on you as you take in the sights and interact with the locals. Pompeii is an easy day-trip. That said, many people bypass Naples and head right for the resorts. These places are all about relaxing—you'll miss the point if you're in a rush.

GETTING HERE

There are up to three trains every hour between Rome and Naples. Both the Alta Velocità Frecciarossa and Italotreno trains (the fastest types of train service) make the trip in a little more than an hour, with the Intercity taking two. All trains to Naples stop at the newly refurbished Stazione Centrale. Naples can also be your entry-point into Italy if you are traveling by air.

GETTING AROUND

Expect to do a lot of walking (take care crossing the chaotic streets); buses are crowded, and taxis often get held up in traffic. Use the funiculars or the metro Line No. 1 to get up and down the hills, and take the quick—but erratic—metro Line No. 2 (the city's older subway system) when crossing the city between Piazza Garibaldi and Pozzuoli. For standard public transit—including the subways, buses, and funiculars—an UnicoNapoli costs €1.30 and is valid for 90 minutes as far as Pozzuoli to the west and Portici to the east; €3.70 buys a *biglietto giornaliero*, good for the whole day (€3.10 on weekends).

When taking a taxi in Naples, trips around the city are unlikely to cost less than €6 or more than €20. Set fares for various destinations within the city should be displayed in the taxi—for instance, in accordance with the new taxi tariff, you should pay €9.50 for travel between the Beverello port and the train station. You need to establish this before the trip begins. Otherwise, make sure the meter is running; extra charges for things like baggage and night service should also be displayed.

During the summer, both buses and ferries connect Naples to the resorts of the Amalfi coast.

TOURS

City Sightseeing ✉ *Piazza Municipio* ☎ *081/5517279* ⊕ *www.napoli. city-sightseeing.it.*

EXPLORING

ROYAL NAPLES

Naples hasn't been a capital for more than 150 years, but it still prides itself on its royal heritage. Most of the modern center of the town owes its look and feel to various members of the Bourbon family, who built their palaces and castles in this area. Allow plenty of time for museum visits; the views of the bay from the Castel dell'Ovo—good at any time—are especially fine at sunset.

Castel dell'Ovo (*Castle of the Egg*). The oldest castle in Naples, the 12th-century Castel dell'Ovo dangles over the Porto Santa Lucia on a thin promontory. Built atop the ruins of an ancient Roman villa, the castle these days shares its views with some of the city's top hotels. Its gigantic rooms, rock tunnels, and belvederes over the bay are among Naples's most striking sights.

As for the castle's name, the poet Virgil is supposed have hidden inside it an egg that had protective powers as long as it remained intact. The belief was taken so seriously that to quell the people's panic after Naples suffered an earthquake, an invasion, and a plague in quick succession, its monarch felt compelled to produce an intact egg, solemnly declaring it to be the Virgilian original. ✉ *Santa Lucia waterfront, Via Eldorado 3, off Via Partenope* ☎ *081/795–6180* 🖃 *Free* ☉ *Mon.–Sat. 8–7:15, Sun. 8–1:45.*

Castel Nuovo. Known to locals as Maschio Angioino, in reference to its Angevin builders, this imposing castle is now used more for marital than military purposes—a portion of it serves as a government registry office. A white four-tiered triumphal entrance arch, ordered by Alfonso of Aragon after he entered the city in 1443 to seize power from the increasingly beleaguered Angevin Giovanna II, upstages the building's looming Angevin stonework. At the arch's top, as if justifying Alfonso's claim to the throne, the Archangel Gabriel slays a demon.

Across the courtyard within the castle is the Sala Grande, also known as the Sala dei Baroni, which has a stunning vaulted ceiling 92 feet high. In 1486 local barons hatched a plot against Alfonso's son, King Ferrante, who reacted by inviting them to this hall for a wedding banquet, which promptly turned into a mass arrest. (Ferrante is also said to have kept a crocodile in the castle as his pet executioner.) You can also visit the Sala dell'Armeria, where a glass floor reveals recent excavations of Roman baths from the Augustan period. ✉ *Piazza Municipio, Toledo* ☎ *081/795–5877* 🖃 *€5* ☉ *Mon.–Sat. 9–7* Ⓜ *Toledo, Piazza Municipio (due 2014).*

Gallerie di Palazzo Zevallos Stigliano. Tucked inside this beautifully restored palazzo, which houses the Banca Intesa San Paolo, one of Italy's major banks, is a small museum that's worth seeking out. Enter the bank through Cosimo Fanzago's gargoyled doorway and take the handsome elevator to the upper floor. The first room to the left holds the star attraction, Caravaggio's last work, *The Martyrdom of Saint Ursula.* The saint here is, for dramatic effect, deprived of her usual retinue of a thousand followers. On the left, a face of pure spite, is the king of the Huns, who has just shot Ursula with an arrow after his proposal of marriage has been rejected. Opposite the painting is an elaborate map of the city of Caravaggio's day, not so different from now. ⊠ *Via Toledo 185, Piazza Plebiscito* ☎ *800/1605–2007* ⊕ *www.palazzozevallos.com* ⊠ *€4* ⊙ *Tues.–Fri. and Sun. 10–6, Sat. 10–8* Ⓜ *Toledo.*

Fodor'sChoice
★
Palazzo Reale. A leading Naples showpiece created as an expression of Bourbon power and values, the Palazzo Reale dates to 1600. Renovated and redecorated by successive rulers, once lorded over by a dim-witted king who liked to shoot his hunting guns at the birds in his tapestries, it is filled with salons designed in the most lavish 18th-century Neapolitan style. The Spanish viceroys originally commissioned the palace, ordering the Swiss architect Domenico Fontana to build a suitable new residence for King Philip III, should he chance to visit Naples. He died in 1621 before ever doing so. The palace saw its greatest moment of splendor in the 18th century, when Charles III of Bourbon became the first permanent resident; the flamboyant Naples-born architect Luigi Vanvitelli redesigned the facade, and Ferdinando Fuga, under Ferdinand IV, created the **Royal Apartments,** sumptuously furnished and full of precious paintings, tapestries, porcelains, and other objets d'art.

To access these 30 rooms, climb the monumental *Scalone d'Onore* (Staircase). On the right is the **Court Theater,** built by Fuga for Charles III and his private opera company. Damaged during World War II, it was restored in the 1950s; note the resplendent royal box. Antechambers lead to Room VI, the **Throne Room,** the ponderous titular object dating to sometime after 1850.

Decoration picks up in the **Ambassadors' Room,** choice Gobelin tapestries gracing the light-green walls. The ceiling painting honoring Spanish military victories is by local artist Belisario Corenzio (1610–20) The **Palatine Chapel,** redone by Gaetano Genovese in the 1830s, is gussied up with an excess of gold, although it has a stunning Technicolor marble intarsia altar from the previous chapel (Dionisio Lazzari, 1678). The sumptuous rooms can still be viewed, and there's a tasteful garden that looks onto Castel Nuovo. ⊠ *Piazza Plebiscito, Toledo* ☎ *081/580–8111, 848/800–288 for schools and guided tours* ⊕ *www.palazzorealenapoli.it* ⊠ *€4, audio guide included* ⊙ *Thurs.–Tues. 9–8* Ⓜ *Toledo, Piazza Municipio (due 2014).*

VOMERO

Heart-stopping views of the Bay of Naples are framed by this gentrified neighborhood on a hill served by the Montesanto, Centrale, and Chiaia funiculars. The upper stations for all three are an easy walk from Piazza

Vanvitelli (on Metro Line No. 2), a good starting point for exploring this thriving district with no shortage of smart bars and trattorias.

Castel Sant'Elmo. Perched on the Vomero, this massive castle is almost the size of a small town. Built by the Angevins in the 14th century to dominate the port and the old city, it was remodeled by the Spanish in 1537. The parapets, configured in the form of a six-pointed star, provide fabulous views. The whole bay lies on one side; on another, the city spreads out like a map, its every dome and turret clearly visible; and to the east, is slumbering Vesuvius. Once a major military outpost, the castle these days hosts occasional cultural events. Its prison, the Carcere alto di Castel Sant'Elmo, is the site of the **Museo del Novecento Napoli,** which traces Naples's 20th-century artistic output, from the futurist period through the 1980s. ⊠ *Largo San Martino, Vomero* ☎ *081/8488–00288* ⊕ *www.polomusealenapoli.beniculturali.it* 🎟 *€5* ۞ *Wed.–Mon. 8:30–7:30* Ⓜ *Vanvitelli.*

Fodor'sChoice **Certosa di San Martino.** Atop a rocky promontory with a fabulous view of
★ the entire city and majestic salons that would please any monarch, the Certosa di San Martino is a monastery that seems more like a palace. In fact, by the 18th century Ferdinand IV was threatening to halt the religious order's government subsidy, so sumptuous was this *certosa,* or charter house, which had been started in 1325. Although the Angevin heritage can be seen in the pointed arches and cross-vaulted ceiling of the **Certosa Church,** over the years dour Gothic was traded in for vari-colored Neapolitan baroque.

The sacristy leads into the **Cappella del Tesoro,** with Luca Giordano's ceiling fresco of Judith holding aloft Holofernes's head and the painting by Il Ribera (the *Pietà* over the altar is one of his masterpieces). The polychrome marble work of the architect and sculptor Cosimo Fanzago (1591–1678) is at its finest here, and he displays a gamut of sculptural skills in the **Chiostro Grande** (Great Cloister). Fanzago's ceremonial portals at each corner of the cloister are among the most spectacular of all baroque creations, aswirl with Michelangelo-esque ornament.

The nearby **Museo dell'Opera,** not always open, contains sociological-themed rooms that add up to a chronological tour of the city. One room has 13 gouaches of Vesuvius, and another has paintings depicting the Plague.

Past the library, with its heavenly majolica-tile floor, comes the **Sezione Presepiale,** the world's greatest collection of Christmas cribs. Pride of place goes to the *Presepe* (Nativity scene) of Michele Cucineniello. Equally amazing in its own way is a crib inside an eggshell. ⊠ *Piazzale San Martino 5, Vomero* ☎ *081/229–4589* ⊕ *www.polomusealenapoli. beniculturali.it* 🎟 *€6* ۞ *Thurs.–Tues. 9–7:30 (ticket office closes at 6:30); Christmas crèches Thurs.–Mon.; some rooms occasionally closed for lack of staffing* Ⓜ *Vanvitelli.*

SPACCANAPOLI AND CAPODIMONTE

Nowhere embodies the spirit of Naples better than the arrow-straight street informally known as Spaccanapoli (literally, "split Naples"). Gazing down it, you can sense where the name comes from—the street resembles a trench, running from Castel Capuano (until recently the

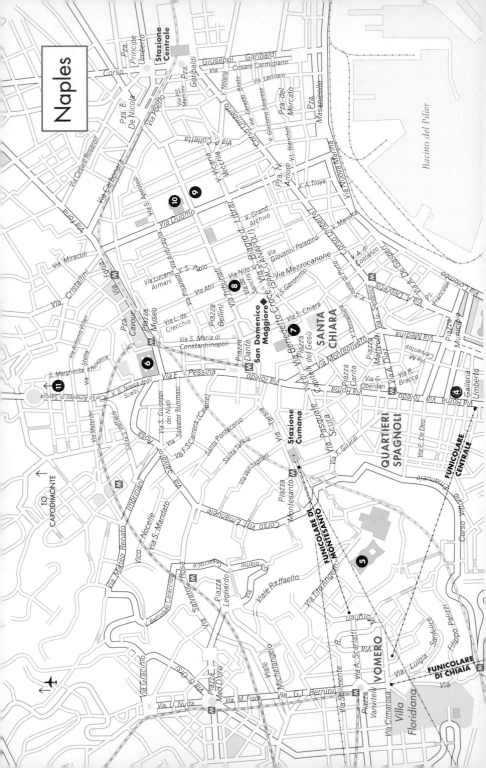

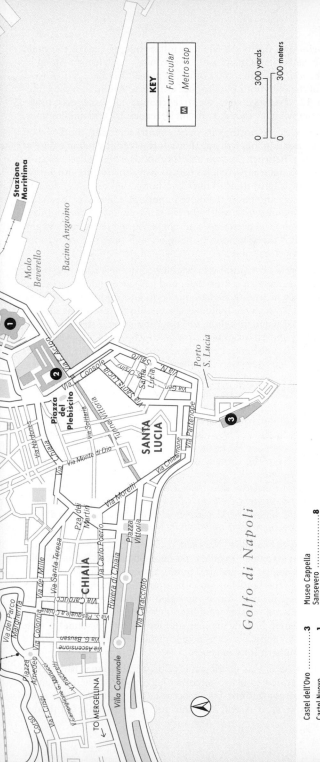

Golfo di Napoli

Stazione Marittima

Molo Beverello

Bacino Angioino

Porto S. Lucia

SANTA LUCIA

Piazza del Plebiscito

CHIAIA

Pza del Martiri

Piazza Vittoria

Villa Comunale

TO MERGELLINA

Piazza Amedeo

KEY

╪ *Funicular*
Ⓜ *Metro stop*

0   300 yards
0   300 meters

city's courthouse) up to the Vomero hill, retracing one of the main arteries of the ancient Greek, and later Roman, settlements. Along its western section, Spaccanapoli is officially named Via Benedetto Croce, in honor of the illustrious philosopher born here in 1866, in the building at No. 12. Over its course, the street changes its name seven times. But no matter what it's called, a vibrant street culture remains constant.

Capodimonte, to the north, was open countryside until the Bourbon kings built a hunting lodge there, after which it rapidly became part of the city proper. Between the two neighborhoods is the Museo Archeologico, Naples's finest museum. It's best to visit shortly after lunchtime, when the crowds have thinned out. Two hours will be just enough to get your bearings and cover the more important collections. Since the Museo di Capodimonte is well lighted—unlike many of the churches and the archaeological museum—and can be viewed in fading daylight, it's best left until the afternoon (leaving enough time to return to the center of town before sunset).

Duomo. Though the cathedral was established in the 1200s, the building you see was erected a century later and has since undergone radical changes—especially during the baroque period. Inside, 110 ancient columns salvaged from pagan buildings are set into the piers that support the 350-year-old wooden ceiling. Off the left aisle you step down into the 4th-century church of **Santa Restituta**, which was incorporated into the cathedral. Though Santa Restituta was redecorated in the late 1600s in the prevalent baroque style, the mosaics in the **Battistero** (Baptistery) are claimed to be the oldest in the Western world.

On the right aisle of the cathedral, in the **Cappella del Tesoro di San Gennaro,** multicolor marbles and frescoes honor Saint Januarius, the miracle-working patron saint of Naples, whose altar and relics are encased in silver. The most spectacular painting on display is Ribera's *San Gennaro in the Furnace* (1647), depicting the saint emerging unscathed from the furnace while his persecutors scatter in disarray. ✉ *Via Duomo 149, Spaccanapoli* ☎ *081/449–097 for Duomo, 081/294–980 for museum* 🎟 *Cathedral €7, baptistery €1.50* ☯ *Cathedral daily 9–6; baptistery weekdays 8:30–12:30 and 3:30–6:30, holidays 8:30–1 and 3:30–6:30; Capella di San Gennaro weekdays 8:30–1 and 3:30–7:30, Sun. 8:30–1 and 4:30–6:30.*

Fodor's Choice   **Museo Archeologico Nazionale** (*National Museum of Archaeology*). Those
★   who know and love this legendary museum—now restyled as MANN (Museo Archeologico Nazionale Napoli), though the name has yet to catch on—have the tendency upon hearing it mentioned to heave a sigh: it's famous not only for its unrivaled collections but also for its cordoned-off rooms, missing identification labels, poor lighting, billows of dust, suffocating heat in summer, and indifferent personnel, a state of affairs seen by some critics as an encapsulation of everything that's wrong with southern Italy in general.

Precisely because of this emblematic value, the National Ministry of Culture has decided to lavish attention and funds on the museum in a complete reorganization. This process has been ongoing for some time and looks as if it will continue for a while longer, although improvements are gradually becoming visible: ticketing has been privatized and opening hours extended—for the core "masterpiece" collection, that is; other rooms are subject to staffing shortages and sometimes close on a rotating basis.

12

Though some rooms may be closed when you visit, world-renowned archaeological finds that put most other museums to shame are always on view. These include the legendary Farnese collection of ancient sculpture, some of the best mosaics and paintings from Pompeii and Herculaneum, and *Iliou Persis* (*The Taking of Troy*), one of several dozen objects returned to Italy by the J. Paul Getty Museum in Los Angeles. ⊠ *Piazza Museo 19, Spaccanapoli* ☎ *081/440–166* ⊕ *cir. campania.beniculturali.it/museoarcheologiconazionale* ⊠ *€8* ⊗ *Wed.– Mon. 9–7:30* Ⓜ *Museo.*

FodorsChoice **Museo Cappella Sansevero** (*Sansevero Chapel Museum*). The dazzling
★ funerary chapel of the Sangro di Sansevero princes combines noble swagger, overwhelming color, and a touch of the macabre—which is to say, it expresses Naples perfectly. The chapel was begun in 1590 by Prince Giovan Francesco di Sangro to fulfill a vow to the Virgin if he were cured of a dire illness. The seventh Sangro di Sansevero prince, Raimondo, had the building modified in the mid-18th century and is generally credited for its current baroque styling, whose noteworthy elements include the splendid marble-inlay floor. A larger-than-life figure, Prince Raimondo was popularly believed to have signed a pact with the devil allowing him to plumb nature's secrets. He commissioned the young sculptor Giuseppe Sammartino to create numerous works, including the chapel's centerpiece: the remarkable *Veiled Christ*, which has a seemingly transparent marble veil some say was produced using a chemical formula provided by the prince. ∎**TIP→ If you have the stomach for it, take a look in the crypt, where some of the anatomical experiments conducted by the prince are gruesomely displayed.** ⊠ *Via Francesco de Sanctis 19, off Vicolo Domenico Maggiore, Spaccanapoli* ☎ *081/551– 8470* ⊕ *www.museosansevero.it* ⊠ *€7 (€5 with Artecard)* ⊗ *Mon. and Wed.–Sat. 10–5:40, Sun. 10–1:10* Ⓜ *Dante.*

Museo di Capodimonte. The grandiose 18th-century Neoclassical Bourbon royal palace houses fine and decorative art. Capodimonte's greatest treasure is the excellent collection of paintings well displayed in the **Galleria Nazionale,** on the palace's first and second floors. Aside from the artworks, part of the royal apartments still has a complement of beautiful antique furniture (most of it on the splashy scale so dear to the Bourbons), and a staggering range of porcelain and majolica from the various royal residences. Most rooms have fairly comprehensive information cards in English, whereas the audio guide is overly selective and somewhat quirky. The main galleries on the first floor are devoted to work from the 13th to the 18th century, including many pieces by Dutch and Spanish masters. On the second floor look for stunning paintings by Simone Martini (circa 1284–1344), Titian (1488/90–1576), and Caravaggio (1573–1610). The palace is in the vast Bosco di Capodimonte (Capodimonte Park), which served as the royal hunting preserve and later as the site of the Capodimonte porcelain works. ⊠ *Via Miano 2, Porta Piccola, Via Capodimonte, Capodimonte* ☎ *199/199–100* *for info and tickets for special exhibitions, 081/749–9111* ⊕ *www. polomusealenapoli.beniculturali.it* ✉ *€7.50* ⊘ *Thurs.–Tues. 8:30–7:30; ticket office closes at 6:30.*

Fodor's Choice
★

Pio Monte della Misericordia. One of Spaccanapoli's defining sites, this octagonal church was built around the corner from the Duomo for a charitable institution seven noblemen founded in 1601. The institution's aim was to carry out acts of Christian charity: feeding the hungry, clothing the poor, nursing the sick, sheltering pilgrims, visiting prisoners, ransoming Christian slaves, and burying the indigent dead—acts immortalized in the history of art by Caravaggio's famous altarpiece depicting the *Sette Opere della Misericordia* (*Seven Acts of Mercy*). In this haunting work the artist has brought the Virgin, borne atop the shoulders of two angels, down into the streets of Spaccanapoli (scholars have suggested a couple of plausible locations) populated by figures in whose spontaneous and passionate movements the people could see themselves. The original church was considered too small and destroyed in 1655 to make way for a new church, designed by Antonio Picchiatti and built between 1658 and 1678. Pride of place is given to the great Caravaggio above the altar, but there are other important baroque-era paintings on view here. Some hang in the church—among them seven other works of mercy depicted individually by Caravaggio acolytes—while other works, including a wonderful self-portrait by Luca Giordano, are in the adjoining *pinacoteca* (picture gallery). ✉ *Via Tribunali 253, Spaccanapoli* ☎ *081/446–973* ⊕ *www.piomontedellamisericordia. it* ✉ *€6, includes audio guide* ⊘ *Daily 9–2* Ⓜ *Piazza Cavour (in construction: Duomo).*

Santa Chiara. Offering a stark and telling contrast to the opulence of the nearby Gesù Nuovo, Santa Chiara is the leading Angevin Gothic monument in Naples. The fashionable house of worship for the 14th-century nobility and a favorite Angevin church from the start, the church of St. Clare was intended to be a great dynastic monument by Robert d'Anjou. His second wife, Sancia di Majorca, added the adjoining convent for the Poor Clares to a monastery of the Franciscan Minors so she could vicariously satisfy a lifelong desire for the cloistered seclusion of a convent. This was the first time the two sexes were combined in a single complex. Built in a Provençal Gothic style between 1310 and 1328 (probably by Guglielmo Primario) and dedicated in 1340, the church had its aspect radically altered, as did so many others, in the baroque period. A six-day fire started by Allied bombs on August 4, 1943, put an end to all that, as well as to what might have been left of the important cycle of frescoes by Giotto and his Neapolitan workshop. The church's most important tomb towers behind the altar. Sculpted by Giovanni and Pacio Bertini of Florence (1343–45), it is, fittingly, the tomb of the founding king: the great Robert d'Anjou, known as the Wise.

Around the left side of the church is the **Chiostro delle Clarisse,** the most famous cloister in Naples. ✉ *Piazza Gesù Nuovo, Spaccanapoli* ☎ *081/551–6673* ⊕ *www.monasterodisantachiara.eu* ✉ *Museum and cloister €6* ⊘ *Church daily 7:30–1 and 4:30–8; museum and cloister Mon.–Sat. 9:30–5:30, Sun. 10–2:30* Ⓜ *Dante, Università.*

WHERE TO EAT

CHIAIA

$$
NEAPOLITAN
Fodor's Choice ★

🍴 **Da Dora.** Despite its location up an unpromising-looking *vicolo* (alley) off the Riviera di Chiaia, this small restaurant has achieved cult status for its seafood platters. It's remarkable what owner-chef Giovanni can produce in his tiny kitchen. Start with linguine *alla Dora,* laden with local seafood and fresh tomatoes, and perhaps follow up with grilled *pezzogna* (blue-spotted bream). Like many restaurants on the seafront, Dora has its own guitarist, who is often robustly accompanied by the kitchen staff. [$] *Average main: €25* ✉ *Via Fernando Palasciano 30* ☎ *081/680–519* ✍ *Reservations essential* ⏲ *Closed Oct.–May. No dinner Sun.*

PIAZZA GARIBALDI

$
PIZZA

🍴 **Da Michele.** You may recognize Da Michele from the movie *Eat, Pray, Love,* but for more than 140 years before Julia Roberts arrived this place was a culinary reference point. Despite offering only two types of pizza—marinara (with tomato, garlic, and oregano) and *Margherita* (with tomato, mozzarella, and basil)—plus a small selection of drinks, it still manages to attract long lines. The prices have something to do with it. But the pizza itself suffers no rivals, so even customers waiting in line are good-humored: the boisterous, joyous atmosphere wafts out with the smell of yeast and wood smoke onto the street. **■TIP→ Get a number at the door, and then hang outside until it's called.** [$] *Average main: €5* ✉ *Via Sersale 1/3, off Corso Umberto, between Piazza Garibaldi and Piazza Nicola Amore* ☎ *081/553–9204* 🌐 *www.damichele.net* 💳 *No credit cards* ⏲ *Closed 2 wks in Aug. and Sun. June–Nov.*

TOLEDO

$
NEAPOLITAN
Fodor's Choice ★

🍴 **Trattoria San Ferdinando.** This cheerful trattoria seems to be run for the sheer pleasure of it. Try the excellent fish or the traditional (but cooked with a lighter modern touch) pasta dishes, especially those with *verdura* (fresh leaf vegetables) or with potatoes and smoked mozzarella (*pasta e patate con la provola*). Close to Teatro San Carlo and aptly decorated with playbills and theatrical memorabilia, both ancient and modern, this is an excellent place to stop after a visit to the opera. **■TIP→ Look for the entrance almost immediately on the right as you go up Via Nardones from Piazza Trieste e Trento—ring the bell outside to be let in.** [$] *Average main: €12* ✉ *Via Nardones 117* ☎ *081/421–964* ⏲ *Closed Sun., Mon., and last 3 wks of Aug. No dinner Sat. and Tues.*

WHERE TO STAY

CHIAIA

$$
HOTEL
Fodor's Choice ★

🏨 **Hotel Palazzo Alabardieri.** Just off the chic Piazza dei Martiri, this is the most fashionable choice among the city's smaller luxury hotels—for some, there is simply no other hotel in Naples. **Pros:** impressive public salons; central yet quiet location; polite, pleasant staff. **Cons:** no sea view; difficult to reach by car. [$] *Rooms from: €145* ✉ *Via Alabardieri 38* ☎ *081/415–278* 🌐 *www.palazzoalabardieri.it* 🛏 *39 rooms* 🍽 *Breakfast.*

SANTA LUCIA

$$$ HOTEL Fodor's Choice ★ **Grand Hotel Vesuvio.** You'd never guess from the modern exterior that this is the oldest of Naples's great seafront hotels—the place where Enrico Caruso died, Oscar Wilde dallied with lover Lord Alfred Douglas, and Bill Clinton charmed the waitresses. **Pros:** luxurious atmosphere; historic setting; directly opposite Borgo Marinaro; traffic-free Lungomare is just outside. **Cons:** spa, pool, and Internet cost extra; reception staff can be snooty; not all rooms have great views. [$] *Rooms from: €230* ✉ *Via Partenope 45* ☎ *081/764–0044* 🌐 *www.vesuvio.it* 🛏 *149 rooms, 21 suites* 🍴 *Breakfast.*

$ HOTEL Fodor's Choice ★ **MGallery Palazzo Caracciolo.** Built in the 1200s, this one-time home of Murat, King of Naples offers royal treatment within walking distance of the train station and centro storico. **Pros:** a tranquil respite; great value; free shuttle service. **Cons:** not an ideal area for evening strolls; some guests have complained of unfriendly staff. [$] *Rooms from: €130* ✉ *Via Carbonara 112, Porta Capuana* ☎ *081/016–0111* 🌐 *www.mgallery.com* 🛏 *139 rooms* 🍴 *Breakfast.*

SPACCANAPOLI

$$ HOTEL Fodor's Choice ★ **Costantinopoli 104.** An oasis of what Italians call *stile liberty* (art-nouveau style), with impressive stained-glass fittings and striking artwork, this serene, elegant hotel is well placed for touring the Museo Archeologico Nazionale and Spaccanapoli. **Pros:** pool (a rarity in Neapolitan hotels) and garden; pleasant service. **Cons:** buildings surround the pool; hotel can be difficult to find (look for the sign that reads Villa Spinelli, the place's former name). [$] *Rooms from: €176* ✉ *Via Costantinopoli 104* ☎ *081/557–1035* 🌐 *www.costantinopoli104.com* 🛏 *19 rooms* 🍴 *Breakfast.*

$$ HOTEL Fodor's Choice ★ **Hotel Palazzo Decumani.** This contemporary upscale hotel near transportation links and Spaccanapoli's major sights occupies an early-20th-century palazzo. **Pros:** convenient to major sights; large rooms and bathrooms; soundproofed windows. **Cons:** can be hard to find—follow signs from Corso Umberto. [$] *Rooms from: €140* ✉ *Piazzetta Giustino Fortunato 8* ☎ *081/420–1379* 🌐 *www.palazzodecumani.com* 🛏 *28 rooms* 🍴 *Breakfast.*

NIGHTLIFE AND THE ARTS

OPERA

Teatro San Carlo. Opera is a serious business in Naples—not in terms of the music so much as the costumes, the stage design, the players, and the politics. What's happening on stage can be secondary to the news of who's there, who they're with, and what they're wearing. Given the circumstances, it's hardly surprising that the city's famous San Carlo Company doesn't offer a particularly innovative repertoire. Nonetheless, the company is usually of very high quality—and if they're not in form the audience lets them know it. Performances take place in the historic Teatro San Carlo, the luxury liner of opera houses in southern Italy. In 2008 the concert hall underwent a massive renovation, with everything from the seats to the gold inlay on the ceiling frescoes replaced, and the statue of the mermaid Parthenope (missing since 1969) restored to its place on the building's facade. ⊠ *Via San Carlo 101–103, Piazza Municipio* ☎ *081/797–2412 for box office, 081/797–2331* ⊕ *www. teatrosancarlo.it.*

NIGHTLIFE

Bars and clubs are found in many areas around Naples. The sophisticated crowd heads to Posillipo and the Vomero, Via Partenope along the seafront, and the Chiaia area (between Piazza dei Martiri and Via dei Mille). A more bohemian contingent makes for the centro storico and the area around Piazza Bellini. The scene is relatively relaxed—you might even be able to sit down at a proper table. Keep in mind that clubs, and their clientele, can change rapidly, so do some investigating before you hit the town.

SHOPPING

Leather goods, jewelry, and cameos are some of the best items to buy in Campania. In Naples you can generally find good deals on handbags, shoes, and clothing. Most boutiques and department stores are open Monday 4:30–8; Tuesday–Saturday 9:15–1 and 4:30–8. The larger chains now open on Sunday, too.

SHOPPING DISTRICTS

Most of the luxury shops in Naples are along a crescent that descends the Via Toledo to Piazza Trieste e Trento and then continues along Via Chiaia to Via Filangieri and on to Piazza Amedeo, as well as continuing south toward Piazza dei Martiri and the Riviera di Chiaia. Within this area, the Via Chiaia probably has the greatest concentration and variety of shops (and café–pastry shop Cimmino, on the corner of Via Filangieri and Via Chiaia, makes for an excellent rest stop en route). The area around Piazza Vanvitelli, and Via Scarlatti in particular, in the Vomero also has a nice selection of shops outside the tourist zone. These can be conveniently reached by funiculars from Piazza Amedeo, Via Toledo, or Montesanto or Metro Line No. 2. Secondhand-book dealers tend to collect in the area between Piazza Dante, Via Port'Alba, and Via Santa Maria di Constantinopoli. Antiques stores can also be found in the latter. The charming shops specializing in Presepi (Nativity scenes) are in Spaccanapoli, on the Via San Gregorio Armeno. Via San Sebastiano, close to the Conservatory, is the kingdom of musical instruments.

RECOMMENDED STORES

Ferrigno. Shops selling Nativity scenes cluster along the Via San Gregorio Armeno in Spaccanapoli, and they're all worth a glance. The most famous is Ferrigno: Maestro Giuseppe Ferrigno died in 2008, but the family business continues, still faithfully using 18th-century techniques. ⊠ *Via San Gregorio Armeno 10, Spaccanapoli* ☎ *081/552–3148* ⊕ *www.arteferrigno.it.*

FAMILY **Ospedale delle Bambole.** This tiny storefront operation with a laboratory across the street is a world-famous "hospital" for dolls. In business since 1850, it's a wonderful place to take kids. ⊠ *Via San Biagio dei Librai 81, Spaccanapoli* ☎ *339/587–2274* ⊕ *www.ospedaledellebambole.it* ⊗ *Weekdays 10–3.*

SIDE TRIP TO POMPEII

Volcanic ash and mud preserved the Roman towns of Herculaneum and Pompeii almost exactly as they were on the day Mt. Vesuvius erupted in AD 79, leaving them not just archaeological ruins but museums of daily life in the ancient world. The two cities and the volcano that buried them can be visited from either Naples or Sorrento, thanks to the Circumvesuviana, the suburban railroad that provides fast, frequent, and economical service.

GETTING HERE AND AROUND

To get to Pompeii by car, take the A3 Napoli–Salerno highway to the "Pompei" exit and follow signs for the nearby "Scavi" excavations. There are numerous guarded car parks near the Porta Marina, Piazza Essedra, and Anfiteatro entrances where you can leave your vehicle for a fee.

Pompeii has two central Circumvesuviana stations served by two separate train lines. The Naples–Sorrento train stops at "Pompei Scavi–Villa dei Misteri," 100 yards from the Porta Marina ticket office of the archaeological site, while the Naples–Poggiomarino train stops at Pompei Santuario, more convenient for the Santuario della Madonna del Rosario and the hotels and restaurants in the modern town center. A third FS (state) train station south of the town center is really only convenient if arriving from Salerno or Rome.

EXPLORING

Fodor's Choice ★ **Pompeii.** The site of Pompeii, petrified memorial to Vesuvius's eruption on August 24, AD 79, is the largest, most accessible, and probably most famous excavation anywhere. A busy commercial center with a population of 12,000–15,000, ancient Pompeii covered about 160 acres on the seaward end of the fertile Sarno Plain. Today it's choked with both the dust of 25 centuries and more than 2 million visitors every year. Only by escaping the hordes and lingering along its silent streets can you truly fall under the site's spell. Come in the late afternoon, when it's nearly deserted, and you'll understand that the true pleasure of Pompeii is not in the seeing but in the feeling.

As you enter the ruins at Porta Marina, the first buildings to the left after you've gone through the ticket turnstiles are the **Terme Suburbane** (Suburban Baths), which, like several other portions of the site, are closed for long-term restoration. Fret not, though, there's still plenty to see here.

Continue up the hill to the **Foro** (Forum), which served as Pompeii's cultural, political, commercial, and religious hub. You can still see some of the two stories of colonnades that used to line two sides of the square. Fronted by an elegant portico on the eastern side of the forum is the **Macellum,** a covered meat and fish market dating to Augustan times. It was also in the Forum that elections were held, politicians let rhetoric fly, official announcements were made, and worshippers crowded the **Tempio di Giove** (Temple of Jupiter), at the northern end of the forum. The nearby **Terme del Foro** (Forum Baths) offered a relaxing respite. It had underground furnaces, the heat from which circulated beneath the floor, rose through flues in the walls, and escaped through chimneys.

On the southwestern corner is the **Basilica,** the city's law court and the economic center. These oblong halls were the model for early Christian churches, which had a nave (central aisle) and two side aisles separated by rows of columns.

Several homes were captured in various states by the eruption of Vesuvius, each representing a different slice of Pompeiian life. The **Casa del Poeta Tragico** (House of the Tragic Poet) is a typical middle-class residence. On the floor is a mosaic of a chained dog and the inscription *cave canem* ("Beware of the dog"). The **Casa dei Vettii** (House of the Vettii) is the best example of a wealthy merchant's home.

There's no more magnificently memorable evidence of Pompeii's devotion to the pleasures of the flesh than the frescoes on view at the **Villa dei Misteri** (Villa of the Mysteries), a palatial abode built at the far northwestern fringe of Pompeii. Unearthed in 1909 this villa had many rooms, all adorned with frescoes—the finest of which are in the *triclinium.*

Pompeii's other major edifice is the **Anfiteatro** (Amphitheater), once the ultimate entertainment venue for locals. It provided a range of experiences, though these essentially involved gladiators rather than wild animals.

To get the most out of Pompeii, rent an audio guide (€6.50 for one, €10 for two; you'll need to leave an ID card) and opt for one of the three itineraries (2 hours, 4 hours, or 6 hours). If hiring a guide, make sure the guide is registered for an English tour and standing inside the gate; agree beforehand on the length of the tour and the price; and prepare yourself for soundbites of English mixed with dollops of hearsay. You can prebook an excellent guide at ⊕ *www.vesuviusvspompeii.com* or ⊕ *www.contexttravel.com.*

A few words about closures: Which excavations are open or closed when you arrive might seem a caprice of the gods adorning many of the buidlings' walls, but the actual determining factors include availability of staff, geological uncertainty, and a greater emphasis on restoration following a recent UNESCO report that criticized the preservation policies at Pompeii. The Villa dei Misteri is always open, however, as is the central core of the city, a visit requiring two or more hours itself. ∎**TIP→ If you're lodging in the town of Pompeii, be aware that a convenient entrance to the ruins can be found near the amphitheater off Piazza Santa Immacolata. Look for the statue of the Virgin in the square.** ☎ *081/857–5347* ⊕ *www.pompeiisites.org* ✉ *€11 for 1 full day, €20 for 3 days including entrance to Herculaneum, Oplontis, Stabia, and one other site* ⊙ *Apr.–Oct., daily 8:30–7:30 (last admission at 6); Nov.–Mar., daily 8:30–5 (last admission at 3:30)* Ⓜ *Pompei–Villa dei Misteri.*

THE AMALFI COAST

One of the most gigglingly gorgeous places on Earth, this corner of Campania tantalizes, almost beyond bearing, the visitor who can stay but a day or two. Poets and millionaires have long journeyed here to see and sense its legendary sights: perfect, precariously perched Positano (a claim that is more than alliteration); Amalfi, a shimmering medieval city; romantic mountain-high Ravello; and ancient Paestum, with its three legendary Greek temples.

Today, the coast's scenic sorcery makes this a top destination and also a honeymoon Shangri-la—it is arguably the most divinely sensual 48-km (30-mile) stretch of water, land, and habitation on Earth.

By the late 19th century, tourism had begun to blossom, giving rise to the creation of the two-lane Amalfi Drive, what has come to be called the "Divina Costiera." A thousand or so gorgeous vistas and a photo-op at nearly every bend appear along these almost 40 km (25 miles), stretching from just outside Sorrento to Vietri, coursing over deep ravines and bays of turquoise-sapphire water, spreading past tunnels and timeless villages.

The justly famed jewels along this coastal necklace are Positano, Amalfi, and Ravello, which fill up in high season, but in the surrounding countryside not much seems to have changed since the Middle Ages: mountains are still terraced and farmed for citrus, olives, wine, and dairy; and the sea is dotted with the gentle reds, whites, and blues of fishermen's boats. Vertiginously high villages, dominated by the spires of *chiese* (churches), are crammed with houses on, into, above, and below hillsides to the bay; crossed by mule paths; and navigated by flights of steps called *scalinatelle* often leading to outlooks and belvederes that take your breath away—in more ways than one.

Semitough realities lurk behind the scenic splendor of the Divina Costiera, most notably the extremes of driving (potentially dangerous, although accidents are reassuringly rare), the endless steps, and virtually nonexistent parking. Furthermore, it often rains in spring, parts of the hills burn dry in summer, museums are few, and until you adjust, people seem to talk at maximum decibels. So what? For a precious little time, you are in a land of unmarred beauty.

PLANNING YOUR TIME

The resorts of the Amalfi coast require at least two or three days. Base yourself in either Positano or Amalfi, the latter being the most conveniently located for transportation, but save time for a trip to the Grotto dello Smeralda and Ravello at least.

POSITANO

57 km (34 miles) south of Naples.

When John Steinbeck lived here in 1953, he wrote that it was difficult to consider tourism an industry because "there are not enough *tourists.*" It's safe to say that Positano, a village of white Moorish-style houses clinging to slopes around a small sheltered bay, has since been

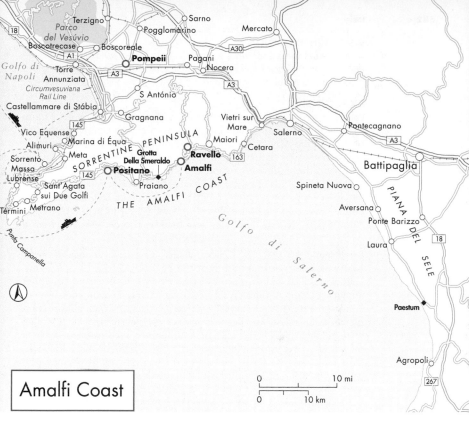

Amalfi Coast

```
0                          10 mi
0              10 km
```

discovered. In the 10th century Positano was part of Amalfi's maritime republic, which rivaled Venice as an important mercantile power. What had been reduced to a forgotten fishing village by the mid-19th century is now the number-one attraction on the coast.

From here you can take escorted bus rides to Ravello and tours of the Grotta dello Smeraldo. If you're staying in Positano, check whether your hotel has a parking area. If not, you'll have to pay for space in a lot, which is almost impossible to find during the high season, from Easter to September.

No matter how much time you spend here, make sure you have some comfortable walking shoes (no heels) and that your back and legs are strong enough to negotiate those daunting scalinatelle. Alternatively, you can ride the municipal bus, which frequently plies along the one-and-only-one-way Via Pasitea: a hairpin road running from Positano's central Piazza dei Mulini to the mountains and back, making a loop through the town every half hour.

GETTING HERE AND AROUND
SitaSud buses leave from the Circumvesuviana train station in Sorrento. Buses also run from Naples and, in summer, Rome. But June to September your best option is the ferry from Naples.

VISITOR INFORMATION
Azienda Autonoma Soggiorno e Turismo ⊠ *Via del Saracino 4* ☎ *089/875–067* ⊕ *www.aziendaturismopositano.it* ☯ *Mon.–Sat. 8:30–4:30 (June–Sept., until 7, plus Sun. morning).*

EXPLORING

Palazzo Murat. Past a bevy of resort boutiques, head to Via dei Mulini to view the prettiest garden in Positano—the 18th-century courtyard of the Palazzo Murat, named for Joachim Murat, who sensibly chose the palazzo as his summer residence. This was where Murat, designated by his brother-in-law Napoléon as King of Naples in 1808, came to forget the demands of power and lead the simple life. Since Murat was a Continental style setter, it couldn't be *too* simple; he built this grand abode (now a hotel, ⇨ *See Where to Stay, below*) near the church of Santa Maria Assunta, just steps from the main beach. ⊠ *Via dei Mulini 23* ☎ *089/875–177* ⊕ *www.palazzomurat.it.*

Santa Maria Assunta. The Chiesa Madre, or parish church of Santa Maria Assunta, lies just south of the Palazzo Murat, its green-and-yellow majolica dome topped by a perky cupola visible from just about anywhere in town. Built on the site of the former Benedictine abbey of Saint Vito, the 13th-century Romanesque structure was almost completely rebuilt in 1700. The last piece of the ancient mosaic floor can be seen under glass behind the altar. Note the carved wooden Christ, a masterpiece of devotional religious art, with its bathetic face and bloodied knees, on view before the altar. At the altar is a Byzantine 13th-century painting on wood of Madonna with Child, known popularly as the Black Virgin, carried to the beach every August 15 to celebrate the Feast of the Assumption. Legend claims that the painting was once stolen by Saracen pirates, who, fleeing in a raging storm, heard from a voice on high saying, *Posa, posa* ("Put it down, put it down"). When they placed the image on the beach near the church, the storm calmed, as did the Saracens. The Oratorio houses historic statues from the Sacristy; renovations to the Crypt have unearthed 1st-century Roman columns. ⊠ *Piazza Flavio Gioia* ☎ *089/875–480* ⊕ *www.chiesapositano.com* ☯ *Church daily 8–noon, in summer also 4–9.*

Spiaggia Grande. The walkway from the Piazza Flavio Gioia leads down to the Spiaggia Grande, or main beach, bordered by an esplanade and some of Positano's best restaurants. Surrounded by the spectacular amphitheater of houses and villas that leapfrog up the hillsides of Monte Commune and Monte Sant'Angelo, this remains one of the most picturesque beaches in the world. Although it faces stiff competition from Spiaggia di Fornillo beach, which is a far bigger and whiter strand of sand, the Spiaggia Grande wins the beauty contest hands down. **Amenities:** food and drink; lifeguards; showers; toilets; water sports. **Best for:** snorkeling, swimming.

Fodor's Choice
★

Via Positanesi d'America. Just before the ferry ticket booths to the right of Spiaggia Grande, a tiny road that is the loveliest seaside walkway on the entire coast, rises up and borders the cliffs leading to the Fornillo beach. The road is named for the town's large number of 19th-century emigrants to the United States—Positano virtually survived during

World War II thanks to the money and packages their descendants sent back home. Halfway up the path lies the Torre Trasìta (Trasìta Tower), the most distinctive of Positano's three coastline defense towers. Now a residence occasionally available for summer rental, the tower was used to spot pirate raids. As you continue along the Via Positanesi d'America, you'll pass a tiny inlet and an emerald cove before Fornillo beach comes into view.

WHERE TO EAT

$$

SOUTHERN
ITALIAN

✕ **La Tagliata.** If your enthusiasm for overpriced seafood dishes is waning, La Tagliata has the answer: local produce provide the ingredients for great antipasti, homemade pastas with rich tomato sauce, and meats grilled before your eyes in the dining room. (Ask for a *piccola porzione* unless you are ravenous.) All this comes with endless views of the Amalfi Coast. The prices are reasonable, and include a jug of red wine; however, aficionados will do better choosing their own bottle. Though it lies between Montepertuso and Nocelle, the restaurant will arrange a shuttle to pick you up from your hotel in Positano. $ *Average main: €35* ✉ *Via Tagliata 22* ☎ *089/875–872* ⊕ *www.latagliata.com* ⚠ *Reservations essential* ⊘ *Closed weekdays Dec.–Feb.*

$

SOUTHERN
ITALIAN
Fodor's Choice
★

✕ **Lo Guarracino.** In a supremely romantic setting, this partly arbor-covered, poised-on-a-cleft aerie is about the most idyllic place to enjoy lemon pasta and a glass of vino as you watch the yachts come and go. Set a few steps above Positano's prettiest seaside path, the terrace vista takes in the cliffs, the sea, Li Galli islands, Spiaggia del Fornillo, and Torre Clavel. The super-charming backroom arbor, beneath thick, twining vines, where tables are covered in cloths that match the tint of the bay, is *the* place to sit. Fine fish specialties are top delights on the menu. The day's catch is often cooked, with potatoes, in the wood-fired pizza oven, which gives it a distinct flavor. $ *Average main: €20* ✉ *Via Positanesi d'America 12* ☎ *089/875–794* ⊕ *www.loguarracino. net* ⊘ *Closed Jan.–Mar.*

WHERE TO STAY

$$

HOTEL
Fodor's Choice
★

🛏 **La Fenice.** This tiny unpretentious hotel on the outskirts of Positano beckons with bougainvillea-laden views, castaway cottages, and a turquoise seawater pool—all perched over a private beach. **Pros:** paradise; 250 steps to private beach. **Cons:** a 10-minute walk to town. $ *Rooms from: €155* ✉ *Via G. Marconi 4* ☎ *089/875–513* ⊕ *www. lafenicepositano.com* ⤵ *14 rooms* ▭ *No credit cards* ⎟⊙⎟ *Breakfast.*

$$$

HOTEL
Fodor's Choice
★

🛏 **Palazzo Murat.** A perfectly central location above the beachside church of Santa Maria Assunta—and an even more perfect entrance through a bougainvillea-draped patio and garden—help make the Murat a top lodging contender. **Pros:** once a regal residence; stunning surroundings. **Cons:** only five rooms have seaside views; constant stream of curious day-trippers. $ *Rooms from: €270* ✉ *Via dei Mulini 23* ☎ *089/875–177* ⊕ *www.palazzomurat.it* ⤵ *31 rooms* ⊘ *Closed Nov.–Mar.* ⎟⊙⎟ *Breakfast.*

GROTTA DELLO SMERALDO

13 km (8 miles) east of Positano

FAMILY **Grotta dello Smeraldo** (*Emerald Grotto*). The tacky road sign and squadron of tour buses may put you off, but this cavern is worth a stop. The karstic cave was originally part of the shore, but the lowest end sank into the sea. Intense greenish light filters into the water from an arch below sea level and is reflected off the cavern walls. You visit the Grotta dello Smeraldo, which is filled with huge stalactites and stalagmites, on a large rowboat. Don't let the boatman's constant spiel detract from the 20-minute experience—just tune out and enjoy the sparkles, shapes, and Harry Winston–esque color. You can take an elevator from the coast road down to the grotto, or you can drive to Amalfi and arrive by boat (€10, excluding the grotto's admission fee). Companies in Positano, Amalfi, and elsewhere along the coast provide service. ■ TIP→ **The light at the grotto is best from noon to 3 pm.** ⊠ *Beyond Punta Acquafetente by boat, or off Amalfi Dr.* ☎ *089/871–107 for Amalfi tourist board* 🖵 *€5* ⏰ *Apr.–mid-Oct., daily 9–4; mid-Oct.–Mar., daily 9–3. Closed in adverse weather conditions.*

AMALFI

17 km (11 miles) east of Positano, 35 km (22 miles) east of Sorrento.

"The sun—the moon—the stars—and Amalfi," Amalfitans used to say. During the Middle Ages, Amalfi was an independent maritime state with a population of 50,000. The republic also brought the art of papermaking to Europe from Arabia. Before World War II there were 13 mills making paper by hand in the Valle dei Molini, but now only two remain. The town is romantically situated at the mouth of a deep gorge and has some good hotels and restaurants. It's also a convenient base for excursions to Capri, Positano, and the Grotta dello Smeraldo. The parking problem here, however, is as bad as that in Positano, although a large parking lot has recently opened a 10-minute walk east of the center. The small lot in the center of town fills quickly. Alternatively, if you're willing to pay the steep prices, make a lunch reservation at one of the hotel restaurants and have your car parked for you.

GETTING HERE AND AROUND

From April to October the optimal way to get to Amalfi is by ferry from Salerno. In the summer months you can also arrive from Naples by fast craft. SitaSud buses run from Naples and Sorrento throughout the year.

VISITOR INFORMATION

Amalfi Tourism Office ⊠ *Corso delle Repubbliche Marinare 27* ☎ *089/871–107* ⊕ *www.amalfitouristoffice.it.*

EXPLORING

Fodor's Choice **Duomo di Sant' Andrea.** Complicated, grand, delicate, and dominating,
★ the 9th-century Amalfi cathedral has been remodeled over the years with Romanesque, Byzantine, Gothic, and baroque elements, but retains a predominantly Arab-Norman style. Cross and crescent seem to be wed here: the campanile, spliced with Saracen colors and the intricate tile

work of High Barbery, looks like a minaret wearing a Scheherazadian turban, the facade conjures up a striped burnoose, and its **Chiostro del Paradiso** (Paradise Cloister) is an Arab-Sicilian spectacular. Built around 1266 as a burial ground for Amalfi's elite, the cloister, the first stop on a tour of the cathedral, is one of southern Italy's architectural treasures. Its flower-and-palm-filled quadrangle has a series of exceptionally delicate intertwining arches on slender double columns.

The chapel at the back of the cloister leads into the earlier (9th century) **basilica.** This section has now been transformed into a museum, housing sarcophagi, sculpture, Neapolitan goldsmiths' artwork, and other treasures from the cathedral complex. ⊠ *Piazza Duomo* ☎ *089/871–324* ⊕ *www.diocesiamalficava.it* ⊠ *€3* ⊙ *Apr.–Sept., daily 9–7:45; Nov.– Jan. 6 and Mar., daily 9–5:45 (closed Jan. 7–Feb. except for daily services).*

FAMILY **Valle dei Mulini** (*Valley of the Mills*). Uphill from town, this was for centuries Amalfi's center for papermaking, an ancient trade learned from the Arabs, who learned it from the Chinese. Beginning in the 12th century, former flour mills were converted to produce paper made from cotton and linen. In 1211 Frederick II of Sicily prohibited this lighter, more readable paper for use in the preparation of official documents, favoring traditional sheepskin parchment. But by 1811 more than a dozen mills here, with more along the coast, were humming. Natural waterpower ensured that the handmade paper was cost-effective. Flooding in 1954, however, closed most of the mills for good, and many have been converted into private housing. The **Museo della Carta** (Museum of Paper) opened in 1971 in a 15th-century mill: paper samples, tools of the trade, old machinery, and the audiovisual presentation are all enlightening. You can also participate in a paper-making laboratory. ⊠ *Via delle Cartiere 23* ☎ *089/830–4561* ⊕ *www.museodellacarta.it* ⊠ *€4, includes guided tour, laboratory €7* ⊙ *Mar.–Oct., daily 10–6:30; Nov.–Feb., Tues.–Sun. 10–2:30.*

WHERE TO EAT

$ | SOUTHERN ITALIAN ✕ **Il Tari.** Locals highly recommend this little ristorante a few minutes' walk north of the Duomo. Named after the ancient coin of the Amalfi Republic, the restaurant occupies a former stable whose space has altered little outwardly since those equine days, though the white walls, appealing local art, crisp tablecloths, large panoramic photos, and tile floors make it cozy enough. Winning dishes on the vast menu include the wood-oven-baked thin-crust pizza and the *scialatielli alla Saracena* (long spaghetti-style pasta laden with tasty treats from the sea). ■ TIP➔ **The prix-fixe options (from €20 to €40) are a great deal.** ⓢ *Average main: €12* ⊠ *Via P. Capuano 9–11* ☎ *089/871–832* ⊕ *www. amalfiristorantetari.it* ⊙ *Closed Tues.*

$$$ | SOUTHERN ITALIAN | Fodor's Choice ★ ✕ **La Caravella.** No wonder this is considered the most romantic restaurant in Amalfi, with lace-covered tables, *ciuccio* (donkey) ceramics, tall candles, and fresh floral bouquets in salons graced with frescoes and marble floors. Opened in 1959, it became the first in Southern Italy to earn a Michelin star in 1966, and once drew a gilded guest list that included such fans as Andy Warhol and Federico Fellini. The menu maintains dishes favored 50 years ago: picture slices of fish grilled

in lemon leaves marinated with an almond and wild fennel sauce. ■TIP➜ A tasting menu is available, but don't miss the antipasti. Ⓢ *Average main: €40* ✉ *Via Matteo Camera 12, near Arsenale* ☎ *089/871–029* ⊕ *www.ristorantelacaravella.it* ⚏ *Reservations essential* ⊘ *Closed Tues. and Nov.–Feb.*

WHERE TO STAY

$
HOTEL
Fodor's Choice
★

⚏ **Albergo Sant'Andrea.** Occupying one of the top spots in town this tiny, family-run *pensione* is just across from the magnificent steps leading to Amalfi's cathedral. **Pros:** on the main square; divine views of the Duomo; friendly staff. **Cons:** steep flight of steps to entrance; very simple rooms. Ⓢ *Rooms from: €100* ✉ *Piazza Duomo* ☎ *089/871–145* ⊕ *www.albergosantandrea.it* ⮑ *8 rooms* ⊘ *Closed Nov.–Mar.* ⦿ *No meals.*

$$$$
HOTEL
Fodor's Choice
★

⚏ **Grand Hotel Convento di Amalfi.** This fabled medieval monastery was lauded by such guests as Longfellow and Wagner, and though recent modernization has sacrificed some of its historic charm, it remains an iconic destination. **Pros:** a slice of paradise; iconic Amalfi. **Cons:** traditionalists will miss its old-world charm; a 10-minute walk to town. Ⓢ *Rooms from: €420* ✉ *Via Annunziatella 46* ☎ *089/873–6711* ⊕ *www.ghconventodiamalfi.com* ⮑ *36 rooms, 17 suites* ⊘ *Closed Nov.–Mar.* ⦿ *Breakfast.*

RAVELLO

Fodor's Choice
★

5 km (3 miles) northeast of Amalfi.

Poised on a ridge high above Amalfi and the neighboring town of Atrani, enchanting Ravello has stupendous views, quiet lanes, two important Romanesque churches, and several irresistibly romantic gardens. Set "closer to the sky than the sea," according to André Gide, the town has been the ultimate aerie ever since it was founded as a smart suburb for the richest families of Amalfi's 12th-century maritime republic. Rediscovered by English aristocrats a century ago, Ravello now hosts one of Italy's most famous music festivals.

GETTING HERE AND AROUND

Buses from Amalfi make the 20-minute trip along white-knuckle roads. From Naples, take the A3 Naples–Salerno motorway; then exit at Angri and follow signs for Ravello. The journey takes about 75 minutes. Save yourself the trouble of driving by hiring a car and driver.

VISITOR INFORMATION

Azienda Autonoma Soggiorno e Turismo ✉ *Via Roma 18b* ☎ *089/857–096* ⊕ *www.ravellotime.it* ⊘ *Nov.–Mar., daily 9:30–5, Apr.–Oct., daily 9:30–7.*

EXPLORING

Fodor's Choice
★

Auditorium Niemeyer. Crowning Via della Repubblica and the hillside, which overlooks the spectacular Bay of Salerno, Auditorium Niemeyer is a startling piece of modernist architecture. Designed with a dramatically curved, all-white roof by the Brazilian architect Oscar Niemeyer (creator of Brasília), it was conceived as an alternative indoor venue for concerts, including those of the famed town music festival, and is now also used as a cinema. The subject of much controversy since its first conception back in 2000, it raised the wrath of some locals who denounced such an ambitious modernist building in medieval Ravello. They need not have worried. The result, inaugurated in 2010, is a design masterpiece—a huge, overhanging canopied roof suspended over a 400-seat concert area, with a giant eye-shape window allowing spectators to contemplate the extraordinary bay vista during performances. ⊠ *Via della Repubblica* ⊕ *www.cinemaravello.it.*

12

Duomo. Ravello's first bishop, Orso Papiro, founded this cathedral, dedicated to San Pantaleone, in 1086. Rebuilt in the 12th and 17th centuries, it retains traces of medieval frescoes in the transept, an original mullioned window, a marble portal, and a three-story 13th-century bell tower playfully interwoven with mullioned windows and arches. Most impressive are the two medieval pulpits. The earlier one (on your left as you face the altar), used for reading the Epistles, is inset with a mosaic scene of Jonah and the whale, symbolizing death and redemption. The more famous one opposite, used for reading the Gospels, was commissioned by Nicola Rufolo in 1272 and created by Niccolò di Bartolomeo da Foggia. It seems almost Tuscan in style, with exquisite mosaic work and bas-reliefs and six twisting columns sitting on lion pedestals. An eagle grandly tops the inlaid marble lectern.

In the crypt is the **Museo del Duomo,** which displays treasures from about the 13th century, during the reign of Frederick II of Sicily. ⊠ *Piazza del Duomo* ☎ *089/858–311* ⊕ *www.chiesaravello.com* ⊠ *€3* ⊙ *Daily 9–7 (between noon and 5:30, access church through museum, to right of steps).*

Fodor's Choice ★ **Villa Cimbrone.** To the west of Ravello's main square, a somewhat hilly 15-minute walk along Via San Francesco brings you to Ravello's showstopper, the Villa Cimbrone, whose dazzling gardens perch 1,500 feet above the sea. The ultimate aerie, this medieval-style fantasy was created in 1905 by England's Lord Grimthorpe and made world-famous in the 1930s when Greta Garbo found sanctuary from the press here. The Gothic *castello-palazzo* sits amid idyllic gardens that are divided by the grand Alleé of Immensity, leading in turn to the literal high point of any trip to the Amalfi Coast—the **Belvedere dell'Infinità** (Belvedere of Infinity). This grand stone parapet, adorned with amusing stone busts, overlooks the entire Bay of Salerno and frames a panorama the late writer Gore Vidal, a longtime Ravello resident, described as the most beautiful in the world. The name Cimbrone derives from the rocky ridge on which the villa stands, first colonized by the ancient Romans and hailed as Cimbronium back then. The villa itself is now a five-star hotel. ⊠ *Via S. Chiara 26* ☎ *089/857–459* ⊕ *www.villacimbrone. it* ⊠ *€7* ⊙ *Daily 9–half hr before sunset.*

Fodor's Choice ★ **Villa Rufolo.** Directly off Ravello's main piazza is the Villa Rufolo, home to some of the most spectacular gardens in Italy, many of which stunningly frame a Cinerama vista of the Bay of Salerno, often called the "bluest view in the world." If the master storyteller Boccaccio is to be believed, the villa was built in the 13th century by Landolfo Rufolo, whose immense fortune stemmed from trade with the Moors and the Saracens. Norman and Arab architecture mingle in a welter of color-filled gardens so lush the composer Richard Wagner used them as inspiration for Klingsor's Garden, the home of the Flower Maidens, in his opera *Parsifal.* Beyond the Arab-Sicilian cloister and the Norman tower lie the two terrace gardens. The lower one, the "Wagner Terrace," is often the site for Ravello Music Festival concerts, with the orchestra perched on a precarious-looking platform constructed over the precipice. Highlights of the house are its Moorish cloister—an Arabic-Sicilian delight with interlacing lancet arcs and polychromatic palmette decoration—and the 14th-century Torre Maggiore, the so-called Klingsor's Tower, renamed in honor of Richard Wagner's landmark 1880 visit. ✉ *Piazza Duomo* ☎ *089/857–621* 🌐 *www.villarufolo.it* 🎫 *€5, extra charge for concerts* ⏲ *Daily 9–9; winter, daily 9–sunset; closes early for rehearsals.*

WHERE TO EAT

$ SOUTHERN ITALIAN Fodor's Choice ★

🍴 **Cumpa' Cosimo.** Lustier-looking than most Ravello spots, Cumpa' Cosimo is run devotedly by Netta Bottone, who tours the tables to ensure her clients are content. Her family has owned this cantina for more than 75 of its 300-plus years, and she has been cooking under the arched ceiling for more than 60 of them. You can't miss with any of the classic Ravellian dishes. A favorite (share it—it's huge) is a *misto* of whatever homemade pasta inspires her, served with a fresh, fragrant pesto. Meats, from Netta's own butcher shop next door, are generally excellent and local wines ease it all down gently. The *funghi porcini* mushroom starter is delicious and the house cheesecake or homemade gelato provide a luscious ending. [$] *Average main: €13* ✉ *Via Roma 46* ☎ *089/857–156* ⏲ *Sometimes closed Mon. in winter.*

WHERE TO STAY

$$$ HOTEL Fodor's Choice ★

🏨 **Hotel Palumbo.** This is the real deal—the only great hotel left in Ravello that's still a monument to the Grand Tour sensibility that first put the town on the map. **Pros:** impossibly romantic; wonderful coastal retreat; incredible Bay of Salerno views. **Cons:** with all this finery it can be difficult to relax; restaurant closed from November to March. [$] *Rooms from: €245* ✉ *Via S. Giovanni del Toro 16* ☎ *089/857–244* 🌐 *www.hotelpalumbo.it* 🛏 *10 rooms, 7 suites* 🍽 *Some meals.*

$$$$ HOTEL Fodor's Choice ★

🏨 **Hotel Villa Cimbrone.** Suspended over the azure sea and set amid legendary rose-filled gardens, this Gothic-style castle was once home to Lord Grimthorpe and a hideaway of Greta Garbo. **Pros:** gorgeous pool and grounds; stay where Garbo chose to "be alone." **Cons:** a longish hike from town center (porters can help with luggage); daily arrival of respectful day-trippers. [$] *Rooms from: €530* ✉ *Via Santa Chiara 26* ☎ *089/857–459* 🌐 *www.villacimbrone.com* 🛏 *19 rooms* ⏲ *Closed Nov.–Mar.* 🍽 *Breakfast.*

VENICE

It's called La Serenissima, "the most serene," a reference to the majesty, wisdom, and monstrous power of this city that was for centuries the unrivaled mistress of trade between Europe and the Orient and the bulwark of Christendom against the tides of Turkish expansion. "Most serene" could also describe the way lovers of this miraculous city feel when they see it, imperturbably floating on its calm blue lagoon.

Built entirely on water by men who defied the sea, Venice is unlike any other town. No matter how many times you've seen it in movies or on TV, the real thing is more dreamlike than you could ever imagine. Its landmarks, the Basilica di San Marco and the Palazzo Ducale, seem hardly Italian: delightfully idiosyncratic, they are exotic mixes of Byzantine, Gothic, and Renaissance styles. Shimmering sunlight and silvery mist soften every perspective here, and you understand how the city became renowned in the Renaissance for its artists' rendering of color.

12

You'll see Venetians going about their daily affairs in *vaporetti* (water buses), aboard the *traghetti* (traditional gondola ferries) that carry them across the Grand Canal, in the *campi* (squares), and along the *calli* (narrow streets). They are nothing if not skilled—and remarkably tolerant—in dealing with the veritable armies of tourists from all over the world who fill the city's streets for most of the year.

PLANNING YOUR TIME

A great introduction to Venice is a ride on *vaporetto* (water bus) Line No. 1 from the train station all the way down the Grand Canal. If you've just arrived and have luggage in tow, you'll need to weigh the merits of taking this trip right away versus getting settled at your hotel first. (Crucial factors: your mood, the bulk of your bags, and your hotel's location.)

Seeing Piazza San Marco and the sights bordering it can fill a day, but if you're going to be around awhile, consider holding off on your visit here—the crowds can be overwhelming, especially when you're fresh off the boat. Instead, spend your first morning at Santa Maria Gloriosa dei Frari and the Scuola Grande di San Rocco, then wander through the Dorsoduro sestiere, choosing between visits to Ca' Rezzonico, the Gallerie dell'Accademia, the Peggy Guggenheim Collection, and Santa Maria della Salute—all A-list attractions. End the afternoon with a gelato-fueled stroll along the Zattere boardwalk. Then tackle San Marco on Day 2.

If you have more time, make these sights your priorities: the Rialto fish and produce markets; Ca' d'Oro and the Jewish Ghetto in Cannaregio; Santa Maria dei Miracoli and Santi Giovanni e Paolo in Castello; and, across the water from Piazza San Marco, San Giorgio Maggiore. (In Venice, there's a spectacular church for every day of the week, and then some.) A day on the outer islands of Murano, Burano, and Torcello is good for a change of pace.

GETTING HERE

From Aeroporto Marco Polo terminal it's a €10 taxi ride or a 10-minute walk to the dock where public and private boats depart for Venice's historic center.

Venice is on the east–west A4 autostrada, which connects with Padua, Verona, Brescia, Milan, and Turin. If you bring a car to Venice, you will have to pay for a garage or parking space.

Venice has rail connections with every major city in Italy and Europe. Note that Venice's station is **Stazione Ferroviaria Santa Lucia,** not to be confused with Stazione Ferroviaria Venezia-Mestre, which is located on the mainland 12 km (7 miles) outside of town. Some continental trains stop only at the Mestre station; in such cases you can catch the next Venice-bound train. Be aware that if you change from a regional train to an Intercity or Eurostar, you'll need to upgrade with a *supplemento* (extra charge) or be liable for a hefty fine. You're also subject to a fine if before boarding you don't validate your ticket in one of the yellow machines found on or near platforms.

Contacts Aeroporto Marco Polo. Venice's Aeroporto Marco Polo is on the mainland, 10 km (6 miles) north of the city. It's served by domestic and international flights, including connections from 21 European cities, plus direct flights from New York's JFK and other U.S. cities. Despite recent expansion, the airport is still too small for the amount of traffic it has to handle. To avoid substantial queues at check-in, it's highly advisable to use online check-in services if provided by your airline. ☎ *041/260–9260* ⊕ *www.veniceairport.it.* **Alilaguna.** This company has regular, scheduled ferry service from predawn until nearly midnight. During most of the day there are two departures from the airport to Venice every hour, at 15 and 45 minutes after the hour. Early morning and evening departures are less frequent, but there is at least one per hour. The charge is €15, including bags, and it takes about 1½ hours to reach the landing near Piazza San Marco; some ferries also stop at Fondamente Nove, Murano, Lido, the Cannaregio Canal, and the Rialto. Slight reductions are possible if you book a round trip on line. ☎ *041/240–1701* ⊕ *www.alilaguna.it.* **ATVO.** Buses run by ATVO make a quick (20-minute) and cheap (€6) trip from the airport to Piazzale Roma, from where you can get a vaporetto to the stop nearest your hotel. Tickets are sold from machines and at the airport ground transportation booth (daily 9–7:30), and on the bus when tickets are otherwise unavailable. The public ACTV Bus No. 5 also runs to the Piazzale Roma in about the same time. Tickets (€6) are available at the airport ground transportation booth. A taxi to Piazzale Roma costs about €35. ☎ *0421/383–672* ⊕ *www.atvo.it.*

GETTING AROUND

A vaporetto ticket for all lines costs €7 one-way (children under four ride free). Another option is a Travel Card: €20 buys 24 hours and €35 buys 72 hours of unlimited travel. For travelers between ages 14 and 29, the 72-hour pass is €18 with the Rolling Venice card. Ask for the card (€4) before buying your tickets. A shuttle ticket allows you to cross a canal, one stop only, for €4.

As your gondola glides away from the fondamenta, a transformation takes place. To some it feels like a Disney ride, but if you insist that your gondolier take you through the tiny side canals, you'll get an intimate glimpse of the city that can't be experienced any other way.

San Marco is loaded with gondola stations, but to get off the circuit, try the San Tomà or Santa Sofia (near Ca' d'Oro) stations. The price of a 40-minute ride is supposed to be fixed at €80 for up to six passengers, rising to €100 between 7:30 pm and 8 am, but these are minimums and you may have difficulty finding a gondolier who will work for that unless the city is empty. Come to terms on cost and duration before you start, and make it clear that you want to see more than just the Grand Canal.

Many tourists are unaware of the two-man gondola ferries that cross the Grand Canal at numerous strategic points. At €0.50, they're the cheapest and shortest gondola ride in Venice, and they can save a lot of walking. Look for "traghetto" signs and hand your fare to the gondolier when you board.

Contact ACTV ☎ 041/2424 ⊕ www.hellovenezia.com.

VISITOR INFORMATION

The multilingual staff of the **Venice tourism office** (☎041/529–8711 ⊕ www.turismovenezia.it) can help you out with directions and up-to-the-minute information about events in the city and sight closures. There are office branches at Marco Polo Airport; the train station; Procurate Nuove, near Museo Correr on Piazza San Marco; Garage Comunale, on Piazzale Roma; the Venice Pavilion, near Ghardini Reali in San Marco; and Santa Maria Elisabetta 6/a, on the Lido. The train-station branch is open daily 8–6:30; other branches generally open at 9:30.

EXPLORING

PIAZZA SAN MARCO

One of the world's most evocative squares, Piazza San Marco (St. Mark's Square) is the heart of Venice, a vast open space bordered by an orderly procession of arcades marching toward the fairy-tale cupolas and marble lacework of the Basilica di San Marco. Perpetually packed by day with people and fluttering pigeons, it can be magical at night, especially in winter, when mists swirl around the lampposts and the Campanile.

Piazzetta San Marco, the "little square" leading from Piazza San Marco to the waters of Bacino San Marco (St. Mark's Basin), is a *molo* (landing) that was once the grand entryway to the republic. It's distinguished by two columns towering above the waterfront. One is topped by the winged lion, a traditional emblem of St. Mark that became the symbol of Venice itself; the other supports St. Theodore, the city's first patron, along with his dragon. Between these columns the republic traditionally executed convicts.

Fodor's Choice ★ **Basilica di San Marco.** The Basilica di San Marco is not only the religious center of a great city, but also an expression of the political, intellectual, and economic aspiration and accomplishments of a city that for centuries was at the forefront of European culture. It is a monument not just to the glory of God, but also to the glory of Venice. The basilica was the doges' personal chapel, linking its religious function to the political life of the city and was endowed with all the riches the Republic's admirals and merchants could carry off from the Orient (as the Byzantine Empire was known), earning it the nickname "Chiesa D'Oro," or "Golden Church."

The dim light, the galleries high above the naves—they served as the *matroneum*, the women's gallery—the massive altar screen, or

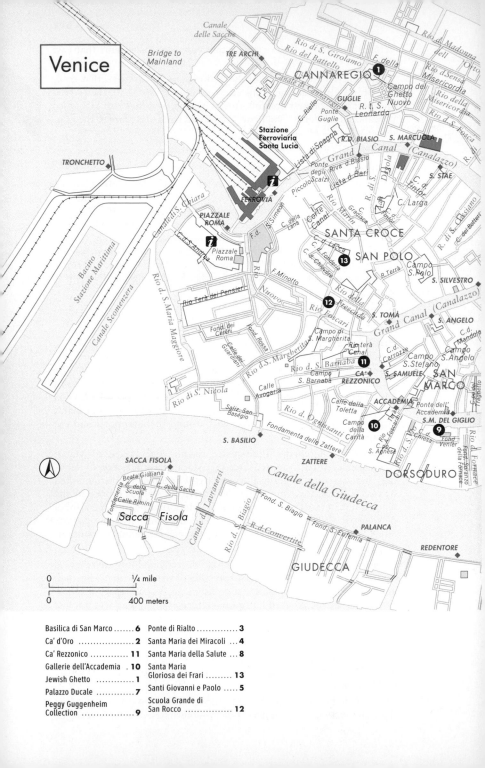

Venice

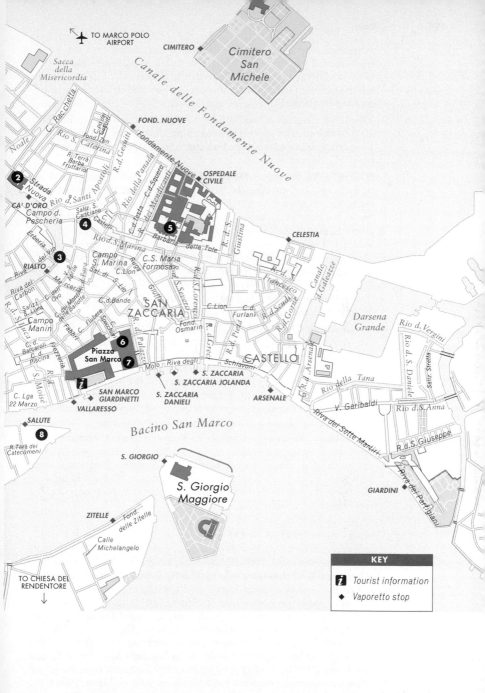

TO MARCO POLO
AIRPORT

CIMITERO

Cimitero
San
Michele

Sacca
della
Misericordia

Canale delle Fondamente Nuove

FOND. NUOVE

C. Racchetta

Noale

Rio S. Caterina

C.d.le
Fond. Zen

R.d. Gesuiti

R. Terrà
Barba
Fruttariol

2

Strada
Nuova

CA' D'ORO

Campo d.
Pescheria

Rio d'Santi Apostoli

Erberia

Saliz. S.
Canciano

4

C.d.Testa

C.d. Squero

Fondamente Nuove

Rio della Panada

Rio dei Mendicanti

OSPEDALE
CIVILE

5

Barbaria

della Tole

R. d. S.

Giustina

CELESTIA

Rio del Vin

3

Riva del

RIALTO

Riod. S. Marina

Campo
S. Marina

C.S. Maria
Formosa

C.d. Bande

Ramo Aprile

Sal. di S. Lio

C. Lion

S. Sauro

S. Lorenzo

R.d. S. Lorenzo

C. Lion

C.d.
Furlani

R.d. Scudi

Rio d. Corte

Fond.
Francesco

Canale
d. Galeazze

Darsena
Grande

Rio d. Vergini

Rio d. S. Daniele

Saliz. Stretta

C. dell'Ovo

Merceria

Calle d.
Fabbri

C. d. Monte
delle Ballotte

C. Fiubera

Spadaria

R. d. Palazzo

Campo
S. Zaccaria

Riva del
Carbon

Riva del
Ferro

Saliz.
S. Luca

R.d. S. Luca

Campo
Manin

C. d.
Barcaroli

Frezzeria

C. d.
Piscina

SAN
ZACCARIA

Giulie

Fond.
Osmarin

R. d'reca

R.d. Pietà

CASTELLO

R.d. Arsenale

R.d. Tana

6

Piazza
San Marco

7

Molo

Riva degli

Schiavoni

i

SAN MARCO
GIARDINETTI

C. Lga
22 Marzo

C. Moisè

R. d.
C. Piscina

VALLARESSO

S. ZACCARIA JOLANDA

S. ZACCARIA

S. ZACCARIA
DANIELI

ARSENALE

Rio della Tana

V. Garibaldi

Riva dei Sette Martiri

Rio d. S. Anna

R. d. S. Giuseppe

SALUTE

8

R. Terrà dei
Catecumeni

Bacino San Marco

GIARDINI

Riva dei Partigiani

S. GIORGIO

S. Giorgio
Maggiore

ZITELLE

Fond.
delle Zitelle

Calle
Michelangelo

TO CHIESA DEL
RENDENTORE

KEY	
i	*Tourist information*
◆	*Vaporetto stop*

iconostasis, the single massive Byzantine chandelier, even the Greek cross ground plan give San Marco an exotic aspect quite unlike that of most Christian churches. The effect is remarkable. Here the pomp and mystery of Oriental magnificence are wedded to Christian belief, creating an intensely awesome impression.

Of course, the glory of the basilica is its medieval mosaic work; about 30% of the mosaics survive in something close to their original form. The earliest date from the late 12th century, but the great majority date from the 13th century.

■ TIP➔ To skip the line at the basilica entrance, reserve your arrival—at no extra cost—on the website. If you check a bag at the nearby checkroom, you can show your check stub to the guard, who will wave you in. Remember that this is a sacred place: guards will deny admission to people in shorts, sleeveless dresses, and tank tops. ⊠ *Piazza San Marco, San Marco 328* ☎ *041/241–3817 for tour info (weekdays 10–noon)* ⊕ *www. basilicasanmarco.it* ⊠ *Basilica free, Treasury €3, Sanctuary and Pala d'Oro €2, Museum €5* ⊘ *Basilica Mon.–Sat. 9:45–5, Sun. and holidays 2–5 (2–4 in winter); Treasury, Sanctuary, Pala d'Oro, and museum close a few minutes earlier. Free guided tours of the Basilica Apr.–Oct.* Ⓜ *Vallaresso/San Zaccaria.*

Fodor's Choice **Palazzo Ducale** *(Doge's Palace).* Rising majestically above the Piazzetta
★ San Marco, this Gothic fantasia of pink-and-white marble is a majestic expression of Venetian prosperity and power. Although the site was the doges' residence from the 10th century, the building began to take its present form around 1340; what you see now is essentially a product of the first half of the 15th century. It served not only as a residence, but also as the central administrative center of the Venetian Republic.

Unlike other medieval seats of authority, the Palazzo Ducale is free of any military defenses—a sign of the Republic's self-confidence. The position of the loggias below instead of above the retaining wall, and the use of pink marble to emphasize the decorative function of that wall, gave the palazzo a light and airy aspect, one that could impress visitors—and even intimidate them, though through opulence and grace rather than fortresslike bulk.

A narrow canal separates the palace's east side from the cramped cell blocks of the **Prigioni Nuove** (New Prisons). High above the water arches the enclosed marble **Ponte dei Sospiri** (Bridge of Sighs), which earned its name in the 19th century, from Lord Byron's *Childe Harold's Pilgrimage.* ■ TIP➔ Reserve your spot for the palazzo's popular Secret Itineraries tour well in advance. You'll visit the doge's private apartments, through hidden passageways to the interrogation (torture) chambers, and into the rooftop *piombi* (lead) prison, named for its lead roofing. Venetian-born writer and libertine Giacomo Casanova (1725–98), along with an accomplice, managed to escape from the piombi in 1756; they were the only men ever to do so. ⊠ *Piazzetta San Marco, Piazza San Marco* ☎ *041/271–5911, 041/520–9070 for Secret Itineraries tour* ⊕ *www.museiciviciveneziani.it* ⊠ *Museums of San Marco Pass €16, includes entry also to the Museo Correr, the Archeological Museum, and the monumental rooms of the Biblioteca Marciana. Free with*

MUVE pass. Secret Itineraries tour €20 ⊙ *Apr.–Oct., daily 8:30–7; Nov.–Mar., daily 8:30–5:30; last entry 1 hr before closing. Secret Itineraries tour in English at 9:55, 10:45, and 11:35* Ⓜ *Vaporetto: San Zaccaria, Vallaresso.*

12

NEED A BREAK?

Caffè Florian. Venice's oldest café, continuously in business since 1720, has served coffee to the likes of Wagner, Casanova, Charles Dickens, and Marcel Proust. Counter seating is less expensive than taking a table, but is, of course, less romantic and you don't have the view of the piazza. This is where many upscale Venetians go when they want to meet a friend for a coffee or spritz around Piazza San Marco. ⊠ *Piazza San Marco 56* ☎ *041/520–5641* ⊕ *www.caffeflorian.com.*

Caffè Quadri. In the Procuratie Vecchie, Caffè Quadri exudes almost as much history as Florian across the way, and is similarly pricey. It was shunned by 19th-century Venetians when the occupying Austrians made it their gathering place. It's closed Monday. ⊠ *Piazza San Marco 121* ☎ *041/522–2105* ⊕ *www.caffequadri.it.*

DORSODURO

The sestiere Dorsoduro (named for its "hard back" solid clay foundation) is across the Grand Canal to the south of San Marco. It is a place of monumental churches, meandering canals, the city's finest art museums, and a boardwalk called the Zattere, where on sunny days you'll swear half the city is out for a *passeggiata*, or stroll. The eastern point of the peninsula, Punta della Dogana, has one of the best views in town. The Stazione Marittima, where in summer cruise ships line the dock, lies at the western end. Midway between these two points, just off the Zattere, is the Squero di San Trovaso, where gondolas have been built and repaired for centuries.

Dorsoduro is also home to the Gallerie dell'Accademia, which has an unparalleled collection of Venetian painting, and Ca' Rezzonico, which houses the Museo del Settecento Veneziano. Another of its landmark sites, the Peggy Guggenheim Collection, has a fine selection of 20th-century art.

Fodor's Choice
★

Ca' Rezzonico. Designed by Baldassare Longhena in the 17th century, this gigantic palace was completed nearly 100 years later by Giorgio Massari and became the last home of English poet Robert Browning (1812–89). Stand on the bridge by the Grand Canal entrance to spot the plaque with Browning's poetic excerpt, "Open my heart and you will see graved inside of it, Italy . . ." on the left side of the palace. The spectacular centerpiece is the eye-popping Grand Ballroom, which has hosted some of the grandest parties in the city's history, from its 18th-century heyday to the 1969 Bal Fantastica (a Save Venice charity event that attracted every notable of the day, from Elizabeth Taylor to Aristotle Onassis) to its balls recreated for Heath Ledger's 2005 film *Casanova*. Today the upper floors of the Ca' Rezzonico are home to the especially delightful **Museo del Settecento** (Museum of Venice in the 1700s). Its main floor successfully retains the appearance of a magnificent Venetian palazzo, decorated with period furniture and tapestries in gilded salons, as well as Tiepolo ceiling frescoes and oil paintings. Upper floors contain a fine collection of paintings by 18th-century Venetian artists, including the famous genre and Pucinella frescoes by Giabattista Tiepolo's son, Giandomenico, moved here from the Villa di Zianigo. There's even a restored apothecary, complete with powders and potions. ⊠ *Fondamenta Rezzonico, Dorsoduro 3136* ☎ *041/241–0100* ⊕ *www.museiciviciveneziani.it* ☜ *€8 (free with MUVE pass)* ⊙ *Wed.–Mon. 10–6* Ⓜ *Vaporetto: Ca' Rezzonico.*

Fodor's Choice ★   **Gallerie dell'Accademia.** The greatest collection of Venetian paintings in the world hangs in these galleries founded by Napoleon back in 1807 on the site of a religious complex he had suppressed. They were carefully and subtly restructured between 1945 and 1959 by the renowned architect Carlo Scarpa.

Jacopo Bellini is considered the father of the Venetian Renaissance, and in Room 2 you can compare his *Madonna and Child with Saints* with such later works as *Madonna of the Orange Tree* by Cima da Conegliano (circa 1459–1517) and *Ten Thousand Martyrs of Mt. Ararat* by Vittore Carpaccio (circa 1455–1525).

■**TIP**➔ **Booking tickets in advance isn't essential but helps during busy seasons and costs only an additional €1.50. Booking is necessary to see the Quadreria, where additional works cover every inch of a wide hallway.** A free map notes art and artists, and the bookshop sells a more informative English-language booklet. In the main galleries a €4 audio guide saves reading but adds little to each room's excellent annotation. ⊠ *Dorsoduro 1050, Campo della Carità just off the Accademia Bridge* ☎ *041/522–2247 for Quadreria reservations, 041/520–0345 for Galleria reservations* ⊕ *www.gallerieaccademia.org* ☜ *€14, includes admission to Palazzo Grimani and special exhibitions* ⊙ *Galleria Tues.–Sun. 8:15–7:15, Mon. 8:15–2; Quadreria Fri. 11–1, Sat. 11–noon* Ⓜ *Vaporetto: Accademia.*

┌
│ **NEED A**
│ **BREAK?**
   Gelateria Nico. Enjoy the Zattere's most scrumptious treat—Nico's famous *gianduiotto*, a slab of chocolate-hazelnut ice cream floating on a cloud of whipped cream—and relax on the big, welcoming deck. Nico's is one of the few places still serving authentic homemade (*artiginale*) ice cream and has been seducing Venetians since 1935. ⊠ *Dorsoduro 922* ☎ *041/522–5293* ⊕ *www.gelaterianico.com.*

FAMILY   **Peggy Guggenheim Collection.** Housed in the surprisingly small and charming Palazzo Venier dei Leoni, this choice selection of 20th-century painting and sculpture represents the taste and extraordinary style of the late heiress Peggy Guggenheim. Through wealth and social connections, Guggenheim (1898–1979) became an important art dealer and collector from the 1930s through the 1950s, and her personal collection here includes works by Picasso, Kandinsky, Pollock, Motherwell, and Ernst (at one time her husband). The museum serves beverages, snacks, and light meals in its refreshingly shady, artistically sophisticated garden. On Sunday at 3 pm the museum offers a free tour and art workshop for children 10 and under; conducted in Italian, anglophone interns are generally on hand to help those who don't *parla italiano.* ✉ *Fondamenta Venier dei Leoni, Dorsoduro 701* ☎ *041/240–5411* ⊕ *www.guggenheim-venice.it* ⊡ *€14* ⊙ *Wed.–Mon.* 10–6 Ⓜ *Vaporetto: Accademia.*

Fodor'sChoice **Santa Maria della Salute.** The most iconic landmark of the Grand Canal,
★ La Salute (as this church is commonly called) is most unforgettably viewed from the Riva degli Schiavoni at sunset or from the Accademia Bridge by moonlight. Outside, this ornate, white Istrian stone octagon is topped by a colossal cupola with snail-like ornamental buttresses—in truth, piers encircled by finely carved "ropes," an allusion to the sail-making industry of the city (or so say today's art historians). Inside, a white-and-gray color scheme is echoed by a polychrome marble floor and the six chapels. The Byzantine icon above the main altar has been venerated as the Madonna della Salute (Madonna of Health) since 1670, when Francesco Morosini brought it here from Crete. Above it is a sculpture showing Venice on her knees before the Madonna as she drives the wretched plague from the city.

Do not leave the church without visiting the **Sacrestia Maggiore,** which contains a dozen works by Titian, including his *San Marco Enthroned with Saints* altarpiece. You'll also see Tintoretto's *The Wedding at Cana.* ✉ *Punta della Dogana* ☎ *041/241–1018* ⊡ *Church free, sacristy €2* ⊙ *Daily 9–noon and 3–5:30* Ⓜ *Vaporetto: Salute.*

SAN POLO AND SANTA CROCE

The two smallest of Venice's six sestieri, San Polo and Santa Croce were named after their main churches, though the Chiesa di Santa Croce was demolished in 1810. The city's most famous bridge, the Ponte di Rialto, unites sestiere San Marco (east) with San Polo (west). The Rialto Bridge takes its name from Rivoaltus, the high ground on which it was built. San Polo has two other major sites, Santa Maria Gloriosa dei Frari and the Scuola Grande di San Rocco, as well as some worthwhile but lesser-known churches.

Shops abound in the area surrounding the Rialto Bridge. On the San Marco side you'll find fashions, on the San Polo side food. Chiesa di San Giacometto, where you see the first fruit vendors as you come off the bridge on the San Polo side, was probably built in the 11th and 12th centuries, about the time the surrounding market came into being. Public announcements were traditionally read in the church's campo; its 24-hour clock, though lovely, has rarely worked.

Fodor'sChoice **Ponte di Rialto** (*Rialto Bridge*). The competition to design a stone bridge
★ across the Grand Canal attracted the best architects of the late 16th century, including Michelangelo, Palladio, and Sansovino, but the job went to the less-famous (but appropriately named) Antonio da Ponte (1512–95). His pragmatic design, completed in 1591, featured shop space and was high enough for galleys to pass beneath. Unlike the classical plans proposed by his more famous contemporaries, Da Ponte's bridge essentially followed the design of its wooden predecessor; it kept decoration and cost to a minimum at a time when the Republic's coffers were low due to continual wars against the Turks and the competition brought about by the Spanish and Portuguese opening of

12

oceanic trade routes. Along the railing you'll enjoy one of the city's most famous views: the Grand Canal vibrant with boat traffic. ⊠ *San Marco* Ⓜ *Vaporetto: Rialto.*

Fodor's Choice **Santa Maria Gloriosa dei Frari.** Completed in 1442, this immense Gothic
★ church of russet-color brick—known locally as *I Frari*—is famous worldwide for its array of spectacular Venetian paintings. Visit the sacristy first, to see Giovanni Bellini's 1488 triptych *Madonna and Child with Saints* in all its mellow luminosity, painted for precisely this spot. The Corner Chapel on the other side of the chancel is graced by Bartolomeo Vivarini's (1415–84) altarpiece *St. Mark Enthroned and Saints John the Baptist, Jerome, Peter, and Nicholas* (1474), which is much more conservative, displaying attention to detail generally associated with late medieval painting.

Titian's beautiful *Madonna di Ca' Pesaro* is in the left aisle. The painting took seven years to complete (finished in 1526), and in it Titian disregarded the conventions of his time by moving the Virgin out of center and making the saints active participants. ⊠ *Campo dei Frari, San Polo* ☎ *041/272–8618, 041/275–0462 for Chorus Foundation* ⊕ *www.chorusvenezia.org* 🎫 *€3 (free with Chorus Pass)* ☉ *Mon.–Sat. 9–6, Sun. 1–6* Ⓜ *Vaporetto: San Tomà.*

Fodor's Choice **Scuola Grande di San Rocco.** Saint Rocco's popularity stemmed from his
★ miraculous recovery from the plague and his care for fellow sufferers. Throughout the plague-filled Middle Ages, followers and donations abounded, and this elegant example of Venetian Renaissance architecture, built between 1517 and 1560 and including the work of at least four architects, built for the essentially secular charitable confraternity bearing the saint's name, was the result. Although San Rocco is bold and dramatic outside, its contents are even more stunning—a series of more than 60 paintings by Tintoretto. In 1564 Tintoretto edged out competition for a commission to decorate a ceiling by submitting not a sketch, but a finished work, which he moreover offered free of charge. *Moses Striking Water from the Rock, The Brazen Serpent*, and *The Fall of Manna* represent three afflictions—thirst, disease, and hunger—that San Rocco and later his brotherhood sought to relieve. ⊠ *Campo San Rocco, San Polo 3052* ☎ *041/523–4864* ⊕ *www.scuolagrandesanrocco. it* 🎫 *€8, includes audio guide* ☉ *Daily 9:30–5:30; last entry ½ hr before closing* Ⓜ *Vaporetto: San Tomà.*

CASTELLO AND CANNAREGIO

Twice the size of tiny San Polo and Santa Croce, Castello and Cannaregio combined spread east to west from one end of Venice to the other. From working-class shipbuilding neighborhoods to the world's first ghetto, here you see a cross section of city life that's always existed beyond the palace walls. There are churches that could make a Renaissance pope jealous and one of the Grand Canal's prettiest palaces, Ca' d'Oro, as well as detour options for leaving the crowds behind.

Fodor's Choice **Ca' d'Oro.** One of the postcard sights of Venice, this exquisite Venetian
★ Gothic palace was once literally a "Golden House," when its marble traceries and ornaments were embellished with gold. It was created by Giovanni and Bartolomeo Bon between 1428 and 1430 for the

12

patrician Marino Contarini, who had read about the Roman emperor Nero's golden house in Rome, and wished to imitate it as a present to his wife. Her family owned the land and the Byzantine *fondaco* (palace-trading house) previously standing on it; you can still see the round Byzantine arches on the entry porch incorporated into the Gothic building. The last proprietor, Baron Giorgio Franchetti, left Ca' d'Oro to the city, after having had it carefully restored and furnished with antiquities, sculptures, and paintings that today make up the **Galleria Franchetti.** ✉ *Calle Ca' d'Oro, Cannaregio 3933* ☎ *041/523–8790* ⊕ *www.cadoro.org* ✉ *€6, plus €1.50 to reserve; €8 when there is a special exhibition.* ⊙ *Tues.–Sun. 8:15–7:15, Mon. 8:15–2. Closed Sun. in Jan.* Ⓜ *Vaporetto: Ca' d'Oro.*

Fodor's Choice
★

Jewish Ghetto. The neighborhood that gave the world the word *ghetto* is today a quiet neighborhood surrounding a large campo. It is home to Jewish institutions, two kosher restaurants, a rabbinical school, and five synagogues. Present-day Venetian Jews live all over the city, and the contemporary Jewish life of the ghetto, with the exception of the Jewish museum and the synagogues, is an enterprise conducted almost exclusively by American Hassidic Jews of Eastern European descent and tradition.

Though Jews may have arrived earlier, the first synagogues weren't built and a cemetery (on the Lido) wasn't founded until the Askenazim, or Northern European Jews, came in the late 1300s. Dwindling coffers may have prompted the Republic to sell temporary visas to Jews, who were over the centuries alternately tolerated and expelled.

In 1516 relentless local opposition forced the Senate to confine Jews to an island in Cannaregio, then on the outer reaches of the city, named for its *geto* (foundry). The term "ghetto" also may come from the Hebrew "ghet," meaning separation or divorce. Gates at the entrance were locked at night, and boats patrolled the surrounding canals. Jews were allowed only to lend money at low interest, operate pawnshops controlled by the government, trade in textiles, or practice medicine. Jewish doctors were highly respected and could leave the ghetto at any hour when on duty. Though ostracized, Jews were nonetheless safe in Venice, and in the 16th century the community grew considerably—primarily with refugees from the Inquisition, which persecuted Jews in southern and central Italy, Spain, and Portugal. The ghetto was allowed to expand twice, but it still had the city's densest population and consequently ended up with the city's tallest buildings. Although the gates were pulled down after Napoleon's 1797 arrival, the ghetto was reinstated during the Austrian occupation. The Jews realized full freedom only in 1866 with the founding of the Italian state. Many Jews fled Italy as a result of Mussolini's 1938 racial laws, so that on the eve of World War II, there were about 1,500 Jews left in the ghetto. Jews continued to flee, and the remaining 247 were deported by the Nazis; only eight returned. ✉ *Campo del Ghetto Nuovo* ✉ *€8.50 Synagogue tour, arranged through the Jewish Museum in the Campo del Ghetto Nuovo; museum €4; combination ticket €10.*

Museo Ebraico. The small but well-arranged museum highlights centuries of Venetian Jewish culture with splendid silver Hanukkah lamps and Torahs, and handwritten, beautifully decorated wedding contracts in Hebrew. Hourly tours in Italian and English (on the half hour) of the ghetto and its five synagogues leave from the museum. ⊠ *Campo del Ghetto Nuovo, Cannaregio 2902/B* ☎ *041/715–359* ⊕ *www.museoebraico.it* ⊠ *Museum €3; guided tour and museum €8.50* ☉ *June–Sept., Sun.–Fri. 10–7; Oct.–May, Sun.–Fri. 10–6. Synagogue tours (in English or Italian): June–Sept., Sun.–Fri. hrly 10:30–6:30; Oct.–May, Sun.–Fri. hrly 10:30–5:30.* Ⓜ *Vaporetto: San Marcuola, Guglie.*

> ### WORD OF MOUTH
>
> "The narrow *calle* of Venice could strike one as either charming or claustrophobic. At different times, we had both reactions." —Suexxyy

Fodor's Choice
★ **Santa Maria dei Miracoli.** Tiny yet harmoniously proportioned, this Renaissance gem, built between 1481 and 1489, is sheathed in marble and decorated inside with exquisite marble reliefs. Architect Pietro Lombardo (circa 1435–1515) miraculously compressed the building into its confined space, then created the illusion of greater size by varying the color of the exterior, adding extra pilasters on the building's canal side, and offsetting the arcade windows to make the arches appear deeper. The church was built to house *I Miracoli,* an image of the Virgin Mary by Niccolò di Pietro (1394–1440) that is said to have performed miracles—look for it on the high altar. ⊠ *Campo Santa Maria Nova* ☎ *041/275–0462 for Chorus Foundation* ⊕ *www.chorusvenezia.org* ⊠ *€3 (free with Chorus Pass)* ☉ *Mon.–Sat. 10–5* Ⓜ *Vaporetto: Rialto.*

Fodor's Choice
★ **Santi Giovanni e Paolo.** A venerated jewel, this gorgeous church looms over one of the most picturesque squares in Venice: the Campo Giovanni e Paolo, centered around the magnificent 15th-century equestrian statue of Bartolomeo Colleoni by the Florentine Andrea Verrocchio. The massive Italian Gothic church itself is of the Dominican order and was consecrated in 1430. Bartolomeo Bon's portal, combining Gothic and classical elements, was added between 1458 and 1462, using columns salvaged from Torcello. The 15th-century stained-glass window near the side entrance is breathtaking for its brilliant colors and beautiful figures; it was made in Murano from drawings by Bartolomeo Vivarini and Gerolamo Mocetto (circa 1458–1531). The second official church of the Republic after San Marco, San Zanipolo is the Venetian equivalent of London's Westminster Abbey, with a great number of important people, including 25 doges, buried here. Artistic highlights include an early (1465) polyptych by Giovanni Bellini (right aisle, second altar) where the influence of Mantegna is still very evident, Alvise Vivarini's *Christ Carrying the Cross* (sacristy), and Lorenzo Lotto's *Charity of St. Antonino* (right transept). Don't miss the *Cappella del Rosario* (Rosary Chapel), off the left transept, built in the 16th century to commemorate the 1571 victory of Lepanto, in western Greece, when Venice led a combined European fleet to defeat the Turkish Navy. ⊠ *Campo dei Santi Giovanni e Paolo* ☎ *041/523–5913* ⊠ *€3* ☉ *Mon.–Sat. 9:30–6, Sun. 1–6* Ⓜ *Vaporetto: Fondamente Nove, Rialto.*

WHERE TO EAT

The catchword in Venice, at both fancy restaurants and holes-in-the-wall, is fish, often at its tastiest when it looks like nothing you've seen before. How do you learn firsthand about the catch of the day? An early-morning visit to the Rialto's *pescheria* (fish market) is more instructive than any book.

12

There's no getting around the fact that Venice has more than its share of overpriced, mediocre eateries that prey on tourists. Avoid places with cajoling waiters standing outside, and beware of restaurants that don't display their prices. At the other end of the spectrum, showy *menu turistico* (tourist menu) boards make offerings clear in a dozen languages, but for the same €15–€20 you'd spend at such places, you could do better at a *bacaro* (the local version of a wine bar) making a meal of *cicchetti* (savory snacks).

CANNAREGIO

$ ✕ **Anice Stellato.** Off the main concourse, on one of the most romantic
VENETIAN *fondamente* (canalside streets) of Cannaregio, this family-run bacaro-trattoria is the place to stop for fairly priced, satisfying fare, though service can feel indifferent and, occasionally but not often, the kitchen is a bit inconsistent. Narrow columns rise from the colorful tile floor, dividing the room into cozy sections. There are also a few outdoor canalside tables. Classics like *seppie in nero* (squid in its ink) are enriched with such offerings as *sarde in beccafico* (sardines rolled and stuffed with breadcrumbs, herbs, and cheese) and tagliatelle with prawns and zucchini flowers. They also serve several meat dishes, including a tender beef filet stewed in Barolo wine. $ *Average main: €18* ⊠ *Fondamenta de la Sensa, Cannaregio 3272* 🕾 *041/720–744* ☾ *Closed Mon. and Tues., 1 wk in Feb., and 3 wks in Aug.* Ⓜ *Vaporetto: San Alvise or San Marcuola.*

$$ ✕ **Vini da Gigio.** Paolo and Laura, a brother-sister team, run this refined
VENETIAN trattoria as if they've invited you to dinner in their home, while keeping
Fodor's Choice the service professional. Deservedly popular with Venetians and visi-
★ tors alike, it's one of the best values in the city. Indulge in pastas such as rigatoni with duck sauce and arugula-stuffed ravioli. Fish is well represented—try the sesame-encrusted tuna—but the meat dishes steal the show. The steak with red-pepper sauce and the *tagliata di agnello* (sautéed lamb filet with a light, crusty coating) are both superb, and you'll never enjoy a better *fegato alla veneziana* (Venetian-style liver with onions). This is a place for wine connoisseurs, as the cellar is one of the best in the city. Come at lunch or for the second sitting in the evening for more relaxed service. $ *Average main: €25* ⊠ *Fondamenta San Felice, Cannaregio 3628/A* 🕾 *041/528–5140* ⊕ *www.vinidagigio. com* ⚠ *Reservations essential* ☾ *Closed Mon. and Tues., 2 wks in Jan., and 3 wks in Aug.* Ⓜ *Vaporetto: Ca' d'Oro.*

DORSODURO

$ ✕ **Cantinone già Schiavi.** A mainstay for anyone living or working in the
WINE BAR area, this beautiful, family-run 19th-century bacaro across from the *squero* (gondola repair shop) of San Trovaso has original furnishings and one of the best wine cellars in town—the walls are covered floor to ceiling by bottles for purchase. Cicchetti here are some of the most

inventive—and freshest—in Venice (feel free to compliment the Signora, who makes them up to twice a day). Try the crostini-style layers of bread, smoked swordfish, and slivers of raw zucchini, or pungent slices of parmigiano, fig, pistachio, and toast. They also have a creamy version of baccalà mantecato spiced with herbs, and there are nearly a dozen open bottles of wine for experimenting at the bar. You'll have no trouble spotting the Cantinone as you approach: it's the one with throngs of chatty patrons enjoying themselves. [$] *Average main: €2* ✉ *Fondamenta Nani, Dorsoduro 992* ☎ *041/523–0034* 💳 *No credit cards* 🕓 *Closed Sun. and 2 wks in Aug.* [M] *Vaporetto: Zattere, Accademia.*

$$$$ NORTHERN ITALIAN

🍴 **Ristorante Riviera.** The impressive panorama from their Zattare terrace attracts travelers yearning for a view, and the Riviera certainly offers that. Choose from contemporary takes on a variety of traditional Venetian dishes, including calf's liver with figs; "guitar string" pasta with shrimp, tiny green beans, and mint; and venison with blueberry sauce. A regional wine list is well matched to the cuisine; don't be surprised if the owner stops by to be sure you're enjoying your meal. Perhaps suited more to travelers than locals (who never worry about a view), while pleasing, the Riviera is definitely a splurge (note the €6 cover). [$] *Average main: €50* ✉ *Zattere, Dorsoduro 1473* ☎ *041/522–7621* 🌐 *www.ristoranteriviera.it* ✍ *Reservations essential* 🕓 *Closed Mon. and 4 wks in Jan. and Feb.* [M] *Vaporetto: San Basilio.*

SAN POLO

$$ MODERN ITALIAN Fodor's Choice ★

🍴 **Al Paradiso.** In a small dining room made warm and cozy by its pleasing and unpretentious decor, proprietor Giordano makes all diners feel like honored guests. Pappardelle "al Paradiso" takes pasta with seafood sauce to new heights, while risotto with shrimp, champagne, and grapefruit puts a delectable twist on a traditional dish. The inspired and original array of entrées includes meat and fish selections such as salmon with honey and balsamic vinegar in a stunning presentation. Unlike many elegant restaurants, Al Paradiso serves generous portions and many of the delicious antipasti and primi are quite satisfying; you may want to follow the traditional Italian way of ordering and wait until you've finished your antipasto or your primo before you order your secondo. [$] *Average main: €26* ✉ *Calle del Paradiso, San Polo 767* ☎ *041/523–4910* ✍ *Reservations essential* 🕓 *Closed Mon. and 3 wks in Jan. and Feb.* [M] *Vaporetto: San Silvestro.*

$$ VENETIAN Fodor's Choice ★

🍴 **Osteria Da Fiore.** The understated atmosphere, simple decor, and quiet elegance featured alongside Da Fiore's modern take on traditional Venetian cuisine certainly merit its international reputation. With such beautifully prepared cuisine, you would expect the kitchen to be manned by a chef with a household name; however the kitchen is headed by none other than owner Maurizio Martin's wife, Mara, who learned to cook from her grandmother. The other surprise is that while this restaurant is in an upper price category, it is hardly among the priciest in Venice. It offers several moderately priced (€50), three-course, prix-fixe luncheon menus, and the prix-fixe dinner menu is €80, which brings it very much into line with most of the more elegant choices in town. The menu is constantly changing, but generally fritto misto or Da Fiore's tender, aromatic version of seppie in nero is almost always available. Reservations, perhaps made a few days in advance in high season, are essential for dinner, but you can try just dropping in for lunch. $ *Average main: €34* ✉ *Calle del Scaleter, San Polo 2002* ☎ *041–721–308* ⊕ *www.dafiore. net* ⚓ *Reservations essential* ⊘ *Closed Sun. and Mon., plus 3 wks in Jan.* Ⓜ *Vaporetto: San Tomà.*

12

SANTA CROCE

$ ✕ **La Zucca.** The simple place settings, lattice-wood walls, and mélange NORTHERN of languages make La Zucca (the pumpkin) feel much like a typical, ITALIAN somewhat sophisticated vegetarian restaurant that you could find in any European city. What makes La Zucca special is the use of fresh, local ingredients (many of which, like the particularly sweet zucca itself, aren't normally found outside northern Italy), and simply great cooking. Though the menu does have superb meat dishes such as the *piccata di pollo ai caperi e limone con riso* (sliced chicken with capers and lemon served with rice), more attention is paid to dishes from the garden: try the radicchio *di Treviso con funghi e scaglie di Montasio* (with mushrooms and shavings of Montasio cheese), the *finocchi piccanti con olive* (fennel in a spicy tomato-olive sauce), or the house's signature dish—the *flan di zucca,* a luscious, naturally sweet, pumpkin pudding topped with slivered, aged ricotta cheese. $ *Average main: €18* ✉ *Calle del Tintor (at Ponte de Megio), Santa Croce 1762* ☎ *041/524–1570* ⊕ *www.lazucca.it* ⚓ *Reservations essential* ⊘ *Closed Sun. and 1 wk in Dec.* Ⓜ *Vaporetto: San Stae.*

WHERE TO STAY

Most of Venice's hotels are in renovated palaces, but space is at a premium—and comes for a price—and even relatively ample rooms may seem cramped by American standards. Also, not all hotels have lounge areas, and because of preservation laws, some hotels are not permitted to install elevators, so if these features are essential, ask ahead of time.

Many travelers assume that a hotel near Piazza San Marco will give them the most convenient location, but keep in mind that Venice is scaled to humans (on foot) rather than automobiles; it's difficult to find a location that's *not* convenient to most of the city. Areas away from San Marco may also offer the benefit of being less overrun by day-trippers whose primary destination is the Piazza.

It is essential to have detailed directions to your hotel when you arrive. Arm yourself with not only a detailed map and postal address (Dorsoduro 825), but the actual street name (Fondamenta San Trovaso).

The public relations arm of **AVA** (*Venetian Hoteliers Association*) has booths where you can make same-day reservations at **Piazzale Roma** (☎ *041/523–1397* ⊘ *Daily 9 am–10 pm*), **Santa Lucia train station** (☎ *041/715–288, 041/715–016* ⊘ *Daily 8 am–9 pm*), and **Marco Polo Airport** (☎ *041/541–5133* ⊘ *Daily 9 am–10 pm*).

CANNAREGIO

$$ 🛏 **3749 Ponte Chiodo.** Attractively appointed guest rooms handy to B&B/INN the Ca' d'Oro vaporetto stop look past geranium-filled windows to the bridge leading to its entrance (one of the only ones without hand

railings remaining) and canals below or the spacious enclosed garden. **Pros:** highly attentive service; warm, relaxed atmosphere; private garden; excellent value. **Cons:** no elevator; some bathrooms are smallish. [$] *Rooms from: €180* ✉ *Calle Racchetta, Cannaregio 3749* ☎ *041/241–3935* 🌐 *www.pontechiodo.it* 🛏 *6 rooms* 🍴 *Breakfast* [M] *Vaporetto: Ca' d'Oro.*

CASTELLO

$ B&B/INN 🏨 **Santa Maria della Pietà.** Though this *casa per ferie* (vacation house) is more spartan than sumptuous, there's more light and space here than in many of Venice's four-star lodgings. **Pros:** space, light, and views at a good price. **Cons:** not luxurious; few amenities; a bit overpriced, especially since rooms do not all have private bathrooms. [$] *Rooms from: €100* ✉ *Calle della Pietà, Castello 3701* ☎ *041/244–3639* 🌐 *www.pietavenezia.org/it/istituto/casa_per_ferie* 🛏 *15 rooms with shared bath* 💳 *No credit cards* 🍴 *Breakfast* [M] *Vaporetto: Arsenale or San Zaccaria.*

DORSODURO

$$ B&B/INN 🏨 **Casa Rezzonico.** Some pleasant if generic guest rooms overlook a sunny fondamenta and canal, and others a spacious private garden, where breakfast is served in good weather. **Pros:** canal views at a reasonable rate; two lively squares nearby; great for families. **Cons:** must reserve well in advance; some rooms are quite small; ground-floor rooms are dark; a/c and heating not totally reliable. [$] *Rooms from: €150* ✉ *Fondamenta Gherardini, Dorsoduro 2813* ☎ *041/277–0653* 🌐 *www.casarezzonico.it* 🛏 *6 rooms* 🍴 *Breakfast* [M] *Vaporetto: Ca' Rezzonico.*

$$$$ HOTEL 🏨 **Hotel American–Dinesen.** The exceptional service here will help you feel at home in spacious guest rooms furnished in Venetian brocade fabrics with lacquered Venetian-style furniture; some front rooms have terraces with canal views. **Pros:** high degree of personal service; on a bright, quiet, exceptionally picturesque canal; free Wi-Fi. **Cons:** no elevator; rooms with a canal view are more expensive; some rooms could stand refurbishing. [$] *Rooms from: €300* ✉ *San Vio, Dorsoduro 628* ☎ *041/520–4733* 🌐 *www.hotelamerican.com* 🛏 *28 rooms, 2 suites* 🍴 *Breakfast* [M] *Vaporetto: Accademia, Salute, and Zattere.*

$$ HOTEL Fodor's Choice ★ 🏨 **La Calcina.** Time-burnished and elegant rooms with parquet floors, original 19th-century furniture, and firm beds enjoy an enviable position along the sunny Zattere, with front rooms offering vistas across the wide Giudecca Canal; a few have private terraces. **Pros:** panoramic views from some rooms; elegant, historic atmosphere. **Cons:** not for travelers who prefer ultramodern surroundings; no elevator; rooms with views are appreciably more expensive. [$] *Rooms from: €180* ✉ *Zattere, Dorsoduro 780* ☎ *041/520–6466* 🌐 *www.lacalcina.com* 🛏 *27 rooms (26 with bath), 5 suites* 🍴 *Breakfast* [M] *Vaporetto: Zattere.*

$$$ HOTEL Fodor's Choice ★ 🏨 **Pensione Accademia Villa Maravege.** Behind iron gates in one of the most densely packed parts of the city you'll find yourself in front of a large and elegant garden and Gothic-style "villa" where accommodations are charmingly decorated with a connoisseur's eye. **Pros:** a unique "villa" in the heart of Venice; one of the city's most enchanting hotels. **Cons:** standard rooms are smaller than is usual in Venice, and seem to

be more sparsely decorated than the more expensive options. $ *Rooms from: €290* ✉ *Fondamenta Bollani, Dorsoduro 1058* ☎ *041/521–0188* ⊕ *www.pensioneaccademia.it* ⮑ *27 rooms, 2 suites* ❍ *Breakfast* Ⓜ *Vaporetto: Accademia.*

SAN MARCO

$$$$ ☷ **Bauer Il Palazzo.** A palazzo with an ornate, 1930s neo-Gothic facade
HOTEL facing the Grand Canal has lavishly decorated guest rooms (large by
Fodor's Choice Venetian standards) featuring high ceilings, tufted walls of Bevilacqua
★ and Rubelli fabrics, Murano glass, marble bathrooms, damask drapes,
and imitation antique furniture. **Pros:** pampering service; high-end
luxury. **Cons:** in one of the busiest areas of the city; you will pay hand-
somely for a room with a canal view; Wi-Fi is additional. $ *Rooms
from: €700* ✉ *Campo San Moisè, San Marco 1413/D* ☎ *041/520–7022*
⊕ *www.ilpalazzovenezia.com* ⮑ *38 rooms, 34 suites* ❍ *Breakfast*
Ⓜ *Vaporetto: Vallaresso.*

$$ ☷ **Ca' dei Dogi.** A quiet courtyard secluded from the San Marco melée
HOTEL offers an island of calm in six individually decorated guest rooms (some
with private terraces) that feature contemporary furnishings and acces-
sories. **Pros:** some rooms have terraces with views of the Doge's Palace.
Cons: rooms are on the small side; furnishings are spartan and look
a bit cheap; located in the middle of the most tourist-frequented part
of Venice. $ *Rooms from: €150* ✉ *Corte Santa Scolastica, Castello
4242* ☎ *041/241–3751* ⊕ *www.cadeidogi.it* ⮑ *6 rooms* ☽ *Closed Dec.*
❍ *Breakfast* Ⓜ *Vaporetto: San Zaccaria.*

NIGHTLIFE AND THE ARTS

CARNEVALE
The first historical evidence of Carnevale (Carnival) in Venice dates
from 1097, and for centuries the city marked the days preceding *qua-
resima* (Lent, the 40 days of abstinence leading up to Palm Sunday)
with abundant feasting and wild celebrations. Carnevale was revived
in the 1970s, and each year over the 10- to 12-day Carnevale period
more than a half-million people attend concerts, theater and street per-
formances, masquerade balls, historical processions, fashion shows,
and contests.

SHOPPING

Alluring shops abound in Venice. You'll find countless vendors of trade-
mark Venetian wares such as glass and lace; the authenticity of some
goods can be suspect. For more sophisticated tastes (and deeper pock-
ets), there are jewelers, antiques dealers, and high-fashion boutiques on
a par with those in Italy's larger cities. There are also some interesting
craft and art studios, where you can find high-quality, one-of-a-kind
articles, from handmade shoes to decorative lamps and mirrors.

It's always a good idea to mark on your map the location of a shop
that interests you; otherwise you may not be able to find it again in
the maze of tiny streets. Regular store hours are usually 9–12:30 and
3:30 or 4–7:30; some stores are closed Saturday afternoon or Monday

morning. Food shops are open 8–1 and 5–7:30, and are closed Wednesday afternoon and all day Sunday. Many tourist-oriented shops are open all day, every day.

SHOPPING DISTRICTS

The **San Marco** area is full of shops and couture boutiques. **Le Mercerie,** along with the Frezzeria and Calle dei Fabbri, leading from Piazza San Marco, are some of Venice's busiest shopping streets. Other good shopping areas surround Calle del Teatro and Campi San Salvador, Manin, San Fantin, and San Bartolomeo. Less expensive shops are between the Rialto Bridge and San Polo.

13

THE NETHERLANDS

Amsterdam, the Bulb Fields, Delft, Rotterdam

WHAT'S WHERE

1 Amsterdam. Built on concentric rings of canals bordered by time-burnished, step-gabled houses, Amsterdam, the principal city of the Netherlands, is custom-made for sightseeing. You almost have to get to know the city from the water to be properly introduced, and glass-roof canal boats make that possible. Helpfully, the city is held together by the linchpins of its great public squares: the Dam, the Rembrandtplein, the Munt, and the Leidseplein.

2 The Bulb Fields. West of Amsterdam, the Bloemen Route (Flower Road) leads from Aalsmeer—one of the greatest floral villages in Europe—to the famed Keuken-hof gardens and the town of Lisse. This is the Holland of tulips, hyacinths, and narcissi, aglow with the colors of Easter in spring and generally a rainbow of color year-round.

3 Delft. The tree-lined canals, humpbacked bridges, and step-gabled houses of Delft preserve the atmosphere of the 16th and 17th centuries better than any other city in the Netherlands. Visit here and you'll recognize it as the scene of paintings by native sons Vermeer and Pieter de Hooch.

4 Rotterdam. Rebuilt almost from scratch follow-ing the devastation of World War II, Europe's biggest port has worked hard to trans-form itself into a showpiece of modern architecture. By contrast, the historic area of Delfshaven—from where the Pilgrim Fathers set sail for their New England—escaped intact.

0   20 miles

0   30 km

North Sea

Voorn

Overflakke

Schouwen

Noord   Duivelanc

Walcheren   Beveland   The

Zuid

Vlissingen   Beveland

Westerschelde

Terneuzen

Schiermonnikoog

Ameland

Terschelling

Delfzijl

Vlieland

Leeuwarden

Groningen

Texel

Waddenzee

Den Helder

Heerenveen

Assen

IJsselmeer

Steenwijk

Emmen

Enkhuizen

Alkmaar

Hoorn

Meppel

Hoogeveen

Edam

IJmuiden

Zaandam

Lelystad

*Oostelijk
Flevoland*

Zwolle

Haarlem

*Zuidelijk
Flevoland*

Almelo

AMSTERDAM

Harderwijk

Deventer

Hengelo

Lisse

Aalsmeer

Hilversum

Apeldoorn

Enschede

Leiden

Alphen

Amersfoort

DEN HAAG
(THE HAGUE)

Utrecht

Lek

Arnhem

Doetinchem

Delft

Gouda

Rotterdam

Waal

Nijmegen

Winterswijk

Beijerland

Dordrecht

s'Hertogenbosch

Breda

Tilburg

Rhein

Roosendaal

Eindhoven

Maas

GERMANY

BELGIUM

Maastricht

NEED TO KNOW

North Sea

NETHERLANDS

Amsterdam

AT A GLANCE

Capital: Amsterdam

Population: 16,804,000

Currency: Euro

Money: ATMs are common; credit cards widely accepted

Language: Dutch

Country Code: ☎ 31

Emergencies: ☎ 112

Driving: On the right

Electricity: 220v/50 cycles; electrical plugs have two round prongs

Time: Six hours ahead of New York

Documents: Up to 90 days with valid passport; Schengen rules apply

Mobile Phones: GSM (900 and 1800 bands)

Major Mobile Companies: KPN, Vodafone, Orange, T-Mobile

WEBSITES

Netherlands: ⊕ holland.com

Amsterdam: ⊕ iamsterdam.com

Amsterdo: ⊕ amsterdo.com

GETTING AROUND

✈ **Air Travel:** The major airport is Amsterdam; Eindhoven and Rotterdam have some intra-Europe flights.

🚌 **Bus and Tram Travel:** Very efficient within the larger cities but limited for getting around the country.

🚗 **Car Travel:** Skip the car in Amsterdam in favor of biking or walking, but consider renting one to reach more rural areas, like the tulip fields and smaller Dutch villages.

🚆 **Train Travel:** Dutch trains are modern, quick, relatively inexpensive, and will get you between nearly every town and city in the Netherlands.

PLAN YOUR BUDGET

	HOTEL ROOM	MEAL	ATTRACTIONS
Low Budget	€120	€15	Oude Kerk, €5
Mid Budget	€165	€22	Rijksmuseum, €15
High Budget	€383	€85	Canal cruise (dinner), €112

WAYS TO SAVE

Snack at the markets. You can make a meal of fresh produce, cheese, haring sandwiches, and stroopwafel for dessert from local markets. Amsterdam's is one of the best. ⊕ www.albertcuypmarkt.nl.

Rent an apartment. A rental often offers more space at a better price, especially in Amsterdam.

Move around like a local. Rent a bike to get around the cities easily and cheaply, or invest in a refillable OV-chipkaart for public transit. ⊕ www.ov-chipkaart.nl.

Buy a discount card. The "I Amsterdam" card offers entry to museums plus a free canal cruise, public transport, and other discounts. ⊕ www.iamsterdam.com.

PLAN YOUR TIME

Hassle Factor	Low. Flights to Amsterdam are frequent, and it's easy to get around the Netherlands by train or car.
3 days	You can sample Amsterdam's top attractions plus take a half-day trip out to the tulip fields, in season.
1 week	Once you're finished thoroughly exploring the charms of Amsterdam, take day-trips to Rotterdam, Delft, and the Storybook Holland villages north of the capital, perhaps biking there if you feel comfortable.
2 weeks	You'll have plenty of time to cover all corners of this small country, with stops in Amsterdam, Rotterdam, Delft, Haarlem, and The Hague, not to mention the picturesque Kinderdijk windmills.

WHEN TO GO

High Season: Tulip season, from mid-March to mid-May, sees crowds of tourists flocking to the bulb fields and visiting the cities. July and August, when the weather is at its most pleasant, also brings an influx to Amsterdam and the rest of the country.

Low Season: Unless you like rain, and snow, and cold, the winter months (November through mid-March) are not the best time to visit the Netherlands. However, if you snuggle up with a blanket outside a *gezellig* (cozy) brown café, *glühwein* (mulled wine) in hand, you may enjoy this quieter time.

Value Season: May and June may still be drizzly, but usually the Netherlands has emerged from the winter's deep freeze. September and October also see fewer tourists but generally nice weather, heading outside on crisp—and, if they're lucky—sunny days.

BIG EVENTS

April: Deck yourself out in orange to celebrate King's Day. ⊕ www.koninginnedagamsterdam.nl

July: The three-day North Sea Jazz Festival brings world-class tunes to Rotterdam. ⊕ www.northseajazz.com

August: Outrageous floats make up the Amsterdam Gay Pride Canal Parade. ⊕ www.amsterdamgaypride.nl

January: On National Tulip Day, Dutch tulip growers create a massive temporary garden in Amsterdam's Dam Square.

READ THIS

■ *Anne Frank: The Diary of a Young Girl,* Anne Frank. An essential classic.

■ *Girl with a Pearl Earring,* Tracy Chevalier. A fictionalized story of Vermeer.

■ *The UnDutchables,* Colin White and Laurie Boucke. A funny and honest look at Dutch culture.

WATCH THIS

■ *Diamonds Are Forever.* Sean Connery's James Bond makes a stop in Amsterdam.

■ *Meet the Fokkens.* Documentary on elderly twin Dutch prostitutes.

■ *Turkish Delight.* Paul Verhoeven's tale of a bohemian Amsterdam sculptor.

EAT THIS

■ **Bitterballen:** fried breadcrumb balls filled with meat, found in every café

■ **Gouda:** the national cheese, eaten young (*jong*) or aged (*oud*)

■ **Herring (haring):** with pickles and onions or wrapped in bread

■ **Poffertjes:** mini pancakes, topped with powdered sugar

■ **Rijsttafel:** Indonesian "rice table" of small and often spicy dishes

■ **Stroopwafel:** sweet *stroop* (*syrup*) between two warm waffles

The Netherlands (only the two provinces that surround Amsterdam and The Hague are technically "Holland") is every cliché you imagine and more. While the clogs may be largely confined to the souvenir shops, this really is a land of windmills, tulips, canals, and bicycles, albeit today with the modern backdrop of a fast-paced 21st-century nation. At its heart is one of Europe's most important capitals, a famously open and tolerant place where almost anything goes, and the pragmatic businesslike approach of the Dutch has even turned its red-light district and coffee shops into tourist attractions and profitable industries.

The Netherlands only assumed its current form in 1830, when Belgium broke away as an independent state, but the country has existed in one form or another for around a thousand years. A proud seafaring nation that built its wealth on international trade, it has also waged a war on the sea itself that is still ongoing. With much of the land lying below sea level, it owes its continued existence to a complex series of dykes, barriers, and polders reclaimed from the waters. This fight, coupled with a population that has always been slightly too large for the available land, has turned the Dutch into perhaps the most pragmatic and practical of all Europeans, as they have learned through the years to make the best of what they had.

While Amsterdam has all the waterways, gabled townhouses, and rusty pushbikes you could possibly shake a stick at, it is only one aspect of the Netherlands. To get the full picture you'll need to head out to the other towns, or to the countryside that is just as flat as you've been told. The country's best-known city may be the national capital, but Rotterdam is where you'll find the modern architecture and melting-pot cultures. Delft is a wonderful, dollhouselike city that also shouldn't be missed, while the brightly colored patchwork of flowers on the Flower Road— if you time your visit to coincide with the spring blooms—is an experience you won't soon forget.

WHEN TO GO

The Netherlands is at its best when the temperatures climb, and cafés and restaurants spill across sidewalks to invite leisurely alfresco meals. Unfortunately, because such weather is so transient, you may find yourself sharing your sun-dappled experience with many others. Spring is the driest time of year, and since it's also when the famous tulip fields bloom (April and May are the prime bloom-viewing months), this is the most popular time to visit Holland.

TOP REASONS TO GO

Great Art. In the country that gave the world Rembrandt, Hals, Vermeer, Van Gogh, and Mondrian, you simply cannot leave without stopping by an art gallery or two—Amsterdam's Rijksmuseum and Van Gogh Museum alone will keep you occupied all day, and Rotterdam's Museum Boijmans van Beuningen is unmissable.

Saying It with Flowers. Visit the Keukenhof, the world's largest flower gardens, and home to millions of colorful blooms during its annual spring season.

Taking to the Water. Water is crucial to Dutch society. There are 50 miles of canals in Amsterdam alone, and what better way to see them than from a boat?

Pottery in Delft. De Koninklijke Porceleyne Fles, established in 1653, is the only remaining factory producing Delft's famous blue-and-white porcelain.

Biking. Go native by renting a bike and taking to two wheels, the preferred form of transportation in this flat land. Cycling Amsterdam is a superb way to avoid crammed trams and pricey taxis.

13

With the approach of summer, museums, galleries, and tourist sights heave with visitors. Some say that if you're making an extended tour of Europe, you should consider scheduling Holland for the beginning or end of your itinerary, saving July and August for exploring less crowded countries.

If you have to visit in high summer, be sure to take a vacation from your Amsterdam vacation with some side trips to outer towns that have historic, quaint Dutch beauty without the crush. The main cultural calendar runs from September through June, but happily there are so many festivals and open-air events scheduled during the summer that no one really notices.

PLANNING

GETTING HERE AND AROUND

AIR TRAVEL
Located 17 km (11 miles) southeast of Amsterdam, Luchthaven Schiphol (pronounced "Shkip-hole") is the main passenger airport for the Netherlands and has frequent nonstop flights from the U.S. and Canada from a variety of airlines. There are several regional airports, but these largely cater to the short-haul and charter routes. With the annual number of passengers using Schiphol topping 50 million, it is ranked among the world's top five best-connected airports. A hotel, a service to aid passengers with disabilities, parking lots, and a main office of the Netherlands tourist board can prove most useful.

Contacts **Amsterdam Schiphol Airport** ⊠ *17 km (11 miles) southwest of Amsterdam* 🖀 *0900/0566 (€0.40 per min), 31/207–940–800 from outside the Netherlands only* ⊕ *www.schiphol.nl.*

BOAT AND FERRY TRAVEL

International ferries link Holland with the United Kingdom. There are two daily Stena Line crossings between the **Hoek van Holland** and Harwich, on a car ferry taking approximately 6½ hours. There is one P&O North Sea overnight crossing between the Europoort in Rotterdam and Hull, which takes about 12 hours, and one DFDS Seaways overnight crossing from Newcastle to IJmuiden, in Amsterdam, taking 15 hours.

Contacts **DFDS Seaways** ⊠ *Sluisplein 33, IJmuiden* 🖀 *0255/546–666 in the Netherlands, 0871/522–9955 in U.K.* ⊕ *www.dfdsseaways.com.* **P&O Ferries** ⊠ *In Holland: Beneluxhaven, Havennummer 5805, Rotterdam/Europoort, Rotterdam* 🖀 *020/200–8333 in the Netherlands, 070/707–771 in Belgium* ⊕ *www. poferries.com.* **Stena Line** ⊠ *In Holland: Hoek van Holland Terminal, Stationsweg 10, Hoek van Holland* 🖀 *0844/770–7070 in U.K., 0900/8123 in NL (€0.10 per min)* ⊕ *www.stenaline.nl.*

BUS TRAVEL

The bus and tram systems within the Netherlands provide excellent transport links within cities. To get around by bus (as well as by tram and metro), you'll need an OV-chipkaart (public transport chip card), an electronic payment system that you hold up to a detector each time you board and leave any bus or tram. Bought preloaded from metro, train, and bus stations or from some magazine kiosks, these credit card–size tickets can be topped up with credit from machines in the stations and are debited according to the distance traveled. You can also buy tickets for individual journeys from bus/tram drivers, although this works out to be more expensive. Visit the OV-chipkaart website (⊕ *www.ov-chipkaart.nl*) or call the help desk (🖀 *0900/500–6010*) for more information.

Contacts **Trains, Buses, Trams, and Ferries.** Information on all public transportation, including schedules, fares for trains, buses, trams, and ferries in the Netherlands. 🖀 *0900/9292 (€0.70 per min)* ⊕ *9292.nl.*

CAR TRAVEL

A network of well-maintained highways and other roads covers the Netherlands, making car travel convenient, although traffic is exceptionally heavy around the bigger cities. There are no tolls on roads or highways. Many of the gas stations in the Netherlands (especially those on the high-traffic motorways) are open 24 hours.

TRAIN TRAVEL

Dutch trains are modern, and the quickest way to travel between city centers. Services are relatively frequent, with a minimum of two departures per hour for each route. Although many Dutch people complain about delays, the trains usually run roughly on time. Most staff speak English. Reserving a seat is not possible. Intercity trains can come double-decker; they stop only at major stations. *Sneltreins* (express trains) also have two decks but take in more stops, so they are a little slower. *Stoptreins* (local trains) are the slowest. Smoking is not permitted on trains, and only permitted in designated zones in stations. On the train you have the choice of first- or second-class. First-class travel costs 50% more, and on local trains gives you a slightly larger seat in a compartment that is less likely to be full. At peak travel times first-class train travel is worth the difference.

Train tickets for travel within the country can be purchased at the last minute. Normal tickets are either *enkele reis* (one-way) or *retour* (round-trip). Round-trip tickets cost approximately 75% of two single tickets. They are valid only on the day you buy them, unless you ask specifically for a ticket with a different date. You can get on and off at will at stops in between your destinations until midnight. You can also use the **OV-chipkaart,** but remember to check in on the platform before you board, and to check out when you leave the train. You can also buy tickets at the yellow touch-screen ticket machines in every railway station. These machines only accept cards with a four-digit PIN code; to use a credit card, you must purchase tickets at the manned ticket desk, where they'll cost slightly more. Note that you can't buy tickets aboard the trains, and you risk a hefty fine if you board and travel without one.

Intercity trains link Amsterdam and Brussels in around three hours. Thalys high-speed trains link Brussels (in 1½ hours) and Amsterdam (4 hours) with Paris. Eurostar operates high-speed passenger trains between stations in London and Brussels (Midi) in 2½ hours.

Contacts Eurostar ⊕ *www.eurostar.com.* **NS–Nederlandse Spoorwegen/ Dutch Railways** ⊕ *www.ns.nl.* **Thalys** ⊕ *www.thalys.com.*

13

HOTELS

The Netherlands has a range of options from major international hotel chains to family-run restored inns. Accommodations in Amsterdam are at a particular premium at any time of year, so book well in advance. Should you arrive without a hotel room, for a small fee the tourist offices can help you find a room.

CLASSIFICATIONS

Dutch hotels are awarded stars (one to five) by the Benelux Hotel Classification System, an independent agency that inspects properties based on their facilities and services. Those with three or more stars feature en suite bathrooms where a shower is standard, whereas a tub is a four-star standard. Rooms in lodgings listed in this guide have a shower unless otherwise indicated.

RATES

Room rates for deluxe and four-star rooms are on a par with those in other European cities. Most cheaper hotels quote room rates including breakfast, while for those at the top end it usually costs extra. Many hotels in Amsterdam appear to be permanently full, so book as far in advance as you can to be sure of getting what you want.

RESTAURANTS

Most restaurants are open for lunch and dinner only. Cafés usually also have a snacks menu (*kleine kaart*), which is available all day. A set-price, three- or four-course menu for lunch is offered in many restaurants. Dinner menus are usually more elaborate and slightly more expensive. Smoking is prohibited in Dutch cafés and restaurants.

MEALS AND MEAL TIMES

Traditional Dutch cuisine is very simple and filling. A typical Dutch *ontbijt* (breakfast) consists of *brood* (bread), *kaas* (cheese), *hard gekookte ei* (hard-boiled eggs), ham, yogurt, jams, and fruit.

Lunch is usually a *boterham* (sandwich) or a *broodje* (soft roll or a baguette). Salads and warm dishes are also popular. One specialty is an *uitsmijter*: two pieces of bread with three fried eggs, ham, and cheese, garnished with pickles and onions. *Pannenkoeken* (pancakes) are a favorite lunch treat, topped with ham and cheese or fruit and a thick *stroop* (syrup).

A popular afternoon snack is *frites* (french fries); try them with curry ketchup and onions (*frites speciaal*), with a *kroket* (a fried, breaded meat roll) on the side. Another snack is whole *haring* (herring) served with raw onions.

Diner (dinner) usually consists of three courses: an appetizer, main course, and dessert, and many restaurants have special prix-fixe deals. Beverages are always charged separately. Dutch specialties include *erwtensoep* (a thick pea soup with sausage), *gerookte paling* (smoked eel), and *hutspot* (beef stew). Steamed North Sea mussels are popular. In general, the standard of the once-dull Dutch cuisine is improving steadily. Chefs have in recent years become more adventurous, and you will find many other more exciting choices (usually French-influenced and/or organic) on menus than were seen a decade ago.

Holland is famous for its cheeses, including Gouda, Edam, and Limburger. Indonesian cuisine is also very popular here, and a favorite lunch or dinner is *rijsttafel,* which literally means "rice table" and refers to a prix-fixe meal that includes a feast of 10–20 small spicy dishes.

Restaurants open for lunch starting at 11, while restaurants opening for dinner will accept guests as early as 5 or 6, closing at 11. Many restaurants are closed Monday.

PAYING

Tipping 15% to 20% of the cost of a meal is not common practice in the Netherlands. Instead, round off the total to a convenient figure, to reward good service. If paying with a credit card, pay the exact amount with your card, and leave a few euros in cash on the table for the waiting staff.

WINES, BEER, AND SPIRITS

When you ask for a beer in Holland, you will get a small (200 mL) glass of draft lager with 5% alcohol, known as *pils*. A number of national breweries turn out similar fare—in Amsterdam it will usually be Heineken, but you may encounter Amstel, Oranjeboom, Grolsch, Bavaria, or another smaller outfit. The argument for serving beer in small glasses is that you can drink it before it gets warm, and that you can also drink more of them. Many bars will serve you a pint (500 mL) if you ask. A number of smaller artisanal breweries attempt different beer styles with ever-improving results—look out for the La Trappe and 't IJ names. You will also find several Belgian standards in most Dutch cafés, including Hoegaarden "white" beer, Westmalle (which comes in brown and blond versions), Kriek, a fruit-flavored beer, and Duvel, a strong blond beer.

HOTEL AND RESTAURANT PRICES

Prices in the restaurant reviews are the average cost of a main course at dinner or, if dinner is not served, at lunch; taxes and service charges are generally included. Prices in the hotel reviews are the lowest cost of a standard double room in high season, excluding taxes, service charges, and meal plans. Prices for rentals are the lowest per-night cost for a one-bedroom unit in high season.

13

PLANNING YOUR TIME

The majority of visitors will be headed for **Amsterdam,** and with good reason—it's one of Europe's most popular and laid-back capitals, and the canals, sights, and museums here will keep you occupied for several days if you want to do more than dip a toe. If you have only one or two days, you would do best to concentrate your efforts here. With a week, you can get a taste of everywhere mentioned here—all are worth spending a few nights getting to know if you can.

Delft is a picture-book example of how a small Dutch city should be, and with its centuries-old charm it is easy to see how Johannes Vermeer could have found inspiration there.

Rotterdam, bombed to the ground in World War II, has nevertheless become one of the world's busiest industrial ports, with a phenomenal skyline and a keepin'-it-real appreciation for the latest culture.

Meanwhile, what could be more Dutch than tulips? So if you arrive in the right season (late March to May), be sure to trip out to see the country burst into color, and in particular make a beeline for the **Keukenhof,** the world's largest flower gardens, located in Lisse, just to the south of Amsterdam.

AMSTERDAM

Amsterdam is a cornucopia of cafés, coffee shops, cozy bars, and outdoor markets. Set on 160 man-made canals (stretching 75 km [50 miles]), it also has the largest historic inner city in Europe. The French writer J. K. Huysmans once called Amsterdam "a dream, an orgy of houses and water." It's true: when compared with other major European cities, this one is uniquely defined by its impressive gabled houses, rather than palaces, estates, and other aristocratic folderol. Most of the 7,000 registered monuments here began as residences and warehouses of humble merchants.

With a mere 820,000 friendly souls and with almost everything a scant 10-minute bike ride away, Amsterdam is actually like a village that happens to pack the cultural wallop of a megalopolis. This is an endlessly fascinating city, where it's remarkably easy to relax and enjoy yourself—just take on the characteristics of the local waterways and go with the flow.

PLANNING YOUR TIME

There is high humidity in the summer and a fair amount of rain, especially in the winter. But moisture aside, Amsterdam's weather is ultimately comfortable, and temperatures are rarely extreme. In the summer Amsterdam can be the most fascinating city in the world; a sun-bleached blend of old and new, crazy and subdued. From October to May, lines for most museums and attractions are smaller, and off-season accommodations are cheaper, but it's colder, rainier, and windier.

The electronic *I amsterdam Card* provides free and discounted admissions to many of Amsterdam's top museums, plus a free canal round trip, free use of public transport, and a discount on various attractions and restaurants. These can be bought online or from tourist offices in Amsterdam, and cost €40, €50, or €60 for one, two, or three days, respectively.

Anyone planning to visit a lot of museums in Amsterdam and the Netherlands should consider investing in a *Museumkaart* (Museum Card). This gives you free entry to more than 400 museums throughout the country for a year, including all the top draws in Amsterdam. It is available upon showing ID at VVV (Netherlands Board of Tourism) offices, online (⊕ *www.museumkaart.nl*), and at participating museums for €49.95.

GETTING HERE AND AROUND
AIRPORT TRANSFERS

The Schiphol Rail Link operates between the airport and the city 24 hours a day, with service to Amsterdam Centraal Station (usually abbreviated to Amsterdam CS). From 6:30 am to 12:30 am, there are four trains each hour; other hours, there is one every hour. The trip takes about 15 minutes and costs €3.90. Schiphol Station is beneath Schiphol Plaza.

Connexxion Schiphol Hotel Shuttle operates a shuttle-bus service between Amsterdam Schiphol Airport and all of the city's major hotels. The trip takes about a half hour and costs €16.50 one-way, or €26.50 round-trip. Hours for this shuttle bus are 6 am to 9:30 pm, every half hour.

Finally, there is a taxi stand directly in front of the arrival hall at Amsterdam Schiphol Airport. A service charge is included, but small additional tips are not unwelcome. Depending on the neighborhood, a trip will cost around €45 or more.

Contacts Connexxion Schiphol Hotel Shuttle ☎ *038/339–4741* ⊕ *www. schipholhotelshuttle.nl.* **Schiphol Rail Link** ☎ *0900/9292 (€0.70 per min)* ⊕ *9292.nl.*

BUS AND TRAM TRAVEL

Although the best way to see Amsterdam is either by bike or on foot, the city's public transport system, GVB, is extremely reliable. It operates the buses, trams, and metro with service 24 hours a day. The trams most frequently used by visitors are Nos. 1, 2, and 5, which start at Centraal Station and stop at the big central Dam Square and, along with Nos. 6, 7, and 10, also stop at Leidseplein square. Numbers 2, 3, 5, and 12 will get you from the station to Museumplein and the Museum District. The GVB also sells 24-, 48-, and 72-hour passes, and family passes.

Contacts **GVB** ✉ *Prins Hendrikkade 108–114, Centrum* ☎ *0900/9292* ⊕ *www. gvb.nl.*

TAXI TRAVEL

Taxis can be difficult to hail on the street; officially, the regular practice is to wait by a taxi stand or phone for one.

Contacts **Taxicentrale Amsterdam** ☎ *020/777-7777* ⊕ *www.tcataxi.nl.* **Wielertaxi** ☎ *06/2824-7550* ⊕ *www.wielertaxi.nl.*

TOURS

Afternoon bus tours of Amsterdam operate daily. Itineraries vary, and prices start at €17. However, it must be said that this city of narrow alleys and canals is not best appreciated from the window of a coach.

From April through October, guided two- to three-hour bike trips through the central area of Amsterdam are available through Yellow Bike.

To see the city from the water, boat tours lasting from 1 to 1 ½ hours leave from various locations across the center at regular intervals, costing around €14.

Contacts **Amsterdam Canal Cruises** ✉ *Stadhouderskade, opposite the Heineken Experience, The Pijp* ☎ *020/679-1370* ⊕ *www.amsterdamcanalcruises. nl.* **Canal Bus** ✉ *Weteringschans 26-1, Leidseplein* ☎ *020/623-9886* ⊕ *www. canal.nl.* **Holland International** ✉ *Prins Hendrikkade, opposite Centraal Station, Centrum* ☎ *020/625-3035* ⊕ *www.hir.nl.* **Rederij Lovers** ✉ *Prins Hendrikkade, opposite Centraal Station, Centrum* ☎ *020/530-1090* ⊕ *www.lovers.nl.* **Yellow Bike** ✉ *Nieuwezijds Kolk 29, Centrum* ☎ *020/620-6940* ⊕ *www.yellowbike.nl.*

VISITOR INFORMATION

Contacts **VVV—Netherlands Board of Tourism** ✉ *Stationsplein 10, Centraal Station, Centrum* ⊕ *www.iamsterdam.com* ✉ *AUB Ticketshop, Leidseplein 26 (terrace-side), Leidseplein* ✉ *Schiphol Airport, Arrivals Building 2 , Luchthaven Schiphol* ✉ *Stationsplein 10, Centraal Station.*

EXPLORING

There are no straight lines in central Amsterdam, but once understood, it's an easy city to navigate—or get lost in. Think of it as an onion whose layers come together at the stem to make a cohesive whole. With Centraal Station as the stem, the Center folds out as layers of the onion, each on a somewhat circular path under the guidance of the Canal Ring. To stay safe, always watch out for bikes and trams. Do not walk on bike paths, which are well paved and often mistaken for sidewalks. Bikers have the right-of-way, so if you hear a bell, move quickly. Trams function similarly, and will also ring their bell (a much louder one) before they move. Just look both ways, and look both ways again before crossing streets.

FAMILY **Amsterdam Museum** (*Amsterdam Historical Museum*). Any city that
Fodor'sChoice began in the 13th century as a boggy swamp to become the trading
★ powerhouse of the world in the 17th century has a fascinating story to tell, and this museum does it superbly. It's housed in a rambling amalgamation of buildings, once a convent, which was used as Amsterdam's Civic Orphanage. Before visiting the actual museum, walk past the entrance and check out the glassed Schuttersgalerij (Civil Guards Gallery) lined with huge portraits of city militias—though not in the same league as *The Night Watch,* you can see them for free. Recently, 21th-century renditions of civil guard paintings have been added to the collection, notably one featuring the "Maid of Amsterdam," with a joint in one hand and Rembrandt's face tattooed on her chest. ⊠ *Kalverstraat 92 and Sint Luciënsteeg 27, Centrum* ☎ *020/523–1822* ⊕ *www. amsterdammuseum.nl* 🎫 *€10* ⊘ *Daily 10–5.*

Fodor'sChoice **Anne Frankhuis** (*Anne Frank House*). Anne Frank, one of the most
★ famous authors of the 20th century, wrote the inspiring diary of a Jewish girl who was forced to hide with her family here in a hidden apartment from the Nazis. In the pages of *The Diary of Anne Frank* (published posthumously in 1947 as *The Annex* by her father—the title she chose) the young Anne recorded two increasingly fraught years living in secret in a warren of rooms at the back of this 1635 canal house. Anne Frank was born in Germany in 1929; when she was four her family moved to the Netherlands to escape growing anti-Jewish sentiment. Otto Frank operated a pectin business and decided to stay in his adopted country when the war finally reached the Netherlands in 1940. In July 1942 he took his wife and daughters, Anne and her sister, Margo, into hiding, and a week later they were joined by the Van Pels family: Auguste, Hermann, and their son, Peter. Four months later, dentist Fritz Pfeffer moved in.

The five adults and three children sought refuge in the attic of the rear annex, or *achterhuis,* of Otto's business in the center of Amsterdam. The entrance to the flat was hidden behind a hinged bookcase. Here, like many *onderduikers* ("people in hiding") throughout Amsterdam, Anne dreamed her dreams, wrote her diary, and pinned up movie-star pictures to her wall (still on view). Five trusted employees provided them with food and supplies. In August 1944, the Franks were betrayed and the Gestapo invaded their hideaway. All the members of the annex were transported to camps. Otto Frank was the only survivor of the annex. Miep Gies, one of the friends who helped with the hiding, found Anne's diary after the raid and kept it through the war. ■**TIP→ The line to get into the Anne Frank House is extremely long, especially in the summer. It moves (sort of) quickly, but it's best to arrive early or book tickets online to avoid the worst crowds.** ⊠ *Prinsengracht 263–267, Centrum* ☎ *020/556– 7105* ⊕ *www.annefrank.nl* 🎫 *€9* ⊘ *Mar.–Sept., daily 9–9 (Sat. until 10); July–Aug., daily 9–10; Sept.–Mar., daily 9–7 (Sat. until 9).*

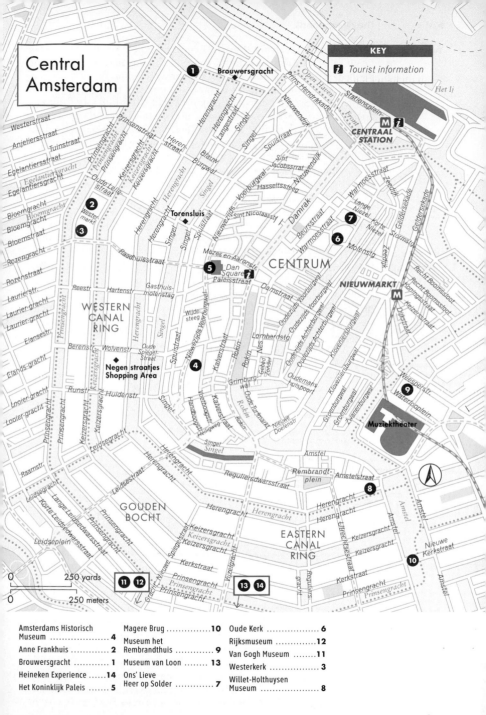

Central Amsterdam

KEY

🛈 *Tourist information*

① Brouwersgracht

Het Ij

CENTRAAL STATION 🛈

Open Haven

Prins Hendrikkade

Stationsplein

Westerstraat

Anjelierstraat

Tuinstraat

Egelantiersstraat

Egelantiersgracht

Egelantiersgracht

Bloemgracht

Bloemgracht

Bloemstraat

Rozengracht

Rozenstraat

Laurierstr.

Laurier-gracht

Laurier-gracht

Elansstr.

Elands-gracht

Looier-gracht

Looier-gracht

Raamstr.

Prinsengracht

Prinsengracht

Prinsenstraat

Keizersgracht

Oude Leliestraat

Herengracht

Herengracht

Blauwburgwal

Heren straat

② Westermarkt

③

Torensluis ◆

Paalhuisstraat

Singel

Spuistraat

Nieuwezijds voorburgwal

Spuistraat

⑤ Dam Square 🛈 Paleisstraat

Damstraat

Singel

Blauwburgwal

Singel

Nieuwendijk

Spuistraat

Sint Jacobsstraat

Nieuwendijk

Hasseltssteeg

Zeedijk

Warmoesstraat

Lange Niezel ⑦

Korte Niezel

Zeedijk

Geldersekade

Stormsteeg

Recht Boomsslot

Koningstraat

Keizersstraat

Damrak

Beursstraat

Warmoesstraat

⑥

Molensteeg

Sint Nicolaasstr

Mozes en Aaronstr

Reestr.

Hartenstr.

Gasthuismolensteeg

WESTERN CANAL RING

Herengracht

Singel

Wijde steeg

CENTRUM

NIEUWMARKT Ⓜ

Oudezijds Voorburgwal

Oudezijds Voorburgwal

Oudezijds Achterburgwal

Oudezijds Achterburgwal

Kloveniersburgwal

Kloveniersburgwal

Recht Boomsslot

Berenstr. Wolvenstr.

Oude Spiegelstraat

◆ Negen straatjes Shopping Area

Runstr.

Huidenstr.

Leidsegracht

Keizersgracht

Prinsengracht

④

Kalverstraat

Rokin

Nes

Lombardstg

Grimburgwal

Oude turfmarkt

Rokin

Gebed Zonder

Oudemanhorspoort

Groenburgwal

Zwanenburgwal

Weesperstr.

⑨ Waterlooplein

Dijkstraat

Voetboogstraat

Handboogstraat

Heiligeweg

Kalverstraat

Nieuwe Doelenstr

Muziektheater

Leidsestraat

Singel Singel

Herengracht

Herengracht

Reguliersdwarsstraat

Amstel

Rembrandtplein

Amstelstraat

Leidsegracht

Lange Leidsedwarsstraat

Korte Leidsedwarsstraat

Leidseplein

Leidsedwarsstraat

Prinsengracht

Prinsengracht

GOUDEN BOCHT

Herengracht

Herengracht

Herengracht

EASTERN CANAL RING

Keizersgracht

Keizersgracht

Amstel

Amstel

Utrechtsestraat

⑧

Nieuwe Kerkstraat

Kerkstraat

Keizersgracht

Keizersgracht

Kerkstraat

⑩

Amstel

Nieuwe Spiegelstraat

Prinsengracht

Prinsengracht

Vijzelgracht

Reguliers gracht

Prinsengracht Prinsengracht

0 ____ 250 yards

0 ____ 250 meters

⑪ ⑫   ⑬ ⑭

Fodor's Choice
★

Brouwersgracht (*Brewers' Canal*). Regularly voted Amsterdam's most beautiful street, this wonderful canal at the northern border of the Jordaan is lined by residences and former warehouses for brewers, fish processors, and tanneries who traded here in the 17th century when Amsterdam was the "warehouse of the world." Without sacrificing the ancient vibe, most of the buildings have been converted into luxury apartments. Of particular note are Nos. 204–212 and their trapezium gables. At No. 162, there are two dried fish above the door. This decoration on a metal screen was the forerunner of the gable stone denoting occupation. The canal provides long views down the grand canals that are perfect for photo-ops. The Brouwersgracht runs westward from the end of the Singel (a short walk along Prins Hendrikkade from Centraal Station) and forms a cap to the western end of the Grachtengordel. On top of the old canal mansions dotting the Brouwersgracht are symbols referring to the breweries that used this waterway to transport their goods to thirsty drinkers hundreds of years ago. ✉ *Jordaan.*

Fodor's Choice
★

Heineken Experience. Founded by Gerard Heineken in 1864, the Heineken label has become one of the world's most famous (and popular) beers. It's no longer brewed here, though you'll see at times that the Heineken horse-drawn dray still clip-clops across town heavy with its kegs. The original brewery has now been transformed into the "Heineken Experience," an interactive center that offers tours of the facilities. Everything from vast copper vats to beer-wagon shire horses are on view, and if you've ever wanted to know what it feels like to be brewed and bottled, the virtual reality ride "Brew U" will clue you in. Others may want to exercise their privilege of drinking multiple beers in a very short time. (Note: this tour is open only to visitors over the age of 18.) ✉ *Stadhouderskade 78, The Pijp* ☎ *020/523–9222* ⊕ *www.heinekenexperience.com* 🎫 *€17 (€15 online)* ⊗ *Sept.–May, daily 11–5:30; June–Aug., daily 10:30–7.*

Fodor's Choice
★

Het Koninklijk Paleis (*Royal Palace*). From the outside, it is somewhat hard to believe that these ponderous premises were declaimed by poet and diplomat Constantijn Huygens as the "Eighth Wonder of the World." It was built between 1648 and 1665 as the largest secular building on the planet. From the inside, its magnificent interior inspires another brand of disbelief: this palace was actually built as a mere city hall. Golden Age artistic greats such as Ferdinand Bol, Govert Flinck and Jan Lievens were called in for the decorating (Rembrandt's sketches were rejected). In the building's public entrance hall, the **Burgerzaal**, the world was placed quite literally at one's feet: two maps inlaid in the marble floor show Amsterdam as the center of the world, and as the center of the universe.

The building has remained the Royal Palace ever since Napoléon's brother squatted there in 1808, and it's one of three palaces at the disposal of King Willem-Alexander, who hosts official receptions and state visits here. The Palace hosts art exhibitions and displays on the history of the building itself. Official occasions mean opening times can vary. ✉ *Dam, Centrum* ☎ *020/620–4060* ⊕ *www.koninklijkhuis.nl* 🎫 *€7.50* ⊗ *Daily 11–5; closed during royal events; check website for details of current opening hours.*

Fodor's Choice **Magere Brug** (*Skinny Bridge*). Of Amsterdam's 60-plus drawbridges,
★ the Magere Brug is the most famous and provides gorgeous views of
the Amstel and surrounding area. It was purportedly first built in 1672
by two sisters living on opposite sides of the Amstel who wanted an
efficient way of sharing that grandest of Dutch traditions: the *gezellige*
(socially cozy) midmorning coffee break. Walk by at night when it's
spectacularly lit. Many replacements to the original bridge have come
and gone, and this, dating from 1969, is just the latest. ✉ *Between
Kerkstraat and Nieuwe Kerkstraat, Centrum.*

13

Fodor's Choice **Museum het Rembrandthuis** (*Rembrandt House Museum*). This is the
★ house that Rembrandt bought, flush with success, for 13,000 guilders
(a princely sum) in 1639, and where he lived and worked until 1656
when declared bankrupt. The inside is a remarkable reconstruction
job, as the contents have been assembled based on inventories made
when Rembrandt was forced to sell everything, including an extravagant collection of art and antiquities (a contributing factor in his money
troubles). He originally chose this house on what was then the main
street of the Jewish Quarter, to experience firsthand the faces he would
use in his Old Testament religious paintings. The house interior has
been restored with contemporaneous elegant furnishings and artwork
in the reception rooms, a collection of rarities that match as closely as
possible the descriptions in the inventory, and the main studio, occasionally used by guest artists, which is kept fully stocked with paints
and canvases. But it doesn't convey much of the humanity of Rembrandt
himself. When he left here, he was not only out of money, but also out
of favor with the city after relationships with servant girls following
the death of his wife, Saskia. The little etching studio is perhaps the
most atmospheric. Littered with tools of the trade, a printing press,
and a line hung with drying prints (there are demonstrations), it's easy
to imagine Rembrandt finding respite here, experimenting with form
and technique, away from uncomfortable schmoozing for commissions
(and loans) in the grander salon. The museum owns a huge collection
of etchings with 260 of the 290 he made represented, and a changing selection is on permanent display. His magisterial "Hundred Guil-
der" and the "Three Crosses" prints show that Rembrandt was almost
more revolutionary in his prints than in his paintings, so this collection
deserves respectful homage, if not downright devotion, by printmak-
ers today. ✉ *Jodenbreestraat 4–6, Centrum* ☎ *020/520–0400* ⊕ *www.
rembrandthuis.nl* 🎫 *€10* ☉ *Daily, 10–5.*

Fodor's Choice **Museum van Loon.** Once home to one of Rembrandt's most successful
★ students, Ferdinand Bol, this house and its twin, No. 674 next door
(home of the Kattenkabinet; a five-room museum dedicated to cats),
were built in 1672 by Adriaan Dortsman and extensively remodeled in
the 18th century by Abraham van Hagan and his wife, Catherina Tripp,
whose names are entwined in the ornate brass balustrade on the staircase. It was occupied by the Van Loon family from 1886 to 1960. After
extensive restoration to take it back to its glory days of the 18th century,
it was opened as a museum in the 1970s. The elegant salons include
many Van Loon portraits and possessions, including paintings known
as *witjes,* illusionistic depictions of landscapes and other scenes. The

symmetrical garden is a gem. Facing the rear of the house, the recently restored Grecian-style coach house holds exhibitions and in the future (hopefully) will serve teas. ✉ *Keizersgracht 672, Centrum* ☎ *020/624– 5255* ⊕ *www.museumvanloon.nl* ▣ *€7* ⊙ *Wed.–Mon. 11–5.*

Fodor's Choice
★

Ons' Lieve Heer op Solder (*Our Lord in the Attic Museum*). With its elegant gray-and-white facade and spout gable, this appears to be just another lovely 17th-century canal house, and on the lower floors it is. But tucked away in the attic is a clandestine place of Catholic worship, a *schuilkerk* (hidden church), one of the very few to survive more or less in its original state. Catholic masses were officially forbidden from 1578, but the Protestant authorities in Amsterdam turned a blind eye provided the churches were not recognizable as such from the outside. The Oude Kerk was decatholicized and stripped of its patron, St. Nicholas, so this little church, consecrated in 1663, was dedicated to him until the St. Nicolaaskerk opened in 1887. The chapel itself is a triumph of Dutch classicist taste, with magnificent marble columns, gilded capitals, a colored-marble altar, and the *Baptism of Christ in the Jordan* (1716) painting by Jacob de Wit presiding over all.

The grandeur continues through the house, which was renovated by merchant Jan Hartan between 1661 and 1663. Even the kitchen and chaplain bedroom remain furnished in the style of the age, and the drawing room, or *sael*, looks as if it were plucked from a Vermeer painting. With its gold chandelier and Solomonic columns, it's one of the most impressive 17th-century rooms left in Amsterdam. Besides boasting canvases by Thomas de Keyser, Jan Wynants, and Abraham de Vries, the house also displays impressive collections of church silver and sculptures. The new part of the museum, on the other side of the alley, hosts temporary exhibitions. ✉ *Oudezijds Voorburgwal 40, Centrum* ☎ *020/624–6604* ⊕ *www.opsolder.nl* ▣ *€8* ⊙ *Mon.–Sat. 10–5, Sun. 1–5.*

Oude Kerk (*Old Church*). Amsterdam's oldest church has evolved over three centuries to look as it does today. What began as a wooden chapel in 1306 was built up to a hall church and then a cross basilica between 1366 and 1566 (and fully restored between 1955 and 1979). It was violently looted during the Reformation and stripped of its altars and images of saints—though the looters did leave the 14th-century paintings still visible on its wooden roof, as well as the Virgin Mary stained-glass windows that had been set in place in 1550. The famed Vater-Müller organ was installed in 1726. Don't miss the carved choir stalls that illustrate proverbs relating to cardinal sins, among other things. Within this open, atmospheric space, there's a gravestone for Rembrandt's wife Saskia van Uylenburgh and also for Kiliaen van Rensselaer, one of the Dutch founders of what is now New York, and by the door, a bronzed hand cupping a naked breast. This is one of a series of sculptures placed throughout Amsterdam in 1982 by an anonymous artist. The Oude Kerk is as much exhibition space as a place of worship, hosting the annual World Press Photography competition and top-notch modern-art shows. Its carillon is played every Tuesday at 2 and every Saturday at 4—the best place to listen is the bridge in front of the church. ✉ *Oudekerksplein 23, Centrum* ☎ *020/625–8284* ⊕ *www. oudekerk.nl* 🖭 *€5* ⊘ *Mon.–Sat. 11–5, Sun. 1–5:30.*

Fodor's Choice **Rijksmuseum** (*State Museum*). The Netherlands' greatest museum, the
★ famed Rijksmuseum is home to Rembrandt's *Night Watch,* Vermeer's
The Milk Maid, and a near infinite selection of world-famous masterpieces by the likes of Steen, Ruisdael, Brouwers, Hals, Hobbema,
Cuyp, Van der Helst, and their Golden Age ilk. Long the nation's pride,
the museum was rent by major changes when it closed for a massive
12-year renovation beginning in 2005, in the interim, keeping a Gallery
of Honor open for the crème de la crème of the collection. As of Spring
2013, however, the revamped museum will finally open its doors, and
viewers will see a lot more than just burnished gold-leafed ceilings and
polished terrazzo-stone floors. For the renewed Rijks has abandoned the
old art/design/history divisions and has now sewn these three previously
disparate collections into one panoply of art and style that is presented
chronologically, from the Middle Ages to the 20th century. Don't be
surprised, in other words, if you see a vase in a 17th-century painting
by Gerard Dou and the same, real Delft blue-and-white vase next to it.
That just the largest of changes wrought in the new revovation.

13

The Rijksmuseum has more than 150 rooms displaying paintings, sculpture, and objects from both the West and Asia, dating from the 9th
through the 19th centuries. The bulk of the collection is of 15th- to
17th-century paintings, mostly Dutch (the Rijksmuseum has the largest
concentration of these masters in the world); there are also extensive
holdings of drawings and prints from the 15th to the 20th century.

If your time is limited, head directly for the Gallery of Honor on the
upper floor, to admire Rembrandt's *Night Watch,* with its central figure,
the "stupidest man in Amsterdam," Frans Banningh Cocq. His militia
buddies that surround him each paid 100 guilders to be included—quite
the sum in those days, so a few of them complained about being lost
in all those shadows. The rest of this "Best of the Golden Age" hall
features other well-known Rembrandt paintings and works by Vermeer,
Frans Hals, and other household names.

Unmissable masterpieces include Vermeer's *The Little Street*—a magical
sliver of 17th-century Delft life—and his incomparable *The Love Letter,* in which a well-appointed interior reveals a mistress and her maid
caught in the emotional eddies of a recently opened and read billet-
doux. Note the calm seascape on the back wall—a quiet sea was seen as
a good omen by the Dutch; inner anxieties, however, are present in the
mistress' face, so much so that the room's clothes hamper, lacemaking
pillow, and broom all lie forgotten. Ostensibly, a more sedate missive
is being read in Vermeer's *Woman in Blue Reading a Letter,* on view
nearby. But is this just a matronly dress or is the woman pregnant and
thinking about a missing husband (note the seafaring map)?

For an institution dedicated to antiquity, the Rijksmuseum has shown
a remarkable technical savvy in making its vast collection more accessible via its incredible website. From the comfort of your home, you
can make a virtual tour, chart out a plan of attack, and absorb vast
chunks of background information. The museum has also introduced an

"ARIA" (Amsterdam Rijksmuseum Inter-Active) system, which allows a visitor to ask for information—which may include visuals, text, film, and/or sound—on 1,250 objects, and then be given directions to find other related objects. These "create-your-own tours" are available in a room directly behind the *Night Watch*. ■ TIP→ Don't leave the country without visiting the minimuseum at Schiphol Airport (✉ *Holland Boulevard between piers E and F behind passport control* 🕾 *020/653–5036* 📧 *Free* ⊙ *Daily 6 am–8 pm*). ✉ *Stadhouderskade 42, Museum District* 🕾 *020/674–7000* ⊕ *www.rijksmuseum.nl* 📧 *€14 (subject to change after the reopening)* ⊙ *Museum daily 9–6; Library, Print Room, and Reading Room (ID required) Tues.–Sat. 10–5.*

Fodor's Choice **Van Gogh Museum.** Opened in 1973, this remarkable light-infused build-
★   ing—based on a design by famed De Stijl architect Gerrit Rietveld—venerates the short, certainly not sweet, but highly productive career of everyone's favorite tortured 19th-century artist. First things first: Vincent was a Dutch boy and therefore his name is not pronounced like the "Go" in Go-Go Lounge but rather like the "Go" uttered when one is choking on a whole raw herring.

While some of the Van Gogh paintings that are scattered throughout the world's high art temples are of dubious providence, this collection's authenticity is indisputable: its roots trace directly back to brother Theo van Gogh, Vincent's artistic and financial supporter. The 200 paintings and 500 drawings on display here can be divided into his five basic periods, the first beginning in 1880 at age 27 after his failure in finding his voice as schoolmaster and lay preacher. These early depictions of Dutch country landscapes and peasants—particularly around the Borinage and Nuenen—were notable for their dark colors and a refusal to romanticize (a stand that perhaps also led in this period to his various failures in romance). The *Potato Eaters* is perhaps his most famous piece from this period.

In 1999, the 200th anniversary of Van Gogh's birth was marked with a new museum extension designed by the Japanese architect Kisho Kurokawa. The new annex is a freestanding, multistory, oval structure, built in a bold combination of titanium and gray-brown stone and connected to the main galleries by an underground walkway. It provides space for a wide range of superbly presented temporary shows of 19th-century art, including changing shows of Van Gogh's drawings (more than 500 are in the collection). With all this new space, you might be tempted to take a break at the museum's cafeteria-style restaurant. ✉ *Paulus Potterstraat 7, Museum District* 🕾 *020/570–5200* ⊕ *www.vangoghmuseum.nl* 📧 *€14* ⊙ *Sat.–Thurs. 10–6, Fri. 10–10.*

Fodor's Choice **Stedelijk Museum of Modern Art.** Amsterdam's celebrated treasurehouse
★   of modern art, the Stedelijk finally reopened (in September 2012) following a massive refurbishment of this wedding-cake n eo-Renaissance structure built in 1895. In true Amsterdam fashion, the locals were quick to nickname the futuristic addition by globally acclaimed local architects Benthem/Crouwel the *"Badkuip"* (Bathtub); it incorporates a glass-walled restaurant (which you can visit, along with the museum shop, without a museum ticket). The new Stedelijk boasts twice the

exhibition space compared to the old, thanks, in part, to the new Bathub, which will now host temporary shows (watch out for the noted South-African-Dutch painter Marlene Dumas in 2014).

As for the Stedelijk's old building, it is now home to the museum's own, fabled collection of modern and contemporary art. While this collection harbors many works by such ancients of modernism as Chagall, Cézanne, Picasso, Monet, Mondriaan, and Malevich, there is a definite emphasis on the post-World War II period: with such local CoBrA boys as Appel and Corneille; American Pop artists as Warhol, Johns, Oldenburg, and Liechtenstein; Abstract Expressionists as de Kooning and Pollock; and contemporary German Expressionists as Polke, Richter, and Baselitz; and displays of Dutch essentials like De Stijl school, including the game-changing *Red Blue Chair* that Gerrit Rietveld designed in 1918 and Mondriaan's 1920 trail-blazing *Composition in Red, Black, Yellow, Blue, and Grey*. ✉ *Paulus Potterstraat 13, Museum District* ☎ *020/573–2911* ⊕ *www.stedelijk.nl* 🎫 *€15* ⊙ *Tues. and Wed. 11–5, Thurs. 11–10, weekends 10–6.*

13

| NEED A BREAK? | **Hoppe.** Several of the bar-cafés and eateries on Spui are good places to take a break. The ancient Hoppe has been serving drinks between woody walls and on sandy floors since 1670. ✉ *Spui 18–20, Centrum* ☎ *020/420–4420.* |

Westerkerk (*Western Church*). Built between 1620 and 1631 by (you guessed it) Hendrick de Keyser, the Dutch Renaissance–style Westerkerk was the largest Protestant church in the world until St. Paul's Cathedral in London was built in 1675. Its 85-meter tower, the tallest in the city, is topped by a gaudy copy of the crown of the Habsburg emperor Maximilian I, who gave Amsterdam the right to use his royal insignia in 1489 in gratitude for support given to the Austro-Burgundian princes.

The church is renowned for its organ and carillon (there are regular concerts). The carillon is played every Tuesday between noon and 1 by a real person (a *carillonneur*) but is automated at other times with different songs tinkling out on the quarter hour, day and night (it drives some locals nuts). Anne Frank described the tunes in her diary. Rembrandt, who lived on Rozengracht during his poverty-stricken last years, and his son, Titus, are buried (somewhere) here. Rembrandt's posthumous reputation inspired some very surreal television three centuries later, when a body was unearthed that was mistakenly thought to be his: while exposed to the glare of the news cameras, the skull turned to dust. The Westertoren (Westerkerk Tower) is a fun climb from April to the end of October. ✉ *Prinsengracht 281 (corner of Westermarkt), Centrum* ☎ *020/624–7766* ⊕ *www.westerkerk.nl* 🎫 *Interior free, Westertoren €6* ⊙ *Apr.–June, weekdays 10–6, Sat. 10–8; July and Aug., Mon.–Sat. 10–8; Sept., weekdays 10–6, Sat. 10–8; Oct., weekdays 10–4, Sat. 10–6.*

Fodor's Choice ★   **Willet-Holthuysen Museum.** Here's a rare chance to experience what it was like to live in a gracious mansion on the Herengracht in the 18th century. In 1895, widow Sandrina Louisa Willet-Holthuysen bequeathed this house to the city, along with all of its contents. It was actually built in 1687 but has been renovated several times and is now under the management of the Amsterdam Museum. Take an hour or so to discover its interiors and artwork, including a sumptuous ballroom and a rarities cabinet. Complete the Dutch luxury experience by lounging in the French-style garden in the back. ✉ *Herengracht 605, Centrum* ☎ *020/523–1822* 🌐 *www.willetholthuysen.nl* 🎫 *€8* 🕐 *Weekdays 10–5, weekends 11–5.*

WHERE TO EAT

$ EUROPEAN Fodor's Choice ★

🍴 **Bakkerswinkel.** This genteel yet unpretentious bakery and tearoom evokes an English country kitchen, one that lovingly prepares and serves breakfasts, high tea, hearty-breaded sandwiches, soups, and divine slabs of quiche. The closely clustered wooden tables don't make for much privacy, but this place is a true oasis if you want to indulge in a healthful breakfast or lunch. The convenient location on busy Zeedijk will only be open until 2014, when the original Bakkerswinkel reopens at Warmoesstraat 69 after renovations. There are several other locations: such as one complete with a garden patio in the Museum District and another at Westergasfabriek, plus a takeout-only counter at Warmoesstraat 133. [$] *Average main: €8* ✉ *Zeedijk 37, Red Light District* ☎ *020/489–8000* 🌐 *www.debakkerswinkel.com* 🕐 *No dinner.*

$ AFRICAN Fodor's Choice ★

🍴 **Bazar Amsterdam.** A golden-angel-capped church provides the singular setting for this kitsch-addled restaurant. Cheap and flavorful North African cooking—covering the range from falafel to mixed grilled meats—is served here in an environment of convivial chaos. Since Bazar is located alongside the country's largest outdoor market, it is also the perfect place to break for coffee (or for breakfast, lunch, or dinner, for that matter) in between rounds of market wandering. [$] *Average main: €13* ✉ *Albert Cuypstraat 182, The Pijp* ☎ *020/675–0544* 🌐 *www.bazaramsterdam.nl.*

$$$ INDONESIAN Fodor's Choice ★

🍴 **Blauw.** Located a bit off the beaten track on the other end of Vondelpark sits Blauw, reputedly—many believe—the best rijstaffel in town. Set along the rising culinary boulevard of Amstelveenseweg, this shrine to one of Holland's favorite taste sensations recently got a make-over: out went the traditional Indonesian batik interior and then arrived an array of lacquered red walls to accent giant blowups of vintage family photos and the like. The result is fun, today, and hip. More color comes from the menu's choices, which range from €26.50 for the vegetarian rijstaffel to €31.25 for the meat, fish, and veggie option; both are fresh, well-spiced, and full of exotic flavors. Note that you can also order à la carte dishes. For those who want memories-in-the-making, ask the waiter to use the staff camera and then check the restaurant's Web site the next day to download a photo of yourself and your party at your table. [$] *Average main: €25* ✉ *Amstelveenseweg 158–160, Museum District* ☎ *020/675–5000* 🌐 *www.restaurantblauw.nl* ✍ *Reservations essential* 🕐 *No lunch.*

$$$ MEDITERRANEAN Fodor's Choice ★

🍴 **Blauw aan de Wal.** In the heart of the Red Light District is a small alley that leads to this charming oasis, complete with the innocent chirping of birds. "Blue on the Quay" is set in a courtyard that once belonged to the Bethanienklooster monastery; it now offers a restful environment with multiple dining areas, each with a unique and serene view. Original wood floors and exposed-brick walls hint at the building's 1625 origins, but the extensive and inspired wine list and the open kitchen employing fresh local ingredients in its Mediterranean-influenced cuisine both have a contemporary chic. After starting with a frothy pea soup with chanterelle mushrooms and pancetta, you may want to indulge in a melt-in-the-mouth, herb-crusted lamb filet. $ *Average main: €31* ⊠ *Oudezijde Achterburgwal 99, Red Light District* ☎ *020/330–2257* ⊕ *www. blauwaandewal.com* ⊘ *Closed Sun. and Mon. No lunch.*

$$ ✕ **Café Luxembourg.** One of the city's top grand cafés, Luxembourg has
CAFÉ a stately interior and a view of a bustling square, both of which are
Fodor's Choice maximized for people-watching. Famous for its brunch, its classic café
★ menu includes a terrific Caesar salad, lobster bisque, and excellent Holtkamp *krokets* (croquettes, these with a cheese, shrimp, or veal filling). The "reading table" is democratically packed with both Dutch and international newspapers and mags. $ *Average main: €18* ⊠ *Spui 24, Centrum* ☎ *020/620–6264* ⊕ *www.luxembourg.nl.*

$$$$ ✕ **De Kas.** This 1926-built municipal "greenhouse" must be the ulti-
MEDITERRANEAN mate workplace for chefs: they can begin the day picking the best and
Fodor's Choice freshest of homegrown produce before building an inspired Mediter-
★ ranean menu around them. For diners it's equally sumptuous, especially since the setting includes two very un-Dutch commodities—lots of light and a giddy sense of vertical space, thanks to the glass roof. The frequently changing €49.50 prix-fixe menu always consists of a selection of small starters, followed by a main course and a dessert. Don't miss out on their fabulous wine selection—their wine pairings are a real treat. $ *Average main: €49* ⊠ *Kamerlingh Onneslaan 3, East of Amstel* ☎ *020/462–4562* ⊕ *www.restaurantdekas.nl* ⚒ *Reservations essential* ⊘ *Closed Sun. No lunch Sat.*

$$$ ✕ **Greetje.** If your Dutch food experiences have consisted of bland pota-
DUTCH toes with even blander balls of fried dough, Greetje could be your reli-
gious awakening. It's certainly not nouvelle: in a truly old-fashioned homey environment, the chef takes rarely seen or forgotten dishes and prepares them with fresh, local, and often organic ingredients. Think grilled sandwiches of Frisian sugar bread (traditional sweet bread from Holland's North) with layers of homemade duck liver terrine and apple syrup, or filet of plaice with carrots, onion, and Dutch shrimp. Service does veer from Dutch tradition—it's efficient and extremely helpful. If you're a licorice fan, don't miss the over-the-top licorice crème brûlée with Dutch black licorice ice cream. $ *Average main: €25* ⊠ *Peperstraat 23, The Waterfront, Centrum* ☎ *020/779–7450* ⊕ *www. restaurantgreetje.nl* ⊘ *No lunch.*

$$$ ✕ **In De Waag.** Although you may wish to sniff out your own favorite
CAFÉ among the many café-restaurants that line this square, only In De Waag occupies such historic surrounds and, at night, even highlights its epic medieval roots with candlelight. $ *Average main: €25* ⊠ *Nieuwmarkt 4, Centrum* ☎ *020/422–7772.*

$$ ✕ **Mamouche.** Romantic and posh, this spot has been a hit with locals.
MOROCCAN This North African restaurant takes delight in the smallest details and
Fodor's Choice prides itself on friendly service—a good thing, then, that all signs of
★ this location's past as a Hell's Angels bar have been erased. Home-runs here include the couscous with saffron-baked pumpkin and the savory

13

lamb tagine. As for desserts, the *Hob El Habiba*—a chocolate-and-date pie—will have chocoholics saying a heartfelt amen. [$] *Average main: €20* ✉ *Quelijnstraat 104, The Pijp* ☎ *020/670–0736* 🌐 *www.restaurantmamouche.nl* 🕒 *No lunch.*

$$ DUTCH 🍴 **The Pancake Bakery.** A Dutch way of keeping eating costs down is to pack one's belly with pancakes. The Pancake Bakery remains one of the best-known places in Amsterdam to try them, with a menu that offers a near infinite range of topping possibilities—from the sweet to the fruity to the truly belly-gelling powers of cheese, pineapple, and bacon. [$] *Average main: €20* ✉ *Prinsengracht 191, Centrum* ☎ *020/625–1333* 🌐 *www.pancake.nl.*

$$$$ EUROPEAN Fodor's Choice ★ 🍴 **Tunes.** Thanks to the exposed brick, industrial lighting, glass-box kitchen, and young, vibrant crowds, you'll swear you're in a mod New York restaurant at this buzzy new rendezvous in the striking Conservatorium Hotel, across from the Stedelijk Museum. But even as the helpful servers explain each Delft-patterned plate of Spanish-inflected Dutch food, your attention will be focused solely on enjoying the sophisticated fusion cooking (the chef spent years in Spain learning the latest in foams, powders, and playful combinations). Particularly excellent are the sweetbreads with peanut sauce and shrimp crackers—a nod to Holland's colonial past in Indonesia—or the zucchini risotto with Dutch cheese and mushrooms. Choose from a three-course set menu for €68, or regular and vegetarian tasting menus, and pair your meal with wines from the smart list. [$] *Average main: €68* ✉ *Conservatorium Hotel Amsterdam, Van Baerlestraat 27, Museum District* ☎ *020/570–0000* 🌐 *www.conservatoriumhotel.com/restaurants_and_bars* ✍ *Reservations essential* 🕒 *Closed Sun. No lunch.*

WHERE TO STAY

$$$ HOTEL Fodor's Choice ★ 🏨 **Ambassade.** Friday's book market on nearby Spui Square lends a literary ambience to these 10 connected, stylishly decorated 17th- and 18th-century houses, where Howard Norman set part of his novel *The Museum Guard* and many well-known writers are regulars. **Pros:** great atmosphere; some guest rooms overlook a picturesque canal; hub for literati; massage salon on premises. **Cons:** somewhat worn; rooms at rear can be small and dark. [$] *Rooms from: €225* ✉ *Herengracht 341, Western Canal Ring* ☎ *020/555–0222* 🌐 *www.ambassade-hotel.nl* 🛏 *58 rooms, 5 suites* 🍽 *No meals.*

$$ HOTEL Fodor's Choice ★ 🏨 **CitizenM.** Trendy travelers on a budget will enjoy the cosmopolitan vibe, lavish public spaces, and airy guest rooms with their high-tech gadgetry—but maybe not the sci-fi-like see-through glass tubes that contain the toilet and shower. **Pros:** luxurious furnishings surpass the price tag; king-size beds and nice ambient lighting; sandwiches and salads available 24/7. **Cons:** guest rooms resemble hospital rooms; out-of-the-way location. [$] *Rooms from: €158* ✉ *Prinses Irenestraat 30, De Pijp and Environs* ☎ *020/811–7090* 🌐 *www.citizenm.com* 🛏 *215 rooms* 🍽 *No meals.*

$$$$ HOTEL Fodor's Choice ★ **Conservatorium Hotel.** An impressive early 20th-century bank turned music school is a visual feast, with a glass-roofed, tree-filled courtyard lobby and dramatically modern guest rooms, many of them duplexes, with huge windows, muted tones, and splashes of color. **Pros:** stunning contemporary surroundings; spacious and beautiful accommodations; spa with lap pool; near museums. **Cons:** quite expensive; a bit removed from city center. [$] *Rooms from: €325* ✉ *Van Baerlestraat 27, Museum District and Environs* ☎ *020/570 0000* 🌐 *www.conservatoriumhotel.com* 🛏 *129 rooms, 42 suites* 🍴 *No meals.*

$$$ HOTEL Fodor's Choice ★ **Estheréa.** Flowery wallpaper, boldly upholstered furniture, antiques, and screaming crystal chandeliers are all put together harmoniously at this gorgeously designed and cozy, family-owned hotel on a picturesque canal. **Pros:** friendly, enthusiastic staff; very comfy public areas; near restaurants; free use of iPads; nice 17th-century details remain. **Cons:** low ceilings; some rooms are small, though stylish. [$] *Rooms from: €180* ✉ *Singel 303–309, Western Canal Ring* ☎ *020/624–5146* 🌐 *www.estherea.nl* 🛏 *92 rooms* 🍴 *No meals.*

$$ B&B/INN FAMILY Fodor's Choice ★ **Hotel Fita.** A favorite with travelers for years is friendly and cozy and getting better all the time—nice improvements like an honor bar enhance such longtime perks as a great breakfast and in-room espresso machines. **Pros:** Dutch flavor; spacious rooms in pleasing contemporary style; beautiful location; family-friendly. **Cons:** no real public areas; no a/c (but ceiling fans). [$] *Rooms from: €134* ✉ *Jan Luykenstraat 37, Museum District and Environs* ☎ *020/679–0976* 🌐 *www.fita.nl* 🛏 *15 rooms* 🍴 *Breakfast.*

$$$ HOTEL Fodor's Choice ★ **Hotel Roemer.** A zest for modern art and design and a sense of travelers' comfort shows up everywhere, from the cozy lounge opening onto a beautiful garden to the stylish, well-equipped guest rooms, where even the bathrooms have flat-screen TVs. **Pros:** elegant and very comfy rooms; extra-long beds; breakfast and drinks included in some rates. **Cons:** fee for Wi-Fi; a bit expensive. [$] *Rooms from: €199* ✉ *Roemer Visscherstraat 10, Museum District and Environ* ☎ *020/589–0800* 🌐 *www.vondelhotels.com* 🛏 *23 rooms* 🍴 *Breakfast.*

$$$ HOTEL Fodor's Choice ★ **Hotel V.** These exquisitely designed lounges and guest rooms are a pleasure to experience, a hip showcase of contemporary furnishings and textiles that lend a spacious, luxurious, and welcoming atmosphere to the center of the old city. **Pros:** free coffee and tea; good value; really helpful staff. **Cons:** slightly off-center location; best rates are nonrefundable. [$] *Rooms from: €169* ✉ *Weteringschans 136, Leidseplein* ☎ *020/662–3233* 🌐 *www.hotelv.nl* 🛏 *48 rooms, 6 apartments* 🍴 *Breakfast.*

$$ HOTEL FAMILY Fodor's Choice ★ **Lloyd Hotel.** A former holding-area home for immigrants, this bohemian hotel is well suited to its current quirky incarnation as an offbeat design showcase, where some rooms have log walls, beds sleep up to seven, and bathtubs stand in the middle of living rooms. **Pros:** historic art-deco building; rooms priced for all budgets; interesting crowd. **Cons:** slightly out-of-the-way location. [$] *Rooms from: €140* ✉ *Oostelijke Handelskade 34, Amsterdam East* ☎ *020/561–3636* 🌐 *www.lloydhotel.com* 🛏 *117 rooms, 9 suites* 🍴 *No meals.*

$$$
HOTEL
FAMILY
Fodor's Choice
★

⊞ **Mövenpick Hotel Amsterdam.** Most of the businesslike rooms in this striking glass skyscraper built on an island within the blossoming docks area offer stunning views of the Amsterdam skyline and beyond. **Pros:** upper-floor suites offer the best views in town; the terrace is a great waterfront spot for refreshments; atmosphere is casual and welcoming. **Cons:** lacks Dutch character; a bit off the beaten path. $ *Rooms from:* €229 ⊠ *Piet Heinkade 11, Eastern Docklands, Station and Docklands* ☎ *020/519–1200* ⊕ *www.moevenpick-amsterdam.com* ⇨ *408 rooms, 31 suites* ⌾| *No meals.*

NIGHTLIFE

Amsterdam's nightlife can have you careening between smoky coffee shops, chic wine bars, mellow jazz joints, laid-back lounges, and clubs either intimate or raucous. The bona fide local flavor can perhaps best be tasted in one of the city's ubiquitous brown café-bars—called "brown" because of their woody walls and nicotine-stained ceilings.

Fodor's Choice
★

't Smalle. Set with Golden Age chandeliers, leaded-glass windows, and the patina of centuries, this charmer is one of Amsterdam's most glorious spots. The after-work crowd always jams the waterside terrace, though you are just as well to opt for the historic interior, once home to one of the city's first *jenever* distilleries. They serve breakfast and lunch. ⊠ *Egelantiersgracht 12, Jordaan* ☎ *020/623-9617* ⊕ *www.t-smalle.nl.*

Fodor's Choice
★

De Rokerij. For over a decade, this coffee shop has managed to maintain a magical-grotto aura that, ironically enough, requires no extra indulgences to induce a state of giddy transcendence. Dim lights, Indian-inspired murals, and low-to-the-ground seating keep the vibe chill regardless of how busy the Leidseplein headquarters can get. De Rokerij's other branches may inspire smaller-scale out-of-body experiences. ⊠ *Lange Leidsedwarsstraat 41, Leidseplein.* ⊠ *Singel 8, The Canal Ring.*

Fodor's Choice
★

Wynand Fockink. This is Amsterdam's most famous—and miraculously least hyped—*proeflokaal* (tasting room). Opened in 1679, this dim-lit, blithely cramped little bar just behind the Hotel Krasnapolsky has a menu of more than 60 Dutch spirits that reads like poetry: *Bruidstranen* (bride's tears) and *Boswandeling* (a walk in the woods) are just two favorites. Call ahead for a guided tour of the distillery. ⊠ *Pijlsteeg 31 and 43, The Old City Center (Het Centrum)* ☎ *020/639–2695* ⊕ *www. wynand-fockink.nl.*

SHOPPING

Just down the road from Centraal Station is **Nieuwendijk.** Besides the national chains, this street has a busy pedestrian mall catering to bargain hunters and a younger crowd. To the south of the Dam is **Kalverstraat,** where you'll find the international chains and favorite Dutch franchises. **Leidsestraat** offers a scaled-down version of Kalverstraat. Just east is the **Spiegelkwartier,** one of Europe's most fabled agglomerations of antiques shops.

Alternatively, go where the locals go. Explore the unique clothing and jewelry boutiques, crafts ateliers, and funky consignment stores dotted along the **Nine Streets,** which radiate from behind the Royal Palace to the periphery of the **Jordaan.** Take time to browse this neighborhood's art galleries, jewelry shops, and purchasable homages to interior design. **P. C. Hooftstraat** is the Madison Avenue of Amsterdam: all the main fashion houses are here, from Armani to Vuitton. Most shops close at 6 but remain open until 9 on Thursdays (*koopavonden*).

13

THE BULB FIELDS

Lisse is 27 km (17 miles) southwest of Amsterdam.

In the spring (late March until mid-May) the bulb fields of South Holland are transformed into a vivid series of Mondrian paintings through the colors of millions of tulips and other flowers. The bulb fields extend from just north of Leiden to the southern limits of Haarlem, with the greatest concentration beginning at the village of Sassenheim and ending between Hillegom and Bennebroek. Floral HQ is the town of Lisse and the fields and glasshouses of the Keukenhof Gardens. It is an unmissable and unforgettable sight. Timing can be volatile, but there's a general progression from crocus in the middle of March, daffodils and narcissi from the end of March to the middle of April, early tulips and hyacinths from the second week of April to the end of the month, and late tulips immediately afterward. An early or late spring can move these approximate dates forward or backward by as much as two weeks.

GETTING HERE AND AROUND

The easiest way to see the Bulb Fields is to get a rental car, but you can also reach the area by train from Amsterdam and then rent or bring a bicycle.

EXPLORING

Fodor's Choice ★ **Bollenstreekroute** (*Bulb District Route*). The Bulb District Route—more popularly known as the Bloemenroute (Flower Route)—is a series of roads that meander through the bulb-growing region. Marked by small blue-and-white signs that say "Bollenstreek," this route was originally designed by Dutch motoring organization ANWB (which began life as a cycling association). Driving from Amsterdam, take the A4 towards Leiden then the N207 signposted Lisse. By train, head for Haarlem and take Bus No. 50 or 51, which allows you to embark and disembark along the route. Tour companies and the local VVVs (tourist information offices) also organize walking and bicycle tours along this route which usually include a visit to Keukenhof. A round-trip tour from Lisse through Hillegom, Noorderwijkerhout, Sassenheim, De Zilk, and Voorhout is approximately 25 km (15 miles). For information about this route consult the VVV in your chosen area.

Fodor's Choice ★ **Keukenhof.** This famed 17-acre park and greenhouse complex was founded in 1950 by Tom van Waveren and other leading bulb growers. It's one of the largest open-air flower exhibitions in the world, and draws huge crowds between the end of March and the end of May.

As many as 7 million tulip bulbs bloom here every spring, either in hothouses or flower beds along the sides of a lake. In the last weeks of April (peak season) you can catch tulips, daffodils, hyacinths, and narcissi all flowering simultaneously. In addition there are blooms on show in the pavilions along with floral demonstrations and exhibitions about the history of tulips. Leading Dutch bulb-growing exporters use it as a showcase for their latest hybrids, which unfortunately means that commercial, not creative, forces are at play here. Some of the planting is of the rather gaudy tulip varieties, and there's no holding back on the bulb-buying opportunities.

It's a lovely—if squashed at times—wander around meandering streams, placid pools, and paved paths. The avenues were designed by Zocher, designer of the Vondelpark in Amsterdam. Keukenhof's roots extend back to the 15th century, when it was the herb farm (Keukenhof means "kitchen courtyard") of one of Holland's richest ladies. Any sense of history has almost been obliterated, though there is a historical garden recreating the oldest botanical garden in the Netherlands in Leiden and at least a nod to contemporary trends in the "Inspiration" section. Head for the windmill for some calm and a vista over the surrounding fields, or view the crowds from a distance with an hour-long boat tour (book this near the windmill, €7.50). This is the Netherlands' most popular springtime attraction, and it's easy to reach from all points of the country. Traveling independently rather than in an organized group should present no problem—just follow the crowds. ⊠ Lisse ☎ 0252/465–555 ⊕ www.keukenhof.nl ⊒ €15 ☉ Late Mar.–late May, daily 8–7:30 (ticket office closes at 6).

DELFT

71 km (44 miles) southwest of Amsterdam.

For many travelers, few spots in Holland are as intimate and attractive as this town. With time-burnished canals and cobblestone streets, Delft possesses a peaceful calm that recalls the quieter pace of the 17th-century Golden Age, back when Johannes Vermeer was counted among its citizens. Imagine a tiny Amsterdam, with smaller canals and narrower bridges, and you have the essence of Old Delft. But even though the city has one foot rooted in the past, another is planted firmly in the present: Delft teems with hip cafés, and being a college town, revelers pile in and out of bars almost every day of the week.

PLANNING YOUR TIME

Delft is lovely at any time of year, but high summer means hordes of visitors; spring and fall can be more pleasant. Most museums tend to close Monday. The city is compact, and you can easily visit the sights on a day trip from Amsterdam. However, staying overnight to experience Delft after the trippers have left can be a real joy.

GETTING HERE AND AROUND

BICYCLE TRAVEL

Once you've arrived in Delft, it's easy to get around by foot or bicycle.

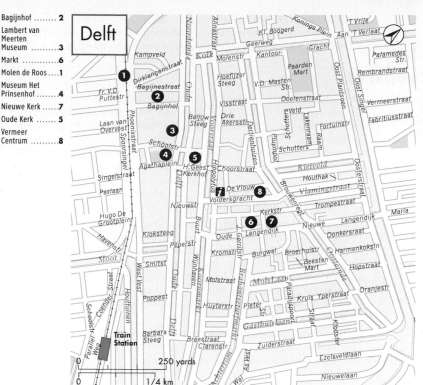

13

Contacts Rijwiel Shop ⊠ *Delft train station (at rear)* ☎ *015/214–3033* 🖂 *From €7.50 per day with a security deposit of €50–€100 (ID required)* ⊘ *Weekdays 5:45–midnight, weekends 6:30–midnight.*

BOAT TRAVEL

Compact and easy to traverse despite its web of canals, Delft is best explored on foot, although water taxis are available in summer. Everything you might want to see is in the old center, with the exception of the Delftware factories, which are an additional 15 minutes' walk or short taxi ride away.

Contacts Rondvaart Delft ⊠ *Koornmarkt 113* ☎ *015/212–6385* ⊕ *rondvaartdelft.nl.*

CAR TRAVEL

If driving, take the A10 and then the A4 south from Amsterdam. The drive will take between 45 minutes and an hour.

TRAIN TRAVEL

Direct trains leave Amsterdam Centraal Station for Delft every half hour throughout the day; the journey time is a little under one hour.

Contacts Public Transportation Information ☎ *0900/9292* ⊕ *www.9292ov.nl.*

VISITOR INFORMATION

Contacts Toeristen Informatie Punt Delft (Delft Tourist Information Point)
✉ *Hippolytusbuurt 4* ☎ *0900/515–1555 (€0.40 per min)* ⊕ *www.delft.nl.*

EXPLORING

Bagijnhof (*Bagijn courtyard*). The city sided with the (Protestant) Dutch rebels during the Eighty Years' War, and when the (Catholic) Spanish were driven out in 1572, the city reverted to Protestantism, leaving many Catholic communities in dire straits. One group of women was permitted to stay and practice their religion, but according to a new law, their place of worship had to be very modest: a drab exterior in the Bagijnhof, a weather-beaten 13th-century Gothic gate on the Oude Delft, just north of the Lambert van Meerten Museum, hides their sumptuously baroque church.

Lambert van Meerten Museum. Within the shadow of the Oude Kerk, this Renaissance-era, canalside mansion has gloriously paneled rooms that provide a noble setting for antique tiles, tin-glazed earthenware, paintings, and an extensive collection of ebony-veneer furniture. Note especially the great collection of tiles, whose subjects range from foodstuffs to warships. The gardens here are alluring, with a spherical sundial, two busts, and a stone gateway leading the eye through to the tangled woods beyond.

The museum is closed for structural and internal renovations, and it is not yet known how long these will take. ✉ *Oude Delft 199* ☎ *015/260–2358* ⊕ *www.lambertvanmeerten-delft.nl* 🎟 *€3.50, combined ticket to Het Prinsenhof, Nusantara, and Lambert van Meerten museums €10* ☉ *Tues.–Sun. 11–5.*

Markt. Delft's main square is bracketed by two town landmarks, the Stadhuis (Town Hall) and the Nieuwe Kerk. Here, too, are cafés, restaurants, and souvenir shops (most selling imitation Delftware) and, on Thursday, a busy general market. Markt 52 is the site of Johannes Vermeer's house, where the 17th-century painter spent much of his youth. Not far away is a statue of Grotius, or Hugo de Groot, born in Delft in 1583 and one of Holland's most famous humanists and lawyers.

Fodor's Choice **Museum Het Prinsenhof.** A former dignitary-hosting convent of St. Agatha,
★ the Prinsenhof Museum is celebrated as the residence of Prince William the Silent, beloved as *Vader des Vaderlands* (Father of the Nation) for his role in the Spanish Revolt and a hero whose tragic end here gave this structure the sobriquet "cradle of Dutch liberty." The complex of buildings was taken over by the government of the new Dutch Republic in 1572 and given to William of Orange for his use as a residence. On July 10, 1584, fevered by monies offered by Philip II of Spain, Bathasar Gerard, a Catholic fanatic, gained admittance to the mansion and succeeded in shooting the prince on the staircase hall, since known as Moordhal (Murder Hall). The fatal bullet holes—the *teykenen der koogelen*—are still visible in the stairwell. Today, the imposing structure is a museum, with a 15th-century chapel, a quaint courtyard, and a bevy of elegantly furnished 17th-century rooms filled with antique pottery,

silver, tapestries, and House of Orange portraits, along with exhibits on Dutch history. ⊠ *Sint Agathaplein 1* ☎ *015/260–2358* ⊕ *www. prinsenhof-delft.nl* 🖳 *€7.50, combined ticket to Het Prinsenhof and Nusantara museums €10* ☉ *Tues.–Sun. 11–5.*

Nieuwe Kerk (*New Church*). Presiding over the Markt, this Late Gothic edifice was built between 1483 and 1510. It represents more than a century's worth of Dutch craftsmanship—it's as though its founders knew it would one day be the last resting place of the man who built the nation, William the Silent, and his descendants of the House of Orange. In 1872 the noted architect P. J. H. Cuypers raised the tower to its current height. There are 22 columns surrounding the ornate black-marble-and-alabaster tomb of William of Orange, which was designed by Hendrick de Keyser and his son. The small dog you see at the prince's feet is rumored to have starved to death after refusing to eat following his owner's death. Throughout the church are paintings, stained-glass windows, and memorabilia associated with the Dutch royal family. There are other mausoleums, most notably that of lawyer-philosopher Hugo de Groot, or Grotius. In summer it is possible to climb the 380-odd steps of the church tower for an unparalleled view that stretches as far as Scheveningen to the north and Rotterdam to the south. ⊠ *Markt 2* ☎ *015/212–3025* 🖳 *Combined ticket for Oude Kerk and Nieuwe Kerk €3.50, tower €3.50* ☉ *Apr.–Oct., Mon.–Sat. 9–6; Nov.–Jan., weekdays 11–4, Sat. 10–5; Feb.–Mar., Mon.–Sat. 10–5.*

Oude Kerk (*Old Church*). At the very heart of historic Delft, the Gothic Oude Kerk, with its tower 6 feet off-kilter, is the last resting place of Vermeer. This is the oldest church in Delft, having been founded in 1200. Building went on until the 15th century, which accounts for the combination of architectural styles, and much of the austere interior dates from the latter part of the work. The tower, dating to 1350, started leaning in the Middle Ages, and today the tilt to the east is somewhat stabilized by the 3-foot tilt to the north but sill prevents ascension by visitors. At the top is the largest carillon bell in the Netherlands, weighing nearly 20,000 pounds and now is used only on state occasions. ⊠ *Heilige Geestkerkhof* ☎ *015/212–3015* 🖳 *Combined ticket to Oude Kerk and Nieuwe Kerk €3.50* ☉ *Apr.–Oct., Mon.–Sat. 9–6; Nov.–Jan., weekdays 11–4, Sat. 10–5; Feb and Mar., Mon.–Sat. 10–5.*

Fodor'sChoice
★ **Vermeer Centrum** (*Vermeer Center*). Housed in the former St. Lucas Guild, where Delft's favorite son was dean for many years, the Center takes visitors on a multimedia journey through the life and work of Johannes Vermeer. Touch screens, projections, and other interactive features are interspersed with giant reproductions of the master's work, weaving a tale of 17th-century Delft and drawing you into the mind of the painter. ☎ *015/213–8588* ⊕ *www.vermeerdelft.nl* 🖳 *€7* ☉ *Daily 10–5.*

WHERE TO EAT

$$
CAFÉ
✕ Café Vlaanderen. At this extensive café, board games keep you entertained on a rainy day but sunny skies will make you head for the tables set under leafy lime trees out front on the Beestenmarkt. Out back is

an equally shady garden. The deluxe fish wrap makes a delicious light lunch, while evening options include a delicious tuna and swordfish brochette. $ *Average main: €12* ✉ *Beestenmarkt 16* ☎ *015/213–3311* ⊕ *www.vlaanderen.nl.*

$ ✕ **De Wijnhaven.** This Delft staple has loyal regulars, drawn by the many
CAFÉ terrace tables on a small square overlooking a narrow canal—and a mean Indonesian satay. There's a smart restaurant on the first floor, but the bar and mezzanine have plenty to offer, with lunch snacks, a reasonable menu for dinner with the latest tracks on the speakers, and great fries and salads. $ *Average main: €9* ✉ *Wijnhaven 22* ☎ *015/214–1460* ⊕ *www.wijnhaven.nl.*

$ ✕ **Stadscafé de Waag.** The ancient brick-and-stone walls of this cavern-
CONTEMPORARY ous former weigh house are adorned with hulking 17th-century balance scales. Tables on the mezzanine in the rear overlook the Wijnhaven canal, while those on the terrace in front nestle under the town's magnificent, looming clock tower. All the while, tastefully unobtrusive music creates a cool vibe for a mixed clientele. Happily, dishes such as Flemish asparagus with ham and egg, or *parelhoen* (guinea fowl) in a rich dark broth, are equal to the fabulous setting. $ *Average main: €10* ✉ *Markt 11* ☎ *015/213–0393* ⊕ *www.de-waag.nl.*

WHERE TO STAY

$ 🏠 **Bridges House.** In this tastefully restored 17th-century inn, once the
HOTEL home of painter Jan Steen, antiques grace each spacious room, all adorned with extra-long beds with custom-made mattresses and some with cozy canal views. **Pros:** central location; canal views; bathrooms with tubs and enormous showerheads for a wake-up blast. **Cons:** parking is difficult. $ *Rooms from: €113* ✉ *Oude Delft 74* ☎ *015/212–4036* ⊕ *www.bridges-house.nl* 🛏 *10 rooms, 2 studio apartments* 🍽 *Breakfast.*

$$ 🏠 **Johannes Vermeer.** You'll be spoiled for choice of old-master views at
HOTEL the first Delft hotel to pay homage to the town's most famous son: the pleasant modern rooms (with beams and other nice touches) at the front overlook a canal, while those at the back have a sweeping city view that takes in three churches. **Pros:** historic building; nice garden. **Cons:** parking is difficult. $ *Rooms from: €125* ✉ *Molslaan 18–22* ☎ *015/212–6466* ⊕ *www.hotelvermeer.nl* 🛏 *25 rooms, 5 suites* 🍽 *Breakfast.*

$ 🏠 **Leeuwenbrug.** Facing one of Delft's quieter waterways, this traditional
HOTEL and well-maintained hotel offers rooms that are large, airy, and taste-
Fodor's Choice fully contemporary in décor; those in the annex are particularly appeal-
★ ing, while those at the front have canal views. **Pros:** friendly; central; atmospheric lounge. **Cons:** some bathrooms are a little old. $ *Rooms from: €99* ✉ *Koornmarkt 16* ☎ *015/214–7741* ⊕ *www.leeuwenbrug.nl* 🛏 *36 rooms* 🍽 *Breakfast.*

SHOPPING

De Porceleyne Fles. It's corny, even sometimes a little tacky (miniature clogs, anyone?), but no visit to Delft would be complete without stopping at a Delft porcelain factory to see plates and tulip vases being

painted by hand and perhaps picking up a souvenir or two. De Porceleyne Fles is the original and most famous home to the popular blue-
and-white pottery. Regular demonstrations of molding and painting
pottery are given by the artisans. On the bottom of each object is a
triple signature: a plump vase topped by a straight line, the stylized
letter "F" below it, and the word "Delft." Blue is no longer the only
official color. In 1948 a rich red cracked glaze premiered, depicting pro-
fuse flowers, graceful birds, and leaping gazelles. There is New Delft,
a range of green, gold, and black hues, whose exquisite minuscule figures are drawn to resemble an old Persian tapestry; the Pynacker Delft,
borrowing Japanese motifs in rich oranges and golds; and the brighter
Polychrome Delft, which can strike a brilliant sunflower-yellow effect.
⊠ *Royal Delftware Factory, Rotterdamseweg 196* ☎ *015/251–2030*
⊕ *www.royaldelft.com* ✆ *Museum €12* ☉ *Mid-Mar.–Oct., daily 9–5;
Nov.–mid-Mar., Mon.–Sat. 9–5.*

De Delftse Pauw. Another favorite place for picking up Delftware is at the
pottery factories of De Delftse Pauw, which, although not as famous as
De Porceleyne Fles, produce work of equally high quality. ⊠ *Delftweg
133* ☎ *015/212–4920* ⊕ *www.delftpottery.com* ✆ *Tours free* ☉ *Apr.–
Oct., daily 9–4:30; Nov.–Mar., weekdays 9–4:30, weekends 11–1.*

De Candelaer. De Candelaer is a smaller pottery, and its city-center location makes it a convenient stop-off for comparisons of Delftware with
other craftsmanship available in Delft. ⊠ *Kerkstraat 14* ☎ *015/213–
1848* ⊕ *www.candelaer.nl.*

ROTTERDAM

*18 km (11 miles) southeast of Delft and 86 km (53 miles) southwest
of Amsterdam.*

Rotterdam looks to the future like almost nowhere else. The decision
to leave the past behind wasn't made entirely through choice, however—the old town disappeared overnight on May 14, 1940, when Nazi
bombs devastated an area greater than one square mile, sweeping away
more than 36,000 buildings in just a few torrid hours.

Since then, a new landscape of concrete, steel, and glass has risen like
a phoenix from the ashes, and today this world port is home to some
of the 21st century's most architecturally important creations. The city
skyline—especially in the areas around the station and by the Maas on
the Kop van Zuid development—is constantly changing, and as each
year passes it lives up more and more to its billing as "Manhattan-on-
the-Maas." Many of the new buildings are commissioned from top-
drawer contemporary architects like Rem Koolhaas and Sir Norman
Foster, and each has a striking identity.

That isn't to say the city is all glass and steel. Areas such as historic
Delfshaven—from where the pilgrim fathers set sail for the New World
aboard the *Speedwell* in 1620—escaped the worst effects of the war,
and still retain their old character and charm. And in between old and
new, the large and leafy Het Park (simply "The Park") has a maze of
paths weaving between small lakes and ponds to provide cool shade in

summer and a welcome break from the urban sprawl at any time of year. As if that wasn't enough reason to visit, Rotterdam also boasts some of the country's best museums and top shopping opportunities.

Thanks to its location on the deltas of the Rhine and Maas rivers, Rotterdam has become the world's largest seaport. Through its harbors and the enormous Europoort pass more tons of shipping than through all of France combined. The rapid expansion of the port in the postwar years created a huge demand for labor, bringing waves of migrants from Italy, Spain, Greece, Turkey, Morocco, Cape Verde, and the Netherlands Antilles, turning Rotterdam into one of the most ethnically diverse cities in Europe.

> ## SAVE EUROS
>
> Fifteen Rotterdam museums participate in the **Museumkaart** (Museum Card), or MJK, program; this gives you free entry to more than 400 museums throughout the country for a year. Alternatively, a **Rotterdam Welcome Card** will get you a 25% discount off entry to 50 local museums and attractions, plus free rides on local buses, trams, and metros. They are available from tourist offices or can be bought online (⊕ *www.rotterdam.info*). They cost €10, €13.50, €17.50 for one, two, or three days, respectively.

ORIENTATION

The city divides itself naturally into a number of main sectors. The **Central** area, south and east of the main railway station, is focused on the pedestrianized zone around the Lijnbaan and Van Oldenbarneveltstraat. This is where the city goes out to shop—all the major department stores and many exclusive boutiques are located here. Along the river are three old harbors, **Delfshaven, Oude Haven,** and **Leuvehaven.** Charming Delfshaven is so narrow it looks like a canal, and is lined with gabled houses dating back centuries, creating a classic Dutch scene. The Oude Haven, by contrast, is surrounded by modern buildings, some of which, like the Blaak Rail Station and Kijk-Kubus, are among Rotterdam's most iconic buildings. To the south of the river, across the Erasmus Bridge, the **Kop van Zuid** and **Entrepot** districts are where famous architects such as Sir Norman Foster and Renzo Piano have been given free rein to design housing projects, theaters, and public buildings to complete the area's transformation into a modern and luxurious commercial and residential district. **Museumpark** is the cultural heart of the city, and home to four museums and bordered by a Sculpture Terrace.

GETTING HERE AND AROUND
BUS AND TRAM TRAVEL

Because the different areas of Rotterdam are fairly spread out, to get between them you may want to make use of the efficient public transport network (taxis are expensive). Buses and trams fan out across the city above ground, while four underground metro lines—one north–south, three east–west—offer an even faster way of getting about. All intersect at Beurs station in the city center for easy transfers. A fifth overground metro line runs from Hofplein (east of the main train station) to The Hague, but this is of less interest to visitors as the main line trains are a much faster means of making the journey. To use the network you'll need an **OV-chipkaart** (public transport chip card). These credit card–size tickets can be loaded up with credit from machines in the railway and metro stations and are debited as you board and leave trains, trams, metros, and buses. There are information and sales points in the Beurs and Centraal Station metro stations, as well as in the main bus station. Or visit ⊕ *www.ov-chipkaart.nl* for more information.

Contacts Public Transportation Information ☎ *0900/9292* ⊕ *www.9292ov.nl.*

13

TAXI TRAVEL
Taxis are available at railway stations, major hotels, and at taxi stands in key locations. You can also order one by phone, but they cannot be hailed on the street. Expect to pay at least €40 for a 30-minute journey between Rotterdam and Delft.

Contacts Rotterdamse Taxi Centrale ☎ *010/462–6060* ⊕ *www.rtcnv.nl.*

TRAIN TRAVEL
Direct trains leave Amsterdam Centraal Station for Rotterdam as often as six times an hour throughout the day and hourly throughout the night—the journey time is around one hour. If driving, take the A10, A4, and A13 freeways south from Amsterdam. The drive will take about one hour, depending on traffic.

TOURS
Spido boat tours. The Nieuwe Maas River has flowed through Rotterdam for 700 years, dividing the city in two and acting as the city's lifeline. A continual procession of some 30,000 oceangoing ships and some 130,000 river barges passes annually through Rotterdam to and from the North Sea. A top option for visitors to see the city's waterfront is to take a 75-minute boat tour (€10.50) with the very popular Spido boat tours. They offer a range of excursions lasting from just over an hour to a full day, while a variety of water taxis and water buses also operates in the Waterstad (the docks and harbors along the banks of the river). ✉ *Willemsplein 85* ☎ *010/275–9988* ⊕ *www.spido.nl.*

VISITOR INFORMATION
For those with an interest in Rotterdam's recent history, pick up a map from the tourist office called "Along the Fire Boundary." It has details of three self-guided walking routes that trace the edge of the area destroyed by the bombing of May 14, 1940, with detailed historical notes.

Contacts VVV Rotterdam ✉ *Binnenwegplein, Coolsingel 195–197* ☎ *010/271–0120* ⊕ *www.rotterdam.info.*

EXPLORING

With a day you can cover pretty much all of Rotterdam's sights. But don't forget to factor in extra time for shopping.

Delfshaven. The last remaining nook of old Rotterdam is the old port area, reconstructed to appear just as it was when originally built—an open-air museum with rows of gabled houses lining the historic waterfront, trendy galleries, cafés, and restaurants. Walk along the Voorhaven, Achterhaven, and neighboring Piet Heynplein and marvel at the

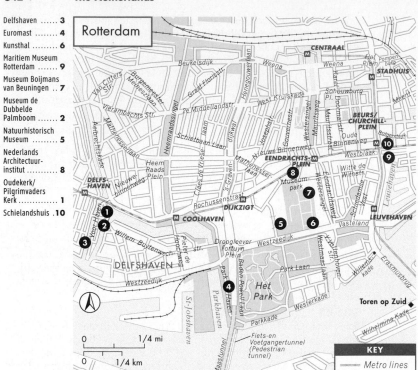

Rotterdam

many historic buildings. For historic sights in the environs, check out the working mill of **Korenmolen de Distilleerketel** (open Wednesday and Saturday only), the fascinating **Museum de Dubbelde Palmboom** on Rotterdam city history, and the **Oudekerk/Pilgrimvaders Kerk.** Tram No. 4 connects Delfshaven with the rest of the city, as does the nearby Delfshaven metro station. ⊠ *Achterhaven and Voorhaven, Delfshaven.*

Euromast. For a bird's-eye view of the contrast between Delfshaven and the majority of the city, as well as a spectacular panorama of city and harbor, visit the 600-foot-high Euromast. Designed by Rotterdam architect Huig Maaskant in 1960, this was the Netherland's tallest building for many years; when a new medical facility for the Erasmus University usurped the honor in 1970, an additional 25 feet were added to the tower in six days, restoring Euromast to its premier position. On a clear day, you can just about see the coast. The main observation deck is at 315 feet, but the **Euroscoop** is a rotating panoramic elevator that will carry you another 300 feet from there to the top of the mast. For the thrill-seekers among us, on weekends from May to September you can skip the elevator and rappel down from the observation deck, or shoot down the rope slide in about 10 seconds on Europe's fastest "zip wire" (make reservations via ⊕ *www.abseilen.nl*). There's also a restaurant at the top. You can even stay up the tower overnight in one of two special suites, but be warned the prices are as high as the experience. Down below, the park at the base of the Euromast is where many Rotterdammers spend time when the weather is good. ✉ *Parkhaven 20, Delfshaven* ☎ *010/436–4811* ⊕ *www.euromast.nl* 🖼 *€9.25, rappelling or rope slide €49.50* ⊘ *Apr.–Sept., daily 9:30 am–11 pm; Oct.–Mar., daily 10 am–11 pm.*

Kunsthal. This "art house" sits at one end of the visitor-friendly museum quarter and hosts major temporary exhibitions. There is no permanent collection, other than the massive, multistory boxlike center itself, designed by architect-prophet Rem Koolhaas. Opinions about the building are sharply divided: some say the design bridging the gap between the Museumpark and the dike is a clever spatial creation; others consider it an ugly mix of facades (part glass, part brick, and part corrugated iron) that has led to rusted iron, stained concrete, and cracks in the central walkway. The biggest complaint is the lack of elevator, compounded by the hazards of the central ramp, whose steep angle makes this a potential ski slope for wheelchair users. Fortunately, the eclectic exhibitions, usually three or four at any one time, are always fascinating, regardless of the setting. ✉ *Westzeedijk 341, Museumpark* ☎ *010/440–0301* ⊕ *www.kunsthal.nl* 🖼 *€11* ⊘ *Tues.–Sat. 10–5, Sun. 11–5.*

FAMILY
Fodor'sChoice
★
Maritiem Museum Rotterdam. A sea lover's delight, the Maritime Museum is Rotterdam's noted nautical collection. Appropriately perched at the head of the Leuvehaven harbor, it was founded by Prince Hendrik in 1874. Set against the background of modern and historical maritime objects, the seafaring ways of old Rotterdammers make more sense. Star attraction of the ground floor is a large model of the Europoort, which shows how the Rotterdam area has developed over the centuries into the major seaport of today. The upper floors are mainly given over to rotating exhibitions on seafaring themes. Children have half a floor dedicated to them, called "Professor Plons" (Professor Plunge), where museum staff are on hand to help with looking through a real periscope, donning a hard hat and taking to the driving seat of a scaled-down crane, and engaging in many other activities dealing with the themes of water and ships. Kids will also love the museum's prize exhibit, the warship *De Buffel*, moored in the harbor outside, dating back to 1868. The ship has been perfectly restored and is fitted out sumptuously, as can be seen in the mahogany-deck captain's cabin. ✉ *Leuvehaven 1, Witte de With* ☎ *010/413–2680* ⊕ *www.maritiemmuseum.nl* 🖼 *€7.50* ⊘ *July and Aug., Mon.–Sat. 10–5, Sun. 11–5; Sept.–June, Tues.–Sat. 10–5, Sun. 11–5.*

Fodor'sChoice
★
Museum Boijmans van Beuningen. Rotterdam's finest shrine to art, with treasures ranging from Pieter Bruegel the Elder's 16th-century *Tower of Babel* to Mondriaan's extraordinary *Composition in Yellow and Blue*, ranks among the greatest art galleries in Europe. The top attraction here is the collection of old masters, which covers West European art from the 14th to the 19th century. In particular 15th- to 17th-century Dutch and Flemish art are well represented, including painters such as Van Eyck, Rubens, Hieronymous Bosch, and Rembrandt. The modern art section runs the gamut from Monet to Warhol and beyond, picking

up Kandinsky, Magritte, and Dalí in between. In the Decorative Art and Design collection, both precious ornamental objects and everyday utensils dating from medieval times are displayed. In the museum café, note the fantastic collection of chairs, each by a different designer. More artworks embellish the museum gardens. ⊠ *Museumpark 18–20, Museumpark* ☎ *010/441–9400* ⊕ *www.boijmans.nl* ⊠ *€12.50* ⊗ *Tues.– Sun. 11–5.*

Museum de Dubbelde Palmboom (*Double Palm Tree Museum*). Devoted to the history of Rotterdam and its role as an international nexus, this museum traces the city's history from prehistoric times to the current day. The focus is on how exotic wares imported by the East India Company affected the city. The building itself is redolent of history: not only do its heavy beams and brick floors waft you back to yesteryear, but there even seems to be a faint smell of grains, recalling the many years the building spent as a warehouse. Ask for the informative guide in English, as all labeling is in Dutch. The first floor has some fascinating archaeological finds: one of the spouted ancient jugs has been traced to a town near Cologne, providing proof that traveling merchants were apparently very active in trading ceramics. ⊠ *Voorhaven 12, Delfshaven* ☎ *010/476–1533* ⊕ *www.museumrotterdam.nl* ⊠ *€6, ticket also valid for a same-day visit to the Schielandshuis* ⊗ *Tues.–Sun. 11–5.*

FAMILY **Natuurhistorisch Museum** (*Natural History Museum*). Located in a historic villalike structure with an enormous glass wing (echoing the hip Kunsthal next door), the Natural History Museum challenges its visitors with skeletal glimpses of creatures you'll be hard put to identify. As soon as you enter the foyer, you are face to face with a mounted scary-hairy gorilla. It doesn't stop there: in one room the skeleton of a giraffe stretches as far up as you can crane your own neck. Continue on to be met by a tiger and arching elephant tusks. There is an "ironic" re-creation of a trophy hunter's display, with turtles mounted on a wall, arranged according to size. In another area, a dinner table is set, with the skulls of a human, a cow, an anteater, a lion, a zebra, and a pig as guests. Before each of them is a plate laden with their respective dining preferences. Children, meanwhile, are drawn to the 40-foot-long skeleton of a sperm whale. ⊠ *Westzeedijk 345, Museumpark* ☎ *010/436– 4222* ⊕ *www.nmr.nl* ⊠ *€6* ⊗ *Tues.–Sat. 10–5, Sun. 11–5.*

Nederlands Architectuurinstituut. Fittingly, for a city of exciting modern architecture, Rotterdam is the home of the NAi, or the Netherlands Architecture Institute. The striking glass-and-metal building—designed by Rotterdam local Joe Conen in 1993—hosts temporary displays on architecture and interior design in seven exhibition spaces, giving a holistic interpretation of the history and development of architecture, especially the urban design and spatial planning of Rotterdam. ⊠ *Museumpark 25, Museumpark* ☎ *010/440–1200* ⊕ *www.nai.nl* ⊠ *€10* ⊗ *Tues.–Sat. 10–5, Sun. 11–5.*

Oudekerk/Pilgrimvaders Kerk (*Pilgrim Fathers' Church*). On July 22, 1620, 16 men, 11 women, and 19 children sailed from Delfshaven on the *Speedwell*. Their final destination was America, where they helped found the Plymouth Colony in Massachusetts. Puritan Protestants fleeing England for religious freedom usually went to Amsterdam, but this group, which arrived in 1608, decided to live in Leiden, then 10 years later opted to travel on to the New World. On July 20, 1620, they left Leiden by boat, and via Delft they reached Delfshaven, where they spent their last night in Holland. After a sermon from their vicar, John Robinson, in what has since become this church, they boarded the *Speedwell,* sailing to Southampton, England, then left on the *Mayflower* on September 5, reaching Cape Cod 60 days later.

The church was built in 1417 as the Chapel of Sint Anthonius, then extended and restyled in the Late Gothic period. However, in 1761 the ceilings were raised, and the current style dates back to this Regency revamp, when an ornate wooden clock tower was also added. Next to the choir is a vestry from 1819, where you can find a memorial plaque to the Pilgrim Fathers on the wall. The bell tower has a tiny balcony. The church is now owned by the Trust for Old Dutch Churches. ✉ *Aelbrechtskolk 20, Delfshaven* ☎ *010/477–4156* 🌐 *www.pelgrimvaderskerk.nl* 🕒 *July–Aug., weekdays 11–3, Sat. 1–4; Sept.–June, Sat. 1–4.*

Schielandshuis (*Schieland House*). Staunchly defending its position against the high-rise Robeco Tower and the giant Hollandse Banke Unie surrounding it, this palatial 17th-century mansion holds its own as a part of Rotterdam's historical museum (the other half is the Dubbelde Palmboom in Delfshaven). Built between 1662 and 1665 in Dutch Neoclassical style by the Schieland family, it burned down in 1864, but the facade survived, and the interior was carefully restored. Another renovation in 2010 has given it a new shine. Inside are baroque- and rococo-style rooms reconstructed from houses in the area, clothing from the 18th century to the present day, and the famous collection of maps, the Atlas von Stolk. Because of the frailty of the paper, only a tiny selection of these vintage documents is on display at any one time, usually under a specific theme. The museum's café is in a lovely garden. ✉ *Korte Hoogstraat 31, Centrum* ☎ *010/217–6767* 🌐 *www.museumrotterdam.nl* 🎟 *€6, ticket also valid for a same-day visit to the Dubbelde Palmboom Museum* 🕒 *Tues.–Fri. 10–5, weekends 11–5.*

WHERE TO EAT

$$ VEGETARIAN 🍴 **Bla Bla.** Just around the corner from the historic heart of Delfshaven, this restaurant is always lively and frequently crowded. There is always a choice of three or four main vegetarian dishes, inspired by cuisines from around the world, and the menu changes often. Make sure you're having dinner on the early side to get the freshest ingredients—and a seat. [$] *Average main: €18* ✉ *Piet Heynsplein 35, Delfshaven* ☎ *010/477–4448* 🌐 *www.bla-bla.nl* 🕒 *Closed Mon. and Tues. No lunch.*

$ CAFÉ 🍴 **Café Dudok.** Lofty ceilings, a cavernous former-warehouse interior, long reading tables stacked with international magazines and papers—little wonder this place attracts an artsy crowd. At its most mellow, the spot is perfect for a lazy afternoon treat of delicious homemade pastries, but you can come here for breakfast, lunch, high tea, dinner, or even a snack after midnight. They offer a small selection for vegetarians. The brasserie, on a mezzanine above the open kitchen at the back, looks out over the Rotte River. Since it's terribly crowded at times, you should get here unfashionably early to avoid disappointment—there's nowhere else like it in Rotterdam. [$] *Average main: €10* ✉ *Meent 88, Centrum* ☎ *010/433–3102* 🌐 *www.dudok.nl.*

$$ INDONESIAN

🍴 **Dewi Sri.** This restaurant has rijsttafel to dream about, with creative takes on traditional Indonesian dishes. Rice table is like Indonesian smorgasbord with samplings from the menu. Choose from a multitude of tantalizing options from Indonesian, Javanese, and Sumatran menus. Some diners may find the mock wood carvings a little heavy, given the subtle flavors of the food being served. All in all, though, this place probably has the best Indonesian food in Rotterdam, so don't let the décor faze you. The large restaurant upstairs could feel quite empty midweek, but the staff is incredibly polite, appearing discreetly at your table just as soon as you feel the need to ask for something. If you can't find space in the Dewi Sri, try the adjacent Warisan restaurant, which serves similarly priced and equally mouthwatering Thai food. [$] *Average main: €15* ✉ *Westerkade 20, Scheepvaartkwartier* ☎ *010/436–0263* 🌐 *www.dewisri.nl* 🕒 *No lunch weekends.*

$$$$ ECLECTIC Fodor's Choice ★

🍴 **Parkheuvel.** Overlooking the Maas, this posh restaurant is run by chef-owner Erik van Loo. It is said to be popular among the harbor barons, who can oversee their dockside territory from the bay windows of this tastefully modern, semicircular building. Tables are covered with cream-color linens, and wood-frame chairs are elegantly upholstered. The service here is as effortlessly attentive as you would expect from one of Holland's top five restaurants. Luxuries such as truffles are added to the freshest ingredients, with the day's menu dictated by the availability of the best produce at that morning's markets. Kudos and salaams are offered up by diners to many of the chef's specialties, including the ravioli of black Bresse chicken with panfried langoustines. [$] *Average main: €45* ✉ *Heuvellaan 21, Centrum* ☎ *010/436–0530* 🌐 *www.parkheuvel.nl* ✍ *Reservations essential* 🕒 *Closed Sun. and 3 wks in Aug. No lunch Sat.*

$$$ SEAFOOD

🍴 **Zeezout.** On an elegant riverfront terrace, the charming "Sea Salt" mirrors the freshness of its sea-based menu in crisp linen tablecloths and its spotlessly clean, open kitchen, where the bustle of the staff whets your appetite. A large fish mosaic on the wall looks out across the river to the floodlighted Erasmus Bridge; a window awning adds to the romance of the view. Try the turbot accompanied by shrimp, aubergine cream, and *rösti* (potato pancakes). [$] *Average main: €27* ✉ *Westerkade 11b, Scheepvaartkwartier* ☎ *010/436–5049* 🌐 *www.restaurantzeezout.nl* ✍ *Reservations essential* 🕒 *Closed Mon. No lunch Sun.*

WHERE TO STAY

$ HOTEL

🏨 **Bazar.** The well-traveled owner has created havens from his wanderings, with hot, deep colors evoking Turkey and Morocco throughout the individually styled rooms on the second floor, and motifs conjuring up Africa and South America on the third and fourth floors. **Pros:** top-floor rooms have balconies. **Cons:** elevator stops on third floor. [$] *Rooms from: €80* ✉ *Witte de Withstraat 16, Witte de With* ☎ *010/206–5151* 🌐 *www.hotelbazar.nl* 🛏 *27 rooms* 🍽 *Breakfast.*

$ 🖭 **Hotel New York.** An atmospheric standout on Rotterdam's business-
HOTEL   oriented hotel scene occupies the former twin-towered, waterside headquarters of the Holland-America Line, offering individually decorated
rooms with high ceilings that contrast with the modernist, vaguely nautical décor, and excellent views. **Pros:** great riverside location; historic
building; nice room décor. **Cons:** away from main sights. $Rooms
from: €110 ⊠ Koninginnenhoofd 1, Kop van Zuid ☎ 010/439–0500
⊕ www.hotelnewyork.nl ⤴ 71 rooms, 1 suite Ⓞ No meals._

$$$ 🖭 **Manhattan Hotel Rotterdam.** The only five-star hotel in the city draws
HOTEL   celebrity guests, and the regal purple corridors, lined with copies of
Fodor's Choice   Dutch masterpieces, and bright spacious rooms fitted out with luxuri-
★   ously huge beds will make you feel like a member of the glitterati yourself.
Pros: sky-high luxury; slick-yet-friendly service; CD players and every
other amenity. **Cons:** sky-high prices. $Rooms from: €189 ⊠ Weena
686, Centrum ☎ 010/430–2000 ⊕ www.manhattanhotelrotterdam.com
⤴ 224 rooms, 7 suites Ⓞ No meals._

$ 🖭 **Van Walsum.** The friendly and gregarious owner proudly restores and
HOTEL   reequips his rooms, floor by floor, on a continuously rotating basis,
with the always-modern décor of each floor determined by that year's
best buys in furniture, carpeting, and bathroom tiles. **Pros:** friendly;
within walking distance of the Museum Boijmans van Beuningen and
other major attractions. **Cons:** away from the nightlife. $Rooms from:
€89 ⊠ Mathenesserlaan 199–201, Centrum ☎ 010/436–3275 ⊕ www.
hotelvanwalsum.nl ⤴ 28 rooms Ⓞ Breakfast._

13

NIGHTLIFE

From hard-core techno—which has been popular here since the early
1990s—to early-hour chill-out cafés, there is a wide gamut of nighttime
entertainment. The best nights tend to be Thursday to Saturday, 11 pm
to 5 am. West Kruiskade (also known as Chinatown) is the place to
go if you want lively bars and music from around the world. Nieuwe
Binnenweg and Witte de Withstraat have many busy late-night cafés
and clubs. Oude Haven is particularly popular with students, and the
Schouwburgplein is favored by visitors to the nearby theaters and cin-
emas. Stadshuisplein has a number of tacky discos and bars.

Breakaway. Breakaway is busy, with a young international crowd, and
the nearest you'll get to a Dutch take on an American bar. ⊠ Karel
Doormanstraat 1, near Centraal Station, Centrum ☎ 010/233–0922
⊕ www.breakaway.nl.

De Schouw. An erstwhile brown café and former journalists' haunt, De
Schouw is now a trendy brown bar with a mix of artists and students.
⊠ Witte de Withstraat 80, Witte de With ☎ 010/412–4253.

Locus Publicus. A favorite with Belgian beer enthusiasts, Locus Publicus
has a menu that tops 200 varieties. Best of all, this one-room café a few
minutes' walk east from Blaak station has an open log fire in winter.
⊠ Oostzeedijk 364, Blaak ☎ 010/433–1761 ⊕ www.locus-publicus.com.

SHOPPING

Rotterdam is the number-one shopping city in South Holland. Its famous Lijnbaan and Beurstraverse shopping centers, as well as the surrounding areas, offer a dazzling variety of shops and department stores. Here you'll find all the biggest chains in Holland, such as Mango, MEXX, Morgan, Invito, and Sacha. The archways and fountains of the Beurstraverse—at the bottom of the Coolsingel—make this newer, pedestrianized area more pleasing to walk around. It is now one of the most expensive places to rent shop space, and has a nickname: *Koopgoot,* which can mean "shopping channel" (if you like it) or "shopping gutter" (if you don't). The Bijenkorf department store has an entrance here on the lower-street level. Van Oldenbarneveldtstraat and Nieuwe Binnenweg are the places to be if you want something different. There is a huge variety of alternative fashion to be found here.

Exclusive shops and boutiques can be found in the Entrepotgebied, Delfshaven, Witte de Withstraat, Nieuwe and Oude Binnenweg, and Van Oldenbarneveldtstraat. West Kruiskade and its vicinity offer a wide assortment of multicultural products in the many Chinese, Surinamese, Mediterranean, and Arabic shops. The shops in the city center are open every Sunday afternoon, and there is late-night shopping—until 9—every Friday.

PORTUGAL

Lisbon, Sintra, Porto

WHAT'S WHERE

1 Lisbon. Portugal's capital, founded more than three millennia ago, is an engaging mixture of modernity and mellow age. It moved into the international limelight by hosting Expo '98, the last great World Exposition of the 20th century, and then the final of soccer's 2004 European championship. A regeneration program has improved the city center, its transportation, and public buildings. The former Expo site—reclaimed shore to the northeast now renamed Parque das Nações (Park of the Nations)—hosts riverside restaurants, shows, a cable-car ride, and the stupendous Oceanarium.

2 Sintra. Along the coastal region west of Lisbon, Sintra is undoubtedly the biggest draw. Described by Lord Byron as "a glorious Eden," this hilly former royal retreat is studded with magnificent palaces, gardens, and luxury *quintas* (manor houses), and is a UNESCO World Heritage Site. The Atlantic coast to its west is often windswept, which means that, while it may not be so conducive to sunbathing, it is excellent for wind- and kite-surfing and sailboarding, as well as stunning coastal drives.

3 Porto. Portugal's northern region is a dramatic patchwork of soaring mountains, rolling hills, and dense forests, centered on Porto. The city is a captivating mix of the medieval and modern, combining a slick commercial hub with the charmingly dilapidated riverfront district—another well-deserved World Heritage Site. Across the water, Vila Nova de Gaia is the headquarters of the thriving Port wine trade.

ATLANTIC OCEAN

← TO THE AZORES

TO MADEIRA ISLAND

Minho Valença

Viana
do Castelo Lima Serra do Gerês Chaves Bragança

Barcelos Braga
Póvoa de Varzim Guimarães Tâmega A4/IP4 Mirandela
Vila do Conde Amarante Vila Real N102/IP2 Mogadouro
Porto Penafiel Douro Sabor Duoro
3
Espinho Oliveira Lamego
dos Azeméis S. Pedro Moimenta
do Sul da Beira
Albergaria-a-Velha Vouga Viseu Pinhel
Aveiro IP5
Mealhada Sta. Comba Guarda
Mira Dão
Cantanhede Mundego Serra da Estrêla
Coimbra Covilhã
Figueira Arganil Fundão
da Foz Zêzere Penamacor
Pombal Serra da
Gardunha
Leiria Castelo
Batalha Ourém Proença- Branco
Nazaré Fátima Tomar a-Nova
Alcobaça Sra. IP6 Abrantes Nisa
do Aire
Torres Tagus
Óbidos Novas Portalegre
Torres Vedras Aveiras de Cima Ponte
Mafra de Sor
2 Sintra Vila Franca Sorraia
de Xira Avis
Cascais ⭐ LISBON Arraiolos Estremoz Elvas Badajoz
Estoril **1**
Seixal Setúbal Sra. de Ossa Vila
Viçosa Guadiana
Cabo Évora
Espichel Alcácer Reguengos
do Sal Sado
Ferreira do
Alentejo Moura
Sines Santiago Vilaverde de Ficalho
Cabo de do Cacem Beja
Sines Serpa
Castro
Verde
Odemira Ourique
Mértola Chança
Guadiana
ALGARVE

0 50 miles
0 50 km

Vila do Bispo IP1 S. Brás de Alportel
Cabo de Lagos Albufeira Tavira Vila Real de
S. Vicente Sagres Faro Olhão S. António

SPAIN

NEED TO KNOW

PORTUGAL

★Lisbon

AT A GLANCE

Capital: Lisbon

Population: 10,000,000

Currency: Euro

Money: ATMs are common

Language: Portuguese

Country Code: ☎ 351

Emergencies: ☎ 112

Driving: On the right

Electricity: 220-240V; electrical plugs have two round prongs

Time: Five hours ahead of New York

Documents: Up to 90 days with valid passport; Schengen rules apply

Mobile Phones: GSM (900 and 1800 bands)

Major Mobile Companies: Optimus, Vodafone, TMN

WEBSITES

Portugal Government: ⊕ www.turismodeportugal.pt

Portugal Tourism: ⊕ www.visitportugal.com

Portugal Tips: ⊕ www.portugal.com

GETTING AROUND

✈ **Air Travel:** The major international airport is Lisbon; Faro and Porto have many intra-Europe flights.

🚌 **Bus Travel:** Comfortable express buses travel between main regions.

🚗 **Car Travel:** Rental cars are popular among tourists and generally a safe, reliable option, but driving in big cities such as Lisbon and Porto is not for the faint-hearted. Never leave valuables visible in the car.

🚆 **Train Travel:** The high-speed Alfa-Pendular train darts between the Algarve, Lisbon, and Porto. Slower regional and urban services travel within regions.

PLAN YOUR BUDGET

	HOTEL ROOM	MEAL	ATTRACTIONS
Low Budget	€100	€15	Jerónimos Monastery, €7
Mid Budget	€150	€25	Oceanarium, €13
High Budget	€300	€150	Yacht trip with dinner for two, €150

WAYS TO SAVE

Grab a takeaway. Take-out shops offer grilled meats like the famous piri-piri chicken, a great meal with fries or rice, a simple salad, and a glass of white wine.

Home Away from Home. There are plenty of lovely family-run guesthouses (called *residenciais*) throughout Portugal at a fraction of the price of a hotel.

Buy travel passes in advance. Buy rail, bus, and metro tickets in advance online.

Party like a local. Join any local festivities, as most will feature traditional food, drink, music and dancing.

PLAN YOUR TIME

Hassle Factor	Medium. There are some nonstop to Lisbon from some U.S. airports (New York, Miami), but more often you will have to connect elsewhere in Europe.
3 days	Explore the history and charm of Lisbon and its surrounding areas like Sintra.
1 week	Explore Lisbon, and then catch the high-speed Alfa-Pendular and spend a night either in the Algarve or in Porto.
2 weeks	After exploring the capital, head south to the Algarve, making sure you stop at a vineyard in the Alentejo. From the Algarve catch a cheap domestic flight all the way north to Porto and spend another few days there before returning to Lisbon.

WHEN TO GO

High Season: June through September is the busiest, hottest, and most expensive time to visit Portugal. While the north of the country remains cooler and quieter, Lisbon and the Algarve can be sweltering. Most Lisbon locals head south for the summer holidays.

Low Season: Winter in Portugal is growing in popularity due to the agreeable temperatures year-round and lower hotel prices. Off-season activities are still varied and plentiful, and while the beach may be off the menu, pleasant strolls and cozy evenings are definitely on it.

Value Season: Spring and autumn are both stunning seasons in which to visit Portugal. In April and October you may be lucky enough to enjoy a bracing dip in the pool or sea. Almond and orange blossoms perfume the air, key regions are quieter, and room prices have not yet peaked.

BIG EVENTS

February: Carnival fever sweeps the country in February, with one of the biggest parades in Torres Vedras. ⊕ www.carnavaldetorres.com

April: Lisbon hosts the Portugal Open tennis tournament at the end of April. ⊕ www.portugalopen.pt

June: Porto explodes on June 23 (St. John the Baptist's Day). ⊕ www.portoturismo.pt

November: Festivities throughout the country celebrate São Martinho (St. Martin), with the focus on chestnuts and wine.

READ THIS

■ *The Food of Portugal,* Jean Anderson. All about Portuguese cuisine.

■ *Journey to Portugal: A Pursuit of Portugal's History and Culture,* José Saramago. The Nobel Prize–winner recalls a trip in 1979.

■ P*ortugal and the Algarve: Now and Then,* Jenny Grainer. Memoirs of a long-time ex-pat.

WATCH THIS

■ *Lisbon Story.* The fictional story of the capital city.

■ *Fados.* Explores the melancholic Portuguese music.

■ *Night Train to Lisbon.* Acclaimed intellectual thriller that explores Portugal's era of dictatorship.

EAT THIS

■ **Bacalhau á Brás:** shredded codf with egg and onion

■ **Paté de Sardinha:** sardine pâté to spread on bread as a starter

■ **Pastel de Nata:** a delicious custard tart

■ **Ensopado de Borrego:** slow-roasted-lamb stew with bread

■ **Peixe Grelhado:** grilled fish, found in abundance in restaurants along the coast

■ **Arroz de Pato:** oven-baked, shredded duck with rice and *chouriça* on top

Portugal's landscape unfolds in astonishing variety from a mountainous, green interior to a sweeping coastline. Celtic, Roman, and Islamic influences are evident in the land, its people, and their tongue. The long Atlantic coastline means that most of Portugal's tumultuous history has centered on the sea. From the charting of the Azores archipelago in 1427 to their arrival in Japan in 1540, Portuguese explorers unlocked sea routes to southern Africa, India, eastern Asia, and the Americas. The great era of exploration, known as the *Descobrimentos,* reached its height during the 15th century under the influence of Prince Henry the Navigator. But the next several centuries saw dynastic instability, extravagant spending by monarchs, natural disasters, and foreign invasion. Order came in the 20th century in the form of a right-wing dictatorship that lasted more than 40 years, until a near-bloodless coup established democracy in 1974.

Today Portugal is politically stable, its people enjoying the prosperity brought by integration into the European Union (EU). The highway system, in particular, has been overhauled with the help of EU money.

PLANNING

WHEN TO GO

If you're planning to visit in summer, particularly July and August, you *must* reserve a hotel room in advance. The best time to experience Lisbon and the south is spring or early fall: the crowds are much thinner than in summer, and if you want to spend time on a beach, it could be warm enough for a brisk swim in April and October. As for Porto and the north, it's best to visit in summer, when the region is comfortably warm, but be prepared for drizzling rain at any time. Coastal temperatures are a few degrees cooler than in the south, but still mild in comparison to the rest of Europe.

Most festivals in Portugal are held in summer. The season starts in June, with the Festa de Santo António (Saint Anthony's Day), celebrated above all in Lisbon. Porto's big day is that of São João, its patron, on June 24. São Pedro de Sintra is a good place to mark the Festa de São Pedro (St. Peter's Day) on June 29.

TOP REASONS TO GO

World Treasures. Located a stone's throw from each other, Lisbon's Mosteiro dos Jerónimos and Torre de Belém, both UNESCO World Heritage sites, are monuments reflecting Portugal's proud seafaring past.

City Sophistication. Lisbon's Museu Colecção Berardo and Porto's Casa da Musica are just two of the ultra-modern institutions that make both cities major cultural centers.

Victorian Style. Explore Lisbon on ancient street trams that wind around narrow cobbled streets where washing hangs from the windows of pastel-colored houses and sardines sizzle on barbecue grills. Trams of a similar vintage ply routes in both Sintra and Porto, too.

Old-Fashioned Hospitality. Even in a modern city such as Lisbon, or the bustling northern business capital of Porto, shopkeepers and café owners tend to move at a slower pace than their counterparts elsewhere in Europe. But even when there's a language barrier, old-fashioned courteousness also tends to prevail.

Buzzing Nightlife. Lisbon and Porto have earned reputations in recent years as great places to hit the town, with bars and dance clubs often located in stunning riverside settings such as adapted former warehouses.

14

GETTING HERE AND AROUND

AIR TRAVEL

The flying time to Lisbon is 6½ hours from New York, 9 hours from Chicago, and 15 hours from Los Angeles. The flight from London to Lisbon (LIS) is about 2½ hours. Both United and TAP Portugal offer nonstop flights from New York–Newark (EWR) to Lisbon, from where you can connect to Porto's Aeroporto Francisco Sá Carneiro (OPO). However, it is sometimes cheaper to fly into London and take an onward budget airline or charter flight. Domestic flights in Portugal are expensive, but there is a daily low-cost domestic flight on Ryanair between Porto and the Algarve that is worth considering. From Lisbon, TAP Portugal also serves Faro.

Contacts Aeroporto de Faro ⊠ *Faro* ☎ *289/800800 for flight information.* **Aeroporto Francisco Sá Carneiro** ⊠ *Oporto* ☎ *229/432400.* **Aeroporto Portela** ⊠ *Lisbon* ☎ *21/841–3500, 21/841–3700.* **ANA** ⊕ *www.ana.pt.*

BUS TRAVEL

Within Portugal, *expressos* are the best cheap long-distance option—they're comfortable direct buses, some with video and food service. Two of the largest bus companies are Rede Expressos, which serves much of the country, and Rodo Norte, which serves the north. Eva Transportes covers the Algarve and also has service to and from major cities, like Évora. Book ahead. Tourism offices can help with schedules, and most travel agents sell tickets.

Contacts Eva Transportes ⊠ *Praça Marechal Humberto Delgado, Estrada das Laranjeiras, Av. República 5, Faro* ☎ *289/899700, 707/223344* ⊕ *www.eva-bus. com.* **Rede Expressos** ⊕ *www.rede-expressos.pt.* **Rodo Norte** ⊕ *www.rodonorte.pt.*

CAR TRAVEL

Your home-country license is valid in Portugal. Roads are mostly good, but drivers alarmingly cavalier. Wear a seatbelt, and note that one glass of wine can put you over the limit. Four-lane *autoestradas* (labeled "A" plus a number) save a lot of time—except late on Sunday when weekenders flock home—but have hefty tolls (almost €20 between Lisbon and Porto). Lanes marked "Via Verde" are for those with a special payment device.

In December 2011 tolls were introduced on the Algarve's only motorway, the Via do Infante/A22, and it costs around €10 to travel the length of the stretch, which runs parallel to the coast covering the entire width of the region.

At intersections, traffic from the right has the right of way; at traffic circles you must yield to vehicles already in the circle. Speed limits are 120 kph (74 mph) on autoestradas, 90 kph (56 mph) on other highways, and 50 kph (30 mph) in urban areas.

Theft is common with rental cars. Contact the agency and police if yours is stolen. Never leave luggage or anything else of value visible in an unattended vehicle.

TRAIN TRAVEL

Portugal's train network, Comboios de Portugal (CP), covers most of the country, though it's thin in the Alentejo region. The cities of Lisbon, Coimbra, Aveiro, Porto, Braga, and Faro are linked by the fast, extremely comfortable Alfa Pendular services.

There are three main classes of long-distance train travel: *regional* trains, which stop at every town and village; reasonably fast *interregional* trains; and express trains appropriately known as *rápido*. The *alfa pendular* is a deluxe, marginally faster train that runs between Lisbon and Porto as well as other major cities. There's also a network of suburban *(suburbano)* train lines.

A direct, nightly train connects Spain and Portugal. The train departs from Madrid's Chamartin station at 9:50 pm and arrives at Lisbon's Santa Apolónia station at 7:30 the following morning; for the reverse trip, the train leaves Lisbon at 9:18 pm, arriving in Madrid at 8:10 am the next day. Passengers can also connect to the train to and from Porto by switching at the Coimbra station; trains depart Porto at 10 pm daily on their way to Madrid, while trains from Madrid arrive in Porto at 6:35 am each day.

A first-class ticket will cost you 40% more than a second-class one and will buy you extra leg- and elbow room but not a great deal more on the Alfa and Intercidade trains. The extra cost is definitely worth it on most regional services, however. Advance booking is mandatory on long-distance trains and is recommended in the case of popular services such as the Alfa trains. Reservations are also advisable for other trains if you want to avoid long lines in front of the ticket window on the day the train leaves. You can avoid a trip to the station to make the reservation by asking a travel agent to take care of it for you.

Contacts CP ☎ *707/201280 from outside Portugal, 808/208208* ⊕ *www.cp.pt.*

HOTELS

Though international chains are present in Portugal, *residenciais* and *pensões* (simple accommodations that serve only breakfast) in former private homes are usually comfortable and affordable. *Pousadas* (inns), many housed in renovated castles or convents, are more atmospheric.

HOTELS

Hotels are graded with one to five stars or with a category rating, based on the amenities offered; a faded establishment with cable television might be rated higher than a new one without. Most rooms have private bathrooms. You generally have a choice of twin beds or a double (never king size). High season means the summer months, Easter week, and during local festivals. In the off-season (generally November through March), rates may tumble by 20%.

14

COUNTRY HOUSES

Throughout the country, *solares* (manors) and *casas de campo* (country houses) have been remodeled to receive guests in a venture called Turismo de Habitação or Turismo Rural. Breakfast is included.

Contacts Central Nacional de Turismo no Espaço Rural ☎ *258/931750* ⊕ *www.center.pt.* **TURIHAB** ☎ *258/741672* ⊕ *www.turihab.pt.*

POUSADAS

Portugal has a network of about 35 of these state-run hotels, which are in restored castles, palaces, monasteries, convents, and other charming buildings. Each pousada is in a particularly scenic and tranquil part of the country and is tastefully furnished with regional crafts, antiques, and artwork. All have restaurants that serve local specialties; you can stop for a meal or a drink without spending the night. Rates are reasonable, considering that most pousadas are four- or five-star hotels, and a stay in one can be the highlight of a visit. Some have only a handful of rooms, so reserve well in advance.

Contacts Pousadas de Portugal ☎ *218/442000 for head office, 218/442001 for central reservations* ⊕ *www.pousadas.pt.*

RESTAURANTS

The best dining in Portugal often is in moderately priced spots, including *churrasqueiras,* serving charcoal-grilled meats and fish. *Marisqueiras* serving fresh fish and shellfish are pricier.

Restaurant menus invariably include a *prato do dia* (dish of the day). An *ementa turística* (tourist menu) can be 80% of the cost of three courses ordered separately, but limits choice. Main dishes are large, and at lunchtime you can request a *meia dose* (half portion). Upmarket restaurants and those in tourist areas will have menus in English.

MEALS AND MEAL TIMES

Breakfast (*pequeno almoço*) is often just a pastry washed down with coffee, either a dark *bica* or a milky *meia de leite.* Lunch (*almoço*) is served between noon and 2:30, dinner from 7 to 10. Unless otherwise noted, restaurants listed are open daily for both.

SPECIALTIES

Thanks to the sea's proximity, *caldeirada* (seafood stew) and *sardinhas grelhadas* (grilled sardines) are usually good choices. Tasty fresh fish includes *salmão grelhado* (grilled salmon), *dourada* (sea bream) and *peixe espada* (scabbard fish). *Bacalhau* (salt cod) served in a reputed 365 different ways, may come *à brás* (with eggs, onions, and potatoes), *com natas* (finely flaked, with cream), and *assado com batatas à murro* (baked with small potatoes, garlic, and olive oil). *Açorda com gambas* is a bread stew with prawns, garlic, and cilantro.

Porco à alentejana mixes marinated pork and clams. You can go whole hog with *leitão da bairrada* (roast suckling pig) or *plumas do porco preto*, from black pigs fed on acorns. Sautéed or grilled *bife à portuguesa* (steak) comes in a port-wine sauce. Steak usually comes rare—*mal passado*; to avoid this, say *"bem passado."*

Cafés serve *tosta mista* (toasted cheese and ham sandwich) and usually also *bifana* (braised pork sandwich) or *prego* (steak sandwich).

Desserts include *baba de camelo* (literally "camel's spit," condensed milk and egg), *molotov* (baked egg whites with caramel), *maçã assada* (baked apple), *arroz doce* (rice pudding), *mousse de chocolate*, and fruit.

WINES, BEER, AND SPIRITS

Red wine accompanies most meals, with the *vinho da casa* (house wine) invariably drinkable. Periquita from the Setúbal region is a bargain. Bairrada, Dão, and sparkling *vinhos verdes* (green wines, so named for their youth) are popular. Portuguese beers such as Super Bock and Sagres are on tap and bottled. They have a good, clean flavor. Local brandies (Macieira, Constantino) are cheap. You must be over 16 to buy alcohol.

HOTEL AND RESTAURANT PRICES

Prices in the restaurant reviews are the average cost of a main course at dinner or, if dinner is not served, at lunch; taxes and service charges are generally included. Prices in the hotel reviews are the lowest cost of a standard double room in high season, excluding taxes, service charges, and meal plans. Prices for rentals are the lowest per-night cost for a one-bedroom unit in high season.

PLANNING YOUR TIME

Portugal is one of Europe's smaller countries—you could drive from one end to the other in seven hours. However, it's also one of one of Europe's more diverse, and to appreciate land and people you will need to take things slowly.

The main population centers cluster along the coast, above all Lisbon and Porto. Though Porto was never the national capital, it has sought to rival Lisbon for centuries. The centralizing tendencies of the modern era have sapped the northern city's influence, but it remains a vibrant cultural center; from Porto you can also take scenic boat or rail trips up the Douro.

Each city has a different feel. If you can, you should overnight in both (they're only some three hours apart by car or train). But if you're in Portugal for less than a week, it may be best to focus on one and, if you have time, explore the surrounding region from there.

Near Lisbon, Sintra is the only must-see. Indeed, many visitors find it so delightful—and restful—that they make it their regional base. But a worthwhile stop on the rail line or highway from Lisbon is Queluz, with its baroque palace set in charming formal gardens. Beyond Sintra are aristocratic follies and pretty villages, spectacular beaches, and a looming cape that is Europe's westernmost point.

LISBON
14

Lisbon bears the mark of an incredible heritage with laid-back pride. Spread over seven hills north of the Rio Tejo (Tagus River) estuary, the city also presents a variety of faces to those who negotiate its switchback streets. In the oldest *bairros* (neighborhoods), stepped alleys are lined with pastel-color houses decked with laundry; here and there *miradouros* (vantage points) afford spectacular views. *Eléctricos* (trams) clank through the streets, and blue-and-white *azulejos* (glazed ceramic tiles) adorn churches and fountains.

Of course, parts of Lisbon lack charm. Even some downtown areas have lost their classic Portuguese appearance as the city has become more cosmopolitan: shiny office blocks have replaced some 19th- and 20th-century art-nouveau buildings. And centenarian trams share the streets with "fast trams" and smoke-belching automobiles.

Some modernization has improved matters, though. In preparing to host the 1998 World Exposition, Lisbon spruced up public buildings, overhauled its subway system, and completed an impressive second bridge across the river. Today the Expo site is an expansive riverfront development known as Parque das Nações, and the city is a popular port of call for cruises, whose passengers disembark onto a revitalized waterfront.

PLANNING YOUR TIME

It's best not to visit at the height of summer, when the city is hot and steamy and lodgings are expensive and crowded. Winters are generally mild and usually accompanied by bright blue skies, and there are plenty of bargains to be had at hotels. For optimum Lisbon weather, visit on either side of summer, in May or late September through October. The city's major festivals are in June; the so-called *santos populares* (popular saints) see days of riotous celebration dedicated to saints Anthony, John, and Peter.

You'll want to give yourself a day at least exploring the *bairro* of Alfama, climbing up to the Castelo de São Jorge (Saint's George's castle) for an overview of the city; another in the monumental downtown area, the Baixa, and in the neighboring fancy shopping district of Chiado, and perhaps also in the funkier shops of the Bairro Alto. Another again could be spent in historic Belém, with its many museums and monuments. Note that many are closed Monday, and that churches often close for a couple of hours at lunchtime.

There are other attractions dotted around the modern city, and families will appreciate the child-friendly attractions of the Parque das Nações, the former Expo site. All in all, there's enough to do and see to fill a week—though if you're staying that long you should think about visiting Sintra or other sights in the hinterland.

GETTING HERE AND AROUND

AIR TRAVEL

Lisbon's small, modern airport, sometimes known as Aeroporto de Portela, is 7 km (4½ miles) north of the center, and getting downtown is simple and inexpensive thanks to a new metro extension that goes via the Gare de Oriente rail station and to the special Aerobus shuttles. Aerobus tickets purchased from the driver cost €3.50, or you can buy them online for €3.15; these are then valid for all local buses for the next 24 hours. Cheaper (€1.80) is Bus No. 744 bound for Praça Marquês de Pombal, which departs every 15 to 30 minutes between 5 am and 12:30 am from the main road in front of airport arrivals. At night (0:30 am to 5:35 am), Bus No. 208 plies a route between Oriente station and Cais do Sodré that takes in the airport. For a taxi, you'll pay €10 to €15 to get downtown, plus a €1.60 surcharge per item of luggage in the trunk. To avoid hassle, a prepaid taxi voucher (from €16 for downtown in daytime) may be bought at the tourist desk in the airport: you'll pay a little more but are sure not to be taken for an extra-long ride.

BUS TRAVEL

Lisbon's main bus terminal is the Gare do Oriente, adjacent to Parque das Nações, also served by rail and metro. Most international and domestic express buses operate from the Sete Rios terminal, beside the metro and suburban train stations of the same name.

CAR TRAVEL

Heading in or out by car, there's rapid access to and from points south and east via the Ponte 25 de Abril bridge across the Rio Tejo (Tagus River), although in rush hour the 17-km-long (11-mile-long) Ponte Vasco da Gama is a better option. To and from Porto, the A1 is the fastest route. The capital's drivers are notorious and parking is difficult, so your rental car is best left in a lot while in town.

FERRY TRAVEL

Ferries across the Rio Tejo are run by Transtejo, from terminals at Belém, Cais do Sodre, and Terreiro do Paço. They offer unique views of Lisbon, and their top decks are a nice way to catch the sun. The €1.5 (loaded onto a 50-cent electronic card) passenger ticket on the car ferry between Belém and Cacilhas contrasts favorably with the €15–€20 price of the Transtejo cruises that depart daily between April and October, one at 3 pm from Terreiro do Paço and the other at 11:15 from Terreiro do Paço and at 11:30 and 4:30 from Cais do Sodré.

Ferry Contact Transtejo ☎ *808/882–4674, 21/0422417 for cruises* ⊕ *www. transtejo.pt.*

PUBLIC TRANSPORTATION TRAVEL

While the best way to see central Lisbon is still on foot since most points of interest are within the well-defined older quarters, at some point you'll want to use the public-transportation system, if only to experience the old trams and *elevadores*: funicular railways and elevators linking high and low parts of the city. Like the buses, they are operated by the public transportation company, Carris.

For all these forms of transport, paying as you board means paying twice to three times as much (€1.80 a ride for the bus, €2.85 the tram, €3.60 for the funicular, and €5 for the elevator), in cash. It's better to buy a €0.50 7 Colinas or Viva Viagem debit card, both of which can also be used on the metro and ferries. Buy them at ticket offices, at Carris kiosks (there's one in Praça de Figueira), and at the foot of the Elevador de Santa Justa.

Lisbon's modern metro system (station entrances are marked with a red "M") is cheap and speedy, though it misses many sights and gets crowded during rush hour and for big soccer matches. You can charge up card with cash or journeys, which are then valid for an hour on metro, buses and trams.

The Lisboa Card, a special pass that allows unlimited travel on all public transportation and entry into 27 museums, monuments, and galleries, is valid for 24 hours (€18.50), 48 hours (€31.50), or 72 hours (€39). It's sold all over the city.

In July 2012 a brand new metro station was inaugurated at the airport, right next to the departures terminal. It now connects the airport to the rest of the city on the Red Line.

Contacts Carris ☎ *21/361–3054* ⊕ *www.carris.pt.* **Metropolitano de Lisboa** ☎ *21/361–3054* ⊕ *www.metrolisboa.pt.*

TRAIN TRAVEL

International and long-distance trains arrive at Santa Apolónia station, to the east of Lisbon's center, after passing through Gare do Oriente, where fast trains from the Algarve also stop. Services to Sintra use Rossio station, a neo-Manueline building just off Rossio square itself. Trains along the Estoril coast terminate at the waterfront Cais do Sodré station.

TOURS

Many companies organize half-day group tours of Lisbon and its environs and full-day trips to more distant places of interest. Reservations can be made through any travel agency or hotel; some tours will pick you up at your door. Half-day tours of Lisbon begin at around €35. As well as its city tram and hop-on, hop-off bus tours, public transport company Carris also does a half-day tour of Sintra, Cascais, and the stunning coast between them. An English-speaking private guide for half day will cost from €55, a full day from €95. The four guides at Lisbon Tour Guides speak English, French, Spanish, and Italian. Lisbon Walker does tailor-made walks and also has the widest range of regular theme tours.

Contacts Lisbon Tour Guides ⊕ *www.lisbontourguides.pt.* **Lisbon Walker** ☎ *21/886–1840, 96/357–5635* ⊕ *www.lisbonwalker.com.*

VISITOR INFORMATION

The Lisbon branch of Portugal's tourist office—National Tourism Office (Turismo de Portugal)—is open daily 9–8. It's in the Palácio Foz, at the Baixa end of Avenida da Liberdade. A much more rewarding place to get information is the Lisbon Welcome Center, though you may have to wait patiently in a long line.

Contacts **Lisbon Welcome Center** ✉ *Praça do Comércio, Baixa* ☎ *21/031–2810, 21/845–0660 for airport branch* ⊕ *www.askmelisboa.com.* **Turismo de Portugal (National Tourism Office)** ✉ *Palácio Foz, Praça dos Restauradores* ☎ *21/346–3314* ⊕ *www.visitportugal.com.*

EXPLORING

THE ALFAMA

The Alfama's timeless alleys and squares have a notoriously confusing layout, but the Alfama is relatively compact, and you'll keep circling back to the same buildings and streets. In the Moorish period this area thrived, and in the 15th century—as evidenced by the ancient synagogue on Beco das Barrelas—it was an important Jewish quarter.

The Alfama's streets and alleys are very steep, and its levels are connected by flights of stone steps, which means it's easier to tour the area from the top down (give yourself two hours, or three if you plan to visit the Museu-Escola de Artes Decorativas). Take a taxi up to the castle or approach it by Tram No. 28 from Rua Conceição in the Baixa or Bus No. 37 from Praça da Figueira. The large terrace next to the church of Santa Luzia, just below the castle, gives a fine overview of the Alfama and the river.

Fodor'sChoice **Castelo de São Jorge.** Although St. George's Castle was constructed by the
★ Moors, the site had previously been fortified by Romans and Visigoths. To your left as you pass through the main entrance is a statue of Dom Afonso Henriques, whose forces in 1147 besieged the castle and drove the Moors from Lisbon. The ramparts offer panoramic views of the city's layout as far as the towering Ponte 25 de Abril suspension bridge; be careful of the uneven footing. Remnants of a palace that was a residence of the kings of Portugal until the 16th century house a snack bar, a small museum showcasing archeological finds, and beyond them a cozy, stately restaurant, the Casa do Leão (☎ *21/888–0154*). From the *periscópio* (periscope) in the Torre de Ulísses, in the castle's keep, you can spy on visitors going about their business below. Beyond the keep, traces of pre-Roman and Moorish houses are visible thanks to recent archeological digs, as well as the remains of a palace founded in the 15th-century. The castle's outer walls encompass a small neighborhood, Castelo, the medieval church of Santa Cruz, restaurants, and souvenir shops. ✉ *Entrance at Largo do Chão da Feira, Alfama* ☎ *21/880–0620* ⊕ *www.castelodesaojorge.pt* 🎟 *Castle €7.50* ⊙ *Mar.–Oct., daily 9–9; Nov.–Feb., daily 9–6.*

Sé. Lisbon's austere Romanesque cathedral, Sé (which stands for *Sedes Episcopalis*), was founded in 1150 to commemorate the defeat of the Moors three years earlier; to rub salt in the wound, the conquerors

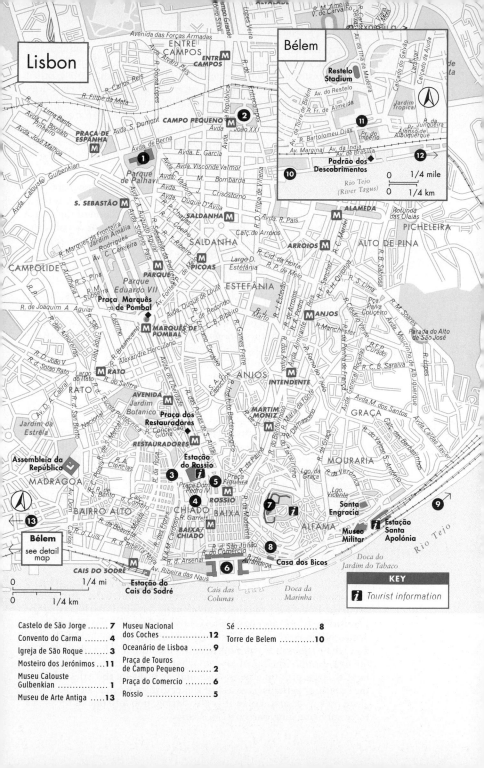

Lisbon

Bélem

Restelo
Stadium

Padrão dos
Descobrimentos

Rio Tejo
(River Tagus)

0   1/4 mile

0   1/4 km

Bélem
see detail
map

0   1/4 mi

0   1/4 km

Avenida das Forças Armadas
ENTRE
CAMPOS
ENTRE
CAMPOS

CAMPO PEQUENO

PRAÇA DE
ESPAÑA

Parque
de Palhavã

S. SEBASTIÃO

SALDANHA

PICOAS

SALDANHA

ARROIOS

ALTO DE PINA

PICHELEIRA

ALAMEDA

Rotunda
das Olaias

CAMPOLIDE

PARQUE

Parque
Eduardo VII

Praça Marquês
de Pombal

ESTEFÂNIA

MARQUÊS DE
POMBAL

RATO

RATO

ANJOS

ANJOS

INTENDENTE

MANJOS

GRAÇA

AVENIDA

Jardim
Botânico

Praça dos
Restauradores

MARTIM
MONIZ

MOURARIA

Jardim da
Estrela

RESTAURADORES

Estação
do Rossio

Praça
Figueira

Santa
Engracia

Assembleia da
República

MADRAGOA

BAIRRO ALTO

Praça Dom
Pedro IV

ROSSIO

CHIADO

BAIXA

ALFAMA

Museu
Militar

Estação
Santa
Apolónia

BAIXA/
CHIADO

CAIS DO SODRÉ

Estação do
Cais do Sodré

Casa dos Bicos

Cais das
Colunas

Doca da
Marinha

Doca do
Jardim do Tabaco

Rio Tejo

KEY

Tourist information

built the sanctuary on the spot where Moorish Lisbon's main mosque once stood. Note the fine rose window, and be sure to visit the 13th-century cloister and the treasure-filled sacristy, which, among other things, contains the relics of the martyr St. Vincent. According to legend, the relics were carried from the Algarve to Lisbon in a ship piloted by ravens; the saint became Lisbon's official patron. ✉ *Largo da Sé, Alfama* ☎ *21/8876628* ⌨ *Cathedral free, cloister and sacristy €2.50* ⊙ *Cathedral daily 9–6:30; cloister Mon.– Sat. 9–6:30, Sun. 9–11 and 2–6:30; sacristy weekdays 10–1 and 2–5, Sat. 10–5* Ⓜ *Terreiro do Paço.*

THE BAIXA

The earthquake of 1755, the massive tidal wave, and subsequent fires killed thousands of people and reduced 18th-century Lisbon to rubble. But within a decade frantic rebuilding under the direction of the king's minister, the Marquês de Pombal, had given the Baixa, or downtown, a neoclassical look. Today full of shops, restaurants, and other commercial enterprises, it stretches from the riverfront Praça do Comércio to the square known as the Rossio. Pombal intended the various streets to house workshops for certain trades and crafts, something that's still reflected in street names such as Rua dos Sapateiros (Cobblers' Street) and Rua da Prata (Silversmiths' Street). Near the neoclassical arch at the bottom of Rua Augusta you'll find street vendors selling jewelry. Northeast of Rossio, the Rua das Portas de Santo Antão has seafood restaurants and two surviving *ginginha* bars—cubbyholes where local characters throw down shots of cherry brandy.

Praça do Comércio. Known also as the Terreiro do Paço, after the royal palace (the Paço) that once stood here, the Praça do Comércio is lined with 18th-century buildings. Down by the river, steps—once used by occupants of the royal barges that docked here—lead up from the water. On the north side, the Arco Triunfal (Triumphal Arch) was the last structure to be completed, in 1873. The equestrian statue in the center is of Dom José I, king at the time of the earthquake and subsequent rebuilding. In 1908, amid unrest that led to the declaration of a republic, King Carlos and his eldest son, Luís Filipe, were assassinated as they rode through the square in a carriage. On Sunday morning a market of old coins and banknotes takes place in the arcades.

Rossio. Lisbon's main square since before the Middle Ages is popularly known as the Rossio, although its official name is Praça Dom Pedro IV (whom the central statue commemorates). Even though it's jammed with traffic, it is a grand space, with ornate French fountains. Public *autos-da-fé* of heretics (a Catholic Mass, prayer, a public procession of those found guilty, a reading of their sentences, and, most often, burning at the stake) were once carried out here; the site of the Palace of the Inquisition, which oversaw these, is now occupied by the 19th-century Teatro Nacional (National Theater). On nearby Largo de São Domingos, where thousands were burned, is a memorial to Jewish victims of the Inquisition. You'll probably do what the locals do when they come here, though: pick up a newspaper and sit at one of the cafés that line the square, or perhaps have a shoe shiner give your boots a polish—just agree on a price first. Later, if you're daring, pop into one of the area's three surviving ginginha bars. Ⓜ *Rossio.*

CHIADO AND BAIRRO ALTO

West of the Baixa is the fashionable shopping district of Chiado. A decade after the calamitous 1988 fire destroyed much of the area, an ambitious rebuilding program restored some fin de siècle facades. And a chic retail complex on the site of the old Armazéns do Chiado— once Lisbon's largest department store—has given the district a modern focus. The most famous of these is Café a Brasileira on Largo do Chiado; with a bronze statue of onetime customer, poet Fernando Pessoa, seated on the esplanade.

Uphill, the Bairro Alto dates back to the 17th century, but most of its buildings are from the 18th and 19th: an appealing mixture of old grocery stores, art galleries, and town houses with wrought-iron balconies. In the daytime, children scuffle amid drying laundry, and old men clog the doorways of bars; at night the area's restaurants, discos, and fado clubs come to life. The neighborhood has always been seen as rather rough-and-ready, and there are alleys where it would be unwise to venture after dark, but on the whole it's safe to walk around this remarkably compact but fascinating area.

Convento do Carmo. The Carmelite Convent—once Lisbon's largest—was all but ruined by the 1755 earthquake. Its sacristy houses the **Museu Arqueológico do Carmo** (Archaeological Museum), a small collection of ceramic tiles, medieval tombs, ancient coins, and other city finds. The tree-shaded square outside—accessible via a walkway from the top of the Elevador da Santa Justa—is a great place to dawdle over a coffee. ⊠ *Largo do Carmo, Chiado* ☎ *21/347–8629* ⊕ *www. museuarqueologicodocarmo.pt* 🎫 *€3.50* ☉ *June–Sept., Mon.–Sat. 10–7; Oct.–May, Mon.–Sat. 10–6* Ⓜ *Baixa-Chiado or Rossio (then Elevador de Santa Justa).*

Igreja de São Roque. Filippo Terzi, the architect who designed São Vicente on the outskirts of the Alfama, also designed this Renaissance church, at the Jesuits' behest. It was completed in 1574. Several side chapels contain statuary and art dating from the early 17th century. The last one on the left is the extraordinary 18th-century Capela de São João Baptista (Chapel of St. John the Baptist): built in Rome, decorated with mosaics that resemble oil paintings, the chapel was taken apart, shipped to Lisbon, and reassembled here in 1747. Adjoining the church, the **Museu de Arte Sacra** (Museum of Sacred Art) displays an engaging collection of rich clerical vestments and liturgical objects. ⊠ *Largo Trindade Coelho, Bairro Alto* ☎ *21/323–5381* 🎫 *Church free, museum €1.50 (free Sun.)* ☉ *Church weekdays 8:30–5, weekends 9:30–5; museum Tues.–Sun. 10–5* Ⓜ *Baixa-Chiado.*

THE MODERN CITY

The 10 parallel rows of trees along the Avenida da Liberdade, which was laid out in 1879, make Lisbon's downtown axis a pleasant place to linger, despite the traffic. Beyond it is the city's central park, Parque Eduardo VII, and then modern Lisbon, stretching into residential suburbs with the occasional attraction. It could take three hours to do justice to the Gulbenkian alone—especially if you have lunch there; add another for walking; and perhaps a fifth for shopping and a coffee.

Fodor's Choice
★ **Museu Calouste Gulbenkian.** On its own lush grounds, the museum of the celebrated Calouste Gulbenkian Foundation, a cultural trust, houses treasures collected by Armenian oil magnate Calouste Gulbenkian. The collection is split in two: one part is devoted to Egyptian, Greek, Roman, Islamic, and Asian art, and the other to European acquisitions. Both holdings are small, but the quality of the pieces is magnificent, and you should aim to spend at least two hours here. English-language notes are available throughout. Varied and interesting temporary exhibitions are also often staged in the Foundation's main building. ⊠ *Avenida de Berna 45, Praça de Espanha* ☎ *21/7823000* ⊕ *www.museu.gulbenkian. pt* ☑ *€4, temporary exhibitions €4–€5, combined ticket museum with Modern Art Center €5, combined ticket for all €7; free Sun.* ☉ *Tues.– Sun. 10–5:45* Ⓜ *São Sebastião or Praça de Espanha.*

Centro de Arte Moderna. In the gardens behind the Fundação Calouste Gulbenkian, sculptures hide in every recess. You may want to spend a little time here before following signs to the Centro de Arte Moderna (Modern Art Center)—the Gulbenkian Foundation's 20th-century art collection, which has at its disposal the finest collection of contemporary and modern Portuguese art, as well as many British works from the same period. There are varied and interesting temporary exhibitions as well as changing displays from this permanent collection. ⊠ *Rua Dr. Nicolau de Bettencourt* ☎ *21/7823474/83* ⊕ *www.cam.gulbenkian.pt* Ⓜ *São Sebastião.*

FAMILY
Fodor's Choice
★ **Oceanário de Lisboa.** Europe's largest indoor aquarium wows children and adults alike with a vast salt-water tank featuring an array of fish, including several types of shark. Along the way you pass through habitats representing the North Atlantic, Pacific, and Indian oceans, where puffins and penguins dive into the water, sea otters roll and play, and tropical birds flit past you. You then descend to the bottom of the tank to watch rays float past gracefully and schools of silvery fish darting this way and that. To avoid the crowds, come during the week or early in the day. The Oceanarium also hosts a range of activities outside normal opening hours, such as Saturday morning concerts for under-3s against the lively backdrop of the central tank. ⊠ *Esplanada D. Carlos I (Doca dos Olivais), Parque das Nações* ☎ *21/891–7002, 21/8917006* ⊕ *www. oceanario.pt* ☑ *€16* ☉ *Apr.–Oct., daily 10–8; Nov.–Mar., daily 10–7; last entry 1 hr before closing* Ⓜ *Oriente.*

Praça de Touros de Campo Pequeno. Built in 1892, Lisbon's circular, red-brick, Moorish-style bullring is an eye-opening site. Encompassing esplanades and an underground mall, the ring holds about 9,000 people who crowd in to watch Portuguese-style bullfights (in which the bull is never killed in the ring), held every Thursday at 10 pm from Easter through September. The arena is also used as a venue for concerts and other events. Tickets for all are sold from a booth in the new shopping mall under the building, which is open daily 10 am–11 pm. (On show nights only, the little ticket windows on either side of the bullring's main gate are also open.) ⊠ *Av. da República* ☎ *21/782–0572 for tickets* ⊕ *www.campopequeno.com* ☑ *Bullfights from €15* Ⓜ *Campo Pequeno.*

BELÉM

Some of Lisbon's grandest monuments and museums are in the district of Belém (Portuguese for Bethlehem), at the city's western edge. It was from here that explorers set out during the period of the discoveries. The wealth brought back helped pay for many neighborhood structures, some of which are fine examples of the uniquely Portuguese late-Gothic architecture known as Manueline. Several buses come here from Lisbon's center, but the 30-minute ride on Tram No. 15 from the Baixa district's Praça do Comércio is scenic and passes other attractions in the Santos and Alcântara districts along the way. Note that most sights are closed Monday, while Sunday sees free or reduced admission to many.

Fodor's Choice **Mosteiro dos Jerónimos.** This UNESCO World Heritage Site is a supreme
★ example of the Manueline style of building (named after King Dom Manuel I), which represented a marked departure from earlier Gothic architecture. Much of it is characterized by elaborate sculptural details, often with a maritime motif. João de Castilho was responsible for the southern portal, which forms the main entrance to the church: the figure on the central pillar is Henry the Navigator. Inside, the spacious interior contrasts with the riot of decoration on the six nave columns and complex latticework ceiling. This is the resting place of both explorer Vasco de Gama and national poet Luís de Camões. Don't miss the Gothic- and Renaissance-style double cloister, also designed to stunning effect by Castilho. ⊠ *Praça do Império, Belém* ☎ *21/362–0034* ⊕ *www. mosteirojeronimos.pt* ⊠ *Church free, cloister €7 (free Sun. till 2), €10 combination ticket includes Torre de Belém, €13 includes Torre de Belém and Palacio de Ajuda* ⊙ *May–Sept., Tues.–Sun. 10–6:30; Oct.– Apr., Tues.–Sun. 10–5:30.*

14

NEEK A BREAK? **Antiga Confeitaria de Belém.** For a real taste of Lisbon, stop at the Antiga Confeitaria de Belém, a bakery shop–café that serves delicious, warm custard pastries sprinkled with cinnamon and powdered sugar. Such *pastéis de nata* are sold throughout Lisbon, but those made here to a secret recipe, since 1837, are reputed to be the best. ⊠ *Rua de Belém 84–92, Belém* ☎ *21/3637423* ⊕ *www.pasteisdebelem.pt.*

Museu de Arte Antiga. On the route from the center of Lisbon to Belém is the Ancient Art Museum, the only institution in the city to approach the status of the Gulbenkian. Housed in a 17th-century palace once owned by the Counts of Alvor and vastly enlarged in 1940 when it took over the Convent of St. Albert, the museum has a beautifully displayed collection of Portuguese art—mainly from the 15th through 19th century The religious works of the Flemish-influenced Portuguese school stand out, especially Nuno Gonçalves' masterpiece, the *St. Vincent Panels.* The museum also boasts early Flemish works that influenced the Portuguese, and other European artists are well represented, such as Hieronymous Bosch, Hans Holbein, Brueghel the Younger, and Diego Velázquez.

Tram No. 15 from Praça do Comércio drops you at the foot of a steep flight of steps below the museum. Otherwise, Buse Nos. 27 and 49 from Praça Marquês de Pombal run straight to Rua das Janelas Verdes, via Rossio; coming from Belém, you can pick them up across from the

Jerónimos monastery. ✉ *Rua das Janelas Verdes, Lapa* ☎ *21/396–2825, 21/396–4151* 🌐 *www.mnarteantiga-ipmuseus.pt* 🎫 *€3* 🕒 *Tues. 2–6, Wed.–Sun. 10–1 and 2–6.*

Museu Nacional dos Coches. In a former royal riding school with a gorgeous painted ceiling, the National Coach Museum has a dazzling collection of gloriously gilded horse-drawn carriages. The oldest on display was made for Philip II of Spain in the late 1500s; the most stunning are three conveyances created in Rome for King John V in 1716. The museum, Portugal's most visited, is right next door to the official residence of the President of the Republic, whose **Museu da Presidência** tells the story of the presidency, profiles the officeholders, and displays gifts they have received on state visits. As of this writing, the Coach Museum was to move across the road into a purpose-built structure designed by Brazilian Pritzker Prize–winner Paulo Mendes da Rocha; visitors are to be able to watch restoration work being carried out on carriages. ✉ *Praça Afonso de Albuquerque, Belém* ☎ *21/361–0850* 🌐 *www.museudoscoches.pt* 🎫 *€5 (free Sun. till 2), €7.50 combined ticket with Ajuda Palace* 🕒 *Tues.–Sun. 10–6; last entry 5:30.*

Torre de Belém. The openwork balconies and domed turrets of the fanciful Belém Tower make it perhaps the country's purest Manueline structure. It was built between 1514 and 1520 on what was an island in the middle of the Rio Tejo, to defend the port entrance, and dedicated to St. Vincent, the patron saint of Lisbon. Today the chalk-white tower stands near the north bank—evidence of the river's changing course. Cross the wood gangway and walk inside, not so much to see the plain interior but rather to climb the steps for a bird's-eye view of river and city. ✉ *Avenida Brasília, Belém* ☎ *21/3620034* 🌐 *www.torrebelem.pt* 🎫 *€5 (free Sun. to 2), €10 combination ticket includes Mosteiro dos Jerónimos, €13 includes Mosteiro dos Jerónimos and Palacio de Ajuda* 🕒 *Oct.–Apr., Tues.–Sun. 10–5:30; May–Sept., Tues.–Sun. 10–6:30.*

WHERE TO EAT

ALFAMA

$$$ ECLECTIC 🍴 **Bica do Sapato.** A favorite among fashionable locals, this riverfront restaurant is known for its stylish interior and furnishings: Knoll, Eero Saarien, and Mies van der Rohe all feature. It serves modern Portuguese fare and nouvelle cuisine. The changing menu might include braised *cherne* (grouper) on spinach with cornmeal and clams seasoned with cilantro, or shoulder of lamb cooked at ultra-low temperatures and served with roast tomato, yam, and *cremoso de nabiças* (turnip tops with cream). There are always a couple vegetarian entrées, too. Desserts include eggy Portuguese classics but also *tarte de alfarroba* (carob tart) and homemade ice creams and sorbets. From September through June, they also do Sunday brunch (€25). Upstairs, a sushi bar offers a range of classic Japanese and fusion dishes (dinner only). [$] *Average main: €24* ✉ *Av. Infante D. Henrique, Armazém B, Cais da Pedra, Avenida Infante D. Henrique, Santa Apolónia* ☎ *21/881–0320* 🌐 *www.bicadosapato.com* 🕒 *No dinner Sun.; no lunch Mon.*

$ ✕ **Santo António de Alfama.** Up some steps from the Travessa do Terreiro
MEDITERRANEAN   do Trigo, you'll find this simple but sophisticated restaurant hung with
black-and-white photos of famous artists. The mushrooms stuffed with
Gorgonzola and deep-fried potato skins are tasty starters. Steak, fish,
or duck accompanied by steamed vegetables are the most popular main
dishes, but there are authentic Portuguese flavors such as *morcela com
grelos* (blood sausage and turnip leaves, sautéed with potatoes). Note
there's less choice at lunch than at dinner, when the kitchen also stays
open till half past midnight. In summer, good use is made of the large
terrace. $ *Average main: €15* ✉ *Beco de São Miguel 7* ☎ *21/8881328*
⊕ *www.siteantonio.com.*

AVENIDA DA LIBERDADE

14

$ ✕ **Os Tibetanos.** Delicious dishes such as *caril de seitan e cenouras* (wheat
VEGETARIAN   gluten and carrot curry), baked *quorn* (made from a relative of mushrooms), and Tibetan *momo* dumplings ensure that there's always a line
for a table in this restaurant's dining room or pleasant garden. Daily
specials cost less than €8, while the fixed-price menus are excellent
value. Desserts, including a range of fruit tarts and cakes, are equally
delicious. Os Tibetanos is part of a Buddhist center: a small shop stocks
books and crafts, incense, homeopathic medicines, and other natural
products, while yoga and meditation classes take place upstairs. $ *Aver-
age main: €9* ✉ *Rua do Salitre 117* ☎ *21/314–2038* ⊕ *www.tibetanos.
com* ▭ *No credit cards* ☾ *Closed Sun.*

BAIRRO ALTO

$ ✕ **Cantinho da Paz.** This place is a joyful mom-and-pop establishment
INDIAN   that specializes in the cuisine of Goa—otherwise surprisingly hard
to find in Lisbon. The spicy veal *balchão* and ginger-and-cardamom-
flavored *xacuti* are particularly rich examples of Goa's unique mix
of Portuguese and Indian influences, but there are also tasty seafood
dishes. English-speaking staff will guide you through the menu. Vegetarians take note: you may have been spoiled for choice in Indian restaurants back home, but there are slim pickings here. This place is on an
alley off the No. 28 tram route from Chiado to Estrela, but take a taxi
if you're worried about getting lost. $ *Average main: €14* ✉ *Rua da
Paz 4, off Rua dos Poiais de São Bento* ☎ *21/390–1963* ☾ *Closed Sun.*

$ ✕ **Casa Faz Frio.** This convivial *adega* (tavern)—complete with wood
PORTUGUESE   beams, stone floors, and bunches of garlic suspended from the ceiling—may look a little faded. But it is now one of just two in Lisbon to
boast *gabinetes*—paneled booths traditionally used for trysts but also
handy for working lunches—and is a great place to sample rustic food
on the cheap. There is a different bacalhau dish every day, and paella
is always on the menu; other house specialties include grilled cuttlefish
and *secretos,* lean meat from the belly of the *porco preto* pig. $ *Average
main: €9* ✉ *Rua de Dom Pedro V 96–98* ☎ *21/3461860* ▭ *No credit
cards* ☾ *Closed Sun.*

$ ✕ **Cervejaria Trindade.** The colorful azulejo wall tiles and vaulted ceiling
PORTUGUESE   of this former monastery hint at its long history, and it's popular with
locals and tourists alike. A homey bar at the entrance will quench your
thirst as you wait—you can also just come here for a drink and some

pastéis de bacalhau (tasty fried cod-and-potato snacks). You might start with *ameijoas à Bulhão Pato* (clams in a garlic-butter and cilantro sauce) before moving on to *bife de vazia à Trindade* (steak with a choice of three sauces) or *bacalhau à Santo Ofício* (baked cod with olive oil). It all tastes great with the house wine. The weekday lunch menus are good value, as is a kids' menu. [$] *Average main: €12* ⌧ *Rua Nova da Trindade 20* ☎ *21/342-3506* ⊕ *www.cervejariatrindade.pt.*

$
PORTUGUESE
Fodor's Choice
★

✕ **Fidalgo.** The local intelligentsia have made this low-key, comfortable restaurant their refuge, though owner Eugenio Fidalgo has been welcoming every sort of patron for four decades now. He'll gladly help you with the Portuguese menu and the excellent, well-priced wine list. Try one of the specialties such as bacalhau or octopus *à lagareiro* (baked in olive oil, with tiny potatoes), or the incredibly succulent *medalhões de javali* (wild boar cutlets). Fidalgo was recently redecorated from top to bottom and is looking better than ever. [$] *Average main: €12* ⌧ *Rua da Barroca 27* ☎ *21/342-2900* ⊕ *www.restaurantefidalgo.com* ⊘ *Closed Sun.*

BAIXA-CHIADO

$$
PORTUGUESE
Fodor's Choice
★

✕ **Aqui Há Peixe.** "There's fish here" is this restaurant's name, and make no mistake: it's one of the most fashionable places in town to eat seafood. At night this informal place attracts a youngish crowd clearly intent on hitting the Bairro Alto's bars later. Popular dishes here include fish stews and tuna steak sautéed with pink peppercorns; you should order a light *vinho verde* or a good white wine to wash them down. There are cheaper lunchtime specials, rustled up from whatever was in the market in the morning. Desserts are homemade—and delicious. [$] *Average main: €18* ⌧ *Rua da Trindade 18A, Chiado* ☎ *21/343-2154* ⊕ *www.aquihapeixe.pt* ⊘ *Closed Mon. No lunch weekends.*

$$$$
ECLECTIC
Fodor's Choice
★

✕ **Belcanto.** José Avillez, one of Portugal's most renowned young chefs, has found his ideal showcase in this cozy haven in front of Lisbon's opera house. The inventive cuisine uses the latest techniques in playing on traditional themes. The à la carte list features signature Avillez dishes such as the heavenly *Pombo à "Convento-de-Alcântara"* (stewed pigeon); and *Raia Jackson Pollock*—skate presented to look just like one of the artist's paintings (a copy is provided for comparison). The olive trilogy (crunchy, spherified, and liquid) is a fun starter, while the petits fours are a divine ender. [$] *Average main: €30* ⌧ *Largo de São Carlos 10, Chiado* ☎ *21/342-0607* ⊕ *www.joseavillez.pt* ⚐ *Reservations essential* ⊘ *Closed Sun. and Mon.*

$$
PORTUGUESE

✕ **Tágide.** In a fine old house that looks out over the Baixa and the Rio Tejo (reserve a table by the window), you can have one of Lisbon's great food experiences. The dining room lined with 18th-century tiles is a charming place to sample Portuguese fare, from both tasting and seasonal à la carte menus. You might start with a platter of cured meats from the Iberian black pig. Then try a signature entrée, such as bacalhau with cured ham, spinach, and chick-pea purée, or veal medallions with Azeitão cheese. Vegetarians are well served here with creamy risottos. Among their desserts, the tiramisu with pear cooked in port wine stands out. On arrival at the restaurant, ring the bell to get in. The downstairs wine bar has similarly panoramic views and a more informal atmosphere. $ *Average main: €16* ✉ *Largo Academia Nacional de Belas Artes 18–20, Chiado* ☎ *21/340–4010* ⊕ *www.restaurantetagide. com* 🍷 *Reservations essential* ☯ *Closed Sun.*

WHERE TO STAY

ALFAMA

$ 🏨 **Albergaria Senhora do Monte.** If you want expansive views of the castle
HOTEL and river, book a room on one of the upper floors of this modern hotel.
Pros: amazing views; in quiet residential neighborhood with restaurants and stores nearby; free WiFi. **Cons:** on a steep hill; limited facilities; little local character. $ *Rooms from: €110* ✉ *Calçada do Monte 39* ☎ *21/8866002* ⊕ *www.albergariasenhoradomonte.com* 🛏 *24 rooms, 4 suites* ❤️ *Breakfast.*

$$$ 🏨 **Olissippo Castelo.** This small, elegant hotel pampers guests with luxuri-
HOTEL ous linens, thick carpeting, elegant furnishings, comfy mattresses, and marble bathrooms. **Pros:** great views; quiet area; free Wi-Fi. **Cons:** up a steep hill; sometimes a wait for breakfast seating; room service till 11 pm only. $ *Rooms from: €240* ✉ *Rua Costa do Castelo 112–116* ☎ *21/8820190* ⊕ *www.hotelolissippocastelo.com* 🛏 *20 rooms, 4 suites* ❤️ *Breakfast.*

$$$$ 🏨 **Solar do Castelo.** In this 18th-century mansion within the walls of a
B&B/INN castle, original architectural features have been lovingly restored and archeological finds put on display. **Pros:** charm to spare; quiet location; free Wi-Fi and Internet terminal. **Cons:** up a steep cobbled road; some rooms only have showers. $ *Rooms from: €265* ✉ *Rua das Cozinhas 2* ☎ *21/880–6050* ⊕ *www.heritage.pt* 🛏 *20 rooms* ❤️ *Breakfast.*

$$$ 🏨 **Solar dos Mouros.** This melon-color town house, owned by an artist,
B&B/INN has a great location near the Castelo de São Jorge. **Pros:** close to the castle; lovely views; funky decor. **Cons:** up a steep hill and with stairs to climb; Wi-Fi free but only in reception; no bar. $ *Rooms from: €240* ✉ *Rua do Milagre de Santo Antonio 6* ☎ *21/885–4940* ⊕ *www. solardosmouros.com* 🛏 *11 rooms, 1 suite* ❤️ *No meals.*

AVENIDA DA LIBERDADE

$$$ 🏨 **Hotel Britânia.** The art-deco touches throughout Hotel Britânia are
HOTEL the key selling point—from the original marble panels in the baths to the "porthole" windows in the facade, the columns and candelabra in the lobby, and the murals in the bar. **Pros:** unique period decoration and furniture; spacious rooms; free Wi-Fi. **Cons:** no restaurant; no exercise facilities. $ *Rooms from: €210* ✉ *Rua Rodrigues Sampaio 17* ☎ *21/315–5016* ⊕ *www.heritage.pt* 🛏 *32 rooms, 1 suite* ❤️ *Breakfast* Ⓜ *Avenida.*

$$$$ 🏨 **Tivoli Lisboa.** There's enough marble in the public areas to make you
HOTEL fear for the future supply of the stone, but grandness gives way to comfort in the rooms, which are characterized by stylish, dark-wood and well-equipped bathrooms. **Pros:** espresso machines in all rooms; metro station out front; garden a real downtown oasis. **Cons:** free Internet access only in common areas; hotel often overrun by conferences. $ *Rooms from: €440* ✉ *Avenida da Liberdade 185* ☎ *21/3198900* ⊕ *www.tivolihotels. com* 🛏 *306 rooms, 48 suites* ❤️ *Breakfast* Ⓜ *Avenida.*

14

BAIRRO ALTO

$$$$ HOTEL
🏨 **Bairro Alto Hotel.** Lisbon's first contemporary boutique hotel, with sleek contemporary design, "the BA" is in the heart of the city. **Pros:** cutting-edge design; central location; attentive staff. **Cons:** some small rooms; few amenities for business travelers. [$] *Rooms from: €440* ✉ *Praça Luís de Camões 2* ☎ *21/340–8288* 🌐 *www.bairroaltohotel.com* 🛏 *51 rooms, 4 suites* 🍴 *Breakfast* [M] *Baixa Chiado.*

$ B&B/INN
🏨 **Casa de São Mamede.** One of the first private houses to be built in Lisbon after the 18th-century earthquake has been transformed into a relaxed guesthouse endowed with antique, country-style furniture; a tiled dining room; a grand staircase; and stained-glass windows. **Pros:** family-friendly; tranquil yet bars and restaurants close by; free Wi-Fi and business center. **Cons:** no parking; perhaps a little staid for younger travelers. [$] *Rooms from: €110* ✉ *Rua da Escola Politécnica 159, Rato* ☎ *21/396–3166* 🌐 *www.casadesaomamede.pt* 🛏 *25 rooms, 1 suite* 🍴 *Breakfast* [M] *Rato.*

BAIXA-CHIADA

$$$$ HOTEL
🏨 **Hotel do Chiado.** Arriving at the entrance, you may assume the taxi—or Jaguar limo that's available on request—has dropped you at an office. **Pros:** fantastic central location and views; comfy café-bar with large terrace; in-room amenities include fax/photocopy machine. **Cons:** no restaurant; in-room Internet access (via dataport) is not free. [$] *Rooms from: €297* ✉ *Rua Nova de Almada 114, Chiado* ☎ *21/325–6100, 21/325–6200* 🌐 *www.hoteldochiado.pt* 🛏 *38 rooms, 2 suites* 🍴 *Breakfast* [M] *Baixa-Chiado.*

$ HOTEL
Fodor's Choice ★
🏨 **Lisboa Carmo Hotel.** This low-key boutique charmer, located in the upscale, hilltop Chiado neighborhood, features a historic setting and Lisbon city views, plus a team that endeavors to be "hotel tailors" who "fit" each guest with a unique experience. **Pros:** affordable; quaint location; local flavor. **Cons:** some rooms are small; restaurant can be inconsistent. [$] *Rooms from: €100* ✉ *Rua da Oliveira ao Carmo, 1, 2, 3, Largo do Carmo, Chiado* ☎ *213/264710* 🌐 *www.lisboacarmohotel.com* 🛏 *45 rooms* 🍴 *No meals.*

LAPA

$$$ B&B/INN
Fodor's Choice ★
🏨 **As Janelas Verdes.** On the same street as the Museu de Arte Antiga, this late-18th-century mansion maintains fittings, furnishings, paintings, and tile work throughout that are in keeping with the building's historic character. **Pros:** elegant and peaceful; unique literary associations; free Internet and Wi-Fi. **Cons:** just five parking spots; limited facilities; away from the city center. [$] *Rooms from: €245* ✉ *Rua das Janelas Verdes 47* ☎ *21/396–8143* 🌐 *www.heritage.pt* 🛏 *29 rooms* 🍴 *Breakfast* [M] *Cais do Sodré.*

NIGHTLIFE

Lisbon has a thriving nightlife scene, and there are listings of concerts, plays, and films in the monthly *Agenda Cultural,* available from the tourist office and in many museums and theaters. The weekly magazine *Time Out Lisboa* is still more comprehensive. Although all written in Portuguese, the listings are easy to decipher.

FADO

Fado is a haunting music that emerged in Lisbon from hotly disputed roots: African, Brazilian, and Moorish are among the contenders. A single singer—male or female—is accompanied by a Spanish guitar and the 12-stringed Portuguese guitar, a closer relative of the lute. Today most *casas de fado* (fado houses) are in the Bairro Alto or Alfama.

They serve traditional Portuguese food, though it's rarely anything special, and the singing starts at 9 or 10 and may continue until 2 am. Reservations for dinner are essential, but if you want to go along later just to listen in, most establishments will let you do so if you buy drinks, usually for around €10 a minimum. Whenever you do arrive, fado etiquette is strict on one point: when the singing starts, all chatter must stop. *Silêncio, canta-se fado!*

14

Lisbon bars don't get going until after midnight, and clubs even later. On weekends, mobs stand shoulder to shoulder in the streets. For a less boisterous night out, visit an *adega típica* (traditional tavern) that has fado shows, or a venue that hosts live music.

ALFAMA

DANCE CLUBS

Most clubs are in Alcântara and along the Avenida 24 de Julho. Some charge a cover of €10–€15 (more on weekends), including one drink; if you come early you may get in free. Clubs are open from about 10 or 11 pm until 4 or 5 am; a few stay open until 8 am.

Lux. Lux is undoubtedly the most stylish club in Lisbon, with two dance floors favored by big-name DJs. ⊠ *Av. Infante D. Henrique near Sta. Apolónia* ☎ *21/882–0890* ⊕ *www.luxfragil.com.*

FADO CLUBS

Fodor's Choice ★ **Baiuca.** At the family-run Baiuca, the quality of both food and singing varies but a great atmosphere is guaranteed. Nights often end with local amateurs literally lining up outside, raring to perform (you can just drop in after dinner if you order a few drinks). ⊠ *Rua de São Miguel 20* ☎ *21/8867284* ☾ *Fado shows Thurs.–Mon.*

BAIRRO ALTO

BARS

The Bairro Alto, long the center of Lisbon's nightlife, is the best place for barhopping. Most bars here are fairly small, and stay open until 2 am or so. Larger designer bars can be found along Avenida 24 de Julho and in the Santos neighborhood, where—because this isn't a residential area—they may stay open until 5 or 6 am. Farther along the riverbank, under the bridge in Alcântara, the Doca do Santo Amaro has terrace-bars and restaurants converted from old warehouses.

Fodor's Choice ★ **Pavilhão Chinês.** For a quiet drink in an intriguing setting, you can't beat this spot. It's filled to the brim with fascinating junk collected over the years—from old toys to statues—and it has two snooker tables. ⊠ *Rua Dom Pedro V 89* ☎ *21/342–4729.*

FADO CLUBS

Adega do Ribatejo. For fado at budget prices, consider a meal here. There's live entertainment nightly, and *fadistas* on the roster might include your cook or waiter. It's a bargain, and also one of the less touristy places to see fado. ⊠ *Rua Diário de Notícias 23* ☎ *21/3468343* ⊘ *Closed Sun.*

SHOPPING

Family-owned stores remain common in Lisbon, especially in Baixa, Chiado, and Bairro Alto, and salespeople are courteous almost everywhere. Apart from designer fashions and high-end antiques, prices are moderate. Most shops are open weekdays 9–1 and 3–7 and Saturday 9–1; malls and supermarkets are often open until 10 and on Sunday. Credit cards—Visa in particular—are widely accepted.

Fodor'sChoice **Feira da Ladra.** One of Lisbon's main shopping attractions is this flea
★ market held on Tuesday morning and all day Saturday. It's fun and you never know what sort of treasure you'll come across. Just be sure to watch your wallet. ⊠ *Campo de Santa Clara, Alfama.*

SINTRA

Fodor'sChoice *30 km (18 miles) northwest of Lisbon.*
★
It was the Moors who first built a castle northwest of the capital at Sintra as a defense against Christian forces, which, under Dom Afonso Henriques, moved steadily southward after the victory at Ourique in 1139. The castle fell to the Christians in 1147, a few days after Lisbon. Sintra's lush hills and valleys later became the summer residence of Portuguese kings and aristocrats, its late medieval palace the greatest expression of royal wealth and power of the time. In the 18th and 19th centuries English travelers, poets, and writers—including an enthusiastic Lord Byron—were drawn by the area's beauty. The poet Robert Southey described Sintra as "the most blessed spot on the whole inhabitable globe." Its historic importance in the Romantic movement in 1995 brought it UNESCO recognition as a World Heritage Site.

Sintra's main attractions are within walking distance or accessible by bus or horse-drawn carriages. There are several marked walks in the surrounding countryside (ideal for escaping the summer crowds), which is crisscrossed by minor roads and marked by old monastic buildings, estates, gardens, and market villages. But it is most easily covered by car, particularly if you want to range as far north as Mafra, with its giant palace-convent. You could also take a guided tour (arranged through the tourist office) or see sights by taxi.

To the west, the Atlantic makes itself felt in windswept beaches and capes, including Cabo da Roca—the westernmost point in Europe, topped by a lighthouse. In the other direction, the town of Queluz, halfway between Lisbon and Sintra, is dominated by its magnificent baroque palace, in gardens dotted with statuary.

GETTING HERE
BUS TRAVEL
Although the best way to reach Sintra and most of the towns on the Estoril Coast is by train from Lisbon, there are some useful bus connections between towns. Tickets are cheap (less than €3.50 for most journeys), and departures are generally every hour (less frequent on weekends); local tourist offices have timetables. Try to arrive 15 minutes before your bus departs.

Contacts **Rede Expressos** ⊠ *Praça Marechal Humberto Delgado—Estrada das Laranjeiras, Lisbon* ☎ *213/581472* ⊕ *www.rede-expressos.pt.* **TST-Transportes Sul do Tejo** ⊠ *Rua Marcos de Portugal—Laranjeiro, Almada* ☎ *211/126200* ⊕ *www.tsuldotejo.pt.*

CAR TRAVEL
By car, Queluz is 20 minutes from Lisbon, signposted off route N249/IC19, making this a good half-day option, or a fine stop on the way to or from Sintra (40 minutes from Lisbon).

PUBLIC TRANSPORTATION
If you don't want to walk, you can take SCOTTurb's Bus No. 434, which loops around the key attractions; all-day tickets are €4.05, and you can hop on and off as long as you don't backtrack.

TRAIN TRAVEL
Trains from Lisbon's Rossio station, between Praça dos Restauradores and Rossio square, run every 15 minutes to Queluz and on to Sintra (40 minutes total). The service operates 6 am–2:40 am, and one-way tickets cost €1.95 to Queluz-Belas, €2.15 to Sintra.

Contacts **Rail information line** ☎ *808/208208* ⊕ *www.cp.pt.*

TOURS
Sintratur offers old-fashioned horse-and-carriage rides in and around the town. A short tour costs €30 for up to four people; longer trips run between €60 and €100 and go as far afield as Pena Palace and Monserrate.

Contacts **Sintratur** ⊠ *Rua João de Deus 82* ☎ *219/241238* ⊕ *www.sintratur.com.*

VISITOR INFORMATION
The local tourist office, the Turismo, has details on opening hours and prices, on walking trails in the countryside, and on tour companies. It also houses an art gallery (the Galeria do Museu Municipal) specializing in works associated with Sintra.

Contacts **Turismo** ⊠ *Praça da República 23* ☎ *219/231157* ⊕ *www.cm-sintra. pt* ☾ *Tues.–Fri. 9–noon and 2–6, weekends 2:30–7* ⊠ *Sintra train station* ☎ *219/241623.*

EXPLORING

Castelo dos Mouros (*Moorish Castle*). The battlemented ruins of this 9th-century castle still give a fine impression of the fortress that finally fell to Christian forces led by Dom Afonso Henriques in 1147. It's visible from various points in Sintra itself, but for a closer look follow the steps that lead up to the ruins from the back of the town center (40 minutes going up, 25 minutes coming down). Alternately, you can catch the SCOTTurb's Bus No. 434 or rent a horse-drawn carriage in town. Panoramic views from the serrated walls explain why the Moors chose the site. ⊠ *Estrada da Pena* ☎ *219/237300* ⊕ *www.parquesdesintra. pt* ⌨ *€5 guided tour* ☉ *Apr.–mid-Sept., daily 9:30–8; mid-Sept.–Mar., daily 10–6; last admission 1 hr before closing.*

FAMILY **Museu do Brinquedo** (*Toy Museum*). The former fire station headquarters has been transformed into the Toy Museum. Based on the collection of João Arbués Moreira, who began hoarding playthings when he was 14, the museum occupies more than four floors and contains thousands of toy planes, trains, and automobiles; dolls' furniture; rare lead soldiers; and puppets. There's also a playroom for kids and a café. A planned cut in government funding has, however, placed a dark cloud over the museum's continued existence. ⊠ *Rua Visconde de Monserrate* ☎ *219/106016* ⊕ *www.museu-do-brinquedo.pt* ⌨ *€4* ☉ *Tues.–Sun. 10–6 (last admission at 5:30).*

Fodor's Choice **Palácio da Pena.** This Disney-like castle is a glorious conglomeration of
★   turrets and domes awash in pastels. In 1503 the Monastery of Nossa Senhora da Pena was constructed here, but it fell into ruins after religious orders were expelled from Portugal in 1832. Seven years later the ruins were purchased by Maria II's consort, Ferdinand of Saxe-Coburg. Inspired by the Bavarian castles of his homeland, Ferdinand commissioned a German architect, Baron Eschwege, to build the castle of his fantasies, in styles that range from Arabian to Victorian. Work was finished in 1885 when he was Fernando II. The surrounding park is filled with trees and flowers from every corner of the Portuguese empire. Portugal's last monarchs used the Pena Palace as a summer home, the last of whom—Queen Amália—went into exile in England after the Republic was proclaimed on October 5, 1910. Inside is a rich, sometimes vulgar, and often bizarre collection of Victorian and Edwardian furniture, ornaments, and paintings. Placards explain each room. A minitrain takes you from the park gate up to the palace. A path beyond an enormous statue (thought to be Baron Eschwege, cast as a medieval knight) on a nearby crag leads to the **Cruz Alta**, a 16th-century stone cross 1,782 feet above sea level, with stupendous views. ⊠ *Estrada da Pena* ☎ *219/910–5340, 219/923–7300 advance booking* ⊕ *www.parquesdesintra.pt* ⌨ *Park €5; combined ticket for park and palace €9 mid-Sept.–Mar., €12 Apr.–mid-Sept. Minitrain €2* ☉ *Mid-Sept.–Mar., daily 10–6 (last admission 5); Apr.–mid-Sept., daily 9:45–7 (last admission 6:15).*

Fodor's Choice **Palácio Nacional de Sintra** (*Sintra Palace*). The conical twin white chim-
★   neys of Sintra Palace are the town's most recognizable landmarks. There has probably been a palace here since Moorish times, although the current structure—also known as the Paço Real—dates from the late 14th century. It is the only surviving royal palace in Portugal from the Middle Ages, and displays a fetching combination of Moorish, Gothic, and Manueline architecture. Bilingual descriptions in each room let you enjoy them at your own pace. The chapel has Mozarabic (Moorish-influenced) azulejos from the 15th and 16th centuries. The ceiling of

the Sala das Armas is painted with the coats of arms of 72 noble families, and the grand Sala dos Cisnes has a remarkable ceiling of painted swans. The Sala das Pegas (magpies) figures in a well-known tale about Dom João I (1385–1433) and his dalliance with a lady-in-waiting. The king had the room painted with as many magpies as there were chattering court ladies, thus satirizing the gossips as loose-tongued birds. ⊠ *Largo Rainha D. Amélia* ☎ *219/910–6840* ⊕ *pnsintra.imc-ip.pt* ▦ *€7 (free Sun. until 2)* ◐ *Daily 9:30–5:30 (last admission at 5).*

NEED A BREAK? Sintra is known for its *queijadas* (cottage-cheese cakes), and one baker with two outlets on the same street is their most renowned purveyor. **Periquita dois.** The larger of the two, Periquita dois has fine views from its terrace. ⊠ *Rua das Padarias 18* ☎ *21/923–1595* ◐ *Closed Tues.*

Fodor's Choice ★ **Quinta da Regaleira.** A five-minute walk along the main road past the tourist office takes you to one of Sintra's most intriguing privately owned mansions. Quinta da Regaleira was built in the early 20th century for a Brazilian mining magnate with a keen interest in freemasonry and the Knights Templar (who made their 11th-century headquarters on this site). The estate includes gardens where almost everything—statues, water features, grottoes, lookout towers—is linked to one or the other of his pet subjects. Spookiest of all is the 100-foot-deep Poço do Iniciático (Initiation Well)—an inverted underground "tower." ⊠ *Rua Barbosa do Bocage 5* ☎ *219/106656* ⊕ *www.regaleira.pt* ▦ *€5, guided tour €10 (call ahead for tours in English)* ◐ *Apr.–Sept., daily 10–8 (last admission at 7); Nov. and Dec., daily 10–5:30 (last admission at 5); Oct., Feb., and Mar., daily 10–6:30 (last admission at 6).*

Sintra Museu de Arte Moderna–Colecção Berardo. In a former palace, this museum is one of several institutions (the main one being in the Lisbon suburb of Belém) that showcase the eclectic taste of Madeiran-born magnate Joe Berardo. The modern art collection, parts of which are often displayed here, includes works by Andy Warhol, Pablo Picasso, Roy Lichtenstein, and Francis Bacon. ⊠ *Av. Heliodoro Salgado* ☎ *219/248170* ⊕ *www.berardocollection.com* ▦ *€3 (free Sun. until 2)* ◐ *Tues.–Sun. 10–6.*

OUTSIDE SINTRA

MONSERRATE
4 km (2½ miles) west of Sintra.

Fodor's Choice ★ **Parque de Monserrate.** This estate, 4 km (2½ miles) west of Sintra, was laid out by Scottish gardeners in the mid-19th century at the behest of a wealthy Englishman, Sir Francis Cook. The centerpiece is the Moorish-style, three-dome **Palácio de Monserrate.** The original palace was built by the Portuguese viceroy of India, and was later home to Gothic novelist William Beckford. A regular ticket allows you to visit the park and part of the palace, and there are guided 1½-hour tours available at various times throughout the day. The gardens, with their streams, waterfalls, and Etruscan tombs, are famed for an array of tree and plant species, though labels are lacking. ⊠ *Estrada da Monserrate, Sintra* ☎ *219/237300* ⊕ *www.parquesdesintra.pt* ▦ *€5, guided tours of palace* *and garden €10 ☉ Apr.–mid-Sept., daily 10–1 and 2–7; mid-Sept.–Mar., daily 10:30–1 and 2–5. Last admission 30 min before closing.*

CONVENTO DOS CAPUCHOS
13 km (8 miles) southwest of Sintra.

Convento dos Capuchos. The plain main entrance to this extraordinarily austere convent, 13 km (8 miles) southwest of Sintra, sets the tone for the severity of the ascetic living conditions within. From 1560 until 1834, when it was abandoned, seven monks—never any more, never any less—prayed in the tiny chapel hewn out of the rock and inhabited the bare cells, which were lined with cork in attempt to maintain a modicum of warmth. Impure thoughts meant a spell in the Penitents' Cell, an excruciatingly small space. Guides for the 45-minute tour bring the history of the place to life with surprising zest and humor. No vehicles are allowed close to the convent, so the peace is disturbed only by birdsong. ✉ *Convento dos Capuchos* 📞 *219/237300* ⊕ *www.parquesdesintra.pt* 💶 *€5, guided tour €10 ☉ Apr.–mid-Sept., daily 9:30–8; mid-Sept.–Mar., daily 10–6; last admission 1 hr before closing.*

SÃO PEDRO DE SINTRA
2 km (1 mile) southeast of Sintra.

This little hillside village is most famous for its fair, the Feira de São Pedro, which dates from the time of the Christian Reconquest. It's held every second and fourth Sunday of the month in the vast Praça Dom Fernando II (also called the Largo da Feira), but it's worth stopping by on other days to see the village church in its enclosed little square, or for a lunch far from the tourist crowds.

Parque da Liberdade. These gardens, off the road between Sintra train station and the National Palace, are a short cut to São Pedro, but you can also catch a local bus from outside Sintra station. ✉ *Volta do Duche, Sintra* 📞 *219/238811* 💶 *Free ☉ June–Sept., weekdays 10–7, weekends 10–8; Oct.–May, daily 10–6.*

CABO DA ROCA
15 km (9 miles) west of Sintra, 20 km (12 miles) northwest of Cascais.

Fodor's Choice
★

The windswept Cabo da Roca and its lighthouse, set in a protected natural park a 40-minute bus ride from Sintra, mark continental Europe's westernmost point, topped by a cross bearing an inscription by Portuguese national poet Luís de Camões. Even if you don't buy a certificate at the gift shop to verify your visit, the memory of this desolate granite cape will linger.

OFF THE BEATEN PATH

The Atlantic Coast. North of Cabo da Roca, the natural parkland extends through the villages of Praia Grande, Praia das Maçãs, and Azenhas do Mar. The first two have good beaches, and all have seafood restaurants. On the way down, the pretty open market with fresh fruit and vegetable stands along the side of a fork in the road makes a nice place to shop with the locals.

QUELUZ

15 km (9 miles) east of Sintra, 15 km (9 miles) northwest of Lisbon.

Fodor's Choice ★ **Palácio Nacional de Queluz** (*Queluz National Palace*). This palace was inspired, in part, by the palace at Versailles. The salmon-pink rococo edifice was ordered as a royal summer residence by Dom Pedro III in 1747. Architect Mateus Vicente de Oliveira took five years to make the place habitable; Frenchman Jean-Baptiste Robillon spent 40 more executing a detailed baroque plan that also comprised imported trees and statues, and azulejo-lined canals and fountains. You can tour the apartments and elegant staterooms, including the frescoed Music Salon, the Hall of Ambassadors, and the mirrored Throne Room with its crystal chandeliers and gilt trim. Some are now used for concerts and state visits, while the old kitchens have been converted into an ordinary café and a fancy restaurant with an imposing open fireplace and a vast oak table. ✉ *Largo do Palácio* ☎ *214/343860* 🌐 *pnqueluz.imc-ip.pt* 🎟 *€7 (free Sun. until 2)* ⏲ *Palace: Wed.–Mon. 9–5 (last admission at 4:30). Palace Gardens: May–Sept., Wed.–Mon. 9–6 (last admission at 5:30), Oct.–Apr., Wed.–Mon. 9–5.*

14

WHERE TO EAT

$ SEAFOOD 🍴 **Neptuno.** Praia das Maçãs is a popular place to go for seafood restaurants on the beach. One of the best is Neptuno, a glassed-in eatery practically on the sand. Hanging on the walls are photos of boats, big catches, and the sea. Try *peixe a bulhão pato* (fish with garlic, olive oil, and coriander) and seafood-rich *arroz de marisco.* [$] *Average main: €15* ✉ *Praia das Maçãs* ☎ *219/291222* ⏲ *Closed Wed. No dinner Tues.*

$ PORTUGUESE 🍴 **Tacho Real.** Locals climb a steep hill to this restaurant for traditional dishes cooked with panache, such as bacalhau *à brás* (with eggs, onions, and sliced potato), steaks, and game in season. The dessert cart allows you to choose from a selection of house-made cakes and tarts. On warm days the small terrace is delightful, and there is live guitar music welcoming you at the door. [$] *Average main: €10* ✉ *Rua do Ferraria 4* ☎ *219/235277* ⏲ *Closed Wed.*

WHERE TO STAY

$ B&B/INN Fodor's Choice ★ 🏨 **Casa Miradouro.** The Belgian owners of this candy-stripe 1890s house at the edge of Sintra have a keen eye for style and comfort. **Pros:** all rooms have views; in-room double-glaze windows and heating an unusual winter bonus in this category; special deals in winter. **Cons:** requires very early booking; no phone or TV in rooms. [$] *Rooms from: €80* ✉ *Rua Sotto Mayor 55* ☎ *91/429–2203* 🌐 *www.casa-miradouro.com* 🛏 *6 rooms* ⏲ *Closed 2 wks in Jan.* 🍽 *Breakfast.*

$$ B&B/INN Fodor's Choice ★ 🏨 **Lawrence's Hotel.** When this 18th-century inn, the oldest on the peninsula, reopened in 1999, the U.S. secretary of state and the Netherlands' Queen Beatrix were among the first guests. **Pros:** rich in historical associations; cozy refuge from what can at times be a chilly local climate; charming rear terrace. **Cons:** no pool, gym, or garden; some rooms barely bigger than their bathrooms. [$] *Rooms from: €150* ✉ *Rua Con-*

siglieri Pedroso 38–40 ☎ *219/910–5500* ⊕ *www.lawrenceshotel.com* ➷ *11 rooms, 5 suites* ○ *Breakfast.*

PORTO

Portugal's second-largest city, with a population of roughly 250,000, considers itself the north's capital and, more contentiously, the country's economic center. Locals support this claim by quoting a typically down-to-earth maxim: "Coimbra sings, Braga prays, Lisbon shows off, and Porto works." There's poverty here, of course, primarily down by the river in the ragged older areas, parts of which are positively medieval. But in the shopping centers, the stately old stock exchange building, and the port-wine trade, Porto oozes confidence.

This emphasis on worth rather than beauty has created a solid rather than graceful city. Largely unaffected by the great earthquake of 1755, Porto has some fine baroque architecture, but its public buildings are generally sober. But its location on a steep hillside above the Rio Douro affords exhilarating perspectives.

The river has influenced the city's development since pre-Roman times, when the town of Cale on the left bank prospered sufficiently to support a trading port, called Portus, on the site of today's city. The 1703 Methuen agreement with England, giving commercial preference to Portuguese wines in detriment to French ones, provided the Douro Valley vineyards with a new market and Porto with a further boost. It was here that Douro wine was first mixed with brandy to preserve it during the journey and to improve its taste over time. The port-wine trade is still big business, based across the river in Vila Nova de Gaia; downtown, the two banks are linked by the impressive two-tier Ponte Dom Luís I (King Luís I Bridge), which was completed in 1886.

Porto is also a cultural hub, thanks to the Serralves Contemporary Art Museum and numerous commercial galleries, many clustered along Rua Miguel Bombarda, and now to the stunning Casa da Musica, or House of Music, designed by Dutch architect Rem Koolhaas and opened in 2005. The restaurants and nightclubs along the riverfront are almost all designed by young Portuguese architects, and Foz do Douro, where the river flows into the Atlantic, is a fashion and design hot spot.

PLANNING YOUR TIME

You'll need a couple of days to experience Porto and its wine lodges and the nearby coastal resorts. Make sure you visit the port-wine lodges, and leave yourself an afternoon or evening free to relax at a riverside bar or restaurant. Art lovers may end up spending hours at the Serralves National Contemporary Art Museum, whose extensive gardens will also charm visitors. And to really appreciate the new Casa da Música, you should take in a concert.

Several more days here would permit a trip out to one of the region's beautiful beaches; up the lovely Douro Valley—rail or boat are options, or rental car, if you want to visit a *quinta* (wine estate); or an excursion to the history-rich towns of Braga, Guimarães, or Amarante.

GETTING HERE AND AROUND

AIR TRAVEL

Porto's Aeroporto Francisco Sá Carneiro, 13 km (8 miles) north of the city, is the gateway to northern Portugal. There's direct service from many European cities and from Lisbon. The airport is now served by the metro system (a 30-minute trip downtown, €1.80). Taxis are also available outside the terminal; the metered fare into town should run €18 to €20, including a surcharge for baggage. Outside the city limits, tariffs are based on kilometers traveled.

Contacts Aeroporto Franciso Sá Carneiro (Porto) ☎ *22/943–2400* ⊕ *www. ana.pt.*

BUS TRAVEL

Rede Expressos operates frequent bus service to and from Lisbon to major towns in the region, with the ride from the capital to Porto, the main regional hub, taking at least three and a half hours and costing €19 one-way. Rodonorte links major towns within the northern region, with the trip from Porto to Amarante taking 50 minutes and costing €7.40 and that from Porto to Bragança taking from three hours and costing €14. Other local operators fill in the gaps. The staff might not speak English, but timetables are easily decipherable with the aid of a dictionary.

Contacts Rede Expressos ✉ *Rua Alexandre Herculano 370* ☎ *969/502050* ⊕ *www.rede-expressos.pt.* **Rodonorte** ✉ *Travessa Passos Manuel* ☎ *259/200–5637* ⊕ *www.rodonorte.pt.*

CAR TRAVEL

Porto is three and a half hours north of Lisbon by highway (via the A1 toll highway) or by express train, so even a short trip to Portugal can include a night or two here. From Porto it's another two hours up the coast to the Spanish border, or three to four hours east through the less visited Trás-os-Montes region to the border there. The densely populated north itself is well served with roads.

Downtown streets are congested or out of bounds, and local drivers manic, so leave your car at your hotel. You can walk around most of the center (though be prepared for steep hills), reaching outlying attractions by bus, taxi, or metro.

PUBLIC TRANSPORTATION

The city has a good network of buses, trams, and funiculars—all run by Sociedade dos Transportes Colectivos do Porto (STCP)—or the metro. Its five lines run from 6 am to 1 am, mostly over ground as a light rail service outside the center but converging underground at the Trindade stop. Bus services are reduced after 9 pm. Maps for all routes are available on the STCP website. The tourist office can provide information; they'll also sell you a Porto Card, which is valid for public transportation and entrance to 21 city sights, and discounts for others, for 24 hours (€8.50), 48 hours (€13.50), or 72 hours (€17.50). There's also a transport-only Andante Tour card valid for 24 hours (€7) or 72 hours (€15) from the first time it is used, when you must validate it at the yellow box at the entry point.

14

Contacts Metro do Porto ☎ *22/508–1000, 808/205060* ⊕ *www.metrodoporto.*
pt. **STCP** ☎ *22/507–1000, 808/200166* ⊕ *www.stcp.pt.*

TRAIN TRAVEL
Long-distance trains arrive at Porto Campanhã station, east of the center. From here you can take a five-minute connection to the central São Bento station. From Spain, the Vigo–Porto train crosses at Tuy/Valença do Minho and then heads south towards Porto, usually stopping at both Campanhã and São Bento. From Porto some of the most scenic lines in the country stretch out into the river valleys and mountain ranges to the northeast. Even if you have rented a car, a scenic daytrip by train is a worthwhile experience. For reservations and schedules, visit São Bento station or the tourist office.

Contacts Estação de Campanhã ✉ *Largo da Estação de Campanhã, Largo da Estação de Campanhã* ☎ *22/105–2700, 808/208208.* **Estação de São Bento** ✉ *Praça Almeida Garrett, Praça Almeida Garrett* ☎ *22/201–9517, 808/208208.*

VISITOR INFORMATION
Contacts Centro de Informação Turística do Porto ✉ *Praça Dom João I 43* ☎ *22/205–7514* ⊕ *www.portoturismo.pt.* **Posto de Turismo Municipal** ✉ *Rua Clube dos Fenianos 25* ☎ *22/339–3470* ⊕ *cm-porto.pt* ✉ *Rua do Infante Dom Henrique 63* ☎ *22/200–9770.*

EXPLORING

FodorsChoice
★
Cais da Ribeira (*Ribeira Pier*). A string of fish restaurants and *tascas* (taverns) are built into the street-level arcade of timeworn buildings along this pier. In the Praça da Ribeira, people sit and chat around an odd, modern, cubelike sculpture; farther on, steps lead to a walkway above the river that's backed by tall houses. The pier also provides the easiest access to the lower level of the middle bridge across the Douro, the Ponte Dom Luis I. Boats docked at Cais da Ribeira and across the river in Vila Nova da Gaia offer various cruises around the bridges and up the river to Peso da Régua and Pinhão.

Estação de São Bento. This train station was built in the early 20th century (King D. Carlos I laid the first brick himself in 1900) and inaugurated in 1915. It sits precisely where the Convent of S. Bento de Avé-Maria was located, and therefore inherited the convent's name—Saint Bento. The atrium is covered with 20,000 azulejos painted by Jorge Colaço (1916) depicting scenes of Portugal's history as well as ethnographic images. It is one of the most magnificent artistic undertakings of the early 20th century. The building was designed by architect Marques da Silva. ✉ *Praça Almeida Garret* ☎ *22/205–1714, 808/208208 for national call center* ⊕ *www.cp.pt.*

Igreja da Misericórdia (*Mercy Church*). Today's building represents a compromise between the church first built during the late 16th century and its reconstruction between 1749 and 1755 by painter and architect Nicolau Nasoni. At the church museum next door you can see *Fons Vitae* (Fountain of Life), a vibrant, anonymous, Renaissance painting depicting the founder of the church, Dom Manuel I, his queen, and their eight children kneeling before a crucified Christ. ✉ *Rua das*

Flores 5 ☎ *22/207–4710* ⊕ *www.scmp.pt* 🖃 *Church free, museum €1.50* ⊘ *Weekdays 9–12:30 and 2–5:30.*

Igreja de São Francisco (*Church of St. Francis*). During the last days of Porto's siege by the absolutist army (the *miguelistas*) in July 1842, there was gunfire by the nearby São Francisco Convent. These shootings caused a fire that destroyed most parts of the convent, sparing only this church. Today the church is the most prominent Gothic monument in Porto. It's a rather undistinguished, late 14th-century Gothic building on the outside, but inside is an astounding interior: gilded carving—added in the mid-18th century—runs up the pillars, over the altar, and across the ceiling. An adjacent museum (Museu de Arte Sacra) houses furnishings from the Franciscan convent. A guided tour (call the day before) includes a visit to the church, museum, and catacombs. ✉ *Rua do Infante Dom Henrique 93* ☎ *22/206–2100* ⊕ *www. ordemsaofrancisco.pt* 🖃 *Free* ⊘ *Nov.–Feb., daily 9–5:30; Mar.–June and Oct., daily 9–7; July–Sept., daily 9–8.*

Fodor's Choice ★ **Museu de Arte Contemporânea.** Designed by Álvaro Siza Vieira, a winner of the Pritzker Prize and Portugal's best-known architect, the Contemporary Art Museum is part of the Serralves Foundation and is surrounded by lovely gardens. It has changing international exhibitions, as well as work from Portuguese painters, sculptors, and designers. Check with the tourist office for the latest information. The original art deco house and its small formal garden is also worth visiting; as well as housing the foundation, it hosts small exhibitions. Various joint tickets are available, including one to the museum and to the Sea Life aquarium in Foz. To get here, take a taxi or catch the metro to Casa da Música and then Bus No. 201, 203, 502, or 504 from the Rotunda da Boavista; or from downtown take Bus No. 201 from Avenida dos Aliados—about a 30-minute ride. ✉ *Rua D. João de Castro 210* ☎ *22/615–6500, 808/200–543* ⊕ *www.serralves.pt* 🖃 *Museum and garden €7 Tues.–Sat., garden €3 (Sun. free until 1)* ⊘ *Museum: Oct.–Mar., Tues.–Fri. 10–5, weekends 10–7; Apr.–Sept., Tues.–Fri. 10–5, weekends 10–8. House: Oct.–Mar., Tues.–Fri. 10–5, weekends 10–7; Apr.–Sept., Tues.–Fri. 10–5, weekends 10–7. Park: Oct.–Mar., Tues.–Sun. 10–7; Apr.–Sept., Tues.–Fri. 10–7, weekends 10–8.*

Museu do Vinho do Porto (*Port Wine Museum*). Not to be confused with the larger, modern port wine museum upriver in Peso da Régua, this small but worthwhile facility has informative exhibits on the history of the trade that made Porto famous. The setting right on the Douro River makes for a spectacular walk in the late afternoon, or a scenic ride by Bus No. 500 or electric Tram No. E1. Displays include implements used in port-wine production—antique glass decanters and textiles, for instance—as well as paintings and engravings depicting the trade. There are occasional tastings as well. ✉ *Rua de Monchique 98* ☎ *22/207–6300* 🖃 *€2.60 (free weekends)* ⊘ *Tues.–Sat. 10–12:30 and 2–5:30, Sun. 2–5:30.*

Palácio da Bolsa. Porto's neoclassical former stock exchange takes up much of the site of the former Franciscan convent at the Igreja de São Francisco. Guided tours (every half hour) are the only way to see the

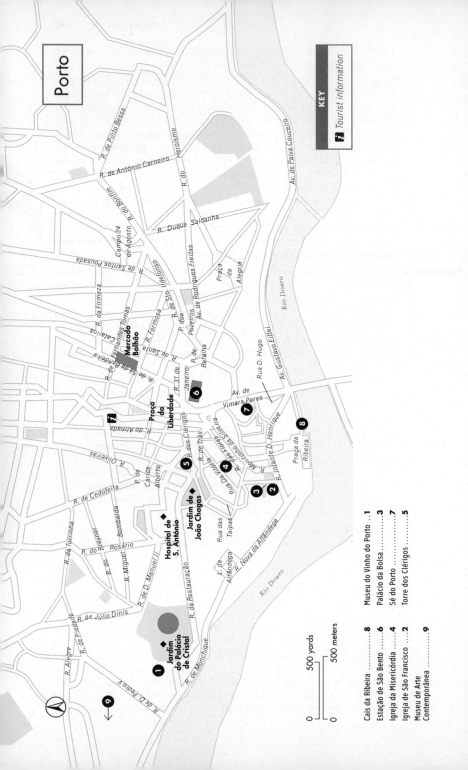

Porto

KEY

ℹ️ *Tourist information*

0 | 500 yards
0 | 500 meters

Cais da Ribeira **8**
Estação de São Bento **6**
Igreja da Misericórdia **4**
Igreja de São Francisco **2**
Museu de Arte
Contemporânea **9**

Museu do Vinho do Porto ..**1**
Palácio da Bolsa **3**
Sé do Porto **7**
Torre dos Clérigos **5**

Rio Douro

Av. de Paiva Couceiro

R. de Pinto Bessa

R. de António Carneiro

R. do Heroísmo

R. Duque Saldanha

R. de Santos Pousada

Campo 24 de Agosto

R. do Bonfim

R. de Sto. Ildefonso

Praça da Alegria

Av. de Rodrigues Freitas

R. da Firmeza

R. de Fernandes Tomás

R. de Santa Catarina

Mercado Bolhão

R. Formosa

R. de 5.ª de la Bandeira

R. 31 de Janeiro

P. de Poveiros

P. dos Poveiros

P. de Santa

P. de Batalha

Rua D. Hugo

Av. Gustavo Eiffel

Rio Douro

Av. de Vimara Peres

7

Sé

R. das Flores

R. do Almada

Praça da Liberdade

6

ℹ️

R. de Oliveiras

P. de Carlos Alberto

R. de Cedofeita

R. dos Clérigos

5

R. de Trás

Rua D. Vitória

R. do Mouzinho da Silveira

4

3

2

R. de Infante D. Henrique

8

Praça da Ribeira

R. Nova da Alfândega

Rua das Taipas

L. da Alfândega

Jardim de João Chagas

Hospital de S. António

R. da Restauração

R. de D. Manuel II

R. do Rosário

R. do Breyner

R. do Miguel Bombarda

R. da Torrinha

R. de Júlio Dinis

R. de Piedade

R. Alegre

R. de D. Pedro V

R. de Monchique

Jardim do Palácio de Cristal

1

9

Rio Douro

interior of this masterpiece of 19th-century Portuguese architecture. The Arab-style ballroom, in particular, is one of the most admired chambers and was designed by civil engineer Gustavo Adolfo Gonçalves e Sousa. ✉ *Rua Ferreira Borges* ☎ *22/339–9013, 22/339–9000* ⊕ *www.palaciodabolsa.pt* ✎ *Tours €7* ⊘ *Apr.–Sept., daily 9–6:30; Oct.–Mar., daily 9–12:30 and 2–5:30.*

Sé do Porto (*Cathedral*). Originally constructed in the 12th century by the parents of Dom Afonso Henriques (Portugal's first king), Porto's granite cathedral has been rebuilt twice: first in the late 13th century and again in the 18th century, when the architect of the Torre dos Clérigos, Nicolau Nasoni, was among those commissioned to work on its expansion. Despite the renovations, it remains a fortresslike structure—an uncompromising testament to medieval wealth and power. Notice a low relief on the northern tower, depicting a 14th-century vessel and symbolizing the city's nautical vocation. Size is the only exceptional thing about the interior; when you enter the two-story, 14th-century cloisters, however, the building comes to life. Decorated with gleaming azulejos, a staircase added by Nasoni leads to the second level and into a richly furnished chapter house, from which there are fine views through narrow windows. Nasoni also designed the Paço dos Arcebispos (Archbishops' Palace) behind the cathedral. It has been converted to offices, so you can only admire its 197-foot-long facade. ✉ *Terreiro da Sé* ☎ *22/205–9028* ⊕ *www.diocese-porto.pt* ✎ *Cathedral free, cloisters €3* ⊘ *Cathedral Nov.–Mar., Mon.–Sat. 9–12:30 and 2:30–6, Sun. 8:30–12:30 and 2:30–6; Apr.–Oct., Mon.–Sat. 9–12:30 and 2:30–7, Sun. 8:30–12:30 and 2:30–7. Cloisters Nov.–Mar., Mon.–Sat. 9–12:15 and 2:30–5:30, Sun. 2:30–5:30; Apr.–Oct., Mon.–Sat. 9–6:30, Sun. 2:30–6:30.*

Torre dos Clérigos. Designed by Italian architect Nicolau Nasoni and begun in 1754, the tower of the church Igreja dos Clérigos reaches an impressive height of 249 feet. There are 225 steep stone steps to the belfry, and the considerable effort required to climb them is rewarded by stunning views of the Old Town, the river, and beyond to the mouth of the Douro. Bincoulars and audio tours are available for an extra charge. The church itself, also built by Nasoni, predates the tower and is an elaborate example of Italianate baroque architecture. ✉ *Rua Senhor Filipe de Nery* ☎ *22/200–1729* ⊕ *www.torredosclerigos.pt* ✎ *Church free, tower €2* ⊘ *Daily 9–7.*

WHERE TO EAT

$$$$
CONTEMPORARY
Fodor's Choice
★

✕ **Bull and Bear.** Even following the departure of celebrated chef Miguel Castro Silva for Lisbon, Bull & Bear remains a star in Porto's restaurant scene. Silva's creative approach to Portuguese and Mediterranean cuisine carries on in this sleek dining room in the Porto stock exchange building. Try the sea bass marinated with fresh herbs, grilled scallops with Avruga caviar and cream of leek soup, and cod with local vegetables and beans. $ *Average main: €35* ✉ *Av. da Boavista 3431* ☎ *22/600–2681, 22/610–7669* ⊕ *www.bbgourmet.net* ⚠ *Reservations essential.*

14

CLOSE UP

Port Wine

Many of the more than 16 companies with caves in Vila Nova de Gaia are foreign owned. They include such well-known names as Sandeman, Osborne, Cockburn, Kopke, Ferreira, Calém, Taylor's, Barros, Ramos-Pinto, Real Companhia Velha, Fonseca, Rozès, Burmester, Offley, Noval, and Graham's. All are signposted and within a few minutes' walk of the bridge and each other; their names are also displayed in huge white letters across their roofs. Each company offers free guided tours, which always end with a tasting of one or two wines and an opportunity to buy bottles from the company store. Children are usually welcome and are often fascinated by the huge warehouses and all sorts of interesting machinery. From April through September, the major lodges are generally open daily 9:30–12:30 and 2–6, although some close on weekends; the rest of the year, tours start a little later and end a little earlier. Tours begin regularly, usually when enough visitors are assembled. The tourist office at Vila Nova de Gaia offers a small map of the main lodges and can advise you on hours of the smaller operations. Some lodges also have restaurants with quite sophisticated menus; a prime example is Taylor's **Barão Fladgate** (✉ *Rua do Choupelo 250* ☎ *22/374–2800* 🌐 *www.tresseculos.pt*), whose location uphill means its garden and terrace afford magnificent views of Porto.

$$$ PORTUGUESE

🍴 **Chez Lapin.** At this Cais da Ribeira restaurant, the service may be slow and the folksy decora bit overdone, but this is definitely a step up from other touristy spots on the riverfront—the food is excellent and the location can't be beat. Grab a seat on the attractive outdoor terrace and order generous portions of such traditional Portuguese dishes as bacalhau *à lagareiro* (baked with potatoes), sardines with rice and beans, and beef medallions with port wine. The restaurant is mainly patronized by foreign visitors, so if you're after authentic Porto cuisine in a less touristy setting, look elsewhere. The family-owned company that owns the restaurant (Douro Acima) offers river excursions on its six traditional boats docked at the quay. [$] *Average main: €25* ✉ *Rua dos Canastreiros 40–42* ☎ *22/200–6418* 🌐 *www.issimo.pt* ✍ *Reservations essential.*

$$$$ PORTUGUESE

🍴 **Dom Tonho.** Seafood is the specialty of this riverfront restaurant owned by veteran musician and Porto native Rui Veloso, which occupies a beautiful and historic building that dates back to the 16th century. Try grilled fish, one of the codfish dishes, *lombo de veado* (loin of venison) or real local specialty *tripas à moda do Porto* (tripe stew with beans and vegetables). There's another Dom Tonho serving similar food just across the Dom Luís bridge in Gaia—affording amazing views of Porto itself. [$] *Average main: €40* ✉ *Cais da Ribeira 13–15* ☎ *22/200–4307* 🌐 *www.dtonho.com.*

$$$ PORTUGUESE

🍴 **O Escondidinho.** In business since 1934, this popular restaurant opened during the first great Portuguese Colonial Exhibition that took place in the Palácio de Cristal. Its long history is evident in the entrance, where hand-painted tiles from the 17th century announce a country-house decor. The menu has French-influenced dishes as well as creative Douro dishes. Steak is prepared no less than six ways (try the smoky version with truffles), and the sole—served with capers or port wine—is always deliciously fresh. The *pudim flan* (egg custard) and *toucinho do céu* (a similar dessert, but with almond and egg yolks) are excellent. [$] *Average main: €25* ✉ *Rua Passos Manuel 142* ☎ *22/200–1079, 93/310–1600* 🌐 *www.escondidinho.com.pt.*

$$$$ ASIAN FUSION Fodor's Choice ★

🍴 **Shis.** On a bluff high above the beach in Foz, you can hear the waves crash below as you dine on a mix of Japanese, Portuguese, and Mediterranean fusion dishes. The sushi menu is probably the most extensive in the city. Top appetizers include a goat cheese "nest" with pepper coulis, fish-and-seaweed soup, and miso with clams and tofu. Among the popular mains, consider chateaubriand with eggplant tempura and ginger sauce, and confit of bacalhau with spring greens and a rich Serra cheese sauce. There are also some very good pastas and risottos. [$] *Average main: €30* ✉ *Praia do Ourigo, Esplanada do Castelo, Foz* ☎ *96/135–6376* 🌐 *www.shisrestaurante.com* ✍ *Reservations essential.*

$$$ PORTUGUESE

🍴 **Tripeiro.** This spacious restaurant is a good place to try ubiquitous stews such as *tripas á moda do Porto* (tripe and beans) or the famous *cozido à portuguesa* (meat, cured sausage, and vegetables), which are nearly always on the menu in one form or another. In case you don't appreciate these, the menu has several meat and fish specialties, too. Along with the typically Portuguese food come typically Portuguese details: wooden ceiling beams, whitewashed walls, and potted plants add plenty of charm. Perhaps as a result, it tends to draw mainly tourists and indeed tour groups; if you want somewhere more favored by locals, head for Abadia do Porto. There's an adjacent bar where you can eat more cheaply. [$] *Average main: €25* ✉ *Rua Passos Manuel 195* ☎ *22/200–5886* 🌐 *www.restaurantetripeiro.com* 🕒 *No dinner Sun.*

WHERE TO STAY

$$ HOTEL

🏨 **Grande Hotel do Porto.** If you enjoy shopping, you can't do better than the stately Grande Hotel do Porto, as it sits on the city's best shopping street. **Pros:** good location; efficient staff; near public transportation. **Cons:** most rooms rather small; restaurant kitchen closes at 10 pm; room safe and Wi-Fi cost extra. [$] *Rooms from: €150* ✉ *Rua de Santa Catarina 197* ☎ *22/207–6690* 🌐 *www.grandehotelporto.com* 🛏 *94 rooms* 🍽 *Breakfast* [M] *Bolhão.*

$$$ HOTEL Fodor's Choice ★

🏨 **Infante Sagres.** Intricately carved wood details, rare area rugs and tapestries, stained-glass windows, and antiques decorate public areas in what on its inauguration in 1951 was Porto's first luxury hotel. **Pros:** oodles of style; central location; fine views from upper floors. **Cons:** no pool or gym; few in-room amenities; bathroom lighting more stylish than effective. [$] *Rooms from: €214* ✉ *Praça D. Filipa de Lencastre 62* ☎ *22/339–8500* 🌐 *www.hotelinfantesagres.pt* 🛏 *62 rooms, 8 suites* 🍽 *Multiple meal plans.*

$ HOTEL

🏨 **Hotel Mercure.** Overlooking one of Porto's central squares, the Praça da Batalha, this upscale chain property is a good choice for location and luxury at a reasonable price. **Pros:** free Wi-Fi; generous breakfast

688 < **Portugal**

included. **Cons:** outer rooms overlooking the square can be noisy on weekends. Ⓢ *Rooms from: €75* ✉ *Praca da Batalha 116* ☎ *22/204–3300* ⊕ *www.mercure.com* ⇨ *145 rooms* ⏻ *Breakfast.*

$$ ⊡ **Pestana Porto.** Right in Porto's historic heart, the Pestana Porto is
HOTEL in a restored former warehouse abutted by a medieval wall, linked to several neighboring former houses; as a result, every room is different and some are unusually shaped. **Pros:** charming historic building; well located for sightseeing in Ribeira and Gaia. **Cons:** few facilities; no restaurant (breakfast only); bus stop is up a steep hill. Ⓢ *Rooms from: €192* ✉ *Praça da Ribeira 1* ☎ *22/340–2300* ⊕ *www.pestana.com* ⇨ *45 rooms, 3 suites* ⏻ *Breakfast.*

$$ ⊡ **Sheraton Porto Hotel & Spa.** Seen by many as the city's top hotel, the
HOTEL Sheraton Porto's declared aim is to blend design and comfort. **Pros:**
FAMILY stunningly stylish; 24-hour luxury spa accessible via VIP lift; smoking
Fodor's Choice areas in bar and restaurant. **Cons:** a little far from center; only pricier
★ rooms have terraces; spa and Wi-Fi/Internet not included with standard room rate. Ⓢ *Rooms from: €120* ✉ *Rua Tenente Valadim 146, Boavista* ☎ *22/040–4000* ⊕ *www.sheratonporto.com* ⇨ *241 rooms, 25 suites* ⏻ *Multiple meal plans* Ⓜ *Francos.*

SHOPPING

The best shopping streets are those off the Praça da Liberdade, particularly Rua 31 de Janeiro, Rua dos Clérigos, Rua de Santa Catarina, Rua Sá da Bandeira, Rua Cedofeita, and Rua das Flores. Traditionally, Rua das Flores has been the street for silversmiths. Gold-plated filigree is also a regional specialty, found along the same street and along Rua de Santa Catarina. Rua 31 de Janeiro and nearby streets are the center of the shoe trade, and many shops create made-to-measure shoes on request.

You'll see port on sale throughout the city. But first taste the wine at either the Museu do Vinho do Porto or the caves at Vila Nova de Gaia. You may want to buy a bottle of the more unusual white port, drunk as an aperitif, as it's not commonly sold in North America or Britain. Try a Portonic, half-tonic water and half-white port served in a special glass that you'll see sold in most shops.

SCANDINAVIA AND THE BALTIC STATES

Denmark, Norway, Sweden,
Finland, Estonia, Latvia, Iceland

WHAT'S WHERE

1 Denmark. The Kingdom of Denmark dapples the Baltic Sea in an archipelago of some 450 islands and the arc of one peninsula. Coziness is a Danish trait, and you'll find lots of it in Copenhagen's canals, cafés, and narrow streets.

2 Norway. Long and narrow, Norway is about 30% clear lakes, lush forests, and rugged mountains. Oslo, the capital and eastern Norway's hub, has a population of about a half million and is a friendly, manageable city, where you can hike away the day and still make it back to town for a nightcap of aquavit.

3 Sweden. With 410,934 square km (158,662 square miles) for only 9 million residents, Sweden's inhabitants have plenty of elbow room. Even capital city Stockholm's 14 small islands—with their bustling boulevards and twisting medieval streets—don't seem too crowded.

4 Finland. One of the most sparsely populated countries in Europe, Finland's vast tracts of forest add to the feeling of remoteness in this northern land. The capital, Helsinki, shows the influence of both Swedish and Russian dominance.

5 Latvia. A compact little country, with more than one-third its population living in the capital Rīga, Latvia is inextricably linked to the Baltic Sea and the German merchants who founded it in the 11th century. In picturesque Rīga, baroque and art-nouveau buildings stand side-by-side along quaint cobbled streets and relaxing waterfront parks.

6 Estonia. With the oldest capital city in northern Europe, Estonia's history is rich and varied. Tallinn—or Reval as it was known for most of the last 600 years—first appeared on a map in 1154. For a city with such history, it has also been described as "as sort Silicon Valley of the Baltic Sea," as the city's modern business district will attest.

7 Iceland. The Land of Fire and Ice holds some of the most stunning and rugged landscape on the planet. The capital, Reykjavik, is the world's most northerly capital city and would barely rank as a city in the U.S. But people don't visit Iceland to see Reykjavik, they come to see its fjords, vast lava fields, erupting geysers and, mostly, dormant volcanoes.

Ísafjordhur

Siglufjordhur

REYKJAVIK
Akureyri

ICELAND

Selfoss

Neskaupstadhur

Arctic Circle

ATLANTIC OCEAN

Hardangerfjord

North Sea

KEY

 Cruise Port

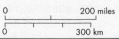

0   200 miles

0   300 km

Barents Sea

TO SVALBARD

Hammerfest

Alta ○   ○ Utsjöki

Karasjok ○

Kautokeino ○   ○ Inari

Tromsø

Harstad   Enonтeкiö ○

Narvik   ○ Muonio   **RUSSIA**

Kiruna ○   ○ Sodankylä

Bodø ○ ○ Fauske   Kemijärvi ○

Jokkmokk   ○ Rovaniemi

Mo i Rana ○   Arjeplog ○   Kalix   ○ Tornio

Mosjøen ○   Sorsele ○   Arvidsjaur ○   ○ Kemi   Pudasjärvi ○

○ Storuman   Piteå ○   Torneå ○

Skellefteå ○   Oulu ○

Lycksele ○   Raahe ○   Kuhmo ○

Pulkkila ○   Oulujärvi

Steinkjer ○   Strömsund ○   Umeå ○   Otanmäki ○   Nurmes ○

Kristiansund ○ Trondheim Meråker ○   **SWEDEN**   Häapajärvi ○   Iisalmi ○ Pielinen

Molde ○   Støren ○   **3**   Kyyjärvi ○   **FINLAND**

Ålesund   Vaasa ○   **4**

Honningsvåg   Oppdal ○ Tynset ○   Sundsvall ○   Seinäjoki ○   Äänekoski ○

Dombås ○   Idre ○   Parkano ○   Jyväskylä ○

Jotunheimen   Koppang ○   ○ Hudiksvall   Tampere ○   Heinola ○ Saimaa

NORWAY   Lillehammer ○ Mora ○   Bollnäs ○   Pori ○   Lahti ○   Kotka ○

Bergen   **2**   Hamar ○ Lake   Rauma ○   Porvoo ○

Voss ○   Geilo ○   Eidsvoll ○   Falun ○   Turku ○ Salo   **HELSINKI**   St. Petersburg

ugesund   Drammen ○ OSLO   Fagersta ○   Avesta ○

Kongsberg ○   Uppsala ○   **Gulf of Finland**

avanger Porsgrunn ○   Fredrikstad ○ Karlstad   Mälaren   **TALLINN**

Evje ○ Larvik ○   Halden ○   **STOCKHOLM**

ndnes   Grimstad ○ Arendal ○   Mellerud ○   Nynäshamn ○   Hiiumaa   **ESTONIA**   **RUSSIA**

Uddevalla ○   Norrköping ○   Baltic   **6**   Pskov

Kristiansand ○   Trollhättan ○   Linköping ○   Sea   Saaremaa

Skagen ○   **Göteborg**   Jönköping ○   Slite ○

Aalborg ○   Borås ○   **Visby**   **RIGA**

Thisted ○   Falkenberg ○   Oskarshamn ○   Gotland   **LATVIA**

DENMARK   Halmstad ○   Kalmar ○   Liepaja ○   **5**

1   Silkeborg ○ **Århus** Helsingborg ○   Karlskrona ○

Esbjerg ○ Fredericia ○   Kristianstad ○

Ribe ○   **COPENHAGEN**   Klaipeda ○   **LITHUANIA**

Flensburg   Malmö ○ Ystad ○

Nakskov ○   Bornholm   **POLAND**   **RUSSIA**   Vilnius ○   **BELARUS**

Norwegian Sea

Skagerrak   *Kattegat*

Barents Sea

NEED TO KNOW

AT A GLANCE

Capitals: Copenhagen, Stockholm, Oslo, Helsinki, Rīga, Tallinn, and Reykjavik

Population: 30,000,000

Currency: See countries

Money: ATMs are common; euro widely accepted

Languages: English widely spoken in Scandinavia, less so in Latvia and Estonia

Country Code: See countries

Emergencies: See countries

Driving: On the right

Electricity: 200v/50 cycles; plus two round prongs

Time: Iceland 4 hours ahead of New York; Denmark, Sweden, Norway 5 hours ahead; Finland, Latvia, 6 hours

Documents: Up to 90 days with valid passport; Schengen rules apply

Mobile Phones: GSM (900 and 1800 bands)

Major Mobile Companies: See countries

WEBSITES

Each country has its own tourism website (see countries)

GETTING AROUND

✈ **Air Travel:** The region's major airports are Copenhagen (CPH), Oslo (OSL), Stockholm-Arland (ARN), Helsinki (HEL), and Reykjavik (RKV); there are also airports in Bergen, Gothenberg, Rīga, and Tallinn.

🚌 **Bus Travel:** Pretty good in general: smaller towns in Estonia and Latvia have less frequent bus service.

🚗 **Car Travel:** Roads are good across the region, especially in Scandinavia. Gas is very expensive in Norway.

🚆 **Train Travel:** Good rail systems link major cities, and commuter trains serve smaller towns. Iceland has no public rail system.

PLAN YOUR BUDGET

	HOTEL ROOM	MEAL	ATTRACTIONS
Low Budget	700 DKK (Copenhagen) –42 (Tallinn)	€12 (Helsinki)–€18 (Riga)	National Gallery of Denmark, free
Mid Budget	€110 (Tallinn)–1,050 SEK (Stockholm)	200 SEK (Stockholm)–€25 (Helsinki)	Iceland Northern Lights Tour, 5,300 ISK
High Budget	1,850 NOK (Oslo)–32,000 ISK (Reykjavik)	960 NOK (Oslo)–€90 (Helsinki)	North Zealand Tour, 560 DKK

WAYS TO SAVE

Rent a bike. Copenhagen, Stockholm, Helsinki, and Oslo are very bicycle-friendly.

Early evening tipple. Alcohol in bars is particularly expensive in Sweden, Iceland, and Norway. Buy a bottle and drink up before going out.

Dine al fresco. The region has great parks. Buy a picnic from one of the many outdoor markets.

PLAN YOUR TIME

Hassle Factor	Low—to Sweden, Denmark, Norway, Finland, and Iceland, to which nonstop flights from the U.S. are frequent. Medium—to Estonia and Latvia, which require connections.
3 days	Take your pick. Any of these northern capitals is easy to cover in two or three days.
1 week	You can easily combine two or even three cities. Helsinki, Tallinn, and Stockholm are easily linked by ferry. Copenhagen to Oslo is a quick flight.
2 weeks	After a short stopover in Reykjavik, you could easily continue to visit two or three additional northern capitals or add a coastal cruise in Norway.

WHEN TO GO

High Season: June and July are peak months, but don't fear the insane chaos of southern Europe's beaches. Many locals head to the country during these months, so though the weather will generally be quite good, the atmosphere in the cities remains relaxed.

Low Season: The relatively temperate climate, at least in relation to cities in Canada and Russia at the same latitude, means January and February will be picture-postcard snowy without the biting Arctic cold.

Value Season: August and September aren't as busy as in earlier in the summer. Mean temperatures of 60°F will empty the beaches, but the towns and cities around the region are still vibrant at this time of year.

BIG EVENTS

May: May 1 is marked across the region and in Sweden. May Day Eve is celebrated as Walpurgis Night with bonfires, a truly Nordic tradition. ⊕ www.sweden.se

June: The second week in June sees Helsinki Week kick off, with Helsinki Day on June 12th. ⊕ www.helsinkiviikko.fi

October/November: The Copenhagen Autumn Jazz Festival runs for four days. ⊕ www.jazz.dk

December/January: Rīga's Christmas Tree Festival continues a 600-year-old custom. ⊕ www.latvia.travel/en

READ THIS

■ *Here under the North Star,* Väinö Linna. Epic tale of three generations of a Finnish family.

■ *Purge,* Sofi Oksanen. A gritty, yet tender tale of Estonian life under communism.

■ *Sophie's World,* Jostein Gaarder. A Norwegian teen embraces philosophy.

WATCH THIS

■ *Fanny and Alexander.* Trials and tribulations of the Swedish upper classes.

■ *Cold Fever.* A Japanese businessman's hilarious road trip across Iceland.

■ *After the Wedding.* A Danish ex-pat's awkward return home.

EAT THIS

■ **Baltic herring:** There are a hundred ways to prepare this fish, and every one is worth a try.

■ **Gravlax:** salmon cured in salt, sugar, and dill

■ **Rye bread:** a dark and hard bread

■ **Pulla/Bulle:** a Finnish and Swedish sweet roll flavored with cardamom

■ **Coffee:** The Nordic countries drink it morning, noon, and night.

■ **Moose:** During hunting season game is popular. (Reindeer is equally delicious.)

Scandinavia and the Baltic States are inescapably intercon-nected by the sea. From Norway, the seafaring adventurer Ingólfur Arnarson settled Reykjavik more than a thousand years ago, giving rise to Iceland's current population. The Danish Viking raiders in their flat-bottomed longboats founded Ireland's capital Dublin and gave their name to France's Normandy. The ambitious Swedes, whose capi-tal city of Stockholm hosts the remains of the *Vasa*—prob-ably the best-preserved 17th-century warship in the world. Some of the largest cruise ships in the world have been built in Finland in recent years. Estonia's capital, Tallinn, was founded by German merchant knights in the 13th century for its coastal position and closeness to ports across the Bal-tic Sea. Rīga has for centuries been a warm-water harbor and haven for ships when the Baltic freezes during winter. All these countries are surrounded by the sea and immersed in its history.

These days Vikings no longer pillage coastal cities across Europe, and the Teutonic Knights are a peaceful religious order, but the influence of the sea is everywhere in these northern lands. The very fjords from where Norwegian raiders sailed now host whale-spotting tours. The islands of Stockholm harbor—where the mighty *Vasa* floundered in 1628—throng with locals and visitors alike, enjoying the sunshine and sailing pleasure craft. Copenhagen's waterfronts and promenades, with their many bicycles and cafés, might recall a less crowded and classier Amsterdam. The impressive Suomenlinna Fortress, once built to defend Helsinki against seaborne attack, is now a UNESCO World Heritage Site visited by nearly a million tourists and locals alike each year. Tal-linn and Rīga, with their medieval old towns, are still important trading ports but are now just as well known as thriving centers of finance and information technology.

It is perhaps this ability to mesh modern and extremely advanced soci-eties seamlessly into thousand-year-old history that marks these north states as special. And though they are very different in character, they each stand among cities consistently ranked as some of the best in the world to live in. The scenery and natural beauty of the region have been preserved in many areas almost exactly as they were when Vikings set out to devastate Europe. An openness to trade and new ideas make

TOP REASONS TO GO

Great Food (Sweden): Industry investment, the finest raw ingredients, and a thirst for the exotic have seen new Swedish cuisine become competitive with the absolute best of Europe's kitchens.

The Great Outdoors (Sweden): The right to roam freely is part of the Swedish constitution, and a couple of days right in Stockholm's archipelago is hard to beat.

Modern Design (Denmark): Denmark's capital is *the* place to experience one of the nation's top exports—in museums like the Dansk Design Center and in shops like Bang & Olufsen, Royal Copenhagen, and Georg Jensen.

Tivoli Gardens (Denmark): It's filled with amusements, restaurants, and people-watching ops. Visit twice: once by day and once by night.

The Fjords (Norway): The Norwegian fjords are known for their beauty, and should top your agenda. One of the most accessible is the Oslofjord, which runs south from Oslo to the sea and is abuzz with locals and visitors all summer long.

City Skiing (Norway): Whether you're after miles upon miles of well-lighted cross-country skiing trails or just some time on a ski simulator at Holmenkollen, Oslo's the place to base yourself.

The Blue Lagoon (Iceland): Perhaps the most famous geothermal spa in the world is just 40 minutes' drive from Reykjavik. Mineral-rich waters heated from the core of the planet are the reason thousands come to soak in the legendary Blue Lagoon.

A Midnight Film Festival (Finland): When the sun never sets in northern Finland, the Midnight Sun Film Festival in Sodankylä is the place to be. The festival shows movies 24 hours a day from guest directors, including Francis Ford Coppola and Terry Gilliam over the years.

A Historic City (Estonia): The old town of Tallinn is a UNESCO World Heritage Site. Its medieval buildings and thick defensive walls can quickly remove you to a bygone time when Germanic knights on horseback cantered down its cobbled streets.

Pristine Forests (Latvia): Rīga may well be the largest and most bustling city in the Baltic States, but Gauja National Park to the city's northeast is a place of breathtaking beauty and worth a visit by hardcore trekkers and novices alike.

15

these destinations that will leave a permanent and pleasant impression on any visitor.

COPENHAGEN

The Kingdom of Denmark is the geographical link between Scandinavia and Europe. Half-timber villages and tidy farms rub shoulders with towns and a few cities, where pedestrians set the pace, not traffic. In the capital, Copenhagen—København in Danish—mothers safely park baby carriages outside bakeries while outdoor cafés fill with cappuccino-sippers, and lanky Danes pedal to work in lanes thick with bicycle traffic. The town was a fishing colony until 1157, when Valdemar the Great gave it to Bishop Absalon, who built a castle on the site of what is now the parliament, Christiansborg. It grew as a center on the Baltic trade route and became known as *købmændenes havn* (merchants' harbor) and eventually København.

In the 15th century it became the royal residence and the capital of Norway and Sweden. From 1596 to 1648 Christian IV, a Renaissance king obsessed with fine architecture, began a building boom that crowned the city with towers and castles, many of which still stand. They're almost all that remain of the city's 800-year history; much of Copenhagen was destroyed by two major fires in the 18th century and by British bombing during the Napoleonic Wars.

Today's Copenhagen has no glittering skylines and little of the high-stress bustle of most capitals. The morning air in the pedestrian streets of the city's core is redolent of baked bread and soap-scrubbed storefronts. If there's such a thing as a cozy city, this is it.

PLANNING

PLANNING YOUR TIME

With just one day in Copenhagen, start at Kongens Nytorv and Nyhavn and walk along the pedestrian street of Strøget in the direction of Rådhus Pladsen. You can see Christiansborg and/or Rosenborg Slot along the way. If you're not up for a walk, one of the guided canal tours will give you a good sense of the city. In summer or around Christmastime, round off your day with a relaxed stroll and nightcap in Tivoli.

With additional days, plan to spend time inside one or more of the following: Nationalmuseet, Dansk Design Center, Statens Museum for Kunst, and Kastellet. You could also head over to Christianshavn, for its café-lined canals and for Christiania, with its hippie culture.

GETTING HERE AND AROUND

AIR TRAVEL

Kastrup International Airport (CPH), 10 km (6 miles) from the center of Copenhagen, is Denmark's air hub. SAS, the main carrier, flies nonstop from several North American cities. The 20-minute taxi ride from the airport to downtown costs DKr 190–250. A sleek subterranean train zips you from the airport to the city's main train station in about 14 minutes. Buy a ticket (DKr 28.50) upstairs in the airport train station at Terminal 3.

Contacts Copenhagen Airport, Kastrup (*CPH*). ☎ (45) 32/31–32–31 ⊕ *www. cph.dk.*

BOAT TRAVEL

DFDS also sails to Oslo from Copenhagen. Fjord Line is another company with service between Denmark and Norway. Scandlines connects Denmark with Sweden and Germany. The Eurail Scandinavia Pass, for travel anywhere within Scandinavia (Denmark, Sweden, Norway, and Finland), is valid on some ferry crossings.

DENMARK AT A GLANCE

■ **Capital:** Copenhagen

■ **Population:** 5,603,000

■ **Currency:** Krone

■ **Money:** ATMs are common, euros widely accepted

■ **Language:** Danish

■ **Country Code:** ☎ 45

■ **Emergencies:** ☎ 112

■ **Driving:** On the right

■ **Electricity:** 200v/50 cycles; electrical plugs have two round prongs

■ **Time:** Five hours ahead of New York

■ **Documents:** Up to 90 days with valid passport; Schengen rules apply

■ **Mobile Phones:** GSM (900 and 1800 bands)

■ **Major Mobile Companies:** TDC, Telia, Telenor and 3

15

Contacts DFDS Seaways ⊕ *www.dfds.com.* **Fjord Lines** ⊕ *www.fjordline.com.* **Scandlines** ⊕ *www.scandlines.dk.*

PUBLIC TRANSPORTATION

Within Copenhagen, Metro trains and buses operate from 5 am (Sunday 6 am) to midnight. Night buses run every half hour from 1 am to 4:30 am from the main bus station at Rådhus Pladsen to most areas. Trains and buses operate on the same ticket system and divide Copenhagen and surrounding areas into three zones. Unlimited travel within two zones (inner city area) for one hour costs DKr 20 for an adult. A discount *klippe kort* (clip card), good for 10 rides, costs DKr 125 for two zones. The card must be stamped in the automatic ticket machines on buses or at stations. (If you don't stamp your clip card, you can be fined up to DKr 600.) Cards can be stamped multiple times for multiple passengers and/or longer rides.

The harbor buses are small ferries that travel along the canal, with stops along the way. The boats are a great way to sightsee and get around the city. They run from 7 am to 11 pm (10 am to 11 pm on weekends). Standard bus fares and tickets apply.

The Metro system runs from 5 am to midnight, and all night on weekends. There are currently two Metro lines in operation. The major Metro hubs in central Copenhagen are Noøreport Station and Kongens Nytorv. Stations are marked with a dark-red Metro logo.

TAXI TRAVEL

The computer-metered Mercedes and Volvo cabs aren't cheap. The base charge is DKr 24–40, plus DKr 11.50–15.80 per kilometer, depending on the hour. A cab is available when it displays the sign *Fri* (free); you can hail cabs, pick them up at stands, or call for one (more expensive). The latter option is your best bet outside the city center.

Contacts Amager Øbro Taxi ☎ *35/51–51–51* ⊕ *www.amagerobrotaxi.dk.* **Koøbenhavns Taxa** ☎ *35/35–35–35.*

TRAIN TRAVEL

Copenhagen's Hovedbanegården (Central Station) is the hub of the DSB rail network and is connected to most major cities in Europe. Intercity trains run regularly (usually every hour) from 6 am to midnight for principal towns in Funen and Jutland.

HOTELS

Copenhagen has a variety of hotel options, but rates are consistently high side and rooms are small. The city has increased its capacity with new design hotels, a luxury all-suite hotel in Tivoli Gardens, and a youth hostel in the city center. Many existing properties have undergone renovation that allows for eco-friendly, sustainable business practices. Note that in Copenhagen, as in the rest of Denmark, most rooms have only showers (while some have showers and tubs); state your preference when booking.

RESTAURANTS

Copenhagen has experienced a gastronomical revolution over the past decade. A rising interest in new Nordic cooking emphasizes using locally sourced raw materials and high-quality seasonal ingredients. Wild game, cured or smoked fish and meats, Limfjord oysters, Læsø langoustine, eel, and plaice are a few examples.

There's also been a revival of authentic Danish fare. Most such meals begin with *sild,* pickled herring of various flavors, served on *rugbrød,* a very dark and dense rye-based bread. This bread is also the basis for *smørrebrød*—open-face sandwiches piled high with various meats, vegetables, and condiments. For dinner, try *flæskesteg,* pork roast with a crispy rind, which is commonly served with *rødkål,* stewed red cabbage, and potatoes.

There are plenty of bistros serving moderately priced meals, and for inexpensive savory noshes in stylish surroundings, consider lingering in a café. Many restaurants offer fixed-priced meals with wine-pairing menus, and most restaurants require reservations. Many restaurants tack a surcharge of between 3.75% and 5.75% onto the bill for the use of foreign credit cards.

HOTEL AND RESTAURANT PRICES

Prices in the restaurant reviews are the average cost of a main course at dinner or, if dinner is not served, at lunch; taxes and service charges are generally included. Prices in the hotel reviews are the lowest cost of a standard double room in high season, excluding taxes, service charges, and meal plans.

VISITOR INFORMATION

Contacts **Danmarks Turistråd** (*Danish Tourist Board*). ☎ *32/88–99–00, 212/885–9700 in New York* ⊕ *www.visitdenmark.com.* **Scandinavian Tourist Board** ⊕ *www.goscandinavia.com.* **Copenhagen Visitor's Centre** ⊠ *Vesterbrog. 4A, Vesterbro* ☎ *70/22–24–42* ⊕ *visitcopenhagen.com.*

EXPLORING

Be it sea or canal, water surrounds Copenhagen. A network of bridges and drawbridges connects the two main islands—Zealand and Amager—on which Copenhagen is built. The seafaring atmosphere is indelible, especially around the districts of Nyhavn and Christianshavn.

Copenhagen is small, with most sights within 2½ square km (1 square mile) at its center. Sightseeing, especially downtown, is best done on foot. Or follow the example of the Danes and rent a bike.

CENTRUM

Centrum (central Copenhagen, aka downtown and city center) is packed with shops, restaurants, and businesses, as well as the crowning architectural achievements of Christian IV. Its boundaries roughly match the fortified borders under his reign (1588–1648), when the city was surrounded by fortified walls and moats.

Centrum is cut by the city's pedestrian spine, called Strøget (pronounced *stroy*-et), Europe's longest pedestrian shopping street (about 2 km [1 mile]). It's actually a series of five streets: Frederiksberggade, Nygade, Vimmelskaftet, Amagertorv, and Østergade. By mid-morning, particularly on Saturday, it's congested with people, baby strollers, and motionless-until-paid mimes. To the north of Strøget, you will find smaller, more peaceful shopping streets.

Fodor's Choice **Christiansborg Slot.** Surrounded by canals on three sides, the massive granite Christiansborg Castle is where the queen officially receives guests. From 1441 until the fire of 1795, it was used as the royal residence. Even though the first two castles on the site were burned, Christiansborg remains an impressive neobaroque and neoclassical compound. It now houses parliament and the prime minister's office. ⊠ *Slotsholmen, (area around Christiansborg, bordered by Boørsgade, Vindebrogade, and Frederiksholms Kanal), Centrum.*

Kongelige Repræsantationslokaler (*Royal Reception Chambers*). At the Kongelige Repræsentationslokaler, you're asked to don slippers to protect the floors in this impossibly grand space. ⊠ *Christiansborg Slot, Slotsholmen, Centrum* ☎ *33/92–64–92* 🖭 *DKr 70* ⊙ *Tours May–Sept., daily at 3; Oct.–Apr., Tues.–Sun. at 3.*

Ruins of Bishop Absalon's castle. While Christiansborg was being rebuilt around 1900, the national museum excavated the ruins of Bishop Absalon's castle beneath it. The resulting dark, subterranean maze contains fascinating models and architectural relics. ⊠ *Christiansborg Slot, Slotsholmen* ☎ *33/92–64–92* 🖭 *DKr 40* ⊙ *May–Sept., daily 10–5; Oct.–Apr., Tues.–Sun., 10–5.*

Kongelige Bibliotek (*Royal Library*). If you like grand architecture and great views, you really should visit the majestic Royal Library. Among its more than 2 million volumes are accounts of Viking journeys to America and Greenland and original manuscripts by Hans Christian Andersen and Karen Blixen (Isak Dinesen). Peer through the glass opening in the door to the old, ornate reading room, which is open only to readers.

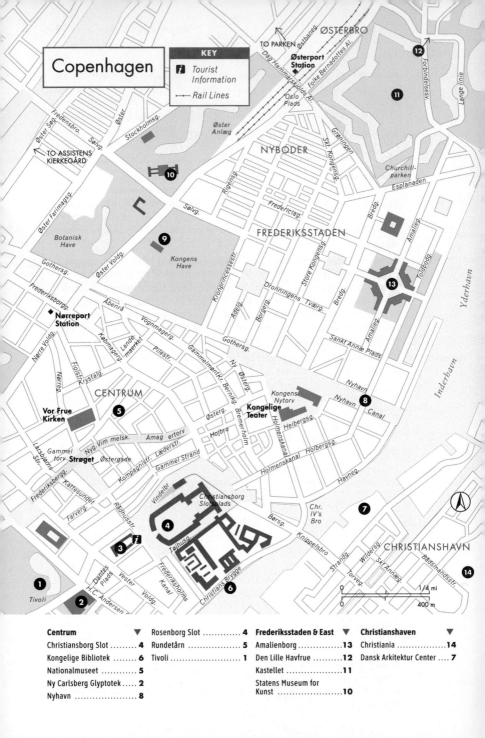

Copenhagen

KEY

i Tourist Information

➞ Rail Lines

ØSTERBRO

TO PARKEN

Østerport Station

Oslo Plads

Øster Anlæg

NYBODER

Churchill-parken

Esplanaden

FREDERIKSSTADEN

TO ASSISTENS KIERKEGÅRD

Botanisk Have

Kongens Have

Nørreport Station

CENTRUM

Vor Frue Kirken

Strøget

Kongens Nytorv

Kongelige Teater

Nyhavn

Christiansborg Slotsplads

Chr. IV's Bro

CHRISTIANSHAVN

Tivoli

1/4 mi

400 m

Escalators that lift you from sea level to the main study areas provide spectacular views of both the harbor and an impressive ceiling mural by the Danish artist Per Kirkeby. The park that lies between the library and the parliament is a lovely place for a stroll or a pensive rest. ⊠ *Søren Kierkegaards Pl. 1, Centrum* ☎ *33/47–47–47* ⊕ *www.kb.dk* ⊠ *Library free, temporary exhibits DKr 40* ☉ *Museum weekdays and Sat. 10–7.*

FAMILY

Fodor'sChoice

★

Nationalmuseet (*National Museum*). One of the best museums of its kind in Europe, the Nationalmuseet is inside a 18th-century royal residence that's peaked by massive overhead windows. Extensive permanent exhibits chronicle Danish cultural history from prehistoric to modern times. The museum has one of the largest collections of Stone Age tools in the world, as well as Egyptian, Greek, and Roman antiquities. The exhibit on Danish prehistory features a great section on Viking times. The children's museum, with replicas of period clothing and a scalable copy of a real Viking ship, makes history fun for those under 12. Displays have English labels, and the do-it-yourself walking tour "History of Denmark in 60 Minutes" offers a good introduction to Denmark; the guide is free at the information desk. ⊠ *Frederiksholms Kanal 12, Centrum* ☎ *33/13–44–11* ⊕ *www.natmus.dk* ⊠ *Free* ☉ *Tues.–Sun. 10–5.*

Ny Carlsberg Glyptotek. The exquisite antiquities and a world-class collection of impressionist masterpieces make this one of Copenhagen's most important museums. The neoclassical building was donated in 1888 by Carl Jacobsen, son of the founder of the Carlsberg Brewery. Surrounding its lush indoor garden, a series of rooms house works by Pissarro, Degas, Monet, Sisley, Rodin, and Gauguin. The museum is also renowned for its extensive assemblage of Egyptian and Greek pieces, not to mention Europe's finest collection of Roman portraits and the best collection of Etruscan art outside Italy. A modern wing, designed by the acclaimed Danish architect Henning Larsen, provides a luminous entry to the French painting section. ⊠ *Dantes Pl. 7, Centrum* ☎ *33/41–81–41* ⊕ *www.glyptoteket.dk* ⊠ *DKr 50 (free on Sun.)* ☉ *Tues.–Sun. 11–5.*

Nyhavn (*New Harbor*). This harborfront neighborhood was built 300 years ago to attract traffic and commerce to the city center. Until 1970 the area was a favorite haunt of sailors. Though restaurants, boutiques, and antiques stores now outnumber tattoo parlors, many old buildings have been well preserved and retain the harbor's authentic 18th-century maritime character; you can even see a fleet of old-time sailing ships from the quay. Hans Christian Andersen lived at various times in the Nyhavn houses at numbers 18, 20, and 67.

Fodor'sChoice

★

Rosenborg Slot. The Dutch Renaissance Rosenborg Castle contains ballrooms, halls, and reception chambers, but for all of its grandeur there's an intimacy that makes you think the king might return any minute. Thousands of objects are displayed, including beer glasses, gilded clocks, golden swords, family portraits, a pearl-studded saddle, and gem-encrusted tables; the underground treasury contains the crown jewels. The castle's setting is equally welcoming: it's in the middle of the Kongens Have (King's Garden), amid lawns, park benches, and shady walking paths.

15

King Christian IV built Rosenborg Castle as a summer residence but loved it so much that he ended up living here until his death. In 1849, when the absolute monarchy was abolished, all the royal castles became state property, except for Rosenborg, which is still passed down from monarch to monarch. ⊠ *Øster Voldgade 4A, Centrum* ☎ *33/15–32–86* ⊕ *www.dkks.dk* ✉ *DKr 80* ⊘ *Castle and Treasury: June–Aug., daily 10–5; Sept.–Oct., daily 10–4. Castle Nov.–mid-Dec., Tues.–Sun. 11–2. Treasury Nov.–mid-Dec., Tues.–Sun. 11–4.*

Rundetårn (*Round Tower*). Instead of climbing the stout Round Tower's stairs, visitors scale a smooth, 600-foot spiral ramp. Supposedly, Peter the Great of Russia once ascended this ramp on a horse alongside his wife, Catherine, who took a carriage. From its top, you enjoy a panoramic view of the twisted streets and crooked roofs of Copenhagen. The unusual building was constructed as an observatory in 1642 by Christian IV and is still maintained as Europe's oldest such structure. ⊠ *Købmagergade 52A, Centrum* ☎ *33/73–03–73* ⊕ *www.rundetaarn. dk* ✉ *DKr 25* ⊘ *Sept. 21–May 20, daily 10–5; May 21–Sept. 20, daily 10–8. Observatory mid-Oct.–mid-Mar., Tues. and Wed. 7 pm–10 pm.*

FAMILY
Fodor's Choice
★

Tivoli. Copenhagen's best-known attraction, conveniently next to its main train station, attracts an astounding 4 million people from mid-April to mid-September. Tivoli is more than just an amusement park: among its attractions are a pantomime theater, an open-air stage, 38 restaurants (some of them very elegant), and frequent concerts, which cover the spectrum from classical to rock to jazz. Fantastic flower exhibits color the lush gardens and float on the swan-filled ponds.

The park was established in the 1840s, when Danish architect George Carstensen persuaded a worried King Christian VIII to let him build an amusement park on the edge of the city's fortifications, reasoning that "when people amuse themselves, they forget politics." The Tivoli Guard, a youth version of the Queen's Royal Guard, performs every day. Try to see Tivoli at least once by night, when 100,000 colored lanterns illuminate the Chinese pagoda and the main fountain. Some evenings there are also fireworks displays. Call to check the season's opening and closing dates as well as family discounts. Tivoli is also open select hours around Halloween and from mid-November until late December. ⊠ *Vesterbrog. 3, on border of Vesterbro district, Centrum* ☎ *33/15–10–01* ⊕ *www.tivoli.dk* ✉ *Grounds DKr 95, unlimited ride pass DKr 199* ⊘ *Apr.–Sept., Sun.–Thurs. 11–10 or 11 pm, Fri. 11 am–12:30 am, Sat. 11–midnight.*

FREDERIKSSTADEN AND EAST

Northeast of Kongens Nytorv is the posh thoroughfare of Bredgade, which intersects Frederiksstaden, a royal quarter commissioned by Frederik V in the mid-1700s. It's home to the castle of Amalienborg. Time your visit with the noon changing of the guard. The old sailors' neighborhood of Nyboder is west of the fortification of Kastellet.

Amalienborg. The four identical rococo buildings occupying this square have housed royals since 1784. It's still the queen's winter residence. The Christian VIII palace across from the royal's wing houses the Amalienborg Museum, which displays the second part of the Royal Collection (the first is at Rosenborg Slot) and chronicles royal lifestyles between 1863 and 1947. Here you can view the study of King Christian IX (1818–1906) and the drawing room of his wife, Queen Louise. Rooms are packed with royal heirlooms and treasures.

In the square's center is a magnificent equestrian statue of King Frederik V by the French sculptor Jacques François Joseph Saly. It reputedly cost as much as all the buildings combined. Every day at noon, the Royal Guard and band march from Rosenborg Slot through the city for the changing of the guard. At noon on Queen Margrethe's birthday, April 16, crowds of Danes gather to cheer their monarch, who stands and waves from her balcony. On Amalienborg's harbor side is the garden of Amaliehaven, at the foot of which the queen's ship often docks. ⊠ *Christian VIII's Palace, Amalienborg Pl., Frederiksberg* ☎ *33/12–21–86* ⊕ *dkks.dk/amalienborgmuseet* ⊠ *Museum DKr 65* ⊙ *Museum May–Oct., daily 10–4; Nov.–Dec., Tues.–Sun. 11–4.*

Den Lille Havfrue (*The Little Mermaid*). Somewhat overhyped, this 1913 statue commemorates Hans Christian Andersen's lovelorn Little Mermaid. Donated to the city by Carl Jacobsen, the son of the founder of Carlsberg Breweries, the innocent waif has also been the subject of some cruel practical jokes, including decapitation and the loss of an arm, but she's currently in one piece. The Langelinie promenade is thronged with Danes and visitors making their pilgrimage to the statue, especially on sunny Sundays. Although the statue itself is modest, the views of the surrounding harbor are not. ⊠ *Langelinie promenade, Østerbro.*

Kastellet. At the end of Amaliegade, the beautiful Churchill Park surrounds the spired Anglican church St. Alban's. From here, walk north on the main path to reach the fortification of Kastellet. The peaceful walking paths, grazing sheep, and greenery welcome joggers and lovebirds to this still-operative military structure. Built in the aftermath of the Swedish siege of the city on February 10, 1659, the double moats were among the improvements made to the city's defense. The Citadel served as the city's main fortress into the 18th century; in a grim reversal during World War II, the Germans used it as headquarters during their occupation. ⊠ *Kastellet 68, Østerbro* ⊠ *Free* ⊙ *Daily 6 am–10 pm.*

FAMILY **Statens Museum for Kunst.** Old-master paintings—including works by Rubens, Rembrandt, Titian, El Greco, and Fragonard—as well as a comprehensive array of antique and 20th-century Danish art make up the National Art Gallery collection. Also notable is the modern art, which includes pieces by Henri Matisse, Edvard Munch, Henri Laurens, Emil Nolde, and Georges Braque. The space also contains a children's museum, which puts on shows for different age groups at kids' eye-level. Wall texts are in English. The bookstore and café are also worth a visit. ⊠ *Sølvgade 48–50, Østerbro* ☎ *33/74–84–94* ⊕ *www.smk.dk* ⊠ *Free, special exhibitions DKr 110* ⊙ *Tues. and Thurs.–Sun. 10–5, Wed. 10–8.*

CHRISTIANSHAVN

Across the capital's main harbor, Inderhavn, is Christianshavn. In the early 1600s this area was mostly a series of shallows between land, which were eventually dammed. Today Christianshavn's colorful boats, cobbled avenues, antique street lamps, shops, and cafés make it one of

15

the toniest parts of town. Its ramparts are edged with green areas and walking paths, making it the perfect neighborhood for an afternoon or evening amble. To get here, walk from the Christiansborg area in Centrum across the Knippelsbro Bridge.

Christiania. If you're nostalgic for 1960s counterculture, head to this anarchists' commune. You can walk here from Christianshavn: take Torvegade and make a left on Prinsessegade, which takes you to the main gate. You can also take Bus No. 2A from Rådhuspladsen, Tivoli, Christiansborg, and Christianshavn Station. Founded in 1971, when students occupied army barracks, it's now a peaceful community of nonconformists who run a number of businesses, including a bike shop, a rock-music club, and good organic eateries. Wall cartoons preach drugs and peace, but the inhabitants are less fond of cameras—photography is forbidden. A group of residents recount their experiences as well as the history of Christiania on daily English-language tours conducted weekends year-round and daily June 26 through August 31. Tours depart at 3 from the main gate and are 1- to 1½-hours long. They cost DKr 40 per person and are a great way to discover the nooks and crannies of this quirky community. ✉ *Prinsessegade and Bådsmansstr., Christianshavn* ☎ *32/57–96–70 for guided tours* 🌐 *www.christiania.org.*

Dansk Arkitektur Center. The Danish Architecture Center occupies an old wharf-side warehouse built in 1880. The center hosts rotating exhibitions that cover trends and trendsetters in architecture and architectural design. The displays are labeled in English, and the museum's website has a guide for discovering noteworthy architecture in Denmark's major cities. ✉ *Strandgade 27B, Christianshavn* ☎ *32/57–19–30* 🌐 *www.dac.dk* 🎟 *DKr 40 (free Wed. 5–9 pm), exhibitions vary* ⏲ *Daily 10–5.*

WHERE TO EAT

CENTRUM

$ SCANDINAVIAN

🍴 **Ida Davidsen.** This five-generations-old, world-renowned lunch spot is synonymous with *smørrebrød,* the Danish open-face sandwich. The often-packed dining area is dimly lighted, with worn wooden tables and news clippings of famous visitors on the walls. Creative sandwiches include the H. C. Andersen, with liver pâté, bacon, and tomatoes. The terrific duck is smoked by Ida's husband, Adam, and served alongside a horseradish-spiked cabbage salad. [$] *Average main: Dkr 200* ✉ *Store Kongensgade 70, Centrum* ☎ *33/91–36–55* 🌐 *www.idadavidsen.dk* ✍ *Reservations essential* ⏲ *Closed weekends and July. No dinner.*

$$ FRENCH
Fodor's Choice ★

🍴 **Le Sommelier.** The grande dame of Copenhagen's French restaurants is appropriately named. The cellar boasts more than 800 varieties of wine, and you can order many of them by the glass—with or without the help of a sommelier. Exquisite French dishes are complemented by an elegant interior of off-white walls, rough-hewn wooden floors, brass chandeliers, and hanging copper pots. Dishes include guinea fowl in a foie-gras sauce or lamb shank and crispy sweetbreads with parsley and garlic. While waiting for your table, head to the burnished dark-wood and brass bar to begin sampling the wine. [$] *Average main: Dkr 225*

✉ *Bredgade 63–65, Centrum* ☎ *33/11–45–15* 🌐 *www.lesommelier.dk* 🕒 *No lunch weekends.*

$ BISTRO 🍴 **Peder Oxe.** On a 17th-century square, this lively, countrified bistro has rustic tables and 15th-century Portuguese tiles. All entrées—among them grilled steaks, fish, and the best burgers in town—come with salad from the excellent self-service bar. Tables are set with simple white linens, heavy cutlery, and opened bottles of hearty French wine. A clever call-light for the waitress is above each table. In spring, when the high northern sun is shining but the warmth still hasn't kicked in, you won't do badly sitting outside in the Gråbrødretorv (Gray Friars' Square) sipping drinks wrapped in one of the blankets left out on the wicker chairs. [$] *Average main: Dkr 195* ✉ *Gråbrødretorv 11, Centrum* ☎ *33/11–00–77* 🌐 *www.pederoxe.dk.*

FREDERIKSSTADEN

$$$$ SCANDINAVIAN Fodor's Choice ★ 🍴 **Geranium.** Don't be put off by the fact that Geranium is located in Parken, Denmark's national football (soccer) stadium; this modern northern European kitchen gives Noma a run for its money. Chefs Rasmus Kofoed and Søren Ledet put a modern touch on classic Scandinavian cooking by using molecular gastronomy and other advanced techniques. They source products from biodynamic farmers (that is, those who follow a system of organic and holistic cultivation) to create vegetable-centric masterpieces. A seven-course menu might include venison covered with a thin layer of smoked lard and served with beets, mushrooms, and forest herbs. For dessert, there's elderberry jelly. An organic vegetarian menu and individual courses are also on offer. All menus can be enjoyed with wine or juice pairings, for an extra charge. [$] *Average main: Dkr 698* ✉ *Per Henrik Lings Allé 4, 8, Østerbro* ☎ *69/96–00–20* 🌐 *www.geranium.dk* ✍ *Reservations essential* 🕒 *Closed Sun.–Tues. No lunch.*

CHRISTIANHAVN

$$$$ SCANDINAVIAN Fodor's Choice ★ 🍴 **noma.** Dark oak tables, wooden floors, and chairs with lamb-fur accents are a rustic interpretation of Nordic luxury that's appropriate to the setting—a former warehouse on the waterfront. This restaurant is at the vanguard of new Nordic cuisine and Denmark's most highly acclaimed. Chef Rene Redzepi and his innovative team pair the best local ingredients like berries, mushrooms, vegetables, and herbs with game, Jutland marsh lamb, Greenlandic musk ox, and Faroe Islands scallops. Dishes from the 20-course tasting menu can be served with wine pairings or a juice menu for an additional charge. Service is irreproachable. Given the hype, it's nearly impossible to book a table—reservations are taken a full three months in advance. So plan well ahead, and be prepared to settle for lunch instead of dinner. [$] *Average main: Dkr 1,500* ✉ *Strandgade 93, Christianshavn* ☎ *32/96–32–97* 🌐 *www.noma.dk* ✍ *Reservations essential* 🕒 *Closed Sun. No lunch Mon.*

WHERE TO STAY

CENTRUM

$$$$ HOTEL [hotel] **First Hotel Skt. Petri.** For the better part of a century, a beloved budget department store nicknamed Dalle Valle occupied this site, which is now a luxury hotel that's a hit with interior designers, fashionistas, and celebrities. **Pros:** great design everywhere; beautiful terrace; sleek cocktail bar. **Cons:** on the pretentious side; small rooms; street noise. [$] *Rooms from: Dkr 2,895* ✉ *Krystalgade 22, Centrum* ☎ *33/45–91–00* 🌐 *www.hotelsktpetri.com* 🛏 *241 rooms, 27 suites* 🍴 *Multiple meal plans.*

$$$$ B&B/INN [hotel] **Hotel Nimb.** It's the first hotel in Tivoli Gardens and the most exclusive one in the city, with prices to match. **Pros:** very comfortable; superb location; great views. **Cons:** sky-high rates; awkward spaces throughout due to building limitations. [$] *Rooms from: Dkr 4,900* ✉ *Bernstorffsgade 5, Centrum* ☎ *88/70–00–00* 🌐 *www.nimb.dk* 🛏 *5 rooms, 9 suites* 🍴 *No meals.*

FREDERIKSSTADEN

$$ HOTEL [hotel] **Copenhagen Admiral Hotel.** A five-minute stroll from Nyhavn, overlooking old Copenhagen and Amalienborg Palace, the massive Admiral was once a grain warehouse (circa 1787). **Pros:** great restaurant; convenient waterfront location. **Cons:** standard rooms aren't that big; all rooms can get stuffy, particularly in summer. [$] *Rooms from: Dkr 1,965* ✉ *Toldbodgade 24–28, Frederiksberg* ☎ *33/74–14–14* 🌐 *www.admiralhotel.dk* 🛏 *314 rooms, 52 suites* 🍴 *Breakfast.*

VESTERBRO

$$$ HOTEL Fodor's Choice ★ [hotel] **Radisson Blu Royal Hotel.** This high-rise was originally designed by Arne Jacobsen in 1960. **Pros:** great views; beautiful Danish design throughout; large fitness area. **Cons:** some furnishings are worn; service can be spotty. [$] *Rooms from: Dkr 2,195* ✉ *Hammerichsgade 1, Vesterbro* ☎ *33/42–60–00* 🌐 *www.radissonblu.com/royalhotel-copenhagen* 🛏 *260 rooms, 24 suites* 🍴 *No meals.*

NIGHTLIFE

Nightspots are concentrated on and around Strøget. Restaurants, cafés, bars, and clubs stay open after midnight, a few until 5 am. Check out *Copenhagen This Week* (🌐 *www.ctw.dk*) and the English newspaper *The Copenhagen Post* (🌐 *www.cphpost.dk*) for listings.

Hviids Vinstue. Around since the 1720s, Hviids Vinstue attracts all kinds, young and old, singles and couples, for a glass of wine or cognac. ✉ *Kongens Nytorv 19, Centrum* ☎ *33/15–10–64* 🌐 *www.hviidsvinstue.dk.*

Icebar Cph. Literally one of the coolest bars in Copenhagen, Icebar Cph is part of the trendy Hotel Twentyseven (which also houses the Honey Ryder lounge, serving "molecular" cocktails). It's basically a –31°C (–23°F) ice box where you drink vodka concoctions in glasses made of ice. Don't worry, a coat is provided during your 40-minute visit.

✉ *Løngangstræde 27, Centrum* ☎ *33/11–70–00* ⊕ *www.icebarcph.com* 🎫 *DKr 150, includes one drink.*

Y's Café and Cocktailbar. Y's Café and Cocktailbar is a low-key cocktail bar with a 110 drinks on its menu, each one concocted by the award-winning mixologist and owner, Yvonne Kubach. ✉ *Nørre Voldgade 102, Centrum* ☎ *33/14–20–44* ⊕ *www.ys-cocktail.dk.*

SHOPPING

A showcase for world-famous Danish design and craftsmanship, Copenhagen seems to have been set up with shoppers in mind. In fact, the city's name means the "merchant's harbor." The best buys are crystal, porcelain, and silver. Throughout summer and into autumn, there are six major markets every weekend, many of which sell antiques and secondhand porcelain, silver, and glassware. Bargaining is expected. Check with the tourist office or the magazine *Copenhagen This Week* (⊕ *www.ctw.dk*) for street markets.

15

GLASSWARE AND PORCELAIN

Royal Copenhagen. The flagship store for Royal Copenhagen beautifully displays its famous porcelain ware and settings fit for a king. The shop also has a museum on the second floor, where you can see the painters in action. ✉ *Amagertorv 6, Centrum* ☎ *33/13–71–81* ⊕ *www. royalcopenhagen.dk.*

Royal Copenhagen Factory Outlet. The Royal Copenhagen Factory Outlet has a good deal of stock, often at reduced prices. You can also buy Holmegaard Glass at the Royal Copenhagen store in Centrum and this factory outlet. ✉ *Søndre Fasanvej 9, Frederiksberg* ☎ *38/34–10–04* ⊕ *www.royalcopenhagen.com* ☾ *Weekdays 10–6, Sat. 10–2.*

SILVER

Georg Jensen. This elegant, austere shop is aglitter with sterling, which is what you'd expect from one of the most recognized names in international silver. Jensen has its own museum next door. ✉ *Amagertorv 4, Centrum* ☎ *33/11–40–80* ⊕ *www.georgjensen.com.*

STOCKHOLM

Sweden requires the visitor to travel far, in both distance and attitude. Approximately the size of California, Sweden reaches as far north as the arctic fringes of Europe, where glacier-topped mountains and thousands of acres of forests are broken only by wild rivers, pristine lakes, and desolate moorland. In the more populous south, roads meander through miles of softly undulating countryside, skirting lakes and passing small villages with sharp-pointed church spires.

Stockholm itself is a city in the flush of its second youth. Since the mid-1990s, Sweden's capital has emerged from its cold, Nordic shadow to take the stage as a truly international city. What started with entry into the European Union in 1995 gained pace with the extraordinary IT boom of the late 1990s, strengthened with the Skype-led IT second wave of 2003, and solidified with the hedge-fund invasion that is still

SWEDEN AT A GLANCE

- **Capital:** Stockholm
- **Population:** 9,556,000
- **Currency:** Krona
- **Money:** ATMs are common. The euro is widely accepted.
- **Language:** Swedish
- **Country Code:** ☎ 46
- **Emergencies:** ☎ 112
- **Driving:** On the right

- **Electricity:** 200v/50 cycles; electrical plugs have two round prongs
- **Time:** Five hours ahead of New York
- **Documents:** Up to 90 days with valid passport; Schengen rules apply
- **Mobile Phones:** GSM (900 and 1800 bands)
- **Major Mobile Companies:** Telia, Tele2, Telenor, 3, and Net 1

happening today as Stockholm gains even more global confidence. And despite more recent economic turmoil, Stockholm's one million or so inhabitants have, almost as one, realized that their city is one to rival Paris, London, New York, or any other great metropolis.

Stockholm also has plenty of history. Positioned where the waters of Lake Mälaren rush into the Baltic, it's been an important Baltic trading site and a wealthy international city for centuries. Built on 14 small islands joined by bridges crossing open bays and narrow channels, Stockholm boasts the story of its history in its glorious medieval old town, grand palaces, ancient churches, sturdy edifices, public parks, and 19th-century museums—its history is soaked into the very fabric of its airy boulevards, built as a public display of trading glory.

PLANNING

PLANNING YOUR TIME

You can manage to see a satisfying amount of Stockholm in a day, though it would be tough to get too much of this place. Start near Stadshuset (City Hall) for a morning trip up to the top of its 348-foot tower. Make your way to Kulturehuset for some art, then relax before heading to Gamla Stan and the Kungliga Slottet. To save on dinner, try picnicking in the beautiful Kungsträdgården, just across Strömsbron.

If you can linger here for a few days, take a day trip into the archipelago. Whether it be a landlubber's stroll along the docks at Strandvägen, venturing onto a commuter ferry for a bit of island hopping, or sea kayaking as far as your arms will let you, get thee to the water.

GETTING HERE AND AROUND
AIR TRAVEL

Stockholm's Arlanda International Airport, 42 km (26 miles) from the city center, is Sweden's air hub. The main regional carrier SAS flies from several North American cities. *Flygbussarna* (airport buses) leave every 10 to 15 minutes from 6:30 am to 11 pm and terminate at Klarabergsviadukten, next to the central railway station.

With taxis, be sure to ask about a *fast pris* (fixed price) between Arlanda and the city. It should be between SKr 490 and SKr 600, to a destination near the center of town. The best bets for cabs are Taxi Stockholm, Taxi 020, and Taxi Kurir. All major taxi companies accept credit cards. Watch out for unregistered cabs, which charge high rates and won't provide the same service.

Alternatively, the yellow-nosed Arlanda Express train takes 20 minutes and leaves every 15 minutes (and every 10 minutes during peak hours). Single tickets cost SKr 220.

Contacts SAS Scandinavian Airlines (⊕ *www.flysas.com*).

BOAT AND FERRY TRAVEL

Silja Line and Viking Line operate massive cruise ship–style ferries daily between Stockholm and Helsinki, either for single journeys or round-trip, two-day cruises. St. Peter Line operates a ferry service between Stockholm and St. Petersburg, Russia, with stops in Tallinn, Estonia; and Helsinki, Finland, along the way.

Contacts St. Peter Line ☎ *08/459–7700* ⊕ *anastasia.stpeterline.com*. **Silja Line** ☎ *08/222140* ⊕ *www.tallinksilja.se*. **Viking Line** ☎ *08/452–4000* ⊕ *www. vikingline.se*.

PUBLIC TRANSPORTATION TRAVEL

The subway system, known as T-banan (Tunnelbanan, with stations marked by a blue-on-white "T"), is the easiest and fastest way to get around. Servicing more than 100 stations and covering more than 96 km (60 miles) of track, trains run frequently between 5 am and 3 am. In 2000 the subway system was bought from SL by Connex, the same company that runs the subways in Paris and London. Tickets for Stockholm subways and buses are interchangeable. Maps and timetables for all city transportation networks are available from the SL information desks at Sergels Torg, the central station, Slussen, and online.

Both long-distance and commuter trains arrive at the central station in Stockholm on Vasagatan. All the major bus services, including Flygbussarna, Swebus Express, Svenska Buss, and Interbus, arrive at Cityterminalen (City Terminal), next to the central railway station. Stockholm has an excellent bus system operated by SL (Stockholm Local Traffic). Tickets work interchangeably on buses and subways in the city. Late-night buses connect certain stations when trains stop running.

Waxholmsbolaget (Waxholm Ferries) offers the Båtluffarkortet (Inter Skerries Card), a discount pass for its extensive commuter network of archipelago boats; the price is SKr 380 for five days of unlimited travel. The Strömma Kanalbolaget operates a fleet of archipelago boats that provide excellent sightseeing tours and excursions.

TAXI TRAVEL

If you call a cab, ask the dispatcher to quote you a fast pris, which is usually lower than the metered fare. A trip of 10 km (6 miles) should cost about SKr 110 between 6 am and 7 pm, SKr 115 at night, and SKr 123 on weekends.

15

Taxi Contacts Taxi 020 ☎ *020/20–20–20* ⊕ *www.taxi020.se.* **Taxi Kurir** ☎ *08/300000* ⊕ *www.taxikurir.se.* **Taxi Stockholm** ☎ *08/150000* ⊕ *www. taxistockholm.se.*

HOTELS

The last few years have brought with them a welcome surge in new hotels, including the Scandic Grand Central Hotel (next to the train station) and Radisson Blu Waterfront Hotel (near the waterfront congress center). While the hotel choices here are often not as trendy as those found elsewhere, they are plentiful and full of variety, from hostels on up to five stars. Most hotels here have a distinctly Scandinavian design sensibility. Who needs the latest designer interior when there are plenty of fresh, nonfussy, reasonably elegant, and endlessly functional places to stay? Although Stockholm has a reputation for prohibitively expensive hotels, fairly good deals can be found in summer, when prices are substantially lower and numerous discounts are available. More than 50 hotels offer the "Stockholm Package," which includes accommodations for one night, breakfast, and the Stockholmskortet, or Stockholm Card entitling the cardholder to free admission to museums and travel on public transport. Details are available from travel agents, tourist bureaus, and the Stockholm Tourism Center.

Contacts Stockholm Tourist Center ✉ *Vasag. 14* ☎ *08/5082–8508* ⊕ *www. visitstockholm.com.*

RESTAURANTS

What was once a dour landscape of overpriced, uninspiring eateries is now a creative hotbed of culinary achievement to rival any major European capital. Industry investment in training, receptivity to international influence, and a flair for creativity all mean that Stockholm's best chefs have stayed way ahead of the game. Increasingly, this achievement is rubbing off on their mid-price colleagues and in terms of culinary experience per krona, mid-range restaurants represent the best value for money in town. Two recent trends have seen many of the city's better restaurants pick up on this and offer more set-price tasting menus and increasing numbers of wines by the glass—making even the most expensive restaurants relatively affordable. In terms of food, New Swedish remains the buzzword, with chefs looking no further than their backyards for fine, seasonal, traditional ingredients, served with a modern twist. Of course, there are also many less expensive restaurants with traditional Swedish cooking. Among Swedish dishes, the best bets are wild game and fish, particularly salmon, and the smorgasbord buffet, which usually offers a good variety at an inexpensive price. Reservations are often necessary.

HOTEL AND RESTAURANT PRICES

Prices in the restaurant reviews are the average cost of a main course at dinner or, if dinner is not served, at lunch; taxes and service charges are generally included. Prices in the hotel reviews are the lowest cost of a standard double room in high season, excluding taxes, service charges, and meal plans.

VISITOR INFORMATION

Contacts Stockholm Information Service ☎ *08/5082–8508* ⊕ *www. visitstockholm.com.* **Stockholm Visitors Board** ✉ *Vasag. 4* ☎ *08/50828508* ⊕ *www.visitstockholm.com.* **Visit Sweden** ☎ *212/885–9700 in New York* ⊕ *www.visitsweden.com.*

EXPLORING

For the inhabitants there's a tribal status to each of the city's islands. But for the visitor, Stockholm's archipelago location primarily helps to dissect the city, both in terms of history and in terms of Stockholm's different characteristics, conveniently packaging the capital into easily handled, ultimately digestible areas.

The central island of Gamla Stan wows visitors with its medieval beauty, winding, narrow lanes and small café-lined squares. To the south, Södermalm challenges with contemporary boutiques, hip hangouts, and left-of-center sensibilities. North of Gamla Stan is Norrmalm, the financial and business heart of the city. Travel west and you'll find Kungsholmen, site of the Stadshuset. Turn east from Norrmalm and Östermalm awaits, an old residential neighborhood with the most money, the most glamour, and the most expensive street on the Swedish Monopoly board. Finally, between Östermalm and Södermalm lies the island of Djurgården, once a royal game preserve, now the site of lovely parks and museums.

15

MODERN STOCKHOLM

The area bounded by Stadshuset, Hötorget, Stureplan, and the Kungliga Dramatiska Teatern (nicknamed Dramaten) is essentially Stockholm's downtown. Shopping, nightlife, business, traffic, dining—all are at their most intense in this part of town. Much of this area was razed to the ground in the 1960s as part of a social experiment to move people to the new suburbs. What came in its place—a series of modernist buildings, concrete public spaces, and pedestrianized walkways—garners support and derision in equal measure.

FAMILY **Kulturhuset** (*Culture House*). Since it opened in 1974, architect Peter Celsing's cultural center, a glass-and-stone monolith on the south side of Sergels Torg, has become a symbol of modernism in Sweden. Stockholmers are divided on the aesthetics of this building—most either love it or hate it. Here there are exhibitions for children and adults, a library, a theater, a youth center, an exhibition center, and a restaurant. Head to Café Panorama, on the top floor, to savor traditional Swedish cuisine and a great view of Sergels Torg down below. ✉ *Sergels Torg 3, City* ☎ *08/5083–1508* ⊕ *www.kulturhuset.stockholm.se* ⊗ *Weekdays 9–7, weekends 11–5.*

Kungsträdgården. Once the Royal kitchen garden, this is now Stockholm's smallest but most central park. It is often used to host festivals and events, but is best seen in its everyday guise: as a pleasant sanctuary from the pulse of downtown. Several neat little glass-cube cafés sell light lunches, coffee, and snacks. ✉ *Kungsträdgården* ☎ *08/5551–0090* ⊕ *www.kungstradgarden.se.*

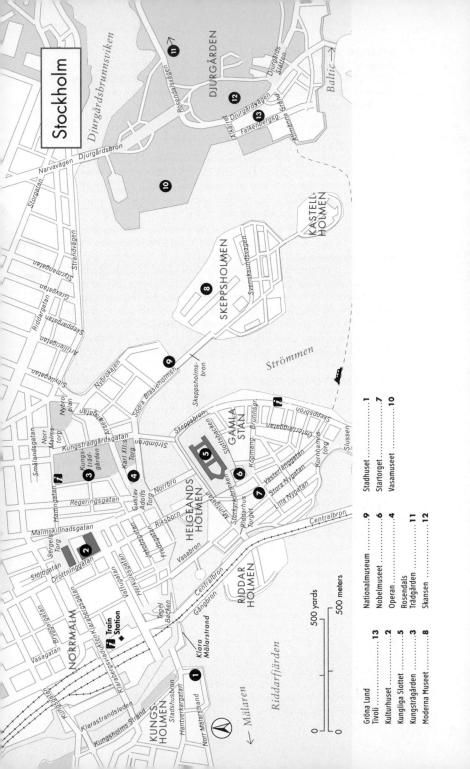

Stockholm

Djurgårdsbrunnsviken

DJURGÅRDEN

Rosendalsvägen

Djurgårds Slätten

Baltic →

Narvavägen Djurgårdsbron

Atkärret Djurgårdsvägen

Falkenbergsg. Grand

Allmänna Grönd

Storgatan

Ststrandvägen

Styrmansgatan

Grevgatan

Ridargatan

Skepparegatan

Artillerigatan

S. Djurgatan

Nybrokajen

Nybro-plan

KASTELL-HOLMEN

SKEPPSHOLMEN

Svensksundsvägen

Strömmen

Skeppsholms-bron

Norr Mälms torg

Kungsträdgårdsgatan

Småjandsgatan

Kungs-träd-gården

Karl XII:s Torg

Strömbron

Norrbro

Skeppsbron

Slottsbacken

Köpmang. Brunnsgr.

Österlånggatan

GAMLA STAN

Kornhamns torg

Skeppsbron

Slussen

Gustav Adolfs Torg

Regeringsgatan

Hamngatan

Sergels torg

Malmskillnadsgatan

Drottninggatan

Stöjdgatan

Jakobsgatan

Fredsgatan

Riksborn

Mynttorget

Stortorsbrinken

Riddarhus Torget

Västerlånggatan

Stora Nygatan

Lilla Nygatan

Centralbron

HELGEANDS HOLMEN

Vasabron

NORRMALM

Vasagatan

Bryggargatan

Klarabergsviadukten Klarabergsgatan

Train Station

Tegel Bäcken

Centralbron

Gångbron

RIDDAR HOLMEN

Klara Mälarstrand

Klarastrandsleden

Kungsholms Strand

Norr Mälarstrand

Hantverkargatan

Stadshusbron

KUNGS-HOLMEN

Mälaren

Riddarfjärden

Gröna Lund Tivoli	13	Nationalmuseum	9	Stadhuset ... 1
Kulturhuset	2	Nobelmuseet	6	Startorget ... 7
Kungliga Slottet	5	Operan	4	Vasamuseet ... 10
Kungsträgården	3	Rosendals Trädgården	11	
Moderna Museet	8	Skansen	12	

500 yards

500 meters

Fodor's Choice
★
Stadshuset (*City Hall*). The architect Ragnar Östberg, one of the founders of the National Romantic movement, completed Stockholm's city hall in 1923. The headquarters of the city council, the building is functional but ornate: its immense **Blå Hallen** (Blue Hall) is the venue for the annual Nobel Prize dinner, Stockholm's main social event. You must take a tour to visit City Hall. You can also take a trip to the top of the 348-foot tower, most of which can be achieved by elevator, to enjoy a breathtaking panorama of the city and Riddarfjärden. ⊠ *Hantverkarg. 1, Kungsholmen* ☎ *08/5082–9058* ⊕ *www.stockholm.se* ≊ *SKr 90, tower Skr 40* ☉ *Tours of City Hall in English, Sept.–May, daily every hr 10–3; June–Aug., daily every 30 mins 9:30–4. Tower May–Sept., daily 9:15–4:30.*

GAMLA STAN AND SKEPPSHOLMEN

Gamla Stan (Old Town) sits between two of Stockholm's main islands, and is the site of the medieval city. Just east of Gamla Stan is the island of Skeppsholmen, whose twisting cobbled streets are lined with superbly preserved old buildings. As the site of the original Stockholm, history, culture, and a dash of Old Europe come thick and fast here. Understandably, Gamla Stan is also a magnet for tourists. Consequently there are plenty of substandard shops and restaurants ready to take your money for shoddy goods and bad food. Because of this, locals often make a big show of dismissing the area, but don't believe them. Secretly they love Gamla Stan and Skeppsholmen. And who wouldn't? Its divine alleys and bars, gorgeous architecture, shops, and restaurants are irresistible.

Fodor's Choice
★
Kungliga Slottet (*Royal Palace*). Designed by Nicodemus Tessin, the Royal Palace was completed in 1760 and replaced the previous palace that had burned down at the location in 1697. The four facades of the palace each have a distinct style: the west is the king's, the east the queen's, the south belongs to the nation, and the north represents royalty in general. Watch the changing of the guard in the curved terrace entrance, and view the palace's fine furnishings and Gobelin tapestries on a tour of the Representationsvän (State Apartments). To survey the crown jewels, which are no longer used in this self-consciously egalitarian country, head to the Skattkammaren (Treasury). The Livrustkammaren (Royal Armory) has an outstanding collection of weaponry, coaches, and royal regalia. Entrances to the Treasury and Armory are on the Slottsbacken side of the palace. ⊠ *Slottsbacken 1, Gamla Stan* ☎ *08/402–6130* ⊕ *www.royalcourt.se* ≊ *SKr 150* ☉ *Mid-May–mid-Sept., daily 10–5; mid-Sept.–mid-May, daily noon-4.*

Moderna Museet (*Museum of Modern Art*). The museum's excellent collection includes works by Picasso, Kandinsky, Dalí, Brancusi, and other international artists. You can also view examples of significant Swedish painters and sculptors and an extensive section on photography. The building itself is striking. Designed by the well-regarded Spanish architect Rafael Moneo, it has seemingly endless hallways of blond wood and walls of glass. ⊠ *Skeppsholmen, Exercisplan, City* ☎ *08/5195–5200* ⊕ *www.modernamuseet.se* ≊ *SKr 120* ☉ *Tues. 10–8, Wed.–Sun. 10–6.*

Fodor's Choice
★
Nationalmuseum. Allow at least an hour if you want to see most of the paintings and sculptures on display at this impressive museum. The

emphasis is on Swedish and Nordic art, but other areas are well represented. Look especially for some fine works by Rembrandt. The print and drawing department is also impressive, with a nearly complete collection of Edouard Manet prints. ■ **TIP→ From summer 2013, the Nationalmuseum will be undergoing major renovations. Many of its works will be temporararily relocated to The Royal Swedish Academy of Fine Arts at Fredsgatan 12, with different hours likely.** ⊠ *Södra Blasieholmshamnen, City* ☎ *08/5195–4410* ⊕ *www.nationalmuseum.se* ⊠ *SKr 100* ⊙ *Jan.– Aug., Tues. 11–8, Wed.–Sun. 11–5; Sept.–Dec., Tues. and Thurs. 11–8, Wed., Fri., and weekends 11–5.*

Nobelmuseet. The Swedish Academy meets at Börshuset (the Stock Exchange) every year to decide the winner of the Nobel Prize for literature. The building is also the home of the Nobel Museum. Along with exhibits on creativity's many forms, the museum displays scientific models, shows films, and has a full explanation of the process of choosing prizewinners. The museum does a good job covering the controversial selections made over the years. It's a must for Nobel Prize hopefuls and others. ⊠ *Börshuset, Stortorget 2, Gamla Stan* ☎ *08/5348–1800* ⊕ *www.nobelmuseum.se* ⊠ *SKr 70* ⊙ *Mid-May–mid-Sept., Wed., Thurs., and Sat.–Mon., 10–6, Tues. and Fri. 10–8; mid-Sept.–mid-May, Tues. 11–8, Wed.–Sun. 11–5.*

Operan (*Opera House*). Stockholm's baroque Opera House is almost more famous for its restaurants and bars than for its opera and ballet productions, but that doesn't mean an evening performance should be missed. There's not a bad seat in the house. For between just SKr 50 and SKr 100 you can even get a listening-only seat (with no view). Still, its food and drink status can't be denied. It has been one of Stockholm's artistic and literary watering holes since the first Operakällaren restaurant opened on the site in 1787. ⊠ *Gustav Adolfs Torg, City* ☎ *08/791–4400* ⊕ *www.operan.se.*

Stortorget (*Great Square*). Here in 1520 the Danish king Christian II ordered a massacre of Swedish noblemen. The slaughter paved the way for a national revolt against foreign rule and the founding of Sweden as a sovereign state under King Gustav Vasa, who ruled from 1523 to 1560. One legend holds that if it rains heavily enough on the anniversary of the massacre, the old stones still run red. ⊠ *Near Kungliga Slottet, Gamla Stan.*

DJURGÅRDEN AND SKANSEN

Throughout history, Djurgården has been Stockholm's pleasure island. There was a time when only the king could enjoy this enormous green space. Today everyone comes here to breathe fresh air, visit the many museums, stroll through the forests and glades, get their pulses racing at the Gröna Lund amusement park, or just relax by the water. You can approach Djurgården from the water aboard the small ferries that leave from Slussen at the southern end of Gamla Stan. In summer, ferries also leave from Nybrokajen, or New Bridge Quay, in front of the Kungliga Dramatiska Teatern.

FAMILY **Gröna Lund Tivoli.** Smaller than Copenhagen's Tivoli or Göteborg's Liseberg, this amusement park has managed to retain much of its historical charm, while making room for some modern, hair-raising rides among the pleasure gardens, amusement arcades, and restaurants. If you're feeling especially daring, try the Power Tower. At 350 feet, it's one of Europe's tallest free-fall amusement-park rides and one of the best ways to see Stockholm, albeit for about three seconds, before you plummet. There isn't an adult who grew up in Stockholm who can't remember the annual excitement of Gröna Lund's April opening. Go and you will see why. ⊠ *Allmänna Gränd 9, Djurgården* ☎ *08/5875–0100* ⊕ *www. gronalund.com* ⊠ *SKr 100 (park entry only; rides and attractions priced separately)* ⊘ *Late Apr.–mid-Sept., daily noon–11 (hrs vary; call ahead).*

Fodor'sChoice
★ **Rosendals Trädgården** (*Rosendal's Garden*). This gorgeous slice of greenery is a perfect place to spend a few hours on a late summer afternoon. When the weather's nice, people flock to the garden café, which is in one of the greenhouses, to enjoy tasty pastries and salads made from the locally grown vegetables. Pick your own flowers from the vast flower beds (paying by weight), stroll through the creative garden displays, or take away produce from the farm shop. ⊠ *Rosendalsterrassen 12, Djurgården* ☎ *08/5458–1270* ⊕ *www.rosendalstradgard.se* ⊠ *Free* ⊘ *May–Sept., weekdays 11–5, weekends 11–6; Oct.–Apr., hrs vary; call ahead.*

FAMILY **Skansen.** The world's first open-air museum, Skansen was founded in 1891 by philologist and ethnographer Artur Hazelius, who is buried here. Drawing from all parts of the country, he preserved examples of traditional Swedish architecture, including farmhouses, windmills, barns, a working glassblower's hut, and churches. Not only is Skansen a delightful trip out of time in the center of a modern city, but it also provides insight into the life and culture of Sweden's various regions. In addition, the park has a zoo, carnival area, aquarium, theater, and cafés. ⊠ *Djurgårdsslätten 49–51, Djurgården* ☎ *08/442–8000* ⊕ *www. skansen.se* ⊠ *Park and zoo: Jan.–Apr. SKr 70, May and Sept. SKr 90, June–Aug. SKr 110. Aquarium SKr 100.* ⊘ *Nov.–Feb., weekdays 10–3, weekends 10–4; Mar., Apr., and Oct., daily 10–4; May–June 19, daily 10–8; June 20–Aug., daily 10–8; Sept., daily 10–8.*

Fodor'sChoice
★ **Vasamuseet** (*Vasa Museum*). The warship *Vasa* sank 10 minutes into its maiden voyage in 1628, consigned to a watery grave until it was raised from the seabed in 1961. Its hull was preserved by the Baltic mud, free of the shipworms (really clams) that can eat through timbers. Now largely restored to her former glory (however short-lived it may have been), the man-of-war resides in a handsome museum. The sheer size of this cannon-laden hulk inspires awe and fear in equal measure. The political history of the world may have been different had she made it out of harbor. Daily tours are available year-round. ⊠ *Galärvarvsv. 14, Djurgården* ☎ *08/5195–4800* ⊕ *www.vasamuseet.se* ⊠ *SKr 110* ⊘ *June–Aug., daily 8:30–6; Sept.–May, Thurs.–Tues. 10–5, Wed. 10–8.*

15

WHERE TO EAT

DOWNTOWN STOCKHOLM AND BEYOND

$$$$
SCANDINAVIAN
Fodor'sChoice
★

✕ **Fredsgatan 12.** Without a doubt, this is one of the most creative restaurants in town. The showpiece is the 11-course tasting menu, with ingredients selected according to a farmers almanac from 1666. The result is dishes such as "The Swell of the Sea" (langoustine on rice bread with dill and ginger) and "The Cooling Shade" (duck liver with white-peach lemonade and toasted seeds). The elegant, neutral-toned dining room oozes class and style; the refreshingly friendly, impressively knowledgeable staff add a pleasant down-to-earth touch to the sky-high prices. This is haute cuisine at its very best—but note that there is a huge difference between lunch and dinner prices: the latter starts around SKr 895. $ *Average main: SKr 425* ✉ *Fredsg. 12, City* ☎ *08/248052* ⊕ *www.f12.se* ⚖ *Reservations essential* ⊙ *Closed Sun. No lunch Sat.*

$$$
STEAKHOUSE
Fodor'sChoice
★

✕ **Grill.** With an interior full of heavy fabrics, vibrant decor, and offbeat period-piece furniture, Grill's love for the Moulin Rouge and French culture in general isn't hard to see. There are five main ways of grilling here: brick oven, rotisserie, smoke, charcoal, and grilling at the table. Share its famous grill plate of lamb, tenderloin, pork loins, farm chicken, and spicy sausage (minimum two people), or a set lunch buffet with meats, pastas, and salads. $ *Average main: SKr 350* ✉ *Drottningg. 89, Vasastan* ☎ *08/314530* ⊕ *www.grill.se* ⚖ *Reservations essential* ⊙ *No lunch on weekends.*

GAMLA STAN, SKEPPSHOLMEN, AND SÖDERMALM

$$
VEGETARIAN
Fodor'sChoice
★

✕ **Hermans.** Hermans is a haven for vegetarians out to get the most bang for their kronor. The glassed-in back deck and open garden both provide breathtaking vistas across the water of Stockholm harbor, Gamla Stan, and the island of Djurgården. The food, served buffet-style, includes various vegetable and pasta salads, warm casseroles, and such entrées as Indonesian stew with peanut sauce and vegetarian lasagna. The fruit pies, chocolate cakes, and cookies are delicious. $ *Average main: SKr 155* ✉ *Fjällg. 23B, Södermalm* ☎ *08/643–9480* ⊕ *www.hermans.se.*

$$$$
SCANDINAVIAN
Fodor'sChoice
★

✕ **Mathias Dahlgren.** From the elegant modern dining room to what's on the plate—simple, artistically rendered local food that its eponymous chef has dubbed "natural cuisine"—this place doesn't disappoint. And for his trouble Dahlgren has picked up two Michelin stars since opening in late 2007. Don't miss this place—and keep in mind that prices in the bar, where lunch is served on weekdays, are much lower than in the dining room. $ *Average main: SKr 1,650* ✉ *Grand Hotel, S Blasieholmshamen 6* ☎ *08/679–3584* ⊕ *www.mathiasdahlgren.com* ⚖ *Reservations essential* ⊙ *Closed Sun. No lunch weekends.*

$$
SCANDINAVIAN
Fodor'sChoice
★

✕ **Pelikan.** Beer, beer, and more beer is the order of the day at this traditional drinking hall, a relic of the days when Södermalm was the dwelling place of the city's blue-collar brigade. Today's more bohemian residents find it just as enticing, with the unvarnished wood-paneled walls, faded murals, and glass globe lights fulfilling all their down-at-the-heel pretensions. The food here is some of the best traditional Swedish fare in the city. The herring, meatballs, and salted bacon with onion sauce are all great choices. $ *Average main: SKr 216* ☒ *Blekingeg. 40, Södermalm* ☎ *08/5560–9090* ⊕ *www.pelikan.se* ☺ *No lunch Fri.–Sun.*

WHERE TO STAY

DOWNTOWN STOCKHOLM

$$
HOTEL

⛴ **Berns Hotel.** This ultramodern hotel was a hot spot when it opened its doors in the late 19th century, and it retains that status today. **Pros:** stylish rooms; fantastic restaurant; great bath products. **Cons:** some rooms are a little small; the bar gets rowdy weekend nights. $ *Rooms from: SKr 2,290* ☒ *Näckströmsg. 8, City* ☎ *08/5663–2200* ⊕ *www. berns.se* ⇆ *65 rooms, 3 suites* �101 *Breakfast.*

$$$$
HOTEL
Fodor's Choice
★

⛴ **Hotel Stureplan.** Housed in a beautiful 18th-century mansion, Stureplan is the perfect mix of modern design, comfortable living, and functional hotel. **Pros:** to-die-for design; great service; perfect location. **Cons:** rooms at the front can be noisy; some rooms are very small. $ *Rooms from: SKr 2,970* ☒ *Birger Jarlsg. 24* ☎ *08/440–6600* ⊕ *www. hotelstureplan.se* ⇆ *90 rooms, 11 suites* �101 *Breakfast.*

$$
HOTEL
Fodor's Choice
★

⛴ **Scandic Grand Central.** The eco-friendly Scandic Grand Central is in an impressive 130-year old building just steps away from the city's main train station, right in the heart of Stockholm's business district. **Pros:** central to everything; everything's new (hotel opened in late 2011). **Cons:** noisy location. $ *Rooms from: SKr 1,650* ☒ *Kungsg. 70, City* ☎ *08/5125–2000* ⊕ *www.scandichotels.com* ⇆ *391 rooms* ⊢⊣ *Breakfast.*

GAMLA STAN AND SKEPPSHOLMEN

$$$$
HOTEL
Fodor's Choice
★

⛴ **Grand Hotel.** At first glance the Grand seems like any other world-class international hotel, and in many ways it is. **Pros:** unadulterated luxury; world-class service; great bar. **Cons:** some rooms are small; faded in parts; very expensive. $ *Rooms from: SKr 3,000* ☒ *Södra Blasieholmshamnen 8* ☎ *08/679–3500* ⊕ *www.grandhotel.se* ⇆ *269 rooms, 31 suites* ⊢⊣ *Breakfast.*

$$
HOTEL

⛴ **Rica Hotel Gamla Stan.** The feel of historical Stockholm living is rarely stronger than in this quiet hotel tucked away on a narrow street in one of the Gamla Stan's 17th-century houses. **Pros:** personal service; most rooms are comfortable. **Cons:** some rooms are small; basic facilities. $ *Rooms from: SKr 1,595* ☒ *Lilla Nyg. 25, Gamla Stan* ☎ *08/723–7250* ⊕ *www.rica.se* ⇆ *51 rooms* ⊢⊣ *Breakfast.*

NIGHTLIFE

Birger Jarlsgatan, Stureplan, and the city end of Kungsträdgården are more upscale and trendy, and thus more expensive. To the south, in Södermalm, things are a bit wilder. Anywhere, a safe bet is wearing black, Stockholm's hue of choice. Things wind down around 3 am. The tourist guide *What's On* (⊕ *www.stockholmtown.com*) lists the month's events in both English and Swedish.

Hotellet. Although originally designed as a hotel, this is now a very chic bar that manages to retain that open-lobby feel for its hot crowd. ☒ *Linnég. 18, Östermalm* ☎ *08/442–8900* ⊕ *www.hotellet.info.*

15

Le Rouge. Le Rouge takes its cue from Le Moulin Rouge. Sit back in sumptuous surroundings of red velvet and heavy drapes and indulge in one of the most interesting cocktail menus in town. ⊠ *Brunnsgränd 2–4, Gamla Stan* ☎ *08/5052–4430* ⊕ *www.lerouge.se.*

Södra Teatern. This combination indoor theater, comedy club, and outdoor café comes with a spectacular view of the city. The crowd here leans toward over-thirty hipsters. ⊠ *Mosebacke torg 1–3, Södermalm* ☎ *08/5319–9400* ⊕ *www.sodrateatern.com.*

BOATING

From May to September sailboats large and small and gorgeous restored wooden boats cruise from island to island. Both types of boats are available for rental. Walk along the water on Strandvägen, where many large power yachts and sailboats (available for charter) are docked. Sea kayaking has also become increasingly popular and is a delightful way to explore the islands.

Strandbryggan. At the end of Strandvägen, before the bridge to Djurgården, is Strandbryggan, an open-air restaurant which also has boats for rent. ⊠ *Strandvägskajen 27, City* ☎ *08/660–3714* ⊕ *www. strandbryggan.se.*

SHOPPING

For souvenirs and crafts, peruse the boutiques and galleries in **Västerlånggatan,** the main street of Gamla Stan. For jewelry, crafts, and fine art, hit the shops that line the raised sidewalk at the start of **Hornsgatan** on Södermalm. Drottninggatan, Birger Jarlsgatan, Biblioteksgatan, Götgatan, and Hamngatan also offer some great shopping.

MARKETS

Fodor'sChoice
★
Hötorgshallen. For a good indoor market hit Hötorgshallen, directly under the Filmstaden movie theater. The market is filled with butcher shops, coffee and tea shops, and fresh-fish markets. It's closed on Sunday. ⊠ *Hötorget, City* ☎ *08/230001* ⊕ *www.hotorgshallen.se.*

Östermalms Saluhall. If you're interested in high-quality Swedish food, try the classic European indoor market Östermalms Saluhall, where you can buy superb fish, game, bread, and vegetables—or just have a glass of wine at one of the bars and watch the world go by. ⊠ *Östermalmstorg, Östermalm* ⊕ *www.ostermalmshallen.se.*

CLOTHING

Filippa K. One of Sweden's hottest designers, Filippa K has stores filled with young women and men grabbing the latest fashions. ⊠ *Grev Tureg. 18, Östermalm* ☎ *08/5458–8888* ⊕ *www.filippa-k.com.*

Hennes & Mauritz (*H&M*). This is one of the few Swedish-owned clothing stores to have achieved international success. At H&M you can find updated designs at reasonable prices. ⊠ *Hamng. 22, City* ☎ *08/5246– 3530* ⊕ *www.hm.com.*

GLASS

Kosta Boda and Orrefors produce the most popular and well-regarded lines of glassware.

Crystal Art Center. Near the central station, this shop has a great selection of small glass items. ✉ *Tegelbacken 4, City* ☎ *08/217169* ⊕ *www.cac.se.*

INTERIOR DESIGN

Sweden is recognized globally for its unique design sense and has contributed significantly to what is commonly referred to as Scandinavian design. All of this makes Stockholm one of the best cities in the world for shopping for furniture and home and office accessories.

Modernity. For something classic, you can't do better than Modernity, where 20th-century Scandinavian design by the likes of Arne Jacobsen, Alvar Aalto, and Poul Henningsen is in full force. ✉ *Sibylleg. 6, Östermalm* ☎ *08/208025* ⊕ *www.modernity.se.*

15

OSLO

One of the world's most beautiful countries, Norway has long been a popular cruising destination, famed for its stunning fjords. Formed during the last ice age's meltdown when the inland valleys carved by huge glaciers filled with seawater, fjords are undoubtedly Norway's top attractions—they shape the country's unique landscape and never fail to take your breath away.

Oslo itself, Norway's capital, is in the east, only a few hours from the Swedish border. What sets Oslo apart from other European cities is not so much its cultural traditions or its internationally renowned museums as its simply stunning natural beauty. How many world capitals have subway service to the forest, or lakes and hiking trails within city limits? But Norwegians will be quick to remind you that Oslo is a cosmopolitan metropolis with prosperous businesses and a thriving nightlife.

Once overlooked by travelers to Scandinavia, Oslo is now a major tourist destination and the gateway to what many believe is Scandinavia's most scenic country. That's just one more change for this city of 600,000—a place that has become good at survival and rebirth throughout its nearly 1,000-year history. In 1348 a plague wiped out half the city's population. In 1624 a fire burned almost the whole of Oslo to the ground. It was redesigned and renamed Christiania by Denmark's royal builder, King Christian IV. After that it slowly gained prominence as the largest and most economically significant city in Norway.

During the mid-19th century, Norway and Sweden were ruled as one kingdom, under Karl Johan. It was then that the grand main street that's his namesake was built, and Karl Johans Gate has been at the center of city life ever since. In 1905 the country separated from Sweden, and in 1925 an act of Parliament finally changed the city's name back to Oslo. Today Oslo is Norway's political, economic, industrial, and cultural capital.

NORWAY AT A GLANCE

- **Capital:** Norway
- **Population:** 5,063,000
- **Currency:** Krone
- **Money:** ATMs are common
- **Language:** Norwegian and Sami
- **Country Code:** ☎ 47
- **Emergencies:** ☎ 112
- **Driving:** On the right
- **Electricity:** 200v/50 cycles; electrical plugs have two round prongs

- **Time:** Five hours ahead of New York
- **Documents:** Up to 90 days with valid passport; Schengen rules apply
- **Mobile Phones:** GSM (900 and 1800 bands)
- **Major Mobile Companies:** Telenor Mobil, NetCom, Tele2

PLANNING

PLANNING YOUR TIME

Oslo is not a huge city, but it offers great museums, top restaurants, and a stunning new opera house. Check out the Royal Palace, at the end of Karl Johans Gate (Oslo's main thoroughfare) before ambling down to Aker Brygge, the trendy area by the harbor. Then visit Vigeland's statue park or the Holmenkollen ski jump, before ending your day in one of Grünerløkka's many buzzing restaurants.

GETTING HERE AND AROUND

AIR TRAVEL

The spacious and bright Oslo Airport in Gardermoen, 45 km (28 miles) north of the city, is a 50-minute car or taxi ride (expensive at around NKr 700 a trip) via the E6 from Oslo's city center. From Oslo S Station, it's a 19-minute ride by Flytoget (express train, NKr 170 one-way) with trains scheduled every 10 minutes (from 4:45 am to 12:05 am every day).

The SAS Flybussen buses depart from Oslo Bussterminalen Galleriet daily every 20 minutes and reach Oslo Airport approximately 40 minutes later (NKr 150 one-way, NKr 250 round-trip).

Contacts Flytoget (*Airport Express Train*). ☎ 81–50–07–77 ⊕ www.flytoget. no. **Oslo Airport Gardermoen** ☎ 06400 in Norway, 91–50–64–00 from abroad ⊕ www.osl.no.

BUS AND TRAIN TRAVEL

The main bus station, Oslo Bussterminalen, is across from the Oslo S Station. You can buy local bus tickets at the terminal or on the bus. Tickets for long-distance routes on Nor-Way Bussekspress can be purchased here or at travel agencies.

Norway's state railway, NSB (Norges Statsbaner), has two train stations downtown—Oslo Sentralstasjon (Oslo S) and a station at Nationaltheatret. Long-distance trains arrive at and leave from Oslo S Station. Suburban commuter trains use one or the other station.

Contacts Bussterminalen Oslo ✉ *Galleri Oslo, Schweigaardsgt. 10* ☎ *23–00– 24–00 for automated, with English-speaking operator available 9–4 daily.* **Nor-Way Bussekspress** ☎ *81–54–44–44* ⊕ *www.nor-way.no.* **NSB Customer Service** ☎ *81–50–08–88* ⊕ *www.nsb.no.*

PUBLIC TRANSIT TRAVEL

Within Oslo, subways and most buses and tramways (*trikk*) start running at 5 am, with the last run after midnight. On weekends, there's night service on certain routes. Trips on all public transportation within Oslo cost NKr 30 (remember to validate your ticket before boarding), with a one-hour free transfer; tickets that cross municipal boundaries have different rates. It often pays to buy a pass or multiple-travel card, which includes transfers. A day card (*dagskort*) costs NKr 75 and a seven-day pass costs NKr 220. Tickets can be used on subways, buses, or tramways.

Tickets are available at numerous kiosks and shops, including Narvesen and 7-Eleven, as well as from machines at the subway stations. The Oslo Pass (from NKr 270 for one day, NKr 395 for two days, and NKr 495 for three days) offers unlimited travel on all public transport in greater Oslo as well as free admission to several museums and sights, discounts at specified restaurants, and other perks. You can buy the cards at tourist offices and hotels.

TAXI TRAVEL

Taxis are dispatched via radio from a central office, and it can take up to 30 minutes to get one during peak hours. There are also taxi stands all over town, usually near Narvesen kiosks. It's possible to hail a cab on the street, but cabs aren't allowed to pick up passengers within 100 yards of a stand. It's not unheard-of to wait for more than an hour at a taxi stand in the wee hours of the morning, after everyone has left the bars. Never take pirate taxis; all registered taxis should have their roof lights on when they're available. Rates start at around NKr 109 for hailed or rank cabs and NKr 91 for ordered taxis, depending on the time of day and the company.

Contacts Oslo Taxi ☎ *02323* ⊕ *www.oslotaxi.no.*

HOTELS

Most lodgings are central, just a short walk from Karl Johans Gate. Many are between the Royal Palace and Oslo S Station, with the newer ones closer to the station. For a quiet stay, choose a hotel in either Frogner or Majorstuen, elegant residential neighborhoods behind the Royal Palace and within walking distance of downtown. Television and phones can be expected in most Oslo hotel rooms, and Internet connection is found in all but budget hotels. Most hotels in Oslo include either a full or continental breakfast in their rates.

RESTAURANTS

Many Oslo chefs have developed menus based on classic Norwegian recipes but with exciting variations, like Asian or Mediterranean cooking styles and ingredients. You may read about "New Scandinavian"

15

cuisine on some menus. It combines seafood and game from Scandinavia with spices and sauces from any other country.

Spend at least one sunny summer afternoon harborside at Aker Brygge eating in one of the many seafood restaurants and watching the world go by. Or buy steamed shrimp off the nearby docked fishing boats and plan a picnic in the Oslo fjords or Vigeland or another of the city's parks. Note that some restaurants close for a week around Easter, in July, and during the Christmas holiday season. Some restaurants are also closed on Sundays.

HOTEL AND RESTAURANT PRICES

Prices in the restaurant reviews are the average cost of a main course at dinner or, if dinner is not served, at lunch; taxes and service charges are generally included. Prices in the hotel reviews are the lowest cost of a standard double room in high season, excluding taxes, service charges, and meal plans.

VISITOR INFORMATION

Contacts **Oslo Tourist Information** ⊠ *By City Hall, or at Jernbanetorget (the main train station)* ☏ *81–53–05–55* ⊕ *www.visitoslo.com.* **VisitNorway** ☏ *22–00–25–00* ⊕ *www.visitnorway.com.*

EXPLORING

Karl Johans Gate, starting at Oslo Sentralstasjon (Oslo Central Station, also called Oslo S Station and simply *Jernbanetorget,* or "railway station" in Norwegian) and ending at the Royal Palace, forms the backbone of downtown Oslo. Many major museums and historic buildings lie between the parallel streets of Grensen and Rådhusgata. West of downtown are Frogner and Majorstuen, residential areas with fine restaurants, shopping, cafés, galleries, and the Vigeland sculpture park. Southwest is the Bygdøy Peninsula, with a castle and five interesting museums that honor aspects of Norway's taste for exploration.

Northwest of town is Holmenkollen, with its stunning bird's-eye view of the city and the surrounding fjords, a world-famous ski jump and museum, and three historic restaurants. On the more multicultural east side, where a diverse immigrant population lives alongside native Norwegians, are the Munch Museum and the Botanisk Hage og Museum (Botanical Gardens and Museum). The trendy neighborhood of Grünerløkka, with lots of cafés and shops, is northeast of the center.

DOWNTOWN: THE ROYAL PALACE TO CITY HALL

Although the city region is huge (454 square km [175 square miles]), downtown Oslo is compact, with shops, museums, historic buildings, restaurants, and clubs concentrated in a small, walkable center that's brightly illuminated at night.

Nasjonalgalleriet (*National Gallery*). The gallery, part of the National Museum of Art, Architecture and Design, houses Norway's largest collection of art created before 1945. The deep-red Edvard Munch room holds such major paintings as *The Dance of Life,* one of two existing oil versions of *The Scream,* and several self-portraits. Classic landscapes by Hans Gude and Adolph Tidemand—including *Bridal Voyage on the*

Oslo

KEY

i Tourist information

Aker Brygge **7**
Akershus Festning
og Slott **5**
Holmenkollbakken og
skimuseet **2**
Munchmuseet **10**
Nasjonalgalleriet **8**
Norsk Folkemuseum **9**

Operahwet **11**
Rådhuset **6**
Slottet (The Royal Palace) ..**8**
Vigelandsparken **1**
Vikingskipshuset **4**

Hardangerfjord—share space in galleries with other works by major Norwegian artists. The museum also has works by Monet, Renoir, Van Gogh, and Gauguin, as well as contemporary works by 20th-century Nordic artists. ✉ *Universitetsgt. 13, Sentrum* ☎ *21–98–20–00* ⊕ *www. nasjonalmuseet.no* ✆ *NKr 50 (free on Sun.)* ☉ *Tues., Wed., and Fri. 10–6, Thurs. 10–7, weekends 11–5.*

Rådhuset (*City Hall*). This redbrick building is best known today for the awarding of the Nobel Peace Prize, which takes place here every December. Inside, many museum-quality masterpieces are on the walls. After viewing the frescoes in the Main Hall, walk upstairs to the Banquet Hall to see the royal portraits. Free drop-in guided tours are available. Meet in the main hall for the 45-minute tour at the noted times. To visit the City Hall Gallery, enter harborside. Special exhibits are hung throughout the year. On festive occasions, the Central Hall is illuminated from outside by 60 large spotlights that simulate daylight. ✉ *Fridtjof Nansens plass, Sentrum* ☎ *02180* ⊕ *www.radhusets-forvaltningstjeneste. oslo.kommune.no/english* ✆ *Free* ☉ *Drop-in guided tours of City Hall: Sept.–May, Wed. at 10, noon, and 2; June–Aug., daily at 10, noon, and 2.*

Slottet (*The Royal Palace*). At one end of Karl Johans gate, the vanilla-and-cream-color neoclassical palace was completed in 1848. The equestrian statue out in front is of Karl Johan, King of Sweden and Norway from 1818 to 1844. The palace is only open to the public in summer, when there are guided tours (in English). ■TIP➔ **Kids of all ages will love the Royal Palace's changing of the guard ceremony, accompanied by the Norwegian Military Band, that takes place daily, rain or shine, at 1:30.** ✉ *Slottsplassen* ☎ *81–53–31–33 for tickets* ⊕ *www.kongehuset.no* ✆ *Tours NKr 95* ☉ *Tours Mid-June–mid-Aug., Mon.–Thurs. and Sat. at noon, 2, and 2:20, Fri. and Sun. at 2, 2:20, and 4.*

KVADRATUREN, AKERSHUS CASTLE, AND AKER BRYGGE

The Kvadraturen is the oldest part of Oslo still standing. Aker Brygge, on the other side of Pipervika, is one of the trendiest areas in Oslo, with several shopping centers and dozens of bars and restaurants lining the waterfront. On a sunny summer day you can sit and relax at one of the many terraces, or hop on a boat for a trip on the Oslo Fjord. The new Opera House, a bit farther to the east in Bjørvika, opened in April 2008. Designed by renowned Norwegian architect firm Snøhetta, the white-marble and glass building has been an instant hit with the public, and quickly established itself as Oslo's new must-see landmark.

Fodor's Choice **Aker Brygge.** This area was the site of a disused shipbuilding yard until
★ redevelopment saw the addition of residential town houses and a commercial sector. Postmodern steel and glass buildings dominate the skyline now. The area has more than 60 shops and 35 restaurants, including upmarket fashion boutiques, pubs, cinemas, a theater, a comedy club, and a shopping mall. There is an open boulevard for strolling. Service facilities include banks, drugstores, and a 1,600-space parking garage. ✉ *Aker Brygge* ☎ *22–83–26–80* ⊕ *www.akerbrygge.no* ✆ *Free* ☉ *Shops weekdays 10–8, Sat. 10–6; grocery store and restaurants are open later.*

Akershus Festning og Slott (*Akershus Fortress and Castle*). Dating to 1299, this stone medieval castle and royal residence was developed into a fortress armed with cannons by 1592. After that time, it withstood a number of sieges and then fell into decay. It was finally restored in 1899. Summer tours take you through its magnificent halls, the castle church, the royal mausoleum, reception rooms, and banqueting halls. Explore Akershus Fortress on your own with the Fortress Trail Map, which you can pick up at the visitor center or download. The castle is closed during official visits, which happen a couple weekends a year. ⊠ *Akershus Festning, Sentrum* ☎ *23–09–35–53* ⊕ *www.forsvarsbygg. no/festningene/Festningene/Akershus-festning* ☒ *Fortress grounds and concerts free. Castle NKr 70, includes audio guide* ☻ *Sept.–Apr., weekends noon–5; May–Aug., Mon.–Sat. 10–4, Sun. noon–4.*

Fodor'sChoice **Munchmuseet** (*Munch Museum*). Edvard Munch, Norway's most famous
★ artist, bequeathed his enormous collection of works (about 1,100 paintings, 3,000 drawings, and 18,000 graphic works) to the city when he died in 1944. The museum is a monument to his artistic genius, housing the largest collection of his works and also mounting changing exhibitions. Munch actually painted four different versions of *The Scream*, the image for which he's best known, and one of them is on display here. While most of the Munch legend focuses on the artist as a troubled, angst-ridden man, he moved away from that pessimistic and dark approach to more optimistic themes later in his career. ⊠ *Tøyengt. 53, Tøyen* ☎ *23–49–35–00* ⊕ *www.munch.museum.no* ☒ *NKr 95* ☻ *Sept.–May, Tues.–Sat. 10–4, Sun. 10–5; June–Aug., daily 10–5.*

Fodor'sChoice **Operahuset.** Oslo's opera house opened in 2008 with a fanfare that
★ included the presence of the Norwegian king and a host of celebrities. The white marble and glass building, designed by renowned Norwegian architect firm Snøhetta, is a stunning addition to the Oslo waterfront, and the pride of Norwegians. It doesn't just look good; acoustics inside the dark oak auditorium are excellent, too. The program includes ballet, orchestra concerts, rock, and opera. Locals and tourists alike enjoy visiting at off hours, eating in the venue's restaurants, and walking on the building's roof. ⊠ *Kirsten Flagstads pl. 1* ☎ *21–42–21–00* ⊕ *www.operaen.no* ☒ *Free, guided tours NKr 100* ☻ *Tours in English in summer.*

FROGNER, MAJORSTUEN, AND HOLMENKOLLEN

Frogner and Majorstuen combine classic Scandinavian elegance with contemporary European chic. Hip boutiques and galleries coexist with embassies and ambassadors' residences on the streets near and around Bygdøy Allé. Holmenkollen, the hill past Frogner Park, has the famous ski jump and miles of ski trails.

Fodor'sChoice **Holmenkollbakken og skimuseet** (*Holmenkollen Ski Jump and Ski*
★ *Museum*). A feat of world-class engineering, this beloved ski jump was first constructed in 1892 and has been rebuilt numerous times, remaining a distinctive part of Oslo's skyline. The cool, futuristic-looking jump you see today was finished in 2010. It offers spectacular views and some repose from Oslo's urbanity, and it still hosts international competitions. The ski-jump simulator puts you in the skis of real jumpers,

15

and the world's oldest ski museum presents 4,000 years of ski history. Check on hours before visiting; they're subject to change, particularly in the fall through spring months. Guided tours of the museum and jump tower are both available. ⊠ *Kongevn. 5, Holmenkollen* ☎ 22–92–32–00 ⊕ *www.holmenkollen.com* 🖾 *Jump tower and museum NKr 110* ⊙ *Oct.–Apr., daily 10–4; May and Sept., daily 10–5; June–Aug, daily 9–8.*

FAMILY
Fodor'sChoice
★

Vigelandsparken (*Vigeland Sculpture Park*). A vast green lung and a favorite hangout for locals, Vigelandsparken has 212 bronze, granite, and wrought-iron sculptures by Gustav Vigeland (1869–1943) as well as ample park space. The 56-foot-high granite *Monolith* is a column of 121 upward-striving nudes surrounded by 36 groups on circular stairs. The *Angry Boy*, a bronze of an enraged cherubic child stamping his foot, draws legions of visitors and has been filmed, parodied, painted red, and even stolen. Kids love to climb on the statues. There's also a museum on-site for those wishing to delve deeper into the artist's work. ⊠ *Frognerparken, Frogner* ☎ 23–49–37–00 ⊕ *www.vigeland.museum. no* 🖾 *Park free, museum NKr 50* ⊙ *Park year-round, dawn–dusk. Museum May–Aug., Tues.–Sun. 10–5; Sept.–Apr., Tues.–Sun. noon–4.*

BYGDØY

Several of Oslo's best-known historic sights are concentrated on the Bygdøy Peninsula (west of the city center), as are several beaches, jogging paths, and the royal family's summer residence. The most pleasant way to get to Bygdøy—available from May to September—is to catch Ferry No. 91 from the rear of the Rådhuset on Pier 3. Times vary, so check with Trafikanten (☎ 177) for schedules. Year-round, Bus No. 30 will take you there from Stortingsgata at Nationaltheatret.

FAMILY
Fodor'sChoice
★

Norsk Folkemuseum (*The Norwegian Museum of Cultural History*). One of the largest open-air museums in Europe, this is a perfect way to see Norway in a day. From the stoic stave church (built in AD 1200) to farmers' houses made of sod, the old buildings here span Norway's regions and most of its recorded history. Indoors, there's a fascinating display of folk costumes. The displays of richly embroidered, colorful *bunader* (national costumes) from every region includes one set at a Telemark country wedding. The museum also has stunning dragon-style wood carvings from 1550 and some beautiful *rosemaling*, or decorative painted floral patterns. The traditional costumes of the Sami (Lapp) people of northern Norway are exhibited around one of their tents. If you're visiting in summer, ask about Norwegian Evening, a summer program of folk dancing, guided tours, and food tastings. On Sundays in December, the museum holds Oslo's largest Christmas market. ⊠ *Museumsvn. 10, Bygdøy* ☎ 22–12–37–00 ⊕ *www.norskfolkemuseum.no* 🖾 *NKr 110* ⊙ *Mid-Sept.–mid-May, weekdays 11–3, weekends 11–4; mid-May–mid-Sept., daily 10–6.*

FAMILY
Fodor'sChoice
★

Vikingskipshuset (*Viking Ship Museum*). The Viking legacy in all its glory lives on at this classic Oslo museum. Chances are you'll come away fascinated by the *Gokstad, Oseberg,* and *Tune,* three blackened wooden Viking ships that date to AD 800. Discovered in Viking tombs around the Oslo fjords between 1860 and 1904, the boats are the best-preserved

Viking ships ever found; they have been on display since the museum's 1957 opening. In Viking times, it was customary to bury the dead with food, drink, useful and decorative objects, and even their horses and dogs. Many of the well-preserved tapestries, household utensils, dragon-style wood carvings, and sledges were found aboard ships. The museum's rounded white walls give the feeling of a burial mound. Avoid summertime crowds by visiting at lunchtime. ⊠ *Huk Aveny 35, Bygdøy* ☎ *22–13–52–80* ⊕ *www.ukm.uio.no/vikingskipshuset* 🖾 *NKr 60* ⊙ *May–Sept., daily 9–6; Oct.–Apr., daily 10–4.*

WHERE TO EAT

DOWNTOWN: ROYAL PALACE TO THE PARLIAMENT

$$$$
ITALIAN
Fodor'sChoice
★

✕**Baltazar Ristorante & Enoteca.** A longtime local favorite, this restaurant is tucked away in the arcades behind the cathedral. It's well worth seeking out. The high-end venue upstairs serves modern Italian food; a more informal enoteca downstairs (with more informal prices; think $ to $$), serves simpler, more traditional dishes. In summer, tables spill out on the big outside terrace and you can enjoy your meal alfresco. Whichever floor you decide to visit, the antipasti are always superb, and so is the homemade pasta; veal with tuna sauce and parmesan is a delicious starter. The stunning wine list features some 450 Italian wines, with all regions well represented, and a choice of vintages for several labels. Our favorite Italian in Oslo. Ⓢ *Average main: NKr 645* ⊠ *Dronningensgt. 27, Domkirkeparken* ☎ *23–35–70–60* ⊕ *www.baltazar.no* ⊙ *Closed Sun. No dinner at Enoteca.*

KVADRATUREN AND AKER BRYGGE

$
AMERICAN
FAMILY

✕**Beach Club.** This diner, its American origins "adjusted to a Norwegian way of life," has been drawing the crowds since it opened in 1989. The classics burgers are all there, but for something a bit different try the "Favourite," with cheese, bacon and chili con carne; or the Zorba (chicken burger with tzatziki); and then a Beach Lime Pie for dessert. Full American-style breakfasts are also available, and there's also a small kids' menu. The original Keith Haring on the walls and the big terrace for sunny days are two more pluses here. Ⓢ *Average main: NKr 150* ⊠ *Bryggetorget 14, Aker Brygge* ☎ *22–83–83–82* ⊕ *www.beachclub.no.*

$$$
NORWEGIAN
Fodor'sChoice
★

✕**Det Gamle Rådhus.** If you're in Oslo for just one night and want an authentic dining experience, head to the city's oldest restaurant— housed in Oslo's first town hall, a building that dates from 1641. It's known for its traditional fish and game dishes such as the moose entrecote or the Røros reindeer. An absolute must, if you're lucky enough to be visiting at the right time, is the house specialty: the pre-Christmas lutefisk platter. The backyard has a charming outdoor area for dining in summer. Ⓢ *Average main: NKr 270* ⊠ *Nedre Slottsgt. 1, Sentrum* ☎ *22–42–01–07* ⊕ *www.gamleraadhus.no* ⊙ *Closed Sun.*

$$$
NORWEGIAN
Fodor'sChoice
★

✕**Solsiden.** With its high ceiling and huge windows, this restaurant, housed in a former warehouse right by the harbor, is the perfect place for dinner on a sunny summer evening. Heed the locals and splash out on a plateau de fruits de mer (the house specialty) or opt for the well-priced menu of the day. Dishes like turbot with mustard purée

15

and lobster sauce, or halibut with mushroom risotto and blue-mussel sauce, come highly recommended. The desserts, from passion-fruit Pavlova to strawberry clafoutis, don't disappoint either. There is also a good wine list with decent by-the-glass options. The restaurant sometimes attracts celebrities (think Rolling Stones and Bruce Springsteen) and often draws sizeable crowds; book ahead. [$] *Average main: NKr 275* ✉ *Søndre Akershus Kai 34* ☎ *22–33–36–30* 🌐 *www.solsiden.no* 🕒 *Closed Sept.–mid-May. No lunch.*

TØYEN AND GRØNLAND

$
NORWEGIAN
FAMILY

🍴 **Asylet.** This popular pub right by Grønland Torg serves homemade traditional Norwegian food in an atmospheric setting. The building, which dates from the 1730s, was once an orphanage. The big lunch menu features a good selection of *smørbrød* (open-faced sandwiches) as well as smoked-salmon salad and the traditional *karbonade* (a sort of open-faced hamburger, served with fried onions). There is a fireplace inside, and a beer garden for enjoying the sun in summer. [$] *Average main: NKr 180* ✉ *Grønland 28* ☎ *22–17–09–39* 🌐 *www.asylet.no.*

FROGNER AND MAJORSTUEN

$$$$
INTERNATIONAL
Fodor's Choice ★

🍴 **Bagatelle.** Bagatelle attracts the who's who of Oslo society, and is widely recognized as one of the city's best restaurants—and also one of the costliest. Artworks by contemporary artists accent the understated, elegant dining room. Bagatelle regained its Michelin star in 2012; next door, the rustic brasserie Lille B has attained a Michelin Bib Gourmand for its good food at moderate prices. [$] *Average main: NKr 1,350* ✉ *Bygdøy Allé 3, Frogner* ☎ *22–44–40–40* 🌐 *www.bagatelle.no* ✍ *Reservations essential* 🕒 *Closed Sun. and Mon. No lunch at Bagatelle.*

HOLMENKOLLEN

$$$$
NORWEGIAN
Fodor's Choice ★

🍴 **De Fem Stuer.** Near the famous Holmenkollen ski jump, in the historic Holmenkollen Park Hotel Rica, this restaurant serves first-rate food in a grand setting, with stunning views over Oslo. Modern Nordic and international dishes blend classic ingredients with more exotic ones. Order the three, five, or seven course meal. Or try carpaccio of whale or sirloin of elk. The restaurant's famous Taste of Norway menu comprises dishes made with ingredients from small-scale Norwegian farmers and local food purveyors. [$] *Average main: NKr 585* ✉ *Holmenkollen Park Hotel Rica, Kongevn. 26, Holmenkollen* ☎ *22–92–20–00* 🌐 *www.holmenkollenparkhotel.no.*

WHERE TO STAY

DOWNTOWN: ROYAL PALACE TO THE PARLIAMENT

$$
HOTEL
Fodor's Choice ★

🏨 **Grand Hotel.** This very central hotel is the choice of visiting heads of state, rock musicians and Nobel Peace Prize winners. **Pros:** period features have been preserved throughout; Ladies Floor, with 13 unique rooms designed for women travelers; beautiful pool and spa. **Cons:** gets busy during festivals and in December, during Nobel Peace Prize week. [$] *Rooms from: NKr 1,440* ✉ *Karl Johans gt. 31, Sentrum* ☎ *23–21–20–00* 🌐 *www.grand.no* 🛏 *238 rooms, 54 suites* 🍽 *Breakfast.*

$$$$ HOTEL Fodor's Choice ★ **Hotel Continental.** History meets modernity at this landmark—it's a sophisticated stay with stylish guest rooms and posh common areas. **Pros:** exemplary service; beautiful, well-appointed rooms; great gym. **Cons:** restaurant and bars are very busy with locals as well as guests; very expensive. [$] *Rooms from: NKr 3,300* ✉ *Stortingsgt. 24–26, Sentrum* ☎ *22–82–40–00* 🌐 *www.hotelcontinental.no* 🛏 *155 rooms, 23 suites* 🍴 *No meals.*

$ HOTEL **Thon Hotel Stefan.** A home away from home, this hotel tries hard to make guests feel well looked after. **Pros:** very central; great breakfast; good value. **Cons:** some rooms are a bit worn (a renovation is in the works); some rooms are noisy from nearby nightlife. [$] *Rooms from: NKr 945* ✉ *Rosenkrantz gt. 1, Sentrum* ☎ *23–31–55–00* 🌐 *www.thonhotels.no/stefan* 🛏 *150 rooms* 🍴 *Breakfast.*

KVADRATUREN AND OSLO S STATION

$ HOTEL **Clarion Royal Christiania Hotel.** What was once bare-bones housing for 1952 Olympians is now a luxurious, 100% no-smoking hotel. **Pros:** welcoming lobby; organic breakfast; on-site parking. **Cons:** location is convenient but not charming; T.G.I. Fridays doesn't offer a very local experience (though the organic Scandinavian breakfast counterbalances its effect). [$] *Rooms from: NKr 790* ✉ *Biskop Gunnerus gt. 3* ☎ *23–10–80–00* 🌐 *www.royalchristiania.no* 🛏 *439 rooms, 64 suites* 🍴 *Breakfast.*

$ B&B/INN **Cochs Pensjonat.** A stone's throw from the Royal Palace and near Bogstadveien (one of Oslo's premier shopping and socializing streets), this no-frills guesthouse has reasonably priced, comfortable, and rather spartan rooms. **Pros:** central location; good value for money, and amiable staff. **Cons:** basic facilities; value rooms are tiny; no on-site restaurant. [$] *Rooms from: NKr 780* ✉ *Parkvn. 25, Majorstuen* ☎ *23–33–24–00* 🌐 *www.cochspensjonat.no* 🛏 *88 rooms* 🍴 *No meals.*

$$ HOTEL **Radisson Blu Plaza Hotel.** The understated elegance helps keep the rooms filled at this business hotel. **Pros:** great top-floor bar; very good breakfast buffet; luxuriously grand bathtubs; excellent location. **Cons:** this is northern Europe's tallest hotel, so it's not very intimate; the breakfast room can get crowded. [$] *Rooms from: NKr 1,495* ✉ *Sonja Henies pl. 3* ☎ *22–05–80–00* 🌐 *www.radissonblu.com/plazahotel-oslo* 🛏 *676 rooms, 20 suites* 🍴 *Breakfast.*

NIGHTLIFE

Into the early hours, people are usually out on Karl Johans Gate. Aker Brygge, the wharf area, has many bars and some nightclubs, attracting mostly tourists, couples on first dates, and other people willing to spend extra for the waterfront location. Grünerløkka and Grønland have even more bars, pubs, and cafés catering to a younger crowd. A more mature upmarket crowd ventures out to the less busy west side of Oslo, to Frogner and Bygdøy.

Drinking out is very expensive, starting at around NKr 70 for a beer or a mixed drink. Some bars in town remain quiet until 11 or midnight when the first groups of *forschpiel* partiers arrive. For nightlife listings, pick up a copy of the free monthly paper *Natt og Dag* or Friday's edition of *Avis 1*.

BARS AND LOUNGES

Bibliotekbaren og Vinterhaven. If you're more partial to lounging than drinking, the Bibliotekbaren og Vinterhaven (Library Bar and Winter Garden) is a stylish hangout with old-fashioned leather armchairs, huge marble columns, and live piano music. Politicians, actors, musicians, journalists and locals have come here for nearly 100 years for informal meetings, quiet chats, or just to enjoy the tempting sandwich and cake buffet. ⊠ *Hotel Bristol, Kristian IVs gt. 7, Sentrum* ☎ 22–82–60–00.

Café Con Bar. With its 1970s theme, Café Con Bar, is one of Oslo's trendy crowd-pleasers. The kitchen closes at 10 and guest DJs spin on weekends. ⊠ *Brugt. 11, Grønland* ☎ 22–05–02–00 ⊕ *www.cafeconbar.no.*

Oslo Mikrobryggeriet. Serious beer-drinkers may find Oslo Mikrobryggeriet worth a stop. Eight different beers are brewed on the premises, including the increasingly popular Oslo Pils. ⊠ *Bogstadvn. 6, Majorstuen* ☎ 22–56–97–76 ⊕ *www.omb.no.*

Stargate Pub. For cheap beer and an informal crowd, visit the popular student hangout Stargate Pub at Brugata, just alongside the bridge. ⊠ *Grønlandsleiret 33, Grønland* ☎ 22–04–13–77.

Underwater Pub. This two-story pubs uses fish tanks and scuba gear to get the theme across. On Tuesday and Thursday there's live opera, with performers from the Norwegian Opera. ⊠ *Dalsbergstien 4, St. Hans Haugen* ☎ 22–46–05–26 ⊕ *underwaterpub.no* ⊠ *Free* ☉ *Closed Sun.*

CAFÉS

As a mark of Oslo's growing cosmopolitanism, the city now has a continental café culture, with bohemian coffeehouses and chic cafés. Grünerløkka especially has lots of cafés to suit every taste; they're great for people-watching and whiling away summer afternoons.

Fru Hagen. For a slightly more bohemian experience, head to Fru Hagen, with its classical-looking chandeliers and elegant velvet-furnished sofas. Aim for a window seat to check out the passing traffic. ⊠ *Thorvald Meyers gt. 40, Grünerløkka* ☎ 45–49–19–04 ⊕ *www.fruhagen.no.*

Kaffebrenneriet. This coffee chain, Oslo's answer to Starbucks (with better coffee, locals would say), has 24 branches throughout the city. ☎ 22–46–13–90 ⊕ *www.kaffebrenneriet.no.*

Tea Lounge. The Tea Lounge serves alcoholic and nonalcoholic tea drinks. It's very stylish, with mellow music, a mosaic tile bar, picture windows, high-backed plush red sofas, and a trendy crowd to match. ⊠ *Thorvald Meyers gt. 33C, Grünerløkka* ☎ 22–37–07–05 ⊕ *www. tealounge.no.*

Theatercafe. Following in the tradition of the grand continental cafés, the Theatercafe in the Continental Hotel is an Oslo institution. ⊠ *Stortingsgt. 24–26, Sentrum* ☎ 22–82–40–50 ⊕ *www.theatercafeen.no.*

SHOPPING

Oslo is the best place in the country for buying anything Norwegian. Popular souvenirs include knitwear, wood and ceramic trolls, cheese slicers, boxes with rosemaling, gold and silver jewelry, items made from pewter, smoked salmon, caviar, akvavit, chocolate, and geitost, the sweet brown goat cheese that can be found in just about every Norwegian kitchen.

Norway is famous for its colorful hand-knit wool sweaters, and even mass-produced (machine-knit) models are of top quality. Prices are regulated, and they are always lower than buying a Norwegian sweater abroad.

Prices in Norway, as in all of Scandinavia, are generally much higher than in other European countries. Prices of handmade articles, such as knitwear, are controlled, making comparison shopping pointless. Otherwise, shops have both sales and specials—look for the words salg and tilbud.

15

SHOPPING NEIGHBORHOODS
Basarhallene, the arcade behind Oslo *domkirke* (cathedral), is worth a browse for glass and crystal and handicrafts made in Norway. Walk 15 minutes west of the city center and you can wander up the tree-lined Bygdøy Allé and browse the fashionable **Frogner** and **Bygdøy** areas, which are brimming with modern and antique-furniture stores, interior design shops, food shops, art galleries, haute couture, and Oslo's beautiful people. The streets downtown around **Karl Johans Gate** draw many of Oslo's shoppers. The concentration of department stores is especially high in this part of town. **Majorstuen** starts at the *T-bane* (subway) station with the same name and proceeds down Bogstadveien to the Royal Palace. Oslo is not famed for its markets, but there's a small flower market on Stortorget in front of the cathedral, and a few stalls selling souvenirs and second-hand records on Youngstorget. Every Saturday, a flea market is open at **Vestkanttorget,** at Amaldus Nilsens plass near Frognerparken. **Grünerløkka,** a 15-minute walk north of the center, is blooming with trendy new and bohemian fashion boutiques, vintage stores, and many other quirky little shops.

HELSINKI

A city of the sea, Helsinki was built along a series of oddly shaped peninsulas and islands jutting into the Baltic coast along the Gulf of Finland. Streets and avenues curve around bays, bridges reach to nearby islands, and ferries ply among offshore islands.

Having grown dramatically since World War II, Helsinki now absorbs more than one-tenth of the Finnish population. The metro area covers 764 square km (474 square miles) and 315 islands. Most sights, hotels, and restaurants cluster on one peninsula, forming a compact central hub. The greater Helsinki metropolitan area, which includes Espoo and Vantaa, has a total population of more than a million people.

FINLAND AT A GLANCE

- **Capital:** Helsinki
- **Population:** 5,435,000
- **Currency:** Euro
- **Money:** ATMs are common
- **Language:** Finnish, Swedish, and Sami
- **Country Code:** ☎ 358
- **Emergencies:** ☎ 112
- **Driving:** On the right

- **Electricity:** 200v/50 cycles; electrical plugs have two round prongs
- **Time:** Six hours ahead of New York
- **Documents:** Up to 90 days with valid passport; Schengen rules apply
- **Mobile Phones:** GSM (900 and 1800 bands)
- **Major Mobile Companies:** Sonera, Elisa, and DNA

Helsinki has some of the purest neoclassical architecture in the world. Add to this the influence of Stockholm and St. Petersburg with the local inspiration of 20th-century Finnish design, and the result is a European capital city that is as architecturally eye-catching as it is distinct from other Scandinavian capitals. You are bound to discover endless engaging details—a grimacing gargoyle; a foursome of males supporting a balcony's weight on their shoulders; a building painted in striking colors with contrasting flowers in the windows. The city's 400 or so parks make it particularly inviting in summer.

Today, Helsinki is still a meeting point of eastern and western Europe, which is reflected in its cosmopolitan image, the influx of Russians and Estonians, and generally multilingual population. Outdoor summer bars (*terrassit* as the locals call them) and cafés in the city center are perfect for people-watching on a summer afternoon.

PLANNING YOUR TIME
Helsinki is a compact city and in a day you can easily see the better tourist attractions with a leisurely stroll. The city's cathedral is on Senate Square and the Russian Orthodox Uspensky Cathedral is just a view minutes' walk. A stroll along Esplanadi is a must, with its chic shops and grand hotels.

If you've got a couple more days, make your way towards the city's main thoroughfare, Mannerhiemintie, taking in the Ateneum Art Museum and the National Museum. The area around Töölö Bay is a pretty and peaceful place to get away from the humdrum and enjoy a picnic. A trip to Suomenlinna is highly recommended, and ferries leave regularly from Kauppatori.

GETTING HERE AND AROUND
AIR TRAVEL
All domestic and international flights to Helsinki use Helsinki-Vantaa International Airport, 20 km (12 miles) north of the city center.

Local Bus No. 615 runs between the airport and the main railway station downtown from 4:50 am to 1:20 am, taking 40 minutes. Finnair buses carry travelers to and from the railway station (Finnair's City Terminal) every 20 minutes, with a stop at the Scandic Hotel Continental Helsinki. Stops requested along the route from the airport to the city are also made. Travel time from the Scandic Hotel Continental to the airport is about 35 minutes from the main railway station.

A limousine ride into central Helsinki will cost €95–€236. A cab ride into central Helsinki costs about €30. Driving time is 20 to 35 minutes, depending on the time of day. Airport Taxi costs €35–€40 for one to four passengers, and it operates shuttles between the city and the airport. If you are going to the airport, you must reserve by 7 pm the day before departure. Leaving from the airport, you do not need a reservation—just look for the Airport Taxi stands in the arrivals halls. The yellow line taxi stand at the airport also offers fixed-rate trips into the city.

Contacts Airport Taxi ☎ 0600/555–555 ⊕ www.airporttaxi.fi ⊙ Weekdays 8–9, weekends noon–9; at Helsinki–Vantaa Airport, daily 6–1:30 am. **Helsinki-Vantaa Airport** ✉ Vantaa ☎ 020/708–000 ⊕ www.helsinki-vantaa.fi. **Limousine Service** ☎ 09/2797–800 in Helsinki ⊕ www.limousineservice.fi.

BOAT TRAVEL

From Stockholm, Silja and Viking Line ships cross to the Finnish Åland Islands (7 hours), Turku (11 hours), and Helsinki (15 hours), generally with one departure daily in each direction. In Helsinki the Tallink Silja Line terminal for ships arriving from Stockholm is at Olympialaituri (Olympic Harbor), on the west side of the South Harbor. The Viking Line terminal for ships arriving from Stockholm is at Katajanokkanlaituri (Katajanokka Harbor), on the east side of the South Harbor.

A ferry to the Suomenlinna fortress island runs about twice an hour, depending on the time of day, and costs €2 one-way and €3.80 round-trip. Ten-trip tickets issued for city public transport can be used on the ferry, too. From June to August, private water buses run from Kauppatori to Suomenlinna, charging €3.50 one-way and €5.50 round-trip.

Contacts Silja Line ☎ 0600/15700 in Helsinki ⊕ www.tallinksilja.com. **Suomenlinna Ferry** ✉ Suomenlinnan Liikenne Oy, Merikasarminkatu 10 ☎ 09/3102–1000 ⊕ www.slloy.fi. **Viking Line** ☎ 0600/41577 in Helsinki ⊕ www. vikingline.fi.

PUBLIC TRANSPORTATION

Bus and tram networks are compact but extensive, and service is frequent, with fewer buses nights and Sunday. Pick up a route map at the tourist office—many stops do not have them. Tickets bought from the driver cost €2.80 for buses and €2 for trams. You can also buy a tourist ticket for unlimited travel on public transportation within the city (€8 one day, €16 three days, €24 five days), or purchase the Travel Card, loaded with an amount or for a time period. Purchase your tickets from the automated machine at stops and stations, rather than onboard, in order to avoid a service charge. Extensive information on routes, fares, and timetables is available from the Helsinki City Transport website.

15

The Helsinki Kortti (Helsinki Card) allows unlimited travel on city public transportation, free entry to many museums, a free sightseeing tour, and other discounts. It's available for one, two, or three days (€36, €46, or €56, respectively). You can buy it at more than 70 places, including airport information desks, ferry terminals, some hotels and travel agencies, Stockmann's department store, the Hotel Booking Centre, the Helsinki City Tourist office, or online through Helsinki Expert.

Contacts Helsinki City Transport ⊠ *HKL Head Office, Toinen linja 7* ☎ *09/310-1071* ⊕ *www.hel.fi/hkl.*

TAXI TRAVEL

There are numerous taxi stands; central stands are at Rautatientori at the station, the main bus station, Linja-autoasema, and in the Esplanade. Taxis can also be hailed, but this can be difficult, as many are on radio call and are often on their way to stands, where late-night lines may be very long. An average taxi ride in Helsinki can cost around €10; a taxi from the airport can cost €30 or more. All taxis in Helsinki go through the Taxi Center, or you can call Kovanen, a private company for taxis, vans, minibuses, and limousine services.

Contacts Kovanen ☎ *0200/6060 (€1.25 per min, plus local charge; 24 hrs)* ⊕ *www.kovanen.com.* **Taxi Center** ☎ *0100/0700 Immediate, €1.15 plus local charge, 0100/0600 Advance, €6.40 added to fare, plus €1.15 per call plus 16 cents per 10 seconds plus local charge* ⊕ *www.taksihelsinki.fi.*

TRAIN TRAVEL

Helsinki's suburbs and most of the rest of southern, western, and central Finland are well served by trains. Travel on trains within the city limits costs the same as all public transport, €2.50 or less if you use a Travel Card (which carries an initial fee of €9 but reduces the cost of each trip; you can buy the card for specific amounts or time periods). A single regional ticket costs €4.50 and is good for 80 minutes, including transfers. Regional tourist tickets are available for one day (€12), three days (€24), and five days (€36).

TOURS

Most major boat tours depart from Kauppatori Market Square. The easiest way to choose one is to go to the square in the morning and read the information boards describing the tours. Most tours run in summer only. You can go as far afield as Porvoo or take a short jaunt to the Helsinki Zoo on Korkeasaari. The Helsinki City Tourist Office employs "Helsinki Helpers," dressed in green and white. From June to August, daily from 8 to 8, they walk the streets in the city center and harbor area, answering questions and giving directions. Helsinki Expert is a multipurpose travel agent and guide-booking center that will arrange personal tour guides. The City Tourist Office also has an excellent brochure, *Helsinki on Foot,* with six walks covering most points of interest.

Helsinki Expert. Bus tours are a good way to get oriented in Helsinki. The Helsinki Expert's 1.75-hour audio tour of central Helsinki sites is free with the Helsinki Card; otherwise it's €28. Recorded commentary is available on a headset. Tours leave from Esplanade Park and the Katajanoka Terminal. Guided city tours, with live commentary in

English and Swedish, are also available; they depart from the Katajanokka and Olympia Ferry terminals and last approximately the same amount of time. ⊠ *Pohjoinen Makasiinikatu 4* ☎ *09/2288–1600* ⊕ *www.helsinkiexpert.fi.*

VISITOR INFORMATION

Contacts Helsinki City Tourist and Convention Bureau ⊠ *Pohjoisespl. 19, Esplanadi* ☎ *09/3101–3300* ⊕ *www.visithelsinki.fi* ⊘ *May 15–Sep. 14, weekdays 9–8, weekends 9–6; Sept. 15–May 14, weekdays 9–6, weekends 10–4.*

EXPLORING

The city center, characterized by its large multistory malls, is densely packed and easily explored on foot, with the main tourist sites grouped in several clusters; nearby islands are easily accessible by ferry. Just west of Katajanokka, Senaatintori and its Tuomiokirkko (Luthern Cathedral) mark the beginning of the city center, which extends westward along Aleksanterinkatu. The wide street Mannerheimintie is comparable to New York's Broadway, moving diagonally past the major attractions of the city center before terminating beside the Esplanade. Southern Helsinki is a tangle of smaller streets, some of them curving and some of them running for just a few blocks before changing their names; carry a good map while exploring this area.

IN AND AROUND KAUPPATORI

The orange tents of the Kauppatori market brighten even the coldest snowy winter months with fresh flowers, fish, crafts, and produce. In warm weather, the bazaar fills with shoppers who stop for the ubiquitous coffee and *munkki* (doughnuts), the seaborne traffic in Eteläsatama or South Harbor a backdrop. From here you can take the local ferry service to Suomenlinna (Finland's Castle); Korkeasaari (Korkea Island), home of the zoo; or take a walk through the neighborhoods of Helsinki, encompassing the harbor; city center shopping district; tree-lined Bulevardi; and the indoor Hietalahden Tori, another marketplace.

Kauppatori (*Market Square*). At this Helsinki institution, open year-round, wooden stands with orange and gold awnings bustle in the mornings when everyone—tourists and locals alike—comes to shop, browse, or sit and enjoy coffee and conversation. You can buy a freshly caught perch for the evening's dinner, a bouquet of bright flowers for a friend, or a fur pelt. In summer the fruit and vegetable stalls are supplemented by an evening arts-and-crafts market. The crêpes, made to order by one of the tented vendors, are excellent. ⊠ *Eteläranta and Pohjoisespl., Keskusta/Kauppatori* ⊘ *Weekdays 6:30–6, Sat. 6:30–4, and in summer, Sun. 10–5.*

Fodor'sChoice **Suomenlinna** (*Finland's Castle*). A former island fortress, Suomenlinna is
★ a perennially popular collection of museums, parks, and gardens, and has been designated a UNESCO World Heritage Site. In 1748 the Finnish army helped build the impregnable fortress, long referred to as the Gibraltar of the North; since then it has expanded into a series of interlinked islands. Although Suomenlinna has never been taken by assault, its occupants surrendered once to the Russians in 1808 and came under

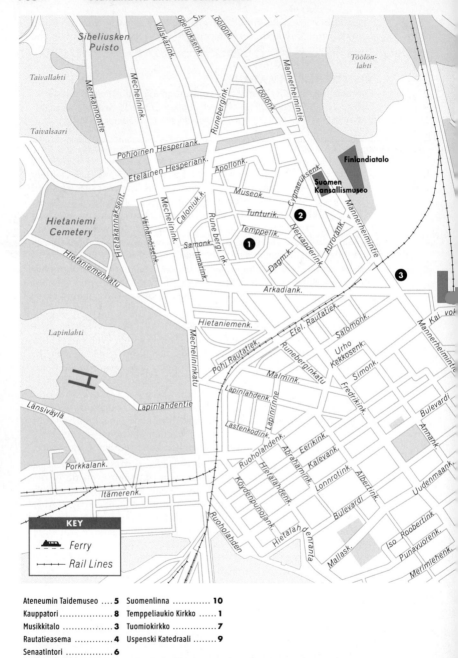

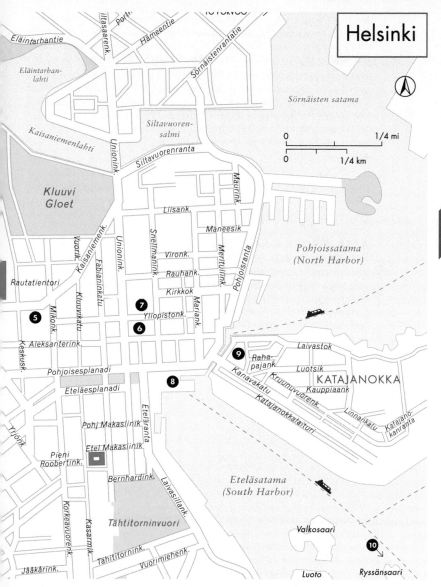

Helsinki

Sörnäisten satama

0   1/4 mi
0   1/4 km

15

fire from British ships in 1855 during the Crimean War. Today Suomenlinna makes a lovely excursion from Helsinki, particularly in early summer when the island is engulfed in a mauve-and-purple mist of lilacs,
introduced from Versailles by the Finnish architect Ehrensvärd.

Suomenlinna is easily reached by public ferry (€2.50 one-way, €3.60
round-trip) or private boat (€3.50 one-way, €5.50 round-trip), both of
which leave from Helsinki's Kauppatori. The ferry ride from South Harbor to Suomenlinna takes about 15 minutes. Plan to spend an afternoon
on the islands; you'll need about four hours to explore the fortress and
museums. Note that days open and hours of sites are limited off-season.

Although its fortification occupied six islands, its main attractions are
now concentrated on three: Iso Mustasaari, Susisaari, and Kustaan-
miekka. There are no street names on the island, so get a map for about
€2 from the Helsinki City Tourist Office before you go, or buy one at
the visitor center on the island. ☎ 029/53–38410 ⊕ www.suomenlinna.
fi/en.

KATAJANOKKA AND SENAATINTORI
Katajanokka is separated from the mainland by a canal and begins
just east of Kauppatori. A charming residential quarter as well as a
cargo- and passenger-ship port, this area also has one of the city's main
landmarks, the dazzling Orthodox Uspenskin Katedraali, one of the
biggest cathedrals in Europe. Not far from Katajanokka is the elegant
Lutheran Cathedral that dominates Senaatintori. The Ateneumin Taidemuseo is also nearby.

Ateneumin Taidemuseo (*Ateneum Art Museum of the Finnish National
Gallery*). The best traditional Finnish art is housed in this splendid neoclassical complex, one of three museums organized under the Finnish
National Gallery umbrella. The gallery holds major European works,
but the outstanding attraction is the Finnish art, particularly the works
of Akseli Gallen-Kallela, inspired by the national epic *Kalevala*. The
rustic portraits by Albert Edelfelt are enchanting, and many contemporary Finnish artists are well represented. The two other museums that
make up the National Gallery are **Kiasma** and **Synebrychoff.** ✉ *Kaivok.
2, Keskusta* ☎ *09/6122–5510 for info* ⊕ *www.fng.fi, www.ateneum.fi*
✉ *€8, extra charge for special exhibits* ☼ *Tues. and Fri. 10–6, Wed. and
Thurs. 10–8, weekends 11–5.*

Rautatieasema (*Central Train Station*). This outdoor square and the
adjoining train station are the city's bustling commuter hub. The station's huge granite figures are by Emil Wikström; the solid building they
adorn was designed by Eliel Saarinen, one of the founders of the early-
20th-century National Romantic style. ✉ *Kaivok. 1, Rautatientori, Keskusta* ☎ *0600/41–902 for info in English (€1 per answered call, plus
local network charge)* ⊕ *www.vr.fi/en* ☼ *Information daily 7–10 pm.*

Senaatintori (*Senate Square*). The harmony of the three buildings flanking Senaatintori exemplifies one of the purest styles of European architecture, as envisioned and designed by German architect Carl Ludvig
Engel. This is the heart of neoclassical Helsinki. On the square's west
side is one of the main buildings of Helsingin Yliopisto (Helsinki University), and up the hill is the university library. On the east side is the

pale yellow Valtionneuvosto (Council of State), completed in 1822 and once the seat of the Autonomous Grand Duchy of Finland's Imperial Senate. At the lower end of the square, stores and restaurants now occupy former merchants' homes. ✉ *Bounded by Aleksanterink. and Yliopistonk., Senaatintori.*

Fodor's Choice **Tuomiokirkko** (*Lutheran Cathedral of Finland*). The steep steps and green
★ domes of the church dominate Senaatintori. Completed in 1852, it is the work of famous architect Carl Ludvig Engel, who also designed parts of Tallinn and St. Petersburg. Wander through the tasteful blue-gray interior, with its white moldings and the statues of German reformers Martin Luther and Philipp Melanchthon, as well as the famous Finnish bishop Mikael Agricola. Concerts are frequently held inside the church. The crypt at the rear is the site of frequent historic and architectural exhibitions and bazaars. ✉ *Unioninkatu 29, Senaatintori* ☎ *09/2340–6120* ⊕ *www.helsinginseurakunnat.fi* ۞ *Sept.–May, daily 9–6; June–Aug., daily 9–midnight.*

Uspenski Katedraali (*Uspenski Orthodox Cathedral*). Perched atop a small rocky cliff over the North Harbor in Katajanokka is the main cathedral of the Orthodox Church in Finland. Its brilliant gold onion domes are its hallmark, but its imposing redbrick edifice, decorated by 19th-century Russian artists, is no less distinctive. The cathedral was built and dedicated in 1868 in the Byzantine-Slavonic style and remains the biggest Orthodox church in Scandinavia. ✉ *Kanavak. 1, Katajanokka* ☎ *0207/220–683* ⊕ *www.ort.fi* ۞ *Oct.–Apr., Tue.–Fri. 9:30–4, Sat. 9.30–2, Sun. noon–3; May–Sept., weekdays 9:30–4, Sat. 9:30–2, Sun. noon–3; closed for weddings and other special events.*

TÖÖLÖ

Most of Helsinki's major cultural buildings—the opera house, concert hall, and national museum—are within a short distance of each other around the perimeter of the inlet from the sea called Töölönlahti. The inlet itself is lovely in all seasons, and the walking and biking paths are well trodden by locals. The winding streets just east of Mannerheimintie enfold the Temppeliaukio Kirkko (Temple Square Church), whose unexceptional facade gives way to an amazing cavernous interior. Also nearby, the Sibelius park cuts a large swath out of the neighborhood and borders the sea.

Musiikkitalo (*Helsinki Music Centre*). Since it opened in 2011, the Helsinki Music Center has been praised for its acoustics and daring design. It's home to the Sibelius Academy and two symphony orchestras. Guided tours are available, but most are in Finnish—check the website for details. The one-hour guided walking tour introduces participants to what happens here, as well as to the architecture, main audience, and the concert hall. ✉ *Mannerheimintie 13 a, Töölö* ☎ *0600/900–900 for tour tickets, 020/707–0421 for service desk* ⊕ *www.musiikkitalo.fi.*

Suomen Kansallismuseo (*National Museum of Finland*). Architect Eliel Saarinen and his partners combined the language of Finnish medieval church architecture with elements of art nouveau to create this vintage example of the National Romantic style. The museum's collection of archaeological, cultural, and ethnological artifacts gives you

15

insight into Finland's past. ✉ *Mannerheimintie 34, Keskusta* ☎ *09/40–501, 09/4050–9544 for ticket office, 09/4050–9552 for guided tours* ⊕ *www.nba.fi/en/nationalmuseum* 🖭 €8 ⊙ *Tue. 11–8, Wed.–Sun. 11–6* Ⓜ *Tram No. 7A/7B, 4, 4T, and 10. to Kansallismuseo/Nationalmuseum (National Museum of Finland).*

Temppeliaukio Kirkko (*Temple Square Church*). Topped with a copper dome, the church looks like a half-buried spaceship from the outside. It's really a modern Lutheran church carved into the rock outcrops below. The sun shines in from above, illuminating a stunning interior with birch pews, modern pipe organ, and cavernous walls. Ecumenical and Lutheran services in various languages are held throughout the week. ✉ *Lutherinkatu 3, Töölö* ☎ *09/2340–5940* ⊕ *www.helsinginseurakunnat.fi* ⊙ *Mon.–Thurs. 10–8, Fri. and Sat. 10–5:45, Sun. 11:45–5:45; closed during weddings, concerts, and services.*

WHERE TO EAT

Helsinki is dotted with cozy yet decidedly modern-looking venues offering reindeer, herring, and pike accompanied by delicious Finnish mushrooms or wild-berry sauces. Don't be turned off by spare menu descriptions such as "reindeer with lingonberry sauce and chanterelles"—it's a classic example of the Finnish tendency toward understatement, and the skill will be evident in the taste. You'll find everything from Mexican to Nepalese (quite popular with locals) in the city, though not at every price point. Expect European-size entrées, excellent location, and service at a steep price. A strong café culture makes it easy to find a tasty, reasonably priced lunch.

AROUND ESPLANADE AND KATAJANOKKA

$$$

EASTERN
EUROPEAN

✕ **Bellevue.** Since 1917, Bellevue has been serving dishes inspired by Russian and Finnish cuisine. Try the *shashlik* (cubed lamb kebab served with mushroom rice) or the ox filet à la Novgorod. The plush interior of this elegant town house has many shining samovars, but only some of them are functional; each table has lighted candles. $ *Average main: €29* ✉ *Rahapajank. 3, Keskusta* ☎ *09/179–560* ⊕ *www.restaurantbellevue.com* ⊙ *Closed Sun. and Mon. No lunch July or Sat. May–Aug.*

$$$

SCANDINAVIAN

✕ **Savotta.** Savotta means "lumber camp," and the hearty food those lumberjacks would want is reflected on the menu. Located on Senate Square, directly across from Helsinki Cathedral, the 250-year-old building is adorned with knickknacks from a bygone era. The food is traditional Finnish food at its best—no effete New Scandinavian nonsense here. Meat dishes predominate, though there are fish and vegetarian options. The Provision Master's menu comes with a starter for two consisting of goat cheese, pâté-like reindeer rillettes, pickled chanterelles, smoked pike, arctic char, smoked salmon roe and a host of other delicious delicacies. Main course is reindeer round top roast and smoked potatoes. Pair it all with the locally brewed strong beer called *tahti*. Dessert is a house-made ice cream flavored with licorice. The cheerful staff are informative when it comes to questions about this very Finnish cuisine. [$] *Average main: €25* ✉ *Aleksanterinkatu 22, Senaatintori* ☎ *09/7425–5588* 🌐 *www.asrestaurants.com* ⏲ *No lunch Sun.*

$$ EUROPEAN 🍴 **Zetor.** Known as the "tractor restaurant," Zetor is a haven for the weary traveler in need of some homey and hearty cooking—choose from meatballs, Karelian stew, sausage, or schnitzel, washed down with the house brew. Wooden tables, farm equipment, and a witty menu make for an entertaining evening. Late nights the restaurant transforms into a bar and disco. [$] *Average main: €17* ✉ *Kaivopiha, Mannerheimintie 3–5, Keskusta/Kaivopiha* ☎ *020/1234–800* 🌐 *www.zetor.net.*

WEST OF MANNERHEIMINTIE

$$$$ FRENCH 🍴 **Demo.** There are not many places where you can really kick back and enjoy pumpkin soup with a tiger prawn mousse starter, or roasted pigeon served with black pudding and pistachios—particularly if you'd like sophisticated dishes like these to be accompanied with the friendliness and relaxed attitude of a corner bar. Opened in 2003 by chefs Tommi Tuominen and Teemu Aura, Demo serves food of the very best quality without the stuffiness of some high-end restaurants; this is a place where you can comfortably laugh out loud. The core menu is classical French, and by far the most popular choices are the 4-, 5- and 6-course chef's menus, which change daily. The wine cellar here might be the best in Finland—some 450 wines and counting, with Burgundy a specialty. [$] *Average main: €36* ✉ *Uudenmaankatu 9–11, Keskusta* ☎ *09/2289–0840* 🌐 *www.restaurantdemo.fi* ⏲ *Closed Sun. and Mon. No lunch.*

$$ BURGER 🍴 **Stone's.** Some of the best burgers in the city emerge from this relaxed and central gastro pub that's open late. Along with classics dishes like pork knuckle and steamed mussels, Stone's serves seven basic, and very different, burgers, all six ounces. The "black and bleu" is a Cajun-blackened burger with Roquefort cheese—it's mouthwatering. "China porky" is a pork burger glazed in an Asian sauce. The beef here is all organic and locally sourced; the buns are cooked on site, and you can taste it. This unpretentious and cozy place nevertheless takes its beer pretty seriously too, with 15 on draft. Every couple months, the two that sell the least are replaced. [$] *Average main: €19* ✉ *Keskuskatu 4, Keskusta/Rautatieasema* ☎ *010/76–63740* 🌐 *www.stonespub.fi.*

WHERE TO STAY

In recent years, Helsinki has been noted for its high-end design hotels, which emphasize room decor, layout, and in-house restaurants and bars. Top hotels are notoriously expensive, generally have small rooms, and mostly cater to business travelers. Standards are high, and the level of service usually corresponds to the price. Rates can plummet by as much as 50% on weekends, and most include a generous breakfast buffet and sauna privileges.

CITY CENTER

$$ HOTEL 🏨 **Holiday Inn Helsinki City Centre.** Some of the comfortable rooms in this central hotel overlook Töölönlahti, and the sleek lobby is partially decked out in bright colors. **Pros:** city center location close to railway station; efficient service. **Cons:** corporate feel. [$] *Rooms from:*

€120 ✉ Elielinaukio 5, Keskusta ☎ 09/5425–5000 🌐 www.holidayinn.com/hotels/us/en/helsinki/helek/hoteldetail 🛏 174 rooms, 26 executive rooms 🍴 Breakfast.

AROUND ESPLANADE AND KATAJANOKKA

$$$$ HOTEL **GLO Hotel Kluuvi.** Well-dressed locals meet in the lobby lounge while a largely international business clientele heads upstairs to unwind in what are Helsinki's slickest hotel rooms. **Pros:** gorgeous rooms; fantastic spa. **Cons:** breakfast, gym and sauna cost extra if in standard room. *$ Rooms from: €200 ✉ Kluuvik. 4 ☎ 010/3444–400 🌐 www.hotelglo.fi/en 🛏 131 rooms, 13 suites 🍴 Multiple meal plans.*

$$$$ HOTEL Fodor's Choice ★ **Hotel Kämp.** Opposite the Esplanade Park stands this splendid, luxurious, late-19th-century cultural landmark, now a member of the Starwood group. **Pros:** lavish rooms; five-star service; fantastic spa. **Cons:** breakfast costs extra; gym and sauna costs €10 extra if in standard room; very high rates. *$ Rooms from: €300 ✉ Pohjoisesplanadi 29, Keskusta ☎ 09/576–111 🌐 www.hotelkamp.fi 🛏 179 rooms 🍴 Multiple meal plans.*

$$$ HOTEL **Scandic Marski Helsinki.** The Marski is favored for its absolutely central location, on the main Mannerheimintie artery and opposite Stockmann's department store. **Pros:** well-appointed rooms; ideal location. **Cons:** parking costs extra; service sometimes inconsistent. *$ Rooms from: €151 ✉ Mannerheim. 10, Keskusta ☎ 09/68–061 🌐 www.scandichotels.com/MARSKI 🛏 289 rooms, 6 suites 🍴 Breakfast.*

$$ HOTEL **Sokos Hotel Torni.** The original part of this hotel was built in 1903, and its towers and internal details still reflect some of the more fanciful touches of Helsinki's Jugendstil period. *$ Rooms from: €115 ✉ Yrjönkatu 26, Keskusta ☎ 020/1234–604 🌐 www.sokoshotels.fi 🛏 138 rooms, 14 suites 🍴 Breakfast.*

NIGHTLIFE

Originally known for its rock and heavy metal clubs, Helsinki has recently developed a suave bar-lounge scene. What began as a love of mojitos is flourishing into a number of carpeted, couch-lined venues combining loungy tunes with magnificent cocktails, some as a separate part of chic restaurants. While the city is generally quiet Sunday to Tuesday nights, a well-dressed, mostly suit-clad clientele begins boozing and schmoozing in earnest on "little Saturday" (aka Wednesday), and you can expect lines at the most popular places starting at 11 on weekends. The compact size of the city center makes it easy to barhop. Almost any place with a terrace or courtyard is sure to be busy in summer, and cover charges, when required, average €5–€10.

SHOPPING

From large, well-organized malls to closet-size boutiques, Helsinki has shopping for every taste. Most sales staff in the main shopping areas speak English and are helpful. Smaller stores are generally open weekdays 9–6 and Saturday 9–1. Small grocery stores are often open on Sunday year-round; other stores are often open on Sunday from June

CLOSE UP

Saunas

An authentic Finnish sauna is an obligatory experience, and not hard to find: there are 1.6 million saunas in this country of just more than 5 million people—even the parliament has its own sauna. The traditional Finnish sauna—which involves relaxing on wooden benches, pouring water onto hot coals, and swatting your neighbor's back with birch branches—is an integral part of cabin life and now city life, too, as apartments are outfitted with small saunas in their bathrooms. Almost every hotel has at least one sauna available free of charge, usually at standard times in the morning or evening for men and women to use separately. Larger hotels offer a private sauna in the higher-class rooms and suites. Public saunas (with swimsuits required) are becoming increasingly popular, even in winter, when sauna-goers momentarily leave the sauna to jump into the sea through a large hole in the ice (called *avantouinti*). Public swimming pools are also equipped with saunas that can be used at no extra charge.

15

through August and December. The Forum and Kamppi complexes and Stockmann's department store are open weekdays 9–9, Saturday 9–6, and (in summer and Christmastime) Sunday noon–6. An ever-expanding network of pedestrian tunnels connects the Forum, Stockmann's, and the train-station tunnel.

The area south and west of Mannerheimintie has been branded Design District Helsinki. It includes roughly 170 venues, most of them smaller boutiques and designer-run shops selling handmade everything from jewelry to clothing to housewares. The majority are located on Fredrikinkatu and Annankatu; look for a black Design District Helsinki sticker in the window. You can pick up a map detailing the shops in the district at most participating stores. Kiosks remain open late and on weekends; they sell such basics as milk, juice, camera film, and tissues. Stores in Asematunneli, the train-station tunnel, are open weekdays 10–10 and weekends noon–10.

DEPARTMENT STORES

Sokos. This high-quality alternative to Stockmann's is in a 1950s landmark building near the train station. ⊠ *Mannerheimintie 9, Rautatieasema* ☎ *010/766–5100* ⊕ *www.sokos.fi*.

Stockmann. Helsinki's premier department store. Head to the fourth floor for accessories and supplies for the sauna. ⊠ *Aleksanterink. 52B, Keskusta* ☎ *09/1211* ⊕ *www.stockmann.fi*.

CLOTHING

Marimekko. Since the 1950s Marimekko has been selling bright, unusual clothes for men, women, and children in quality fabrics. Though the products are expensive, they're worth a look even if you don't plan to buy. There are four locations in central Helsinki. ⊠ *Pohjoisespl. 2, Esplanadi* ☎ *09/686–0240* ⊕ *www.marimekko.com* ⊠ *Pohjoisespl. 33, Kämp Galleria, Esplanadi* ☎ *09/686–0240* ⊠ *Kamppi shopping center, Urho Kekkosen Katu 1, Keskusta* ☎ *010/344–3300*.

CLOSE UP

Marimekko

When the world's fashion-conscious think "Finland," they think Marimekko. Founded by a Finnish couple in 1951, the company got its big international break when Jacqueline Kennedy appeared in front of JFK on the cover of *Sports Illustrated* magazine wearing a Marimekko dress during the 1960 presidential campaign. More recently, Manolo Blahnik took the company's prints as one of the inspirations for his spring/summer 2008 collection. One of its best-known designs is artist Marija Isola's "Unikko," comprising large poppies in bright, bold colors, created in 1964 and still in production on items from dresses to bedding. Another of the company's timeless designs is "Piccolo," a vivid striped pattern that first took the form of the "Jokapoika" shirt (1956) and is today printed on clothing and accessories found in Marimekko stores. The company introduces dozens of new fabric designs every year, with an emphasis on bold, uncluttered patterns.

RĪGA

Rīga has an upscale, big-city feel unmatched in the region. The capital (almost as large as Tallinn and Vilnius combined) is the business center of the area, while original, high-quality restaurants and hotels have earned Rīga some bragging rights among its Western European counterparts. The city also doesn't lack for beauty—Rīga's Old Town (now a UNESCO World Heritage site) is one of Europe's most striking examples of the art-nouveau architectural style. Long avenues of complex and sometimes whimsical Jugendstil facades hint at Rīga's grand past. Many were designed by Mikhail Eisenstein, the father of Soviet director Sergei. This style dominates the city center; you can see the finest examples at Alberta 2, 2a, 4, 6, 8, and 13; Elizabetes 10b; and Strēlnieku 4a.

PLANNING

PLANNING YOUR TIME
Rīga's Old Town is full of little squares ideal for enjoying a beer and watching the world go by. The Latvian National Opera building is a 19th-century masterpiece definitely worth a visit. Further down the street is the Orthodox Nativity of Christ Cathedral just beside Esplanade Park.

If you have a little more time the Ethnographic Open Air Museum on the city's eastern edge displays old wooden farm buildings representative of Latvia's five historic regions. An hour or two in the Musee Art Nouveau is time well spent for an authentic feeling of the era.

GETTING HERE AND AROUND
AIR TRAVEL
There are no nonstop flights from the U.S. to Latvia, but several airlines offer connections within Europe.

LATVIA A GLANCE

- **Capital:** Rīga
- **Population:** 2,013,000
- **Currency:** Euro
- **Money:** ATMs are common
- **Language:** Latvian
- **Country Code:** ☎ 371
- **Emergencies:** ☎ 112
- **Driving:** On the right
- **Electricity:** 200v/50 cycles; electrical plugs have two round prongs

- **Time:** Six hours ahead of New York
- **Documents:** Up to 90 days with valid passport; Schengen rules apply
- **Mobile Phones:** GSM (900 and 1800 bands)
- **Major Mobile Companies:** Latvian Mobile Telephone, Tele2, BITE Latvia

15

BUS TRAVEL

Public transportation runs from 5:30 am to midnight (or until 1 am for some routes). Other routes have 24-hour service. A convenient e-ticket system is used with plastic passes; long-term blue e-tickets can be bought in "Rīgas satiksme" outlets only, but can be recharged in vending machines or kiosks. There are also short-term passes, suitable for tourists and visitors that consist of yellow e-tickets good for a specific number of rides, and these can be bought almost anywhere. If you have not purchased your e-ticket in advance, you can always get a more expensive single-journey paper ticket from the driver. Prices and schedules can be found in English at ⊕ *www.rigassatiksme.lv/en.*

Information Bus Station ⊠ *Prāgas 1* ☎ *900–0009* ⊕ *www.autoosta.lv.*

CAR TRAVEL

An international or national driver's license bearing a photograph is acceptable in Latvia. Drive on the right and be aware that roads are not up to Western standards. Gas costs about €1.5 per liter.

Cars may be rented from €57 a day; lower rates are available for longer rental terms.

Major Agencies Avis ⊠ *Riga International Airport, Marupes Pag.* ☎ *6/720–7353* ⊕ *www.rigaairportcarhire.com.* **Hertz** ⊠ *Riga International Airport, Marupes Pag.* ☎ *6/720–7980* ⊕ *www.rigaairportcarhire.com.* **National** ⊠ *Riga International Airport, Marupes Pag.* ☎ *720–7710* ⊕ *ww.rigaairportcarhire.com.*

TAXI TRAVEL

Taxis are expensive around Rīga's hotels and ferry, bus, and train stations but cheaper within the city center; for best results, telephone for one. An average trip within the city should not cost more than €4.25 Ls; some taxis charge a flat fee of €15 Ls to and from the airport. Drivers must display an operating license and a meter. Stick to the state cabs with orange and black markings. Insist that the meter be turned on; if there is no meter, choose another taxi or decide on a price beforehand.

Rīga Taxi and Rīgas Taksometru Parks are by and large trustworthy taxi companies.

Information **Rīga Taxi** ☎ *800–1010.* **Rīgas Taksometru Parks** ☎ *800–1313.* ⊕ *www.rtp.lv.*

HOTELS

Rīga's hotels run the gamut, but many are modern and luxurious (and cheaper than a comparable hotel would be in any other major European capital). Breakfast is usually included in hotel rates, and all prices include V.A.T.

RESTAURANTS

Latvian cuisine includes elements found in both Russian and German cuisines; it has less of a Scandinavian influence than that of some of the other countries in the region. Menus offer seasonal produce but are often heavy on wild game and pork. Both food and drink tend to be significantly cheaper than those in other European destinations. Restaurant bills may include service; if not, tip about 10%.

HOTEL AND RESTAURANT PRICES

Prices in the restaurant reviews are the average cost of a main course at dinner or, if dinner is not served, at lunch; taxes and service charges are generally included. Prices in the hotel reviews are the lowest cost of a standard double room in high season, excluding taxes, service charges, and meal plans.

VISITOR INFORMATION

Contacts **Latvia Tourism** ⊕ *www.latvia.travel/en.*

EXPLORING

FAMILY **Brīvdabas muzejs.** The Open-Air Ethnographic Museum is well worth the 9-km (5-mile) trek from downtown. At this countryside living museum, farmsteads and villages have been crafted to look like those in 18th- and 19th-century Latvia, and costumed workers engage in traditional activities (beekeeping, smithing, and so on). ⊠ *Brīvības 440* ☎ *6799–4515* ⊕ *www.brivdabasmuzejs.lv* ☐ *€4.27* ⊘ *Daily 10–5.*

Brīvības piemineklis. The central Freedom Monument, a 1935 statue whose upheld stars represent Latvia's united peoples (the Kurzeme, Vidzeme, and Latgale), was the rallying point for many nationalist protests during the late 1980s and early 1990s. Watch the changing of the guard every hour on the hour between 9 and 6. ⊠ *Brīvības and Raina.*

Doma baznīca (*Dome Cathedral*). In Doma laukums (Dome Square), the nerve center of the Old Town, the stately 1210 cathedral dominates. Reconstructed over the years with Romanesque, Gothic, and baroque elements, this place of worship is astounding as much for its architecture as for its size. The massive 6,768-pipe organ is among the largest in Europe, and it is played nearly every evening at 7. Check at the cathedral for schedule and tickets. ⊠ *Doma laukums* ☎ *6/722–7573* ⊕ *www. doms.lv* ⊘ *Tues.–Fri. 1–5, Sat. 10–2.*

Melngalvju Nams. The fiercely Gothic Blackheads House was built in 1344 as a hotel for wayfaring merchants (who wore black hats).

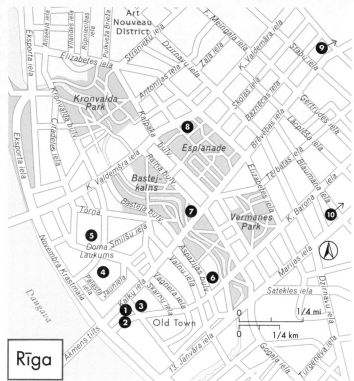

Partially destroyed during World War II and leveled by the Soviets in 1948, the extravagant, ornate building was renovated and reopened in 2000 for Rīga's 800th anniversary. The facade is a treasured example of Dutch Renaissance work. ⊠ *Ratslaukums 7* ☎ *6/7043678* ⊕ *www. melngalvjunams.lv* ⊙ *Tues.–Sun. 10–5.*

Nacionālā Opera. Latvia's restored 18th-century National Opera House, where Richard Wagner once conducted, is worthy of a night out. ⊠ *Aspazijas 3* ☎ *6/707-3777* ⊕ *www.opera.lv* ⊙ *Mon.–Sat. 10–7, Sun. 11–7.*

Okupācijas muzejs. The Latvian Occupation Museum details the devastation of Latvia at the hands of the Nazis and Soviets during World War II, as well as the Latvians' struggle for independence in September 1991. In front of the museum is a monument to the Latvian sharpshooters who protected Lenin during the 1917 revolution. ⊠ *Strēlnieku laukums 1* ☎ *6/721-2715* ⊕ *www.okupacijasmuzejs.lv/en* ⊠ *Donations accepted* ⊙ *May–Sept., daily 11–6; Oct.–Apr., Tues.–Sun. 11–5.*

Pētera baznīca. Towering St. Peter's Church, originally built in 1209, had a long history of annihilation and conflagration before being destroyed most recently in 1941. Rebuilt by the Soviets, it lacks authenticity but has a good observation deck on the 200-foot spire. ⊠ *Skārnu 19* ☎ *6/722-9426* ⊕ *www.peterbaznica.lv* ⊙ *Tues.–Sun. 10–7.*

Rīgas motormuzejs. At the Motor Museum, the Western cars on display can impress, but the Soviet models—including Stalin's iron-plated limo and a Rolls-Royce totaled by Brezhnev himself—are the most fun. ✉ *Eizensteina 6* ☎ *6/7025888* 🌐 *www.motormuzejs.lv* 🎟 *€1.71* ⏲ *Daily 10–6.*

Trīs Brāli. The Three Brothers—a trio of houses on Mazā Pils—show what the city looked like before the 20th century. The three oldest stone houses in the capital (No. 17 is the oldest, dating from the 15th century) span several styles, from the medieval to the baroque. The building at No. 19 is the city's **architecture museum**. The third is at No. 21. ✉ *Mazā Pils 19* ☎ *6/722–0779* 🌐 *www.archmuseum.lv* ⏲ *Mon. 9–6, Tues.–Thurs. 9–5, Fri. 9–4.*

Valsts mākslas muzejs. The National Art Museum has a gorgeous interior, with imposing marble staircases linking several large halls of 19th- and 20th-century Latvian paintings. ✉ *K. Valdemāra 10a* ☎ *6732–4461* 🌐 *www.lnmm.lv* 🎟 *€3.56* ⏲ *Mon., Wed., Thurs., and weekends 11–5, Fri. 11–8.*

WHERE TO EAT

$ MEXICAN 🍴 **A. Suns.** "Andalusian Dog" has long been an expat hangout in Rīga—and why not? With an art-house cinema upstairs, a breezy restaurant downstairs, and a wall of windows perfect for people-watching, the restaurant is decidedly hip, with a tasty Tex-Mex menu. [$] *Average main: €10* ✉ *Elizabetes 83–85* ☎ *6728–8418* 🌐 *www.andaluzijassuns.lv.*

$$ CONTEMPORARY 🍴 **Charlestons.** This restaurant has achieved a level of informal class and hearty good taste from breakfast to dinner. The front café is perfect for a quiche or croissant and coffee, and the main dining room and summer terrace invite long, leisurely lunches and dinners. [$] *Average main: €14* ✉ *Blaumaņa 38/40* ☎ *777–0573* 🌐 *www.restaurant-riga.com.*

$ MEDITERRANEAN 🍴 **Cydonia.** One of Rīga's premier dining establishments, Cydonia gastropub serves outstanding Mediterranean cuisine, with an emphasis on seafood, as well as light soups and salads. The dining room is furnished in a fashionable Scandinavian style—simple yet cozy, with an abundance of natural materials like wood and stone. There's also a lovely kids' corner with toys and crayons. [$] *Average main: €7* ✉ *Berga Bazārs, Dzirnavu 84/1* ☎ *6/7282055* 🌐 *www.cydonia.lv.*

$ EASTERN EUROPEAN 🍴 **Staburags.** Found in the art-nouveau Hotel Viktorija in downtown Rīga, this may be the capital's best place to sample Latvian national cuisine, with such offerings as roast leg of pork, sauerkraut, an assortment of potato dishes, and smoked chicken. [$] *Average main: €7* ✉ *Hotel Viktorija, Caka 55* ☎ *6729–9787* 🌐 *www.hotelviktorija.lv.*

$$$ ECLECTIC Fodor's Choice ★ 🍴 **Vincent's.** Named for van Gogh, this restaurant serves sensational international delicacies and subscribes to the growing "slow food" movement, focusing on preserving traditional and regional cuisine as well as local ecosystems. Numbered among its clientele are Mstislav Rostropovich, José Carreras, and the princes and princesses of Europe. [$] *Average main: €26* ✉ *Elizabetes 19* ☎ *6/733–2634* 🌐 *www.restorans.lv* ⏲ *Closed Sun.*

WHERE TO STAY

$$ HOTEL 🏨 **Grand Palace Hotel.** Outstanding amenities, 19th-century furnishings, and an enviable location in the heart of Rīga make this a grand place in which to relax in luxury. **Pros:** Old World elegance; outstanding service. **Cons:** some guests might be bothered by the smoke from the hotel's bar. [$] *Rooms from: €171* ✉ *Pils 12* ☎ *6/704–4000* 🌐 *www.grandpalaceriga.com* 🛏 *56 rooms* 🍴 *Breakfast.*

$ HOTEL 🏨 **Konventa Sēta.** In a charming complex of buildings dating from the Middle Ages, this hotel has rooms with a clean, white Scandinavian aesthetic and medieval details. **Pros:** good value; very clean. **Cons:** some rooms (street-side) may be noisy; amenities are a little dated. [$] *Rooms from: €71* ✉ *Kalēju 9/11* ☎ *6/708–7507* 🌐 *www.hotelkolonna.com/konventa-seta* 🛏 *140 rooms* 🍴 *Breakfast.*

$ B&B/INN 🏨 **Krišjānis & Gertrūde.** Just five rooms occupy this British-style bed-and-breakfast that features friendly owners and comfortable rooms with cable TV and coffee and tea sets. **Pros:** near the railway station; very affordable. **Cons:** slightly dated; thin walls mean it can get noisy. [$] *Rooms from: €43* ✉ *K. Barona 391* ☎ *6/750–6604* 🌐 *www.kg.lv* 🛏 *5 rooms* 🍴 *Breakfast.*

$ HOTEL 🏨 **Radi un Draugi.** This small hotel offers a great location for a low price; it's efficiently run and simple. **Pros:** comfortable and friendly; centrally located. **Cons:** breakfast room is a little drab (although breakfast itself is good); possible late-night noise from the street. [$] *Rooms from: €55* ✉ *Mārstaļu 1/3* ☎ *6/782-0200* 🌐 *www.hotelradiundraugi.lv* 🛏 *47 rooms* 🍴 *Breakfast.*

NIGHTLIFE

Most of Rīga's better bars and nightclubs are around the **Old Town** north of Old Rīga Palace Hotel. The Old Town's network of streets and alleys host some great neighborhood bars frequented by locals and tourists alike. On weekends most bars will close only after the last patron has left the place, but on weekdays, sadly, plenty of bars close their doors at midnight. Some of the more "adult" nightspots may attempt to extort money from tourists, so beware of what you're paying for before you part with your credit card.

TALLINN

Estonia's history is sprinkled liberally with long stretches of foreign domination, beginning in 1219 with the Danes, followed without interruption by the Germans, Swedes, and Russians. Only after World War I, with Russia in revolutionary wreckage, was Estonia able to declare its independence. Shortly before World War II, in 1940, that independence was usurped by the Soviets, who—save for a brief three-year occupation by Hitler's Nazis—proceeded to suppress all forms of national Estonian pride for the next 50 years. Estonia finally regained independence in 1991. In the early 1990s, Estonia's own Riigikogu (Parliament), not some other nation's puppet ruler, handed down from the Upper City reforms that forced Estonia to blaze its post-Soviet trail to the European

15

ESTONIA AT A GLANCE

- **Capital:** Tallinn
- **Population:** 1,287,000
- **Currency:** Euro
- **Money:** ATMs are common
- **Language:** Estonian
- **Country Code:** ☎ 372
- **Emergencies:** ☎ 112
- **Driving:** On the right
- **Electricity:** 200v/50 cycles; electrical plugs have two round prongs

- **Time:** Six hours ahead of New York
- **Documents:** Up to 90 days with valid passport; Schengen rules apply
- **Mobile Phones:** GSM (900 and 1800 bands)
- **Major Mobile Companies:** EMT, Elisa, and Tele2

Union. Estonia has been a member of the EU since 2004, and in 2011, the country and its growing economy joined the Eurozone. Tallinn was also named the European City of Culture in 2011, cementing its growing reputation as a cultural hotspot.

PLANNING

GETTING HERE AND AROUND

AIR TRAVEL

There are no direct flights between Estonia and the United States. Estonian Air operates from Copenhagen, Frankfurt, Hamburg, Helsinki, Kiev, London, Moscow, Rīga, Stockholm, Vienna, Vilnius, and Warsaw. American carriers partnered with Austrian Airlines, Finnair, LOT, and SAS have good connections. Estonian Air is the national carrier. Copterline helicopters fly the 18-minute trip between Helsinki and Tallinn daily.

Contacts Copterline helicopters ☎ *200/18181* ⊕ *www.copterline.com.* **Estonian Air** ☎ *640/1162* ⊕ *www.estonian-air.com/en.*

BOAT AND FERRY TRAVEL

Passenger ships—including frequent ferries and hydrofoils—connect Tallinn with Helsinki and Stockholm. Boat service to and from Tallinn is minimal and dependent on weather from October to March. Call the Tallinn Harbor for schedules; travel agencies for tickets.

Information Tallinn Harbor information ☎ *631/8550* ⊕ *www.portoftallinn.com.*

BUS TRAVEL

Public transportation tickets purchased from nearly any kiosk cost €1. Purchased from the driver, they are €1.60. A single type of ticket is valid on buses, trolleys, and streetcars. A carnet of 10 tickets costs €8. Upon boarding the bus, punch your ticket in the machine or be fined €40. You can also buy a 24-hour pass (€4), or a 72-hour pass (€6). Public transportation operates 6 am–midnight.

Information Bus station ⊠ *Lastekodu 46* ☎ *680/12550* ⊕ *www.bussijaam.ee/ eng.*

CAR TRAVEL

An international or national driver's license bearing a photograph is acceptable in Estonia. Drive on the right. Most roads are not up to Western standards, but major thoroughfares tend to be in better condition than secondary roads, where potholes and unpaved ways are common. Gas costs about €1.40 per liter. Note that Tallinn is a pedestrian city and driving can be impractical as parking is generally scarce and expensive.

Cars may be rented from Avis, Budget, Hertz, or National, or other local agencies, with prices starting at €25 a day.

Major Agencies Avis ⊠ *Tallin Airport, Tartu mnt. 101* ☎ *605–148* ⊕ *www.sixt. ee.* **Budget** ⊠ *Tallinn Airport, Tartu mnt. 101* ☎ *605–8223* ⊕ *www.budget.ee.* **Europcar** ⊠ *Tallinn Airport, Tartu mnt. 101* ☎ *605–8031* ⊕ *www.europcar.ee.* **Hertz** ⊠ *Tallinn Airport, Tartu mnt. 101* ☎ *605–8923* ⊕ *www.hertz.ee.* **National** ☎ *605–8031* ⊕ *www.nationalcar.co.uk.*

TAXI TRAVEL

Taxis are expensive around hotels and major transportation hubs and cheaper within the city center; it's best to telephone for one. Taxi fares generally start at €2.50 and increase by €0.40 or €1 per kilometer (½ mile) in the daytime and slightly more at night. Drivers are bound by law to display an operating license and a meter.

Contacts Tulika ☎ *612/0001* ⊕ *www.tulika.ee.*

HOTELS

Talinn's hotels run the gamut, but many are modern and luxurious (and significantly cheaper than a comparable hotel would be in any other major European capital). Free Wi-Fi is expected, and some hotels even have Skype phones (Skype was invented in Estonia). Breakfast is usually included in hotel rates, but at cheaper establishments you should verify that.

RESTAURANTS

Estonian cuisine includes elements found in both Scandinavian and German cuisines, and there is still a lingering Russian influence. Menus offer seasonal produce but are often heavy on wild game, but another local delicacy is eel. Restaurant bills always include 20% V.A.T. and service, so an additional tip is not expected in most cases.

HOTEL AND RESTAURANT PRICES

Prices in the restaurant reviews are the average cost of a main course at dinner or, if dinner is not served, at lunch; taxes and service charges are generally included. Prices in the hotel reviews are the lowest cost of a standard double room in high season, excluding taxes, service charges, and meal plans.

TOURS

Contacts Reisiekspert ⊠ *Roosikrantsi 8B, Tallinn* ☎ *610–8600* ⊕ *www. reisiekspert.ee.*

15

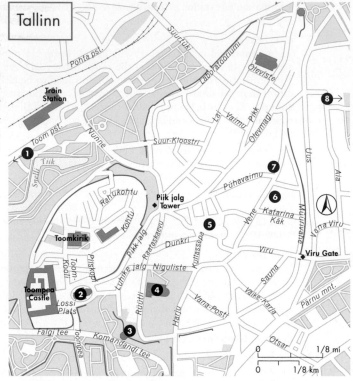

VISITOR INFORMATION

Contacts **Talinn City Tourist Office** ⊕ *www.tourism.tallinn.ee/eng.* **Visit Estonia** ⊕ *www.visitestonia.com/en.*

EXPLORING

Tallinn's tiny Old Town, the most impressive in the region, has romantic towers, ankle-wrenching cobblestone streets, cozy nooks, city-wall cafés, and a dozen other attractions—all within 1 square km (½ square mile). In the 1990s, Vanalinn (the lower Old Town)—historically the domain of traders, artisans, and ordinary citizens—sprouted glitzy neon signs in otherwise charming alleys and sights. The stately, sedate Toompea (Upper Town), a hillock that was the site of the original Estonian settlement, is on the burial mound of Kalev, the epic hero of Estonia. Toompea Castle, crowning the hill, is now the seat of the country's parliament and is not open to visitors. Summer visitors can experience the unforgettable white nights, when the sun never completely sets.

Aleksandr Nevski Khram. The 19th-century Russian Orthodox Alexander Nevsky Cathedral, with the country's largest bell, is a symbol of the centuries of Russification endured by Estonia. ✉ *Lossi pl. 10, Toompea* ☎ *644–3484* ⊘ *Daily 8–7.*

Dominiiklaste Kloostri Muuseum. Wander through the ages in the ancient stone galleries and narrow hallways of the Dominican Monastery Museum, founded in 1246 and now displaying 15th- and 16th-century stone carvings. At 5 pm enjoy a half-hour baroque music concert. ⊠ *Vene 16, Vanalinn* ☎ *644–4606* ⊕ *www.kloostri.ee* ⊙ *Daily 10–6.*

Kadriorg Palace Foreign Art Museum. The baroque palace, built for Catherine I by her husband Peter the Great in 1721, merits a visit not just for its impressive and thorough exhibition of 16th- to 20th-century art, but also for the palace's architectural beauty and manicured gardens. Kadriorg Palace offers a glimpse into history, from Russian imperial splendor to Soviet Socialist Realist art, with Estonian and European masterpieces along the way. ⊠ *Weizenbergi 37* ☎ *606–6400* ⊕ *www. kadriorumuuseum.ee/en* ⊠ *€4.80* ⊙ *May–Sept., Tues.–Sun. 10–5; Oct.–Apr., Wed.–Sun. 10–5.*

Kiek-in-de-Kök. At the southern end of the Old Town looms this magnificent, six-story tower church (the name is Low German for "peep in the kitchen"), so called because during the 15th century one could peer into the kitchens of lower town houses from here. The tower has a museum of contemporary art and ancient maps and weapons. ⊠ *Komandandi 2, Vanalinn* ☎ *644–6686* ⊕ *www.linnamuuseum.ee/kok* ⊠ *€4.50* ⊙ *Mar.–Oct., Tues.–Sun. 10:30–6; Nov.–Feb., Tues.–Sun. 10:30–5.*

Niguliste Kirik. The 15th-century Church of St. Nicholas, part of the Estonian Art Museum, is famed for its fragment of a treasured frieze, Bernt Notke's (1440–1509) *Danse Macabre*, a haunting depiction of death. ⊠ *Niguliste 3, Vanalinn* ☎ *631–4330* ⊕ *www.nigulistemuuseum. ee/en* ⊠ *€3.50* ⊙ *Wed.–Sun. 10–5.*

Paks Margareeta. The stocky guardian of the northernmost point of the Old Town, Fat Margaret, is a 16th-century fortification named for a particularly hefty cannon it contained. Now it houses the Maritime Museum and a roof with a view of Old Town. ⊠ *Pikk 70, Vanalinn* ☎ *641–1408* ⊕ *www.meremuuseum.ee* ⊠ *€4* ⊙ *Wed.–Sun. 10–6.*

Fodor's Choice
★
Raekoja Plats. Tallinn's Town Hall Square has a long history of intrigue, executions, and salt (Tallinn's main export in the Middle Ages). You can tour the only surviving Gothic **town hall** in northern Europe. Old Thomas, its weather vane, has been atop the town hall since 1530. Near the center of the square, an L-shape stone marks the site of a 17th-century execution, where a priest was beheaded for killing a waitress who had offered him a rock-hard omelet. Across the square stands the town **apothecary,** which dates from 1422. ⊠ *Raekoja plats 11* ☎ *645–7900 for town hall, 631–4860 for apothecary* ⊠ *Town Hall: €4* ⊙ *Town Hall Mon.–Sat. 10–4.*

FAMILY **Rocca al Mare.** A 15-minute taxi ride from the center, the 207-acre Open-Air Ethnographic Museum provides a breath of fresh air and an informative look into Estonia's past, from farm architecture to World War II–era deportations. ⊠ *Vabaõhumuuseumi 12* ☎ *654–9101* ⊕ *www. evm.ee/keel/eng* ⊠ *€3* ⊙ *Late Apr.–late Sept., daily 10–8; late Sept.–late Apr., daily 10–5.*

15

WHERE TO EAT

$$$ ECLECTIC

🍴 **Gloria.** The art-nouveau interior compliments the French-influenced menu of highbrow European food like beef Stroganoff or tournedos Rossini. To maintain its tradition of decadence, Gloria offers a *tabacalera* (tobacco shop) complete with Cuban cigars and an extensive wine cellar. [$] *Average main: €25* ✉ *Müürivahe 2* ☎ *640–6800* 🌐 *www.gloria.ee* ✍ *Reservations essential* 👔 *Jacket and tie* ⏲ *Closed Sun. No lunch Sat.*

$$ EASTERN EUROPEAN

🍴 **Maiasmokk.** A top-notch restoration has revived this fine Estonian restaurant's 19th-century feel. Founded in 1864, the property has been restored to its old, refined glory, with an equally refined menu of such delicacies as lamprey, deer, wild boar, and elk, with accompaniments ranging from lingonberries to mead sauce. It is also a traditional café, with coffees and excellent cakes. [$] *Average main: €15* ✉ *Pikk 16* ☎ *646–40–79* 🌐 *www.kalev.eu/maiasmokk/kohvik* ✍ *Reservations essential.*

$$ EASTERN EUROPEAN Fodor's Choice ★

🍴 **Olde Hansa.** In a 15th-century building in the Old Town, this restaurant recreates medieval times with waiters in period costume, candlelit tables, and historic Eastern European recipes for such dishes as nobleman's smoked filet mignon in mushroom sauce and wild boar with game sauce and forest berries. The honey beer is out of this world, and the old-fashioned food is always fresh and tasty. [$] *Average main: €15* ✉ *Vanaturg 1* ☎ *627–9020* 🌐 *www.oldehansa.ee.*

$$ EASTERN EUROPEAN

🍴 **Vanaema Juures.** Just as the name suggests, Grandma's Place is a cozy and homey place to sample Estonian favorites such as roast elk. Filled with antiques, sepia photographs, and the sounds of the 1920s and '30s, the restaurant gets high marks for authenticity and warmth. [$] *Average main: €15* ✉ *Rataskaevu 10* ☎ *626–9080* 🌐 *www.vonkrahl.ee/et/toit/vanaemajuures.*

WHERE TO STAY

$$$$ HOTEL Fodor's Choice ★

🏨 **Hotel Schlössle.** In three medieval warehouses in the Old Town, Tallinn's most luxurious hotel has unparalleled service and historic decor. **Pros:** lots of charm; excellent location. **Cons:** no a/c. [$] *Rooms from: €190* ✉ *Pühavaimu 13–15* ☎ *699–7700* 🌐 *www.schlossle-hotels.com* 🛏 *23 rooms* 🍽 *Breakfast.*

$ B&B/INN

🏨 **Johanna Hostel.** More like a guesthouse than a youth hostel, Johanna Hostel makes for an excellent budget choice for its Old Town central location, with its spic-and-span rooms and friendly service. **Pros:** centrally located; inexpensive. **Cons:** might be too basic for some; can be a bit noisy. [$] *Rooms from: €55* ✉ *Väike-Karja 1* ☎ *631–3252* 🌐 *www.hostel.ee* 🛏 *9 rooms* 🍽 *Breakfast.*

$$ HOTEL

🏨 **Kreutzwald Hotel.** With little extras like flat-screen TVs, in-room computers with Internet, and tea and coffee makers, this five-story hotel on the outskirts of Old Town sets itself apart from other midrange options. **Pros:** modern and bright; thoughtful in-room amenities. **Cons:** some rooms may be noisy; 15-minute walk to the Old Town. [$] *Rooms from: €110* ✉ *Endla 23* ☎ *666–4800* 🌐 *www.uniquestay.com* 🛏 *61 rooms* 🍽 *Breakfast.*

$ HOTEL 🏨 **Radisson Blu Olümpia.** This high-rise has some rooms with great views of the Old Town, but even if you don't land one of those, you'll still have access to a fitness room and sauna overlooking the city and a splendid breakfast buffet. **Pros:** free Wi-Fi in rooms; reliable Radisson Blu comfort and service. **Cons:** very business-oriented with little "local" feeling; some amenities are slightly dated. [$] *Rooms from: €100* ✉ *Liivalaia 33* ☎ *631–5333* 🌐 *www.radissonblu.com/olumpiahotel-tallinn* 🛏 *405 rooms* 🍴 *Breakfast.*

$ HOTEL 🏨 **Tallink-Express Hotel.** Just a few minutes walk from the center of the Old Town, the Express Hotel is extremely democratic: all rooms here are identical and cost exactly the same price. **Pros:** great value; convenient base for exploring the city. **Cons:** some might find the decor a little impersonal. [$] *Rooms from: €42* ✉ *Sadama 9* ☎ *667–8700* 🌐 *www.tallinkhotels.com/en* 🛏 *166 rooms* 🍴 *Breakfast.*

NIGHTLIFE

The **Old Town** square hosts a number of lively bars, but most of Tallinn's nightclubs lie outside the Old Town walls. One thing you won't be stuck for is choice, as the city is pretty packed full of bars and clubs. **Club Baila** is one the few nightclubs within the Old Town and is a tropical island–themed spot with Latin beats and an extensive range of cocktails. **Shooters,** on Suur-Karja, has a running special now for a number of years of five shots for €5.50.

SHOPPING

Tallinn has a wide range of crafts on sale. Fragrant juniper wood is carved into bowls and dolomite stone is fashioned into candlesticks and coasters. A whole range of handblown glass, ceramics, delicate wrought iron, and art is sold in tiny galleries. Hand-knitted sweaters, gloves, and socks keep the locals snug in winter and are signature souvenirs here. Warming quilts are also available, as well as a good range of leather goods. Sweet tooths will love the chocolates made by Kalev and the hand-painted marzipan that's sold in presentation boxes. The **Old Town** is the place to browse, with some excellent shops around **Katerina käik** (Catherine Passage).

REYKJAVIK

Sprawling Reykjavik, Iceland's nerve center and government seat, is home to half the island's population. On a bay overlooked by proud Mt. Esja (pronounced *eh*-shyuh), with its ever-changing hues, Reykjavik presents a colorful sight, its concrete houses painted in light colors and topped by vibrant red, blue, and green roofs.

Reykjavik's name comes from the Icelandic words for smoke, *reykur,* and bay, *vík*. In AD 874, Norseman Ingólfur Arnarson saw Iceland rising out of the misty sea and came ashore at a bay eerily shrouded with plumes of steam from nearby hot springs. Today most of the houses in Reykjavik are heated by near-boiling water from the hot springs.

15

ICELAND AT A GLANCE

- **Capital:** Reykjavik
- **Population:** 321,800
- **Currency:** Krona
- **Money:** ATMs are common
- **Language:** Icelandic
- **Country Code:** ☎354
- **Emergencies:** ☎112
- **Driving:** On the right
- **Electricity:** 200v/50 cycles; electrical plugs have two round prongs

- **Time:** Four hours ahead of New York
- **Documents:** Up to 90 days with valid passport; Schengen rules apply
- **Mobile Phones:** GSM (900 and 1800 bands)
- **Major Mobile Companies:** Siminn, Vodafone Iceland, and Nova

Natural heating avoids air pollution; there's no smoke around. You may notice, however, that the hot water brings a slight sulfur smell to the bathroom.

Prices have been adjusted upward in some cases (particularly for exported goods) after the economic collapse and are on par with major cities in Europe, but they still favor Americans and Europeans at this writing. A practical money-saving option is to purchase a Reykjavik Tourist Card at the Tourist Information Center; the card permits unlimited bus usage and admission to any of the city's seven pools, the Family Park and Zoo, and city museums.

PLANNING

PLANNING YOUR TIME
Though Reykjavik is quite spread out and much less dense than other Nordic capitals, within relatively short walking distance you can visit Hallgrímskirkja—the largest church in Iceland and a remarkable building architecturally—and climb to the viewing platform on top, which offers stunning views of the city and its surroundings. Reykjavik City Museum on Kistuhyl displays some fascinating exhibitions portraying life for the early settlers of Iceland. If you have a couple of days a trip to the Blue Lagoon Geothermal Spa, just a 40-minute drive from the city, is a must. Another alternative is to rent a car and drive "Route 1," the main highway that circles the island.

GETTING HERE AND AROUND
AIR TRAVEL
Virtually all international flights originate from and arrive at Keflavik Airport 50 km (31 miles) south of Reykjavik. Reykjavik Airport is mostly a domestic airport, although some flights to Greenland, Vestmannaeyjar, and the Faroe Islands leave from there.

The Reykjavik FlyBus leaves Keflavik (from directly outside the terminal building) and arrives in Reykjavik at the BSÍ bus terminal. Connections are provided from there to the larger hotels and guesthouses, or you can take a taxi to your final destination. FlyBuses are scheduled in connection with flight arrivals and departures. A taxi from the Keflavik Airport to Reykjavik is a little faster than the FlyBus and costs ISK 10,500 during daytime and ISK 13,500 in the evenings for a smaller car. A large car, which seats five to eight passengers, costs ISK 13,500 during the day and ISK 17,800 at night. If you share it with others, you can split the cost. There are direct phones to taxi companies in the arrivals hall.

Contacts Keflavík Airport ☎ *425–6000* ⊕ *www.keflavikairport.com.* **Reykjavík Airport** ☎ *424–4000* ⊕ *www.isavia.is.* **Reykjavík FlyBus** ☎ *580–5400* ⊕ *www. flybus.is.*

BUS TRAVEL
The municipal bus service, affectionately nicknamed Stræto (pronounced *stry*-toe), provides extensive, cheap, and reliable service throughout Reykjavik and its surrounding municipalities.

Buses are yellow with an "S" logo on a red circular background, and run starting around 6:30 am, with last buses tending to depart around 11 pm. Express buses run every 15 minutes during peak times and every half hour during the evenings and weekends. Route booklets are available at the main terminals of Lækjartorg, Hlemmur, Mjódd, and Ártún, as well as at most tourist information centers. The flat fare within the sprawling capital area is ISK 350, payable to the driver in exact change on boarding. You can buy strips of tickets at a lower price from the driver or at the main terminals. The fare allows you to travel any distance in the metro area; depending on your destination, you may have to change buses. If so, ask for *skiptimiða* (skiff-teh-mee-tha), a transfer ticket that you give the second bus driver.

If you plan an extended stay in the Reykjavik area, it may be worthwhile to spend ISK 7,700 on the Green Card, a monthly pass valid on all routes. For shorter stays, a practical investment is the Reykjavik Welcome Card, available from the Tourist Information Center, which permits unlimited bus usage and admission to any of the capital city's seven pools, the Family Park and Zoo, the ferry to Viðey Island, and city-run museums.

Contact Stræto ☎ *540–2700* ⊕ *www.bus.is.*

TAXI TRAVEL
Most cabs are new, fully equipped passenger sedans. They have small "taxi" signs on top and can be hailed anywhere on the street; the "laus" sign indicates that the cab is available. There are taxi stands in a few locations around the city, but it is common to order a taxi by phone. Normally you have to wait only a few minutes. Most taxis accept major credit and debit cards. Fares are regulated by meter; rides around Reykjavik run between ISK 1,000 and ISK 1,500. There is no tipping.

Contacts BSR Taxi ☎ *561–0000* ⊕ *www.bsr.is.* **Hreyfill Taxi** ☎ *588–5522* ⊕ *www.hreyfill.is.*

HOTELS

Lodgings range from modern, first-class Scandinavian-style hotels to inexpensive guesthouses and B&Bs offering basic amenities at relatively low prices. Iceland's climate makes air-conditioning unnecessary. Most hotel rooms have televisions, though not always cable TV. Lower-price hotels sometimes have a television lounge in lieu of TV in each room. Ask if your hotel offers complimentary admission tickets to the closest swimming pool.

RESTAURANTS

The dining scene in Reykjavik has been diversifying: traditional Icelandic restaurants now face competition from restaurants serving Asian, Italian, Mexican, Indian, and vegetarian fare. A recent trend has seen the emergence of several upscale establishments emphasizing locally grown ingredients.

HOTEL AND RESTAURANT PRICES

Prices in the restaurant reviews are the average cost of a main course at dinner or, if dinner is not served, at lunch; taxes and service charges are generally included. Prices in the hotel reviews are the lowest cost of a standard double room in high season, excluding taxes, service charges, and meal plans.

TOURS

The Iceland Tour Guide Association can provide the names of qualified guides who work in a variety of languages and have different specialties. During the summer, several free walking tours of the city run from Lækjartorg and the Old Harbour. Several bus companies, including Reykjavik Excursions and Iceland Excursions, also run bus tours that include museums and art galleries, shopping centers, and the like in around three hours. Reykjavik Excursions also operates a hop-on/hop-off bus service in the city during the summer. Iceland Travel operates trips from Reykjavik to Akureyri and Lake Mývatn.

Ferðafélag Íslands, or the Iceland Touring Association, owns and operates numerous mountain huts where hikers and other travelers can get a sleeping bag accommodation (pre-booking necessary). The ITA also offers a variety of tours year-round: day tours (hiking, cross-country skiing or bus tours), weekend tours (Friday evening through Sunday), and longer tours.

Arcanum offers snowmobiling tours and Dog Sledding Iceland offers dog-sled tours; both companies can take you to see a glacier.

Contacts Arcanum. Snowmobiling is possible in summer on a glacial tongue of the Mýrdalsjökull Glacier, which looms over Vík, through Arcanum. ⊠ *Sólheimaskála, Vík* ☎ *487–1500* ⊕ *www.snow.is.* **Dog Sledding Iceland** ⊠ *Selfoss* ☎ *899–1791* ⊕ *www.dogsledding.is.* **Ferðafélag Íslands** (*Iceland Touring Association*). ⊠ *Mörkin 6* ☎ *568–2533* ⊕ *www.fi.is.* **Iceland Excursions Allrahanda** ⊠ *Höfðatún 12* ☎ *540–1313* ⊕ *www.icelandexcursions.is.* **Iceland Tour Guide Association** ⊠ *Mörkin 6* ☎ *588–8670* ⊕ *www.touristguide.is.* **Reykjavík Excursions** ⊠ *BSÍ Bus Terminal, Vatnsmýrarvegi 10* ☎ *580–5040* ⊕ *www.re.is* ⊙ *Daily 4 am–11 pm.* **Útivist Travel Association** ⊠ *Laugavegur 178* ☎ *562–1000* ⊕ *www.utivist.is.*

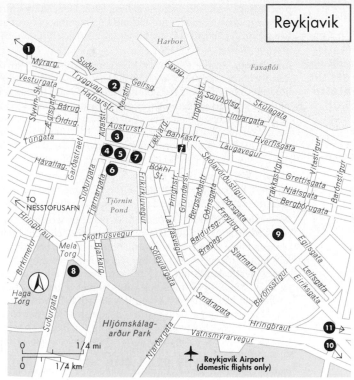

VISITOR INFORMATION

The Reykjavik Tourist Information Center, in the classic Geysishús at Aðalstræti 2, is open daily 8:30–7, June through September 15. For the rest of the year, it's open weekdays 9–6, Saturday 10–4, and Sunday 10–2.

Contacts Reykjavík Tourist Information Center ✉ *Geysishús, Aðalstræti 2* ☎ *590–1550* ⊕ *www.visitreykjavik.is* ⊗ *June–Sept., daily 8:30–7; Sept.–May, weekdays 9–6, Sat. 9–4, Sun. 9–2.*

EXPLORING

Any part of town can be reached by city bus, but take a walk around to get an idea of the present and past. The best way to see Reykjavik is on foot. Many of the interesting sights are in the city center, within easy walking distance of one another. In the Old Town, classic wooden buildings rub shoulders with modern timber-and-concrete structures.

OLD TOWN AND HARBOR

Alþingishús (*Parliament House*). Built in 1880–81, this structure is one of the country's oldest stone buildings. Iceland's Alþingi held its first session in AD 930 and therefore can lay claim to being the oldest representative parliament in the world. You can view the parliament proceedings from the visitor's gallery here. Depending on the urgency of the agenda, any number of Iceland's 63 members of parliament, from five political parties, may be present. ☒ *Austurvöllur Sq.* ☏ *563–0500* ⊕ *www.althingi.is.*

OFF THE
BEATEN
PATH

Árbæjarsafn. At the Open-Air Municipal Museum, 19th- and 20th-century houses furnished in old-fashioned style display authentic household utensils and tools for cottage industries and farming. During the summer you can see demonstrations of farm activities and taste piping-hot *lummur* (chewy pancakes) cooked over an old farmhouse stove. To get to the museum, take Bus No. 12 or 19. ☒ *Ártúnsblettur, Kistuhyl 4* ☏ *411–6300* ⊕ *www.minjasafnreykjavikur.is* ☑ *ISK 1100* ☯ *June–Aug., daily 10–5; Sept.–May, guided tours daily at 1.*

Austurvöllur Square. East Field is a peculiar name for a west-central square. The reason: it's just east of the presumed spot where first settler Ingólfur Arnarson built his farm, today near the corner of Aðalstræti.

Dómkirkjan (*Lutheran Cathedral*). A place of worship has existed on this site since AD 1200. The small, charming church, built 1788–96, represents the state religion, Lutheranism. It was here that sovereignty and independence were first blessed and endorsed by the church. It's also where Iceland's national anthem, actually a hymn, was first sung in 1874. Since 1845, members and cabinet ministers of every Alþing parliament have gathered here for a service before the annual session. Among the treasured items inside is a baptismal font carved and donated by the famous 19th-century master sculptor Bertel Thorvaldsen, who was half Icelandic. ☒ *Austurvöllur* ☏ *520–9700* ⊕ *www.domkirkjan.is/enska.html* ☯ *Weekdays 10–4:30, except for services.*

Ingólfur Arnarson statue. Ingólfur Arnarson is renowned as the first Nordic settler in Iceland. Beyond this statue lies the city's architectural mélange: 18th-century stone houses, 19th-century small wooden houses, and office blocks from the '30s and '40s. ☒ *Arnarhóll.*

Listasafn Reykjavíkur (*Reykjavík Art Museum*). Also known as Hafnar-hús, this former warehouse of the Port of Reykjavík now houses the city's art museum. The six galleries occupy two floors, and there's a courtyard and "multipurpose" space. The museum's permanent collection includes a large number of works donated by the contemporary Icelandic artist, Erró. There are also regular temporary exhibitions. ☒ *Tryggvagata 17* ☏ *590–1200* ⊕ *www.artmuseum.is* ☑ *ISK 1100* ☯ *Fri.–Wed. 10–5, Thurs. 10–8.*

OFF THE
BEATEN
PATH

Perlan. On top of Öskjuhlíð, the hill overlooking Reykjavík Airport, Perlan (the Pearl) was opened in 1991 as a monument to Iceland's invaluable geothermal water supplies. Among the indoor and outdoor spectacles are art exhibits, musical performances, markets, a permanent Viking history exhibit, and fountains that spurt water like geysers. Above the six vast tanks, which once held 24 million liters of hot water, the panoramic viewing platform offers telescopes and a cafeteria complete with ice-cream parlor. The crowning glory is a revolving restaurant under the glass dome; it's pricey, but the view is second to none ☒ *Öskjuhlíð Hill* ☏ *562–0200* ⊕ *www.perlan.is* ☯ *Daily 10–9.*

Ráðhús (*City Hall*). Modern architecture and nature converge at this building overlooking Tjörnin Lake. Inside is a visitor information desk and coffee bar with Internet access. A three-dimensional model of Iceland, over 819 square feet in size, is usually on display in the gallery, which often hosts various temporary exhibitions. ✉ *Bounded by Fríkirkjuvegur, Vonarstræti, and Tjarnargata* ☎ *411–1000* ⊕ *www.reykjavik.is* ⊙ *Weekdays 8–7, weekends noon–6.*

OFF THE BEATEN PATH

Víkin Sjóminjasafnið í Reykjavík (*Víkin Maritime Museum*). Housed in an old fish factory with great views of the harbor, the maritime museum features an exhibition on Icelandic fisheries, trading vessels, and displays a whole Costal Guard Vessel which can be explored. ✉ *Grandargarði 8* ☎ *517–9400* ⊕ *www.maritimemuseum.is* 🖬 *ISK 1200* ⊙ *June–Sept. 15, daily 10–5; Sept. 16–May, Tues–Sun. 11–5.*

MUSEUMS AND THE UNIVERSITY

Art-lovers can keep busy in what is still called Reykjavik's "eastern" quarter—even though it is now geographically in the west and center, as the city has been expanding to the east.

15

Hallgrímskirkja (*Hallgrímur's Church*). Completed in 1986 after more than 40 years of construction, the church is named for the 17th-century hymn writer Hallgrímur Pétursson. It has a stylized concrete facade recalling both organ pipes and the distinctive columnar basalt formations you can see around Iceland. You may luck into hearing a performance or practice on the church's huge pipe organ. In front of Hallgrímskirkja is a statue of Leifur Eiríksson, the Icelander who discovered America 500 years before Columbus. (Leif's father was Eric the Red, who discovered Greenland.) The statue, by American sculptor Alexander Calder, was presented to Iceland by the United States in 1930 to mark the millennium of the Alþing parliament. ✉ *At the top of Skólavörðustígur* ☎ *510–1000* ⊕ *www.hallgrimskirkja.is* 🖬 *Tower ISK 600* ⊙ *Daily 9–5.*

Þjóðminjasafn (*National Museum*). Viking treasures and artifacts, silver work, wood carvings, and some unusual whalebone carvings are on display here, as well as maritime objects, historical textiles, jewelry, and crafts. There is also a coffee shop. ✉ *Suðurgata 41* ☎ *530–2200* ⊕ *www.natmus.is* 🖬 *ISK 1200* ⊙ *May–Sept. 15, daily 10–5; Sept. 16–Apr., Tues.–Sun. 11–5.*

WHERE TO EAT

OLD TOWN

$$$$
STEAKHOUSE

✕ **Argentína.** If you want to try the best steaks in Iceland, come here. Like all Icelandic meat, everything is organic, and the classy atmosphere is warm and inviting. There are also great wines to match. $ *Average main: ISK 5,900* ✉ *Barónstígur 11a* ☎ *551–9555* ⊕ *www.argentina.is* ⊙ *No lunch.*

$
FAST FOOD

✕ **Bæjarins beztu.** Facing the harbor in a parking lot, this tiny but famous fast-food hut is famous for serving the original Icelandic hot dog; one person serves about a thousand hot dogs a day from the window. Ask for *AYN-ah-med-UTL-lou*, which will get you "one with everything":

mustard, tomato sauce, rémoulade, and chopped raw and fried onions. $ *Average main: ISK 320* ✉ *Tryggvagata and Pósthússtræti* 🕾 *894–4515* ⊕ *www.bbp.is* ⊙ *Sun.–Thurs., 10 am–12:30 am; Fri.–Sat., 10 am–4:30 am.*

$$$$
EUROPEAN
Fodor's Choice
★

✕ **Grillmarket.** A collaborative project by well-known culinary innovators Hrefna Rós Sætran (founder/owner of the Fish Market) and Guðlaugur P. Frímannsson, Grillmarkaðurinn emphasizes seasonal, organic, locally grown ingredients in a beautifully designed interior that's heavy on natural materials such as wood and stone. The menu is equally "earthy" featuring lots of smoked, grilled, and barbecued meat dishes. For something classic, try the grilled chicken wings or grilled pork ribs; for something more unique, order the Minke whale steak. $ *Average main: ISK 4,495* ✉ *Lækjargata 2a* 🕾 *571–7777* ⊕ *www.grillmarkadurinn.is.*

$$$$
ITALIAN

✕ **Hornið.** This welcoming bistro is light and airy, with lots of natural wood, potted plants, and cast-iron bistro tables. The emphasis is on pizzas and pasta, but there's also a selection of meat and fish dishes. Try the seafood soup, a favorite for lunch. Their delicious cakes can be enjoyed with the obligatory espresso at any time of day. $ *Average main: ISK 3,790* ✉ *Hafnarstræti 15* 🕾 *551–3340* ⊕ *www.hornid.is.*

$$$$
ECLECTIC

✕ **Lækjarbrekka.** Set in one of the oldest houses in Reykjavik (built in 1834), this restaurant serves a wide range of food, from salads and soups to meat and fish dishes. Among the menu's treats are the Icelandic lobster and the mountain lamb. The restaurant's interior features antique furniture and lace curtains. $ *Average main: ISK 5,340* ✉ *Bankastræti 2* 🕾 *551–4430* ⊕ *www.laekjarbrekka.is* ⊙ *Daily 11:30–11:30.*

$$$$
SEAFOOD

✕ **Þrír Frakkar.** In an unassuming building in an older part of town, this restaurant serves truly traditional Icelandic food, with an emphasis on seafood. Whale-meat sashimi and smoked puffin are just some of the novelties here. The bright annex overlooks a tiny, tree-filled park. $ *Average main: ISK 3,825* ✉ *Baldursgata 14, at Nönnugata* 🕾 *552–3939* ⊕ *www.3frakkar.com/* ⊙ *No lunch weekends.*

$$$$
SEAFOOD

✕ **Við Tjörnina.** Opened in 1986, this was the first Icelandic restaurant to specialize in seafood, though they sell meat too now. Visitors enter through a classic wooden doorway and go up a flight of stairs and back in time in this early-20th-century house with a hand-carved bar and chairs, embroidered tablecloths, and crocheted drapes. The baked salt cod and smoked pork belly is a perennial favorite, though if you're feeling adventurous try the three- or four-course surprise menu. $ *Average main: ISK 5,640* ✉ *Templarasund 3* 🕾 *551–8666* ⊕ *vidtjornina.is/.*

$$$$
INTERNATIONAL

✕ **VOX.** The restaurant's award-winning chef creates some unique international-themed dishes at this chic restaurant, and the wine list is one of the city's most impressive. The main menu features items such as reindeer and smoked puffin, and the weekend brunch, while less inventive, is generous and subsequently popular (ISK 3,450 per person). $ *Average main: ISK 5,775* ✉ *Suðurlandsbraut 2* 🕾 *444–5050.*

WHERE TO STAY

OLD TOWN AND EAST

$$$$
HOTEL
Fodor's Choice
★

Hótel Borg. In contrast to the ultramodern glass and chrome architecture around Reykjavík, the Borg—the city's oldest hotel—is pure 1930's art deco, from the black marble statues in the entryway to the brass-and-wood railing on the stairs to the square little coffee cups in the rooms. **Pros:** central location; lovely art-deco design; good service. **Cons:** street noise can be an issue on the lower floors; some visitors find the beds too firm. $Rooms from: ISK 37,000 ⊠ Pósthússtræti 11 ☎ 551–1440 ⊕ www.hotelborg.is ⇰ 48 rooms, 8 suites ⏹ Breakfast.

$$$
HOTEL

Hótel Reykjavík Centrum. Situated downtown, this hotel opened its doors in the spring of 2005. **Pros:** central location; friendly staff; historical building. **Cons:** no free Wi–Fi. $Rooms from: ISK 30,600 ⊠ Aðalstræti 16 ☎ 514–6000 ⊕ www.hotelcentrum.is ⇰ 84 rooms, 1 suite, 4 apartments ⏹ Breakfast.

$
RENTAL

Room with a View. Highly recommended by Fodor's readers, Room with a View offers a number of self-catering apartments in the center of town for those who prefer to cook their own meals and would like extra space. **Pros:** well-established; friendly staff; independent atmosphere. **Cons:** no on-call staff; no concierge. $Rooms from: ISK 18,900 ⊠ Laugavegur 18 ☎ 552–7262 ⊕ www.roomwithaview.is ⇰ 40 apartments ⏹ No meals.

MUSEUMS, THE UNIVERSITY AND BEYOND

$$
HOTEL
Fodor's Choice
★

Hótel Holt. This quietly elegant member of the prestigious World Hotels group has impeccable service, an excellent restaurant (Gallery), and free Wi–Fi throughout the hotel, all of which make it a favorite among business travelers. **Pros:** large rooms; excellent restaurant and bar; professional service. **Cons:** bathrooms can be small; slightly formal atmosphere. $Rooms from: ISK 29,000 ⊠ Bergstaðastræti 37 ☎ 552–5700 ⊕ www.holt.is ⇰ 40 rooms, 4 suites ⏹ Breakfast.

$$
HOTEL

Hotel Óðinsvé. Four buildings in a calm corner in an older part of town make up this hotel. **Pros:** central but quiet; good restaurant; professional service. **Cons:** some rooms are better than others. $Rooms from: ISK 28,500 ⊠ Þórsgata 1 ☎ 511–6200 ⊕ www.hotelodinsve.is ⇰ 35 rooms, 8 suites ⏹ Breakfast.

15

NIGHTLIFE AND THE ARTS

Reykjavik has an active cultural life through most of the year, and is especially strong in music and the visual arts. The classical performing-arts scene tends to quiet down somewhat in summer, though a growing number of rock and jazz concerts as well as a new chamber music festival held in Harpa, called **Reykjavik Midsummer Music,** have been helping to fill in the lull. The **Reykjavik Arts Festival** is an annual event held in May. Past festivals have drawn Luciano Pavarotti and David Bowie, among other stars. Check out *The Reykjavik Grapevine* (⊕ *www.grapevine.is*) for up-to-date listings; it's biweekly in summer, monthly in winter.

Nightlife in Reykjavik essentially means two types of establishments: pubs and nightclubs with dancing and live music. Icelanders tend to dress up for nightspots, but visitors can get away with being a bit more casual. On weekends, unless you start before 11 pm, be prepared to wait in line, especially if summer weekend weather is good. Avoid downtown after midnight during the first weekends of summer, when excessive drinking can result in some raucous and aggressive behavior. Suffice it to say, Icelanders party en masse.

SHOPPING

The main shopping downtown is on and around Austurstræti, Aðalstræti, Hafnarstræti, Hverfisgata, Bankastræti, Laugavegur, and Skólavörðustígur.

MALLS

Kringlan Mall. There are a number of good clothing stores and a movie theater, as well good places to get souvenirs. The mall is on the east side of town at the intersection of Miklabraut and Kringlumýrarbraut; Kringlan's Shuttle Bus is a free ride to Kringlan departing from the Tourist Information Centre, Aðalstræti 2 at 11 am and 2 pm (Mon.–Sat.). Return trips from Kringlan are at 1:30 pm (weekdays). ⊠ *Kringlun 4–12* ☎ *517–9000* ⊕ *www.kringlan.is* ⊙ *Mon–Wed. 10–6:30, Thurs. 9 am–9:30 pm, Fri.–Sat. 10–7, Sun. noon–7.*

ART GALLERIES

You can find crafts workshops and galleries all around town.

Gallery Fold. There are a large selection of prints, drawings, paintings, and sculpture by contemporary Icelandic artists, as well as some older Icelandic art. ⊠ *Rauðarárstígur 12–14* ☎ *551–0400* ⊕ *www.myndlist. is* ⊙ *Weekdays 10–6, Sat. 11–2* .

CRAFTS

Sheepskin rugs and Viking-inspired jewelry are popular souvenirs. An amble along **Skólavörðustígur** from Laugavegur to Hallgrímskirkja church takes you past many tempting woolen, jewelry, and crafts shops, as well as art galleries.

Handprjónasambandið. The Handknitting Association of Iceland, Handprjónasambandið, has its own outlet, selling, of course, only hand-knit items of various kinds. ⊠ *Skólavörðurstígur 19* ☎ *552–1890* ⊕ *www. handknit.is* ⊙ *Mon.–Sat. 9–6, Sun. 11–5.*

Islandia. A range of woolens, giftware, and souvenirs are available. ⊠ *Kringlan Mall* ☎ *540–2315.*

Rammagerðin. Many hand- and machine-knitted woolen garments are sold at Rammagerðin. They have a smaller version in the Keflavik Airport as well. ⊠ *Hafnarstræti 19* ☎ *551–1122* ⊕ *www.icelandgiftstore. com* ⊙ *Daily 9–7.*

JEWELRY

Laugavegur and Skólavörðustígur streets are both filled with jewelry stores that craft unique pieces, often incorporating gold or silver with materials found in Iceland, like lava rock, creating a very eye-catching effect.

Anna María design. Founded in 1986, this workshop and store sells a variety of jewelry for both men and women, made from a variety of materials that encompass silver, gold, and Icelandic stones. ✉ *Skólavörðustígur 3* ☎ *551–0036* 🌐 *www.annamariadesign.is.*

DAY TRIPS FROM REYKJAVIK

HAFNARFJÖRÐUR

10 km (6 miles) south of Reykjavik.

"Harbor fjord" had an important commercial port centuries before Reykjavik did, and today there's still healthy competition between the two. Iceland's **International Summer Solstice Viking Festival** is held here.

GETTING HERE AND AROUND

To get to the town, take Bus No. S1 from Lækjatorg Plaza or Hlemmur station.

VISITOR INFORMATION

Hafnarfjörður Tourist Information Center. The center has maps of the town's sites and possibly elfin homes. ✉ *Town Hall, Strandgata 6* ☎ *585–5500* 🌐 *www.visithafnarfjordur.is* 🕒 *Summer, weekdays 8–4.*

EXPLORING

Hafnarborg Center of Culture and Fine Art. Permanent exhibits focus on the work of prominent Icelandic artists, but there are rotating exhibits that bring in other artwork as well. There are concerts, and tours are offered in English upon request. ✉ *Strandgata 34* ☎ *585–5790* 🌐 *www.hafnarborg.is* 🎟 *Free* 🕒 *Fri.–Mon. and Wed. noon–5, Thurs. noon–9.*

Hafnarfjörður Museum. The museum is housed in several buildings and is dedicated to documenting the history and culture of Hafnarfjörður. ✉ *Vesturgata 8* ☎ *565–5420* 🌐 *www2.hafnarfjordur.is/museum* 🎟 *Free.*

Hellisgerði. Hafnarfjörður residents are serious about their respect for hidden folk said to live in local lava formations. As part of that respect, this local park is home to the world's northernmost bonsai garden and other rare floriculture. ✉ *Corner of Hellisgata and Reykjavikurvegur.*

Viking Festival Hafnarfjörður. An annual summer event celebrating all things Viking with clothing, instruments, jewelry, crafts, and food and drink. ✉ *Strandgata 55* 🌐 *www.fjorukrain.is.*

WHERE TO EAT

$$$ ECLECTIC 🍴 **Fjörukráin Restaurant.** Immerse yourself in everything Viking—from the style of architecture to the menu. Excellent seafood and meat dishes are served for those leery of traditional fare. It's next to the Viking Hotel. [$] *Average main: ISK 3,950* ✉ *Strandgata 55* ☎ *565–1213* 🌐 *www.fjorukrain.is* 🕒 *No lunch.*

BLUE LAGOON

The Blue Lagoon Geothermal Spa is Iceland's most visited tourist attraction and is located just 22 km (14 miles) from Keflavík Airport and 47 km (29 miles) from Reykjavik (turn off the airport road toward the village of Grindavík).

The lagoon's warm waters are rich in minerals and are said to cure a host of skin diseases and other ailments. The naturally heated water of the bathing area averages 37–39°C (98–102°F). There is a strict code of hygiene and guests are required to shower before and after bathing.

GETTING HERE AND AROUND

Buses run from the BSÍ bus terminal in Reykjavik to the Blue Lagoon twice daily and three times a day in July and August, or you can get to the Blue Lagoon from the airport on your own by taking a special FlyBus.

EXPLORING

Fodor's Choice **Blue Lagoon.** This world-renowned therapeutic wonder is now in a shel-
★ tered site where man-made structures blend with geologic formations. A reception area includes food concessions and boutiques where you can buy health products made from the lagoon's mineral-rich ingredients. Bathing suits are available to rent, and futuristic bracelets keep track of your locker code, any other purchases, and the length of your visit (all of which no doubt make useful marketing statistics). Buses run from the BSÍ bus terminal in Reykjavík to the Blue Lagoon twice daily and three times a day in July and August, or you can get to the airport on your own by taking a special FlyBus. ⊠ *Bláalóniδ, Grindavík* ☎ *420–8800* ⊕ *www.bluelagoon.com* ⊠ *ISK 4,800* ⊙ *Sept.–May, daily 10–8; June–Aug., daily 9–9.*

SLOVENIA

Ljubljana, the Karst Region

WHAT'S WHERE

1 Ljubljana. Slovenia's charming capital lies astride the tiny, emerald-green Ljubljanica River that winds its way through the Old Town. The river is lined on both sides with cafés, restaurants, and tiny streets that wend their way through historic squares. High above the rivers stands historic Ljubljanski grad (Ljubljana Castle), a focal point for the city.

2 Karst Region. The Karst is a geological and geographic term referring to the large limestone plateau that stretches out south and west of Ljubljana, nearly all the way to the Adriatic. Below ground, the Karst is typified by sinkholes, caves, and streams, while above ground it resembles Tuscany, with a rolling landscapes and vineyards.

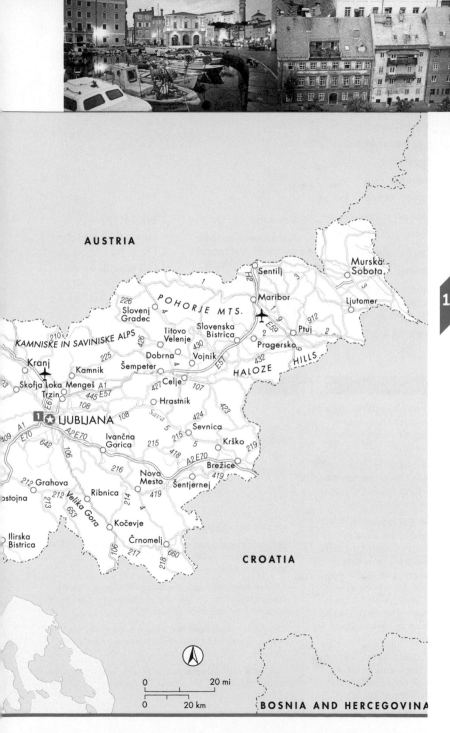

AUSTRIA

Murská Sobota

Šentilj

Maribor

Ljutomer

226
Slovenj Gradec

POHORJE MTS.

Slovenska Bistrica

912

Ptuj

210
KAMNIŠKE IN SAVINJSKE ALPS

Titovo Velenje
430

Pragersko

2

225
Kranj

Dobrna

Vojnik

432

HALOZE HILLS

Kamnik

Šempeter

Škofja Loka Mengeš A1
Trzin   445 E57
             108

427 Celje

107

Hrastnik

424

LJUBLJANA

108

Sava

Sevnica

A1
E70
409 E70   A2 E70
642   106

Ivančna Gorica

215

Krško

219

216

418

A2 E70

Brežice
419

212 Grahova

212 Velika Gora

Ribnica

214

Nova Mesto

Šentjernej

419

ostojna

213

653

Kočevje

Ilirska Bistrica

106

Črnomelj

217   218

660

CROATIA

0   20 mi

0   20 km

BOSNIA AND HERCEGOVINA

NEED TO KNOW

AT A GLANCE

Capital: Ljubljana

Population: 2,058,000

Currency: Euro

Money: ATMs are common

Language: Slovenian

Country Code: ☎ 386

Emergencies: ☎ 112

Driving: On the right

Electricity: 200v/50 cycles; electrical plugs have two round prongs

Time: Six hours ahead of New York

Ljubljana
★
SLOVENIA

Documents: Up to 90 days with valid passport; Schengen rules apply

Mobile Phones: GSM (900 and 1800 bands)

Major Mobile Companies: Mobitel, Simobil

WEBSITES

Slovenia: ⊕ www.slovenia.info

Ljubljana: ⊕ www.ljubljana.info

More Slovenia: ⊕ www.slovenia.si

GETTING AROUND

✈ **Air Travel:** The country's only major international airport is at Brnik, near Ljubljana.

🚌 **Bus Travel:** The best option for getting to smaller regional towns and exploring the Adriatic coast.

🚗 **Car Travel:** You won't need to rent a car, as transport options are excellent, but a car is handy for exploring at your own pace. If you bring a car into Slovenia, be sure to get a highway sticker as fines are steep for driving without one.

🚆 **Train Travel:** Train travel is handy for traveling to Bled; cross-country trains are frequent and fast.

PLAN YOUR BUDGET

	HOTEL ROOM	MEAL	ATTRACTIONS
Low Budget	€60	€1o	Ljubljana City Museum, €4
Mid Budget	€100	€20	Ljubljana Castle, €8
High Budget	€150	€50	Classical concert ticket, €25

WAYS TO SAVE

Eat your meals picnic-style. Take advantage of Ljubljana's wonderful outdoor market for fresh breads, meats, fruits, and cheeses.

Choose takeaway spots for lunch. Ljubljana's central market has stand-up fish stands, where you can get a plate of fresh calamari grilled or fried.

Choose low-tech activities. Slovenia is very green, and nature is free. Hike in the mountains or relax on the coast.

Opt for a rental apartment. A private rental can save money, especially for a family or group.

Hassle Factor	Medium. There are no nonstop flights from the U.S., but Slovenia is small, and getting around is easy by bus or train.
3 days	This is a perfect amount of time for seeing the capital, allowing time for a day trip to one of the caves, either Postojna or Škocjan.
1 week	Spend three to four days in the capital, take a day-trip to the caves, and move to the coast for the beach and to see the Karst region.
2 weeks	Divide your first week between Ljubljana and the Alps (including Lake Bled). Spend the second week on a leisurely exploration of the Karst and coast.

WHEN TO GO

High Season: On the coast and in Ljubljana, the high season runs May through September. Expect warm temps and lots of sunshine. Swimming weather normally lasts through mid-September. In the mountains, ski season runs from mid-December through March, with the most crowded month being February.

Low Season: Winter is quiet for tourists in Ljubljana and on the coast. Some areas along the Adriatic shut down for the season. In the mountains, summer is a nice time to visit. Warm weather is perfect for mountain hikes.

Value Season: Spring and fall are often the best seasons for any part of the country, bringing generally decent weather (though always prepare for rain), but without any of the crowds. Note that snow comes to the mountains by November, and mountain passes are usually inaccessible to cars from November to June.

BIG EVENTS

February: Kurentovanje in Ptuj is how Slovenians celebrate the pre-Lentan carnival. ⊕ *www.kurentovanje.net*

April: The town of Kamnik erupts in color at the Spring Flower Show. ⊕ *www.arboretum-vp.si*

July: The Ljubljana Festival brings high-end arts to the capital. ⊕ *www.ljubljanafestival.si*

August: Enjoy the Radovljica Festival of Classic Music, not far from the capital. ⊕ *www.festival-radovljica.si*

READ THIS

■ *Conversations With Žižek,* Slavoj Žižek. On the controversial philosopher.

■ *Black Lamb and Grey Falcon,* Rebecca West. Yugoslavia on the eve of WWII.

■ *The Fall of Yugoslavia,* Misha Glenny. The best modern history.

WATCH THIS

■ *Black Cat, White Cat.* Classic Balkan comedy from Emir Kusturica.

■ *Underground.* A satirical look at Yugoslav history from Kusturica.

■ *Dance in the Rain.* In French New Wave style, a great Slovenian film.

EAT THIS

■ **Ajda:** buckwheat groats (hulled seeds), a typical and filling Slovenian side dish

■ **Pršut:** dry-cured ham, which pairs perfectly with red wine and fresh bread

■ **Prekmurska gibanica:** a popular dessert of apples, pastry, nuts, and cream

■ **Burek:** cheese- or meat-filled pastries—the country's most popular street food

■ **Bučno olje:** organic pumpkin-seed oil, delicious in salads or with bread

■ **Žlikrofi:** tasty pasta pockets stuffed with potato and served as a side with meat dishes

Slovenia may be the best-kept secret in Europe. Just half the size of Switzerland, the country is often treated as fly-over—or drive-through—territory by travelers heading to better-known places in Croatia or Italy. That's good news for anyone choosing Slovenia as a destination, either in its own right or as a highlight during a visit to the region. It means fewer crowds—even in the peak summer touring months—fewer hassles, and in many ways a more relaxed travel experience with a chance to get to know the friendly and sophisticated Slovenian people.

While Slovenia's beautiful artistic monuments and charming towns may lack the grandeur and historical importance found in neighboring Italy or Austria, they still cast a captivating spell. And when it comes to natural beauty, Slovenia easily competes with other European countries. The Julian Alps northwest of the capital are every bit as spectacular as their sister Alpine ranges in Austria, Italy, and Switzerland, while the magnificent countryside and the quietly elegant charm of Ljubljana await those with the imagination to choose a destination that is off the beaten path.

HISTORY

The territory of Slovenia has been inhabited for thousands of years with archaeological finds dating back to 4000 BC. Although mythology attributes the founding of Ljubljana to Jason and the Argonauts, the country's recorded history begins with the arrival of the Romans in the 1st century BC. They built villas along the coast and founded the inland military and later urban centers of Emona (Ljubljana) and Poetovio (Ptuj). The 6th century AD saw the first influx of Slav migrants, the ancestors of present-day Slovenes, who set up an early Slav state.

In 1335 the Habsburgs took control of Slovenia, making it into the Austrian crown land of Carniola. Slovenia remained under the Habsburgs until 1918, with the exception of a brief period of semi-independence from 1809 to 1813, when it became part of Napoléon's Illyrian Provinces.

In the aftermath of World War I and Austria-Hungary's defeat, Italy seized control of the coastal towns, whereas inland Slovenia became part of the Kingdom of Serbs, Croats, and Slovenes; in 1929, the name of the kingdom was changed to Yugoslavia.

Nazi Germany declared war on Yugoslavia in 1941, and shortly afterward, Axis forces occupied the country. Slovenia was divided between Germany, Italy, and Hungary. When the war ended in 1945, Slovenia became one of the six constituent republics of Yugoslavia.

The Yugoslav years were mostly kind to Slovenia, but in early 1990, buoyed by the recent anti-communist revolutions across Eastern Europe, demands for increased autonomy from Yugoslavia were stepped up. A referendum was held, and nearly 90% of the electorate voted for independence. Slovenia proclaimed independence in 1991, and the so-called 10-Day War followed. Yugoslav federal troops moved in, but there was little violence to compare with the heavy fighting in the rest of Yugoslavia.

In 1992, Slovenia gained its independence. In May 2004, Slovenia, along with seven other Central and Eastern European countries, was admitted into the European Union; it adopted the euro in 2007.

PLANNING

WHEN TO GO

The country offers things to do year-round so the best time to visit depends on what you plan to do during your stay. Ljubljana is vibrant the whole year through. Many visitors want to head straight for the coast. Those in search of sea, sun, and all-night parties will find what they're looking for in peak season (July and August), including cultural events, open-air dancing, busy restaurants, and crowded beaches. If you want to avoid the crowds, hit the Adriatic in June or September, when it should be warm enough to swim and easier to find a place to put your beach towel.

16

In the mountains there are two distinct seasons: winter is dedicated to skiing; summer to hiking, rafting, and biking. Some hotels close in November and March to mark a break between the two periods. Conditions for more strenuous walking and biking are optimal in April, May, September, and October, although the summer in Slovenia is seldom as uncomfortably warm as it is in neighboring countries.

Lovers of fine food and wine should visit Slovenia during fall. The grape harvest concludes with the blessing of the season's young wine on St. Martin's Day (Nov. 11). In rural areas autumn is the time to make provisions for the hard winter ahead: wild mushrooms are gathered, firewood is chopped, and *koline* (sausages and other pork products) are prepared by hand.

GETTING HERE AND AROUND

AIR TRAVEL

There are no direct flights between North America and Slovenia. The Slovenian national carrier, Adria Airways, flies from many Western European cities to Ljubljana Airport and is a regional carrier of the Star Alliance. Be aware, however, that since Slovenia is not a major airline destination, fares between other European cities and Ljubljana tend to be high, regardless of where in Europe you're flying from. It may, in fact, be cheaper to fly to Ljubljana via London than via Vienna or Venice, or to fly to Vienna or Venice and use ground transportation to reach Slovenia.

The Ljubljana Airport is at Brnik, 25 km (16 miles) north of the city. Public bus service runs regularly between the airport and Ljubljana's main bus station in the city center. Buses depart from the airport every hour on the hour weekdays and slightly less frequently on weekends. Tickets cost around €4. A private airport shuttle makes the same trip in slightly less time; departures average every 90 minutes or so. A taxi costs approximately €30; the ride takes about 30 minutes.

Contacts Ljubljana Airport ✉ *Brnik* ☎ *04/206–1981* ⊕ *www.lju-airport.si.*
Ljubljana Airport Shuttle. Shuttle buses depart regularly from Ljubljana Airport to Ljubljana and many other destinations in Slovenia. Check the website for schedules, prices, and to purchase tickets. ☎ *01/234–4600* ⊕ *www.lju-airport. si/eng.*

CAR TRAVEL

From Budapest and Vienna the Slovenian border is no more than a two-hour drive. A tunnel speeds traffic through the Karavanke Alps between Slovenia and Austria. From Vienna the passage is by way of Maribor to Ljubljana, with a four-lane highway most of the way. Slovenia's roads also connect with Italy's autostrada.

You don't need a car if you are not planning to leave Ljubljana; autos are, in fact, prohibited in the old city. However, traveling by car undoubtedly gives you the chance to reach remote areas of the country when and as you wish and will also allow you to appreciate the country's natural beauty. If you're bringing a car into Slovenia, be sure to buy a highway toll sticker, a vignette, at the border. It's required to drive on any highway, and fines are steep if you're caught without one. Short-term stickers are available. Any rental car hired in Slovenia should already have one.

TAXI TRAVEL

Private taxis operate 24 hours a day. Phone from your hotel or hail one in the street. Drivers are bound by law to display and run a meter.

TRAIN TRAVEL

There are daily trains from Vienna (six hours) and Budapest (eight hours). The train station is just north of the city center. There's no longer a direct rail connection between Venice and Ljubljana, although you can get from Venice to Ljubljana by train, with stopovers in Klagenfurt, Austria (6 hours). You can also travel by minivan, which leaves Venice from near the Mestre train station once a day and takes three hours to reach Slovenia. Book your tickets in advance at ⊕ *www.drd.si* as seats tend to fill up quickly.

Contacts Ljubljana Train station ✉ *Trg OF 6, Ljubljana* ☎ *01/291–3332* ⊕ *www.slo-zeleznice.si.*

HOTELS

Lodging prices are similar to what you see in Western Europe, although there are some less expensive options. During peak season (July and August), many hotels—particularly those on the coast—are fully booked. Hotels are generally clean and well run. Establishments built under communism are often equipped with extras such as saunas and sports facilities, but tend to be gargantuan structures lacking in soul. Hotels dating from the turn of the 20th century are more romantic, as are the castle hotels, but even here the rooms tend to have been modernized; they are comfortable and well equipped, but generally lack the charm that the hotels' facades and common rooms promise.

RESTAURANTS

Slovenia's traditional dining institution is the *gostilna*, essentially an inn or tavern but cleaner, warmer, and more inviting than the English translation suggests. These are frequently family-run, especially in the smaller towns and villages, with Mom in the kitchen and Pop out front pouring beers and taking orders. The staff is usually happy to suggest local or regional specialties. Some of the better gostilna are situated alongside vineyards or farms. In Ljubljana, these are usually on the outskirts of the city; the ones in the city center tend to be oriented toward the tourist trade, since urban Ljubljaners usually prefer lighter, more modern fare.

Slovenian cuisine is highly regionalized, with offerings quite similar to dishes of neighboring countries and cultures. The Adriatic coast features Italian-influenced grilled fish and pasta, while the inland regions will offer cuisine very similar to that of Austria and Hungary. From the former Yugoslavia (and originally from Turkey), you'll find grilled meats and a popular street food called *burek,* a little pastry pocket stuffed with cheese or meat.

HOTEL AND RESTAURANT PRICES

Prices in the restaurant reviews are the average cost of a main course at dinner or, if dinner is not served, at lunch; taxes and service charges are generally included. Prices in the hotel reviews are the lowest cost of a standard double room in high season, excluding taxes, service charges, and meal plans (except at all-inclusives).

16

VISITOR INFORMATION

Contacts **Slovenian Tourist Information Center** ⊠ *Krekov trg 10, Ljubljana* ☎ *01/306-4575* ⊕ *www.slovenia.info.* **Turistično Informacijski Center kiosk** ⊠ *Stritareva 1, Ljubljana* ☎ *01/306-4576* ⊕ *www.slovenia.info.*

TOP REASONS TO GO	
Go Caving. Slovenia's Karst region is filled with some amazing limestone caves.	**Expose yourself to art.** Ljubljana is filled with a wide variety of excellent museums for a city its size.
Swim the Adriatic. Slovenia's small Adriatic coastline is lined with bays, inlets, and tiny, secluded beaches.	**Eat and drink.** As southern Europeans, Slovenians love simple pleasures like good food, wine, and coffee.
Experience the Alps. The Julian Alps, north of Ljubljana, are real mountains, with ample chances for hiking or rafting mountain rivers.	

LJUBLJANA

Slovenia's small but exceedingly charming capital has enjoyed a tourism renaissance in recent years, as easier access from larger European countries has brought in a dramatic influx of visitors and helped the country earn its status as one of the top urban destinations in Central Europe.

The city center is immediately captivating and among the most beautiful urban areas in Europe. Part of the charm is doubtless the crystalline Ljubljanica River that winds its way through the Old Town, providing a focal point and the perfect backdrop to the cafés and restaurants that line the banks. Partly, too, it's the beautifully restored baroque and neoclassical houses that line the riverbanks, streets, and many squares of the old city. There are few modern additions and those that have been added are frequently the work of internationally recognized architects, like the homegrown master Jože Plečnik. His meticulously designed pillars, orbs, and obelisks lend the city an element of whimsy and a feeling of good cheer that's immediately infectious.

The heart of the Old Town dates back centuries. The earliest settlement was founded by the Romans and called Emona. A section of the walls and a complex of foundations—complete with mosaics—can still be seen today. In the 12th century, a new settlement, Laibach, was built on the right bank of the river, below Castle Hill, by the dukes of Carniola. In 1335, the Habsburgs gained control of the region, and it was they who constructed the castle fortification system, part of which is still there.

The 17th and 18th centuries saw an increase of baroque architecture, strongly influenced by movements in Austria and Italy. Walk along the cobblestones of the Mestni trg (Town Square) and the Stari trg (Old Square) to see the oldest part of Ljubljana, with its colored baroque town houses and Francesco Robba's delightful Fountain of the Three Carniolan Rivers.

PLANNING

PLANNING YOUR TIME

For short stays of two to three days, base yourself in Ljubljana. Spend at least one day taking in the attractions of the capital and the other day or two on day trips, such as to the Postojna or Škocjan Caves. If you have one other day to spend, you might consider dividing your time between Ljubljana and a town like Koper on the Adriatic coast.

GETTING HERE AND AROUND

Central Ljubljana is tiny and compact. You'll find yourself walking from place to place. Take taxis or city buses if you need to cover more ground. Taxis are ample and affordable, and the city bus route is extensive.

TOURS

For a private guided tour of the city, contact the Tourist Information Centre Ljubljana. Tours must be arranged in advance and are offered in several languages.

Contacts **Tourist Information Centre Ljubljana.** The general municipal tourist information office provides two-hour guided tours of the city if booked in advance over the telephone or the office's website. ✉ *Adamič Lundrovo nabrežje 2* ☎ *1/306–1230* ⊕ *www.visitljubljana.com.*

16

EXPLORING

Much of Ljubljana's architecture from the period between the two world wars is the work of Jože Plečnik (1872–1957). Born in Ljubljana, Plečnik studied architecture in Vienna under Otto Wagner and was an important member of the Viennese Secessionist School. It was Plečnik who added many of the decorative touches to the city's parks, squares, and bridges. Some of his finest projects include the Triple Bridge, the open-air market on Vodnik Square, the University Library, and the plans for the Križanke Summer Theater. Although Plečnik survived World War II, he fell out of favor with government officials, since his Roman Catholicism conflicted with the ideologies of the socialist state under Tito. Be on the lookout for his masterpieces. The city center is concentrated within a small area, so you can cover all the sights on foot.

Cankarjevo nabrežje. Numerous cafés line this pretty riverside walkway. When the weather is good, tables are placed outside overlooking the water. ✉ *Between Tromostovje and Čevljarski most.*

Čevljarski most (*Cobblers' Bridge*). The most southerly of the historic bridges linking the old and new sides of town, this romantic pedestrian bridge was built in 1931 according to plans by the architect Jože Plečnik. The name refers to a wooden structure lined with shoemakers' huts that once stood here.

City Museum of Ljubljana. Situated in the grand Auersberg Palace, this museum and its beautifully designed exhibits trace the history of the city from pre-Roman times through the Austrian domination, the World Wars, the Tito years, and finally the establishment of independent Slovenia. In the basement, you can walk on a piece of the ancient Roman road and see a cross-sectioned excavation that shows the burning of

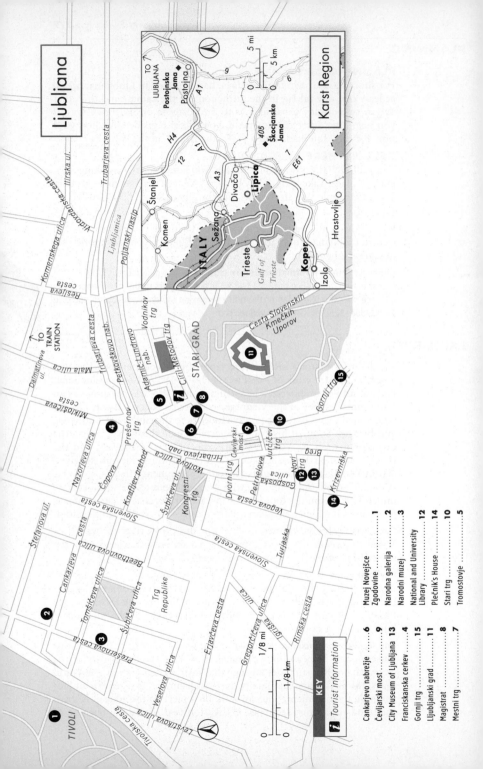

Ljubljana

Karst Region

TIVOLI

TO TRAIN STATION

STARI GRAD

Tivolska cesta
Levstikova ulica
Cankarjeva cesta
Streljarova ul.
Tomšičeva ulica
Prešernova cesta
Subičeva ulica
Veselova ulica
Beethovnova ulica
Nazorjeva ulica
Čopova
Knafljev prehod
Slovenska cesta
Wolfova ulica
Dvorni trg
Vegova cesta
Turjaška
Gregorčičeva ulica
Erjavčeva cesta
Rimska cesta
Igrišča
Kongresni trg
Trg Republike
Subičeva ul.
Prešernov trg
Miklošičeva cesta
Trubarjeva cesta
Resljeva cesta
Komenskega ulica
Vidovdanska cesta
Illirska ul.
Dalmatinova ul.
Mala ulica
Petkovškovo nab.
Adamič-Lundrovo nab.
Vodnikov trg
Cyril-Metodov trg
Hribarjevo nab.
Ljubljanica
Poljanski nasip
Ciril-Metodov trg
Čevljarski most
Jurčičev trg
Gosposka ulica
Petrnelova
Novi trg
Breg
Križevniška
Cesta Slovenskih Kmečkih Uporov
Gornji trg

KEY
ⓘ Tourist information

Cankarjevo nabrežje	6
Čevljarski most	9
City Museum of Ljubljana	13
Franciskanska cerkev	4
Gornji trg	15
Ljubljanski grad	11
Magistrat	8
Mestni trg	7
Muzej Novejše	1
Zgodovine	1
Narodna galerija	2
Narodni muzej	3
National and University	
Library	12
Plečnik's House	14
Stari trg	10
Tromostovje	5

0 1/8 mi
0 1/8 km

Karst Region

ITALY
SLOVENIA

TO LJUBLJANA
Postojnska Jama
Postojna
Štanjel
Komen
Sežana
Divača
Lipica
Škocjanske Jama
405
Trieste
Gulf of Trieste
Koper
Izola
Hrastovlje

A1
H4
12
A1
A3
E61
7
6
9

0 5 km
0 5 mi

Emona by Attila the Hun through a black, charred stratum. If you're interested, you can arrange for a museum guide to take you to other ancient Roman sites around the city. The city museum also houses the world's oldest wooden wheel, dating from 4000 BC. ⊠ *Gosposka ulitca 15* ☎ *01/241-2500* ⊕ *www.mgml.si* ⊠ *€4* ۞ *Tues.–Sun. 10–6, Thurs. 10–9.*

Franciskanska cerkev (*Franciscan Church*). This imposing, pink, high-baroque church was built between 1646 and 1660 for Augustinian priests; the Franciscans took it over in the 18th century and painted it red, the color of their order (although the outside facade has now faded to pink). The main altar, by Francesco Robba (1698–1757), dates from 1736. The three sets of stairs in front are a 19th century addition added after the ground was leveled in the plaza and now serve as a popular meeting place for students. ⊠ *Prešernov trg 4* ☎ *01/425–3007* ۞ *Daily 8–12:30 and 1:30–8.*

Gornji trg (*Upper Square*). This cobbled street, just around the corner from Stari trg, is where you'll find some of the capital's finest restaurants and a small but growing collection of design and art studios. ⊠ *Gornji trg.*

Ljubljanski grad (*Ljubljana Castle*). Ljubljana's hilltop castle affords views over the river and the Old Town's terra-cotta rooftops, spires, and green cupolas. On a clear day, the distant Julian Alps are a dramatic backdrop. The castle walls date from the early 16th century, although the tower was added in the mid-19th century. The surrounding park was landscaped by Plečnik in the 1930s. The castle also houses a virtual museum showcasing Slovenian history through digital technology. ⊠ *Studentovska ul, uphill from Vodnikov trg, Grajska planota 1* ☎ *01/306–4293* ⊕ *www.ljubljanskigrad.si* ⊠ *€8, includes cable car* ۞ *Apr.–Oct., daily 9–9; Nov.–Mar., daily 10–7.*

16

Magistrat (*Town Hall*). The current town hall is the work of the Ljubliana architect Gregor Maček, who substantially renovated the 1484 original building from 1717 to 1719. The interior was completely reworked in the 19th and 20th centuries and now frequently hosts temporary art exhibits. ⊠ *Mestni trg 1* ☎ *Free* ۞ *Daily 9–6.*

Mestni trg (*Town Square*). Right up the street from the Old Town end of the Triple Bridge, this cobbled square extends into the oldest part of the city. Baroque town houses, now divided into functional apartments, present marvelously ornate facades: carved oak doors with great brass handles are framed within columns, and upper floors are decorated with balustrades, statuary, and intricate ironwork. Narrow passageways connect with inner courtyards in one direction and run to the riverfront in the other. The street-level floors contain boutiques, antiques shops, and art galleries.

Muzej Novejše Zgodovine (*Museum of Modern History*). The permanent exhibition on Slovenes in the 20th century takes you from the days of Austria-Hungary, through World War II, the victory of the Partisan liberation movement and the ensuing Tito period, and up to the present day. Relics and memorabilia are combined with a dramatic sound-and-video presentation (scenes from World War II are projected on the walls and ceiling, accompanied by thundering gunfire, screams, and singing). You'll find the museum in a pink-and-white baroque villa in Tivoli Park. ⊠ *Celovška 23* ☎ *01/300–9610* ⊕ *www.muzej-nz.si* 🖾 *€3.50* ◷ *Tues.– Sun. 10–6.*

Narodna galerija (*National Gallery*). This massive building houses a large collection of Slovenian art from the 13th through the early 20th century, and a smaller but impressive collection of European paintings. It also houses the original of Francesco Robba's *Fountain of the Three Rivers.* ⊠ *Prešernova 24* ☎ *01/241–5418* ⊕ *www.ng-slo.si* 🖾 *€7* ◷ *Tues.–Sun. 10–6.*

Narodni muzej (*National Museum*). The centerpiece here is a bronze urn from the late 5th or 6th century BC known as the Vace Situle. Discovered in Vace, Slovenia, it is a striking example of Illyrian workmanship and is decorated with friezes representing a procession with men, horses, and chariots. ⊠ *Prešernova 20* ☎ *01/241–4400* ⊕ *www. nms.si* 🖾 *€3, €5 combined ticket with the Natural History Museum* ◷ *Fri.–Wed. 10–6, Thurs. 10–8.*

National and University Library. Built from 1936 to 1941, the National Library is architect Jože Plečnik's secular masterpiece. The external facades present a modernist version of an Italian reanaissance palazzo, using brick, stone, and even archeological remains from excavations around Ljubljana. However, these are not arranged in registers as in a traditional palazzo, but rather are scattered haphazardly over the entire exterior, creating a dynamic and three-dimensional look that makes the massive building seem light and airy. Inside, there is a beautiful collonaded black marble staircase and a reading room with huge windows at either end to let in light. The austere furniture in the reading room was also designed by Plečnik. Don't miss the beautiful horsehead door handles on the main entrance. ⊠ *Turjaška ulitca 1* ☎ *01/200–1121* ⊕ *www.nuk.uni-lj.si* ◷ *Reading Room weekdays 9–8, Sat. 9–2.*

Plečnik's House. Architecture enthusiasts will enjoy a visit to architect Jože Plečnik's house, still as he left it, to see his studio, home, and garden. You'll be struck by the strange combination of refined aestheticism and severe, almost monastic, asceticism that pervades the residence of the man who played a large part in transforming Ljubjana between the two World Wars. From the Križanke Summer Theater, cross Zoisova cesta, and then follow Emonska to Karunova. ⊠ *Karunova 4, Trnovo* ☎ *01/280–1600* ⊕ *www.mgml.si/plecnikova-zbirka* 🖾 *€4* ◷ *Daily 10–5, guided tours on the hr.*

Stari trg (*Old Square*). Now more a narrow street than a square, the Old Square once extended all the way down to the river during the Middle Ages. Today, it's lined with small restaurants and elegant houses. Note the Schweiger house, built in 1749 for Franc Karl Schweiger by the promanent architect Candido Zulliani; it is considered one of the finest baroque homes in the city. A figure above the door has his finger to his lips, urging silence—a visual pun on the name of the house's owner (Schweiger means "a silent man" in German). Be sure to also check out the Stična Mansion, one of the oldest and most beautiful houses on the square, built in 1630. ⊠ *Between Mestni trg and Gornji trg.*

Tromostovje (*Triple Bridge*). This striking structure spans the River Ljubljanica from Prešernov trg to the Old Town. The three bridges started as a single span, and in 1931 the two graceful outer arched bridges, designed by Plečnik, were added.

WHERE TO EAT

You can eat fairly well in Ljubljana. The surrounding hills supply the capital with first-class meat and game, dairy produce, fruit, and vegetables. At some of the more modern restaurants, the menus may verge on nouvelle cuisine, featuring imaginative and beautifully presented dishes. The portions, however, are almost always more ample than their counterparts in other countries. Complement your meal with a bottle of good Slovenian wine; the waiter can help you choose an appropriate one. For a lunchtime snack visit the market in Vodnik Square. Choose from tasty fried squid and whitebait in the riverside arcade or freshly baked pies and *kròf* (jelly-filled doughnuts) at the square's bakeries.

$$$ STEAKHOUSE 🍴 **Gostilna As.** This refined restaurant—not to be confused with the on-premises beer garden and after-hours club of the same name—is *the* place to enjoy excellent, well-aged steaks, complemented by a first-rate wine list. As—or "Ace"—is tucked away in a courtyard just off Wolfova ulic, with a sleek and elegant ambience to match the creative and modern dishes. [$] *Average main: €22* ✉ *Knafljev prehod 5a* ☎ *01/425–8822* 🌐 *www.gostilnaas.si* ✍ *Reservations essential.*

$ SLOVENIAN 🍴 **Gostilna na Gradu.** This polished but traditional Slovenian restaurant, located in the hilltop Ljubljana Castle, is the perfect place to try the famous *kranjska klobasa* (boiled Slovenian sausage). It also has a great selection of Slovenian pastries and cheeses, and, of course, an ample selection of Slovenian wines. [$] *Average main: €12* ✉ *Grajska planota 1* ☎ *08/205–1930* 🌐 *www.nagradu.si* ✍ *Reservations essential* 🕒 *No dinner Sun.*

$ PIZZA 🍴 **Ljubljanski Dvor.** Situated close to Čevljarski most and overlooking the river, this restaurant doubles as a pizzeria (which remains open on Sunday, when the restaurant is closed). The summer terrace makes it a convenient stopping point for lunch. [$] *Average main: €12* ✉ *Dvorni trg 1* ☎ *01/251–6555* 🕒 *Closed Sun.*

$$$ MEDITERRANEAN 🍴 **Špajza.** Towards the end of the Gornji trg, you'll find a restaurant with a series of romantic candlelit rooms and refined folkloric decor. The inviting atmosphere helps create a great place for quiet conversation over an elegantly served meal. The menu features interesting updates on traditional Slovenian cuisine. [$] *Average main: €24* ✉ *Gornji trg 28* ☎ *01/425–3094* ✍ *Reservations essential* 🕒 *Closed Sun.*

$$ EUROPEAN 🍴 **Zlata Ribica.** Although there is a good range of Slovenian and Italian specialties, it's not the food that's the main draw here—it's the riverside location near the Triple Bridge. On a warm summer evening, there's no better table in town. Despite the name, which translates as "goldfish," there's not much in the way of seafood here—instead the focus is on salads, grilled meats, and game. [$] *Average main: €20* ✉ *Cankarjevo nabrezje 5.*

WHERE TO STAY

Most of the listed hotels are clustered conveniently around Miklošičeva cesta, the main axis running from the train station down to Tromostovje (Triple Bridge). Although high compared to Central and Eastern European prices, Ljubljana's hotels are slightly less expensive than their Western European equivalents. The standards here usually are high, but rooms, even in older historic hotels, tend to be modern and somewhat devoid of charm. In summer you can get good deals through private accommodations or university dorms. Ask about these options at the tourist information kiosk in the town center.

$ HOTEL 🏨 **Best Western Slon Hotel.** Close to the city's historic center, this high-rise hotel stands on the site of a famous 16th-century inn and maintains an atmosphere of traditional hospitality. **Pros:** good breakfast. **Cons:** run-of-the-mill rooms. [$] *Rooms from: €100* ✉ *Slovenska 34* ☎ *01/470–1131* 🌐 *www.hotelslon.com* 🛏 *185 rooms* 🍴 *Breakfast.*

$ HOTEL 🏨 **City Hotel.** Rooms at this hotel are contemporary and streamlined, with a variety of rooms and apartments that can meet any budget. **Pros:** convenient location; free Internet in the lobby. **Cons:** despite creative use of color, design in most rooms is pretty basic; primarily a business hotel. [$] *Rooms from: €87* ✉ *Dalmatinova 15* ☎ *01/239–0000* 🌐 *www.cityhotel.si* 🛏 *123 rooms* 🍴 *Breakfast.*

$ HOTEL 🏨 **Emonec.** A considerable bargain for its location, Emonec fills a long-time gap in the market for a clean, affordable hotel in the center of Ljubljana. **Pros:** decent value for money; free Wi-Fi and cable Internet in most rooms. **Cons:** small and spartan, although clean and comfortable, rooms. [$] *Rooms from: €69* ✉ *Wolfova 12* ☎ *01/200–1520* 🌐 *www.hotel-emonec.com* 🛏 *26 rooms* 🍴 *Breakfast.*

$$$ HOTEL 🏨 **Grand Hotel Union.** The pricier "Executive" section of this bustling hotel complex in central Ljubljana occupies a Secessionist-style building where the interior and public space furnishings remain typically turn-of-the-20th-century Vienna. **Pros:** great location; tasty breakfast; massage services available. **Cons:** rooms lack personality; some bathrooms could use updating. [$] *Rooms from: €225* ✉ *Miklošičeva 1* ☎ *01/308–1270* 🌐 *www.gh-union.si* 🛏 *297 rooms, 12 suites* 🍴 *Breakfast.*

$$ HOTEL 🏨 **Hotel Lev.** Formerly a nondescript modern building with a 10-minute walk to city center, the Lev has turned into the country's leading hotel, making up for its location with stunning views of Tivoli Park and the Julian Alps. **Pros:** great packages and offers; excellent views. **Cons:** little atmosphere; best for business travelers. [$] *Rooms from: €150* ✉ *Vošnjakova 1* ☎ *01/433–2155* 🌐 *www.hotel-lev.si* 🛏 *170 rooms* 🍴 *Breakfast.*

NIGHTLIFE AND THE ARTS

Although they were considered the workaholics of Yugoslavia, Slovenes do know how to enjoy themselves. One in 10 of the capital's inhabitants is a student, hence the proliferation of trendy cafés and small art galleries. Each year the International Summer Festival breathes new life into the Ljubljana cultural scene, sparking off a lively program of concerts and experimental theater.

NIGHTLIFE

The listed bars and clubs are all situated within walking distance of the center. However, during summer the all-night party scene moves to the Adriatic coast, where open-air dancing and rave parties abound.

CAFÉS

The most idyllic way to close a summer evening is with a nightcap on the terrace of one of the riverside cafés in the Old Town.

Café Galerija. Café Galerija serves stylish cocktails by candlelight in a hip hideout that doubles as an art gallery. ⊠ *Mestni trg 5* ☎ *041/728–818* ⏱ *Mon.–Sat. 9 am–3 am, Sun. 9 am–10 pm.*

Café Maček. With a large terrace and glamorous clientele, Café Maček is the place to be seen down by the river. It's perhaps the oldest café along the river, and still one of the most popular. Sit outside on the terrace and watch sophisticated Ljubljana go by. ⊠ *Krojaška 5* ☎ *01/425–3791* ⏱ *Mon.–Sat. 9 am–1 am, Sun. 9 am–11 pm.*

MUSIC

Casa del Papa. Literary fans should be sure to visit Casa del Papa and its three floors of exotic food, drinks, and entertainment in tribute to Ernest Hemingway. The individual rooms evoke the atmosphere of Hemingway's famous haunts: Cuba, Key West, and Paris. But Hemingway also has a connection to Ljubljana; he was hospitalized near here while fighting in World War I and his wartime experiences in Slovenia's Soča Valley are recalled in *A Farewell to Arms.* ⊠ *Celovška 54A* ☎ *01/434–3158* ⊕ *www.casadelpapa.si* ⏱ *Daily noon–midnight.*

Jazz Club Gajo. For live jazz visit Jazz Club Gajo, which attracts stars from home and abroad. Clark Terry, Sheila Jordan, and Woody Shaw have all performed here. There are also jam sessions on Monday nights. ⊠ *Beethovnova 8* ☎ *01/425–3206* ⊕ *www.jazzclubgajo.com.*

K4. The student-run club K4 hosts visiting DJs and plays a mix of musical styles—house, hip-hop, surf—throughout the week. It attracts a young and alternative crowd; Sunday is gay night. Check the website for a schedule of concerts and entrance fees. ⊠ *Kersnikova 4* ☎ *01/483–0300* ⊕ *www.klubk4.org.*

BARS AND CLUBS

Metelkova. At one time this was an army barracks that was occupied by students and transformed into a multipurpose venue for shows and happenings. Today it is the center of the Slovenian alternative culture scene. Check the website for schedules of openings and activities. ⊠ *Metelkova, Tabor* ⊕ *www.metelkovamesto.org.*

Romeo. If you get hunger pangs after a night in the bars in the Old Town, head to Romeo for great sandwiches and quesadillas. It's open until midnight. ⊠ *Stari trg 6* ☎ *040/706–070.*

THE ARTS

ANNUAL EVENTS

Each year in June, the International Jazz Festival and the Druga Godba (a festival of alternative and ethnic music) are staged at the Križanke Summer Theater. For schedules and tickets contact the box office at Cankarjev dom.

16

International Summer Festival. Ljubljana's International Summer Festival is held each year from late June until mid-September in the open-air Križanke Summer Theater. Musical, theatrical, and dance performances attract acclaimed artists from all over the world. Check the website for schedules and reservations. ⊠ *Trg Francoske Revolucije 1–2* ☎ *01/241–6000* ⊕ *www.ljubljanafestival.si.*

CLASSICAL MUSIC

Ljubljana has plenty of events for classical-music lovers. The season, which runs from September through June, includes weekly concerts by the Slovenian Philharmonic Orchestra and the RTV Slovenia Orchestra, as well as performances by guest soloists, chamber musicians, and foreign symphony orchestras.

Slovenska Filharmonija (*Slovenian Philharmonic*). The 19th-century performance hall housing concerts by the Slovenska Filharmonija is a traditional classical-music venue. Check their website for a schedule of performances and to make reservations. ⊠ *Kongresni trg 10* ☎ *01/241–0800* ⊕ *www.filharmonija.si.*

THEATER, DANCE AND OPERA

Ljubljana has a long tradition of experimental and alternative theater, frequently incorporating dance as well. Contemporary dance plays by the internationally recognized choreographers Matjaz Faric and Iztok Kovac and performances by the dance troupes Betontanc and En Knap are ideal for those who don't understand Slovenian.

SNG Opera in Balet (*Slovene National Opera & Ballet Theater*). From September through June the SNG Opera in Balet stages everything from classical to modern and alternative productions. ⊠ *Cankarjeva 11/1* ☎ *01/241–1700* ⊕ *www.opera.si.*

SHOPPING

Shopping isn't huge in Ljubljana like in other European cities, but there are still plenty of places to scope out the latest fashions or pick up a traditional Slovenian souvenir.

Anappurna. If you want to do some hiking but have come unprepared, Anappurna has a good selection of mountaineering equipment. ⊠ *Krakovski Nasip 10* ☎ *031/740–838* ⊕ *www.annapurna.si.*

Ljubljana Flea Market. You can pick up antiques and memorabilia at the Ljubljana Flea Market, held on the Breg Embankment each Sunday morning. ⊠ *Breg Embankment.*

Open-air Market. The most interesting shopping experience is undoubtedly a visit to the open-air market, where you can find fresh fruit and vegetables as well as dried herbs and locally produced honey. ⊠ *Vodnikov trg.*

THE KARST REGION AND THE ADRIATIC COAST

As you move south and west from Ljubljana toward the Adriatic, the breeze feels warmer, the air smells saltier, and the landscape looks less like Austria and more like Italy.

The word "karst," or in Slovenian *Kras,* is both a geological and geographic term referring to the large limestone plateau stretching roughly from Nova Gorica in the north to well beyond Divača in the south. It extends from the Italian frontier in the west to the fertile, wine-producing Vipava valley in the east. The Karst is typified by sinkholes, underground caves, and streams. Two caves—Postojna and especially Škocjan—are particularly well known for their jaw-dropping beauty and size.

To most Slovenians, the word "karst" conjures up two things: *pršut* (air-cured ham, a Slovenian version of *prosciutto*) and blood-red Teran wine, made from the refosco grape. The two pair beautifully, especially with a plate of cheese and a basket of homemade bread taken at a traditional *osmica,* a small farmhouse restaurant. Teran gets its name from the *terra rossa,* or red soil, that typifies the Karst.

For visitors, the Karst is ideal for low-key exploration. The gentle terrain and the many wine roads (look for the sign that reads *vinska cesta*) are perfect for leisurely walks or bike rides. Several wine roads can be found in the area around the town of Komen and along the main road from Komen to Dutovlje. The pretty towns—with their old stone churches and red-tiled roofs—are a delight. If you have wheels, visit Stanjel to the east of Komen. It's a nearly abandoned hilltop village that's found new life as a haven for artists. The Lipica stud farm—the original breeding ground of the famed Lipizzaner horses of Vienna's Spanish Riding School—is an excellent base.

A little farther on, Slovenia's tiny piece of the Adriatic coast gives tourists a welcome chance to swim and sunbathe. Backed by hills planted with olive groves and vineyards, the small strip is only 47 km (29 miles) long and dominated by the towns of Koper, Izola, Piran, and Portorož.

Following centuries of Venetian rule, the coast remains culturally connected to Italy, and Italian is still widely spoken. The medieval port of Piran is certainly worth a visit just for its nearly perfectly preserved Venetian core. Portorož is a classic fun-and-sun resort. Koper, Slovenia's largest port, and Izola, its biggest fishery, are workaday towns that nevertheless retain a lot of historical charm. For beachgoers the best-equipped beach is at Bernadin, between Piran and Portorož. The most unspoiled stretch of coast is at the Strunjan Nature Reserve—which also has an area reserved for nudists—between Piran and Izola.

PLANNING

PLANNING YOUR TIME

Piran and Portorož are very different in character, but either can serve as an excellent base depending on what you plan to do. Choose Portorož if your primary interest is swimming and sunbathing, or if you're seeking a modern hotel with all of the amenities. Pick Piran if you're looking for something quainter, quieter, and more austerely beautiful. Whatever you choose, you can travel easily between the two—buses make the 10-minute trip at least once an hour in season.

Both Piran and Portorož fill to capacity in July and August, so try to arrange accommodation in advance. If you show up without a room, inquire at one of the privately run travel agencies. Along the coast, these are likely to be more helpful than the local tourist information centers.

GETTING HERE AND AROUND

BUS TRAVEL

Several buses a day connect Ljubljana to Koper and Piran, passing through Postojna and Divača on the way. There is also a daily service connecting the coastal towns to Trieste, Italy.

A network of local buses connects all listed sights, with the exception of those in Štanjel and Lipica. Schedules vary depending on the time of year, so contact a local bus station for information.

CAR TRAVEL

A car is advisable for touring the Karst region. However, parking can be a problem along the coast during summer, when town centers are closed to traffic. The E63 highway connects Ljubljana to the coast, passing through the Karst region en route.

TRAIN TRAVEL

Four trains daily link Ljubljana and Koper, passing through Postojna and Divača en route.

VISITOR INFORMATION

Information Koper Tourist Information ⊠ *Titov trg 3, Koper* 🕿 *05/664–6403* ⊕ *www.koper.si.* Izola Tourist Information ⊠ *Sončno nab. 4, Izola* 🕿 *05/640–1050* ⊕ *www.izola.si.* Lipica Tourist Information ⊠ *Lipica 5, Sežana* 🕿 *05/739–1580* ⊕ *www.lipica.org.* Postojna Tourist Information ⊠ *Ljubjanska cesta 4, Postojna* 🕿 *05/728–0788* ⊕ *www.postojna.si.*

POSTOJNSKA JAMA

44 km (27 miles) southwest of Ljubljana.

FAMILY **Postojnska Jama** (*Postojna Cave*). Postojnska Jama conceals one of the largest networks of caves in the world, with 23 km (14 miles) of underground passageways. A miniature train takes you through the first 7 km (4½ miles), to reveal a succession of well-lighted rock formations. This strange underground world is home of the snakelike "human fish" on view in an aquarium in the Great Hall. Eyeless and colorless because of countless millennia of life in total darkness, these amphibians can live for up to 60 years. Temperatures average 8°C (46°F) year-round, so bring a sweater, even in summer. Tours leave every hour on the hour throughout the year. ⊠ *Jamska 30, Postojna* 🕿 *05/700–0163* ⊕ *www.postojna-cave.com* 🎫 *€22.90* ⊗ *May–Sept., daily 8:30–6; Apr. and Oct., daily 8:30–5; Nov.–Mar., weekdays 9:30–1:30, weekends 9:30–3.*

ŠKOCJANSKE JAMA

26 km (16 miles) from Postojna, 76 km (47 miles) from Ljubljana.

FAMILY

Fodor'sChoice

★

Škocjanske Jama (*Škocjanske Caves*). The 11 interconnected chambers that make up the Škocjan Jama stretch for almost 6 km (about 4 miles) through a dramatic, subterranean landscape so unique that UNESCO has named them a World Heritage Site. The 90-minute walking tour of the two chilly main chambers—the Silent Cave and the Murmuring Cave—winds past otherworldly dripstone sculptures, massive sinkholes, and stalactites and stalagmites that resemble the horns of some mythic creature. The highlight is Europe's largest cave hall, a gorge 479 feet high, 404 feet wide, and 984 feet long, spanned by a narrow bridge lighted with footlights. Far below, the brilliant jade waters of the Reka River rush by on their underground journey. The view is nothing short of mesmerizing. ⊠ *Škocjan 2, Divača* ☎ *05/763–2840* ⊕ *www. park-skocjanske-jame.si* ⊠ *€20, includes Mahorčić and Marinić caves* ☉ *Guided tour only: Apr.–May and Oct. daily at 10, 1, and 3; June– Sept., daily 10–5; Nov.–Mar., daily at 10 and 1.*

LIPICA

16

5 km (3 miles) west of Divača, 30 km (19 miles) south of Stanjel, 80 km (50 miles) from Ljubljana.

Lipica is best known as the home of the *Kobilarna Lipica,* the Lipica Stud farm, where the fabled white Lipizzaner horses were first bred by the Habsburg monarchy. The horse farm is still the primary reason most people come here, though the area has developed into a modern sports complex, with an excellent nine-hole golf course.

FAMILY

Kobilarna Lipica (*Lipica Stud Farm*). The Kobilarna Lipica was founded in 1580 by the Austrian archduke Karl II. It's where the white Lipizzaners—the majestic horses of the famed Spanish Riding School in Vienna—originated. Today the farm no longer sends its horses to Vienna, but breeds them for its own performances and riding instruction. The impressive stables and grounds are open to the public. Riding classes are available, but lessons are geared toward experienced riders and must be booked in advance. ⊠ *Lipica 5, Sežana* ☎ *05/739–1708* ⊕ *www.lipica.org* ☉ *Dressage performances June–Oct., Tues., Fri., and Sun. at 3. Stable tours July and Aug., daily 9–6; Apr.–June and Sept. and Oct., daily 10–5; Nov.–Mar., daily 11–3.*

KOPER

50 km (31 miles) southwest of Divača (Lipica), 105 km (65 miles) southwest of Ljubljana.

Today a port town surrounded by industrial suburbs, Koper nevertheless warrants a visit. The Republic of Venice made Koper the regional capital during the 15th and 16th centuries, and the stately architecture of the Old Town bears witness to the spirit of those times.

The most important buildings are clustered around **Titov trg,** the central town square. Here stands the **Cathedral,** which can be visited daily from

7 to noon and 3 to 7, with its Gothic facade. Be sure to step inside to see the gorgeous *Sacra Conversazione* painted by Vittore Carpaccio in 1516. Across the square the splendid **Praetor's Palace,** formerly the seat of the Venetian Grand Council, combines Gothic and Renaissance styles. From the west side of Titov trg, the narrow, cobbled **Kidriceva ulica** brings you down to the seafront.

EXPLORING

Loggia Cafe. Stop for coffee or a glass of wine at the elegant but affordable Loggia Cafe, housed within the Venetian Gothic loggia built in 1463. In summer there are tables out on the terrace overlooking the town square. ✉ *Titov trg 1* ☎ *05/627–3213.*

WHERE TO EAT

$$$ SEAFOOD 🍴 **Skipper.** Noted for its vast summer terrace overlooking the marina, Skipper is popular with the yachting fraternity. The menu includes pasta dishes, risottos, grilled meats, and fish. [$] *Average main: €30* ✉ *Kopališko nab 3* ☎ *05/626–1810.*

SPAIN

Madrid, Barcelona, Bilbao, Andalusia

WHAT'S WHERE

1 Madrid. Its boundless energy makes sights and sounds larger than life. The Prado, Reina Sofia, and Thyssen-Bornemisza museums pack thousands of Spanish and European masterworks into half a mile of art heaven, while the cafés and wine bars of Plaza Mayor and Cava Baja are always buzzing. Sunday's crowded flea market in El Rastro is thick with overpriced oddities.

2 Toledo. An hour from Madrid by bus, Toledo is a city of dreamy spires and rambling, narrow streets perched on the banks of the Rio Tajo.

3 Barcelona. Its Rambla is a mass of strollers, artists, street entertainers, vendors, and vamps, all preparing you for the city's startling architectural landmarks. Antoni Gaudí's sinuous Casa Milà and unique Sagrada Familia church are masterpieces of the *moderniste* movement.

4 Bilbao. Greener, cloudier, and stubbornly independent in spirit, the Basque region is a country within a country, proud of its own language, one of Europe's oldest. Its capital, Bilbao, overlooking the Bay of Biscay, is a hotbed of architectural endeavor, exciting urban regeneration projects, and culinary excellence.

5 Andalusia. Eight provinces, five of which are coastal (Huelva, Cádiz, Málaga, Granada, and Almería) and three that are landlocked (Seville, Córdoba, and Jaén) compose this southern autonomous community known for its Moorish influences. Highlights are the romantic Alhambra and seductive Seville.

FRANCE

Bay of Biscay

Ribadesella   Santander

San
Sebastián

viedo

PICOS DE
EUROPA

4 Bilbao

Vitoria

Roncesvalles

ANDORRA

PYRENEES

Figueres

León

Burgos

Logroño

Pamplona

Jaca

Huesca

Palencia

avente

Valladolid

Tordesillas

Soria

Ducro

SIERRA DE
GUADARRAMA

Tudela

Ebro

Zaragoza

Lleida

Manresa

Vic

COSTA BRAVA

Montserrat

3

Barcelona

amanca

Adanero

Segovia

Calatayud

Daroca

Medinaceli

Caminreal

Alcañiz

Tarragona

COSTA DORADA

Avila

Guadalajara

Tajo

Monreal
del Campo

Tortosa

SIERRA
E GREDOS

MADRID **1**

Cuenca

Teruel

La Jana

Vinaròs

TO
MINORCA →

Toledo **2**

Talavera
de la Reina

Aranjuez

Tarancón

Castellón
de la Plana

COSTA DEL AZAHAR

Balearic
Sea

Tajo

lo, Guadalupe

Alcázar de
San Juan

Sagunto

Palma

Guadiana

Abenójar

Valdepeñas

Requena

Valencia

Majorca

Albacete

Ibiza

BALEARIC
ISLANDS

Almadén

SIERRA MORENA

Alcaraz

Hellín

Eivissa

Córdoba

Linares

Ubeda

Bailén

Baeza

Cazorla

Alicante

Orihuela

Elche

COSTA BLANCA

Formentera

Jaén

Segura

Murcia

Manga del
Mar Menor

Minorca
Ciutadella

Baena

Cartagena

Mahón

Ecija

Guadalquivir

Granada **5**

SIERRA NEVADA

Antequera

Loja

Almería

Mediterranean
Sea

Ronda

Nerja

Motril

COSTA DE ALMERÍA

Málaga

Marbella

COSTA DEL SOL

ALGERIA

eciras

Gibraltar

ROCCO

0   100 miles

0   150 km

NEED TO KNOW

Bay of Biscay

⊙ Madrid

SPAIN

Mediterranean Sea

AT A GLANCE

Capital: Madrid

Population: 46,704,000

Currency: Euro

Money: ATMs are common; credit cards widely accepted

Language: Spanish

Country Code: ☎ 34

Emergencies: ☎ 112

Driving: On the right

Electricity: 220v/50 cycles; electrical plugs have two round prongs

Time: Six hours ahead of New York

Documents: Up to 90 days with valid passport; Schengen rules apply

Mobile Phones: GSM (900 and 1800 bands)

Major Mobile Companies: Movistar, Orange, Vodafone

WEBSITES

Spain: ⊕ *www.spain.info*

Spanish Paradores: ⊕ *www.parador.es*

Spanish Airports: ⊕ *www.aena.es*

GETTING AROUND

✈ **Air Travel:** The major airports are Madrid, Barcelona, and Málaga.

🚌 **Bus Travel:** The best and cheapest way to get around but beware of complicated journeys if you're traveling off the main tourist trail.

🚗 **Car Travel:** Rent a car to explore at your own pace and see the hidden Spain. Gas and toll highways are expensive.

🚆 **Train Travel:** Fast AVE trains link Madrid with major cities like Barcelona, Valencia, Seville, and Málaga, but book early for the best fares. Otherwise, train services are slow or nonexistent.

PLAN YOUR BUDGET

	HOTEL ROOM	MEAL	ATTRACTIONS
Low Budget	€60	€15	Reina Sofia Museum, €4
Mid Budget	€150	€30	Alhambra, €16
High Budget	€250	€100	Barça football match, €80

WAYS TO SAVE

Lunch on the *menú del día*. Take advantage of daily prix-fixe menus (usually with a drink) offered at many bars and restaurants. Go off the tourist trail for the best values.

Book a rental apartment. For space and a kitchen, consider a furnished rental—a good bet for families.

Book rail tickets in advance. For the cheapest AVE rail fares, book online without a fee 90 days before travel (⊕ www.renfe.com).

Look for free museums. Many museums are free, and even those that aren't may be free on the first or last Sunday.

Hassle Factor	Low. Flights to Madrid are frequent, and the AVE trains take you to most big cities quickly.
3 days	You can get a good feel for Madrid or Barcelona and perhaps take a day trip out to Toledo or Bilbao.
1 week	Combine two or three days in Madrid with a trip to Andalusia to take in Seville and Granada, plus a day trip to Toledo.
2 weeks	You have time to center on Madrid and Barcelona for a few days each. In between, include a trip in Andalusia to soak up Spain's Moorish roots and take in the southern highlights, including the Alhambra and Córdoba's mosque.

WHEN TO GO

High Season: June through mid-September is the most expensive and popular time to visit the coast and islands; July and August are especially crowded. Inland cities are quieter but hot, and many businesses close for August. Sunshine is guaranteed almost everywhere except in the north, where weather is changeable.

Low Season: Winter offers the least appealing weather, though it's the best time for airfares and hotel deals. The Mediterranean coast can be balmy during the daytime even in December — and there are no crowds — but nighttime temperatures drop.

Value Season: May, June, and September are lovely with warm weather, saner airfares, and good hotel offers. You can hang with the locals without the tourist crowds. October still has great weather, though temperatures start to fall by November. Bring an umbrella in March and April.

BIG EVENTS

February/March: Second only to Rio, Spain celebrates Carnaval before Lent. Highlights are Santa Cruz de Tenerife and Cádiz.

March/April: Holy Week events range from solemn processions to enactments of the Passion throughout Spain.

April: Celebrations at Seville's Feria de Abril are a week of dance, song, and joie de vivre.

October: October 12 is the national day honoring Spain's patron, the Virgen del Pilar.

READ THIS

■ **Spain . . . A Culinary Road Trip,** Mario Batali and Gwyneth Paltrow. Best dishes from all over Spain.

■ **For Whom the Bell Tolls,** Ernest Hemingway. A classic fictional account of the Spanish Civil War.

■ **The New Spaniards,** John Hooper. A portrait of modern Spain.

WATCH THIS

■ **Volver.** Rural and urban family feuds as seen by Pedro Almódovar.

■ **Belle Époque.** Rural Spain in the liberal 1930s.

■ **Flamenco Trilogy.** Carlos Saura's take on three Spanish classics.

EAT THIS

■ **Churros:** deep-fried batter sticks: the ultimate comfort food

■ **Cocido:** a winter classic of pork, vegetables, and garbanzo beans

■ **Fritura:** fish and shellfish fried to a crisp, washed down with a glass of fino

■ **Gazpacho:** a refreshingly cool tomato-and-cucumber salad in soup form

■ **Paella:** rice with meat (chicken, pork, or rabbit), fish, or shellfish

■ **Tortilla española:** potato (and often onion) omelet: a nationwide staple

17

The word *Spain* conjures images of flamenco dancers, bull-fighters, and white hillside villages. Beyond these traditional associations you'll find that Spain is really several countries within a country, with cutting-edge art museums, green highland valleys, soaring cathedrals, medieval towns, designer cuisine, raucous nightlife, and an immense treasury of paintings and sculptures.

At the center of it all, sprawling over the parched plains of Castille, is one of Europe's liveliest capitals, Madrid. Beyond its designer boutiques and chic restaurants, you'll discover the noisy cafés and rustic taverns of a typical Castilian town. Food lovers will appreciate the fact that delicious seafood is packed into trucks and brought over daily from the coast. Arts lovers will swoon over the world-famous Prado, Reina Sofia, and Thyssen-Bornemisza museums, all collected on one half-mile stretch of leafy promenade. Madrid inherited its capital status from Toledo, a short side trip away, in whose labyrinthine *casco antiguo* (Old Town) Jews, Moors, and Christians lived and worked together to inspire Europe's intellectual and cultural renaissance. A virtual open-air museum, Toledo is often referred to as Spain's spiritual capital.

Nowhere are tradition and history more beautifully preserved than in Andalusia, where rolling hills dotted with whitewashed villages and olive trees seem to encapsulate the romance of Spain. Jutting out into the Atlantic, Cádiz, with its gold-domed cathedral and ramshackle streets, is almost African in appearance, while Córdoba, center of Western art and culture between the 8th and 11th centuries, is dominated by the ochre-red archways of its mosque-cum-cathedral, scene of an epic clash of baroque and Moorish styles. Granada is synonymous with the opulent, frescoed rooms, and the spectacular snow-capped backdrop of its Alhambra Palace. Seville is known for flamenco, for beautiful women in ruffled polka-dot dresses at its April Fair, and the solemn procession of penitents during Semana Santa (Holy Week). Go to Andalusia's famous tiled bars and you can expect generous mounds of fried fish and shellfish—called *frituras*—olives, and serrano ham, all washed down with the sherries of Jerez.

Catalonia, with a population of 6 million Catalan speakers, is Spain's richest and most industrial region. Its capital, Barcelona, rivals Madrid for power, and edges it in culture and style. Its tree-lined streets, art-nouveau architecture, and renovated waterfront still gleam from a face-lift received for the 1992 Olympic Games, an event that not only focused the world's attention on this Mediterranean port but also provided the city with new museums, sports facilities, and restaurants. Barcelona's museums, including the Picasso Museum and innovative science extravaganza, CosmoCaixa, receive around 7 million visitors a year. The spirit of modern architect Antoni Gaudí lives on in the surreal spires of his work-in-progress cathedral, La Sagrada Familia, and in the Catalan passion for radical, playful design, illustrated in the MACBA modern art center.

Industrious, artistic Bilbao, famous for its cuisine and fierce sense of local identity, is now beginning to emerge from the shadows of Barcelona and Madrid. Here you'll find one of the world's most talked-about buildings, Frank Gehry's Guggenheim, as well as mouthwatering culinary concoctions—Bilbao's pintxo chefs are taking the world by storm with their innovative cooking.

Since joining the European Union (EU) in 1986, Spain has come up to speed technologically with rest of Western Europe. The most obvious improvements for travelers are the nationwide network of superhighways and the high-speed AVE trains linking Madrid with Barcelona, Córdoba, Málaga, Seville, and Valencia. Spain's progress, happily, has not nudged aside cherished old traditions: Shops still shut at around 2 pm for a siesta, and three-hour lunches are commonplace. Young adults often still live with their parents until marriage. Bullfights continue despite protests from animal-rights activists. And flamenco is being fused successfully with everything from rock music to rap.

Most exciting for any visitor is the national insistence on enjoying life. Whether it be strolling in the park with the family on a Sunday afternoon, lingering over a weekday lunch, or socializing with friends until dawn, living life to its fullest is what Spain does best.

17

PLANNING

GETTING HERE AND AROUND

AIR TRAVEL

Most flights into Spain go to Madrid or Barcelona, though certain destinations in Andalusia are popular with carriers traveling from England and other European countries. Flying time from New York to Madrid is about seven hours; from London, it's just over two hours. Regular nonstop flights serve Spain from major cities in the eastern United States; flying from other North American cities usually involves a stop. There are a few solid package flight options for travel to and within Spain. If you buy a round-trip transatlantic ticket on Iberia, you might want to purchase an Iberiabono air pass, which provides access to economy-class travel across Spain. The pass must be purchased before arrival in Spain, and all flights must be booked in advance.

Contacts Barcelona–El Prat de Llobregat ☎ *902/404704* ⊕ *www.aena.es.* **Madrid–Barajas** ☎ *902/404704* ⊕ *www.aena.es.*

BOAT AND FERRY TRAVEL

Regular car ferries connect the United Kingdom with northern Spain. Brittany Ferries sails from Plymouth and Portsmouth to Santander and Bilbao. Trasmediterránea and Balearia connect mainland Spain to the Balearic and Canary islands.

TOP REASONS TO GO

La Alhambra. Nothing can prepare you for the Moorish grandeur of Andalusia's greatest monument. The ornamental palace is set around sumptuous courtyards and gardens with bubbling fountains, magnificent statues, and fragrant flowerbeds.

Toledo. Castile's crowning glory, Toledo is often cited as Spain's spiritual capital. This open-air city is an architectural tapestry of medieval buildings, churches, mosques, and synagogues threaded by narrow cobbled streets and squares.

La Sagrada Familia, Barcelona. *The* symbol of Barcelona, Gaudí's extraordinary unfinished cathedral should be included on everyone's must-see list. The pointed spires, with organic shapes that resemble a honeycombed stalagmite, give the whole city a fairytale quality.

Guggenheim Museum, Bilbao. All swooping curves and rippling forms, the innovative museum—one of architect Frank Gehry's most breathtaking projects—was built on the site of the city's former shipyards, its inspiration the shape of a ship's hull.

Museo del Prado, Madrid. Set in a magnificent neoclassical building on one of the capital's most elegant boulevards, the Prado is Spain's answer to the Louvre and a regal home to Spanish masterpieces.

Festa de Sant Jordi, Barcelona. Valentine's Day with a Catalan twist. Celebrating St. George, the patron saint of Barcelona, who saved a princess from a dragon, local tradition dictates that men buy their true love a rose and, since the festival shares a date with International Book Day, women reciprocate by buying their beau a book.

Drink like a Madrileño. In the capital an aperitif is a crucial part of daily life. In fact, there are more bars per square mile than in any other capital in Europe, so finding a venue poses no great challenge.

Feria de Abril, Seville. Seville's April Fair features sultry, foot-stomping señoritas wearing traditional, brilliantly colored dresses. From 1 to 5 every afternoon, Sevillan society parades around in carriages drawn by glossy high-stepping horses.

Contacts Balearia ☎ *902/160180* ⊕ *www.balearia.com.* **Brittany Ferries** ☎ *0871/244–0744 in U.K., 902/108147 in Spain* ⊕ *www.brittany-ferries.com.* **Trasmediterránea** ☎ *902/454645* ⊕ *www.trasmediterranea.com.*

BUS TRAVEL

The bus is usually much faster than the train to smaller destinations, and bus fares tend to be lower. Service is extensive, though less frequent on weekends. Various bus companies service the country, but Spain's major national bus line is Alsa-Enatcar.

Contacts Alsa ☎ *902/422242* ⊕ *www.alsa.es.* **Eurolines Spain** ☎ *902/405040, 93/367–4400* ⊕ *www.eurolines.es.*

CAR TRAVEL

All the major international car-rental brands have branches at major Spanish airports and in large cities. Smaller, regional companies and wholesalers offer lower rates. The online outfit Pepe Car has been a big hit with travelers; in general, the earlier you book, the less you pay.

Pickups at center-city locations are considerably cheaper than at the airports. All agencies have a range of models, but virtually all cars in Spain have manual transmission. ■**TIP→ If you don't want a stick shift, reserve weeks in advance and specify automatic transmission, then call to reconfirm your automatic car before you leave for Spain.** Children under 10 may not ride in the front seat, and seat belts are mandatory for all passengers. Follow speed limits. Rental cars are frequently targeted by police monitoring speeding vehicles.

Contacts Pepe Car ☎ *807/414243 (premium call charge)* ⊕ *www.pepecar.com.*

TRAIN TRAVEL

RENFE trains are economical if they're short routes with convenient schedules (such as the commuter trains around Madrid and Barcelona); or take the AVE, Spain's high-speed train, which is wonderfully fast—it can go from Madrid to Seville in under three hours. Most Spaniards buy train tickets in advance at the train station's *taquilla* (ticket office). The lines can be long, so give yourself plenty of time. For popular train routes, you will need to reserve tickets more than a few days in advance and pick them up at least a day before traveling. The ticket clerks at the stations rarely speak English, so if you need help or advice in planning a more complex train journey, you may be better off going to a travel agency that displays the blue-and-yellow RENFE sign. A small commission (€2.50) should be expected. For shorter, regional train trips, you can often buy your tickets from machines in the train station, though machines may accept only chip-and-pin credit cards.

17

Contacts RENFE ☎ *902/320320 for information, 902/109420 for tickets* ⊕ *www.renfe.es.*

HOTELS

For a slice of Spanish culture, check out the *paradores*; to indulge your pastoral fantasies, a *casa rural* (country house), Spain's version of a bed-and-breakfast. On the other end of the spectrum are luxurious high-rise hotels along the coastline, and chain hotels in the major cities.

In big cities or popular tourist areas it's best to book in advance. In smaller towns and rural areas you can usually find something on the spot, except when local fiestas are on—for those dates you may have to book months in advance.

RESTAURANTS

MEALS AND MEAL TIMES

Most restaurants in Spain do not serve breakfast (*desayuno*); for coffee and carbs, head to a bar or *cafetería*. Outside major hotels, which serve morning buffets, breakfast in Spain is usually limited to coffee and toast or a roll. Lunch (*comida* or *almuerzo*) traditionally consists of an appetizer, a main course, and dessert, followed by coffee and perhaps a liqueur. Between lunch and dinner the best way to snack is to sample some *tapas* (appetizers) at a bar; normally you can choose from quite a variety. Dinner (*cena*) is somewhat lighter, with perhaps only one course. In addition to an à la carte menu, most restaurants offer a daily fixed-price menu (*menú del día*) consisting of a starter, main plate, drink (wine, beer, water, soda, etc.), and usually either coffee or dessert at a very attractive price (usually between €6 and €12). If your waiter does not suggest the menú del día when you're seated, ask, *Hay menú del día, por favor?* Restaurants in many of the larger tourist areas will have the menú del día posted outside. The menú del día is traditionally offered only at lunch, but increasingly it's also offered at dinner in popular tourist destinations.

Mealtimes in Spain are later than elsewhere in Europe, and later still in Madrid and the southern region of Andalusia. Lunch starts around 2 or 2:30 (closer to 3 in Madrid), and dinner after 9 (later in Madrid). Weekend eating times, especially dinner, can begin upward of about an hour later. In areas with heavy tourist traffic, some restaurants open a bit earlier.

PAYING
Credit cards are widely accepted in Spanish restaurants, but some smaller establishments do not take them. If you pay by credit card and you want to leave a small tip above and beyond the service charge, leave it in cash.

RESERVATIONS AND DRESS
Regardless of where you are, it's a good idea to make a reservation. For popular restaurants, book as far ahead as you can (often 30 days), and reconfirm as soon as you arrive. We mention dress only when men are required to wear a jacket or a jacket and tie.

WINES, BEER, AND SPIRITS
Apart from its famous wines, Spain produces many brands of lager, the most popular of which are San Miguel, Moritz, Cruzcampo, Aguila, Voll Damm, Mahou, and Estrella. Jerez de la Frontera is Europe's largest producer of brandy, and is a major source of sherry. Catalonia produces most of the world's *cava* (sparkling wine). Spanish law prohibits the sale of alcohol to people under 18.

HOTEL AND RESTAURANT PRICES
Prices in the restaurant reviews are the average cost of a main course at dinner or, if dinner is not served, at lunch; taxes and service charges are generally included. Prices in the hotel reviews are the lowest cost of a standard double room in high season, excluding taxes, service charges, and meal plans (except at all-inclusives). Prices for rentals are the lowest per-night cost for a one-bedroom unit in high season.

PLANNING YOUR TIME

Spain is anchored by two great cities, Madrid and Barcelona. If you have time you should visit both, but if you're in Spain for a week or less, you're better off choosing one and planning excursions to the surrounding region. Madrid will give you world-class art and much more of a sense of a workaday Spanish city. From here you can also make a short side trip to Spain's capital of old, Toledo, where 2,000 years of architectural styles clash, from the Roman to the Visigothic to the baroque and beyond. Cosmopolitan Barcelona has Gaudí, Catalan cuisine, and its special Mediterranean atmosphere. This city is in itself worth longer than just a several-day sojourn, and has the Pyrenees at hand for side trips. The northern city of Bilbao, to the west of the Pyrenees, is a must for foodies and culture vultures, thanks to its pintxo bars and cutting-edge architecture.

If you're interested in the Moorish influence on Spain or seduced by the rhythm of flamenco, make time for a trip south to Andalusia. The area is large, however, and if you don't have more than a week, it will be hard to visit all of its principal attractions, but absolutely essential are stops in the old Moorish strongholds of Granada, Seville, and Córdoba, all easily accessible to each other by car, bus, or rail.

An ideal way to organize a trip around Spain if arriving by air in Madrid would be to start in Madrid before moving south to discover Andalusia and then heading northeast to Barcelona and Bilbao, before returning to Madrid. If arriving by car or train from France, begin with Bilbao, before heading to Barcelona and then doing Madrid and the South.

MADRID

Sitting on a plateau 2,165 feet above sea level and bordered to the north by a mountain range, swashbuckling Madrid celebrates itself and life in general around the clock. A vibrant crossroads, Madrid—the Spanish capital since 1561—has an infectious appetite for art, music, and epicurean pleasure, and it's turned into a cosmopolitan, modern urban center while fiercely preserving its traditions. The rapid political and economic development of Spain following the arrival of democracy in 1977, the integration of the country in the European Union a decade later, and the social upheaval brought in by the many immigrants settling here after the new millennium have put Madrid back on the world stage with an energy redolent of its 17th-century golden age, when painters and playwrights swarmed to the flame of Spain's brilliant royal court.

17

PLANNING YOUR TIME

Madrid's most valuable art treasures are all on display within a few blocks of Paseo del Prado. This area is home to the Prado, with its astounding selection of masterworks from Velázquez, Goya, El Greco, and others; the Centro de Arte Reina Sofía, with an excellent collection of contemporary art; and the Thyssen-Bornemisza Museum, with a singular collection that stretches from the Renaissance to the 21st century. Each can take a number of hours to explore, so it's best to alternate museum visits with less overwhelming attractions. If you're running short on time and want to pack everything in, replenish your energy at any of the tapas bars or restaurants in the Barrio de las Letras (behind the Paseo del Prado, across from the Prado Museum).

Any visit to Madrid should include a walk in the old area between Puerta del Sol and the Royal Palace.

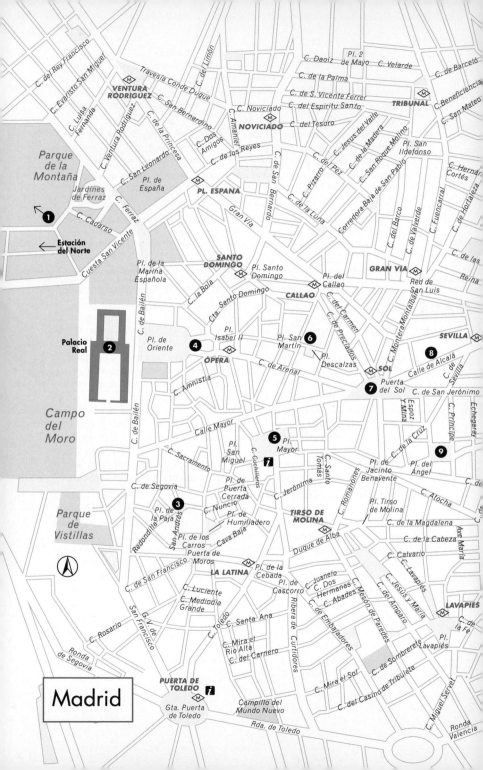

Madrid

17

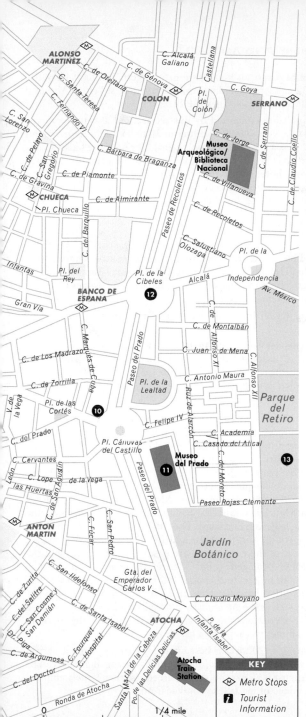

KEY

Ⓜ Metro Stops

🛈 Tourist Information

GETTING HERE AND AROUND
AIR TRAVEL
Madrid's Barajas Airport is Europe's fourth largest. Terminal 4 handles flights from 32 carriers, including American Airlines, British Airways, and Iberia. All other U.S. airlines use Terminal 1.

Airport terminals are connected by bus service and also to the metro (Línea 8) and take you to the city center in 30 to 45 minutes for around €5 (€1.50–€2 plus a €3 airport supplement). For €5 there's also a convenient bus to Avenida de América, where you can catch the subway or a taxi to your hotel. (Note that bus drivers don't take bills greater than €20.) A taxi to your hotel can be expensive but makes sense if you have a lot of luggage, but there is a surcharge on all fares of €5.50 to or from the airport.

BUS TRAVEL
Buses are generally less popular than trains, though they're sometimes faster. Madrid has no central bus station: most of southern and eastern Spain (including Toledo) is served by the Estación del Sur. Estación de Avenida de América and Estación del Sur have subway stops (Avenida de América and Méndez Álvaro).

Red city buses (€1.50 for a one-way ticket) run from about 6 am to 11:30 pm.

Contacts Estación del Avenida de América ⊠ Av. de América 9, Salamanca Ⓜ Av. de América. Estación del Sur ⊠ Méndez Álvaro s/n, Atocha ⊕ www.estaciondeautobuses.com Ⓜ Méndez Álvaro. Intercambiador de Moncloa ⊠ Princesa 89, Moncloa Ⓜ Moncloa.

CAR TRAVEL
Felipe II made Madrid the capital of Spain because it was at the very center of his peninsular domains, and to this day many of the nation's highways radiate from Madrid like the spokes of a wheel. Originating at Kilometer 0—marked by a brass plaque on the sidewalk of the Puerta del Sol—these highways include the A6 (Segovia, Salamanca, Galicia); A1 (Burgos and the Basque Country); the A2 (Guadalajara, Barcelona, France); the A3 (Cuenca, Valencia, the Mediterranean coast); the A4 (Aranjuez, La Mancha, Granada, Seville); the A42 (Toledo); and the A5 (Talavera de la Reina, Portugal). The city is surrounded by the M30 (the inner ring road), and the M40 and M50 (the outer ring roads), from which most of these highways are easily picked up. To fight the heavy traffic leaving and getting into Madrid, the government set up an infrastructure plan that includes radial toll highways (marked R1, R2, R3, R4, and R5) that bypass the major highways by 50 to 60 km (31 to 37 miles), as well as the A41, a new toll highway connecting Madrid and Toledo. These options are worth considering, especially if you're driving on a summer weekend or a holiday.

That said, driving in Madrid is best avoided. Parking is nightmarish, traffic is heavy almost all the time, and the city's daredevil drivers can be frightening. August is an exception; the streets are then largely emptied by the mass exodus of madrileños on vacation.

METRO AND TAXI TRAVEL

Once in Madrid you'll find that all the historic neighborhoods are in close proximity and can best be enjoyed when explored on foot. However, the metro, which runs frequently, is a fast and in expensive alternative. The metro costs from €1.50 to a maximum of €2, depending on how far you're traveling within the city; you can also buy a 10-ride Metrobus ticket (€12.20) or a daily ticket for €8.40 that can also be used on buses. The **Abono Turístico** (Tourist Pass) allows unlimited use of public buses and the subway for one to seven days. Buy it at tourist offices, metro stations, or select newsstands. The metro runs from 6 am to 1:30 am, though a few entrances close earlier.

Taxis work under three different tariff schemes. Tariff 1 is for the city center from 6 am to 9 pm; meters start at €2.30. Supplements include €5.50 to or from the airport and €3 to or from bus and train stations. Tariff 2 is from 9 pm to 6 am in the city center (and 6 am to 10 pm in the suburbs); the meter runs faster and charges more per kilometer. Tariff 3 runs at night beyond the city limits. All tariffs are listed on taxi windows.

TRAIN TRAVEL

Madrid has three main train stations: Chamartín, Atocha, and Norte, the last primarily for commuter trains. Remember to confirm which station you need when arranging a trip. Generally speaking, Chamartín, near the northern tip of Paseo de la Castellana, serves destinations north and west, including San Sebastián, Burgos, León, Oviedo, La Coruña, and Salamanca, as well as France and Portugal and the night train to Barcelona. Atocha, at the southern end of Paseo del Prado, serves towns near Madrid, including El Escorial, Segovia, and Toledo, and southern and eastern cities such as Seville, Málaga, Córdoba, Valencia, and Castellón, and the daily trains to Barcelona. Atocha also sends AVE (high-speed) trains to Córdoba, Seville, Zaragosa, Toledo, Segovia, Huesca, Lleida, Málaga, and Barcelona. For some destinations, however, you can depart from either Atocha or Chamartín (this is the case for Toledo, Segovia, El Escorial, and Alcalá de Henares).

Contacts Estación de Atocha ⊠ *Glorieta del Emperador Carlos V, Atocha* ☎ *91/528–4630* Ⓜ *Atocha.* **Estación Chamartín** ⊠ *C. Agustín de Foxá s/n, Chamartín* ☎ *91/315–9976* Ⓜ *Chamartín.* **Estación de Príncipe Pío (Norte)** ⊠ *Paseo de la Florida s/n, Moncloa* ☎ *902/240202 RENFE* Ⓜ *Príncipe Pío.* **RENFE** ☎ *902/320320 for information, 902/109420 for tickets* ⊕ *www.renfe.es.*

EXPLORING

The real Madrid is not to be found along major arteries like the Gran Vía and the Paseo de la Castellana. To find the quiet, intimate streets and squares that give the city its true character, duck into the warren of villagelike byways in the downtown area that extends 2 km (1 mile) from the Royal Palace to the Parque del Buen Retiro and from Plaza de Lavapiés to the Glorieta de Bilbao. Broad *avenidas,* twisting medieval alleys, grand museums, stately gardens, and tiny tile taverns are all jumbled together, creating an urban texture so rich that walking is really the only way to soak it in.

Fodor'sChoice
★ **Centro de Arte Reina Sofía** (*Queen Sofía Art Center*). Madrid's museum of modern art was once a hospital, but today the classical granite austerity of the space is somewhat relieved (or ruined, depending on your point of view) by the playful pair of glass elevator shafts on its facade. Three separate buildings joined by a common vault were added to the original complex in 2005—the first contains an art bookshop and a public library, the second a center for contemporary exhibitions, and the third an auditorium and restaurant-cafeteria. The latter, although expensive, makes an excellent stop for refreshment, be it a cup of tea or coffee, a snack, or even a cocktail, and in summer they also set up a popular snack bar in the gardens.

The permanent art collection features 1,000 works on four floors (the second and fourth floor of the Sabatini building and the ground and first floor of the Nouvel annex) and, despite concentrating on painting, puts a much higher emphasis on other art forms such as photography and cinema. The new collection breaks from the traditional habit of grouping works by major artistic movement and individual artist: instead, the current director has chosen to contextualize the works of the great modern masters—Picasso, Miró, and Salvador Dalí—and of other big local names, such as Juan Gris, Jorge Oteiza, Pablo Gargallo, Julio Gonzalez, Eduardo Chillida, and Antoni Tàpies, into broader narratives that attempt to explain better the evolution of modern art.

The museum's showpiece is Picasso's *Guernica,* in Room No. 206 on the second floor. The huge black-and-white canvas—suitably lit and without distracting barriers—depicts the horror of the Nazi Condor Legion's bombing of the ancient Basque town of Gernika in 1937, during the Spanish Civil War. The work, something of a national shrine, was commissioned from Picasso by the Republican government for the Spanish pavilion at the 1937 World's Fair in an attempt to gather sympathy for the Republican side during the civil war—the museum rooms adjacent to *Guernica*'s now reconstruct the artistic significance of the Spanish participation in the World's Fair, with works from other artists such as Miró, Josep María Sert, and Alexander Calder. *Guernica* did not reach Madrid until 1981, as Picasso had stipulated in his will that the painting return to Spain only after democracy was restored. ⊠ *Santa Isabel 52, Lavapiés* ☎ *91/467–5062* ⊕ *www.museoreinasofia.es* ⛱ *€8 (free Mon. and Wed.–Sat. after 7, Sun. 3–7), combined Paseo del Arte (Art Walk) ticket for the Prado, Reina Sofía, and Thyssen-Bornemisza €21.60* ☉ *Mon. and Wed.–Sat. 10–9, Sun. 10–7 (after 2:30 only the temporary exhibition can be visited)* Ⓜ *Atocha.*

Ermita de San Antonio de la Florida (Goya's tomb). Built between 1792 and 1798 by the Italian architect Francisco Fontana, this neoclassical church was financed by King Carlos IV, who also commissioned Goya to paint the vaults and the main dome. He took 120 days to complete his assignment, painting alone except for a little boy who stirred his pigments. This gave him absolute freedom to depict events of the 13th century (e.g., St. Anthony of Padua resurrecting a dead man) as if they had happened five centuries later with naturalistic images never used before to paint religious scenes. Opposite the image of the frightening dead man on the main dome, Goya painted himself as a man covered with a black cloak. The frescoes' third restoration phase ended in 2005, and visitors can now admire them in their full splendor. Goya, who died in Bordeaux in 1828, is buried here (without his head, since it was stolen in France) under an unadorned gravestone. ⊠ *Glorieta de San Antonio de la Florida 5, Príncipe Pío* ☎ *91/542–0722* ⓔ *Free* ⓥ *Tues.–Sun. 9:30–8* Ⓜ *Príncipe Pío.*

Monasterio de las Descalzas Reales (*Monastery of the Royal Discalced, or Barefoot, Nuns*). This 16th-century building was restricted for 200 years to women of royal blood. Its plain, brick-and-stone facade hides paintings by Francisco de Zurbarán, Titian, and Pieter Brueghel the Elder—all part of the dowry the novices had to provide when they joined the monastery—as well as a hall of sumptuous tapestries crafted from drawings by Peter Paul Rubens. The convent was founded in 1559 by Juana of Austria, one of Felipe II's sisters, who ruled Spain while he was in England and the Netherlands. It houses 33 different chapels—the age of Christ when he died and the maximum number of nuns allowed to live at the monastery at the same time—and more than 100 sculptures of Jesus as a baby. About 30 nuns (not necessarily of royal blood) still live here, cultivating their own vegetables in the convent's garden. ∎**TIP➜ You must take a tour in order to visit the convent; it's conducted in Spanish only.** ⊠ *Pl. de las Descalzas Reales 3, Palacio* ☎ *91/454–8800* ⓔ *€7, combined ticket with Convento de la Encarnación €10* ⓥ *Tues.–Sat. 10–2 and 4–6:30, Sun. 10–15; last ticket sold 1 hr before closing* Ⓜ *Sol.*

Fodor's Choice ★ **Museo del Prado** (*Prado Museum*). When the Prado was commissioned by King/Mayor Carlos III, in 1785, it was meant to be a natural science museum. The king wanted the museum, the adjoining botanical gardens, and the elegant Paseo del Prado to serve as a center of scientific enlightenment. By the time the building was completed in 1819, its purpose had changed to exhibiting the art gathered by Spanish royalty since the time of Ferdinand and Isabella. The museum's long-awaited facelift was begun in 2002 and completed after five years of work. It features a massive new wing together with a new building around the remains of the Cloister of the San Jerónimo el Real, designed by Rafael Moneo, that has resurrected long-hidden works by Zurbarán and Antonio de Pereda and more than double the number of paintings on display from the permanent collection.

The Prado's jewels are its works by the nation's three great masters: Goya, Velázquez, and El Greco. The museum also holds masterpieces by Flemish, Dutch, German, French, and Italian artists, collected when their lands were part of the Spanish Empire. The museum benefited greatly from the anticlerical laws of 1836, which forced monasteries, convents, and churches to forfeit many of their artworks for public display. ⊠ *Paseo del Prado s/n, Retiro* ☎ *91/330–2800* ⊕ *www.museodelprado. es* ⓔ *€14 (permanent collection free Mon.–Sat. 6–8 pm, Sun. 5–7 pm)* ⓥ *Mon.–Sat. 10–8, Sun. and holidays 10–7* Ⓜ *Banco de España, Atocha.*

Fodor's Choice ★ **Museo Thyssen-Bornemisza.** Opened in 1992, the Thyssen occupies spacious galleries filled with natural light in the late-18th-century Villahermosa Palace (itself finished in 1771). This ambitious collection of

17

almost 1,000 paintings traces the history of Western art with examples from every important movement, from the 13th-century Italian Gothic through 20th-century American pop art. The works were gathered from the 1920s to the 1980s by Swiss industrialist Baron Hans Heinrich Thyssen-Bornemisza and his father. At the urging of his wife, the baron donated the entire collection to Spain in 1993, and a renovation in 2004 increased the number of paintings on display to include the baroness's personal collection (considered of lesser quality). Critics have described the museum's paintings as the minor works of major artists and the major works of minor artists, but the collection still traces the development of Western humanism as no other in the world.

One of the high points is Hans Holbein's *Portrait of Henry VIII* (purchased from the late Princess Diana's grandfather, who used the money to buy a Bugatti sports car). American artists are also well represented; look for the Gilbert Stuart portrait of George Washington's cook, and note how closely the composition and rendering resemble the artist's famous painting of the Founding Father. Two halls are devoted to the impressionists and post-impressionists, including many works by Camille Pissarro and a few each by Pierre-Auguste Renoir, Claude Monet, Edgar Degas, Vincent van Gogh, and Paul Cézanne. You can buy tickets in advance online. ⊠ *Paseo del Prado 8, Cortes* ☎ *91/369–0151* ⊕ *www.museothyssen.org* ⊠ *Permanent collection €9 (free Mon.), temporary exhibition €8, combined €14; combined Paseo del Arte ticket for the Prado, Reina Sofía, and Thyssen-Bornemisza €21.60* ⊘ *Mon. noon–4, Tues.–Sun. 10–7* Ⓜ *Banco de España.*

Fodor's Choice ★   **Palacio Real.** Emblematic of the oldest part of the city and intimately related to the origins of Madrid—it rests on the terrain where the Muslims built their defensive fortress in the 9th century—the Royal Palace awes visitors with its sheer size and monumental presence that unmistakably stands out against the city's silhouetted background. The palace was commissioned in the early 18th century by the first of Spain's Bourbon rulers, Felipe V.

Outside, you can see the classical French architecture on the graceful **Patio de Armas:** Felipe was obviously inspired by his childhood days at Versailles with his grandfather Louis XIV. Look for the stone statues of Inca prince Atahualpa and Aztec king Montezuma, perhaps the only tributes in Spain to these pre-Columbian American rulers. Notice how the steep bluff drops west to the Manzanares River—on a clear day, this vantage point commands a view of the mountain passes leading into Madrid from Old Castile; it's easy to see why the Moors picked this spot for a fortress.

Inside, 2,800 rooms compete with each other for over-the-top opulence. A two-hour guided tour in English winds a mile-long path through the palace; highlights include the **Salón de Gasparini,** King Carlos III's private apartments, with swirling, inlaid floors and curlicued stucco wall and ceiling decoration, all glistening in the light of a 2-ton crystal chandelier; the **Salón del Trono,** a grand throne room with the royal seats of King Juan Carlos and Queen Sofía; and the **banquet hall,** the palace's largest room, which seats up to 140 people for state dinners.

⊠ *C. Bailén s/n, Palacio* ☎ *91/454–8800* 🎟 *€10 (€17 with guided tour), Royal Armory only €3.40, Painting Gallery only €2* ⊙ *Apr.–Sept., daily 10–8, Sun. 9–3; Oct.–Mar., daily 10–6* Ⓜ *Ópera.*

FAMILY
Fodor's Choice
★

Parque del Buen Retiro (*The Retreat*). Once the private playground of royalty, Madrid's crowning park is a vast expanse of green encompassing formal gardens, fountains, lakes, exhibition halls, children's play areas, outdoor cafés, and a **Puppet Theater** featuring free slapstick routines that even non–Spanish speakers will enjoy. Shows take place on Saturday at 1 and on Sunday at 1, 6, and 7. The park is especially lively on weekends, when it fills with street musicians, jugglers, clowns, gypsy fortune-tellers, and sidewalk painters, along with hundreds of Spaniards out for some jogging, rollerblading, bicycling, or just a walk.

West of the Rosaleda, look for a statue called the **Ángel Caído** (Fallen Angel), which madrileños claim is the only one in the world depicting the prince of darkness before (during, actually) his fall from grace. ⊠ *Puerta de Alcalá, Retiro* 🎟 *Free* Ⓜ *Retiro.*

Plaza de la Cibeles. A tree-lined walkway runs down the center of Paseo del Prado to the grand Plaza de la Cibeles, where the famous Fuente de la Cibeles (Fountain of Cybele) depicts the nature goddess driving a chariot drawn by lions. Even more than the officially designated bear and arbutus tree of Madrid's coat of arms, this monument, beautifully lighted at night, has come to symbolize Madrid—so much so that during the civil war, patriotic madrileños risked life and limb to sandbag it as Nationalist aircraft bombed the city. ⊠ *Cortes* Ⓜ *Banco de España.*

Plaza de la Paja. At the top of the hill, on Costanilla San Andrés, the Plaza de la Paja was the most important square in medieval Madrid. The plaza's jewel is the **Capilla del Obispo** (Bishop's Chapel), built between 1520 and 1530; this was where peasants deposited their tithes, called *diezmas*—literally, one-tenth of their crop. The stacks of wheat on the chapel's ceramic tiles refer to this tradition. Architecturally, the chapel marks a transition from the blocky Gothic period, which gave the structure its basic shape, to the Renaissance, the source of the decorations. It houses an intricately carved polychrome altarpiece by Francisco Giralta, with scenes from the life of Christ. To visit the chapel (⊙ *Tues. 9:30–12:30, Thurs. 4–5:30*) reserve in advance (☎ *91/559–2874 or* ✎ *reservascapilladelobispo@archimadrid.es*). ⊠ *La Latina* Ⓜ *La Latina.*

Plaza Mayor. Austere, grand, and often surprisingly quiet compared with the rest of Madrid, this public square, finished in 1620 under Felipe III—whose equestrian statue stands in the center—is one of the largest in Europe, measuring 360 feet by 300 feet. It's seen it all: *autos-da-fé* (trials of faith, i.e., public burnings of heretics); the canonization of saints; criminal executions; royal marriages, such as that of Princess María and the King of Hungary in 1629; bullfights (until 1847); masked balls; and all manner of other events. Special events still take place here.

This space was once occupied by a city market, and many of the surrounding streets retain the charming names of the trades and foods once headquartered there. The plaza's oldest building is the one with the brightly painted murals and the gray spires, called Casa de la Panadería (Bakery House) in honor of the bread shop over which it was built; it

17

is now the tourist office. Opposite is the Casa de la Carnicería (Butcher Shop), now a police station.

The plaza is closed to motorized traffic, making it a pleasant place to sit at one of the sidewalk cafés, watching alfresco artists, street musicians, and madrileños from all walks of life. Sunday morning brings a stamp and coin market. Around Christmas the plaza fills with stalls selling trees, ornaments, and nativity scenes. ⊠ *Sol* Ⓜ *Sol.*

Plaza Santa Ana. This plaza was the heart of the theater district in the 17th century—the Golden Age of Spanish literature—and is now the center of Madrid's thumping nightlife. A statue of 17th-century playwright Pedro Calderón de la Barca faces the **Teatro Español,** where playwrights such as Félix Lope de Vega, Tirso de Molina, Pedro Calderón de la Barca, and Ramón del Valle-Inclán released some of their plays. (Opposite the theater and off to the side of a hotel is the diminutive **Plaza del Ángel,** with one of Madrid's best jazz clubs, the **Café Central.**) One of Madrid's most famous cafés, **Cervecería Alemana,** is on Plaza Santa Ana and is still catnip to writers and poets; it's a good spot for a beer but for eating check out our listings for Tapas Bars and Where to Eat. ⊠ *Cortes* Ⓜ *Sevilla.*

Puerta del Sol. Crowded with people but pedestrian-friendly, the Puerta del Sol is the nerve center of Madrid. The city's main subway interchange is below, and buses fan out from here. A brass plaque in the sidewalk on the south side of the plaza marks Kilometer 0, the spot from which all distances in Spain are measured. The restored 1756 French-neoclassical building near the marker now houses the offices of the regional government, but during Franco's reign it was the headquarters of his secret police, and it's still known colloquially as the Casa de los Gritos (House of Screams). Across the square are a bronze statue of Madrid's official symbol, a bear with a *madroño* (strawberry tree), and a statue of King-Mayor Carlos III on horseback. ⊠ *Sol* Ⓜ *Sol.*

Real Academia de Bellas Artes de San Fernando (*St. Ferdinand Royal Academy of Fine Arts*). Designed by José Churriguera in the waning baroque years of the early 18th century, this museum showcases 500 years of Spanish painting, from José Ribera and Bartolomé Esteban Murillo to Joaquín Sorolla and Ignacio Zuloaga. The tapestries along the stairways are stunning. Because of a lack of personnel, only the first floor is now open, displaying paintings up to the 18th century, including some by Goya. Guided tours are available on Tuesday, Thursday, and Friday at 11, except during August. The same building houses the **Instituto de Calcografía** (Prints Institute), which sells limited-edition prints from original plates engraved by Spanish artists. Check listings for classical and contemporary concerts in the small upstairs hall. ⊠ *Alcalá 13, Sol* ☎ *91/524–0864* ⊕ *www.realacademiabellasartessanfernando.com* ⌨ *€5 (free Wed.)* ⊙ *Tues.–Sun. 9–3* Ⓜ *Sol.*

Teatro Real (*Royal Theater*). Built in 1850, this neoclassical theater was long a cultural center for madrileño society. A major restoration project has left it filled with golden balconies, plush seats, and state-of-the-art stage equipment for operas and ballets. ⊠ *Pl. de Isabel II, Palacio* ☎ *91/516–0660* ⊕ *www.teatro-real.com* Ⓜ *Ópera.*

CLOSE UP

Tapas

Originally a lid used to *tapar* (cover or close) a glass of wine, a *tapa* is a kind of hors d'oeuvre that sometimes comes free with a drink: the term supposedly came from pieces of ham or cheese laid across glasses of wine to keep flies out and to keep stagecoach drivers sober. The history of tapas goes back to the 7th- to 15th-century Moorish presence on the Iberian Peninsula. The Moors brought with them exotic ingredients, such as saffron, almonds, and peppers, and a taste for small delicacies that eventually became Spain's best-known culinary innovation.

Often miniature versions of classic Spanish dishes, the individual *pinchos* or tapas, or the larger *raciones*, which usually feed a few, allow you to sample different kinds of food and wine with minimal intoxication, especially on a *tapeo*, the Spanish version of a pub crawl: you walk off your wine and tapas as you move from bar to bar. In the tapas bars, you can test the food without committing to a sit-down meal. Here are a few standards to watch for: *croquetas* (béchamel and meat with a fried bread-crumb crust), *tortilla de patata* (Spanish potato omelet), *chorizo* (hard pork sausage), *gambas* (shrimp grilled or cooked in parsley, oil, and garlic), *patatas bravas* (potatoes in spicy sauce), and *boquerones en vinagre* (fresh anchovies marinated in salt and vinegar).

17

WHERE TO EAT

$$$$ ECLECTIC Fodor's Choice ★ 🍴 **Asiana.** Young chef Jaime Renedo surprises even the most jaded palates in this unique setting—his mother's Asian antiques furniture store, which used to be a ham-drying shed, where seats are amid a Vietnamese bed, a life-size Buddha, and other merchandise for sale. Renedo brings to his job a contagious enthusiasm for cooking and experimentation as well as painstaking attention to detail, and the eclectic 15-dish fixed sampler menu (€85, and the only menu on offer) perfectly balances Spanish, East Asian, Peruvian, and Japanese cooking traditions. If you're willing to forfeit exclusiveness but want to indulge in a milder version of the chef's creations, try the adjacent and much more affordable Asiana Next Door. [$] *Average main: €85* ✉ *Travesía de San Mateo 4, Chueca* ☎ *91/310–4020, 91/310–0965* 🌐 *www.restauranteasiana.com* ✍ *Reservations essential* ⏲ *Closed Sun. and Mon., and Aug. No lunch* [M] *Tribunal.*

$$$$ SPANISH Fodor's Choice ★ 🍴 **Casa Benigna.** Owner Don Norberto takes gracious care in what he does, providing a carefully chosen and health conscious menu and painstakingly selected wines to devoted customers. Evidence of craftsmanship is alive in every corner of the casual and understated hideaway, from the best rice in the city (cooked with extra-flat paella pans especially manufactured for the restaurant) to the ceramic plates from Talavera, but the star attraction is the chef and his astounding knowledge of food (he has his own brand of tuna, olive oil, and balsamic vinegar). He generously talks (and often sings) to his guests without ever looking at his watch. [$] *Average main: €26* ✉ *Benigno Soto 9, Chamartín*

☎ *91/416–9357* ✍ *Reservations essential* ⏲ *Closed Christmas and Easter wks. No dinner Sun. and Mon.* [M] *Concha Espina, Prosperidad.*

$$$$ STEAKHOUSE Fodor's Choice ★

🍴 **Casa Paco.** This Castilian tavern wouldn't have looked out of place two or three centuries ago, and today you can still squeeze past the old, zinc-top bar, crowded with madrileños downing Valdepeñas red wine, and into the tiled dining rooms. Feast on thick slabs of red meat, sizzling on plates so hot the meat continues to cook at your table. The Spanish consider overcooking a sin, so expect looks of dismay if you ask for your meat well done (*bien hecho*). You order by weight, so remember that a *medio kilo* is more than a pound. To start, try the *pisto manchego* (La Mancha version of ratatouille) or the Castilian *sopa de ajo* (garlic soup). [$] *Average main: €24* ✉ *Puerta Cerrada 11, La Latina* ☎ *91/366–3166* ✍ *Reservations essential* ⏲ *Closed 1st wk of Aug. No dinner Sun.* [M] *Tirso de Molina.*

$$$$ SPANISH Fodor's Choice ★

🍴 **Goizeko Wellington.** Aware of the more sophisticated palate of Spain's new generation of diners, the owners of the traditional madrileño dreamland that is Goizeko Kabi opened this other restaurant that shares the virtues of its kin but has none of its stuffiness. The menu here delivers the same quality fish, house staples such as the *kokotxas de merluza* (hake jowls) either grilled or sautéed with herbs and olive oil, and the *chipirones en su tinta* (line-caught calamari cooked in its own ink); as well as pastas, a superb lobster and crayfish risotto, and some hearty bean stews. The interior of the restaurant is warm and modern with citrus-yellow walls. [$] *Average main: €29* ✉ *Hotel Wellington, Villanueva 34, Salamanca* ☎ *91/577–6026* ✍ *Reservations essential* ⏲ *Closed Sun. No lunch Sat. in July and Aug.* [M] *Retiro, Príncipe de Vergara.*

$$ SPANISH Fodor's Choice ★

🍴 **Las Tortillas de Gabino.** Few national dishes raise more intense debates among Spaniards than the *tortilla de patata* (Spanish omelet). A deceivingly simple dish, it has many variations: some like it soft with the eggs runny, others prefer a spongy, evenly cooked result. At this lively restaurant you'll find crowds of Spaniards gobbling up one of the city's finest traditional versions of the tortilla, as well as some unconventional ones—potatoes with octopus, potato chips with *salmorejo* (a gazpacho-like soup), tortillas with garlic soup, with codfish and leek stew, with truffles (when available), and with a potato mousse, to name just a few—that are best enjoyed when shared by everyone at the table. The menu includes plenty of equally succulent non-egg choices and a green-apple sorbet that shouldn't be missed. [$] *Average main: €15* ✉ *Rafael Calvo 20, Chamberí* ☎ *91/319–7505* 🌐 *lastortillasdegabino.com* ⏲ *Closed Sun.* [M] *Rubén Darío.*

$$$$ ECLECTIC Fodor's Choice ★

🍴 **La Terraza–Casino de Madrid.** This rooftop terrace just off Puerta del Sol is in one of Madrid's oldest, most exclusive clubs (the *casino* is a club for gentlemen, not gamblers; it's members only, but the restaurant is open to all). When it opened the food was inspired and overseen by celebrity chef Ferran Adriá, but as the years have gone by, chef Francisco Roncero has built a reputation of his own. Try any of the light and tasty mousses, foams, and liquid jellies, or indulge in the unique tapas—experiments of flavor, texture, and temperature, such as the salmon *ventresca* in miso with radish ice cream or the spherified sea urchin. There's also a sampler menu. [$] *Average main: €35* ✉ *Alcalá 15,*

Sol ☎ *91/521–8700* 🌐 *www.casinodemadrid.es* ✍ *Reservations essential* 🕒 *Closed Sun. and Mon., and Aug.* [M] *Sol.*

$$$$ ECLECTIC Fodor's Choice ★ 🍴 **Sergi Arola Gastro.** Celebrity chef Sergi Arola—Ferran Adrià's most popular disciple—vaulted to the top of the Madrid dining scene at La Broche, then left (in 2007) to go solo. The result is a smaller, less minimalist though equally modern bistro space crafted to enhance the dining experience, 30 customers at a time. At the height of his career and surrounded by an impeccable team—which now also includes a talented and talkative bartender in the lounge—Arola offers two sampler menus ranging from five courses (€105) to eight (€135) in the namesake "Sergi Arola" menu, as well as some limited à la carte options. The choices include some of the chef's classic surf-and-turf dishes (such as rabbit filled with giant scarlet shrimp) and nods to his Catalonian roots (sautéed broad beans and peas with blood sausage). The wine list has more than 600 labels, mostly from small producers, all available by the glass. [$] *Average main: €40* ✉ *Zurbano 31, Chamberí* ☎ *91/310–2169* 🌐 *www.sergiarola.es* ✍ *Reservations essential* 🕒 *Closed Sun. and Mon.* [M] *Alonso Martínez.*

$$$$ BASQUE Fodor's Choice ★ 🍴 **Zalacaín.** This restaurant, decorated in dramatic dark wood, gleaming silver, and apricot hues, introduced nouvelle Basque cuisine to Spain in the 1970s and has since become a Madrid classic. It's particularly known for using the best and freshest seasonal products available as well as for having the best service in town. Making use of ingredients such as various fungi, game, and hard-to-find seafood, the food here tends to be unusual—it's not one of those places where they cook with liquid nitrogen, yet you won't find these dishes elsewhere. [$] *Average main: €36* ✉ *Alvarez de Baena 4, Salamanca* ☎ *91/561–4840* 🌐 *www.restaurantezalacain.com* ✍ *Reservations essential* 👔 *Jacket and tie* 🕒 *Closed Sun., Easter wk., and Aug. No lunch Sat.* [M] *Gregorio Marañón.*

WHERE TO STAY

CHAMBERÍ, RETIRO, AND SALAMANCA

$$$$ HOTEL Fodor's Choice ★ 🏨 **AC Palacio del Retiro.** A palatial early-20th-century building, once owned by a noble family with extravagant habits (the elevator carried their horses up and down from the rooftop exercise ring), this spectacular hotel epitomizes tasteful modern style. **Pros:** spacious, stylish rooms; within walking distance of the Prado; bathrooms stocked with all sorts of complimentary products. **Cons:** pricey breakfast; lower rooms facing the park can get noisy. [$] *Rooms from: €265* ✉ *Alfonso XII 14, Retiro* ☎ *91/523–7460* 🌐 *www.ac-hotels.com* 🛏 *50 rooms, 8 suites* 🍽 *No meals* [M] *Retiro.*

BARRIO DE LAS LETRAS AND SANTA ANA

$$$$ HOTEL Fodor's Choice ★ 🏨 **Hotel Urban.** This is the hotel that best conveys Madrid's new cosmopolitan spirit, with its stylish mix of authentic ancient artifacts and daring sophistication. **Pros:** excellent restaurant and happening bar; rooftop swimming pool. **Cons:** some rooms are small; rooms near the elevator can be noisy. [$] *Rooms from: €240* ✉ *Carrera de San Jerónimo 34, Barrio de las Letras* ☎ *91/787–7770* 🌐 *www.derbyhotels.com* 🛏 *96 rooms, 7 suites* 🍽 *No meals* [M] *Sevilla.*

$$ HOTEL Fodor's Choice ★ **Room Mate Alicia.** The all-white lobby with curving walls, ceiling, and lamps, and the fancy gastrobar facing Plaza Santa Ana set the hip mood for the mostly young urbanites who stay in this former trench coat factory. **Pros:** great value; chic design; laid-back atmosphere; unbeatable location. **Cons:** standard rooms are small; some might not care for the zero-privacy bathroom spaces. [$] *Rooms from: €115* ✉ *Prado 2, Barrio de las Letras* ☎ *91/389–6095* 🌐 *www.room-matehoteles.com* 🛏 *34 rooms, 3 suites* 🍴 *No meals* [M] *Sevilla.*

CHUECA AND MALASAÑA

$$ HOTEL Fodor's Choice ★ **Room Mate Óscar.** Bold, bright, and modern, the flagship Room Mate is undeniably hip and glamorous. **Pros:** friendly staff; hip guests; fashionable facilities. **Cons:** noisy street; may be *too* happening for some. [$] *Rooms from: €110* ✉ *Pl. Vázquez de Mella 12, Chueca* ☎ *91/701–1173* 🌐 *www.room-matehoteles.com* 🛏 *69 rooms, 6 suites* 🍴 *Breakfast* [M] *Chueca.*

SOL AND THE ROYAL PALACE

$$$ HOTEL Fodor's Choice ★ **De Las Letras.** Modern-pop interior design seamlessly respects and accents the original details of this 1917 building on the bustling Gran Vía. **Pros:** young vibe; gym with personal trainers; happening rooftop bar. **Cons:** lower rooms facing noisy Gran Vía could be better insulated. [$] *Rooms from: €140* ✉ *Gran Vía 11, Sol* ☎ *91/523–7980* 🌐 *www.hoteldelasletras.com* 🛏 *103 rooms, 7 suites* 🍴 *No meals* [M] *Banco de España.*

$ HOTEL Fodor's Choice ★ **Hostal Adriano.** Tucked away on a street with dozens of bland competitors a couple of blocks from Sol, this hotel really stands out for its price and quality. **Pros:** friendly service; great value; charming touches. **Cons:** short on facilities. [$] *Rooms from: €69* ✉ *De la Cruz 26, 4th fl., Sol* ☎ *91/521–1339* 🌐 *www.hostaladriano.com* 🛏 *22 rooms* 🍴 *No meals* [M] *Sol.*

$$$ HOTEL **Hotel Intur Palacio San Martín.** In an unbeatable location across from one of Madrid's most celebrated monuments (the Convent of Descalzas), this hotel, once the U.S. embassy and later a luxurious residential building crowded with noblemen, still exudes a kind of glory. **Pros:** charming location; spacious rooms. **Cons:** average-quality restaurant. [$] *Rooms from: €150* ✉ *Pl. de San Martín 5, Palacio* ☎ *91/701–5000* 🌐 *www.intur.com* 🛏 *94 rooms, 8 suites* 🍴 *No meals* [M] *Ópera, Callao.*

NIGHTLIFE AND THE ARTS

THE ARTS

As Madrid's reputation as a vibrant, contemporary arts center has grown, artists and performers have been arriving in droves. Consult the daily listings and Friday city-guide supplements in any of the leading newspapers—*El País, El Mundo,* or *ABC,* all of which are fairly easy to understand even if you don't read much Spanish.

Seats for the classical performing arts can usually be purchased through your hotel concierge, on the Internet, or at the venue itself.

DANCE AND MUSIC PERFORMANCES

Auditorio Nacional de Música. This is Madrid's main concert hall, with spaces for both symphonic and chamber music. ⊠ *Príncipe de Vergara 146, Salamanca* ☎ *91/337–0140* ⊕ *www.auditorionacional.mcu.es.*

Matadero Madrid. The city's newest and biggest arts center is in the city's old slaughterhouse—a massive early-20th-century neo-Mudejar compound of 13 buildings—and has a theater, multiple exhibition spaces, workshops, and a lively bar. ⊠ *Paseo de la Chopera 14, Legazpi* ☎ *91/517–7309* ⊕ *www.mataderomadrid.org.*

Teatro Real. This resplendent theater is the venue for opera and dance performances. ⊠ *Pl. de Isabel II, Palacio* ☎ *91/516–0660* ⊕ *www.teatro-real.com.*

FLAMENCO

Although the best place in Spain to find flamenco is Andalusia, there are a few possibilities in Madrid. Note that *tablaos* (flamenco venues) charge around €25–€35 for the show only (with a complimentary drink included), so save money by dining elsewhere. If you want to dine at the tablaos anyway, note that Carboneras and Café de Chinitas also offer a show-plus-fixed-menu option that's worth considering.

Café de Chinitas. It's expensive, but the flamenco is the best in Madrid. Make reservations because shows often sell out. The restaurant opens at 8 and there are performances at 8 and 10:30 Monday through Saturday. ⊠ *Torija 7, Palacio* ☎ *91/559–5135* ⊕ *www.chinitas.com.*

Casa Patas. Along with tapas, this well-known space offers good, relatively authentic (according to the performers) flamenco. Prices are more reasonable than elsewhere. Shows are at 10:30 pm Monday through Wednesday, at 8 and 10:30 pm on Thursday, and at 9 pm and midnight on Friday and Saturday. ⊠ *Canizares 10, Lavapiés* ☎ *91/369–0496* ⊕ *www.casapatas.com.*

Las Carboneras. A prime flamenco showcase, this venue rivals Casa Patas as the best option in terms of quality and price. Performers here include both the young, less commercial artists and more established stars on tour. The show is staged at 8:30 and 10:30 Monday through Thursday and at 8:30 and 11 Friday and Saturday. ⊠ *Pl. del Conde de Miranda 1, Centro* ☎ *91/542–8677* ⊕ *www.tablaolascarboneras.com* ☯ *Closed Sun.*

NIGHTLIFE

Nightlife—or *la marcha*—reaches legendary heights in Madrid. It's been said that madrileños rarely sleep, largely because they spend so much time in bars—not drunk, but socializing in the easy, sophisticated way that's unique to this city. This is true of old as well as young, and it's not uncommon for children to play on the sidewalks past midnight while multigenerational families and friends convene over coffee or cocktails at an outdoor café.

BARS AND NIGHTCLUBS

Bar Cock. Resembling a room at a very exclusive club (with all the waiters in suits), this bar with a dark wood interior and cathedral-like ceilings serves about 20 different cocktails (hence the name). It caters to an older, more classic crowd. ⊠ *Reina 16, Chueca* ☎ *91/532–2826.*

17

Café Central. Madrid's best-known jazz venue is chic, and the musicians are often internationally known. Nightly performances are usually from 10 to midnight. ⊠ *Pl. de Ángel 10, Barrio de las Letras* ☎ *91/369–4143* ⊕ *www.cafecentralmadrid.com.*

Coquette. This is the most authentic blues bar in the city, with live music Tuesday to Thurday at 11, barmen with jeans and leather jackets, and bohemian executives who've left their suits at home and parked their Harley-Davidsons at the door. ⊠ *Torrecilla del Leal 18, Lavapiés* ☎ *91/530–8095.*

La Realidad. Artists, musicians, aspiring filmmakers—they all flock to this bar with the free-spirited vibe for which Malasaña is famous. Locals come here to chat with friends over tea, delve into their Macs or, later in the day, sip an inexpensive gin and tonic. ⊠ *Corredera Baja de San Pablo 51, Malasaña.*

Museo Chicote. This landmark cocktail bar–lounge is said to have been one of Hemingway's haunts. Much of the interior can be traced back to the 1930s, but modern elements (like the in-house DJ) keep this spot firmly in the present. ⊠ *Gran Vía 12, Chueca* ☎ *91/532–6737* ☉ *Closed Sun.*

Reina Bruja. Magical and chameleonlike thanks to the use of LED lighting and the undulating shapes of the columns and walls, this is the place to go if you want a late-night drink—it opens at 11 and closes at 5:30 am—without the thunder of a full–blown disco. ⊠ *Jacometrezo 6, Palacio* ☎ *91/445–6886* ☉ *Closed Sun.–Wed.*

DISCOS

Azúcar. Salsa has become a fixture in Madrid; check out the most spectacular moves here. ⊠ *Paseo Reina Cristina 7, Retiro* ☎ *91/501–6107.*

Cocó Madrid. Dizzyingly colorful, this club has a large dance floor, a bar specializing in fancy cocktails, and different house music sessions which cater to the city's most glamorous and refined. ⊠ *Alcalá 20, Sol* ☎ *91/445–7938* ⊕ *www.cocomadrid.com* ☉ *Closed Mon.–Wed.*

El Sol. Madrid's oldest disco, and one of the hippest clubs for all-night dancing to an international music mix, is open until 5:30 am. There's live music starting at around midnight, Thursday through Saturday. ⊠ *Jardines 3, Sol* ☎ *91/532–6490.*

Golden Boite. This happening spot is hot from midnight on. ⊠ *Duque de Sesto 54, Retiro* ☎ *91/573–8775.*

Stella. Come here for funky rhythms. On Thursday and Saturday, starting after midnight, it hosts the famous Mondo session (electronic, house, and Afro music). ⊠ *Arlabán 7, Barrio de las Letras* ☎ *91/531–6378* ☉ *Closed Sun.–Wed.*

Teatro Barceló. A landmark enclave that until 2013 carried the legendary label Pachá in its name, it's been running for over three decades with the same energetic vibe and the blessing of the local crowd. ⊠ *Barceló 11, Malasaña* ☎ *91/447–0128* ☉ *Closed Sun.–Wed.*

SHOPPING

Spain has become one of the world's centers for design of every kind. You'll have no trouble finding traditional crafts, such as ceramics, guitars, and leather goods, albeit not at countryside prices—at this point, the city is more like Rodeo Drive than the bargain bin. Known for contemporary furniture and decorative items as well as chic clothing, shoes, and jewelry, Spain's capital has become stiff competition for Barcelona. Keep in mind that many shops, especially those that are small and family run, close during lunch hours, on Sunday, and on Saturday afternoon. Shops generally accept most major credit cards.

Madrid has three main shopping areas. The first, the area that stretches from Callao to Puerta del Sol (Calle Preciados, Gran Vía on both sides of Callao, and the streets around the Puerta del Sol), includes the major department stores (El Corte Inglés and the French music-and-book chain FNAC) and popular brands such as H&M and Zara.

The second area, far more elegant and expensive, is in the eastern Salamanca district, bounded roughly by Serrano, Juan Bravo, Jorge Juan (and its blind alleys), and Velázquez; the shops on Goya extend as far as Alcalá. The streets just off the Plaza de Colón, particularly Calle Serrano and Calle Ortega y Gasset, have the widest selection of designer goods—think Prada, Loewe, Armani, and Louis Vuitton—as well as other mainstream and popular local designers (Purificación García, Pedro del Hierro, Adolfo Domínguez, or Roberto Verino). Hidden within Calle Jorge Juan, Calle Lagasca, and Calle Claudio Coello is the widest selection of smart boutiques from renowned young Spanish designers, such as Sybilla, Josep Font, and Victorio & Lucchino.

Finally, for hipper clothes, Chueca, Malasaña, and what's now called the Triball (the triangle formed by Fuencarral, Gran Vía, and Corredera Baja, with Calle Ballesta in the middle) are your best bets. Calle Fuencarral, from Gran Vía to Tribunal, is the street with the most shops in this area. On Fuencarral you can find name brands such as Diesel, Gas, and Billabong, but also local brands such as Homeless, Adolfo Domínguez U (selling the Galician designer's younger collection), and Custo, as well as some makeup stores (Madame B and M.A.C). Less mainstream and sometimes more exciting is the selection you can find on nearby Calles Hortaleza, Almirante, and Piamonte and in the Triball area.

CERAMICS
CENTRO
Antigua Casa Talavera. This is the best of Madrid's many ceramics shops. Despite the name, the finest wares sold here are from Manises, near Valencia, but the blue-and-yellow Talavera ceramics are also excellent. ✉ *Isabel la Católica 2, Palacio* ☎ *91/547–3417.*

CLOTHING
SALAMANCA
Adolfo Domínguez. This Galician designer creates simple, sober, and elegant lines for both men and women. Of the eight other locations in the city, the one at Calle Fuencarral 5, a block away from Gran Vía,

17

is geared toward a younger crowd, with more affordable and colorful clothes. ✉ *C. Serrano 5* ☎ *91/577–4744* ⊕ *www.adolfodominguez.com.*

Jocomomola. At Sybilla's younger and more affordable second brand, Jocomomola, you'll find plenty of informal, provocative, and colorful pieces, as well as some accessories. ✉ *Colón 4, Malasaña* ☎ *91/ 575–0005.*

Pedro del Hierro. This madrileño designer has built himself a solid reputation for his sophisticated but uncomplicated clothes for both sexes. ✉ *C. Serrano 24, 29, and 40* ☎ *91/575–6906.*

Sybilla. One of Spain's best-known female designers, with fluid dresses and hand-knit sweaters that are sought after by anyone who is fashion savvy, including Danish former supermodel and now editor and designer Helena Christensen. ✉ *Jorge Juan 12, at end of one of two cul-de-sacs* ☎ *91/578–1322* ⊕ *www.sybilla.es.*

CHUECA AND MALASAÑA

Custo. Brothers Custodio and David Dalmau are the creative force behind the success of this chain, whose eye-catching T-shirts can be found in the closets of such stars as Madonna and Julia Roberts. They have expanded their collection to incorporate pants, dresses, and accessories, never relinquishing the traits that have made them famous: bold colors and striking graphic designs. ✉ *Mayor 37, Sol* ☎ *91/354–0099* ✉ *Fuencarral 29, Chueca* ☎ *91/360–4636* ✉ *Serrano 16, Salamanca* ☎ *91/577–2663.*

H.A.N.D. Chueca's trademark is its multibrand boutiques and small multibrand fashion shops, often managed by eccentric and outspoken characters. This is a good example—a cozy, tasteful store owned by two Frenchmen: Stephan and Thierry. They specialize in feminine, colorful, and young French prêt-à-porter designers (Stella Forest, La Petite, Tara Jarmon). ✉ *Hortaleza 26, Chueca* ☎ *91/521–5152.*

DEPARTMENT STORES

El Corte Inglés. Spain's largest department store carries the best selection of everything, from auto parts to groceries, electronics, lingerie, and designer fashions. It also sells tickets for major sports and arts events and has its own travel agency, a restaurant (usually the building's top floor), and a great gourmet store. Madrid's biggest branch is the one on the corner of Calle Raimundo Fernández Villaverde and Castellana, which is not a central location. Try instead the one at Sol-Callao (split into three separate buildings), or the ones at Serrano or Goya (each of these has two independent buildings). ✉ *Preciados 1, 2, and 3, Sol* ☎ *91/379–8000, 90/112–2122 for general info, 90/240–0222 for tickets* ⊕ *www.elcorteingles.es* ✉ *Callao 2, Sol* ☎ *91/379–8000* ✉ *C. Goya 76 and 85, Salamanca* ☎ *91/432–9300* ✉ *Princesa 41, 47, and 56, Moncloa* ☎ *91/454–6000* ✉ *C. Serrano 47, Salamanca* ☎ *91/432–5490* ✉ *Raimundo Fernández Villaverde 79, Cuatro Caminos* ☎ *91/418–8800.*

FLEA MARKETS

On Sunday morning Calle de Ribera de Curtidores is closed to traffic and jammed with outdoor booths selling everything under the sun—the weekly transformation into the **El Rastro** flea market, Madrid's most popular outdoor market.

TOLEDO

88 km (55 miles) southwest of Madrid.

Long the spiritual capital of Spain, Toledo perches atop a rocky mount with steep ocher hills rising on either side, bound on three sides by the Río Tajo (Tagus River). When the Romans came in 192 BC they fortified the highest point of the rock, where you now see the Alcázar. This stronghold was later remodeled by the Visigoths. In the 8th century, the Moors arrived.

Today the Moorish legacy is evident in Toledo's strong crafts tradition, the mazelike arrangement of the streets, and the predominance of brick rather than stone.

Alfonso VI, aided by El Cid ("Lord Conqueror"), captured the city in 1085 and styled himself emperor of Toledo. Under the Christians, the town's strong intellectual life was maintained, and Toledo became famous for its school of translators, who spread to the West knowledge of Arab medicine, law, culture, and philosophy. Today Toledo is conservative, prosperous, and expensive.

17

EXPLORING

Alcázar. Originally a Moorish citadel (*alcázar* is Arabic for "fortress") and occupied from the 10th century until the Reconquest, Toledo's Alcázar is on a hill just outside the walled city, dominating the horizon. The south facade—the building's most severe—is the work of Juan de Herrera, of El Escorial fame, while the east facade incorporates a large section of battlements. The finest facade is the northern, one of many Toledan works by Covarrubias, who did more than any other architect to introduce the Renaissance style here. The building's architectural highlight is Covarrubias's Italianate courtyard, which, like most other parts of the building, was largely rebuilt after the civil war, when the Alcázar was besieged by the Republicans. The Alcázar now houses the **Museo del Ejército** (Military Museum), which was formerly in Madrid. ■ TIP→ Be sure to keep your ticket—it's needed when you exit the museum. ⊠ *Cuesta Carlos V 2* ☎ *925/238800* ⊕ *www.museo.ejercito.es* ☑ *€5 (€8 with audio guide), free Sun. 10–3. Additional fee may be charged for temporary exhibitions* ☉ *Thurs.–Tues. 11–5; last tickets sold 30 mins before closing.*

Fodor'sChoice **Cathedral.** One of the most impressive structures in all of Spain, this
 ★ is a must-see on any visit to the city. The elaborate structure owes its impressive Mozarabic chapel, with an elongated dome crowning the west facade, to Jorge Manuel Theotokópoulos. The rest of the facade, however, is mainly early 15th century; it features a depiction of Mary

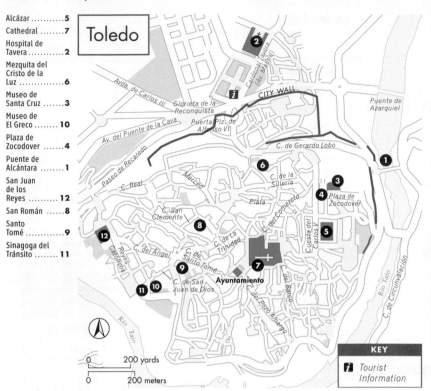

presenting her robe to Ildefonsus, Toledo's patron saint, a Visigoth who was archbishop of the city in the 7th century. Chartres and other Gothic cathedrals in France inspired the cathedral's 13th-century architecture, but the squat proportions give it a Spanish feel, as do the weight of the furnishings and the elaborate choir in the center of the nave. Immediately to your right as you enter the building is a beautifully carved plateresque doorway by Covarrubias, marking the entrance to the Treasury. The latter houses a small Crucifixion by the Italian painter Cimabue and an extraordinarily intricate late-15th-century monstrance by Juan del Arfe, a silversmith of German descent; the ceiling is an excellent example of Mudejar (11th- to 16th-century Moorish-influenced) workmanship. ✉ *C. Cardenal Cisneros 1* ☎ *925/222241 for general info* ⊕ *www.catedralprimada.es* ✉ *€8 cathedral and museums (€11 with tower)* ⊙ *Mon.–Sat. 10–6:30, Sun. and holidays 2–6:30.*

Hospital de Tavera. Architect Alonso de Covarrubias's last work, this hospital lies outside the city walls, beyond Toledo's main northern gate. Reopened after renovations in early 2013, the building is a fine example of Spanish Renaissance architecture. It also houses the **Museo de Duque de Lema** in its southern wing. The most important work in the museum's miscellaneous collection is a painting by the 17th-century artist José Ribera. The hospital's monumental chapel holds El Greco's

Baptism of Christ and the exquisitely carved marble tomb of Cardinal Tavera, the last work of Alonso de Berruguete. Descend into the crypt to experience some bizarre acoustical effects. A full ticket includes the hospital, museum, old pharmacy, and Renaissance patios. A partial ticket includes everything except the museum. Guided tours are available at 45-minute intervals. ⊠ *C. Duque de Lerma 2 (also known as C. Cardenal Tavera)* ☎ *925/220451* ⊕ *www.fundacionmedinaceli.org* ⊠ *€4.50 full ticket, €3.50 partial ticket* ☉ *Mon.–Sat. 10–1:30 and 3–6:30, Sun. and holidays 10–2:30; ticket office closes 45 mins before the museum.*

Mezquita del Cristo de la Luz (*Mosque of Christ of the Light*). This mosque-chapel is nestled in a park above the city's ramparts. Originally a tiny Visigothic church, the chapel was transformed into a mosque during the Moorish occupation. The Islamic arches and vaulting survived, making this the most important relic of Moorish Toledo. The chapel got its name when Alfonso VI's horse, striding triumphantly into Toledo in 1085, fell to its knees out front (a white stone marks the spot). It was then discovered that a candle had burned continuously behind the masonry the whole time the Muslims had been in power. Allegedly, the first Mass of the Reconquest was held here, and later a Mudejar apse was added. Archaeological excavations are underway to reveal the remnants of a Roman house in the yard nearby. ⊠ *Cuesta de los Carmelitas Descalzas 10* ☎ *925/254191* ⊠ *€2.50* ☉ *Mid-Oct.–Feb., daily 10–2 and 3:30–5:45; Mar.–mid-Oct., daily 10–2 and 3:30–6:45.*

Fodor's Choice
★

Museo de El Greco (*El Greco Museum*). This house that once belonged to Peter the Cruel's treasurer, Samuel Levi, is said to have later been El Greco's home, though there's little historical evidence to prove the artist lived here. Nevertheless, the interior is decorated to resemble a "typical" house of El Greco's time. The house is now incorporated into a revamped El Greco museum with several of the artist's paintings, including a panorama of Toledo with the Hospital of Tavera in the foreground, and works of several other 16th- and 17th-century artists. There are also medieval caves excavated at the site, and a beautiful garden in which to take refuge from Toledo's often scorching summer heat. ⊠ *Paseo del Tránsito s/n* ☎ *925/223665* ⊕ *museodelgreco.mcu. es or elgreco2014.com* ⊠ *€3 (free Sat. after 4 pm and all day Sun.)* ☉ *Apr.–Sept., Tues.–Sat. 9:30–8, Sun. and holidays 10–3; Oct.–Mar., Tues.–Sat. 9:30–6:30, Sun. and holidays 10–3. Last tickets sold 15 mins before closing.*

Museo de Santa Cruz. In a beautiful Renaissance hospital with a stunning classical-plateresque facade, this museum is open all day without a break (unlike many of Toledo's other sights). Aside from some small renovations in early 2013, the light and elegant interior has changed little since the 16th century. Works of art have replaced the hospital beds, and among the displays is El Greco's *Assumption* of 1613, the artist's last known work. A small **Museo de Arqueología** (Museum of Archaeology) is in and around the hospital's delightful cloister. ⊠ *C. Cervantes 3* ☎ *925/221036* ⊠ *Free* ☉ *Mon.–Sat. 10–7, Sun. 10–2:30.*

Plaza de Zocodover. Toledo's main square was built in the early 17th century as part of an unsuccessful attempt to impose a rigid geometry on the chaotic Moorish streets. Over the centuries, this tiny plaza has hosted bullfights, executions by the Spanish Inquisition, and countless street fairs. Today it's home to the largest and oldest marzipan store in town, Santo Tomé. You can catch inner-city buses here, and the tourist office is just around the corner.

Puente de Alcántara. Roman in origin, this is the city's oldest bridge. Next to it is a heavily restored castle built after the Christian capture of 1085 and, above this, a vast and severe military academy, a typical example of fascist architecture under Franco. From the other side of the Tagus River, the bridge offers unparalleled views of Toledo's historic center and the Alcázar. ☒ *C. Gerardo Lobo.*

San Juan de los Reyes. This convent church in western Toledo was erected by Ferdinand and Isabella to commemorate their victory at the Battle of Toro in 1476. (It was also intended to be their burial place, but their wish changed after Granada was recaptured from the Moors in 1492, and their actual tomb is in that city's Capilla Real.) The building is largely the work of architect Juan Guas, who considered it his masterpiece and asked to be buried here himself. In true plateresque fashion, the white interior is covered with inscriptions and heraldic motifs. ☒ *Av. de los Reyes Católicos 17* ☎ *925/223802* ⊕ *www.sanjuandelosreyes. org* ▣ *€2.50* ⊙ *Oct.–Mar., daily 10–5:30; Apr.–Sept., daily 10–6:30.*

San Román. Hidden in a virtually unspoiled part of Toledo, this early-13th-century Mudejar church is now the **Museo de los Concilios y de la Cultura Visigótica,** with exhibits of statuary, manuscript illustrations, jewelry, and an extensive collection of frescoes. The church tower is adjacent to recently opened ruins of Roman baths. ☒ *C. San Roman* ☎ *925/221036 (shared with Museo de Santa Cruz)* ▣ *Free, but a small charge may be introduced in 2014* ⊙ *Tues.–Sat. 10–2:30 and 4–7, Sun. 10–2:30.*

Santo Tomé. Not to be confused with the marzipan shop of the same name, the real Santo Tomé is a chapel topped with a Mudejar tower, and built specially to house El Greco's most famous painting, *The Burial of Count Orgaz.* The painting portrays the benefactor of the church being buried with the posthumous assistance of St. Augustine and St. Stephen, who have appeared at the funeral to thank the count for his donations to religious institutions named after the two saints. Though the count's burial took place in the 14th century, El Greco painted the onlookers in contemporary 16th-century costumes and included people he knew; the boy in the foreground is one of El Greco's sons, and the sixth figure on the left is said to be the artist himself. Santo Tomé is Toledo's most-visited church besides the Cathedral so to avoid crowds in summer, plan to visit as soon as the building opens. ☒ *Pl. del Conde 4, C. Santo Tomé* ☎ *925/256098* ⊕ *www.santotome.org* ▣ *€2.50* ⊙ *Mar.–mid-Oct., daily 10–6:45; mid-Oct.–Feb., daily 10–5:45.*

Fodor's Choice ★   **Sinagoga del Tránsito.** Financed by Samuel Levi, this 14th-century rectangular synagogue is plain on the outside, but the inside walls are embellished with intricate Mudejar decoration, as well as Hebraic inscriptions glorifying God, Peter the Cruel, and Levi himself. It's said that Levi imported cedars from Lebanon for the building's construction, à la

Solomon when he built the First Temple in Jerusalem. Adjoining the main hall is the **Museo Sefardí,** a small but excellent museum of Jewish culture in Spain. ✉ *C. Samuel Levi 2* ☎ *925/223665* 🌐 *museosefardi.mcu.es* 🎟 *€3 (free Sat. afternoon and Sun.)* 🕒 *Oct.–Mar., Tues.–Sat. 9:30–6:30, Sun. and holidays 10–3; Apr.–Sept., 9:30–8, Sun. and holidays 10–3.*

WHERE TO EAT

$$$$ SPANISH Fodor'sChoice ★ 🍴 **Adolfo Restaurant.** Steps from the cathedral but discreetly hidden, this restaurant has an intimate interior with a coffered ceiling that was painted in the 14th century. From the entryway you can see game, fresh produce, and traditional Toledan recipes being prepared in the kitchen, which combines local tastes with Nueva Cocina tendencies. The *tempura de flor de calabacín* (tempura-battered zucchini blossoms in a saffron sauce) makes for a tasty starter; King Juan Carlos I has declared Adolfo's partridge stew the best in Spain. Finish with a Toledan specialty, *delicias de mazapán* (marzipan sweets). The restaurant runs its own winery and is affiliated with the Toledo culinary arts school. [$] *Average main: €50* ✉ *C. del Hombre de Palo 7* ☎ *925/227321, 925/252694 for reservations* 🌐 *www.adolforestaurante.com* ✍ *Reservations essential* 🕒 *No dinner Sun.*

$ SPANISH 🍴 **Bar Ludeña.** Locals and visitors come together at this bar to have a beer and share the typical Toledan *carcamusas,* a meat stew with peas and tomatoes served in a hot dish. A couple of steps from the Zocodover square, the bar is famous for heaping plates of free tapas that come with your drink—helping make it a favorite for students, too. [$] *Average main: €12* ✉ *Pl. de la Magdalena 10* ☎ *925/223384* 🕒 *Closed Wed.*

WHERE TO STAY

$ HOTEL 🏨 **Hotel del Cardenal.** Built in the 18th century (restored in 1972) as a summer palace for Cardinal Lorenzana, this quiet and beautiful hotel is fully outfitted with antique furniture and other nice touches. **Pros:** lovely courtyard; convenient dining. **Cons:** restaurant often full; parking is pricey. [$] *Rooms from: €85* ✉ *Paseo de Recaredo 24* ☎ *925/224900* 🌐 *www.hostaldelcardenal.com* 🛏 *27 rooms* 🍽 *Breakfast.*

$$ HOTEL 🏨 **Hotel Pintor El Greco Sercotel.** Next door to the painter's house, this former 17th-century bakery is now a chic, contemporary hotel. **Pros:** parking garage adjacent. **Cons:** street noise in most rooms; elevator goes to the second floor only. [$] *Rooms from: €100* ✉ *Alamillos del Tránsito 13* ☎ *925/285191* 🌐 *www.hotelpintorelgreco.com* 🛏 *60 rooms* 🍽 *Multiple meal plans.*

$$$ HOTEL FAMILY 🏨 **Parador de Toledo.** This modern building with Mudejar-style touches on Toledo's outskirts has an unbeatable panorama of the town from the rooms' terraces and adjacent swimming pool, where you can sit and watch the sunset. **Pros:** outdoor swimming pool. **Cons:** Long walk from the city center; swimming pool only open June 15–Sept. 15. [$] *Rooms from: €180* ✉ *Cerro del Emperador* ☎ *925/221850, 902/547979 for reservations* 🌐 *www.parador.es* 🛏 *77 rooms* 🍽 *Breakfast.*

SHOPPING

The Moors established silver work, damascening (metalwork inlaid with gold or silver), pottery, embroidery, and marzipan traditions here, and next to San Juan de los Reyes a turn-of-the-20th-century art school keeps these crafts alive. For inexpensive pottery, stop at the large emporia on the outskirts of town, on the main road to Madrid.

Museo Cerámica Ruiz de Luna. Most of the region's pottery is made in Talavera de la Reina, 76 km (47 miles) west of Toledo. At this museum you can watch artisans throw local clay, then trace the development of Talavera's world-famous ceramics, chronicled through about 1,500 tiles, bowls, vases, and plates dating back to the 15th century. It's closed on Monday, and there's a small admission fee of €0.60. ⊠ *Pl. de San Agustín, Talavera de la Reina* ☎ *925/800149.*

BILBAO

397 km (247 miles) north of Madrid, 610 km (380 miles) northwest of Barcelona.

Time in Bilbao (*Bilbo,* in Euskera) may soon need to be identified as "BG" or "AG" (Before Guggenheim, After Guggenheim). Never has a single monument of art and architecture so radically changed a city—or, for that matter, a nation, and in this case two: Spain and Euskadi. Frank Gehry's stunning museum, Norman Foster's sleek subway system, the glass Santiago Calatrava footbridge, and the leafy park and commercial complex in Abandoibarra have all helped foment a cultural revolution in the commercial capital of the Basque Country. Greater Bilbao encompasses almost 1 million inhabitants, nearly half the total population of the Basque Country.

Bilbao's new attractions get more press, but the city's old treasures still quietly line the banks of the rust-color Nervión River. The Casco Viejo (Old Quarter)—also known as Siete Calles (Seven Streets)—is a charming jumble of shops, bars, and restaurants on the river's Right Bank, near the Puente del Arenal bridge. Throughout the old quarter are ancient mansions emblazoned with family coats of arms, noble wooden doors, and fine ironwork balconies. Bilbao's cultural institutions include, along with the Guggenheim, a major museum of fine arts (the Museo de Bellas Artes) and an opera society (ABAO: Asociación Bilbaina de Amigos de la Opera) with 7,000 members from all over Spain and parts of southern France. In addition, epicureans have long ranked Bilbao's culinary offerings among the best in Spain.

EXPLORING

The **Casco Viejo** *(Old Quarter)* is folded into an elbow of the Nervión River behind Bilbao's grand, elaborately restored theater. While exploring, don't miss the colossal food market **El Mercado de la Ribera** at the edge of the river, the Renaissance town house **Palacio Yohn** at the corner of Sant Maria and Perro, and the library and cultural center **Biblioteca Municipal Bidebarrieta** at Calle Bidebarrieta 4.

Ayuntamiento (*City Hall*). Architect Joaquín de Rucoba built this city hall in 1892, on the site of the San Agustín convent destroyed during the 1836 Carlist War. Sharing the belle-époque style of de Rucoba's Teatro Arriaga, the Ayuntamiento is characterized by the same brash, slightly aggressive attitude to which most *bilbainos* confess without undue embarrassment. The Salón Árabe, the highlight of the interior, was designed by the same architect who built the Café Iruña, as their mutual neo-Mudejar motifs suggest. ✉ *Paseo Campo de Volantín s/n, El Arenal* ☎ *944/204200, 944/205298 for tours* 🔖 *Tour free* ⊙ *Tours weekdays 9–11 am by appointment* Ⓜ *Abando.*

Basílica de Nuestra Señora de Begoña. Bilbao's most cherished religious sanctuary, dedicated to the patron saint of Vizcaya, can be reached by the 313 stairs from Plaza de Unamuno or by the gigantic elevator (the Ascensor de Begoña) looming over Calle Esperanza 6 behind the San Nicolás church. The church's Gothic nave was begun in 1519 on the site of an early hermitage, where the Virgin Mary was alleged to have appeared long before. Finished in 1620, the basilica was completed with the economic support of the shipbuilders and merchants of Bilbao, many of whose businesses are commemorated on the inner walls of the church. The high ground the basilica occupies was strategically important during the Carlist Wars of 1836 and 1873, and as a result La Begoña suffered significant damage that was not restored until the beginning of the 20th century. ✉ *C. Virgen de Begoña 38, Begoña* ☎ *944/127091* ⊕ *www.basilicadebegona.com* 🔖 *Free* ⊙ *Mon.–Sat. 10:30–1:30 and 5:30–8:30, Sun. for mass only* Ⓜ *Casco Viejo.*

Catedral de Santiago (*St. James's Cathedral*). Bilbao's earliest church was a pilgrimage stop on the coastal route to Santiago de Compostela. Work on the structure began in 1379, but fire delayed completion until the early 16th century. The florid Gothic style with Isabelline elements features a nave in the form of a Greek cross, with ribbed vaulting resting on cylindrical columns. The notable outdoor arcade, or *pórtico,* was used for public meetings of the early town's governing bodies. ✉ *Pl. de Santiago 1, Casco Viejo* ☎ *944/153627* ⊕ *catedraldebilbao.blogspot. com.es* 🔖 *Free* ⊙ *Weekdays 11–1 and 5–7:30, weekends and holidays 11–noon* Ⓜ *Casco Viejo.*

Fodor'sChoice ★ **Mercado de la Ribera.** This triple-decker ocean liner with its prow headed down the estuary toward the open sea is one of the best markets of its kind in Europe, as well as one of the biggest, with more than 400 retail stands covering 37,950 square feet. Like the architects of the Guggenheim and the Palacio de Euskalduna nearly 75 years later, the architect here was playful with this well-anchored, ocean-going grocery store in the river. From the stained-glass entryway over Calle de la Ribera to the tiny catwalks over the river or the diminutive restaurant on the second floor, the market is an inviting place. Look for the farmers' market on the top floor, and down on the bottom floor ask how fresh a fish is some morning and you might hear, "Oh, that one's not too fresh: caught last night." ✉ *C. de la Ribera 20, Casco Viejo* ☎ *946/023791* ⊕ *www. mercadodelaribera.net* ⊙ *Mon.–Thurs. 9:30–1 and 3:30–6, Fri.–Sat. 9–3* Ⓜ *Casco Viejo.*

17

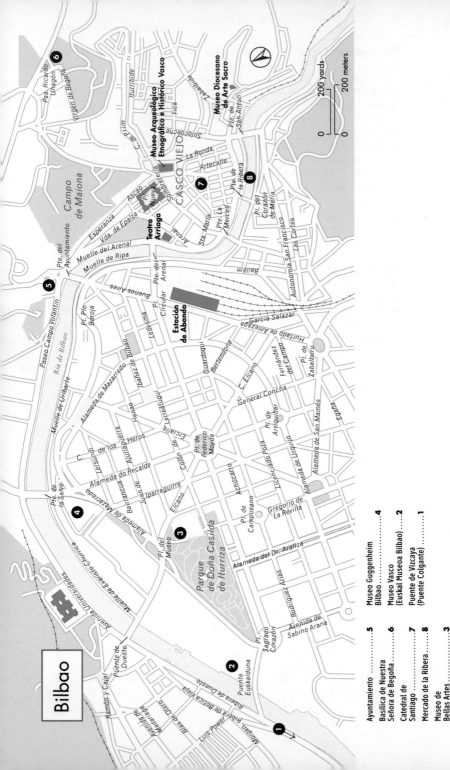

Bilbao

Ayuntamiento **5**

Basílica de Nuestra
Señora de Begoña **6**

Catedral de
Santiago **7**

Mercado de la Ribera **8**

Museo de
Bellas Artes **3**

Museo Guggenheim
Bilbao **4**

Museo Vasco
(Euskal Museoa Bilbao) **2**

Puente de Vizcaya
(Puente Colgante) **1**

CASCO VIEJO

Museo Arqueológico
Etnográfico e Histórico Vasco

Museo Diocesano
de Arte Sacro

Teatro
Arriaga

Estación
de Abando

Campo
de Maiona

Parque
de Doña Casilda
de Iturriza

Ría de Bilbao

Pza. Ricardo
Uhagón

0   200 yards

0   200 meters

Fodor's Choice **Museo de Bellas Artes** (*Museum of Fine Arts*). Considered one of the top
★ five museums in a country that has a staggering number of museums
and great paintings, the Museo de Bellas Artes is like a mini-Prado,
with representatives from every Spanish school and movement from
the 12th through the 20th centuries. The museum's fine collection of
Flemish, French, Italian, and Spanish paintings includes works by El
Greco, Francisco de Goya y Lucientes, Diego Velázquez, Zurbarán,
José Ribera, Paul Gauguin, and Antoni Tàpies. One large and excellent
section traces developments in 20th-century Spanish and Basque art
alongside works by better-known European contemporaries, such as
Fernand Léger and Francis Bacon. Look especially for Zuloaga's famous
portrait of La Condesa Mathieu de Moailles and Joaquín Sorolla's portrait of Basque philosopher Miguel de Unamuno. A statue of Zuloaga
outside greets visitors to this sparkling collection at the edge of Doña
Casilda Park and on the left bank end of the Deusto bridge, five minutes from the Guggenheim. Three hours might be barely enough to
appreciate this international and pan-chronological painting course.
The museum's excellent Arbolagaña restaurant offers a stellar lunch to
break up the visit. ⊠ *Parque de Doña Casilda de Iturrizar, Museo Plaza
2D, El Ensanche* ☏ *94/4396060* ⊕ *www.museobilbao.com* 🖃 *€6 (free
Wed.), Bono Artean combined ticket with Guggenheim €13.50 (valid
1 yr);* ☉ *Tues.–Sun. 10–8* Ⓜ *Moyúa.*

Fodor's Choice **Museo Guggenheim Bilbao.** Described by the late Spanish novelist Manuel
★ Vázquez Montalbán as a "meteorite," the Guggenheim, with its erup-
tion of light in the ruins of Bilbao's scruffy shipyards and steelworks,
has dramatically reanimated this onetime industrial city.

Frank Gehry's gleaming brainchild, opened in 1997 and in its first year
attracted 1.4 million visitors, three times the number expected and more
than both Guggenheim museums in New York during the same period.

The enormous atrium, more than 150 feet high, connects to the 19
galleries by a system of suspended metal walkways and glass elevators.
Vertical windows reveal the undulating titanium flukes and contours
of this beached whale. The free Audio Guía explains everything you
always wanted to know about modern art, contemporary art, and the
Guggenheim.

The collection, described by Krens as "a daring history of the art of the
20th century," consists of more than 250 works, most from the New
York Guggenheim and the rest acquired by the Basque government. The
second and third floors reprise the original Guggenheim collection of
abstract expressionist, cubist, surrealist, and geometrical works. Artists
whose names are synonymous with the art of the 20th century (Was-
sily Kandinsky, Pablo Picasso, Max Ernst, Georges Braque, Joan Miró,
Jackson Pollock, Alexander Calder, Kazimir Malevich) and European
artists of the 1950s and 1960s (Eduardo Chillida, Tàpies, Jose Maria
Iglesias, Francesco Clemente, and Anselm Kiefer) are joined by contemporary figures (Bruce Nauman, Juan Muñoz, Julian Schnabel, Txomin
Badiola, Miquel Barceló, Jean-Michel Basquiat).

On holidays and weekends lines may develop, though between the
playful clarinetist making a well-deserved killing on the front steps

17

and the general spell of the place (who can be irked in the shadow of Jeff Koons's flower-covered, 40-foot-high *Puppy*), no one seems too impatient. You can buy tickets in advance online and from Servicaixa ATMs or, in the Basque Country, the BBK bank machines—a great way to miss the line. Failing that (sometimes they run out), go around closing time and buy tickets for the next few days. The museum has no parking of its own, but underground lots throughout the area provide alternatives; check the website for information. ⊠ *Abandoibarra Etorbidea 2, El Ensanche* ☎ *944/359080* ⊕ *www.guggenheim-bilbao. es* ⊠ *€13 (includes audio guide), Bono Artean combined ticket with Museo de Bellas Artes €13.50* ⏱ *July and Aug., daily 10–8; Sept.–June, Tues.–Sun. 10–8* Ⓜ *Moyúa.*

Fodor'sChoice
★
Museo Vasco (Euskal Museoa Bilbao) (*Basque Museum of Bilbao*). One of the standout, not-to-miss visits in Bilbao, this museum occupies an austerely elegant 16th-century convent. The collection centers on Basque ethnography, Bilbao history, and comprehensive displays from the lives of Basque shepherds, fishermen, and farmers—everything you ever wanted to know about this fascinating and little-known culture. Highlights include *El Mikeldi* in the cloister, a pre-Christian, Iron Age, stone, animal representation that may be 4,000 years old; the room dedicated to Basque shepherds and the pastoral way of life; the Mar de los Vascos (Sea of the Basques) exhibit featuring whaling, fishing, and maritime activities; the second-floor prehistoric exhibit featuring a wooden harpoon recovered in the Santimamiñe caves at Kortezubi that dates from the 10th century BC; and the third-floor scale model of Vizcaya province with the *montes bocineros* (bugling mountains), showing the five peaks of Vizcaya used for calling the different *anteiglesias* (parishes) with bonfires or *txalaparta* (percussive sticks) to the general assemblies held in Gernika. ⊠ *Pl. Unamuno 4, Casco Viejo* ☎ *94/4155423* ⊠ *€3, free Thurs.* ⏱ *Tues.–Sat. 11–5, Sun. 11–2* Ⓜ *Casco Viejo.*

Fodor'sChoice
★
Puente de Vizcaya. Commonly called the "Puente Colgante" ("Hanging Bridge"), this has been one of Bilbao's most extraordinary sights ever since it was built in 1893. The bridge, a transporter hung from cables, ferries cars and passengers across the Nervión, uniting two distinct worlds: exclusive, bourgeois Las Arenas and Portugalete, a much older, working-class town. Portugalete is a 15-minute walk from Santurce, where the quayside Hogar del Pescador serves simple fish specialties. *Besugo* (sea bream) is the traditional choice, but the grilled sardines are hard to surpass. To reach the bridge, take the subway to Areeta, or drive across the Puente de Deusto, turn left on Avenida Lehendakari Aguirre, and follow signs for Las Arenas; it's a 10- or 15-minute drive from downtown. ☎ *944/801012* ⊕ *www.puente-colgante.com* ⊠ *Pedestrians €0.35, car €1.35 (5 am–10 pm; price increases after 10 pm); tour with audio guide €9; observation deck €7* Ⓜ *Areeta.*

WHERE TO EAT

$$$$
CONTEMPORARY
Fodor'sChoice
★
✕ **Arbolagaña.** On the top floor of the Museo de Bellas Artes, this elegant space has bay windows overlooking the lush Parque de Doña Casilda. A devotee of the "slow food" movement, chef Aitor Basabe's modern cuisine offers innovative versions of Basque classics such as

codfish on toast, venison with wild mushrooms, or rice with truffles and shallots. The €45 *menú de degustación* (tasting menu) is a superb affordable luxury, while the abbreviated *menú de trabajo* (work menu) provides a perfect light lunch. [$] *Average main: €30* ✉ *Museo de Bellas Artes, Alameda Conde Arteche s/n, El Ensanche* ☎ *944/424657* 🌐 *www.arbolagana.com* ✍ *Reservations essential* ⏲ *Closed Mon. No dinner Tues., Wed., and Sun.* [M] *Moyúa.*

$ CAFÉ Fodor's Choice ★ 🍴 **Café Iruña.** Managed by the same owners as the historic Café La Granja, this is an essential Bilbao haunt on the Ensanche's most popular garden and square, Los Jardines de Albia. Famous for its interior design and boisterous ambience, the neo-Mudejar dining room overlooking the square is the place to be (if they try to stuff you in the back dining room, resist or come back another time). The bar has two distinct sections: the elegant side near the dining room, and the older, more bare-bones Spanish side on the Calle Berástegui, with its plain marble counters and *pintxos morunos de carne de cordero* (lamb brochettes) as the house specialty. [$] *Average main: €12* ✉ *C. Berástegui 4, El Ensanche* ☎ *944/249059* 🌐 *www.grupoiruña.net* [M] *Moyúa.*

$$$ BASQUE Fodor's Choice ★ 🍴 **Casa Rufo.** Charming and cozy, this place is more than 100 years old, a Bilbao institution that's actually a series of nooks and crannies tucked into a fine food, wine, olive-oil, cheese, and ham emporium. It has become famous for its *txuleta de buey* (beef or ox chops). Let the affable owners size you up and bring on what you crave. The house wine is an excellent *crianza* (two years in oak, one in bottle) from La Rioja, but the 1,000-strong wine list offers a good selection from Ribera de Duero, Somantano, and El Priorat as well. [$] *Average main: €18* ✉ *C. Hurtado de Amézaga 5, El Ensanche* ☎ *944/432172* 🌐 *www.casarufo.com* ✍ *Reservations essential* ⏲ *Closed Sun.* [M] *Abando.*

$$$$ BASQUE Fodor's Choice ★ 🍴 **Guetaria.** With a wood paneled dining room decorated with antiques, this family operation is a longtime local favorite for fresh fish and meats cooked over coals, and is known for first-rate ingredients lovingly prepared. Named for the famous fishing village just west of San Sebastián long known as *la cocina de Guipúzcoa* (the kitchen of Guipúzcoa province), Bilbao's Guetaria does its namesake justice. The kitchen, open to the clientele, cooks lubina, besugo, dorada, txuletas de buey, and *chuletas de cordero* (lamb chops) to perfection in a classic *asador* (barbecue) setting. [$] *Average main: €50* ✉ *Colón de Larreátegui 12, El Ensanche* ☎ *944/243923, 944/232527* 🌐 *www.guetaria.com* ✍ *Reservations essential* ⏲ *Closed Easter wk* [M] *Moyúa.*

$$$$ BASQUE Fodor's Choice ★ 🍴 **Kiskia.** A modern take on the traditional cider house, this rambling tavern near the San Mamés soccer stadium serves the classical *sidrería* menu of chorizo sausage cooked in cider, codfish omelet, txuleta de buey, Idiazabal with quince jelly and nuts, and as much cider as you can drink. Actors, sculptors, writers, soccer stars, and Spain's who's who frequent this boisterous marvel. [$] *Average main: €25* ✉ *C. Pérez Galdós 51, San Mamés* ☎ *944/413469* 🌐 *www.sidreria-kiskia-bilbao.com* [M] *San Mamés.*

WHERE TO STAY

$$$$ HOTEL Fodor's Choice ★

🏨 **Castillo de Arteaga.** Built in the mid-19th century for Empress Eugenia de Montijo, wife of Napoleon III, this neo-Gothic limestone castle with rooms in the watchtowers and defensive walls is one of the most extraordinary lodging options in or around Bilbao. **Pros:** excellent wine and local food product tastings; views over the wetlands. **Cons:** somewhat isolated from village life and a half-hour drive to Bilbao. [$] *Rooms from: €190* ✉ *Calle Gaztelubide 7, 40 km (24 miles) northwest of Bilbao, Gautegiz de Arteaga* ☎ *946/270440* 🌐 *www.castillodearteaga.com* 🛏 *7 rooms, 6 suites* 🍴 *Some meals.*

$$$$ HOTEL Fodor's Choice ★

🏨 **Hotel Carlton.** This illustrious hotel exudes old-world grace and charm along with a sense of history—which it has aplenty. **Pros:** historic, old-world surroundings that remind you that Bilbao has an illustrious past. **Cons:** surrounded by plenty of concrete and urban frenzy. [$] *Rooms from: €250* ✉ *Pl. Federico Moyúa 2, El Ensanche* ☎ *944/162200* 🌐 *www.hotelcarlton.es* 🛏 *136 rooms, 6 suites* 🍴 *Breakfast* [M] *Moyúa.*

$ B&B/INN Fodor's Choice ★

🏨 **Iturrienea Ostatua.** Extraordinarily beautiful, with charm to spare, this hotel is in a traditional Basque town house one flight above the street in Bilbao's Old Quarter. **Pros:** budget-friendly; all no-smoking; exquisite rustic style; free Wi-Fi. **Cons:** nocturnal noise on the front side, especially on summer weekend nights—try for an interior room or bring earplugs. [$] *Rooms from: €70* ✉ *Santa María 14, Casco Viejo* ☎ *944/161500* 🌐 *www.iturrieneaostatua.com* 🛏 *19 rooms* 🍴 *No meals* [M] *Casco Viejo.*

BARCELONA

621 km (386 miles) east of Madrid; approximately 3 hrs by high-speed train.

Capital of Catalonia, 2,000-year-old Barcelona commanded a vast Mediterranean empire when Madrid was still a dusty Moorish outpost on the Spanish steppe. One of Europe's most visually stunning cities, Barcelona balances the medieval intimacy of its Gothic Quarter with the grace and distinction of the wide boulevards in the moderniste Eixample—just as the Mediterranean Gothic elegance of the church of Santa Maria del Mar provides a perfect counterpoint to Gaudí's riotous Sagrada Família. Mies van der Rohe's pavilion seems even more minimalist after a look at the art-nouveau Palau de la Música Catalana, while such exciting contemporary creations as Bofill's neoclassical Parthenon-under-glass Teatre Nacional de Catalunya, Frank Gehry's waterfront goldfish, Norman Foster's Torre de Collserola, and Jean Nouvel's Torre Agbar all add spice to Barcelona's visual soup. Meanwhile, Barcelona's fashion industry is pulling even with those of Paris and Milan, and FC (Futbol Club) is Barcelona's perennial contender for European championships and the world's most glamorous soccer club.

PLANNING YOUR TIME

La Rambla is the focal point of most trips to Barcelona, from Plaça Catalunya, and moving toward the Port, and don't miss the Boqueria market with all its colors and aromas of Mediterranean life. Other must-sees include the Liceu opera house, Plaça Reial, and Gaudí's masterworks, the Palau Güell and the Sagrada Família church. The Gothic Quarter is a warren of Roman and medieval alleys. Once the Roman forum, Plaça Sant Jaume opens up between the municipal and Catalonian government palaces. Across Via Laietana, the Ribera-Born neighborhood is centered on the exquisite Mediterranean Gothic Santa Maria del Mar basilica, a step away from the Picasso Museum. A 15-minute walk east from Santa Maria del Mar is Barceloneta, the traditional fishermen's quarter, with a dozen good seafood restaurants.

El Raval, home of the medieval hospital, one of the city's finest Gothic spaces, is a good morning's hike. Gràcia and Sarrià are both interesting half-day explorations, while Montjuïc has the Museu Nacional d'Art de Catalunya, the Miró Fundació, and the Mies van der Rohe Pavilion.

WHEN TO GO
Summer can be uncomfortably hot in Barcelona, and many of the finest restaurants and musical venues are closed. On the other hand, El Grec, the summer music festival, is a delight, and the August Gràcia Festa Major is a major block party, while the whole city becomes an extension of the Barceloneta beach, which is not without its attractions. October through June is the time to come to observe Barcelona's daily hum, with mid-November–early April pleasantly cool and the rest of the time ideally warm. Late September's Festa de la Mercé is a fiesta not to miss; winter's Carnaval and *calçot* (long-stemmed onions) season are spectacular and delicious, and April and May are best of all: the Sant Jordi lovers' day on April 23 and the Sant Ponç celebration of natural produce on May 11 are among the most magical moments of the year.

GETTING HERE AND AROUND
AIR TRAVEL
The major gateway to Catalonia is Spain's second-largest airport, Barcelona's spectacular glass, steel, and marble El Prat de Llobregat (BCN), which handles some 35 million passengers a year. Terminal 1, opened in 2009, is a sleek ultramodern facility that uses solar panels for sustainable energy and offers a spa, a fitness center, excellent restaurants and cafés, and more VIP lounges. Some low-cost flights land in Girona, 92 km (55 miles) north of the city. Bus and train connections from Girona to Barcelona work well and cheaply, provided you have the time.

Some hotels in Barcelona provide airport-shuttle service; otherwise, you can get into town via train, bus, or taxi. The Aerobus leaves the airport for Plaça de Catalunya every 10 or 20 minutes between 6 am and 1 am, depending on the time of day. The fare is €5.90 one-way and €10.20 round-trip. It is important to remember that Aerobuses for Terminal 1 and for Terminal 2 stop at the same bus stops. If you are traveling to Barcelona Airport, make sure that you take the right Aerobus. The Aerobus for Terminal 1 is two-tone light and dark blue. The Aerobus for Terminal 2 is dark blue and yellow.

Cab fare from the airport into town runs €30–€35, depending on traffic, the part of town you're heading to, and the number of large bags you're carrying (the first is free; €3 is charged for each additional). The train's only drawback is that it's a 10- to 15-minute walk from your gate through Terminal 2 over the bridge. From Terminal 1 a shuttle bus drops you at the train.

Contacts Aeroport de Girona-Costa Brava (*GRO*). ⊠ *Girona* ☎ *91/321–1000.* **El Prat de Llobregat** (*BCN*). ☎ *91/321–1000.*

PUBLIC TRANSPORTATION

City buses run daily 5:30 am–11:30 pm. Route maps are displayed at bus stops. Schedules are available at bus and metro stations or at ⊕ *www.bcn.es/guia/welcomea.htm.*

Barcelona's new tramway system is divided into two subsectors: Trambaix serves the western end of the Diagonal, and Trambesòs serves the eastern end.

The subway is the fastest, cheapest, and easiest way to get around Barcelona. Metro lines are color coded, and the FGC trains (Ferrocarriles de la Generalitat de Catalunya, part of the city underground system) are marked with a reclining-S-like blue-and-white icon. All the lines run weekdays 5 am–midnight. On Friday, Saturday, and holiday evenings all trains run until 2 am. The FGC Generalitat trains run until 12:30 am on weekdays and Sunday and until 2:15 am on weekends and eves of holidays. The Montjuïc Funicular runs from the junction of Avinguda del Paral.lel and Nou de la Rambla to the Miramar station on Montjuïc. It operates daily 10 am–9:00 pm in summer and on weekends and holidays, and 10 am–6 pm in winter; the fare is €2.

Bus, subway, and tram fares are a flat fee of €2 no matter how far you travel (with free transfers for up to 75 minutes), but it's more economical to buy a Tarjeta T-10 (valid for bus or metro FGC Generalitat trains, the Tramvía Blau blue tram, and the Montjuïc Funicular; 10 rides for €9.80). The Dia T-1 pass is valid for one day of unlimited travel on all subway, bus, and FGC lines, but the Tarjeta T-10 is generally a better value than the Día T-1 if you'll be in town more than a day.

Contacts Transports Metropolitans de Barcelona (TMB) ☎ *93/298–7000 for lost-and-found and general info* ⊕ *www.tmb.cat/en.*

TRAIN TRAVEL

Almost all long-distance trains arrive and depart from Estació de Sants. En route to or from Sants, some trains stop at another station on Passeig de Gràcia at Carrer Aragó. The Estació de França, near the port, now handles only a few long-distance trains within Spain. The air shuttle (or a scheduled flight) between Madrid and Barcelona can, if all goes well, get you door to door in less than three hours for less then the cost of a train. The AVE, the high-speed RENFE train, now connects Barcelona and Madrid in 2 hours, 45 minutes (or 3 hours, 10 minutes for some trains with more stops in between), for between €90 and €120; upmarket *preferente* seats are €176.

TAXI TRAVEL

In Barcelona, taxis are black and yellow and show a green rooftop light on the front right corner when available for hire. The meter currently starts at €2 and rises in increments of €0.90 every kilometer. These rates apply 6 am to 10 pm weekdays. At hours outside of these, the rates rise 20%. There are official supplements for luggage, and for trips to Estació de Sants and the airport. Cab stands (*parades*, in Catalan) are all over town, and you can also hail cabs on the street. Drivers do not expect a tip, though rounding up in their favor is the norm.

VISITOR INFORMATION

Turisme de Barcelona ✉ *Pl. de Catalunya 17–S, Eixample* ☎ *93/285–3834* ⊕ *www.barcelonaturisme.com.*

EXPLORING

Barcelona has long had a frenetically active cultural life. It was the home of architect Antoni Gaudí, whose buildings are the most startling statements of Modernisme. Other leading moderniste architects of the city include Lluís Domènech i Montaner and Josep Puig i Cadafalch, and the painters Joan Miró, Salvador Dalí, and Antoni Tàpies are also strongly identified with Catalonia. Pablo Picasso spent his formative years in Barcelona, and one of the city's treasures is a museum devoted to his works. Barcelona's opera house, the Liceu, is the finest in Spain, and the city claims such native Catalan musicians as cellist Pablo (Pau, in Catalan) Casals, opera singers Montserrat Caballé and José (Josep) Carreras, and early-music viola da gamba master Jordi Savall.

LA RAMBLA

Barcelona's best-known promenade is a constant and colorful flood of humanity that flows past flower stalls, bird vendors, mimes, musicians, newspaper kiosks, and outdoor cafés; traffic plays second fiddle to the endless *paseo* (stroll) of locals and travelers alike. Federico García Lorca called this street the only one in the world that he wished would never end. The whole avenue is referred to as Las Ramblas (Les Rambles, in Catalan) or La Rambla, but each section has its own name: Rambla Santa Monica is at the southeastern, or port, end; Rambla de les Flors in the middle; and Rambla dels Estudis is at the top, near Plaça de Catalunya.

Font de Canaletes. This fountain is a key spot in Barcelona, the place where all great sports victories are celebrated by jubilant (and often unruly) Barça fans. It was originally known for the best water in Barcelona, brought in by *canaletes* (small canals) from the mountains. The bronze plaque on the pavement in front of the fountain explains in Catalan that if you drink from these waters, you will fall under Barcelona's spell and return forevermore—so beware. ✉ *Top of Rambla* Ⓜ *Catalunya.*

Fodor's Choice
★
La Boqueria. Barcelona's most spectacular food market, also known as the Mercat de Sant Josep, is an explosion of life and color sprinkled with delicious little bar-restaurants. A solid polychrome wall of fruits, herbs, wild mushrooms, vegetables, nuts, candied fruits, cheeses, hams, fish, poultry, and provender of every imaginable genus and strain greets you as you turn in from La Rambla and breathe air alive with the aromas of fresh produce and reverberating with the din of commerce. Within this steel hangar the market occupies a neoclassical square built in 1840 by architect Francesc Daniel Molina. The Ionic columns visible around the edges of the market were part of the mid-19th-century neoclassical

17

Barcelona

0 — 450 yards
0 — 450 meters

Plaça Pius XII!

Plaça de la Reina María Cristina

Plaça Prat de la Riba

Ronda del General Mitré

C. de Modolell

Via Augusta

C. de les Escoles Pías

C. de Ganduxer

Calle de Sant Elíes

C. Deu i Mata

C. de Numància

C. de Calvet

C. de Santaló

C. de Muntaner

C. Gran de Gràcia

Travessera de les Corts

Pl. de Francesc Macià

C. de Loreto

C. d'Enrenza

Avda. de J. Tarradellas

C. de Berlín

C. de París

C. de Villarroel

Avda. Diagonal

C. de Tuset

Travessera de Gràcia

Plaça de Joan Carles I

C. de Joan Güell

C. del Vallespir

C. de Còrsega

C. del Rosselló

C. de Provença

C. de Muntaner

C. d'Aribau

C. de Còrsega

27

Estació Central-Sants

Pl. Països Catalans

Avda. de Roma

EIXAMPLE

C. de Balmes

Pg. de Gràcia

Rambla de Catalunya

C. de Pau Claris

C. de la Creu Coberta

C. de Valencia

Enrença

C. de Rocafort

C. de Calàbria

C. de Viladomat

C. del Comte Borrell

C. del Comte d'Urgell

C. de Villarroel

C. de Casanova

C. de Mallorca

12

C. d'Aragó

C. de la Diputació

C. de la Diputació

Plaça d'Espanya

Gran Via de les Corts Catalanes

Plaça Universitat

Gran Via de les Corts Catalanes

Pl. Urquinaona

Pl. de les Cascades

Avda. Reina M. Cristina

Avda. de Lleida

Avda. del Paral·lel

C. de Sepúlveda

C. de Floridablanca

C. de Tamarit

C. de Manso

Ronda Sant Antoni

C. dels Tallers

Ronda Universitat

Pelai

8

RAVAL

Pl. de Catalunya

13

Jonqueres

14

S.

Pg. de les Cascades

1

C. de Blai

C. de Magdalenes

Rda. de Sant Pau

C. de Sant Antoni

Joaquín Costa

Carretes

C. del Carme

C. Hospital

Portaferrisa

BARRI GÒTIC

RIBERA

9

10

Avda. Catedral

18

Pl. de l'Angel

16

Jardins de Joan Maragall

3

MONTJUÏC

Les Flors

5

C. de Sant Pau

LA RAMBLA

C. de Ferran

17

Pl. de Ciutat

Avda. de Miramar

2

Camí dels Tres Pins

C. la Unió

Rambla

Passeig Isabel II

Pl. d'Antoni López

Parc de Montjuïc

Pg. de Montjuïc

C. Nou de la Rambla

C. Ample

Pg. de Colom

Portal de la Pau

6

7

Moll de la Fusta

Jardins de Miramar

Castell de Montjuïc

4

Moll de Sant Bertrán

TORRE DE JAUME I

Moll d'Espanya

31

KEY
Funicular
Metro Stations
Railway Lines
Telefèric
Tourist Information
Tram stops
Parc Güell
30
Plaça de Lesseps
Trav. de Dalt
C. de Sant Salvador
C. de la Providència
C. Menéndez Pelayo
C. de Verdi
C. de L'Escorial
Plaça Alfons el Savi
Ronda del Guinardó
C. de Pi i Margall
GRÀCIA
Travessera de Gràcia
29
C. Sant Antoni Marìa Claret
C. de Indústria
C. de Sardenya
C. de Marina
C. de Cartagena
C. de Bailèn
Passeig de S. Joan
C. del Rosselló
Avda. de Gaudí
C. de Provença
28
C. de Mallorca
C. de Roger Llúria
C. de Valencia
Avda. Diagonal
C. d'Aragó
Consell de Cent
C. de Consell de Cent
C. de Roger de Flor
C. de Nàpols
C. de Sicília
Plaça Tetuán
C. del Bruc
C. de Girona
C. de Casp
C. de Ribes
C. d'Ausias Marc
Ronda S. Pere
Estació Norte-Vilanova (Bus Station)
26
Pere Més Alt
BORN
S. Pere Més Baix
C. Dels
C. de Tànger
C. dels Almogàvers
Avda. de la Meridiana
C. de Sancho de Avila
Passeig de Lluís Companys
Passeig Pujadas
C. de Pere IV
15
C. Princesa
C. del Comerç
19
Passeig del Born
Pg. Picasso
Parc de la Ciutadella
C. de Wellington
C. de Pujades
C. d'Alaba
21
Avda. M. de l'Argentera
20
C. de Llull
Estació de França
C. de Pamplona
Passeig D. Joan de Borbó
BARCELONETA
22
23
24
25

Antic Hospital de la Santa Creu i Sant Pau 8
Arc del Triomf 26
Barceloneta 22
Casa Milá 27
Castell de Montjuïc 4
Cooperative Oborera La Fraternit 23
Estadi Olímpic 2
Font de Canaletes 11
Fundació Miró 3
La Boqueria 10
Manzana de la Discòrdia 12
Museu d'Art Contemporani de Barcelona 9
Museu d' Història de la Ciutat 16
Museu Marítim 6
Museu Nacional d'Art de Catalunya 1
Museu Picasso 19
Palau de la Mùsica Catalana 14
Palau del Lloctinent 15
Parc de la Ciutadella 20
Park Güell 30
Plaça de Catalunya 13
Plaça Sant Jaume 18
Plaça Sant Just 17
Port 7
Port Olímpic 25
Port Vell 24
Recinte Modernista de Sant Pau 29
Santa Maria del Mar 21
Sant Pau del Camp 5
Temple Expiatori de la Sagrada Família 28
Tibidabo 31

square constructed here after the Sant Josep convent was torn down. The columns were uncovered in 2001 after more than a century of being buried in the busy market. Highlights include the sunny green-grocer's market outside (to the right if you've come in from la Rambla), along with **Pinotxo** (Pinocchio), just inside to the right, which has won international acclaim as a food sanctuary. Pinotxo—marked with a ceramic portrait of the wood-nosed prevaricator himself—is typically overbooked. But take heart; the **Kiosko Universal**, over toward the port side of the market, or **Quim de la Boqueria** offer delicious alternatives. Don't miss the herb- and wild-mushroom stand at the back of the Boqueria, with its display of *fruits del bosc* (fruits of the forest): wild mushrooms, herbs, nuts, and berries. ⊠ *Rambla 91* ⊕ *www.boqueria. info* ⊘ *Mon.–Sat. 8–8* Ⓜ *Liceu.*

Fodor'sChoice
★
Museu d'Art Contemporani de Barcelona (*Barcelona Museum of Contemporary Art, MACBA*). Designed by American architect Richard Meier in 1992, this gleaming explosion of light and geometry in the darkest corner of Raval houses a permanent collection of contemporary art as well as traveling exhibits. With barely a nod to Gaudí (via the amorphous tower in front of the main facade), Meier's exercise in minimalism (resembling, to some degree, a bathroom turned inside out) has been much debated in Barcelona. Basque sculptor Jorge Oteiza's massive bronze *La Ola* (*The Wave*) on the MACBA's front porch is popular with skateboarders, while the late Eduardo Chillida's *Barcelona* climbs the wall to the left of the main entrance in the sculptor's signature primitive blocky black geometrical patterns. The MACBA's 20th-century art collection (Calder, Rauschenberg, Oteiza, Chillida, Tàpies) is excellent, as is the guided tour carefully introducing the philosophical bases of contemporary art as well as the pieces themselves. ⊠ *Pl. dels Àngels s/n, El Raval* ☎ *93/412–0810* ⊕ *www.macba.es* 🎟 *€7.50* ⊘ *Mon. and Wed.–Fri. 11–7:30, Sat. 10–9, Sun. 10–3; free guided tours daily at 6, Sun. at noon* Ⓜ *Catalunya.*

FAMILY
Fodor'sChoice
★
Museu Marítim. The superb Maritime Museum is housed in the 13th-century **Drassanes Reials** (Royal Shipyards), at the foot of la Rambla adjacent to the harbor front. This vast covered complex launched the ships of Catalonia's powerful Mediterranean fleet directly from its yards into the port (the water once reached the level of the eastern facade of the building). Today these are the world's largest and best-preserved medieval shipyards; centuries ago, at a time when Greece was a province of the House of Aragón (1377–88), they were of crucial importance to the sea power of Catalonia (then the heavyweight in an alliance with Aragón). On the Avinguda del Paral.lel side of Drassanes is a completely intact section of the 14th- to 15th-century walls—Barcelona's third and final ramparts—that encircled the Raval along the Paral.lel and the Rondas de Sant Pau, Sant Antoni, and Universitat.

Though the shipyards seem more like a cathedral than a naval construction site, the Maritime Museum is filled with vessels, including a spectacular collection of ship models. The life-size reconstruction of the galley of Juan de Austria, commander of the Spanish fleet in the Battle of Lepanto, is perhaps the most impressive display in the museum. The cafeteria is Barcelona's hands-down winner for dining in the midst of medieval elegance. Don't miss the small bronze reproduction of a sailing ship, commemorating the 1571 Battle of Lepanto, out on the Rambla corner nearest the port. ⊠ *Av. de les Drassanes s/n* ☎ *93/342–9920* ⊕ *www.mmb.cat* ⊡ *€3.50 (free on Sun.)* ⊙ *Daily 10–8* Ⓜ *Drassanes.*

Plaça de Catalunya. Barcelona's main transport hub, Plaça de Catalunya, is the frontier between the Old City and the post-1860 Eixample. Comparable in size to Paris's Place de l'Étoile or to Rome's St. Peter's Square, Plaça de Catalunya is generally an unavoidable place to scurry across at high speed on your way to somewhere quieter, shadier, and generally gentler on the senses. The only relief in sight is **Café Zurich,** at the head of the Rambla and the mouth of the metro, which remains the classic Barcelona rendezvous point. The block behind the Zurich, known as El Triangle, houses a strip of megastores, including FNAC and Habitat, among others.

The underground **tourist office** on the northeast corner is the place to pick up free maps of the city and check on walking tours (some in English) that originate there. The most interesting features in this large but mostly uncharming square are the sensual and exuberant sculptures. Ⓜ *Catalunya.*

Port. Beyond the Columbus monument—behind the ornate Duana (now headquarters for the Barcelona Port Authority)—is the **Rambla de Mar,** a boardwalk with a drawbridge designed to allow boats into and out of the inner harbor. The Rambla de Mar extends out to the **Moll d'Espanya,** with its Maremagnum shopping center, IMAX theater, and the excellent aquarium. Next to the Duana you can board a Golondrina boat for a tour of the port and the waterfront or, from the Moll de Barcelona on the right, take a cable car to Montjuïc or Barceloneta. Trasmediterránea and the fleeter Buquebus passenger ferries leave for Italy and the Balearic Islands from the Moll de Barcelona, while at the end of the quay is Barcelona's World Trade Center and the Eurostars Grand Marina Hotel. Ⓜ *Drassanes.*

CIUTAT VELLA: EL BARRI GÒTIC AND RIBERA-BORN

Fodor's Choice **Antic Hospital de la Santa Creu i Sant Pau.** Founded in the 10th century, ★ this is one of Europe's earliest medical complexes, and contains some of Barcelona's most stunningly graceful Gothic architecture, built mostly in the 15th and 16th centuries. Approached through either the Casa de la Convalescència entry on Carrer del Carme or through the main door on Carrer Hospital, the cluster of medieval architecture surrounds a garden courtyard and a midtown orange grove. The first stone was laid by King Martí el Humà (Martin the Humane) in 1401. As you approach from Carrer del Carme, the first door on the left is the **Reial Acadèmia de Cirurgia i Medecina** (Royal Academy of Surgery and Medicine), a neoclassical 18th-century building of carved stone. (The academy is open to the public on Wednesdays from 10 am to noon. Guided tours by appointment: call *93/317–1686.*)

Past the door to the Biblioteca Infantil, the children's library, on both sides of the courtyard is the 1.5-million-volume **Biblioteca de Catalunya** (⊠ *Carrer del Carme 47* ☎ *93/270–2300* ⊕ *www.bnc.cat* ⊙ *Weekdays 9–8, Sat. 9–2*), Catalonia's national library and Spain's second in scope

17

after Madrid's Biblioteca Nacional.This was the hospital where Antoni Gaudí was taken after he was struck by a trolley on June 7, 1926. Among the library's collections are archives recording Gaudí's admittance and photographs of the infirmary and the private room where he died. ⊠ *Carrer Hospital 56 (or Carrer del Carme 45), El Raval* 🕾 *93/270–2300* Ⓜ *Liceu.*

Fodor's Choice **Museu d'Història de la Ciutat** (*City History Museum*). This fascinating
★ museum just off the Plaça del Rei traces Barcelona's evolution from its first Iberian settlement through its Roman and Visigothic times and beyond. Antiquity is the focus here: Romans took the city during the Punic Wars, and the striking underground remains of their *Colonia Favencia Julia Augusta Paterna Barcino (Favored Colony of the Father Julius Augustus Barcino)*, through which you can roam on metal walkways, are the museum's main treasure. Archaeological finds include Roman houses, parts of walls and fluted columns as well as recovered busts and vases. The visit includes tours of treasures around **Plaça del Rei** including the **Palau Reial Major,** the splendid **Saló del Tinell,** and the chapel of **Santa Àgata.** ⊠ *Palau Padellàs, Carrer del Veguer 2, Barri Gòtic* 🕾 *93/256–2122* ⊕ *www.museuhistoria.bcn.cat* ⊠ *€7, includes admission to Monestir de Pedralbes, Centre d'Interpretació del Park Güell, Centre d'Interpretació del Call, Centre d'Interpretació Històrica, Refugi 307, and Museu-Casa Verdaguer* ⊙ *Tues.–Sat. 10–7, Sun. 10–8* Ⓜ *Catalunya, Liceu, Jaume I.*

Fodor's Choice **Museu Picasso.** The Picasso Museum is housed in five adjoining pal-
★ aces on Carrer Montcada, a street known for Barcelona's most elegant medieval palaces. Picasso spent his key formative years in Barcelona (1895–1904), and this collection, while it does not include a significant number of the artist's best paintings, is particularly strong on his early work. The museum was begun in 1962 on the suggestion of Picasso's crony Jaume Sabartés, and the initial donation was from the Sabartés collection. Later Picasso donated his early works, and in 1981 his widow, Jaqueline Roque, added 141 pieces.

Displays include childhood sketches, works from Picasso's Rose and Blue periods, and the famous 1950s Cubist variations on Velázquez's *Las Meninas* (in Rooms 22–26). The lower-floor sketches, oils, and schoolboy caricatures and drawings from Picasso's early years in La Coruña are perhaps the most fascinating part of the whole museum, showing the facility the artist seemed to possess almost from the cradle. His *La Primera Communión (First Communion)*, painted at the age of 16, gives an idea of his early accomplishment. On the second floor you meet the beginnings of the mature Picasso and his Blue Period in Paris, a time of loneliness, cold, and hunger for the artist. ⊠ *Carrer Montcada 15–19, Born-Ribera* 🕾 *93/319–6310* ⊕ *www.museupicasso. bcn.cat* ⊠ *€11 (free 1st Sun. of month, free Sun. 3–8* ⊙ *Tues.–Sun. 10–8)* Ⓜ *Jaume I.*

Fodor's Choice **Palau de la Música Catalana.** One of the world's most extraordinary music
★ halls, with facades that are a riot of color and form, the Music Palace is a landmark of Carrer Amadeus Vives, set just across Via Laietana, a five-minute walk from Plaça de Catalunya. From its polychrome-ceramic

ticket windows on the Carrer de Sant Pere Més Alt side to its overhead busts of (from left to right) Palestrina, Bach, Beethoven, and (around the corner on Carrer Amadeus Vives) Wagner, the Palau is a flamboyant tour de force designed in 1908 by Lluís Domènech i Montaner.

The exterior is remarkable in itself. The Miquel Blay sculptural group over the corner of Amadeu Vives and Sant Pere Més Alt is Catalonia's popular music come to life, with everyone included from St. George the dragon slayer (at the top) to women and children, fishermen with oars over their shoulders, and every strain and strata of popular life and music, the faces of the past fading into the background.

The Palau's interior is, well, a permanent uproar before the first note of music is ever heard. The visuals alone make music sound different here, and at any important concert the excitement is palpably thick. ✉ *Carrer Sant Pere Més Alt 4–6, Sant Pere* ☎ *93/295–7200* ⊕ *www. palaumusica.org* 🎫 *Tour €17* ☉ *Sept.–June, tours daily 10–4:30; July and Aug., tours daily 10–7* Ⓜ *Urquinaona.*

Palau del Lloctinent (*Lieutenant's Palace*). The three facades of this fine building face the Carrer dels Comtes de Barcelona on the cathedral side, the Baixada de Santa Clara, and the Plaça del Rei. Typical of late Gothic–early Renaissance Catalan design, it was constructed by Antoni Carbonell in 1557, and remains one of the Gothic Quarter's most graceful buildings. The heavy stone arches over the entry, the central patio, and the intricately coffered wooden roof over the stairs are all good examples of noble 16th-century architecture. The door on the stairway is a 1975 Josep Maria Subirachs work portraying scenes from the life of Sant Jordi and the history of Catalonia. The Palau del Lloctinent was inhabited by the king's official emissary or viceroy to Barcelona during the 16th and 17th centuries, and now offers an excellent exhibit on the life and times of Jaume I, one Catalonia's most important founding fathers. ✉ *Carrer dels Comtes de Barcelona, 2, Barri Gòtic* ☎ *93/485–4285* Ⓜ *Jaume I.*

Plaça Sant Jaume. This central hub a couple of blocks east of the Cathedral is the site of Catalonia's government building, the **Generalitat de Catalunya** in the Palau de La Generalitat, and Barcelona's City Hall, the **Casa de la Ciutat–Ayuntamiento de Barcelona.** This was the site of the Roman forum 2,000 years ago, though subsequent construction filled the space with buildings. The square was cleared in the 1840s, but the two imposing (and often opposing) government buildings facing each other across it are much older. ⊕ *www.bcn.es, www.gencat.cat/gener-alitat/cat/guia/palau/index.htm for reservations* ☉ *Ayuntamiento tours (in English) Mon.–Sat. at 11; Generalitat tours 2nd and 4th weekends of the month 9–1* Ⓜ *Jaume I.*

Plaça Sant Just. Off to the left side of city hall down Carrer Hèrcules (named for the mythical founder of Barcelona) are this square and the site of the Església de Sant Just i Pastor, one of the city's oldest Christian churches, dating from the 4th century. Christian catacombs are reported to have been found beneath Plaça Sant Just. The Gothic fountain was built in 1367 by famed Barcelona councilman Joan Fiveller. Fiveller had discovered a spring in the Collserola hills, and had the water piped

17

straight to Barcelona. The fountain bears an image of St. Just and city and sovereign count-kings' coats of arms, along with a pair of falcons. The church is dedicated to the boy martyrs Just and Pastor; the Latin inscription over the door translates into English almost in reverse syntax as, "Our pious patron is the black and beautiful Virgin, together with the sainted children Just and Pastore." Ⓜ *Jaume I.*

> ## WANT TO KNOW MORE?
>
> *La Catedral del Mar* (published in 2006 and translated as *The Cathedral of the Sea*), by Ildefonso Falcones, is a fascinating novel chronicling the life and times of a boy stevedore who participated in the construction of Santa del Mar in 14th-century Barcelona.

Fodor's Choice
★
Santa Maria del Mar. The most beautiful example of early Catalan Gothic architecture, Santa Maria del Mar is extraordinary for its unbroken lines and elegance. The lightness of the interior is especially surprising considering the blocky exterior. The site, originally outside the 1st- to 4th-century Roman walls at what was then the water's edge, was home to a Christian cult from the late 3rd century. Built by a mere stonemason who chose, fitted, and carved each stone hauled down from the same Montjuïc quarry that provided the sandstone for the 4th-century Roman walls, Santa Maria del Mar is breathtakingly and nearly hypnotically symmetrical. The medieval numerological symbol for the Virgin Mary, the number eight (or multiples thereof) runs through every element of the basilica: The 16 octagonal pillars are 6½ feet in diameter and spread out into rib vaulting arches at a height of 52 feet. The painted keystones at the apex of the arches are 105 feet from the floor. Furthermore, the central nave is twice as wide as the lateral naves (26 feet each), whose width equals the difference (26 feet) between their height and that of the main nave. The result of all this proportional balance and harmony is a sense of uplift that, especially in baroque and moderniste Barcelona, is both exhilarating and soothing.

Set aside at least a half hour to see Santa Maria del Mar. *La Catedral del Mar* (*The Cathedral of the Sea*) by Ildefonso Falcons chronicles the construction of the basilica and 14th-century life in Barcelona. Check the schedule for concerts in Santa Maria del Mar. Either arrive early to get seats in the front rows or sit on the stone steps in the side chapels near the front of the basilica to avoid getting lost in the six-second acoustic delay. ✉ *Pl. de Santa Maria, Born-Ribera* ☎ *93/310–2390* ☉ *Daily 9–1:30 and 4:30–8* Ⓜ *Jaume I.*

Fodor's Choice
★
Sant Pau del Camp. Barcelona's oldest church was originally outside the city walls (*del camp* means "in the fields") and was a Roman cemetery as far back as the 2nd century, according to archaeological evidence. A Visigothic belt buckle found in the 20th century confirmed that Visigoths used the site as a cemetery between the 2nd and 7th centuries. What you see now was built in 1127 and is the earliest Romanesque structure in Barcelona, redolent of the pre-Romanesque Asturian churches or of the pre-Romanesque Sant Michel de Cuxà in Prades, Catalunya Nord (Catalonia North, aka southern France). Elements of the church—the classical marble capitals atop the columns in the main entry—are thought to be from the 6th and 7th centuries. The hulking

mastodonic shape of the church is a reminder of the church's defensive posture in the face of intermittent Roman persecution and, later, Moorish invasions and sackings. The tiny cloister is Sant Pau del Camp's best feature, and one of Barcelona's semisecret treasures. Sculpted capitals portraying biblical scenes support tri-lobed Mudejar arches; birdlike sirens tempt monks from prayer on the southwestern corner capital. This penumbral sanctuary, barely a block from the frantic Avinguda del Paral.lel, is a gift from time. ⊠ *Sant Pau 99, El Raval* ☏ *93/441–0001* ⊠ *Cloister: €3* ⊙ *Cloister: Mon.–Sat. 10–1:30, 4–7; Sun. Mass at 10:30, 12:30, and 8 pm* Ⓜ *Paral.lel.*

BARCELONETA, LA CIUTADELLA, AND PORT OLIMPIC

Arc del Triomf. This imposing, exposed-redbrick arch was built by Josep Vilaseca as the grand entrance for the 1888 Universal Exhibition. Similar in size and sense to the traditional triumphal arches of ancient Rome, this one refers to no specific military triumph anyone can recall. In fact, Catalunya's last military triumph of note may have been Jaume I el Conqueridor's 1229 conquest of the Moors in Mallorca—as suggested by the bats (always part of Jaume I's coat of arms) on either side of the arch itself. The Josep Reynés sculptures adorning the structure represent Barcelona hosting visitors to the Exhibition on the west (front) side, while the Josep Llimona sculptures on the east side depict the prizes being given to its outstanding contributors. ⊠ *Passeig de Sant Joan, La Ciutadella* Ⓜ *Arc de Triomf.*

Barceloneta. Once Barcelona's pungent fishing port, Barceloneta retains much of its salty maritime flavor. It's an exciting and colorful place to walk through, with narrow streets with lines of laundry snapping in the breeze. Barceloneta's surprisingly clean and sandy beach, though overcrowded in midsummer, offers swimming, surfing, and a lively social scene from late May through September.

Cooperative Obrera La Fraternitat (*Brotherhood Workers Cooperative*). This strikingly ornate building in the otherwise humble fishermen's quarter, the only art-nouveau building in Barceloneta, housed the progressive workers' organization La Fraternitat, founded in 1879. Begun as a low-cost outlet to help supply workers and their families with basic necessities at cut-rate prices, the cooperative soon became a social and cultural center that included a public library. The present cooperative building was inaugurated in 1918 and is now, once again, Barceloneta's library. ⊠ *Carrer Comte de Santa Clara 8, Barceloneta* ☏ *93/225–3574* Ⓜ *Barceloneta.*

FAMILY **Parc de la Ciutadella** (*Citadel Park*). Once a fortress designed to consolidate Madrid's military occupation of Barcelona, the Ciutadella is now the city's main downtown park. The clearing dates from shortly after the War of the Spanish Succession in the early 18th century, when Felipe V demolished some 1,000 houses in what was then the Barri de la Ribera to build a fortress and barracks for his soldiers and a *glacis,* or open space, between rebellious Barcelona and his artillery positions. The fortress walls were pulled down in 1868 and replaced by gardens laid out by Josep Fontseré. In 1888 the park was the site of the Universal Exposition that put Barcelona on the map as a truly European

17

city; today it is home to the Castell dels Tres Dragons, built by architect Lluís Domènech i Montaner as the café and restaurant for the exposition (the only building to survive that project, now a botanical research center), the Catalan parliament, and the city zoo. ⊠ *La Ciutadella* Ⓜ *Barceloneta, Ciutadella.*

Port Olímpic. Choked with yachts, restaurants, tapas bars, and megarestaurants serving reasonably decent fare continuously from 1 pm to 1 am, the Olympic Port is 2 km (1 mile) up the beach, marked by the mammoth shimmering goldfish sculpture by Frank Gehry of Bilbao Guggenheim fame (Bilbao got a leviathan; Barcelona got a goldfish). In the shadow of Barcelona's first real skyscraper, the Hotel Arts, the Olympic Port rages on Friday and Saturday nights, especially in summer, with hundreds of young people of all nationalities contributing to a scene characterized by go-go girls (and boys), fast-food chains, ice-cream parlors, and a buzz redolent of spring break in Cancún. Ⓜ *Ciutadella, Vila Olímpica.*

> ### CATALAN FOR BEGINNERS
>
> Catalan is derived from Latin and Provençal French, whereas Spanish is heavy on Arabic vocabulary and phonetics. For language exchange (*intercambios*), check the bulletin board at the central university Philosophy and Letters Faculty on Gran Via or any English bookstore for free half-hour exchanges of English for Catalan (or Spanish), a great way to get free private lessons and meet locals. Who knows? With the right chemistry, *intercambios* can lead to cross-cultural friendships and even romance. Who said the language of love is French?

Port Vell (*Old Port*). From Pla del Palau, cross to the edge of the port, where the Moll d'Espanya, the Moll de la Fusta, and the Moll de Barceloneta meet. (*Moll* means docks.) Just beyond the colorful Roy Lichtenstein sculpture in front of the post office, the modern Port Vell complex—an IMAX theater, aquarium, and Maremagnum shopping mall—looms seaward on the Moll d'Espanya. The Palau de Mar, with its five somewhat pricey and impersonal quayside terrace restaurants, stretches down along the Moll de Barceloneta (try Llevataps or the Merendero de la Mari; even better is El Magatzem, by the entrance to the Museu de Història de Catalunya in the Palau de Mar). Key points in the Maremagnum complex are the grassy hillside (for lovers, especially, on April 23, Sant Jordi's Day, Barcelona's variant of Valentine's Day); and the *Ictineo II* replica of the submarine created by Narcis Monturiol (1819–85)—the world's first, launched in the Barcelona port in 1862. Ⓜ *Barceloneta.*

THE EIXAMPLE

Fodor's Choice
★

Casa Milà. Usually referred to as **La Pedrera** (The Stone Quarry), with a wavy, curving stone facade that undulates around the corner of the block, this building is one of Gaudí's most celebrated yet initially reviled designs. Topped by chimneys so eerie they were nicknamed *espantabruxes* (witch-scarers), the Casa Milà was unveiled in 1910 to the horror of local residents. Other observers were undone by the facade, complaining, as one critic put it, that the rippling, undressed stone made you feel "as though you are on board a ship in an angry sea."

Seemingly defying the laws of gravity, the exterior has no straight lines, and is adorned with winding balconies covered with wrought-iron foliage sculpted by Josep Maria Jujol.

Gaudí's rooftop chimney park, alternately interpreted as veiled Saharan women or helmeted warriors, is as spectacular as anything in Barcelona, especially in late afternoon, when the sunlight slants over the city into the Mediterranean. Inside, the handsome **Espai Gaudí** (Gaudí Space) in the attic has excellent critical displays of Gaudí's works from all over Spain, as well as explanations of theories and techniques, including an upside-down model (a reproduction of the original in the Sagrada Família museum) of the Güell family crypt at Santa Coloma made of weighted hanging strings.

Guided tours of Casa Milà are offered in various languages, weekdays at 6 pm, weekends at 11 am; email ✉ *grupslapedrera@oscatalunyacaixa. com* for bookings (essential) and information. On *Nits d'Estiu* (Summer Nights: Thurs., Fri., and Sat., Jun. 20–Sept. 7) the Espai Gaudí and the roof terrace are open for drinks and jazz concerts; the doors open at 9:45 pm and concerts begin at 10:30. Admission is €27. ✉ *Passeig de Gràcia 92* ☎ *902/202138* 🎫 *€16.50* ☉ *Nov.–Feb., daily 9–6:30; Mar.– Oct., daily 9–8* Ⓜ *Diagonal, Provença.*

Fodor'sChoice **Manzana de la Discòrdia.** The name is a pun on the Spanish word *man-*
★ *zana,* which means both "apple" and "city block," alluding to the three-way architectural counterpoint on this street and to the classical myth of the Apple of Discord (which played a part in that legendary tale about the Judgment of Paris and the subsequent Trojan War). The houses here are spectacular and encompass three monuments of Modernisme—Casa Lleó Morera, Casa Amatller, and Casa Batlló. Of the three competing buildings (four if you count Sagnier i Villavecchia's comparatively tame 1910 Casa Mulleras at No. 37), Casa Batlló is clearly the star attraction and the only one of the three offering visits to the interior—though the Casa Amatller does have a gallery and a gift shop on the ground floor, where you can buy some of the excellent chocolate that made the family fortune.

Casa Batlló. Gaudí at his most spectacular, the colorful and bizarre Casa Batlló, with its mottled facade resembling anything from an abstract pointillist painting to a rainbow of colored sprinkles on an ice-cream cone, is usually easily identifiable by the crowd of tourists snapping photographs on the sidewalk. ✉ *Passeig de Gràcia 43* ☎ *93/216–0306* 🌐 *www.casabatllo.es* 🎫 *€18* ☉ *Daily 9–8* Ⓜ *Passeig de Gràcia.*

Casa Lleó Morera. The ornate Casa Lleó Morera was extensively rebuilt (1902–06) by Palau de la Música Catalana architect Domènech i Montaner and is a treasure house of Catalan Modernisme. The facade is covered with ornamentation and sculptures depicting female figures using the modern inventions of the age: the telephone, the telegraph, the photographic camera, and the Victrola. ✉ *Passeig de Gracia 35* Ⓜ *Passeig de Gracia.*

Casa Amatller. The neo-Gothic, pseudo-Flemish Casa Amatller was built by Josep Puig i Cadafalch in 1900, when the architect was 33 years old. Eighteen years younger than Domènech i Montaner and 15 years younger than Gaudí, Puig i Cadafalch was one of the leading statesmen of his generation, mayor of Barcelona and, in 1917, president of Catalonia's first home-rule government since 1714, the Mancomunitat de Catalunya. ⊠ *Passeig de Gràcia 41* ☎ *93/487–7217* ⊕ *www.amatller. org* Ⓜ *Passeig de Gràcia.*

FodorsChoice
★
Recinte Modernista de Sant Pau. Among the more recent tourist attractions in Barcelona, the Recinte Modernista (Modernist Complex) is set in what was surely one of the most beautiful public projects in the world: the Hospital de Sant Pau. A World Heritage site, the Complex is extraordinary in its setting and style, and in the idea that inspired it. Architect Lluis Domènech i Montaner believed that trees and flowers and fresh air were likely to help people recover from what ailed them more than anything doctors could do in emotionally sterile surroundings. The hospital wards were set among gardens, their brick facades topped with polychrome ceramic tile roofs in extravagant shapes and details. Domènech also believed in the therapeutic properties of form and color, and decorated the hospital with Pau Gargallo sculptures and colorful mosaics, replete with motifs of hope and healing and healthy growth. Begun in 1900, this monumental production won Domènech i Montaner his third Barcelona "Best Building" award in 1912. Tours of the Complex are offered in English daily at 10:15 and 12:15. ⊠ *Carrer Sant Antoni Maria Claret 167* ☎ *93/553–7801* ⊕ *www. santpaubarcelona.org* 🎫 *Tour €5* Ⓜ *Hospital de Sant Pau.*

FodorsChoice
★
Temple Expiatori de la Sagrada Família. Barcelona's most emblematic architectural icon, Antoni Gaudí's Sagrada Família, is still under construction 130 years after it was begun. This striking and surreal creation was conceived as nothing short of a Bible in stone, a gigantic representation of the entire history of Christianity, and it continues to cause responses from surprise to consternation to wonder. No building in Barcelona and few in the world are more deserving of the investment of a few hours to the better part of a day in getting to know it well. In fact, a quick visit can be more tiring than an extended one, as there are too many things to take in at once. However long your visit, it's a good idea to bring binoculars.

"My client is not in a hurry," Gaudí was fond of replying to anyone curious about the timetable for the completion of his mammoth project. And it's a lucky thing, because the Sagrada Família was begun in 1882 under architect Francesc Villar, passed on in 1891 to Gaudí (who worked on the project until his death in 1926), and is still thought to be 15 or 20 years from completion, despite the ever-increasing velocity of today's computerized construction techniques. ⊠ *Pl. de la Sagrada Família s/n* ☎ *93/207–3031* ⊕ *www.sagradafamilia.org* 🎫 *€13.50 (€18 with audio guide), bell-tower elevator €4.50* ☯ *Oct.–Mar., daily 9–6; Apr.–Sept., daily 9–8* Ⓜ *Sagrada Família.*

UPPER BARCELONA

FAMILY
FodorsChoice
★
Park Güell. This park is one of Gaudí's, and Barcelona's, most pleasant and stimulating places to spend a few hours. Whereas Gaudí's landmark Sagrada Família can be exhaustingly bright and hot in its massive energy

and complexity, Park Güell is invariably light and playful, uplifting and restorative. Alternately shady, green, floral, or sunny, the park always has a delicious corner for whatever one needs. Named for and commissioned by Gaudí's main patron, Count Eusebi Güell, it was originally intended as a gated residential community based on the English Garden City model, centered on an open-air theater built over a covered marketplace. Only two of the houses were ever built (one of which, designed by Gaudí assistant Francesc Berenguer, became Gaudí's home from 1906 to 1926 and now houses the park's Gaudí museum). Ultimately, as Barcelona's bourgeoisie seemed happier living closer to "town," the Güell family turned the area over to the city as a public park.

Other Gaudí highlights include the **Casa-Museu Gaudí** (the house where Gaudí lived), the Room of a Hundred Columns and the fabulous serpentine, polychrome bench that snakes along the main square. The bench is one of Gaudí assistant Josep Maria Jujol's most memorable creations, and one of Barcelona's best examples of the *trencadis* technique of making colorful mosaics with broken bits of tile. From the metro at Plaça de Lesseps, or the Bus Turistic stop on Travessera de Dalt, take Bus No. 24 to the park entrance, or make the steep 10-minute climb uphill on Carrer de Lallard. ⊠ *Carrer d'Olot s/n, Gràcia* ⊕ *www.parkguell.es* ⊙ *Daily 10–9* Ⓜ *Lesseps.*

FAMILY **Tibidabo.** One of Barcelona's two promontories, this hill bears a distinctive name, generally translated as "To Thee I Will Give" and referring to the Catalan legend that this was the spot from which Satan tempted Christ with all the riches of the earth below (namely, Barcelona). When the wind blows the smog out to sea, the views from this 1,789-foot peak are legendary. Tibidabo's skyline is marked by a neo-Gothic church, the work of Enric Sagnier in 1902, and—off to one side, near the village of Vallvidrera—the 854-foot communications tower, the **Torre de Collserola,** designed by Sir Norman Foster. Youngsters in tow? Take the cute little San Francisco-style Tramvía Blau (Blue Trolley) cable car from Plaça Kennedy to the overlook at the top, and transfer to the funicular to the 100-year-old amusement park at the summit. ⊠ *Pl. Tibidabo 3–4, Tibidabo* ⊕ *www.tibidabo.cat* 🎫 *All rides €28.50* ⊙ *Hrs vary* Ⓜ *Tibidabo.*

La Venta. The restaurant La Venta at the base of the funicular is excellent and a fine place to sit in the sun in cool weather (straw sun hats are provided). ⊠ *Pl. Doctor Andreu s/n, Vallvidrera* ☎ *93/212–6455.*

El Mirador de la Venta. El Mirador de la Venta has great views and contemporary cuisine to match. ⊠ *Pl. Doctor Andreu s/n, Vallvidrera* ☎ *93/212–6455.*

Mirablau. The bar Mirablau, overlooking the city lights, is a popular late-night hangout. ⊠ *Pl. Doctor Andreu s/n* ☎ *93/418–5879.*

MONTJUÏC

Castell de Montjuïc. Built in 1640 by rebels against Felipe IV, the castle has had a dark history as a symbol of Barcelona's military domination by foreign powers, usually the Spanish army. The fortress was stormed several times, most famously in 1705 by Lord Peterborough for Archduke Carlos of Austria. After the 1936–39 Spanish Civil War,

17

the castle was used as a dungeon for political prisoners. Lluís Companys, president of the Generalitat de Catalunya during the civil war, was executed by firing squad here on October 14, 1940. In 2007 the fortress was formally ceded back to Barcelona. The present uses of the space include an Interpretation Center for Peace, a Space for Historical Memory, and a Montjuïc Interpretation Center, along with cultural and educational events and activities. A popular weekend park and picnic area, the moat contains attractive gardens, with one side given over to an archery range, and the various terraces have panoramic views over the city and out to sea. ⊠ *Ctra. de Montjuïc 66* ☎ *93/329–8613* 🖃 *€3.50* ⊗ *Tues.–Sun. 9:30–8.*

Estadi Olímpic. The Olympic Stadium was originally built for the International Exhibition of 1929, with the idea that Barcelona would then host the 1936 Olympics (ultimately staged in Hitler's Berlin). After failing twice to win the nomination, the city celebrated the attainment of its long-cherished goal by renovating the semiderelict stadium in time for 1992, providing seating for 70,000. The **Galeria Olímpica,** a museum about the Olympic movement in Barcelona, displays objects and shows audiovisual replays from the 1992 Olympics. An information center traces the history of the modern Olympics from Athens in 1896 to the present. Next door and just downhill stands the futuristic **Palau Sant Jordi Sports Palace,** designed by the noted Japanese architect Arata Isozaki. The Isozaki structure has no pillars or beams to obstruct the view, and was built from the roof down—the roof was built first, then hydraulically lifted into place. ⊠ *Passeig Olímpic 17–19* ☎ *93/426–2089* ⊕ *www.fundaciobarcelonaolimpica.es* 🖃 *Gallery €5* ⊗ *Tues.–Sat. 10–2 and 4–7.*

Fodor'sChoice
★
Fundació Miró. The Miró Foundation, a gift from the artist Joan Miró to his native city, is one of Barcelona's most exciting showcases of contemporary art. The airy, white building, with panoramic views north over Barcelona, was designed by the artist's close friend and collaborator Josep Lluís Sert and opened in 1975; an extension was added by Sert's pupil Jaume Freixa in 1988. Miró's playful and colorful style, filled with Mediterranean light and humor, seems a perfect match for its surroundings, and the exhibits and retrospectives that open here tend to be progressive and provocative. Look for Alexander Calder's fountain of moving mercury. Miró himself rests in the cemetery on Montjuïc's southern slopes. During the Franco regime, which he strongly opposed, Miró first lived in self-imposed exile in Paris, then moved to Majorca in 1956. When he died in 1983, the Catalans gave him a send-off amounting to a state funeral. ⊠ *Av. Miramar 71* ☎ *93/443–9470* ⊕ *www.fundaciomiro-bcn.org* 🖃 *€11* ⊗ *Tues., Wed., Fri., and Sat. 10–7, Thurs. 10–9:30, Sun. 10–2:30.*

Fodor'sChoice
★
Museu Nacional d'Art de Catalunya (*Catalonian National Museum of Art, MNAC*). Housed in the imposingly domed, towered, frescoed, and columned **Palau Nacional,** built in 1929 as the centerpiece of the International Exposition, this superb museum was renovated in 1995 by Gae Aulenti, architect of the Musée d'Orsay in Paris. In 2004 the museum's three collections—Romanesque, Gothic, and the Cambó Collection, an eclectic trove, including a Goya, donated by Francesc

Cambó—were joined by the 19th- and 20th-century collection of Catalan impressionist and moderniste painters. Also now on display is the Thyssen-Bornemisza collection of early masters, with works by Zurbarán, Rubens, Tintoretto, Velázquez, and others. With this influx of artistic treasure, the MNAC becomes Catalonia's grand central museum. Pride of place goes to the Romanesque exhibition, the world's finest collection of Romanesque frescoes, altarpieces, and wood carvings, most of them rescued from deterioration, theft, and art dealers. ✉ *Palau Nacional* ☎ *93/622–0360* ⊕ *www.mnac.cat* ✄ *€12, valid for day of purchase and one other day in same month* ☯ *Jun.–Sept., Tues.–Sat. 10–8, Sun. 10–3; Oct.–May, Tues.–Sat. 10–6, Sun. 10–3.*

WHERE TO EAT

CIUTAT VELLA (OLD CITY)

$$$$
CATALAN
Fodor's Choice
★

✕ **Ca l'Isidre.** A favorite with Barcelona's creative crowd, this place is hung with pictures and engravings, some original, by Dalí and other prominent artists. Just inside the Raval from Avinguda del Paral.lel, the restaurant relies on fresh produce from the nearby Boqueria for its traditional Catalan cooking. The wines are invariably novelties from all over the Iberian Peninsula; ask for Isidre's advice and you'll get a great wine as well as an enology, geography, and history course delivered with charm, brevity, and wit. The slight French accent in cuisine is evident in superb homemade foie gras. Come and go by cab at night; it's not easy to find and the streets here can be iffy. $ *Average main: €38* ✉ *Les Flors 12, El Raval* ☎ *93/441–1139* ⊕ *www.calisidre.com* ⌀ *Reservations essential* ☯ *Closed Sun., Easter wk, and 1st 2 wks of Aug.* Ⓜ *Paral.lel.*

$$$$
CATALAN
Fodor's Choice
★

✕ **Casa Leopoldo.** In a hard-to-find pocket of the Raval, west of the Rambla, this family-run restaurant serves fine seafood and Catalan fare. To get here, approach along Carrer Hospital, take a left through the Passatge Bernardí Martorell, and go 50 feet right on Sant Rafael to the front door. Try the *revuelto de ajos tiernos y gambas* (eggs scrambled with young garlic and shrimp) or the famous *cap-i-pota* (stewed head and hoof of pork). Albariños and Priorats are among owner Rosa Gil's favorite wines. The dining room, lined in blue-and-yellow tiles, has an appropriately Mediterranean feel. $ *Average main: €38* ✉ *Sant Rafael 24, El Raval* ☎ *93/441–3014* ⊕ *www.casaleopoldo.com* ☯ *Closed Mon. No dinner Sun.* Ⓜ *Liceu.*

$$$$
CATALAN
Fodor's Choice
★

✕ **Comerç 24.** Artist, aesthete, and chef Carles Abellán playfully reinterprets traditional Catalan favorites and creates new ones at this artfully decorated dining spot on Carrer Comerç. Try the *arroz d'ànec amb foie* (rice with duck and foie gras). For dessert, don't miss the postmodern version of the traditional Spanish after-school snack of chocolate, olive oil, salt, and bread. Abellán trained under superstar Ferran Adrià and is as original as the master; the best way to experience his creativity is to throw budget to the winds and order one of the two tasting menus (€84 and €106, without wine). $ *Average main: €32* ✉ *Carrer Comerç 24, Born-Ribera* ☎ *93/319–2102* ⊕ *www.projectes24.com* ⌀ *Reservations essential* ☯ *Closed Sun. and Mon.* Ⓜ *Arc de Triomf.*

17

$$ CATALAN

🍴 **Cometacinc.** In an increasingly chic neighborhood of artisans and antiquers, this stylish place in the Barri Gòtic is a fine example of Barcelona's new-over-old architecture and interior-design panache. Although the 30-foot, floor-to-ceiling, wooden shutters are already a visual feast, the carefully prepared interpretations of old standards such as the *xai al forn* (roast lamb) or the more surprising *raviolis de vieiras* (scallop raviolis) awaken the palate brilliantly. The separate dining room, for a dozen to two-dozen diners, is a perfect place for a private party. [$] *Average main: €17* ✉ *Carrer Cometa 5, Barri Gòtic* ☎ *93/310–1558* ⏲ *Closed Tues.* [M] *Jaume I.*

$$ TAPAS Fodor'sChoice ★

🍴 **Quimet-Quimet.** A foodie haunt, this tiny place is hugely popular with locals and in-the-know visitors alike. If you come too late, you might not be able to get in. Come before 1:30 pm and 7:30 pm, and you will generally find a stand-up table. Chef-owner Quimet improvises ingenious canapés. All you have to do is orient him toward cheese, anchovies, or whatever it is you might crave, and Quimet masterfully does the rest *and* recommends the wine to go with it. [$] *Average main: €15* ✉ *Poeta Cabanyes 25, Poble Sec* ☎ *93/442–3142* ⏲ *Weekdays noon–4 and 7–10:30, Sat. noon–4* [M] *Paral.lel.*

BARCELONETA AND THE PORT OLÍMPIC

Barceloneta and the Port Olímpic (Olympic Port) have little in common beyond their seaside location: the former is a traditional fishermen's quarter, the latter is a crazed disco strip with 1,000-seat restaurants.

$$$$ SEAFOOD FAMILY Fodor'sChoice ★

🍴 **Can Majó.** At the edge of the beach in Barceloneta is one of Barcelona's premier seafood restaurants. House specialties are *caldero de bogavante* (a cross between paella and lobster bouillabaisse) and *suquet* (fish stewed in its own juices), but whatever you choose will be excellent. In summer, the terrace overlooking the Mediterranean is a pleasantly upscale version of the Barceloneta *chiringuitos* (shanty restaurants) that used to line the beach here. Even so, there's nothing "shanty" about the decor: a white-tablecloth experience with soft pendant lighting inside. [$] *Average main: €26* ✉ *Almirall Aixada 23, Barceloneta* ☎ *93/221–5455* 🌐 *www.canmajo.es* ⏲ *Closed Mon. No dinner Sun.* [M] *Barceloneta.*

$$ MEDITERRANEAN FAMILY

🍴 **Can Manel la Puda.** The first choice for a budget-friendly paella in the sun, year-round, Can Manel is near the end of the main road out to the Barceloneta beach. Any time before 4 o'clock will do (It reopens again at 7 pm.) *Arròs a banda* (rice with peeled shellfish) and paella *marinera* (with seafood) or *fideuá* (with noodles) are all delicious. The paella, prepared for a minimum of two diners, will easily feed three (or even four if you're planning to dine a few more times that day). [$] *Average main: €16* ✉ *Passeig Joan de Borbó 60, Barceloneta* ☎ *93/221–5013* 🌐 *www.pudacanmanel.com* ⏲ *Closed Mon.* [M] *Barceloneta.*

$$$$ SEAFOOD FAMILY

🍴 **Els Pescadors.** A kilometer northeast of the Olympic Port in the interesting Sant Martí neighborhood, this handsome late-19th-century bistro-style dining room has a lovely terrace on a little square shaded by immense ficus trees. Kids can play safely in the traffic-free square while their parents concentrate on well-prepared seafood specialties such as paella, fresh fish, or fideuá. [$] *Average main: €26* ✉ *Pl. de Prim 1,*

Sant Martí ☎ *93/225–2018* ⊕ *www.elspescadors.com* ⊙ *Closed Mon.* Ⓜ *Poblenou.*

$$$$

MEDITERRANEAN

✕ **Torre d'Alta Mar.** Location, location, location: at a height of 250 feet over the Barcelona waterfront in the Eiffel-tower-like Sant Sebastià cable-car station over the far side of the port, this restaurant has spectacular 360-degree views of Barcelona as well as far out into the Mediterranean. Seafood of every stripe, spot, fin, and carapace emanates from the kitchen here, but the filet mignon under a colossal slab of foie gras never fails to delight carnivores. Ⓢ *Average main: €33* ✉ *Torre de San Sebastián, Passeig Joan de Borbó 88, Barceloneta* ☎ *93/221–0007* ⊕ *www.torredealtamar.com* ⚐ *Reservations essential* ⊙ *Closed Mon. No lunch Sun.* Ⓜ *Barceloneta.*

EIXAMPLE

$$$$

MEDITERRANEAN

✕ **Casa Calvet.** It's hard to pass up the opportunity to break bread in a Gaudí-designed building. Completed in 1900, the art-nouveau Casa Calvet includes a graceful dining room decorated in moderniste ornamentation, from looping parabolic door handles to polychrome stained glass, etched glass, and wood carved in floral and organic motifs. The Catalan and Mediterranean fare is light and contemporary, seasonal and market-inspired. Ⓢ *Average main: €30* ✉ *Casp 48* ☎ *93/412–4012* ⊕ *www.casacalvet.es* ⊙ *Closed Sun.* Ⓜ *Urquinaona.*

$$$$

CATALAN

Fodor's Choice

★

✕ **Cinc Sentits.** The engaging Artal clan—led by master chef Jordi—is a Catalan-Canadian family who provides a unique Barcelona experience: cutting-edge, contemporary cooking explained eloquently in English. Three tasting menus—*Essències* is the simplest, *Sensacions* is more creative, *Gastronomic* is top of the line—with wine pairings, provide a wide range of experimental tastes and textures, which are also invariably delicious. (Expect to spend from €49 to a budget-busting €109, depending on which menu you select.) At the end of the meal, diners receive a printout reprising the various courses and wines that have just crossed their palates. This is foodie nirvana. Ⓢ *Average main: €36* ✉ *Aribau 58* ☎ *93/323–9490* ⊕ *cincsentits.com* ⊙ *Closed Sun. and Mon.* Ⓜ *Provença.*

$$$

CATALAN

Fodor's Choice

★

✕ **Manairó.** A *manairó* is a mysterious Pyrenean elf and Jordi Herrera may be the culinary version. A demon with meat cooked *al clavo ardiente* (à la burning nail)—filets warmed from within by red-hot spikes producing meat both rare and warm and never undercooked—Jordi also serves an unforgettable version of squid with blowtorch-fried eggs (*calamari de huevo frito*) and a palate-cleansing gin and tonic with liquid nitrogen, gin, and lime. The intimate and edgy design of the dining room is a perfect reflection of the cuisine. Ⓢ *Average main: €20* ✉ *Diputació 424* ☎ *93/231–0057* ⊕ *www.manairo.com* ⚐ *Reservations essential* ⊙ *Closed Sun. and 1st wk of Jan.* Ⓜ *Monumental.*

GRÁCIA

$$$$

SPANISH

Fodor's Choice

★

✕ **Botafumeiro.** On Gràcia's main thoroughfare, Barcelona's best-known Galician restaurant has maritime motifs, snowy tablecloths, wood paneling, and fleets of waiters in spotless white outfits all moving at the speed of light. The bank-breaking *Mariscada Botafumeiro* is a seafood medley from shellfish to fin fish to cuttlefish to caviar. An assortment of

17

media ración (half-ration) selections is available at the bar, where *pulpo a feira* (squid on slices of potato), *jamón ibérico de bellota* (acorn-fed Iberian ham), and *pan con tomate* (toasted bread topped with olive oil and tomato) make peerless late-night snacks. [$] *Average main: €26* ✉ *Gran de Gràcia 81* ☎ *93/218–4230* 🌐 *www.botafumeiro.es* ✍ *Reservations essential* [M] *Gràcia.*

SARRIA-PEDRALBES AND SANT GERVASI

$$$$ MEDITERRANEAN Fodor's Choice ★

🍴 **Neichel.** Originally from Alsace, chef Jean-Louis Neichel skillfully manages a vast variety of exquisite ingredients such as foie gras, truffles, wild mushrooms, herbs, and the best seasonal vegetables. With his son Mario now at the burners, and his identical triplet daughters taking turns serving tables, Neichel is fully a family operation. His flawless Mediterranean delicacies include *ensalada de gambas de Palamós al sésamo con puerros* (shrimp from Palamós with sesame-seed and leeks) and *espardenyes amb salicornia* (sea cucumbers with saltwort) on sun-dried tomato paste. The dining room is classically elegant with bold red accent walls and contrasting crisp white tablecloths. [$] *Average main: €27* ✉ *Carrer Bertran i Rózpide 1, Pedralbes* ☎ *93/203–8408* 🌐 *www.neichel.es* ✍ *Reservations essential* ⏲ *Closed Sun., Mon., Jan.1–8 and Aug. 1–21* [M] *Maria Cristina.*

WHERE TO STAY

CIUTAT VELLA (OLD CITY)

$$$$ HOTEL Fodor's Choice ★

🏨 **Hotel Neri.** Built into an 18th-century palace over one of the Gothic Quarter's smallest and most charming squares, Plaça Sant Felip Neri, this hotel marries ancient and avant-garde design. **Pros:** central location; hip design; roof terrace for cocktails and breakfast. **Cons:** noise from the echo-chamber square can be a problem on summer nights (and winter-morning school days); impractical hanging bed lights. [$] *Rooms from: €420* ✉ *St. Sever 5, Barri Gòtic* ☎ *93/304–0655* 🌐 *www.hotelneri.com* 🛏 *22 rooms* 🍽 *No meals* [M] *Liceu, Catalunya.*

$ HOTEL Fodor's Choice ★

🏨 **Jardí.** Perched over the traffic-free and charming Plaça del Pi and Plaça Sant Josep Oriol, this charming budget hotel has rooms with views of the Gothic church of Santa Maria del Pi and outfitted with simple pine furniture. **Pros:** central location; good value; impeccable bathrooms. **Cons:** flimsy beds and furnishings; scarce amenities, including no room service. [$] *Rooms from: €90* ✉ *Pl. Sant Josep Oriol 1, Barri Gòtic* ☎ *93/301–5900* 🌐 *www.hoteljardi-barcelona.com* 🛏 *40 rooms* 🍽 *No meals* [M] *Liceu, Catalunya.*

BARCELONETA AND THE PORT OLÍMPIC

$$$$ HOTEL Fodor's Choice ★

🏨 **Hotel Arts.** This luxurious Ritz-Carlton–owned, 44-story skyscraper overlooks Barcelona from the Olympic Port, providing stunning views of the Mediterranean, the city, and the Sagrada Familia, and the mountains behind. **Pros:** excellent views over Barcelona; impeccable service; fine restaurants; general comfort and technology. **Cons:** a 20-minute hike, at least, from central Barcelona. [$] *Rooms from: €325* ✉ *Calle de la Marina 19–21, Port Olímpic* ☎ *93/221–1000* 🌐 *www.hotelartsbarcelona.com* 🛏 *397 rooms, 58 suites, 28 apartments* 🍽 *No meals* [M] *Ciutadella–Vil.la Olímpica.*

$$$$ HOTEL Fodor's Choice ★ 🏨 **W Barcelona.** Opened in 2009, this towering sail-shape monolith is the most dominant and iconic shape on the Barcelona waterfront. **Pros:** unrivaled views and general design excitement and glamour; excellent restaurants; rooms are bright, clean-lined, and have nonpareil views in all directions. **Cons:** the high-rise icon could seem garish to some; a good hike from the Gothic Quarter. [$] *Rooms from: €360* ✉ *Pl. de la Rosa del Vents 1 (Moll de Llevant), Barceloneta* ☎ *93/295–2800* 🌐 *www.starwoodhotels.com* 🛏 *473 rooms, 67 suites* 🍴 *No meals* [M] *Barceloneta.*

EIXAMPLE

$$$ HOTEL Fodor's Choice ★ 🏨 **Claris.** Acclaimed as one of Barcelona's best hotels, the Claris is a mélange of design and tradition, as is evident from the building itself: a late-20th-century glass-and-steel upper annex that seems to have sprouted from the stone and concrete 19th-century town house below. **Pros:** elegant service and furnishings; central location for shopping and moderniste architecture; facilities and technology perfect. **Cons:** on a noisy corner; bathrooms are designer chic but impractical. [$] *Rooms from: €160* ✉ *Carrer Pau Claris 150* ☎ *93/487–6262* 🌐 *www.derbyhotels.com/es/hotel-claris* 🛏 *80 rooms, 40 suites* 🍴 *No meals* [M] *Passeig de Gràcia.*

$$$ HOTEL Fodor's Choice ★ 🏨 **Condes de Barcelona.** One of Barcelona's most popular hotels, the Condes de Barcelona retains a grand charm with a marble-floored pentagonal lobby and the original columns and courtyard dating from the 1891 building. **Pros:** elegant moderniste building with subdued contemporary furnishings; prime spot in the middle of the Eixample. **Cons:** too large for much of a personal touch; staff somewhat overextended; restaurant Lasarte difficult to book. [$] *Rooms from: €180* ✉ *Passeig de Gràcia 73–75* ☎ *93/445–0000* 🌐 *www.condesdebarcelona.com* 🛏 *232 rooms, 3 suites* 🍴 *No meals* [M] *Passeig de Gràcia.*

$$$ HOTEL 🏨 **Hotel Granvía.** A 19th-century town house and moderniste enclave with a hall-of-mirrors breakfast room and an ornate staircase, the Granvia allows you to experience Barcelona's art-nouveau even while you're sleeping. **Pros:** waking up surrounded by Barcelona's famous moderniste design; only a 15-minute walk from the Gothic Quarter. **Cons:** somewhat antiquated; service a little tourist-weary. [$] *Rooms from: €170* ✉ *Gran Via 642* ☎ *93/318–1900* 🌐 *www.nnhotels.es* 🛏 *53 rooms* 🍴 *Breakfast* [M] *Passeig de Gràcia.*

$$ HOTEL Fodor's Choice ★ 🏨 **Hotel Granados 83.** Billed as an NYC loft in Barcelona, this hotel pairs exposed brick, steel, and glass to lend it a downtown cool. **Pros:** quiet semi-pedestrianized street; elegant building with chic "downtown" design; polished service. **Cons:** room prices here vary wildly according to availability and season. [$] *Rooms from: €120* ✉ *Carrer Enric Granados 83* ☎ *93/492–9670* 🌐 *www.derbyhotels.es/hotel-granados-83* 🛏 *70 rooms, 7 suites* 🍴 *No meals* [M] *Provença.*

$$$$ HOTEL Fodor's Choice ★ 🏨 **Hotel Omm.** A team of designers sought to create a playful-but-peaceful hotel, mirroring its name, and the result is this postmodern architectural stunner. **Pros:** a perfect location for the upper Eixample; a design triumph; great nightlife scene around the bar on weekends. **Cons:** slightly pretentious staff; the restaurant, Moo, is pricey and a little pre-

17

cious. $ *Rooms from: €270* ✉ *Roselló 265* ☎ *93/445–4000* ⊕ *www.hotelomm.es* ⇝ *83 rooms, 8 suites* ᴵ◎ᴵ *No meals* Ⓜ *Diagonal, Provença.*

$$$$
HOTEL
Fodor'sChoice
★

⊡ Majestic Hotel & Spa. With an unbeatable location on Barcelona's most stylish boulevard, surrounded by fashion emporiums of every denomination, this hotel is a near-perfect place to stay. **Pros:** perfectly placed in the center of the Eixample; good balance between technology and charm. **Cons:** facing one of the city's widest, brightest, noisiest, most commercial thoroughfares; parking fees are a bit steep. $ *Rooms from: €269* ✉ *Passeig de Gràcia 68* ☎ *93/488–1880* ⊕ *www.hotelmajestic.es* ⇝ *288 rooms, 47 suites* ᴵ◎ᴵ *No meals* Ⓜ *Passeig de Gràcia.*

GRÀCIA

$$$$
HOTEL
Fodor'sChoice
★

⊡ Casa Fuster. This hotel offers one of two chances (the other is the Hotel España) to stay in an art-nouveau building designed by Lluís Domènech i Montaner, architect of the sumptuous Palau de la Música Catalana. **Pros:** well placed for exploring Gràcia as well as the Eixample; equidistant from the port and upper Barcelona's Tibidabo. **Cons:** the design can feel a little heavy and loud; in-room facilities, given the rack rates here, could be better. $ *Rooms from: €365* ✉ *Passeig de Gràcia 132* ☎ *93/255–3000* ⊕ *www.hotelescenter.com/casafuster* ⇝ *67 rooms, 39 suites* ᴵ◎ᴵ *Some meals* Ⓜ *Diagonal.*

NIGHTLIFE AND THE ARTS

Barcelona's art and nightlife scenes start early and never quite stop. To find out what's on, look in newspapers or the weekly *Guía del Ocio,* which has a section in English, and is available at newsstands all over town.

THE ARTS

CLASSICAL MUSIC

Fodor'sChoice
★

Gran Teatre del Liceu. Barcelona's famous opera house on the Rambla, in all its gilt and stained-glass and red plush glory, runs a full season from September through June, combining the Liceu's own chorus and orchestra with first-tier, invited soloists from Roberto Alagna and Rolando Villazón to Nicole Cabell and Anna Netrebko. For most operas in any given season, there are also "popular" performances, with lesser-known but promising singers in the leading roles, at substantially lower prices. In addition, touring dance companies—ballet, flamenco, and modern dance—appear here. The downstairs foyer holds early-evening recitals, puppet shows for children on weekends, and occasional analytical discussions. The Espai Liceu under the opera house includes an excellent café; a gift shop for music-related DVDs, CDs, books, instruments, and knickknacks; and a tiny 50-seat theater projecting fragments of operas and a video of the history of the Liceu. Seats can be expensive and hard to get; reserve well in advance. ✉ *La Rambla 51–59, Rambla* ☎ *93/485–9913* ⊕ *www.liceubarcelona.cat* Ⓜ *Liceu.*

L'Auditori de Barcelona. Minimal, like the inside of a guitar, the Auditori schedules a full program of classical music with occasional jazz or pop concerts near Plaça de les Glòries. Orchestras that perform here include the Orquestra Simfònica de Barcelona i Nacional de Catalunya (OBC) and the Orquestra Nacional de Cambra de Andorra. ✉ *Lepant 150, Eixample* ☎ *93/247–9300* ⊕ *www.auditori.cat* Ⓜ *Marina, Monumental.*

Fodor'sChoice **Palau de la Música Catalana.** Barcelona's most spectacular concert hall is
★ a moderniste masterpiece in the Ciutat Vella, off the Barri Gòtic. Performances run year-round, with 11 am Sunday concerts a popular tradition. The calendar here is packed—everyone from Madredeus to the Buena Vista Social Club has performed here, while the house troupe, the Orfeó Catalá, holds choral concerts several times a year. Tickets range from €6 (for concerts in the small hall) all the way to €190, and are best purchased well in advance. The ticket office is open weekdays 11 am–1 pm and 5 pm–8 pm, Saturday 5 pm–8 pm only. Tours in English of this artnouveau masterpiece (€17) are offered daily, on the hour, from 10 am to 3 pm (to 6 pm April–September). ✉ *Carrer Sant Pere Més Alt 4–6, Urquinaona* ☎ *902/442882* ⊕ *www.palaumusica.cat* Ⓜ *Urquinaona.*

DANCE

El Mercat de les Flors. Near Plaça de Espanya, this theater makes a traditional setting for modern dance as well as theater. ✉ *Lleida 59, Eixample* ☎ *93/426–1875* ⊕ *www.mercatflors.org* Ⓜ *Poble Sec.*

Los Tarantos. This standby spotlights some of Andalusia's best flamenco, and has been staging serious artists in a largely nontouristy environment for the last quarter century. The flamenco shows upstairs give way to disco action downstairs at the Jamboree Dance Club by 1 am or so. ✉ *Pl. Reial 17, Barri Gòtic* ☎ *93/318–3067* Ⓜ *Liceu.*

17

THEATER

Barcelona is known for avant-garde theater and troupes that specialize in mime, large-scale performance art, and special effects (La Fura dels Baus, Els Joglars, Els Comediants). Most plays are performed in Catalan, though some are in Spanish. Teatre Lliure has English subtitles on Wednesday, to make theater accessible for visitors, and other theaters are beginning to follow this lead. Call ahead for details. Several theaters along Avinguda Paral.lel specialize in musicals.

Mercat de les Flors. Near Plaça de Espanya, this is one of the city's most traditional dance and theater venues. ✉ *Lleida 59, Montjuïc* ☎ *93/426–1875* ⊕ *www.mercatflors.org* Ⓜ *Poble Sec.*

Teatre Lliure. Gràcia's branch of the Fundació Teatre Lliure stages theater, dance, and musical events. ✉ *Montseny 47, Gràcia* ☎ *93/218–9251* ⊕ *www.teatrelliure.cat* Ⓜ *Fontana.*

Teatre Nacional de Catalunya. Near Plaça de les Glòries, at the eastern end of the Diagonal, this glass-enclosed classical temple was designed by Ricardo Bofill, architect of Barcelona's airport. Programs cover everything from Shakespeare to ballet to avant-garde theater. ✉ *Carrer l'Art 1, Eixample* ☎ *93/306–5700* ⊕ *www.tnc.cat* Ⓜ *Maragall.*

Teatre Poliorama. Just below Plaça de Catalunya, this famous and traditional theater nearly always has a hot-ticket show. ✉ *Rambla 15, Rambla* ☎ *93/317–7599* Ⓜ *Catalunya.*

NIGHTLIFE
JAZZ AND BLUES
Harlem Jazz Club. Good acts play every Tuesday and Thursday at 10 pm, Friday and Saturday at 11, at this small but exciting music venue a five-minute walk from Plaça Reial. The band Shine holds forth every Tuesday, playin' the blues; catch Sazonando on Saturday night, for Afro-Cuban jazz. ⊠ *Comtessa de Sobradiel 8, Barri Gòtic* ☎ *93/310– 0755* ⊕ *www.harlemjazzclub.es* ⊙ *Mon.–Sat. 8 pm–4 am* Ⓜ *Jaume I, Liceu.*

Jamboree-Jazz and Dance-Club. This pivotal nightspot, another happy fief-dom of the imperial Mas siblings, is a center for jazz, rock, and flamenco in the evening's early stages (11 pm) and turns into a wild and woolly dance club after performances. Jazz greats Joe Smith, Jordi Rossy, Billy McHenry, Gorka Benítez, and Llibert Fortuny all perform here regu-larly, while in Los Tarantos, the upstairs space, some of Barcelona's finest flamenco can be heard. ⊠ *Pl. Reial 17, Rambla* ☎ *93/301–7564* ⊕ *www.connectclub.com* ⊙ *Mon.–Sun. 10:30 pm–5 am* Ⓜ *Liceu.*

Jazz Sí Club. Run by the Barcelona contemporary music school next door, this workshop and (during the day) café is a forum for musicians, teachers, and fans to listen and debate their art. There is jazz on Mon-day; pop, blues, and rock jam sessions on Tuesday; jazzmen jamming on Wednesday; Cuban salsa on Thursday; flamenco on Friday; and rock and pop on weekends. The small cover charge (€4–€9), depending on which night you visit) includes a drink; no cover charge Wednesday. ⊠ *Requesens 2, El Raval* ☎ *93/329–0020* ⊕ *www.tallerdemusics.com* ⊙ *Weekdays 9 pm–11 pm, weekends 7 pm–11 pm* Ⓜ *Sant Antoni.*

BARS
Bar Almirall. The twisted wooden fronds framing the bar's mirror and art-nouveau touches from curvy door handles to organic-shape table lamps to floral chair design make this one of the prettiest bars in Bar-celona, and also the second-oldest, dating from 1860. (The oldest is the Marsella, another Raval favorite.) It's a good spot for drinks after hitting the nearby the MACBA (Museu d'Art Contemporani de Bar-celona). ⊠ *Joaquín Costa 33, El Raval* ☎ *93/318–9917* ⊙ *Mon.–Sun. 7 pm–3 am* Ⓜ *Universitat.*

Bar Pastis. Near the bottom of the Rambla, just above the Santa Mònica art center, this tiny hole-in-the-wall has live performances every day of the week, ranging from Dixieland and swing to rumba and South Amer-ican folk music, with Tuesdays reserved for tango. When performers are not on stage, clients are treated to an encyclopedic tour of every Edith Piaf song ever recorded. There is no cover charge. ⊠ *Santa Mònica 4, Rambla* ☎ *93/318–7980, 634/938–422* ⊕ *www.barpastis.com* ⊙ *Week-days midnight–2:30 am, weekends 7 pm–3 am* Ⓜ *Drassanes.*

Cata 1.81. Wine tasting (*la cata*) in this contemporary design space comes with plenty of friendly advice about enology and some of the world's most exciting new vintages. Small delicacies such as macaroni with sobrasada (spiced pork paté) make this streamlined sliver of a bar a gourmet haven as well. If you come in a group, be sure to reserve the table in the wine cellar in the back. Tapas are a little pricey, at €7 apiece, but well worth it. ⊠ *Valencia 181, Eixample* ☎*93/323–6818* ⊕*www.cata181.com* ⊘ *Mon.–Sat. 5:30 pm–12 am* Ⓜ*Provença.*

FodorśChoice
★

Eclipse Bar. On the 26th floor of the seaside W Hotel, Eclipse is undoubtedly the bar with the best view in all of Barcelona. Owned by a London hospitality group experienced in satisfying a demanding clientele, its slick interior design and roster of international DJs attract scores of beautiful people every day of the week. All this comes with a price tag, of course, but the bar staff will make sure you won't regret it. ⊠*Pl. de la Rosa dels Vents 1* ☎*93/295–2800* ⊕*www.eclipsebars.com.*

L'Ovella Negra. With heavy wooden tables, stone floors, and some cozy nooks and crannies to drink in, this bar is the city's top student tavern, especially for the barely legal. Aromas of brews gone by never completely abandon the air in this cavernous hangout; the raucous crowd is usually a good match for the surroundings. ⊠ *Carrer de les Sitges 5, El Raval* ☎*93/317–1037* ⊕ *www.ovellanegra.com* ⊘ *Weekdays 9 pm–3 am, weekends 5 pm–3 am* Ⓜ*Catalunya.*

London Bar. The trapeze (often in use) suspended above the bar adds even more flair to this art-nouveau circus haunt in the Barrio Chino. Stop in at least for a look, as this is one of the Raval's old standards, which has entertained generations of Barcelona visitors and locals. ⊠*Nou de la Rambla 34, El Raval* ☎*93/318–5261* ⊘ *Weekdays 10 pm–3 am, weekends 6 pm–3:30 am* Ⓜ*Liceu, Drassanes.*

DANCE CLUBS

Bikini Barcelona. This haven for postgraduates offers three ecosystems: Espai BKN with music from the '80s and '90s along with funk, dance-pop, and house; Espai Arutanga with salsa and Latin fusion; and Dry Bikini, which serves cocktails, sandwiches, and, of course, *bikinis* (Spanish for grilled-cheese sandwiches). Bikini opens at midnight; cover charges vary, depending on the night you visit. ⊠*Deu i Mata 105, at Entença, Eixample* ☎*93/322–0800* ⊕*www.bikinibcn.com* ⊘ *Wed.–Sat. midnight–6 am* Ⓜ*Les Corts.*

CDLC. Surely the glitziest of Barcelona's waterfront clubs, the Carpe Diem Lounge Club embraces all the clichés of Ibizan over-the-top decor: replica terra-cotta Chinese warriors, golden Buddhas from who knows where, Moorish filigreed arches, VIP divans compartmentalized off with billowy white drapes. The music is electronic; cocktails are exotic—and pricey. If there are celebrities in town, sooner or later they show up here. ⊠*Passeig Maritim 22, Marina Beach, Port Olímpic* ☎*93/224–0470, 647/779 for VIP services* ⊕*www.cdlcbarcelona.com* ⊘ *Mon.–Sun. 3 pm–3 am* Ⓜ*Ciutadella–Vil.la Olímpica.*

Otto Zutz. Just off Via Augusta, above the Diagonal, this nightclub and disco is a perennial Barcelona favorite that keeps attracting a glitzy mix of Barcelona movers and shakers, models, ex-models, wannabe models, and the hoping-to-get-lucky mob that predictably follows this sort of pulchritude. Music is usually recorded, with occasional live performers. ⊠ *Lincoln 15, Eixample* ☎ *93/238–0722* ⊕*www.ottozutz.com* ⊘ *Wed.–Sat. midnight–6 am* Ⓜ*Sant Gervasi, Plaça Molina.*

Sala Razzmatazz. Razzmatazz stages weeknight concerts featuring international draws from James Taylor to Moriarty. The small-format

17

environment is extraordinarily intimate and beats out sports stadiums or the immense Palau Sant Jordi as a top venue for concerts. It shares its Friday and Saturday club madness with neighboring sister venture the Loft around the corner. ⊠ *Almogavers 122, Poble Nou* ☎ *93/320–8200* ⊕ *www.salarazzmatazz.com* ۞ *Wed.–Thurs. midnight–5 am, Fri.–Sun. 1–6 am* Ⓜ *Marina, Bogatell.*

Shôko. The hottest of the glitzerati spots below the Hotel Arts and the Frank Gehry fish, this is the place to see and be seen in Barcelona these days. The excellent restaurant morphs into a disco around midnight and continues until the wee hours of the morning, with all manner of local and international celebrities perfectly liable to make an appearance at one time or another. ⊠ *Passeig Marítim de la Barceloneta 36, Port Olímpic-Barceloneta* ☎ *93/225–9200* ⊕ *www.shoko.biz* ۞ *Restaurant daily noon–midnight, lounge club daily midnight–3 am* Ⓜ *Ciutadella–Vila Olímpica.*

Up and Down. Locally pronounced "pen-*dow,*" this has been a classic for well-heeled party animals for more than 30 years, and it's still kicking out the jams. The club is so named for its two separate spaces, one downstairs for younger carousers and one upstairs for more mature and accomplished night owls. The FC Barcelona soccer team is apt to let off steam here after great triumphs, while upper-Barcelona's beautiful people make this their downhill base camp for nocturnal pursuits. ⊠ *Av. Doctor Marañón 17, Les Corts–Diagonal* ☎ *93/448–6115* ⊕ *www.upanddownbarcelona.com* ۞ *9 pm–4 am* Ⓜ *Maria Cristina.*

SHOPPING DISTRICTS

Barcelona's prime shopping districts are the Passeig de Gràcia, Rambla de Catalunya, Plaça de Catalunya, Porta de l'Àngel, and Avinguda Diagonal up to Carrer Ganduxer.

For high fashion, browse along **Passeig de Gràcia** and the **Diagonal** between Plaça Joan Carles I and Plaça Francesc Macià. There are two dozen antiques shops in the Gothic Quarter, another 70 shops off Passeig de Gràcia on Bulevard dels Antiquaris, and still more in Gràcia and Sarrià. For old-fashioned Spanish shops, prowl the Gothic Quarter, especially **Carrer Ferran.** The area surrounding **Plaça del Pi,** from the Boqueria to Carrer Portaferrissa and Carrer de la Canuda, is thick with boutiques, jewelry, and design shops. The **Barri de la Ribera,** around Santa Maria del Mar, especially El Born area, has a cluster of design, fashion, and food shops.

On Plaça de Catalunya you can also find the international book and music store **FNAC** and the furniture and household design goods store **Habitat,** also on Carrer Tuset at the Diagonal.

The headquarter of antiques shopping is the Gothic Quarter, where **Carrer de la Palla** and **Carrer Banys Nous** are lined with shops full of prints, maps, books, paintings, and furniture. An antiques market is held in front of the Catedral de la Seau every Thursday from 10 to 8.

CLOTHING BOUTIQUES AND JEWELRY

Adolfo Domínguez. One of Barcelona's longtime fashion giants, this is one of Spain's leading clothes designers, with four locations around town. Famed as the creator of the Iberia Airlines uniforms, Adolfo Domínguez has been in the not-too-radical mainstream and forefront of Spanish clothes design for the last quarter century. ⊠ *Passeig de Gràcia 89, Eixample* ☎ *93/487–4170* ⊕ *www.adolfodominguez.com* Ⓜ *Diagonal.*

Bulevard Rosa. This alleyway off Passeig de Gràcia, as much a social event as a shopping venue, is composed of more than 100 clothing, jewelry, perfume, and footwear shops. Lunch is a major element in the shopping process, and the Fishop restaurant down the stairway under this raging commercial maelstrom is an opportunity to see and be seen and recharge acquisitive batteries. ⊠ *Passeig de Gràcia 53–55, Eixample* ☎ *93/378–9191* Ⓜ *Passeig de Gràcia.*

DEPARTMENT STORES

El Corte Inglés. Otherwise known as ECI, this iconic and ubiquitous Spanish department store has its main Barcelona branch on Plaça Catalunya, with an annex 100 yards away in Porta de l'Àngel. Shopping at Spain's most powerful and comprehensive clothing and general goods emporium (its name means "The English Cut") can be a lesson in how not to provide good customer service, but you can find just about anything you're looking for. The encyclopedic range of quality items here can save you hours of questing around town. ⊠ *Pl. de Catalunya 14, Eixample* ☎ *93/306–3800* Ⓜ *Catalunya* ⊠ *Portal de l'Àngel 19–21, Barri Gòtic* ☎ *93/306–3800* Ⓜ *Catalunya* ⊠ *Pl. Francesc Macià, Av. Diagonal 471, Eixample* ☎ *93/419–2020* Ⓜ *La Bonanova* ⊠ *Av. Diagonal 617, Diagonal/Les Corts* ☎ *93/419–2828* Ⓜ *Maria Cristina.*

FOOD AND FLEA MARKETS

Boqueria. The oldest of its kind in Europe, Barcelona's most colorful and bustling food market appears here on the Rambla between Carrer del Carme and Carrer de Hospital. Open Monday through Saturday until 8:30 pm, it's most active before 2 pm, though many of the stalls remain open all day. Standout stalls include Petràs, the wild mushroom guru in the back of the market on Plaça de la Gardunya, and Juanito Bayen of the world-famous collection of bar stools known as Pinotxo. ⊠ *Rambla 91, Rambla* ☎ *93/318–2017* ⊕ *www.boqueria.info* Ⓜ *Liceu, Catalunya.*

Els Encants. Barcelona's biggest flea market, an event with distinctly Bohemian allure, spreads out at the end of Carrer Dos de Maig. The center of the circular Plaça de les Glòries Catalanes also fills with ill-gotten goods of all kinds. Keep close track of your wallet or you might come across it as an empty item for sale. ⊠ *Dos de Maig 177, Eixample* ☎ *93/246–3030* ⊙ *Mon., Wed., Fri., and Sat. 9–5* Ⓜ *Glòries.*

Mercat Gòtic. A browser's bonanza, this market for antique books and art objects occupies the plaza in front of the cathedral, on Thursdays. ⊠ *Pl. de la Seu s/n, Barri Gòtic* ⊕ *www.mercatgotic.com* Ⓜ *Jaume I, Urquinaona.*

17

GIFTS AND MISCELLANY

Fodor'sChoice **La Manual Alpargatera.** If you appreciate old-school craftsmanship in
★   footwear, visit this boutique just off Carrer Ferran. Handmade rope-sole
sandals and espadrilles are the specialty, and this shop has sold them to
everyone—including the Pope. The beribboned espadrilles model used
for dancing the sardana is also available, but these artisans are capable
of making any kind of creation you can think of. ✉ *Avinyó 7, Barri
Gòtic* ☎ *93/301–0172* ⊕ *www.lamanual.net* ⊙ *Mon.–Sat. 9:30–1:30
and 4:30–8* Ⓜ *Liceu, Jaume I.*

ANDALUSIA

Andalusia—for 781 years (711–1492) a Moorish empire and named for
Al-Andalus (Arabic for "Land of the West")—is where the authentic
history and character of the Iberian Peninsula and Spanish culture are
most palpably, visibly, audibly, and aromatically apparent.

Though church- and Franco regime–influenced historians endeavor to
sell a sanitized, Christians-versus-infidels portrayal of Spanish history,
what most distinctively imprinted and defined Spanish culture—and
most singularly marked the art, architecture, language, thought, and
even the cooking and dining customs of most of the Iberian Peninsula—
was the almost eight-century reign of the Arabic-speaking peoples who
have become known collectively as the Moors.

All the romantic images of Andalusia, and Spain in general, spring vividly to life in Seville. Spain's fourth-largest city is a cliché of matadors,
flamenco, tapas bars, gypsies, geraniums, and strolling guitarists. So
tantalizing is this city that many travelers spend their entire Andalusian
time here. It's a good start, for an exploration of Andalusia must begin
with the cities of Seville, Córdoba, and Granada as the fundamental
triangle of interest and identity. The smaller cities of Cádiz—the Western world's oldest metropolis, founded by Phoenicians more than 3,000
years ago—and Jerez, with its sherry cellars and purebred horses, have
much to recommend themselves as well.

PLANNING YOUR TIME

A week in Andalusia should include visits to Córdoba, Seville, and
Granada to see, respectively, the Mezquita, the Cathedral and its
Giralda, and the Alhambra. Two days in each city nearly fills the week,
though the extra day would be best spent in Seville, by far Andalusia's
most vibrant concentration of art, architecture, culture, and excitement.

A week or more in Seville alone would be well spent, especially during
the Semana Santa celebration when the city, though crowded, becomes
a giant street party. With more time on your hands, Cádiz and Jerez de
la Frontera form a three- or four-day jaunt through flamenco, sherry,
Andalusian equestrian culture, and tapas emporiums.

GETTING HERE AND AROUND
AIR TRAVEL

Andalusia's regional airports can be reached via Spain's domestic flights
or from major European hubs. Málaga Airport is one of Spain's major
hubs and a good access point for exploring this part of Andalusia. The

region's second-largest airport, after Málaga, is in Seville. The smaller Aeropuerto de Jerez is 7 km (4 miles) northeast of Jerez on the road to Seville. Buses run from the airport to Jerez and Cádiz. Flying into Granada's airport is also a good option if you want to start your trip in Andalusia. It's easy to get into Granada from the airport.

Contacts Aeropuerto de Granada (*Aeropurto Federico García Lorca*). ☎ *958/245200.*

BUS TRAVEL

The best way to get around Andalusia, if you're not driving, is by bus. Buses serve most small towns and villages and are faster and more frequent than trains. Alsa is the major bus company; tickets can be booked online.

Contacts Alsa ☎ *902/422242* ⊕ *www.alsa.es.*

CAR TRAVEL

If you're planning to exploring beyond Seville, a car makes travel convenient. Driving in western Andalusia is easy—the terrain is mostly flat land or slightly hilly, and the roads are straight and in good condition. With the exception of parts of the Alpujarras, most roads in this region are smooth, and touring by car is one of the most enjoyable ways to see the countryside.

TRAIN TRAVEL

From Madrid, the best approach to Andalusia is via the high-speed railroad connection, the AVE. In under three hours, the spectacular ride winds from Madrid's Atocha Station through the olive groves and rolling fields of the Castilian countryside to Córdoba and on to Seville. Another option, especially if you plan to go outside Seville, Granada, and Córdoba, is to travel by car. The main road south from Madrid is the A4/E5.

17

SEVILLE

550 km (340 miles) southwest of Madrid.

Seville's whitewashed houses bright with bougainvillea, its ocher-colored palaces, and its baroque facades have long enchanted both *sevillanos* and travelers. Lord Byron's well-known line, "Seville is a pleasant city famous for oranges and women," may be true, but is far too tame. Yes, the orange trees are pretty enough, but the fruit is too bitter to eat except as Scottish-made marmalade. As for the women, stroll down the swankier pedestrian shopping streets and you can't fail to notice just how good-looking *everyone* is. Aside from being blessed with even features and flashing dark eyes, sevillanos exude a cool sophistication of style about them that seems more Catalan than Andalusian.

EXPLORING

Fodor's Choice ★ **Alcázar.** The Plaza del Triunfo forms the entrance to the Mudejar palace built by Pedro I (1350–69) on the site of Seville's former Moorish *alcázar* (fortress). Don't mistake the Alcázar for a genuine Moorish palace like Granada's Alhambra—it may look like one, and it was designed and built by Moorish workers brought in from Granada, but it was

Alcázar **6**

Casa de Pilatos ..**3**

Cathedral **4**

Convento de
Santa Paula **2**

Jewish Quarter ..**5**

Museo de
Bellas Artes **1**

Parque de
María Luisa **7**

CENTRO

BARRIO DE
LA MACARENA **2**

TO
EL CORTE
INGLES

J. Rabadán

Torneo

Castellar

C. Santa
Paula

C. Baños

C. de Santa Clara

C. de Trajano

Cervantes

Gerona

Tavera

C. Sol

Gotes

C. San Vicente

Teodosio Jesús

Jesús del Gran Poder

C. de Dios

Amor de Dios

Pl.
Gavidia

Pl.
Encarnación

Santiago

Centro Comercial
Plaza
de Armas

Calle de Alfonso XII

Pl.
Duque

Larañа

Pl. Cristo
de Burgos

TO
ESTACIÓN
SANTA JUSTA

1

Gravina

Bailén

San Eloy

Teluán

Pl. del
Salvador

P. Galdós

3

Marqués de Paradas

Canalejas

CENTRO

Pl.
Pilatos

Arjona

Tastámara

C. de San Pablo

Pl.
Nueva

Pl. de
S. Francisco

Conde de Ibarra

Reyes
Católicos

Pastor y Landero

C. de Zaragoza

Avda. de la Constitución

Mateos Gago

5

BARRIO
DE SANTA
CRUZ

Pte. de
Isabel II

Adriano

Paseo de Colón

Vinuesa

Pl. Virgen
de los Reyes

4

Pl.
Alianza

Pl. Santa
Cruz

Avda. Menéndez Pelayo

Dos
de Mayo

Santo
tomás

Pl. de los
Venerables

6

Agua

Guadalquivir

TRIANA

Calle Betis

C. Rodrigo de Triana

EL ARENAL

Almirante
Lobo

P. de
Jerez

C. San Fernando

Estación de
Autobuses

Pagés del Corro

Pte.
de
San
Telmo

Avda. de Roma

Palos de
la Frontera

Pl. D. Juan
de Austria

Avda. de
Carlos V

Avda. Portugal

Pl. de
Cuba

Sebastián

Paseo de las Delicias

Gta. San
Diego

Avda. República Argentina

Asunción

Elcano

Teatro Lope
de Vega

Avda. María Luisa

Pl. de
España

Avda. Isabel la Católica

Gta.
de los
Marineros
Voluntarios

Parque de
María
Luisa

Gta.
Covadonga

Pte. del
Generalísimo

7

Avda. Don Pelayo

Feria
de Abril

Seville

0   1/4 mile

0   400 meters

KEY

i Tourist
Information

commissioned and paid for by a Christian king more than 100 years after the reconquest of Seville. The palace is the official residence of the king and queen when they're in town.

Entering the Alcázar through the Puerta del León (Lion's Gate) and the high, fortified walls, you'll first find yourself in a garden courtyard, the **Patio del León** (Courtyard of the Lion). Off to the left are the oldest parts of the building, the 14th-century **Sala de Justicia** (Hall of Justice) and, next to it, the intimate **Patio del Yeso** (Courtyard of Plaster), the only part of the original 12th-century Almohad Alcázar. Cross the **Patio de la Montería** (Courtyard of the Hunt) to Pedro's Mudejar palace, arranged around the beautiful **Patio de las Doncellas** (Court of the Damsels), resplendent with delicately carved stucco. Opening off this patio, the **Salón de Embajadores** (Hall of the Ambassadors), with its cedar cupola of green, red, and gold, is the most sumptuous hall in the palace.

In the **gardens,** inhale the fragrances of jasmine and myrtle, wander among terraces and baths, and peer into the well-stocked goldfish pond. From here, a passageway leads to the **Patio de las Banderas** (Court of the Flags), which has a classic view of the Giralda. ⊠ *Pl. del Triunfo, Santa Cruz* ☎ *954/502323* ⊕ *www.alcazarsevilla.org* ⊡ *€8.75* ⊗ *Apr.– Sept., daily 9:30–7; Oct.–Mar., daily 9:30–5.*

Fodor's Choice **Casa de Pilatos.** This palace was built in the first half of the 16th cen-
★ tury by the dukes of Tarifa, ancestors of the present owner, the Duke of Medinaceli. It's known as Pilate's House because Don Fadrique, first marquis of Tarifa, allegedly modeled it on Pontius Pilate's house in Jerusalem, where he had gone on a pilgrimage in 1518. With its fine patio and superb azulejo decorations, the palace is a beautiful blend of Spanish Mudejar and Renaissance architecture; it's considered a prototype of an Andalusian mansion. The upstairs apartments, which you can see on a guided tour, have frescoes, paintings, and antique furniture. Admission prices include an audio guide in English. ⊠ *Pl. de Pilatos 1, Barrio de Santa Cruz* ☎ *954/225298* ⊡ *€6 1st floor only, €8 both floors* ⊗ *Daily 9–6.*

Fodor's Choice **Cathedral.** Seville's cathedral can be described only in superlatives: it's
★ the largest and highest cathedral in Spain, the largest Gothic building in the world, and the world's third-largest church, after St. Peter's in Rome and St. Paul's in London. After Ferdinand III captured Seville from the Moors in 1248, the great mosque begun by Yusuf II in 1171 was reconsecrated to the Virgin Mary and used as a Christian cathedral. In 1401 the people of Seville decided to erect a new cathedral, one that would equal the glory of their great city. They pulled down the old mosque, leaving only its minaret and outer courtyard, and built the existing building in just over a century—a remarkable feat for the time.

The cathedral's dimly illuminated interior, aside from the well-lighted high altar, can be disappointing: Gothic purity has been largely submerged in ornate baroque decoration. In the central nave rises the **Capilla Mayor** (Main Chapel). Its magnificent *retablo* (altarpiece) is the largest in Christendom (65 feet by 43 feet). It depicts some 36 scenes from the life of Christ, with pillars carved with more than 200 figures. Restoration of the altarpiece is set to start in March 2014 and will continue until the fall.

17

The Christians could not bring themselves to destroy the tower when they tore down the mosque, so they incorporated it into their new cathedral. In 1565–68 they added a lantern and belfry to the old minaret and installed 24 bells, one for each of Seville's 24 parishes and the 24 Christian knights who fought with Ferdinand III in the reconquest. They also added the bronze statue of Faith, which turned as a weather vane—*el giraldillo,* or "something that turns," thus the whole tower became known as the **Giralda.** With its baroque additions, the slender Giralda rises 322 feet. Inside, instead of steps, 35 sloping ramps—wide enough for two horsemen to pass abreast—climb to a viewing platform 230 feet up. Admission also includes the visit to the Iglesia del Salvador. ⊠ *Pl. Virgen de los Reyes, Centro* ☎ *954/214971* 🖃 *Cathedral and Giralda €8* ⊙ *Mon.–Sat. 11:30–5:30, Sun. 2:30–6.*

Fodor'sChoice
★
Convento de Santa Paula. This 15th-century Gothic convent has a fine facade and portico, with ceramic decoration by Nicolaso Pisano. The chapel has some beautiful azulejos and sculptures by Martínez Montañés. It also contains a small museum and a shop selling delicious cakes and jams made by the nuns. ⊠ *C. Santa Paula 11, La Macarena* ☎ *954/536330* 🖃 *€3* ⊙ *Tues.–Sun. 10–1.*

Fodor'sChoice
★
Jewish Quarter. The twisting alleyways and traditional whitewashed houses add to the tourist charm of this *barrio.* On some streets, bars alternate with antiques and souvenir shops, but most of the quarter is quiet and residential. On the Plaza Alianza, pause to enjoy the antiques shops and outdoor cafés. In the Plaza de Doña Elvira, with its fountain and azulejo benches, young sevillanos gather to play guitars. Just around the corner from the hospital, at Callejón del Agua and Jope de Rueda, Gioacchino Rossini's Figaro serenaded Rosina on her Plaza Alfaro balcony. Adjoining the Plaza Alfaro, in the Plaza Santa Cruz, flowers and orange trees surround a 17th-century filigree iron cross, which marks the site of the erstwhile church of Santa Cruz, destroyed by Napoléon's General Jean-de-Dieu Soult.

Fodor'sChoice
★
Museo de Bellas Artes (*Museum of Fine Arts*). This museum is second only to Madrid's Prado for Spanish art. It's in the former convent of La Merced Calzada, most of which dates from the 17th century. The collection includes works by Murillo and the 17th-century Seville school, as well as by Zurbarán, Diego Velázquez, Alonso Cano, Valdés Leal, and El Greco; outstanding examples of Sevillian Gothic art; and baroque religious sculptures in wood (a quintessentially Andalusian art form). In the rooms dedicated to Sevillian art of the 19th and 20th centuries, look for Gonzalo Bilbao's *Las Cigarreras,* a group portrait of Seville's famous cigar makers. ⊠ *Pl. del Museo 9, El Arenal/Porvenir* ☎ *954/786491* ⊕ *www.museosdeandalucia.es* 🖃 *€1.50* ⊙ *Tues.–Sat. 10–8:30, Sun. 10–5:30.*

Fodor'sChoice
★
Parque de María Luisa. Formerly the garden of the Palacio de San Telmo, this park blends formal design and wild vegetation. In the burst of development that gripped Seville in the 1920s, it was redesigned for the 1929 World's Fair, and the impressive villas you see now are the fair's remaining pavilions, many of them consulates or schools; the old Casino holds the Teatro Lope de Vega, which puts on mainly musicals.

Note the Anna Huntington **statue of El Cid** (Rodrigo Díaz de Vivar, 1043–99), who fought both for and against the Muslim rulers during the Reconquest. The statue was presented to Seville by the Massachusetts-born sculptor for the 1929 World's Fair. ✉ *Main entrance: Glorieta San Diego, El Arenal.*

WHERE TO EAT

$$$ SPANISH Fodor's Choice ★ 🍴 **Becerrita.** The affable Jesús Becerra runs this cozy establishment, where several small dining rooms are decorated with traditional columns, tiles, and colorful paintings of Seville by local artists. Diligent service and tasty modern treatments of such classic Spanish dishes as *bacalao gratinado con Idiazábal sobre una salsa de piquillos* (Basque-cheese grilled cod on pepper sauce) and *lágrima de buey Wagyu con boletus* (slow-stewed Wagyu beef served with funghi) have won the favor of sevillanos, as have the signature oxtail croquettes. Smaller appetites can try such tasty tapas as stuffed calamari and garlic-spiked prawns. The restaurant has parking for clients. [$] *Average main: €22* ✉ *C. Recaredo 9, Santa Cruz/Santa Catalina* ☎ *954/412057* 🌐 *www.becerrita.com* ✍ *Reservations essential* ⏲ *No dinner Sun.*

$$$ SPANISH Fodor's Choice ★ 🍴 **Enrique Becerra.** Excellent tapas (€3.50—try the lamb kebab with dates and couscous), a lively bar, and an extensive wine list await at this restaurant run by the fifth generation of a family of celebrated restaurateurs (Enrique's brother Jesús owns Becerrita). The menu focuses on traditional, home-cooked Andalusian dishes, such as *pez espada al amontillado* (swordfish cooked in dark sherry) and *cordero a la miel con espinacas y piñones* (honey-glazed lamb stuffed with spinach and pine nuts). Don't miss the fried eggplant stuffed with prawns. If you want a quiet meal, call to reserve a table in one of the small upstairs rooms. [$] *Average main: €21* ✉ *C. Gamazo 2, El Arenal* ☎ *954/213049* ⏲ *Closed Sun. and Aug.*

$ TAPAS Fodor's Choice ★ 🍴 **Eslava Bar de Tapas.** The crowds gathered outside this local favorite off the Alameda de Hercules may be off-putting at first, but the creative, inexpensive tapas (from €2.50) are well worth the wait. Try delicacies like the *solomillo al eneldo* or *con cabrales* (sirloin with fennel or Cabrales cheese) or *montaditos* (basically an open-face sandwich) like the *huevo sobre bizcocho boletus y vino caramelizado* (egg on mushroom pie with caramelized wine). The house specialty, however, is the Basque dessert, Sokoa, so be sure to leave some room. Tables at the tapas bar can't be booked (a call will get you a reservation at the next-door Eslava restaurant), so arrive early to avoid a wait. [$] *Average main: €12* ✉ *C. Eslava 3, La Alameda* ☎ *954/906568* ✍ *Reservations not accepted* ⏲ *Closed Mon. No dinner Sun.*

$$$$ SPANISH 🍴 **Taberna de Alabardero.** In a magnificent manor house with a stunning patio, this restaurant's upstairs dining rooms are set around a central arcade, with tables arranged under the tinkling crystal of chandeliers. Exquisite paintings and a pale green and yellow color scheme add to the charm. The cuisine is innovative and sophisticated, with dishes like crab pancake in white wine, and roasted duck breast with mandarins and asparagus. The ground-level bistro offers a good-value lunchtime menú del día. [$] *Average main: €23* ✉ *C. Zaragoza 20, Arenal* ☎ *954/502721* ⏲ *Closed Aug.*

17

$ ✕ **Vineria San Telmo.** Whether you eat in the dimly lit dining room or on
SPANISH   the street-level terrace, prepare to spend some time perusing a menu that
Fodor'sChoice   is full of surprises. All dishes are superb and sophisticated, especially the
★   foie gras with apple, the Iberian pork with curried pumpkin and rocket,
and the oxtail in filo pastry. Dishes come as tapas, half portions, or full
portions—ideal for sharing—and the Argentinean-owned restaurant's
vast glass-fronted wine cellar includes an extensive choice of Spanish
vinos. It's near the touristy Alcazar and its popularity sometimes works
to its detriment—it can get very crowded and noisy at times, when it
would not be the ideal place for a romantic meal for two. $ *Average
main: €12* ⊠ *Paseo Catalina de Ribera 4, Santa Cruz* ☎ *954/410600.*

WHERE TO STAY

$$$$ ▦ **Casa Número 7.** Dating from 1850, this converted town house retains
B&B/INN   an elegant but lived-in feel, with family photographs, original oil paint-
Fodor'sChoice   ings, and plush furnishings throughout. **Pros:** the personal touch of a
★   B&B; delightfully different; great location. **Cons:** on the pricey side.
$ *Rooms from: €275* ⊠ *C. Virgenes 7, Santa Cruz* ☎ *954/221581*
⊕ *www.casanumero7.com* ⤴ *6 rooms* ⦿| *Breakfast.*

$$$$ ▦ **Hotel Alfonso XIII.** Inaugurated by King Alfonso XIII in 1929 and
HOTEL   restored in 2011, this grand hotel is a splendid, historic, Mudejar-style
Fodor'sChoice   palace, built around a central patio and surrounded by ornate brick
★   arches. **Pros:** both stately and hip; impeccable service. **Cons:** a tour-
ist colony; expensive. $ *Rooms from: €390* ⊠ *C. San Fernando 2, El
Arenal* ☎ *954/917000* ⊕ *www.luxurycollection.com/alfonsoxiii* ⤴ *132
rooms, 19 suites* ⦿| *Multiple meal plans.*

$$ ▦ **Hotel Amadeus La Música de Sevilla.** With pianos in some of the sound-
HOTEL   proof rooms, other instruments for guests to use, a music room off
Fodor'sChoice   the central patio, and regular classical concerts, this acoustic oasis is
★   ideal for touring professional musicians and music fans in general.
Pros: small but charming rooms; roof terrace. **Cons:** certain rooms
are noisy and lack privacy; ground-floor rooms can be dark. $ *Rooms
from: €112* ⊠ *C. Farnesio 6, Santa Cruz* ☎ *954/501443* ⊕ *www.
hotelamadeussevilla.com* ⤴ *30 rooms* ⦿| *No meals.*

$$$ ▦ **Hotel Casa 1800.** This classy boutique hotel, in a refurbished 19th-
B&B/INN   century mansion, is an oasis in bustling Santa Cruz. **Pros:** top-notch
Fodor'sChoice   amenities; great service. **Cons:** the rooms facing the patio can be noisy;
★   no restaurant; prices skyrocket for a three-week period around Easter.
$ *Rooms from: €150* ⊠ *C. Rodrigo Caro 6, Santa Cruz* ☎ *954/561800*
⊕ *www.hotelcasa1800sevilla.com* ⤴ *23 rooms, 1 suite* ⦿| *No meals.*

NIGHTLIFE AND THE ARTS

BULLFIGHTING

Bullfighting season is Easter through Columbus Day; most *corridas*
(bullfights) are held on Sunday. The highlight is the April Fair, with
Spain's leading *toreros*; other key dates are Corpus Christi (date varies;
about seven weeks after Easter), Assumption (August 15), and the last
weekend in September.

Plaza de Toros Real Maestranza (*Royal Maestranza Bullring*). Sevillanos
have spent many a thrilling evening in this bullring, built between 1760
and 1763. Painted a deep ocher, the stadium is the one of the oldest and

loveliest *plazas de toros* in Spain. The 20-minute tour (in English) takes in the empty arena, a museum with elaborate costumes and prints, and the chapel where matadors pray before the fight. Bullfights take place in the evening Thursday through Sunday from April through July and in September. Tickets can be booked online or by phone. ✉ *Paseo de Colón 12, El Arenal* ☎ *954/210315 for visits, 954/501382 for bullfights* ⊕ *www. realmaestranza.es* ☑ *€6.50* ⊘ *Tours daily 9–7; on bullfight days call ahead.*

FLAMENCO
Seville has a handful of commercial *tablaos* (flamenco clubs), patronized more by tourists than locals. Spontaneous flamenco is often found for free in *peñas flamencas* (flamenco clubs) and flamenco bars in Triana.

Casa Anselma. In the heart of Triana, this is an unmarked bar on the corner of Antillano Campos where Anselma and her friends sing and dance for the pure joy and catharsis that are at the heart of flamenco. ✉ *C. Pagés del Corro 49, Triana* ☑ *Free* ⊘ *Shows Mon.–Sat. at 11.*

Fodor'sChoice ★ **Casa de la Memoria de Al-Andalus.** This club set in an 18th-century palace has a nightly show plus classes for the intrepid. It's a small venue so book to be sure of a seat. ✉ *Calle Cuna 6, Santa Cruz* ☎ *954/560670* ⊕ *www.casadelamemoria.es* ☑ *€16* ⊘ *Shows nightly at 7:30 and 9.*

La Carbonería. This rambling former coal yard is usually packed since the flamenco is spontaneous. There's no entry charge. ✉ *C. Levíes 18, Santa Cruz* ☎ *954/214460.*

Los Gallos. This intimate club in the heart of Santa Cruz attracts mainly tourists. Performances are entertaining and reasonably authentic. ✉ *Pl. Santa Cruz 11, Santa Cruz* ☎ *954/216981* ⊕ *www.tablaolosgallos.com* ☑ *€35, includes one drink* ⊘ *Shows nightly at 8:15 and 10:30.*

CLASSICAL MUSIC AND OPERA
Teatro de la Maestranza. Long prominent in the opera world, Seville is proud of its opera house. Tickets go quickly, so book (online is best) well in advance. ✉ *Paseo de Colón 22, El Arenal* ☎ *954/223344 for info, 954/226573 for tickets* ⊕ *www.teatrodelamaestranza.es.*

Teatro Lope de Vega. Classical music, ballet, and musicals are performed here. ✉ *Av. María Luisa s/n, Parque de María Luisa* ☎ *954/472828 for info, 955/472822 for tickets* ⊕ *www.teatrolopedevega.org.*

Teatro Central. This modern venue stages theater, dance, and classical and contemporary music. Tickets can be bought via ⊕ *www.ticketmaster. es* or at Caixa ATMs. ✉ *C. José de Gálvez 6, Isla de la Cartuja* ☎ *955/ 037200 for info, 902/150025 for tickets.*

17

JEREZ DE LA FRONTERA

97 km (60 miles) south of Seville.

Jerez, world headquarters for sherry, is surrounded by vineyards of chalky soil, whose palomino grapes have funded a host of churches and noble mansions. Names such as González Byass, Domecq, Harvey, and Sandeman are inextricably linked with Jerez. The word "sherry," first used in Great Britain in 1608, is an English corruption of the town's old Moorish name, Xeres. Both sherry and horses are the domain of

Jerez's Anglo-Spanish aristocracy, whose Catholic ancestors came here from England centuries ago.

EXPLORING

Alcázar. Once the residence of the caliph of Seville, the 12th-century Alcázar and its small, octagonal **mosque** and **baths** were built for the Moorish governor's private use. The baths have three sections: the *sala fria* (cold room), the larger *sala templada* (warm room), and the *sala caliente* (hot room) for steam baths. In the midst of it all is the 17th-century **Palacio de Villavicencio**, built on the site of the original Moorish palace. A camera obscura, a lens-and-mirrors device that projects the outdoors onto a large indoor screen, offers a 360-degree view of Jerez. ⊠ *C. Alameda Vieja* ☎ *956/149955* ⊠ *€5 (€7 including camera obscura)* ⊙ *July–mid-Sept., weekdays 9:30–8, weekends 9:30–3; Mar.–June and mid-Sept.–Oct., weekdays 9:30–6, weekends 9:30–3; Nov.–Feb., daily 9:30–3.*

Catedral de Jerez. Across from the Alcázar and around the corner from the González Byass winery, the cathedral has an octagonal cupola and a separate bell tower, as well as Zurbarán's canvas *La Virgen Niña* (The Virgin as a Young Girl). ⊠ *Pl. de la Encarnación* ☎ *956/169059* ⊠ *€5* ⊙ *Mon.–Sat. 10–6:30.*

Museo Arqueológico. Diving into the maze of streets that form the scruffy San Mateo neighborhood east of the town center, you come to one of Andalusia's best archaeological museums, which reopened in 2012 after extensive restoration. The collection is strongest on the pre-Roman period and the star item, found near Jerez, is a Greek helmet dating from the 7th century BC. ⊠ *Pl. del Mercado s/n* ☎ *956/149561* ⊠ *€5* ⊙ *Tues.–Fri. 10–2 and 4–7, weekends 10–2.*

FAMILY **Real Escuela Andaluza del Arte Ecuestre** (*Royal Andalusian School of*
Fodor'sChoice *Equestrian Art*). This prestigious school operates on the grounds of
★ the Recreo de las Cadenas, a 19th-century palace. The school was masterminded by Alvaro Domecq in the 1970s, and every Thursday (and at various other times throughout the year) the Cartujana horses—a cross between the native Andalusian workhorse and the Arabian—and skilled riders in 18th-century riding costume demonstrate intricate dressage techniques and jumping in the spectacular show "Cómo Bailan los Caballos Andaluces" (roughly, "The Dancing Horses of Andalusia"). Reservations are essential. Admission price depends on how close to the arena you sit; the first two rows are the priciest. At certain other times you can visit the stables and tack room, and watch the horses being schooled. ⊠ *Av. Duque de Abrantes* ☎ *956/319635 for info* ⊕ *www.realescuela.org* ⊠ *Shows €21–€27, stables tour and training sessions €11* ⊙ *Times for shows, tours, and training sessions vary throughout the year; check website for up-to-date details.*

WHERE TO EAT

$$ ✕ **Sabores.** The walled garden at this eatery, widely regarded as the best
SPANISH restaurant in town, is a cool spot on a warm night. The staff's enthu-
Fodor'sChoice siasm and culinary knowledge will help guide your choice. Consider
★ kick-starting your meal with the creative tapas, such as mushroom and pistachio croquettes, and octopus roasted in beer with black rice.

Innovative main dishes include fish of the day with a red bean purée, carrots and curry, and duck breast with pesto noodles. $ *Average main:* *€16* ✉ *Chancilleria Hotel, C. Chancilleria 21* ☎ *956/329835* ◬ *Reservations essential* ۩ *No lunch Mon.*

WHERE TO STAY

$
B&B/INN
Fodor's Choice
★

⌂ **Hotel Palacio Garvey.** Dating from 1850, this luxurious boutique hotel was once the home of the prestigious Garvey family, and the original neoclassical architecture and interior decoration has been exquisitely restored. **Pros:** in the center of town; fashionable and contemporary feel. **Cons:** breakfast offers few choices; inadequate parking. $ *Rooms from: €85* ✉ *C. Tornería 24* ☎ *956/326700* ⊕ *www.sferahoteles.com* ⊷ *7 rooms, 9 suites* ⎮⎮ *Breakfast.*

CÁDIZ

32 km (20 miles) southwest of Jerez, 149 km (93 miles) southwest of Seville.

Fodor's Choice
★

Surrounded by the Atlantic Ocean on three sides, Cádiz was founded as Gadir by Phoenician traders in 1100 BC and claims to be the oldest continuously inhabited city in the Western world. Hannibal lived in Cádiz for a time, Julius Caesar first held public office here, and Columbus set out from here on his second voyage, after which the city became the home base of the Spanish fleet. In the 18th century, when the Guadalquivir silted up, Cádiz monopolized New World trade and became the wealthiest port in Western Europe. Most of its buildings—including the cathedral, built in part with gold and silver from the New World—date from this period.

EXPLORING

Museo de Cádiz (*Provincial Museum*). On the east side of the Plaza de Mina is Cadiz's provincial museum. Notable pieces include works by Murillo and Alonso Cano as well as the *Four Evangelists* and a set of saints by Zurbarán. The archaeological section contains Phoenician sarcophagi from the time of this ancient city's birth. ✉ *Pl. de Mina* ☎ *956/203368* ▣ *€1.50* ۩ *Tues. 2:30–8:30, Wed.–Sat. 9–8:30, Sun. 9–2:30.*

FAMILY
Fodor's Choice
★

Torre Tavira. At 150 feet, this is the highest point in the old city. More than a hundred such watchtowers were used by Cádiz ship owners to spot their arriving fleets. A camera obscura gives a good overview of the city and its monuments; the last show is a half hour before closing time. ✉ *C. Marqués del Real Tesoro 10* ☎ *956/212910* ▣ *€5* ۩ *Mid-Sept.–mid-June, daily 10–6; mid-June–mid-Sept., daily 1–8.*

Cádiz Cathedral. Five blocks southeast of the Torre Tavira are the gold dome and baroque facade of Cádiz's cathedral, begun in 1722, when the city was at the height of its power. The Cádiz-born composer Manuel de Falla, who died in 1946 at the age of 70, is buried in the **crypt**. The cathedral **museum,** on Calle Acero, displays gold, silver, and jewels from the New World, as well as Enrique de Arfe's processional cross, which is carried in the annual Corpus Christi parades. The cathedral is known as the New Cathedral because it supplanted the original 13th-century structure next door, which was destroyed by the British in

17

1592, rebuilt, and rechristened the church of **Santa Cruz** when the New Cathedral came along. ✉ *Pl. Catedral* ☎ *956/286154* 🎟 *€5, includes crypt, museum, and church of Santa Cruz* ⏲ *Museum, crypt, and Santa Cruz Mon.–Sat. 10–6:30, Sun. 11:30–12:30 and 1–6; Cathedral Mass Sun. at noon.*

WHERE TO EAT

$$$ SPANISH 🍴 **El Faro.** This famous fishing-quarter restaurant near Playa de la Caleta is deservedly known as one of the best in the province. From the outside, it's one of many whitewashed houses with ocher details and shiny black lanterns; inside, it's warm and inviting, with half-tile walls, glass lanterns, oil paintings, and photos of old Cádiz. Fish dishes dominate the menu, of course, but meat and vegetarian options are always available. If you don't want to go for the full splurge (either gastronomically or financially), there's an excellent tapas bar. [$] *Average main: €19* ✉ *C. San Felix 15* ☎ *956/211068.*

WHERE TO STAY

$$$$ HOTEL 🏨 **Parador de Cádiz.** Totally reformed and reopened in 2013, this parador has a privileged position overlooking the bay. **Pros:** great views of the bay; central location; bright and cheerful. **Cons:** could be too modern for some. [$] *Rooms from: €210* ✉ *Av. Duque de Nájera 9* ☎ *956/226905* 🌐 *www.parador.es* 🛏 *106 rooms, 18 suites* 🍽 *No meals.*

SHOPPING

Traditional Andalusian handicrafts, especially ceramics and wicker, are plentiful in Cádiz.

CÓRDOBA

166 km (103 miles) northwest of Granada, 407 km (250 miles) southwest of Madrid, 239 km (143 miles) northeast of Cádiz, 143 km (86 miles) northeast of Seville.

Strategically located on the north bank of the Guadalquivir River, Córdoba was the Roman and Moorish capital of Spain, and its old quarter, clustered around its famous mezquita), remains one of the country's grandest and yet most intimate examples of its Moorish heritage.

The city's artistic and historical treasures begin with the *mezquita-catedral* (mosque-cathedral), as it is ever-more-frequently called, and continue through the winding, whitewashed streets of the Judería (the medieval Jewish quarter); the jasmine-, geranium-, and orange blossom–filled patios; the Renaissance palaces; and the two-dozen churches, convents, and hermitages built by Moorish artisans directly over former mosques.

EXPLORING

Alcázar de los Reyes Cristianos (*Fortress of the Christian Monarchs*). Built by Alfonso XI in 1328, the Alcázar is a Mudejar-style palace with splendid gardens. (The original Moorish Alcázar stood beside the Mezquita, on the site of the present Bishop's Palace.) This is where, in the 15th century, the Catholic Monarchs held court and launched their conquest of Granada. Boabdil was imprisoned here in 1483, and for nearly 300 years the Alcázar served as the Inquisition's base. The most important sights here are the Hall of the Mosaics and a Roman stone sarcophagus from the 2nd or 3rd century. ⊠ *Pl. Campo Santo de los Mártires, Judería* ☎ *957/420151* ☜ *€4.50* ⏱ *June 15–Sept. 15, Tues.– Sun. 8:30–3:30; Sept. 16–June 14, Tues.–Fri. 8:30 am–8:45 pm, Sat. 8:30–4, Sun. 8:30–2:30.*

Calleja de las Flores. You'd be hard pressed to find prettier patios than those along this tiny street, a few yards off the northeastern corner of the Mezquita. Patios, many with ceramics, foliage, and iron grilles, are key to Córdoba's architecture, at least in the old quarter, where life is lived behind sturdy white walls—a legacy of the Moors, who honored both the sanctity of the home and the need to shut out the fierce summer sun. Córdoba's tourist office publishes an itinerary of the best patios in town (downloadable from ⊕ *www.turismodecordoba.org*)—note that most are open only in the late afternoon on weekdays but all day on weekends.

Fodor's Choice **Madinat Al-Zahra** (*Medina Azahara*). Built in the foothills of the Sierra
★ Morena by Abd ar-Rahman III for his favorite concubine, az-Zahra (the Flower), this once-splendid summer pleasure palace was begun in 936. Historians say it took 10,000 men, 2,600 mules, and 400 camels 25 years to erect this fantasy of 4,300 columns in dazzling pink, green, and white marble and jasper brought from Carthage. A palace, a mosque, luxurious baths, fragrant gardens, fish ponds, an aviary, and a zoo stood on three terraces here, and for around 70 years the Madinat was the de facto capital of al-Andalus, until, in 1013, it was sacked and destroyed by Berber mercenaries. In 1944 the Royal Apartments were rediscovered, and the throne room carefully reconstructed. The outline of the mosque has also been excavated. The only covered part of the site is the Salon de Abd ar-Rahman III (currently being restored); the rest is a sprawl of foundations and arches that hint at the splendor of the original city-palace. Visits begin at the nearby museum, which provides background information and a 3-D reconstruction of the city, and continue with a walk among the ruins, where you can only imagine the bustle and splendor of days gone by. There's no public transportation, but a tourist bus runs twice daily (three times on Saturday); the tourist office can provide details of stops and schedule. ⊠ *Ctra. de Palma del Río, Km 5.5, 8 km (5 miles) west of Córdoba on C431* ☎ *957/352860* ⊕ *www.juntadeandalucia.es/cultura/museos/CAMA* ☜ *€1.50* ⏱ *Mid-Sept.–Apr., Tues.–Sat. 9–6:30, Sun. 10–5; May–mid-Sept., Tues.–Sat. 9–8:30, Sun. 10–5.*

Fodor's Choice **Mezquita** (*Mosque*). Built between the 8th and 10th centuries, Córdoba's
★ mosque is one of the earliest and most transportingly beautiful examples of Spanish Islamic architecture. The plain, crenellated exterior walls do little to prepare you for the sublime beauty of the interior. As you enter through the **Puerta de las Palmas** (Door of the Palms), some 850 columns rise before you in a forest of jasper, marble, granite, and onyx. The pillars are topped by ornate capitals taken from the Visigothic church that was razed to make way for the mosque. Crowning these, red-and-white-stripe arches curve away into the dimness, and the ceiling is carved of delicately tinted cedar. The Mezquita has served as a cathedral since 1236, but its origins as a mosque are clear. Built in four stages, it

17

was founded in 785 by Abd ar-Rahman I (756–88) on a site he bought from the Visigoth Christians. He pulled down their church and replaced it with a mosque, one-third the size of the present one, into which he incorporated marble pillars from earlier Roman and Visigothic shrines. Under Abd ar-Rahman II (822–52), the Mezquita held an original copy of the Koran and a bone from the arm of the prophet Mohammed and became a Muslim pilgrimage site second only in importance to Mecca. ⊠ *C. de Torrijos, Judería* ☏ *957/470512* ⌨ *€8* ☉ *Mon.–Sat. 10–7, Sun. 8:30–10 and 2–7 (mass at 11 and 1).*

Fodor'sChoice   **Museo de Bellas Artes.** Hard to miss because of its deep-pink facade, Cór-
★   doba's Museum of Fine Arts, in a courtyard just off the Plaza del Potro, belongs to a former Hospital de la Caridad (Charity Hospital). It was founded by Ferdinand and Isabella, who twice received Columbus here. The collection includes paintings by Murillo, Valdés Leal, Zurbarán, Goya, and Joaquín Sorolla y Bastida. ⊠ *Pl. del Potro 1, San Francisco* ☏ *957/103639* ⊕ *www.juntadeandalucia.es/cultura/museos/MBACO* ⌨ *€1.50* ☉ *Tues.–Sun. 10–8:30.*

Museo Taurino (*Museum of Bullfighting*). Two adjoining mansions on the Plaza Maimónides (or Plaza de las Bulas) house this museum, and it's worth a visit, as much for the chance to see a restored mansion as for the posters, art-nouveau paintings, bull's heads, suits of lights (bullfighting outfits), and memorabilia of famous Córdoban bullfighters, including the most famous of all, Manolete. To the surprise of the nation, Mano-lete, who was considered immortal, was killed by a bull in the ring at Linares in 1947. ⊠ *Pl. de Maimónides 1, Judería* ☏ *957/201056.*

Synagogue. The only Jewish temple in Andalusia to survive the expul-sion and inquisition of the Jews in 1492, Córdoba's synagogue is also one of only three ancient synagogues left in all of Spain (the other two are in Toledo). Though it no longer functions as a place of worship, it's a treasured symbol for Spain's modern Jewish communities. The outside is plain, but the inside, measuring 23 feet by 21 feet, contains some exquisite Mudejar stucco tracery. Look for the fine plant motifs and the Hebrew inscription saying that the synagogue was built in 1315. The women's gallery, not open for visits, still stands, and in the east wall is the ark where the sacred scrolls of the Torah were kept. ⊠ *C. Judíos, Judería* ☏ *957/202928* ⌨ *€0.30* ☉ *Tues.–Sun. 9:30–2 and 3:30–5:30.*

WHERE TO EAT

$$ ✕ **Bodegas Campos.** A block east of the Plaza del Potro, this traditional
SPANISH   old wine cellar is the epitome of all that's great about Andalusian cui-
Fodor'sChoice   sine and high quality service. The dining rooms are in barrel-heavy
★   rustic rooms and leafy traditional patios (take a look at some of the signed barrels—you may recognize a name or two, such as the former UK prime minister Tony Blair. Magnificent vintage flamenco posters decorate the walls. Regional dishes include *solomillo del Valle de los Pedroches dos salsas y patatas a lo pobre* (local pork with two sauces—green and sherry—and creamy potatoes) and *dados de bacalao frtio con ali-oli* (fried dices of cod with garlic mayonnaise). Vegetables come from the restaurant's own market garden. There's also an excellent tapas

bar (from €3). $ *Average main: €16* ✉ *C. Los Lineros 32, San Pedro* ☎ *957/497500* ☾ *No dinner Sun.*

$$$
SPANISH
Fodor's Choice
★

✕ **El Caballo Rojo.** This is one of the most famous traditional restaurants in Andalusia, frequented by royalty and society folk. The interior resembles a cool, leafy Andalusian patio, and the dining room is furnished with stained glass and dark wood; the upstairs terrace overlooks the Mezquita. The menu combines traditional specialties, such as *rabo de toro* (oxtail stew) and *salmorejo* (a thick version of gazpacho), with more modern versions, such as *alcachofas a la Montillana* (artichoke in sweet Montilla wine) and *pez espada a la cordobesa con gambas* (swordfish Córdoba-style with prawns). A delicious selection of homemade tarts and flans are served from a trolley. $ *Average main: €20* ✉ *C. Cardenal Herrero 28, Judería* ☎ *957/475375* ⊕ *www. elcaballorojo.com* ⚓ *Reservations essential.*

$$
SPANISH
Fodor's Choice
★

✕ **El Choco.** The city's most exciting restaurant, awarded a Michelin star in 2012, El Choco has renowned chef Kisko Garcia at the helm whipping up innovative dishes with a twist of traditional favorites such as *cochinillo cruiente con crema de ajos y naranjas* (crispy suckling pig with cream of garlic and oranges) and *atún fresco de Almadraba que quiso ser cerdo ibérico* (traditionally-caught fresh tuna that wished it were an Iberian pig -fresh tuna cooked in pork stock and roasted on an oak log fire). The fresh Gellardeau oysters served with Iberian ham and cream of avocado are a highly acclaimed starter. The restaurant has a minimalist interior, with charcoal-color walls and glossy parquet floors. El Choco is outside the city center to the east and not easy to find, so take a taxi. $ *Average main: €17* ✉ *Compositor Serrano Lucena 14, Centro* ☎ *957/264863* ☾ *Closed Mon. No dinner Sun.*

$
TAPAS

✕ **Taberna Sociedad de Plateros.** On a narrow side street just steps away from the Plaza del Potro, this delightful spot dates from the 17th century. One of the city's most historic inns, it has a large patio that adjoins a traditional marble bar where locals meet. Photographs of iconic local bullfighter Manolete line the walls, and the patio is decorated with giddily patterned tiles and bricks plus a giant flat-screen television. The food is solid home-style cooking, with choices including fried green peppers, Spanish potato omelet, and hearty oxtail stew. Choose from tapas (€2) or full portions. $ *Average main: €7* ✉ *C. San Francisco 6, Pl. de la Corredera* ☎ *957/470042* ☾ *Closed Mon. Sept.–mid-May, and Sun. mid-May–Aug.*

WHERE TO STAY

$
B&B/INN

▦ **Casa de los Azulejos.** This 17th-century house still has original details like the majestic vaulted ceilings and, with the use of stunning azulejos—hence the name—it mixes Andalusian and Latin American influences. **Pros:** interesting architecture; friendly staff. **Cons:** hyper-busy interior design; limited privacy. $ *Rooms from: €78* ✉ *C. Fernando Colón 5, Centro* ☎ *957/470000* ⊕ *www.casadelosazulejos.com* ⚓ *7 rooms, 2 suites* ▢ *Breakfast.*

$$$
B&B/INN
Fodor's Choice
★

▦ **Hospederia de El Churrasco.** This small hotel, occupying a collection of houses just a stone's throw from the Mezquita, combines enchanting antique furnishings with modern amenities, but its greatest asset is its exceptionally helpful staff. **Pros:** beautiful interiors; rooms are equipped

17

with computers. **Cons:** rooms facing street can be noisy. [$] *Rooms from: €178* ✉ *C. Romero 38, Judería* ☎ *957/294808* 🛏 *9 rooms* 🍴 *Breakfast.*

$$$$ HOTEL Fodor's Choice ★ 🏨 **Hospes Palacio del Bailío.** This tastefully renovated 17th-century mansion, one of the city's top lodging options, is built over the ruins of a Roman house (visible beneath glass floors) in the historic center of town. **Pros:** dazzling interiors; impeccable comforts. **Cons:** not easy to access by car. [$] *Rooms from: €350* ✉ *C. Ramírez de las Casas Deza 10–12, Plaza de la Corredera* ☎ *957/498993* 🌐 *www.hospes.es* 🛏 *49 rooms, 4 suites* 🍴 *No meals.*

$ HOTEL 🏨 **Hotel Maestre.** Around the corner from the Plaza del Potro, this is an affordable hotel in which Castilian-style furniture, gleaming marble, and high-quality oil paintings add elegance to excellent value. **Pros:** good location; great value. **Cons:** no elevator and lots of steps; ancient plumbing. [$] *Rooms from: €56* ✉ *C. Romero Barros 4–6, San Pedro* ☎ *957/472410* 🌐 *www.hotelmaestre.com* 🛏 *26 rooms* 🍴 *No meals.*

$$$ HOTEL 🏨 **NH Amistad Córdoba.** Two 18th-century mansions overlooking Plaza de Maimónides in the heart of the Judería have been melded into a modern business hotel with a cobblestone Mudejar courtyard, carved-wood ceilings, and a plush lounge. **Pros:** pleasant and efficient service; great value. **Cons:** parking is difficult; access via steep steps with no ramp. [$] *Rooms from: €155* ✉ *Pl. de Maimónides 3, Judería* ☎ *957/420335* 🌐 *www.nh-hoteles.com* 🛏 *83 rooms* 🍴 *No meals.*

$$$ HOTEL FAMILY 🏨 **Parador de Córdoba.** On the slopes of the Sierra de Córdoba, on the site of Abd ar-Rahman I's 8th-century summer palace, this modern parador has sunny rooms and nice views. **Pros:** wonderful views from south-facing rooms; sleek interiors; quality traditional cuisine. **Cons:** characterless modern building; far from main sights. [$] *Rooms from: €161* ✉ *Av. de la Arruzafa 39, 5 km (3 miles) north of city, El Brillante* ☎ *957/275900* 🌐 *www.parador.es* 🛏 *89 rooms, 5 suites* 🍴 *No meals.*

NIGHTLIFE AND THE ARTS

FESTIVALS AND EVENTS

During the **Patio Festival,** held the second and third weeks of May, the city fills with flamenco dancers and singers. The **Festival de Córdoba-Guitarra** attracts Spanish and international guitarists for more than two weeks of great music in July. Orchestras perform in the Alcázar's garden on Sunday throughout the summer. The **Feria de Mayo** (the last week of May) draws popular musical performers to the city.

FLAMENCO

Tablao Cardenal. Córdoba's most popular flamenco club is worth the trip just to see the courtyard of the 16th-century building, which was Córdoba's first hospital. Admission is €20 and the 90-minute show takes place Monday to Saturday at 10:30 pm. ✉ *C. Torrijos 10, Judería* ☎ *957/483320.*

GRANADA

430 km (265 miles) south of Madrid, 261 km (162 miles) east of Seville, and 160 km (100 miles) southeast of Córdoba.

The Alhambra and the tomb of the Catholic Monarchs are the pride of Granada. The city rises majestically from a plain onto three hills, dwarfed—on a clear day—by the Sierra Nevada. Atop one of these hills perches the reddish-gold Alhambra palace. The stunning view from the palace promontory takes in the sprawling medieval Moorish quarter, the caves of the Sacromonte, and, in the distance, the fertile *vega* (plain), rich in orchards, tobacco fields, and poplar groves. Granada was the Moors' last stronghold; the city fell to Catholic monarchs in January 1492.

ALHAMBRA

Fodor's Choice
★

Alhambra. With more than 3 million visitors a year, the Alhambra is Spain's most popular attraction. Walking *to* the Alhambra can be as inspiring as walking *around* it. If you're up to a long, and rather steep, scenic approach, start in the Plaza Nueva and climb the Cuesta de Gomérez—through the slopes of green elms planted by the Duke of Wellington—to reach the Puerta de las Granadas (Gate of the Pomegranates), a Renaissance gateway built by Carlos V and topped by three pomegranates, symbols of Granada. The complex has three main parts: the Alcazaba, the Palacios Nazaríes (Nasrid Palaces), and the Generalife, the ancient summer palace.

Construction of the Alhambra was begun in 1238 by Ibn el-Ahmar, the first king of the Nasrids. The great citadel once comprised a complex of houses, schools, baths, barracks, and gardens surrounded by defense towers and seemingly impregnable walls. Today, only the Alcazaba and the Palacios Nazaríes, built chiefly by Yusuf I (1334–54) and his son Mohammed V (1354–91), remain. The palace is an endless, intricate conglomeration of patios, arches, and cupolas made from wood, plaster, and tile; lavishly colored and adorned with marquetry and ceramics in geometric patterns and topped by delicate, frothy profusions of lacelike stucco and *mocárabes* (ornamental stalactites). Built of perishable materials, it was never intended to last but to be forever replenished and replaced by succeeding generations. By the early 17th century, ruin and decay had set in, and the Alhambra was abandoned by all but tramps and stray dogs. Napoléon's troops commandeered it in 1812, but their attempts to destroy it were, happily, foiled. In 1862, Granada finally launched a complete restoration program that has been carried on ever since. ⊠ *Cuesta de Gomérez, Alhambra* ⊕ *www.alhambra-patronato. es* 🏛 *Alhambra and Generalife €13, Generalife and Alcazaba €7, Fine Arts Museum €1.50, Museum of the Alhambra and Palace of Carlos V free* ⊙ *Alhambra, Alcazaba, Generalife, and Palace of Carlos V: Oct. 15–Mar. 14, daily 8:30–6; Mar. 15–Oct. 14, daily 8:30–8. Museum of the Alhambra Tues.–Sun. 8:30–2. Museum of Fine Arts Tues. 2:30–8, Wed.–Sat. 9–8, Sun. 9–2:30.*

SACROMONTE

Abadía de Sacromonte. The caverns on Sacromonte are thought to have sheltered early Christians; 15th-century treasure hunters found bones inside and assumed they belonged to San Cecilio, the city's patron saint. Thus, the hill was sanctified—*sacro monte* (holy mountain)—and an abbey built on its summit, the Abadía de Sacromonte. ⊠ *C. del Sacromonte, Sacromonte* 🕾 *958/221445* 🏛 *€4* ⊙ *Tues.–Sat. 10–1 and 4–6, Sun. 11–1 and 4–6; guided tours every ½ hr (Spanish only).*

17

ALBAYZÍN

Covering a hill of its own, across the Darro ravine from the Alhambra, this ancient Moorish neighborhood is a mix of dilapidated white houses and immaculate *cármenes* (private villas in gardens enclosed by high walls). It was founded in 1228 by Moors who fled Baeza after Saint King Ferdinand III captured the city. Full of cobblestone alleyways and secret corners, the Albayzín guards its old Moorish roots jealously, though its 30 mosques were converted to baroque churches long ago. A stretch of the Moors' original city wall runs beside the Cuesta de la Alhacaba. If you're walking—the best way to explore—you can enter the Albayzín from either the Cuesta de Elvira or the Plaza Nueva. One of the highest points in the quarter, the plaza in front of the church of San Nicolás—called the **Mirador de San Nicolás**—has one of the finest views in all of Granada: on the hill opposite, the turrets and towers of the Alhambra form a dramatic silhouette against the snowy peaks of the Sierra Nevada.

El Bañuelo (*Little Bath House*). These 11th-century Arab steam baths might be a little dark and dank now, but try to imagine them some 900 years ago, filled with Moorish beauties. Back then, the dull brick walls were backed by bright ceramic tiles, tapestries, and rugs. Light comes in through star-shape vents in the ceiling, à la bathhouse in the Alhambra. ✉ *Carrera del Darro 31, Albayzín* ☎ *958/229738* 💲 *Free* ⊘ *Tues.–Sat. 10–2:30.*

CENTRO

Capilla Real (*Royal Chapel*). Catholic Monarchs Isabella of Castile and Ferdinand of Aragón are buried at this shrine. The couple originally planned to be buried in Toledo's San Juan de los Reyes, but Isabella changed her mind when the pair conquered Granada in 1492. When she died in 1504, her body was first laid to rest in the Convent of San Francisco (now a parador), on the Alhambra hill. The architect Enrique Egas began work on the Royal Chapel in 1506 and completed it 15 years later, creating a masterpiece of the ornate Gothic style now known in Spain as Isabelline. In 1521 Isabella's body was transferred to a simple lead coffin in the Royal Chapel crypt, where it was joined by that of her husband, Ferdinand, and later other relatives. The **crypt** containing the five lead coffins is quite simple, but it's topped by elaborate marble **tombs** showing Ferdinand and Isabella lying side by side (commissioned by their grandson Carlos V and sculpted by Domenico Fancelli). The **altarpiece,** by Felipe Vigarini (1522), comprises 34 carved panels depicting religious and historical scenes; the bottom row shows Boabdil surrendering the keys of the city to its conquerors and the forced baptism of the defeated Moors. The **sacristy** holds Ferdinand's sword, Isabella's crown and scepter, and a fine collection of Flemish paintings once owned by Isabella. ✉ *C. Oficios, Centro* ☎ *958/229239* ⊕ *www. capillarealgranada.com* 💲 *€4* ⊘ *Apr.–Oct., Mon.–Sat. 10:15–1:30 and 4–7:30, Sun. 11–1.30 and 4–7:30; Nov.–Mar., Mon.–Sat. 10:30–1:30 and 3:30–6:30, Sun. 10:30–1:30 and 3:30–6:30.*

Cathedral. Carlos V commissioned the cathedral in 1521 because he considered the Royal Chapel "too small for so much glory" and wanted to house his illustrious late grandparents someplace more worthy. Carlos undoubtedly had great intentions, as the cathedral was created by some of the finest architects of its time: Enrique Egas, Diego de Siloé, Alonso Cano, and sculptor Juan de Mena. Alas, his ambitions came to little, for the cathedral is a grand and gloomy monument, not completed until 1714 and never used as the crypt for his grandparents (or parents). Enter through a small door at the back, off the Gran Vía. Old hymnals are displayed throughout, and there's a museum, which includes a 14th-century gold-and-silver monstrance (used for communion) given to the city by Queen Isabella. Audio guides are available for an extra €3. ✉ *Gran Vía, Centro* ☎ *958/222959* 🎫 *€4* 🕒 *Apr.–Oct., Mon.–Sat. 10:45–1:15 and 4–7:45, Sun. 4–7:45; Nov.–Mar., Mon.–Sat. 10:45–1:15 and 4–6:45, Sun. 4–6:45.*

OUTSKIRTS OF TOWN

Monasterio de La Cartuja. This Carthusian monastery in northern Granada (2 km [1 mile] from the center of town and reached by the No. 8 bus) was begun in 1506 and moved to its present site in 1516, though construction continued for the next 300 years. The exterior is sober and monolithic, but inside are twisted, multicolor marble columns; a profusion of gold, silver, tortoiseshell, and ivory; intricate stucco; and the extravagant sacristy—it's easy to see why it has been called the Christian answer to the Alhambra. Among its wonders are the trompe l'oeil spikes, shadows and all, in the Sanchez Cotan cross over the *Last Supper* painting at the west end of the refectory. If you're lucky you may see small birds attempting to land on these faux perches. ✉ *C. de Alfacar, Cartuja* ☎ *958/161932* 🎫 *€4* 🕒 *Apr.–Oct., daily 10–1 and 4–8; Nov.–Mar., daily 10–1 and 3–6.*

17

WHERE TO EAT

$$$ SPANISH 🍴 **Damasqueros.** The modern, wood-paneled dining room and warm light form the perfect setting for the creative Andalusian cuisine served here. The concise menu includes dishes like fresh tuna with pumpkin ravioli, pesto, and fried almonds, and Iberian pork with couscous, apricots, and yoghurt. Thanks to its slightly hidden location in the Realejo, Damasqueros is not highly frequented by tourists. [$] *Average main: €20* ✉ *C. Damasqueros 3, Realejo* ☎ *958/210550* 🕒 *Closed Mon. No dinner Sun.*

$ TAPAS 🍴 **Los Diamantes.** This cheap and cheerful bar is a big favorite with locals and draws crowds whatever the time of year. Specialties include fried fish and seafood—try the *surtido de pescado* (assortment of fried fish) to sample the best—as well as *mollejas fritas* (fried lambs brains). No reservations are taken and there's no seating so arrive early (1:30 pm or 8 pm) to be sure of some bar space or a tall table outside. Even when it's crowded, the service comes with a smile. [$] *Average main: €12* ✉ *C. Navas 28, Centro* ☎ *958/222572.*

$$$ SPANISH 🍴 **Mirador de Morayma.** Buried in the Albayzín, this hard-to-find restaurant might appear to be closed, so ring the doorbell. Once inside, you'll have unbeatable views across the gorge to the Alhambra, particularly from the wisteria-laden outdoor terrace. In colder weather you can enjoy the open fireplace and attractive dining space inside. The menu has some surprising sweet-savory mixes such as *bacalao gratinado con alioli de manzana* (grilled cod with apple garlic mayonnaise), and *presa ibérica con salsa de higos, vino dulce, membrillo y puerros* (Iberian pork

with fig and sweet wine sauce, quince, and leeks). Service is sometimes a little on the slow side. The restaurant has several flights of steps. $ *Average main: €20* ⊠ *C. Pianista García Carrillo 2, Albayzín* ☎ *958/228290* ⊗ *No dinner Sun.*

$$
SPANISH

✕ **Oliver.** The interior may look a bit bare, but whatever this fish restaurant lacks in warmth it makes up for with the food. Less pricey than its neighbor Cunini, it serves simple but high-quality dishes like grilled mullet, dorada baked in salt, prawns with garlic, and monkfish in saffron sauce. The tapas (€1.50) bar, which is more popular with locals than the dining room, offers classic dishes like *migas* (fried bread crumbs), beans with serrano ham, and tortilla *del Sacromonte* (with lamb testicles and brains, as traditionally prepared by the Sacromonte's gypsies). Granada visitors on Fodor's website community highlight the good, friendly service here. $ *Average main: €15* ⊠ *Pl. Pescadería 12, Centro* ☎ *958/262200* ⊗ *Closed Sun.*

WHERE TO STAY

$$$
B&B/INN
Fodor's Choice
★

▦ **Carmen de la Alcubilla del Caracol.** In a traditional Granadino villa on the slopes of the Alhambra, this privately run lodging is one of Granada's most stylish hotels. **Pros:** great views; personal service; impeccable taste. **Cons:** tough climb in hot weather. $ *Rooms from: €140* ⊠ *C. Aire Alta 12, Alhambra* ☎ *958/215551* ⊕ *www.alcubilladelcaracol.com* ⇖ *7 rooms* ⊗ *Closed Aug.* ⎰⊙⎱ *No meals.*

$$
B&B/INN
Fodor's Choice
★

▦ **Casa Morisca.** The architect who owns this 15th-century building transformed it into a hotel so distinctive that he received Spain's National Restoration Award for his preservation of original architectural elements, including barrel-vaulted brickwork, wooden ceilings, and the original pool. **Pros:** historic location; award-winning design; easy parking; free Wi-Fi. **Cons:** stuffy interior rooms; no full restaurant on site. $ *Rooms from: €125* ⊠ *Cuesta de la Victoria 9, Albayzín* ☎ *958/221100* ⊕ *www.hotelcasamorisca.com* ⇖ *12 rooms, 2 suites* ⎰⊙⎱ *No meals.*

$$$$
HOTEL

▦ **Hotel Alhambra Palace.** Built by a local duke in 1910, this neo-Moorish hotel is on leafy grounds at the back of the Alhambra hill, and 2012 saw completion of the restoration of its very Arabian Nights interior (think orange-and-brown overtones, multicolor tiles, and Moorish-style arches and pillars). **Pros:** bird's-eye views, location near (but not in) the Alhambra. **Cons:** steep climb up from Granada; doubles as a popular convention center—there are five spacious meeting rooms—so often packed with business folk. $ *Rooms from: €200* ⊠ *Pl. Arquitecto García de Paredes 1, Alhambra* ☎ *958/221468* ⊕ *www.h-alhambrapalace. es* ⇖ *115 rooms, 11 suites* ⎰⊙⎱ *Breakfast.*

$$$$
HOTEL
Fodor's Choice
★

▦ **Parador de Granada.** This is Spain's most expensive and most popular parador, right within the walls of the Alhambra. **Pros:** good location; lovely interiors; garden restaurant. **Cons:** no views in some rooms; removed from city life. $ *Rooms from: €336* ⊠ *C. Real de la Alhambra, Alhambra* ☎ *958/221440* ⊕ *www.parador.es* ⇖ *35 rooms, 5 suites* ⎰⊙⎱ *No meals.*

SWITZERLAND

Zurich, Berner Oberland, Luzern

WHAT'S WHERE

1 Zurich. This rich banking center and bastion of Swiss-Germanism has actually become cool and found its voice with a vibrant restaurant, art, and design scene that offers lively counterpoints to its fascinating history. Straddling the Limmat River, Zurich's center is made up primarily of medieval churches, guildhalls, and town houses.

2 Luzern. A mere 23 square km (23 square miles) in size, it encompasses much of Switzerland in a nutshell: a well-preserved medieval Old Town, a lakeshore promenade with breathtaking Alpine views, great shops, restaurants, and museums. It also offers a world-class concert hall.

3 Berner Oberland: The Jungfrau Region. Valleys, lakes, and peaks—including the Jungfraujoch, an almost alien landscape slathered in whipped-cream snow all year round, and at 3,475 meters (11,400 feet) the most accessible high-altitude peak in Europe. This is among the most popular destinations in Switzerland, and with good reason.

FRANCE

JURA MOUNTAINS

La Chaux-de-Fonds
Neuchâtel

Lac de Neuchâtel

Yverdon

Payerne

Lausanne

Gruyèr
Vevey

Nyon

Lac Léman

Montreu

Geneva

Martig

0   40 miles

0   60 km

GERMANY

Schaffhausen

Rhine   Kreuzlingen
                                    Bodensee
        Basel   Brugg Winterthur Frauenfeld   Rorschach
                        Baden   Arbon
  orrentruy Olten   Wil
             Aarau   St.Gallen
Solothurn   Zürich **1** Küsnacht   Appenzell   AUSTRIA
                                      Buchs Vaduz
  Biel   Zug   Sargans   LIECHTENSTEIN
        BERN   Langnau Lüzern **2** Schwyz   Glarus
   urten   Sarnen   Altdorf   GLARNER ALPS   Chur
  ibourg   Thun   Davos   Scuol
        Interlaken Meiringen   Wassen   Zernez
             3 Grindelwald Andermatt
         Wengen   St. Moritz
  Gstaad   ENGADINE
     BERNER ALPS Jungfraujoch   RHAETIAN ALPS ALPS
        Rhône Rhône Brig   LEPONTINE ALPS
           Sierre Visp   Biasca
   Sion   Simplon   Bellinzona
                   Pass
   erbier PENNINE ALPS Zermatt   Locarno
        Matterhorn   Ascona
  nd St. Bernard Pass   Lugano

                            ITALY

NEED TO KNOW

AT A GLANCE

Capital: Bern

Population: 8,039,100

Currency: Swiss franc (CHF)

Money: ATMs are common; credit cards widely accepted

Language: German, French, Italian, Romansh

Country Code: ☎ 41

Emergencies: ☎ 117

Driving: On the right

Electricity: 200v/50 cycles; electrical plugs have two or three round prongs

● Bern

SWITZERLAND

Time: Six hours ahead of New York

Documents: Up to 90 days with valid passport; Schengen rules apply

Mobile Phones: GSM (900 and 1800 bands)

Major Mobile Companies: Swisscom, Orange, Sunrise

WEBSITES

Switzerland: ⊕ www.myswitzerland.com

Swiss Railways: ⊕ www.sbb.ch

Swiss Travel: ⊕ www.swisstravelsystem.com

GETTING AROUND

✈ **Air Travel:** The major airports are Geneva Cointrin and Zurich Airport.

🚌 **Bus Travel:** Good for traveling between smaller regional towns to and from isolated villages.

🚗 **Car Travel:** Rent a car to explore at your own pace, buy a *vignette* for the autobahn if your rental doesn't already have one (40 SF at the border or in gas stations).

🚆 **Train Travel:** The Swiss train network is exemplary; Swiss Rail passes also include buses, boats, city trams, and discounts on cable cars and funicular trains up to most alpine peaks.

PLAN YOUR BUDGET

	HOTEL ROOM	MEAL	ATTRACTIONS
Low Budget	118 CHF	20 CHF	Grossmünster Tower, Zurich, 4 CHF
Mid Budget	340 CHF	40 CHF	Kunsthaus Zurich, 25 CHF
High Budget	1250 CHF	150 CHF	Opera ticket, 250 CHF

WAYS TO SAVE

Eat lunch picnic-style. Take advantage of Coop and Migros supermarkets. Prices for perishables often drop 25% to 50% after 5 pm. Then have a picnic.

Ski in the afternoon. Most mountain resorts offer a cheaper half-day ski pass. With runs usually closing between 4 or 5 pm.

Buy a rail pass. Transit passes let you explore the country by rail, boat, bus, and city tram. ⊕ www.tellpass.ch, ⊕ www.swisstravelsystem.com.

Experience markets and festivals. Every town has a festival ("Dorffest") between June and September; markets are held weekly.

PLAN YOUR TIME

Hassle Factor	Low. Flights to Zurich are frequent, and Switzerland has a great transport network.
3 days	You can see some of the magic of Zurich and perhaps take a half-day trip out to Winterthur or Luzern.
1 week	Combine a short trip to Zurich with at least one day trip to Luzern or Interlaken as well as an additional day or two in a place within easy reach like Geneva or Lugano.
2 weeks	You have time to move around and for the highlights, including a stop in Zurich, excursions to Lake Lucerne, and a trip to take in the highlights of atmospheric Graubünden and ritzy Montreux.

WHEN TO GO

High Season: July, August, and December are the most expensive and popular times to visit Switzerland. In December, the Bernese Oberland is crowded with skiers; the season runs from December to March. July/August is busy in Luzern. Zurich is busiest from May through October.

Low Season: November is quiet, which also means many family-run hotels are closed. The lowlands (Zurich, Luzern) go gray and foggy in November, but above that there are blue skies and fabulous mountain views. November to March is pretty much gray and wet anywhere under 914 meters (3,000 feet).

Value Season: September and October still have great weather, though temperatures start to drop by late October. Late April and May is a good time to visit, before the masses arrive but when the fields are green and dotted with flowers.

BIG EVENTS

January: The White Turf horse race in St. Moritz attracts international high society. ⊕ www.whiteturf.ch

May: Cows are led to pasture with great pomp and circumstance for the traditional Alpine ascent. ⊕ www.appenzell.info

July: The legendary Montreux Jazz Festival offers three weeks of exemplary music. ⊕ www.montreuxjazz.com

September/October: The Zurich Film Festival is an intimate place to rub shoulders with filmmakers. ⊕ www.zff.com

READ THIS

- *In the Cradle of Liberty,* Mark Twain. A witty report on Twain's mid-19th-century trip to Switzerland.

- *Jakob von Gunten,* Robert Walser. A classic novel from a writer deemed a genius by J. M. Coetzee.

- *Dunant's Dream: War, Switzerland and the History of the Red Cross,* Caroline Moorehead. The title says it all.

WATCH THIS

- *On Her Majesty's Secret Service.* Bond and Blofeld match wits in the Bernese Oberland.

- *The Swissmakers.* A satirical comedy about xenophobia in Switzerland.

- *Vitus.* A pianist wunderkind rebels against his parents' plan for his future.

EAT THIS

- **Fondue:** Cheese mixtures vary according to region.

- **Zürcher Geschnetzeltes:** veal strips in cream sauce

- **Pike-perch:** fresh from local lakes

- **Cheese:** every region has its own variety.

- **Birchermüesli:** authentic with wheat germ, fresh berries, and cream

- **Chocolate:** Zurich especially has a wealth of specialty shops.

18

The paradox of Switzerland pitches rustic homeyness against high-tech urban efficiency. While digital screens tick off beef futures in Zurich, the crude harmony of cowbells echoes in the velvet mountain pastures of the Berner Oberland. While fur-clad socialites raise jeweled fingers to bid at auctions in Geneva, the women of Appenzell, in Central Switzerland, stand beside the men on the Landsgemeindeplatz and raise their hands to vote—a right not won until 1991.

Switzerland is a haven of private banking, serious shopping, major music festivals, fabulous art collections, palace hotels, state-of-the-art spas, some of the finest gastronomy in the world—from the hautest French and even molecular cuisine to traditional foods like fondue and Rösti—and a burgeoning contemporary scene of filmmakers, architects, artists, and designers making international names for themselves.

The country's Roman ruins, decorated medieval facades, castles, churches, and ornately carved wooden chalets point to its rich history, as do folk traditions like "banishing winter," where bell ringing, whip cracking, fire, and fearsome costumes are meant to frighten off the old spirits and usher in the spring.

This home of William Tell, heartland of the Reformation, birthplace of the Red Cross, and one of the world's oldest democracies also boasts extraordinary scenery—lakes and valleys, craggy peaks.

PLANNING

WHEN TO GO

Ski season starts before Christmas, with the peak season being over the Christmas and New Year's holidays, carrying through to about the end of March.

Otherwise, any time of year is good to travel in Switzerland. You may wish to check ahead if you're planning to visit cities, because a big event—like the annual Street Parade dance festival in Zurich—can mean hotels are full for miles around and even if you find space it'll be for top-most dollar.

Spring and fall weather can be rainy but is usually mild.

Summers tend to last into October and bring out a "Riviera" feel in many Swiss cities, giving them a laid-back, sometimes almost Mediterranean ambience, with people sunbathing along lake and river shores and filling sidewalk cafés.

TOP REASONS TO GO

Scenery. Whether you're on the water, in the air, lowlands or mountains, the scenery is breathtaking—and from cities, the sight of silent snowy peaks rising up over urban buildings offers a poignant contrast to cosmopolitan concerns.

Food and Wine. Some of the highest concentrations of Michelin-starred restaurants anywhere are here, but if gastronomic French is not your thing, then discover Swiss cuisine, which, like the country's excellent wines, is characterized by strong regional differences.

Museums. There are world-class collections of art in Switzerland. For Impressionists and classical moderns like Picasso, Chagall, Miró: in Zurich alone, there's the art museum and the Bührle Collection. Luzern has the Rosengart Collection.

Great Outdoors. Winter and mountain sports aside, this is a country where detailed maps are available for walkers, hikers, cyclists, and even those touring on horseback. There's rafting on the rivers, sailing on the

lakes, and paragliding and hang gliding for some of the most stupendous takes ever on all that glorious scenery.

Shopping. Swiss contemporary design (sometimes using the Swiss flag as an iconic feature) just keeps getting better and better. Whether it's lifestyle accessories, clothes, or watches from Swatch to Patek Philippe (Zurich's Bahnhofstrasse offers all the luxury watches you'll ever want), the shopping's great—if not necessarily cheap.

Diversity. Finding such distinct regions with their own languages and traditions in such a compact country exercises a fascination of its own—multiplied by the startling contrasts between urban sophistication and the time-warp, rural simplicity of mountain folk.

Festivals and Folk Traditions. World-class music festivals are huge drawing crowds—as are increasingly folk traditions that take place largely in Central Switzerland.

18

City winters are relatively mild with little snow (although watch out for occasional glacial winds, like the *Bise*) but the higher you go into the mountains the colder it gets, particularly at night. It can be chilly at night up there in the summer, too.

GETTING HERE AND AROUND

AIR TRAVEL

The major gateways are Zurich Airport (ZRH) and Geneva's Cointrin Airport (GVA), 10 km (8 miles) and 5 km (3 miles) outside the respective cities. You can connect to the cities (and the rest of the country) via train from the airport, or you can have a rental car waiting for you. SWISS serves seven airports in the U.S.: Boston (BOS), Chicago (CDG), Newark (EWR), New York (JFK), Los Angeles (LAX), Miami (MIA), and San Francisco (SFO).

Contacts Cointrin Airport (*GVA*). ☎ *022/717–7105* ⊕ *www.gva.ch.* **Swiss** ☎ *877/359–7947, 0848/700700 in Switzerland* ⊕ *www.swiss.com.* **Zürich Airport** (*ZRH*). ☎ *043/816–2211* ⊕ *www.zurich-airport.com.*

CAR TRAVEL

If you want to explore more remote areas of the country, driving is certainly the best option. Road maps are available at gas stations, but a rule of thumb if you're looking for the fastest way to get from place to place is follow the green *autoroute/autobahn* signs.

There are no tolls in Switzerland; however, to use semi-expressways and expressways you must display a sticker, or *vignette,* on the windshield. You can buy one at the border or in gas stations for 40 SF. Cars rented within Switzerland already have these stickers.

Have some 10 SF and 20 SF notes available, as many gas stations (especially in the mountains) have vending-machine pumps that operate even when they're closed. Simply slide in a bill and fill your tank. Many of these machines also accept major chip-and-PIN credit cards. You can request a receipt (*Quittung* in German, *quittance* in French) from the machine.

BUS TRAVEL

Switzerland's famous yellow postbuses (called *Postautos* or *cars post-aux*), with their stentorian tritone horns, link main cities with villages off the beaten track and even crawl over the highest mountain passes.

Both postbuses and city buses follow posted schedules to the minute: you can set your watch by them. You can pick up a free schedule for a particular route in most postbuses; full schedules are included in train schedule books. Postbuses cater to hikers: walking itineraries are available at some postbus stops. Be sure to ask whether reservations are required, as is the case for some Alpine pass routes.

Contacts Swiss Post ☎ *0848/888888* ⊕ *www.postbus.ch.*

TRAIN TRAVEL

Trains described as Inter-City or Express are the fastest, stopping only in principal towns. Regional trains stop at all the small stations along the way. There are numerous train passes available. The Swiss Pass is the best value, offering unlimited travel on Swiss Federal Railways, postbuses, lake steamers, and the local bus and tram services of 38 cities.

Contacts Swiss Federal Railways ☎ *0900/300300 (1.19 SF per min)* ⊕ *www. sbb.ch.*

HOTELS

The Swiss Hotel Association (SHA), a rigorous and demanding organization, maintains a specific rating system for lodging standards. Four out of five Swiss hotels belong to this group and take their stars seriously. In contrast to more casual European countries, stars in Switzerland have precise meaning: a five-star hotel is required to have a specific staff–guest ratio, a daily change of bed linens, and extended hours for room service. In contrast, a two-star hotel must have telephones in the rooms, soap in the bathrooms, and fabric tablecloths in the restaurant.

But the SHA standards cannot control the quality of the decor and the grace of service. Thus you may find a five-star hotel that meets the technical requirements but has shabby appointments, leaky plumbing, or a rude concierge, or a good, family-run two-star pension that makes you feel like royalty.

Contacts Swiss Hotel Association ✉ *Monbijoustr. 130, Bern* ☎ *031/370–4111* ⊕ *www.swisshotels.com.*

INNS
Travelers on a budget can find help from the *Check-in E & G Hotels* guide (E & G stands for *einfach und gemütlich*: roughly, "simple and cozy"), available through Switzerland Tourism. These comfortable little hotels have banded together to dispel Switzerland's intimidating image as an elite, overpriced vacation spot and offer simple two-star standards in memorable, atmospheric inns.

BED AND BREAKFASTS
You can get information about B&Bs from the user-friendly site of Bed & Breakfast Switzerland (⊕ *www.bnb.ch*).You can make reservations online.

RESTAURANTS

While the standard Swiss breakfast consists of coffee, bread, jam, and sometimes *Birchermüesli* (oat flakes mixed with berries, nuts and yogurt), many hotel restaurants offer a larger spread, which can include eggs, toast, cheese, cold cuts and sausage, potatoes, and pancakes or waffles.

18

Popular specialties for lunch and dinner include cheese fondue and raclette (melted cheese served with potatoes in their skins, and pickles); order a plate of air-dried beef from Graubünden or Valais to enjoy beforehand. You can get fondue in most parts of the country, but it is not customary for Swiss to eat it during the warmer months. However—especially for tourists—some restaurants serve it anyway.

The French-speaking cantons pride themselves on *filets de perche* (fried perch fillets), served with various sauces, or just lemon, and French fries.

German-speaking Switzerland made its mark in culinary history with the ubiquitous *Rösti,* a grated potato pancake. If served on its own as a main dish, it is often spruced up with herbs, bacon, or cheese. Just plain, it is served with nearly any meat but tastes particularly good with *Leberli* (sautéed calf's liver) or *Geschnezeltes*, a Zurich specialty of veal strips in cream sauce.

Risotto, gnocchi, polenta, and pasta dishes that reflect both Italian and Swiss-Italian cooking are available in eateries all over the nation, as are some of the better-known Graubünden specialties like air-dried beef (*Bündnerfleisch* or *viande des Grisons*) and walnut tart.

MEALS AND MEAL TIMES
Restaurants serve lunch between noon and 2, and dinner usually from 7 to 10, but in some places (especially the farther out in the countryside you are) service may stop earlier than that.

RESERVATIONS AND DRESS

It's a good idea to reserve a table, but essential (do it several months ahead) for a famed restaurant—even if said restaurant is in a hotel that you are a guest at. Casual smart will be fine for almost any restaurant, even the gastronomic venues.

MONEY-SAVING TIPS

Müesli is available in most supermarkets (such as Migros and Coop) and can make a hearty lunch, especially when eaten with plain or fruit yogurt instead of milk and fresh fruit.

Lunch is also a good opportunity to sample the fare at some of the more expensive venues, as almost all restaurants offer a fixed-price lunch special that includes soup or salad and a main course for far less than dinner prices.

Food halls like Globus delicatessen in Zurich or Manor Food or the Halle de Rive in Geneva can be great places to wander through, buying small quantities of cheese, sausage, breads, and baked goods that make it possible to sample a lot of prime Swiss specialties for very little money.

HOTEL AND RESTAURANT PRICES

Prices in the restaurant reviews are the average cost of a main course at dinner or, if dinner is not served, at lunch; taxes and service charges are generally included. Prices in the hotel reviews are the lowest cost of a standard double room in high season, excluding taxes, service charges, and meal plans.

PLANNING YOUR TIME

Unless you specifically want to land in Geneva, you'll find that most flights land in Zurich.

In Zurich: explore the Old Town, its hip shops and galleries, the Frau-münster church with stained-glass windows by Marc Chagall, and stroll down Bahnhofstrasse—Zurich's equivalent to 5th Avenue in New York City. Stop in for coffee and pastry at Sprüngli, on Paradeplatz where the big banks are located. Art lovers will want to check out not only the Kunstmuseum but the Bührle Collection.

If mountains have a "home," it is truly Switzerland—a summit of summits. In the Berner Oberland, you have the Lauterbrunnen Valley, which looks more like a painting than real life, with the jaw-dropping vista threaded by 72 waterfalls that plummet from sky-high cliffs.

Moving on to Luzern and Central Switzerland: this is gentler country, with the lake and rolling hills surrounded by Alps. A must here is a steamer cruise to explore the William Tell legend, but also just how the Swiss Confederation began way back in 1291. Check the concert schedules—world-class symphony orchestras and soloists perform here.

ZURICH

Zurich, located by the Limmat River at the point where it emerges from the Zürichsee (Lake of Zurich), is a beautiful city with vistas of snowy mountains in the distance and a charming *Altstadt* (Old Town). The

Romans came here in the 1st century BC but were expelled in the 5th century by the Germanic Alemanni, ancestors of present-day Zurichers. Zurich was renowned as a center of commerce from the 12th century. The Reformation defined its soul: from his pulpit in the Grossmünster, Ulrich Zwingli ingrained in Zurichers a devotion to thrift and industriousness. Today the Zurich stock exchange is the fourth-largest in the world, and the city's extraordinary museums and galleries and luxurious shops along Bahnhofstrasse attest to its position as Switzerland's money and cultural—if not political—capital. The latest addition to the city's profile is Zurich West, where former factories now house restaurants, bars, art galleries, and dance clubs.

PLANNING YOUR TIME

The Limmat River neatly bisects Zurich, crisscrossed by lovely, low bridges. On the left bank is the grander, more genteel part of the Old Town; the main train station; and Bahnhofplatz, an urban crossroads off which the world-famous luxury shopping street, Bahnhofstrasse, feeds. The right bank constitutes the livelier old section, divided into the Oberdorf (Upper Village) and the Niederdorf (Lower Village). Scattered throughout the town are 13 medieval guildhalls, or *Zunfthäuser,* which once formed the backbone of Zurich's commercial society.

Just walk around the city, on both sides of the river: it's the best way to take it all in—see most of the listed sites, even if only from the outside, and the shops. Museum buffs will want to visit both the Kunstmuseum and the Bührle Collection.

GETTING HERE AND AROUND

AIR TRAVEL

Zurich Airport is Switzerland's most important airport and the 10th busiest in the world. Some 60 airlines, including American, United, and, of course, Swiss International Air Lines, known as SWISS, serve this airport, located 11 km (7 miles) north of the city.

CAR TRAVEL

Switzerland's highway system also networks through Zurich: if you're traveling by car, it's best to pick up a rental only when you're ready to leave town. Since most streets in Zurich that aren't pedestrian zones are liable to be one-way—you'll find it easier to explore the city on foot or by public transportation, which is excellent.

TRAIN TRAVEL

For train travel, the Swiss Federal Railway manages everything. Trains arrive hourly from Geneva (84 SF one-way) and Luzern (24 SF one-way).

TRAM TRAVEL

Zurich ZVV, the tram service in Zurich, runs from 5:30 am to midnight, every 6 minutes at peak hours, every 12 minutes at other times.

VISITOR INFORMATION

Contacts **Zürich Tourist Service** ⊠ *Hauptbahnhof, Bahnhofpl., Kreis 1* ☎ *044/2154000* ⊕ *www.zuerich.com.*

18

Zürich

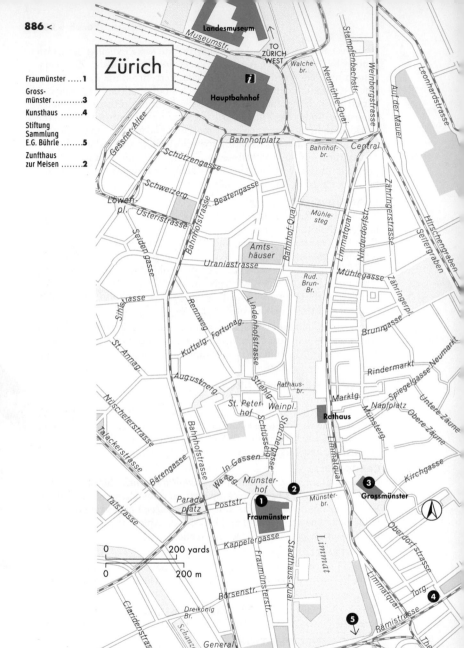

KEY

🛈 *Tourist Information*

⚋⚋ *Tram lines*

EXPLORING

Fraumünster (*Church of Our Lady*). Of the church spires that are Zürich's signature, the Fraumünster's is the most delicate, a graceful sweep to a narrow spire. It was added to the Gothic structure in 1732; the remains of Louis the German's original ninth-century abbey are below. Its Romanesque choir is a perfect spot for meditation beneath the ocher, sapphire, and ruby glow of the 1970 stained-glass windows by the Russian-born Marc Chagall, who loved Zürich. The Graubünden sculptor Alberto Giacometti's cousin, Augusto Giacometti, executed the fine painted window, made in 1930, in the north transept. ✉ *Stadthausquai, Kreis 1* ⊕ *www.fraumuenster.ch* ◷ *Nov.–Mar., daily 10–4; Apr.–Oct., daily 10–6.*

Fodor's Choice ★ **Grossmünster** (*Great Church*). This impressive cathedral is affectionately known to English speakers as the "Gross Monster." Executed on the plump twin towers (circa 1781) are classical caricatures of Gothic forms bordering on the comical. The core of the structure was built in the 12th century on the site of a Carolingian church dedicated to the memory of martyrs Felix and Regula, who allegedly carried their severed heads to the spot. Charlemagne is said to have founded the church after his horse stumbled over their burial site. On the side of the south tower an enormous stone Charlemagne sits enthroned; the original statue, carved in the late-15th century, is protected in the crypt. ✉ *Zwinglipl., Kreis 1* ☎ *044/2513860* ⊕ *www.grossmuenster.ch* ◷ *Mar.–Oct., daily 10–6, Nov.–Feb., daily 10–5; cloister weekdays 9–6.*

Fodor's Choice ★ **Kunsthaus** (*Museum of Art*). With a varied and high-quality permanent collection of paintings—medieval, Dutch and Italian baroque, and impressionist—the Kunsthaus is Zürich's best art museum. The collection includes some fascinating Swiss works; others might be an acquired taste. Besides works by Ferdinand Hodler, with their mix of realism and stylization, there's a superb room full of Johann Heinrich Füssli paintings, which hover between the darkly ethereal and the grotesque. And then there's Picasso, Klee, Degas, Matisse, Kandinsky, Chagall, and Munch, all satisfyingly represented. ✉ *Heimpl. 1, Kreis 1* ☎ *044/2538484* ⊕ *www.kunsthaus.ch* 🎟 *Varies by exhibition* ◷ *Wed.–Fri. 10–8, Sat., Sun., and Tues. 10–6.*

Fodor's Choice ★ **Stiftung Sammlung E. G. Bührle.** A stunning array of Cézannes, Manets, Monets, and Degas make this eye-popping collection one of the best art museums in Europe—unfortunately, since a spectacular robbery in 2008, visits are possible only on the first Sunday of each month. There are plans, however, to move the entire collection to Zürich's Kunsthaus by 2017. This fabled collection was put together in the space of a single decade. During the 1950s, Zürich industrialist E. G. Bührle purchased the finest offerings from the world's most prestigious art dealers, winding up with a collection studded with legendary Impressionist and Postimpressionist works, including Cézanne's *Self Portrait with Palette,* Renoir's *Little Irene,* and Degas's *Little Dancer.* Take Tram No. 11 from Bellevue, then Bus No. 77 from Hegibachplatz to the Altenhofstrasse stop. ✉ *Zollikerstr. 172, Kreis 8* ☎ *044/4220086* ⊕ *www.buehrle.ch* 🎟 *25 SF* ◷ *1st Sun. of each month.*

18

Zunfthaus zur Meisen. Set on the bank of the Limmat across the river from the towering Fraumünster is Zürich's most beautiful guildhall, comprising a magnificent suite of reception salons, several of which are topped by extravagant baroque stucco ceilings. Erected for the city's wine merchants in the 18th century, the Zunfthaus today is a fitting showplace for the Swiss National Museum's ceramics collection. The Kilchberg-Schooren porcelain works flourished in Zürich from 1763 to 1790 and their masterwork—a 300-piece dining service created for the monastery Einsiedeln in 1775—takes center stage, along with exquisite figurines and table decor. Also on view are Nyon porcelains, Swiss pottery, and faience. Enter on the Fraumünster side. ✉ *Münsterhof 20, Kreis 1* ☎ *044/2212807* 🌐 *www.musee-suisse.ch* 🎟 *3 SF* ⏲ *Thurs.–Sun. 11–4.*

WHERE TO EAT

$$$$ SWISS

🍴 **Haus zum Rüden.** The most ambitious of the city's many Zunfthaus dining places, this fine restaurant is also the most spectacular, combining a wooden barrel-vaulted ceiling and 30-foot beams. Slick modern improvements—including a glassed-in elevator—manage to blend intelligently with the ancient decor and old-world chandeliers. Innovative entrées might include lobster-coconut bisque with dried prawns and mangos, or sautéed goose liver on balsamico grapes. The river views are especially impressive at night; ask for a window table. [$] *Average main: 65 SF* ✉ *Limmatquai 42, Kreis 1* ☎ *044/2619566* 🌐 *www.hauszumrueden.ch* ⏲ *Closed weekends and mid-July–mid-Aug.*

$$$ SWISS Fodor's Choice ★

🍴 **Kaiser's Reblaube.** Get the most out of the Altstadt experience by eating in one of its most beautiful medieval buildings, which dates back to 1260. Goethe slept here, in a room named after him now used as an extra dining room, the "Goethe Stübli." For the full effect, come for the economical four-course Business Lunch (usually around 35 SF), which may include cold apricot-tomato soup, duck-liver mousse with steamed mushrooms, lamb filet with lentils, and—if you have room left—crème brûlée. [$] *Average main: 50 SF* ✉ *Glockeng. 7, Kreis 1* ☎ *044/2212120* 🌐 *www.kaisers-reblaube.ch* ✍ *Reservations essential* ⏲ *Closed Sunday.*

$$$ SWISS Fodor's Choice ★

🍴 **Kronenhalle.** From Stravinsky, Brecht, and Joyce to Nureyev, Deneuve, and Saint-Laurent, this beloved landmark has always drawn a stellar crowd. Every panel of gleaming wood wainscoting frames works by Picasso, Braque, Miró, Chagall, or Matisse, collected by patroness-hostess Hulda Zumsteg, who owned the restaurant from 1921 until her death in 1985. The tradition is carried on by the family trust, and robust cooking is still served in hefty portions: veal steak in morel sauce, duck à l'orange with red cabbage, and Spätzli. Unless you're a recognizable celebrity, make sure to insist on a table in the main dining room; ordinary mortals are otherwise seated in a less exciting room upstairs. [$] *Average main: 65 SF* ✉ *Rämistr. 4, Kreis 1* ☎ *044/2629900* 🌐 *www.kronenhalle.com* ✍ *Reservations essential.*

$$ SWISS

🍴 **Zum Kropf.** Under the mounted boar's head and restored century-old murals depicting gallivanting cherubs, businesspeople, workers, and shoppers share crowded tables to feast on generous hot dishes and a great selection of sausages. The *Leberknödli* (liver dumplings) are tasty, the potato croquettes are filled with farmer's cheese and garnished with a generous fresh salad, and the *Apfelküchli* (fried apple slices) are tender and sweet. The bustle and clatter provide a lively, sociable experience, and you'll more than likely get to know your neighbor. [$] *Average main: 30 SF* ✉ *In Gassen 16, Kreis 1* ☎ *044/2211805* ⊗ *Closed Sun.*

WHERE TO STAY

$$$$ HOTEL Fodor's Choice ★ 🏨 **Dolder Grand Hotel.** Zürich has a new pinnacle of hotel luxury—or should we say a new old pinnacle: this 1899 building, resplendent with towering turrets and timbered balconies, has been completely refurbished and is now flanked by two glass-and-steel wings that mirror the natural surroundings. **Pros:** gorgeous views; high-end service; very good restaurants. **Cons:** off the beaten track; a bit pricey; standard rooms are small, considering the cost. [$] *Rooms from: 970 SF* ✉ *Kurhausstr. 65, Kreis 7* ☎ *044/4566000* 🌐 *www.thedoldergrand.com* 🛏 *114 rooms, 59 suites* 🍴 *No meals.*

$$$ HOTEL 🏨 **Haus zum Kindli.** This charming little bijou hotel is as artfully styled as a magazine ad, with subtle grays and beiges underscoring the inviting white bed linens and original bath fixtures refurbished to match modern needs. **Pros:** just steps from where the town was founded; run home to the bathroom while you're shopping—it's that close. **Cons:** no parking; a little dark during winter. [$] *Rooms from: 400 SF* ✉ *Pfalzg. 1, Kreis 1* ☎ *043/8887676* 🌐 *www.kindli.ch* 🛏 *20 rooms* 🍴 *Breakfast.*

$ B&B/INN Fodor's Choice ★ 🏨 **Kafischnaps.** Away from the throb of downtown but only a 15-minute walk back, this is the best deal in town for anyone on a budget. **Pros:** beautifully designed rooms; very hip café; great value. **Cons:** far from the madding crowd; check-in can be slow if the café is busy. [$] *Rooms from: 118 SF* ✉ *Kornhausstr. 57, Kreis 6* ☎ *043/5388116* 🌐 *www.kafischnaps.ch* 🛏 *5 rooms* 🍴 *No meals.*

$$$ HOTEL 🏨 **Seehof.** Offering the best of both worlds, this lodging is in a quiet neighborhood, yet is conveniently close to the opera, theaters, and the lake. **Pros:** small but very nice bathrooms; surrounded by good restaurants. **Cons:** on a narrow and charmless side street. [$] *Rooms from: 330 SF* ✉ *Seehofstr. 11, Kreis 1* ☎ *044/2545757* 🌐 *www.hotelseehof.ch* 🛏 *19 rooms* 🍴 *Breakfast.*

$$$$ HOTEL Fodor's Choice ★ 🏨 **Widder.** Zürich's most captivating hotel was created when 10 adjacent medieval houses were gutted and combined—now steel fuses with ancient stone and timeworn wood. **Pros:** the spectacular Room 210; the more modern Room 509. **Cons:** there are no "cons," since this place is perfect. [$] *Rooms from: 755 SF* ✉ *Rennweg 7, Kreis 1* ☎ *044/2242526* 🌐 *www.widderhotel.ch* 🛏 *42 rooms, 7 suites* 🍴 *No meals.*

18

NIGHTLIFE AND THE ARTS

NIGHTLIFE

Of all the Swiss cities, Zurich has the liveliest nightlife. The Niederdorf is Zurich's well-known nightlife district, but the locales are a shade hipper in Zurich West. In winter things wind down between midnight and 2 am, but come summer most places stay open until 4 am.

BARS

Café Central Bar. In the Hotel Central, Café Central Bar is a popular neo–art deco café by day and a piano bar by night. ⊠ *Central 1, Kreis 1* ☎ *044/2515555* ⊕ *www.central.ch*.

Jules Verne Panorama Bar. This wine bar boasts a wraparound view of downtown. ⊠ *Uraniastr. 9, Kreis 1* ☎ *043/8886666* ⊕ *www.jules-verne.ch*.

Kronenhalle. The narrow bar at the Kronenhalle draws mobs of well-heeled locals and internationals for its prize-winning cocktails. ⊠ *Rämistr. 4, Kreis 1* ☎ *044/2511597* ⊕ *www.kronenhalle.ch*.

Purpur. At this Moroccan-style lounge you can enjoy your drinks lying down on a heap of throw pillows while DJs mix ambient sounds. ⊠ *Seefeldstr. 9, Kreis 8* ☎ *044/4192066* ⊕ *www.purpurzurich.ch*.

SHOPPING

Many of Zurich's designer boutiques lie hidden along the narrow streets between Bahnhofstrasse and the Limmat River. Quirky bookstores and antiques shops lurk in the sloping cobblestone alleyways leading off Niedorfstrasse and Oberdorfstrasse. The fabled Bahnhofstrasse is dominated by large department stores and extravagantly priced jewelry shops.

LUZERN

51 km (32 miles) southwest of Zurich.

With the mist rising off the waves and the mountains looming above the clouds, it's easy to understand how Wagner could have composed his *Siegfried Idyll* here. It was on Lake Lucerne, after all, that Wilhelm Tell—the beloved, if legendary, Swiss national hero—supposedly leaped from the tyrant Gessler's boat to freedom. And it was in a meadow on the western shore of Lake Lucerne that the world's oldest still-extant democracy was born. Every August 1, the Swiss national holiday, citizens gather in the meadow in remembrance, and the sky glows with the light of hundreds of mountaintop bonfires.

Wilhelm Tell played an important role in that early rebellion, and here, around the villages of Altdorf, Bürglen, and the stunningly picturesque lakeside Tell Chapel, thousands come to honor the memory of the rebellious archer.

Yet for all its potential for drama, central Switzerland and the area surrounding Lake Lucerne are tame enough turf: neat little towns, accessible mountains, smooth roads, resorts virtually glamour-free—and modest, graceful Luzern astride the River Reuss much as it has been since the Middle Ages.

PLANNING YOUR TIME

Luzern is a convenient home base for excursions all over central Switzerland. The countryside here is easy to access, and the vast Vierwaldstättersee offers a prime opportunity for the lake steamer cruise. Where the River Reuss flows out of Lake Lucerne, the Old Town straddles the narrow waters. There are a couple of discount passes available for museums and sites in the city to take advantage of.

GETTING HERE AND AROUND

AIR TRAVEL
The nearest airport to Luzern is Zurich Airport, which is approximately 54 km (33 miles) to the northeast.

BOAT TRAVEL
It would be a shame to see this historic region only from the shore; some of its most impressive landscapes are framed along the waterfront, as seen from the decks of one of the cruise ships that ply the lake. Rides on these are included in a Swiss Pass or a Swiss Boat Pass. Individual tickets can be purchased at Luzern's departure docks; the fee is based on the length of your ride.

Contacts Schifffahrtsgesellschaft des Vierwaldstättersees ✉ *Werftestr. 5* ☎ *041/3676767* ⊕ *www.lakelucerne.ch/en.html.*

CAR TRAVEL
It's easy to reach Luzern from Zurich by road, approaching from national expressway A3 south, connecting to A4 via the secondary E41 in the direction of Zug, and continuing on A4, which turns into the A14, to the city. Parking is limited, and the Old Town is pedestrian only; it is best to park your car and walk. All destinations in this region mentioned here are small, reachable by train or boat, and can easily be traveled on foot once you get there.

TRAIN TRAVEL
Luzern's centrally located main station brings hourly trains in from Zurich (23 SF one-way). Directly outside the station's entrance is the quay where lake boats that form part of the public transit system can take you to a variety of towns along the Vierwaldstättersee.

Contacts Bahnhof Luzern ✉ *Zentralstr. 5* ☎ *0900/300–300* ⊕ *www.sbb.ch.*

VISITOR INFORMATION
The principal tourist bureau for the whole of central Switzerland, including the lake region, is Zentralschweiz Tourismus (Central Switzerland Tourism; ⊕ *www.lakeluzern.ch*). There are also local tourist offices in many of the region's towns, often near the train station.

18

EXPLORING

Altes Rathaus (*Old Town Hall*). In 1606 the town council held its first meeting in this late-Renaissance-style building, built between 1602 and 1606. It still meets here today. ✉ *Kornmarkt 3.*

Historisches Museum (*History Museum*). Housed in the late-Gothic armory dating from 1567, this stylish institution exhibits numerous city icons, including the original Gothic fountain that stood in the Weinmarkt. Reconstructed rooms depict rural and urban life. ✉ *Pfisterg. 24* ☎ *041/2285424* ⊕ *www.hmluzern.ch* 🖃 *10 SF* ☉ *Tues.–Sun. and most holidays 10–5.*

Fodor's Choice ★ **Jesuitenkirche** (*Jesuit Church*). Constructed in 1666–77, this baroque church with a symmetrical entrance is flanked by two onion-dome

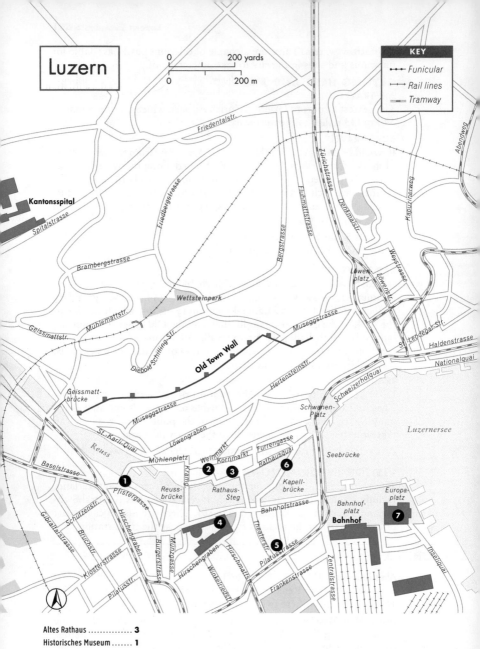

Luzern

KEY
- ••• Funicular
- ┼┼ Rail lines
- ══ Tramway

0			200 yards
0			200 m

Kantonsspital

Spitalstrasse

Bramber, grstrasse

Friedbergstrasse

Friedentalstr.

Zürichstrasse

Denkmalstr.

Kapuzinerweg

Abendweg

Bergstrasse

Flühmattstrasse

Löwen-platz

Weinstrasse

Löwenstr.

Löwenhof

St.-Leodegar-Str.

Haldenstrasse

Nationalquai

Wettsteinpark

Museggstrasse

Geissmattstr.

Mühlemattstr.

Diebold-Schilling-Str.

Old Town Wall

Hertensteinstr.

Schwanen-Platz

Schweizerhofquai

Luzernersee

Geissmatt-brücke

Museggstrasse

Löwengraben

St.-Karli-Quai

Reuss

Baselstrasse

Mühlenplatz

Weinmarkt

Kornmarkt

Furrengasse

Rathausquai

Seebrücke

❶ ❷ ❸ ❻

Reuss-brücke

Rathaus-Steg

Kapell-brücke

Bahnhofstrasse

Bahnhof-platz

Bahnhof

Europa-platz

❼

Pfistergasse

Kramgasse

Theaterstr.

❹ ❺

Gibraltarstrasse

Schützenstr.

Bruchstr.

Hirschengraben

Münzgasse

Burgerstrasse

Hirschengraben

Winkelriedstr.

Pilatusstrasse

Frankenstrasse

Zentralstrasse

Inseliquai

Klosterstrasse

Pilatusstr.

towers, added in 1893. Inside, its vast interior, restored to its original splendor, is a dramatic explosion of gilt, marble, and epic frescoes. Nearby is the Renaissance **Regierungsgebäude** (Government Building), seat of the cantonal government. ⊠ *Bahnhofstr. 11a* ☎ *041/2100756* ⊕ *www.jesuitenkirche-luzern.ch* ⊘ *Daily 6 am–6:30 pm.*

Fodor's Choice **Kapellbrücke** (*Chapel Bridge*). The oldest wooden bridge in Europe
★ snakes diagonally across the Reuss. When it was constructed in the early-14th century, the bridge served as a rampart in case of attacks from the lake. Its shingle roof and grand stone water tower are to Luzern what the Matterhorn is to Zermatt, but considerably more vulnerable, as a 1993 fire proved. Almost 80% of this fragile monument was destroyed, including many of the 17th-century paintings inside. However, a walk through this dark, creaky landmark will take you past polychrome copies of 110 gable panels, painted by Heinrich Wägmann in the 17th century and depicting Luzern and Swiss history, stories of St. Leodegar and St. Mauritius, Luzern's patron saints, and coats of arms of local patrician families. ⊠ *Between Seebrücke and Rathaus-Steg, connecting Rathausquai and Bahnhofstr..*

Kultur- und Kongresszentrum (*Culture and Convention Center*). Architect Jean Nouvel's stunning glass-and-steel building manages both to stand out from as well as to fuse with its ancient milieu. The lakeside center's roof is an oversized, cantilevered, flat plane; shallow water channels thread inside, and immense glass plates mirror the surrounding views. The main draw is the concert hall, which opened in 1998. Although the lobbies are rich in blue, red, and stained wood, the hall itself is refreshingly pale, with brilliant acoustics. Among the annual music events is the renowned International Music Festival. A museum focuses on rotating exhibits of new international artists. ⊠ *Europapl. 1* ☎ *041/2267070* ⊕ *www.kkl-luzern.ch.*

Sammlung Rosengart (*Rosengart Collection*). A father-and-daughter team amassed this amazing group of works by major late-19th- and 20th-century artists. Now housed in a former bank building, the collection reveals their intensely personal approach; the Rosengarts acquired according to their own tastes instead of investment potential. Here you can see Miró's *Dancer,* Léger's *Contraste de formes,* and works by Cézanne, Monet, Matisse, Klee, and Chagall. There's an especially rich selection of Picassos; the artist painted the daughter, Angela Rosengart, five times. ⊠ *Pilatusstr. 10, New Town* ☎ *041/2201660* ⊕ *www. rosengart.ch* ⊠ *18 SF* ⊘ *Apr.–Oct., daily 10–6; Nov.–Mar., daily 11–5.*

Weinmarkt (*Wine Market*). What is now the loveliest of Luzern's several fountain squares was famous across Europe for the passion plays staged here in the 15th to 17th centuries. Its Gothic central fountain depicts St. Mauritius (patron saint of soldiers), and its surrounding buildings are flamboyantly frescoed in 16th-century style. ⊠ *West of Kornmarkt.*

18

ON AND AROUND LAKE LUCERNE

WEGGIS

Boats come from Luzern every 1 to 1 ½ hours during daylight hours. Weggis is a summer resort town known for its mild, almost subtropical climate. The famed **Mt. Rigi** (1,798 meters [5,900 feet]) is just a cable-car ride away: follow signs for the Rigibahn, a station high above the resort (a 15-minute walk). From here you can ride a large cable car to **Rigi-Kaltbad**, a small resort on a spectacular plateau; walk across to the electric rack-and-pinion railway station and ride the steep tracks of the Vitznau–Rigi line to the summit of the mountain. Take an elevator to the **Rigi-Kulm** hotel to enjoy the views indoors or walk to the crest (45 minutes) to see as far as the Black Forest in one direction and Mt. Säntis in the other. Or consider climbing to the top, staying in the hotel, and getting up early to see the sun rise over the Alps—a view that astounded both Victor Hugo and Mark Twain.

RÜTLI MEADOW

The lake steamers from Luzern make frequent stops here.

About 10 minutes beyond the **Schillerstein,** a spectacular natural rock obelisk extending nearly 26 meters (85 feet) up out of the lake, the steamer pulls up at the quaint, 19th-century landing dock for perhaps the most historically significant site in central Switzerland: the Rütli Meadow, where the confederates of Schwyz, Unterwalden, and Uri are said to have met in 1307 to renew the 1291 Oath of Eternal Alliance.

Head up the hillside for a five-minute walk to emerge on a grassy plateau where you'll find a rock and flagpole to honor the sacred spot. Afterwards, head back down, watch the video presentation, and stop in the time-burnished, 19th-century chalet snack shop, with its lovely stained-glass salons and picturesque wood verandas.

THE TELLSKAPELLE

This magnificently picturesque lakeside chapel at the foot of the Axen mountain is a shrine to Wilhelm Tell. The adjacent **Tellsplatte,** was the rocky ledge onto which Tell, the rebellious archer, leaped to escape from Gessler's boat, pushing the boat back into the stormy waves as he jumped. Originally built in 1500, the chapel contains frescoes of the Tell legend. This is but one of the many scenic highlights that line the lake shore, some of which are incorporated into the Weg der Schweiz (Swiss Path; ⊕ *www.weg-der-schweiz.ch*), a historic foot trail, which covers 35 km (21½ miles) of lakefront lore offering spectacular vistas and lakeside perches.

ALTDORF

Schiller's play *Wilhelm Tell* sums up the tale for the Swiss, who perform his play religiously in venues all over the country—including the town of Altdorf, just up the lake from the Rütli Meadow. Leave the steamer at Flüelen, the farthest point of the boat ride around the lake, and connect by bus to Altdorf, the capital of the canton Uri and, by popular if not scholarly consensus, the setting for Tell's famous apple-shooting scene.

There's an often-reproduced **Tell monument** in the village center, showing a proud father with crossbow on one shoulder, the other hand grasping his son's hand.

BÜRGLEN

Tell was supposedly from the tiny, turreted town of Bürglen, just up the road from Altdorf.

Tell-Museum. The Tell-Museum displays documents and art related to the legendary man. ✉ *Postpl., Bürglen* ☎ *041/8704155* 🌐 *www.tellmuseum.ch* 🎫 *5.50 SF* 🕒 *May 15–June, daily 10–11:30 and 1:30–5; July and Aug., daily 10–5; Sept.–Oct., daily 10–11:30 and 1:30–5.*

WHERE TO EAT

$$ SWISS
🍴 **Galliker.** Step past the ancient facade and into a room roaring with local action. Brisk waitresses serve up the dishes that *Mutti* (Mom) used to make: fresh *Kutteln* (tripe) in rich white-wine sauce with cumin seeds; real *Kalbs-kopf* (chopped fresh veal head) served with heaps of green onions and warm vinaigrette; and authentic Luzerner *Kügelipaschtetli* (puff-pastry nests filled with finely ground beef, savory herbs, and cream sauce). Occasional experiments in a modern mode—such as steak with wasabi sauce—prove that Peter Galliker's kitchen is no museum. Desserts may include raspberries with peppermint ice cream. [$] *Average main: 36 SF* ✉ *Schützenstr. 1* ☎ *041/2401002* 🕒 *Closed Sun., Mon., and mid-July–mid-Aug.*

$$$ SWISS
🍴 **Old Swiss House.** This popular establishment has been feeding travelers since 1931. Originally built as a farmhouse in 1858, it pleases crowds with its beautifully contrived collection of 17th-century antiques, leaded glass, and an old-world style, now pleasantly burnished by more than 80 years of service. The standing menu includes specialties from around the country: cubed filet of beef in a green-pepper mustard sauce with fresh buttered noodles, pike-perch with ratatouille and potatoes, and chocolate mousse. In warm weather you can enjoy your meal in the outdoor seating area, which spills out into the pedestrian zone. [$] *Average main: 48 SF* ✉ *Löwenpl. 4* ☎ *041/4106171* 🌐 *www.oldswisshouse.ch/en* 🕒 *Closed Mon. and Feb.*

18

$$ SWISS
🍴 **Pfistern.** One of the architectural focal points of the Old Town waterfront, this floridly decorated guild house provides an authentic medieval setting in which to sample reasonably priced local fare (the guild's origins can be traced back to 1341). Lake fish with steamed new potatoes or *Pastetli* (meat pies with puff pastry) are worthy local options. The interior is woody and publike; in summer the small first-floor balcony or the airy cobblestone riverside arcade provides one of the best seats in town. [$] *Average main: 35 SF* ✉ *Kornmarkt 4* ☎ *041/4103650* 🌐 *www.restaurant-pfistern.ch.*

$$ SWISS
🍴 **Rebstock/Hofstube.** Formerly a 16th-century tavern, this spot is a favorite meeting place for Luzern's art and media crowd. The lively brasserie hums with locals lunching by the bar, and the more formal old-style restaurant glows with wood and brass under a low-beamed parquetry ceiling. Fresh market ingredients are combined for modern, international fare, including chicken simmered in white wine, rabbit

stewed with rosemary, classic garlic snails, and the signature dessert, Vogelheu: batter-fried croissants sprinkled with sugar and cinnamon. There is ample outside seating when it's warm, including a small garden. [$] *Average main: 40 SF* ✉ *St. Leodegarstr. 3, Old Town* ☎ *041/4171819* 🌐 *www.rebstock-luzern.ch/rebstock_02.php.*

WHERE TO STAY

$$$ HOTEL 🏨 **Hotel Des Balances.** Built in the 19th century on the site of two ancient guildhalls, this waterfront lodging is full of style. **Pros:** all rooms have great views; the river terrace is exceptional. **Cons:** top-floor rooms are very small. [$] *Rooms from: 350 SF* ✉ *Weinmarkt* ☎ *041/4182828* 🌐 *www.balances.ch* 🛏 *56 rooms, 9 suites* 🍴 *No meals.*

$$$$ 🏨 **Palace Hotel.** This waterfront hotel drinks in the broadest possible lake views. **Pros:** lakefront setting, right off the promenade; grand interiors. **Cons:** backs onto a main thoroughfare. [$] *Rooms from: 540 SF* ✉ *Haldenstr. 10, Old town* ☎ *041/4161616* 🌐 *www.palace-luzern.com* 🛏 *73 rooms, 57 suites* 🍴 *No meals.*

$ HOTEL 🏨 **Schlüssel.** This crisp, no-nonsense lodging on the Franziskanerplatz attracts a young crowd in search of a bargain. **Pros:** staff makes that extra effort. **Cons:** be prepared for insistent morning church bells. [$] *Rooms from: 190 SF* ✉ *Franziskanerpl. 12* ☎ *041/2101061* 🌐 *www.schluessel-luzern.ch* 🛏 *10 rooms* 🍴 *Breakfast.*

$$ HOTEL 🏨 **Wilden Mann.** The city's best-known hotel, the gracious and atmospheric Wilden Mann has stone walls, coffered ceilings, brass fittings, and burnished wood everywhere. **Pros:** friendly service; medieval architecture straight out of Middle Earth. **Cons:** some ceilings are a bit low. [$] *Rooms from: 250 SF* ✉ *Bahnhofstr. 30* ☎ *041/2101666* 🌐 *www.wilden-mann.ch* 🛏 *42 rooms, 9 suites* 🍴 *Breakfast.*

SHOPPING

The best shopping in town is concentrated along **Hertensteinstrasse.** Although Luzern no longer produces embroidery or lace, it still offers a wide variety of Swiss handicrafts as well as the luxury goods. This pedestrian zone is packed with boutiques and department stores.

BERNER OBERLAND: THE JUNGFRAU REGION

There are times when the reality of Switzerland puts postcard idealization to shame, and those times happen most often in the Berner Oberland, with its awesome mountain panoramas, massive glaciers, crystalline lakes, gorges and waterfalls, chic ski resorts, dense pine forests, and charming gingerbread chalets.

The region's main resort city, Interlaken, lies in green lowlands between the gleaming twin pools of the Brienzersee and the Thunersee. Behind them to the south loom craggy, forested foothills, and behind those foothills stand some of Europe's noblest peaks, most notably the snowy crowns of the Eiger (3,970 meters [13,022 feet]), the Mönch (4,098 meters [13,445 feet]), and the fiercely beautiful Jungfrau (4,157 meters

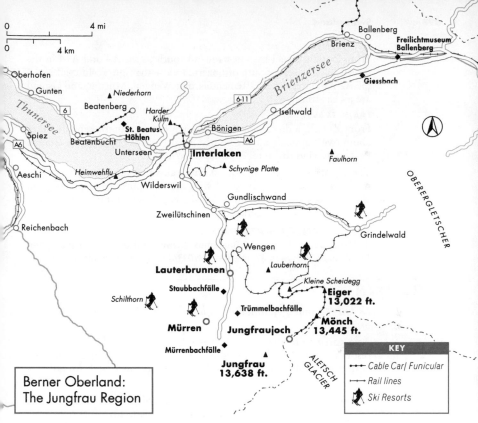

Berner Oberland:
The Jungfrau Region

KEY

••••• *Cable Car/ Funicular*

—— *Rail lines*

🎿 *Ski Resorts*

[13,638 feet]). The area offers an efficient network of boats, trains, and funiculars, a variety of activities and attractions, and a wide range of accommodations.

PLANNING YOUR TIME

The central, urban-Victorian resort of Interlaken makes a good base for excursions for visitors who want to experience the entire Jungfrau region, which includes the craggy, bluff-lined Lauterbrunnen Valley and the opposing resorts that perch high above it: car-free Mürren and Wengen.

GETTING HERE AND AROUND

AIR TRAVEL

Belp Airport in Bern brings you within an hour via train of Interlaken, the hub of the Berner Oberland. Zurich Airport is 2½ hours away.

BUS TRAVEL

Postbuses (called postautos or postcars) travel into much of the area not served by trains, including most smaller mountain towns.

CAR TRAVEL

From Zurich, travel by autobahn A3 south to the A4 and A14 in the direction of Luzern. South of Luzern, follow the signs to Interlaken on the A2 and later the A8. Remember that Wengen, Mürren, and Gstaad are all car-free.

TRAIN TRAVEL

From Zurich, a direct line leads through Bern to Interlaken and takes about two hours, departing hourly; a more scenic trip over the Golden Pass route via Luzern takes about three hours.

The Berner Oberland is riddled with railways, funiculars, cogwheel trains, and cable lifts designed with the sole purpose of getting you closer to its spectacular views. A Swiss Pass lets you travel free on federal trains and lake steamers.

VISITOR INFORMATION

Contacts Berner Orberland Tourismus 🌐 *www.berneroberland.ch.* **Interlaken Tourismus** ✉ *Höheweg 37, Interlaken* ☎ *033/8265300* 🌐 *www.interlaken.ch.*

INTERLAKEN

68 km (42 miles) southwest of Luzern, 117 km (73 miles) southwest of Zurich.

As a gateway to the entire Berner Oberland, this bustling Victorian resort town is the obvious home base for travelers planning to visit both the region's two lakes and the mountains towering behind them.

EXPLORING

Fodor's Choice ★ **Schynige Platte.** For a most splendid overview of the region, head to this 6,454-foot plateau for a picnic, or wander down any of its numerous footpaths, or visit its Alpine Botanical Garden, where more than 600 varieties of mountain flowers grow. A cogwheel train dating from 1893 takes you on the round-trip journey, though you may opt to walk either up or (more comfortably) down. Make sure to specify when you buy your ticket. Trains run from approximately 7:25 am to 4:45 pm. To get here, take the four-minute ride on the Bernese Oberland Railway from Interlaken East to Wilderswil. ✉ *Wilderswil* ☎ *033/8287233* 🌐 *www.jungfrau.ch* 🎟 *35 SF one-way, 60 SF round-trip* 🕓 *Late May or early June–late Oct., daily, depending on snow conditions.*

WHERE TO EAT

$$ SWISS 🍴 **Alpenblick.** This carved wood-and-shingle 17th-century landmark attracts both locals and travelers with its two restaurants. The Dorfstube serves old-style Swiss cuisine—try the *Felchen* (a kind of whitefish) from nearby Lake Brienz, or an Alpenblick Rösti. The Gourmetstübli, a showcase for chef Richard Stöckli's renowned international fare, may include fish and mussels in a saffron pepper sauce or veal ravioli and vegetables. The established wine cellar offers Swiss and international wines; should you have a few too many glasses there is always the option of staying over, as the Alpenblick is also a hotel, with rooms spread over two chalets. The place is in Wilderswil, 2 km (1 mile) south of Interlaken. [$] *Average main: 36 SF* ✉ *Oberdorfstr. 8, Wilderswil* ☎ *033/8283550* 🌐 *www.hotel-alpenblick.ch* 🕓 *Closed Mon. and Tues.*

$
ECLECTIC

✗**Schuh.** With a luxurious shady terrace spilling into the Höhematte in summer and mellow piano sounds enhancing the classically elegant interior, this café-restaurant serves rich, hot Swiss meals (as well as some Chinese and Thai dishes). The recipes may date all the way back to 1818, but most of the dishes are freshly made in-house on a daily basis. Leave room for the chocolate specialties and pastries, like the glossy strawberry tarts, which you'll also find in the adjoining shop. Ⓢ *Average main: 22 SF* ⊠ *Höheweg 56, Interlaken* ☎ *033/8888050* ⊕ *www. schuh-interlaken.ch* ☾ *Closed Mon.*

WHERE TO STAY

$
B&B/INN

⌂**Alphorn.** Completely renovated in 2011, this modern bed-and-breakfast sits on a quiet side street between Interlaken West and the Heimwehfluh. **Pros:** free Internet in every room; peaceful location; pets stay free. **Cons:** some rooms are tiny. Ⓢ *Rooms from: 180 SF* ⊠ *Rothornstrasse 29a, Interlaken* ☎ *033/8223051* ⊕ *www.hotel-alphorn.ch* ⤶ *13 rooms* ☾ *Early Jan.–early Mar.* ❢◯❢ *Breakfast.*

$$
HOTEL
Fodor$Choice
★

⌂**Hotel Interlaken.** The oldest hotel in town, the Hotel Interlaken has been hosting overnight guests since 1323—first as a hospital, then as a cloister, and by the early 15th century as a tavern. **Pros:** in the historic part of Interlaken, close to the train station; friendly, helpful service. **Cons:** no a/c. Ⓢ *Rooms from: 224 SF* ⊠ *Höheweg 74, Interlaken* ☎ *033/8266868* ⊕ *www.interlakenhotel.ch* ⤶ *55 rooms, 5 suites* ❢◯❢ *Breakfast.*

$$$$
RESORT
Fodor$Choice
★

⌂**Victoria-Jungfrau Grand Hotel & Spa.** Restoration has taken this 1865 grand dame firmly into the 21st century, with glitzy touches such as the burled-wood entryway and a vast belle-époque lobby that spirals off into innumerable bars and tea salons. **Pros:** location with view of Jungfrau; wonderful spa. **Cons:** so gargantuan that you can feel like a mouse among many; some call this place overpriced. Ⓢ *Rooms from: 650 SF* ⊠ *Höheweg 41, Interlaken* ☎ *033/8282828* ⊕ *www.victoria-jungfrau.ch* ⤶ *212 rooms, 95 suites* ❢◯❢ *Multiple meal plans.*

THE ARTS
THEATER

Fodor$Choice
★

Tellfreilichtspiele. For a real introduction to the local experience, don't miss the Tellfreilichtspiele, an outdoor pageant presented in Interlaken every summer by a cast of Swiss amateurs. Wrapped in a rented blanket and seated in a 2,200-seat sheltered amphitheater that opens onto illuminated woods and a permanent "medieval" village set, you'll see 250 players in splendid costumes acting out the epic tale of Swiss hero Wilhelm Tell. The text is Schiller's famous play, performed in German with the guttural singsong of a Schwyzerdütsch accent—but don't worry; with galloping horses, flower-decked cows, bonfires, parades, and, of course, the famous apple-shooting climax, the operatic story tells itself. Tickets range from 36 SF to 62 SF. ⊠ *Interlaken* ☎ *033/8223722* ⊕ *www.tellspiele.ch.*

18

LAUTERBRUNNEN

Fodor's Choice
★

10 km (6 miles) south of Interlaken.

The Lauterbrunnen Valley is often ranked as one of the five most beautiful places in Switzerland. What really sets this mountainous masterpiece apart are the more than 70 waterfalls (Lauterbrunnen means "only springs") that line the length of the 3-km-long (2-mile-long) valley. The relentlessly picturesque panorama opens up as you get off the train. This tidy town of weathered chalets also serves as a starting point for the region's two most famous excursions: to the Schilthorn and to the Jungfraujoch. Super-efficient parking and a rail terminal allow long- and short-term parking for visitors heading for Wengen, Mürren, and the Jungfraujoch. Consider choosing this valley as a home base for day trips by train, funicular, or cable, thereby saving considerably on hotel rates. But don't ignore its own wealth of hiking options through some of the most awe-inspiring scenery in Europe.

Staubbachfälle (*Staubbach Falls*). Magnificent waterfalls adorn the length of the Lauterbrunnen Valley, the most famous being the 974-foot Staubbachfälle, which are illuminated at night and visible from town. These falls draw you like a magnet through the village of Lauterbrunnen itself, past a bevy of roadside cafés and the town center (marked by a church and a small Museum of the Lauterbrunnen Valley). Just opposite the falls is a centuries-old graveyard.

MÜRREN

Fodor's Choice
★

7 km (4 miles) southwest of Lauterbrunnen, 16 km (10 miles) south of Interlaken, plus a 5-min cable car ride from Stechelberg.

Birthplace of downhill and slalom skiing (in the 1920s), Mürren offers extraordinarily peaceful mountain nights and an unrivaled panorama of the Jungfrau, Mönch, and Eiger, all set so close you feel you can almost reach out and touch them. Skiers may want to settle here for daredevil year-round skiing at the top (the annual Inferno Race in January is the longest downhill in the world); hikers can combine blufftop trails with staggering views. Mürren is usually accessed from the center of Lauterbrunnen village by an aerial cable car and Bergbahn cogwheel rail (round-trip 30.80 SF) from Grütschalp; alternatively, take the bus to Stechelberg—located at the far end of the valley—where two even more dizzying cable cars (round-trip 21.60 SF) have you reaching for the sky in no time. Upon arrival, Mürren splays out along a long mountain ridge road lined with hotels, restaurants, shops, a few historic chalets, and a large **Sportzentrum** sports center. The village is not overly picturesque, but having your Kaffee und Kuchen on a nearly levitating restaurant terrace will give you that top-of-the-world feeling.

VISITOR INFORMATION
Wengen-Mürren-Lauterbrunnen ☎ *033/8568568* ⊕ *www.wengen-muerren.ch.*

EXPLORING

Bergbahn Lauterbrunnen-Mürren. To reach Mürren from Lauterbrunnen take the aerial cable car across the street from the Lauterbrunnen train station. You then connect to the cogwheel rail from Grütschalp, which runs along the cliff and affords some magnificent views. The whole trip takes about 30 minutes and drops you at the Mürren rail station, at the opposite end of town from the cable-car stop and a nice walk away. There are departures every 15 to 30 minutes. As you ascend, point your binoculars at the gleaming dome on the Jungfraujoch across the valley: you can almost hear the winds howling off the Aletsch Glacier. ✉ *Lauterbrunnen* ☎ *033/8287233* 🌐 *www.jungfrau.ch* 🎟 *30.80 SF round-trip.*

Schilthorn. Mürren boasts some of the longest downhill runs because it is at the foot of the Schilthorn (9,748 feet) mountain, famed for its role in the James Bond movie *On Her Majesty's Secret Service.* The peak of this icy megalith is accessed by a four-stage cable-lift ride past bare-rock cliffs and stunning slopes. At each level you step off the cable car, walk across the station, and wait briefly for the next cable car. At the top is the much-photographed revolving restaurant Piz Gloria, where you can see clips of the film. The cable-car station is in the town of Stechelberg, near the spectacular Mürrenbachfälle (Mürrenbach Falls). ✉ *Stechelberg* ☎ *033/8260007* 🌐 *www.schilthorn.ch* 🎟 *Cable car 98.60 SF round-trip* 🕒 *Departures daily year-round, twice hrly 7:25–4:25.*

SKIING

Swiss Ski & Snowboard School. For lessons, contact Mürren's Swiss Ski & Snowboard School at Chalet Finel, directly behind the Hotel Jungfrau. ✉ *Chalet Finel, Mürren* ☎ *033/8551247.*

18

WHERE TO STAY

$$ HOTEL 🏨 **Alpenruh.** Clad in time-burnished pine, fitted with gables, and sporting some great gingerbread trim, the Alpenruh is as picturesque a hotel as you can get in Mürren. **Pros:** views straight out of a postcard; tasteful interiors at relatively low prices. **Cons:** nearby cable-car girders mar the view from some rooms; only three bathrooms have bathtubs—if you like a long hot soak après-ski be sure to book one of them. [$] *Rooms from: 240 SF* ✉ *Eggli, Mürren* ☎ *033/8568800* 🌐 *www.alpenruh-muerren.ch* 🛏 *26 rooms* 🍴 *Multiple meal plans.*

$$ RESORT Fodor's Choice ★ 🏨 **Hotel Eiger.** With a front-row perch directly across from the Eiger, Mönch, and Jungfrau, this is the most stylish hotel in Mürren. **Pros:** fantastic views; plush and cozy environment; adjacent to the Bergbahn clifftop station. **Cons:** the location is all about peace and tranquility, not excitement. [$] *Rooms from: 288 SF* ✉ *Aegerten, Mürren* ☎ *033/8565454* 🌐 *www.hoteleiger.com* 🛏 *39 rooms, 10 suites* 🍴 *Multiple meal plans.*

JUNGFRAUJOCH

Fodor's Choice ★ *Half-day cog railway excursion out of Interlaken or Lauterbrunnen.*

The granddaddy of all high-altitude excursions, the famous journey to the Jungfraujoch, site of the highest railroad station in Europe, is one of the most popular rides in Switzerland. From the station at

Lauterbrunnen you take the green cogwheel Wengernalp Railway nearly straight up the wooded mountainside and watch as the valley and the village shrink below. From the hilltop resort of **Wengen** the train climbs up steep grassy slopes past the timberline to **Kleine Scheidegg,** a tiny, isolated resort settlement surrounded by vertiginous scenery. Here you change to the **Jungfraubahn,** another train, which tunnels straight into the rock of the Eiger, stopping briefly for views out enormous picture windows blasted through its stony face.

The **Jungfraujoch terminus** stands at an elevation of 3,475 meters (11,400 feet); you may feel a bit light-headed from the altitude. Follow signs to the Top of Europe restaurant, a gleaming white glass-and-steel pavilion. The expanse of rock and ice you see from here is simply blinding.

If you're not sated with the staggering views from the Jungfraujoch terminus, you can reach yet another height by riding a high-tech 90-second elevator up 111 meters (364 feet) to the **Sphinx Terrace:** to the south crawls the vast Aletsch Glacier, to the northeast stand the Mönch and the Eiger, and to the southwest—almost close enough to touch—towers the tip of the Jungfrau herself. Note: even in low season you may have to wait in line for the elevator.

More than views are offered to the hordes that mount the Jungfraujoch daily. From June to the middle of September you can sign up for a beginner's ski lesson or a dogsled ride, or tour the chill blue depths of the **Ice Palace,** a novelty reminiscent of a wax museum, full of incongruous and slightly soggy ice sculptures. Admission to the attraction is included in the price of the excursion.

TURKEY

Istanbul

WHAT'S WHERE

1 Sultanahmet: The Historic Center. The Blue Mosque, Topkapı Sarayı, Aya Sofya, and the Istanbul Archaeological Museums are just some of the impressive attractions in historic Istanbul. This is tourist central, so be prepared for crowds.

2 The Bazaar Area and Environs. Bargain your way through the Grand Bazaar, then follow narrow streets down to the Egyptian Bazaar and the docks on the Golden Horn. On your way, visit the Süleymaniye and other magnificent imperial mosques that rank among the most outstanding examples of Ottoman architecture.

3 The Western Districts. A gem of Byzantine art, the former Chora Church is the highlight of the western districts, which also include the historically Greek and Jewish neighborhoods of Fener and Balat. At the tip of the Golden Horn, Eyüp Sultan Camii is a place of pilgrimage for Muslims.

4 Beyoğlu: Istanbul's "New Town". With its elegant 19th- and early-20th-century apartment buildings, Beyoğlu is the place to see for yourself that "new" is a relative term in this city. The main pedestrian thoroughfare, İstiklal Caddesi, is lined with shops and cafés.

5 Karaköy and Beşiktaş. The Istanbul Museum of Modern Art and Dolmabahçe Palace, the lavish home of the last Ottoman sultans, are among the attractions in these waterside quarters. A perfect pastime is sipping tea and watching the ships go by.

6 The Bosphorus. Hop on a ferry and zigzag back and forth between Asia and Europe, past grand palaces, ancient fortresses, fishing villages, and beautiful old wooden villas.

7 The Asian Shore. The pleasant neighborhoods on Istanbul's Asian side have fewer "sights" but there are interesting enclaves to explore, away from the throngs of tourists.

8 Princes' Islands. This nine-island archipelago in the Sea of Marmara has pine forests, gardens, beaches, and a welcome absence of motorized traffic—the perfect antidote to the noise and chaos of the big city.

KURTULUŞ

KULAKSIZ
MEZARLIĞI

Kasımpaşa
Zindanarkası
Mezarlığı

Fatih Sultan Minber Cad.

Piyale Paşa Bulvarı

Dolapdere Caddesi

Ömer Hayam

YENİŞEHİR

Taksim Caddesi

Cumhuriyet Caddesi

Taşkışla

Maçka
Parkı

Kadırgalar Cad.

İnönü
Stadium

Taksim
Parkı

Gazhane Bostanı Sk.

Mete Caddesi

İstanbul Teknik
University

KASIMPAŞA

TEPEBAŞI

Tarlabaşı Bulvarı

Kasımpaşa Haşköy Yolu

Golden Horn

Sıraselviler Cad.

Şahkulu Caddesi

BEYOĞLU

Meşrutiyet Cad.

İstiklal Caddesi

GALATASARAY

Yeni Çarşı Cad.

İstiklal Cad.

İnönü Cad.

KABATAŞ

Necatibey Cad.

Kabataş
Vapur İskelesi

Kasımpaşa Vapur
İskelesi

Evliya Çelebi Cad.

4

Metro
Stop

Boğazkesen
Cad.

CİHANGİR

Aykapı Vapur İskelesi

Yolcuzade İskender
Cad.

Okçu Musa
Cad.

Küçük Kaldırım Cad.

Necatibey Cad.

5

Cibali Vapur İskelesi

Tersane Caddesi

Galata Kül Tünel

Kemeraltı Cad.

Necatibey Cad.

TOPHANE

köprüler Paşa Cad.

Atatürk Bridge

GALATA

Kemankeş Cad.

6

UNKAPANI

Prof.

Metro
Stop

Rıh Tım

7 →

KÜÇÜKPAZAR

Ragıp Gümüşpala Cad.

Küçükpazar Cad.

EMINONU

Galata Bridge

Deniz Otobüsü İskelesi

Karaköy Vapur İskelesi

Atatürk Bulvarı Hacı Kadın
Caddesi

Sobacılar Cad.

Kutucular Cad.

Reşadiye Cad.

Şehirhattı
İskelesi

Eminönü İskelesi

Sirkeci Feribot İskelesi

19

VEFA

Süleymaniye Cad.

Cadırcılar Cad.

Örücüler Cad.

SİRKECİ

Sirkeci
Station

Statue
of Atatürk

Vezneciler Cad.

İstanbul
University

CAGALOGLU

Gülhane
Parkı

Topkapı
Sarayı

Alemdar Cad.

BEYAZIT Cad.

Bakıralar Cad.

Babıali Cad.

2

Yeniçeriler Caddesi

Gedikpaşa Cad.

SULTANAHMET

Aya
Sofya

1

Kennedy Caddesi (Sahil Yolu)

Türkeli Cad.

Kadırga Limanı Cad.

Atmeydanı
Sokak

Sultanahmet
Parkı

Kabasakal
Cad.

KUMKAPI

Blue Mosque

8 ↙

0   1,000 m

Kennedy Caddesi (Sahil Yolu)

0   1,000 yd

Kennedy Caddesi (Sahil Yolu)

NEED TO KNOW

AT A GLANCE

Capital: Ankara

Population: 75,627,384

Currency: Turkish lira (TL)

Money: ATMs are common; cash is still king in bazaars

Language: Turkish

Country Code: ☎ 90

Emergencies: ☎ 155

Driving: On the right

Electricity: 200v/50 cycles; electrical plugs have two round prongs

Ankara ★

TURKEY

Time: Seven hours ahead of New York

Documents: Up to 90 days out of a 180-day period with valid passport; U.S. citizens must purchase e-visa for $20 in advance

Mobile Phones: GSM (900 and 1800 bands)

Major Mobile Companies: Turkcell, Vodafone, Avea

WEBSITES

Turkey: ⊕ www.goturkey. com

e-Visa: ⊕ www.evisa.gov.tr

Travel Planner: ⊕ www. turkeytravelplanner.com

GETTING AROUND

✈ **Air Travel:** Istanbul's Atatürk Airport is the main hub for international flights, with connections to regional airports around Turkey.

🚌 **Bus Travel:** A robust, and generally quite comfortable, bus system crisscrosses the country.

🚗 **Car Travel:** Rent a car to get off the beaten path in Cappadocia, eastern Turkey, and the coasts, but avoid driving in Istanbul. Gas is expensive, and rural roads are rough and poorly lit.

🚆 **Train Travel:** Train-travel options are limited and slow, though a high-speed rail line between Istanbul and Ankara is expected to be open in 2014.

PLAN YOUR BUDGET

	HOTEL ROOM	MEAL	ATTRACTIONS
Low Budget	€50	31 TL	Basilica Cistern, 10 TL
Mid Budget	€130	120 TL	Bosphorus tour on city ferry, 70 TL
High Budget	£235	330 TL	72-hour Museum Pass Istanbul, €30

WAYS TO SAVE

Fill up at lunchtime. Simple *lokanta* restaurants close early but serve some of the best and cheapest food.

Look for home-style lodgings. Apartments can be your best bet in pricey Istanbul; elsewhere, family-run *pansiyons* (guesthouses) are simple but welcoming.

Hop on the bus. Long-haul bus travel in Turkey is affordable and comfortable. In Istanbul, buy an Ýstanbulkart—these transport passes can be used by multiple people and save you 1 TL per ride.

Go gallery-hopping in Istanbul. Contemporary art spaces like SALT and Arter offer a free alternative to museums.

PLAN YOUR TIME	
Hassle Factor	Medium. Flights to Istanbul can be pricey, and European train travel slows dramatically as it nears Turkey.
3 days	Hit the main historic sights in Istanbul, take a short Bosphorus cruise, and get a taste of the city's food, culture, and nightlife scenes.
1 week	Combine three or four days in Istanbul with a trip to the surreal landscape of Cappadocia (two or three days minimum) or the ruins of Ephesus (one or two days is enough).
2 weeks	If you keep moving, you can hit all the highlights of western Turkey—Istanbul, Ephesus, Cappadocia, and bits of the Aegean and or Mediterranean coast, perhaps stopping over in Ankara or Konya as well.

WHEN TO GO

High Season: July and August are the busiest, hottest, and priciest months to visit Turkey. The Aegean and Mediterranean will be packed with beachgoers, but it's a good time to explore the often-rainy Black Sea.

Low Season: Prices and crowds are significantly reduced in winter, which is wet and gray in Istanbul and can be brutally cold in central and eastern Turkey. The Mediterranean coast and southeast Turkey stay relatively mild, though beach towns partially shut down.

Value Season: Spring and fall are pleasant and lively in Istanbul, though it can be rainy into April. Eastern Turkey won't fully thaw out until May or June, but the Mediterranean stays warm well into October.

BIG EVENTS

April: The Istanbul International Film Festival is a highlight. ⊕ film.iksv.org/en

June or July: Only in Turkey: watching greased-up men grapple for the title at the Historic Kýrkpýnar Oil Wrestling Festival.

September and October: Art parties abound during the Istanbul Biennial (next held in 2015). ⊕ bienal.iksv.org/en

December: The Mevlâna Festival in Konya is a must for fans of Rumi and the whirling dervishes.

READ THIS

- **Birds Without Wings,** Louis de Bernières. Weaves together personal and political dramas.

- **Constantinople: City of the World's Desire 1453–1924,** Philip Mansel. A comprehensive and history of Ottoman-era Istanbul.

- **Istanbul: Memories of a City,** Orhan Pamuk. The Nobel-winner's memoir.

WATCH THIS

- **Crossing the Bridge.** A love letter to Istanbul's vibrant music scene.

- **Distant (Uzak).** Melancholy drama by one of the Turkey's leading lights.

- **From Russia with Love.** James Bond's second film outing co-stars colorful 1960s Istanbul.

EAT THIS

- **Baklava:** The şöbiyet variety is filled with pistachios and cream.

- **Börek:** buttery pastries stuffed with cheese, spinach, potatoes, or meat

- **Kebab:** Turks love their grilled meat in a restaurant or streetside.

- **Meze:** Turkish tapas showcase the country's bounty of fresh fish and vegetables.

- **Turkish breakfast:** a feast of sweet and savory nibbles

With the lion's share of Turkey's population, its richest array of cultural activities, and migrants from all over the country bringing their culinary traditions to the city with them, Istanbul is the logical destination for a first trip to Turkey—and the best jumping-off point to travel elsewhere in the country. The only city in the world that can lay claim to straddling two continents, Istanbul—once known as Constantinople, capital of the Byzantine and then the Ottoman Empire—has for centuries been a bustling metropolis with one foot in Europe and the other in Asia. Istanbul embraces this enviable position with both a certain chaos and inventiveness, ever evolving as one of the world's most cosmopolitan crossroads.

It's often said that Istanbul is the meeting point of East and West, but visitors to this city built over the former capital of two great empires are likely to be just as impressed by the juxtaposition of old and new. Office towers creep up behind historic palaces, women in chic designer outfits pass others wearing long skirts and head coverings, peddlers' pushcarts vie with battered old Fiats and shiny BMWs for dominance of the noisy, narrow streets, and the Grand Bazaar competes with modern shopping malls. At dawn, when the muezzin's call to prayer resounds from ancient minarets, there are inevitably a few hearty revelers still making their way home from nightclubs and bars.

PLANNING

GETTING HERE AND AROUND

AIR TRAVEL
Most international and domestic flights arrive at Istanbul's Atatürk Airport, although an increasing number fly into the newer Sabiha Gökçen Airport on the Asian side of the city. The Havataş shuttle bus (10 TL from Atatürk, 13 TL from Sabiha Gökçen) serves Taksim Square from both airports. From Atatürk Airport you can also take a metro to Aksaray and then a tram to Sultanahmet, which is cheap but slow.

Contacts Atatürk Airport ☎ *212/463-3000* ⊕ *www.ataturkairport.com.* **Sabiha Gökçen Airport** ☎ *216/585-5000* ⊕ *www.sgairport.com.*

BOAT TRAVEL
The main ferry docks on Istanbul's European side are at Eminönü and Karaköy (on either side of the Galata Bridge) and at Kabataş, while Üsküdar and Kadıköy are the most important docks on the Asian side.

With the exception of Bosphorus cruises, ferries are most useful for crossing the Bosphorus (rather than going up and down it) and for getting to the Princes' Islands. Longer-distance trips across the Marmara Sea to Yalova and Bursa depart from the Yenikapı port.

BUS AND DOLMUŞ TRAVEL

Bus service within the city is frequent, with a set fare for most rides of 3 TL with a jeton (token) and 1.95 TL with an İstanbulkart. The bus system is supplemented by private *dolmuşes,* typically bright yellow minibuses that run set routes, leave when full, and make fewer stops than a bus. Dolmuş stands are marked by signs, but you can sometimes hail one on the street; the destination is shown on a roof sign or a card in the front window, and the fare, which varies by distance traveled, is payable only in cash.

Turkey also has an extensive system of intercity buses for travel around the country, departing from Istanbul's large, chaotic Esenler Otogar and the smaller Harem bus station on the Asian side. Many of the bus companies operate their own shuttle buses, known as a *servis,* that collect passengers from various downtown Istanbul locations.

CAR TRAVEL

Istanbul is notorious for congested traffic, a cavalier attitude to traffic regulations, poor signposting, and a shortage of parking spaces. In short, don't even think about renting a car for travel in the city.

PUBLIC TRANSPORTATION

Istanbul's two short underground funiculars are convenient for avoiding the steep, uphill walk to Taksim and İstiklal Caddesi from Karaköy or Kabataş, both near the tram line, which runs right through Sultanahmet. The city also has two underground metro lines: one starts in Şişhane (near Tünel), passes through Taksim, and continues north to the business districts, while the other connects Aksaray, west of Sultanahmet, with the airport and Esenler Otogar.

TAXI TRAVEL

Taxis are metered and relatively cheap—a ride from Sultanahmet to Taksim is about 10–15 TL. Many drivers don't speak English, so it may be helpful to write your destination on a piece of paper, and to bring the business card of your hotel with you so you don't have problems getting back later. Ask your hotel to call a taxi or find a stand in front of a hotel—you'll be more likely to get a driver who won't take you the long way around.

HOTELS

With the number of visitors to Turkey growing every year, there are plenty more lodging options than there were in the past, but Istanbul is not the travel bargain it used to be. Some hotels, though, will offer a 5% to 10% discount for payment in cash, and most lodgings, save four- and five-star hotels, include a full Turkish breakfast with the room rate.

The majority of visitors to Istanbul stay in the Sultanahmet area—home to most of the major historic sites—which has the city's widest selection of hotels, *pansiyons* (guesthouses), and some charmingly stylish inns.

The stiff competition usually means better prices too. The downside to Sultanahmet is that the area is overrun most of the year not only with tourists but also touts.

An increasingly popular alternative is the Beyoğlu area, only a 10-minute cab ride or 20-minute tram ride from Sultanahmet. There's a fast-growing array of both upscale and boutique hotels around Taksim Square, down Meşrutiyet Caddesi, and in the hip Galata, Cihangir/Çukurcuma, and Karaköy neighborhoods. Staying in Beyoğlu puts you closer to Istanbul's best restaurants and nightspots and also gives you a chance to stroll through the area's lively backstreets.

RESTAURANTS

From humble kebab joints to fancy fish restaurants, Istanbullus take their food seriously, though places that cater to tourists (including most eateries in Sultanahmet) are often disappointing.

A classic Istanbul meal, usually eaten at one of the rollicking *meyhanes* in the Beyoğlu area, starts off with a selection of small appetizers called *meze*—just point at what you'd like—and then moves on to a main course of grilled fish, all of it accompanied by the anise-flavored spirit rakı. Though Istanbul is famous for seafood, fish can be expensive, so check prices and ask what's in season before ordering.

Other venues specialize in grilled meats, home-style stewed dishes, or regional cooking from throughout Turkey. International cuisine is generally pricey and not terribly authentic.

Reservations are essential at most of the city's better restaurants, especially if you want to snag a coveted outside table during the summer months. For the most part, dining is casual, although locals enjoy dressing smartly when they're out.

Beer, wine, and rakı are widely available, and at more upscale venues you can also find cocktails. Because of high taxes, however, alcoholic drinks—particularly anything imported—will usually be considerably more expensive than in North America or Europe.

HOTEL AND RESTAURANT PRICES

Prices in the restaurant reviews are the average cost of a main course at dinner or, if dinner is not served, at lunch; taxes and service charges are generally included. Prices in the hotel reviews are the lowest cost of a standard double room in high season, excluding taxes, service charges, and meal plans.

PLANNING YOUR TIME

With just a few days in Turkey, focus on Istanbul, the cultural hub of the country and home to some of its most important historic sites. The city's top attractions—the Blue Mosque, Aya Sofya, and Topkapı Sarayı (as well as the Archaeological Museums and the Basilica Cistern)—are conveniently clustered within a short walking distance of each other.

It's also well worthwhile to get out of Sultanahmet and explore some of the city's diverse neighborhoods: from the conservative western districts (featuring the stunning Byzantine frescoes at the Kariye Müzesi) to posh Bosphorus "villages" like Bebek to lively Beyoğlu, chock-a-block with bars, restaurants, cafés, shops, galleries, and people. No trip to Istanbul is complete without a view of the city from the water. If you don't have time for a full-day Bosphorus tour, either take a short, privately run cruise, or hop on an evening commuter ferry to relax after a hard day's sightseeing.

TOURS

It's generally better to make tour arrangements through a travel agency or your hotel. If you join a group, a "classic tour" of the Aya Sofya, Blue Mosque, Hippodrome, and Grand Bazaar should cost about 85 TL for a half day. For a full-day tour that also includes the Topkapı Palace and Süleymaniye Camii, as well as lunch, expect to pay about 160 TL. Bosphorus tours include a cruise and excursions to sights like Rumeli Hisarı and the Dolmabahçe or Beylerbeyi palaces. Rates for private tours with a guide and driver are higher, and more cost-effective if you have a large party; for two people, expect to pay at least 250 TL per person for a full day, and about a third less per person if you have four or more people. Keep in mind that admission fees and meals are generally not included in private tour rates, so this alternative ends up being considerably more costly.

VISITOR INFORMATION

There are several tourism information offices in Istanbul run by the Turkish Ministry of Culture and Tourism, including at both airports.

Contacts Turkish Culture and Tourism Office ⊕ *www.goturkey.com.*

ISTANBUL

Most visitors to this sprawling city of more than 14 million will first set foot in the relatively compact Old City, where the legacy of the Byzantine and Ottoman empires can be seen in monumental works of architecture like the brilliant Hagia Sophia and the beautifully proportioned mosques built by the great architect Sinan. Though it would be easy to spend days, if not weeks, exploring the wealth of attractions in the historical peninsula, visitors should make sure also to venture elsewhere, in order to experience the vibrancy of contemporary Istanbul. With a lively nightlife propelled by its young population and an exciting arts scene that's increasingly on the international radar, Istanbul is truly a city that never sleeps.

EXPLORING

Istanbul is a city divided. The Bosphorus—the 31-km-long (17-mile-long) waterway joining the Black Sea to the Sea of Marmara—separates the European side of the city from the Asian side. The European side is itself divided by the Golden Horn, an 8-km-long (5-mile-long)

TOP REASONS TO GO

Cruising the Bosphorus. Taking a boat ride past scenic waterfront neighborhoods and wooded slopes studded with mansions and fortresses is quintessentially Istanbul.

Shopping in the bazaars. Bargain like the locals do in the Grand Bazaar and Egyptian Bazaar—it may be a bit touristy, but it's fun.

Admiring beautiful architecture. From the stunning Aya Sofya to the sumptuous Topkapı Palace, the city's greatest works of imperial architecture never cease to impress.

Soaking in a hamam. Steam and scrub your cares away in one of Istanbul's historic (and often beautiful) Turkish baths.

Pleasing your palate. Taste the best of what Turkey's rich cuisine has to offer—from sublimely simple street food to lavish Ottoman-style meals.

inlet that lies between historic Sultanahmet to the south and the New Town, known as Beyoğlu, to the north. In Beyoğlu, the 14th-century Galata Tower dominates the hillside that rises north of the Golden Horn; just beyond, high-rise hotels and other landmarks of the modern city radiate out from Taksim Meydanı (Taksim Square), not far above the Bosphorus-side neighborhood of Beşiktaş. To the north, the European suburbs line the western shore of the Bosphorus. The Asian suburbs are on the eastern shore.

SULTANAHMET: THE HISTORIC CENTER

Sultanahmet is the heart of Old Istanbul, where many of the city's must-see attractions are located: an incredible concentration of art and architecture spanning millennia is packed into its narrow, winding streets.

Fodor'sChoice
★
Aya Sofya (*Hagia Sophia, Church of the Holy Wisdom*). This soaring edifice is perhaps the greatest work of Byzantine architecture and for almost a thousand years, starting from its completion in 537, it was the world's largest and most important religious monument. As Emperor Justinian may well have intended, the impression that will stay with you longest, years after a visit, is the sight of the dome. As you enter, the half domes trick you before the great space opens up with the immense dome, almost 18 stories high and more than 30 meters (100 feet) across, towering above—look up into it and you'll see the spectacle of thousands of gold tiles glittering in the light of 40 windows. Only Saint Peter's in Rome, not completed until the 17th century, surpasses Hagia Sophia in size and grandeur. It was the cathedral of Constantinople, the heart of the city's spiritual life, and the scene of imperial coronations. It was also the third church on this site: the second, the foundations of which you can see at the entrance, was burned down in the antigovernment Nika riots of 532. Justinian then commissioned a new church and, in response to his dictum that Aya Sofya be the grandest place of worship ever built—far greater than the temples whose columns were incorporated in the church—his master architects devised a magnificent

dome. Over the centuries Hagia Sophia has survived additional earthquakes, looting Crusaders, and the conquest of the city by Mehmet the Conqueror in 1453.

Mehmet II famously sprinkled dirt on his head before entering the church after the conquest as a sign of humility. His first order was for Hagia Sofia to be turned into a mosque and, in keeping with the Islamic proscription against figural images, mosaics were plastered over. Successive sultans added the four minarets, *mihrab* (prayer niche), and *minbar* (pulpit for the imam) that visitors see today, as well as the large black medallions inscribed in Arabic with the names of Allah, Muhammad, and the early caliphs. In 1935, Atatürk turned Hagia Sophia into a museum and a project of restoration, including the uncovering of mosaics, began.

Recent restoration efforts have, among other things, uncovered the large, beautifully preserved mosaic of a seraph, or six-winged angel, in the northeast pendentive of the dome, which had been plastered over 160 years earlier. The 9th-century mosaic of the Virgin and Child in the apse is also quite impressive: though it looks tiny, it is actually 16 feet high. To the right of the Virgin is the archangel Gabriel, while Michael, on the left, is almost totally lost. The upstairs galleries are where the most intricate of the mosaics are to be found. On your way out of the church, through the "vestibule of the warriors," a mirror reminds you to look back at the mosaic of Justinian and Constantine presenting Hagia Sophia and Constantinople, respectively, to the Virgin Mary. ✉ *Aya Sofya Sq., Sultanahmet* ☎ *212/522–1750* 💲 *25 TL* ☉ *Summer, Tues.–Sun. 9–7; winter, Tues.–Sun. 9–5; last entry 1 hr before closing time.*

Fodor's Choice **Ayasofya Hürrem Sultan Hamamı.** This hamam, which reopened in 2011
★ following a several-year, $10-million restoration after decades of disuse, is the sleekest and most luxurious in the Old City. It has a prestigious history, having been built by Ottoman architect Sinan in 1556 on the order of Sultan Süleyman the Magnificent, in honor of his wife Roxelana (Hürrem). The setup here is more like that of a modern spa: there is no self-service option, reservations are strongly encouraged, and you'll certainly feel pampered (particularly by the redbud-scented bath amenities). The prices are on par with this level of service —the cheapest treatment is a whopping $110 (about 200 TL). In addition to traditional hamam services, more modern treatments such as aromatherapy massage are offered. ✉ *Babıhümayun Cad. 1, Sultanahmet* ☎ *212/517–3535* ⊕ *www.ayasofyahamami.com.*

Fodor's Choice **Blue Mosque** (*Sultan Ahmet Camii*). Only after you enter the Blue
★ Mosque do you understand the name. The inside is covered with 20,000 shimmering blue-green İznik tiles interspersed with 260 stained-glass windows; calligraphy and intricate floral patterns are painted on the ceiling. After the dark corners and stern faces of the Byzantine mosaics in Aya Sofya, this mosque feels gloriously airy and full of light. Indeed, this favorable comparison was the intention of architect Mehmet Ağa (a former student of the famous Ottoman architect Sinan), whose goal was to surpass Justinian's crowning achievement (Aya Sofya). At the

19

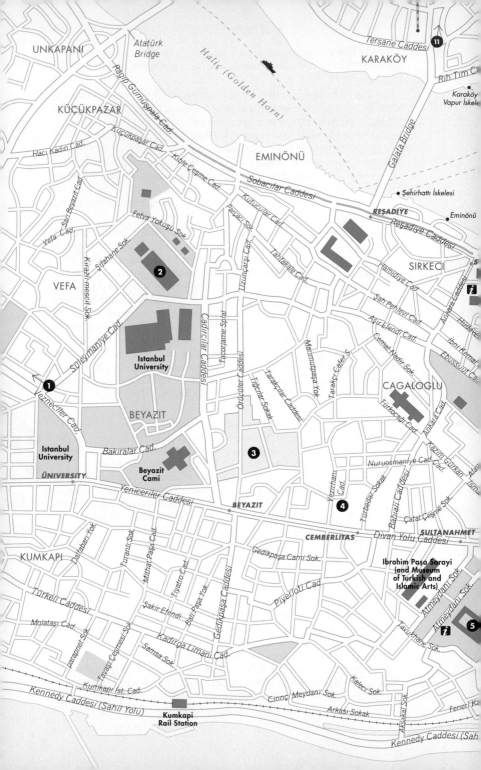

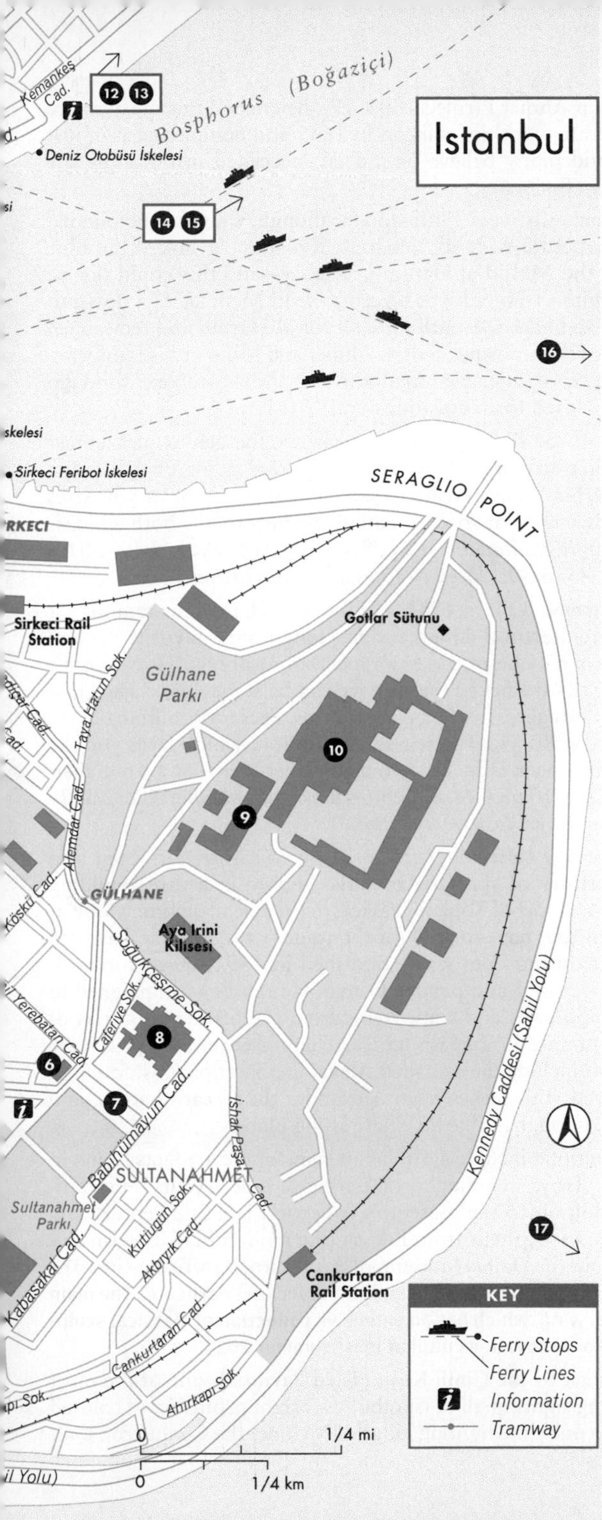

Istanbul

Bosphorus (Boğaziçi)

Deniz Otobüsü İskelesi

Sirkeci Feribot İskelesi

SERAGLIO POINT

RKECI

Sirkeci Rail Station

Gülhane Parkı

Gotlar Sütunu

Gülhane

Aya İrini Kilisesi

SULTANAHMET

Sultanahmet Parkı

Cankurtaran Rail Station

Kabasakal Cad.

Kennedy Caddesi (Sahil Yolu)

19

KEY

Ferry Stops
Ferry Lines
Information
Tramway

1/4 mi

1/4 km

behest of Sultan Ahmet I (ruled 1603–17), he created this masterpiece of Ottoman craftsmanship, starting in 1609 and completing it in just eight years, and many believe he indeed succeeded in outdoing the splendor of Aya Sofya.

Mehmet Ağa actually went a little too far though, when he surrounded the massive structure with six minarets: this number linked the Blue Mosque with the Masjid al-Haram in Mecca—and this could not be allowed. So Sultan Ahmet I was forced to send Mehmet Ağa down to the Holy City to build a seventh minaret for al-Haram and reestablish the eminence of that mosque. Sultan Ahmet and some of his family are interred in the *türbe* (mausoleum) at a corner of the complex, although the tombs are closed for renovations until 2015.

From outside of the Blue Mosque you can see the genius of Mehmet Ağa, who didn't attempt to surpass the massive dome of Aya Sofya across the way, but instead created a secession of domes of varying sizes to cover the huge interior space, creating an effect that is both whimsical and uplifting. ⊠ *Sultanahmet Sq., Sultanahmet* ☉ *Daily 8:30–12:15, 2–4:30, and 5:45–6:30; closed to tourists during prayer times.*

Çemberlitaş Hamamı. Built in 1584, Çemberlitaş Hamamı is famous for its beautiful architectural design and has long been a favorite hamam with visitors, as it's one of the city's most atmospheric. However, it's become so heavily trafficked that service can be somewhat rushed and attendants can be aggressive in asking for tips. Fees for scrubbing by an attendant start at 80 TL. The self-service option, which gives you the chance to linger longer, is 54 TL. Avoid going between 4 and 8 pm, their busiest time. ⊠ *Vezirhan Cad. 8, Çemberlitaş, Sultanahmet* ☎ *212/522–7974* ⊕ *www.cemberlitashamami.com.*

FAMILY
Fodor'sChoice
★

Istanbul Archaeology Museums (*İstanbul Arkeoloji Müzeleri*). Step into this vast repository of spectacular finds, housed in a three-building complex in a forecourt of Topkapı Palace, to get a head-spinning look at the civilizations that have thrived for thousands of years in and around Turkey. The main museum was established in 1891, when forward-thinking archaeologist and painter Osman Hamdi Bey campaigned to keep native antiquities and some items from the former countries of the Ottoman Empire in Turkish hands. The most stunning pieces are sarcophagi that include the so-called Alexander Sarcophagus, found in Lebanon, carved with scenes from Alexander the Great's battles, and once believed, wrongly, to be his final resting place.

Exhibits on Anatolia include a display of some of the artifacts found in excavations at Troy, including a smattering of gold jewelry. A significant recent addition to the museum's collection is a 2nd-century AD Roman mosaic of Orpheus from Edessa (the modern-day Turkish city of Şanlıurfa) that the Dallas Museum of Art returned to Turkey in 2012 after it was determined to have been looted decades earlier. △ **The main building's south wing, which has an extensive collection of classical sculpture, is closed for renovations until at least summer 2014.**

Don't miss a visit to the **Çinili Köşk** (Tiled Pavilion), one of the most visually pleasing sights in all of Istanbul—a bright profusion of colored tiles covers this one-time hunting lodge of Mehmet the Conqueror, built

Hammam Etiquette

A favorite pastime for visitors to Istanbul is to spend time in a Turkish bath, or *hamam*, some of which are in exquisite buildings more than 500 years old. Hamams were born out of necessity—this was how people kept clean before there was home plumbing—but they also became an important part of Ottoman social life. Now that people bathe at home, hamams are becoming less central in Turkish life, and many wouldn't survive without steady tourist traffic.

Nearly all hamams have separate facilities or hours for men and women. Each has a *camekan*, a large, domed room with small cubicles where you can undress, wrap yourself in a thin cloth called a *peştemal*, and put on slippers or wooden sandals—all provided. The main action happens in a hot, steamy chamber where you can douse yourself with water from a marble washbasin while waiting your turn for a vigorous massage and scrub while lying on the heated marble platform in the center of the room.

After you've been worked over, you can relax (and recover) in the same room or head back to your changing cubicle, which typically has a small bed where you can lie down and sip tea or juice brought by an attendant. Before you leave, it's good etiquette to tip your masseur or masseuse.

---

in 1472. Inside are ceramics from the early Seljuk and Ottoman empires, as well as brilliant tiles from İznik, the city that produced perhaps the finest ceramics in the world during the 16th and 17th centuries. ⊠ *Gülhane Park, next to Topkapı Sarayı, Sultanahmet* ☎ *212/520–7740* ⊕ *www.istanbularkeoloji.gov.tr* ⌨ *10 TL for 3 museums* ⊙ *Apr.–Oct., Tues.–Sun. 9–7; Nov.–Mar., 9–5; ticket sales until 1 hr before closing.*

Fodor'sChoice **Topkapı Palace** (*Topkapı Sarayı*). This vast palace on Sarayburnu ("Sera-
★ glio Point"), above the confluence of the Bosphorus and the Golden Horn, was the residence of sultans and their harems, in addition to being the seat of Ottoman rule from the 1460s until the mid-19th century. Few other royal residences match this hilltop compound when it comes to mystery, intrigue, and the lavish intricacies of court life.

Sultan Mehmet II built the original Topkapı Palace, known simply as the New Palace, between 1459 and 1465, shortly after his conquest of Constantinople. Over the centuries, sultan after sultan added ever more elaborate architectural frills and fantasies, until the palace had acquired four courtyards and quarters for some 5,000 full-time residents, including slaves, concubines, and eunuchs. Many of its inhabitants lived their entire adult lives behind its walls, and the palace was often the scene of intrigue, bloodshed, and drama as members of the sultan's entourage plotted and schemed to advance their favorites, sometimes even deposing and assassinating the sultan himself. Topkapı was finally abandoned in 1856, when Sultan Abdülmecid I moved his court to Dolmabahçe Palace on the Bosphorus.

The **Harem**, a maze of 400 halls, terraces, rooms, wings, and apartments grouped around the sultan's private quarters, evokes all the exoticism

19

of Orientalist fantasies of the Ottoman Empire. Yet seeing the 40 or
so Harem rooms that have been
restored and open to the public
brings to mind not just luxury but
also the regimentation, and even
barbarity, of life in this enclosed
enclave. A separate ticket must be
purchased to visit the Harem.

Beyond the Harem is the **Third
Courtyard,** shaded by regal old
trees and dotted by some of the
most ornate of the palace's pavilions. (From the Harem, you enter

> **MONEY-SAVING
> MUSEUM PASS**
>
> The 72-hour Istanbul Museum
> Pass (⊕ www.muze.gov.tr) costs 85
> TL and grants you entrance to 12
> of Istanbul's top museums, includ-
> ing the Hagia Sophia and Topkapı
> Palace, and allows you to skip
> ticket lines, which can be long
> during the high season. It also
> offers discounts to several private
> museums and attractions.

to the side of the courtyard, but to
see this beautiful space to best advantage, make your way to its main
gate, the **Bab-üs Saadet,** or Gate of Felicity, exit, and reenter—and
consider yourself privileged to do so, because for centuries only the
sultan and grand vizier were allowed to pass through this gate.) Foreign
ambassadors once groveled in the Arz Odası (Audience Chamber), but
access to the courtyard was highly restricted, in part because it housed
the **Treasury,** four rooms filled with imperial thrones and lavish gifts
bestowed upon generations of sultans, and spoils garnered from centuries of war and invasions. The glittering prizes here are the jewels. The
most famous pieces are the 86-carat Spoonmaker's Diamond and the
emerald-studded Topkapı Dagger. Two uncut emeralds, each weighing
about eight pounds (!), once hung from the ceiling, but are now displayed behind glass. Other pavilions show off a curious assortment of
treasures, among them relics of the prophet Muhammad (including hair
from his beard), considered especially holy by Muslims, and sultans'
garments, from the lavish wardrobes of the first to the last ruler. Some
of these robes are bloodstained and torn from assassins' daggers; other
garments are stiff with gold and silver thread, tooled leather, and gold,
silver, and jewels. ⊠ *Babıhümayun Cad., Gülhane Park, near Sultanahmet Sq., Sultanahmet* ☎ *212/512–0480* ⊕ *www.topkapisarayi.gov.
tr* ▣ *Palace 25 TL, Harem 15 TL* ☉ *Palace: Apr.–Oct., Wed.–Mon.
9–7; Nov.–Mar., Wed.–Mon. 9–5 (last entry 1 hr before closing time).
Harem: Apr.–Oct., Wed.–Mon. 9–6; Nov.–Mar., Wed.–Mon. 9–5.*

FAMILY
Fodor's Choice
★
Yerebatan Sarnıcı *(Basilica Cistern).* The major problem with the site
of Byzantium was the lack of fresh water, and so for the city to grow,
a great system of aqueducts and cisterns was built, the most famous
of which is the Basilica Cistern, whose present form dates to the reign
of Justinian in the 6th century. A journey through this ancient underground waterway takes you along dimly lit walkways that weave
around 336 marble columns rising 26 feet to support Byzantine arches
and domes, from which water drips unceasingly. The two most famous
columns feature upturned Medusa heads. The cistern was always kept
full as a precaution against long sieges, and fish, presumably descendants of those that arrived in Byzantine times, still flit through the dark
waters. A hauntingly beautiful oasis of cool, shadowed, cathedrallike

stillness (with Turkish instrumental music playing softly in the background), the cistern is a particularly relaxing place to get away from the hubbub of the Old City. Come early to avoid the long lines and have a more peaceful visit. ⊠ *Yerebatan Cad. at Divan Yolu, Sultanahmet* ☎ *212/522–1259* ⊕ *www.yerebatan.com* ▤ *10 TL* ⊙ *Apr–Oct., daily 9–6:30; Nov.–Mar., daily 9–5:30.*

THE BAZAAR AREA AND ENVIRONS

The area between the Grand Bazaar and the Egyptian Bazaar (also known as the Spice Market) was historically the city's center of business and trade, and the streets here still teem with tradespeople and shoppers.

Fodor'sChoice
★
Grand Bazaar (*Kapalı Çarşı*). Take a deep breath and plunge into this maze of 65 winding, covered streets crammed with 4,000 tiny shops, cafés, restaurants, mosques, and courtyards. It's said that this early version of a shopping mall is the largest concentration of stores under one roof anywhere in the world, and that's easy to believe; it's also easy to believe that some of the most aggressive salesmanship in the world takes place here, which is why you should take that deep breath and also put up your guard before entering. Oddly enough, though, the sales pitches, the crowds, and the sheer volume of junky trinkets on offer can be hypnotizing, and you'll probably find it hard to spend less than a couple of hours wandering through the maze. Originally built by Mehmet II (the Conqueror) in 1461 over the main Byzantine shopping streets, the Grand Bazaar was ravaged twice by fire in relatively recent years—once in 1954 when it was almost destroyed, and previously in 1943, in a smaller conflagration. In both cases, the bazaar was quickly rebuilt into something resembling the original style, with its arched passageways and brass-and-tile fountains at regular intervals.

The amazingly polylingual sellers are all anxious to reassure you that you do not have to buy.just drink a glass of tea while you browse through leather goods, carpets, fabric, clothing (including counterfeit brand names), brassware, furniture, ceramics, and gold and silver jewelry. A sizable share of the goods are trinkets tailored for the tourist trade, but a separate section for antiques at the very center of the bazaar, called the *iç bedestan*—once a secure fortress in the heart of the bazaar for the most expensive items—always has some beautiful items on offer; look for the double-headed Byzantine eagle over the door. Outside the western gate of the bazaar and through a doorway is the **Sahaflar Çarşısı**, the Old Book Bazaar, where you can buy new editions as well as antique volumes in Turkish and other languages. Remember, whether you're bargaining for a pair of shoes or an antique carpet, the best prices are offered when the would-be seller thinks you are about to slip away.

To help find your way around, look at the signs overhead, which state where you are and what streets and exits are in which direction—though you'll inevitably get lost, so don't worry too much. ⊠ *Yeniçeriler Cad. and Çadırcılar Cad.* ☎ *212/519–1248* ⊕ *www.kapalicarsi.org.tr* ⊙ *Mon.–Sat. 8:30–7.*

19

Fodor's Choice **Süleymaniye Camii** (*Mosque of Süleyman*). Perched on a hilltop opposite
★ Istanbul University, Süleymaniye Camii is perhaps the most magnifi-
cent mosque in Istanbul and is considered one of the architect Sinan's
masterpieces. The architectural thrill of the mosque, which was built
between 1550 and 1557, is the enormous dome, the highest of any Ottoman mosque. Supported by four square columns and arches, as well as
exterior walls with smaller domes on either side, the soaring space gives
the impression that it's held up principally by divine cooperation. Sinan
was guided by a philosophy of simplicity in designing this mosque and,
except for around the mihrab, there is little in the way of tile work—
though the extremely intricate stained-glass windows and baroque decorations painted on the domes (added later) more than make up for
that. Thanks to a multimillion-dollar restoration project completed in
late 2010, the Süleymaniye can now be seen in its full glory. The tomb of
Sinan is just outside the walls, on the northern corner, while those of his
patron, Süleyman the Magnificent, and the sultan's wife, Roxelana, are
housed in the cemetery adjacent to the mosque. The *külliye*, or mosque
complex, still includes a hospital, library, hamam, several schools, and
other charitable institutions that mosques traditionally operate, so take
a stroll around the beautiful grounds—and don't miss the wonderful
views of the Golden Horn. ⊠ *Süleymaniye Cad., near Istanbul University's north gate* ⊙ *Daily sunrise–sunset, except during prayer times.*

WESTERN DISTRICTS

The historical peninsula's western districts, most notably Eyüp, Fener,
and Balat, are farther off the beaten path than the heavily tourist-trod
Sultanahmet and bazaar areas, but the rewards of visiting are a number
of interesting sights—including the impressive old city walls of Constantinople—and a more authentic atmosphere.

Fodor's Choice **Kariye Müzesi** (*Kariye Museum or Church of the Holy Savior in Chora*).
★ The dazzling mosaics and frescoes in the former Church of the Holy
Savior in Chora are considered to be among the finest Byzantine artworks in the world. Most of the mosaics, in 50 panels, depict scenes
from the New Testament and date from the 14th century. They are
in splendid condition, having been plastered over when the church
became a mosque in the 16th century and not uncovered until the
1940s. "Chora" comes from the Greek word for countryside; the original church here was outside the city walls that were built by Constantine the Great, but at the beginning of the 5th century AD Theodosius
built new fortifications to expand the growing city, which brought the
church inside the walls. The current edifice is believed to have been
built in the 12th century.

The easiest way to reach Kariye Müzesi is by taxi (about 10–15 TL from
Eminönü), or take an Edirnekapı-bound bus from Eminönu or Taksim
Square. The tree-shaded café outside the church and Asitane Restau-
rant next door are both pleasant spots for lunch before you trek back
into town. ⊠ *Kariye Türbesi Sokak (a short walk north of Fevzi Paşa
Cad., near Edirnekapı in Old City walls)* ☎ 212/631–9241 🖃 15 TL
⊙ *Apr.–Oct., Thurs.–Tues. 9–7 (ticket sales until 6); Nov.–Mar., 9–4:30.*

BEYOĞLU: ISTANBUL'S "NEW TOWN"

Beyoğlu, the neighborhood on the hill above Galata, has traditionally been thought of as the "New Town," and this is where you will feel the beating pulse of the modern city: the district is a major destination for eating and drinking, shopping, and arts and culture.

İstiklal Caddesi (*Independence Avenue*). Running for almost a mile between Taksim Square and Tünel Square, İstiklal Caddesi is the heart of modern Istanbul. The street was once known as "La Grande Rue de Péra," after the Pera neighborhood. (The name "Pera" means "across" in Greek, and it was used because the area was on the other side of the Golden Horn from the city proper.) In the 19th century, palatial European embassies were built here, away from the dirt and chaos of the Old City. The wealthy city folk soon followed, particularly after the short funicular called the Tünel—the first underground urban rail line in continental Europe—was built in 1875 to carry them up the hill from their workplaces in the banks and trading houses of Karaköy. The area was traditionally non-Muslim, and the Greek, Armenian, Catholic, and Protestant churches here are more prominent than the mosques. The impressive building behind the massive iron gates halfway down the street is Galatasaray, a French-language high school founded in 1868 that for a time was the most prestigious institution of learning in the Ottoman Empire.

Today İstiklal is a lively pedestrian thoroughfare, filled with shops (an increasing number of them international chains), restaurants, cafés, and one or two cinemas. Turks love to promenade here, and at times it can turn into one great flow of humanity; even in the wee hours of the morning it's still alive with people. This is the Istanbul that never sleeps.

KARAKÖY AND BEŞIKTAŞ

19

The lower-Bosphorus neighborhoods on the city's European side offer an eclectic mix of attractions, from symbols of late-Ottoman power to cutting-edge art spaces.

FodorsChoice **Dolmabahçe Palace** (*Dolmabahçe Sarayı*). The name Dolmabahçe means
★ "filled-in garden," from the fact that Sultan Ahmet I (ruled 1603–17) had an imperial garden planted here on land reclaimed from the sea. Abdülmecid I, whose free-spending lifestyle later bankrupted the empire, had this palace built from 1843 to 1856 as a symbol of Turkey's march toward European-style modernization. He gave father and son Garabet and Nikoğos Balyan—from a prominent Armenian family of late-Ottoman architects—complete freedom and an unlimited budget, the only demand being that the palace "surpass any other palace of any other potentate anywhere in the world." The result, an extraordinary mixture of Turkish and European architectural and decorative styles, is a riot of rococo: marble columns with gilt Corinthian capitals, huge mirrors, trompe-l'oeil painted ceilings, inlaid parquet floors, rich brocade. Abdülmecid's bed is solid silver, the tub and basins in his marble-paved bathroom are translucent alabaster, and more than 200 kilos (420 pounds) of gold were used throughout the palace.

Dolmabahçe is divided into the public "Selamlık" and the private "Harem," which can only be seen on separate, oversized guided tours, which together take about 90 minutes. The Selamlık is far more opulent, befitting its ceremonial purpose, while the Harem shows how traditional social hierarchies and living arrangements continued despite the outwardly European decor. Atatürk, the founder of the Turkish Republic, spent his last days here, and visitors are shown his deathbed in the Harem; all the clocks in the palace remain permanently stopped at 9:05 am, the hour of his death on November 10, 1938.

After the tour(s), take time to stroll along the palace's nearly ½-km-long (¼-mile-long) waterfront facade and through the formal gardens. Two small buildings set back from the palace can be visited without a tour: the ornate Crystal Pavilion, which boasts a crystal piano and glass conservatory with a crystal fountain, and the Clock Museum, which has some of the most elaborate clocks you have ever seen. ■ TIP➜ The palace has a daily visitor quota, so call the reservation number, ☎ 212/327–2626 (Mon.–Sat.), at least a day in advance to reserve tickets and to avoid lines of up to an hour long at the ticket booth. ✉ Dolmabahçe Cad., Beşiktaş ☎ 212/236–9000 ☜ Selamlık 30 TL, Harem 20 TL, joint ticket 40 TL ☉ Tues.–Wed. and Fri.–Sun. 9–4; last tickets sold at 3.

Fodor's Choice
★ **Istanbul Modern.** Housed in a converted warehouse on the shores of the Bosphorus, the Istanbul Museum of Modern Art showcases modern and contemporary painting, sculpture, photography, and works in other media from Turkey and around the world. The permanent collection tells the story of modern Turkish art from its late-19th-century beginnings up through the present day, while a top-notch program of temporary exhibitions features significant local and international contemporary artists, with one gallery devoted exclusively to photography. A free guided tour (Thursday and Sunday at 5 pm; reservations required) can give you a good introduction to the art scene in Turkey. The museum also has a sculpture garden, small cinema, and design store, while the Istanbul Modern Restaurant offers beautiful views of the Sea of Marmara and the Old City. ✉ Meclis-i Mebusan Cad. Liman İşletmeleri Sahası, Antrepo No. 4 ☎ 212/334–7300 ⊕ www.istanbulmodern.org ☜ 15 TL ☉ Tues., Wed., and Fri.–Sun. 10–6, Thurs. 10–8.

THE BOSPHORUS

Whether explored on foot or seen from the vantage point of a boat on the water, the Bosphorus shores are home to some of the prettiest parts of the city. Both sides of the strait are dotted with palaces, fortresses, and waterfront neighborhoods and fishing villages lined with the old wooden summer homes, called *yalıs* (waterside mansions), which were built for the city's wealthier residents in the Ottoman era. Ortaköy, Arnavutköy, Bebek, Emirgan, and Sariyer on the European side and Kanlıca and Anadolu Kavaği on the Asian side are among the more popular destinations. As you cruise up the Bosphorus, you'll have the chance to disembark at some of these waterside enclaves for a stroll.

FAMILY **Rumeli Hisarı** (*Castle of Europe*). Built on a hill overlooking the water, Rumeli Hisarı is the best preserved of all the fortresses on the Bosphorus and well worth a visit. Constructed in just four months in 1452, these eccentric-looking fortifications were ordered built by Mehmet the Conqueror directly across from Anadolu Hisarı, at the narrowest point of the strait. This allowed the Ottomans to take control of the waterway, and Mehmet and his troops conquered Constantinople the following year. The real fun here is in climbing on and around the towers and crenellated walls, which offer fabulous views of the Bosphorus and the nearby Fatih Sultan Mehmet Bridge. ⊠ *Yahya Kemal Cad. 42, Rumelihisarı* ☎ *212/263–5305* ☞ *5 TL* ☉ *Summer, Thurs.–Tues. 9–7; winter, Thurs.–Tues. 8:30-6.*

Sakıp Sabancı Museum *(Sakıp Sabancı Müzesi).* The Sakıp Sabancı Museum is one of Istanbul's premier private museums, thanks to its world-class exhibits and stunning location in a historic villa overlooking the water in the leafy suburb of Emirgan. The permanent collection includes an excellent display of late-19th-century Orientalist and early Republican Turkish paintings, rare examples of Ottoman calligraphy, and antique furnishings such as exquisite Sèvres vases, all from the private collection of the industrialist Sabancı family. The biggest draws, though, are the temporary installations—of a caliber equal to that seen at top museums around the world—which range from retrospectives on major artists like Picasso and leading contemporary names such as Anish Kapoor to exhibits on Anatolian archaeology and masterpieces of Islamic art. Housed in the museum, Müzedechanga restaurant is a foodie destination in itself. The beautiful grounds, which boast 150-year-old monumental trees and a variety of rare plants from around the world, are perfect for a stroll after viewing the art. ⊠ *Sakıp Sabancı Cad. 42, Emirgan* ☎ *212/277–2200* ⊕ *muze.sabanciuniv.edu* ☞ *15 TL (free on Wed.)* ☉ *Tues. and Thurs.–Sun. 10–6, Wed. 10–8.*

THE ASIAN SHORE

19

Spread out along the shoreline of the lower Bosphorus and the Sea of Marmara, the main residential districts on the Asian side have few "sights" as such but offer a pleasant change of pace from the faster tempo of the European side—as well as a welcome escape from the tourist crowds.

Kadıköy. Though there's no visible evidence of its beginnings as the ancient Greek colony of Chalcedon, the relaxed, suburban neighborhood of Kadıköy is a pleasant area to explore on foot. As you approach by ferry, look for the beautiful neoclassical-style **Haydarpaşa train station,** built out over the water on piles at the north end of the harbor. Built in 1908, the terminal is one of the most notable pieces of architecture on the Asian side and a classic Istanbul landmark. You can get off here, at the tiled Ottoman-era quay, or stay on the boat for a few more minutes until it reaches Kadıköy proper.

The area just up from the Kadıköy dock, to the south of busy Söğütlü Çeşme Caddesi, is known as the Çarşı, or "market"—a grid of narrow, pedestrian-only lanes filled with a small open-air food market, shops, cafés, nightlife venues, and a few modern churches. Güneşlibahçe Sokak, home to an assortment of fish restaurants and some bars, is particularly lively. Several streets up and farther to the right, Kadife Sokak, dubbed Barlar Sokağı, or "bars street," is the center of Kadıköy's nightlife, lined with small, wooden rowhouses occupied by bars with a casual, laid-back vibe. A few streets north of Kadife Sokak towards Söğütlü Çeşme Caddesi, Osmancık Sokak (just off Serasker Caddesi) is another popular nightlife street that becomes a sort of miniversion of Beyoğlu's Nevizade Sokak in the summer, lined with small bars with sidewalk seating.

General Asım Gündüz Caddesi, which runs perpendicular to Söğütlü Çeşme Caddesi, has branches of well-known Turkish and international clothing stores, movie theaters, and some eateries. On Tuesdays, near the intersection of these two streets (look for the bronze sculpture of a bull), there begins a lively, open-air street market, selling mostly food and clothes. A tiny nostalgic tram runs in a clockwise direction up General Asım Gündüz, from where it loops down to the lovely waterfront neighborhood of Moda before stopping at the Kadıköy dock. If you've come this far on foot, it's nice to ride the tram back to the dock. ⊠ *Asian Shore.*

Üsküdar. One of the oldest inhabited areas on the Asian Shore, Üsküdar takes its name from the 7th-century BC settlement of Scutari, though nothing now remains of that ancient town. Today, Üsküdar is a conservative residential district with a handful of noteworthy Ottoman mosques. The waterfront looks set to change dramatically with the opening of the long-awaited Marmaray, a rail tunnel under the Bosphorus that is to transport passengers from Üsküdar to Sirkeci in just four minutes. The ferry landing is dominated by Sinan's pretty, if somewhat dark, Mihrimah Sultan Camii, also known as the İskele Camii (built 1548). The large Yeni Valide Camii from 1710 and another Sinan mosque, the small, beautifully situated Şemsi Paşa Camii, are a short walk southwest along the waterfront.

The most architecturally significant mosque in the district, Sinan's **Atık Valide Camii** from 1583, is a 20-minute gradually uphill walk from the waterfront on Hakimiyeti Milliye Caddesi and then on Dr. Fahri Atabey Caddesi. There's a pleasant tea garden in the mosque courtyard, and several other buildings in the complex are in the process of being restored. Another couple hundred yards to the left and then up Çavuşdere Caddesi is the 17th-century Çinili Cami, or "Tiled Mosque," which has splendid İznik tiles. Though the mosque itself is usually kept locked to protect the tiles, it's possible to access the porticos and peak in through the windows. ⊠ *Asian Shore.*

WHERE TO EAT

SULTANAHMET

$$$ ✕ **Asitane.** One of Istanbul's most distinctive restaurants serves season-
TURKISH ally changing menus based on the traditional cuisine of the Ottoman court, which the venue's owners have carefully researched over the past two decades. Dishes feature unusual combinations of ingredients, such as eggplant stuffed with quail, or baked melon with a pilaf and ground meat filling. The historical versions of more familiar contemporary

Turkish dishes, like stuffed grape leaves with sour cherries, also make appearances. The atmosphere is elegant, service exceptional, and there's a pleasant, shaded courtyard open in summer. Asitane is conveniently located next to the Kariye Müzesi. [$] *Average main: 36 TL* ✉ *Kariye Camii Sok. 6, Edirnekapı, Western Districts* ☎ *212/635–7997* 🌐 *www.asitanerestaurant.com* ✍ *Reservations essential.*

$$$$ SEAFOOD Fodor's Choice ★

🍴 **Giritli.** Popular with locals and visitors alike, Giritli offers a prix-fixe multicourse dinner menu of well-prepared Cretan specialties that includes unlimited local alcoholic drinks (wine or rakı). At least 15 different cold mezes—such as sea-bass ceviche, herb-covered cubes of feta cheese with walnuts and olives, and various uncommon wild greens—are followed by hot starters like fried calamari or octopus leg in olive oil. The main course is a choice among several grilled fish, followed by dessert. With its whitewashed walls, colored lights, and blue trim, the restaurant's relaxed garden feels like a slice of the Greek islands in Istanbul. A limited lunch menu is also available. [$] *Average main: 125 TL* ✉ *Keresteci Hakkı Sok.* ☎ *212/458–2270* 🌐 *www.giritlirestoran.com* ✍ *Reservations essential.*

$$ TURKISH

🍴 **Khorasani.** One of Sultanahmet's most outstanding restaurants emphasizes the Arab- and Kurdish-influenced cuisine of southeastern Turkey, from where the restaurant's owners hail. This translates to delicious mezes like hummus, *muhammara* (hot pepper and walnut spread), and thyme salad, as well as tasty kebabs like the lamb shish. Interesting non-kebab main dishes include lamb stew, which has chunks of meat in a thick sauce of onions, carrots, and prunes. Diners can sit outdoors on the cobblestoned sidewalk or get a table inside to watch the chefs prepare kebabs over the large charcoal grill. [$] *Average main: 30 TL* ✉ *Ticarethane Sok. 39/41* ☎ *212/519–5959* 🌐 *www.khorasanirestaurant.com* ✍ *Reservations essential.*

NIŞANTAŞI

$$ TURKISH Fodor's Choice ★

🍴 **Kantin.** A sort of Turkish Alice Waters, Şemza Denizsel finds the freshest ingredients for her daily menus, written on chalkboards, that feature simply prepared but delicious Turkish dishes emphasizing meat and vegetables. Prices are a bit high for the portion size, but you're paying for local, mostly organic foods, such as sourdough bread made with heirloom Anatolian wheat. The venue is especially popular at lunchtime with local professionals; if you can't land a seat in the upstairs dining rooms or on the pleasant backyard deck, consider making a picnic from the side dishes and delectable baked goods sold at Kantin's street-level food shop (entrance is separate from the restaurant). No alcohol is served. [$] *Average main: 24 TL* ✉ *Akkavak Sok. 30* ☎ *212/219–3114* 🌐 *www.kantin.biz* ✍ *Reservations not accepted* 🕒 *Closed Sun.*

19

BOSPHORUS

$$$$ ECLECTIC Fodor's Choice ★

🍴 **Müzedechanga.** A beautiful, lush setting just a stone's throw from the Bosphorus, a Mediterranean-inspired menu, and a sophisticated ambiance makes this restaurant in the Sakıp Sabancı Museum a draw in its own right. Particularly recommendable are the small plates, which include reinterpretations of traditional Turkish mezes, such as grilled halloumi cheese in vine leaves or fried zucchini flowers stuffed with lor cheese. Overseen by award-winning London-based chef Peter Gordon, the menu also shows international influences, like the sea bass with creamy basil sauce or catfish served with potato salad. The venue is especially relaxing in summer, when seating is on the open-air terrace. [$] *Average main: 54 TL* ✉ *Sakıp Sabancı Cad. 42, Emirgan* ☎ *212/323–0901* 🌐 *www.changa-istanbul.com* ✍ *Reservations essential* ⏲ *Closed Mon.*

BEYOĞLU

$$$ TURKISH Fodor's Choice ★

🍴 **Lokanta Maya.** At her highly regarded restaurant, New York–trained chef Didem Şenol offers what could be called "nouvelle Turkish" cuisine, based on seasonal, local, and primarily organic ingredients. A daily-changing menu features a range of tasty appetizers, like grilled octopus with red onions and zucchini fritters with cucumber sauce, and a handful of main course options, such as caramelized sea bass with apricots. The wine list consists of Turkish labels, both established and new. Hip yet unpretentious, with contemporary furniture, light-colored woods, and warm lighting, it's located on one of the main streets in fast-gentrifying Karaköy. [$] *Average main: 38 TL* ✉ *Kemankeş Cad. 35A, Karaköy* ☎ *212/252–6884* 🌐 *www.lokantamaya.com* ✍ *Reservations essential* ⏲ *Closed Sun.*

$$$$ CONTEMPORARY Fodor's Choice ★

🍴 **Mikla.** With sleek, contemporary decor and a stunning 360-degree view of Istanbul from its perch on the top floor of the 18-story Marmara Pera Hotel, Mikla is the dramatic setting for prestigious American-trained Turkish-Finnish chef Mehmet Gürs's modern Anatolian cuisine. Sophisticated dishes of domestically sourced ingredients offer unique flavor combinations rarely seen in traditional Turkish cuisine, such as dentex served with artichokes, fennel, couscous, and lemon confit, or a dessert of sour-cherry compote with bulgur wheat. One of Istanbul's most wide-ranging—though expensive—wine lists features some 40 pages of labels from Turkey and around the world. Diners can choose between a three-course prix-fixe menu (150 TL) or a seven-course tasting menu (225 TL), with or without wine pairings. [$] *Average main: 150 TL* ✉ *Meşrutiyet Cad. 15* ☎ *212/293–5656* 🌐 *www.miklarestaurant.com* ✍ *Reservations essential* ⏲ *Closed Sun. in Nov.–Mar. and July–Aug. No lunch.*

$$$ TURKISH Fodor's Choice ★

🍴 **Münferit.** Owner Ferit Sarper's menu gives traditional meyhane fare a twist that's as contemporary as the upscale surroundings, creating dishes that are innovative and remarkable, but not too experimental. Traditional "Circassian chicken" is made here with duck breast, while feta cheese is served baked in paper with porcini mushrooms and truffle oil; other standout mezes include grilled jumbo shrimp with hummus and a sea bass carpaccio. The extensive wine list features both Turkish and international labels, and desserts are worth saving room for, particularly the house-made ice cream in flavors like tahini and sage. Seating is on the popular outdoor patio—if you can get a table—or in the chic, private-club-like interior. [$] *Average main: 40 TL* ✉ *Yeni Çarşı Cad. 19* ☎ *212/252–5067* ✍ *Reservations essential* ⏲ *Closed Sun.*

ASIAN SHORE

$ 🍴 **Çiya.** Three no-frills branches on the same street comprise one of
TURKISH Istanbul's most popular foodie destinations, and the reputation is well-
Fodor's Choice ★ deserved. Chef-owner Musa Dağdeviren, who hails from the southeastern Turkish city of Gaziantep, is something of a culinary anthropologist, serving recipes from around Turkey that you're unlikely to find elsewhere. His original venue, Çiya Kebap, makes a range of top-notch kebabs, but the biggest draw is the selection of seasonal and daily specials—both meat-based and vegetarian—featuring unusual flavor combinations. Equally memorable desserts include candied olives, tomatoes, or eggplant, served with sweet clotted cream. Nearby Çiya Sofrası offers home-style dishes only, while Çiya Kebap 2 just does kebabs. Alcohol is only served at Çiya Sofrası; at the other locations, try the *şerbet,* a traditional drink made from various fruits. [$] *Average main: 19 TL* ✉ *Güneşlibahçe Sok. 48B, Kadıköy* ☎ *216/336–3013* 🌐 *www.ciya.com.tr.*

WHERE TO STAY

SULTANAHMET

$$ 🏨 **Dersaadet Hotel.** *Dersaadet* means "place of happiness" in Ottoman
B&B/INN Turkish and this small, cozy hotel lives up to its name—rooms have an
Fodor's Choice ★ elegant, even plush, feel, with colorful rugs on the floor, antique furniture, and ceilings hand-painted with traditional motifs. **Pros:** extraordinary level of service; lovely terrace; good value. **Cons:** some rooms are on the small side; no view from rooms on lower floors; walls can be thin. [$] *Rooms from: $150* ✉ *Küçükayasofya Cad., Kapıağası Sok. 5* ☎ *212/458–0760* 🌐 *www.dersaadethotel.com* 🛏 *14 rooms, 3 suites* 🍽 *Breakfast.*

$ 🏨 **Esans Hotel.** The emphasis at this delightful family-run bed-and-
B&B/INN breakfast is on guest satisfaction, and the eight rooms in the restored
Fodor's Choice ★ wooden house are decorated with thoughtful attention to detail, like lovely Ottoman-Victorian-style wallpaper, upholstery, and linens, real wooden floors and ceilings, and old-fashioned furniture. **Pros:** great value; located on quiet street; staff go out of their way to assist. **Cons:** no elevator; breakfast served in rather dimly lit reception area. [$] *Rooms from: $130* ✉ *Yeni Saraçhane Sok. 4* ☎ *212/516–1902* 🌐 *www.esanshotel.com* 🛏 *8 rooms* 🍽 *Breakfast.*

$$$$ 🏨 **Four Seasons Hotel Istanbul at Sultanahmet.** What a rehabilitation suc-
HOTEL cess story: a former prison just steps from Topkapı Palace and Aya
Fodor's Choice ★ Sofya is now one of Istanbul's premier accommodations, where rooms and suites are luxuriously outfitted and overlook the Sea of Marmara, the Old City, or a manicured interior courtyard. **Pros:** historic building surrounded by major tourist attractions; luxurious accommodations; exceptional service. **Cons:** limited fitness facilities; no view from rooms on lower floors; expensive rates and food. [$] *Rooms from: $690* ✉ *Tevkifhane Sok. 1* ☎ *212/402–3000* 🌐 *www.fourseasons.com/istanbul* 🛏 *54 rooms, 11 suites* 🍽 *No meals.*

$$ 🏨 **Hotel İbrahim Pasha.** What was once the home of an extended Arme-
HOTEL nian family offers comfortable, stylishly decorated rooms—a few look
Fodor's Choice ★ out toward the Sea of Marmara—with vintage-looking wood and leather furniture, colorfully patterned Turkish carpets and textiles, and

contemporary Middle-Eastern touches. **Pros:** location just off Hippodrome; personable staff; inviting public areas and roof terrace. **Cons:** standard rooms can be cramped; most rooms don't have a view; rates for standard rooms a bit high for what is offered. $ *Rooms from: $240* ✉ *Terzihane Sok. 7* ☎ *212/518-0394* ⊕ *www.ibrahimpasha.com* ⇗ *24 rooms* ⦿ *Breakfast.*

TAKSIM

$$$$ 🏨 **Divan Istanbul.** An Istanbul institution established in 1956, the Divan HOTEL has been completely rebuilt and redesigned to offer grand luxury that brings together authentic Turkish style and contemporary design elements. **Pros:** first-class service; beautiful half-Olympic-size indoor pool; excellent breakfast (not included). **Cons:** fairly uninteresting views from most rooms; expensive food and beverages; fee for Internet use. $ *Rooms from: $422* ✉ *Asker Ocağı Cad. 1* ☎ *212/315-5500* ⊕ *www. divan.com.tr* ⇗ *149 rooms, 42 suites* ⦿ *No meals.*

BOSPHORUS

$$$$ 🏨 **Çırağan Palace Kempinski Istanbul.** Once a residence for the Ottoman HOTEL sultans, the late 19th-century Çırağan Palace (pronounced chi-rahn) **Fodor's Choice** is Istanbul's most luxurious hotel, with ornate public spaces that feel ★ absolutely decadent and a breathtaking setting right on the Bosphorus—the outdoor infinity pool seems to hover on the water's edge and most rooms, full of Ottoman-inspired wood furnishings and textiles in warm colors, have balconies overlooking the Bosphorus as well. **Pros:** grand setting in incredible Bosphorus-front location; over-the-top feeling of luxury. **Cons:** exorbitant price of food and drinks; high rates, especially for rooms that have no Bosphorus view. $ *Rooms from: $683* ✉ *Çırağan Cad. 32* ☎ *212/326-4646* ⊕ *www.kempinski.com/istanbul* ⇗ *282 rooms, 31 suites* ⦿ *No meals.*

BEYOĞLU

$$$ 🏨 **Pera Palace Hotel Jumeirah.** Extensive restoration has brought this HOTEL Istanbul landmark—founded in 1892 to provide upscale accommoda-**Fodor's Choice** tions for travelers arriving on the Orient Express—back to its former ★ glory, with beautifully outfitted rooms and plenty of period decorations and antique furniture. **Pros:** historic venue; luxurious facilities. **Cons:** some rooms have small bathrooms; rooms on back side look onto street with lots of traffic; expensive food and drinks. $ *Rooms from: $318* ✉ *Meşrutiyet Cad. 52, Tepebaşı* ☎ *212/377-4000* ⊕ *www.jumeirah. com* ⇗ *99 rooms, 16 suites* ⦿ *No meals.*

$$$$ 🏨 **Tomtom Suites.** A restored 1901 residence that once housed Francis-HOTEL can nuns offers superb accommodations and authentic character, with **Fodor's Choice** guest rooms furnished with warm woods, textiles in natural colors, high ★ ceilings, and original artwork. **Pros:** historic building with romantic ambiance; on quiet street; helpful, welcoming staff. **Cons:** only upper room categories have sea views; reached via steep streets; rather high rates, especially considering lack of fitness facilities. $ *Rooms from: $416* ✉ *Boğazkesen Cad., Tomtom Kaptan Sok. 18* ☎ *212/292-4949* ⊕ *www.tomtomsuites.com* ⇗ *20 suites* ⦿ *Breakfast.*

ASIAN SHORE

$$$$ HOTEL Fodor's Choice ★ 🏨 **Sumahan on the Water.** What was once a derelict distillery on the Asian waterfront of the Bosphorus is now one of Istanbul's most chic and original places to stay, with comfortable rooms and suites—all with incredible views of the water and decorated in a contemporary style with a few Turkish touches. **Pros:** stunning waterfront location; stylish and inviting public areas; secluded, romantic atmosphere. **Cons:** far from sights and commercial center; somewhat inconvenient to get to without the launch. [$] *Rooms from: $422* ✉ *Kuleli Cad. 43, Çengelköy* ☎ *216/422–8000* 🌐 *www.sumahan.com* 🛏 *11 rooms, 13 suites* 🍴 *Breakfast.*

NIGHTLIFE AND THE ARTS

Istanbul's nightlife still revolves, in many ways, around its meyhanes, jovial tavernlike restaurants—mostly found in the lively Beyoğlu area—where long nights are spent nibbling on meze and sipping the anise-flavored rakı. But there are lots of other options, too, again mostly in Beyoğlu, which has everything from dive bars to sophisticated lounges, live-music venues and dance clubs. In warm weather, much of the city's nightlife action shifts to the Bosphorus shore, where chic (and pricey) summer-only nightclubs play host to Istanbul's rich and famous—and those who want to rub shoulders with them.

For tips about what to do in Istanbul, pick up a copy of the monthly *Time Out Istanbul* or bimonthly *The Guide,* both of which are English-language publications with listings of hotels, bars, restaurants, and events, as well as features about Istanbul. The English-language *Hürriyet Daily News* and *Today's Zaman* are also good resources for listings and for keeping abreast of what's happening in Turkish and international politics.

BARS AND LOUNGES

The side streets leading off from İstiklal Caddesi in Beyoğlu are full of small bars. Many cater to a student crowd, with cheap beer and loud music, but there are also comfortable and inviting lounges, as well as rooftop bars like Balkon and NuTeras that usually have stunning views and fresh breezes. Kadıköy on the Asian Shore has a lively, up-and-coming bar scene, with Karga Bar among the most established and popular venues. For more upscale bars, head to the neighborhoods and hotels (such as the W Hotel, with its W Lounge) along the Bosphorus. Nightlife opportunities in Sultanahmet are limited to hotel bars and a few touristy pubs.

LIVE MUSIC

Whether you want to hear Turkish pop, contemporary jazz, or good old rock-and-roll, Beyoğlu is the place to be. Babylon, garajistanbul, Ghetto, Nardis Jazz Club, and Salon İKSV are some of the best live-music venues in the area.

WHIRLING DERVISHES

The Mevlevi, a Sufi brotherhood originally founded in Konya, are best known around the world as the whirling dervishes, mystics who believe ritual spinning will bring them closer to God. If you can't make it to Konya to see the *sema* ceremony in the place where it all began, there are a couple of venues at which to see them in Istanbul. It should be noted that these ceremonies—at least in Istanbul—have essentially turned into performances staged for tourists, lacking much religious context. Nonetheless, seeing the dervishes whirl tends to entrance even the least spiritual of people, and gives a window onto an interesting aspect of traditional Turkish culture.

Hodjapasha Culture Center. Housed in a nicely restored 15th-century hamam, the Hodjapasha Culture Center hosts whirling-dervish ceremonies most nights of the week. The hourlong event starts with a performance of classical Turkish music before the dervishes whirl. Though some are captivated by the whirling, others may find it excessively slow and hypnotic, so consider whether this sort of cultural experience is your cup of tea. Note that photography is not allowed during the sema ceremony. Hodjapasha also offers two different dance shows that are considerably more lively; one features traditional Turkish folk dancing and the other is a theatrical performance that combines bellydancing and modern dance. Tickets are 60 TL for the dervishes and 70 TL for the dance shows. ⊠ *Hocapaşa Hamamı Cad. 3/B, Sirkeci, The Bazaar Area and Environs* ☎ *212/511–4686* ⊕ *www.hodjapasha.com.*

Mevlâna Education and Culture Society. A local dervish group, the Mevlâna Education and Culture Society (MEKDER), holds sema ceremonies one Sunday per month at the Galata Mevlevihanesi. The ceremonies last about an hour and include traditional Mevlevi music and ritual whirling. Tickets cost 40 TL. ⊠ *Galata Mevlevihanesi, Galip Dede Cad. 15, Beyoğlu* ☎ *216/336–1662* ⊕ *www.mekder.org.*

SHOPPING

Istanbul has been a shopper's town for, well, centuries—the sprawling Grand Bazaar, open since 1461, could easily be called the world's oldest shopping mall—but this is not to say that the city is stuck in the past. Along with its colorful bazaars and outdoor markets, Istanbul also has a wide range of modern shopping options, from the enormous new malls that seem to be sprouting up everywhere to small independent boutiques. Either way, it's almost impossible to leave Istanbul without buying something. Whether you're looking for trinkets and souvenirs, kilims and carpets, brass and silverware, leather goods, old books, prints and maps, or furnishings and clothes (Turkish textiles are among the best in the world), you can find them here.

İstiklal Caddesi is a pedestrian-only boulevard with everything from global brands like Mango and the Gap and big-name Turkish companies such as Mavi to small shoe stores and bookstores, while many young designers are increasingly taking up residence in the trendy **Galata** area nearby. The **Çukurcuma** neighborhood, also in Beyoğlu, is a hub for quirky antique stores. The high-fashion district is the upscale **Nişantaşı**

neighborhood, 1 km (½ mile) north of İstiklal Caddesi—this is where you'll find the boutiques of established Turkish fashion designers, as well as the flagship stores of high-end international brands such as Armani, DKNY, and Louis Vuitton—though because of the high import taxes, travelers coming from the United States probably won't nab any bargains. Kanyon in Levent, City's in Nişantaşı and İstinye Park are among the most popular upscale malls; Cevahir in Şişli is a little easier on the wallet.

SIDE TRIPS TO PRINCES' ISLANDS

20 km (12 miles) off the coast of Istanbul from Sultanahmet.

GETTING HERE AND AROUND
Ferries (3 TL) and faster Seabuses (8 TL) depart from Katabaş, and take 90 minutes and 45 minutes, respectively. Schedules change with the seasons, so check beforehand for departure times (⊕ *www.ido.com. tr/en*). In summer the early-evening ferries returning to the mainland are often very crowded, particularly on weekends.

No cars are allowed on the islands, so you'll do most of your exploring on foot. The cost of horse-drawn carriage tours varies by distance: it's about 20 TL to go to the Monastery of St. George, and 60 TL or 70 TL for a full-island circle tour. You can rent bicycles (10 TL per hour) from one of the shops near the clock tower on Büyükada: definitely a more fun (and more strenuous) way to get around. To get from one of the Princes' Islands to the other, hop aboard any of several daily ferries.

EXPLORING
The Princes' Islands, known simply as Adalar in Turkish, are everything that Istanbul isn't: quiet, green, and carless. They are primarily a relaxing getaway from the noise and traffic of the big city, though can be quite crowded on sunny weekends. Restrictions on development and a ban on automobiles help maintain the old-fashioned peace and quiet—transportation here is only by horse-drawn carriage or bicycle. There are no real sights, per se; the attraction is the relaxed, peaceful atmosphere. Of the nine islands, four have regular ferry service, but only the two largest, Büyükada and Heybeliada, are of real interest to the general traveler. Both are hilly and wooded, and the fresh breeze is gently pine-scented. They make fun day trips from Istanbul thanks to frequent ferries—both the atmospheric old boats and the faster, less atmospheric catamarans known as sea buses—from Katabaş, near Taksim at the end of the tram line.

From the ferry you can see the two smallest, uninhabited, islands, known in Greek and Turkish as the "pointy" Oxya/Sivri and the "flat" Plate/Yassı. Sivri's main claim to fame was that in the 19th and early 20th centuries Istanbul's stray dogs would be occasionally rounded up and dumped there, while Yassı was the site of the trial and execution of Prime Minister Adnan Menderes after the 1960 military coup. Two of the other inhabited islands are Kınalıada, popular with the city's Armenians, and Burgaz Ada, known to be more Greek, though neither have any significant sights.

19

BÜYÜKADA

Büyükada is the largest of the Princes' Islands and generally the one with the most to offer. To the left as you leave the ferry, you'll see a handful of restaurants. **Yörük Ali Plaj,** the public beach on the west side of the island, is an easy walk from the harbor and also has a little restaurant. To see the island's splendid old Victorian houses, walk to the clock tower and bear right. The most famous of these is the İzzet Paşa Köşkü, at Çankaya Caddesi 55, where Trotsky lived while exiled here. To explore the island, carriages are available at the clock tower square, or there are many places to rent bikes. The carriage tour winds up hilly lanes lined with gardens filled with jasmine, mimosa, and imported palm trees. After all of Istanbul's mosques and palaces, the frilly pastel houses come as something of a surprise. You can have your buggy driver wait while you make the 20- to 30-minute hike up Yücetepe Hill to the **Greek Monastery of St. George (Aya Yorgi),** a 19th-century church built on Byzantine foundations and with a view that goes on and on. As you walk up the path, notice the pieces of cloth, string, and paper that visitors have tied to the bushes and trees in hope of a wish coming true. This is a popular Orthodox Christian pilgrimage site. The outdoor restaurant next to the monastery, Yücetepe Kir Gazinosu, is known for its homemade wine, once made by the monks themselves but now made by a family on the Aegean island of Bozcaada.

WHERE TO EAT

There is little difference from one spot on Büyükada's restaurant row to the next. Generally, the prices are more expensive the closer to the docks. The best bet is to look at a menu and ask to see the dishes on display. **İskele Caddesi,** one street behind the shore road, has some cheaper cafés.

UNITED KINGDOM

London, Oxford, Stratford, Bath
& Stonehenge, Cambridge,
Edinburgh, The Great Glen

WHAT'S WHERE

1 **London.** Britain's capital city is an ancient metropolis energized with contemporary cool. Lovers of palaces and pageantry will delight in Buckingham Palace and, outside town, Hampton Court Palace and Windsor Castle. Besides its renowned monuments and museums, London retains intriguing villagelike neighborhoods that you can explore on its iconic double-decker buses.

2 **Oxford.** This university town is wonderfully walkable, with one golden-stone building after another to discover. Beyond the tidy quadrangles and graceful spires, Oxford has a lively selection of pubs and restaurants. An easy excursion is to the vast, ornate, extraordinary Blenheim Palace.

3 **Stratford-upon-Avon.** One hundred miles northwest of London, Stratford is the place to see Shakespeare's birthplace and watch his plays.

4 **Bath.** This Georgian town is one of England's most harmonious cities, adorned with graceful 18th- and 19th-century architecture. At its heart is a complex of beautifully preserved Roman baths, built around the country's only hot spring. You can also make a side trip to Stonehenge,

the world's most famous prehistoric stone circle.

5 **Cambridge.** The home of the famous university is perfect for ambling around the ancient colleges and museums. Don't miss the entrancing King's College Chapel, a Gothic masterpiece. The best views of the university's colleges and immaculate lawns (and some famous bridges) are from a punt on the River Cam.

6 **Edinburgh.** Scotland's capital captivates many people at first sight, with a skyline dominated by Edinburgh Castle and an array of Georgian and Victorian architecture. The Scottish Parliament is a new addition. Far from being locked in the past, this is a modern, cosmopolitan city, its ancient Old Town and 18th-century New Town enlivened by first-class restaurants and bars.

7 **The Great Glen.** An awe-inspiring valley laced with rivers and streams defines this part of the country. The malt whisky trail begins here, in Forres. Those who believe in Nessie, Scotland's famous monster, can follow the throngs to Loch Ness. Inverness, the capital of the Highlands, is useful as a base for exploring.

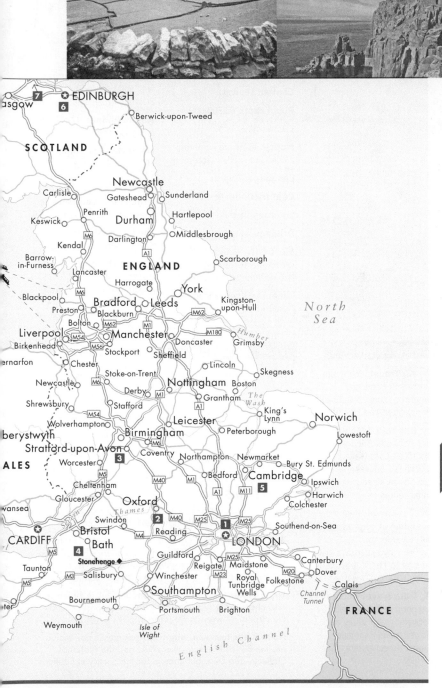

EDINBURGH

asgow

Berwick-upon-Tweed

SCOTLAND

Carlisle
Newcastle
Gateshead
Sunderland

Keswick
Penrith
Durham
Hartlepool

Kendal
Darlington
Middlesbrough

Barrow-
in-Furness
Lancaster
ENGLAND
Scarborough

Harrogate

Blackpool
York
Preston
Bradford
Leeds
Kingston-
upon-Hull

North
Sea

Blackburn

Bolton
Liverpool
Manchester
Doncaster
Grimsby

Birkenhead
Stockport
Sheffield

ernarfon
Chester
Stoke-on-Trent
Lincoln
Skegness

Newcastle
Derby
Nottingham
Boston

Shrewsbury
Stafford
Grantham
The
Wash

Wolverhampton
Leicester
King's
Lynn
Norwich

berystwyth
Birmingham
Peterborough
Lowestoft

Stratford-upon-Avon
Coventry

ALES
Worcester
Northampton
Newmarket
Bury St. Edmunds

Cheltenham
Bedford
Cambridge
Ipswich

vansea
Gloucester
Oxford
Harwich
Colchester

Swindon
Thames

CARDIFF
Bristol
Reading
LONDON
Southend-on-Sea

Bath

Stonehenge
Guildford
Maidstone
Canterbury

Taunton
Reigate
Dover

Salisbury
Winchester
Royal
Tunbridge
Wells
Folkestone
Calais

Bournemouth
Southampton
Channel
Tunnel

Weymouth
Portsmouth
Brighton
FRANCE

Isle of
Wight

English Channel

NEED TO KNOW

Scotland

Northern
Ireland

UNITED
KINGDOM

England

London ★

AT A GLANCE

Capital: London

Population: 63,700,000

Currency: Pound

Money: ATMs are common; credit cards widely accepted

Language: English

Country Code: ☎ 44

Emergencies: ☎ 999

Driving: On the left

Electricity: 220–240v/50 cycles; electrical plugs have two or three square prongs

Time: Five hours ahead of New York

Documents: Six months with valid passport; Schengen rules apply

Mobile Phones: GSM (900 and 1800 bands)

Major Mobile Companies: EE, 3, Vodafone, O2

WEBSITES

Official U.K. Tourism site: ⊕ www.visitbritain.com

The National Trust: ⊕ www.nationaltrust.org.uk

London Theatre Guide: ⊕ www.officiallondontheatre.co.uk

GETTING AROUND

✈ **Air Travel:** The major airports are London Heathrow, London Gatwick, Manchester, and Edinburgh.

🚌 **Bus Travel:** An extensive network of long-distance buses (called "coaches") offers such luxuries as sleeper seats on some routes.

🚗 **Car Travel:** Rent a car to explore at your own pace, but never in London. Gas can be very expensive; also be sure to check regulations if you park in a town.

🚆 **Train Travel:** There are good fast train links between major cities and slower trains to smaller towns. However, fares can be high.

PLAN YOUR BUDGET

	HOTEL ROOM	MEAL	ATTRACTIONS
Low Budget	£120	£15	Tate Modern, free
Mid Budget	£200	£27	Tower of London ticket, £21.45
High Budget	£300	£100	West End Theatre ticket, £80

WAYS TO SAVE

Go for a fixed-price lunch. Many restaurants offer good prix-fixe lunch deals (Indian restaurants especially).

Book a Wolsey Lodge. If you're touring the countryside, Wolsey Lodges offer B&B rooms in comfortable private homes, some historic or with beautiful grounds, at reasonable prices. ⊕ www.wolseylodges.com.

Buy a Visitor Oyster Card for London. This is the easiest and cheapest way to pay for public transport around the capital. ⊕ www.visitorshop.tfl.gov.uk.

Go to a free museum. Many London museums—including the British Museum, the V&A, and the National Gallery—are free, but charge for temporary exhibitions.

Hassle Factor	Low. Flights to London are frequent, and travel links for onward travel are good.
3 days	You can see some of London's historic sights and perhaps take a day trip out to Windsor Castle or Oxford.
1 week	Combine a short trip to London with a one day-trip to Stonehenge and then travel on to Salisbury Cathedral and the grand estates of Stourhead and Longleat, or else head south to Jane Austen's house, the New Forest, and the Jurassic Coast.
2 weeks	This gives you time for a stop in London plus excursions farther north to the beautiful Lake District, the wild moors of Brontë Country in Yorkshire, and Scotland.

WHEN TO GO

High Season: You'll find good weather, sports events, and a busy music festival calendar from June through August. This is also the most expensive and popular time to visit Britain, though the natives tend to desert London in August.

Low Season: Rain and cold make this the best time for airfares and hotel deals—and to escape the crowds. However, London is mobbed with Christmas shoppers in December.

Value Season: September has the most settled weather, plus saner airfares and the buzz of the new season's cultural events. The weather is still good in October, though temperatures start to drop in November. Late April and May is a great time to visit: fewer crowds, lower prices, and a glorious display of flowers. March and early April weather can be changeable and wet.

BIG EVENTS

May: Meet leading writers at the huge Hay Festival in Wales's lovely Brecon Beacon National Park. ⊕ www.hayfestival.com

June: Wimbledon starts the last week and goes into July. ⊕ www.wimbledon.com

August: A galaxy of arts luminaries perform at the Edinburgh International Festival. ⊕ www.edinburghfestivals.co.uk

September: The Open House Weekend is a rare chance to explore many of London's most beautiful structures. ⊕ www.londonopenhouse.org

READ THIS

■ *London: The Biography,* Peter Ackroyd. A magisterial history of the city.

■ *The English: A Portrait of a People,* Jeremy Paxman. A BBC star wryly examines his compatriots.

■ *Notes from a Small Island,* Bill Bryson. An American's look at his adopted home.

WATCH THIS

■ *Notting Hill.* A rose-colored view of London.

■ *Local Hero.* A close-knit Scottish community tries to fend off developers.

■ *Tamara Drewe.* Comic modern reworking of Hardy's *Far from the Madding Crowd.*

EAT THIS

■ **Roast lamb with mint:** a traditional Sunday lunch

■ **"Full English" breakfast:** eggs, back bacon, beans, toast, mushrooms, and tomatoes

■ **English asparagus:** If you're in the U.K. during May and June, don't miss it.

■ **Shepherd's Pie:** minced lamb with vegetables under a mashed potato crust

■ **Cheese:** Blue Stilton and Wensleydale are especially prized.

■ **Fish and chips:** cod or haddock fried in a beer-batter crust with fries

20

From soaring medieval cathedrals to the latest postmodern structures, from prehistoric Stonehenge to Regency Bath, from London's pubs to Edinburgh's buzzing eateries, Great Britain is a spectacular tribute to the strength—and flexibility—of tradition. Alongside the grand country mansions and grim fortified castles, you'll find cutting-edge art, stylistic innovation, and up-to-the-minute shopping.

Nowhere is this meeting of heritage and contemporary flair more evident than in the nation's capital, London, where the city's turn-of-the-millennium building frenzy produced a slew of goodies, including the gigantic Tate Modern art gallery and the British Museum's sparkling glass-roofed Great Court. Consequently, don't be surprised to find glass-and-steel tower blocks marching two abreast the length of the River Thames, or, riding high and white over the city skyline, the stately dome of St. Paul's Cathedral being nudged by glittering skyscrapers.

With all of London's cosmopolitan pizzazz, you're more likely to find Britain's more traditional character outside the metropolis. Anyone wishing to penetrate the mystique of the British monarchy should visit Windsor, the Thames-side town that is home to the medieval and massive Windsor Castle. Centuries-old customs collide with a lively student vibe amid the scholarly quadrangles and graceful spires of Oxford and Cambridge. Conducive to relaxed strolling and long coffee breaks, these are arguably the world's most attractive university towns. To the west, exquisitely Georgian Bath still centers around the hot mineral springs that made it the fashionable spa for the wealthy in the 18th and early 19th centuries. Here, you'll find streets lined with Palladian buildings made of golden limestone, an ancient abbey, ruined Roman baths, tea shops, and boutiques.

Finally, it is important to remember that the United Kingdom consists of three nations—England, Scotland, and Wales—and that 400 miles north of London lies Scotland's capital city of Edinburgh, whose streets and monuments bear witness to the often turbulent and momentous history of the Scottish people. Edinburgh Castle and the Palace of Holyroodhouse are key sights, but there's more to the city than its past. Check out the modern Parliament building, the artistic treasures of the National Museum of Scotland and the National Gallery of Scotland, and the vibrant restaurant scene—as well as the city's famous arts festivals, including the Edinburgh International Festival.

TOP REASONS TO GO

Houses of Parliament and Big Ben: One of the world's most famous sights, the gold-tipped towers of Parliament and the famous clock tower stand at the center of British power, and at the heart of London.

Westminster Abbey: Steeped in history, this church is the final resting place of the men and women who built Britain. Its great Gothic hall has hosted nearly every coronation since 1308.

British Museum: The self-appointed protector of treasures from around the globe, this vast and varied museum in London is packed to bursting with antiquities and alluring objects. Among the greatest hits are the Parthenon Marbles, the Rosetta Stone, and Egyptian mummies.

Windsor Castle: The mystique of eight successive royal houses of the British monarchy permeates Windsor, where a fraction of the current queen's vast wealth is displayed in heraldic splendor.

Christ Church, Oxford: Nothing encapsulates the special atmosphere of this "city of dreaming spires" better than Christ Church, home of Oxford's largest quadrangle and the must-see Christ Church Picture Gallery.

Roman Baths, Bath: Take a break from the town's Georgian elegance and return to its Roman days on a fascinating tour around this beautifully preserved bath complex, built around the country's only hot spring.

King's College Chapel, Cambridge: The famous university town is perfect for aimless ambling, but prepare to be awestruck by King's College Chapel, one of England's greatest monuments.

Royal Mile, Edinburgh: Take a trip north of the border and stroll along this famous thoroughfare, overlooked by the mighty profile of Edinburgh Castle.

Whisky Trail: The two westernmost distilleries on the Malt Whisky Trail are in Forres.

PLANNING

20

WHEN TO GO

Generally, the climate in England is temperate but damp. Summer temperatures can reach the 80s, with high humidity. Scotland is usually three or four degrees cooler than southern England. In winter there can be heavy frost, thin snow, thick fog, and rain, rain, rain.

The British tourist season peaks from mid-April to mid-October, and many historic houses outside London and other major cities close from October to Easter. During July and August, accommodations in popular resorts and areas are in high demand and at their most expensive. The winter cultural season in London and Edinburgh is lively. Hotel rates are lower then, too. Spring and fall can be good alternatives, as prices are still below high-season rates, and the crowds are thinner.

GETTING HERE AND AROUND

AIR TRAVEL

Most international flights arrive at either London's Heathrow Airport (LHR), 15 miles west of London, or at Gatwick Airport (LGW), 27 miles south of the capital. A third, much smaller airport, Stansted (STN), 35 miles northeast of the city, handles mainly European and domestic traffic, as does Luton Airport (LLA).

London has excellent bus and train connections between its airports and downtown. From Heathrow, for example, you can take the less expensive Underground (50 minutes); National Express buses take over an hour, and the Heathrow Express trains take 15 minutes but cost £20 one way. Taxis are pricey (£60 to £80 from Heathrow); your hotel may be able to recommend a car service if this is your preference.

Contacts **Gatwick Airport** ☎ 0844/892–0322 ⊕ www.gatwickairport.com. **Heathrow Airport** ☎ 0844/335–1801 ⊕ www.heathrowairport.com. **Luton Airport** ☎ 01582/405100 ⊕ www.london-luton.co.uk. **Stansted Airport** ☎ 0844/355–1803 ⊕ www.stanstedairport.com.

BOAT TRAVEL

There are regular ferries between Britain and France, Spain, Ireland, and Scandinavia, operated by a number of companies. Sailings can be rough. For fares and schedules, contact the companies directly.

Boat Contacts **DFDS Seaways** ☎ 0871/574–7235 ⊕ www.dfdsseaways.co.uk. **Ferry Cheap** ☎ 01304/501100 ⊕ www.ferrycheap.com. **P&O** ☎ 0871/664–2121 ⊕ www.poferries.com. **Seaview** ☎ 01442/843–050 ⊕ www.seaview.co.uk. **Stena Line** ☎ 0137/040–100 ⊕ www.stenaline.co.uk.

BUS TRAVEL

Britain has a comprehensive bus (multistop public transportation) and coach (the British term for private short- or long-distance buses) network. National Express is the major coach operator, and Victoria Coach Station, near Victoria Station in central London, is the hub of the National Express network. Megabus is a discount coach service between major cities; book tickets online. Coach tickets can be as low as half the price of a train ticket, but many services take twice as long as trains.

Contacts **Megabus** ☎ 0900/160–0900 ⊕ uk.megabus.com. **National Express** ☎ 0871/781–8178 ⊕ www.nationalexpress.com. **Victoria Coach Station** ✉ 164 Buckingham Palace Rd., London ☎ 0207/027–2520 ⊕ www.tfl.gov.uk.

CAR TRAVEL

With a road system designed in part for horse-drawn carriages and where people drive on the left side of the road, Britain can be a challenging place in which to drive. There's no reason to rent a car for a stay in desperately congested London or for traveling between the main centers, since there is adequate public transportation in both cases. Rental rates are generally reasonable, and insurance costs are relatively low. However, gas is very expensive in the U.K.

TRAIN TRAVEL

Eurostar operates a fast and efficient rail service through the Channel Tunnel. Travel time is 35 minutes between Folkestone and Calais, 2 hours and 15 minutes between London's St. Pancras Station and Paris's Gare du Nord, and 2 hours between St. Pancras and Brussels.

With all major cities and many small towns in Britain served by trains, rail travel is the most pleasant way to cover long distances, though fares can be high. For trips of less than 200 miles, trains are usually cheaper and quicker than planes. Buying tickets in advance can save you a substantial amount. Call National Rail Enquiries for information on all services as well as regional rail passes. BritRail passes, purchased before your trip, can save you money; Eurail passes cannot be used in Britain.

Contacts Eurostar ☎ *0843/218–6186* ⊕ *www.eurostar.com.* **National Rail Enquiries** ☎ *0845/748–4950, 020/7278–5240 outside U.K.* ⊕ *www.nationalrail. co.uk.* **Rail Europe** ☎ *800/622–8600 in U.S., 0844/848–4064 in U.K.* ⊕ *www. raileurope.com.*

HOTELS

Britain has everything from luxurious retreats in converted country houses to budget chain hotels and bed-and-breakfasts. In many towns and villages you will find former coaching inns from the stagecoach era. Some older hotels can be in need of refurbishment, but they're usually cheaper. B&Bs are popular with British travelers and can be a great way to meet locals. Some B&Bs are gorgeous, and many are in handy locations; others are neither, so be careful.

Hotels, guesthouses, inns, and B&Bs in the United Kingdom are all graded from one to five stars by the tourism board, VisitBritain. Basically, the more stars a property has, the more facilities it has, and the facilities will be of a higher standard.

Especially in London, rooms and bathrooms may be smaller than what you find in the United States. Most places offer "en suite" (attached) bathrooms, although some older ones may have only washbasins in the rooms; in this case, showers and bathtubs (and toilets) are usually just down the hall. A "private bathroom" is one for your exclusive use, but not attached. When you book a room in the mid-to-lower price categories, it's best to confirm your request for a room with en-suite or private facilities.

Unless otherwise noted, all lodgings listed have an elevator, a private bathroom, a room phone, and a TV. Air-conditioning is often the exception rather than the rule in the U.K.

20

RESTAURANTS

MEALS AND MEAL TIMES

Outside London almost every accommodation option in Britain includes breakfast in the bill. This could mean a "full English breakfast," consisting of eggs, bacon, grilled tomato, and tea or coffee; but more often it is a lighter "continental breakfast" option—rolls, croissants, or pastries.

At lunch you can grab a sandwich between sights, pop into the local pub, or sit down in a restaurant. Note that most pubs do not have any waitstaff and that you are expected to go to the bar, order a beverage and your meal, and inform them of your table number.

Breakfast is generally served between 7:30 and 9, lunch between noon and 2, dinner or supper between 7:30 and 9:30, sometimes earlier, seldom later except in large cities. Tea shops are often open all day in touristy areas, offering drinks and snacks. Many pubs do not serve lunch after 2 or 3, or dinner after 9. Since 2007, smoking has been banned in pubs, clubs, and restaurants throughout Britain.

WINE, BEER, AND SPIRITS

Among the hundreds of British beers, the traditional brew is known as bitter and is not carbonated; it's usually served at room temperature. Locally brewed "real ales" are worth seeking out. Chilled, fizzy American-style beer is called lager. Stouts like Guinness and Murphy's are thick, pitch-black brews you'll either love or hate; ciders, made from apples (or sometimes pears), are an alcoholic drink in Britain; shandies are a low-alcohol mix of beer and lemon soda. The legal drinking age is 18. Most pubs tend to be child-friendly, but others have restricted hours for children. If you're in doubt, ask the bartender.

PAYING

Be sure that you don't double-pay a service charge. Some restaurants exclude service charges from the printed menu, then add 10% to 15% to the check. Others will stamp "service not included" along the bottom of the bill, in which case you should add 10% to 15%. Credit cards are widely accepted in restaurants, but many pubs still require cash.

RESERVATIONS AND DRESS

We mention reservations only when these are essential or when they are not accepted. For popular restaurants, book as far ahead as you can (often 30 days); large parties should always call ahead. We mention dress only if men are required to wear a jacket or a jacket and tie.

HOTEL AND RESTAURANT PRICES

Prices in the restaurant reviews are the average cost of a main course at dinner or, if dinner is not served, at lunch; taxes and service charges are generally included. Prices in the hotel reviews are the lowest cost of a standard double room in high season, excluding taxes, service charges, and meal plans (except at all-inclusives).

PLANNING YOUR TIME

For many, London is the main priority of any visit to Britain, and with good reason. The capital has a concentration of everything that most visitors associate with the country: colorful pageantry, time-burnished monuments, and some of the world's greatest museums, not to mention cutting-edge art, fashion, and nightlife. The city's charms could easily swallow up an entire holiday without exhausting its marvels.

However, there are good reasons for limiting your time here and moving outside the metropolis. London is one of the most expensive spots on the planet, for a start. Secondly, the chances of getting properly

DISCOUNTS AND DEALS

All national collections (such as the Natural History Museum, Science Museum, and the Victoria & Albert Museum—all in London) are free, a real bargain for museumgoers.

If you plan to visit castles, gardens, and historic houses during your stay, look into discount passes or organization memberships. Match what the pass or membership offers against your itinerary to see if it's worthwhile. VisitBritain's English Heritage Overseas Visitors Pass is £24 for 9 days, £28 for 16 days for one adult. The National Trust Touring Pass, for overseas visitors, is £24 for 7 days, £29 for 14 days. These passes are sold online and at major tourist information centers in Britain. Family passes are available. Annual membership in the National Trust (through the Royal Oak Foundation, the U.S. affiliate) is $55 a year, versus £46 if you join in Britain.

Contacts English Heritage ☎ 0870/333–1181 ⊕ www. english-heritage.org.uk. **National Trust** ☎ 0844/800–1895 ⊕ www. nationaltrust.org.uk. **Royal Oak Foundation** ☎ 212/480–2889, 800/913–6565 ⊕ www.royal-oak.org.

acquainted with the country and its population are slim—in fact, there are some places where locals may seem pretty thin on the ground. But the best reason of all to venture beyond the confines of London is to sample the diverse attractions that Britain has to offer away from the noise and crowds of the capital. You can immerse yourself in the rarefied, history-soaked atmosphere of Oxford and Cambridge, or dip into the elegance and vivacity of Bath. For a once-in-a-lifetime play-going experience, there is no substitute for seeing an authentic slice of Shakespeare in his hometown of Stratford-upon-Avon. Each of these places is comparatively close to London (1½–2½ hours' driving) and could be visited on a day excursion, though a stay of a night or two would allow a deeper appreciation.

If you want a leisurely tour of a day or more outside of London, you could base yourself in either Bath or Stratford.

With more time, you could detach yourself entirely from London's ambit to experience another side of Britain, in Edinburgh. A surprise awaits those for whom these northern reaches conjure images of a harsh and bleak country. There is plenty of dramatic splendor in Edinburgh Castle, as well as rousing spirit at events such as the Edinburgh Festival. Scotland offers a genuine friendliness that sometimes seems lacking in fast-moving London. A couple of days would be sufficient to appreciate Edinburgh's individual character. However, you would have to factor in the travel time required to reach it.

20

LONDON

London is an ancient city whose history greets you at every turn; it's also one of the coolest cities in the world. To gain a sense of its continuity, stand on Waterloo Bridge at sunset. To the east, the great globe of St. Paul's Cathedral glows golden in the fading sunlight as it has since the 17th century, still majestic amid the modern glass towers. To the west stand the Victorian-Gothic splendor of the Palace of Westminster, home to the "Mother of Parliaments." Past them both snakes the swift, dark Thames, which flowed past the Roman settlement of Londinium nearly 2,000 years ago. If London contained only its famous landmarks—the Tower of London, Big Ben, Westminster Abbey, Buckingham Palace—it would still rank as one of the world's top cities. But London is so much more.

The capital beckons with great museums, royal pageantry, and history-steeped houses. It has a unique mixture of Georgian terraces sitting next to cutting-edge modern skyscrapers, while parks and squares provide unexpected oases of greenery in the urban density. Modern-day London largely reflects its medieval layout, a willfully difficult tangle of streets. Even Londoners, most of whom own a dog-eared copy of an indispensable A–Z street finder or a smartphone, get lost in their own city. But the bewildering street patterns will be a plus for anyone who likes wandering on foot down atmospheric streets.

Today the city's art, style, fashion, and restaurant scenes make headlines around the world. London's chefs have become internationally influential, its fashion designers and art stars set global trends, its nightlife continues to produce exciting new bands, and its theater remains celebrated for both superb classical and innovative productions."

PLANNING YOUR TIME

London is sprawling, so you might focus a day's efforts in adjacent areas. It's easy, for example, to spend a day or more in the dense concentration of sights around Westminster and Royal London. If you're heading east to see St. Paul's Cathedral in the City, you might visit the Tower of London, which is nearby. You can make a day out of the major museums, but take a break in one of London's beloved parks. To get the most out of London, set aside time for random wandering. Walk in the city's backstreets and mews, around Park Lane and Kensington. Pass up Buckingham Palace for Kensington Palace, and abandon the city's standard-issue chain stores for its wonderful markets.

GETTING HERE AND AROUND
BUS TRAVEL

Buses, or "coaches," as long-distance services are known here, operate mainly from London's Victoria Coach Station to more than 1,200 major towns and cities.

In central London, buses are traditionally bright-red double- and single-deckers. You must purchase tickets from machines at bus stops along the routes before you board. Bus stops are clearly indicated. When the word "request" is written across the sign, you must flag the bus down. Buses are a good way to see the town, but don't take one if you're in a hurry.

A flat-rate fare of £2.40 applies for all bus fares. You can get a Visitor Oyster card, an electronic smart card that you load with money, which is then deducted each time you use the card on buses or the tube: a single Oyster card fare is £1.40. A 7-Day Bus Pass for Zones 1–4 is £19.60

but must be bought before boarding from one of the machines at bus stops, most newsagents, or underground stations.

If you're traveling on the tube (subway) as well as the bus, consider an off-peak one-day Travelcard (£7.30), which allows unrestricted travel on buses *and* tubes inZones 1 and 2 after 9:30 am and all day on weekends and national holidays. "Peak" Travelcards—those for use before 9:30 am—are more expensive (£8.80 for Zones 1 and 2). Children under 11 travel free on the tube and buses after 9:30 am, while children ages 11–15 travel free on buses as long as they order an Oyster card at least four weeks before they travel.

CAR TRAVEL

The major approach roads to London are six-lane motorways. Motorways (from Heathrow, M4; from Gatwick, M23 to M25, then M3; Stansted, M11) are usually the faster option for getting in and out of town, although rush-hour traffic is horrendous.

The simple advice about driving in London is: don't. If you must drive in London, remember to drive on the left and stick to the speed limit (30 mph on most city streets, 20 mph in Islington, Camden, and some other boroughs). A £10 "congestion charge" is levied on all vehicles entering central London (bounded by the Inner Ring Road; street signs and "C" road markings note the area) on weekdays from 7 to 6:30, excluding bank holidays. Pay in advance (by phone, mail, or Internet) or on that day until 10 pm if you're entering the central zone. There are no tollbooths; cameras monitor the area. For current information, check ⊕ *www.cclondon.com.*

TAXI TRAVEL

Taxis are expensive, but if you're with several people they can be practical. Hotels and main tourist areas have taxi ranks; you can also hail taxis on the street. If the yellow "for hire" sign is lighted on top, the taxi is available. Drivers often cruise at night with their signs unlighted, so if you see an unlighted cab, keep your hand up. Generally fares start at £2.20 and increase according to distance. Tips are extra, usually 10% to 15% per ride. The average cost for a 15-minute journey within central London is £12. To get to a surrounding area—Islington or Chelsea, for example—expect to pay approximately £20.

TRAIN TRAVEL

London has eight major train stations, each serving a different area of the country, all accessible by Underground or bus. Trains are operated by a number of private companies, but National Rail Enquiries acts as a central rail information number.

Contacts National Rail Enquiries ☎ *0845/748–4950, 020/7278–5240 outside U.K.* ⊕ *www.nationalrail.co.uk.*

TUBE TRAVEL

London's extensive Underground (tube) system has color-coded routes, clear signs, and extensive connections. Trains run out into the suburbs, and all stations are marked with the London Underground circular symbol. (In Britain, the word "subway" means "pedestrian underpass.") Some lines have branches (Central, District, Northern, Metropolitan,

20

and Piccadilly), so be sure to note which branch is needed for your destination. Electronic platform signs tell you the final stop and route of the next train and how many minutes until it arrives.

London is divided into six concentric zones. The more zones your trip crosses, the higher the fare. Most tourist sights are within Zone 1. If you inadvertently travel into a zone for which you do not have the right ticket, you can purchase an "extension" to your own ticket at the ticket office by the barriers. This usually costs a pound, and merely equalizes your fare. Buy a Visitor Oyster card for fare reductions; it can be a huge money-saver.

The tube begins running just after 5 am Monday through Saturday; the last services leave central London between midnight and 12:30 am. On Sunday, trains start two hours later and finish about an hour earlier.

Contacts Transport for London ☎ *0843/222–1234* ⊕ *www.tfl.gov.uk.*

TOURS

Year-round, but more frequently from April to October, boats cruise the Thames, offering a different view of the London skyline. Most leave from Westminster Pier, Charing Cross Pier, and Tower Pier.

Guided sightseeing tours from the top of double-decker buses, which are open-top in summer, are a good introduction to the city, as they cover all the main central sights. Numerous companies run daily bus tours that depart from central points. You may board or alight at any of the numerous stops to view the sights, and reboard on the next bus. Tickets can be bought from the driver and are good all day. The typical price is £20.

Green Line, Evan Evans, and National Express offer day excursions by bus to places within easy reach of London, such as Hampton Court, Oxford, Stratford, and Bath.

Boat Tours Thames Cruises ☎ *020/7928–9009* ⊕ *www.thamescruises.com.* **Thames River Boats** ☎ *020/7930–2062* ⊕ *www.wpsa.co.uk.*

Bus Tours Big Bus Tours ☎ *020/7233–9533* ⊕ *www.bigbustours.com.* **Evan Evans** ☎ *020/7950–1777, 800/422–9022 in U.S.* ⊕ *www.evanevanstours.co.uk.* **Green Line** ☎ *0844/801–7261* ⊕ *www.greenline.co.uk.* **National Express** ☎ *0871/781–8178* ⊕ *www.nationalexpress.com.* **Original London Sightseeing Tour** ☎ *020/8877–1722* ⊕ *www.theoriginaltour.com.*

VISITOR INFORMATION

Contacts London Tourist Information Centre ⊠ *Victoria Station Forecourt, Victoria.* **VisitLondon** ⊠ *Victoria* ⊕ *www.visitlondon.com.*

EXPLORING

Westminster and the City contain many of the grand buildings that have played a central role in British history: Westminster Abbey and the Houses of Parliament, Buckingham Palace and the older royal palace of St. James's, and the Tower of London and St. Paul's Cathedral.

Within a few minutes' walk of Buckingham Palace lie St. James's and Mayfair, neighboring quarters of elegant town houses built for the nobility during the 17th and early 18th centuries and now notable for shopping opportunities. Hyde Park and Kensington Gardens, preserved by past kings and queens for their own hunting and relaxation, create a swath of parkland across the city center. A walk across Kensington Gardens brings you to the museum district of South Kensington, with the Natural History Museum, the Science Museum, and the Victoria & Albert Museum. The South Bank has many cultural highlights: the theaters of the South Bank Centre, the Tate Modern, and the reconstruction of Shakespeare's Globe theater. The London Eye observation wheel here gives stunning city views.

WESTMINSTER AND ROYAL LONDON

If you have time to visit only one part of London, this is it. Westminster and Royal London might be called "London for Beginners." If you went no farther than these few acres, you would have seen many of the famous sights, from the Houses of Parliament, Big Ben, Westminster Abbey, and Buckingham Palace, to two of the world's greatest art collections, in the National Gallery and Tate Britain. You can truly call this area Royal London, since it is bounded by the triangle of streets that make up the route that the queen usually takes when journeying from Buckingham Palace to Westminster Abbey or to the Houses of Parliament on state occasions. The three points on this royal triangle are Trafalgar Square, Parliament Square, and Buckingham Palace.

Trafalgar Square—easy to access and smack dab in the center of the action—is a good place to start. Take the Tube to Embankment (District and Circle lines) and walk north until you cross the Strand, or alight at Charing Cross (Bakerloo, Jubilee, and Northern lines), where the Northumberland Avenue exit deposits you on the southeast corner of the Square.

Fodor's Choice
★
Buckingham Palace. It's rare to get a chance to see how the other half—well, the other minute fraction—lives and works. But when the Queen heads off to Scotland on her annual summer holiday (you can tell because the Union Jack flies above the palace instead of the Royal Standard), the palace's 19 State Rooms open up to visitors, although the north wing's private apartments remain behind closed doors. With fabulous gilt moldings and walls adorned with masterpieces by Rembrandt, Rubens, and other old masters, the State Rooms are the grandest of the palace's 775 rooms.

20

The **Changing the Guard,** also known as **Guard Mounting,** remains one of London's best free shows and culminates in front of the palace. Marching to live bands, the old guard proceeds up the Mall from St. James's Palace to Buckingham Palace. Shortly afterward, the new guard approaches from Wellington Barracks. Then within the forecourt, the captains of the old and new guards symbolically transfer the keys to the palace.

Admission is by timed ticket with entry every 15 minutes throughout the day. Allow up to two hours. Get there by 10:30 to grab a spot in the best viewing section for the Changing the Guard (⊕ *www.changing-the-guard.com*), daily at 11:30 from May until the end of July (varies according to troop deployment requirements) and on alternate days for

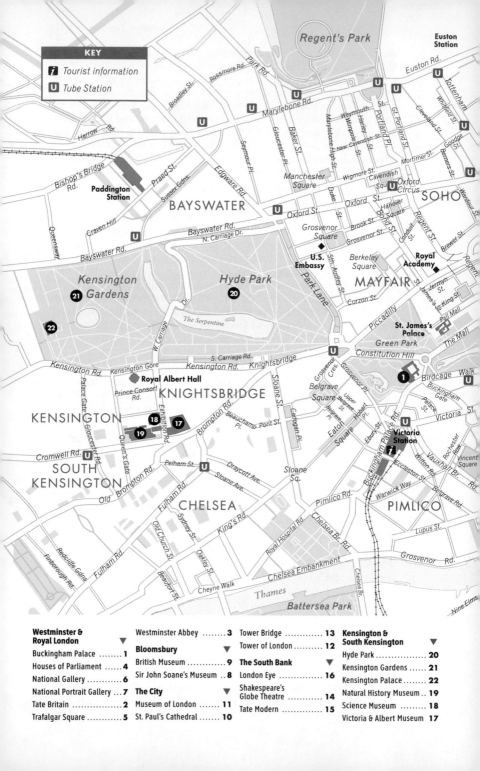

KEY

🄸 Tourist information
🅄 Tube Station

Regent's Park

Euston Station

BAYSWATER

Paddington Station

SOHO

Kensington Gardens

Hyde Park

The Serpentine

MAYFAIR

U.S. Embassy

Berkeley Square

Royal Academy

St. James's Palace

Green Park

Piccadilly

KNIGHTSBRIDGE

Royal Albert Hall

KENSINGTON

Belgrave Square

Victoria Station

Buckingham Gate

SOUTH KENSINGTON

CHELSEA

PIMLICO

Sloane Sq.

Vincent Square

Battersea Park

Thames

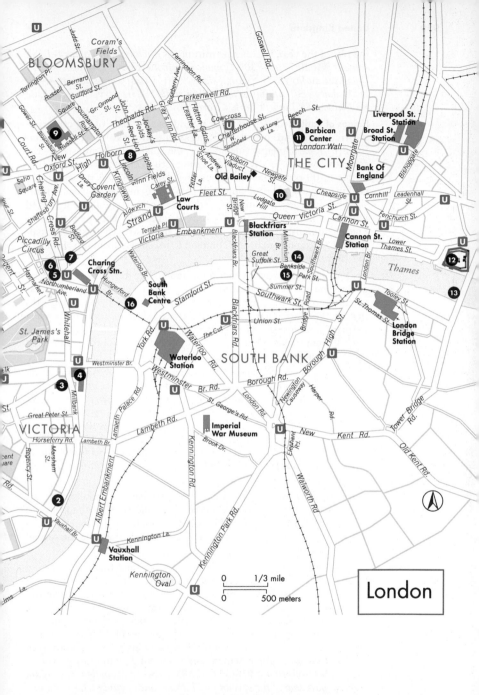

London

BLOOMSBURY

Coram's Fields

Judd St.

Torrington Pl.

Russell St.
Bernard St.
Guilford St.
Square
Gower St.
Southampton Row
Gr. Ormond St.
John St.
Theobalds Rd.
Jockey's Fields
Gray's Inn Rd.
Red Lion St.
Clerkenwell Rd.
Roseberry Ave.
Farringdon Rd.
Hatton Gdns.
Leather La.

Goswell Rd.

9

New Oxford St.
High Holborn
8
Lincoln's Inn Fields

Court Rd.
Bloomsbury
Charing Cross Rd.

Cowcross
Charterhouse St.
W. Smithfield
W. Long La.
Holborn Viaduct
Old Bailey ◆
Newgate St.

Beech St.
11 **Barbican Center**
London Wall
Liverpool St. Station
Broad St. Station

THE CITY

Moorgate
Bishopsgate
Bank Of England

Soho Square
Charing Cross Rd.
Shaftesbury Ave.

Drury La.
Covent Garden
Kingsway
Aldwych
Strand
Law Courts
Temple Pl.

Carey St.
Fetter La.
St. Andrew St.
Shoe La.
Fleet St.
New Bridge St.
Ludgate Hill
10

Queen Victoria St.
Cannon St.
Cheapside
Cornhill
Leadenhall St.
Fenchurch St.

Piccadilly Circus

7
6
5
Northumberland Ave.
Haymarket
Regent St.
Charing Cross Stn.

Bedford St.
Victoria Embankment
Blackfriars Station

Waterloo Br.
Hungerford Br.

South Bank Centre
16

Great Suffolk St.
Bankside
14
15
Park St.
Summer St.
Southwark St.
Southwark Br.
Blackfriars Br.
Millennium Br.

Cannon St. Station
Lower Thames St.
London Br.

Thames

12

13

St. James's Park

Whitehall

4

3

2

Westminster Br.

York Rd.
Stamford St.
The Cut
Blackfriars Rd.
Union St.
Waterloo Br.

Waterloo Station

SOUTH BANK

Borough Rd.
London Rd.
Borough High St.
Newington Causeway
Harper Rd.

Bridge Rd.
St. Thomas St.
Tooley St.

London Bridge Station

Lower Bridge Rd.

Westminster Br. Rd.
St. George's Rd.

VICTORIA

Great Peter St.
Horseferry Rd.
Lambeth Br.
Marsham St.
Regency St.
Millbank
Albert Embankment
Lambeth Rd.
Lambeth Palace Rd.
Lambeth Rd.

Imperial War Museum ▪
Brook Dr.
Kennington Rd.
Elephant Rd.
Walworth Rd.
Kennington Park Rd.

New Kent Rd.
Kent Rd.
Old Kent Rd.

Kennington La.
Vauxhall Station
Vauxhall Br.

Kennington Oval

0   1/3 mile
0   500 meters

the rest of the year, weather permitting. ⊠ *Buckingham Palace Rd., St. James's* ☎ *020/7766–7300* ⊕ *www.royalcollection.org.uk/visit* ▣ *£19 (includes audio tour)* ☉ *Aug., daily 9:30–7 (last admission at 4:45); Sept., daily 9:30–6:30 (last admission at 3:45). Hrs vary; check website* Ⓜ *Victoria, St. James's Park, Green Park.*

Houses of Parliament. If you want to understand some of the centuries-old traditions and arcane idiosyncrasies that make up constitution-less British parliamentary democracy, the Palace of Westminster, as the complex is still properly called, is the place to come. The architecture in this 1,100-room labyrinth impresses, but the real excitement lies in stalking the corridors of power. A palace was first established on this site by Edward the Confessor in the 11th century. William II started building a new palace in 1087, and this gradually became the seat of English administrative power. However, fire destroyed most of the palace in 1834, and the current complex dates largely from the middle of the 19th century.

Visitors aren't allowed to snoop too much, but the **Visitors' Galleries** of the House of Commons do afford a view of democracy in process when the banks of green-leather benches are filled by opposing MPs (members of Parliament). Nonresidents are able to watch debates when Parliament is in session if they wait in line for tickets. Embassies and High Commissions often have a quota of debate tickets available to their citizens, which can help you avoid long lines.

The only guided tour nonresidents can go on is the tour offered on Saturday, or Monday through Saturday during August and September (book through ⊕ *www.ticketmaster.co.uk*). ⊠ *St. Stephen's Entrance, St. Margaret St., Westminster* ☎ *020/7219–4272 for info, 0844/847–1672 for public tours* ⊕ *www.parliament.uk/visiting* ▣ *Free, tours £15 (book in advance)* ☉ *Tours: Aug., Mon., Tues., Fri., and Sat. 9:15–4:30, Wed. and Thurs. 1:15–4:30; Sept., Mon., Fri., and Sat. 9:15–4:30, Tues., Wed., and Thurs. 1:15–4:30. Call to confirm hrs for Visitors Galleries.* Ⓜ *Westminster.*

FAMILY **National Gallery.** Standing proudly on the north side of Trafalgar Square,
Fodor'sChoice this is truly one of the world's supreme art collections, with more than
★ 2,300 masterpieces on show. Picasso, van Gogh, Michelangelo, Leonardo, Monet, Turner, and more—all for free. Watch out for special temporary exhibitions too.

Color coding throughout the galleries helps you keep track of the period in which you're immersed. Begin at an "Art Start" terminal in the Sainsbury Wing or East Wing Espresso Bar. The interactive screens give you access to information on all of the museum's holdings; you can choose your favorites, and print out a free personal tour map. One-hour free, guided tours start at the Sainsbury Wing daily at 11:30 and 2:30 (also Friday at 7 pm). If you are eager for even more insight into the art, pick up a themed audio guide, which takes in about 20 paintings. ⊠ *Trafalgar Sq., Westminster* ☎ *020/7747–2885* ⊕ *www.nationalgallery.org.uk* ▣ *Free, plus charge for special exhibitions; audio guide £3.50* ☉ *Sun.– Thurs. 10–6, Fri. 10–9* Ⓜ *Charing Cross, Embankment, Leicester Sq.*

FAMILY
Fodor's Choice
★

National Portrait Gallery. Tucked around the corner from the National Gallery, the National Portrait Gallery was founded in 1856 with a single aim: to gather together portraits of famous (and infamous) British men and women. More than 150 years and 160,000 portraits later, it is an essential stop for all history and literature buffs. The spacious galleries make it a pleasant place to visit, and you can choose to take in a little or a lot. Need to rest those legs? Then use the Portrait Explorer in the Digital Space on the ground-floor mezzanine for interactive, computer-aided exploration of the gallery's extensive collection. If you visit with little ones, ask at the desk about the excellent Family Trails, which make exploring the galleries with children much more fun. On the top floor, the Portrait Restaurant (check website for details) will delight skyline aficionados. ■ TIP→ The restaurant vista will reveal stately London at its finest: a panoramic view of Nelson's Column and the backdrop along White-hall to the Houses of Parliament.

Look for the four Andy Warhol *Queen Elizabeth II* silkscreens from 1985 and Maggi Hambling's surreal self-portrait. Contemporary portraits range from the iconic (*Julian with T-shirt*—an LCD screen on a continuous loop—by Julian Opie) to the creepy (Marc Quinn's *Self*, a realization of the artist's head in frozen blood) and the eccentric (Tim Noble's ghoulish *Head of Isabella Blow*). ⊠ *St. Martin's Pl., Westminster* ☎ *020/7312–2463, 020/730–0555 for recorded switchboard information* ⊕ *www.npg.org.uk* ⊠ *Free, plus charge for special exhibitions; audiovisual guide £3* ⊗ *Mon.–Wed. and weekends 10–6, Thurs. and Fri. 10–9; last admission 1 hr before closing* Ⓜ *Charing Cross, Leicester Sq.*

FAMILY
Fodor's Choice
★

Tate Britain. The stately neoclassical institution may not be as ambitious as its sibling Tate Modern on the South Bank, but Tate Britain's bright galleries lure only a fraction of the Modern's crowds and are a great place to explore British art from 1500 to the present. From early 2014, much more of the Tate's collection will be on permanent display as part of a major re-development of the galleries. So you'll have no excuse not to pop in and view classic works by John Constable, Thomas Gainsborough, David Wilkie, Francis Bacon, Duncan Grant, Barbara Hepworth, and Ben Nicholson and an outstanding display from J. M. W. Turner in the Clore Gallery, including many later vaporous and light-infused works such as *Sunrise with Sea Monsters*. Sumptuous Pre-Raphaelite pieces are a major drawcard while the Contemporary British Art galleries bring you face to face with Damien Hirst's *Away from the Flock* and other recent conceptions. ■ TIP→ Craving more art? Head down the river on the Tate to Tate (£5.50 one-way) to the Tate Modern, running between the two museums every 40 minutes. A River Roamer ticket (£13.60) permits a day's travel, with stops including the London Eye and the Tower of London. ⊠ *Millbank, Westminster* ☎ *020/7887–8888* ⊕ *www.tate.org.uk/britain* ⊠ *Free, special exhibitions £9–£15* ⊗ *Sat.–Thurs. 10–6 (last entry at 5:15), Fri. 10–10 (last entry at 9:15)* Ⓜ *Pimlico.*

20

Trafalgar Square. This is literally the center of London: a plaque on the corner of the Strand and Charing Cross Road marks the spot from which distances on U.K. signposts are measured. **Nelson's Column** stands at the heart of the square (which is named after the great admiral's most important victory), guarded by haughty lions designed by Sir Edwin

Landseer and flanked by **statues of Charles Napier and Henry Have-lock,** two generals who helped establish the British Empire in India. The fourth plinth is given over to rotating works by contemporary artists. The square is a magnet for national celebrations and protests—V.E. Day, New Year's Eve, sporting triumphs, political demonstrations—and is, thankfully, more pleasant to visit since the pedestrianization of its northern side. Although Chinese tourists know it as Pigeon Square, feeding the birds is now banned and the gray flocks have flown.

At the southern point of the square, en route to Whitehall, is the **equestrian statue of Charles I.** After the Civil War and the king's execution, Oliver Cromwell, the anti-Royalist leader, commissioned a scrap dealer, brazier John Rivett, to melt the statue. The story goes that Rivett buried it in his garden and made a fortune peddling knickknacks wrought, he claimed, from its metal, only to produce the statue miraculously unscathed after the restoration of the monarchy—and to make more cash reselling it to the authorities. In 1667 Charles II had it placed where it stands today, near the spot where his father was executed in 1649. Each year, on January 30, the day of the king's death, the Royal Stuart Society lays a wreath at the foot of the statue. ⊠ *Westminster* Ⓜ *Charing Cross.*

Fodor's Choice **Westminster Abbey.** A monument to the nation's rich—and often bloody—
★ history, the abbey is one of London's most iconic sites. The atmospheric gloom of the lofty medieval interior is home to more than 600 statues, tombs, and commemorative tablets. About 3,300 people, from kings to composers to wordsmiths, are buried in the abbey. It has hosted 38 coronations—beginning in 1066 with William the Conqueror—and no fewer than 16 royal weddings, the latest being that of Prince William and Kate Middleton in 2011.

But be warned: there's only one way around the abbey, and as a million visitors flock through its doors each year, you'll need to be alert to catch the highlights. Enter by the north door then turn around and look up to see the **painted-glass rose window,** the largest of its kind. Step into the small Chapel of St. Michael, where a tomb effigy of Joseph Gascoigne Nightingale fights off a sheet-draped figure of death. Next enter the adjacent Tomb of St. John the Baptist past a lovely statue of the Virgin Mary and child.

Arrive early if possible, but be prepared to wait in line to tour the abbey. Photography is not permitted. ⊠ *Broad Sanctuary, Westminster* ☎ *020/7222–5152* ⊕ *www.westminster-abbey.org* 🖃 *Abbey and museum £16, audio tour free* ⊘ *Abbey: Mon., Tues., Thurs., Fri. 9:30–4:30, Wed. 9:30–7, Sat. 9:30–2.30 (last admission is 1 hr before closing); Sun. for worship only. Museum Mon.–Sat. 10:30–4. Cloisters daily 8–6. College Garden: Apr.–Sept., Tues.–Thurs. 10–6; Oct.–Mar., Tues.–Thurs. 10–4. Chapter House daily 10:30–4. Services may affect hrs, so call ahead* Ⓜ *Westminster, St James's Park.*

BLOOMSBURY

The hub of intellectual London, Bloomsbury is anchored by the British Museum, the University of London, and nearby Russell Square. You can see students engaged in heated conversation, while academics and collectors browse the shelves of the antiquarian bookstores nearby. The leafy squares are fun to explore, and the neighborhood is adjacent to the restaurants and pubs of Soho.

Tottenham Court Road on the Northern and Central lines or Russell Square (Piccadilly Line) are best for the British Museum.

Fodor'sChoice **British Museum.** With a facade like a great temple, this celebrated treasure
★ house, filled with plunder of incalculable value and beauty from around the globe, occupies an immense, imposing, neo-classical building in the heart of Bloomsbury. Inside are some of the greatest relics of human-kind: the Parthenon Sculptures (Elgin Marbles), the Rosetta Stone, the Sutton Hoo Treasure—almost everything, it seems, but the Ark of the Covenant. The three rooms that make up the **Sainsbury African Galleries** are a must-see in the Lower Gallery—together they present 200,000 objects, highlighting such ancient kingdoms as the Benin and Asante. The museum's focal point is the **Great Court,** a brilliant modern design with a vast glass roof that reveals the museum's covered courtyard. The revered **Reading Room** has a blue-and-gold dome and hosts temporary exhibitions. If you want to navigate the highlights of the almost 100 galleries, join the free **eyeOpener** 30- to 40-minute tours by museum guides (details at the information desk). Or, alternatively, hire a mul-timedia guide for £5.

Upstairs are some of the most popular galleries, especially beloved by children, like Rooms 62–63, where the **Egyptian mummies** live. Nearby are the glittering 4th-century **Mildenhall Treasure** and the equally splen-did 8th-century Anglo-Saxon **Sutton Hoo Treasure** (with magnificent helmets and jewelry). A more prosaic exhibit is that of Pete Marsh, sentimentally named by the archaeologists who unearthed the **Lindow Man** from a Cheshire peat marsh; poor Pete was ritually slain in the 1st century, and lay perfectly pickled in his bog until 1984. The **Korean Foundation Gallery** (Room 67) delves into the art and archaeology of the country, including a reconstruction of a *sarangbang*, a traditional scholar's study. ⊠ *Great Russell St., Bloomsbury* ☎ *020/7323–8299* ⊕ *www.britishmuseum.org* ⊠ *Free; donations encouraged* ⊙ *Galleries Sat.–Thurs. 10–5:30, Fri. 10–8:30. Great Court Sat.–Thurs. 9–6, Fri. 9–8:30* Ⓜ *Russell Sq., Holborn, Tottenham Court Rd.*

20

Fodor'sChoice **Sir John Soane's Museum.** A wonderful, eccentric jewel of a place, Sir
★ John (1753–1837), architect of the Bank of England, bequeathed his house to the nation on one condition: that nothing be changed. It's a house full of surprises. In the Picture Room, for instance, two of Hogarth's *Rake's Progress* series are among the paintings on panels that swing away to reveal secret gallery pockets with even more paintings. Everywhere, mirrors and colors play tricks with light and space, and split-level floors worthy of a fairground fun house disorient you. In a basement chamber sits the vast 1300 BC sarcophagus of Seti I, lit by a domed skylight two stories above. (When Sir John acquired this price-less object for £2,000, after it was rejected by the British Museum, he celebrated with a three-day party.) The elegant, tranquil courtyard gar-dens are also open to the public, and a below-street-level passage joins two of the courtyards to the museum. Because of the small size of the

museum, limited numbers are allowed entry at any one time, so you may have a short wait outside—but it's worth it. Hourlong tours are offered (check the website for details), and on the first Tuesday of the month the museum offers a very popular candle-light evening opening, from 6 to 9 pm. ⊠ *13 Lincoln's Inn Fields, Bloomsbury* ☎ *020/7405–2107* ⊕ *www.soane.org* ✉ *Free, tours £10* ☉ *Tues.–Sat. 10–5 (also 6–9 on 1st Tues. of month)* Ⓜ *Holborn.*

THE CITY

The City, as opposed to the city, is the capital's fast-beating financial heart. Behind a host of imposing neoclassical facades lie the banks and exchanges whose frantic trade determines the fortunes that underpin London—and the country. But the "Square Mile" is much more than London's Wall Street—the capital's economic engine room also has currency as a religious and political center. St. Paul's Cathedral has looked after Londoners' souls since the seventh century, and the Tower of London—that moat-surrounded royal fortress, prison, and jewel house—has specialized in beheading them.

The pedestrian-only Millennium Bridge connects the area with the South Bank; it's well worth the walk.

The City is well served by Underground stops: St Paul's and Bank on the Central Line; and Mansion House, Cannon Street, and Monument on the District and Circle lines.

FAMILY   **Museum of London.** If there's one place to absorb the history of London, from 450,000 BC to the present day, it's here: Oliver Cromwell's death mask, Queen Victoria's crinoline gowns, Selfridges' art deco elevators, the London's Burning exhibition, fans, guns and jewelry, an original Newgate Prison Door, and the incredible late-18th-century Blackett Dolls House—7,000 objects to wonder at in all. The museum appropriately shelters a section of the 2nd- to 4th-century London wall, which you can view through a window, and permanent displays highlight Pre-Roman, Roman, Medieval, and Tudor London. The Galleries of Modern London are equally enthralling: experience the "Expanding City," "People's City," and "World City," each gallery dealing with a section of London's history from 1666 until the 21st century. Innovative interactive displays abound, and you can even wander around a 19th-century London street with impressively detailed shopfronts and interiors, including a pawnbrokers, a pub, a barber, and a bank manager's office, in case you're running short on holiday money. There's also a fine schedule of temporary exhibitions. ⊠ *London Wall, The City* ☎ *020/7001–9844* ⊕ *www.museumoflondon.org.uk* ✉ *Free* ☉ *Mon.– Sun. 10–6 (last admission at 5:30)* Ⓜ *Barbican, St. Paul's.*

Fodor'sChoice   **St. Paul's Cathedral.** St. Paul's is simply breathtaking, especially now that
  ★   the scaffolding has been removed, after 15 years of major restoration work. The structure is Sir Christopher Wren's masterpiece, completed in 1710 after 35 years of building, and, much later, miraculously spared (mostly) by World War II bombs. Wren's first plan, known as the New Model, did not make it past the drawing board. The second, known as the Great Model, got as far as a 20-foot oak rendering—now displayed in the Trophy Room—before it also was rejected.

The third plan was accepted, with the fortunate proviso that the architect be allowed to make changes as he saw fit. Without that, there would be no dome, because the approved design had a steeple—and St. Paul's simply would not be St. Paul's as we know it without the dome, the third largest in the world. Even so, from inside the vast cathedral the dome may seem smaller than you'd expect—the inner dome is 60 feet lower than the lead-covered outer dome. Beneath the lantern is Wren's famous and succinct epitaph, which his son composed and had set into the pavement, *Lector, si monumentum requiris, circumspice* ("Reader, if you seek his monument, look around you"). The epitaph also appears on Wren's memorial in the Crypt.

Up 163 spiral steps is the **Whispering Gallery,** an acoustic phenomenon; you whisper something to the wall on one side, and a second later it transmits clearly to the other side, 107 feet away. Ascend to the **Stone Gallery,** which encircles the base of the dome. Farther up (280 feet from ground level) is the small **Golden Gallery,** the dome's highest point. From both these galleries (if you have a head for heights) you can walk outside for a spectacular panorama of London.

Among the famous figures whose remains lie in the **Crypt** are the Duke of Wellington and Admiral Lord Nelson. The Crypt also has a gift shop and a café. ⊠ *St. Paul's Churchyard, The City* ☎ *020/7236–4128* ⊕ *www.stpauls.co.uk* ✒ *£15 (includes multimedia guides and guided tours)* ⊘ *Mon.–Sat. 8:30–4; shop Mon.–Sat. 9–5, Sun. 10–4.30; Crypt Café Mon.–Sat. 9–5, Sun. 12–4* Ⓜ *St. Paul's.*

FAMILY
Fodor's Choice
★
Tower Bridge. Despite its medieval, fairy-tale appearance, this is a Victorian youngster. Constructed of steel, then clothed in Portland stone, the Horace Jones masterpiece was deliberately styled in the Gothic persuasion to complement the Tower next door, and it's famous for its enormous bascules— the 1,200-ton "arms" that open to allow large ships to glide beneath. This still happens occasionally (the website has details), but when river traffic was dense, the bascules were raised about five times a day.

The **Tower Bridge Exhibition** is a child-friendly tour where you can discover how one of the world's most famous bridges actually works before heading out onto the walkways for the wonderful city views. First, take in the romance of the panoramas from the east and west walkways between those grand turrets. On the east are the modern superstructures of the Docklands, and on the west is the Tower of London, St. Paul's, the Monument, and the steel-and-glass "futuristic mushroom" that is Greater London Assembly's City Hall. Then it's back down to explore the Victorian engine rooms and discover the inner workings, which you learn about through hands-on displays and films. ⊠ *Tower Bridge Rd., The City* ☎ *020/7403–3761* ⊕ *www.towerbridge. org.uk* ✒ *£8* ⊘ *Apr.–Sept., daily 10–6; Oct.–Mar., daily 9:30–5.30. Last admission 30 mins before closing* Ⓜ *Tower Hill.*

20

Fodor's Choice
★
Tower of London. Nowhere else does London's history come to life so vividly as it does in this minicity of 20 towers filled with heraldry and treasure, the intimate details of lords and dukes and princes and sovereigns etched into the walls (literally, in some places), and quite a few

pints of royal blood spilled on the stones. This is one of Britain's most popular sights—the Crown Jewels are here—and you can avoid lines by buying a ticket in advance online, by phone, at any tube station, or from the automatic kiosks on arrival. The visitor center provides an introduction to the Tower. Allow at least three hours for exploring, and take time to stroll along the battlements for a wonderful overview. The Crown Jewels are worth the inevitable wait, the White Tower is essential, and the Medieval Palace and Bloody Tower should at least be breezed through.

Today's Tower has seen everything, as a palace, barracks, a mint for producing coins, an archive, an armory, and the Royal Menagerie (which formed the basis of the London Zoo). Most of all, though, the Tower is known for death: it's been a place of imprisonment, torture, and execution for the realm's most notorious traitors, and a few innocents as well.

Free tours depart every half hour or so from the Middle Tower. They are conducted by the Yeoman Warders, better known as Beefeaters, dressed in resplendent navy-and-red (scarlet-and-gold on special occasions) Tudor outfits. Beefeaters have been guarding the Tower since Henry VII appointed them in 1485. One of them, the Yeoman Warder Raven Master, is responsible for making life comfortable for the ravens (six birds plus reserves) that live in **Lanthorn Tower**. It's an important duty, because if the ravens were to desert the Tower, goes the legend, the kingdom would fall. Today, the Tower takes no chances: The ravens' wings are clipped.

The most famous exhibits are, of course, the **Crown Jewels**, in the Jewel House, Waterloo Barracks. This is the Tower's biggest draw, perfect for playing pick-your-favorite-crown from the wrong side of bullet-proof glass. Not only are these crowns, staffs, and orbs encrusted with heavy-duty gems, they are invested with the authority of monarchical power in England, dating back to the 1300s. Included is the famous Koh-i-noor, or "Mountain of Light." The legendary diamond, which was supposed to bring luck to women, came from India, and was given to Queen Elizabeth, the Queen Mother.

For free tickets to the 700-year-old Ceremony of the Keys (locking of main gates, nightly between 9:30 and 10), write several months in advance; check the tower website for details. Also, check for winter twilight tours of the Tower on selected evenings. ⊠ *Tower Hill, The City* ☎ *0844/482-7777, 0844/482-7799* ⊕ *www.hrp.org.uk* ⌨ *£19.50* ☾ *Mar.–Oct., Tues.–Sat. 9–5:30, Sun. and Mon. 10–5:30 (last admission at 5); Nov.–Feb., Tues.–Sat. 9–4:30, Sun. and Mon. 10–4:30 (last admission at 4)* Ⓜ *Tower Hill.*

THE SOUTH BANK

For decades, tourists rarely ventured south of the Thames. But now it is a leading destination in its own right. Culture, history, markets—the South Bank has it all. Installed in a converted 1930s power station, the Tate Modern is the star attraction, with the eye-catching Millennium Bridge connecting it to the City across the river. Near the cultural venues of the South Bank Centre, the London Eye observation wheel gives you a bird's-eye view of the city.

It's fitting that so much of London's artistic life should once again be centered on the South Bank—in the past, Southwark was known for its inns, prisons, bear-baiting arenas, and theaters. The Globe, which housed the company Shakespeare wrote for and performed with, was one of several here.

For the South Bank, use Embankment on the District, Circle, Northern, and Bakerloo lines, from where you can walk across Hungerford Bridge; or Waterloo on the Northern, and Bakerloo lines, from where it's a five-minute walk to the Royal Festival Hall (slightly longer from the Jubilee line station).

FAMILY **London Eye.** To mark the start of the new millennium, architects David Marks and Julia Barfield conceived a beautiful and celebratory structure that would allow people to see this great city from a completely new perspective. They came up with a giant Ferris wheel, which, as well as representing the turn of the century, would also be a symbol of regeneration. The London Eye is the largest cantilevered observation wheel ever built and among the tallest structures in London. The 25-minute slow-motion ride inside one of the enclosed passenger capsules is so smooth you'd hardly know you were suspended over the Thames. On a clear day you can see for up to 25 miles, with a bird's-eye view over London's most famous landmarks as you circle through 360 degrees. If you're looking for a special place to celebrate, champagne and canapés can be arranged ahead of time. ■TIP➔ **Buy your ticket online to avoid the long lines and get a 10% discount. For an extra £10, you can save even more time with a Fast Track flight for which you check in 15 minutes before your "departure."** ✉ *Westminster Bridge Rd., Riverside Bldg., County Hall, South Bank* ☎ *0870/990–8883* ⊕ *www.londoneye.com* 🎫 *£18.90, cruise £12.50* 🕙 *June and Sept., daily 10–9; July and Aug., daily 10–9:30; Oct.–Mar., daily 10–8:30* Ⓜ *Waterloo.*

FAMILY
Fodor's Choice
★
Shakespeare's Globe Theatre. This spectacular theater is a replica of Shakespeare's open-roof, wood-and-thatch Globe Playhouse (built in 1599 and burned down in 1613), where most of the Bard's greatest works premiered. American actor and director Sam Wanamaker worked ceaselessly for several decades to raise funds for the theater's reconstruction 200 yards from its original site, using authentic materials and techniques, a dream realized in 1997. "Groundlings"—patrons with £5 standing-only tickets—are not allowed to sit during the performance. Fortunately, you can reserve an actual seat on any one of the theater's three levels, but you will want to rent a cushion for £1 (or bring your own) to soften the backless wooden benches. The show must go on, rain or shine, warm or chilly—so come prepared for anything. Umbrellas are banned, but you can bring a raincoat or buy a cheap Globe rain poncho, which doubles as a great souvenir.

Shakespeare's Globe Exhibition, a museum under the theater (the entry is adjacent), provides background material on the Elizabethan theater and the construction of the modern-day Globe. Admission to the museum also includes a tour of the theater. On matinee days, the tour visits the archaeological site of the nearby (and older) Rose Theatre. ✉ *21 New Globe Walk, Bankside* ☎ *020/7902–1400 for box office,*

20

020/7401–9919 for exhibition ⊕ www.shakespearesglobe.com ✉ Exhibition and Globe Theatre tour £13.50 (£2 reduction with valid performance ticket). Tickets for plays £5–£39 ⊙ Exhibition: May–early Oct., daily 10–5; mid-Oct.–Apr., daily 9–12:30 and 1–5. Plays: Apr. 23–Oct., call for schedule Ⓜ London Bridge; Mansion House, then cross Southwark Bridge.

FAMILY
Fodor's Choice
★

Tate Modern. This spectacular renovation of a mid-20th-century power station is one of the most-visited museums of modern art in the world. Its great permanent collection, which starts in 1900 and ranges from Modern masters like Matisse to the most cutting-edge contemporary artists, is arranged thematically—Landscape, Still Life, and the Nude. Its blockbuster temporary exhibitions showcase the work of individual artists like Gaugin, Roy Lichtenstein, and Gerhard Richter.

The vast **Turbine Hall** is a dramatic entrance point used to showcase big, audacious installations that tend to generate a lot of publicity. Past highlights include Olafur Eliasson's massive glowing sun and Carsten Holler's huge metal slides.

Join one of the free, 45-minute guided tours. Each one covers a different gallery: Poetry and Dream at 11, Transformed Visions at noon, Structure and Clarity at 2, and Energy and Process at 3. No need to book; just show up in the appropriate room. Levels 2 and 3 include temporary exhibitions, for which there's usually a charge of around £15. Bypass these if you're just here to see the main collection, which is free. ✉ Bankside ☎ 020/7887–8888 ⊕ www.tate.org.uk/modern ✉ Free, charge for special exhibitions ⊙ Sun.–Thurs. 10–6, Fri. and Sat. 10–10 (last entry 45 mins before close) Ⓜ Southwark, Mansion House, St. Paul's.

KENSINGTON AND SOUTH KENSINGTON

Splendid houses with pillared porches, as well as fascinating museums, stylish squares, and expensive boutiques, line the streets of the Royal Borough of Kensington. Also here is Kensington Palace (the former home of both Diana, Princess of Wales, and Queen Victoria), which put the district literally on the map back in the 17th century. To Kensington's east is one of the highest concentrations of important artifacts anywhere, the "museum mile" of South Kensington, with the rest of Kensington offering peaceful strolls and a busy main street.

South Kensington and Gloucester Road on the District, Circle, and Piccadilly lines are convenient stops for the South Kensington museums.

FAMILY
Fodor's Choice
★

Hyde Park. Along with the smaller St. James's and Green parks to the east, Hyde Park started as Henry VIII's hunting grounds. Along its south side runs Rotten Row, once Henry's royal path to the hunt—the name is a corruption of *Route du Roi* (route of the king). It's still used by the Household Cavalry, who live at the Hyde Park Barracks—a highrise and a low, ugly, red block—to the left. This is where the brigade that mounts the guard at Buckingham Palace resides, and you can see them leave to perform their duty, in full regalia, at about 10:30, or await the return of the guard around noon. Hyde Park is wonderful for strolling, watching the locals, or just relaxing by the Serpentine, the long body of water near its southern border. On the south side, by the 1930s **Serpentine Lido**, is the site of the **Diana Princess of Wales**

Memorial Fountain, which opened in 2003 and is a good spot to refuel at one of the cafés. On Sunday, Speakers' Corner, in the park near Marble Arch, is an unmissable spectacle of vehement, sometimes comical, and always entertaining orators. ⊠ *Hyde Park* ☎ *030/0061–2000* ⊕ *www.royalparks.gov.uk* ⊙ *Daily 5 am–midnight* Ⓜ *Hyde Park Corner, Knightsbridge, Lancaster Gate, Marble Arch.*

The Serpentine. You can rent paddleboats and rowboats here for use on the Serpentine. ☎ *020/7262–1330* ⌸ *£10 per person per hr* ⊙ *Apr.–Oct., daily 10–dusk*

Serpentine Lido. It's technically a beach on a lake, but on a hot day in Hyde Park this is surreally reminiscent of the seaside. There are changing facilities, and the swimming section is chlorinated. There is also a paddling pool, sandpit, and a kids' entertainer in the afternoons. ⊠ *Kensington* ☎ *020/7706–7098* ⊕ *www.royalparks.org.uk* ⌸ *£4 (£3.50 after 4 pm)* ⊙ *May, weekends 10–6; June–Sept., daily 10–6* Ⓜ *Knightsbridge*

FAMILY

Fodor'sChoice

★

Kensington Gardens. Laid out in 1689 by William III, who commissioned Christopher Wren to build Kensington Palace, the gardens are a formal counterpart to neighbouring Hyde Park. Just to the north of the palace itself is the Dutch-style **Sunken Garden.** Nearby, the 1912 bronze statue of *Peter Pan* commemorates the boy in J. M. Barrie's story who lived on an island in the Serpentine and never grew up. The lovely **Diana Princess of Wales Memorial Playground** has sections inspired by Peter's other imaginary home, *Neverland.* Beside the playground, the **Elfin Oak** is a 900 year-old tree trunk that was carved with scores of tiny elves, fairies, and other fanciful creations in the 1920s. The **Italian Gardens** (1860) comprise several ornamental ponds and fountains, while the **Round Pond** is a magnet for model-boat enthusiasts. The park's most striking monument, the **Albert Memorial,** is a high-Gothic edifice dedicated to Queen Victoria's husband. The central freize depicts 169 different artists, while the heroic figures on the marble corner statues present an archetypally Victorian vision of Europe, Asia, Africa, and the Americas. Nearby, the **Serpentine Gallery** holds often controversial exhibitions of contemporary works. ⊠ *Kensington* ☎ *030/0061–2000* ⊕ *www.royalparks.gov.uk* ⊙ *Daily 6 –dusk* Ⓜ *High Street Kensington, Lancaster Gate, Queensway, South Kensington.*

Kensington Palace. Neither as imposing as Buckingham Palace nor as charming as Hampton Court, Kensington Palace is something of a Royal Family commune, with various close relatives of the Queen occupying large apartments in the private part of the palace. Bought in 1689 by Queen Mary and King William III, it was converted into a palace by Sir Christopher Wren and Nicholas Hawksmoor, and Royals have been in residence ever since. Its most famous resident, Princess Diana, lived here with her sons after her divorce, and this is where Prince William now lives with his wife, Catherine, Duchess of Cambridge.

The State Apartments, however, are open to the public, and galleries showcase three permanent exhibitions that delve into palace history: Queen Victoria (with the theme "love, duty, and loss"); William and Mary and Queen Anne ("the private life of the Queen"); and George II

20

("the curious world of the court"). There is also a changing temporary exhibition during the summer months.

The palace now has a wheelchair-accessible elevator, and Kensington Gardens has electric buggies for mobility-impaired visitors. If you also plan to visit the Tower of London, Hampton Court Palace, Banqueting House, or Kew Palace, become a member of Historic Royal Palaces. It costs £43 per person, or £83 for a family, and gives you free entry to all five sites for a year. ⊠ *The Broad Walk, Kensington Gardens, Kensington* ☎ *0844/482–7799 for advance booking, 0844/482–7777 for info, 0203/166–6000 from outside U.K.* ⊕ *www.hrp.org.uk* ⊠ *£14.50 (subject to change)* ⊙ *Mar.–Sept., daily 10–6; Oct.–Feb., daily 10–5; last admission 1 hr before closing* Ⓜ *Queensway, High Street Kensington.*

FAMILY
Fodor's Choice
★

Natural History Museum. The ornate terracotta facade of this enormous Victorian museum is strewn with relief panels depicting living creatures to the left of the entrance and extinct ones to the right (although some species have subsequently changed categories). It's an appropriate design, for within these walls lie more than 70 million different specimens. Only a small percentage is on public display, but you could still spend a day here and not come close to seeing everything. The museum is full of cutting-edge exhibits, with all the wow-power and interactives necessary to secure interest from younger visitors.

"Nature Live" is a program of free, informal talks given by scientists, covering a wildly eclectic range of subjects, usually at 2:30 (and on some days at 12:30) in the David Attenborough Studio in the Darwin Centre. The museum has an outdoor ice-skating rink from November to January, and a popular Christmas fair. Free, daily behind-the-scenes Spirit collection tours of the museum can be booked on the day, but space is limited so come early; recommended for children over eight years old. Got kids under seven with you? Check out the museum's free "Explorer Backpacks." They contain a range of activity materials to keep the little ones amused, including a pair of binoculars and an explorer's hat. ⊠ *Cromwell Rd., South Kensington* ☎ *0207/942–5000* ⊕ *www.nhm.ac.uk* ⊠ *Free (some fees for special exhibitions)* ⊙ *Daily 10–5:50, last admission at 5:30* Ⓜ *South Kensington.*

Science Museum. One of the three great South Kensington museums, the Science Museum stands next to the Natural History Museum in a far plainer building. It has lots of hands-on painlessly educational exhibits, with entire schools of children apparently decanted inside to interact with them, but don't dismiss the Science Museum as just for kids. Highlights include the Launch Pad gallery, which demonstrates basic laws of physics; *Puffing Billy,* the oldest steam locomotive in the world; and the actual *Apollo 10* capsule. The six floors are devoted to subjects as diverse as the history of flight, space exploration, steam power, medicine, and a sublime exhibition on science in the 18th century. Overshadowed by a three-story blue-glass wall, the Wellcome Wing is an annex to the rear of the museum, devoted to contemporary science and technology. It contains a 450-seat IMAX theater and the Legend of Apollo—an advanced motion simulator that combines seat vibration with other technical gizmos to re-create the experience of a moon landing. ⊠ *Exhibition Rd., South Kensington* ☎ *0870/870–4868* ⊕ *www.sciencemuseum.org.uk* ✉ *Free; charge for special exhibitions, cinema shows and simulator rides* ☉ *Daily 10–6 (10–7 during school holidays; check website)* Ⓜ *South Kensington.*

FAMILY
Fodor's Choice
★
Victoria & Albert Museum. Known to all as the V&A, this huge museum is devoted to the applied arts of all disciplines, all periods, and all nationalities. Full of innovation, it's a wonderful, generous place in which to get lost. First opened as the South Kensington Museum in 1857, it was renamed in 1899 in honor of Queen Victoria's late husband and has since grown to become one of the country's best-loved cultural institutions.

Many collections at the V&A are presented not by period but by category—textiles, sculpture, jewelry, and so on. Nowhere is the benefit of this more apparent than in the **Fashion Gallery** (Room 40), where formal 18th-century court dresses are displayed alongside the haute couture styles of contemporary designers, creating an arresting sense of visual continuity.

The V&A is a tricky building to navigate, so be sure to use the free map. As a whirlwind introduction, you could take a free one-hour tour (10:30, 11:30, 12:30, 1:30, 2:30, or 3:30). There are also tours devoted just to the British Galleries at 12:30 and 2:30. Whatever time you visit, the spectacular sculpture hall will be filled with artists, both amateur and professional, sketching the myriad of artworks on display there. Don't be shy; bring a pad and join in. Although the permanent collection is free—and there's enough there to keep you busy for a week—the V&A also hosts high-profile special exhibitions that run for several months. ⊠ *Cromwell Rd., South Kensington* ☎ *020/7942-2000* ⊕ *www.vam.ac.uk* ✉ *Free; charge for some special exhibitions (from £5)* ☉ *Sat.–Thurs. 10–5:45, Fri. 10–10* Ⓜ *South Kensington.*

DAY TRIPS FROM LONDON

Upstream, the royal palaces and grand houses that dot the area were built not as town houses but as country residences with easy access to London by river; Hampton Court Palace and Windsor Castle are the best and biggest of all.

HAMPTON COURT PALACE

20 miles southwest of central London.

FAMILY
Fodor's Choice
★
Hampton Court Palace. The beloved seat of Henry VIII's court, sprawled elegantly beside the languid waters of the Thames, this beautiful palace really gives you two for the price of one: the magnificent Tudor red-brick mansion, begun in 1514 by Cardinal Wolsey to curry favor with the young Henry, and the larger 17th-century baroque building, which was partly designed by Christopher Wren (of St. Paul's fame). The earliest buildings on this site belonged to a religious order founded in the 11th century and were expanded over the years by its many subsequent residents, until George II moved the royal household closer to London in the early 18th century.

Don't miss the famous **maze** (the oldest hedge maze in the world), its half mile of pathways among clipped hedgerows still fiendish to

20

negotiate. There's a trick, but we won't give it away here: It's much more fun just to go and lose yourself.

Choose which parts of the palace to explore based on a number of self-guided audio walking tours. Come Christmas time, there's ice-skating on a rink before the West Front of the palace.

Are you brave enough to explore the Haunted Gallery by candlelight? Evening ghost tours (£25 per person) are held throughout the year. Not only are they entertainingly spooky, but they're a great opportunity way to see the older parts of the palace without the crowds. Call or go online to check dates. ✉ *Hampton Court Rd., East Molesley, Surrey* ☎ *0844/482–7799 for tickets, 0844/482–7777 for info (24 hrs)* ⊕ *www.hrp.org.uk/hamptoncourtpalace* ✑ *Palace, maze, and gardens £17; maze only £3.85; gardens only £5.50 (free Oct.–Mar.)* ☉ *Late Mar.–Oct., daily 10–6; Nov.–late Mar., daily 10–4:30; last admission 1 hr before closing (last entry to maze 45 mins before closing); check website before visiting* Ⓜ *Richmond, then Bus No. R68. National Rail: Hampton Court Station, 35 mins from Waterloo (most trains require change at Surbiton).*

WINDSOR CASTLE
12 miles west of London.

Fodor's Choice ★ **Windsor Castle.** From William the Conqueror to Queen Victoria, the kings and queens of England added towers and wings to this brooding, imposing castle, visible for miles and now the largest inhabited castle in the world. Despite the multiplicity of hands involved in its design, the palace manages to have a unity of style and character. The most impressive view of Windsor Castle is from the A332 road, coming into town from the south. Admission includes an audio guide and, if you wish, a guided tour of the castle precincts. Entrance lines can be long in season and you're likely to spend at least half a day here, so come early.

William the Conqueror began work on the castle in the 11th century, and Edward III modified and extended it in the mid-1300s. One of Edward's largest contributions was the enormous and distinctive **Round Tower.** Later, between 1824 and 1837, George IV transformed the still-essentially-medieval castle into the fortified royal palace you see today. Most of England's kings and queens have demonstrated their undying attachment to the castle, the only royal residence in continuous use by the Royal Family since the Middle Ages.

As you enter the castle, **Henry VIII's gateway** leads uphill into the wide castle precincts, where you're free to wander. Across from the entrance is the exquisite **St. George's Chapel** (closed Sunday). Here lie 10 of the kings of England, including Henry VI, Charles I, and Henry VIII (Jane Seymour is the only one of his six wives buried here).

The **North Terrace** provides especially good views across the Thames to Eton College, perhaps the most famous of Britain's exclusive "public" boys' schools. From the terrace, you enter the **State Apartments,** which are open to the public most days. On display to the left of the entrance to the State Apartments in Windsor Castle, **Queen Mary's Dolls' House** is a perfect miniature Georgian palace-within-a-palace, created in 1923. Electric lights glow, the doors all have tiny keys, and a miniature library holds Lilliputian-size books written especially for the young queen by famous authors of the 1920s. Five cars, including a Daimler and Rolls-Royce, stand at the ready.

■ TIP→ To see the castle come magnificently alive, check out the Changing of the Guard, which takes place daily at 11 am from April through July and on alternate days at 11 am from August through March. Confirm the exact schedule before traveling to Windsor. When the Queen is in town, the guard and a regimental band parade through town to the castle gate; when she's away, a drum-and-fife band takes over. ✉ *Castle Hill* ☎ *020/7766–7304 for tickets, 01753/831118 for recorded info* 🌐 *www.royalcollection.org.uk* 🎟 *£17.75 for Precincts, State Apartments, Gallery, St. George's Chapel, and Queen Mary's Dolls' House; £9.70 when State Apartments are closed* ⏲ *Mar.–Oct., daily 9:45–5:15 (last admission at 4); Nov.–Feb., daily 9:45–4:15 (last admission at 3).*

WHERE TO EAT

Swinging London rivals New York and Tokyo as one of the best places to eat in the world right now. The sheer diversity of restaurants here is unparalleled. Among the city's 6,700 restaurants are see-and-be-seen hot spots, casual ethnic eateries, innovative gastro-pubs, and temples to haute cuisine.

Two caveats: first, an outright ban on smoking in public places—such as restaurants—was enacted in 2007. Second, beware of Sunday. Many restaurants are closed, especially in the evening; likewise, public holidays. Over the Christmas period, London virtually shuts down—it seems only hotels are prepared to feed travelers. When in doubt, call ahead. It's a good idea to book a table at all times.

BLOOMSBURY

$$ BRASSERIE

🍴 **Galvin Bistrot de Luxe.** The accomplished brothers Chris and Jeff Galvin blaze a trail for the French bistrot-de-luxe approach on a fast-moving stretch of Baker St. Seasoned fans and a more discerning crowd go for the impeccable food and service in a handsome slate-floor, bentwood chair, and mahogany-paneled Parisian-style salon. There's no finer Dorset crab lasagna in town, and mains consistently punch above their weight: Cornish brill, calves' livers with Alsace bacon, stuffed pig's trotter, and sumptious daube of venison with quince and chestnuts are all devilishly tasty, each one a superbly executed gastro triumph. The £19.50 three-course set lunches and £21.50 early evening dinners (6–7 pm) are top values. Look out for occasional live Sunday afternoon jazz. [$] *Average main: £19* ✉ *66 Baker St., Marylebone, London* ☎ *020/7935–4007* 🌐 *www.galvinrestaurants.com* ✍ *Reservations essential* [M] *Baker St.*

SOHO

$ BRASSERIE FAMILY Fodor's Choice ★

🍴 **Brasserie Zédel.** Vichyssoise soupe du jour with sliced baguette, butter, and a jug of water for £2.25? A prix fixe with steak haché and frites in a silver cup for £8.75? Or a three-course daily set meal with salade Mâche, duck confit, a glass of red, and coffee for £19.75? *And* just off Piccadilly, in a glam-and-gilded art deco/Beaux Arts gastro and jazz-bar basement emporium? *Surely* some mistake? But no, these are a few indecently priced steals on offer at restaurateurs Corbin and King's magnifique take on an all-day Parisian-style brasserie ("Chartier by way of La Coupole," says King), just north of Piccadilly Circus. Save centimes on a classic céleri rémoulade for £2.95 or soupe de poisson for £4.95 in a soaring salon of leather banquettes, marbled columns, mirrors, and stained birch tops. You'll also find decent onglet steak, seafood vol-au-vent, or *choucroute Alsacienne* with pork belly and frankfurters, plus nifty profiteroles or nougat glacé. Afterwards, imbibe at the swank Bar Américain, or enjoy live jazz or cabaret at the in-house Crazy Coqs. [$] *Average main: £8* ✉ *20 Sherwood St., Soho* ☎ *020/7734–4888* 🌐 *www.brasseriezedel.com* [M] *Piccadilly Circus.*

$ THAI FAMILY 🍴 **Busaba Eathai.** It's top Thai nosh for little moolah at this sleek and sultry modern Thai canteen in the heart of Soho. Fitted with dark-wood bench seats and hardwood tables, this flagship restaurant has communal dining, rapid service, low lighting, and often fast-moving queues out front. Pour yourself a lemongrass tea, then try ginger beef with Thai pepper, classic crunchy green papaya salad, chicken with shiitake mushrooms, jungle curry, vermicelli with prawns, squid, and scallops, or other tasty winners. You'll escape for about £15 a head, and all in all, this makes for a top-value tummy-filler and a fine pit stop during a West End shopping safari. [$] *Average main: £11* ✉ *106–110 Wardour St., Soho* ☎ *020/7255–8686* 🌐 *www.busaba.com* ✍ *Reservations not accepted* [M] *Tottenham Court Rd.*

COVENT GARDEN

$ VEGETARIAN FAMILY 🍴 **Food for Thought.** Covent Garden's hippy-vibey '70s-style subterranean BYO vegetarian café has a cult veggie and vegan following, so be prepared to queue onto Neal St. with the best of them. You'll find cramped wooden communal tables and a daily changing menu of wholesome soups, salads, pulses, stews, quiches, stir-fries, bakes, and casseroles—from mushroom Stroganoff to Rajistani red lentil curry. Wheat-free, gluten-free, GM-free, free-range, Fair Trade, vegan, and organic options are available throughout, and leave room for such puddings as their famous oat-based strawberry and banana "Scrunch." There's take-away, but note that it's only open from noon until 8:30 pm Monday through Saturday, and from noon until 5:30 pm on Sundays. [$] *Average main: £8* ✉ *31 Neal St., Covent Garden, London* ☎ *020/7836–9072* 🌐 *www.foodforthought-london.co.uk* ✍ *Reservations not accepted* 💳 *No credit cards* [M] *Covent Garden.*

$$$ FRENCH 🍴 **L'Atelier de Joël Robuchon.** A few doors down from The Ivy and arguably one of London's least publicized best restaurants, L'Atelier attracts both glitterati and food cognoscenti to sit side-by-side at the ground-floor open kitchen. This is the seductive staging post of French non-plus-ultra superchef Joël Robuchon and the lure is being able to graze tapas-style on his famous creations. Framed with a leafy-green wall, James Bond lighting, and signature red glasses and raised counter seats, this space is custom-made for those who want to splurge on an unparalleled orgy of exquisite French tapas—from frogs' legs and egg cocotte to foie gras, pig's trotters, scallops, langoustines, and roast quail with buttery truffle mash. The £129 eight-course "*decouverte*" menu is a

WHERE TO REFUEL AROUND TOWN

When you're on the go or don't have time for a leisurely meal—and Starbucks simply won't cut it—you might want to try a good local chain restaurant or sandwich bar.

Café Rouge: A classic 30-strong French bistro chain that's been around for eons—so "uncool" that it's now almost fashionable. ⊕ *www. caferouge.co.uk*

Carluccio's Caffé: Affable TV chef Antonio Carluccio's chain of 12 all-day traditional Italian café/bar/ food shops are freshly sourced and make brilliant stops on a shopping spree. ⊕ *www.carluccios.com*

Gourmet Burger Kitchen (aka GBK): Peter Gordon's line of burger joints is wholesome and handy, with Aberdeen Angus beef, lamb, or venison burgers. ⊕ *www.gbkinfo. co.uk*

Pizza Express: Serving tasty but utterly predictable pizzas, Pizza Express seems to be everywhere (there are 95 in London). Soho's branch has a cool live-jazz program. ⊕ *www.pizzaexpress.com*

Pret a Manger: London's take-out supremo isn't just for sandwiches: there are wraps, noodles, sushi, salads, and tea cakes as well. ⊕ *www.pretamanger.com*

Strada: Stop here for authentic pizzas baked over a wood fire, plus simple pastas and risottos. It's stylish, cheap, and packed. ⊕ *www. strada.co.uk*

Wagamama: Londoners drain endless bowls of noodles at this chain of high-tech, high-turnover, high-volume Japanese canteens. ⊕ *www.wagamama.com*

---

wanton way to blow the bank, but the £28 and £33 lunch and pre-theater deals are an altogether more sensible way to go. There's a formal restaurant, La Cuisine, on the first floor, and a cozy, open-fire snug bar, too. $ *Average main: £27* ✉ *13–15 West St., Covent Garden, London* ☎ *020/7010–8600* ⊕ *www.joel-robuchon.net* ⚓ *Reservations essential* Ⓜ *Leicester Sq.*

KNIGHTSBRIDGE

$$$$
INDIAN

✗ **Rasoi.** Indian chef-owner Vineet Bhatia conjures up Michelin-star modern Indian cuisine at this tony special-occasion Chelsea town house off the King's Road, where new-wave curry fans with chubby wallets swoon over chili scallop-prawn brochettes, mango chicken tikka, tandoori paneer, Keralean lamb lasagne, and grilled duck with curry-leaf foam. Average price of dinner for two: £200. $ *Average main: £33* ✉ *10 Lincoln St., Knightsbridge, London* ☎ *020/7225–1881* ⊕ *www. rasoi-uk.com* ☽ *No lunch Sat.* Ⓜ *Sloane Sq.*

MAYFAIR

$$
MODERN ITALIAN

✗ **Cecconi's.** Spot the odd A-list celeb and revel in all-day buzz at this ever-fashionable up-scale Italian brasserie wedged handsomely between Old Bond St., Cork St., and Savile Row, and across from the Royal Academy of Arts. The vaguely familiar and important-looking Miu Miu, off-shore tax exile, and private jet set spill out onto the street for breakfast, brunch, and *cicchetti* (Italian tapas), and return later in the

20

day for something more substantial. À la mode designer Ilse Crawford's luxe green-and-brown interior is a stylish backdrop for classics like stuffed baby squid, Umbrian sausages, lobster spaghetti, and a flavorful pick-me-up tiramisu. It's just the spot for a high-end pit stop during an ill-advised kamikaze West End shopping spree. [$] *Average main: £23* ✉ *5A Burlington Gardens, Mayfair, London* ☎ *020/7434–1500* 🌐 *www.cecconis.co.uk* ✍ *Reservations essential* [M] *Green Park, Piccadilly Circus.*

$$$$ FRENCH
🍴 **Le Gavroche.** Enthusiastic "MasterChef" judge Michel Roux Jr. thrives and works the floor at this clubby basement national institution in Mayfair—established by his uncle and father in 1967—and which many still rate to this day as the best formal dining in London. With silver domes and old-fashioned unpriced ladies' menus, Roux's mastery of technically precise and classical French cuisine hypnotizes all comers with signature dishes like foie gras with cinnamon-scented crispy duck pancake, langoustine with snails and Hollandaise, pig's trotters, or saddle of rabbit with Parmesan cheese. Desserts like Roux's famous chocolate omelet soufflé or upside-down apple tart are searingly accomplished. Weekday three-course set lunches (£52) are the best and sanest way to experience such unashamed overwrought flummery—with a half bottle of wine, coffee, and petit fours thrown in. The decor is 80s-traditional-luxe: some might find it dated, but the V.I.P.s here must adore it. [$] *Average main: £40* ✉ *43 Upper Brook St., Mayfair, London* ☎ *020/7408–0881* 🌐 *www.le-gavroche.co.uk* ✍ *Reservations essential* 👔 *Jacket required* ⏰ *Closed Sun. and 10 days at Christmas* [M] *Marble Arch, Bond St.*

$ BURGER FAMILY
🍴 **The Riding House Café.** Stuffed squirrel lamp holders peer down on trendy London diners at this groovy New York–style small-plates-and-luxe-burgers all-day brasserie just north of Oxford Circus. Everything's appropriately salvaged or bespoke here, so you'll find stuffed birds and other taxidermy dotted around, reclaimed theater seats at the long counter bar, bright orange leather banquettes, or old snooker table legs holding up your dining table. Opt for the £5 small plates of sea bass ceviche with lime and chili or veal-and-pork meatballs with pomarola sauce, and then head for the poached egg–chorizo hash browns, pearl-barley salt-marsh lamb broth, a decadent cheeseburger with gherkin and chips—a bargain at £12.50—or their famed tummy-filling lobster lasagna (£18.80). Service is NYC-standard friendly, and you'll find all-day breakfasts, hard shakes, and cocktails, plus sundaes on the kids' menu. [$] *Average main: £14* ✉ *43–51 Great Titchfield St., Noho* ☎ *020/7927–0840* 🌐 *www.ridinghousecafe.co.uk* ✍ *Reservations essential* [M] *Oxford Circus.*

NOTTING HILL

$$$ MODERN FRENCH Fodor's Choice ★
🍴 **The Ledbury.** Sensational Aussie chef Brett Graham wins hearts and minds—and global accolades—at this high-ceilinged destination dining landmark on the crumbier edges of Notting Hill. In a handsome four-square room full of drapes, mirrored walls, and plush seats, you won't find a more inventive vegetable dish than Graham's ash-baked celeriac with hazelnut and wood sorrel, and it's impossible to best his roast quail with walnut cream, roe deer with bone marrow, or Cornish turbot with fennel and elderflower. Besides an obsessive interest in game, Graham's

also famous for incredible desserts, so why not finish with thinly sliced figs with ewes milk yogurt and fig-leaf ice cream? Pro service and a top sommelier round out this winning proposition, now considered one of London's very best eateries by many foodies. $ *Average main: £31* ⊠ *127 Ledbury Rd., Notting Hill, London* ☎ *0207/7792–9090* ⊕ *www. theledbury.com* ⌖ *Reservations essential* ☉ *No lunch Mon.* Ⓜ *Westbourne Park, Ladbroke Grove.*

ST. JAMES'S

$$
AUSTRIAN
FAMILY
Fodor'sChoice
★

× **The Wolseley.** The whole of beau London comes for the always-on-show spectacle and soaring elegance at this Viennese-style Mitteleuropa grand café on Piccadilly. Framed with black laquerware, silver service, and a few doors down from the Ritz, this all-day brasserie begins its long decadent days with breakfast at 7 and serves until midnight. Don't be shy to pop in on spec (they hold seats back for walk-ins) to enjoy such highlights as Hungarian goulash, Austrian pork belly, chicken soup with salt beef sandwich, eggs Benedict, kedgeree, or the breaded Wiener schnitzel. For dessert, plump for the luscious *Kaiserschmarren*—caramalized pancake with stewed fruit and raisins—and don't forget to book a return table to savor the Viennoiserie pastries at one of their classy £9.75 to £32.50 afternoon teas. $ *Average main: £18* ⊠ *160 Piccadilly, St. James's, London* ☎ *020/7499–6996* ⊕ *www.thewolseley. com* ⌖ *Reservations essential* Ⓜ *Green Park.*

SOUTH BANK

$$
MODERN BRITISH

× **Anchor & Hope.** Hearty meaty dishes at wallet-friendly prices emerge from the open kitchen at this permanently packed, no-reservations leading gastropub on The Cut (between Waterloo and Southwark Tube), a few doors down from the excellent Young Vic contemporary theater. Pot-roast duck, Herefordshire beef, deep-fried pig's head, pumpkin gratin, and cuttlefish with bacon stand out. Bear in mind that it's noisy, cramped, informal, and always overflowing. That said, the kitchen is highly original, and there are great dishes for groups—like the famous slow-roasted shoulder of lamb. Eager diners wait for a table over a drink in the pub's convivial saloon bar, and be prepared to share a wooden dining table with others once seated, too. $ *Average main: £17* ⊠ *36 The Cut, South Bank, London* ☎ *020/7928–9898* ⌖ *Reservations not accepted* ☉ *No dinner Sun.; no lunch Mon.* Ⓜ *Waterloo, Southwark.*

20

PUBS AND AFTERNOON TEA

PUBS

The list below offers a few pubs selected for central location, historical interest, a pleasant garden, music, or good food—but you might just as happily adopt your own temporary local.

Fodor'sChoice
★

Black Friar. A step from Blackfriars Tube station, this spectacular pub has an Arts and Crafts interior that is entertainingly, satirically ecclesiastical, with inlaid mother-of-pearl, wood carvings, stained glass, and marble pillars all over the place. In spite of the finely lettered temperance tracts on view just below the reliefs of monks, fairies, and friars, there is a nice group of ales on tap from independent brewers. The

20th-century poet Sir John Betjeman once led a successful campaign to save the pub from demolition. ✉ *174 Queen Victoria St., The City, London* ☎ *020/7236–5474* ⊕ *www.nicholsonspubs.co.uk/theblackfriarblackfriarslondon* Ⓜ *Blackfriars.*

WORD OF MOUTH

"My favorite pub in London is the Black Friar. The beer's good and the pub is an absolutely gorgeous Art Nouveau masterpiece. It is a cathedral of drink, no joke. Crowded immediately after work, not at other times." —fnarf999

Museum Tavern. Across the street from the British Museum, this friendly and classy Victorian pub makes an ideal resting place after the rigors of the culture trail. Karl Marx unwound here after a hard day in the Library. He could have spent his *Kapital* on any of seven well-kept beers available on tap. ✉ *49 Great Russell St., Bloomsbury, London* ☎ *020/7242–8987* Ⓜ *Tottenham Court Rd.*

Prospect of Whitby. Named after a ship, this is London's oldest riverside pub, dating from around 1520. Once upon a time it was called the Devil's Tavern because of the lowlife criminals—thieves and smugglers—who congregated here. Ornamented with pewter ware and nautical objects, this much-loved "boozer" has a terrace with views of the Thames, from where boat trips often point it out. ✉ *57 Wapping Wall, East End, London* ☎ *020/7481–1095* ⊕ *www.taylor-walker.co.uk* Ⓜ *Wapping. DLR: Shadwell.*

White Hart. Claiming to be the oldest licensed pub in London, this elegant, family-owned place on Drury Lane had already been here for more than 500 years when it served highwayman Dick Turpin in 1739, just before he was hanged. Nowadays it is one of the best places to mix with cast and crew of the stage. A female-friendly environment, a cheery skylight above the lounge area, and above-average pub fare make the White Hart a particularly sociable spot for a drink. ✉ *191 Drury La., Covent Garden, London* ☎ *020/7242–2317* Ⓜ *Holborn, Covent Garden, Tottenham Court Rd.*

AFTERNOON TEA

Fodor's Choice ★ **Fortnum & Mason.** Although F&M is popularly known as the Queen's grocer, and the impeccably mannered staff wear traditional tailcoats, its celebrated food hall stocks gifts for all budgets, such as loads of irresistibly packaged luxury foods stamped with the gold "By Appointment" crest for less than £5. Try the teas, preserves (unusual products include rose-petal jelly), condiments, or Gentleman's Relish (anchovy paste). The store's famous hampers are always a welcome gift. The gleaming food hall spans two floors and includes a sleek wine bar designed by David Collins, with the rest of the store devoted to upscale homewares, men and women's clothing and accessories, toiletries, women's jewelry and cosmetics, and clothing and toys for children. If you start to flag, break for afternoon tea at one of the four other restaurants (one's an indulgent ice-cream parlor)—or a treatment in the Beauty Rooms. ✉ *181 Piccadilly, St. James's, London* ☎ *020/7734–8040* ⊕ *www.fortnumandmason.com* Ⓜ *Green Park.*

WHERE TO STAY

It's hard to get a bargain on a London hotel. If money is no object, though, you can have the most indulgent luxury imaginable: when it comes to pampering, few do it better than the British.

WHICH NEIGHBORHOOD?

Where you stay can affect your experience. Hotels in Mayfair and St. James's are central and yet distant in both mileage and sensibility from funky, youthful neighborhoods such as Shoreditch and from major tourist sights. On the edges of the West End, Soho and Covent Garden are crammed with eateries and entertainment options. South Kensington, Kensington, Chelsea, and Knightsbridge are patrician and peaceful. From Bloomsbury it's a stroll to the shops and restaurants of Covent Garden, to Theatreland, and to the British Museum; Marylebone and Clerkenwell are close enough to explore easily, too. Bayswater is an affordable haven north of Hyde Park. The South Bank, with all its cultural attractions, is an affordable option.

PRICES AND MONEY-SAVING OPTIONS

Finding a cheap but tolerable double room is a real coup. Look around Russell Square in Bloomsbury, around Victoria and King's Cross stations, on the South Bank, in Bayswater or Earl's Court, or farther out in Shepherd's Bush. Your cheapest option is a B&B or a dorm bed in a hostel; apartments are an increasingly popular choice.

University residence halls offer a cheap alternative during university vacation periods. Whatever the price, *don't* expect a room that's large by American standards.

$
B&B/INN
London School of Economics Vacations. London School of Economics Vacations costs around £50 for a double with shared bathroom, or £72 for a double with private bathroom. $ *Rooms from: £52 ⊠ Sardinia House, Houghton St., Bloomsbury, London* ☎ *020/7955–7676* ⊕ *www.lsevacations.co.uk* ❌ *No meals.*

$
B&B/INN
University College London. University College London opens up its accommodations from mid-June to mid-September (for two-night minimum stays only). $ *Rooms from: £44 ⊠ Residence Manager, Campbell House, 5–10 Taviton St., London* ☎ *020/7837–6704* ⊕ *www.ucl.ac.uk/residences* ❌ *No meals.*

20

In any event, you should confirm *exactly* what your room costs before checking in. British hotels are obliged by law to display a price chart at the reception desk; study it carefully. In January and February you can often find reduced rates, and large hotels with a business clientele have frequent weekend packages. The usual practice these days in all but the cheaper hotels is for quoted prices to cover room alone; breakfast, whether continental or "full English," costs extra. V.A.T. (Value Added Tax—sales tax) follows the same rule, with the most expensive hotels excluding a hefty 17.5%; middle-of-the-range and budget places include it in the initial quote.

BLOOMSBURY AND HOLBORN

$$$ HOTEL Fodor's Choice ★ **The Zetter.** The dizzying five-story atrium, art-deco staircase, and slick European restaurant hint at the delights to come in this converted warehouse—a breath of fresh air with its playful color schemes, elegant wallpapers, and wonderful views of The City from the higher floors. **Pros:** huge amounts of character; big rooms; free Wi-Fi; gorgeous "Rainforest" showers. **Cons:** rooms with good views cost more. [$] *Rooms from: £234* ✉ *86–88 Clerkenwell Rd., Holborn, London* ☎ *020/7324–4444* 🌐 *www.thezetter.com* 🛏 *59 rooms* 🍴 *Breakfast* [M] *Farringdon.*

KING'S CROSS

$$ HOTEL **The Megaro.** Directly across the street from St. Pancras International station (for Eurostar), the snazzy, well-designed, modern bedrooms here surround guests with startlingly contemporary style and amenities that include powerful showers and espresso machines. **Pros:** comfortable beds; great location for Eurostar; short hop on Tube to city center. **Cons:** neighborhood isn't great; standard rooms are small; interiors may be a bit stark for some. [$] *Rooms from: £160* ✉ *Belgrove St., King's Cross* ☎ *020/7843–2222* 🌐 *www.hotelmegaro.co.uk* 🛏 *49 rooms* 🍴 *Breakfast.*

COVENT GARDEN

$$$$ HOTEL Fodor's Choice ★ **Covent Garden Hotel.** It's little wonder this is now the London home-away-from-home for off-duty celebrities, actors, and style mavens, with its Covent Garden location and guest rooms that are *World of Interiors* stylish. **Pros:** great for star-spotting; super-trendy. **Cons:** you can feel you don't matter if you're not famous; setting in Covent Garden can be a bit boisterous. [$] *Rooms from: £315* ✉ *10 Monmouth St., Covent Garden, London* ☎ *020/7806–1000, 800/553–6674 in U.S.* 🌐 *www.firmdale.com* 🛏 *55 rooms, 3 suites* 🍴 *Some meals* [M] *Covent Garden.*

KENSINGTON AND SOUTH KENSINGTON

$ HOTEL **easyHotel South Kensington.** London's first "pod hotel" has tiny rooms with a double bed, private shower room, and little else, each brightly decorated in the easyGroup's trademark orange and white (to match their budget airline easyJet). **Pros:** amazing price; safe and pleasant space. **Cons:** not for the claustrophobic; most rooms have no windows; six floors and no elevator. [$] *Rooms from: £44* ✉ *14 Lexham Gardens, Kensington, London* ☎ *020/7216–1717* 🌐 *www.easyhotel.com* 🛏 *34 rooms* 🍴 *No meals* [M] *Gloucester Rd.*

$$$ HOTEL **Number Sixteen.** Guest rooms at this lovely luxury guesthouse, just around the corner from the Victoria & Albert Museum, look like they come from the pages of *Architectural Digest,* and the delightful garden is an added bonus. **Pros:** just the right level of helpful service; interiors are gorgeous. **Cons:** no restaurant; small elevator. [$] *Rooms from: £285* ✉ *16 Sumner Pl., South Kensington, London* ☎ *020/7589–5232, 888/559–5508 in U.S.* 🌐 *www.firmdale.com* 🛏 *42 rooms* 🍴 *Breakfast* [M] *South Kensington.*

KNIGHTSBRIDGE AND CHELSEA

$$$$ HOTEL Fodor's Choice ★ **Mandarin Oriental Hyde Park.** Built in 1880, the Mandarin Oriental welcomes you with one of the most exuberantly Victorian facades in town, then fast-forwards you to high-trend modern London, thanks to striking and luxurious guest rooms filled with high-tech gadgets. [$] *Rooms from: £570* ✉ *66 Knightsbridge, Knightsbridge, London* ☎ *020/7235–2000* 🌐 *www.mandarinoriental.com/london* 🛏 *177 rooms, 23 suites* 🍴 *Breakfast* [M] *Knightsbridge.*

$$ HOTEL **myhotel chelsea.** Rooms at this small, chic charmer—tucked away down a side street in an upscale neighborhood—are bijou tiny but sophisticated, with mauve satin throws atop crisp-white down comforters. **Pros:** stylish rooms made for relaxation; good neighborhood. **Cons:** price a bit high for what you get; tiny rooms; no restaurant. [$] *Rooms from: £200* ✉ *35 Ixworth Pl., Chelsea, London* ☎ *020/7225–7500* 🌐 *www.myhotels.com* 🛏 *45 rooms, 9 suites* 🍴 *Breakfast* [M] *South Kensington.*

MAYFAIR AND ST. JAMES'S

$$ B&B/INN **22 York Street.** This Georgian town house has a cozy, family feel, with polished pine floors and plenty of quilts and French antiques in the homey, individually furnished bedrooms. **Pros:** outstanding location for shoppers; friendly hosts; very flexible check-in times; entirely no-smoking. **Cons:** if you take away the great location, you're paying a lot for a B&B; not everyone enjoys socializing with strangers over breakfast. [$] *Rooms from: £130* ✉ *22 York St., Mayfair, London* ☎ *020/7224–2990* 🌐 *www.22yorkstreet.co.uk* 🛏 *10 rooms* 🍴 *Breakfast* [M] *Baker St.*

$$$$ HOTEL FAMILY Fodor's Choice ★ **Claridge's.** The well-heeled have been meeting—and eating—at Claridge's for generations, and the tradition continues at Gordon Ramsay's famed restaurant and in the original art-deco public spaces of this super-glamorous London institution. **Pros:** see-and-be-seen dining and drinking; serious luxury everywhere—this is an old-money hotel; comics, books, and DVDs to help keep kids amused. **Cons:** better pack your designer wardrobe if you want to fit in with the locals. [$] *Rooms from: £390* ✉ *Brook St., St. James's, London* ☎ *020/7629–8860, 866/599–6991 in U.S.* 🌐 *www.claridges.co.uk* 🛏 *203 rooms* 🍴 *Breakfast* [M] *Bond St.*

$$ HOTEL **Radisson Blu Edwardian Berkshire Hotel.** In a dangerously good location for shopaholics, central to Oxford Street, this pleasant and well-run outpost of the Radisson chain offers a similar level of service to some of the more established hotels in the neighborhood, at a less eye-watering rate. **Pros:** great location; good restaurant; free Wi-Fi; worthwhile deals and promotions. **Cons:** walk-in rate is still quite expensive; small bedrooms. [$] *Rooms from: £198* ✉ *350 Oxford St., Mayfair* ☎ *020/7629–7474, 0800/374–411 toll-free in U.K., 800/333–3333 toll-free in U.S.* 🌐 *www.radissonblu-edwardian.com* 🛏 *145 rooms, 2 suites* 🍴 *Some meals* [M] *Bond St., Oxford Circus.*

SOUTH BANK

$$ HOTEL [🏨] **Premier Travel Inn Southwark (Borough Market).** This excellent branch of the huge Premier Travel Inn chain is a bit out of the way on the South Bank, but is convenient for visits to the Tate Modern, Shakespeare's Globe Theatre, and Borough Market. **Pros:** ideally placed for visiting the Tate Modern or the Globe Theatre. **Cons:** small rooms; uninspiring building; limited extras or services; rooms near elevators can be a little noisy (ask for one farther down the hall). [$] *Rooms from: £132* ✉ *34 Park St., Southwark, London* ☎ *0871/527–8676* 🌐 *www.premiertravelinn.com* 🛏 *56 rooms* 🍴 *Breakfast* [M] *London Bridge.*

NIGHTLIFE AND THE ARTS

London is a must-go destination for both nightlife enthusiasts and culture vultures. Whether you prefer a refined evening at the opera or ballet, funky rhythm and blues in a Soho club, hardcore techno in east London, a pint and gourmet pizza at a local gastropub, or cocktails and sushi at a chic Mayfair bar, the U.K. capital has entertainment to suit all tastes.

One of the special experiences the city has to offer is great theater. London's theater scene consists, broadly, of the state-subsidized companies, including the Royal National Theatre and the Royal Shakespeare Company; the commercial West End, equivalent to Broadway; and the Fringe—small, experimental companies. Most of the West End theaters are in the neighborhood nicknamed Theatreland, around the Strand and Shaftesbury Avenue.

Theatergoing isn't cheap. Tickets under £10 are a rarity; in the West End you should expect to pay from £20 for a seat in the upper balcony to at least £60 for a good one in the stalls (orchestra) or dress circle (mezzanine). Fringe and subsidized companies are less. However, as the vast majority of theaters have some tickets (returns and house seats) available on the night of performance, you may find some good deals. Tickets may be booked through ticket agents, at individual theater box offices, or over the phone by credit card. Be sure to inquire about any extra fees. Be *very* careful of scalpers (known locally as "ticket touts") and unscrupulous ticket agents outside theaters and in the line at TKTS.

To find out what's showing on the cultural scene, check the weekly magazine *Time Out*. The *Evening Standard* also carries listings, especially in the Thursday supplement "Metro Life," as do London's free newspapers, many Sunday papers, and the Saturday *Independent, Guardian,* and *Times.*

BARS AND PUBS

American Bar. Festooned with a chin-dropping array of club ties, signed celebrity photographs, sporting mementos, and baseball caps, this sensational hotel cocktail bar has superb martinis. The name dates from the 1930s, when hotel bars in London started to cater to growing numbers of Americans crossing the Atlantic in ocean liners, but it wasn't until the 1970s, when a customer left a small carved wooden eagle, that the collection of paraphernalia was started. ✉ *Stafford Hotel,*

16–18 St. James's Pl., St. James's, London ☎ *020/7493–0111* ⊕ *www. thestaffordhotel.co.uk* ☉ *Daily 11:30 am–1 am* Ⓜ *Green Park.*

Barfly Club. At one of the finest small clubs in the capital, punk, indie guitar bands, and new metal rock attract a nonmainstream crowd. Weekend club nights upstairs host DJs (and live bands) who rock the decks. ⊠ *49 Chalk Farm Rd., Camden Town, London* ☎ *020/7424–0800 for venue, 0870/9070–999 for tickets* ⊕ *www.barflyclub.com* 🖃 *£5–£11* ☉ *Mon. and Tues. 7–midnight, Wed. and Thurs. 7 pm–2 am, Fri. and Sat. 7 pm–3 am* Ⓜ *Camden Town, Chalk Farm.*

Cargo. Housed under a series of old railroad arches, this vast brick-wall bar, restaurant, dance floor, and live-music venue pulls a young, international crowd with its hip vibe and diverse selection of music. Long tables bring people together, as does the food, which draws on global influences and is served tapas-style. Drinks, though, are expensive. ⊠ *83 Rivington St., Shoreditch, London* ☎ *020/7739–3440* ⊕ *www. cargo-london.com* 🖃 *Free–£20* ☉ *Mon.–Thurs. 6 pm–1 am, Fri. 6 pm–3 am, Sat. 6 pm–3 am, Sun. 6 pm–midnight (restaurant opens at noon)* Ⓜ *Old St.*

Jazz Café. A palace of high-tech cool in bohemian Camden, this remains an essential hangout for fans of both the mainstream end of the jazz repertoire and hip-hop, funk, world music, and Latin fusion. It's also the unlikely venue for Saturday "I Love the 80s" nights. Book ahead if you want a prime table in the balcony restaurant overlooking the stage. ⊠ *5 Parkway, Camden Town, London* ☎ *020/7688–8899 for restaurant reservations, 020/7485–6834 for venue info, 0844/847–2514 for tickets (Ticketmaster)* ⊕ *venues.meanfiddler.com/jazz-cafe/home* 🖃 *£6–£35* ☉ *Daily 7 pm–2 am* Ⓜ *Camden Town.*

CLASSICAL MUSIC

Royal Albert Hall. Built in 1871, this splendid iron-and-glass–dome auditorium hosts music programs in a wide range of genres. Its terra-cotta exterior surmounted by a mosaic frieze depicting figures engaged in artistic, scientific, and cultural pursuits, this domed, circular 5,223-seat auditorium was made possible by the Victorian public, who donated the money to build it. After funds were diverted toward the Albert Memorial (opposite), more money was raised by selling 999-year leases for 1,276 "Members'" seats at £100 apiece—today a box with five Members' Seats goes for half a million pounds. The notoriously poor acoustics were fixed after a 2004 renovation and the sightlines are excellent. ⊠ *Kensington Gore, Kensington* ☎ *020/7589–8212, 0845/401–5034 for box office* ⊕ *www.royalalberthall.com* Ⓜ *South Kensington.*

FAMILY **St. Martin-in-the-Fields.** One of London's best-loved and most welcoming of churches is more than just a place of worship. Named after the saint who helped beggars, St Martin's has long been a welcome sight for the homeless, who have sought soup and shelter at the church since 1914. The church is also a haven for music lovers; the internationally known Academy of St. Martin-in-the-Fields was founded here, and a popular program of concerts continues today. (Although the interior is a wonderful setting for a recital, beware the hard wooden benches!) The crypt is a hive of activity, with a popular café and shop, plus the **London**

20

Brass-Rubbing Centre, where you can make your own life-size souvenir knight, lady, or monarch from replica tomb brasses, with metallic waxes, paper, and instructions from about £5. Also watch out for a new alfresco café that opened in summer 2013. ⊠ *Trafalgar Sq., Westminster, London* ☎ *020/7766–1100, 020/7839–8362 for brass rubbings, 020/7766–1122 for evening concerts* ⊕ *www.smitf.org* ⊞ *Free; concerts £7–£30* ⊙ *Open all day for worship; sightseeing: Mon., Tue., and Fri. 8:30–1 and 2–6, Wed. 8:30–1:15 and 2–5, Thurs. 8:30–1:15 and 2–6, Sat. 9:30–6, Sun. 9:30–5* Ⓜ *Charing Cross, Leicester Sq.*

Fodor's Choice
★
Wigmore Hall. Hear chamber music and song recitals in this charming hall with near-perfect acoustics. Don't miss the Sunday morning concerts (11:30 am). ⊠ *36 Wigmore St., Marylebone, London* ☎ *020/7935–2141* ⊕ *www.wigmore-hall.org.uk* Ⓜ *Bond St.*

THEATER

Almeida Theatre. This Off–West End venue premieres excellent new plays and exciting twists on the classics, often featuring high-profile actors. There's a good café and a licensed bar that serves "sharing dishes" as well as tasty main courses. ⊠ *Almeida St., Islington, London* ☎ *020/7359–4404* ⊕ *www.almeida.co.uk* Ⓜ *Angel, Highbury & Islington.*

Fodor's Choice
★
Donmar Warehouse. Hollywood stars often perform in this not-for-profit theatre in diverse and daring new works, bold interpretations of the classics, and small-scale musicals. Nicole Kidman, Gwyneth Paltrow, and Ewan McGregor have all been featured. ⊠ *41 Earlham St., Seven Dials, Covent Garden, London* ☎ *0844/871–7624* ⊕ *www.donmarwarehouse.com* Ⓜ *Covent Garden.*

National Theatre. When this theater, designed by Sir Denys Lasdun, opened in 1976 Londoners weren't all so keen on the low-slung, multilayered Brutalist block. Prince Charles described the building as "a clever way of building a nuclear power station in the middle of London without anyone objecting." But whatever its merits or demerits as a feature on the landscape, the National Theatre's interior spaces are definitely worth a tour. Interspersed with the three theaters—the 1,120-seat Olivier, the 890-seat Lyttelton, and the 300-seat Cottesloe—is a multilayered foyer with exhibitions, bars, and restaurants, and free entertainment. Musicals, classics, and new plays are all performed by top-flight professionals. Some shows offer £12 ticket deals. ⊠ *Belvedere Rd., South Bank, London* ☎ *020/7452–3000 for box office, 020/7452–3400 for info* ⊕ *www.nationaltheatre.org.uk* ⊞ *Tour £8.50* ⊙ *Foyer Mon.–Sat. 9:30 am–11 pm; 75-min tour backstage up to 6 times daily weekdays, twice on Sat., often on Sun.* Ⓜ *Waterloo.*

Royal Court Theatre. Britain's undisputed epicenter of new theatrical works, the RCT is now 50 years old and continues to produce gritty British and international drama. ■TIP➜ Don't miss the best deal in town—four 10-pence standing tickets go on sale one hour before each performance, and £10 tickets are available on Monday. ⊠ *Sloane Sq., Chelsea, London* ☎ *020/7565–5000* ⊕ *www.royalcourttheatre.com* Ⓜ *Sloane Sq.*

SHOPPING

As befits one of the great trading capitals of the world, London has a shop for almost everything, from ratified couture to busy street markets. Apart from bankrupting yourself, the only problem you may encounter is exhaustion, traveling between London's many far-flung shopping areas. If you have limited time, zoom in on one of the city's specialty shops or grand department stores, or browse through one of the markets.

SHOPPING NEIGHBORHOODS

COVENT GARDEN
This neighborhood has chain clothing stores and top designers, craft stalls, and shops selling gifts of every type—bikes, kites, tea, herbs, beads, hats—you name it.

KENSINGTON
Kensington's main drag, Kensington High Street, houses some small, classy shops, with a few larger stores at the eastern end. Try Kensington Church Street for expensive antiques, plus a little fashion.

KNIGHTSBRIDGE
Knightsbridge, east of Kensington, has Harrods but also fashionista temple Harvey Nichols, and many expensive designer boutiques along Sloane Street, Walton Street, and Beauchamp Place.

MAYFAIR
In Mayfair are the two Bond streets, Old and New, with desirable dress designers, jewelers, and fine art. Top international designers are found on Mount Street, while South Moulton Street has more affordable boutiques.

NOTTING HILL
Go westward from the Portobello Road market and explore the Ledbury Road–Westbourne Grove axis, Clarendon Cross, and Kensington Park Road for a mix of antiques and up-to-the-minute must-haves for body and lifestyle.

REGENT STREET
At right angles to Oxford Street is Regent Street, with possibly London's most pleasant department store, Liberty, plus Hamleys, the capital's favorite toy store. A revitalized Redchurch Street in Spitalfields is home to London's hippest boutiques and galleries.

ST. JAMES'S
Here the English gentleman buys everything but the suit (which is from Savile Row): handmade hats, shirts and shoes, silver shaving kits, and hip flasks. Nothing in this neighborhood is cheap, in any sense.

DEPARTMENT STORES
Harrods. With an encyclopedic assortment of luxury brands, this Knightsbridge institution has more than 300 departments and 20 restaurants, all spread over 1 million square feet on a 5-acre site. If you approach Harrods as a tourist attraction rather than as a fashion hunting ground, you won't be disappointed. Focus on the spectacular food halls, the huge ground-floor perfumery, the revamped toy and technology departments, the excellent Urban Retreat spa, and the Vegas-like

20

Egyptian Room. At the bottom of the nearby Egyptian escalator, there's a bronze statue depicting the late Princess Diana and Dodi Fayed, son of the former owner, dancing beneath the wings of an albatross. Nevertheless, standards of taste are enforced with a customer dress code (no shorts, ripped jeans, or flip-flops). ■**TIP→ Be prepared to brave the crowds (avoid visiting on a Saturday if you can), and be prepared to pay if you want to use the bathroom on some floors (!).** ✉ *87–135 Brompton Rd., Knightsbridge, London* ☎ *020/7730–1234* ⊕ *www.harrods.com* Ⓜ *Knightsbridge.*

Harvey Nichols. While visiting tourists flock to Harrods, true London fashionistas shop at Harvey Nichols, aka "Harvey Nicks." The womenswear and accessories departments are outstanding, featuring of-the-moment designers like Roland Mouret, Peter Pilotto, and 3.1 Phillip Lim. The furniture and housewares are equally gorgeous (and pricey), though they become somewhat more affordable during the twice-annual sales in January and July. The Fifth Floor restaurant is the place to see and be seen, but if you're just after a quick bite, there's also a more informal café on the same floor or sushi-to-go from Yo! Sushi. ✉ *109–125 Knightsbridge, Knightsbridge, London* ☎ *020/7235–5000* ⊕ *www.harveynichols.com* Ⓜ *Knightsbridge.*

Fodor's Choice | **Selfridges.** This giant, bustling store (the second-largest in the U.K. after
★ | Harrods) gives Harvey Nichols a run for its money as London's most fashionable department store. Packed to the rafters with clothes ranging from midprice lines to the latest catwalk names, the store continues to break ground with its innovative retail schemes, especially the high-fashion Superbrands section, the ground-floor Wonder Room showcasing extravagant jewelry and luxury gifts, and the Concept Store, which features a rotating series of themed displays. There are so many zones that merge into one another—from youth-oriented Miss Selfridge to audio equipment to the large, comprehensive cosmetics department—that you practically need a map. Don't miss the Shoe Galleries, the world's largest shoe department filled with more than 5,000 pairs from 120 brands, displayed like works of art under spotlights. ■**TIP→ Take a break with a glass of wine from the Wonder Bar, or pick up some rare tea in the Food Hall as a gift.** ✉ *400 Oxford St., Marylebone, London* ☎ *0800/123–400* ⊕ *www.selfridges.com* Ⓜ *Bond St.*

STREET MARKETS

Fodor's Choice | **Bermondsey Antiques Market.** The early bird catches the worm here, so
★ | come before dawn on a Friday (flashlight recommended) to bag a bargain at London's largest antiques market. Dealers arrive as early as 4 am to snap up the best curios and silver, paintings, objets d'art, and furniture. The early start grew out of wrinkle in the law under which stolen goods bought here during the hours of darkness when provenance could not be determined did not have to be returned. ✉ *Long La. and Bermondsey Sq., Bermondsey, London* ⊙ *Fri. 4 am–1 pm* Ⓜ *London Bridge.*

Covent Garden. Covent Garden is actually three markets. Forty stalls selling jewelry, clothes, pottery, and other unique hand-crafted items congregate in the covered area, originally designed by Inigo Jones, known as the **Apple Market**. The **Jubilee Market**, in Jubilee Hall toward Southampton Street, tends toward the more pedestrian (kitschy T-shirts, unremarkable household goods, and the like) on Tuesday through Friday, but offers a selection of vintage collectibles on Monday and worthwhile handmade goods on weekends. The **East Colonnade** market specializes in handmade items ranging from soaps to leather goods and children's clothing, while the surrounding arcades house upscale chains (including the world's largest Apple Store). Covent Garden is something of a tourist magnet, which may be reflected in the prices, but don't miss the magicians, musicians, and escape artists who perform in the open-air piazza. Covent Garden has recently started aiming for a more sophisticated image with the opening of upscale restaurants such as a branch of New York's Balthazar. ⊠ *The Piazza, off Wellington St., Covent Garden, London* ⊕ *www.coventgardenlondonuk.com* ⊙ *Daily 9–7* Ⓜ *Covent Garden.*

Old Spitalfields Market. This fine example of a Victorian market hall (once the East End's wholesale fruit and vegetable market), now restored to its original splendor, is at the center of the area's gentrified revival. The original building is now largely occupied by shops with traders' stalls in the courtyard, and a modern shopping precinct under a Norman Foster–designed glass canopy adjoins the old building, home to a large number of independent traders' stalls. Wares include crafts, retro clothing, handmade rugs, jewelry, aromatherapy oils, fashion-forward clothes by new designers, hand-carved toy trains, unique baby clothes, vintage art prints, rare vinyl records, and cakes, though you may have to wade through a certain number of stalls selling cheap imports to find the good stuff. Thursday is particularly good for antiques. And, from Spanish tapas to Thai satays, the food outlets (mostly small, upscale chains but some independent stallholders as well) offer cuisines from around the world. ⊠ *16 Horner Sq., Brushfield St., Spitalfields, London* ☎ *020/7247–8556* ⊕ *www.spitalfields.co.uk* ⊙ *Stalls Tues.–Fri. 10–5, Sun. 9–5; restaurants weekdays 11–11, Sun. 9–11; retail shops daily 10–7* Ⓜ *Liverpool St. London Overground: Shoreditch High Street.*

Fodor'sChoice   **Portobello Market.** London's most famous market still wins the prize
★   (according to some) for the all-round best, stretching almost two miles from fashionable Notting Hill to the lively cultural melting pot of North Kensington, changing character as it goes.

The southern end, starting at Chepstow Villas, is lined with shops, stalls, and arcades selling antiques, silver, and bric-a-brac on Saturday; the middle, above Westbourne Grove, is devoted on weekdays to fruit and veg, interspersed with excellent hot food stalls; On Friday and Saturday, the area between Talbot Road and the elevated highway (called the Westway) becomes more of a flea market specializing in household and mass-produced goods sold at a discount, while north of the Westway are more stalls selling even cheaper household goods. Scattered throughout but mostly concentrated under the Westway are clothing stalls—everything from vintage to emerging designers, custom T-shirts and super-cool baby clothes, plus jewelry. As well, new and established designers are found in the boutiques of the Portobello Green Arcade.

20

Some say Portobello Road has become a tourist trap, but if you acknowledge that it's a circus and get into the spirit, it's a lot of fun. Perhaps you won't find many bargains, but this is such a fascinating part of town that just hanging out is a good enough excuse to come. There are some food and flower stalls throughout the week (try the Hummingbird Bakery for delicious cupcakes) but Saturday is when the market is in full swing. Serious shoppers avoid the crowds and go on Friday morning. ■TIP→ Bring cash (several vendors don't take credit cards) but keep an eye on it. ⊠ *Portobello Rd., Notting Hill, London* ⊕ *www.portobellomarket.org* ⊗ *Mon.–Wed., Fri.–Sat. 8–6:30, Thurs. 8–1* Ⓜ *Notting Hill Gate.*

OXFORD

With arguably the most famous university in the world, Oxford has been a center of learning since 1167; only the Sorbonne is older. Alumni of Oxford University include 47 Nobel Prize winners, 25 British prime ministers, and 28 foreign presidents, along with poets, authors, and artists. Victorian writer Matthew Arnold described Oxford's "dreaming spires," a phrase that has become famous. Students rush past you on the sidewalks on the way to their exams, clad with marvelous antiquarian style in their requisite mortar caps, flowing dark gowns, stiff collars, and crisp white bow ties.

The university is not one easily identifiable campus but a sprawling mixture of more than 39 colleges scattered around the city center, each with its own distinctive identity and focus. Oxford students live and study at their own college, and also use the centralized resources of the over-arching university. Most of the grounds and magnificent dining halls and chapels of the individual colleges are open to visitors, though the opening times (displayed at the entrance gates) vary greatly.

Oxford is 55 miles northwest of London, at the junction of the Thames and Cherwell rivers. The city is more cosmopolitan than Cambridge, and also bigger, though the interest is all at the center, where the Old Town curls around the grand stone buildings, good restaurants, and historic pubs. Eight miles northwest of Oxford, Blenheim Palace, one of the grandest houses in England, is well worth a side trip.

PLANNING YOUR TIME

You can explore major sights in town in a day or so, but you'll need more than a day to spend an hour in all of the key museums and absorb the scene at the colleges. Some colleges are open only in the afternoon during university terms; when the undergraduates are in residence, access is often restricted to the chapels, dining rooms, and libraries, too. All are closed certain days during exams, usually from mid-April to late June.

GETTING HERE AND AROUND

Megabus, Oxford Bus Company, and Oxford Tube all have buses traveling from London 24 hours a day. In London, Megabus departs from Victoria Coach Station, and Oxford Bus Company and Oxford Tube have pickup points near Victoria Station and Baker Street and Marble

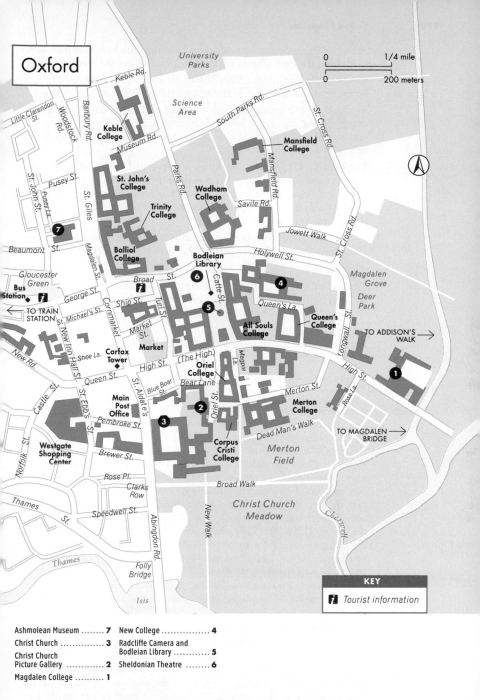

Oxford

University Parks

Science Area

Keble Rd.

Keble College

Museum Rd.

Mansfield College

Little Clarendon St.

Woodstock Rd.

Banbury Rd.

South Parks Rd.

St. Cross Rd.

Pusey St.

St. Giles

St. John St.

St. John's College

Parks Rd.

Wadham College

Mansfield Rd.

Savile Rd.

Trinity College

Jowett Walk

Beaumont St.

Magdalen St.

Balliol College

Bodleian Library

Holywell St.

Magdalen Grove Deer Park

Gloucester Green

Bus Station

George St.

Cornmarket

Broad St.

Catte St.

Queen's La.

Longwall

TO ADDISON'S WALK

TO TRAIN STATION

St. Michael's St.

Ship St.

Turl St.

Market St.

All Souls College

Queen's College

New Inn Hall St.

Shoe La.

Market

Carfax Tower

Oriel College

Magpie La.

High St.

New Rd.

Queen St.

High St. (The High)

Bear Lane

Oriel St.

Rose La.

Castle St.

St. Ebb's

St. Aldate's

Blue Boar St.

Merton St.

Merton College

TO MAGDALEN BRIDGE

Main Post Office

Pembroke St.

Corpus Cristi College

Dead Man's Walk

Merton Field

Norfolk St.

Westgate Shopping Center

Brewer St.

Rose Pl.

Clarks Row

Broad Walk

Christ Church Meadow

Cherwell

Thames St.

Speedwell St.

Abingdon Rd.

New Walk

Thames

Folly Bridge

Isis

0 — 1/4 mile
0 — 200 meters

KEY

i Tourist information

Arch Underground stations. Most of the companies have multiple stops in Oxford, the final stop being the most convenient for travelers.

Trains to Oxford depart from London's Paddington station. Oxford Station is just at the edge of the historic town center on Botley Road.

By car, the M40 heads northwest from London. It's an hour's drive, except during rush hour, when it can take twice as long. St. Clement's parking lot before the roundabout that leads to Magdalen Bridge is the best option for public parking.

Bordered by High Street, St. Giles Street, and Long Wall Road, the town center is quite compact and walkable, with most of Oxford University's most famous buildings within this area. The public bus route No. 20 runs (usually every half hour) between Oxford and Woodstock (for Blenheim Palace).

Bus Contacts **Oxford Bus Company** ☎ *01865/785400* ⊕ *www.oxfordbus.co.uk.* **Stagecoach Oxford Tube** ☎ *01865/772250* ⊕ *www.oxfordtube.com.*

TOURS
The Oxford Tourist Information Centre has up to five two-hour guided walking tours of the university. This is the best way of gaining access to the collegiate buildings.

VISITOR INFORMATION
Contacts **Oxford Tourist Information Centre** ✉ *15/16 Broad St.* ☎ *01865/252200* ⊕ *www.visitoxfordandoxfordshire.com.*

EXPLORING

Fodor'sChoice **Ashmolean Museum.** Britain's oldest public museum displays its rich
★ and varied collections from the Neolithic to the present day over five floors. Innovative and spacious galleries on the theme of "Crossing Cultures, Crossing Time" explore connections between the priceless Egyptian, Greek, Roman, Chinese, and Indian artifacts, and also display a superb art collection. Among the highlights are drawings by Raphael, the shell-encrusted mantle of Powhatan (father of Pocahontas), the lantern belonging to Guy Fawkes, and the Alfred Jewel. This ancient piece features a large semiprecious stone set in gold carved with the words, *Aelfred mec heht gewyrcan,* which translate from old English as, "Alfred ordered me to be made." The piece dates from the reign of King Alfred the Great (ruled 871–899). ■ TIP→ **There's too much to see in one visit, but the free admission makes return trips easy.** The Ashmolean Dining Room, Oxford's first rooftop restaurant, is a good spot for refreshments. ✉ *Beaumont St.* ☎ *01865/278002* ⊕ *www.ashmolean. org* ✉ *Free* ☉ *Tues.–Sun. and national holidays 10–6.*

Christ Church. Built in 1546, the college of Christ Church is referred to by its members as "The House." This is the site of Oxford's largest quadrangle, Tom Quad, named after the huge bell (6¼ tons) that hangs in the Christopher Wren–designed gate tower and rings 101 times at five past nine every evening in honor of the original number of Christ Church scholars. The vaulted, 800-year-old chapel in one corner has been Oxford's cathedral since the time of Henry VIII. The college's medieval dining hall, re-created for the Harry Potter films, contains portraits of many famous alumni, including 13 of Britain's prime ministers. ■TIP➔ Plan carefully, as the dining hall is only open weekdays 10:30–11:40 and 2:30–4:30 and weekends 2:30–4:30. Lewis Carroll, author of *Alice in Wonderland,* was a teacher of mathematics here for many years; a shop opposite the meadows on St. Aldate's sells Alice paraphernalia. ⊠ *St. Aldate's* ☎ *01865/276492* ⊕ *www.chch.ox.ac.uk* ⊠ *£8 (£8.50 in July and Aug.)* ☾ *Mon.–Sat. 10–5, Sun. 2–5; last admission 30 mins before closing.*

Christ Church Picture Gallery. This connoisseur's delight in Canterbury Quadrangle exhibits works by the Italian masters as well as Hals, Rubens, and Van Dyck. Drawings in the 2,000-strong collection are shown on a changing basis. ⊠ *Oriel Sq.* ☎ *01865/276172* ⊕ *www.chch. ox.ac.uk* ⊠ *£3* ☾ *June, Mon. and Wed.–Sat. 10:30–5, Sun. 2–5; July–Sept., Mon.–Sat. 10:30–5, Sun. 2–5; Oct.–May, Mon. and Wed.–Sat. 10:30–1 and 2–4:30, Sun. 2–4:30.*

Fodor'sChoice ★ **Magdalen College.** Founded in 1458, with a handsome main quadrangle and a supremely monastic air, Magdalen (pronounced *maud*-lin) is one of the most impressive of Oxford's colleges and attracts its most artistic students. Alumni include such diverse people as P. G. Wodehouse, Oscar Wilde, and John Betjeman. The school's large, square tower is a famous local landmark. ■TIP➔ To enhance your visit, take a stroll around the Deer Park and along Addison's Walk; then have tea in the Old Kitchen, which overlooks the river. ⊠ *High St.* ☎ *01865/276000* ⊕ *www.magd.ox.ac.uk* ⊠ *£5* ☾ *July–Sept., daily noon–7 or dusk; Oct.–June, daily 1–6 or dusk.*

New College. One of the university's best-known and oldest colleges (dating to 1379), New College stands alongside New College Lane, known for its Italianate Bridge of Sighs. Its grounds are big and enticing, with acres of soft green grass and pristinely maintained gardens. The college buildings, in ivory stone, are partly enclosed by the medieval city wall, and feature one of the city's best displays of Gothic gargoyles. ⊠ *Holywell St.* ☎ *01865/279253* ⊕ *www.new.ox.ac.uk* ⊠ *Easter–Sept. £3, Oct.–Easter free* ☾ *Easter–Sept., daily 11–5; Oct.–Easter, daily 2–4.*

20

Radcliffe Camera and Bodleian Library. A vast library, the domed Radcliffe Camera is Oxford's most spectacular building, built in 1737–49 by James Gibbs in Italian baroque style. It's usually surrounded by tourists with cameras trained at its golden-stone walls. The Camera contains part of the Bodleian Library's enormous collection, begun in 1602. Much like the Library of Congress in the United States, the Bodleian contains a copy of every book printed in Great Britain and grows by 5,000 items a week. Tours reveal the magnificent Duke Humfrey's Library, which was the original chained library and completed in 1488. (The ancient tomes are dusted once a decade.) Guides will show you the spots used for Hogwarts School in the Harry Potter films. ■TIP➔ Arrive early to secure tickets for the three to six daily tours. These are sold on a first-come, first-served basis (except for the extended tour on Wednesday and Saturday, which can be prebooked). Audio tours, the only tours open to kids under 11, don't require reservations. Call ahead to confirm tour times. ⊠ *Broad St.* ☎ *01865/277216* ⊕ *www.bodleian.ox.ac.uk* ⊠ *Audio tour*

£2.50, minitour £5, standard tour £7, extended tour £13 ⏲ *Weekdays 9–5, Sat. 9–4:30, Sun. 11–5.*

Sheldonian Theatre. This fabulously ornate theater is where Oxford's impressive graduation ceremonies are held, conducted almost entirely in Latin. Dating to 1663, it was the first building designed by Sir Christopher Wren when he served as professor of astronomy. The D-shape auditorium has pillars, balconies, and an elaborately painted ceiling. The stone pillars outside are topped by 18 massive stone heads. Climb the stairs to the cupola for the best view of the city's "dreaming spires." ✉ *Broad St.* ☎ *01865/277299* 🌐 *www.sheldon.ox.ac.uk* 🎟 *£2.50* ⏲ *Mon.–Sat. 10–1 and 2–4:30. Closed for 10 days at Christmas and Easter.*

WHERE TO EAT

$ FRENCH 🍴 **Brasserie Blanc.** Raymond Blanc's sophisticated brasserie in the Jericho neighborhood, a hipper cousin of Le Manoir aux Quat' Saisons in Great Milton, is one of the best places to eat in Oxford. Wood floors, pale walls, and large windows keep the restaurant open and airy. The changing menu always lists innovative, visually stunning adaptations of bourgeois French fare, sometimes with Mediterranean or Asian influences. Try the pasta with Jervaulx blue cheese, chestnut, and apple or the chicken stuffed with Armagnac-soaked prunes. There's a good selection of steaks as well. The £11.50 fixed-price lunch is a good value, and kids have their own menu. [$] *Average main: £15* ✉ *71–72 Walton St.* ☎ *01865/510999* 🌐 *www.brasserieblanc.com.*

$$ SEAFOOD 🍴 **Fishers.** Everything is remarkably fresh at what is widely viewed as the city's best fish restaurant. Seafood is prepared with a European touch and frequently comes with butter, cream, and other sauces: bream is served with fennel and black olive butter, for instance. Hot and cold shellfish platters are popular, as are the mussels on white wine and oysters in shallot vinegar. The interior has a casual nautical theme with wooden floors and tables, porthole windows, and red sails overhead. Lunch is a very good value. [$] *Average main: £16* ✉ *36–37 St. Clement's St.* ☎ *01865/243003* 🌐 *www.fishers-restaurant.com.*

$ CAFÉ 🍴 **Grand Café.** Golden-hue tiles, towering columns, and antique marble tables make this café both architecturally impressive and an excellent spot for sandwiches, salads, or other light fare. It's packed with tourists and the service can be slow, but this is still a pretty spot for afternoon tea. From Thursday through Saturday night, it transforms into a popular cocktail bar. [$] *Average main: £8* ✉ *84 High St.* ☎ *01865/204463* 🌐 *www.thegrandcafe.co.uk.*

WHERE TO STAY

Oxford is pricey; for the cheapest lodging, contact the tourist information office for B&Bs in locals' homes.

$ B&B/INN 🏨 **Newton House.** This handsome Victorian mansion, a five-minute walk from all of Oxford's action, is a sprawling, friendly place on three floors. **Pros:** great breakfasts; handy parking lot. **Cons:** on a main road; no elevator. [$] *Rooms from: £90* ✉ *82 Abingdon Rd.* ☎ *01865/240561* 🌐 *www.oxfordcity.co.uk/accom/newton* 🛏 *14 rooms (13 with bath)* 🍴 *Breakfast.*

$$$ HOTEL 🏨 **Old Parsonage.** A 17th-century gabled stone house in a small garden next to St. Giles Church, the Old Parsonage is a dignified retreat. **Pros:** interesting building; complimentary walking tours. **Cons:** pricey given what's on offer; some guest rooms on small side. [$] *Rooms from: £220* ✉ *1 Banbury Rd.* ☎ *01865/310210* 🌐 *www.oldparsonage-hotel.co.uk* 🛏 *26 rooms, 4 suites* 🍴 *Breakfast.*

SIDE TRIP TO BLENHEIM PALACE

Fodor's Choice ★ **Blenheim Palace.** This grandiose palace was named a World Heritage Site, the only historic house in Britain to receive the honor. Designed by Sir John Vanbrugh in the early 1700s in collaboration with Nicholas Hawksmoor, Blenheim was given by Queen Anne and the nation to General John Churchill, first duke of Marlborough, in gratitude for his military victories (including the Battle of Blenheim) against the French in 1704. The exterior is mind-boggling, with its huge columns, enormous pediments, and obelisks, all exemplars of English baroque. Inside, lavishness continues in monumental extremes: you can join a free guided tour or simply walk through on your own. In most of the opulent rooms family portraits look down at sumptuous furniture, elaborate carpets, fine Chinese porcelain, and immense pieces of silver. Exquisite tapestries in the three state rooms illustrate the first duke's victories. ■ **TIP→ Book a tour of the current duke's private apartments for a more intimate view of ducal life.** For some visitors, the most memorable room is the small, low-ceiling chamber where Winston Churchill (his father was the younger brother of the then-duke) was born in 1874; he's buried in nearby Bladon.

Sir Winston wrote that the unique beauty of Blenheim lay in its perfect adaptation of English parkland to an Italian palace. Its 2,000 acres of grounds, the work of Capability Brown, 18th-century England's best-known landscape gardener, are arguably the best example of the "cunningly natural" park in the country. Blenheim's formal gardens include notable water terraces and an Italian garden with a mermaid fountain, all built in the 1920s.

The Pleasure Gardens, reached by a miniature train that stops outside the palace's main entrance, contain some child-pleasers, including a butterfly house, a hedge maze, and giant chess set. The herb-and-lavender garden is also delightful. Blenheim Palace stages a concert of Beethoven's *Battle Symphony* in mid-July, combined with a marvelous fireworks display. There are many other outdoor events throughout the summer, including jousting tournaments. ✉ *Off A4095, Woodstock* ☎ *0800/849–6500 for info* 🌐 *www.blenheimpalace.com* 🎟 *Palace, park, and gardens £21; park and gardens £12* 🕒 *Palace mid-Feb.–Oct., daily 10:30–4:45; Nov.–mid-Dec., Wed.–Sun. 10:30–4:45. Park mid-Feb.–mid-Dec., daily 9–6 or dusk.*

20

STRATFORD-UPON-AVON

100 miles northwest of London, 37 miles southeast of Birmingham.

Even under the weight of busloads of visitors coming to see the Shakespeare sights or plays at the Royal Shakespeare Theatre, Stratford, on the banks of the slow-flowing River Avon, has somehow hung on to much of its ancient character. It can, on a good day, still feel like an English market town.

It doesn't take long to figure out who's the center of attention here. Born in a half-timber, early-16th-century building in the center of Stratford on April 23, 1564, William Shakespeare died on April 23, 1616, his 52nd birthday, in a more imposing house at New Place. Although he spent much of his life in London, the world still associates him with "Shakespeare's Avon." You can see his whole life here, from his birthplace on Henley Street to his burial place in Holy Trinity Church.

PLANNING YOUR TIME

If you have only a day in Stratford-upon-Avon, arrive early and confine your visit to two or three Shakespeare Birthplace Trust properties, a few other town sights, a pub lunch, and a walk along the river, capped off by a stroll to the Anne Hathaway's Cottage. Avoid visiting on weekends and school holidays, and take in the main Shakespeare shrines in the early morning to see them at their least frenetic. One high point of Stratford's calendar is the Shakespeare Birthday Celebrations, usually on the weekend nearest to April 23. You would do well to avoid weekends in the busier areas of the Cotswolds, but during the week, even in summer, you may hardly see a soul in the more remote spots.

GETTING HERE AND AROUND

Stratford's train station is at the edge of the town center on Alcester Road. There are usually taxis to pick up arriving passengers—alternatively it's an easy walk into town. You can travel by train *and* bus using the Shakespeare Connection Road & Rail Link from London's Euston Station, taking around two hours. There's a train to London after theater performances. Call National Rail Enquiries for information.

Bus Contacts **Castleways** ☎ *01242/602949* ⊕ *www.castleways.co.uk.* **First** ☎ *0871/200–2233* ⊕ *www.firstgroup.com.* **National Express** ☎ *0871/781–8178* ⊕ *www.nationalexpress.com.* **Pulham's Coaches** ☎ *01451/820369* ⊕ *www. pulhamscoaches.com.* **Stagecoach** ☎ *0871/200–2233* ⊕ *www.stagecoachbus. com.* **Swanbrook** ☎ *01452/712386* ⊕ *www.swanbrook.co.uk.* **Traveline** ☎ *0871/200–2233* ⊕ *www.traveline.info.*

Train Contacts **National Rail Enquiries** ☎ *0845/748–4950* ⊕ *www. nationalrail.co.uk.*

VISITOR INFORMATION

Contacts **Stratford-upon-Avon Tourist Information Centre** ✉ *Bridgefoot* ☎ *01789/264293* ⊕ *www.shakespeare-country.co.uk.*

EXPLORING

Most sights cluster around Henley Street, High Street, and Waterside, which skirts the public gardens through which the River Avon flows. Bridge Street and Sheep Street (parallel to Bridge) are Stratford's main thoroughfares and the site of most banks, shops, and eating places. The town's tourist office lies at Bridgefoot, next to Clopton Bridge.

The Shakespeare Birthplace Trust runs the main places of Shakespearean interest: Anne Hathaway's Cottage, Hall's Croft, Mary Arden's House, Nash's House and New Place, and Shakespeare's Birthplace. They have similar opening times. ■ TIP→ **You can buy a money-saving combination ticket to the three in-town properties or to all five properties, or pay separate entry fees if you're visiting only one or two. Family tickets are an option too.** You can check out special events at the properties, from talks about Tudor life to performances of Shakespeare's plays.

Fodor's Choice ★ **Anne Hathaway's Cottage.** The most picturesque of the Shakespeare Trust properties, on the western outskirts of Stratford, was the family home of the woman Shakespeare married in 1582. The "cottage," actually a substantial Tudor farmhouse, has latticed windows and a grand thatch roof. Inside is period furniture, including the settle where Shakespeare reputedly conducted his courtship, and a rare carved Elizabethan bed; outside is a garden planted in lush Victorian style with herbs and flowers. A stroll through the adjacent orchard takes you to willow cabins where you can listen to sonnets, view sculptures with Shakespearean themes, and try a yew and a heart-shaped lavender maze. ■ TIP→ **The best way to get here is on foot, especially in late spring when the apple trees are in blossom.** The signed path runs from Evesham Place (an extension of Grove Road) opposite Chestnut Walk. Pick up a leaflet with a map from the tourist office; the walk takes a good half hour. ⊠ *Cottage La., Shottery* ☎ *01789/295517* ⊕ *www.shakespeare.org.uk* 🎫 *£9; £22.50 with the Five House Pass which includes Anne Hathaway's Cottage & Gardens, Hall's Croft, Mary Arden's Farm, Nash's House & New Place, Shakespeare's Birthplace, Shakespeare's Grave* ☉ *Apr.–Oct., daily 9–5; Nov.–Mar., daily 10–4; last admission 30 mins before closing.*

20

Holy Trinity Church. The burial place of William Shakespeare, this 13th-century church sits on the banks of the Avon, with a graceful avenue of lime trees framing its entrance. Shakespeare's final resting place is in the chancel, rebuilt in 1465–91 in the late Perpendicular style. He was buried here not because he was a famed poet but because he was a lay rector of Stratford, owning a portion of the township tithes. On the north wall of the sanctuary, over the altar steps, is the famous marble bust created by Gerard Jansen in 1623 and thought to be a true likeness of Shakespeare. The bust offers a more human, even humorous, perspective when viewed from the side. Also in the chancel are the graves of Shakespeare's wife, Anne; his daughter Susanna; his son-in-law John Hall; and his granddaughter's husband, Thomas Nash. Nearby, the Parish Register is displayed, containing Shakespeare's baptismal entry (1564) and his burial notice (1616). ⊠ *Trinity St.* ☎ *01789/266316* ⊕ *www.stratford-upon-avon.org* 🎫 *£2 for chancel* ☉ *Mar. and Oct., Mon.–Sat. 9–5, Sun. 12:30–5; Apr.–Sept., Mon.–Sat. 8:30–6, Sun.*

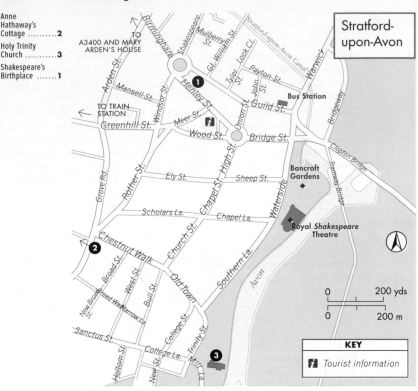

12:30–5; Nov.–Feb., Mon.–Sat. 9–4, Sun. 12:30–5; last admission 20 mins before closing.

Fodor's Choice ★ **Shakespeare's Birthplace.** A half-timber house typical of its time, the playwright's birthplace is a much-visited shrine that has been altered and restored since he lived here. Entering through the modern visitor center, you are immersed in an entertaining but basic introduction to Shakespeare through a "Life, Love, and Legacy" visual and audio exhibition; this can be crowded. You can see a First Folio and what is reputedly Shakespeare's signet ring, listen to the sounds of the Forest of Arden, and watch snippets of contemporary Shakespearean films. The house itself is across the garden from this large modern center. Colorful wall decorations and the furnishings in the actual house reflect comfortable, middle-class Elizabethan domestic life. Shakespeare's father, John, a glove maker and wool dealer, purchased the house; a reconstructed workshop shows the tools of the glover's trade. Mark Twain and Charles Dickens were earlier pilgrims here, and you can see the signatures of Thomas Carlyle and Walter Scott scratched into Shakespeare's windowpanes. In the garden, actors present excerpts from the plays. There's also a café and bookshop on the grounds. ⊠ Henley St. ☎ 01789/201822 ⊕ www.shakespeare.org.uk 🖭 £14.95, includes entry *to Hall's Croft and Nash's House* ⏲ *Apr.–June and Sept.–Oct., daily 9–5; July and Aug., daily 9–6; Nov.–Mar., daily 10–4.*

WHERE TO EAT

$ BRITISH Fodor's Choice ★ 🍴 **The Black Swan/The Dirty Duck.** The only pub in Britain to be licensed under two names (the more informal one came courtesy of American GIs who were stationed here during World War II), this is one of Stratford's most celebrated pubs—it's attracted actors since the 18th-century thespian David Garrick's days. A little veranda overlooks the theaters and the river here. Along with your pint of bitter, you can choose from the extensive menu of daily specials, wraps, ciabattas, steaks, burgers, and grills. Few people come here for the food, though you will need to book ahead for dinner: the real attraction is the ambience and your fellow customers. [$] *Average main: £10* ✉ *Waterside* ☎ *01789/297312* 🌐 *www.dirtyduck-pub-stratford-upon-avon.co.uk.*

WHERE TO STAY

$$ HOTEL 🏨 **Mercure Shakespeare Hotel.** Built in the 1400s, this Elizabethan town house in the heart of town is a vision right out of *The Merry Wives of Windsor,* with its nine gables and long, stunning, black-and-white half-timber facade. **Pros:** historic building; relaxing lounge. **Cons:** some very small bedrooms; charge for parking. [$] *Rooms from: £130* ✉ *Chapel St.* ☎ *01789/294997* 🌐 *www.mercure.com* 🛏 *63 rooms, 10 suites* 🍽 *Breakfast.*

$$ HOTEL Fodor's Choice ★ 🏨 **White Swan.** None of the character of this black-and-white timbered hotel, which claims to be the oldest building in Stratford, has been lost in its swanky, but sympathetic update. **Pros:** antiquity; generous bathrooms; friendly service. **Cons:** tricky to stop with car; no parking on site; stripey carpet may cause dizziness. [$] *Rooms from: £150* ✉ *Rother St.* ☎ *01789/297022* 🌐 *www.white-swan-stratford.co.uk* 🛏 *37 rooms, 4 suites* 🍽 *Breakfast.*

ARTS AND ENTERTAINMENT

Fodor's Choice ★ **Royal Shakespeare Company (RSC).** One of the finest repertory troupes in the world and long the backbone of the country's theatrical life, the company performs plays year-round in Stratford and at venues around Britain. The stunning Royal Shakespeare Theatre, home of the RSC, has a thrust stage based on the original Globe Theater in London. The Swan Theatre, part of the theater complex and also built in the style of Shakespeare's Globe, stages plays by Shakespeare and contemporaries such as Christopher Marlowe and Ben Jonson, as well as works by contemporary playwrights. Prices usually are £14 to £60. ■ **TIP→ Seats book up fast, but day-of-performance and returned tickets are often available.** ✉ *Waterside* ☎ *0844/800–1110 for tickets* 🌐 *www.rsc.org.uk.*

BATH

"I really believe I shall always be talking of Bath . . . Oh! who can ever be tired of Bath," enthused Catherine Morland in Jane Austen's *Northanger Abbey*, and today plenty of people agree with these sentiments. In Bath you are surrounded by magnificent 18th-century architecture, a lasting reminder of the vanished world described by Austen.

Bath is no museum, though: it's lively, with good dining and shopping, excellent art galleries and museums, the remarkable excavated Roman baths, and theater, music, and other performances all year. Many people rush through Bath in a day, but there's enough to do to merit an overnight stay—or more.

The Romans put Bath on the map in the 1st century, when they built a temple here, in honor of the goddess Minerva, and a sophisticated network of baths to make full use of the mineral springs that gush from the earth at a constant temperature of 116°F (46.5°C). ■TIP→Don't miss the remains of these baths, one of the city's glories. Visits by Queen Anne in 1702 and 1703 brought attention to the town, and soon 18th-century "people of quality" took it to heart. Bath became the most fashionable spa in Britain. The architects John Wood and John Wood the Younger created a harmonious city, building graceful terraces (row houses), crescents (curving rows of houses), and villas of the same golden local limestone used by the Romans.

PLANNING YOUR TIME

Schedule a visit to Bath during the week, as weekends see an influx of visitors. The city gets similarly crowded during its various festivals, though the added conviviality and cultural activity during these events are big draws in themselves. Early morning and late afternoon are the best times to view nearby Stonehenge at its least populated.

GETTING HERE AND AROUND

Bath lies 115 miles west of London and 13 miles southeast of Bristol. Frequent trains from Paddington and National Express buses from Victoria connect Bath with London. The bus and train stations are close to each other south of the center. From Bath numerous private companies operate tours to Stonehenge.

By car, M4 is the main route west from London to Bath; expect about a two-hour drive. From Exit 18, take A46 south to Bath. Public parking lots in the historic area fill up early, but the Park and Ride lots on the outskirts provide inexpensive shuttle service into the center, which is pleasant to stroll around. Drivers from Bath to Stonehenge should take A36/A303, and from London to Stonehenge, M3/A303.

TOURS

City Sightseeing runs 50-minute guided tours of Bath on open-top buses year-round, leaving three or four times an hour from High Street, near the Abbey. Mad Max Tours runs full-day tours to Stonehenge.

Contacts **City Sightseeing** ☎ *01225/444102* ⊕ *www.city-sightseeing.com.* **Mad Max Tours** ☎ *0799/050–5970* ⊕ *www.madmaxtours.co.uk.* **Mayor of Bath's Honorary Guides** ☎ *01225/477411* ⊕ *www.bathguides.org.uk.*

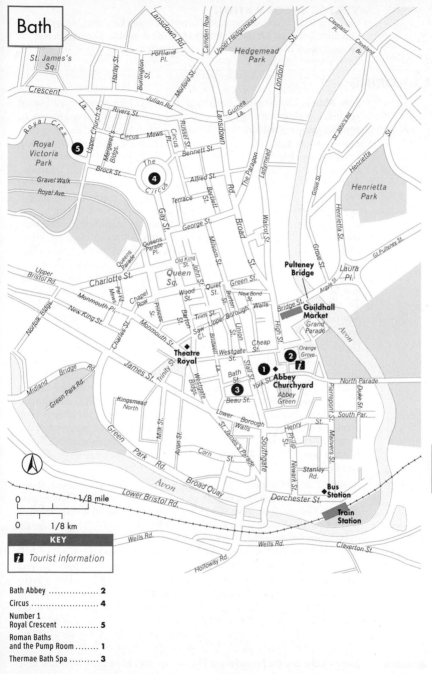

Bath

St. James's Sq.

Crescent

Hedgemead Park

Royal Victoria Park

Royal Cres.

Gravel Walk

Royal Ave.

The Circus

Henrietta Park

Pulteney Bridge

Laura Pl.

Queen Sq.

Guildhall Market

Grand Parade

Theatre Royal

Abbey Churchyard

Abbey Green

Bus Station

Train Station

20

0 ———— 1/8 mile

0 ———— 1/8 km

KEY

 Tourist information

Bath Abbey **2**

Circus **4**

Number 1
Royal Crescent **5**

Roman Baths
and the Pump Room **1**

Thermae Bath Spa **3**

VISITOR INFORMATION

Contacts **Bath Tourist Information Centre** ✉ *Abbey Chambers, Abbey Churchyard* ☎ *0844/847–5257, 0844/847–5256 for booking accommodation service* ⊕ *www.visitbath.co.uk.*

EXPLORING

Bath Abbey. Dominating Bath's center, this 15th-century edifice of golden, glowing stone has a splendid west front, with carved figures of angels ascending ladders on either side. Notice, too, the miter, olive tree, and crown motif, a play on the name of the building's founder, Bishop Oliver King. More than 50 stained-glass windows fill about 80% of the building's wall space, giving the interior an impression of lightness. The abbey was built in the Perpendicular (English late-Gothic) style on the site of a Saxon abbey, and the nave and side aisles contain superb fan-vaulted ceilings. Look for the expressively carved angels on the choir screens. There are five services on Sunday, including choral evensong at 3:30. Forty-five-minute **tower tours**, allowing close-up views of the massive bells and panoramic cityscapes from the roof, take place daily except Sundays; the 212 dizzying steps demand a level of fitness. ✉ *Abbey Churchyard* ☎ *01225/422462* ⊕ *www.bathabbey.org* ✉ *Abbey £2.50 suggested donation, tower tours £6* ⊗ *Abbey Mon. 9:30–6, Tues–Sat. 9–6, Sun. 1–2:30 and 4:30–5:30. Tower tours Apr., May, Sept., and Oct., Mon.–Sat. 10–4 hrly; June–Aug., Mon.–Sat. 10–5 hrly; Nov.–Mar., Mon.–Sat. 11, noon, and 2.*

Circus. John Wood designed the masterful Circus, a circle of curving, perfectly proportioned Georgian houses interrupted just three times for intersecting streets. Wood died shortly after work began; his son, the younger John Wood, completed the project. Notice the carved acorns atop the houses: Wood nurtured the myth that Prince Bladud founded Bath, ostensibly with the help of an errant pig rooting for acorns (this is one of a number of variations of Bladud's story). A garden fills the center of the Circus. The painter Thomas Gainsborough (1727–88) lived at No. 17 from 1760 to 1774. ✉ *Intersection of Bennett, Brock, and Gay sts.*

Fodor'sChoice **Number 1 Royal Crescent.** The majestic arc of the Royal Crescent, much
★ used as a film location, is the crowning glory of Palladian architecture in Bath. The work of John Wood the Younger, these 30 houses fronted by 114 columns were laid out between 1767 and 1774. The first house to be built, on the corner of Brock Street and the Royal Crescent, was Number 1 Royal Crescent. Having undergone substantial refurbishment in 2013, it has been reunited with its original servants' annex, and the museum now crystallizes a view of the English class system in the 18th century—status, wealth and elegance of the main house reflected in and contrasted with the servants' quarters and kitchen, set apart in the service wing. ✉ *Royal Crescent* ☎ *01225/428126* ⊕ *www. bath-preservation-trust.org.uk* ✉ *£8.50* ⊗ *Mid-Feb.–mid-Dec., Mon. 12–4:30, Tues.–Sun. 10:30–5:30; last admission 1 hr before closing.*

Fodor'sChoice **Roman Baths and the Pump Room.** The hot springs have drawn people here
★ since prehistoric times, so it's quite appropriate to begin an exploration

of Bath at this excellent museum on the site of the ancient city's primary "watering hole." Roman patricians would gather to immerse themselves, drink the mineral waters, and socialize. With the departure of the Romans, the baths fell into disuse. When bathing again became fashionable at the end of the 18th century, this magnificent Georgian building was erected.

Adjacent to the Roman bath complex is the famed **Pump Room**, built in 1792–96, a rendezvous for members of 18th- and 19th-century Bath society. Here Catherine Morland and Mrs. Allen "paraded up and down for an hour, looking at everybody and speaking to no one," to quote from Jane Austen's *Northanger Abbey*. Today you can take in the elegant space—or you can simply, for a small fee, taste the fairly vile mineral water. Charles Dickens described it as tasting like warm flatirons. ■**TIP**➔ The tourist office offers a £63.50 package that includes a visit to the Roman Baths, a three-course lunch or champagne afternoon tea, and a two-hour spa session. ⊠ *Abbey Churchyard* ☎ *01225/477785* ⊕ *www. romanbaths.co.uk* ⊠ *Roman Baths £12.75 (£13.25 in July and Aug.), £16.25 combined ticket includes the Fashion Museum and Assembly Rooms* ⊗ *Mar.–June, Sept., and Oct., daily 9–6; July and Aug., daily 9 am–10 pm; Nov.–Feb., daily 9:30–5:30; last admission 1 hr before closing.*

Thermae Bath Spa. The only place in Britain where you can bathe in natural hot-spring water, and in an open-air rooftop location as well, this striking complex designed by Nicholas Grimshaw consists of a Bath-stone building surrounded by a glass curtain wall. The only difficulty is in deciding where to spend more time—in the sleekly luxurious, light-filled Minerva Bath, with its curves and gentle currents, or in the smaller, open-air rooftop pool for the unique sensation of bathing with views of Bath's operatic skyline—twilight is atmospheric here. Two 18th-century thermal baths, the Cross Bath and the Hot Bath, are back in use, too (the latter for treatments only). End your session in the crisp third-floor café and restaurant. ■**TIP**➔ It's essential to book spa treatments ahead. Towels, robes, and slippers are available for rent. Note that changing rooms are co-ed. Weekdays are the quietest time to visit. You must be 18 to book a spa treatment. A separate, free **Visitor Centre** (April through October, Monday through Saturday 10–5, Sunday 11–4) opposite the entrance gives an overview of the project and provides audio guides (£2) for a brief tour of the exterior. ⊠ *Hot Bath St.* ☎ *0844/888–0844* ⊕ *www.thermaebathspa.com* ⊠ *£26 for 2 hrs, £36 for 4 hrs, £56 all day* ⊗ *Daily 9 am–10 pm; last admission at 7.*

20

WHERE TO EAT

$ ✕**Pump Room.** The 18th-century Pump Room, with views over the
BRITISH Roman Baths, serves morning coffee, substantial lunches, and afternoon tea, to music by a pianist or string trio who play every day. The stately setting is the selling point rather than the food, but do sample the West Country cheese board and the homemade cakes and pastries. There's a fixed-price menu at lunchtime, and the place is usually open for dinners in July, August, and December and during the major festivals

(reservations are essential). Be prepared to wait in line for a table during the day. [$] *Average main: £12* ✉ *Abbey Churchyard* ☎ *01225/444477* 🌐 *www.romanbaths.co.uk* ⏲ *No dinner Jan.–June and Sept.–Nov.*

$ BRITISH 🍴 **Sally Lunn's.** Small and slightly twee, this tourist magnet near Bath Abbey occupies the oldest house in Bath, dating to 1482. It's famous for the Sally Lunn bun, actually a semisweet bread served here since 1680. You can choose from more than 30 sweet and savory toppings to accompany your bun, or turn it into a meal with such dishes as duck with orange-and-cinnamon sauce. There are also economical lunch and early-evening menus. Daytime diners can view the small kitchen museum in the cellar (30p for nondining visitors). [$] *Average main: £12* ✉ *4 N. Parade Passage* ☎ *01225/461634* 🌐 *www.sallylunns.co.uk.*

WHERE TO STAY

$ B&B/INN 🏨 **Albany Guest House.** Homey and friendly, this Edwardian house close to the Royal Crescent has simply furnished rooms decorated with neutral shades of beige and cream. **Pros:** spotless rooms; convenient location; excellent breakfasts. **Cons:** some rooms are very small; limited parking. [$] *Rooms from: £85* ✉ *24 Crescent Gardens* ☎ *01225/313339* 🌐 *www.albanybath.co.uk* 🛏 *5 rooms* 🍽 *Breakfast.*

$$$ HOTEL 🏨 **Queensberry Hotel.** Intimate and elegant, this boutique hotel in a residential street near the Circus occupies three 1772 town houses built by John Wood the Younger for the marquis of Queensberry; it's a perfect marriage of chic sophistication, homey comforts, and attentive service. **Pros:** efficient service; tranquil ambience; valet parking. **Cons:** occasional street noise; no tea/coffee-making facilities in rooms; breakfast extra. [$] *Rooms from: £165* ✉ *7 Russel St.* ☎ *01225/447928* 🌐 *www.thequeensberry.co.uk* 🛏 *26 rooms, 3 suites* 🍽 *No meals.*

$$ B&B/INN 🏨 **Three Abbey Green.** Just steps from Bath Abbey, a gorgeous square dominated by a majestic plane tree is home to this welcoming B&B. **Pros:** superb location; airy rooms. **Cons:** some noise from pubgoers; only two suites have bathtubs; no parking. [$] *Rooms from: £120* ✉ *3 Abbey Green* ☎ *01225/428558* 🌐 *www.threeabbeygreen.com* 🛏 *7 rooms* 🍽 *Breakfast.*

STONEHENGE

STONEHENGE

Fodor's Choice ★ **Stonehenge.** Mysterious and ancient, Stonehenge has baffled archaeologists for centuries. One of England's most visited monuments, the circle of giant stones standing starkly against the wide sweep of Salisbury Plain still has the capacity to fascinate and move those who view it. This World Heritage Site is now enclosed by barriers due to incidents of vandalism and growing fears that its popularity could threaten its existence, and visitors are kept on a paved path a short distance away from the stones. But if you visit in the early morning before the crowds have arrived, or in the evening, when the sky is heavy with scudding clouds, you can experience Stonehenge as it once was: a mystical, awe-inspiring place. ■ **TIP→ English Heritage arranges access to the stone**

**circle outside of normal hours. These tours require a payment of £16.30.
Book well in advance.**

Stonehenge was begun about 3000 BC, and it continued to undergo changes until around 2500 BC, in use until around 1600 BC. It was made up of an outer circle of 30 sarsen stones, huge sandstone blocks weighing up to 25 tons, which are believed to have originated from the Marlborough Downs, and an earlier inner circle of bluestones that was constructed around 2500 BC. Within these circles was a horseshoe-shape group of sarsen trilithons (two large vertical stones supporting a third stone laid horizontally across it) and within that another horseshoe-shape grouping of bluestones. The sarsens used in the trilithons averaged 45 tons. Many of the huge stones were brought here from great distances before the invention of the wheel, and it's not certain what ancient form of transportation was used to move them. The bluestones, for example, are thought to have come from the Preseli Hills on the Atlantic coast of Wales, and may have been moved by raft over sea and river, and then dragged on rollers across country despite weighing as much as 4 tons each—a total journey of 149 miles as the crow flies. However, every time a reconstruction of the journey has been attempted, it has failed. The labor involved in quarrying, transporting, and carving these stones is astonishing, all the more so when you realize that it was accomplished about the same time as the construction of Egypt's major pyramids. Stonehenge (the name derives from the Saxon term for "hanging stones") has been excavated several times over the centuries, but, the primary reason for its erection remains unknown. It's fairly certain that it was a religious site, and that worship here involved the cycles of the sun; the alignment of the stones on the axis of the midsummer sunrise and midwinter sunset makes this clear. The Druids certainly had nothing to do with the construction: the monument had already been in existence for nearly 2,000 years by the time they appeared. To fully engage your imagination, or to get that magical photo, it's worth exploring all aspects of the site, both near and far. It has a particularly romantic aspect at dawn and dusk, or by a full moon. Your ticket entitles you to an informative audio tour, but in general, visitor amenities at Stonehenge have been limited, especially for such a major tourist attraction. An improved visitor center 1½ miles away is scheduled to open by early 2014, with improved exhibits, a café, and a shop. In addition, traffic on a busy road nearby will be re-routed by mid-2014. ⊠ *Jct. of A303 and A360, Amesbury* ☎ *0870/333–1181, 01722/343830 for private tours* ⊕ *www.english-heritage.org.uk* ✎ *£8* ⊙ *Late Mar.–May and Sept.–mid-Oct., daily 9:30–6; June–Aug., daily 9–7; mid-Oct.–mid-Mar., daily 9:30–4; last admission 30 mins before closing.*

20

CAMBRIDGE

With the spires of its university buildings framed by towering trees and expansive meadows, its medieval streets and passages enhanced by gardens and riverbanks, the city of Cambridge is among the loveliest in England. The city predates the Roman occupation of Britain, but there's confusion about when the university was founded. One story attributes its founding to impoverished students from Oxford, who came in search of eels—a cheap source of nourishment.

Cambridge embodies a certain genteel, intellectual, and sometimes anachronistically idealized image of Englishness. The exquisite King's College choir defines the traditional English Christmas, when the Festival of Nine Lessons and Carols is broadcast live on Christmas Eve. Filled with tiny gardens, ancient courtyards, imposing classic buildings, alleyways that lead past medieval churches, and wisteria-hung facades, the city remains an extraordinary center of learning and research where innovation and discovery still happen behind its ancient walls.

Keep in mind that there is no recognizable campus: the scattered colleges *are* the university. Each of the 25 oldest colleges is built around a series of courts, or quadrangles, whose velvety lawns are the envy of many a gardener. Since students and fellows (faculty) live and work in these courts, access is restricted. Visitors are not normally allowed into college buildings other than chapels, dining halls, and some libraries; some colleges charge admission for certain buildings. Public visiting hours vary from college to college, and it's best to call, check with the city tourist office or consult the university's website, ⊕ *www.cam.ac.uk*.

■**TIP**➜ When the colleges are open, the best way to gain access is to join a walking tour led by an official Blue Badge guide—many areas are off-limits unless you do. The two-hour tours (£9–£10) leave up to four times daily from the city tourist office.

Perhaps the best views are from the Backs, the green parkland that extends along the River Cam behind several colleges. This broad, sweeping openness, a result of the larger size of the colleges and from the lack of industrialization in the city center, is just what distinguishes Cambridge from Oxford. The other traditional view of the colleges is gained from a punt—the boats propelled by pole on the River Cam.

PLANNING YOUR TIME

Colleges close to visitors during the main exam time, late May to mid-June. Term time (when classes are in session) means roughly October to December, January to March, and April to June. During the summer vacation (July to September) and over the Easter and Christmas holidays, Cambridge is devoid of students, its heart and soul. Summer, however, is enlivened by festivals, notably the Strawberry Fair (June) and the Folk Festival and Arts Festival (both July). The May Bumps, intercollegiate boat races, are, confusingly, held the first week of June in Cambridge.

GETTING HERE AND AROUND

Good bus (2 hours) and train (1 to 1½ hours) services connect London and Cambridge. The train station is a mile or so southeast of the center and is connected by city bus service 3 to Emmanuel Street, which is just around the corner from the long-distance bus terminus on Drummer Street. If you're driving, don't attempt to venture very far into the center—parking is scarce and pricey. The center is amenable to explorations on foot, or you could join the throng by renting a bicycle.

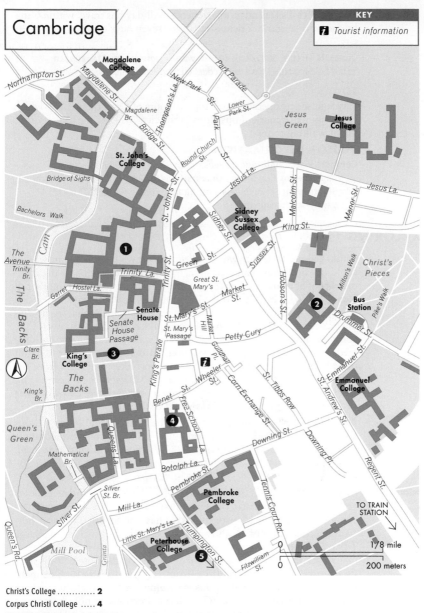

Cambridge

KEY

i Tourist information

Stagecoach sells Dayrider (£3) tickets for all-day bus travel within Cambridge, and Megarider tickets (£10) for seven days of travel within the city.

Contacts First ☎ *0845/410–4444* ⊕ *www.firstgroup.com.* **Stagecoach** ☎ *0871/834–0010* ⊕ *www.stagecoachbus.com/cambridge.*

TOURS

City Sightseeing operates open-top bus tours of Cambridge (£10), which can be joined at marked bus stops in the city. Also ask the tourist office about walking tours.

VISITOR INFORMATION

Contacts Visit Cambridge ✉ *Peas Hill* ☎ *0871/226–8006* ⊕ *www. visitcambridge.org.* **Cambridge University** ☎ *01223/337733* ⊕ *www.cam.ac.uk.* **City Sightseeing** ✉ *Cambridge Train Station, Station Rd.* ☎ *01223/423578* ⊕ *www.city-sightseeing.com.*

EXPLORING

Christ's College. To see the way a college has grown over the centuries you could not do better than visit here. The main gateway bears the enormous coat of arms of its patroness, Lady Margaret Beaufort, mother of Henry VII, who established the institution in 1505. It leads into a fine courtyard, with the chapel framed by an ancient magnolia. In the dining hall hang portraits of John Milton and Charles Darwin, two of the college's more famous students. You next walk past a fellows' building credited to Inigo Jones, to the spacious garden (once a favorite haunt of Milton), and finally to a modern ziggurat-like confection from the 1960s. ✉ *St. Andrew's St.* ☎ *01223/334900* ⊕ *www.christs.cam.ac.uk* 🎫 *Free* ☉ *Grounds daily 9–4; gardens weekdays 9–4; closed during exam periods (typically early May–mid Jun.).*

Corpus Christi College. Founded in 1352, the beautiful and serene Corpus Christi College is the longest continuously inhabited college quadrangle in Cambridge. ✉ *King's Parade* ☎ *01223/338000* ⊕ *www.corpus.cam. ac.uk* 🎫 *July–Sept. £2.50; Oct.–June free* ☉ *July–Sept., daily 10:30– 4:30; Oct.–late Dec. daily 2–4; Jan.–late Apr., daily 10–4.*

Fodor'sChoice ★ **Fitzwilliam Museum.** In a Classical Revival building renowned for its grand Corinthian portico, the Fitzwilliam, founded by the seventh viscount Fitzwilliam of Merrion in 1816, has one of Britain's most outstanding collections of art and antiquities. Highlights include two large Titians, an extensive collection of French impressionist painting, and many paintings by Matisse and Picasso. The opulent interior displays its treasures to marvelous effect, from Egyptian pieces such as inch-high figurines and painted coffins, to sculptures from the Chinese Han dynasty of the 3rd century BC. Other collections of note here are a fine assortment of medieval illuminated manuscripts and a fascinating room full of armor and muskets. ✉ *Trumpington St.* ☎ *01223/332900* ⊕ *www.fitzmuseum.cam.ac.uk* 🎫 *Free* ☉ *Tues.–Sat. 10–5, Sun. noon–5.*

Fodor'sChoice ★ **King's College Chapel.** Based on Sainte-Chapelle, the 13th-century royal chapel in Paris, this house of worship is perhaps the most glorious flowering of Perpendicular Gothic in Britain. Henry VI, the king after whom the college is named, oversaw the work. From the outside, the most prominent features are the massive flying buttresses and the finger-like spires that line the length of the building. Inside, the most obvious impression is of great space—the chapel was once described as "the noblest barn in Europe"—and of light flooding in from its huge windows. The brilliantly colored bosses (carved panels at the intersections of the roof ribs) are particularly intense, although hard to see without binoculars. An exhibition in the chantries, or side chapels, explains more about the chapel's construction. Behind the altar is *The Adoration of the Magi,* an enormous painting by Peter Paul Rubens. **■ TIP→ The chapel, unlike the rest of King's College, stays open during exam periods.** Every Christmas Eve, a festival of carols is sung by the chapel's famous choir. To compete for the small number of tickets available, join the line at the college's main entrance early—doors open at 7 am. ✉ *King's Parade* ☎ *01223/331212* 🌐 *www.kings.cam.ac.uk* 🎟 *£7.50, includes college and grounds* 🕒 *During term, weekdays 9:30–3:30, Sat. 9:30–3:15, Sun. 1:15–2:30; out of term, daily 9:30–4:30. Chapel occasionally closed for services and private events; call or check online.*

Trinity College. Founded in 1546 by Henry VIII, Trinity replaced a 14th-century educational foundation and is the largest college in either Cambridge or Oxford, with nearly 700 undergraduates. In the 17th-century great court, with its massive gatehouse, is **Great Tom,** a giant clock that strikes each hour with high and low notes. The college's greatest masterpiece is Christopher Wren's **library,** colonnaded and seemingly constructed with as much light as stone. Among the things you can see here is A. A. Milne's handwritten manuscript of *The House at Pooh Corner.* Trinity alumni include Isaac Newton, William Thackeray, Lord Byron, Alfred Tennyson, and 31 Nobel Prize winners. ✉ *St. John's St.* ☎ *01223/338400* 🌐 *www.trin.cam.ac.uk* 🎟 *£1* 🕒 *College and chapel daily 10–4, except exam period and event days; great court and library weekdays noon–2, Sat. during term 10:30–12:30.*

WHERE TO EAT

$$$$ FRENCH

🍴 **Midsummer House.** Beside the River Cam on the edge of Midsummer Common, this gray-brick building holds an elegant restaurant with a comfortable conservatory and a handful of tables under fruit trees in a lush, secluded garden. Fixed-price menus for lunch and dinner include innovative French and Mediterranean dishes. Choices might include roasted sea bass or venison with blue cheese and cocoa nibs. [$] *Average main: £40* ✉ *Midsummer Common* ☎ *01223/369299* 🌐 *www.midsummerhouse.co.uk* ✍ *Reservations essential* 🕒 *Closed Sun. and Mon. No lunch Tues.*

$$ MODERN BRITISH

🍴 **River Bar & Kitchen.** Across the river from Magdalene College, this popular waterfront bar and grill serves delicious steak and burgers, plus specialties such as lobster macaroni and cheese and blackened salmon with soy and ginger greens. Light lunches are served in the afternoon, and the evening cocktail list is small but elegant. Try the French 75, which is gin with lemon juice, sugar, and sparkling wine. [$] *Average main: £17*

✉ *Quayside, Thompsons Ln., off Bridge St.* ☎ *01223/307030* 🌐 *www.riverbarsteakhouse.com* ✍ *Reservations essential.*

$$ ITALIAN 🍴 **Three Horseshoes.** This early-19th-century pub-restaurant in a thatched cottage has an elegant dining space in the conservatory and more casual tables in the airy bar. The tempting, beautifully presented, and carefully sourced dishes are modern Italian with a British accent. Appetizers might include beetroot risotto with creamed goat cheese and orange oil, and among the main courses you might find beef shin with risotto, or haunch of venison with blackened leeks and dauphinoise potatoes. The wine list is enormous and predominantly Italian, but there are also some good New World choices. It's 5 miles west of Cambridge, about a 10-minute taxi ride. [$] *Average main: £18* ✉ *High St., Madingley* ☎ *01954/210221* 🌐 *www.threehorseshoesmadingley.co.uk.*

WHERE TO STAY

$$ HOTEL 🏨 **Regent Hotel.** A rare small hotel in central Cambridge, this handsome Georgian town house has wooden sash windows that look out over a tree-lined park called Parker's Piece. **Pros:** good view from top rooms; close to bars and restaurants. **Cons:** no parking; a tad scruffy; disappointing breakfasts. [$] *Rooms from: £102* ✉ *41 Regent St.* ☎ *01223/351470* 🌐 *www.regenthotel.co.uk* 🛏 *22 rooms* 🍽 *Breakfast.*

EDINBURGH

Although Scotland and England have been united in a single kingdom since 1603, Scotland retains its own marked political and social character, with separate legal and educational systems quite distinct from those of England and, since 1999, a Parliament of its own. Scotland's proud capital is one of the world's stateliest cities, and is built—like Rome—on seven hills. Its spectacular buildings, with Doric, Ionic, and Corinthian pillars, add touches of neoclassical grandeur to the overall Presbyterian sobriety. Named UNESCO's first City of Literature, Edinburgh is known worldwide for its International Festival, which attracts lovers of all the arts in August and September.

Take time to explore the streets—peopled by the spirits of Mary, Queen of Scots, Sir Walter Scott, and Robert Louis Stevenson—and pay your respects to the world's best-loved terrier, Greyfriars Bobby. In the evening you can enjoy a pub or a folk *ceilidh* (a traditional Scottish dance with music [pronounced *kay*-lee]), though you should remember that you haven't earned your porridge until you've climbed Arthur's Seat.

PLANNING YOUR TIME

If you have just two days here, don't miss the four key sights of Edinburgh Castle, the Palace of Holyroodhouse, the National Museum of Scotland, and the National Gallery of Scotland for the quintessential Edinburgh experience. But for those who have more time, make sure you see both halves of the city, the Old Town and the New Town. You need a good part of a day to weave through the Old Town and down the Royal Mile, the city's historic thoroughfare. Beyond Princes Street, the spacious New Town also needs a day.

GETTING HERE AND AROUND

AIR TRAVEL

Edinburgh Airport, 7 miles west of the city center, offers only a few transatlantic flights. It does, however, have air connections to London's Gatwick and Heathrow airports and other U.K. and European destinations. Glasgow Airport, 50 miles west of Edinburgh, serves as the major point of entry into Scotland for transatlantic flights.

The airport is connected by the Airlink express bus to Waverley Station via Haymarket; the trip takes 25–50 minutes. A single-fare ticket costs £3.50, a return £6. Taxis are readily available outside the terminal. The trip takes 25–35 minutes to the city center. The fare is roughly £20.

Contacts Edinburgh Airport ☎ 0844/444–8833 ⊕ www.edinburghairport.com. **Glasgow Airport** ☎ 0844/481–5555 ⊕ www.glasgowairport.com.

BUS TRAVEL

Megabus (book online) and National Express provide bus service to and from London and other major towns and cities. The main terminal, St. Andrew Square bus station, is a couple of minutes (on foot) north of Waverley station. Long-distance coaches must be booked in advance. Edinburgh is approximately 10 hours by bus from London.

Lothian Buses is the main operator within Edinburgh. You can buy tickets on the bus. The Day Ticket (£3.50) allows unlimited one-day travel on the city's buses.

Contacts Lothian Buses ☎ 0131/555–6363 ⊕ www.lothianbuses.com. **Megabus** ☎ 0900/160–0900 ⊕ www.megabus.co.uk. **National Express** ☎ 08717/818178 ⊕ www.nationalexpress.com.

CAR TRAVEL

Metered parking in the city center is scarce and expensive, and the local traffic wardens are a feisty bunch. Illegally parked cars are routinely towed away, and getting your car back will be expensive. After 6 pm the parking situation improves considerably.

TAXI TRAVEL

The following taxi stands are the most convenient: the west end of Princes Street; South St. David Street, and North St. Andrew Street (both just off St. Andrew Square); Princes Mall; Waterloo Place; and Lauriston Place. Alternatively, hail any taxi displaying an illuminated "for hire" sign.

TRAIN TRAVEL

Edinburgh's main train hub is Waverley Station. Travel time from Edinburgh to London by train is as little as 4½ hours for the fastest service. Edinburgh's other main station is Haymarket, about four minutes (by rail) beyond the west end of Princes Street. All Glasgow and other western and northern services stop here.

Contacts ScotRail ☎ 0845/601–5929 ⊕ www.scotrail.co.uk. **National Rail Enquiries** ☎ 08457/484950 ⊕ www.nationalrail.co.uk.

20

TOURS

City Sightseeing and the vintage bus MacTours are both open-top tours and cost £9 including multilingual commentary. All tours take you to the main attractions. Tickets are sold on board and, departing from Waverley Bridge, the tours are hop-on/hop-off services.

Contacts Edinburgh Bus Tours ☎ *0131/220-0770* ⊕ *www.edinburghtour.com.*

VISITOR INFORMATION

Visitor Information Edinburgh and Scotland Information Centre ✉ *3 Princes St., East End* ☎ *0131/473-3868* ⊕ *www.edinburgh.org.*

EXPLORING

The key to understanding Edinburgh is to make the distinction between the Old and New Towns. Until the 18th century the city was confined to the rocky crag on which its castle stands, straggling between the fortress at one end and the royal residence, the Palace of Holyroodhouse, at the other. In the 18th century, during a time of expansion known as the Scottish Enlightenment, the city fathers fostered the construction of another Edinburgh, one a little to the north, the elegant New Town. Apart from the Old and New Towns in central Edinburgh, some outlying neighborhoods are also worth a visit. Leith, Edinburgh's port, throbs with chic bars and restaurants, while Dean Village is home to the Scottish National Gallery of Modern Art. ■ TIP➜ Don't forget that some attractions have special hours during the Edinburgh International Festival: check the schedule ahead of time.

OLD TOWN

East of Edinburgh Castle, the historic castle esplanade becomes the street known as the Royal Mile. It leads from the castle down through Old Town to the Palace of Holyroodhouse and is made up of one thoroughfare that bears, in consecutive sequence, different names—Castlehill, Lawnmarket, Parliament Square, High Street, and Canongate. Before the 18th-century expansions to the south and north, everybody lived here; the richer folk on the lower floors of houses, with less well-to-do families on the middle floors—the higher up, the poorer. Time and progress (of a sort) have swept away some of the narrow closes and tall tenements of the Old Town, but enough survive for you to be able to imagine the original profile of Scotland's capital.

FAMILY **Edinburgh Castle.** The crowning glory of the Scottish capital, Edin-
Fodor'sChoice burgh Castle is popular not only because it's the symbolic heart of
★ Scotland but also because of the views from its battlements: on a clear day the vistas—stretching to the "kingdom" of Fife—are breathtaking. ■ TIP➜ There's so much to see that you need at least three hours to do the site justice, especially if you're interested in military sites.

You enter across the **Esplanade,** the huge forecourt built in the 18th century as a parade ground. The area comes alive with color and music each August when it's used for the Military Tattoo, a festival of magnificently outfitted marching bands and regiments. Heading over the drawbridge and through the gatehouse, past the guards, you can find the rough stone walls of the **Half-Moon Battery,** where the one-o'clock gun is fired

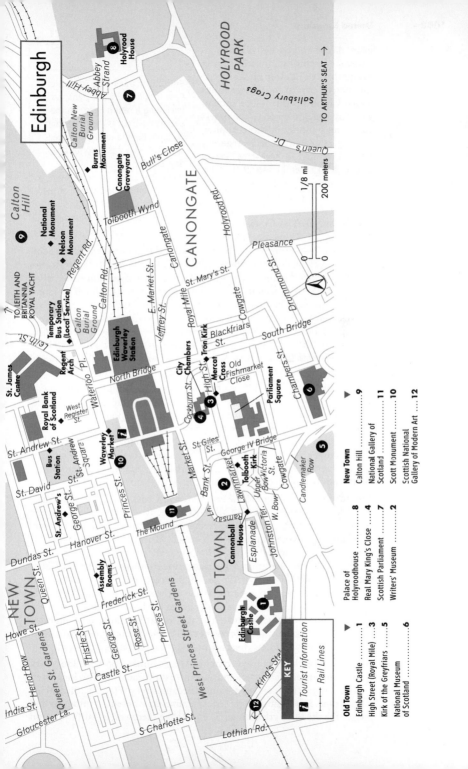

Edinburgh

Old Town

Edinburgh Castle **1**
High Street (Royal Mile) **3**
Kirk of the Greyfriars **5**
National Museum
of Scotland **6**

Palace of
Holyroodhouse **8**
Real Mary King's Close **4**
Scottish Parliament **7**
Writers' Museum **2**

New Town

Calton Hill **9**
National Gallery of
Scotland **11**
Scott Monument **10**
Scottish National
Gallery of Modern Art **12**

KEY

🛈 Tourist Information
+–+–+ Rail Lines

1/8 mi
0
200 meters
0

TO ARTHUR'S SEAT →

every day in an impressively anach-
ronistic ceremony; these curving
ramparts give Edinburgh Castle its
distinctive appearance from miles
away. Climb up through a second
gateway and you come to the oldest
surviving building in the complex,
the tiny 11th-century **St. Margaret's
Chapel,** named in honor of Saxon
queen Margaret (1046–93), who
had persuaded her husband, King
Malcolm III (circa 1031–93), to
move his court from Dunfermline
to Edinburgh. The **Crown Room,**
a must-see, contains the "Honours

of Scotland"—the crown, scepter, and sword that once graced the Scot-
tish monarch. Upon the **Stone of Scone,** also in the Crown Room,
Scottish monarchs once sat to be crowned. In the section now called
Queen Mary's Apartments, Mary, Queen of Scots, gave birth to James
VI of Scotland. The **Great Hall** displays arms and armor under an
impressive vaulted, beamed ceiling. Scottish parliament meetings were
conducted here until 1840. ⊠ *Castle Esplanade and Castlehill, Old
Town* ☎ *0131/225–9846 for Edinburgh Castle, 0131/226–7393 for
War Memorial* ⊕ *www.edinburghcastle.gov.uk* ☑ *£14* ☉ *Apr.–Sept.,
daily 9:30–6; Oct.–Mar., daily 9:30–5; last entry 1 hr before closing.*

High Street. Some of Old Town's most impressive buildings and sights
are on High Street, one of the five streets making up the Royal Mile.
Also here are other, less obvious historic relics. Near Parliament Square,
look on the west side for a **heart** set in cobbles. This marks the site of
the vanished Tolbooth, the center of city life from the 15th century until
the building's demolition in 1817. The ancient civic edifice housed the
Scottish parliament and was used as a prison—it also inspired Sir Walter
Scott's novel *The Heart of Midlothian.*

Just outside Parliament House is the **Mercat Cross** (*mercat* means "market"), a great landmark of Old Town life. It was an old mercantile
center, where in the early days executions were held, and where royal
proclamations were—and are still—read. Most of the present cross is
comparatively modern, dating from the time of William Ewart Glad-
stone (1809–98), the great Victorian prime minister and rival of Ben-
jamin Disraeli (1804–81). Across High Street from the High Kirk of
St. Giles stands the **City Chambers,** now the seat of local government.
Built by John Fergus, who adapted a design of John Adam in 1753, the
chambers were originally known as the Royal Exchange and intended
to be where merchants and lawyers could conduct business. Note how
the building drops 11 stories to Cockburn Street on its north side.

A *tron* is a weigh beam used in public weigh houses, and the **Tron Kirk**
was named after a salt tron that used to stand nearby. The kirk itself
was built after 1633, when St. Giles's became an Episcopal cathedral for
a brief time. In this church in 1693, a minister offered an often-quoted
prayer for the local government: "Lord, hae mercy on a' [all] fools and

idiots, and particularly on the Magistrates of Edinburgh." ⊠ *Between Lawnmarket and Canongate, Old Town.*

Kirk of the Greyfriars. Greyfriars Church, built circa 1620 on the site of a medieval monastery, was where the National Covenant, declaring that the Presbyterian Church in Scotland was independent of the monarch and not Episcopalian in government, was signed in 1638. The covenant plunged Scotland into decades of civil war. Informative panels tell the story. Be sure to search out the graveyard—one of the most evocative in Europe. Its old, tottering, elaborate tombstones mark the graves of some of Scotland's most respected heroes and despised villains. Nearby, at the corner of George IV Bridge and Candlemaker Row, stands one of the most photographed sites in Scotland, the Greyfriars Bobby statue. ⊠ *Greyfriars Pl., Old Town* ☎ *0131/225–1900* ⊕ *www.greyfriarskirk. com* ⊠ *Free* ⊙ *Easter–Oct., weekdays 10:30–4:30, Sat. 11–2; Nov.– Easter, Thurs. 1:30–3:30.*

FAMILY
Fodor's Choice
★
National Museum of Scotland. This museum traces the country's fascinating story from the oldest fossils to the most recent popular culture, making it a must-see for first-time visitors to Scotland or anyone interested in history. One of the most famous treasures is the Lewis Chessmen, 11 intricately carved ivory chess pieces found in the 19th century on one of Scotland's Western Isles. An extensive renovation of the basement has created a dramatic, cryptlike entrance. Visitors now rise to the light-filled, birdcage wonders of the Victorian grand hall and the upper galleries in glass elevators. Highlights include the hanging hippo and sea creatures of the Wildlife Panorama, a life-size skeleton cast of a Tyrannosaurus rex, Viking brooches, Pictish stones, Jacobite relics, the Stevenson family's inventions, including lighthouse optics, and Queen Mary's *clarsach* (harp). ⊠ *Chambers St., Old Town* ☎ *0300/123–6789* ⊕ *www.nms.ac.uk* ⊠ *Free* ⊙ *Daily 10–5.*

Fodor's Choice
★
Palace of Holyroodhouse. Once the haunt of Mary, Queen of Scots, and the setting for high drama—including at least one notorious murder, several major fires, and centuries of the colorful lifestyles of larger-than-life, power-hungry personalities—this is now Queen Elizabeth's official residence in Scotland. A doughty and impressive palace standing at the foot of the Royal Mile in a hilly public park, it's built around a graceful, lawned central court at the end of Canongate. When the queen or royal family is not in residence you can take a tour. The free audio guide is excellent.

Many monarchs, including Charles II, Queen Victoria, and George V, have left their mark on its rooms, but it's Mary, Queen of Scots, whose spirit looms largest. For some visitors, the most memorable room here is the little chamber in which David Rizzio (1533–66), secretary to Mary, Queen of Scots, met an unhappy end in 1566. In part because Rizzio was hated at court for his social-climbing ways, Mary's second husband, Lord Darnley (Henry Stewart, 1545–65), burst into the queen's rooms with his henchmen, dragged Rizzio into an antechamber, and stabbed him more than 50 times; a bronze plaque marks the spot. Darnley himself was murdered the next year, which made way for the queen's marriage to her lover, the Earl of Bothwell. ■ TIP→ There's plenty to see

20

here, so make sure you have at least two hours to tour the palace, gardens, and the ruins of the 12th-century abbey.

Behind the palace lie the open grounds and looming crags of Holyrood Park, the hunting ground of early Scottish kings. From the top of Edinburgh's minimountain, **Arthur's Seat** (822 feet), views are breathtaking. ⊠ *Abbey Strand, Old Town* ☎ *0131/556–5100* ⊕ *www.royalcollection. org.uk* 🖃 *£11, £15.50 includes the Queen's Gallery* ⊙ *Apr.–Oct., daily 9:30–6; Nov.–Mar., daily 9:30–4:30; last admission 1 hr before closing. Closed during royal visits.*

FAMILY
Fodor's Choice
★
Real Mary King's Close. Hidden beneath the City Chambers, this narrow, cobbled *close,* or lane, named after a former landowner, is said to be one of Edinburgh's most haunted sites. The close was sealed off in 1645 to quarantine residents who became sick when the bubonic plague swept through the city, and many victims were herded there to die. After the plague passed, the bodies were removed and buried, and the street was reopened. A few people returned, but they soon reported ghostly goings-on and departed, leaving the close empty for decades. In 1753 city authorities built the Royal Exchange (later the City Chambers) directly over the close, sealing it off and, unwittingly, ensuring it remained intact, except for the buildings' upper stories, which were destroyed. Today you can walk among the remains of the shops and houses. People still report ghostly visions and eerie sounds, such as the crying of a young girl. Over the years visitors have left small offerings for her, such as dolls, pieces of ribbon, or candy. ■**TIP→ Although kids like the spookiness of this attraction, it's not for the youngest ones. In fact, children under age five are not admitted.** ⊠ *Writers' Court, Old Town* ☎ *0845/070–6244* ⊕ *www.realmarykingsclose.com* 🖃 *£12.95* ⊙ *Apr.–Oct., daily 10–9; Nov.–Mar., weekdays 10–5, weekends 10–9.*

Scottish Parliament. Scotland's somewhat controversial Parliament building is dramatically modern, with irregular curves and angles that mirror the twisting shapes of the surrounding landscape. The structure's artistry is most apparent when you step inside, where the gentle slopes, forest's worth of oak, polished concrete and granite, and walls of glass create an understated magnificence. It's worth taking a free tour to see the main hall and debating chamber, a committee room, and other areas. ■**TIP→ Call well in advance to get a free ticket to view Parliament in action.** Originally conceived by the late Catalan architect Enric Miralles, who often said the building was "growing out of the ground," the design was completed by his widow, Benedetta Tagliabue, in August 2004. ⊠ *Horse Wynd, Old Town* ☎ *0131/348–5200* ⊕ *www.scottish. parliament.uk* 🖃 *Free* ⊙ *Mon.–Sat. 10–5:30.*

Writers' Museum. Down a close off Lawnmarket is the 1662 Lady Stair's House, a fine example of 17th-century urban architecture. Inside, the Writer's Museum evokes Scotland's literary past with such exhibits as the letters, possessions, and original manuscripts of Sir Walter Scott, Robert Louis Stevenson, and Robert Burns. The Stevenson collection is particularly compelling. ⊠ *Lady Stair's Close, Old Town* ☎ *0131/529– 4901* ⊕ *www.edinburghmuseums.org.uk* 🖃 *Free* ⊙ *Sept.–July, Mon.– Sat. 10–5; Aug., Mon.–Sat. 10–5, Sun. noon–5.*

NEW TOWN

It was not until the Scottish Enlightenment, a civilizing time of expansion in the 1700s, that the city fathers decided to break away from the Royal Mile's rocky slope and create a new Edinburgh below the castle, a little to the north. This was to become the New Town, with elegant squares, classical facades, wide streets, and harmonious proportions. The plan of architect James Craig (1744–95) called for a grid of three main east–west streets, balanced at either end by two grand squares. These streets survive today, though some of the buildings that line them have been altered by later development.

Save time by riding the free galleries bus, which connects the National Gallery of Scotland, Scottish National Portrait Gallery, Scottish National Gallery of Modern Art, and Dean Gallery daily from 11 to 5. You can board or leave the bus at any of the galleries.

OFF THE BEATEN PATH

Britannia. Moored on the waterfront at Leith, Edinburgh's port north of the city center, is the former Royal Yacht *Britannia,* launched in Scotland in 1953 and now retired to her home country. The Royal Apartments and the more functional engine room, bridge, galleys, and captain's cabin are all open to view. The land-based visitor center within the huge Ocean Terminal shopping mall has exhibits and photographs about the yacht's history. ⊠ *Ocean Terminal, Leith* 🕾 *0131/555–5566* ⊕ *www.royalyachtbritannia.co.uk* 🖾 *£12* ☉ *Mar.–Oct., daily 9:30–4; Nov.–Feb., daily 10–3:30.*

Calton Hill. Robert Louis Stevenson's favorite view of his beloved city was from the top of this hill. The architectural styles represented by the extraordinary collection of monuments here include mock Gothic—the Old Observatory, for example—and neoclassical. Under the latter category falls the monument by William Playfair (1789–1857) designed to honor his talented uncle, the geologist and mathematician John Playfair (1748–1819), as well as his cruciform **New Observatory.** The piece that commands the most attention, however, is the so-called **National Monument,** often referred to as "Scotland's Disgrace." Intended to mimic Athens's Parthenon, this monument to the dead of the Napoleonic Wars was started in 1822 to the specifications of a design by Playfair. But in 1830, only 12 columns later, money ran out, and the facade became a monument to high aspirations and poor fund-raising. The tallest monument on Calton Hill is the 100-foot-high **Nelson Monument,** completed in 1815 in honor of Britain's naval hero Horatio Nelson (1758–1805); you can climb its 143 steps for sweeping city views. The **Burns Monument** is the circular Corinthian temple below Regent Road. Devotees of Robert Burns may want to visit one other grave—that of Mrs. Agnes McLehose, or "Clarinda," in the Canongate Graveyard. ⊠ *Bounded by Leith St. to the west and Regent Rd. to the south, New Town* 🕾 *0131/556–2716* ⊕ *www.edinburghmuseums.org.uk* 🖾 *Nelson Monument £4* ☉ *Nelson Monument Oct.–Mar., Mon.–Sat. 10–3; Apr.–Sept., daily 10–7.*

Fodor's Choice ★ **National Gallery of Scotland.** Opened to the public in 1859, the National Gallery presents a wide selection of paintings from the Renaissance to the postimpressionist period within a grand neoclassical building. Most

20

famous are the old-master paintings bequeathed by the Duke of Sutherland, including Titian's *Three Ages of Man*. Many masters are here; works by Velázquez, El Greco, Rembrandt, Goya, Poussin, Turner, Degas, Monet, and Van Gogh, among others, complement a fine collection of Scottish art, including Sir Henry Raeburn's *Reverend Robert Walker Skating on Duddingston Loch* and other works by Ramsay, Raeburn, and Wilkie. The Weston Link connects the National Gallery of Scotland to the Royal Scottish Academy and includes a restaurant, bar, café, shop, and information center. ⊠ *The Mound, New Town* ☎ *0131/624–6336* ⊕ *www.nationalgalleries.org* ⌨ *Free* ☉ *Fri.–Wed. 10–5, Thurs. 10–7.*

> ## LEITH, EDINBURGH'S SEAPORT
>
> Just north of the city, Leith sits on the south shore of the Firth of Forth and was a separate town until it merged with the city in 1920. After World War II and up until the 1980s, the declining seaport had a reputation for poverty and crime. In recent years, however, it has been revitalized with the restoration of commercial buildings as well as the construction of new luxury housing, bringing a buzz of trendiness.

Scott Monument. What appears to be a Gothic cathedral spire chopped off and planted in the east end of the Princes Street Gardens is the nation's tribute to Sir Walter—a 200-foot-high monument looming over Princes Street. Built in 1844 in honor of Scotland's most famous author, Sir Walter Scott, the author of *Ivanhoe*, *Waverley*, and many other novels and poems, it's centered on a marble statue of Scott and his favorite dog, Maida. It's worth taking the time to explore the immediate area, including Princes Street Gardens, one of the prettiest city parks in Britain. In the open-air theater, amid the park's trim flowerbeds, stately trees, and carefully tended lawns, brass bands occasionally play. Here, too, is the famous **monument to David Livingstone,** whose African meeting with H. M. Stanley is part of Scots-American history. ⊠ *Princes St., New Town* ☎ *0131/529–4068* ⊕ *www.edinburghmuseums.org.uk* ⌨ *£4* ☉ *Apr.–Sept., Mon.–Sat. 10–7, Sun. 10–6; Oct.–Mar., Mon.–Sat 9–4, Sun. 10–6.*

Fodor'sChoice
★

Scottish National Gallery of Modern Art. This handsome former school building, close to the New Town, displays paintings and sculptures by Pablo Picasso, Georges Braque, Henri Matisse, and André Derain, among others. The gallery houses an excellent restaurant in the basement and lavender-filled garden. Across the street in a former orphanage is the **Gallery of Modern Art Two** (formerly the Dean Gallery), which has Scots-Italian Sir Eduardo Paolozzi's intriguing re-created studio and towering sculpture Vulcan. ⊠ *Belford Rd., Dean Village* ☎ *0131/624–6200* ⊕ *www.nationalgalleries.org* ⌨ *Free* ☉ *Daily 10–5.*

WHERE TO EAT

$
MODERN BRITISH

✕ **David Bann.** In the heart of the Old Town, this ultrahip eatery serving vegetarian and vegan favorites attracts young locals with its light, airy, modern dining room. Drinking water comes with mint and strawberries;

the sizable and creative dishes include mushroom risotto and Jerusalem artichoke in puff pastry. The food is so flavorful that carnivores may forget they're eating vegetarian, especially with dishes like mushroom strudel with celeriac sauce. [$] *Average main: £12* ✉ *56–58 St. Mary's St., Old Town* ☎ *0131/556–5888* 🌐 *www.davidbann.com.*

$ BRITISH

🍴 **Doric Tavern.** Edinburgh's original gastropub offers a languid bistro environment and serves reliable Scots favorites. The menu has such daily-changing items as honey-baked salmon with oatcakes, and specialties include haggis, neeps and tatties, and grilled steaks. Try the creamy Cullen skink soup for a filling, good-value lunchtime choice. The stripped-wood interiors upstairs have been spruced up. The Doric is handy for rail travelers, as it's near Waverley Station. Sunday lunch includes a traditional roast of Border beef with all the trimmings. [$] *Average main: £13* ✉ *15/16 Market St., Old Town* ☎ *0131/225–1084* 🌐 *www.the-doric.com* ✍ *Reservations essential.*

$ VEGETARIAN

🍴 **Henderson's.** Edinburgh's pioneering canteen-style vegetarian restaurant opened in 1962, long before it was fashionable to serve healthy, meatless creations. The salad bar has more than a dozen different offerings each day, and a massive plateful costs £8. Tasty hot options include Moroccan stew with couscous and moussaka. Live mellow music plays six nights a week, and there's an art gallery as well. Around the corner on Thistle Street is the Bistro, from the same proprietors; it serves snacks, meals, and decadent desserts such as chocolate fondue. **■ TIP→ Drop by the fabulous deli for picnic supplies, including wonderful organic bread and pastries.** [$] *Average main: £8* ✉ *94 Hanover St., New Town* ☎ *0131/225–2605* 🌐 *www.hendersonsofedinburgh.co.uk* ⏰ *Closed Sun.*

$$$$ FRENCH

Fodor's Choice ★

🍴 **Martin Wishart.** Slightly out of town but worth every penny of the taxi fare, this restaurant's well-known chef woos diners with an impeccable and varied menu of beautifully presented, French-influenced dishes. Shoulder filet of beef with Devonshire snails, chervil root, and parsley typify the cuisine, which costs £75 for three courses. For the very sweet of tooth there's a dessert tasting menu combing all three daily choices for an extra £7.50. On weekdays, the three-course lunch is £28. Reservations are essential on Friday and Saturday night. [$] *Average main: £65* ✉ *54 The Shore, Leith* ☎ *0131/553–3557* 🌐 *www.martin-wishart.co.uk* ⏰ *Closed Sun. and Mon.*

$$$ MODERN BRITISH

🍴 **The Witchery.** The hundreds of "witches" who were executed on Castlehill, just yards from where you'll be seated, are the inspiration for this outstanding and atmospheric restaurant. The cavernous interior, complete with flickering candlelight, is festooned with cabalistic insignia and tarot-card characters. Gilded and painted ceilings reflect the close links between France and Scotland, as does the menu, which includes steak tartare, roasted quail with braised endive, shellfish bisque, and herb-baked scallops. Two-course pre- and posttheater (5:30–6:30 and 10:30–11:30) specials let you sample the exceptional cuisine for just £15.95. [$] *Average main: £27* ✉ *Castlehill, Old Town* ☎ *0131/225–5613* 🌐 *www.thewitchery.com* ✍ *Reservations essential.*

WHERE TO STAY

Rooms are harder to find in August and September, when the festivals take place, so reserve at least three months in advance.

$$$$

HOTEL

Fodor's Choice

★

☷ Balmoral Hotel. The attention to detail in the elegant rooms—colors were picked to echo the country's heathers and moors—and the sheer élan that has re-created the Edwardian splendor of this grand, former railroad hotel make staying at the Balmoral a special introduction to Edinburgh. **Pros:** big and beautiful building; top-hatted doorman; quality bathroom goodies. **Cons:** small pool; spa books up fast; restaurants can be very busy. $ *Rooms from: £380* ⊠ *1 Princes St., New Town* ☎ *0131/556–2414* ⊕ *www.thebalmoralhotel.com* ↬ *168 rooms, 20 suites* ⚭ *Breakfast.*

$$$

HOTEL

Fodor's Choice

★

☷ The Bonham. There's a clubby atmosphere throughout this hotel, which carries on a successful, sophisticated flirtation with modernity. **Pros:** thorough yet unobtrusive service; excellent restaurant. **Cons:** few common areas; can feel like a business hotel. $ *Rooms from: £165* ⊠ *35 Drumsheugh Gardens, West End* ☎ *0131/226–6050* ⊕ *www. thebonham.com* ↬ *42 rooms, 6 suites* ⚭ *Multiple meal plans.*

$$

B&B/INN

☷ Gerald's Place. Although he is not a native of the city, Gerald Della-Porta is one of those B&B owners to whom Edinburgh owes so much. **Pros:** the advice and thoughtfulness of the owner; spacious rooms. **Cons:** stairs are difficult to manage; an uphill walk to the city center; no credit cards. $ *Rooms from: £150* ⊠ *21B Abercromby Pl.* ☎ *0131/558–7017* ⊕ *www.geraldsplace.com* ↬ *2 rooms* ▭ *No credit cards* ⚭ *Breakfast.*

$$$

RENTAL

FAMILY

☷ Knight Residence. About 10 minutes from the Grassmarket, the Knight is made up of 19 different apartments that offer good value and convenient locations. **Pros:** comfortable apartments; secure location; good for families needing space and privacy. **Cons:** lack of staff won't suit everyone; better for stays of two or more nights. $ *Rooms from: £168* ⊠ *12 Lauriston St., Old Town* ☎ *0131/622–8120* ⊕ *www.theknightresidence. co.uk* ↬ *19 apartments* ⚭ *No meals.*

$$$$

HOTEL

Fodor's Choice

★

☷ The Scotsman. A magnificent turn-of-the-20th-century building, with a marble staircase and a fascinating history—it was once the headquarters of the *Scotsman* newspaper—now houses this modern, luxurious hotel. **Pros:** gorgeous surroundings; personalized service. **Cons:** no a/c; spa can be noisy. $ *Rooms from: £270* ⊠ *20 N. Bridge, Old Town* ☎ *0131/556–5565* ⊕ *www.thescotsmanhotel.co.uk* ↬ *56 rooms, 13 suites* ⚭ *Multiple meal plans.*

$$

B&B/INN

☷ Victorian Town House. In a leafy crescent, this handsome house once belonged to a cousin of Robert Louis Stevenson, and the celebrated writer would doubtless be happy to lay his head in this good-value B&B. **Pros:** serene surroundings near Water of Leith; gracious staff. **Cons:** no parking nearby; distance from Old Town. $ *Rooms from: £110* ⊠ *14 Eglinton Terr., Haymarket* ☎ *0131/337–7088* ⊕ *www. thevictoriantownhouse.co.uk* ↬ *3 rooms* ⚭ *Breakfast.*

NIGHTLIFE

The List, a publication available from city-center bookstores and newsstands, has information about all types of events. The Edinburgh International Festival and the Edinburgh Fringe Festival bring thousands into the city every August for a wide range of theater and performing arts events. Also in August, the Edinburgh Military Tattoo is a celebration of martial music and skills and is also wildly popular. Plus, it's a real piece of Scottish culture.

BARS AND PUBS

Café Royal. This café serves good Scottish lagers and ales, and simple lunch items and, of course, oysters. The 18th-century building has bags of character, with ornate tiles, stained-glass windows and—allegedly—its own ghost. ⊠ *19 W. Register St., New Town* ☏ *0131/556–1884* ⊕ *www.caferoyaledinburgh.co.uk.*

Cloisters. The Cloisters prides itself on the absence of music, gaming machines, and all other modern pub gimmicks. Instead, it specializes in real ales, malt whiskies, and good food, all at reasonable prices. ⊠ *26 Brougham St., Tollcross* ☏ *0131/221–9997.*

Milne's Bar. This spot is known as the poets' pub because of its popularity with Edinburgh's literati. Pies and baked potatoes go well with seven real ales and various guest beers (meaning anything besides the house brew). Victorian advertisements and photos of old Edinburgh give the place an old-time feel. ⊠ *35 Hanover St., New Town* ☏ *0131/225–6738.*

SHOPPING

Despite its renown, **Princes Street** may disappoint some visitors with its average chain stores. One block north of Princes Street, **Rose Street** has many smaller specialty shops. **George Street** shops are fairly upscale, with names such as Jaegar and Penhaligons.

The streets crossing George Street—Hanover, Frederick, and Castle— are also worth exploring. **Dundas Street,** the northern extension of Hanover Street, beyond Queen Street Gardens, has several antiques shops. **Thistle Street** has several boutiques and more antiques shops. **Stockbridge is** an oddball shopping area of some charm, particularly on St. Stephen Street.

Many shops along the **Royal Mile** sell what may be politely or euphemistically described as tourist-ware—whiskies, tartans, and tweeds.

20

THE GREAT GLEN

Defined by a striking geological feature, the Great Glen brings together mountains and myths, battles and whisky—and there's a great view around nearly every bend in the road. The city of Inverness sits at the northern end of the glen, and Loch Ness, home to the legendary Loch Ness Monster, stretches south. Daunting mountain ranges and expansive coasts flank the Great Glen and make for scenic traveling. There's also plenty here for history buffs, as the area was the site of the massacre at Glencoe in 1692 and the defeat of the Jacobites at Culloden in 1746.

Inverness has a growing reputation for excellent restaurants, and from here nearly everything in the Great Glen is an easy day trip. Just south of the city, the iconic 13th-century ruined Urquhart Castle sits on the shores of the deep, murky Loch Ness.

The Malt Whisky Trail begins in Forres and follows the wide, fast River Spey south until it butts against the Cairngorm Mountains and the old Caledonian forests, with their diverse and rare wildlife.

PLANNING YOUR TIME

The Great Glen is an enormous area, so a short trip requires focus. Inverness makes for a good starting point or at least a base from which you can explore a bit of the Whisky Trail and Loch Ness.

GETTING HERE AND AROUND

AIR TRAVEL

Inverness Airport has flights from London, Edinburgh, and Glasgow.

Airport Contacts Inverness Airport ⊠ *Dalcross, Inverness* ☎ *01667/464000* ⊕ *www.hial.co.uk/inverness-airport.*

BUS TRAVEL

Inverness is well served from the central belt of Scotland by bus service. Discount carrier Megabus (book online to avoid phone charges) has service to Inverness from various cities.

Contacts Inverness Coach Station ⊠ *Margaret St., Inverness* ☎ *01463/233371.* **Megabus** ☎ *0900/160–0900* ⊕ *www.megabus.com.* **Scottish Citylink** ☎ *0871/266–3333* ⊕ *www.citylink.co.uk.*

CAR TRAVEL

As in all areas of rural Scotland, a car is a great asset for exploring the Great Glen, especially since the best of the area is away from the main roads. You can use the smaller B862/B852 roads to explore the much quieter east side of Loch Ness. The best sights are often hidden from the main road, which is an excellent reason to favor peaceful rural byways and to avoid as much as possible the busy A96 and A9, which carry much of the traffic in the area.

TRAIN TRAVEL

ScotRail has connections from London to Inverness and Fort William (including overnight sleeper service), as well as reliable links from Glasgow and Edinburgh. There's train service between Glasgow (Queen Street) and Inverness, via Aviemore, which gives access to the heart of Speyside.

Although there's no rail connection among towns within the Great Glen, this area has the West Highland Line, which links Fort William to Mallaig. This train, run by ScotRail, remains the most enjoyable way to experience the rugged hills and loch scenery between these two places. The Jacobite Steam Train is an exciting summer (mid-May–mid-October) option on the same route.

Contacts Jacobite Steam Train ☎ *0844/850–4685* ⊕ *www.westcoastrailways. co.uk.* **ScotRail** ☎ *0845/755–0033* ⊕ *www.scotrail.co.uk.*

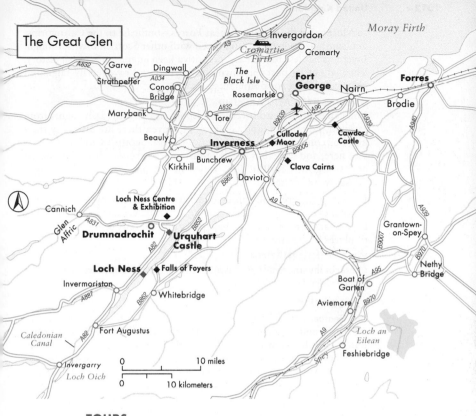

The Great Glen

TOURS

Inverness Tours runs the occasional boat cruise but is mainly known for tours around the Highlands in well-equipped vehicles, which are led by expert guides and heritage enthusiasts. James Johnstone, a personal guide, is based in Inverness but will drive you anywhere; he has a particularly good knowledge of the Highlands and islands, including the Outer Isles.

Contacts Inverness Tours ☎ *01667/455699* ⊕ *www.invernesstours.com.*
James Johnstone ☎ *01463/798372* ⊕ *www.jajcd.com.*

VISITOR INFORMATION

Inverness has a year-round tourist office. Other tourist centers are open seasonally.

Visitor Information Visit Highlands ⊕ *www.visithighlands.com.*

INVERNESS

176 miles north of Glasgow, 109 miles northwest of Aberdeen, 161 miles northwest of Edinburgh.

The city makes a great base for exploring the region, and you can fan out in almost any direction from Inverness for interesting day trips: east to Moray and the distilleries near Forres, southeast to the Cairngorms, and south to Loch Ness. Compared with other Scottish towns, though, Inverness has less to offer visitors with a keen interest in Scottish history. Throughout its past the town was burned and ravaged by Highland clans competing for dominance.

GETTING HERE AND AROUND

You can easily fly into Inverness Airport, as there are daily flights from London, Edinburgh, and Glasgow. However, there are also easy train and bus connections from Glasgow Airport. Scottish Citylink has service here, and Megabus has long-distance bus service from Edinburgh and Glasgow. ScotRail runs trains here from London, Edinburgh, Glasgow, and other cities.

Once you're here, you can explore much of the city by foot. A rental car makes exploring the surrounding area much easier. But if you don't have a car, there are bus and boat tours from the city center to a number of places in the Great Glen.

VISITOR INFORMATION

Contacts Inverness ✉ *Castle Wynd* ☎ *01463/252401* 🌐 *www.inverness-scotland.com.*

EXPLORING

Fort George. After the fateful battle at Culloden, the nervous government in London ordered the construction of a large fort on a promontory reaching into the Moray Firth. Fort George was started in 1748 and completed some 20 years later. It's one of the best-preserved 18th-century military fortifications in Europe. The on-site Highlanders Museum gives you a glimpse of the fort's history. The fort is 14 miles northeast of Inverness. ✉ *Old Military Rd., Ardersier* ☎ *01667/460232* 🌐 *www.historic-scotland.gov.uk* 🎟 *£8.90* ⏲ *Apr.–Sept., daily 9:30–5:30; Oct.–Mar., daily 10–4:30; last admission 45 mins before closing.*

Inverness Castle. One of Inverness's few historic landmarks is reddish sandstone Inverness Castle (now the local Sheriff Court), nestled above the river off Castle Road on Castle Hill. The current structure is Victorian, built after a former fort was blown up by the Jacobites in the 1745 campaign. The castle isn't open to the public, but you are free to wander the grounds. ✉ *41 Castle St.*

WHERE TO EAT

$$ MODERN BRITISH 🍴 **Cafe 1.** Locals recommend this restaurant before any other, so it's no surprise that a well-dressed and diverse crowd fills the dining room. The decor is refined, with thin-legged metal chairs, lacquered wood-topped tables, and Celtic knot mirrors. The menu includes bistro-style dishes like sea bass with rosemary and garlic polenta chips, or classic Angus steak with peppercorn sauce. The tiny bar at the front has a great view of the castle. [$] *Average main: £18* ✉ *75 Castle St.* ☎ *01463/226200* 🌐 *www.cafe1.net.*

$ BRITISH 🍴 **Dores Inn.** Off a pretty country road on the eastern shore of Loch Ness, this low-slung, white-stone eatery is the perfect place to stop for lunch or dinner. The menu is a combination of well-prepared old favorites—fish-and-chips, perhaps, or neeps and tatties (turnips and potatoes)—together with steaks, lamb, and seafood. It's busy during the summer and on weekends, so book ahead. [$] *Average main: £12* ✉ *Off B862, Dores* ☎ *01463/751203* 🌐 *www.thedoresinn.co.uk.*

$ PIZZA 🍴 **Riva.** Facing Inverness Castle, Riva has views over the River Ness from its window seats. The dining room has subtly lighted deep-red walls lined with black-and-white photographs of Italian cityscapes. Tasty Italian dishes include pasta carbonara (with eggs, cream, and pancetta), as well as more unusual concoctions like tagliatelle with smoked salmon and a tomato cream sauce. There is a separate pizzeria upstairs from the main dining room. [$] *Average main: £14* ✉ *4–6 Ness Walk* ☎ *01463/237377* 🌐 *www.rivarestaurant.co.uk* 🕓 *No lunch Sun.*

$$ BRASSERIE 🍴 **Rocpool Restaurant.** Highly recommended by locals, the Rocpool has a frequently changing menu of modern bistro classics, with a few modern twists. Main dishes could include sea bream fillet with a roasted pepper salad, or lamb cutlets with polenta cakes. The early evening menu is excellent value. [$] *Average main: £20* ✉ *1 Ness Walk* ☎ *01463/717274* 🌐 *www.rocpoolrestaurant.com* 🕓 *Closed Sun.*

WHERE TO STAY

There are many places to stay in Inverness, but if your goal is to explore the countryside, a hotel outside the center may be a good choice.

$ B&B/INN 🏨 **Avalon.** A 20-minute walk from the city center, this neat and modern B&B is a rare find. **Pros:** friendly and well run; good-size rooms. **Cons:** slightly far outside the city; minimum stay on some dates. [$] *Rooms from: £75* ✉ *79 Glenarquhart Rd.* ☎ *01463/239075* 🌐 *www.inverness-loch-ness.co.uk* 🛏 *6 rooms* 🍽 *Breakfast.*

$ B&B/INN 🏨 **Strathness House.** Standing on the banks of the River Ness, this 12-room guesthouse is a quick walk from the well-regarded Eden Court Theatre and the rest of the attractions of the city center. **Pros:** overlooks the river; close to the city center; free Wi-Fi. **Cons:** parking can be difficult. [$] *Rooms from: £80* ✉ *4 Ardross Terr.* ☎ *01463/232765* 🌐 *www.strathnesshouse.com* 🛏 *12 rooms* 🍽 *Breakfast.*

$$ B&B/INN 🏨 **Trafford Bank.** A 15-minute walk from downtown Inverness, this delightful little B&B is the perfect place to base yourself. **Pros:** welcoming atmosphere; stylish rooms; relaxing vibe. **Cons:** rooms on the small side. [$] *Rooms from: £110* ✉ *96 Fairfield Rd.* ☎ *01463/241414* 🌐 *www.traffordbankguesthouse.co.uk* 🛏 *5 rooms* 🍽 *Breakfast.*

NIGHTLIFE AND THE ARTS

Hootenany. Hootenany is an odd combination of Scottish pub, concert hall, and Thai restaurant. The excellent pub has a warm atmosphere and serves food that comes highly recommended by locals. ✉ *67 Church St.* ☎ *01463/233651* 🌐 *www.hootanannyinverness.co.uk.*

GOLF

Inverness Golf Club. Established in 1883, Inverness Golf Club welcomes visitors to its parkland course 1 mile from downtown. Overlooking the Beauly Firth, it's a tree-lined course that requires a good deal of accuracy. ✉ *Culcabock Rd.* ☎ *01463/239882* 🌐 *www.invernessgolfclub.co.uk* 💷 *Green Fee: £18–£42* ⛳ *18 holes, 6256 yds, par 69.*

SHOPPING

Although Inverness has the usual indoor shopping malls and department stores—including Marks & Spencer—the most interesting goods are in the specialty outlets in and around town.

Duncan Chisholm and Sons. This shop specializes in Highland dress and tartans. Mail-order and made-to-measure services are available. ⊠ 47–51 Castle St. ☎ 01463/234599 ⊕ www.kilts.co.uk.

Leakey's Secondhand Bookshop. This shop claims to be the biggest secondhand bookstore in Scotland. When you get tired of leafing through the 100,000 or so titles, climb to the mezzanine café and study the cavernous church interior. Antique prints and maps are housed on the balcony. ⊠ Greyfriars Hall, Church St. ☎ 01463/239947 ⊙ Closed Sun.

FORRES

10 miles east of Nairn.

The burgh of Forres is everything a Scottish medieval town should be, with a handsome tollbooth (the former courthouse and prison) and impressive gardens as its centerpiece. It's remarkable how well the old buildings have adapted to their modern retail uses. With two distilleries—one still operating, the other preserved as a museum—Forres is a key point on the Malt Whisky Trail. Brodie Castle is also nearby. Just 6 miles north you'll find Findhorn Ecovillage and a sandy beach stretches along the edge of the semi-enclosed Findhorn Bay, which is excellent bird-watching territory.

GETTING HERE AND AROUND

Forres is easy to reach by car from Inverness on the A96. Daily ScotRail trains run here from Inverness and Aberdeen.

EXPLORING

Benromach Distillery. The smallest distillery in Moray, Benromach Distiller was founded in 1898. It's now owned by whisky specialist Gordon and MacPhail, and it stocks a vast range of malts. An informative hourly tour ends with a tutored nosing and tasting. ⊠ Invererne Rd. ☎ 01309/675968 ⊕ www.benromach.com ⊠ £5 ⊙ May and Sept., Mon.–Sat. 9:30–5; June–Aug., Mon.–Sat. 9:30–5, Sun. noon–4; Oct.–Dec. and Feb.–Apr., weekdays 10–4; last tour 1 hr before closing.

Brodie Castle. This medieval castle was rebuilt and extended in the 17th and 19th centuries. Fine examples of late-17th-century plasterwork are preserved in the Dining Room and Blue Sitting Room; an impressive library and a superb collection of pictures extend into the 20th century. The castle is about 24 miles east of Inverness, making it a good day trip. ⊠ Off A96, 2 miles west of Forres, Brodie ☎ 0844/493–2156 ⊕ www.nts.org.uk ⊠ Castle £10, grounds free ⊙ Castle: late Mar., Apr., Sept., and Oct., daily 10:30–4:30; May and June, Sun.–Thurs. 10:30–4:30; July and Aug., daily 10:30–5. Last tour 1 hr before closing. Grounds daily 10:30–sunset.

Dallas Dhu Historic Distillery. The final port of call on the Malt Whisky Trail, the Dallas Dhu Historic Distillery was the last distillery built in the 19th century. No longer a working distillery, the structure is a small

museum that tells the story of Scotland's national drink. ⊠ *Mannachie Rd.* ☎ *01309/676548* ⊕ *www.dallasdhu.com* ☒ *£6* ⊘ *Apr.–Sept., daily 9:30–5:30; Oct., daily 9:30–4:30; Nov.–Mar., Sat.–Wed. 9:30–4:30.*

Findhorn Ecovillage. This education center is dedicated to developing "new ways of living infused with spiritual values." Drawing power from wind turbines, locals farm and garden to sustain themselves. A tour affords a thought-provoking glimpse into the lives of the ultra-independent villagers. See homes made out of whisky barrels, and the Universal Hall, filled with beautiful engraved glass. The Phoenix Shop sells organic foods and handmade crafts, and the Blue Angel Café serves organic and vegetarian fare. ⊠ *The Park, off B9011, 6 miles from Forres, Findhorn* ☎ *01309/690311* ⊕ *www.findhorn.org* ☒ *Free, tours £5* ⊘ *Visitor center: May–Sept., weekdays 10–5, weekends 1–4; Oct.–Apr., weekdays 10–5. Tours: Apr., Oct., and Nov., Mon., Wed., and Fri. at 2; May–Sept., Fri.–Mon. and Wed. at 2.*

LOCH NESS

Though not considered as beautiful as many other lochs, Loch Ness attracts numerous visitors thanks to its famous legendary monster. Heading south from Inverness, you can travel along the loch's quiet east side or the more touristy west side. A pleasant morning can be spent at Urquhart Castle, in the monster-gazing town of Drumnadrochit. As you travel south and west, the landscape opens up and the Nevis Range comes into view.

Loch Ness. From the A82 you get many views of the formidable and famous Loch Ness, which has a greater volume of water than any other Scottish loch, a maximum depth of more than 800 feet, and its own monster—at least according to popular myth. Early travelers who passed this way included English lexicographer Dr. Samuel Johnson (1709–84) and his guide and biographer, James Boswell (1740–95), who were on their way to the Hebrides in 1783. They remarked at the time about the poor condition of the population and the squalor of their homes. Another early travel writer and naturalist, Thomas Pennant (1726–98), noted that the loch kept the locality frost-free in winter. Even General Wade came here, his troops blasting and digging a road up much of the eastern shore. None of these observant early travelers ever made mention of a monster. Clearly, they had not read the local guidebooks.

20

DRUMNADROCHIT

14 miles south of Inverness.

More tourist hub than cultural center, Drumnadrochit is nevertheless a magnet for "Nessie" spotters. There aren't many good restaurants, but there are some solid hotels.

GETTING HERE AND AROUND

It's easy to get here from Fort Augustus or Inverness via the A82, either by car or by local bus.

EXPLORING

Urquhart Castle. About 2 miles southeast of Drumnadrochit, this castle is a favorite Loch-Ness-monster-watching spot. This romantically broken-down fortress stands on a promontory overlooking the loch, as it has since the Middle Ages. Because of its central and strategic position in the Great Glen line of communication, the castle has a complex history involving military offense and defense, as well as its own destruction and renovation. The castle was begun in the 13th century and was destroyed before the end of the 17th century to prevent its use by the Jacobites. A visitor center gives an idea of what life was like here in medieval times. ✉ *A82* ☎ *01456/450551* 🌐 *www.historic-scotland.gov.uk/places* 🎟 *£8* 🕓 *Apr.–Sept., daily 9:30–6; Oct., daily 9:30–5; Nov.–Mar., daily 9:30–4:30; last admission 45 mins before closing.*

WHERE TO STAY

$$$ B&B/INN Fodor's Choice ★ 🏨 **Loch Ness Lodge.** Run by siblings Scott and Iona Sutherland, Loch Ness Lodge is an exquisite place: opulent, classy, and welcoming. **Pros:** excellent staff; superb views; lovely rooms. **Cons:** near a busy road; no restaurant. [$] *Rooms from: £210* ✉ *A82, Brachla* ☎ *01456/459469* 🌐 *www.loch-ness-lodge.com* 🛏 *7 rooms* 🍴 *Some meals.*

INDEX

PHOTO CREDITS

NOTES

NOTES

NOTES

Fodor's ESSENTIAL EUROPE

Publisher: Amanda D'Acierno, *Senior Vice President*

Editorial: Arabella Bowen, *Editor in Chief*; Linda Cabasin, *Editorial Director*

Design: Fabrizio La Rocca, *Vice President, Creative Director*; Tina Malaney, *Associate Art Director*; Chie Ushio, *Senior Designer*; Ann McBride, *Production Designer*

Photography: Melanie Marin, *Associate Director of Photography*; Jessica Parkhill and Jennifer Romains, *Researchers*

Maps: Rebecca Baer, *Senior Map Editor*; Mark Stroud (Moon Street Cartography), David Lindroth, *Cartographers*

Production: Linda Schmidt, *Managing Editor*; Evangelos Vasilakis, *Associate Managing Editor*; Angela L. McLean, *Senior Production Manager*

Sales: Jacqueline Lebow, *Sales Director*

Marketing & Publicity: Heather Dalton, *Marketing Director*; Katherine Fleming, *Senior Publicist*

Business & Operations: Susan Livingston, *Vice President, Strategic Business Planning*; Sue Daulton, *Vice President, Operations*

Fodors.com: Megan Bell, *Executive Director, Revenue & Business Development*; Yasmin Marinaro, *Senior Director, Marketing & Partnerships*

Copyright © 2014 by Fodor's Travel, a division of Random House LLC

Editors: Douglas Stallings (Lead Editor), Steven Montero

Editorial Contributors: Mark Baker, Brendan de Beer, David Dunne, Matthew Ellis, Jane Foster, Natasha Giannousi, Katrin Gygax, Jennifer Hattam, Anto Howard, Liz Humphreys, Jennifer Ladonne, Diane Naar-Elphee, Giulia Pines, Amanda Ruggieri, Ellin Stein, Joanna Styles
Production Editor: Carrie Parker

2nd Edition

ISBN 978-0-8041-4210-6

ISSN 1943-006X

All details in this book are based on information supplied to us at press time. Always confirm information when it matters, especially if you're making a detour to visit a specific place. Fodor's expressly disclaims any liability, loss, or risk, personal or otherwise, that is incurred as a consequence of the use of any of the contents of this book.

914.0456
F
2014

SPECIAL SALES

This book is available at special discounts for bulk purchases for sales promotions or premiums. For more information, e-mail specialmarkets@randomhouse.com

PRINTED IN THE UNITED STATES OF AMERICA

10 9 8 7 6 5 4 3 2 1

ABOUT OUR WRITERS

Fodor's aims to give you the best local insights by using writers who live in the destinations they cover. Essential Europe is the work of the following Europe-based team:

Austria: Diane Naar-Elphee (destination specialist, Vienna), Ulrich Ehrhardt (Innsbruck), Karin Hanta (Vienna), Horst E. Reischenböck (Salzburg).

Belgium: Liz Humphreys (destination specialist), Tim Skelton (Belgium)

Croatia: Jane Foster (destination specialist).

Czech Republic: Mark Baker (destination specialist, Prague), Jennifer Rigby (Prague Shopping, Arts & Nightlife, Side Trips).

France: Jennifer Ladonne (destination specialist, Ile de France, Paris Shopping, Dining, Arts & Nightlife), Linda Hervieux (Paris), Nancy Heslin (Provence, French Riviera), Christopher Mooney (Normandy), Bryan J. Pirolli (Paris), Victoria Tang (Paris Hotels), Jack Vermee (Normandy).

Germany: Giulia Pines (destination specialist, Berlin Dining, Arts & Nightlife), Lee A. Evans (Saxony), Catherine Moser Horlacher (Excursions from Munich), Evelyn Kanter (Heidelberg), Jeff Kavanash (Hamburg), Sally McGrane (Berlin), Paul Wheatley (Munich, the Bavarian Alps).

Greece: Natasha Giannousi (destination specialist, Athens, Delphi & Apollo Coast), Jeffrey and Elizabeth Carson (Mykonos, Santorini).

Hungary: Matthew Ellis (destination specialist).

Ireland: Anto Howard (destination specialist, Dublin), Paul Clements (Belfast), Alannah Hopkin (County Cork, Ring of Kerry).

Italy: Amanda Ruggieri (destination specialist, Rome), Peter Blackman (Tuscany), Bruce Leimsidor (Venice), Patricia Rucidlo (Florence, Tuscany), Mark Walters (Naples, Amalfi Coast).

Netherlands: Liz Humphreys (destination specialist, Amsterdam Dining), Floris Dogterom (Amsterdam Exploring & Vicinity), Marie-Claire Melzer (Amsterdam Hotels, Shopping, Arts & Nightlife).

Portugal: Brendan de Beer (destination specialist, Lisbon Environs), Carrie-Marie Bratley (Lisbon Environs), Lauren Frayer (Porto), Alison Roberts (Lisbon).

Scandinavia: David Dunne (destination specialist, Estonia, Finland, Latvia), Lola Akinmade-Åkerström (Sweden) Anne-Sophie Redisch (Norway), Paul Sullivan (Iceland), Gelu Sulugiuc (Denmark).

Slovenia: Mark Baker (destination specialist)

Spain: Joanna Styles (destination specialist, Andalusia), Lauren Frayer (Bilbao, Toledo), Ignacio Gómez (Madrid), Jared Lubarsky (Barcelona)

Switzerland: Katrin Gygax (destination specialist)

Turkey: Jennifer Hattam (destination specialist, Istanbul), Vanessa H. Larson (Istanbul).

United Kingdom: Ellin Stein (destination specialist, London), Julius Honnor, Kate Hughes (Bath, Oxford, Stratford), Jack Jewers (London, Cambridge), James O'Neill (London), Alex Wijeratna (London).